Strategic Management

Planning for Domestic & Global Competition

Strategic Management

Planning for Domestic & Global Competition

Thirteenth Edition

John A. Pearce II
Villanova School of Business
Villanova University

Richard B. Robinson, Jr.
Darla Moore School of Business
University of South Carolina

The McGraw·Hill Companies

STRATEGIC MANAGEMENT: PLANNING FOR DOMESTIC & GLOBAL COMPETITION, THIRTEENTH EDITION

Published by McGraw-Hill, a business unit of The McGraw-Hill Companies, Inc., 1221 Avenue of the Americas, New York, NY 10020.

This book is printed on acid-free paper.

1 2 3 4 5 6 7 8 9 0 DOW/DOW 1 0 9 8 7 6 5 4 3 2

ISBN 978-0-07-802929-5
MHID 0-07-802929-5

Vice President & Editor-in-Chief: *Brent Gordon*
Vice President of Specialized Publishing: *Janice M. Roerig-Blong*
Editorial Director: *Paul Ducham*
Executive Editor: *Michael Ablassmeir*
Editorial Coordinator: *Andrea Heirendt*
Marketing Manager: *Anke Weekes*
Senior Project Manager: *Lisa A. Bruflodt*
Design Coordinator: *Margarite Reynolds*
Cover Designer: *Studio Montage, St. Louis, Missouri*
Cover Images Credits: *From top to bottom, © Stockbyte/Getty Images; ©John Lund/Drew Kelly/Blend Images LLC; blue jean images/Getty Images; © Image 100/Corbis; Klaus Tiedge/Blend Images/Getty Images; Steve Cole/Getty Images*
Buyer: *Kara Kudronowicz*
Media Project Manager: *Balaji Sundararaman*
Compositor: *MPS Limited, a Macmillan Company*
Typeface: *10/12 Times New Roman*
Printer: *R. R. Donnelley*

Library of Congress Cataloging-in-Publication Data

Pearce, John A.
Strategic management : planning for domestic & global competition / John A. Pearce II, Richard B. Robinson, Jr.—13th ed.
p. cm.—(Strategic management)
ISBN 978-0-07-802929-5 (alk. paper)
1. Strategic planning. I. Robinson, Richard B. (Richard Braden), 1947– II. Title.
HD30.28.P3395 2013
658.4'012—dc23

2011042826

www.mhhe.com

To Susan McCartney Pearce, David Donham Pearce, Mark McCartney Pearce, Sage Ast, Rowan Ast, Anjali Ast, and Oakley Robinson—for the love, joy, and vitality that they give to our lives.

About the Authors

John A. Pearce II *Villanova University*

John A. Pearce II, Ph.D., holds the Villanova School of Business Endowed Chair in Strategic Management and Entrepreneurship at Villanova University. In 2009, he received the Fulbright Senior Specialist Award for work at Simon Fraser University's Segal Graduate School of Business in Vancouver, Canada. In 2004, he was the Distinguished Visiting Professor at ITAM in Mexico City. Previously, Professor Pearce was the Eakin Endowed Chair in Strategic Management at George Mason University and a State of Virginia Eminent Scholar. He received the 1994 Fulbright U.S. Professional Award, which he served at INTAN in Malaysia. Dr. Pearce has taught at Penn State University, West Virginia University, the University of Malta as the Fulbright Senior Professor in International Management, and at the University of South Carolina where he was Director of Ph.D. Programs in Strategic Management. He received a Ph.D. degree in Business Administration and Strategic Management from the Pennsylvania State University.

Professor Pearce is coauthor of 40 books and has authored more than 250 articles and refereed professional papers. The articles have appeared in journals that include *Academy of Management Executive, Academy of Management Journal, Academy of Management Review, Business Horizons, California Management Review, Entrepreneurship Theory and Practice, Journal of Applied Psychology, Journal of Business Venturing, Long-Range Planning, Organizational Dynamics, MIT-Sloan Management Review,* and *Strategic Management Journal.* Several of these publications have resulted from Professor Pearce's work as a principal on research projects funded for more than $2 million.

Professor Pearce is the recipient of several awards in recognition of his accomplishments in teaching, research, scholarship, and professional service, including three Outstanding Paper Awards from the Academy of Management and the 2003 Villanova University Outstanding Faculty Research Award. A frequent leader of executive development programs and an active consultant to business and industry, Dr. Pearce's client list includes domestic and multinational firms engaged in manufacturing and service industries.

Richard B. Robinson, Jr. *University of South Carolina*

Richard B. Robinson, Jr., Ph.D., is a Distinguish Professor Emeritus at the Darla Moore School of Business, University of South Carolina. He also serves as Director Emeritus of the Faber Entrepreneurship Center at USC. Dr. Robinson received his Ph.D. in Business Administration from the University of Georgia. He graduated from Georgia Tech in Industrial Management.

Professor Robinson has authored or coauthored numerous books, articles, professional papers, and case studies addressing strategic management and entrepreneurship issues that students and managers use worldwide. His research has been published in major journals including the *Academy of Management Journal, Academy of Management Review, Strategic Management Journal, Entrepreneurship Theory and Practice, Business Horizons, Academy of Entrepreneurship Journal,* and the *Journal of Business Venturing.*

Dr. Robinson has previously held executive positions with companies in the pulp and paper, hazardous waste, building products, lodging, and restaurant industries. He currently serves as a director or adviser to entrepreneurial companies that are global leaders in niche markets in the animation and visualization software industries. Dr. Robinson also advises more than 250 students each year who undertake field consulting projects and internships with entrepreneurial companies worldwide.

Preface

This thirteenth edition of *Strategic Management* has a refined message and a new subtitle: *Planning for Domestic & Global Competition.* This new edition is specially designed to accommodate the needs of strategy students worldwide in our fast-changing twenty-first century. We complement our focus on strategic planning for success within U.S. borders with unprecedented attention on how U.S. firms can leverage their domestic success by forming international partnerships and can achieve international success by becoming actively involved in global trade. These are exciting times, and they are reflected in this book. This preface describes what we have done to make the thirteenth edition uniquely effective in preparing students for strategic decisions in the fast-paced global business arena. They include NEW or revised chapter material, 30 NEW cases, and dozens of NEW illustrations examining:

- Globalization as a central theme integrated and illustrated throughout this book and in a separate chapter on the global business environment that every business faces.
- Business ethics and corporate social responsibility, featuring an award-winning model of successful CRS activities.
- Strategies that enable managers to to use innovation and entrepreneurship to shape their companies' futures more proactively.
- Structuring networked, boundaryless organizational structures to face twenty-first century challenges.
- Frameworks that help managers adapt to the accelerating pace of global and technological change in their industries, companies, and markets.
- Ways for strategists to identify and leverage their firm's strengths in rapidly changing industries.
- Examination of the challenges and advantages of using global supply chains and outsourcing parts of a firm's product or service offerings.
- Investigation of the increased importance of companies founded and managed by women and minorities worldwide.

We are also pleased to offer:

- 30 Global Strategy in Action boxes that detail how businesses large and small have designed strategies that have enabled then to successfully compete in global markets.
- 15 Top Strategist boxes highlighting leaders worldwide who are examples of good strategic leadership and thinking.
- 30 new, comprehensive cases covering business situations from around the world in both large and small companies.
- More than 50 Strategy in Action boxes illustrating key concepts in each chapter.
- Literally hundreds of new, twenty-first-century examples woven into the 14 chapters of the text.

The thirteenth edition of *Strategic Management* is divided into 14 chapters. We provide thorough, state-of-the-art treatments of the critical business skills needed to plan and manage strategic activities. While the text continues a solid academic connection, students will find the text material to be practical, skills oriented, and relevant to their jobs and career aspirations.

All of the material in this edition is based on a proven model-based treatment of strategic management that allows for self-study and an easy-to-understand presentation. We have also significantly reduced the page length in this edition, providing a very focused presentation that is also the most cost-effective offering from McGraw-Hill/Irwin for students and instructors of strategic management.

AN OVERVIEW OF OUR TEXT MATERIAL

The thirteenth edition uses a model of the strategic management process as the basis for the organization of the text material. Adopters have identified this model as a key distinctive competence for our text because it offers a logical flow, distinct elements, and an easy-to-understand guide to strategic management. The model reflects strategic analysis at different organizational levels as well as the importance of innovation in the strategic management process. The model and parallel chapter organization provides a student-friendly approach to the study of strategic management.

Chapters

The first chapter provides an overview of the strategic management process and explains what students will find as they use this book. The remaining 13 chapters cover each part of the strategic management process and techniques that aid strategic analysis, decision making, implementation, control, and renewal. The thirteenth edition includes several upgrades designed to incorporate major developments from both these sources. These cutting-edge concepts add to our emphasis on straightforward and logical presentation so that students can grasp these new ideas without additional reading.

Global Strategy in Action Modules and Strategy in Action Modules

Each chapter provides Global Strategy in Action modules and Strategy in Action modules, a key pedagogical feature. We have drawn on the work of prestigious business magazine field correspondents worldwide to fill more than 50 new modules with short, hard-hitting current illustrations of key chapter topics. They add excitement, interest, and practical illustration value to the essential cutting-edge theory that provides the foundation of this text.

Top Strategist Boxes

Adding to the Strategy in Action modules, we have included Top Strategist boxes in each chapter that tell the personal story of a company or industry leader whose behavior, practices, or actions illustrate a key concept in the strategic management process. These boxes help personalize the lessons in the chapter through a vignette about a recognized expert.

CASES IN THE THIRTEENTH EDITION

We are pleased to offer 30 excellent cases in this edition. These cases present companies, industries, and situations that are easily recognized, current, and interesting. We have a good mixture of global and domestically focused companies. The cases involve service, retail, manufacturing, technology, and diversified activities. We explore companies in the United States, Europe, Asia, and Middle East economies.

OUR WEB SITE

A substantial Web site is designed to aid your use of this book. It includes areas accessible only to instructors and areas specifically designed to assist students. The instructor section includes supplement files, which include detailed teaching notes, PowerPoint slides, and case teaching notes for all 30 case studies, which keep your work area less cluttered and let you quickly obtain information. Students are provided company and related business periodical Web site linkages to aid and expedite their case research and preparation efforts. Practice quizzes are provided to help students prepare for tests on the text material and attempt to lower their anxiety in that regard. We expect students will find the Web site useful and interesting. Please visit us at www.mhhe.com/pearce13e.

SUPPLEMENTS

Components of our teaching package include a comprehensive instructor's manual, PowerPoint presentations, and a computerized test bank. These are all available to qualified adopters of the text.

Acknowledgments

We have benefited from the help of many people in the evolution of this project over thirteen editions. Students, adopters, colleagues, reviewers, and business contacts have provided hundreds of insightful comments, suggestions, and contributions that have progressively enhanced this book and its supplements. We are indebted to the researchers and practicing managers who have accelerated the development of the literature on strategic management.

We are particularly indebted to the talented case researchers who have produced the cases used in this book, as well as to case researchers dedicated to the revitalization of case research as an important academic endeavor. First-class case research is a major avenue through which top strategic management scholars should be recognized.

Several reviewers provided constructive suggestions and feedback, which helped facilitate useful revisions, the addition of numerous current examples throughout the text, and a new case selection we find compelling. We extend particular thanks to the following who offered exceptionally comprehensive coverage:

Thomas D. Ashman
Eckerd College

Samuel H. Clovis Jr.
Morningside College

Matt C. Dwyer
Olivet Nazarene University

Phyllis Flott
Tennessee State University

Donald Grunewald
Iona College

Michael Harvey
Washington College

Nabil Ibrahim
Augusta State University

Donald J. Kopka Jr.
Towson University

Steven G. Morrissette, PhD
University of St. Francis

Jeffrey R. Nystrom
University of Colorado Denver

Dr. Michael D. Santonino III
Bethune-Cookman University

Greg Schultz
Carroll University

Sally Sledge
Norfolk State University

We are affiliated with two separate universities, both of which provide environments that deserve thanks. As the Villanova School of Business Endowed Chair at Villanova University, Jack is able to combine his scholarly and teaching activities with his coauthorship of this text. He is grateful to Villanova University and his colleagues for the support and encouragement they provide.

Richard appreciates the support provided within the Darla Moore School of Business by Dean Hildy Teegen, Deputy Dean Scott Koewer, Associate Dean Greg Neihaus, Dr. Brian Klaas, Mr. Dean Kress, Ms. Cheryl Fowler, Ms. Carol Lucas, and Sandra Bringley.

We want to thank Dr. Ram Subramanian, Montclair State University, for his outstanding contributions in the instructor's manual and ancillaries for this thirteenth edition. His dedication and attention to detail make this a better book.

Leaders at McGraw-Hill/Irwin deserve our utmost thanks and appreciation. Gerald Saykes, John Black, John Biernat, and Craig Beytein contributed to our early success. The editorial leadership of Michael Ablassmeir helps to assure that it will continue in this thirteenth edition. Editorial Coordinator Andrea Heirendt helped us stay on schedule, arranged permissions, and tirelessly and professionally helped us to produce a much improved book. The McGraw-Hill/Irwin field organization deserves particular recognition and thanks for their ongoing worldwide adoption results for this text. We particularly wish to express appreciation to and acknowledge the hard work and excellent support provided to us by Sandy Wolbers, Kathleen Sutterlin, Stacey Flowerree, Brooke Briggs, Nick Miggans, Kevin Eichelberger, Colin Kelley, Steve Tomlin, Bryan Sullivan, Clark White, Meghan Manders, Lori Ziegenfuss, Jessica King, Rosalie Skears, Lisa Huinker, Bob Noel, Adam Rooke, John Wiese, Carlin Robinson, Courtney Kieffer, Rosario Valenti, Anni Lundgren, Deborah Judge-Watt, Nate Kehoe, David Wulff, Kim Freund, Joni Thompson, and Mary Park. Their professionalism and dedication to the professors and instructors they serve sets a standard we have worked very hard to match by making the thirteenth edition a text deserving of their representation.

We hope that you will find our book and ancillaries all that you expect. We welcome your ideas and recommendations about our material, and we wish you the utmost success in teaching and studying strategic management.

Dr. John A. Pearce II
Villanova School of Business
Villanova University
Villanova, PA 19085–1678

Dr. Richard Robinson
Darla Moore School of Business
University of South Carolina
Columbia, SC 29208

Brief Contents

Table of Contents

Chapter 5
The Global Environment 122

Chapter 6
Internal Analysis 147

Chapter 7
Long-Term Objectives and Strategies 190

Chapter 11
Organizational Structure 316

Chapter 12
Leadership and Culture 352

Chapter 13
Strategic Control 381

Chapter 14
Innovation and Entrepreneurship 398

PART FOUR
CASES 425

Part **One**

Overview of Strategic Management

The first chapter of this book introduces strategic management, the set of decisions and actions that result in the design and activation of strategies to achieve the objectives of an organization. The chapter provides an overview of the nature, benefits, and terminology of and the need for strategic management. Subsequent chapters provide greater detail.

The first major section of Chapter 1, "The Nature and Value of Strategic Management," emphasizes the practical value and benefits of strategic management for a firm. It also distinguishes between a firm's strategic decisions and its other planning tasks.

The section stresses the key point that strategic management activities are undertaken at three levels: corporate, business, and functional. The distinctive characteristics of strategic decision making at each of these levels affect the impact of activities at these levels on company operations. Other topics dealt with in this section are the value of formality in strategic management and the alignment of strategy makers in strategy formulation and implementation. The section concludes with a review of the planning research on business, which demonstrates that the use of strategic management processes yields financial and behavioral benefits that justify their costs.

The second major section of Chapter 1 presents a model of the strategic management process. The model, which will serve as an outline for the remainder of the text, describes approaches currently used by strategic planners. Its individual components are carefully defined and explained, as is the process for integrating them into the strategic management process. The section ends with a discussion of the model's practical limitations and the advisability of tailoring the recommendations made to actual business situations.

Chapter **One**

Strategic Management

After reading and studying this chapter, you should be able to

1. Explain the concept of strategic management.
2. Describe how strategic decisions differ from other decisions that managers make.
3. Name the benefits and risks of a participative approach to strategic decision making.
4. Understand the types of strategic decisions for which managers at different levels of the company are responsible.
5. Describe a comprehensive model of strategic decision making.
6. Appreciate the importance of strategic management as a process.
7. Give examples of strategic decisions that companies have recently made.

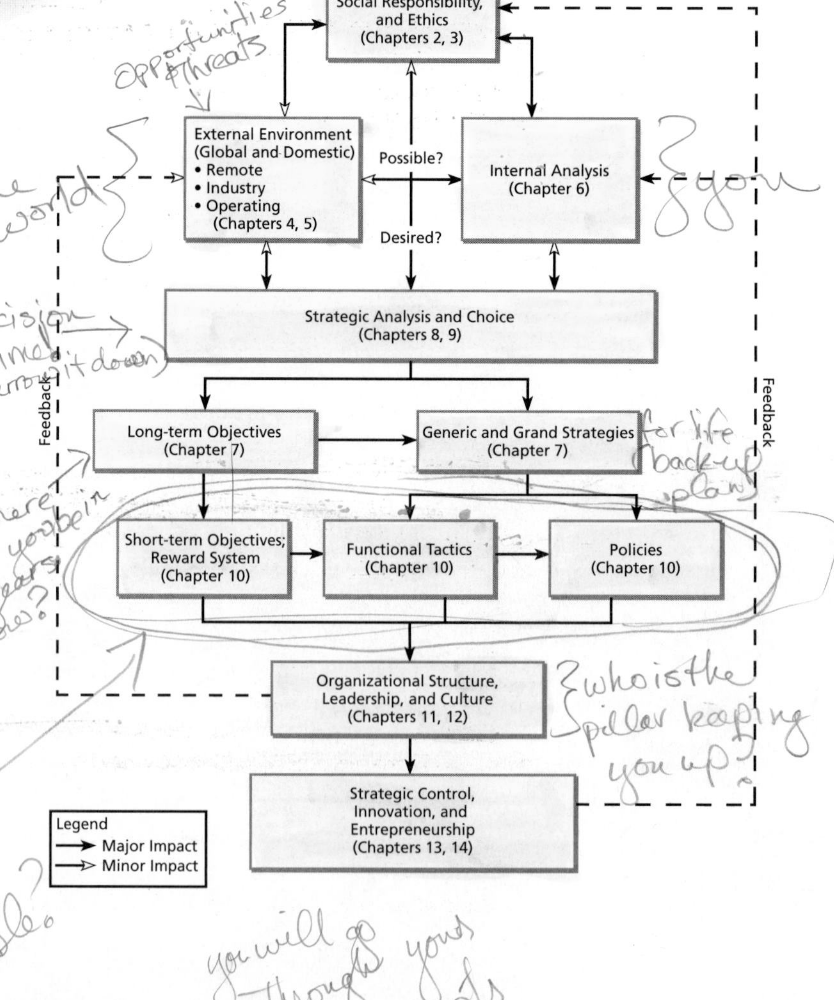

Strategy in Action — Exhibit 1.1

Strategic Blunder: Xerox's Sale of Insider Information to Apple

In the early 1970s, Xerox developed world-changing computer technology, including the mouse and the graphical user interface. (Modern GUIs include Microsoft Windows and Mac OS X.) One of the devices was called the Xerox Alto, a desktop personal computer that Xerox never bothered to market. A decade later, several Apple employees, including Steve Jobs, visited the Xerox PARC research and development facility for three days in exchange for $1 million in Apple's still–privately held stock. That educational field trip was well worth the price of admission (Apple gave Xerox shares of Apple stock as an admission fee that was worth $3.5 billion in 2008), given that it helped Jobs build a company worth $110 billion in 2008. In the late 1980s, Xerox sued Apple for using GUI technology in its Macintosh computer, but the case was dismissed—the statute of limitations on the dispute had passed. Size of Blunder: $107 billion.

Source: Excerpted from Melanie Lindner, "The 10 Biggest Blunders Ever in Business," *Forbes,* March 25, 2008, http://www.Forbes.com

THE NATURE AND VALUE OF STRATEGIC MANAGEMENT

Managing activities internal to the firm is only part of the modern executive's responsibilities. The modern executive also must respond to the challenges posed by the firm's immediate and remote external environments. The immediate external environment includes competitors, suppliers, increasingly scarce resources, government agencies and their ever more numerous regulations, and customers whose preferences often shift inexplicably. The remote external environment comprises economic and social conditions, political priorities, and technological developments, all of which must be anticipated, monitored, assessed, and incorporated into the executive's decision making. However, the executive often is compelled to subordinate the demands of the firm's internal activities and external environment to the multiple and often inconsistent requirements of its stakeholders: owners, top managers, employees, communities, customers, and country. To deal effectively with everything that affects the growth and profitability of a firm, executives employ management processes that they feel will position it optimally in its competitive environment by maximizing the anticipation of environmental changes and of unexpected internal and competitive demands. For an intriguing example of how a failure to anticipate the consequences of competitive dynamics resulted in a major strategic blunder by Xerox, read Exhibit 1.1, Strategy in Action.

To earn profits, firms need to perfect processes that respond to increases in the size and number of competing businesses; to the expanded role of government as a buyer, seller, regulator, and competitor in the free enterprise system; and to greater business involvement in international trade. Perhaps the most significant improvement in these management processes came when "long-range planning," "planning, programming, budgeting," and "business policy" were blended with increased emphasis on environmental forecasting and external considerations in formulating and implementing plans. This all-encompassing approach is known as strategic management.

strategic management
The set of decisions and actions that result in the formulation and implementation of plans designed to achieve a company's objectives.

Strategic management is defined as the set of decisions and actions that result in the formulation and implementation of plans designed to achieve a company's objectives. It comprises nine critical tasks:

1. Formulate the company's mission, including broad statements about its purpose, philosophy, and goals.
2. Conduct an analysis that reflects the company's internal conditions and capabilities.

Strategy in Action — Exhibit 1.2

JCP's Aggressive Strategic Plan for Growth

JCPenney has an aggressive five-year growth strategy that focuses on further enhancement of its dot com, mobile and social networking media; improving productivity in lagging product areas; and attracting more of the consumer base that is 25 to 44 years old with the goal of hitting $23 billion by 2014. Myron (Mike) Ullman III, chairman and CEO, outlined specific targets designed to achieve these goals: stepping up style across the board; digital marketing, leadership development and an expansion of its exclusive in-store Sephora departments.

The company's five-year agenda is centered on a new look in attitude—primarily offering style and quality at a "killer price," Ullman said. At the same time, the company has identified two other categories for performance and emphasis: "moderate"—which involves inventory, SG&A, Cap-Ex reflected in the diminished store opening program especially; and "maintain," which includes customer experience, brand launches, newness and merchandise flow.

Overall, Ullman said the company's objectives are "five, five, five" which is "a five-year plan, an additional $5 billion in sales, and $5 for EPS." The sales growth will be primarily organic. There will be few new store openings, with remodels the key for the first years of the plan.

Source: Excerpted from "JCP Plans Aggressive Growth," *Home Textiles Today,* April 26, 2010, p. 1. http://proquest.umi.com/pqdweb?did=2020546621&Fmt=3&clientId=3260&RQT=309&VName=PQD

3. Assess the company's external environment, including both the competitive and the general contextual factors.
4. Analyze the company's options by matching its resources with the external environment.
5. Identify the most desirable options by evaluating each option in light of the company's mission.
6. Select a set of long-term objectives and grand strategies that will achieve the most desirable options.
7. Develop annual objectives and short-term strategies that are compatible with the selected set of long-term objectives and grand strategies.
8. Implement the strategic choices by means of budgeted resource allocations in which the matching of tasks, people, structures, technologies, and reward systems is emphasized.
9. Evaluate the success of the strategic process as an input for future decision making.

strategy
Large-scale, future-oriented plans for interacting with the competitive environment to achieve company objectives.

As these nine tasks indicate, strategic management involves the planning, directing, organizing, and controlling of a company's strategy-related decisions and actions. By **strategy,** managers mean their large-scale, future-oriented plans for interacting with the competitive environment to achieve company objectives. A strategy is a company's game plan. Although that plan does not precisely detail all future deployment of people, finances, material, and information, it does provide a framework for managerial decisions. A strategy reflects a company's awareness of how, when, and where it should compete; against whom it should compete; and for what purposes it should compete. Exhibit 1.2, Strategy in Action provides an overview of the strategic plan of JCPenney. It stresses a time period, a revenue objective, a general marketing approach, and a target return for investors.

Dimensions of Strategic Decisions

What decisions facing a business are strategic and therefore deserve strategic management attention? Typically, strategic issues have the following dimensions.

Strategic Issues Require Top-Management Decisions Because strategic decisions overarch several areas of a firm's operations, they require top-management involvement. Usually only top management has the perspective needed to understand the broad implications of such decisions and the power to authorize the necessary resource allocations. As top manager of Volvo GM Heavy Truck Corporation, Karl-Erling Trogen, president, wanted to push the company closer to the customer by overarching operations with service and customer relations empowering the workforce closest to the customer with greater knowledge and authority. This strategy called for a major commitment to the parts and service end of the business where customer relations was first priority. Trogen's philosophy was to so empower the workforce that more operating questions were handled on the line where workers worked directly with customers. He believed that the corporate headquarters should be more focused on strategic issues, such as engineering, production, quality, and marketing.

Strategic Issues Require Large Amounts of the Firm's Resources Strategic decisions involve substantial allocations of people, physical assets, or moneys that either must be redirected from internal sources or secured from outside the firm. They also commit the firm to actions over an extended period. For these reasons, they require substantial resources. Whirlpool Corporation's "Quality Express" product delivery program exemplified a strategy that required a strong financial and personnel commitment from the company. The plan was to deliver products to customers when, where, and how they wanted them. This proprietary service uses contract logistics strategy to deliver Whirlpool, Kitchen Aid, Roper, and Estate brand appliances to 90 percent of the company's dealer and builder customers within 24 hours and to the other 10 percent within 48 hours. In highly competitive service-oriented businesses, achieving and maintaining customer satisfaction frequently involve a commitment from every facet of the organization.

Strategic Issues Often Affect the Firm's Long-Term Prosperity Strategic decisions ostensibly commit the firm for a long time, typically five years; however, the impact of such decisions often lasts much longer. Once a firm has committed itself to a particular strategy, its image and competitive advantages usually are tied to that strategy. Firms become known in certain markets, for certain products, with certain technologies. They would jeopardize their previous gains if they shifted from these markets, products, or technologies by adopting a radically different strategy. Thus, strategic decisions have enduring effects on firms—for better or worse. For example, Commerce One created an alliance with SAP to improve its position in the e-marketplace for business to business (B2B) sales. After taking three years to ready its e-portals, Commerce One and SAP were ready to take on the market. Unfortunately, the market changed. The "foolproof strategy" got to the market too late and the alliance failed.

Strategic Issues Are Future Oriented Strategic decisions are based on what managers forecast, rather than on what they know. In such decisions, emphasis is placed on the development of projections that will enable the firm to select the most promising strategic options. In the turbulent and competitive free enterprise environment, a firm will succeed only if it takes a proactive (anticipatory) stance toward change. Microsoft's Bill Gates, who gained fame as a future-oriented strategic decision maker, often succeeds at the expense of short-sighted competitors as described in Exhibit 1.3, Strategy in Action.

Strategic Issues Usually Have Multifunctional or Multibusiness Consequences Strategic decisions have complex implications for most areas of the firm. Decisions about such matters as customer mix, competitive emphasis, or organizational structure necessarily involve a number of the firm's strategic business units (SBUs), divisions, or program units. All of these areas will be affected by allocations or reallocations of responsibilities and resources that result from these decisions.

Strategic Issues Require Considering the Firm's External Environment All businesses exist in an open system. They affect and are affected by external conditions that are largely beyond their control. Therefore, to successfully position a firm in competitive situations,

Strategy in Action — Exhibit 1.3

Strategic Blunder: Seattle Computer Products' Sale of the DOS Operating System

In 1980, Tim Paterson, a 24-year-old programmer at Seattle Computer Products, spent four months writing the 86-DOS operating system. Meanwhile, Bill Gates was on a hunt for operating software that Microsoft could license to IBM; Big Blue had the money and factories to build computers, but not the operating system to run them. Gates bought the DOS system for a pittance: $50,000. When Seattle Computer figured out what it had let slip through its fingers, it accused Microsoft of swindling the company by not revealing that IBM was its customer; Microsoft settled by compensating Seattle Computer an additional $1 million in 1986. Big deal—the market for the rest of Microsoft's cool software had been born, and there was no looking back. Arguably, this key deal ultimately propelled Microsoft to software domination—and its current $253 billion valuation. Size of Blunder: $253 billion.

Source: Excerpted from Melanie Lindner, "The 10 Biggest Blunders Ever in Business," *Forbes,* March 25, 2008, http://www.msnbc.msn.com/id/23677510/

its strategic managers must look beyond its operations. They must consider what relevant others are likely to do, including competitors, customers, suppliers, creditors, government, and labor.

Three Levels of Strategy

The decision-making hierarchy of a firm typically contains three levels. At the top of this hierarchy is the corporate level, composed principally of a board of directors and the chief executive and administrative officers. They are responsible for the firm's financial performance and for the achievement of nonfinancial goals, such as enhancing the firm's image and fulfilling its social responsibilities. To a large extent, attitudes at the corporate level reflect the concerns of stockholders and society at large. In a multibusiness firm, corporate-level executives determine the businesses in which the firm should be involved. They also set objectives and formulate strategies that span the activities and functional areas of these businesses. Corporate-level strategic managers attempt to exploit their firm's distinctive competencies by adopting a portfolio approach to the management of its businesses and by developing long-term plans, typically for a three- to five-year period. A key corporate strategy of Airborne Express's operations involved direct sale to high-volume corporate accounts and developing an expansive network in the international arena. Instead of setting up operations overseas, Airborne's long-term strategy was to form direct associations with national companies within foreign countries to expand and diversify their operations.

Another example of the portfolio approach involved a plan by state-owned Saudi Arabian Oil to spend $1.4 billion to build and operate an oil refinery in Korea with its partner, Ssangyong. To implement their program, the Saudis embarked on a new "cut-out-the-middleman" strategy to reduce the role of international oil companies in the processing and selling of Saudi crude oil.

In the middle of the decision-making hierarchy is the business level, composed principally of business and corporate managers. These managers must translate the statements of direction and intent generated at the corporate level into concrete objectives and strategies for individual business divisions, or SBUs. In essence, business-level strategic managers determine how the firm will compete in the selected product-market arena. They strive to identify and secure the most promising market segment within that arena. This segment is the piece of the total market that the firm can claim and defend because of its competitive advantages.

At the bottom of the decision-making hierarchy is the functional level, composed principally of managers of product, geographic, and functional areas. They develop annual objectives and short-term strategies in such areas as production, operations, research and

EXHIBIT 1.4
Alternative Strategic Management Structures

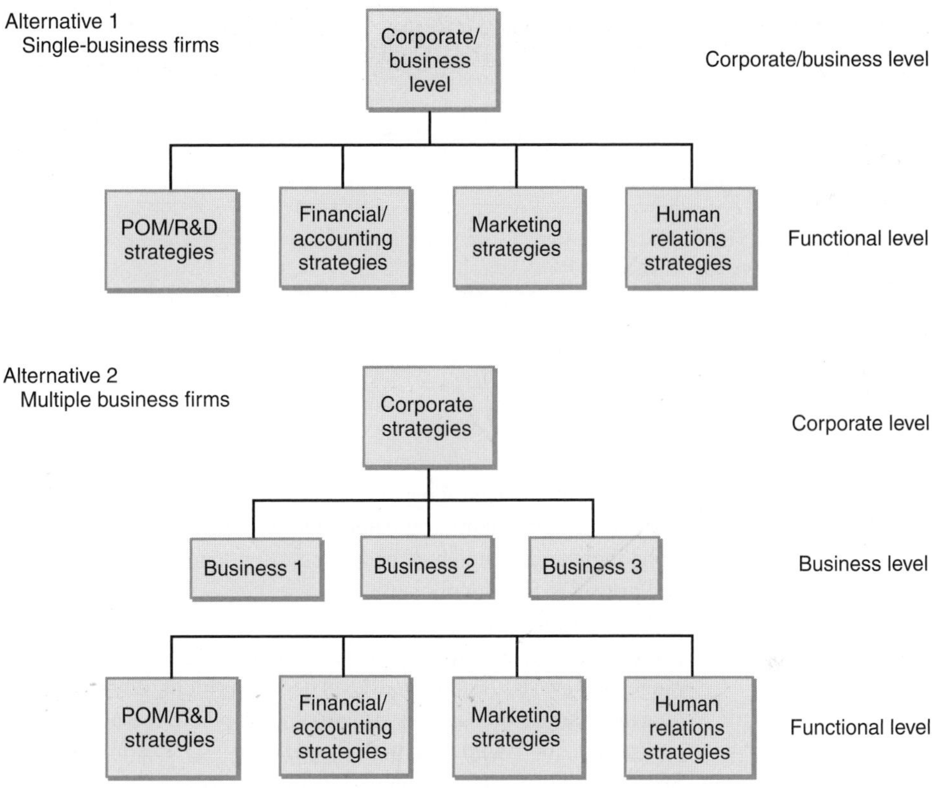

development, finance and accounting, marketing, and human relations. However, their principal responsibility is to implement or execute the firm's strategic plans. Whereas corporate- and business-level managers center their attention on "doing the right things," managers at the functional level center their attention on "doing things right." Thus, they address such issues as the efficiency and effectiveness of production and marketing systems, the quality of customer service, and the success of particular products and services in increasing the firm's market shares.

Exhibit 1.4 depicts the three levels of strategic management as structured in practice. In alternative 1, the firm is engaged in only one business and the corporate- and business-level responsibilities are concentrated in a single group of directors, officers, and managers. This is the organizational format of most small businesses.

Alternative 2, the classical corporate structure, comprises three fully operative levels: the corporate level, the business level, and the functional level. The approach taken throughout this text assumes the use of alternative 2. Moreover, whenever appropriate, topics are covered from the perspective of each level of strategic management. In this way, the text presents a comprehensive discussion of the strategic management process.

Characteristics of Strategic Management Decisions

The characteristics of strategic management decisions vary with the level of strategic activity considered. As shown in Exhibit 1.5, decisions at the corporate level tend to be more value oriented, more conceptual, and less concrete than decisions at the business or functional level. For example, at Alcoa, the world's largest aluminum maker, chairman Paul O'Neill made Alcoa one of the nation's most centralized organizations by imposing a dramatic management reorganization that wiped out two layers of management. He found

EXHIBIT 1.5 Hierarchy of Objectives and Strategies

Ends (What is to be achieved?)	Means (How is it to be achieved?)	Strategic Decision Makers: Board of Directors	Corporate Managers	Business Managers	Functional Managers
Mission, including goals and philosophy		✓✓	✓✓	✓	
Long-term objectives	Grand strategy	✓	✓✓	✓✓	
Annual objectives	Short-term strategies and policies		✓	✓✓	✓✓

Note: ✓✓ indicate a principal responsibility; ✓ indicates a secondary responsibility.

that this effort not only reduced costs but also enabled him to be closer to the front-line operations managers. Corporate-level decisions are often characterized by greater risk, cost, and profit potential; greater need for flexibility; and longer time horizons. Such decisions include the choice of businesses, dividend policies, sources of long-term financing, and priorities for growth.

Functional-level decisions implement the overall strategy formulated at the corporate and business levels. They involve action-oriented operational issues and are relatively short range and low risk. Functional-level decisions incur only modest costs, because they depend on available resources. They usually are adaptable to ongoing activities and, therefore, can be implemented with minimal cooperation. For example, the corporate headquarters of Sears Holding Company spent $60 million to automate 6,900 clerical jobs by installing 28,000 computerized cash registers at its 868 stores in the United States. Although this move eliminated many functional-level jobs, top management believed that reducing annual operating expenses by at least $50 million was crucial to competitive survival.

Because functional-level decisions are relatively concrete and quantifiable, they receive critical attention and analysis even though their comparative profit potential is low. Common functional-level decisions include decisions on generic versus brand-name labeling, basic versus applied research and development (R&D), high versus low inventory levels, general-purpose versus specific-purpose production equipment, and close versus loose supervision.

Business-level decisions help bridge decisions at the corporate and functional levels. Such decisions are less costly, risky, and potentially profitable than corporate-level decisions, but they are more costly, risky, and potentially profitable than functional-level decisions. Common business-level decisions include decisions on plant location, marketing segmentation and geographic coverage, and distribution channels.

Formality in Strategic Management

formality
The degree to which participation, responsibility, authority, and discretion in decision making are specified in strategic management.

The formality of strategic management systems varies widely among companies. **Formality** refers to the degree to which participants, responsibilities, authority, and discretion in decision making are specified. It is an important consideration in the study of strategic management, because greater formality is usually positively correlated with the cost, comprehensiveness, accuracy, and success of planning.

A number of forces determine how much formality is needed in strategic management. The size of the organization, its predominant management styles, the complexity of its environment, its production process, its problems, and the purpose of its planning system all play a part in determining the appropriate degree of formality.

entrepreneurial mode
The informal, intuitive, and limited approach to strategic management associated with owner-managers of smaller firms.

planning mode
The strategic formality associated with large firms that operate under a comprehensive, formal planning system.

adaptive mode
The strategic formality associated with medium-sized firms that emphasize the incremental modification of existing competitive approaches.

In particular, formality is associated with the size of the firm and with its stage of development. Some firms, especially smaller ones, follow an **entrepreneurial mode.** They are basically under the control of a single individual, and they produce a limited number of products or services. In such firms, strategic evaluation is informal, intuitive, and limited. Very large firms, on the other hand, make strategic evaluation part of a comprehensive, formal planning system, an approach that is called the **planning mode.** A third approach, labelled the **adaptive mode,** is associated with medium-sized firms in relatively stable environments. For firms that follow the adaptive mode, the identification and evaluation of alternative strategies are closely related to existing strategy. It is not unusual to find different modes within the same organization. For example, ExxonMobil might follow an entrepreneurial mode in developing and evaluating the strategy of its solar subsidiary but follow a planning mode in the rest of the company.

The Strategy Makers

The ideal strategic management team includes decision makers from all three company levels (the corporate, business, and functional)—for example, the chief executive officer (CEO), the product managers, and the heads of functional areas. In addition, the team obtains input from company planning staffs, when they exist, and from lower-level managers and supervisors. The latter provide data for strategic decision making and then implement strategies.

Because strategic decisions have a tremendous impact on a company and require large commitments of company resources, top managers must give final approval for strategic action. Exhibit 1.5 aligns levels of strategic decision makers with the kinds of objectives and strategies for which they are typically responsible.

Planning departments, often headed by a corporate vice president for planning, are common in large corporations. Medium-sized firms often employ at least one full-time staff member to spearhead strategic data-collection efforts. Even in small firms or less progressive larger firms, strategic planning often is spearheaded by an officer or by a group of officers designated as a planning committee.

Precisely what are managers' responsibilities in the strategic planning process at the corporate and business levels? Top management shoulders broad responsibility for all the major elements of strategic planning and management. They develop the major portions of the strategic plan and reviews, and they evaluate and counsel on all other portions. General managers at the business level typically have principal responsibilities for developing environmental analysis and forecasting, establishing business objectives, and developing business plans prepared by staff groups.

A firm's president or CEO characteristically plays a dominant role in the strategic planning process. In many ways, this situation is desirable. The CEO's principal duty often is defined as giving long-term direction to the firm, and the CEO is ultimately responsible for the firm's success and, therefore, for the success of its strategy. In addition, CEOs are typically strong-willed, company-oriented individuals.

However, when the dominance of the CEO approaches autocracy, the effectiveness of the firm's strategic planning and management processes is likely to be diminished. For this reason, establishing a strategic management system implies that the CEO will allow managers at all levels to participate in the strategic posture of the company.

In implementing a company's strategy, the CEO must have an appreciation for the power and responsibility of the board, while retaining the power to lead the company with the guidance of informed directors. The interaction between the CEO and board is key to any corporation's strategy. Empowerment of nonmanagerial employees has been a recent trend across major management teams. For example, in 2003, IBM replaced its 92-year-old executive board structure with three newly created management teams: strategy, operations, and technology. Each team combined top executives, managers, and engineers going down six levels in some cases. This new team structure was responsible for guiding the creation of IBM's strategy and for helping to implement the strategies once they were authorized.

Benefits of Strategic Management

Using the strategic management approach, managers at all levels of the firm interact in planning and implementing. As a result, the behavioral consequences of strategic management are similar to those of participative decision making. Therefore, an accurate assessment of the impact of strategy formulation on organizational performance requires not only financial evaluation criteria but also nonfinancial evaluation criteria—measures of behavior-based effects. In fact, promoting positive behavioral consequences also enables the firm to achieve its financial goals. However, regardless of the profitability of strategic plans, several behavioral effects of strategic management improve the firm's welfare:

1. Strategy formulation activities enhance the firm's ability to prevent problems. Managers who encourage subordinates' attention to planning are aided in their monitoring and forecasting responsibilities by subordinates who are aware of the needs of strategic planning.
2. Group-based strategic decisions are likely to be drawn from the best available alternatives. The strategic management process results in better decisions because group interaction generates a greater variety of strategies and because forecasts based on the specialized perspectives of group members improve the screening of options.
3. The involvement of employees in strategy formulation improves their understanding of the productivity-reward relationship in every strategic plan and, thus, heightens their motivation.
4. Gaps and overlaps in activities among individuals and groups are reduced as participation in strategy formulation clarifies differences in roles.
5. Resistance to change is reduced. Though the participants in strategy formulation may be no more pleased with their own decisions than they would be with authoritarian decisions, their greater awareness of the parameters that limit the available options makes them more likely to accept those decisions.

THE STRATEGIC MANAGEMENT PROCESS

Businesses vary in the processes they use to formulate and direct their strategic management activities. Sophisticated planners, such as General Electric, Procter & Gamble, and IBM, have developed more detailed processes than less formal planners of similar size. Small businesses that rely on the strategy formulation skills and limited time of an entrepreneur typically exhibit more basic planning concerns than those of larger firms in their industries. Understandably, firms with multiple products, markets, or technologies tend to use more complex strategic management systems. However, despite differences in detail and the degree of formalization, the basic components of the models used to analyze strategic management operations are very similar.

Because of the similarity among the general models of the strategic management process, it is possible to develop an eclectic model representative of the foremost thought in the strategic management area. This model is shown in Exhibit 1.6. It serves three major functions: (1) It depicts the sequence and the relationships of the major components of the strategic management process. (2) It is the outline for this book. This chapter provides a general overview of the strategic management process, and the major components of the model will be the principal theme of subsequent chapters. Notice that the chapters of the text that discuss each of the strategic management process components are shown in each

EXHIBIT 1.6
Strategic Management Model

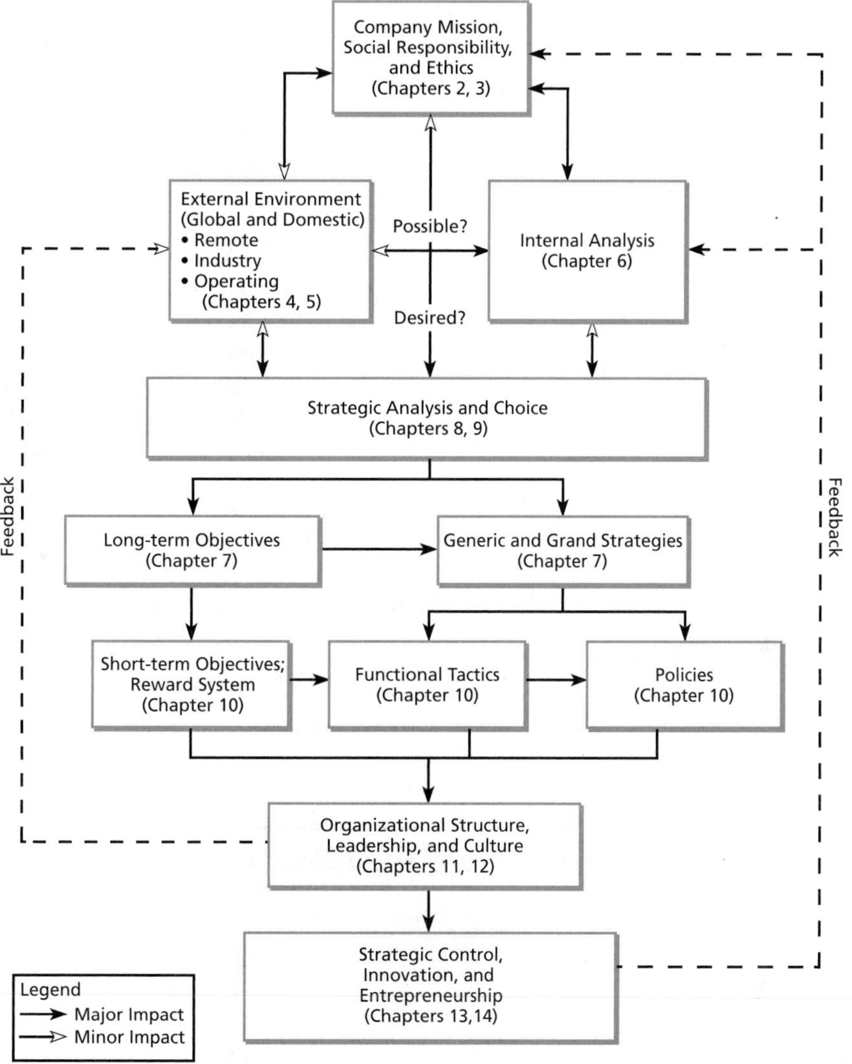

block. (3) The model offers one approach for analyzing the case studies in this text and thus helps the analyst develop strategy formulation skills.

Components of the Strategic Management Model

This section will define and briefly describe the key components of the strategic management model. Each of these components will receive much greater attention in a later chapter. The intention here is simply to introduce them.

Company Mission

company mission
The unique purpose that sets a company apart from others of its type and identifies the scope of its operations.

The mission of a company is the unique purpose that sets it apart from other companies of its type and identifies the scope of its operations. In short, the **company mission** describes the company's product, market, and technological areas of emphasis in a way that reflects the values and priorities of the strategic decision makers. For example, Lee Kun-Hee, the former chairman of the Samsung Group, revamped the company mission by stamping his own brand of management on Samsung. Immediately, Samsung separated Chonju Paper

Manufacturing and Shinsegae Department Store from other operations. This corporate act of downscaling reflected a revised management philosophy that favored specialization, thereby changing the direction and scope of the organization.

Social responsibility is a critical consideration for a company's strategic decision makers because the mission statement must express how the company intends to contribute to the societies that sustain it. A firm needs to set social responsibility aspirations for itself, just as it does in other areas of corporate performance.

Internal Analysis

The company analyzes the quantity and quality of the company's financial, human, and physical resources. It also assesses the strengths and weaknesses of the company's management and organizational structure. Finally, it contrasts the company's past successes and traditional concerns with the company's current capabilities in an attempt to identify the company's future capabilities.

External Environment

A firm's external environment consists of all the conditions and forces that affect its strategic options and define its competitive situation. The strategic management model shows the external environment as three interactive segments: the remote, industry, and operating environments.

Strategic Analysis and Choice

Simultaneous assessment of the external environment and the company profile enables a firm to identify a range of possibly attractive interactive opportunities. These opportunities are *possible* avenues for investment. However, they must be screened through the criterion of the company mission to generate a set of possible and *desired* opportunities. This screening process results in the selection of options from which a *strategic choice* is made. The process is meant to provide the combination of long-term objectives and generic and grand strategies that optimally position the firm in its external environment to achieve the company mission.

Strategic analysis and choice in single or dominant product/service businesses center around identifying strategies that are most effective at building sustainable competitive advantage based on key value chain activities and capabilities—core competencies of the firm. Multibusiness companies find their managers focused on the question of which combination of businesses maximizes shareholder value as the guiding theme during their strategic analysis and choice.

Long-Term Objectives

long-term objectives
The results that an organization seeks to achieve over a multiyear period.

The results that an organization seeks over a multiyear period are its **long-term objectives.** Such objectives typically involve some or all of the following areas: profitability, return on investment, competitive position, technological leadership, productivity, employee relations, public responsibility, and employee development.

Generic and Grand Strategies

generic strategies
Fundamental philosophical options for the design of strategies.

grand strategies
The means by which objectives are achieved.

Many businesses explicitly and all implicitly adopt one or more **generic strategies** characterizing their competitive orientation in the marketplace. Low cost, differentiation, or focus strategies define the three fundamental options. Enlightened managers seek to create ways their firm possesses both low cost and differentiation competitive advantages as part of their overall generic strategy. They usually combine these capabilities with a comprehensive, general plan of major actions through which their firm intends to achieve its long-term objectives in a dynamic environment. Called the **grand strategy,** this statement of means indicates how the objectives are to be achieved. Although every grand strategy is, in fact, a unique package of long-term strategies, 15 basic approaches can be identified: concentration,

Global Strategy in Action — Exhibit 1.7

Philips Healthcare: Keeping the Supply Chain Recession-Ready

Philips Healthcare (PHC), a leading supplier of diagnostic imaging systems and patient monitoring and cardiac devices, has implemented several supply chain practices to minimize the impact of recessions while maintaining high product quality.

"We use supplier-managed and -owned inventory programs that combine vendor-owned inventories and CPFR," says Steve Saunders, PHC's supply chain programs manager. "Philips shares its forecast information with its suppliers and provides visibility into its inventory and production schedules. We allow the suppliers to store supplier-owned inventory in a Philips warehouse. Philips takes ownership of the material only when it is pulled to the manufacturing line."

PHC also negotiates risk management contracts with suppliers to avoid having to make so many long-term, non-cancellable commitments. The company also actively monitors its suppliers' financial health. If the risks seem to be growing beyond what is acceptable, PHC is ready with risk mitigation plans such as alternate sourcing or temporary inventory increases. At the same time, the company runs a significant customer service organization that supports its installed base of equipment. This service business generally remains stable regardless of economic conditions.

The company also ensures that its cost structure is flexible. Explains Saunders: "We try to minimize fixed overhead and have a variable cost structure. While we still perform most final assembly and test, we procure virtually all major materials, such as circuit boards, plastics and sheet metal. In addition, we outsource a wide variety of supply chain support functions such as warehousing, security and building maintenance. And by using a contingent work force in most production operations, we have upside and downside flexibility as demand fluctuates."

Those approaches helped PHC expand sales 4–8 percent a year between 2005 and 2009, while earnings before interest, taxes, and amortization expenses have grown to more than 13 percent of revenue. In 2009, PHC commanded more than 22 percent of the global market for such healthcare equipment.

Source: Excerpted from Bruce Arntzen, "How to Recession-Proof Your Supply Chain," *Supply Chain Management Review* 13, no. 3 (April 2009), p. 12.

market development, product development, innovation, horizontal integration, vertical integration, joint venture, strategic alliances, consortia, concentric diversification, conglomerate diversification, turnaround, divestiture, bankruptcy, and liquidation.

Each of these grand strategies will be covered in detail in Chapter 7.

Short-Term Objectives

Short-term objectives are the desired results that a company seeks over a period of one year or less. They are logically consistent with the firm's long-term objectives. Companies typically have many **short-term objectives** to provide guidance for their functional and operational activities. Thus, there are short-term marketing activity, raw material usage, employee turnover, and sales objectives, to name just four.

short-term objectives
Desired results that provide specific guidance for action during a period of one year or less.

Action Plans

Action plans translate generic and grand strategies into "action" by incorporating four elements. First, they identify specific actions to be undertaken in the next year or less as part of the business's effort to build competitive advantage. Second, they establish a clear time frame for completion of each action. Third, action plans create accountability by identifying who is responsible for each "action" in the plan. Fourth, each "action" has one or more specific, immediate objectives that the action should achieve. Philips Healthcare describes its action plans for its supply chain in the event of a recession in Exhibit 1.7, Global Strategy in Action.

Functional Tactics

Within the general framework created by the business's generic and grand strategies, each business function needs to undertake activities that help build a sustainable competitive

functional tactics
Short-term, narrow scoped plans that detail the "means" or activities that a company will use to achieve short-term objectives.

advantage. These short-term, limited-scope plans are called **functional tactics.** A radio ad campaign, an inventory reduction, and an introductory loan rate are examples of tactics. Managers in each business function develop tactics that delineate the functional activities undertaken in their part of the business and usually include them as a core part of their action plan. Functional tactics are detailed statements of the "means" or activities that will be used to achieve short-term objectives and establish competitive advantage.

Policies That Empower Action

policies
Predetermined decisions that substitute for managerial discretion in repetitive decision making.

Speed is a critical necessity for success in today's competitive, global marketplace. One way to enhance speed and responsiveness is to force/allow decisions to be made whenever possible at the lowest level in organizations. **Policies** are broad, precedent-setting decisions that guide or substitute for repetitive or time-sensitive managerial decision making. Creating policies that guide and "preauthorize" the thinking, decisions, and actions of operating managers and their subordinates in implementing the business's strategy is essential for establishing and controlling the ongoing operating process of the firm in a manner consistent with the firm's strategic objectives. Policies often increase managerial effectiveness by standardizing routine decisions and empowering or expanding the discretion of managers and subordinates in implementing business strategies.

The following are examples of the nature and diversity of company policies:

A requirement that managers have purchase requests for items costing more than $5,000 cosigned by the controller.

The minimum equity position required for all new McDonald's franchises.

The standard formula used to calculate return on investment for the six strategic business units of General Electric.

A decision that Sears service and repair employees have the right to waive repair charges to appliance customers they feel have been poorly served by their Sears appliance.

Restructuring, Reengineering, and Refocusing the Organization

Until this point in the strategic management process, managers have maintained a decidedly market-oriented focus as they formulate strategies and begin implementation through action plans and functional tactics. Now the process takes an internal focus—getting the work of the business done efficiently and effectively so as to make the strategy successful. What is the best way to organize ourselves to accomplish the mission? Where should leadership come from? What values should guide our daily activities—what should the organization and its people be like? How can we shape rewards to encourage appropriate action? The intense competition in the global marketplace has made this traditionally "internally focused" set of questions—how the activities within their business are conducted—recast themselves with unprecedented attentiveness to the marketplace. *Downsizing, restructuring,* and *reengineering* are terms that reflect the critical stage in strategy implementation wherein managers attempt to recast their organization. The company's structure, leadership, culture, and reward systems may all be changed to ensure cost competitiveness and quality demanded by unique requirements of its strategies.

The elements of the strategic management process are evident in the recent activities at Ford Motor Company. In 2008, Ford undertook to create a strategy to lower costs, increase efficiency, improve designs, and increase brand appeal. These improvements were needed to keep cash flows up to cover rising pension costs. For Ford to accomplish this new strategy it had to improve operations. New executives were brought in to lead product development and financial controls. To break down the bureaucratic boundaries, a committee was created that included employees from the major functional areas, and it was given the assignment to reduce the time needed to develop a new-concept vehicle.

Strategic Control and Continuous Improvement

strategic control
Tracking a strategy as it is being implemented, detecting problems or changes in its underlying premises, and making necessary adjustments.

continuous improvement
A form of strategic control in which managers are encouraged to be proactive in improving all operations of the firm.

Strategic control is concerned with tracking a strategy as it is being implemented, detecting problems or changes in its underlying premises, and making necessary adjustments. In contrast to postaction control, strategic control seeks to guide action on behalf of the generic and grand strategies as they are taking place and when the end results are still several years away. The rapid, accelerating change of the global marketplace of the last 10 years has made continuous improvement another aspect of strategic control in many organizations. **Continuous improvement** provides a way for managers to provide a form of strategic control that allows their organization to respond more proactively and timely to rapid developments in hundreds of areas that influence a business's success.

Continuous improvement includes preparing for contingencies. An extended period of economic decline brought on by a recession is an example. Exhibit 1.8, Strategy in Action provides guidelines for improvements that a company can make on an ongoing basis to recession-proof its supply chain.

In 2003, Yahoo!'s strategy was to move into the broadband and Internet search markets. However, even in its early implementation stages the strategy required revisions. Yahoo! had formed an alliance with SBC to provide the broadband service, but SBC had such limited capabilities that Yahoo! had to find new ways to reach users. Yahoo! also needed to continuously improve its new Internet search market, given competitors' upgrades and rapidly rising customer expectations. Additionally, for Yahoo! to increase its market share, it needed to continually improve its branding, rather than rely largely on its technological capabilities.

Strategic Management as a Process

process
The flow of information through interrelated stages of analysis toward the achievement of an aim.

stakeholders
Influential people who are vitally interested in the actions of the business.

A **process** is the flow of information through interrelated stages of analysis toward the achievement of an aim. Thus, the strategic management model in Exhibit 1.6 depicts a process. In the strategic management process, the flow of information involves historical, current, and forecast data on the operations and environment of the business. Managers evaluate these data in light of the values and priorities of influential individuals and groups—often called **stakeholders**—that are vitally interested in the actions of the business. The interrelated stages of the process are the 11 components discussed in the previous section. Finally, the aim of the process is the formulation and implementation of strategies that work, achieving the company's long-term mission and near-term objectives.

Viewing strategic management as a process has several important implications. First, a change in any component will affect several or all of the other components. Most of the arrows in the model point two ways, suggesting that the flow of information usually is reciprocal. For example, forces in the external environment may influence the nature of a company's mission, and the company may in turn affect the external environment and heighten competition in its realm of operation. A specific example is a power company that is persuaded, in part by governmental incentives, to include a commitment to the development of energy alternatives in its mission statement. The company then might promise to extend its research and development (R&D) efforts in the area of coal liquefaction. The external environment has affected the company's mission, and the revised mission signals a competitive condition in the environment.

A second implication of viewing strategic management as a process is that strategy formulation and implementation are sequential. The process begins with development or reevaluation of the company mission. This step is associated with, but essentially followed

Strategy in Action **Exhibit 1.8**

Continuous Improvement to Recession-Proof Your Supply Chain

When a recession hits, customers can reduce your revenues and stop your outbound product flow faster than you can trim expenses and halt your inbound flow of raw materials. Working capital becomes stressed as your materials pipeline backs up and profits take a hit. To reduce the severity of these problems, here are six steps to take to improve operations in preparation for a downturn.

CHALLENGE 1: CUSTOMERS CANCEL ORDERS AND FINISHED GOODS INVENTORY BUILDS UP

Build a robust CPFR program. A healthy, ongoing CPFR program will encourage customers to discuss their plans with you, collaborate on risk-taking and work with you during the hard times.

Forge risk-aware contracts with customers. Too often in expansionary times, managers don't imagine how contentious material supply contracts can become if the customer stops buying. All contracts with customers should spell out very clearly what will happen to the material flow and cash flow if their forecasts turn out to be significantly in error.

Use demand-driven, lean manufacturing. By using build-to-order and "pull" manufacturing techniques with small lot sizes and just-in-time (JIT) replenishment, it is much easier to prevent supply from overshooting demand.

CHALLENGE 2: CUSTOMERS SLOW DOWN BILL PAYMENT, STRETCH OUT PAYABLES

Don't give away terms blithely. Control the sales teams' ability to give away terms. Whatever terms you do give will likely be stretched out during a recession. Focusing management on the cash-to-cash cycle time is a great way to call attention to the terms issue. After all, a dollar of accounts receivable counts as much toward working capital as a dollar of inventory.

Provide payment options through financing. It's smart to persuade customers to agree to attractive flexible financing and payment options during good times so a formal financing mechanism is in place when recession hits. The financing arms of organizations such as GMAC and GE Capital offer an array of payment options. The customer can choose the number of months to pay off the purchase and must agree to the interest rate. Later, if money is tight, they cannot unilaterally stretch payments, as they could during a "conventional" sale transaction.

CHALLENGE 3: RAW INVENTORY BUILDS UP AS MATERIAL KEEPS ARRIVING

Rely on VOI or VMI. The best situation, if you can do it, is to set up nearby stocking with vendor-owned (VOI) or vendor-managed (VMI) inventory programs that provide JIT delivery to your site.

Place cancellable orders. All contracts need to have a reasonable "way out," yet many do not. Standard contracts are almost always heavily biased in favor of the large company and provide no risk-sharing and no reasonable exit for the smaller partner.

by, development of a company profile and assessment of the external environment. Then follow, in order, strategic choice, definition of long-term objectives, design of the grand strategy, definition of short-term objectives, design of operating strategies, institutionalization of the strategy, and review and evaluation.

The apparent rigidity of the process, however, must be qualified.

First, a firm's strategic posture may have to be reevaluated in response to changes in any of the principal factors that determine or affect its performance. Entry by a major new competitor, the death of a prominent board member, replacement of the chief executive officer, and a downturn in market responsiveness are among the thousands of changes that can prompt reassessment of a firm's strategic plan. However, no matter where the need for a reassessment originates, the strategic management process begins with the mission statement.

Second, not every component of the strategic management process deserves equal attention each time planning activity takes place. Firms in an extremely stable environment may find that an in-depth assessment is not required every year. Companies often are satisfied with their original mission statements even after a decade of operation and spend only a minimal amount of time addressing this subject.

Establish CPFR systems with your suppliers. Giving suppliers as much forewarning as possible helps them react faster to your need to stem the inbound flow of raw materials.

CHALLENGE 4: PARTS SHORTAGES BECOME CRITICAL WHEN A SUPPLIER COLLAPSES

A detailed review of the supplier's financial health should be part of the quarterly business analysis discussed with each supplier. You can further reduce the risk of supply-chain disruption by using more industry-standard parts, thereby making it easier to find alternate sources.

Keep extra inventory on hand. In a push to create lean supply chains, many companies depend on rapid resupply from suppliers. But recessions make even dependable suppliers undependable, and parts we take for granted in good times may become critical-path if supplies are interrupted. Keeping some extra inventory of critical parts is a smart insurance policy.

CHALLENGE 5: DIRECT LABOR SPENDING STAYS HIGH

Move to a variable cost structure. Outsource operations based on a cost per piece. This approach could be used, for example, with contract manufacturing, common carriers, third-party logistics providers, and contract repair centers. Many of these providers are much more practiced at ramping up and down and shifting resources around than are typical large OEMs.

Deploy a more flexible workforce. Rethink your labor resources so they can more easily scale up and down based on need. Arrange this flexibility with workers during good times when the issue is less contentious so it will be in place when you need it.

CHALLENGE 6: OVERHEAD SPENDING STAYS HIGH

Implement a variable cost structure. Employees with flexible hours will enjoy overtime during good years and provide cost relief during lean years. In addition, call centers and a host of back-office functions can be outsourced as variable costs.

Install firm purchasing controls. Central control of spending and approved supplier lists are needed to enforce policies consistently to modulate spending in hard times. Employees must be required to get spending approved by someone accountable for the budget.

Source: Excerpted from Bruce Arntzen, "How to Recession-Proof Your Supply Chain," *Supply Chain Management Review* 13, no. 3 (April 2009), p. 12. http://proquest.umi.com/pqdweb?did=1737280001&Fmt=3&clientId=3260&RQT=309&VName=PQD

feedback
The analysis of postimplementation results that can be used to enhance future decision making.

dynamic
The term that characterizes the constantly changing conditions that affect interrelated and interdependent strategic activities.

A third implication of viewing strategic management as a process is the necessity of feedback from institutionalization, review, and evaluation to the early stages of the process. **Feedback** can be defined as the analysis of postimplementation results that can be used to enhance future decision making. Therefore, as indicated in Exhibit 1.6, strategic managers should assess the impact of implemented strategies on external environments. Thus, future planning can reflect any changes precipitated by strategic actions. Strategic managers also should analyze the impact of strategies on the possible need for modifications in the company mission.

A fourth implication of viewing strategic management as a process is the need to regard it as a dynamic system. The term **dynamic** characterizes the constantly changing conditions that affect interrelated and interdependent strategic activities. Managers should recognize that the components of the strategic process are constantly evolving but that formal planning artificially freezes those components, much as an action photograph freezes the movement of a swimmer. Since change is continuous, the dynamic strategic planning process must be monitored constantly for significant shifts in any of its components as a precaution against implementing an obsolete strategy. An example of the potentially devastating consequences of such dynamism is seen in the failure of the merger between AOL and Time Warner, as described in Exhibit 1.9, Strategy in Action.

Strategy in Action — Exhibit 1.9

Strategic Blunder: The Merger of AOL and Time Warner

On February 11, 2000, Internet portal America Online, then valued at $108 billion, swallowed media stalwart Time Warner, worth $111 billion, for $164 billion in an all-stock deal. AOL owned 55 percent of the new, combined company; Time Warner, 45 percent. The tech wreck of 2001, followed by the rise of stiff competitors Yahoo! and Google, changed the competitive dynamics. As cultures clashed and the stock price tanked, the company in 2002 reported a one-time write-off of $99 billion—at the time, the largest corporate loss ever reported. At its nadir, the firm boasted a meager market cap of $48 billion—$171 billion less than at the time of the merger. Time Warner was worth only $53 billion in 2008. Size of Blunder: $196 billion.

Source: Excerpted from Melanie Lindner, "The 10 Biggest Blunders Ever in Business," *Forbes,* March 25, 2008, http://www.msnbc.msn.com/id/23677510/

Summary

Strategic management is the set of decisions and actions that result in the formulation and implementation of plans designed to achieve a company's objectives. Because it involves long-term, future-oriented, complex decision making and requires considerable resources, top-management participation is essential.

Strategic management is a three-tier process involving corporate-, business-, and functional-level planners, and support personnel. At each progressively lower level, strategic activities were shown to be more specific, narrow, short-term, and action oriented, with lower risks but fewer opportunities for dramatic impact.

The strategic management model presented in this chapter will serve as the structure for understanding and integrating all the major phases of strategy formulation and implementation. The chapter provided a summary account of these phases, each of which is given extensive individual attention in subsequent chapters.

The chapter stressed that the strategic management process centers on the belief that a firm's mission can be best achieved through a systematic and comprehensive assessment of both its internal capabilities and its external environment. Subsequent evaluation of the firm's opportunities leads, in turn, to the choice of long-term objectives and grand strategies and, ultimately, to annual objectives and operating strategies, which must be implemented, monitored, and controlled.

Key Terms

adaptive mode, *p.* 9
company mission, *p.* 11
continuous improvement, *p.* 15
dynamic, *p.* 17
entrepreneurial mode, *p.* 9
feedback, *p.* 17
formality, *p.* 8
functional tactics, *p.* 14
generic strategies, *p.* 12
grand strategies, *p.* 12
long-term objectives, *p.* 12
planning mode, *p.* 9
policies, *p.* 14
process, *p.* 15
short-term objectives, *p.* 13
stakeholders, *p.* 15
strategic control, *p.* 15
strategic management, *p.* 3
strategy, *p.* 4

Questions for Discussion

1. Read an article in the business press about a major action taken by a corporation. Be prepared to briefly describe this action to your professor and to name the key strategic management terms that the author used in the article.
2. In what ways do you think the subject matter in this strategic management–business policy course will differ from that of previous courses you have taken?

3. After graduation, you are not likely to move directly to a top-level management position. In fact, few members of your class will ever reach the top-management level. Why, then, is it important for all business majors to study the field of strategic management?
4. Do you expect outstanding performance in this course to require a great deal of memorization? Why or why not?
5. You undoubtedly have read about individuals who seemingly have given single-handed direction to their corporations. Is a participative strategic management approach likely to stifle or suppress the contributions of such individuals?
6. Think about the courses you have taken in functional areas, such as marketing, finance, production, personnel, and accounting. What is the importance of each of these areas to the strategic planning process?
7. Discuss with practicing business managers the strategic management models used in their firms. What are the similarities and differences between these models and the one in the text?
8. In what ways do you believe the strategic planning approach of not-for-profit organizations would differ from that of profit-oriented organizations?
9. How do you explain the success of firms that do not use a formal strategic planning process?
10. Think about your postgraduation job search as a strategic decision. How would the strategic management model be helpful to you in identifying and securing the most promising position?

Part **Two**

Strategy Formulation

Strategy formulation guides executives in defining the business their firm is in, the ends it seeks, and the means it will use to accomplish those ends. The approach of strategy formulation is an improvement over that of traditional long-range planning. As discussed in the next eight chapters—about developing a firm's competitive plan of action—strategy formulation combines a future-oriented perspective with concern for the firm's internal and external environments.

The strategy formulation process begins with definition of the company mission, as discussed in Chapter 2, which defines the purpose of its business and values. In Chapter 3 social responsibility is discussed as a critical consideration for a company's strategic decision makers because the mission statement must express how the company intends to contribute to the societies that sustain it. Central to the idea that companies should be operated in socially responsible ways is the belief that managers will behave in an ethical manner. Management ethics are discussed in this chapter with special attention to the utilitarian, moral rights, and social justice approaches.

Chapter 4 deals with the principal factors in a firm's external environment that strategic managers must assess so they can anticipate and take advantage of future business conditions. It emphasizes the importance to a firm's planning activities of factors in the firm's remote, industry, and operating environments.

Chapter 5 describes the key differences in strategic planning among domestic, multinational, and global firms. It gives special attention to the new vision that a firm must communicate when it multinationalizes.

Chapter 6 shows how firms evaluate their company's strengths and weaknesses to produce an internal analysis. Strategic managers use such profiles to target competitive advantages they can emphasize and competitive disadvantages they should correct or minimize.

Chapter 7 examines the types of long-range objectives strategic managers set and specifies the qualities these objectives must have to provide a basis for direction and evaluation. The chapter also examines the generic and grand strategies that firms use to achieve long-range objectives.

Comprehensive approaches to the evaluation of strategic opportunities and to the final strategic decision are the focus of Chapter 8. The chapter shows how a firm's strategic options can be compared in a way that allows selection of the best available option. It also discusses how a company can create competitive advantages for each of its businesses.

Chapter 9 extends the attention on strategic analysis and choice by showing how managers can build value in multibusiness companies.

Chapter Two

Company Mission

After reading and studying this chapter, you should be able to

1. Describe a company mission and explain its value.
2. Explain why it is important for the mission statement to include the company's basic product or service, its primary markets, and its principal technology.
3. Explain which goal of a company is most important: survival, profitability, or growth.
4. Discuss the importance of company philosophy, public image, and company self-concept to stockholders.
5. Give examples of the newest trends in mission statement components: customer emphasis, quality, and company vision.
6. Describe the role of a company's board of directors.
7. Explain agency theory and its value in helping a board of directors improve corporate governance.

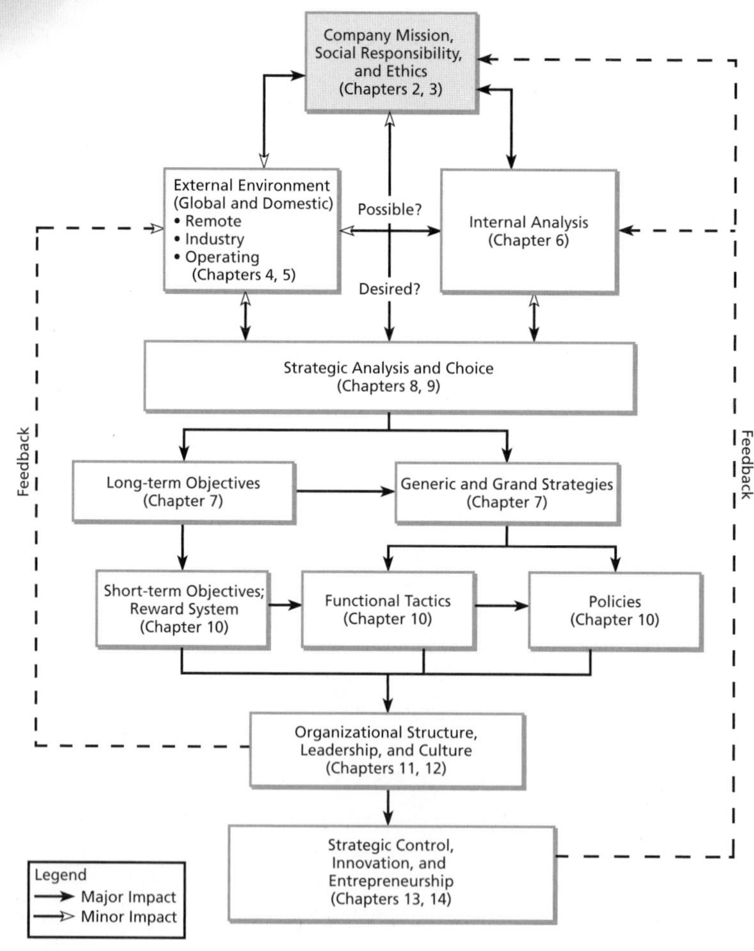

Strategy in Action — Exhibit 2.1

Mission Statement of Nicor Inc.

PREAMBLE

We, the management of Nicor Inc., here set forth our belief as to the purpose for which the company is established and the principles under which it should operate. We pledge our effort to the accomplishment of these purposes within these principles.

BASIC PURPOSE

The basic purpose of Nicor Inc. is to perpetuate an investor-owned company engaging in various phases of the energy business, striving for balance among those phases so as to render needed satisfactory products and services and earn optimum, long-range profits.

WHAT WE DO

The principal business of the company, through its utility subsidiary, is the provision of energy through a pipe system to meet the needs of ultimate consumers. To accomplish its basic purpose, and to ensure its strength, the company will engage in other energy-related activities, directly or through subsidiaries or in participation with other persons, corporations, firms, or entities.

All activities of the company shall be consistent with its responsibilities to investors, customers, employees, and the public and its concern for the optimum development and utilization of natural resources and for environmental needs.

WHERE WE DO IT

The company's operations shall be primarily in the United States, but no self-imposed or regulatory geographical limitations are placed upon the acquisition, development, processing, transportation, or storage of energy resources, or upon other energy-related ventures in which the company may engage. The company will engage in such activities in any location where, after careful review, it has determined that such activity is in the best interest of its stockholders.

Utility service will be offered in the territory of the company's utility subsidiary to the best of its ability, in accordance with the requirements of regulatory agencies and pursuant to the subsidiary's purposes and principles.

Source: Nicor Inc., http://www.nicor.com/

WHAT IS A COMPANY MISSION?

company mission
The unique purpose that sets a company apart from others of its type and identifies the scope of its operations in product, market, and technology terms.

Whether a firm is developing a new business or reformulating direction for an ongoing business, it must determine the basic goals and philosophies that will shape its strategic posture. This fundamental purpose that sets a firm apart from other firms of its type and identifies the scope of its operations in product and market terms is defined as the company mission. As discussed in Chapter 1, the **company mission** is a broadly framed but enduring statement of a firm's intent. It embodies the business philosophy of the firm's strategic decision makers, implies the image the firm seeks to project, reflects the firm's self-concept, and indicates the firm's principal product or service areas and the primary customer needs the firm will attempt to satisfy. In short, it describes the firm's product, market, and technological areas of emphasis, and it does so in a way that reflects the values and priorities of the firm's strategic decision makers. An excellent example is the company mission statement of Nicor Inc., shown in Exhibit 2.1, Strategy in Action.

The Need for an Explicit Mission

No external body requires that the company mission be defined, and the process of defining it is time-consuming and tedious. Moreover, it contains broadly outlined or implied objectives and strategies rather than specific directives. Characteristically, it is a statement, not of measurable targets but of attitude, outlook, and orientation.

The mission statement is a message designed to be inclusive of the expectations of all stakeholders for the company's performance over the long run. The executives and board who prepare the mission statement attempt to provide a unifying purpose for the company that will provide a basis for strategic objective setting and decision making. In general terms, the mission statement addresses the following questions:

Why is this firm in business?

What are our economic goals?

What is our operating philosophy in terms of quality, company image, and self-concept?

What are our core competencies and competitive advantages?

What customers do and can we serve?

How do we view our responsibilities to stockholders, employees, communities, environment, social issues, and competitors?

FORMULATING A MISSION

The process of defining the company mission for a specific business can perhaps be best understood by thinking about the business at its inception. The typical business begins with the beliefs, desires, and aspirations of a single entrepreneur. Such an owner-manager's sense of mission usually is based on the following fundamental beliefs:

1. The product or service of the business can provide benefits at least equal to its price.
2. The product or service can satisfy a customer need of specific market segments that is currently not being met adequately.
3. The technology that is to be used in production will provide a cost- and quality-competitive product or service.
4. With hard work and the support of others, the business can not only survive but also grow and be profitable.
5. The management philosophy of the business will result in a favorable public image and will provide financial and psychological rewards for those who are willing to invest their labor and money in helping the business to succeed.
6. The entrepreneur's self-concept of the business can be communicated to and adopted by employees and stockholders.

As the business grows or is forced by competitive pressures to alter its product, market, or technology, redefining the company mission may be necessary. If so, the revised mission statement will contain the same components as the original. It will state the basic type of product or service to be offered, the primary markets or customer groups to be served; the technology to be used in production or delivery; the firm's fundamental concern for survival through growth and profitability; the firm's managerial philosophy; the public image the firm seeks; and the self-concept those affiliated with the firm should have of it. This chapter will discuss in detail these components. The examples shown in Exhibit 2.2, Strategy in Action, provide insights into how some major corporations handle them.

Basic Product or Service: Primary Market; Principal Technology

Three indispensable components of the mission statement are specification of the basic product or service, specification of the primary market, and specification of the principal technology for production or delivery. These components are discussed under one heading because only in combination do they describe the company's business activity. A good example of the three components is to be found in the business plan of ITT Barton,

Strategy in Action — Exhibit 2.2

Identifying Mission Statement Components: A Compilation of Excerpts from Actual Corporate Mission Statements

1. Customer-market	We believe our first responsibility is to the doctors, nurses, and patients, to mothers and all others who use our products and services. (Johnson & Johnson) To anticipate and meet market needs of farmers, ranchers, and rural communities within North America. (CENEX)
2. Product-service	AMAX's principal products are molybdenum, coal, iron ore, copper, lead, zinc, petroleum and natural gas, potash, phosphates, nickel, tungsten, silver, gold, and magnesium. (AMAX)
3. Geographic domain	We are dedicated to total success of Corning Glass Works as a worldwide competitor. (Corning Glass)
4. Technology	Control Data is in the business of applying microelectronics and computer technology in two general areas: computer-related hardware and computing-enhancing services, which include computation, information, education, and finance. (Control Data) The common technology in these areas relates to discrete particle coatings. (NASHUA)
5. Concern for survival	In this respect, the company will conduct its operation prudently, and will provide the profits and growth which will assure Hoover's ultimate success. (Hoover Universal)
6. Philosophy	We are committed to improve health care throughout the world. (Baxter Travenol) We believe human development to be the worthiest of the goals of civilization and independence to be the superior condition for nurturing growth in the capabilities of people. (Sun Company)
7. Self-concept	Hoover Universal is a diversified, multi-industry corporation with strong manufacturing capabilities, entrepreneurial policies, and individual business unit autonomy. (Hoover Universal)
8. Concern for public image	We are responsible to the communities in which we live and work and to the world community as well. (Johnson & Johnson) Also, we must be responsive to the broader concerns of the public, including especially the general desire for improvement in the quality of life, equal opportunity for all, and the constructive use of natural resources. (Sun Company)

a division of ITT. Under the heading of business mission and area served, the following information is presented:

> The unit's mission is to serve industry and government with quality instruments used for the primary measurement, analysis, and local control of fluid flow, level, pressure, temperature, and fluid properties. This instrumentation includes flow meters, electronic readouts, indicators, recorders, switches, liquid level systems, analytical instruments such as titrators, integrators, controllers, transmitters, and various instruments for the measurement of fluid properties (density, viscosity, gravity) used for processing variable sensing, data collecting, control, and transmission. The unit's mission includes fundamental loop-closing control and display devices, when economically justified, but excludes broadline central control room instrumentation, systems design, and turnkey responsibility.
>
> Markets served include instrumentation for oil and gas production, gas transportation, chemical and petrochemical processing, cryogenics, power generation, aerospace, government, and marine, as well as other instrument and equipment manufacturers.

In only 129 words, this segment of the mission statement clearly indicates to all readers—from company employees to casual observers—the basic products, primary markets, and principal technologies of ITT Barton.

Often the most referenced public statement of a company's selected products and markets appears in "silver bullet" form in the mission statement; for example, "Dayton-Hudson Corporation is a diversified retailing company whose business is to serve the American consumer through the retailing of fashion-oriented quality merchandise." Such an abstract of company direction is particularly helpful to outsiders who value condensed overviews.

Company Goals: Survival; Growth; Profitability

Three economic goals guide the strategic direction of almost every business organization. Whether or not the mission statement explicitly states these goals, it reflects the firm's intention to secure *survival* through *growth* and *profitability*.

A firm that is unable to survive will be incapable of satisfying the aims of any of its stakeholders. Unfortunately, the goal of survival, like the goals of growth and profitability, often is taken for granted to such an extent that it is neglected as a principal criterion in strategic decision making. When this happens, the firm may focus on short-term aims at the expense of the long run. Concerns for expediency, a quick fix, or a bargain may displace the assessment of long-term impact. Too often, the result is near-term economic failure owing to a lack of resource synergy and sound business practice. For example, Consolidated Foods, maker of Shasta soft drinks and L'eggs hosiery, sought growth through the acquisition of bargain businesses. However, the erratic sales patterns of its diverse holdings forced it to divest itself of more than four dozen companies. This process cost Consolidated Foods millions of dollars and hampered its growth.

Profitability is the mainstay goal of a business organization. No matter how profit is measured or defined, profit over the long term is the clearest indication of a firm's ability to satisfy the principal claims and desires of employees and stockholders. The key phrase here is "over the long term." Obviously, basing decisions on a short-term concern for profitability would lead to a strategic myopia. Overlooking the enduring concerns of customers, suppliers, creditors, ecologists, and regulatory agents may produce profit in the short term, but, over time, the financial consequences are likely to be detrimental.

The following excerpt from the Hewlett-Packard statement of mission ably expresses the importance of an orientation toward long-term profit:

> To achieve sufficient profit to finance our company growth and to provide the resources we need to achieve our other corporate objectives.
>
> In our economic system, the profit we generate from our operation is the ultimate source of the funds we need to prosper and grow. It is the one absolutely essential measure of our corporate performance over the long term. Only if we continue to meet our profit objective can we achieve our other corporate objectives.

A firm's growth is tied inextricably to its survival and profitability. In this context, the meaning of growth must be broadly defined. Although product impact market studies (PIMS) have shown that growth in market share is correlated with profitability, other important forms of growth do exist. Growth in the number of markets served, in the variety of products offered, and in the technologies that are used to provide goods or services frequently lead to improvements in a firm's competitive ability. Growth means change, and proactive change is essential in a dynamic business environment.

AOL's strategy provides an example. In 2003, some analysts believed that AOL Time Warner should change to a survival strategy because of the amount of debt that it was carrying. They believed that AOL should try to reduce debt and regain some market share that it had lost over the previous year. AOL did decide to reduce its $7 billion debt by the end of 2004, but not simply to survive. AOL was trying to position itself for the acquisition of either Adelphia or Cablevision. AOL felt that if it could acquire one of these two companies or possibly both, it could increase its footprint in the market. AOL believed that growth for its company would have to come from the cable TV market and that the only way to grow was to serve more markets. Luckily, AOL's top competitor, Comcast, was in the same debt position as AOL and could not immediately preempt the acquisitions.

Hewlett-Packard's mission statement provides another excellent example of corporate regard for growth:

> Objective: To let our growth be limited only by our profits and our ability to develop and produce technical products that satisfy real customer needs.
>
> We do not believe that large size is important for its own sake; however, for at least two basic reasons, continuous growth is essential for us to achieve our other objectives.
>
> In the first place, we serve a rapidly growing and expanding segment of our technological society. To remain static would be to lose ground. We cannot maintain a position of strength and leadership in our field without growth.
>
> In the second place, growth is important in order to attract and hold high-caliber people. These individuals will align their future only with a company that offers them considerable opportunity for personal progress. Opportunities are greater and more challenging in a growing company.

The issue of growth raises a concern about the definition of the company mission. How can a firm's product, market, and technology be specified sufficiently to provide direction without precluding the exercise of unanticipated strategic options? How can a firm so define its mission that it can consider opportunistic diversification while maintaining the parameters that guide its growth decision? Perhaps such questions are best addressed when a firm's mission statement outlines the conditions under which the firm might depart from ongoing operations. General Electric Company's extensive global mission provided the foundation for its GE Appliances (GEA) in Louisville, Kentucky. GEA did not see consumer preferences in the world market becoming Americanized. Instead, its expansion goals allowed for flexibility in examining the unique characteristics of individual foreign markets and tailoring strategies to fit them.

The growth philosophy of Dayton-Hudson also embodies this approach:

> The stability and quality of the corporation's financial performance will be developed through the profitable execution of our existing businesses, as well as through the acquisition or development of new businesses. Our growth priorities, in order, are as follows:
>
> 1. Development of the profitable market preeminence of existing companies in existing markets through new store development or new strategies within existing stores.
> 2. Expansion of our companies to feasible new markets.
> 3. Acquisition of other retailing companies that are strategically and financially compatible with Dayton-Hudson.
> 4. Internal development of new retailing strategies.
>
> Capital allocations to fund the expansion of existing Dayton-Hudson operating companies will be based on each company's return on investment (ROI), in relationship to its ROI objective and its consistency in earnings growth and on the ability of its management to perform up to the forecasts contained in its capital requests. Expansion via acquisition or new venture will occur when the opportunity promises an acceptable rate of long-term growth and profitability, an acceptable degree of risk, and compatibility with Dayton-Hudson's long-term strategy.

Company Philosophy

company creed
A company's statement of its philosophy.

The statement of a company's philosophy, often called the **company creed,** usually accompanies or appears within the mission statement. It reflects or specifies the basic beliefs, values, aspirations, and philosophical priorities to which strategic decision makers are committed in managing the company. Fortunately, the philosophies vary little from one firm to another. Owners and managers implicitly accept a general, unwritten, yet pervasive code of behavior

Global Strategy in Action — Exhibit 2.3

Cadbury Position on Sustainability

Cadbury PLC is a leading global confectionery company with a portfolio of chocolate, gum and candy brands. It has number one or number two positions in over 20 of the world's 50 largest confectionery markets. Cadbury also has the largest and most broadly spread emerging markets business of any confectionery company. Cadbury's brands include Cadbury, Creme Egg, Flake, and Green & Black's in chocolate; Trident, Clorets, Dentyne, Hollywood, Bubbaloo, and Stimorol in gum; and Halls, Cadbury Eclairs, and The Natural Confectionery Company in candy.

Cadbury's new approach to CSR includes:

- Sustainability is fully integrated into the Cadbury business strategy
- Clear roadmaps and goals established in the form of Sustainability Commitments
- Creation of new significant, leading edge programmes in "Purple Goes Green" and the "Cadbury Cocoa Partnership"
- Specific training in sustainable business practices for colleagues and key suppliers

ENVIRONMENT

Cadbury's revolutionary "Purple Goes Green" programme sets aggressive environmental targets for 2020. Cadbury is the only food manufacturer to commit to a 50% absolute reduction in carbon emissions. The company has also set targets for packaging and water-use reduction.

CADBURY COCOA PARTNERSHIP

Cocoa is a key crop for Cadbury and in the centenary year of sourcing cocoa beans from Ghana the company has committed to invest over £45 million over 10 years into the Cadbury Cocoa Partnership.

ENJOYING CONFECTIONERY RESPONSIBLY

Cadbury leads wellbeing competitors in the confectionary category. In 2007, 30% of net sales revenues came from wellbeing confectionery compared with a market average of 18%. And sugar-free gum accounts for 70% of their gum sales globally.

INDEPENDENT REVIEW

Cadbury continues to submit data on progress on the company's goals and commitments to key third parties for review and scrutiny. This includes:

- The Dow Jones Sustainability Index—in 2008 Cadbury received a score of 75%, the highest ever score for the company and against an industry average of 48%
- The Carbon Disclosure Project—in 2008 Cadbury performance was rated as "best in class" and the company has been reporting since launch of the project in 2003
- FTSE4Good—Cadbury has been submitting data to the index since its launch in 2001

Source: Excerpted from "Cadbury Reconfirms Leadership Position on Sustainability," November 6, 2008. http://www.csrwire.com/press_releases/13807

that governs business actions and permits them to be largely self-regulated. Unfortunately, statements of company philosophy are often so similar and so platitudinous that they read more like public relations handouts than the commitment to values they are meant to be.

Encouragingly there are an increasing number of exceptions. Cadbury PLC, a leading global confectionery company, provides an example of a company that is working hard to communicate its commitment to sustainability. As shown in Exhibit 2.3, Global Strategy in Action, Cadbury's new approach to sustainability is fully integrated into the business strategy, provides roadmaps and goals established in the form of Sustainability Commitments, and includes well-developed programs and specific training in sustainable business practices for employees and key suppliers, and third parties' reviews of the company's performance in sustainability.

Company executives attempt more than ever to provide a distinctive and accurate picture of the firm's managerial outlook. One such statement of company philosophy is that of AIM Private Asset Management, Inc. As Exhibit 2.4, Strategy in Action, shows, AIM's board of directors and executives have established especially clear directions for company decision making and action based on growth.

Strategy in Action — Exhibit 2.4

Growth Philosophy at AIM Private Asset Management Inc.

AIM's growth philosophy focuses on earnings—a tangible measure of a company's growth. Because stock prices can gyrate widely on rumors, we use earnings to weed out "high-flying" speculative stocks.

In selecting investments, we look for:

- Quality earnings growth—because we believe earnings drive stock prices.
- Positive earnings momentum—stocks with greater positive momentum will rise above the crowd.

Our growth philosophy adheres to four basic rules:

- Remain fully invested.
- Focus on individual companies rather than industries, sectors or countries.
- Strive to find the best earnings growth.
- Maintain a strong sell discipline.

Why growth philosophy?

- Investment decisions are based on facts, not guesses or big-picture economic forecasts.
- Earnings—not emotions—dictate when we should buy and sell.
- AIM's investment managers have followed the same earnings-driven philosophy for decades.
- This approach has proven itself in domestic and foreign markets.

Source: AIM Private Asset Management Inc., http://sma.aiminvestments.com/

As seen in Exhibit 2.5, Global Strategy in Action, the philosophy of Nissan Motor Manufacturing is expressed by the company's People Principles and Key Corporate Principles. These principles form the basis of the way the company operates on a daily basis. They address the principal concepts used in meeting the company's established goals. Nissan focuses on the distinction between the role of the individual and the corporation. In this way, employees can link their productivity and success to the productivity and success of the company. Given these principles, the company is able to concentrate on the issues most important to its survival, growth, and profitability.

Exhibit 2.6, Strategy in Action, provides an example of how General Motors uses a statement of company philosophy to clarify its environmental principles.

Ronald A. Williams has led a multipronged strategy as CEO at Aetna since 2001 to provide affordable health care to the masses—the foundation of his company's mission. The components of his strategy include physician transparency acquisitions and communication among patients, employers, public officials, and the health care industry, as is explained in Exhibit 2.7, Top Strategist.

Public Image

Both present and potential customers attribute certain qualities to particular businesses. Gerber and Johnson & Johnson make safe products; Cross Pen makes high-quality writing instruments; Étienne Aigner makes stylish but affordable leather products; Corvettes are power machines; and Izod Lacoste stands for the preppy look. Thus, mission statements should reflect the public's expectations, because this makes achievement of the firm's goals more likely. Gerber's mission statement should not open the possibility for diversification into pesticides, and Cross Pen's should not open the possibility for diversification into $0.59 brand-name disposables.

On the other hand, a negative public image often prompts firms to reemphasize the beneficial aspects of their mission. For example, in response to what it saw as a disturbing trend in public opinion, Dow Chemical undertook an aggressive promotional campaign to

Global Strategy in Action — Exhibit 2.5

Principles of Nissan Motor Manufacturing (UK) Ltd.

	People Principles (All other objectives can only be achieved by people)
Selection	Hire the highest caliber people; look for technical capabilities and emphasize attitude.
Responsibility	Maximize the responsibility; staff by devolving decision making.
Teamwork	Recognize and encourage individual contributions, with everyone working toward the same objectives.
Flexibility	Expand the role of the individual: multiskilled, no job description, generic job titles.
Kaizen	Continuously seek 100.1 percent improvements; give "ownership of change."
Communications	"Every day, face to face."
Training	Establish individual "continuous development programs."
Supervisors	Regard as "the professionals at managing the production process"; give them much responsibility normally assumed by individual departments; make them the genuine leaders of their teams.
Single status	Treat everyone as a "first class" citizen; eliminate all illogical differences.
Trade unionism	Establish single union agreement with AEU emphasizing the common objective for a successful enterprise.

	Key Corporate Principles
Quality	Building profitably the highest quality car sold in Europe.
Customer	Achieve target of no. 1 customer satisfaction in Europe.
Volume	Always achieve required volume.
New products	Deliver on time, at required quality, within cost.
Suppliers	Establish long-term relationship with single-source suppliers; aim for zero defects and just-in-time delivery; apply Nissan principles to suppliers.
Production	Use "most appropriate" technology; develop predictable "best method" of doing job; build in quality.
Engineering	Design "quality" and "ease of working" into the product and facilities; establish "simultaneous engineering" to reduce development time.

Source: Nissan Motor Co. Ltd., http://www.nissanmotors.com/

fortify its credibility, particularly among "employees and those who live and work in [their] plant communities." Dow described its approach in its annual report:

> All around the world today, Dow people are speaking up. People who care deeply about their company, what it stands for, and how it is viewed by others. People who are immensely proud of their company's performance, yet realistic enough to realize it is the public's perception of that performance that counts in the long run.

Firms seldom address the question of their public image in an intermittent fashion. Although public agitation often stimulates greater attention to this question, firms are concerned about their public image even in the absence of such agitation. The following excerpt from the mission statement of Intel Corporation is an example of this attitude:

> We are sensitive to our *image with our customers and the business community*. Commitments to customers are considered sacred, and we are upset with ourselves when we do not meet

Strategy in Action — Exhibit 2.6

General Motors Environmental Principles

As a responsible corporate citizen, General Motors is dedicated to protecting human health, natural resources, and the global environment. This dedication reaches further than compliance with the law to encompass the integration of sound environmental practices into our business decisions.

The following environmental principles provide guidance to General Motors personnel worldwide in the conduct of their daily business practices:

1. We are committed to actions to restore and preserve the environment.
2. We are committed to reducing waste and pollutants, conserving resources, and recycling materials at every stage of the product life cycle.
3. We will continue to participate actively in educating the public regarding environmental conservation.
4. We will continue to pursue vigorously the development and implementation of technologies for minimizing pollutant emissions.
5. We will continue to work with all governmental entities for the development of technically sound and financially responsible environmental laws and regulations.
6. We will continually assess the impact of our plants and products on the environment and the communities in which we live and operate with a goal of continuous improvement.

Source: General Motors Corporation, http://www.gm.com/

our commitments. We strive to demonstrate to the business world on a continuing basis that we are credible in describing the state of the corporation, and that we are well organized and in complete control of all things that determine the numbers.

Exhibit 2.8, Strategy in Action, presents a marketing translation of the essence of the mission statements of six high-end shoe companies. The impressive feature of the exhibit is that it shows dramatically how closely competing firms can incorporate subtle, yet meaningful, differences into their mission statements.

Company Self-Concept

A major determinant of a firm's success is the extent to which the firm can relate functionally to its external environment. To achieve its proper place in a competitive situation, the firm realistically must evaluate its competitive strengths and weaknesses. This idea—that the firm must know itself—is the essence of the company self-concept. The idea is not commonly integrated into theories of strategic management; its importance for individuals has been recognized since ancient times.

Both individuals and firms have a crucial need to know themselves. The ability of either to survive in a dynamic and highly competitive environment would be severely limited if they did not understand their impact on others or of others on them.

In some senses, then, firms take on personalities of their own. Much behavior in firms is organizationally based; that is, a firm acts on its members in other ways than their individual interactions. Thus, firms are entities whose personality transcends the personalities of their members. As such, they can set decision-making parameters based on aims different and distinct from the aims of their members. These organizational considerations have pervasive effects.

Ordinarily, descriptions of the company self-concept per se do not appear in mission statements. Yet such statements often provide strong impressions of the company self-concept. For example, ARCO's environment, health, and safety (EHS) managers were adamant about emphasizing the company's position on safety and environmental performance as a part of the mission statement. The challenges facing the ARCO EHS managers included dealing with concerned environmental groups and a public that has become environmentally aware.

Top Strategist
CEO Ronald A. Williams Leads to Fulfill Aetna's Mission

Exhibit 2.7

Ronald A. Williams joined Aetna in 2001 as chief of health operations and helped build the Health-Fund network. The consumer-directed program consists of employer-funded health savings accounts; pretax employee-funded flexible spending accounts; and Aetna Navigator, where members can track expenditures. Williams's success in implementing this program catapulted his career, enabling him to oversee more initiatives in pursuit of the company's mission.

As president of Aetna, Williams guided his team to create Aexcel in 2003. Aexcel outlined physicians' effective care delivery and was crafted after obtaining feedback from various stakeholders and anonymous physician reviewers. The program was expanded to include physician-specific costs, clinical quality, and cost comparisons among hospitals, surgical centers, and free-standing health providers.

Williams's transition to CEO led him to use corporate acquisitions as a primary strategic tool. In August 2007, Aetna acquired Schaller Anderson, a health care management services company that specialized in Medicaid offerings. In October 2007, Aetna acquired Goodhealth Worldwide to provide expanded services to U.S. citizens working outside the country.

Company growth and member expansion bolstered Williams's health care reform agenda. He presented ideas for future expansion to the U.S. Senate in 2008, and outlined how to provide health care to more people. He stated, "Fundamentally it is about having a society in which everyone really has access to high-quality health care services."*

As an example of Aetna's commitment to its mission, Williams has, at critical times, temporarily lifted medical and pharmacy policy requirements for victims of natural disasters and relief workers who aid these victims. These victims and workers can obtain prescription refills without the normal 30-day restriction and are covered for doctor visits that are outside their network without referrals. This modification of Aetna policies has helped those exposed to hurricanes Katrina, Dolly, Rita, Wilma, Ike, and Gustav and to Southern California wildfires.

Sources: Aetna Mission & Values, http://www.aetna.com/about/aetna/ms/

* C. Freeland, "View from the Top," *Financial Times*, September 12, 2008, p. 10.

They hoped to motivate employees toward safer behavior while reducing emissions and waste. They saw this as a reflection of the company's positive self-image.

The following excerpts from the Intel Corporation mission statement describe the corporate persona that its top management seeks to foster:

> Management is self-critical. The leaders must be capable of recognizing and accepting their mistakes and learning from them.
>
> Open (constructive) confrontation is encouraged at all levels of the corporation and is viewed as a method of problem solving and conflict resolution.
>
> Decision by consensus is the rule. Decisions once made are supported. Position in the organization is not the basis for quality of ideas.
>
> A highly communicative, open management is part of the style.
>
> Management must be ethical. Managing by telling the truth and treating all employees equitably has established credibility that is ethical.
>
> We strive to provide an opportunity for rapid development.
>
> Intel is a results-oriented company. The focus is on substance versus form, quality versus quantity.

Strategy in Action — Exhibit 2.8

Mission Statements for the High-End Shoe Industry

ALLEN-EDMONDS
Allen-Edmonds provides high-quality shoes for the affluent consumer who appreciates a well-made, finely crafted, stylish dress shoe.

BALLY
Bally shoes set you apart. They are the perfect shoe to complement your lifestyle. Bally shoes project an image of European style and elegance that ensures one is not just dressed, but well dressed.

BOSTONIAN
Bostonian shoes are for those successful individuals who are well-traveled, on the "go" and want a stylish dress shoe that can keep up with their variety of needs and activities. With Bostonian, you know you will always be well dressed whatever the situation.

COLE HAAN
Cole Haan offers a line of contemporary shoes for the man who wants to go his own way. They are shoes for the urban, upscale, stylish man who wants to project an image of being one step ahead.

FLORSHEIM
Florsheim shoes are the affordable classic men's dress shoes for those who want to experience the comfort and style of a solid dress shoe.

JOHNSTON & MURPHY
Johnston & Murphy is the quintessential business shoe for those affluent individuals who know and demand the best.

Source: "Thinking on Your Feet, the Johnston & Murphy Guerrilla Marketing Competition" (Johnston & Murphy, a GENESCO Company).

We believe in the principle that hard work, high productivity is something to be proud of.

The concept of assumed responsibility is accepted. (If a task needs to be done, assume you have the responsibility to get it done.)

Commitments are long term. If career problems occur at some point, reassignment is a better alternative than termination.

We desire to have all employees involved and participative in their relationship with Intel.

Newest Trends in Mission Components

Three issues have become so prominent in the strategic planning for organizations that they are now integral parts in the development and revisions of mission statements: sensitivity to consumer wants, concern for quality, and statements of company vision.

Customers

"The customer is our top priority" is a slogan that would be claimed by the majority of businesses in the United States and abroad. For companies including Caterpillar Tractor, General Electric, and Johnson & Johnson this means analyzing consumer needs before as well as after a sale. The bonus plan at Xerox allows for a 40 percent annual bonus, based on high customer reviews of the service that they receive, and a 20 percent penalty if the feedback is especially bad. For these firms and many others, the overriding concern for the company has become consumer satisfaction.

In addition many U.S. firms maintain extensive product safety programs to help ensure consumer satisfaction. GE, Sears, and 3M boast of such programs. Other firms including Calgon Corporation, Amoco, Mobil Oil, Whirlpool, and Zenith provide toll-free telephone lines to answer customer concerns and complaints.

The focus on customer satisfaction is demonstrated by retailer JCPenney in this excerpt from its statement of philosophy: "The Penney Idea is (1) To serve the public as nearly as we can to its complete satisfaction; (2) To expect for the service we render a fair remuneration, and not all the profit the traffic will bear; (3) To do all in our power to pack the customer's dollar full of value, quality, and satisfaction."

A focus on customer satisfaction causes managers to realize the importance of providing quality customer service. Strong customer service initiatives have led some firms to gain competitive advantages in the marketplace. Hence, many corporations have made the customer service initiative a key component of their corporate mission.

Quality

"Quality is job one!" is a rallying point not only for Ford Motor Corporation but for many resurging U.S. businesses as well. Two U.S. management experts fostered a worldwide emphasis on quality in manufacturing. W. Edwards Deming and J. M. Juran's messages were first embraced by Japanese managers, whose quality consciousness led to global dominance in several industries including automobile, TV, audio equipment, and electronic components manufacturing. Deming summarizes his approach in 14 now well-known points:

1. Create constancy of purpose.
2. Adopt the new philosophy.
3. Cease dependence on mass inspection to achieve quality.
4. End the practice of awarding business on price tag alone. Instead, minimize total cost, often accomplished by working with a single supplier.
5. Improve constantly the system of production and service.
6. Institute training on the job.
7. Institute leadership.
8. Drive out fear.
9. Break down barriers between departments.
10. Eliminate slogans, exhortations, and numerical targets.
11. Eliminate work standards (quotas) and management by objective.
12. Remove barriers that rob workers, engineers, and managers of their right to pride of workmanship.
13. Institute a vigorous program of education and self-improvement.
14. Put everyone in the company to work to accomplish the transformation.

Firms in the United States responded aggressively. The new philosophy is that quality should be the norm. For example, Motorola's production goal is 60 or fewer defects per every billion components that it manufactures.

Exhibit 2.9, Strategy in Action, presents the integration of the quality initiative into the mission statements of three corporations. The emphasis on quality has received added emphasis in many corporate philosophies since the Congress created the Malcolm Baldrige Quality Award. Each year up to two Baldrige Awards can be given in three categories of a company's operations: manufacturing, services, and small businesses.

Vision Statement

vision statement
A statement that presents a firm's strategic intent designed to focus the energies and resources of the company on achieving a desirable future.

Whereas the mission statement expresses an answer to the question "What business are we in?" a company **vision statement** is sometimes developed to express the aspirations of the executive leadership. A vision statement presents the firm's strategic intent that focuses the energies and resources of the company on achieving a desirable future. However, in actual practice, the mission and vision statement are frequently combined into a single statement. When they are separated, the vision statement is often a single sentence, designed to be memorable. For examples, see Exhibit 2.10, Strategy in Action.

Strategy in Action Exhibit 2.9

Visions of Quality

CADILLAC

The Mission of the Cadillac Motor Company is to engineer, produce, and market the world's finest automobiles known for uncompromised levels of distinctiveness, comfort, convenience, and refined performance. Through its people, who are its strength, Cadillac will continuously improve the quality of its products and services to meet or exceed customer expectations and succeed as a profitable business.

MOTOROLA

Dedication to quality is a way of life at our company, so much so that it goes far beyond rhetorical slogans. Our ongoing program is one of continued improvement reaching out for change, refinement, and even revolution in our pursuit of quality excellence.

It is the objective of Motorola Inc. to produce and provide products and services of the highest quality. In its activities, Motorola will pursue goals aimed at the achievement of quality excellence. These results will be derived from the dedicated efforts of each employee in conjunction with supportive participation from management at all levels of the corporation.

ZYTEC

Zytec is a company that competes on value; is market driven; provides superior quality and service; builds strong relationship with its customers; and provides technical excellence in its products.

Vision statements can also be used to refocus the attention of investors and the public. In 2011, following a series of car recalls that damaged Toyota's reputation for quality, the company issued a vision statement to assure car buyers that the company had recognized its shortcomings and was committed to superior future performance, as explained in Exhibit 2.11, Global Strategy in Action.

An Exemplary Mission Statement

When BB&T merged with Southern Bank, the board of directors and officers undertook the creation of a comprehensive mission statement that was designed to include most of the topics that we discussed in this chapter. The company updated its statement and mailed the resulting booklet to its shareholders and other interested parties. The foreword to the document expresses the greatest values of such a public pronouncement and was signed by BB&T's chairman and CEO, John A. Allison:

> In a rapidly changing and unpredictable world, individuals and organizations need a clear set of fundamental principles to guide their actions. At BB&T we know the content of our business will, and should, experience constant change. Change is necessary for progress. However, the context, our fundamental principles, is unchanging because these principles are based on basic truths.
>
> BB&T is a mission-driven organization with a clearly defined set of values. We encourage our employees to have a strong sense of purpose, a high level of self-esteem and the capacity to think clearly and logically.
>
> We believe that competitive advantage is largely in the minds of our employees as represented by their capacity to turn rational ideas into action towards the accomplishment of our mission.

The Chapter 2 Appendix presents BB&T's vision, mission, and purpose statement in its entirety. It also includes detailed expressions of the company's values and views on the role of emotions, management style, the management concept, attributes of an outstanding employee, the importance of positive attitude, obligations to its employees, virtues of an outstanding credit culture, achieving the company goal, the nature of a "world standard"

and wildlife habitats as well as the Gulf's fishing and tourism industries. The U.S. government named BP as the responsible party and holds the company accountable for all cleanup costs and damage. In part because of this disaster, BP released a Sustainability Review in 2010 to clarify its values, the duties of its board of directors, and its position on corporate governance and risk management. A key excerpt from that review appears as Exhibit 2.12, Global Strategy in Action.

This chapter considers the board of directors because the board's greatest impact on the behavior of a firm results from its determination of the company mission. The philosophy espoused in the mission statement sets the tone by which the firm and all of its employees will be judged. As logical extensions of the mission statement, the firm's objectives and strategies embody the board's view of proper business demeanor. Through its appointment of top executives and its decisions about their compensation, the board reveals its priorities for organizational achievement.

AGENCY THEORY

agency theory
A set of ideas on organizational control based on the belief that the separation of the ownership from management creates the potential for the wishes of owners to be ignored.

Whenever there is a separation of the owners (principals) and the managers (agents) of a firm, the potential exists for the wishes of the owners to be ignored. This fact, and the recognition that agents are expensive, established the basis for a set of complex but helpful ideas known as **agency theory.** Whenever owners (or managers) delegate decision-making authority to others, an agency relationship exists between the two parties. Agency relationships, such as those between stockholders and managers, can be very effective as long as managers make investment decisions in ways that are consistent with stockholders' interests. However, when the interests of managers diverge from those of owners, then managers' decisions are more likely to reflect the managers' preferences than the owners' preferences.

In general, owners seek stock value maximization. When managers hold important blocks of company stock, they too prefer strategies that result in stock appreciation. However, when managers better resemble "hired hands" than owner-partners, they often prefer strategies that increase their personal payoffs rather than those of shareholders. Such behavior can result in decreased stock performance (as when high executive bonuses reduce corporate earnings) and in strategic decisions that point the firm in the direction of outcomes that are suboptimal from a stockholder's perspective.

If, as agency theory argues, self-interested managers act in ways that increase their own welfare at the expense of the gain of corporate stockholders, then owners who delegate decision-making authority to their agents will incur both the loss of potential gain that would have resulted from owner-optimal strategies and/or the costs of monitoring and control systems that are designed to minimize the consequences of such self-centered management decisions. In combination, the cost of agency problems and the cost of actions taken to minimize agency problems are called **agency costs.** These costs can often be identified by their direct benefit for the agents and their negative present value. Agency costs are found when there are differing self-interests between shareholders and managers, superiors and subordinates, or managers of competing departments or branch offices.

agency costs
The cost of agency problems and the cost of actions taken to minimize them.

moral hazard problem
An agency problem that occurs because owners have limited access to company information, making executives free to pursue their own interests.

How Agency Problems Occur

Because owners have access to only a relatively small portion of the information that is available to executives about the performance of the firm and cannot afford to monitor every executive decision or action, executives are often free to pursue their own interests. This condition is known as the **moral hazard problem.** It is also called shirking to suggest "self-interest combined with smile."

Exhibit 2.12

Corporate Governance and Risk Management

Our governance framework includes the principles that guide our board and management team, as well as a system of controls that defines how we work.

THE BOARD

The board is responsible for the direction and oversight of BP p.l.c. on behalf of shareholders; it is accountable to them, as owners, for all aspects of BP's business. It focuses its activities on strategy development, the oversight of risk and monitoring the performance of the business.

The board sets the tone from the top, and has established a set of board governance principles, which delegate management authority to the group chief executive within defined limits. These include a requirement that the group chief executive will not engage in any activity without regard to health, safety and environmental consequence.

The board reviews key group risks and how they are managed as part of its agendas.

On 1 January 2011, the board was composed of the chairman, three executive directors and 11 non-executive directors.

BP's Management of Sustainability Risks and Issues

Shareholders

External Stakeholders ⇄

BP Board	
Direction and oversight of BP on behalf of the shareholders for all aspects of BP's business, including sustainability performance. Comprised of the chairman, executive directors and non-executive directors.	
Safety, Ethics and Environment Assurance Committee	**Gulf of Mexico Committee**
Reviews BP's processes to identify and mitigate significant non-financial risks and receives assurance that they are appropriate in design and effective in implementation.	Monitors BP's spill response and delivery of commitments in the Gulf region through oversight of the new Gulf Coast Restoration Organization.

Executive team	
Supports the group chief executive (GCE) in his accountability to the board for BP's overall business, including sustainability performance. Comprised of the GCE and the heads of businesses and certain functions, including safety and operational risk (S&OR).	
Group Operations Risk Committee	**Group People Committee**
Monitors HSE performance across the group. Representation from S&OR.	Overall responsibility for policy decisions relating to employees.

Group Functions	Local Operations
Functions, such as safety and operational risk, define and support implementation of group-wide standards.	Specialists and line management identify risks and implement our group-wide operating management system and other standards.

BOARD COMMITTEES

The board delegates some of its oversight and monitoring activities to its committees, composed entirely of non-executives. The chair of each committee provides updates on committee activities to the wider board.

One of the five permanent committees—the safety, ethics and environment assurance committee (SEEAC)—monitors the management of non-financial risk, which includes regular reviews of information and reports from executive risk committees, such as our group operations risk committee, as well as from the safety and operational risk function and other parts of the business. SEEAC is monitoring BP's global implementation of the measures recommended in BP's investigation after the Deepwater Horizon accident.

EXTERNAL INFORMATION AND ADVICE

The board and its committees also receive information from external sources, as needed. For example, the board and SEEAC work with the Independent Expert to review the progress made in implementing the recommendations of the BP US Refineries Independent Safety Review Panel. An international advisory board advises the chairman, group chief executive and board of BP p.l.c. on strategic and geopolitical issues relating to the long-term development of the company.

BOARD ACTIVITIES IN 2010

The Deepwater Horizon accident dominated the focus and work of the board. Non-executive members of our board, including the chairman and the chair of SEEAC, visited the Gulf of Mexico during this period.

(*continued*)

Exhibit 2.12 cont.

During 2010, the board appointed four new non-executive directors, who together bring deep experience in the oil and gas industry, global strategy, accounting and audit, and the management and monitoring of organizational safety.

In July, the board established the Gulf of Mexico committee to monitor BP's response to the Deepwater Horizon accident through oversight of the new Gulf Coast Restoration Organization. The committee oversees BP's activities and responsibilities with respect to the Gulf Coast Claims Facility, the $20-billion trust, remediation work, community outreach, and response to fines and penalties.

OUR SYSTEM OF INTERNAL CONTROL

BP uses a comprehensive set of management systems, organizational structures, processes, standards and behaviours to conduct our business and deliver returns for shareholders. The board is responsible for maintaining a sound system of internal control, and delegates the establishment and maintenance of this system to the group chief executive. Everyone who works for BP needs to meet the aspects of the system relevant to them in what they do. It is the job of leaders to ensure that aspects of the system relevant to their team are understood and followed in such a way that risks are managed appropriately at all levels in BP.

RISK MANAGEMENT

Our businesses identify, prioritize, manage, monitor and improve the management of risks on a day-to-day basis to equip them to deal with hazards and uncertainties. We report the key risks, and how they are managed, up through the line in a consistent manner to assist with business planning, appropriate intervention and knowledge sharing.

The board reviews material risks to the group and their recognition in the company's annual plan. The board committees review the reporting by business and function which includes the safety and environmental performance of projects.

We are examining what can be learnt from our experiences in 2010 to further improve BP's risk processes.

Source: BP Sustainability Review 2010, BP.com/sustainability, p. 15.

As a result of moral hazards, executives may design strategies that provide the greatest possible benefits for themselves, with the welfare of the organization being given only secondary consideration. For example, executives may presell products at year-end to trigger their annual bonuses even though the deep discounts that they must offer will threaten the price stability of their products for the upcoming year. Similarly, unchecked executives may advance their own self-interests by slacking on the job, altering forecasts to maximize their performance bonuses; unrealistically assessing acquisition targets' outlooks in order to increase the probability of increasing organizational size through their acquisition; or manipulating personnel records to keep or acquire key company personnel.

adverse selection
An agency problem caused by the limited ability of stockholders to precisely determine the competencies and priorities of executives at the time they are hired.

The second major reason that agency costs are incurred is known as **adverse selection.** This refers to the limited ability that stockholders have to precisely determine the competencies and priorities of executives at the time that they are hired. Because principals cannot initially verify an executive's appropriateness as an agent of the owners, unanticipated problems of nonoverlapping priorities between owners and agents are likely to occur.

The most popular solution to moral dilemma and adverse selection problems is for owners to attempt to more closely align their own best interests with those of their agents through the use of executive bonus plans. Foremost among these approaches are stock option plans, which enable executives to benefit directly from the appreciation of the company's stock just as other stockholders do. In most instances, executive bonus plans are unabashed attempts to align the interests of owners and executives and to thereby induce executives to support strategies that increase stockholder wealth. While such schemes are unlikely to eliminate self-interest as a major criterion in executive decision making, they help to reduce the costs associated with moral dilemmas and adverse selections.

Problems That Can Result from Agency

From a strategic management perspective there are five different kinds of problems that can arise because of the agency relationship between corporate stockholders and their company's executives:

1. Executives pursue growth in company size rather than in earnings. Shareholders generally want to maximize earnings, because earnings growth yields stock appreciation. However, because managers are typically more heavily compensated for increases in firm size than for earnings growth, they may recommend strategies that yield company growth such as mergers and acquisitions.

In addition, managers' stature in the business community is commonly associated with company size. Managers gain prominence by directing the growth of an organization, and they benefit in the forms of career advancement and job mobility that are associated with increases in company size.

Finally, executives need an enlarging set of advancement opportunities for subordinates whom they wish to motivate with nonfinancial inducements. Acquisitions can provide the needed positions.

2. Executives attempt to diversify their corporate risk. Whereas stockholders can vary their investment risks through management of their individual stock portfolios, managers' careers and stock incentives are tied to the performance of a single corporation, albeit the one that employs them. Consequently, executives are tempted to diversify their corporation's operation, businesses, and product lines to moderate the risk incurred in any single venture. While this approach serves the executives' personal agendas, it compromises the "pure play" quality of their firm as an investment. In other words, diversifying a corporation reduces the beta associated with the firm's return, which is an undesirable outcome for many stockholders.

3. Executives avoid risk. Even when, or perhaps especially when, executives are willing to restrict the diversification of their companies, they are tempted to minimize the risk that they face. Executives are often fired for failure, but rarely for mediocre corporate performance. Therefore, executives may avoid desirable levels of risk if they anticipate little reward and opt for conservative strategies that minimize the risk of company failure. If they do, executives will rarely support plans for innovation, diversification, and rapid growth.

However, from an investor's perspective, risk taking is desirable when it is systematic. In other words, when investors can reasonably expect that their company will generate higher long-term returns from assuming greater risk, they may wish to pursue the greater payoff, especially when the company is positioned to perform better than its competitors that face the same nominal risks. Obviously, the agency relationship creates a problem—should executives prioritize their job security or the company's financial returns to stockholders?

4. Managers act to optimize their personal payoffs. If executives can gain more from an annual performance bonus by achieving objective 1 than from stock appreciation resulting from the achievement of objective 2, then owners must anticipate that the executives will target objective 1 as their priority, even though objective 2 is clearly in the best interest of the shareholders. Similarly, executives may pursue a range of expensive perquisites that have a net negative effect on shareholder returns. Elegant corner offices, corporate jets, large staffs, golf club memberships, extravagant retirement programs, and limousines for executive benefit are rarely good investments for stockholders.

5. Executives act to protect their status. When their companies expand, executives want to ensure that their knowledge, experience, and skills remain relevant and central to the strategic direction of the corporation. They favor doing more of what they already do well. In

contrast, investors may prefer revolutionary advancement to incremental improvement. For example, when confronted with Amazon.com, competitor Barnes & Noble initiated a joint venture Web site with Bertelsmann. In addition, Barnes & Noble used vertical integration with the nation's largest book distributor, which supplies 60 percent of Amazon's books. This type of revolutionary strategy is most likely to occur when executives are given assurances that they will not make themselves obsolete within the changing company that they create.

Solutions to the Agency Problem

In addition to defining an agent's responsibilities in a contract and including elements like bonus incentives that help align executives' and owners' interests, principals can take several other actions to minimize agency problems. The first is for the owners to pay executives a premium for their service. This premium helps executives to see their loyalty to the stockholders as the key to achieving their personal financial targets.

A second solution to agency problems is for executives to receive backloaded compensation. This means that executives are paid a handsome premium for superior future performance. Strategic actions taken in year one, which are to have an impact in year three, become the basis for executive bonuses in year three. This lag time between action and bonus more realistically rewards executives for the consequences of their decision making, ties the executive to the company for the long term, and properly focuses strategic management activities on the future.

Finally, creating teams of executives across different units of a corporation can help to focus performance measures on organizational rather than personal goals. Through the use of executive teams, owner interests often receive the priority that they deserve.

Summary

Defining the company mission is one of the most often slighted tasks in strategic management. Emphasizing the operational aspects of long-range management activities comes much more easily for most executives. But the critical role of the mission statement repeatedly is demonstrated by failing firms whose short-run actions have been at odds with their long-run purposes.

The principal value of the mission statement is its specification of the firm's ultimate aims. A firm gains a heightened sense of purpose when its board of directors and its top executives address these issues: "What business are we in?" "What customers do we serve?" "Why does this organization exist?" However, the potential contribution of the company mission can be undermined if platitudes or ambiguous generalizations are accepted in response to these questions. It is not enough to say that Lever Brothers is in the business of "making anything that cleans anything" or that Polaroid is committed to businesses that deal with "the interaction of light and matter." Only if a firm clearly articulates its long-term intentions can its goals serve as a basis for shared expectations, planning, and performance evaluation.

A mission statement that is developed from this perspective provides managers with a unity of direction transcending individual, parochial, and temporary needs. It promotes a sense of shared expectations among all levels and generations of employees. It consolidates values over time and across individuals and interest groups. It projects a sense of worth and intent that can be identified and assimilated by outside stakeholders, that is, customers, suppliers, competitors, local committees, and the general public. Finally, it asserts the firm's commitment to responsible action in symbiosis with the preservation and protection of the essential claims of insider stakeholders' survival, growth, and profitability.

Key Terms

adverse selection, *p. 40*
agency costs, *p. 38*
agency theory, *p. 38*
board of directors, *p. 36*
company creed, *p. 27*
company mission, *p. 23*
moral hazard problem, *p. 38*
vision statement, *p. 34*

Questions for Discussion

1. Reread Nicor Inc.'s mission statement in Exhibit 2.1, Strategy in Action. List five insights into Nicor that you feel you gained from knowing its mission.
2. Locate the mission statement of a company not mentioned in the chapter. Where did you find it? Was it presented as a consolidated statement, or were you forced to assemble it yourself from various publications of the firm? How many of the mission statement elements outlined in this chapter were discussed or revealed in the statement you found?
3. Prepare a two-page typewritten mission statement for your school of business or for a firm selected by your instructor.
4. List five potentially vulnerable areas of a firm without a stated company mission.
5. Mission statements are often criticized for being lists of platitudes. What can strategic managers do to prevent their statements from appearing to be simple statements of obvious truths?
6. What evidence do you see that mission statements are valuable?
7. How can a mission statement be an enduring statement of values and simultaneously provide a basis of competitive advantage?
8. If the goal of survival refers to ability to maintain a specific legal form, what are the comparative advantages of sole proprietorships, partnerships, and corporations?
9. In the 1990s many Nasdaq firms favored growth over profitability; in the 2012s the goal of profitability is displacing growth. How might each preference be explained?
10. Do you agree that a mission statement provides substantive guidance while a vision statement provides inspirational guidance? Explain.

Chapter 2 Appendix

BB&T Vision, Mission, and Purpose

BB&T Vision

To create the best financial institution possible: *"The Best of The Best."*

BB&T Mission

To make the world a better place to live by: helping our clients achieve economic success and financial security; creating a place where our employees can learn, grow and be fulfilled in their work; making the communities in which we work better places to be; and thereby: optimizing the long-term return to our shareholders, while providing a safe and sound investment.

BB&T Purpose

Our ultimate purpose is to create superior long-term economic rewards for our shareholders.

This purpose is defined by the free market and is as it should be. Our shareholders provide the capital that is necessary to make our business possible. They take the risk if the business is unsuccessful. They have the right to receive economic rewards for the risk which they have undertaken.

However, our purpose, to create superior long-term economic rewards for our shareholders, can only be accomplished by providing excellent service to our clients, as our clients are our source of revenues.

To have excellent client relations, we must have outstanding employees to serve our clients. To attract and retain outstanding employees, we must reward them financially and create an environment where they can learn and grow.

Our economic results are significantly impacted by the success of our communities. The community's "quality of life" impacts its ability to attract industry for growth.

Therefore, we manage our business in a long-term context, as an integrated whole, with the ultimate objective of rewarding the shareholders for their investment, while realizing that the cause of this result is quality client service. Excellent service will be delivered by motivated employees working as an integrated team. These results will be impacted by our capacity to contribute to the growth and well-being of the communities we serve.

Values

"Excellence is an art won by training and habituation.We are what we repeatedly do. Excellence then is not an act, but a habit."—Aristotle

The great Greek philosophers saw values as guides to excellence in thinking and action. In this context, values are standards which we strive to achieve. Values are practical habits that enable us as individuals to live, be successful and achieve happiness. For BB&T, our values enable us to achieve our mission and corporate purpose.

To be useful, values must be consciously held and be consistent (noncontradictory). Many people have conflicting values which prevent them from acting with clarity and self-confidence.

There are 10 primary values at BB&T. These values are consistent with one another and are integrated. To fully act on one of these values, you must also act consistently with the other values. Our focus on values grows from our belief that ideas matter and that an individual's character is of critical significance.

Values are important at BB&T!

1. Reality (Fact-Based)

What is, is. If we want to be better, we must act within the context of reality (the facts). Businesses and individuals often make serious mistakes by making decisions based on what they "wish was so," or based on theories which are disconnected from reality. The foundation for quality decision making is a careful understanding of the facts.

There is a fundamental difference between the laws of nature (reality), which are immutable, and the man-made. The law of gravity is the law of gravity. The existence of the law of gravity does not mean man cannot create an airplane. However, an airplane must be created within the context of the law of gravity. At BB&T, we believe in being "reality grounded."

2. Reason (Objectivity)

Mankind has a specific means of survival, which is his ability to think, i.e., his capacity to reason logically from the facts of reality as presented to his five senses. A lion has claws to hunt. A deer has swiftness to avoid the hunter. Man has his ability to think. There is only one "natural resource"—the human mind.

Clear thinking is not automatic. It requires intellectual discipline and begins with sound premises based on observed facts. You must be able to draw general conclusions in a rational manner from specific examples (induction) and be able to apply general principles to the solution of specific problems (deduction). You must be able to think in an integrated way, thereby avoiding logical contradictions.

We cannot all be geniuses, but each of us can develop the mental habits which ensure that when making decisions we carefully examine the facts and think logically without contradiction in deriving a conclusion. We must learn to think in terms of what is essential, i.e., about what is important. Our goal is to objectively make the best decision to accomplish our purpose.

Rational thinking is a learned skill which requires mental focus and a fundamental commitment to consistently improving the clarity of our mental processes. At BB&T, we are looking for people who are committed to constantly improving their ability to reason.

3. Independent Thinking

All employees are challenged to use their individual minds to their optimum to make rational decisions. In this context, each of us is *responsible* for what we do and who we are. In addition, creativity is strongly encouraged and only possible with independent thought.

We learn a great deal from each other. Teamwork is important at BB&T (as will be discussed later). However, each of us thinks alone. Our minds are not physically connected. In this regard, each of us must be willing to make an independent judgment of the facts based on our capacity to think logically. Just because the "crowd" says it is so, does not make it so.

In this context, each of us is responsible for our own actions. Each of us is responsible for our personal success or failure; that is, it is not the bank's fault if someone does not achieve his objectives.

All human progress by definition is based on creativity, because creativity is the source of positive change. Creativity is only possible to an independent thinker. Creativity is not about just doing something different. It is about doing something better. To be better, the new method/process must be judged by its impact on the whole organization, and as to whether it contributes to the accomplishment of our mission.

There is an infinite opportunity for each of us to do whatever we do better. A significant aspect of the self-fulfillment which work can provide comes from creative thought and action.

4. Productivity

We are committed to being producers of wealth and well-being by taking the actions necessary to accomplish our mission. The tangible evidence of our productivity is that we have rationally allocated capital through our lending and investment process, and that we have provided needed services to our clients in an efficient manner resulting in superior profitability.

Profitability is a measure of the differences in the economic value of the products/services we produce and the cost of producing these products/services. In a long-term context and in a free market, the bigger the profit, the better. This is true not only from our shareholders' perspective (which would be enough justification), but also in terms of the impact of our work on society as a whole. Healthy profits represent productive work. At BB&T we are looking for people who want to create, to produce, and who are thereby committed to turning their thoughts into actions that improve economic well-being.

5. Honesty

Being honest is simply being consistent with reality. To be dishonest is to be in conflict with reality, which is therefore self-defeating. A primary reason that individuals fail is because they become disconnected from reality, pretending that facts are other than they are.

To be honest does not require that we know everything. Knowledge is always contextual and man is not omniscient. However, we must be responsible for saying what we mean and meaning what we say.

6. Integrity

Because we have developed our principles logically, based on reality, we will always act consistently with our principles. Regardless of the short-term benefits, acting inconsistently with our principles is to our long-term detriment. We do not, therefore, believe in compromising our principles in any situation.

Principles provide carefully thought-out concepts which will lead to our long-term success and happiness. Violating our principles will always lead to failure. BB&T is an organization of the highest integrity.

7. Justice (Fairness)

Individuals should be evaluated and rewarded objectively (for better or worse) based on their contributions toward accomplishing our mission and adherence to our values. Those who contribute the most should receive the most.

The single most significant way in which employees evaluate their managers is in determining whether the manager is just. Employees become extremely unhappy (and rightly so) when they perceive that a person who is not contributing is overrewarded or a strong contributor is underrewarded.

If we do not reward those who contribute the most, they will leave and our organization will be less successful. Even more important, if there is no reward for superior performance, the average person will not be motivated to maximize his productivity.

We must evaluate whether the food we eat is healthy, the clothes we wear attractive, the car we drive functional, etc., and we must also evaluate whether relationships with other people are good for us or not.

In evaluating other people, it is critical that we judge based on essentials. At BB&T we do not discriminate based on nonessentials such as race, sex, nationality, etc. We do discriminate based on competency, performance and character. We consciously reject egalitarianism and collectivism. Individuals must be judged individually based on their personal merits, not their membership in any group.

8. Pride

Pride is the psychological reward we earn from living by our values, that is, from being just, honest, having integrity, being an independent thinker, being productive and rational.

Aristotle believed that "earned" pride (not arrogance) was the highest of virtues, because it presupposed all the others. Striving for earned pride simply reinforces the importance of having high moral values.

Each of us must perform our work in a manner as to be able to be justly proud of what we have accomplished. BB&T must be the kind of organization with which each employee and client can be proud to be associated.

9. Self-Esteem (Self-Motivation)

We expect our employees to earn positive self-esteem from doing their work well. We expect and want our employees to act in their rational, long-term self-interest. We want employees who have strong personal goals and who expect to be able to accomplish their goals within the context of our mission.

A necessary attribute for self-esteem is self-motivation. We have a strong work ethic. We believe that you receive from your work in proportion to how much you contribute. If you do not want to work hard, work somewhere else.

While there are many trade-offs in the content of life, you need to be clear that BB&T is the best place, all things considered, for you to work to accomplish your long-term goals. When you know this, you can be more productive and happy.

10. Teamwork/Mutual Supportiveness

While independent thought and strong personal goals are critically important, our work is accomplished within teams. Each of us must consistently act to achieve the agreed-upon objectives of the team, with respect for our fellow employees, while acting in a mutually supportive manner.

Our work at BB&T is so complex that it requires an integrated effort among many people to accomplish important tasks. While we are looking for self-motivated and independent thinking individuals, these individuals must recognize that almost nothing at BB&T can be accomplished without the help of their team members. One of the responsibilities of leadership in our organization is to ensure that each individual is rewarded based on their contribution to the success of the total team. We need outstanding individuals working together to create an outstanding team.

Our values are held consciously and are logically consistent. To fully execute on any one value, you must act consistently with all 10 values. At BB&T values are practical and important.

The Role of Emotions

Often people believe that making logical decisions means that we should be unemotional and that emotions are thereby unimportant. In fact, emotions are important. However, the real issue is how rational are our emotions. Emotions are mental habits which are often developed as children. Emotions give us automatic responses to people and events; these responses can either be very useful or destructive indicators. Emotions as such are not means of decision or of knowledge; the issue is: How were your emotions formed? The real question is, Are we happy when we should be happy, and unhappy when we should be unhappy, or are we unhappy when we should be happy?

Emotions are learned behaviors. The goal is to "train up" our emotions so that our emotions objectively reinforce the best decisions and behaviors toward our long-term success and happiness. Just because someone is unemotional does not mean that they are logical.

Concepts That Describe BB&T

1. Client-Driven

"World class" client service organization.
Our clients are our partners.
Our goal is to create win/win relationships.
"You can tell we want your business."
"It is easy to do business with BB&T."
"Respect the individual, value the relationship."

We will absolutely never, ever, take advantage of anyone, nor do we want to do business with those who would take advantage of us. Our clients are long-term partners and should be treated accordingly. One of the attributes of partnerships is that both partners must keep their agreements. We keep our agreements. When our partners fail to keep their agreements, they are terminating the partnership.

There are an infinite number of opportunities where we can get better together, where we can help our clients achieve their financial goals and where our client will enable us to make a profit in doing so.

2. Quality Oriented

Quality must be built into the process.

In every aspect of our business we want to execute and deliver quality. It is easier and less expensive to do things correctly than to fix what has been done incorrectly.

3. Efficient

"Waste not, want not."
Design efficiency into the system.

4. Growing Both Our Business and Our People

Grow or die.
Life requires constant, focused thought and actions towards one's goals.

5. Continuous Improvement

Everything can be done better.
Fundamental commitment to innovation.
Every employee should constantly use their reasoning ability to do whatever they do better every day. All managers of systems/processes should constantly search for better methods to solve problems and serve the client.

6. Objective Decision Making

Fact-based and rational.

BB&T Management Style

Participative
Team Oriented
Fact-Based
Rational
Objective

Our management process, by intention, is designed to be participative and team oriented. We work hard to create consensus. When people are involved in the decision process, better information is available to make decisions. The participant's understanding of the decision is greater and, therefore, execution is better.

However, there is a risk in participative decision making: the decision process can become a popularity contest. Therefore, our decision process is disciplined. Our decisions will be made based on the facts using reason. The best objective decision will be the one which is enacted.

Therefore, it does not matter whom you know, who your friends are, etc.; it matters whether you can offer the best objective solution to accomplishing the goal or solving the problem at hand.

BB&T Management Concept

Hire excellent people
Train them well
Give them an appropriate level of authority and responsibility
Expect a high level of achievement
Reward their performance

Our concept is to operate a highly autonomous, entrepreneurial organization. In order to execute this concept, we must have extremely competent individuals who are "masters" of BB&T's philosophy and who are "masters" in their field of technical expertise.

By having individuals who are "masters" in their field, we can afford to have less costly control systems and be more responsive in meeting the needs of our clients.

Attributes of an Outstanding BB&T Employee

Purpose
Rationality
Self-esteem

Consistent with our values, successful individuals at BB&T have a sense of purpose for their lives; that is, they believe that their lives matter and that they can accomplish something meaningful through their work. We are looking for people who are rational and have a high level of personal self-esteem. People with a strong personal self-esteem get along better with others, because they are at peace with themselves.

BB&T Positive Attitude

Since we build on the facts of reality and our ability to reason, we are capable of achieving both success and happiness.

We do not believe that "realism" means pessimism. On the contrary, precisely because our goals are based on and consistent with reality, we fully expect to accomplish them.

BB&T'S Obligations to Its Employees

We will do our best to:

Compensate employees fairly in relation to internal equity and market-comparable pay practices—performance-based compensation.

Provide a comprehensive and market-competitive benefit program.

Create a place where employees can learn and grow—to become more productive workers and better people.

Train employees so they are competent to do the work asked of them. (Never ask anyone to do anything they are not trained to do.)

Evaluate and recognize performance objectively, fairly and consistently based on the individual's contribution to the accomplishment of our mission and adherence to our values.

Treat each employee as an individual with dignity and respect.

Virtues of an Outstanding Credit Culture

Just as individuals need a set of values (virtues) to guide their actions, systems should be designed to have a set of attributes which optimize their performance towards our goals. In this regard, our credit culture has seven fundamental virtues:

1. Provides fundamental insight to help clients achieve their economic goals and solve their financial problems: We are in the high-quality financial advice business.
2. Responsive: The client deserves an answer as quickly as possible, even when the answer is no.
3. Flexible (Creative): We are committed to finding better ways to meet the client's financial needs.
4. Reliable: Our clients are selected as long-term partners and treated accordingly. BB&T must continue to earn the right to be known as the most reliable bank.
5. Manages risk within agreed-upon limits: Clients do not want to fail financially, and the bank does not want a bad loan.
6. Ensures an appropriate economic return to the bank for risk taken: The higher the risk, the higher the return. The lower the risk, the lower the return. This is an expression of justice.
7. Creates a "premium" for service delivery: The concept is to provide superior value to the client through outstanding service quality. A rational client will fairly compensate us when we provide sound financial advice, are responsive, creative and reliable, because these attributes are of economic value to the client.

Strategic Objectives

Create a high performance financial institution that can survive and prosper in a rapidly changing, highly competitive, globally integrated environment.

Achieving Our Goal

The key to maximizing our probability of being both independent and prosperous over the long term is to create a superior earnings per share (EPS) growth rate without sacrificing the fundamental quality and long-term competitiveness of our business and without taking unreasonable risk.

While being fundamentally efficient is critical, the "easy" way to rapid EPS growth is to artificially cut cost. However, not investing for the future is long-term suicide, as it destroys our capability to compete.

The intelligent process to achieve superior EPS growth is to grow revenues by providing (and selling) superior quality service while systematically enhancing our margins, improving our efficiency, expanding our profitable product offerings and creating more effective distribution channels.

The "World Standard" Revenue-Driven Sales Organization

At BB&T, selling is about identifying our clients' legitimate financial needs and finding a way to help the client achieve economic goals by providing the right products and services.

Effective selling requires a disciplined approach in which the BB&T employee asks the client about financial goals and problems and has a complete understanding of how our products can help the client achieve objectives and solve financial problems.

It also requires exceptional execution by support staffs and product managers, since service and sales are fundamentally connected and creativity is required in product design and development.

"World Standard" Client Service Community Banks

BB&T operates as a series of "Community Banks." The "Community Bank" concept is the foundation for local decision making and the basis for responsive, reliable and empathetic client service.

By putting decision making closer to the client, all local factors can be considered, and we can ensure that the client is being treated as an individual.

To operate in this decentralized decision-making fashion, we must have highly trained employees who understand BB&T's philosophy and are "masters" of their areas of responsibility.

Commitment to Education/Learning

Competitive advantage is in the minds of our employees. We are committed to making substantial investments in employee education to create a "knowledge-based learning organization" founded on the premise that knowledge (understanding), properly applied, is the source of superior performance.

We believe in systematized learning founded on Aristotle's concept that "excellence is an art won by training and habituation." We attempt to train our employees with the best knowledge/methods in their fields and to habituate those behaviors through consistent management reinforcement. The goal is for each employee to be a "master" of his or her role, whether it be a computer operator, teller, lender, financial consultant or any other job responsibility.

Our Passions

To create the best financial institution possible.

To consistently provide the client with better value through rational innovation and productivity improvement.

At BB&T we have two powerful passions. Our fundamental passion is our Vision: To Create the Best Financial Institution Possible—The "World Standard"—The "Best of the Best." We believe that the best can be objectively evaluated by rational performance standards in relation to the accomplishment of our mission.

To be the best of the best, we must constantly find ways to deliver better value to our clients in a highly profitable manner. This requires us to keep our minds focused at all times on innovative ways to enhance our productivity.

Chapter Three

Corporate Social Responsibility and Business Ethics

After reading and studying this chapter, you should be able to

1. Understand the importance of the stakeholder approach to social responsibility.
2. Explain the continuum of social responsibility and the effect of various options on company profitability.
3. Describe a social audit and explain its importance.
4. Discuss the effect of the Sarbanes-Oxley Act on the ethical conduct of business.
5. Compare the advantages of collaborative social initiatives with alternative approaches to CSR.
6. Explain the five principles of collaborative social initiatives.
7. Compare the merits of different approaches to business ethics.
8. Explain the relevance of business ethics to strategic management practice.

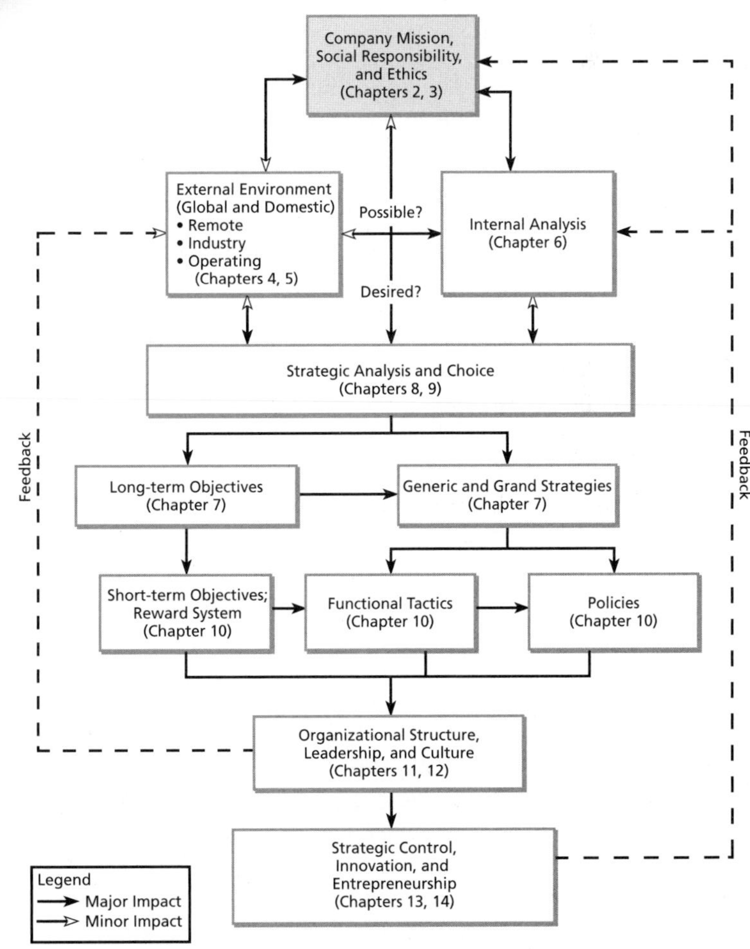

THE STAKEHOLDER APPROACH TO SOCIAL RESPONSIBILITY

In defining or redefining the company mission, strategic managers must recognize the legitimate rights of the firm's claimants. These include not only stockholders and employees but also outsiders affected by the firm's actions, sometimes referred to as stakeholders. Such outsiders commonly include customers, suppliers, governments, unions, competitors, local communities, and the general public. Each of these interest groups has justifiable reasons for expecting (and often for demanding) that the firm satisfy their claims in a responsible manner. In general, stockholders claim appropriate returns on their investment; employees seek broadly defined job satisfactions; customers want what they pay for; suppliers seek dependable buyers; governments want adherence to legislation; unions seek benefits for their members; competitors want fair competition; local communities want the firm to be a responsible citizen; and the general public expects the firm's existence to improve the quality of life.

According to a survey of 2,361 directors in 291 of the largest southeastern U.S. companies,

1. Directors perceived the existence of distinct stakeholder groups.
2. Directors have high stakeholder orientations.
3. Directors view some stakeholders differently, depending on their occupation (CEO directors versus non-CEO directors) and type (inside versus outside directors).

The study also found that the perceived stakeholders were, in the order of their importance, customers and government, stockholders, employees, and society. The results clearly indicated that boards of directors no longer believe that the stockholder is the only constituency to whom they are responsible.

However, when a firm attempts to incorporate the interests of these groups into its mission statement, broad generalizations are insufficient. These steps need to be taken:

1. Identification of the stakeholders.
2. Understanding the stakeholders' specific claims vis-à-vis the firm.
3. Reconciliation of these claims and assignment of priorities to them.
4. Coordination of the claims with other elements of the company mission.

Identification The left-hand column of Exhibit 3.1 lists the commonly encountered stakeholder groups, to which the executive officer group often is added. Obviously, though, every business faces a slightly different set of stakeholder groups, which vary in number, size, influence, and importance. In defining the company, strategic managers must identify all of the stakeholder groups and weigh their relative rights and their relative ability to affect the firm's success.

Understanding The concerns of the principal stakeholder groups tend to center on the general claims listed in the right-hand column of Exhibit 3.1. However, strategic decision makers should understand the specific demands of each group. They then will be better able to initiate actions that satisfy these demands.

Reconciliation and Priorities Unfortunately, the claims of various stakeholder groups often conflict. For example, the claims of governments and the general public tend to limit profitability, which is the central claim of most creditors and stockholders. Thus, claims must be reconciled in a mission statement that resolves the competing, conflicting, and contradicting claims of stakeholders. For objectives and strategies to be internally consistent and precisely focused, the statement must display a single-minded, though multidimensional, approach to the firm's aims.

EXHIBIT 3.1
A Stakeholder View of Company Responsibility

Stakeholder	Nature of the Claim
Stockholders	Participation in distribution of profits, additional stock offerings, assets on liquidation; vote of stock; inspection of company books; transfer of stock; election of board of directors; and such additional rights as have been established in the contract with the corporation.
Creditors	Legal proportion of interest payments due and return of principal from the investment. Security of pledged assets; relative priority in event of liquidation. Management and owner prerogatives if certain conditions exist with the company (such as default of interest payments).
Employees	Economic, social, and psychological satisfaction in the place of employment. Freedom from arbitrary and capricious behavior on the part of company officials. Share in fringe benefits, freedom to join union and participate in collective bargaining, individual freedom in offering up their services through an employment contract. Adequate working conditions.
Customers	Service provided with the product; technical data to use the product; suitable warranties; spare parts to support the product during use; R&D leading to product improvement; facilitation of credit.
Suppliers	Continuing source of business; timely consummation of trade credit obligations; professional relationship in contracting for, purchasing, and receiving goods and services.
Governments	Taxes (income, property, and so on); adherence to the letter and intent of public policy dealing with the requirements of fair and free competition; discharge of legal obligations of businesspeople (and business organizations); adherence to antitrust laws.
Unions	Recognition as the negotiating agent for employees. Opportunity to perpetuate the union as a participant in the business organization.
Competitors	Observation of the norms for competitive conduct established by society and the industry. Business statesmanship on the part of peers.
Local communities	Place of productive and healthful employment in the community. Participation of company officials in community affairs, provision of regular employment, fair play, reasonable portion of purchases made in the local community, interest in and support of local government, support of cultural and charitable projects.
The general public	Participation in and contribution to society as a whole; creative communications between governmental and business units designed for reciprocal understanding; assumption of fair proportion of the burden of government and society. Fair price for products and advancement of the state-of-the-art technology that the product line involves.

Source: William R. King and David I. Cleland, *Strategic Planning and Policy*, © 1978 Litton Educational Publishing, Inc., p. 153.

There are hundreds, if not thousands, of claims on any firm—high wages, pure air, job security, product quality, community service, taxes, occupational health and safety regulations, equal employment opportunity regulations, product variety, wide markets, career opportunities, company growth, investment security, high ROI, and many, many more. Although most, perhaps all, of these claims may be desirable ends, they cannot be pursued with equal emphasis. They must be assigned priorities in accordance with the relative emphasis that the firm will give them. That emphasis is reflected in the criteria that the firm uses in its strategic decision making; in the firm's allocation of its human, financial, and physical resources; and in the firm's long-term objectives and strategies.

Coordination with Other Elements The demands of stakeholder groups constitute only one principal set of inputs to the company mission. The other principal sets are the managerial operating philosophy and the determinants of the product-market offering. Those determinants constitute a reality test that the accepted claims must pass. The key question is, How can the firm satisfy its claimants and at the same time optimize its economic success in the marketplace?

The Dynamics of Social Responsibility

As indicated in Exhibit 3.2, the various stakeholders of a firm can be divided into inside stakeholders and outside stakeholders. The insiders are the individuals or groups that are stockholders or employees of the firm. The outsiders are all the other individuals or groups that the firm's actions affect. The extremely large and often amorphous set of outsiders makes the general claim that the firm be socially responsible.

Perhaps the thorniest issues faced in defining a company mission are those that pertain to social responsibility. Corporate social responsibility is the idea that a business has a duty to serve society in general as well as the financial interests of its stockholders. The stakeholder approach offers the clearest perspective on such issues. Broadly stated, outsiders often demand that insiders' claims be subordinated to the greater good of the society; that is, to the greater good of outsiders. They believe that such issues as pollution, the disposal of solid and liquid wastes, and the conservation of natural resources should be principal considerations in strategic decision making. Also broadly stated, insiders tend to believe that the competing claims of outsiders should be balanced against one another in a way that protects the company mission. For example, they tend to believe that the need of consumers for a product should be balanced against the water pollution resulting from its production if the firm cannot eliminate that pollution entirely and still remain profitable. Some insiders also argue that the claims of society, as expressed in government regulation, provide tax money that can be used to eliminate water pollution and the like if the general public wants this to be done.

EXHIBIT 3.2
Inputs to the Development of the Company Mission

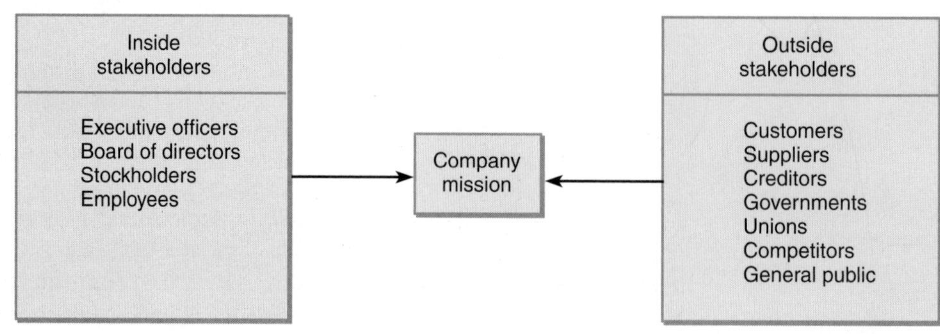

The issues are numerous, complex, and contingent on specific situations. Thus, rigid rules of business conduct cannot deal with them. Each firm *regardless of size* must decide how to meet its perceived social responsibility. While large, well-capitalized companies may have easy access to environmental consultants, this is not an affordable strategy for smaller companies. However, the experience of many small businesses demonstrates that it is feasible to accomplish significant pollution prevention and waste reduction without big expenditures and without hiring consultants. Once a problem area has been identified, a company's line employees frequently can develop a solution. Other important pollution prevention strategies include changing the materials used or redesigning how operations are bid out. Making pollution prevention a social responsibility can be beneficial to smaller companies. Publicly traded firms also can benefit directly from socially responsible strategies.

Different approaches adopted by different firms reflect differences in competitive position, industry, country, environmental and ecological pressures, and a host of other factors. In other words, they will reflect both situational factors and differing priorities in the acknowledgment of claims. Obviously, winning the loyalty of the growing legions of consumers will require new strategies and new alliances in the twenty-first century. Exhibit 3.3, Global Strategy in Action, discusses a wide range of socially responsible actions in which corporations are currently engaged.

Occidental Petroleum faces issues of corporate social responsibility in addressing the needs of the many stakeholders involved in the firm's oil exploration in developing countries. Many parties have the potential to be affected by the company's endeavors, including local inhabitants and government, environmental groups, and institutional investors.

Despite differences in their approaches, most American firms now try to assure outsiders that they attempt to conduct business in a socially responsible manner. Many firms, including Abt Associates, Dow Chemical, Eastern Gas and Fuel Associates, ExxonMobil, and the Bank of America, conduct and publish annual social audits. Such audits attempt to evaluate a firm from the perspective of social responsibility. Private consultants often conduct them for the firm and offer minimally biased evaluations on what are inherently highly subjective issues.

TYPES OF SOCIAL RESPONSIBILITY

To better understand the nature and range of social responsibilities for which they must plan, strategic managers can consider four types of social commitment: economic, legal, ethical, and discretionary social responsibilities.

economic responsibilities
The duty of managers, as agents of the company owners, to maximize stockholder wealth.

Economic responsibilities are the most basic social responsibilities of business. As we have noted, some economists see these as the only legitimate social responsibility of business. Living up to their economic responsibilities requires managers to maximize profits whenever possible. The essential responsibility of business is assumed to be providing goods and services to society at a reasonable cost. In discharging that economic responsibility, the company also emerges as socially responsible by providing productive jobs for its workforce, and tax payments for its local, state, and federal governments.

legal responsibilities
The firm's obligations to comply with the laws that regulate business activities.

Legal responsibilities reflect the firm's obligations to comply with the laws that regulate business activities. The consumer and environmental movements focused increased public attention on the need for social responsibility in business by lobbying for laws that govern business in the areas of pollution control and consumer safety. The intent of consumer legislation has been to correct the "balance of power" between buyers and sellers in the marketplace. Among the most important laws are the Federal Fair Packaging and Labeling

Global Strategy in Action — Exhibit 3.3

Who's Doing Well by Doing Good

Automobiles	
Toyota	The maker of the top-selling Prius hybrid leads in developing efficient gas-electric vehicles.
Volkswagen	A market leader in small cars and clean diesel technologies.
Computers and Peripherals	
Toshiba	At forefront of developing eco-efficient products, such as fuel cells for notebook PC batteries.
Dell	Among the first U.S. PC makers to take hardware back from consumers and recycle it for free.
Health Care	
Fresenius Medical Care	Discloses costs of its patient treatment in terms of energy and water use and waste generated.
Quest Diagnostics	Diversity program promotes businesses owned by minorities, women, and veterans.
Oil and Gas	
Norsk Hydro	Cut greenhouse gas emissions 32 percent since 1990; strong in assessing social, environmental impact.
Suncor Energy	Ties with aboriginals help it deal with social and ecological issues in Canada's far north.
Retail	
Marks & Spencer	Buys local product to cut transit costs and fuel use; good wages and benefits help retain staff.
Aeon	Environmental accounting has saved $5.6 million; good employee policies in China and Southeast Asia.
Communications Equipment	
Nokia	Makes phones for handicapped and low-income consumers; a leader in phasing out toxic materials.
Ericsson	Eco-freindly initiatives include wind- and fuel-cell-powered telecom systems in Nigerian villages.
Financial Services	
ABN Amro	Involved in carbon-emissions trading; finances everything from micro-enterprises to biomass fuels.
ING	Weighs sustainability in project finance; helps developing nations improve financial institutions.
Household Durables	
Philips Electronics	Top innovator of energy-saving appliances, lighting, and medical gear and goods for developing world.
Matsushita Electric	State-of-the-art green products; eliminated 96 percent of the most toxic substances in its global operations.
Pharmaceuticals	
Novo Nordisk	Spearheads efforts in leprosy and bird flu and is a leading player in lower-cost generics.
Glaxo-SmithKline	Devotes R&D to malaria and TB; first to offer AIDS drugs at cost.
Utilities	
FPL	Largest U.S. solar generator.
Scottish & Southern	Aggressively discloses environmental risk, including air pollution and climate change.

Source: From "Beyond the Green Corporation," by Pete Engardino. Reprinted from January 29, 2007 issue of *BusinessWeek* by special permission.

Act that regulates labeling procedures for business, the Truth in Lending Act that regulates the extension of credit to individuals, and the Consumer Product Safety Act that protects consumers against unreasonable risks of injury in the use of consumer products.

The environmental movement has had a similar effect on the regulation of business. This movement achieved stricter enforcement of existing environmental protections and it spurred the passage of new, more comprehensive laws such as the National Environmental Policy Act, which is devoted to preserving the United States' ecological balance and making environmental protection a federal policy goal. It requires environmental impact studies whenever new construction may threaten an existing ecosystem, and it established the Council on Environmental Quality to guide business development. Another product of the environmental movement was the creation of the federal Environmental Protection Agency, which interprets and administers the environmental protection policies of the U.S. government.

Clearly, these legal responsibilities are supplemental to the requirement that businesses and their employees comply fully with the general civil and criminal laws that apply to all individuals and institutions in the country. Yet, strangely, individual failures to adhere to the law have recently produced some of the greatest scandals in the history of American free enterprise. Probably the most disgraceful of these high-profile cases involved the Enron Corporation, an American company with headquarters in Houston, Texas. Enron was one of the world's largest electricity, natural gas, pulp and paper, and communication companies, before its bankruptcy in 2001. It had been named "America's Most Innovative Company" for six consecutive years and "100 Best Companies to Work For in America" by *Fortune* magazine. Its revenue in 2000 was $101 billion, making it the seventh largest corporation in the United States.

Enron's bankruptcy was caused by willful and creatively planned accounting fraud masterminded by three Enron executives. Kenneth Lay (founder, former chairman, and CEO), Jeffrey Skilling (former president, CEO, and chief operating officer [COO]), and Andrew Fastow (former chief financial officer [CFO]) received lengthy prison sentences for crimes including conspiracy, securities fraud, false statements, and insider trading.

It was revealed in court hearings that the majority of Enron's profits and revenue came from deals with special-purpose entities, while the majority of Enron's debts and losses were not reported in its financial statements. As the scandal was exposed to the general public, Enron's blue chip stock plummeted from more than $90 to pennies per share. Enron's accounting firm, Arthur Andersen, was found guilty of obstruction of justice for destroying documents related to Enron, was forced to stop auditing public companies, and suffered irreparable damage to its reputation. In 2007, Enron changed its name to Enron Creditors Recovery Corporation to reflect the reorganization and liquidation of remaining operations and assets of the company.

Exhibit 3.4, Strategy in Action, presents an overview of seven other major criminal or ethical violations that involved executives from Adelphia Communications, Arthur Andersen, Global Crossing, ImClone Systems, Merrill Lynch, WorldCom, and Xerox.

ethical responsibilities
The strategic managers' notion of right and proper business behavior.

Ethical responsibilities reflect the company's notion of right and proper business behavior. Ethical responsibilities are obligations that transcend legal requirements. Firms are expected, but not required, to behave ethically. Some actions that are legal might be considered unethical. For example, the manufacture and distribution of cigarettes is legal. But in light of the often-lethal consequences of smoking, many consider the continued sale of cigarettes to be unethical. The topic of management ethics receives additional attention later in this chapter.

Strategy in Action

Exhibit 3.4

An Overview of Corporate Scandals*

ADELPHIA COMMUNICATIONS

On July 24, 2002, John Rigas, the 77-year-old founder of the country's sixth largest cable television operator, was arrested, along with two of his sons, and accused of looting the now-bankrupt company. Several other former Adelphia executives were also arrested. The Securities and Exchange Commission (SEC) brought a civil suit against the company for allegedly fraudulently excluding billions of dollars in liabilities from its financial statements, falsifying statistics, inflating its earnings to meet Wall Street's expectations, and concealing "rampant self-dealing by the Rigas family." The family, which founded Adelphia in 1952, gave up control of the firm in May, and on June 25 the company filed for bankruptcy protection. The company was delisted by NASDAQ in June 2002.

ARTHUR ANDERSEN

On June 15, 2002, a Texas jury found the accounting firm guilty of obstructing justice for its role in shredding financial documents related to its former client Enron. Andersen, founded in 1913, had already been largely destroyed after admitting that it sped up the shredding of Enron documents following the launch of an SEC investigation. Andersen fired David Duncan, who led its Houston office, saying he was responsible for shredding the Enron documents. Duncan admitted to obstruction of justice, turned state's evidence, and testified on behalf of the government.

GLOBAL CROSSING

The SEC and the Federal Bureau of Investigation (FBI) are probing the five-year-old telecom company Global Crossing regarding alleged swaps of network capacity with other telecommunications firms to inflate revenue. The company ran into trouble by betting that it could borrow billions of dollars to build a fiber-optic infrastructure that would be in strong demand by corporations. Because others made the same bet, there was a glut of fiber optics and prices plunged, leaving Global Crossing with massive debts. It filed for bankruptcy on January 28, 2002. Chairman Gary Winnick, who founded Global Crossing in 1997, cashed out $734 million in stock before the company collapsed. Global Crossing was delisted from the New York Stock Exchange (NYSE) in January 2002.

IMCLONE SYSTEMS

The biotech firm is being investigated by a congressional committee that is seeking to find out if ImClone correctly informed investors that the Food and Drug Administration (FDA) had declined to accept for review its key experimental cancer drug, Erbitux. Former CEO Samuel Waksal pled guilty in June 2003 to insider trading charges related to Erbitux and was sentenced to seven years in prison. Also, federal investigators filed charges against home decorating diva Martha Stewart for using insider information on the cancer drug when she sold 4,000 ImClone shares one day before the FDA initially said it would reject the drug.

MERRILL LYNCH

On May 21, 2002, Merrill Lynch agreed to pay $100 million to settle New York Attorney General Eliot Spitzer's charges that the nation's largest securities firm knowingly peddled Internet stocks to investors to generate lucrative investment banking fees. Internal memos written by Merrill's feted Internet analyst Henry Blodgett revealed that company analysts thought little of the Web stocks that they urged investors to buy. Merrill agreed to strengthen firewalls between its research and investment-banking divisions, ensuring advice given to investors is not influenced by efforts to win underwriting fees.

WORLDCOM

The nation's second largest telecom company filed for the nation's biggest ever bankruptcy on July 21, 2002. WorldCom's demise accelerated on June 25, 2002, when it admitted it hid $3.85 billion in expenses, allowing it to post net income of $1.38 billion in 2001, instead of a loss. The company fired its CFO, Scott Sullivan, and on June 28 began cutting 17,000 jobs, more than 20 percent of its workforce. CEO Bernie Ebbers resigned in April amid questions about $408 million of personal loans he received from the company to cover losses he incurred in buying its shares. WorldCom was delisted from NASDAQ in July 2002.

XEROX

Xerox said on June 28, 2002, that it would restate five years of financial results to reclassify more than $6 billion in revenues. In April, the company settled SEC charges that it used "accounting tricks" to defraud investors, agreeing to pay a $10 million fine. The firm admitted no wrongdoing. Xerox manufactures imaging products, such as copiers, printers, fax machines, and scanners.

*This section was derived in its entirety from "A Guide to Corporate Scandals," MSNBC, www.msnbc.com/news/corpscandal front.

discretionary responsibilities
Responsibilities voluntarily assumed by a business, such as public relations, good citizenship, and full corporate responsibility.

Discretionary responsibilities are those that are voluntarily assumed by a business organization. They include public relations activities, good citizenship, and full corporate social responsibility. Through public relations activities, managers attempt to enhance the image of their companies, products, and services by supporting worthy causes. This form of discretionary responsibility has a self-serving dimension. Companies that adopt the good citizenship approach actively support ongoing charities, public service advertising campaigns, or issues in the public interest. A commitment to full corporate responsibility requires strategic managers to attack social problems with the same zeal with which they attack business problems. For example, teams in the National Football League provide time off for players and other employees afflicted with drug or alcohol addictions who agree to enter rehabilitation programs.

It is important to remember that the categories on the continuum of social responsibility overlap, creating gray areas where societal expectations of organizational behavior are difficult to categorize. In considering the overlaps among various demands for social responsibility, however, managers should keep in mind that in the view of the general public, economic and legal responsibilities are required, ethical responsibility is expected, and discretionary responsibility is desired.

Corporate Social Responsibility and Profitability

CSR and the Bottom Line

corporate social responsibility (CSR)
The idea that business has a duty to serve society in general as well as the financial interest of stockholders.

The goal of every firm is to maintain viability through long-run profitability. Until all costs and benefits are accounted for, however, profits may not be claimed. In the case of **corporate social responsibility (CSR)**, costs and benefits are both economic and social. While economic costs and benefits are easily quantifiable, social costs and benefits are not. Managers therefore risk subordinating social consequences to other performance results that can be more straightforwardly measured.

The dynamic between CSR and success (profit) is complex. While one concept is clearly not mutually exclusive of the other, it is also clear that neither is a prerequisite for the other. Rather than viewing these two concepts as competing, it may be better to view CSR as a component in the decision-making process of business that must determine, among other objectives, how to maximize profits.

Attempts to undertake a cost-benefit analysis of CSR have not been very successful. The process is complicated by several factors. First, some CSR activities incur no dollar costs at all. For example, Second Harvest, the largest nongovernment, charitable food distributor in the nation, accepts donations from food manufacturers and food retailers of surplus food that would otherwise be thrown out due to overruns, warehouse damage, or labeling errors. In 10 years, Second Harvest has distributed more than 2 billion pounds of food. Gifts in Kind America is an organization that enables companies to reduce unsold or obsolete inventory by matching a corporation's donated products with a charity's or other nonprofit organization's needs. In addition, a tax break is realized by the company. In the past, corporate donations have included 130,000 pairs of shoes from Nike, 10,000 pairs of gloves from Aris Isotoner, and 480 computer systems from Apple Computer.

In addition, philanthropic activities of a corporation, which have been a traditional mainstay of CSR, are undertaken at a discounted cost to the firm since they are often tax deductible. The benefits of corporate philanthropy can be enormous as is shown by the many national social welfare causes that have been spurred by corporate giving. While such acts of benevolence often help establish a general perception of the involved companies within society, some philanthropic acts bring specific credit to the firm.

Strategy in Action — Exhibit 3.5

Mission Statement: Johnson & Johnson

"We believe our first responsibility is to the doctors, nurses and patients, to mothers and fathers and all others who use our products and services. In meeting their needs everything we do must be of high quality. We must constantly strive to reduce our costs in order to maintain reasonable prices. Customers' orders must be serviced promptly and accurately. Our suppliers and distributors must have an opportunity to make a fair profit.

We are responsible to our employees, the men and women who work with us throughout the world. Everyone must be considered as an individual. We must respect their dignity and recognize their merit. They must have a sense of security in their jobs. Compensation must be fair and adequate, and working conditions clean, orderly and safe. Employees must feel free to make suggestions and complaints. There must be equal opportunity for employment, development and advancement for those qualified. We must provide competent management, and their actions must be just and ethical.

We are responsible to the communities in which we live and work and to the world community as well. We must be good citizens—support good works and charities and bear our fair share of taxes. We must encourage civic improvements and better health and education. We must maintain in good order the property we are privileged to use, protecting the environment and natural resources.

Our final responsibility is to our stockholders. Business must make a sound profit. We must experiment with new ideas. Research must be carried on, innovative programs developed and mistakes paid for. New equipment must be purchased, new facilities provided and new products launched. Reserves must be created to provide for adverse times. When we operate according to these principles, the stockholders should realize a fair return."

Source: Johnson & Johnson, http://www.jnj.com

Second, socially responsible behavior does not come at a prohibitive cost. One needs only to look at the problems of A. H. Robbins Company (Dalkon Shield), Beech-Nut Corporation (apple juice), Drexel Burnham (insider trading), and Exxon (*Valdez*) for stark answers on the "cost" of social responsibility (or its absence) in the business environment.

Third, socially responsible practices may create savings and, as a result, increase profits. SET Laboratories uses popcorn to ship software rather than polystyrene peanuts. It is environmentally safer and costs 60 percent less to use. Corporations that offer part-time and adjustable work schedules have realized that this can lead to reduced absenteeism, greater productivity and increased morale. DuPont opted for more flexible schedules for its employees after a survey revealed 50 percent of women and 25 percent of men considered working for another employer with more flexibility for family concerns.

Proponents argue that CSR costs are more than offset in the long run by an improved company image and increased community goodwill. These intangible assets can prove valuable in a crisis, as Johnson & Johnson discovered with the Tylenol cyanide scare in 1982. Because it had established a solid reputation as a socially responsible company before the incident, the public readily accepted the company's assurances of public safety. Consequently, financial damage to Johnson & Johnson was minimized, despite the company's $100 million voluntary recall of potentially tainted capsules. CSR may also head off new regulation, preventing increased compliance costs. It may even attract investors who are themselves socially responsible. Proponents believe that for these reasons, socially responsible behavior increases the financial value of the firm in the long run. The mission statement of Johnson & Johnson is provided as Exhibit 3.5, Strategy in Action.

Performance To explore the relationship between socially responsible behavior and financial performance, an important question must first be answered: How do managers measure the financial effect of corporate social performance?

Critics of CSR believe that companies that behave in a socially responsible manner, and portfolios comprising these companies' securities, should perform more poorly financially than those that do not. The costs of CSR outweigh the benefits for individual firms, they suggest. In addition, traditional portfolio theory holds that investors minimize risk and maximize return by being able to choose from an infinite universe of investment opportunities. Portfolios based on social criteria should suffer, critics argue, because they are by definition restrictive in nature. This restriction should increase portfolio risk and reduce portfolio return.

CSR Today

CSR has become a priority with American business. In addition to a commonsense belief that companies should be able to "do well by doing good," at least three broad trends are driving businesses to adopt CSR frameworks: the resurgence of environmentalism, increasing buyer power, and the globalization of business.

The Resurgence of Environmentalism In March 1989, the Exxon *Valdez* ran aground in Prince William Sound, spilling 11 million gallons of oil, polluting miles of ocean and shore, and helping to revive worldwide concern for the ecological environment. Six months after the *Valdez* incident, the Coalition for Environmentally Responsible Economies (CERES) was formed to establish new goals for environmentally responsible corporate behavior. The group drafted the CERES Principles to "establish an environmental ethic with criteria by which investors and others can assess the environmental performance of companies. Companies that sign these Principles pledge to go voluntarily beyond the requirements of the law."

The most prevalent forms of environmentalism are efforts to preserve natural resources and eliminating environmental pollution, often referred to as the concern for "greening." The Heinz Corporation is a company that is praised for its strong green stance. Some details of its aggressive sustainability program are provided in Exhibit 3.6, Top Strategist.

Increasing Buyer Power The rise of the consumer movement has meant that buyers—consumers and investors—are increasingly flexing their economic muscle. Consumers are becoming more interested in buying products from socially responsible companies. Organizations such as the Council on Economic Priorities (CEP) help consumers make more informed buying decisions through such publications as *Shopping for a Better World,* which provides social performance information on 191 companies making more than 2,000 consumer products. CEP also sponsors the annual Corporate Conscience Awards, which recognize socially responsible companies. One example of consumer power at work is the effective outcry over the deaths of dolphins in tuna fishermen's nets.

Investors represent a second type of influential consumer. There has been a dramatic increase in the number of people interested in supporting socially responsible companies through their investments. Membership in the Social Investment Forum, a trade association serving social investing professionals, has been growing at a rate of about 50 percent annually. As baby boomers achieve their own financial success, the social investing movement has continued its rapid growth.

While social investing wields relatively low power as an individual private act (selling one's shares of ExxonMobil does not affect the company), it can be very powerful as a collective public act. When investors vote their shares on behalf of pro-CSR issues, companies may be pressured to change their social behavior. The South African divestiture movement is one example of how effective this pressure can be.

The Vermont National Bank has added a Socially Responsible Banking Fund to its product line. Investors can designate any of their interest-bearing accounts with a

Top Strategist
Heinz CEO Bill Johnson Stresses Corporate Social Responsibility

Exhibit 3.6

During a National Press Club luncheon in Washington, D.C., Bill Johnson, the CEO of Heinz Corp, was named the CEO Pioneer of 2008 for his work in establishing Heinz as a leader in corporate social responsibility.

Johnson and his management team established a very aggressive strategic plan encompassing eight major global sustainability goals:

Greenhouse gas	Emissions	Decrease by 20%
Energy use in manufacturing	Usage	Decrease by 20%
Water use in manufacturing	Water consumption	Decrease by 20%
Solid waste	Waste from Heinz operations	Decrease by 20%
Packaging	Total packaging	Decrease by 15%
Transportation	Fossil fuel consumption	Decrease by 10%
Renewable energy	Renewable energy resources	Increase by 15%
Sustainable agriculture	Carbon footprint	Decrease by 15%
	Water usage	Decrease by 15%
	Field yield	Increase by 5%

These environmental goals were viewed by Johnson as an extension of the original vision of Henry J. Heinz, who believed that food safety regulations made a significant contribution to society.

The overarching theme of Johnson's corporate social responsibility plan was a 20 percent reduction of greenhouse gas emissions by the year 2015. He stated, "To achieve these goals we are executing numerous global initiatives to reduce non-value-added packaging, increase the use of recycled materials, lower energy consumption, conserve water, and increase our use of renewable energy sources at some of our largest plants."* Examples of successes in achieving his plan included a European plastics consumption reduction of 340 tons and a solid waste reduction in an Ohio plant of 800,000 pounds.

* *H.J. Heinz Corp. Web site,* 2011, http://www.heinz.com/sustainability/environment.aspx

Source: *2008 Annual Report*, H.J. Heinz Corporation, June 19, 2008, p. 14.

$500 minimum balance to be used by the fund. This fund then lends these monies for purposes such as low-income housing, the environment, education, farming, or small business development. Although it has had a "humble" beginning of approximately 800 people investing about $11 million, the bank has attracted out-of-state depositors and is growing faster than expected.

Social investors comprise both individuals and institutions. Much of the impetus for social investing originated with religious organizations that wanted their investments to mirror their beliefs. At present, the ranks of social investors have expanded to include educational institutions and large pension funds.

Large-scale social investing can be broken down into the two broad areas of guideline portfolio investing and shareholder activism. Guideline portfolio investing is the largest and fastest-growing segment of social investing. Individual and institutional guideline portfolio investors use ethical guidelines as screens to identify possible investments in stocks, bonds, and mutual funds. The investment instruments that survive the social screens are then layered over the investor's financial screens to create the investor's universe of possible investments.

Screens may be negative (e.g., excluding all tobacco companies) or they may combine negative and positive elements (e.g., eliminating companies with bad labor records while seeking out companies with good ones). Most investors rely on screens created by investment firms such as Kinder, Lydenberg Domini & Co. or by industry groups such as the Council on Economic Priorities. In addition to ecology, employee relations, and community development, corporations may be screened on their association with "sin" products (alcohol, tobacco, gambling), defense/weapons production, and nuclear power.

In contrast to guideline portfolio investors, who passively indicate their approval or disapproval of a company's social behavior by simply including or excluding it from their portfolios, shareholder activists seek to directly influence corporate social behavior. Shareholder activists invest in a corporation hoping to improve specific aspects of the company's social performance, typically by seeking a dialogue with upper management. If this and successive actions fail to achieve the desired results, shareholder activists may introduce proxy resolutions to be voted upon at the corporation's annual meeting. The goal of these resolutions is to achieve change by gaining public exposure for the issue at hand. While the number of shareholder activists is relatively small, they are by no means small in achievement: shareholder activists, led by such groups as the Interfaith Center on Corporate Responsibility, were the driving force behind the South African divestiture movement. Currently, there are more than 35 socially screened mutual funds available in the United States alone.

The Globalization of Business Management issues, including CSR, have become more complex as companies increasingly transcend national borders: It is difficult enough to come to a consensus on what constitutes socially responsible behavior within one culture, let alone determine common ethical values across cultures. In addition to different cultural views, the high barriers facing international CSR include differing corporate disclosure practices, inconsistent financial data and reporting methods, and the lack of CSR research organizations within countries. Despite these problems, CSR is growing abroad. The United Kingdom has 30 ethical mutual funds and Canada offers 6 socially responsible funds.

One of the most contentious social responsibility issues confronting multinational firms pertains to human rights. For example, many U.S. firms reduce their costs either by relying on foreign manufactured goods or by outsourcing their manufacturing to foreign manufacturers. These foreign manufacturers, often Chinese, offer low pricing because they pay very low wages by U.S. standards, even though they are extremely competitive by Chinese pay rates.

While Chinese workers are happy to earn manufacturer wages and U.S. customers are pleased by the lower prices charged for foreign manufactured goods, others are unhappy. They believe that such U.S. firms are failing to satisfy their social responsibilities. Some U.S. workers and their unions argue that jobs in the United States are being eliminated or devalued by foreign competition. Some human rights advocates argue that the working conditions and living standards of foreign workers are so substandard when compared with U.S. standards that they verge on inhumane. A troubling twist on American corporations' role in the human rights debate about conditions in China arises from the sale of software to the Chinese government. Developed by Cisco, Oracle, and other U.S. companies, the software is used by China's police to monitor the activities of individuals that the Chinese government labels as criminals and dissidents.

Exhibit 3.8 cont.

the company, nor be an officer, director, partner, or employee of the company.

- The audit committee must have the authority to engage the outside auditing firm.
- The audit committee must establish procedures for the treatment of complaints regarding accounting controls or auditing matters. They are responsible for employee complaints concerning questionable accounting and auditing.
- The audit committee must disclose whether at least one of the committee members is a "financial expert." If not, the committee must explain why not.

NEW CRIMES AND INCREASED CRIMINAL PENALTIES

- Tampering with records with intent to impede or influence any federal investigation or bankruptcy will be punishable by a fine and/or prison sentence up to 20 years.
- Failure by an accountant to maintain all auditing papers for five years after the end of the fiscal period will be punishable by a fine and/or up to 10-year prison sentence.
- Knowingly executing, or attempting to execute, a scheme to defraud investors will be punishable by a fine and/or prison sentence of up to 25 years.
- Willfully certifying a report that does not comply with the law can be punishable with a fine up to $5,000,000 and/or a prison sentence up to 20 years.

NEW CIVIL CAUSE OF ACTION AND INCREASED ENFORCEMENT POWERS

- Protection will be provided to whistle-blowers who provide information or assist in an investigation by law enforcement, congressional committee, or employee supervisor.
- Bankruptcy cannot be used to avoid liability from securities laws violations.
- Investors are able to file a civil action for fraud up to two years after discovery of the facts and five years after the occurrence of fraud.
- The SEC can receive a restraining order prohibiting payments to insiders during an investigation.
- The SEC can prevent individuals from holding an officer's or director's position in a public company as a result of violation of the securities law.

AUDITOR INDEPENDENCE

- All audit services must be preapproved by the audit committee and must be disclosed to investors.
- The lead audit or reviewing audit partner from the auditing accounting firm must change at least once every five fiscal years.
- The registered accounting firms must report to the audit committee all accounting policies and practices used, alternative uses of the financial information within GAAP that has been discussed with management, and written communications between the accounting firm and management.
- An auditing firm is prohibited from auditing a company if the company's CEO or CFO was employed by the auditing firm within the past year.

A Public Company Accounting Oversight Board is established by the SEC to oversee the audits of public companies. The board will register public accounting firms, establish audit standards, inspect registered accounting firms, and discipline violators of the rules. No person can take part in an audit if not employed by a registered public accounting firm.

the company's financial condition and result of operations for the period represented. The certification also makes the officers responsible for establishing and maintaining internal controls such that they are aware of any material information relating to the company. The officers must also evaluate the effectiveness of the internal controls within 90 days of the release of the report and present their conclusions of the effectiveness of the controls. Also, the officers must disclose any fraudulent material, deficiencies in the reporting of the financial reports, or problems with the internal control to the company's auditors and auditing committee. Finally, the officers must indicate any changes to the internal controls or factors that could affect them.

The Sarbanes-Oxley Act includes provisions restricting the corporate control of executives, accounting firms, auditing committees, and attorneys. With regard to executives, the act bans personal loans. A company can no longer directly or indirectly issue, extend, or maintain a personal loan to any director or executive officer. Executive officers and directors are not permitted to purchase, sell, acquire, or transfer any equity security during any pension fund blackout period. Executives are required to notify fund participants of any blackout period and the reasons for the blackout period. The SEC will provide the company's executives with a code of ethics for the company to adopt. Failure to meet the code must be disclosed to the SEC.

The act limits some and issues new duties of the registered public accounting firms that conduct the audits of the financial statements. Accounting firms are prohibited from performing bookkeeping or other accounting services related to the financial statements, designing or implementing financial systems, appraising, internal auditing, brokering banking services, or providing legal services unrelated to the audit. All critical accounting policies and alternative treatments of financial information within generally accepted accounting principles (GAAP), and written communication between the accounting firm and the company's management must be reported to the audit committee.

The act defines the composition of the audit committee and specifies its responsibilities. The members of the audit committee must be members of the company's board of directors. At least one member of the committee should be classified as a "financial expert." The audit committee is directly responsible for the work of any accounting firm employed by the company, and the accounting firm must report directly to the audit committee. The audit committee must create procedures for employee complaints or concerns over accounting or auditing matters. Upon discovery of unlawful acts by the company, the audit committee must report and be supervised in its investigation by a Public Company Accounting Oversight Board.

The act includes rules for attorney conduct. If a company's attorneys find evidence of securities violations, they are required to report the matter to the chief legal counsel or CEO. If there is not an appropriate response, the attorneys must report the information to the audit committee or the board of directors.

Other sections of the Sarbanes-Oxley Act stipulate disclosure periods for financial operations and reporting. Relevant information relating to changes in the financial condition or operations of a company must be immediately reported in plain English. Off-balance-sheet transactions, correcting adjustments, and pro-forma information must be presented in the annual and quarterly financial reports. The information must not contain any untrue statements, must not omit material facts, and must meet GAAP standards.

Stricter penalties have been issued for violations of the Sarbanes-Oxley Act. If a company must restate its financial statements due to noncompliance, the CEO and CFO must relinquish any bonus or incentive-based compensation or realized profits from the sale of securities during the 12-month period following the filing with the SEC. Other securities fraud, such as destruction or falsification of records, results in fines and prison sentences up to 25 years.

The New Corporate Governance Structure

A major consequence of the 2000–2002 accounting scandals was the Sarbanes-Oxley Act of 2002, and a major consequence of Sarbanes-Oxley has been the restructuring of the governance structure of American corporations. The most significant change in the restructuring is the heightened role of corporate internal auditors, as depicted in Exhibit 3.9, Strategy in Action. Auditors have traditionally been viewed as performing a necessary but

Strategy in Action — Exhibit 3.9

The New Corporate Governance Structure

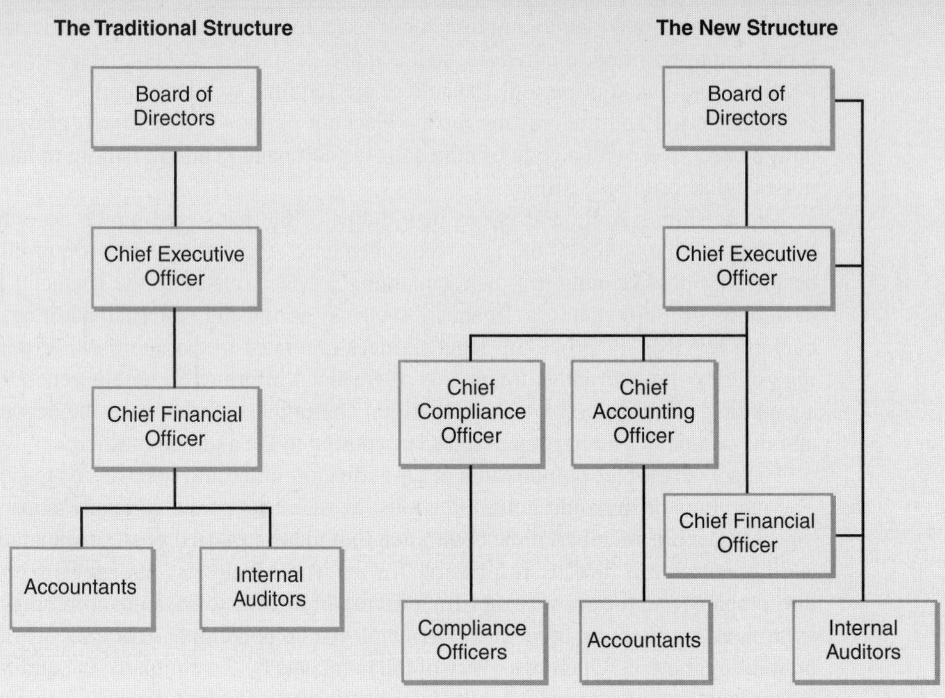

perfunctory function, namely to probe corporate financial records for unintentional or illicit misrepresentations. Although a majority of U.S. corporations have longstanding traditions of reporting that their auditors operated independently of CFO approval and that they had direct access to the board, in practice, the auditors' work usually traveled through the organization's hierarchical chain of command.

In the past, internal auditors reviewed financial reports generated by other corporate accountants. The auditors considered professional accounting and financial practices, as well as relevant aspects of corporate law, and then presented their findings to the chief financial officer (CFO). Historically, the CFO reviewed the audits and determined the financial data and information that was to be presented to top management, directors, and investors of the company.

However, because Sarbanes-Oxley requires that CEOs and audit committees sign off on financial results, auditors now routinely deal directly with top corporate officials, as shown in the new structure in Exhibit 3.9, Strategy in Action. Approximately 75 percent of senior corporate auditors now report directly to the Board of Directors' audit committee. Additionally, to eliminate the potential for accounting problems, companies are establishing direct lines of communication between top managers and the board and auditors that inform the CFO but that are not dependent on CFO approval or authorization.

The new structure also provides the CEO information provided directly by the company's chief compliance and chief accounting officers. Consequently, the CFO, who is responsible for ultimately approving all company payments, is not empowered to be the sole provider of data for financial evaluations by the CEO and board.

CSR's Effect on the Mission Statement

The mission statement not only identifies what product or service a company produces, how it produces it, and what market it serves, it also embodies what the company believes. As such, it is essential that the mission statement recognize the legitimate claims of its external stakeholders, which may include creditors, customers, suppliers, government, unions, competitors, local communities, and elements of the general public. This stakeholder approach has become widely accepted by U.S. business. For example, a survey of directors in 291 of the largest southeastern U.S. companies found that directors had high stakeholder orientations. Customers, government, stockholders, employees, and society, in that order, were the stakeholders these directors perceived as most important.

In developing mission statements, managers must identify all stakeholder groups and weigh their relative rights and abilities to affect the firm's success. Some companies are proactive in their approach to CSR, making it an integral part of their raison d'être (e.g., Ben & Jerry's ice cream); others are reactive, adopting socially responsible behavior only when they must (e.g., Exxon after the *Valdez* incident).

Social Audit

social audit
An attempt to measure a company's actual social performance against its social objectives.

A **social audit** attempts to measure a company's actual social performance against the social objectives it has set for itself. A social audit may be conducted by the company itself. However, one conducted by an outside consultant who will impose minimal biases may prove more beneficial to the firm. As with a financial audit, an outside auditor brings credibility to the evaluation. This credibility is essential if management is to take the results seriously and if the general public is to believe the company's public relations pronouncements.

Careful, accurate monitoring and evaluation of a company's CSR actions are important not only because the company wants to be sure it is implementing CSR policy as planned but also because CSR actions by their nature are open to intense public scrutiny. To make sure it is making good on its CSR promises, a company may conduct a social audit of its performance.

Once the social audit is complete, it may be distributed internally or both internally and externally, depending on the firm's goals and situation. Some firms include a section in their annual report devoted to social responsibility activities; others publish a separate periodic report on their social responsiveness. Companies publishing separate social audits include General Motors, Bank of America, Atlantic Richfield, Control Data, and Aetna Life and Casualty Company. Nearly all *Fortune* 500 corporations disclose social performance information in their annual reports.

Large firms are not the only companies employing the social audit. Boutique ice cream maker Ben & Jerry's, a CSR pioneer, publishes a social audit in its annual report. The audit, conducted by an outside consultant, scores company performance in such areas as employee benefits, plant safety, ecology, community involvement, and customer service. The report is published unedited.

The social audit may be used for more than simply monitoring and evaluating firm social performance. Managers also use social audits to scan the external environment, determine firm vulnerabilities, and institutionalize CSR within the firm. In addition, companies themselves are not the only ones who conduct social audits; public interest groups and the media watch companies who claim to be socially responsible very closely to see if they practice what they preach. These organizations include consumer groups and socially responsible investing firms that construct their own guidelines for evaluating companies.

The Body Shop learned what can happen when a company's behavior falls short of its espoused mission and objectives. The 20-year-old manufacturer and retailer of naturally based hair and skin products had cultivated a socially responsible corporate image based on a reputation for socially responsible behavior. However, *Business Ethics* magazine published an exposé claiming that the company did not "walk the talk." It accused The Body Shop of using nonrenewable petrochemicals in its products, recycling far less than it claimed, using ingredients tested on animals, and making threats against investigative journalists. The Body Shop's contradictions were noteworthy because Anita Roddick, the company's founder, made CSR a centerpiece of the company's strategy.[1]

SATISFYING CORPORATE SOCIAL RESPONSIBILITY[2]

William Ford Jr. angered Ford Motor Co. executives and investors when he wrote that "there are very real conflicts between Ford's current business practices, consumer choices, and emerging views of (environmental) sustainability." In his company's citizenship report, the grandson of Henry Ford, then the automaker's nonexecutive chairman, even appeared to endorse a Sierra Club statement declaring that "the gas-guzzling SUV is a rolling monument to environmental destruction."

Bill Ford moderated his strongest environmental beliefs since assuming the company's CEO position. Nevertheless, while he strives to improve Ford's financial performance and restore trust among its diverse stakeholders, he remains strongly committed to corporate responsibility and environmental protection. In his words, "A good company delivers excellent products and services, and a great company does all that and strives to make the world a better place."[3] Today, Ford is a leader in producing vehicles that run on alternative sources of fuel, and it is performing as well as or better than its major North American rivals, all of whom are involved in intense global competition. The company is successfully pursuing a strategy that is showing improved financial performance, increased confidence in the brand, and clear evidence that the car company is committed to contributing more broadly to society. Among Ford's more notable outreach efforts are an innovative HIV/AIDS initiative in South Africa that is now expanding to India, China, and Thailand; a partnership with the U.S. National Parks Foundation to provide environmentally friendly transportation for park visitors; and significant support for the Clean Air Initiative for Asian Cities.

Ford's actions are emblematic of the corporate social responsibility initiatives of many leading companies. Corporate-supported social initiatives are now a given. Many *Fortune* 500 corporations have senior manager titles dedicated to helping their organizations "give back" more effectively. CSR is now almost universally embraced by top managers as an integral component of their executive roles, whether motivated by self-interest, altruism, strategic advantage, or political gain. Their outreach is usually plain to see on the companies' corporate Web sites. CSR is high on the agenda at major executive gatherings such as the World Economic Forum. It is very much in evidence during times of tragedy and it is the subject of many conferences, workshops, newsletters, and more. "Consultancies have sprung up to advise companies on how to do corporate social responsibility and how to let it be known that they are doing it," noted *The Economist* in a survey on CSR.

Executives face conflicting pressures to contribute to social responsibility while honoring their duties to maximize shareholder value. They face many belligerent critics who challenge the idea of a single-minded focus on profits—witness the often violent antiglobalization protests in recent years. They also face skeptics who contend that CSR

[1] Jon Entine, "Shattered Image," *Business Ethics* 8, no. 5 (September/October 1994), pp. 23–28.

[2] This section was excerpted from J. A. Pearce II and J. Doh, "Enhancing Corporate Responsibility through Skillful Collaboration," *Sloan Management Review* 46, no. 3 (2005), pp. 30–39.

[3] "Ford Motor Company Encourages Elementary School Students to Support America's National Parks," www.ford.com/en/company/nationalParks.htm

Top Strategist
Starbucks CEO Howard Schultz on CSR

Exhibit 3.10

Starbucks supports coffee farmers by paying premium prices for the highest quality coffee beans and by maintaining its position as the largest purchaser, roaster, and distributor of Fair Trade Certified™ coffee in North America (it is also among the largest worldwide). In addition, Starbucks is a long-time partner of Conservation International (CI). Together, the two organizations developed environmental and social practice standards (C.A.F.E. Practices) for coffee farmers and implemented a rewards system for farmers who adhere to these practices.

The partnership has had a major impact on coffee farmers worldwide. For example, the Association of Kilimanjaro Specialty Coffee Growers, an association of 8,000 smallholder coffee growers in Tanzania, receives support from Starbucks because it is C.A.F.E.-certified. As a result, the association is able to add environmentally sustainable technology to increase coffee quality, which in turn improves the profitability of its farmer members.

Since he came out of retirement to be reappointed as Starbucks' CEO in January 2008, Howard Schultz has taken action to further solidify the company's support of coffee farmers. Schultz partnered with Peter Seligmann, CI's chairman and CEO, to take support of coffee farmers to the next level by protecting the land surrounding coffee farms. The effort involves an effort to help the farmers get a piece of the fast-growing $70 billion carbon finance business. Starbucks finances CI's efforts to work with local growers to protect the landscapes around the coffee farms. Farmers agree to preserve forests to replant trees so that they become eligible for carbon credits from companies that are voluntarily offsetting their emissions.

Under Schultz's leadership, Starbucks has also extended its direct financial support of coffee farmers. In 2008, Starbucks, Transfair USA, and the Fairtrade Labeling Organizations (FLO) International announced Starbucks' commitment to doubling its purchases of Fair Trade™ coffee to 40 million pounds in 2009. This commitment made Starbucks the worldwide largest purchaser of Fair Trade Certified™ coffee.

initiatives are chiefly a convenient marketing gloss. However, the reality is that most executives are eager to improve their CSR effectiveness. The issue is not whether companies will engage in socially responsible activities, but how. For most companies, the challenge is how best to achieve the maximum social benefit from a given amount of resources available for social projects.

Starbucks CEO Howard Schultz believes that he has found a way to make CSR produce benefits both for others and for his firm. Starbucks invests to support coffee farmers through a new initiative with partner Conservation International—and through Starbucks purchase commitments of premium coffee beans. The details are provided in Exhibit 3.10, Top Strategist.

Studies of dozens of social responsibility initiatives at major corporations show that senior managers struggle to find the right balance between "low-engagement" solutions such as charitable gift-giving and "high-commitment" solutions that run the risk of diverting attention from the company's core mission. In this section, we will see that collaborative social initiatives (CSIs)—a form of engagement in which companies provide ongoing and sustained commitments to a social project or issue—provide the best combination of social and strategic impact.

The Core of the CSR Debate

The proper role of CSR—the actions of a company to benefit society beyond the requirement of the law and the direct interests of shareholders—has generated a century's worth of philosophically and economically intriguing debates. Since steel baron Andrew Carnegie published *The Gospel of Wealth* in 1899, the argument that businesses are the trustees of societal property that should be managed for the public good has been seen as one end of a continuum with, at the other end, the belief that profit maximization is management's only legitimate goal. The CSR debates were largely confined to the background for most of the twentieth century, making the news after an oil spill or when a consumer product caused harm, or when ethics scandals reopened the question of business's fundamental purpose.

The debates surfaced in more positive ways in the last 30 years as new businesses set up shop with altruism very much in mind and on display. Firms such as ice cream maker Ben & Jerry's argued that CSR and profits do not clash; their stance was that doing good leads to making good money. That line of thinking has gained popularity as more executives have come to understand the value of their companies' reputations with customers—and with investors and employees. But only recently have business leaders begun to get a clearer understanding of the appropriate role of CSR and its effect on financial performance.

In the past, research on the financial effect of CSR produced inconsistent findings, with some studies reporting a positive relationship, others a negative one, and others no relationship at all. Since the mid-1990s, improvements in theory, research designs, data, and analysis have produced empirical research with more consistent results.[4] Importantly, a recent meta-analysis (a methodological technique that aggregates findings of multiple studies) of more than 10 studies found that on balance, positive relationships can be expected from CSR initiatives but that the primary vehicle for achieving superior financial performance from social responsibility is via reputation effects.[5]

There is no shortage of options with which businesses can advance their CSR goals. The greater challenge is finding the right balance. Philanthropy without active engagement—cash donations, for instance—has been criticized as narrow, self-serving, and often motivated to improve the corporation's reputation and keep nongovernmental organization (NGO) critics and other naysayers at bay.[6] However, redirecting the company toward a socially responsible mission, while seemingly attractive, may have the unintended consequences of diverting both managers and employees from their core mission. Exhibit 3.11 presents a simple illustration of the range of options available to corporations as they consider their CSR commitments.

What managers need is a model that they can use to guide them in selecting social initiatives and through which they can exploit their companies' core competencies for the maximum positive impact. As a starting point, research confirms that a business must determine the social causes that it will support and why and then decide how its support should

[4] J. J. Griffin and J. F. Mahon,"The Corporate Social Performance and Corporate Financial Performance Debate: Twenty-Five Years of Incomparable Research," *Business and Society* 36 (1997), pp. 5–31; R. M. Roman, S. Hayibor, and B. R. Agle, "The Relationship between Social and Financial Performance: Repainting a Portrait," *Business and Society* 38 (1999), pp. 109–125; and J. D. Margolis and J. P. Walsh,"Misery Loves Companies: Rethinking Social Initiatives by Business," *Administrative Science Quarterly* 48 (2003), pp. 268–305.

[5] M. Orlitzky, F. L. Schmidt, and S. L. Rynes, "Corporate Social and Financial Performance: A Meta-Analysis," *Organization Studies* 24, no. 3 (2003), pp. 403–441.

[6] B. Husted,"Governance Choices for Corporate Social Responsibility: To Contribute, Collaborate or Internalize?" *Long Range Planning* 36, no. 5 (2003), pp. 481–498.

EXHIBIT 3.11
Continuum of Corporate Social Responsibility Commitments

be organized.[7] According to one perspective, businesses have three basic support options: donations of cash or material, usually to a nongovernmental or nonprofit agency; creation of a functional operation within the company to assist external charitable efforts; and development of a collaboration approach, whereby a company joins with an organization that has particular expertise in managing the way benefits are derived from corporate support.[8]

Mutual Advantages of Collaborative Social Initiatives

The term *social initiative* describes initiatives that take a collaborative approach. Research on alliances and networks among companies in competitive commercial environments tells us that each partner benefits when the other brings resources, capabilities, or other assets that it cannot easily attain on its own. These *combinative capabilities* allow the company to acquire and synthesize resources and build new applications from those resources, generating innovative responses to rapidly evolving environments.

The same is true with collaborative social initiatives. While neither companies nor nonprofits are well equipped to handle escalating social or environmental problems, each participant has the potential to contribute valuable material resources, services, or individuals' voluntary time, talents, energies, and organizational knowledge. Those cumulative offerings are vastly superior to cash-only donations, which are a minimalist solution to the challenges of social responsibility. Social initiatives involve ongoing information and operational exchanges among participants and are especially attractive because of their potential benefits for both the corporate and not-for-profit partners.

There is strong evidence to show that CSR activities increasingly confer benefits beyond enhanced reputation. For some participants, they can be a tool to attract, retain, and develop managerial talent. The PricewaterhouseCoopers (PwC) Project Ulysses is a leadership development program that sends small teams of PwC partners to developing countries to apply their expertise to complex social and economic challenges. The cross-cultural PwC teams collaborate with nongovernmental organizations (NGOs), community-based organizations, and intergovernmental agencies, working pro bono in eight-week assignments in communities struggling with the effects of poverty, conflict, and environmental degradation. The Ulysses program was designed in part to respond to a growing challenge confronting professional services companies: identifying and training up-and-coming leaders who can find nontraditional answers to intractable problems.

All 24 Ulysses graduates still work at PwC; most say they have a stronger commitment to the firm because of the commitment it made to them and because they now have a different view of PwC's values. For PwC, the Ulysses program provides a tangible message to its primary stakeholders that the company is committed to making a difference in the world. According to Brian McCann, the first U.S.-based partner to participate in Ulysses, "This is a real differentiator—not just in relation to our competitors, but to all global organizations."

[7] N. C. Smith. "Corporate Social Responsibility: Whether or How?" *California Management Review* 45, no. 4 (2003), pp. 52–76.

[8] Husted,"Governance Choices for Corporate Social Responsibility."

Strategy in Action — Exhibit 3.12

Five Principles of Successful Corporate Social Responsibility Collaboration

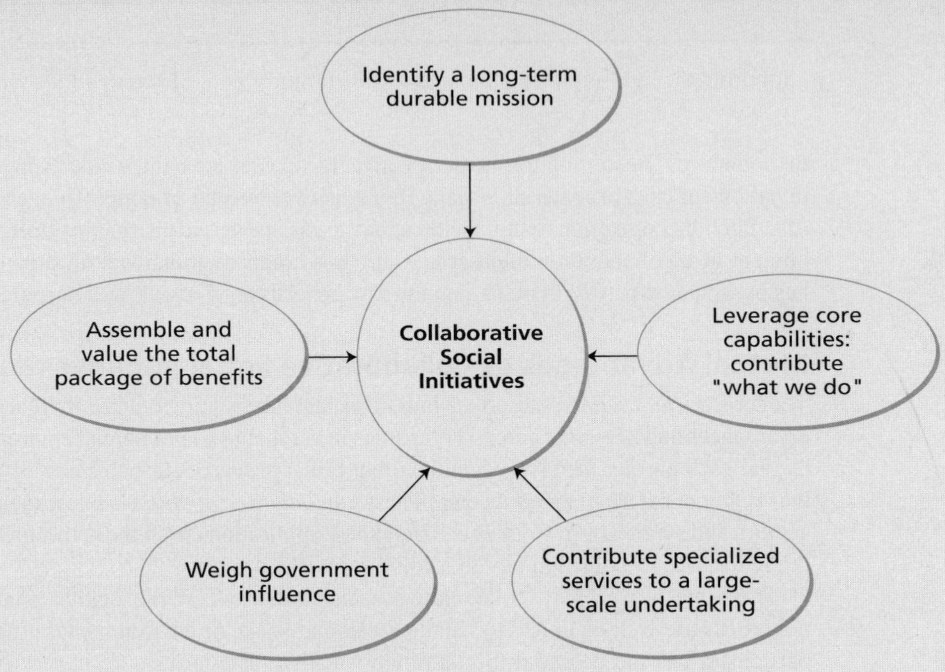

Five Principles of Successful Collaborative Social Initiatives

Corporate social responsibility has become a vital part of the business conversation. The issue is not whether companies will engage in socially responsible activities, but how. For most companies, the challenge is how best to achieve the maximum social benefit from a given amount of resources available for social projects. Research points to five principles that facilitate better outcomes for society and for corporate participants, as shown in Exhibit 3.12, Strategy in Action. When CSR initiatives include most or all of these elements, companies can indeed maximize the effects of their social contributions while advancing broader strategic goals. While most CSIs will not achieve complete success with all five elements, some progress with each is requisite for success. Here are the five principles, along with examples of companies that have adhered to them well:

1. Identify a Long-Term Durable Mission

Companies make the greatest social contribution when they identify an important, long-standing policy challenge and they participate in its solution over the long term. Veteran *Wall Street Journal* reporter and author Ron Alsop argues that companies that are interested in contributing to corporate responsibility and thus burnishing their reputations should "own the issue."[9] Companies that step up to tackle problems that are clearly important to society's welfare and that require substantial resources are signaling to internal and external constituencies that the initiative is deserving of the company's investment.

Among the more obvious examples of social challenges that will demand attention for years to come are hunger, inadequate housing, ill health, substandard education, and degradation

[9] R. Alsop, *The 18 Immutable Laws of Corporate Reputation* (New York: Free Press, 2004).

of the environment. While a company's long-term commitment to any one of those problems embeds that issue in the fabric of the company, it is more important that the company can develop competencies that allow it to become better at its social activities yet be able to keep investing in those outputs. It is also important to identify limited-scope projects and shorter-term milestones that can be accomplished through direct contributions by the company. Solving global hunger is a worthy goal, but it is too large for any individual company to make much of a dent.

Avon Products Inc., the seller of beauty and related products, offers a fine example of a long-term commitment to a pervasive and longstanding problem. In 1992, the company's Avon Foundation—a public charity established in 1955 to improve the lives of women and their families—launched its Breast Cancer Crusade in the United Kingdom. The program has expanded to 50 countries. Funds are raised through a variety of programs, product sales, and special events, including the Avon Walk for Breast Cancer series. The company distinguishes itself from other corporations that fund a single institution or scientific investigator because it operates as part of a collaborative, supporting a national network of research, medical, social service, and community-based organizations, each of which makes its own unique contribution to helping patients or advancing breast cancer research. The Crusade has awarded more than $300 million to breast cancer research and care organizations worldwide. In its first 10 years, The Avon Walks program raised more than $250 million for research, awareness, detection, and treatment.

Another example of a powerful CSI is found in IBM Corp.'s Reinventing Education initiative. Since 1994, IBM has worked with nonprofit school partners throughout the world to develop and implement innovative technology solutions designed to solve some of education's toughest problems: from coping with shrinking budgets and increasing parental involvement to moving to team teaching and developing new lesson plans. This initiative responds to a nearly universal agreement that education—especially education of young girls and women—provides the essential foundation for addressing a range of social and economic challenges in developing countries. Overcoming the existing educational deficit requires a long-term commitment to achieve school reform, such as methods for measuring learning.

One element of the Reinventing Education initiative is a Web-based "Change Toolkit" developed by IBM and Harvard Business School professor Rosabeth Moss Kanter, with sponsorship from the Council of Chief State School Officers, the National Association of Secondary School Principals, and the National Association of Elementary School Principals. The program has been lauded as a compelling model for systemic school reform.

The Home Depot has identified housing as its principal CSI. In 2002, the company set up its Home Depot Foundation with the primary mission of building "affordable, efficient, and healthy homes." Thirty million Americans face some sort of challenge in securing dependable housing, including living in substandard or overcrowded housing; lacking hot water, electricity, toilet, or bathtub/shower; or simply paying too high a percentage of their income on housing. Hence, Home Depot's long-term commitment in this area is unassailable. Its foundation works closely with Home Depot suppliers and with a variety of nonprofits, placing a strong emphasis on local volunteer efforts.

2. Contribute "What We Do"

Companies maximize the benefits of their corporate contributions when they leverage core capabilities and contribute products and services that are based on expertise used in or generated by their normal operations. Such contributions create a mutually beneficial relationship between the partners; the social-purpose initiatives receive the maximum gains while the company minimizes costs and diversions. It is not essential that these services be synonymous with those of the company's business, but they should build upon some aspect of its strategic competencies.

The issue was aired at the recent World Economic Forum gathering in Davos, Switzerland. "We see corporate social responsibility as part and parcel of doing business, part of our core skills," said Antony Burgmans, chairman of consumer-products giant Unilever NV. "The major value for Unilever is the corporate reputation it helps create."

The thinking is similar at IBM, where, as part of its Reinventing Education initiative, the company contributes financial resources, researchers, educational consultants, and technology to each site to find new ways for technology to spur and support fundamental school restructuring and broad-based systemic change to raise student achievement. In effect, IBM leverages its technological and systems expertise, and its experience providing systems solutions to educational clients, to meet a broader educational challenge. Says Stanley Litow, vice president of Corporate Community Relations at IBM: "IBM believes that a strong community is a key to a company's success . . . To this end, a key focus of our work has been on raising the quality of public education and bridging the digital divide."[10] IBM gains significant goodwill and brand identity with important target markets, in some ways repeating Apple Computer Inc.'s successful strategy in the 1980s under which it donated computers to schools as a way to gain recognition.

There are many comparable initiatives on the procurement side. Retailers such as Starbucks Coffee Company now source much of their bean supply directly from producers, thereby ensuring that those farmers receive fair compensation without being exploited by powerful middlemen. Many retail supermarkets have followed with their own versions of the "fair trade" model.

3. Contribute Specialized Services to a Large-Scale Undertaking

Companies have the greatest social impact when they make specialized contributions to large-scale cooperative efforts. Those that contribute to initiatives in which other private, public, or nonprofit organizations are also active have an effect that goes beyond their limited contributions. Although it is tempting for a company to identify a specific cause that will be associated only with its own contributions, such a strategy is likely to be viewed as a "pet project" and not as a contribution to a larger problem where a range of players have important interests.

A good example is The AES Corp.'s carbon offset program. AES, headquartered in Arlington, Virginia, is one of the world's largest independent power producers, with 30,000 employees and generation and distribution businesses in 27 countries. Some years ago, the company recognized that it could make a contribution to the battle against global warming—a significant environmental threat with serious consequences such as habitat and species depletion, drought, and water scarcity. AES developed a program that offsets carbon emissions, creating carbon "sinks," a practical and effective means of combating this global problem.

Researchers have concluded that planting and preserving trees (technically "forest enhancement") provides the most practical and effective way to address the CO_2 emissions problem. Trees absorb CO_2 as they grow and convert it to carbon that is locked up (sequestered) in biomass as long as they live. AES leaders believed that if their company could contribute to increasing the standing stock of trees, the additional trees might be able to absorb enough CO_2 to offset the emissions from an AES cogeneration plant. This approach became one of the many mitigation measures now accepted in the global climate change treaty—the Kyoto Protocol—as a means of achieving legally binding emissions reduction targets.

For its part, packaged-foods giant ConAgra Foods Inc. helps to fight hunger in partnership with America's Second Harvest, an organization that leads the food recovery effort in the United States. Set up as the nationwide clearinghouse for handling the donations of prepared and perishable foods, ConAgra's coordination efforts enable smaller, local programs

[10] "Reinventing Education," www.ibm.com/ibm/ibmgives/grant/education/programs/reinventing/re_school_reform.shtml

to share resources, making the food donation and distribution process more effective. In October 1999, ConAgra joined with food bank network America's Second Harvest in a specific initiative, the Feeding Children Better program, distributing food to 50,000 local charitable agencies, which, in turn, operate more than 94,000 food programs.

4. Weigh Government's Influence

Government support for corporate participation in CSIs—or at least its willingness to remove barriers—can have an important positive influence. Tax incentives, liability protection, and other forms of direct and indirect support for businesses all help to foster business participation and contribute to the success of CSIs.

For instance, in the United States, ConAgra's food recovery initiatives can deduct the cost (but not market value) of the donated products plus one half of the product's profit margin; the value of this deduction is capped at twice the cost of the product. To encourage further participation of businesses in such food recovery programs, America's Second Harvest generated a series of recommendations for the U.S. government. The recommendations seek to improve the tax benefits associated with food donation, including a proposal that tax deductions be set at the fair market value of donations. Tax deductions provide economic enticement for companies to consider participation, as Boston Market, KFC, and Kraft Foods have publicly acknowledged. Donating food also allows companies to identify the amount of food wasted because it is tracked for tax purposes.

Similar efforts are being applied to reforms that will ease businesses' concerns about their liability from contributing to social enterprises. The Bill Emerson Good Samaritan Food Donation Act, enacted in 1996, protects businesses from liability for food donations except in the case of gross negligence. Building on this federal U.S. act, all 50 states and the District of Columbia have enacted "good Samaritan" laws to protect donors except in cases evidencing negligence. Many companies and nonprofits would like to see more comprehensive tort reform to support their efforts.

Government endorsements are invaluable too. The Home Depot's partnership with Habitat for Humanity is actively supported by the U.S. Department of Housing and Urban Development (HUD). This support takes the form of formal endorsement, logistical facilitation, and implicit acknowledgement that the partnership's initiatives complement HUD's own efforts. Home Depot is assured that the agency will not burden the program with red tape. In the case of AES's efforts in the area of global warming, organizations such as the World Bank, the Global Environmental Facility, and the U.N. Environment and Development Program endorse and encourage offsets via grants, loans, and scientific research.

5. Assemble and Value the Total Package of Benefits

Companies gain the greatest benefits from their social contributions when they put a price on the total benefit package. The valuation should include both the social contributions delivered and the reputation effects that solidify or enhance the company's position among its constituencies. Positive reputation—by consumers, suppliers, employees, regulators, interest groups, and other stakeholders—is driven by genuine commitment rather than episodic or sporadic interest; consumers and other stakeholders see through nominal commitments designed simply to garner short-term positive goodwill. "The public can smell if [a CSR effort] is not legitimate," said Shelly Lazarus, chairman and CEO of advertising agency Ogilvy & Mather USA. Hence, social initiatives that reflect the five principles discussed here can generate significant reputation benefits for participating companies.

AES's commitment to carbon offsets has won it several awards and generates favorable consideration from international financial institutions such as the World Bank, International Finance Corporation, and Inter-American Development Bank, as well as from governments, insurers, and NGOs. In the consumer products sector, Avon receives extensive media recognition from the advertising and marketing of cancer walks, nationwide special events including a gala fund-raising concert, and an awards ceremony. Avon has become so closely associated with the breast cancer cause that many consumers now identify the company's commitment—and the trademark pink ribbon—as easily as its traditional door-to-door marketing and distribution systems.

While difficult to quantify precisely, the potential value of the pink ribbon campaign, and the brand awareness associated with it, generates economic benefits for Avon in the form of goodwill and overall reputation. Avon's strategy of focusing on a cause that women care about, leveraging its contributions, and partnering with respected NGOs has enabled it to gain trust and credibility in the marketplace. "There needs to be a correlation between the cause and the company," said Susan Heany, director for corporate social responsibility at Avon. "The linkage between corporate giving and the corporate product creates brand recognition. Both buyers and sellers want to achieve the same goal: improving women's health care worldwide."[11]

Assembling the Components

A range of corporate initiatives lend themselves to the CSI model because they share most of the five key attributes we have described here: they have long-term objectives, they are sufficiently large to allow a company to specialize in its contributions, they provide many opportunities for the company to contribute from its current activities or products, they enjoy government support, and they provide a package of benefits that adds value to the company. Exhibit 3.13, Strategy in Action, summarizes five very successful CSI programs and their performance against each of the five principles.

Of the five principles, the most important by far is the second one. Companies must apply what they do best in their normal commercial operations to their social responsibility undertakings. This tenet is consistent with research that argues that social activities most closely related to the company's core mission are most efficiently administered through internalization or collaboration. It is applicable far beyond the examples in this chapter; to waste management companies and recycling programs, for instance, or to publishing companies and after-school educational initiatives, or pharmaceutical companies and local immunization and health education programs.

The Limits of CSR Strategies

Some companies such as Ben & Jerry's have embedded social responsibility and sustainability commitments deeply in their core strategies. Research suggests that such single-minded devotion to CSR may be unrealistic for larger, more established corporations. For example, some analysts have suggested that the intense focus on social responsibility goals by the management team at Levi Strauss & Co. may have diverted the company from its core operational challenges, accelerating the company's closure of all of its North American manufacturing operations.

Larger companies must move beyond the easy options of charitable donations but also steer clear of overreaching commitments. This is not to suggest that companies should not think big—research shows that projects can be broad in scale and scope and still succeed. Rather, it suggests that companies need to view their commitments to corporate responsibility as one important part of their overall strategy but not let the commitment obscure their broad strategic business goals. By starting with a well-defined CSR strategy and developing

[11] "Corporate Social Responsibility in Practice Casebook," *The Catalyst Consortium*, July 2002, p. 8. Available at www.rhcatalyst.org

Strategy in Action — Exhibit 3.13

Five Successful Collaborative Social Initiatives

Program	Pursue a Long-Term, Durable Mission	Contribute "What We Do"	Contribute Specialized Resources to a Large Scale Undertaking	Weigh Government Influence	Assemble and Value Total Package of Benefits
ConAgra Foods' Feeding Children Better	Individuals needing food from charity in the United States grew to more than 23 million in 2001. In the United Kingdom, the total was 4 million people in 2003.	ConAgra uses its electronic inventory control systems and refrigerated trucks to assist America's Second Harvest's food rescue programs.	ConAgra fights child hunger in America by assembling a powerful partnership with America's Second Harvest, Brandeis University's Center on Hunger and Poverty, and the Ad Council.	The Bill Emerson Good Samaritan Food Donation Act protects businesses from liability for food donations.	ConAgra's brand-sponsored support of food rescue programs sustains its image as provider of "the largest corporate initiative dedicated solely to fighting child hunger in America."
Avon's Breast Cancer Crusade	Breast cancer is the second-leading cause of death in women in the United States and the most common cancer among women.	Avon's commitment to being "the company for women" is shown by their 550,000 sales representatives who sell Crusade "pink ribbon" items.	Avon distinguishes itself by supporting a national network of research, medical, social service, and local organizations to advance cancer research.	Government agencies often match individual contributions; local governments provide logistical support for fundraising walks.	Avon receives media recognition from the advertising and marketing of cancer walks and nationwide special events, including a gala fundraising concert and awards ceremony.
IBM's Reinventing Education	Education in developing countries requires a long-term commitment to school reform, such as methods for measuring learning.	IBM uses its leading researchers, educational consultants, and technology to spur and support fundamental school restructuring.	IBM monitors the program with rigorous, independent evaluations from the Center for Children & Technology in conjunction with the Harvard Business School.	IBM teams with the U.S. Department of Education and the U.K. Department of Education and Employment on many reinvention projects.	IBM views a commitment to education as a strategic business investment. By investing in its future workforce and its customers, IBM feels that it promotes its own success.
Home Depot's In Your Community	30 million Americans face housing problems, such as overcrowding, no hot water, no electricity, and no toilet, bathtub, or shower.	Home Depot offers help with the construction of homes, plus donations and volunteers to help provide affordable housing for low-income families.	More than 1,500 Home Depot stores have Team Depot volunteer programs to support Habitat for Humanity, Rebuilding Together, and KaBOOM with the help of its 315,000 company associates.	Home Depot's partnership with Habitat for Humanity is actively supported by the U.S. Department of Housing and Urban Development.	Home Depot's volunteer programs and "how-to" clinics "invite the community into their stores." Hundreds of thousands of potential customers participate each year.
AES's Carbon Offsets Program	Global warming is an environmental threat. Carbon offsets or "sinks" are one proven, effective means of combating this problem.	AES is a leading international power producer with extensive knowledge of developing countries and their resources, including the dangers from cogeneration plants.	AES has teamed with the World Resources Institute, Nature Conservancy, and CARE to find and evaluate appropriate forestry-based offset projects.	The Environmental Protection Agency, European environmental organizations, U.N. Development Program, and other agencies support carbon offsets.	AES has committed $12 million to carbon offset projects to offset 67 million tons of carbon emitted over the next 40 years—the equivalent of the emissions from a 1,000-MW coal facility over its lifetime.

the collaborative initiatives that support that strategy by meeting the five criteria we have identified, companies and their leaders can make important contributions to the common good while advancing their broader financial and market objectives.

CSR strategies can also run afoul of the skeptics, and the speed with which information can be disseminated via the Web—and accumulated in Web logs—makes this an issue with serious ramifications for reputation management. Nike has been a lightning rod for CSR activists for its alleged tolerance of hostile and dangerous working conditions in its many factories and subcontractors around the world. Despite the considerable efforts the company has made to respond to its critics, it has consistently been on the defensive in trying to redeem its reputation.

Touching on this issue at the World Economic Forum, Unilever chief Antony Burgmans noted the importance of "making people who matter in society aware of what you do." His point was amplified by Starbucks CEO Orin Smith, who invited the authors of an NGO report critical of Starbucks' sourcing strategies to the company's offices and showed them the books. "In many instances we ended up partnering with them," he said.

The Future of CSR

CSR is firmly and irreversibly part of the corporate fabric. Managed properly, CSR programs can confer significant benefits to participants in terms of corporate reputation; in terms of hiring, motivation, and retention; and as a means of building and cementing valuable partnerships. And of course, the benefits extend well beyond the boundaries of the participating organizations, enriching the lives of many disadvantaged communities and individuals and pushing back on problems that threaten future generations, other species, and precious natural resources.

That is the positive perspective. The more prickly aspect of CSR is that for all of their resources and capabilities, corporations will face growing demands for social responsibility contributions far beyond simple cash or in-kind donations. Aggressive protesters will keep the issues hot, employees will continue to have their say, and shareholders will pass judgment with their investments—and their votes.

The challenge for management, then, is to know how to meet the company's obligations to all stakeholders without compromising the basic need to earn a fair return for its owners. As research shows, a collaborative approach is the foundation for the most effective CSR initiatives. By then adhering to the five key principles outlined in this section, business leaders can maintain ongoing commitments to carefully chosen initiatives that can have positive and tangible effects on social problems while meeting their obligations to shareholders, employees, and the broader communities in which they operate.

MANAGEMENT ETHICS

The Nature of Ethics in Business

Central to the belief that companies should be operated in a socially responsive way for the benefit of all stakeholders is the belief that managers will behave in an ethical manner. The term **ethics** refers to the moral principles that reflect society's beliefs about the actions of an individual or a group that are right and wrong. Of course, the values of one individual, group, or society may be at odds with the values of another individual, group, or society. Ethical standards, therefore, reflect not a universally accepted code, but rather the end product of a process of defining and clarifying the nature and content of human interaction.

ethics
The moral principles that reflect society's beliefs about the actions of an individual or group that are right and wrong.

Unfortunately, the public's perception of the ethics of corporate executives in America is near its all-time low. A major cause is a spate of corporate scandals prompted by

Strategy in Action — Exhibit 3.14

HR Professionals Believe Ethical Conduct Not Rewarded in Business

A major survey indicates that nearly half of human resources (HR) professionals believe ethical conduct is not rewarded in business today. Over the past five years, HR professionals have felt increasingly more pressure to compromise their organizations' ethical standards; however, they also indicate personally observing fewer cases of misconduct.

The Society for Human Resource Management (SHRM) and the Ethics Resource Center (ERC) jointly conducted the 2003 Business Ethics Survey, with 462 respondents. The survey results show the following:

- 79 percent of respondent organizations have written ethics standards.
- 49 percent say that ethical conduct is not rewarded in business today.
- 35 percent of HR professionals often or occasionally personally observed ethics misconduct in the last year.
- 24 percent of HR professionals feel pressured to compromise ethics standards. In comparison, 13 percent indicated they felt pressured in 1997.
- The top five reasons HR professionals compromise an organization's ethical standards are the need to follow the boss's directives (49 percent); meeting overly aggressive business/financial objectives (48 percent); helping the organization survive (40 percent); meeting schedule pressures (35 percent); and wanting to be a team player (27 percent).

Source: Society for Human Resource Management, www.shrm.org/press

self-serving, and often criminal, executive action that resulted in the loss of stakeholder investments and employee jobs. The goal of every company is to avoid scandal through a combination of high moral and ethical standards and careful monitoring to assure that those standards are maintained. However, when problems arise, the management task of restoring the credibility of the company becomes paramount.

External stakeholders are not the only critics of the current state of business ethics. Exhibit 3.14, Strategy in Action, presents the findings of a major survey of human resource managers in which they indicate that strategic managers have much work to do to establish high ethical standards in their organizations.

Even when groups agree on what constitutes human welfare in a given case, the means they choose to achieve this welfare may differ. Therefore, ethics also involve acting to attain human goals. For example, many people would agree that health is a value worth seeking—that is, health enhances human welfare. But what if the means deemed necessary to attain this value for some include the denial or risk of health for others, as is commonly an issue faced by pharmaceutical manufacturers? During production of some drugs, employees are sometimes subjected to great risk of personal injury and infection. For example, if contacted or inhaled, the mercury used in making thermometers and blood pressure equipment can cause heavy metal poisoning. If inhaled, ethylene oxide used to sterilize medical equipment before it is shipped to doctors can cause fetal abnormalities and miscarriages. Even penicillin, if inhaled during its manufacturing process, can cause acute anaphylaxis or shock. Thus, although the goal of customer health might be widely accepted, the means (involving jeopardy to production employees) may not be.

Although McDonald's faced a great deal of public criticism for the presumed poor nutritional balance of its food products that could contribute to poor consumer health, the law did not require the company or any of its competitors to disclose the exact nutritional contents of its products. However, in 2005, McDonald's broke ranks with its competitors and voluntarily provided the information on its labels.

Toyota is also concerned about the business ethics that it projects. Exhibit 3.15, Global Strategy in Action discusses five powerful lessons that the company learned after suffering

Global Strategy in Action — Exhibit 3.15

Toyota Recalls: Solidifying the Company's Business Ethics

Toyota's announcement of a technical fix for its sticky gas pedals—which can lead to sudden acceleration problems—is not likely to bring a quick end to the company's current recall nightmare. Having already halted sales and production of eight of its top-selling cars in the United States—and recalled more than 9 million cars worldwide, in two separate recalls—Toyota faces the prospect of billions of dollars in charges and operating losses. The Toyota brand, once almost synonymous with top quality, has taken a heavy hit.

It is clear that Toyota's crisis did not emerge full-blown overnight. Fixing the problem and ensuring that something like it does not happen again will require an all-out effort, from assembly line to the boardroom. Even then, there are no guarantees. Maintaining a good corporate reputation in the 21st century is tricky business indeed.

Toyota's case offers a number of valuable lessons for other business people and companies to consider. Here, for starters, are two:

ACCEPT RESPONSIBILITY

This is one area where Toyota seems to be doing a good job, albeit maybe a year or more too late. Toyota seems to be avoiding the appearance of passing the buck. When pressed by the *New York Times* about problems that might have been caused by supplier CTS, for example, Toyota spokesman Mike Michels said: "I don't want to get into any kind of a disagreement with CTS. Our position on suppliers has always been that Toyota is responsible for the cars."

Accountability matters enormously. Johnson & Johnson's 1982 recall of its painkiller Tylenol, following the deaths of seven people in the Chicago area, has earned it a permanent place in the annals of crisis management. But that recall stemmed from the deadly act of an outsider, not any problem with the product itself, as is the case with Toyota.

TAKE THE LONG VIEW

The three leading factors burnishing corporate reputation these days are "quality products and services, a company I can trust and transparency of business practices," writes public relations executive Richard Edelman, who authors an annual corporate "Trust Barometer."

That is unfortunate news for Toyota. But the company does not have much choice. By one estimate, auto industry recalls conservatively cost an average of $100 per car—suggesting that Toyota might be on the hook for at least a one billion dollar charge. That does not include lost revenue to Toyota and its dealers from the production shutdown. And competitors are already trying to woo customers away and capitalize on Toyota's misfortune.

Reputation can be easily lost—and Toyota's reputation is indeed threatened—but it is highly unlikely the company will collapse completely. And that may be one of the one of the biggest lessons for other companies as they study how Toyota emerges from this recall crisis. The reality is that Toyota is positioned for recovery about as well as it could be—owing, in large measure, to the reputation for quality products and corporate responsibility it has developed over the last two decades. That reputation is a valuable asset, and one that Toyota will undoubtedly be citing and calling upon, in the weeks and months ahead.

Source: Excerpted from Michael Connor, "Toyota Recall: Five Critical Lessons," *Business Ethics*, January 31, 2010.

serious damage to its reputation for automotive design and manufacturing, and the actions that it took to reestablish its business ethics.

The spotlight on business ethics is a widespread phenomenon. For example, a survey by the Institute of Business Ethics helps to clarify how companies use their codes of ethics.[12] It found that more than 90 percent of Financial Times Stock Exchange (FTSE) companies in the United Kingdom have an explicit commitment to doing business ethically in the form of a code of ethical conduct. The respondents also reported that 26 percent of boards of directors are taking direct responsibility for the ethical programs of companies. The main reasons for having a code of ethics were to provide guidance to staff (38 percent) and to reduce legal liability (33 percent). Many of the managers (41 percent) also reported that

[12] Accessed in 2005 from http://www.ibe.org.uk/ExecSumm.pdf

they had used their code in disciplinary procedures in the last three years, usually on safety, security, and environmental ethical issues.

Approaches to Questions of Ethics

Managers report that the most critical quality of ethical decision making is consistency. Thus, they often try to adopt a philosophical approach that can provide the basis for the consistency they seek. There are three fundamental ethical approaches for executives to consider: the utilitarian approach, the moral rights approach, and the social justice approach.

utilitarian approach
Judging the appropriateness of a particular action based on a goal to provide the greatest good for the greatest number of people.

Managers who adopt the **utilitarian approach** judge the effects of a particular action on the people directly involved, in terms of what provides the greatest good for the greatest number of people. The utilitarian approach focuses on actions, rather than on the motives behind the actions. Potentially positive results are weighed against potentially negative results. If the former outweigh the latter, the manager taking the utilitarian approach is likely to proceed with the action. That some people might be adversely affected by the action is accepted as inevitable. For example, the Council on Environmental Quality conducts cost-benefit analyses when selecting air pollution standards under the Clean Air Act, thereby acknowledging that some pollution must be accepted.

moral rights approach
Judging the appropriateness of a particular action based on a goal to maintain the fundamental rights and privileges of individuals and groups.

Managers who subscribe to the **moral rights approach** judge whether decisions and actions are in keeping with the maintenance of fundamental individual and group rights and privileges. The moral rights approach (also referred to as deontology) includes the rights of human beings to life and safety, a standard of truthfulness, privacy, freedom to express one's conscience, freedom of speech, and private property.

social justice approach
Judging the appropriateness of a particular action based on equity, fairness, and impartiality in the distribution of rewards and costs among individuals and groups.

Managers who take the **social justice approach** judge how consistent actions are with equity, fairness, and impartiality in the distribution of rewards and costs among individuals and groups. These ideas stem from two principles known as the liberty principle and the difference principle. The *liberty principle* states that individuals have certain basic liberties compatible with similar liberties of other people. The *difference principle* holds that social and economic inequities must be addressed to achieve a more equitable distribution of goods and services.

In addition to these defining principles, three implementing principles are essential to the social justice approach. According to the *distributive-justice principle,* individuals should not be treated differently on the basis of arbitrary characteristics, such as race, sex, religion or national origin. This familiar principle is embodied in the Civil Rights Act. The *fairness principle* means that employees must be expected to engage in cooperative activities according to the rules of the company, assuming that the company rules are deemed fair. The most obvious example is that, in order to further the mutual interests of the company, themselves, and other workers, employees must accept limits on their freedom to be absent from work. The *natural-duty principle* points up a number of general obligations, including the duty to help others who are in need or danger, the duty not to cause unnecessary suffering, and the duty to comply with the just rules of an institution.

CODES OF BUSINESS ETHICS

To help ensure consistency in the application of ethical standards, an increasing number of professional associations and businesses are establishing codes of ethical conduct. Associations of chemists, funeral directors, law enforcement agents, migration agents, hockey players, Internet providers, librarians, military arms sellers, philatelists, physicians, and

Global Strategy in Action — Exhibit 3.16

Nike, Inc. Code of Conduct

At Nike, we believe that although there is no finish line, there is a clear starting line.

Understanding that our work with contract factories is always evolving, this Code of Conduct clarifies and elevates the expectations we have of our factory suppliers and lays out the minimum standards we expect each factory to meet.

It is our intention to use these standards as an integral component to how we approach NIKE, Inc. sourcing strategies, how we evaluate factory performance, and how we determine with which factories Nike will continue to engage and grow our business.

As we evolve our business model in sourcing and manufacturing, we intend to work with factories who understand that meeting these minimum standards is a critical baseline from which manufacturing leadership, continuous improvement and self-governance must evolve.

Beyond the Code, Nike is committed to collaborating with our contract factories to help build a leaner, greener, more empowered and equitable supply chain. And we will continue to engage with civil society, governments, and the private sector to affect systemic change to labor and environmental conditions in countries where we operate.

We expect our contract factories to share Nike's commitment to the goals of reducing waste, using resources responsibly, supporting workers' rights, and advancing the welfare of workers and communities. We believe that partnerships based on transparency, collaboration and mutual respect are integral to making this happen.

Our Code of Conduct binds our contract factories to the following specific minimum standards that we believe are essential to meeting these goals.

EMPLOYMENT IS VOLUNTARY

The contractor does not use forced labor, including prison labor, indentured labor, bonded labor or other forms of forced labor. The contractor is responsible for employment eligibility fees of foreign workers, including recruitment fees.

EMPLOYEES ARE AGE 16 OR OLDER

Contractor's employees are at least age 16 or over the age for completion of compulsory education or country legal working age, whichever is higher. Employees under 18 are not employed in hazardous conditions.

CONTRACTOR DOES NOT DISCRIMINATE

Contractor's employees are not subject to discrimination in employment, including hiring, compensation, promotion or discipline, on the basis of gender, race, religion, age, disability, sexual orientation, pregnancy, marital status, nationality, political opinion, trade union affiliation, social or ethnic origin or any other status protected by country law.

FREEDOM OF ASSOCIATION AND COLLECTIVE BARGAINING ARE RESPECTED

To the extent permitted by the laws of the manufacturing country, the contractor respects the right of its employees to freedom of association and collective bargaining. This includes the right to form and join trade

psychologists all have such codes. So do companies such as Amazon.com, Colgate, Honeywell, New York Times, Nokia, PricewaterhouseCoopers, Sony Group, and Riggs Bank.

Nike faces the problems of a large global corporation in enforcing a code of conduct. Nike's products are manufactured in factories owned and operated by other companies. Nike's supply chain includes more than 660,000 contract manufacturing workers in more than 900 factories in more than 50 countries, including the United States. The workers are predominantly women, ages 19 to 25. The geographic dispersion of its manufacturing facilities is driven by many factors including pricing, quality, factory capacity, and quota allocations.

With such cultural, societal, and economic diversity, the ethics challenge for Nike is to "do business with contract factories that consistently demonstrate compliance with standards we set and that operate in an ethical and lawful manner." To help in this process, Nike has developed its own code of ethics, which it calls a Code of Conduct. It is a set of ethical principles intended to guide management decision making. Nike's code is presented in Exhibit 3.16, Global Strategy in Action.

Exhibit 3.16 cont.

unions and other worker organizations of their own choosing without harassment, interference or retaliation.

COMPENSATION IS TIMELY PAID

Contractor's employees are timely paid at least the minimum wage required by country law and provided legally mandated benefits, including holidays and leaves, and statutory severance when employment ends. There are no disciplinary deductions from pay.

HARASSMENT AND ABUSE ARE NOT TOLERATED

Contractor's employees are treated with respect and dignity. Employees are not subject to physical, sexual, psychological or verbal harassment or abuse.

WORKING HOURS ARE NOT EXCESSIVE

Contractor's employees do not work in excess of 60 hours per week, or the regular and overtime hours allowed by the laws of the manufacturing country, whichever is less. Any overtime hours are consensual and compensated at a premium rate. Employees are allowed at least 24 consecutive hours rest in every seven-day period.

REGULAR EMPLOYMENT IS PROVIDED

Work is performed on the basis of a recognized employment relationship established through country law and practice. The contractor does not use any form of home working arrangement for the production of Nike-branded or affiliate product.

THE WORKPLACE IS HEALTHY AND SAFE

The contractor provides a safe, hygienic and healthy workplace setting and takes necessary steps to prevent accidents and injury arising out of, linked with or occurring in the course of work or as a result of the operation of contractor's facilities. The contractor has systems to detect, avoid and respond to potential risks to the safety and health of all employees.

ENVIRONMENTAL IMPACT IS MINIMIZED

The contractor protects human health and the environment by meeting applicable regulatory requirements including air emissions, solid/hazardous waste and water discharge. The contractor adopts reasonable measures to mitigate negative operational impacts on the environmental and strives to continuously improve environmental performance.

THE CODE IS FULLY IMPLEMENTED

As a condition of doing business with Nike, the contractor shall implement and integrate this Code and accompanying Code Leadership Standards and applicable laws into its business and submit to verification and monitoring. The contractor shall post this Code, in the language(s) of its employees, in all major workspaces, train employees on their rights and obligations as defined by this Code and applicable country law; and ensure the compliance of any sub-contractors producing Nike branded or affiliate products.

Source: Nike Biz, August 2010. www.nike.com

Major Trends in Codes of Ethics

The increased interest in codifying business ethics has led to both the proliferation of formal statements by companies and to their prominence among business documents. Not long ago, codes of ethics that existed were usually found solely in employee handbooks. The new trend is for them to also be prominently displayed on corporate Web sites, in annual reports, and next to Title VII posters on bulletin boards.

A second trend is that companies are adding enforcement measures to their codes, including policies that are designed to guide employees on what to do if they see violations occur and sanctions that will be applied, including consequences on their employment and civil and criminal charges. As a consequence, businesses are increasingly requiring all employees to sign the ethics statement as a way to acknowledge that they have read and understood their obligations. In part this requirement reflects the impact of the Sarbanes-Oxley rule that CEOs and CFOs certify the accuracy of company financials. Executives want employees at all levels to recognize their own obligations to pass accurate information up the chain of command.

The third trend is increased attention by companies in improving employees' training in understanding their obligations under the company's code of ethics. The objective is to emphasize the consideration of ethics during the decision-making process. Training, and subsequent monitoring of actual work behavior, is also aided by computer software that identifies possible code violations, which managers can then investigate in detail.

Summary

Given the amount of time that people spend working, it is reasonable that they should try to shape the organizations in which they work. Inanimate organizations are often blamed for setting the legal, ethical, and moral tones in the workplace when, in reality, people determine how people behave. Just as individuals try to shape their neighborhoods, schools, political and social organizations, and religious institutions, employees need to help determine the major issues of corporate social responsibility and business ethics.

Strategic decisions, indeed all decisions, involve trade-offs. We choose one thing over another. We pursue one goal while subordinating another. On the topic of corporate social responsibility, individual employees must work to achieve the outcomes that they want. By volunteering for certain community welfare options they choose to improve that option's chances of being beneficial. Business ethics present a parallel opportunity. By choosing proper behaviors, employees help to build an organization that can be respected and economically viable in the long run.

Often, the concern is expressed that business activities tend to be illegal or unethical and that the failure of individuals to follow the pattern will leave them at a competitive disadvantage. Such claims, often prompted by high-profile examples, are absurd. Rare but much publicized criminal activities mask the meaningful reality that business conduct is as honest and honorable as any other activity in our lives. The people who are involved are the same, with the same values, ideals, and aspirations.

In this chapter, we have studied corporate social responsibility to understand it and to learn how our businesses can occasionally use some of their resources to make differential, positive impacts on our society. We also looked at business ethics to gain an appreciation for the importance of maintaining and promoting social values in the workplace.

Key Terms

corporate social responsibility (CSR), *p. 57*
discretionary responsibilities, *p. 57*
economic responsibilities, *p. 53*
ethical responsibilities, *p. 55*
ethics, *p. 78*
legal responsibilities, *p. 53*
moral rights approach, *p. 81*
Sarbanes-Oxley Act of 2002, *p. 62*
social audit, *p. 67*
social justice approach, *p. 81*
utilitarian approach, *p. 81*

Questions for Discussion

1. Define the term *social responsibility*. Find an example of a company action that was legal but not socially responsible. Defend your example on the basis of your definition.
2. Name five potentially valuable indicators of a firm's social responsibility and describe how company performance in each could be measured.
3. Do you think a business organization in today's society benefits by defining a socially responsible role for itself? Why or why not?
4. Which of the three basic philosophies of social responsibility would you find most appealing as the chief executive of a large corporation? Explain.

5. Do you think society's expectations for corporate social responsibility will change in the next decade? Explain.
6. How much should social responsibility be considered in evaluating an organization's overall performance?
7. Is it necessary that an action be voluntary to be termed socially responsible? Explain.
8. Do you think an organization should adhere to different philosophies of corporate responsibility when confronted with different issues, or should its philosophy always remain the same? Explain.
9. Describe yourself as a stakeholder in a company. What kind of stakeholder role do you play now? What kind of stakeholder roles do you expect to play in the future?
10. What sets the affirmative philosophy apart from the stakeholder philosophy of social responsibility? In what areas do the two philosophies overlap?
11. Cite examples of both ethical and unethical behavior drawn from your knowledge of current business events.
12. How would you describe the contemporary state of business ethics?
13. How can business self-interest also serve social interests?

The External Environment

After reading and studying this chapter, you should be able to

1. Describe the three tiers of environmental factors that affect the performance of a firm.
2. List and explain the five factors in the remote environment.
3. Give examples of the economic, social, political, technological, and ecological influences on a business.
4. Explain the five forces model of industry analysis and give examples of each force.
5. Give examples of the influences of entry barriers, supplier power, buyer power, substitute availability, and competitive rivalry on a business.
6. List and explain the five factors in the operating environment.
7. Give examples of the influences of competitors, creditors, customers, labor, and direct suppliers on a business.

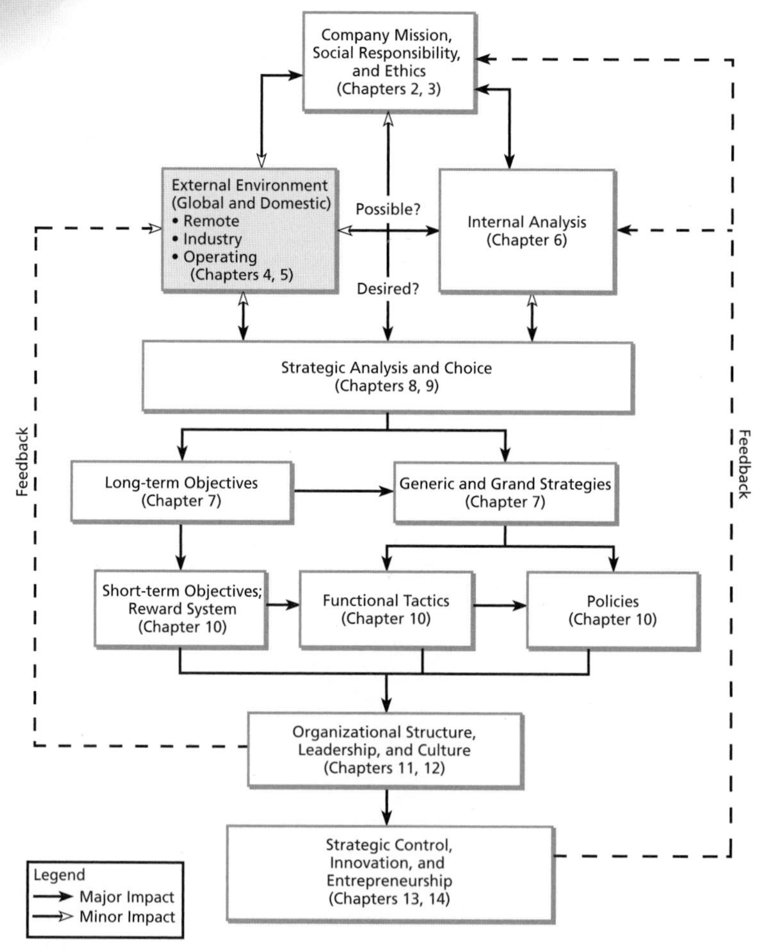

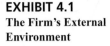

EXHIBIT 4.1
The Firm's External Environment

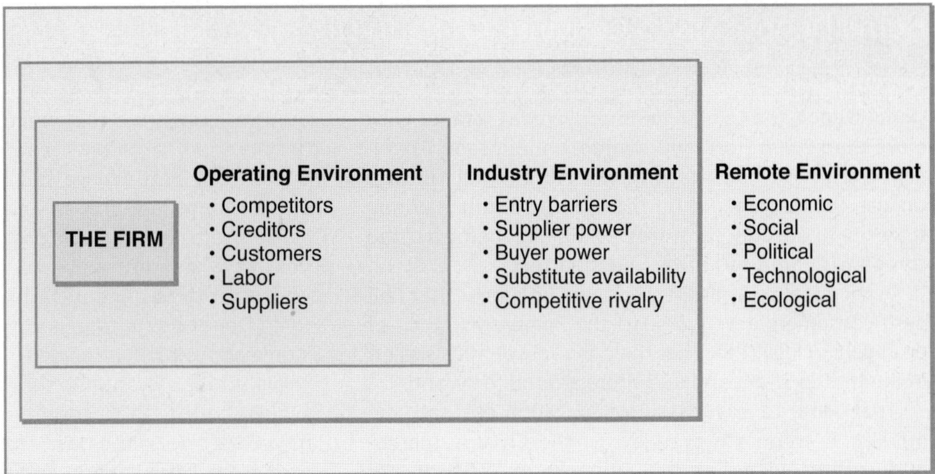

THE FIRM'S EXTERNAL ENVIRONMENT

external environment
The factors beyond the control of the firm that influence its choice of direction and action, organizational structure, and internal processes.

A host of external factors influence a firm's choice of direction and action and, ultimately, its organizational structure and internal processes. These factors, which constitute the **external environment,** can be divided into three interrelated subcategories: factors in the remote environment, factors in the industry environment, and factors in the operating environment. This chapter describes the complex necessities involved in formulating strategies that optimize a firm's market opportunities. Exhibit 4.1 suggests the interrelationship between the firm and its remote, its industry, and its operating environments. In combination, these factors form the basis of the opportunities and threats that a firm faces in its competitive environment.

REMOTE ENVIRONMENT

remote environment
Economic, social, political, technological, and ecological factors that originate beyond, and usually irrespective of, any single firm's operating situation.

The **remote environment** comprises factors that originate beyond, and usually irrespective of, any single firm's operating situation: (1) economic, (2) social, (3) political, (4) technological, and (5) ecological factors. That environment presents firms with opportunities, threats, and constraints, but rarely does a single firm exert any meaningful reciprocal influence. For example, when the economy slows and construction starts to decrease, an individual contractor is likely to suffer a decline in business, but that contractor's efforts in stimulating local construction activities would be unable to reverse the overall decrease in construction starts. The trade agreements that resulted from improved relations between the United States and China and the United States and Russia are examples of political factors that impact individual firms. The agreements provided individual U.S. manufacturers with opportunities to broaden their international operations.

Economic Factors

Economic factors concern the nature and direction of the economy in which a firm operates. Because consumption patterns are affected by the relative affluence of various market segments, each firm must consider economic trends in the segments that affect its industry. On both the national and international level, managers must consider the general availability of credit, the level of disposable income, and the propensity of people to spend.

Global Strategy in Action — Exhibit 4.2

Home Depot Fails to Convince China to DIY

Home Depot, the U.S. home-improvement retailer with more than 2,200 stores worldwide, announced in January 2011 that it had closed its last store in Beijing. The closure cut its presence on the mainland down to one store in Xi'an and six stores in Tianjin, home to the company's China corporate headquarters.

In the case of Home Depot, it would appear that Chinese consumers never took to the company's ethos of do-it-yourself (DIY) that has been the source of its success in the United States and elsewhere around the world.

That isn't to say that Home Depot misread the market. A corporate overview of the Chinese market underscored many of the compelling statistics and trends that made China a target for Home Depot and many other global home-improvement companies.

China in the last decade has become a market of new homeowners, many of whom are buying homes that developers have left unfinished and require significant investment in home improvement. Tour a new shiny residential high-rise anywhere in the country and you will often find apartments that lack light fixtures, proper flooring and even doorbells.

These conditions paired with a rapidly growing middle-class seemed to create an ideal opening for Home Depot's primary product: home construction expertise and quality installation services.

The problem was, while demand and need had been factored into Home Depot's equation, one human element appeared to have not: will. In a nation with a sizable pool of unskilled labor floating around cities and countless small-time construction companies available for hire, it is simply more convenient and cheaper to outsource such jobs to others.

Alan, a landlord who has lived and worked in the United States and has been to Home Depots in both countries, suggested that while price point was a serious consideration, trust and familiarity also played a role. "I want the best service but lowest price," said Alan, "Home Depot in China, I think it's not attractive to me. If I decorate again, I will probably have a friend who lives in the area introduce me to a company so I know I can trust it to give me a fair price and service . . . I think Home Depot needs to invest money in teaching Chinese people about DIY," he added.

Will China's gradually shrinking migrant labor pool give rise to the "DIY" conditions Home Depot needs to thrive? It's one of the new economic realities that have come from globalization and the Sino-U.S. relationship today: more and more American businesses are seeing their growth and profits coming from China rather than the United States.

While Home Depot was unsuccessful in catching the home-improvement wave this time, the company's epitaph has yet to be written. It still has a presence in China and is currently focused on the rapidly developing second- and third-tier cities that are transforming at unseen speeds. Perhaps with a focus on a lower price-point and greater consumer education, Home Depot could come out of this setback a stronger and bolder company than the one that cautiously stepped into the market in 2006.

In addition, as China's surplus labor pool continues to shrink and building prices go up, it is entirely possible that regular Chinese will be simply forced to take on the home construction projects many Americans routinely perform.

Source: Excerpted from Ed Flannagan, "Home Depot Fails to Convince China to DIY," NBC News, February 8, 2011. http://behindthewall.msnbc.msn.com/_news/2011/02/08/6009194-home-depot-fails-to-convince-china-to-diy

Prime interest rates, inflation rates, and trends in the growth of the gross national product are other economic factors they should monitor.

Changes in economic factors can be difficult to interpret. The tremendous economic growth in China has meant sharp increases in the financial wealth of many Chinese. Home ownership is growing at a historically high rate. Consequently, Home Depot saw the opportunity to enter the Chinese market as a supplier of home remodeling products. The story of the company's failure in China is explained in Exhibit 4.2, Global Strategy in Action.

For example, in 2003, the depressed economy hit Crown Cork & Seal Co. especially hard because it had $2 billion in debt due in the year and no way to raise the money to pay it. The down market had caused its stock price to be too low to raise cash as it normally would. Therefore, Crown Cork managers turned to issuing bonds to refinance its debt. With the slow market, investors were taking advantage of such bonds because they could safely gain higher returns over stocks. Not only were investors getting a deal, but Crown Cork and other companies were seeing the lowest interest rates on bonds in years and by issuing bonds could reorganize their balance sheets.

The emergence of new international power brokers has changed the focus of economic environmental forecasting. Among the most prominent of these power brokers are the European Economic Community (EEC, or Common Market), the Organization of Petroleum Exporting Countries (OPEC), and coalitions of developing countries.

The EEC, whose members include most of the West European countries, eliminated quotas and established a tariff-free trade area for industrial products among its members. By fostering intra-European economic cooperation, it has helped its member countries compete more effectively in non-European international markets.

Social Factors

The social factors that affect a firm involve the beliefs, values, attitudes, opinions, and lifestyles of persons in the firm's external environment, as developed from cultural, ecological, demographic, religious, educational, and ethnic conditioning. As social attitudes change, so too does the demand for various types of clothing, books, leisure activities, and so on. Like other forces in the remote external environment, social forces are dynamic, with constant change resulting from the efforts of individuals to satisfy their desires and needs by controlling and adapting to environmental factors. Teresa Iglesias-Solomon hopes to benefit from social changes with *Niños*, a children's catalog written in both English and Spanish. The catalog features books, videos, and Spanish cultural offerings for English-speaking children who want to learn Spanish and for Spanish-speaking children who want to learn English. *Niños'* target market includes middle- to upper-income Hispanic parents, consumers, educators, bilingual schools, libraries, and purchasing agents. Iglesias-Solomon has reason to be optimistic about the future of *Niños*, because the Hispanic population is growing five times faster than the general U.S. population and ranks as the nation's largest minority.

One of the most profound social changes in recent years has been the entry of large numbers of women into the labor market. This has not only affected the hiring and compensation policies and the resource capabilities of their employers; it has also created or greatly expanded the demand for a wide range of products and services necessitated by their absence from the home. Firms that anticipated or reacted quickly to this social change offered such products and services as convenience foods, microwave ovens, and day care centers.

A second profound social change has been the accelerating interest of consumers and employees in quality-of-life issues. Evidence of this change is seen in recent contract negotiations. In addition to the traditional demand for increased salaries, workers demand such benefits as sabbaticals, flexible hours or four-day workweeks, lump-sum vacation plans, and opportunities for advanced training.

A third profound social change has been the shift in the age distribution of the population. Changing social values and a growing acceptance of improved birth control methods are expected to raise the mean age of the U.S. population, which was 27.9 in 1970, and 34.9 in the year 2000 to 43.7 years by 2030. This trend will have an increasingly unfavorable effect on most producers of predominantly youth-oriented goods and will necessitate a shift in their long-range marketing strategies. Producers of hair and skin care preparations already have begun to adjust their research and development to reflect anticipated changes in demand.

A consequence of the changing age distribution of the population has been a sharp increase in the demands made by a growing number of senior citizens. Constrained by fixed incomes, these citizens have demanded that arbitrary and rigid policies on retirement age be modified and have successfully lobbied for tax exemptions and increases in Social Security benefits. Such changes have significantly altered the opportunity-risk equations of many firms—often to the benefit of firms that anticipated the changes.

Cutting across these issues is concern for individual health. The fast-food industry has been the target of a great deal of public concern. A great deal of popular press attention has been directed toward Americans'concern over the relationship between obesity and health. As documented by the hit movie *Supersize Me*, McDonald's was caught in the middle of this new social concern because its menu consisted principally of high-calorie, artery-clogging foods. Health experts blamed the fast-food industry for the rise in obesity, claiming that companies like McDonald's created an environment that encouraged overeating and discouraged physical activity. Specifically, McDonald's was charged with taking advantage of the fact that kids and adults were watching more TV, by targeting certain program slots to increase sales.

McDonald's responded aggressively and successfully. The company's strategists soon established McDonald's Corp. as an innovator in healthy food options. By 2005, the world's largest fast-food chain launched a new promotional campaign touting healthy lifestyles, including fruit and milk in Happy Meals, activity programs in schools, and a new partnership with the International Olympic Committee. At the time of the announcement, McDonald's was enjoying its longest ever period of same-store sales growth in 25 years, with 24 consecutive months of improved global sales resulting from new healthy menu options, later hours, and better customer service, such as cashless payment options. McDonald's healthy options included a fruit and walnut salad, Paul Newman's brand lowfat Italian dressing, and premium chicken sandwiches in the United States and chicken flatbread and fruit smoothies in Europe.

Translating social change into forecasts of business effects is a difficult process, at best. Nevertheless, informed estimates of the impact of such alterations as geographic shifts in populations and changing work values, ethical standards, and religious orientation can only help a strategizing firm in its attempts to prosper.

Political Factors

The direction and stability of political factors are a major consideration for managers on formulating company strategy. Political factors define the legal and regulatory parameters within which firms must operate. Political constraints are placed on firms through fair-trade decisions, antitrust laws, tax programs, minimum wage legislation, pollution and pricing policies, administrative jawboning, and many other actions aimed at protecting employees, consumers, the general public, and the environment. Because such laws and regulations are most commonly restrictive, they tend to reduce the potential profits of firms. However, some political actions are designed to benefit and protect firms. Such actions include patent laws, government subsidies, and product research grants. Often, different stakeholders take different sides on important issues that affect business operations. They then work to influence legislators to vote for the position that they favor. The attempt of labor unions to influence President Barack Obama as payback for their support at the polls is a well-publicized example, as described in Exhibit 4.3, Strategy in Action.

Political factors either may limit or benefit the firms they influence. For example, in a pair of surprising decisions, the Federal Communications Commission (FCC) ruled that local phone companies had to continue to lease their lines to the long-distance carriers at what the locals said was below cost. At the same time, the FCC ruled that the local companies were not required to lease their broadband lines to the national carriers. These decisions

Strategy in Action — Exhibit 4.3

Obama and Unions: Many in Labor Movement Frustrated with President

Two years into a presidency that carried immense promises for the labor movement, this is how it has gone for President Barack Obama. Some unions remain firmly by his side, while others think he has reneged on promises or—as he seeks to mend relationships with business leaders—abandoned them altogether.

"He's basically trying to be everything to everybody," said Rose Ann DeMoro, executive director of National Nurses United, a nursing union that claims 160,000 members and is an affiliate of the AFL-CIO. "Until you look at the policies, and then it's clear he's there for the corporate sector." The union arranged a protest when Obama addressed the U.S. Chamber of Commerce, accusing him of cozying up to big businesses.

Officials from another AFL-CIO affiliate, the International Association of Machinists and Aerospace Workers, said that tens of thousands of its members have been laid off and that they don't see the White House advocating for them. "They may be lost to the Democratic cause," said Rick Sloan, a spokesman for the union.

The tensions underscore a careful political balance faced by Obama, who has frustrated many union leaders and activists after courting their support in his 2008 campaign. A major disappointment was the failure to win passage of legislation that would have made it easier for unions to organize. Obama pledged to support the measure, but it was stymied in the Democratic-controlled Senate. Obama's support for free-trade deals has irked some labor activists, who recall that as a candidate he was deeply critical of the North American Free Trade Agreement and opposed the George W. Bush–backed South Korea free-trade deal.

He has satisfied labor on some fronts. In 2009, he imposed a tariff on Chinese-made tires, winning praise from the United Steelworkers union, which represents workers in U.S. tire plants. And his renegotiation of the South Korea deal scored popular concessions.

Now, many union leaders are bristling at White House efforts to reset its relationship with corporate America. Unions were opposed to the extension of tax cuts for the wealthy in the December deal Obama struck with Republicans. Some have criticized his call for a review of regulations. And most unions oppose the South Korea deal.

Source: Excerpted from Peter Wallsten, "Obama and Unions: Many in Labor Movement Frustrated with President," *Washington Post*, February 19, 2011.

were good and bad for the local companies because, although they would lose money by leasing to the long-distance carriers, they could regain some of that loss with their broadband services that did not have to be leased.

The decisions did not mean that the local carriers had to remove existing lines and replace them with broadband lines. Instead, the local carriers would have to run two networks to areas where they want to incorporate broadband because the long-distance carriers had a right to the conventional lines as ruled in the decision. These regulations caused the local carriers to alter their strategies. For example, they often chose to reduce capital investments on new broadband lines because they had to maintain old lines as well. The reduction in capital investments was used to offset the losses they incurred in subsidizing their current lines to the long-distance carriers.

There are many political factors that profoundly affect the nature and potential of business operations in a country, including government policy with regard to industry cooperation, antitrust activities, foreign trade, depreciation, environmental protection, deregulation, and foreign trade barriers. However, executives often point to a nation's corporate tax structure as the most important consideration in their deliberation about international expansion. Exhibit 4.4, Global Strategy in Action describes how international tax maneuvering saves Google billions of dollars annually.

The direction and stability of political factors are a major consideration when evaluating the remote environment. Consider piracy. Microsoft's performance in the Chinese market is greatly affected by the lack of legal enforcement of piracy and also by the policies of

Global Strategy in Action — Exhibit 4.4

"Dutch Sandwich" Saves Google Billions in Taxes

The heart of Google's international operations is a silvery glass office building in central Dublin, a block from the city's Grand Canal. In 2009, the office was credited with 88 percent of the search juggernaut's $12.5 billion in sales outside the U.S. Most of the profits, however, went to the tax haven of Bermuda.

To reduce its overseas tax bill, Google uses a complicated legal structure that has saved it $3.1 billion in 2007–2009 and boosted 2009's overall earnings by 26 percent. Google has managed to lower its overseas tax rate more than its peers in the technology sector. Its rate since 2007 has been 2.4 percent.

According to company disclosures, Apple, Oracle, Microsoft and IBM—which together with Google make up the top five technology companies by market capitalization—reported tax rates between 4.5 percent and 25.8 percent on their overseas earnings from 2007 to 2009.

"It's remarkable that Google's effective rate is that low," says Martin A. Sullivan, a tax economist who formerly worked for the U.S. Treasury Department. "This company operates throughout the world mostly in high-tax countries where the average corporate rate is well over 20 percent."

In Bermuda there's no corporate income tax at all. Google's profits travel to the island's white sands via a convoluted route known to tax lawyers as the "Dutch Sandwich." In Google's case, it generally works like this: When a company in Europe, the Middle East or Africa purchases a search ad through Google, it sends the money to Google Ireland. The Irish government taxes corporate profits at 12.5 percent, but Google mostly escapes that tax because its earnings don't stay in the Dublin office, which reported a pretax profit of less than 1 percent of revenues in 2008.

Irish law makes it difficult for Google to send the money directly to Bermuda without incurring a large tax hit, so the payment makes a brief detour through the Netherlands, since Ireland doesn't tax certain payments to companies in other European Union states. Once the money is in the Netherlands, Google can take advantage of generous Dutch tax laws. Its subsidiary there, Google Netherlands Holdings, is just a shell (it has no employees) and passes on about 99.8 percent of what it collects to Bermuda.

All of these arrangements are legal. Google Ireland licenses its search and advertising technology from Google headquarters in Mountain View, CA. The licensing agreement allows Google to attribute its overseas profits to its Irish operations instead of the U.S., where most of the technology was developed. The subsidiary is supposed to pay an "arm's length" price for the rights, or the same amount an unrelated company would. Yet because licensing fees from the Irish subsidiary generate income that is taxed at 35 percent, one of the highest corporate rates in the world, Google has an incentive to set the licensing price as low as possible. The effect is to shift some of its profits overseas in an arrangement known as "transfer pricing."

This, too, is legal. In 2006 the IRS approved Google's transfer pricing arrangements, which began in 2003. Transfer pricing arrangements are popular with technology and pharmaceutical companies in particular because they rely on intellectual property, which is easily transportable across borders.

Source: Excerpted from Jesse Drucker, "'Dutch Sandwich' Saves Google Billions in Taxes," *Bloomburg Businessweek*, Msnbc.com, October 22, 2010. http://www.msnbc.msn.com/id/39784907

the Chinese government. Likewise, the government's actions in support of its competitor, Linux, have limited Microsoft's ability to penetrate the Chinese market.

Political activity also has a significant impact on two governmental functions that influence the remote environment of firms: the supplier function and the customer function.

Supplier Function

Government decisions regarding the accessibility of private businesses to government-owned natural resources and national stockpiles of agricultural products will affect profoundly the viability of the strategies of some firms.

Customer Function

Government demand for products and services can create, sustain, enhance, or eliminate many market opportunities. For example, the Kennedy administration's emphasis on landing a man on the moon spawned a demand for thousands of new products; the Carter administration's emphasis on developing synthetic fuels created a demand for new skills, technologies, and products; the Reagan administration's strategic defense initiative (the "Star Wars" defense) sharply accelerated the development of laser technologies; Clinton's federal block grants to the states for welfare reform led to office rental and lease opportunities; and the war against terrorism during the Bush administration created enormous investment in aviation.

Technological Factors

The fourth set of factors in the remote environment involves technological change. To avoid obsolescence and promote innovation, a firm must be aware of technological changes that might influence its industry. Creative technological adaptations can suggest possibilities for new products or for improvements in existing products or in manufacturing and marketing techniques.

A technological breakthrough can have a sudden and dramatic effect on a firm's environment. It may spawn sophisticated new markets and products or significantly shorten the anticipated life of a manufacturing facility. Thus, all firms, and most particularly those in turbulent growth industries, must strive for an understanding both of the existing technological advances and the probable future advances that can affect their products and services. This quasi-science of attempting to foresee advancements and estimate their impact on an organization's operations is known as **technological forecasting.**

technological forecasting
The quasi-science of anticipating environmental and competitive changes and estimating their importance to an organization's operations.

Technological forecasting can help protect and improve the profitability of firms in growing industries. It alerts strategic managers to both impending challenges and promising opportunities. As examples: (1) advances in xerography were a key to Xerox's success but caused major difficulties for carbon paper manufacturers, and (2) the perfection of transistors changed the nature of competition in the radio and television industry, helping such giants as RCA while seriously weakening smaller firms whose resource commitments required that they continue to base their products on vacuum tubes.

The key to beneficial forecasting of technological advancement lies in accurately predicting future technological capabilities and their probable impacts. A comprehensive analysis of the effect of technological change involves study of the expected effect of new technologies on the remote environment, on the competitive business situation, and on the business-society interface. In recent years, forecasting in the last area has warranted particular attention. For example, as a consequence of increased concern over the environment, firms must carefully investigate the probable effect of technological advances on quality-of-life factors, such as ecology and public safety.

For example, by combining the powers of Internet technologies with the capability of downloading music in a digital format, Bertelsmann has found a creative technological adaptation for distributing music online to millions of consumers whenever or wherever they might be. Bertelsmann, AOL Time Warner, and EMI formed a joint venture called Musicnet. The ease and wide availability of Internet technologies is increasing the marketplace for online e-tailers. Bertelsmann's response to the shifts in technological factors enables it to distribute music more rapidly through Musicnet to a growing consumer base.

ecology
The relationships among human beings and other living things and the air, soil, and water that supports them.

Ecological Factors

pollution
Threats to life-supporting ecology caused principally by human activities in an industrial society.

The most prominent factor in the remote environment is often the reciprocal relationship between business and the ecology. The term **ecology** refers to the relationships among human beings and other living things and the air, soil, and water that support them. Threats to our life-supporting ecology caused principally by human activities in an industrial society are commonly referred to as **pollution.** Specific concerns include global warming, loss of habitat and biodiversity, as well as air, water, and land pollution.

Global Strategy in Action — Exhibit 4.5

Devastating Global Droughts Predicted

Increasingly dry conditions across much of the globe—including in the United States—are likely over the next 30 years. The study from the National Center for Atmospheric Research projects serious impacts as soon as the 2030s. Impacts by century's end could go beyond anything in the historical records.

Areas likely to experience significant drying include:

- the western two-thirds of the United States;
- much of Latin America, especially large parts of Mexico and Brazil;
- regions bordering the Mediterranean Sea;
- large parts of southwest Asia;
- southeast Asia, including China and neighboring countries;
- most of Africa and Australia.

While Earth is expected to get dryer overall, some areas will see a lowering of the drought risk. These include: much of northern Europe; Russia; Canada; Alaska; and some areas of the Southern Hemisphere.

To get an idea of how severe droughts might get, scientists use a measure called the Palmer Drought Severity Index, or PDSI. A positive score is wet, a negative score is dry and a score of zero is neither overly wet nor dry. The most severe drought in recent history, in the Sahel region of western Africa in the 1970s, had a PDSI of –3 or –4. By contrast, the study indicates that by 2100 some parts of the United States could see –8 to –10 PDSI, while Mediterranean areas could see drought in the –15 or –20 range.

Source: Excerpted from "Future Droughts Will Be Shockers, Study Says," October 19, 2010. MSNBC.com, http://www.msnbc.msn.com/cleanprint/CleanPrintProxy.aspx?1299168008916

Frequent severe droughts plague parts of many nations. As described in Exhibit 4.5, Global Strategy in Action, businesses interested in locating operations internationally need to consider the likelihood of a dependable water supply for their operations.

The global climate has been changing for ages; however, it is now evident that humanity's activities are accelerating this tremendously. A change in atmospheric radiation, due in part to ozone depletion, causes global warming. Solar radiation that is normally absorbed into the atmosphere reaches the earth's surface, heating the soil, water, and air.

Another area of great importance is the loss of habitat and biodiversity. Ecologists agree that the extinction of important flora and fauna is occurring at a rapid rate and, if this pace is continued, could constitute a global extinction on the scale of those found in fossil records. The earth's life-forms depend on a well-functioning ecosystem. In addition, immeasurable advances in disease treatment can be attributed to research involving substances found in plants. As species become extinct, the life support system is irreparably harmed. The primary cause of extinction on this scale is a disturbance of natural habitat. For example, current data suggest that the earth's primary tropical forests, a prime source of oxygen and potential plant "cure," could be destroyed in only five decades.

Air pollution is created by dust particles and gaseous discharges that contaminate the air. Acid rain, or rain contaminated by sulfur dioxide, which can destroy aquatic and plant life, is believed to result from coal-burning factories in 70 percent of all cases. A health-threatening "thermal blanket" is created when the atmosphere traps carbon dioxide emitted from smokestacks in factories burning fossil fuels. This "greenhouse effect" can have disastrous consequences, making the climate unpredictable and raising temperatures.

Water pollution occurs principally when industrial toxic wastes are dumped or leak into the nation's waterways. Because fewer than 50 percent of all municipal sewer systems are in compliance with Environmental Protection Agency requirements for water safety, contaminated waters represent a substantial present threat to public welfare. Efforts to keep from contaminating the water supply are a major challenge to even the most conscientious of manufacturing firms.

Land pollution is caused by the need to dispose of ever-increasing amounts of waste. Routine, everyday packaging is a major contributor to this problem. Land pollution is more dauntingly caused by the disposal of industrial toxic wastes in underground sites. With approximately 90 percent of the annual U.S. output of 500 million metric tons of hazardous industrial wastes being placed in underground dumps, it is evident that land pollution and its resulting endangerment of the ecology have become a major item on the political agenda.

As a major contributor to ecological pollution, business now is being held responsible for eliminating the toxic by-products of its current manufacturing processes and for cleaning up the environmental damage that it did previously. Increasingly, managers are being required by the government or are being expected by the public to incorporate ecological concerns into their decision making. For example, between 1975 and 1992, 3M cut its pollution in half by reformulating products, modifying processes, redesigning production equipment, and recycling by-products. Similarly, steel companies and public utilities have invested billions of dollars in costlier but cleaner-burning fuels and pollution control equipment. The automobile industry has been required to install expensive emission controls in cars. The gasoline industry has been forced to formulate new low-lead and no-lead products. And thousands of companies have found it necessary to direct their R&D resources into the search for ecologically superior products, such as Sears's phosphate-free laundry detergent and Pepsi-Cola's biodegradable plastic soft-drink bottle.

Environmental legislation impacts corporate strategies worldwide. Many companies fear the consequences of highly restrictive and costly environmental regulations. However, some manufacturers view these new controls as an opportunity, capturing markets with products that help customers satisfy their own regulatory standards. Other manufacturers contend that the costs of environmental spending inhibit the growth and productivity of their operations.

Despite cleanup efforts to date, the job of protecting the ecology will continue to be a top strategic priority—usually because corporate stockholders and executives choose it, increasingly because the public and the government require it. As evidenced by Exhibit 4.6, the government has made numerous interventions into the conduct of business for the purpose of bettering the ecology.

Benefits of Eco-Efficiency

Many of the world's largest corporations are realizing that business activities must no longer ignore environmental concerns. Every activity is linked to thousands of other transactions and their environmental impact; therefore, corporate environmental responsibility must be taken seriously and environmental policy must be implemented to ensure a comprehensive organizational strategy. Because of increases in government regulations and consumer environmental concerns, the implementation of environmental policy has become a point of competitive advantage. Therefore, the rational goal of business should be to limit its impact on the environment, thus ensuring long-run benefits to both the firm and society. To neglect this responsibility is to ensure the demise of both the firm and our ecosystem.

Responding to this need, General Electric unveiled plans to double its research funds for technologies that reduce energy use, pollution, and emissions tied to global warming. GE said it would focus even more on solar and wind power as well as other environmental technologies it is involved with, such as diesel-electric locomotives, lower emission aircraft engines, more efficient lighting, and water purification. The company's "ecomagination" plans for 2010 include investing $1.5 billion annually in cleaner technologies research; and doubling revenues to $20 billion from environmentally friendly products and services.

eco-efficiency
Company actions that produce more useful goods and services while continuously reducing resource consumption and pollution.

Stephen Schmidheiny, chairman of the Business Council for Sustainable Development, has coined the term **eco-efficiency** to describe corporations that produce more-useful goods

EXHIBIT 4.6
Federal Ecological Legislation

National Environmental Policy Act, 1969 Established Environmental Protection Agency; consolidated federal environmental activities under it. Established Council on Environmental Quality to advise president on environmental policy and to review environmental impact statements.

Air Pollution:

Clean Air Act, 1963 Authorized assistance to state and local governments in formulating control programs. Authorized limited federal action in correcting specific pollution problems.
Clean Air Act, Amendments (Motor Vehicle Air Pollution Control Act), 1965 Authorized federal standards for auto exhaust emission. Standards first set for 1968 models.
Air Quality Act, 1967 Authorized federal government to establish air quality control regions and to set maximum permissible pollution levels. Required states and localities to carry out approved control programs or else give way to federal controls.
Clean Air Act Amendments, 1970 Authorized EPA to establish nationwide air pollution standards and to limit the discharge of six principal pollutants into the lower atmosphere. Authorized citizens to take legal action to require EPA to implement its standards against undiscovered offenders.
Clean Air Act Amendments, 1977 Postponed auto emission requirements. Required use of scrubbers in new coal-fired power plants. Directed EPA to establish a system to prevent deterioration of air quality in clean areas.

Solid Waste Pollution:

Solid Waste Disposal Act, 1965 Authorized research and assistance to state and local control programs.
Resource Recovery Act, 1970 Subsidized construction of pilot recycling plants; authorized development of nationwide control programs.
Resource Conservation and Recovery Act, 1976 Directed EPA to regulate hazardous waste management, from generation through disposal.
Surface Mining and Reclamation Act, 1976 Controlled strip mining and restoration of reclaimed land.

Water Pollution:

Refuse Act, 1899 Prohibited dumping of debris into navigable waters without a permit. Extended by court decision to industrial discharges.
Federal Water Pollution Control Act, 1956 Authorized grants to states for water pollution control. Gave federal government limited authority to correct specific pollution problems.
Water Quality Act, 1965 Provided for adoption of water quality standards by states, subject to federal approval.
Water Quality Improvement Act, 1970 Provided for federal cleanup of oil spills. Strengthened federal authority over water pollution control.
Federal Water Pollution Control Act Amendments, 1972 Authorized EPA to set water quality and effluent standards; provided for enforcement and research.
Safe Drinking Water Act, 1974 Set standards for drinking water quality.
Clean Water Act, 1977 Ordered control of toxic pollutants by 1984 with best available technology economically feasible.

and services while continuously reducing resource consumption and pollution. He cites a number of reasons for corporations to implement environmental policy: customers demand cleaner products, environmental regulations are increasingly more stringent, employees prefer to work for environmentally conscious firms, and financing is more readily available for eco-efficient firms. In addition, the government provides incentives for environmentally responsible companies.

Setting priorities, developing corporate standards, controlling property acquisition and use to preserve habitats, implementing energy-conserving activities, and redesigning products (e.g., minimizing packaging) are a number of measures the firm can implement to enhance an eco-efficient strategy. One of the most important steps a firm can take in achieving a competitive position with regard to the eco-efficient strategy is to fully capitalize on technological developments as a method of gaining efficiency.

There are four key characteristics of eco-efficient corporations:

- Eco-efficient firms are proactive, not reactive. Policy is initiated and promoted by business because it is in their own interests and the interest of their customers, not because it is imposed by one or more external forces.
- Eco-efficiency is designed in, not added on. This characteristic implies that the optimization of eco-efficiency requires every business effort regarding the product and process to internalize the strategy.
- Flexibility is imperative for eco-efficient strategy implementation. Continuous attention must be paid to technological innovation and market evolution.
- Eco-efficiency is encompassing, not insular. In the modern global business environment, efforts must cross not only industrial sectors but national and cultural boundaries as well.

International Environment

Monitoring the international environment, perhaps better thought of as the international dimension of the global environment, involves assessing each nondomestic market on the same factors that are used in a domestic assessment. While the importance of factors will differ, the same set of considerations can be used for each country. For example, Exhibit 4.7, Global Strategy in Action, lists economic, political, legal, and social factors used to assess international environments. However, there is one complication to this process, namely, that the interplay among international markets must be considered. For example, in recent years, conflicts in the Middle East have made collaborative business strategies among firms in traditionally antagonistic countries especially difficult to implement.

INDUSTRY ENVIRONMENT

industry environment
The general conditions for competition that influence all businesses that provide similar products and services.

Harvard professor Michael E. Porter propelled the concept of **industry environment** into the foreground of strategic thought and business planning. The cornerstone of his work first appeared in the *Harvard Business Review,* in which Porter explains the five forces that shape competition in an industry. His well-defined analytic framework helps strategic managers to link remote factors to their effects on a firm's operating environment.

With the special permission of Professor Porter and the *Harvard Business Review,* we present in this section of the chapter the major portion of his seminal article on the industry environment and its impact on strategic management.[1]

HOW COMPETITIVE FORCES SHAPE STRATEGY

The essence of strategy formulation is coping with competition. Yet it is easy to view competition too narrowly and too pessimistically. While we sometimes hear executives complaining to the contrary, intense competition in an industry is neither coincidence nor bad luck.

[1]M. E. Porter, "How Competitive Forces Shape Strategy," *Harvard Business Review,* March–April 1979, pp. 137–45.

Global Strategy in Action — Exhibit 4.7

Used to Assess the International Environment

ECONOMIC ENVIRONMENT
- Level of economic development
- Population
- Gross national product
- Per capita income
- Literacy level
- Social infrastructure
- Natural resources
- Climate
- Membership in regional economic blocs (EU, NAFTA, LAFTA)
- Monetary and fiscal policies
- Wage and salary levels
- Nature of competition
- Currency convertibility
- Inflation
- Taxation system
- Interest rates

LEGAL ENVIRONMENT
- Legal tradition
- Effectiveness of legal system
- Treaties with foreign nations
- Patent trademark laws
- Laws affecting business firms

POLITICAL SYSTEM
- Form of government
- Political ideology
- Stability of government
- Strength of opposition parties and groups
- Social unrest
- Political strife and insurgency
- Governmental attitude towards foreign firms
- Foreign policy

CULTURAL ENVIRONMENT
- Customs, norms, values, beliefs
- Language
- Attitudes
- Motivations
- Social institutions
- Status symbols
- Religious beliefs

Source: From Arvind V. Phatak, *International Management,* South-Western College Publishing, 1997, p. 6. Reprinted with permission of Arvind V. Phatak.

Moreover, in the fight for market share, competition is not manifested only in the other players. Rather, competition in an industry is rooted in its underlying economics, and competitive forces exist that go well beyond the established combatants in a particular industry. Customers, suppliers, potential entrants, and substitute products are all competitors that may be more or less prominent or active depending on the industry.

The state of competition in an industry depends on five basic forces, which are diagrammed in Exhibit 4.8. The collective strength of these forces determines the ultimate profit potential of an industry. It ranges from intense in industries like tires, metal cans, and steel, where no company earns spectacular returns on investment, to mild in industries like oil-field services and equipment, soft drinks, and toiletries, where there is room for quite high returns.

In the economists' "perfectly competitive" industry, jockeying for position is unbridled and entry to the industry very easy. This kind of industry structure, of course, offers the worst prospect for long-run profitability. The weaker the forces collectively, however, the greater the opportunity for superior performance.

Whatever their collective strength, the corporate strategist's goal is to find a position in the industry where his or her company can best defend itself against these forces or can influence them in its favor. The collective strength of the forces may be painfully apparent to all the antagonists; but to cope with them, the strategist must delve below the surface and analyze the sources of competition. For example, what makes the industry vulnerable to entry? What determines the bargaining power of suppliers?

EXHIBIT 4.8 **Forces Driving Industry Competition**

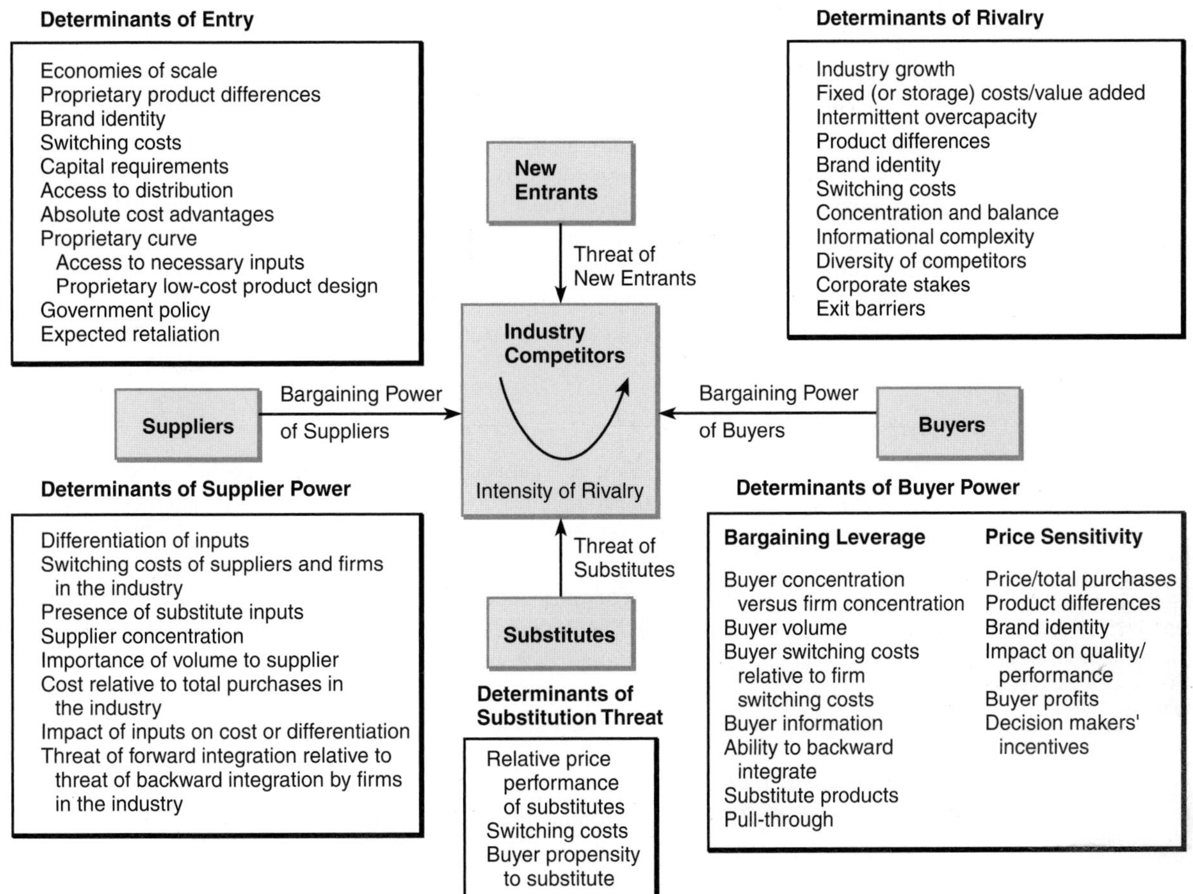

Source: Reprinted by permission of *Harvard Business Review*. Exhibit from "How Competitive Forces Shape Strategy," by M.E. Porter, March–April 1979.

Knowledge of these underlying sources of competitive pressure provides the groundwork for a strategic agenda of action. They highlight the critical strengths and weaknesses of the company, animate the positioning of the company in its industry, clarify the areas where strategic changes may yield the greatest payoff, and highlight the places where industry trends promise to hold the greatest significance as either opportunities or threats.

Understanding these sources also proves to be of help in considering areas for diversification.

CONTENDING FORCES

The strongest competitive force or forces determine the profitability of an industry and so are of greatest importance in strategy formulation. For example, even a company with a strong position in an industry unthreatened by potential entrants will earn low returns if it faces a superior or a lower-cost substitute product—as the leading manufacturers of vacuum tubes and coffee percolators have learned to their sorrow. In such a situation, coping with the substitute product becomes the number one strategic priority.

Different forces take on prominence, of course, in shaping competition in each industry. In the ocean-going tanker industry, the key force is probably the buyers (the major oil companies), while in tires it is powerful OEM buyers coupled with tough competitors. In the steel industry the key forces are foreign competitors and substitute materials.

Every industry has an underlying structure, or a set of fundamental economic and technical characteristics, that gives rise to these competitive forces. The strategist, wanting to position his or her company to cope best with its industry environment or to influence that environment in the company's favor, must learn what makes the environment tick.

This view of competition pertains equally to industries dealing in services and to those selling products. To avoid monotony, we refer to both products and services as *products.* The same general principles apply to all types of business.

A few characteristics are critical to the strength of each competitive force. They will be discussed in this section.

Threat of Entry

New entrants to an industry bring new capacity, the desire to gain market share, and often substantial resources. Similarly, companies diversifying through acquisition into the industry from other markets often leverage their resources to cause a shake-up, as Philip Morris did with Miller beer.

The seriousness of the threat of entry depends on the barriers present and on the reaction from existing competitors that the entrant can expect. If **barriers to entry** are high and a newcomer can expect sharp retaliation from the entrenched competitors, he or she obviously will not pose a serious threat of entering.

barriers to entry
The conditions that a firm must satisfy to enter an industry.

There are six major sources of barriers to entry.

Economies of Scale

These economies deter entry by forcing the aspirant either to come in on a large scale or to accept a cost disadvantage. Scale economies in production, research, marketing, and service are probably the key barriers to entry in the mainframe computer industry, as Xerox and GE sadly discovered. **Economies of scale** also can act as hurdles in distribution, utilization of the sales force, financing, and nearly any other part of a business.

economies of scale
The savings that companies achieve because of increased volume.

Economies of scale refer to the savings that companies within an industry achieve due to increased volume. Simply put, when the volume of production increases, the long-range average cost of a unit produced will decline.

Economies of scale result from technological and nontechnological sources. The technological sources of these economies are higher levels of mechanization or automation and a greater modernization of plant and facilities The nontechnological sources include better managerial coordination of production functions and processes, long-term contractual agreements with suppliers, and enhanced employee performance arising from specialization.

Economies of scale are an important determinant of the intensity of competition in an industry. Firms that enjoy such economies can charge lower prices than their competitors. They also can create barriers to entry by reducing their prices temporarily, or permanently, to deter new firms from entering the industry.

Product Differentiation

Product differentiation, or brand identification, creates a barrier by forcing entrants to spend heavily to overcome customer loyalty. Advertising, customer service, being first in the industry, and product differences are among the factors fostering brand identification. It is perhaps the most important entry barrier in soft drinks, over-the-counter drugs, cosmetics, investment banking, and public accounting. To create high fences around their business, brewers couple brand identification with economies of scale in production, distribution, and marketing.

product differentiation
The extent to which customers perceive differences among products and services.

Strategy in Action — Exhibit 4.9

The Experience Curve as an Entry Barrier

In recent years, the experience curve has become widely discussed as a key element of industry structure. According to this concept, unit costs in many manufacturing industries (some dogmatic adherents say in all manufacturing industries) as well as in some service industries decline with "experience," or a particular company's cumulative volume of production. (The experience curve, which encompasses many factors, is a broader concept than the better-known learning curve, which refers to the efficiency achieved over time by workers through much repetition.)

The causes of the decline in unit costs are a combination of elements, including economies of scale, the learning curve for labor, and capital-labor substitution. The cost decline creates a barrier to entry because new competitors with no "experience" face higher costs than established ones, particularly the producer with the largest market share, and have difficulty catching up with the entrenched competitors.

Adherents of the experience curve concept stress the importance of achieving market leadership to maximize this barrier to entry, and they recommend aggressive action to achieve it, such as price cutting in anticipation of falling costs in order to build volume. For the combatant that cannot achieve a healthy market share, the prescription is usually, "Get out."

Is the experience curve an entry barrier on which strategies should be built? The answer is, not in every industry. In fact, in some industries, building a strategy on the experience curve can be potentially disastrous. That costs decline with experience in some industries is not news to corporate executives. The significance of the experience curve for strategy depends on what factors are causing the decline.

A new entrant may well be more efficient than the more experienced competitors: if it has built the newest plant, it will face no disadvantage in having to catch up. The strategic prescription, "You must have the largest, most efficient plant," is a lot different from "You must produce the greatest cumulative output of the item to get your costs down."

Whether a drop in costs with cumulative (not absolute) volume erects an entry barrier also depends on the sources of the decline. If costs go down because of technical advances known generally in the industry or because of the development of improved equipment that can be copied or purchased from equipment suppliers, the experience curve is not an entry barrier at all—in fact, new or less-experienced competitors may actually enjoy a cost advantage over the leaders. Free of the legacy of heavy past investments, the newcomer or less-experienced competitor can purchase or copy the newest and lowest cost equipment and technology.

If, however, experience can be kept proprietary, the leaders will maintain a cost advantage. But new entrants may require less experience to reduce their costs than the leaders needed. All this suggests that the experience curve can be a shaky entry barrier on which to build a strategy.

Capital Requirements

The need to invest large financial resources to compete creates a barrier to entry, particularly if the capital is required for unrecoverable expenditures in upfront advertising or R&D. Capital is necessary not only for fixed facilities but also for customer credit, inventories, and absorbing start-up losses. While major corporations have the financial resources to invade almost any industry, the huge capital requirements in certain fields, such as computer manufacturing and mineral extraction, limit the pool of likely entrants.

Cost Disadvantages Independent of Size

Entrenched companies may have cost advantages not available to potential rivals, no matter what their size and attainable economies of scale. These advantages can stem from the effects of the learning curve (and of its first cousin, the experience curve), proprietary technology, access to the best raw materials sources, assets purchased at preinflation prices, government subsidies, or favorable locations. Sometimes cost advantages are enforceable legally, as they are through patents. (For analysis of the much-discussed experience curve as a barrier to entry, see Exhibit 4.9, Strategy in Action.)

Access to Distribution Channels

The new boy or girl on the block must, of course, secure distribution of his or her product or service. A new food product, for example, must displace others from the supermarket shelf via price breaks, promotions, intense selling efforts, or some other means. The more limited the wholesale or retail channels are and the more that existing competitors have these tied up, obviously the tougher that entry into the industry will be. Sometimes this barrier is so high that, to surmount it, a new contestant must create its own distribution channels, as Timex did in the watch industry.

Government Policy

The government can limit or even foreclose entry to industries, with such controls as license requirements, limits on access to raw materials, and tax incentives. Regulated industries like trucking, liquor retailing, and freight forwarding are noticeable examples; more subtle government restrictions operate in fields like ski-area development and coal mining. The government also can play a major indirect role by affecting entry barriers through such controls as air and water pollution standards and safety regulations.

The potential rival's expectations about the reaction of existing competitors also will influence its decision on whether to enter. The company is likely to have second thoughts if incumbents have previously lashed out at new entrants, or if

The incumbents possess substantial resources to fight back, including excess cash and unused borrowing power, productive capacity, or clout with distribution channels and customers.

The incumbents seem likely to cut prices because of a desire to keep market shares or because of industrywide excess capacity.

Industry growth is slow, affecting its ability to absorb the new arrival and probably causing the financial performance of all the parties involved to decline.

Powerful Suppliers

Suppliers can exert bargaining power on participants in an industry by raising prices or reducing the quality of purchased goods and services. Powerful suppliers, thereby, can squeeze profitability out of an industry unable to recover cost increases in its own prices. By raising their prices, soft-drink concentrate producers have contributed to the erosion of profitability of bottling companies because the bottlers—facing intense competition from powdered mixes, fruit drinks, and other beverages—have limited freedom to raise their prices accordingly.

The power of each important supplier (or buyer) group depends on a number of characteristics of its market situation and on the relative importance of its sales or purchases to the industry compared with its overall business.

A *supplier* group is powerful if

1. It is dominated by a few companies and is more concentrated than the industry it sells.

2. Its product is unique or at least differentiated, or if it has built-up switching costs. Switching costs are fixed costs that buyers face in changing suppliers. These arise because, among other things, a buyer's product specifications tie it to particular suppliers, it has invested heavily in specialized ancillary equipment or in learning how to operate a supplier's equipment (as in computer software), or its production lines are connected to the supplier's manufacturing facilities (as in some manufacturing of beverage containers).

3. It is not obliged to contend with other products for sale to the industry. For instance, the competition between the steel companies and the aluminum companies to sell to the can industry checks the power of each supplier.

4. It poses a credible threat of integrating forward into the industry's business. This provides a check against the industry's ability to improve the terms on which it purchases.

5. The industry is not an important customer of the supplier group. If the industry is an important customer, suppliers' fortunes will be tied closely to the industry, and they will want to protect the industry through reasonable pricing and assistance in activities like R&D and lobbying.

Powerful Buyers

Customers likewise can force down prices, demand higher quality or more service, and play competitors off against each other—all at the expense of industry profits.

A *buyer* group is powerful if

1. It is concentrated or purchases in large volumes. Large-volume buyers are particularly potent forces if heavy fixed costs characterize the industry—as they do in metal containers, corn refining, and bulk chemicals, for example—which raise the stakes to keep capacity filled.

2. The products it purchases from the industry are standard or undifferentiated. The buyers, sure that they always can find alternative suppliers, may play one company against another, as they do in aluminum extrusion.

3. The products it purchases from the industry form a component of its product and represent a significant fraction of its cost. The buyers are likely to shop for a favorable price and purchase selectively. Where the product sold by the industry in question is a small fraction of buyers' costs, buyers are usually much less price sensitive.

4. It earns low profits, which create great incentive to lower its purchasing costs. Highly profitable buyers, however, are generally less price sensitive (i.e., of course, if the item does not represent a large fraction of their costs).

5. The industry's product is unimportant to the quality of the buyers' products or services. Where the quality of the buyers' products is very much affected by the industry's product, buyers are generally less price sensitive. Industries in which this situation exists include oil field equipment, where a malfunction can lead to large losses, and enclosures for electronic medical and test instruments, where the quality of the enclosure can influence the user's impression about the quality of the equipment inside.

6. The industry's product does not save the buyer money. Where the industry's product or service can pay for itself many times over, the buyer is rarely price sensitive; rather, he or she is interested in quality. This is true in services like investment banking and public accounting, where errors in judgment can be costly and embarrassing, and in businesses like the mapping of oil wells, where an accurate survey can save thousands of dollars in drilling costs.

7. The buyers pose a credible threat of integrating backward to make the industry's product. The Big Three auto producers and major buyers of cars often have used the threat of self-manufacture as a bargaining lever. But sometimes an industry so engenders a threat to buyers that its members may integrate forward.

Most of these sources of buyer power can be attributed to consumers as a group as well as to industrial and commercial buyers; only a modification of the frame of reference is necessary. Consumers tend to be more price sensitive if they are purchasing products that are undifferentiated, expensive relative to their incomes, and of a sort where quality is not particularly important.

The buying power of retailers is determined by the same rules, with one important addition. Retailers can gain significant bargaining power over manufacturers when they can influence consumers' purchasing decisions, as they do in audio components, jewelry, appliances, sporting goods, and other goods.

Because its heavy reliance on a few large customers, MasterCard's corporate strategy is strongly influenced by buyer power. MasterCard Inc. generates revenue by charging fees to process payments from banks to consumers who swipe MasterCard-brand credit and debit cards, making the banks, not individual consumers, MasterCard's customers. MasterCard issues 916 million cards through 25,000 financial institutions in more than 200 countries.

Rapid consolidation within the banking industry, combined with a 28 percent market share in global credit and debit card transactions compared with main-rival Visa's 68 percent share, means that MasterCard has to work hard to win and keep bank business. Further, MasterCard's dependence on four large customers, which make up 30 percent of annual revenues (J.P. Morgan Chase, Citigroup, Bank of America, and HSBC), makes it vulnerable to attack.

Substitute Products

By placing a ceiling on the prices it can charge, substitute products or services limit the potential of an industry. Unless it can upgrade the quality of the product or differentiate it somehow (as via marketing), the industry will suffer in earnings and possibly in growth.

Manifestly, the more attractive the price-performance trade-off offered by substitute products, the firmer the lid placed on the industry's profit potential. Sugar producers confronted with the large-scale commercialization of high-fructose corn syrup, a sugar substitute, learned this lesson.

Substitutes not only limit profits in normal times but also reduce the bonanza an industry can reap in boom times. The producers of fiberglass insulation enjoyed unprecedented demand as a result of high energy costs and severe winter weather. But the industry's ability to raise prices was tempered by the plethora of insulation substitutes, including cellulose, rock wool, and Styrofoam. These substitutes are bound to become an even stronger force once the current round of plant additions by fiberglass insulation producers has boosted capacity enough to meet demand (and then some).

Substitute products that deserve the most attention strategically are those that *(a)* are subject to trends improving their price-performance trade-off with the industry's product or *(b)* are produced by industries earning high profits. Substitutes often come rapidly into play if some development increases competition in their industries and causes price reduction or performance improvement.

Jockeying for Position

Rivalry among existing competitors takes the familiar form of jockeying for position—using tactics like price competition, product introduction, and advertising price-cutting. This type of intense rivalry is related to the presence of a number of factors:

1. Competitors are numerous or are roughly equal in size and power. In many U.S. industries in recent years, foreign contenders, of course, have become part of the competitive picture.

2. Industry growth is slow, precipitating fights for market share that involve expansion-minded members.

3. The product or service lacks differentiation or switching costs, which lock in buyers and protect one combatant from raids on its customers by another.

4. Fixed costs are high or the product is perishable, creating strong temptation to cut prices. Many basic materials businesses, like paper and aluminum, suffer from this problem when demand slackens.

5. Capacity normally is augmented in large increments. Such additions, as in the chlorine and vinyl chloride businesses, disrupt the industry's supply–demand balance and often lead to periods of overcapacity and price-cutting.

6. Exit barriers are high. Exit barriers, like very specialized assets or management's loyalty to a particular business, keep companies competing even though they may be earning low or even negative returns on investment. Excess capacity remains functioning, and the profitability of the healthy competitors suffers as the sick ones hang on. If the entire industry suffers from overcapacity, it may seek government help—particularly if foreign competition is present.

7. The rivals are diverse in strategies, origins, and "personalities." They have different ideas about how to compete and continually run head-on into each other in the process.

As an industry matures, its growth rate changes, resulting in declining profits and (often) a shakeout. In the booming recreational vehicle industry of the early 1970s, nearly every producer did well; but slow growth since then has eliminated the high returns, except for the strongest members, not to mention many of the weaker companies. The same profit story has been played out in industry after industry—snowmobiles, aerosol packaging, and sports equipment are just a few examples.

An acquisition can introduce a very different personality to an industry, as has been the case with Black & Decker's takeover of McCullough, the producer of chain saws. Technological innovation can boost the level of fixed costs in the production process, as it did in the shift from batch to continuous-line photo finishing.

While a company must live with many of these factors—because they are built into the industry economics—it may have some latitude for improving matters through strategic shifts. For example, it may try to raise buyers' switching costs or increase product differentiation. A focus on selling efforts in the fastest growing segments of the industry or on market areas with the lowest fixed costs can reduce the impact of industry rivalry. If it is feasible, a company can try to avoid confrontation with competitors having high exit barriers and, thus, can sidestep involvement in bitter price-cutting.

INDUSTRY ANALYSIS AND COMPETITIVE ANALYSIS

Designing viable strategies for a firm requires a thorough understanding of the firm's industry and competition. The firm's executives need to address four questions: (1) What are the boundaries of the industry? (2) What is the structure of the industry? (3) Which firms are our competitors? (4) What are the major determinants of competition? The answers to these questions provide a basis for thinking about the appropriate strategies that are open to the firm.

Industry Boundaries

industry
A group of companies that provide similar products and services.

An **industry** is a collection of firms that offer similar products or services. By "similar products," we mean products that customers perceive to be substitutable for one another. Consider, for example, the brands of personal computers (PCs) that are now being marketed. The firms that produce these PCs, such as Hewlett-Packard, IBM, Apple, and Dell, form the nucleus of the microcomputer industry.

Suppose a firm competes in the microcomputer industry. Where do the boundaries of this industry begin and end? Does the industry include desktops? Laptops? These are the kinds of questions that executives face in defining industry boundaries.

Why is a definition of industry boundaries important? First, it helps executives determine the arena in which their firm is competing. A firm competing in the microcomputer industry participates in an environment very different from that of the broader electronics business. The microcomputer industry comprises several related product families, including personal computers, inexpensive computers for home use, and workstations. The unifying characteristic of these product families is the use of a central processing unit (CPU) in a microchip. On the other hand, the electronics industry is far more extensive; it includes computers, radios, supercomputers, superconductors, and many other products.

The microcomputer and electronics industries differ in their volume of sales, their scope (some would consider microcomputers a segment of the electronics industry), their rate of growth, and their competitive makeup. The dominant issues faced by the two industries also are different. Witness, for example, the raging public debate being waged on the future of the "high-definition TV." U.S. policy makers are attempting to ensure domestic control of that segment of the electronics industry. They also are considering ways to stimulate "cutting-edge" research in superconductivity. These efforts are likely to spur innovation and stimulate progress in the electronics industry.

Second, a definition of industry boundaries focuses attention on the firm's competitors. Defining industry boundaries enables the firm to identify its competitors and producers of substitute products. This is critically important to the firm's design of its competitive strategy.

Third, a definition of industry boundaries helps executives determine key factors for success. Survival in the premier segment of the microcomputer industry requires skills that are considerably different from those required in the lower end of the industry. Firms that compete in the premier segment need to be on the cutting edge of technological development and to provide extensive customer support and education. On the other hand, firms that compete in the lower end need to excel in imitating the products introduced by the premier segment, to focus on customer convenience, and to maintain operational efficiency that permits them to charge the lowest market price. Defining industry boundaries enables executives to ask these questions: Do we have the skills it takes to succeed here? If not, what must we do to develop these skills?

Finally, a definition of industry boundaries gives executives another basis on which to evaluate their firm's goals. Executives use that definition to forecast demand for their firm's products and services. Armed with that forecast, they can determine whether those goals are realistic.

Problems in Defining Industry Boundaries

Defining industry boundaries requires both caution and imagination. Caution is necessary because there are no precise rules for this task and because a poor definition will lead to poor planning. Imagination is necessary because industries are dynamic—in every industry, important changes are under way in such key factors as competition, technology, and consumer demand.

Defining industry boundaries is a very difficult task. The difficulty stems from three sources:

1. The evolution of industries over time creates new opportunities and threats. Compare the financial services industry as we know it today with that of the 1990s, and then try to imagine how different the industry will be in the year 2020.

2. Industrial evolution creates industries within industries. The electronics industry of the 1960s has been transformed into many "industries"—TV sets, transistor radios, micro and macrocomputers, supercomputers, superconductors, and so on. Such transformation allows some firms to specialize and others to compete in different, related industries.

3. Industries are becoming global in scope. Consider the civilian aircraft manufacturing industry. For nearly three decades, U.S. firms dominated world production in that industry. But small and large competitors were challenging their dominance by 1990. At that time, Airbus Industries (a consortium of European firms) and Brazilian, Korean, and Japanese firms were actively competing in the industry.

Exhibit 4.10, Global Strategy in Action provides a professional analysis of the automotive industry in 2011. Looking back, you can now assess how insightful the analysis was

Global Strategy in Action — Exhibit 4.10

Analysis of the Automotive Industry in 2011

Among industrial companies, the automotive sector merits special mention, given its historical significance and its position at the epicenter of the globalization battleground. After an unprecedented downturn, the American automotive industry is beginning to recover. The dislocations of bankruptcy and restructuring are mostly finished, credit is becoming more readily available, and many observers expect demand to grow as the cars already on the road age. Long-term industry fundamentals are improving now that the Detroit Three have greatly reduced legacy costs and are introducing more competitive passenger vehicles. Further, Toyota appears to be recovering from its recall crisis, and South Korean automaker Hyundai is gaining market share with an impressive line of new products.

Suppliers are enjoying a similar turnaround. Several large Tier One suppliers have emerged from Chapter 11 bankruptcy, and some suppliers are benefiting from the revival in industry volumes and improved product portfolios, which are generating solid profitability and cash flow. Yet automakers in North America and elsewhere still face significant obstacles to achieving sustainable profitability over the long term. Competition is fierce across most segments. Hyundai has launched a compelling lineup at attractive prices. Honda is fighting back with aggressive lease deals on its aging Accord, and Toyota is working to reestablish its reputation for industry-leading quality while using incentives to maintain share and volume.

The Detroit Three face a separate set of obstacles. GM, Ford, and Chrysler still confront the difficult task of closing the cost gap with advantaged global competitors. Despite union concessions, wages and benefits for current hourly workers are still well above benchmarks established by new North American plants. In addition, the unions are working hard to reverse recent concessions, which could erase hard-won gains.

The Detroit Three also have a quality perception gap to overcome. Although the quality, reliability, and durability (QRD) statistics for U.S. automakers are closer than ever to those of their Japanese counterparts, Booz & Company research shows that car buyers can take as long as 10 years to catch up to the quality data. Finally, GM and Chrysler need to rebuild their financing capabilities and dealer relationships, which were both badly damaged during the bankruptcy process.

In the United States, GM and Chrysler will also have to rebuild their finance capabilities. They must heal the wounds in their dealer networks caused by bankruptcy-driven closures. Finally, incumbent automakers everywhere will need to get ready for new international competitors with inherently lower cost structures. Most of these will come from countries with exploding markets, notably Korea, China, and India. Competing successfully in this industry will require continuous improvement in products, technologies, costs, investment economics, and business models.

Source: Excerpted from Scott Corwin, John Loehr, and Evan Hirsh. "Five Industries Hit by the Reset Button, Automotives," *Strategy + Business*, January 14, 2011. http://www.strategy-business.com/article/00060?pg=all

in forecasting the competitive challenges of the global industry and, in particular, of the strategic requirements on the Big Three auto makers in the United States.

Developing a Realistic Industry Definition

Given the difficulties just outlined, how do executives draw accurate boundaries for an industry? The starting point is a definition of the industry in global terms; that is, in terms that consider the industry's international components as well as its domestic components.

Having developed a preliminary concept of the industry (e.g., computers), executives flesh out its current components. This can be done by defining its product segments. Executives need to select the scope of their firm's potential market from among these related but distinct areas.

To understand the makeup of the industry, executives adopt a longitudinal perspective. They examine the emergence and evolution of product families. Why did these product families arise? How and why did they change? The answers to such questions provide executives with clues about the factors that drive competition in the industry.

Global Strategy in Action — Exhibit 4.11

A Year of Change in the Philippine Telecommunications Industry

To say that 2011 would be a difficult year for the Philippine telecommunications industry is an understatement. The industry's dynamics are changing dramatically. While consumers rejoice about the barrage of unlimited and bucket priced offerings that brought down the costs of text messaging and mobile voice calls, the revenues of telecommunications companies suffered.

Globe Telecom president and CEO Ernest Cu said the company's financial results are reflective of the challenges facing the industry, whereby traffic is growing, but revenues are declining with the market's increasing preference for unlimited services. Despite an increase in traffic and over-all usage, Globe's mobile revenues were lower with sustained price pressures resulting from intense competition and subscribers' increasing preference for lower-yield bucket and unlimited promotions.

Globe's Super All Txt 20 is one such bucket priced offering. For only P20 a day, a subscriber gets to send 200 text messages to any network which means that each SMS costs only 10 centavos. The company's Unli Txt All Day allows one to send unlimited text messages to Globe/TM subscribers for one day. Many of these promos are offered for a limited time only, but they are usually renewed.

The mobile telephony sector is now a matured one. The cellular penetration rate has now exceeded 80%. This triggered the search for new revenue streams and the rise of broadband Internet services as the new revenue driver.

But even the cost of mobile Internet access has significantly gone down, thanks to bucket price and unlimited offerings. For just P50 a day, a Globe subscriber is given unlimited access to the Internet using a Globe Tattoo Broadband USB or mobile phone for one day. Smart also offers unlimited mobile surfing for P50 per day while Smart Broadband has its unlimited Internet access promo at P200 good for five days. With the entry of a new player, San Miguel Corp./Liberty Telecom's Wi-Tribe, expect the cost of Internet access to go down even further.

Now here's a look at how the industry's decision makers viewed prospects for 2011:

- PLDT planned to preserve "margins by strengthening cost management given the modest top-line growth. . . . Demand for bucket and unlimited offers in the cellular space will continue. We expect that broadband will keep growing given the growing popularity of social networking and new access devices such as tablets and smartphones. PLDT will continue to invest in its network in order to fortify its market leadership."
- In 2011". . . we expect further developments in 3.5G. New Android phones are also getting exciting. We are optimistic both about the telco industry and the economy in general. . . . In 2011, we are confident we can achieve robust growth in both 2G and 3.5G as we continue our strong rollout of cellsites. By end of 2011, Sun should be even in number of cellsites as the other two telco players in almost all regions of the country." —James Go, president, Digital Telecommunications Phils. Inc. (Digitel)
- "Our growth drivers next year would continue to be data and Internet services for both consumer and corporate sectors. On the consumer side, we will continue to focus on Internet services as we leverage on our cooperation within the Lopez Group to deliver relevant and compelling communication and content services. At the same time, Bayan has been strong in the corporate data sector servicing banks and BPOs, and we hope to gain on the opportunities." —Rafael Aguado, chief operations officer, Bayan Telecommunications
- "The device business will continue to grow in leaps and bounds with the mobile phones still leading the way and new affordable devices such as smart phones and tablets coming in strong in the second half of the year. MyPhone will continue to invest in expanding our retail chains and service centers to maintain its excellent quality and after-sales service reputation." —David Lim, chairman, Solid Group, makers of MyPhone

Source: Exerpted from Mary Ann L. Reyes, "2010: A Year of Changing Telecommunications Market Dynamics," *The Philippine Star*, December 30, 2010.

Exhibit 4.11, Global Strategy in Action provides an example of the changing industry dynamics in the Philippine telecommunications industry in 2011. Increased rivalry resulting from the maturing of the industry, heightened price competition, and product improvements all add to the challenges of the industry's strategic planners.

Executives also examine the companies that offer different product families, the overlapping or distinctiveness of customer segments, and the rate of substitutability among product families.

EXHIBIT 4.12
Common Shape of a Power Curve

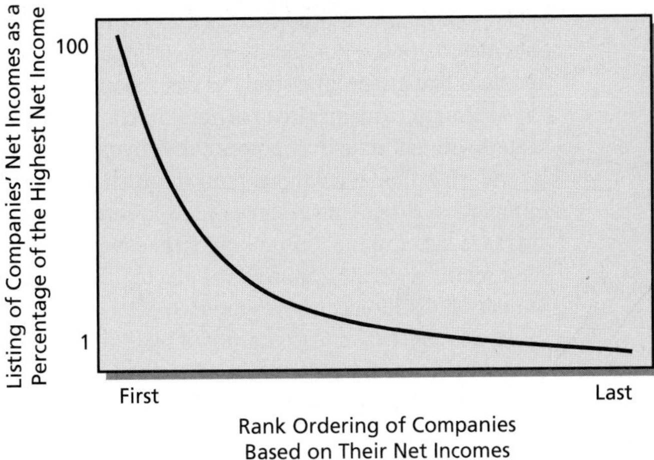

To realistically define their industry, executives need to examine five issues:

1. Which part of the industry corresponds to our firm's goals?
2. What are the key ingredients of success in that part of the industry?
3. Does our firm have the skills needed to compete in that part of the industry? If not, can we build those skills?
4. Will the skills enable us to seize emerging opportunities and deal with future threats?
5. Is our definition of the industry flexible enough to allow necessary adjustments to our business concept as the industry grows?

Power Curves

Strategic managers have a new tool that helps them assess industry structure, which refers to the enduring characteristics that give an industry its distinctive character. According to Michele Zanini of the McKinsey Group, from whose work this discussion is derived, power curves depict the fundamental structural trends that underlie an industry.[2] While major economic events like the worldwide recession of 2008 are extremely disruptive to business activity, they do little to change the relative position of most businesses to one another over the long term.

What would you guess is the typical shape of the distribution of companies in an industry? Is it bell shaped, with a few superlarge firms, many companies of medium size, and a few extremely small competitors? Or, is it linear, with a few large companies and progressively larger numbers of smaller firms? Do you think that company strategies should be different if one of these models is right and the other wrong?

In many industries, the top firm is best described as a mega-institution—a company of unprecedented scale and scope that has an undeniable lead over competitors. Wal-Mart, Best Buy, McDonald's, and Starbucks are examples. However, even among these firms, there is a clear difference in size and performance. When the distribution of net incomes of the global top 150 corporations in 2005 was plotted, the result was a "power curve," which implies that most companies, even in the set of superstars, are below average in performance. This power curve is shown in Exhibit 4.12.

[2] Michele Zanini, "'Using Power Curves' to Assess Industry Dynamics," *The McKinsey Quarterly*, November 2008.

A power curve is described as exhibiting a small set of companies with extremely large incomes, followed quickly by a much larger array of companies with significantly smaller incomes that are progressively smaller than one another, but only slightly.

As Zanini explains, low barriers to entry and high levels of rivalry are positively associated with an industry's power curve dynamics. The larger the number of competitors in an industry, the larger the gap on the vertical axis usually is between the top and median companies. When entry barriers are lowered, such as occurs with deregulation, revenues increase faster in the top-ranking firms, creating a steeper power curve. This greater openness seems to create a more level playing field at first, but greater differentiation and consolidation tend to occur over time.

Power curves are also promoted by intangible assets such as software and biotechnology, which generate increasing returns to scale and economies of scope. By contrast, more labor- or capital-intensive sectors, such as chemicals and machinery, have flatter curves.

In industries that display a power curve—including insurance, machinery, and U.S. banks and savings institutions—intriguing implications suggest that strategic thrusts rather than incremental strategies are required to improve a company's position significantly. Zanini defends this idea with evidence from the retail mutual fund industry. The major players at the top of the power curve can extend their lead by exploiting network effects, such as cross-selling individual retirement accounts (IRAs), to a large installed base of 401(k) plan holders as they roll over their assets. A financial crisis, like the recession of 2008, increases the likelihood of this opportunity as weakened financial institutions sell their asset-management units to raise capital.

Power curves can be useful to strategic managers in understanding their industry's structural dynamics and in benchmarking its performance. Because an industry's curve evolves over many years, a large deviation in the slope can indicate some exceptional occurrence, such as unusual firm performance or market instability.

As Zanini concludes, power curves suggest that companies generally compete against one another and against an industry structure that becomes progressively more unequal. For most companies, this possibility makes power curves an important strategic consideration.

Competitive Analysis

How to Identify Competitors

In identifying their firm's current and potential competitors, executives consider several important variables:

1. How do other firms define the scope of their market? The more similar the definitions of firms, the more likely the firms will view each other as competitors.

2. How similar are the benefits the customers derive from the products and services that other firms offer? The more similar the benefits of products or services, the higher the level of substitutability between them. High substitutability levels force firms to compete fiercely for customers.

3. How committed are other firms to the industry? Although this question may appear to be far removed from the identification of competitors, it is in fact one of the most important questions that competitive analysis must address, because it sheds light on the long-term intentions and goals. To size up the commitment of potential competitors to the industry, reliable intelligence data are needed. Such data may relate to potential resource commitments (e.g., planned facility expansions).

Common Mistakes in Identifying Competitors

Identifying competitors is a milestone in the development of strategy. But it is a process laden with uncertainty and risk, a process in which executives sometimes make costly mistakes. Examples of these mistakes are:

1. Overemphasizing current and known competitors while giving inadequate attention to potential entrants.
2. Overemphasizing large competitors while ignoring small competitors.
3. Overlooking potential international competitors.
4. Assuming that competitors will continue to behave in the same way they have behaved in the past.
5. Misreading signals that may indicate a shift in the focus of competitors or a refinement of their present strategies or tactics.
6. Overemphasizing competitors' financial resources, market position, and strategies while ignoring their intangible assets, such as a top management team.
7. Assuming that all of the firms in the industry are subject to the same constraints or are open to the same opportunities.
8. Believing that the purpose of strategy is to outsmart the competition, rather than to satisfy customer needs and expectations.

OPERATING ENVIRONMENT

operating environment
Factors in the immediate competitive situation that affect a firm's success in acquiring needed resources.

The **operating environment,** also called the *competitive* or *task environment,* comprises factors in the competitive situation that affect a firm's success in acquiring needed resources or in profitably marketing its goods and services. Among the most important of these factors are the firm's competitive position, the composition of its customers, its reputation among suppliers and creditors, and its ability to attract capable employees. The operating environment is typically much more subject to the firm's influence or control than the remote environment. Thus, firms can be much more proactive (as opposed to reactive) in dealing with the operating environment than in dealing with the remote environment.

Competitive Position

Assessing its competitive position improves a firm's chances of designing strategies that optimize its environmental opportunities. Development of competitor profiles enables a firm to more accurately forecast both its short- and long-term growth and its profit potentials. Although the exact criteria used in constructing a competitor's profile are largely determined by situational factors, the following criteria are often included:

1. Market share.
2. Breadth of product line.
3. Effectiveness of sales distribution.
4. Proprietary and key account advantages.
5. Price competitiveness.
6. Advertising and promotion effectiveness.
7. Location and age of facility.
8. Capacity and productivity.
9. Experience.
10. Raw materials costs.
11. Financial position.
12. Relative product quality.
13. R&D advantages position.
14. Caliber of personnel.
15. General images.
16. Customer profile.
17. Patents and copyrights.
18. Union relations.
19. Technological position.
20. Community reputation.

EXHIBIT 4.13
Competitor Profile

Key Success Factors	Weight	Rating*	Weighted Score
Market share	0.30	4	1.20
Price competitiveness	0.20	3	0.60
Facilities location	0.20	5	1.00
Raw materials costs	0.10	3	0.30
Caliber of personnel	0.20	1	0.20
	1.00†		3.30

*The rating scale suggested is as follows: very strong competitive position (5 points), strong (4), average (3), weak (2), very weak (1).
†The total of the weights must always equal 1.00.

Once appropriate criteria have been selected, they are weighted to reflect their importance to a firm's success. Then the competitor being evaluated is rated on the criteria, the ratings are multiplied by the weight, and the weighted scores are summed to yield a numerical profile of the competitor, as shown in Exhibit 4.13.

This type of competitor profile is limited by the subjectivity of its criteria selection, weighting, and evaluation approaches. Nevertheless, the process of developing such profiles is of considerable help to a firm in defining its perception of its competitive position. Moreover, comparing the firm's profile with those of its competitors can aid its managers in identifying factors that might make the competitors vulnerable to the strategies the firm might choose to implement.

Customer Profiles

Perhaps the most vulnerable result of analyzing the operating environment is the understanding of a firm's customers that this provides. Developing a profile of a firm's present and prospective customers improves the ability of its managers to plan strategic operations, to anticipate changes in the size of markets, and to reallocate resources so as to support forecast shifts in demand patterns. The traditional approach to segmenting customers is based on customer profiles constructed from geographic, demographic, psychographic, and buyer behavior information.

Enterprising companies have quickly learned the importance of identifying target segments. In recent years, market research has increased tremendously as companies realize the benefits of demographic and psychographic segmentation. Research by American Express (AMEX) showed that competitors were stealing a prime segment of the company's business, affluent business travelers. AMEX's competing companies, including Visa and Mastercard, began offering high-spending business travelers frequent flier programs and other rewards including discounts on new cars. In turn, AMEX began to invest heavily in rewards programs, while also focusing on its strongest capabilities, assets, and competitive advantage. Unlike most credit card companies, AMEX cannot rely on charging interest to make money because most of its customers pay in full each month. Therefore, the company charges higher transaction fees to its merchants. In this way, increases in spending by AMEX customers who pay off their balances each month are more profitable to AMEX than to competing credit card companies.

Assessing consumer behavior is a key element in the process of satisfying your target market needs. Many firms lose market share as a result of assumptions made about target segments. Market research and industry surveys can help to reduce a firm's chances of relying on illusive assumptions. Firms most vulnerable are those that have had success with one or more products in the marketplace and as a result try to base consumer behavior on past data and trends.

Geographic

It is important to define the geographic area from which customers do or could come. Almost every product or service has some quality that makes it variably attractive to buyers from different locations. Obviously, a Wisconsin manufacturer of snow skis should think twice about investing in a wholesale distribution center in South Carolina. On the other hand, advertising in the *Milwaukee Journal-Sentinel* could significantly expand the geographically defined customer market of a major Myrtle Beach hotel in South Carolina.

Demographic

Demographic variables most commonly are used to differentiate groups of present or potential customers. Demographic information (e.g., information on sex, age, marital status, income, and occupation) is comparatively easy to collect, quantify, and use in strategic forecasting, and such information is the minimum basis for a customer profile.

Psychographic

Personality and lifestyle variables often are better predictors of customer purchasing behavior than geographic or demographic variables. In such situations, a psychographic study is an important component of the customer profile. Advertising campaigns by soft-drink producers—Pepsi-Cola ("the Pepsi generation"), Coca-Cola ("the real thing"), and 7UP ("America's turning 7UP")—reflect strategic management's attention to the psychographic characteristics of their largest customer segment—physically active, group-oriented nonprofessionals.

Buyer Behavior

Buyer behavior data also can be a component of the customer profile. Such data are used to explain or predict some aspect of customer behavior with regard to a product or service. Information on buyer behavior (e.g., usage rate, benefits sought, and brand loyalty) can provide significant aid in the design of more accurate and profitable strategies.

Suppliers

Dependable relationships between a firm and its suppliers are essential to the firm's long-term survival and growth. A firm regularly relies on its suppliers for financial support, services, materials, and equipment. In addition, it occasionally is forced to make special requests for such favors as quick delivery, liberal credit terms, or broken-lot orders. Particularly at such times, it is essential for a firm to have had an ongoing relationship with its suppliers.

In the assessment of a firm's relationships with its suppliers, several factors, other than the strength of that relationship, should be considered. With regard to its competitive position with its suppliers, the firm should address the following questions:

Are the suppliers' prices competitive? Do the suppliers offer attractive quantity discounts?

How costly are their shipping charges? Are the suppliers competitive in terms of production standards?

In terms of deficiency rates, are the suppliers' abilities, reputations, and services competitive?

Are the suppliers reciprocally dependent on the firm?

Creditors

Because the quantity, quality, price, and accessibility of financial, human, and material resources are rarely ideal, assessment of suppliers and creditors is critical to an accurate evaluation of a firm's operating environment. With regard to its competitive position with its creditors, among the most important questions that the firm should address are the following:

Do the creditors fairly value and willingly accept the firm's stock as collateral?

Do the creditors perceive the firm as having an acceptable record of past payment?

A strong working capital position? Little or no leverage?

Are the creditors' loan terms compatible with the firm's profitability objectives?

Are the creditors able to extend the necessary lines of credit?

The answers to these and related questions help a firm forecast the availability of the resources it will need to implement and sustain its competitive strategies.

Human Resources: Nature of the Labor Market

A firm's ability to attract and hold capable employees is essential to its success. However, a firm's personnel recruitment and selection alternatives often are influenced by the nature of its operating environment. A firm's access to needed personnel is affected primarily by four factors: the firm's reputation as an employer, local employment rates, the ready availability of people with the needed skills, and its relationship with labor unions.

Reputation

A firm's reputation within its operating environment is a major element of its ability to satisfy its personnel needs. A firm is more likely to attract and retain valuable employees if it is seen as permanent in the community, competitive in its compensation package, and concerned with the welfare of its employees, and if it is respected for its product or service and appreciated for its overall contribution to the general welfare.

Employment Rates

The readily available supply of skilled and experienced personnel may vary considerably with the stage of a community's growth. A new manufacturing firm would find it far more difficult to obtain skilled employees in a vigorous industrialized community than in an economically depressed community in which similar firms had recently cut back operations.

Availability

The skills of some people are so specialized that relocation may be necessary to secure the jobs and the compensation that those skills commonly command. People with such skills include oil drillers, chefs, technical specialists, and industry executives. A firm that seeks to hire such a person is said to have broad labor market boundaries; that is, the geographic area within which the firm might reasonably expect to attract qualified candidates is quite large. On the other hand, people with more common skills are less likely to relocate from a considerable distance to achieve modest economic or career advancements. Thus, the labor market boundaries are fairly limited for such occupational groups as unskilled laborers, clerical personnel, and retail clerks.

Many manufacturers in the United States attempt to minimize the labor cost disadvantage they face in competing with overseas producers by outsourcing to lower-cost foreign locations or by hiring immigrant workers. Similarly, companies in construction and other labor-intensive industries try to provide themselves with a cost advantage by hiring temporary, often migrant, workers.

Labor Unions

Approximately 12 percent of all workers in the United States belong to a labor union; and almost half of these are government employees. The percentages are higher in Japan and western Europe at about 25 and 40 percent, respectively, and extremely low in developing nations. Unions represent the workers in their negotiations with employers through the process of collective bargaining. When managers' relationships with their employees are complicated by the involvement of a union, the company's ability to manage and motivate the people that it needs can be compromised.

EMPHASIS ON ENVIRONMENTAL FACTORS

This chapter has described the remote, industry, and operating environments as encompassing five components each. While that description is generally accurate, it may give the false impression that the components are easily identified, mutually exclusive, and equally applicable in all situations. In fact, the forces in the external environment are so dynamic and interactive that the impact of any single element cannot be wholly disassociated from the effect of other elements. For example, are increases in OPEC oil prices the result of economic, political, social, or technological changes? Or are a manufacturer's surprisingly good relations with suppliers a result of competitors', customers', or creditors' activities or of the supplier's own activities? The answer to both questions is probably that a number of forces in the external environment have combined to create the situation. Such is the case in most studies of the environment.

Strategic managers are frequently frustrated in their attempts to anticipate the environment's changing influences. Different external elements affect different strategies at different times and with varying strengths. The only certainty is that the effect of the remote and operating environments will be uncertain until a strategy is implemented. This leads many managers, particularly in less powerful or smaller firms, to minimize long-term planning, which requires a commitment of resources. Instead, they favor allowing managers to adapt to new pressures from the environment. While such a decision has considerable merit for many firms, there is an associated trade-off, namely that absence of a strong resource and psychological commitment to a proactive strategy effectively bars a firm from assuming a leadership role in its competitive environment.

There is yet another difficulty in assessing the probable impact of remote, industry, and operating environments on the effectiveness of alternative strategies. Assessment of this kind involves collecting information that can be analyzed to disclose predictable effects. Except in rare instances, however, it is virtually impossible for any single firm to anticipate the consequences of a change in the environment; for example, what is the precise effect on alternative strategies of a 2 percent increase in the national inflation rate, a 1 percent decrease in statewide unemployment, or the entry of a new competitor in a regional market?

Still, assessing the potential impact of changes in the external environment offers a real advantage. It enables decision makers to narrow the range of the available options and to eliminate options that are clearly inconsistent with the forecast opportunities. Environmental assessment seldom identifies the best strategy, but it generally leads to the elimination of all but the most promising options.

Exhibit 4.14 provides a set of key strategic forecasting issues for each level of environmental assessment—remote, industry, and operating. While the issues that are presented are not inclusive of all of the questions that are important, they provide an excellent set of questions with which to begin. Chapter 4 Appendix, Sources for Environmental Forecasting, is provided to help identify valuable sources of data and information from which answers and subsequent forecasts can be constructed. It lists governmental and private marketplace intelligence that can be used by a firm to gain a foothold in undertaking a strategic assessment of any level of the competitive environment.

EXHIBIT 4.14
Strategic Forecasting Issues

Key Issues in the Remote Environment Economy

What are the probable future directions of the economies in the firm's regional, national, and international market? What changes in economic growth, inflation, interest rates, capital availability, credit availability, and consumer purchasing power can be expected? What income differences can be expected between the wealthy upper middle class, the working class, and the underclass in various regions? What shifts in relative demand for different categories of goods and services can be expected?

Society and demographics

What effects will changes in social values and attitudes regarding childbearing, marriage, lifestyle, work, ethics, sex roles, racial equality, education, retirement, pollution, and energy have on the firm's development? What effects will population changes have on major social and political expectations—at home and abroad? What constraints or opportunities will develop? What pressure groups will increase in power?

Ecology

What natural or pollution-caused disasters threaten the firm's employees, customers, or facilities? How rigorously will existing environment legislature be enforced? What new federal, state, and local laws will affect the firm, and in what ways?

Politics

What changes in government policy can be expected with regard to industry cooperation, antitrust activities, foreign trade, taxation, depreciation, environmental protection, deregulation, defense, foreign trade barriers, and other important parameters? What success will a new administration have in achieving its stated goals? What effect will that success have on the firm? Will specific international climates be hostile or favorable? Is there a tendency toward instability, corruption, or violence? What is the level of political risk in each foreign market? What other political or legal constraints or supports can be expected in international business (e.g., trade barriers, equity requirements, nationalism, patent protection)?

Technology

What is the current state of the art? How will it change? What pertinent new products or services are likely to become technically feasible in the foreseeable future? What future impact can be expected from technological breakthroughs in related product areas? How will those breakthroughs interface with the other remote considerations, such as economic issues, social values, public safety, regulations, and court interpretations?

Key Issues in the Industry Environment

New entrants

Will new technologies or market demands enable competitors to minimize the impact of traditional economies of scale in the industry? Will consumers accept our claims of product or service differentiation? Will potential new entrants be able to match the capital requirements that currently exist? How permanent are the cost disadvantages (independent of size) in our industry? Will conditions change so that all competitors have equal access to marketing channels? Is government policy toward competition in our industry likely to change?

Bargaining power of suppliers

How stable are the size and composition of our supplier group? Are any suppliers likely to attempt forward integration into our business level? How dependent will our suppliers be in the future? Are substitute suppliers likely to become available? Could we become our own supplier?

EXHIBIT 4.14
(continued)

Substitute products or services

Are new substitutes likely? Will they be price competitive? Could we fight off substitutes by price competition? By advertising to sharpen product differentiation? What actions could we take to reduce the potential for having alternative products seen as legitimate substitutes?

Bargaining power of buyers

Can we break free of overcommitment to a few large buyers? How would our buyers react to attempts by us to differentiate our products? What possibilities exist that our buyers might vertically integrate backward? Should we consider forward integration? How can we make the value of our components greater in the products of our buyers?

Rivalry among existing firms

Are major competitors likely to undo the established balance of power in our industry? Is growth in our industry slowing such that competition will become fiercer? What excess capacity exists in our industry? How capable are our major competitors of withstanding intensified price competition? How unique are the objectives and strategies of our major competitors?

Key Issues in the Operating Environment

Competitive position

What strategic moves are expected by existing rivals—inside and outside the United States? What competitive advantage is necessary in selected foreign markets? What will be our competitors' priorities and ability to change? Is the behavior of our competitors predictable?

Customer profiles and market changes

What will our customer regard as needed value? Is marketing research done, or do managers talk to each other to discover what the customer wants? Which customer needs are not being met by existing products? Why? Are R&D activities under way to develop means for fulfilling these needs? What is the status of these activities? What marketing and distribution channels should we use? What do demographic and population changes portend for the size and sales potential of our market? What new market segments or products might develop as a result of these changes? What will be the buying power of our customer groups?

Supplier relationships

What is the likelihood of major cost increases because of dwindling supplies of a needed natural resource? Will sources of supply, especially of energy, be reliable? Are there reasons to expect major changes in the cost or availability of inputs as a result of money, people, or subassembly problems? Which suppliers can be expected to respond to emergency requests?

Creditors

What lines of credit are available to help finance our growth? What changes may occur in our creditworthiness? Are creditors likely to feel comfortable with our strategic plan and performance? What is the stock market likely to feel about our firm? What flexibility would our creditors show toward us during a downturn? Do we have sufficient cash reserves to protect our creditors and our credit rating?

Labor market

Are potential employees with desired skills and abilities available in the geographic areas in which our facilities are located? Are colleges and vocational/technical schools that can aid in meeting our training needs located near our plant or store sites? Are labor relations in our industry conducive to meeting our expanding needs for employees? Are workers whose skills we need shifting toward or away from the geographic location of our facilities?

Summary

A firm's external environment consists of three interrelated sets of factors that play a principal role in determining the opportunities, threats, and constraints that the firm faces. The remote environment comprises factors originating beyond, and usually irrespective of, any single firm's operating situation—economic, social, political, technological, and ecological factors. Factors that more directly influence a firm's prospects originate in the environment of its industry, including entry barriers, competitor rivalry, the availability of substitutes, and the bargaining power of buyers and suppliers. The operating environment comprises factors that influence a firm's immediate competitive situation—competitive position, customer profiles, suppliers, creditors, and the labor market. These three sets of factors provide many of the challenges that a particular firm faces in its attempts to attract or acquire needed resources and to profitably market its goods and services. Environmental assessment is more complicated for multinational corporations (MNCs) than for domestic firms because multinationals must evaluate several environments simultaneously.

Thus, the design of business strategies is based on the conviction that a firm able to anticipate future business conditions will improve its performance and profitability. Despite the uncertainty and dynamic nature of the business environment, an assessment process that narrows, even if it does not precisely define, future expectations is of substantial value to strategic managers.

Key Terms

barriers to entry, *p. 100*
eco-efficiency, *p. 95*
ecology, *p. 93*
economies of scale, *p. 100*
external environment, *p. 87*
industry, *p. 105*
industry environment, *p. 97*
operating environment, *p. 111*
pollution, *p. 93*
product differentiation, *p. 100*
remote environment, *p. 87*
technological forecasting, *p. 93*

Questions for Discussion

1. Briefly describe two important recent changes in the remote environment of U.S. business in each of the following areas:
   a. Economic.
   b. Social.
   c. Political.
   d. Technological.
   e. Ecological.
2. Describe two major environmental changes that you expect to have a major impact on the wholesale food industry in the next 10 years.
3. Develop a competitor profile for your college and for the college geographically closest to yours. Next, prepare a brief strategic plan to improve the competitive position of the weaker of the two colleges.
4. Assume the invention of a competitively priced synthetic fuel that could supply 25 percent of U.S. energy needs within 20 years. In what major ways might this change the external environment of U.S. business?
5. With your instructor's help, identify a local firm that has enjoyed great growth in recent years. To what degree and in what ways do you think this firm's success resulted from taking advantage of favorable conditions in its remote, industry, and operating environments?
6. Choose a specific industry and, relying solely on your impressions, evaluate the impact of the five forces that drive competition in that industry.
7. Choose an industry in which you would like to compete. Use the five-forces method of analysis to explain why you find that industry attractive.
8. Many firms neglect industry analysis. When does this hurt them? When does it not?

9. The model below depicts industry analysis as a funnel that focuses on remote-factor analysis to better understand the impact of factors in the operating environment. Do you find this model satisfactory? If not, how would you improve it?

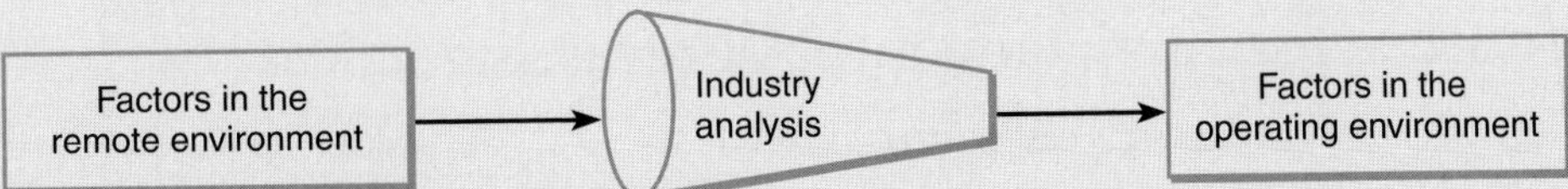

10. Who in a firm should be responsible for industry analysis? Assume that the firm does not have a strategic planning department.

Chapter 4 Appendix

Sources for Environmental Forecasting

Remote and Industry Environments

A. Economic considerations:
  1. *Predicasts* (most complete and up-to-date review of forecasts)
  2. National Bureau of Economic Research
  3. *Handbook of Basic Economic Statistics*
  4. *Statistical Abstract of the United States* (also includes industrial, social, and political statistics)
  5. Publications by Department of Commerce agencies:
     a. Office of Business Economics (e.g., *Survey of Business*)
     b. Bureau of Economic Analysis (e.g., *Business Conditions Digest*)
     c. Bureau of the Census (e.g., *Survey of Manufacturers* and various reports on population, housing, and industries)
     d. Business and Defense Services Administration (e.g., *United States Industrial Outlook*)
  6. Securities and Exchange Commission (various quarterly reports on plant and equipment, financial reports, working capital of corporations)
  7. The Conference Board
  8. *Survey of Buying Power*
  9. *Marketing Economic Guide*
  10. *Industrial Arts Index*
  11. U.S. and national chambers of commerce
  12. American Manufacturers Association
  13. *Federal Reserve Bulletin*
  14. *Economic Indicators*, annual report
  15. *Kiplinger Newsletter*
  16. International economic sources:
     a. *Worldcasts*
     b. Master key index for business international publications
     c. Department of Commerce
        (1) Overseas business reports
        (2) Industry and Trade Administration
        (3) Bureau of the Census—*Guide to Foreign Trade Statistics*
  17. *Business Periodicals Index*

B. Social considerations:
  1. Public opinion polls
  2. Surveys such as *Social Indicators and Social Reporting*, the annals of the American Academy of Political and Social Sciences
  3. Current controls: Social and behavioral sciences
  4. Abstract services and indexes for articles in sociological, psychological, and political journals
  5. Indexes for *The Wall Street Journal, New York Times*, and other newspapers
  6. Bureau of the Census reports on population, housing, manufacturers, selected services, construction, retail trade, wholesale trade, and enterprise statistics
  7. Various reports from such groups as the Brookings Institution and the Ford Foundation
  8. World Bank Atlas (population growth and GNP data)
  9. World Bank–World Development Report

C. Political considerations:
  1. *Public Affairs Information Services Bulletin*
  2. CIS Index (Congressional Information Index)
  3. Business periodicals
  4. Funk & Scott (regulations by product breakdown)
  5. Weekly compilation of presidential documents
  6. *Monthly Catalog of Government Publications*
  7. *Federal Register* (daily announcements of pending regulations)
  8. *Code of Federal Regulations* (final listing of regulations)
  9. Business International Master Key Index (regulations, tariffs)
  10. Various state publications
  11. Various information services (Bureau of National Affairs, Commerce Clearing House, Dow Jones)

D. Technological considerations:
  1. *Applied Science and Technology Index*
  2. *Statistical Abstract of the United States*
  3. Scientific and Technical Information Service
  4. University reports, congressional reports
  5. Department of Defense and military purchasing publishers
  6. Trade journals and industrial reports
  7. Industry contacts, professional meetings
  8. Computer-assisted information searches
  9. National Science Foundation annual report
  10. *Research and Development Directory* patent records

E. Industry considerations:
  1. *Concentration Ratios in Manufacturing* (Bureau of the Census)
  2. *Input-Output Survey* (productivity ratios)
  3. *Monthly Labor Review* (productivity ratios)
  4. *Quarterly Failure Report* (Dun & Bradstreet)
  5. *Federal Reserve Bulletin* (capacity utilization)
  6. *Report on Industrial Concentration and Product Diversification in the 1,000 Largest Manufacturing Companies* (Federal Trade Commission)

7. Industry trade publications
8. Bureau of Economic Analysis, Department of Commerce (specialization ratios)

Industry and Operating Environments

A. Competition and supplier considerations:
   1. Target Group Index
   2. U.S. Industrial Outlook
   3. Robert Morris annual statement studies
   4. Troy, Leo *Almanac of Business & Industrial Financial Ratios*
   5. *Census of Enterprise Statistics*
   6. Securities and Exchange Commission (10-K reports)
   7. Annual reports of specific companies
   8. *Fortune 500 Directory, The Wall Street Journal, Barron's, Forbes, Dun's Review*
   9. Investment services and directories: Moody's, Dun & Bradstreet, Standard & Poor's, Starch Marketing, Funk & Scott Index
   10. Trade association surveys
   11. Industry surveys
   12. Market research surveys
   13. *Country Business Patterns*
   14. *Country and City Data Book*
   15. Industry contacts, professional meetings, salespeople
   16. *NFIB Quarterly Economic Report for Small Business*

B. Customer profile:
   1. *Statistical Abstract of the United States*, first source of statistics
   2. *Statistical Sources* by Paul Wasserman (a subject guide to data—both domestic and international)
   3. *American Statistics Index* (Congressional Information Service Guide to statistical publications of U.S. government—monthly)
   4. Office of the Department of Commerce:
      a. Bureau of the Census reports on population, housing, and industries
      b. *U.S. Census of Manufacturers* (statistics by industry, area, and products)
      c. *Survey of Current Business* (analysis of business trends, especially February and July issues)
   5. Market research studies (*A Basic Bibliography on Market Review*, compiled by Robert Ferber et al., American Marketing Association)
   6. *Current Sources of Marketing Information: A Bibliography of Primary Marketing Data* by Gunther & Goldstein, AMA
   7. *Guide to Consumer Markets*, The Conference Board (provides statistical information with demographic, social, and economic data—annual)
   8. *Survey of Buying Power*
   9. *Predicasts* (abstracts of publishing forecasts of all industries, detailed products, and end-use data)
   10. *Predicasts Basebook* (historical data from 1960 to present, covering subjects ranging from population and GNP to specific products and services; series are coded by Standard Industrial Classifications)
   11. *Market Guide* (individual market surveys of over 1,500 U.S. and Canadian cities; includes population, location, trade areas, banks, principal industries, colleges and universities, department and chain stores, newspapers, retail outlets, and sales)
   12. *Country and City Data Book* (includes bank deposits, birth and death rates, business firms, education, employment, income of families, manufacturers, population, savings, and wholesale and retail trade)
   13. *Yearbook of International Trade Statistics* (UN)
   14. *Yearbook of National Accounts Statistics* (UN)
   15. *Statistical Yearbook* (UN—covers population, national income, agricultural and industrial production, energy, external trade, and transport)
   16. *Statistics of (Continents): Sources for Market Research* (includes separate books on Africa, America, Europe)

C. Key natural resources:
   1. *Minerals Yearbook, Geological Survey* (Bureau of Mines, Department of the Interior)
   2. *Agricultural Abstract* (Department of Agriculture)
   3. Statistics of electric utilities and gas pipeline companies (Federal Power Commission)
   4. Publications of various institutions: American Petroleum Institute, Atomic Energy Commission, Coal Mining Institute of America, American Steel Institute, and Brookings Institution

The Global Environment

After reading and studying this chapter, you should be able to

1. Explain the importance of a company's decision to globalize.
2. Describe the four main strategic orientations of global firms.
3. Understand the complexity of the global environment and the control problems that are faced by global firms.
4. Discuss major issues in global strategic planning, including the differences for multinational and global firms.
5. Describe the market requirements and product characteristics in global competition.
6. Evaluate the competitive strategies for firms in foreign markets, including niche market exporting, licensing and contract manufacturing, franchising, joint ventures, foreign branching, private equity, and wholly owned subsidiaries.

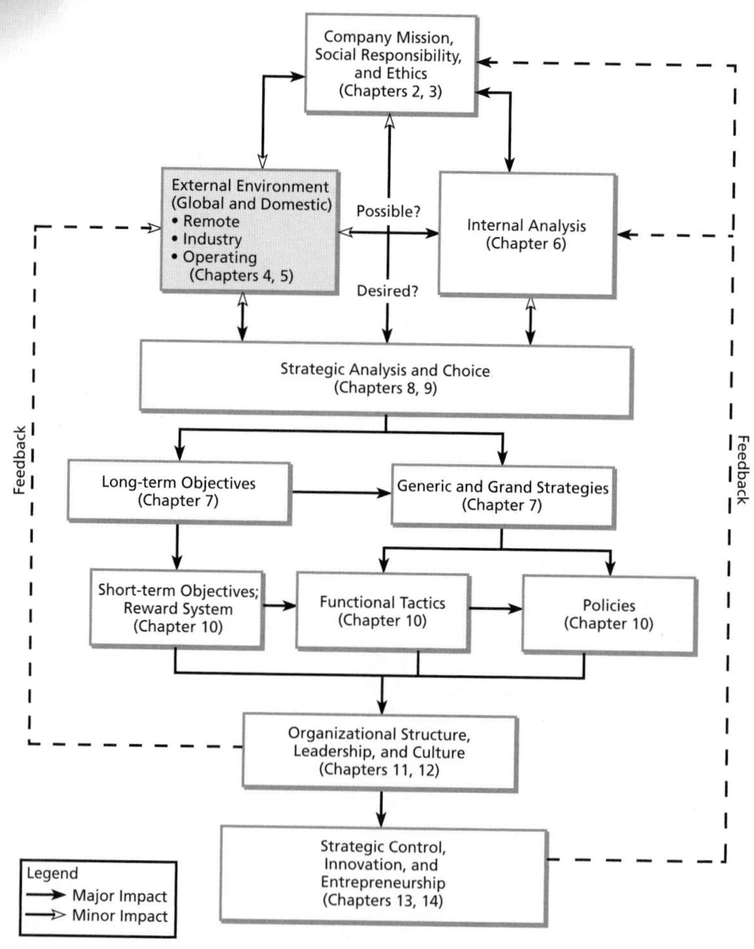

GLOBALIZATION

globalization
The strategy of pursuing opportunities anywhere in the world that enable a firm to optimize its business functions in the countries in which it operates.

Globalization refers to the strategy of pursuing opportunities anywhere in the world that enable a firm to optimize its business functions in the countries in which it operates. A company with global sales may have its high value-added software design activity done in Ireland, while it may achieve its lowest manufacturing costs by outsourcing those activities to India.

There are two main theories concerning the introduction of a product globally: standardization and customization. Standardization is the use of a common product, service, and message across all markets to create a strong brand image. The constantly improving communication technology in the twentieth century led to an ever-more-homogenous global customer base that allowed for strategic success with a standardized product. Standardization performed well until the late 1990s, when global brand owners saw their share prices drop as consumers reached for local products that were better aligned with their cultural identities. The change in customer purchase behavior was the beginning of an evolution in international strategy.

Since then, standardization is steadily being replaced by customization, which is the development of modified products and services, and the use of somewhat tailor-made messages, to meet the demands of a local population.

While serving as Coca-Cola's CEO, Douglas Daft famously argued that globalization strategies had to adapt to the times, saying that multinational firms needed to "Think global. Act local." His approach, which combines global standardization with some local customization, is now widely accepted within the Coca-Cola Corporation, as well as by other global superstars, including McDonald's and Wal-Mart. The approach allows the company to build a global brand image while creating products to meet the local demands of the target market. For Coca-Cola, this strategy has resulted in a ranking as the number one global brand in carbonated beverages, while producing more than 450 localized brands in more than 200 countries. Refer to Exhibit 5.1, Global Strategy in Action, to read about Coke's recent major globalization efforts.

Awareness of the strategic opportunities faced by global corporations and of the threats posed to them is important to planners in almost every domestic U.S. industry. Among corporations headquartered in the United States that receive more than 50 percent of their annual profits from foreign operations are Citicorp, Coca-Cola, ExxonMobil, Gillette, IBM, Otis Elevator, and Texas Instruments. In fact, the 100 largest U.S. globals earn an average of 37 percent of their operating profits abroad. Equally impressive is the effect of foreign-based globals that operate in the United States. Their "direct foreign investment" in the United States now exceeds $90 billion, with Japanese, German, and French firms leading the way.

Understanding the myriad and sometimes subtle nuances of competing in global markets or against global corporations is rapidly becoming a required competence of strategic managers. For example, experts in the advertising community contend that Korean companies only recently recognized the importance of making their names known abroad. In the 1980s, there was very little advertising of Korean brands, and the country had very few recognizable brands abroad. Korean companies tended to emphasize sales and production more than marketing. The opening of the Korean advertising market in the 1990s indicated that Korean firms had acquired a new appreciation for the strategic competencies that are needed to compete globally and created an influx of global firms like Saatchi and Saatchi, J. W. Thompson, Ogilvy and Mather, and Bozell. Many of them established joint ventures or partnerships with Korean agencies. An excellent example

Global Strategy in Action — Exhibit 5.1

Coca-Cola-Follows Its Motto: "Think global. Act local."

In 2008, Coca-Cola Co. bought China Huiyuan Juice Group Ltd. for $2.4 billion. The price reflected a value for Huiyuan of 45 times the company's estimated annual earnings. This is a valuable asset for Coca-Cola due to Huiyuan's position as the leading fruit and vegetable juice company in China. Huiyuan Juice produces more than 220 brands of fruit and vegetable juice and enjoys an industry-leading market share of 10.3 percent, with Coca-Cola in second place with 9.7 percent of the market. Coca-Cola's strategy in China is a prime example of "Think global. Act local."

The acquisition of Huiyuan helps with the localization aspect of Coca-Cola's strategy in China. Although Coca-Cola is best known for its carbonated beverage, the Chinese population prefers the tastes of juice to Coca-Cola's traditional products. The 2008 demand for juice in China was 10 billion liters compared to only 9.6 billion liters of soda. At the time, Euromonitor International estimated that fruit and vegetable juice sales would grow by 16 percent, which was more than double the growth of carbonated drinks. The projected growth was based on the health consciousness of Chinese consumers, who often opt for healthier teas and juices over carbonated beverages.

Source: Stephanie Wong, "Coca-Cola to Buy China's Huiyuan for $2.3 Billion," *Bloomberg.com,* September 3, 2008.

of such a strategic approach to globalization by Philip Morris's KGFI is described in Exhibit 5.2, Global Strategy in Action. The opportunities for corporate growth often seem brightest in global markets. Exhibit 5.3, Global Strategy in Action reports on the growth in national shares of the world's outputs and growth in national economies to the year 2020. While the United States had a commanding lead in the size of its economy in 1992, it was caught by China in the year 2000 and will be far surpassed by 2020. Overall, in less than 20 years, rich industrial countries will be overshadowed by developing countries in their produced share of the world's output.

Because the growth in the number of global firms continues to overshadow other changes in the competitive environment, this section will focus on the nature, outlook, and operations of global corporations.

DEVELOPMENT OF A GLOBAL CORPORATION

The evolution of a global corporation often entails progressively involved strategy levels. The first level, which often entails export-import activity, has minimal effect on the existing management orientation or on existing product lines. The second level, which can involve foreign licensing and technology transfer, requires little change in management or operation. The third level typically is characterized by direct investment in overseas operations, including manufacturing plants. This level requires large capital outlays and the development of global management skills. Although the domestic operations of a firm at this level continue to dominate its policy, such a firm is commonly categorized as a true multinational corporation (MNC). The most involved strategy level is characterized by a substantial increase in foreign investment, with foreign assets comprising a significant portion of total assets. At this level, the firm begins to emerge as a global enterprise with global approaches to production, sales, finance, and control.

To get a more complete understanding of the many elements of a multinational environment that need to be considered by strategic planners, study the Chapter 5 Appendix. It contains lists of important competitive issues that will help you to see the complexity of the multinational landscape and to better appreciate the complicated and sophisticated nature of strategic planning.

Global Strategy in Action

Exhibit 5.2

The Globalization of Philip Morris's KGFI

Outside of its core Western markets, Kraft General Foods International's (KGFI) food products have a growing presence in one of the most dynamic business environments in the world—the Asia-Pacific region. Its operations there are expanding rapidly, often aided by links with local manufacturers and distributors.

Japan and Korea are important examples. In both countries, local alliances can be crucial to market entry and success. Realizing this fact in the early 1970s, General Foods established joint ventures in both Japan and Korea. These joint ventures, combined with Kraft General Foods International's (KGFI) stand-alone operations, generate more than $1 billion in revenues. In the aggregate, their combined food operations in Japan and Korea are larger than many *Fortune* 500 companies.

Whereas soluble coffee accounts for just over 25 percent of the coffee consumed in U.S. homes, it fills more than 70 percent of the cups consumed in the homes of convenience-minded Japan. Additionally, Japan is the origin of a unique form of packaged coffee—liquid—and a unique channel of distribution—vending machines. Japanese consumers have purchased packaged liquid coffee for years, and it amounts to a $5 billion category. Some 2 million vending machines dispense 9 billion cans of liquid coffee annually—an average of 75 cans per person.

Japan offers a culturally unique distribution channel for coffee products—the gift-set market. Many Japanese exchange specially packaged food or beverage assortments at least twice a year to commemorate holidays as well as special personal or business occasions. The gift-set business has helped Maxim products reinforce their quality image; it also will be a launching pad and support vehicle for Carte Noire coffees.

Outside the Ajinomoto General Foods joint venture, KGFI is developing a freestanding food business under the name Kraft Japan. It is building a cheese business with imported Philadelphia Brand cream cheese, the leading cream cheese in the Tokyo metropolitan market, as well as locally manufactured and licensed Kraft Milk Farm cheese slices. The cheese market is expected to grow approximately 5 percent per year. This is a rapid growth rate for a large food category. In addition to cheese, KGFI also imports Oscar Mayer prepared meats and Jacobs Suchard chocolates.

KGFI's joint venture in Korea, Doug Suh Foods Corporation, is one of the top 10 food companies in the country. Doug Suh manufactures coffees and cereals and has its own distribution network. One of Doug Suh's other businesses in Korea, Post Cereals, is also a strong number two, with a 42 percent category share.

Korea's $400 million coffee market is the fastest-growing major coffee market in the world, expanding at an average annual rate of 14 percent. Growing with the market, Maxim and Maxwell soluble coffees, in both traditional "agglomerate" and freeze-dried forms, account for more than 70 percent of the country's soluble coffee sales. The strength of these brands also brings the company a strong number one position in coffee mix, a mixture of soluble coffee, creamer, and sugar. In addition, its Frima brand leads the market in the nondairy creamer segment.

Beyond Japan and Korea, KGFI is targeting many other countries for geographic expansion. In Indonesia, for instance, KGFI has established a rapidly growing cheese business through a licensee and introduced other KGFI products. In Taiwan, the joint venture company, PremierFoods Corporation, holds a 34 percent share of the soluble coffee market and is aggressively developing a Kraft cheese and Jacobs Suchard import business. KGFI Philippines, a wholly owned subsidiary, has a leading position in the cheese and powdered soft-drink markets in its country. In the People's Republic of China, the company produces and markets Maxwell House coffees and Tang powdered soft drinks through two successful and rapidly growing joint ventures.

Some firms downplay their global nature (to never appear distracted from their domestic operations), whereas others highlight it. For example, General Electric's formal statement of mission and business philosophy includes the following commitment:

> To carry out a diversified, growing, and profitable worldwide manufacturing business in electrical apparatus, appliances, and supplies, and in related materials, products, systems, and services for industry, commerce, agriculture, government, the community, and the home.

A similar global orientation is evident at IBM, which operates in 125 countries, conducts business in 30 languages and more than 100 currencies, and has 23 major manufacturing facilities in 14 countries.

Global Strategy in Action — Exhibit 5.3

Projected Economic Growth

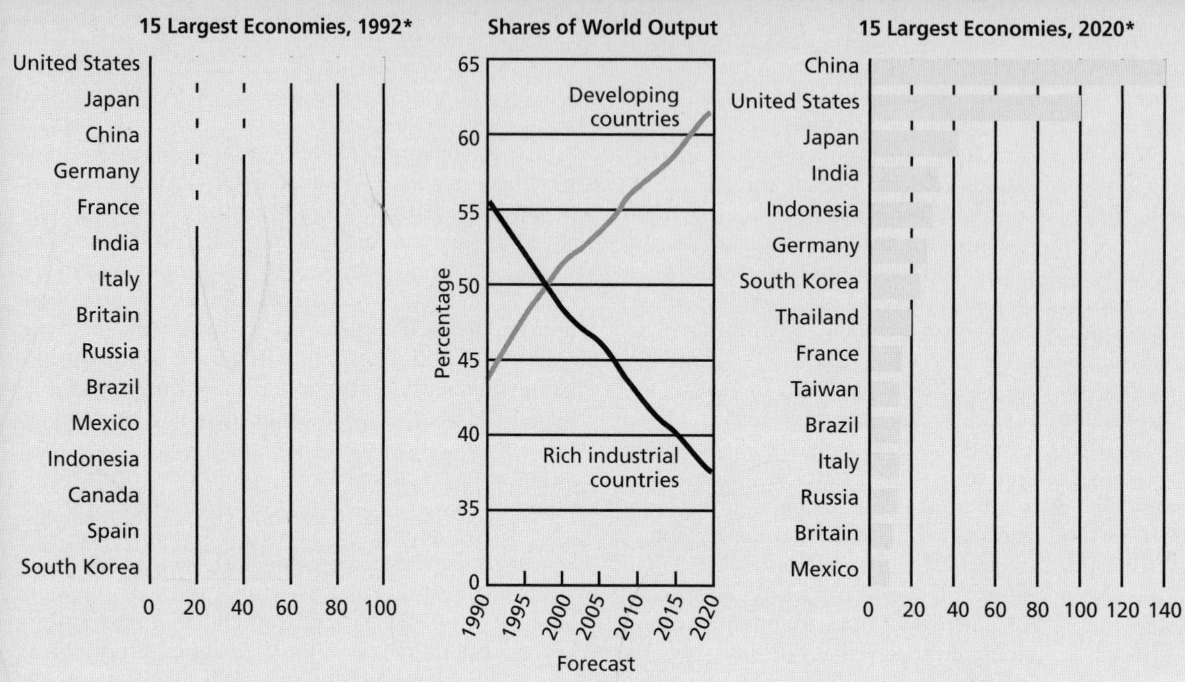

Source: World Bank, *Global Economic Prospects and the Developing Countries.*

WHY FIRMS GLOBALIZE

The technological advantage once enjoyed by the United States has declined dramatically during the past 30 years. In contrast, France is making impressive advances in electric traction, nuclear power, and aviation. Germany leads in chemicals and pharmaceuticals, precision and heavy machinery, heavy electrical goods, metallurgy, and surface transport equipment. Japan leads in optics, solid-state physics, engineering, chemistry, and process metallurgy. Eastern Europe and the former Soviet Union, the so-called COMECON (Council for Mutual Economic Assistance) countries, generate 30 percent of annual worldwide patent applications. However, the United States is regaining some of its lost technological advantage. Through globalization, U.S. firms often can reap benefits from industries and technologies developed abroad. Even a relatively small service firm that possesses a distinct competitive advantage can capitalize on large overseas operations.

Diebold Inc. once operated solely in the United States, selling automated teller machines (ATMs), bank vaults, and security systems to financial institutions. However, with the U.S. market saturated, Diebold needed to expand internationally to continue its growth. The firm's globalization efforts led to both the development of new technologies in emerging markets and opportunistic entry into entirely new industries that significantly improved Diebold's sales.

In many situations, global development makes sense as a competitive weapon. Direct penetration of foreign markets can drain vital cash flows from a foreign competitor's domestic operations. The resulting lost opportunities, reduced income, and limited production can impair the competitor's ability to invade U.S. markets. A case in point is IBM's move to establish a position of strength in the Japanese mainframe computer industry before two key competitors, Fugitsu and Hitachi, could dominate it. Once IBM had achieved a substantial share of the Japanese market, it worked to deny its Japanese competitors the vital cash and production experience they needed to invade the U.S. market.

Firms that operate principally in the domestic environment have an important decision to make with regard to their globalization: Should they act before being forced to do so by competitive pressures or after? Should they (1) be proactive by entering global markets in advance of other firms and thereby enjoy the first-mover advantages often accruing to risk-taker firms that introduce new products or services or (2) be reactive by taking the more conservative approach and following other companies into global markets once customer demand has been proven and the high costs of new-product or new-service introductions have been absorbed by competitors?

ethnocentric orientation
When the values and priorities of the parent organization guide the strategic decision making of all its international operations.

polycentric orientation
When the culture of the country in which the strategy is to be implemented is allowed to dominate a company's international decision-making process.

regiocentric orientation
When a parent company blends its own predisposition with those of its international units to develop region-sensitive strategies

geocentric orientation
When an international firm adopts a systems approach to strategic decision making that emphasizes global integration.

Strategic Orientations of Global Firms

Multinational corporations typically display one of four orientations toward their overseas activities. They have a certain set of beliefs about how the management of foreign operations should be handled. A company with an **ethnocentric orientation** believes that the values and priorities of the parent organization should guide the strategic decision making of all its operations. If a corporation has a **polycentric orientation,** then the culture of the country in which a strategy is to be implemented is allowed to dominate the decision-making process. In contrast, a **regiocentric orientation** exists when the parent attempts to blend its own predispositions with those of the region under consideration, thereby arriving at a region-sensitive compromise. Finally, a corporation with a **geocentric orientation** adopts a global systems approach to strategic decision making, thereby emphasizing global integration.

American firms often adopt a regiocentric orientation for pursing strategies in Europe. U.S. e-tailers have attempted to blend their own corporate structure and expertise with that of European corporations. For example, Amazon has been able to leverage its experience in the United States while developing regionally and culturally specific strategies overseas. By purchasing European franchises that have had regional success, E*Trade is pursuing a foreign strategy in which they insert their European units into their corporate structure. This strategy requires the combination and use of culturally different management styles and involves major challenges for upper management.

Exhibit 5.4, Global Strategy in Action shows the effects of each of the four orientations on key activities of the firm. It is clear from the figure that the strategic orientation of a global firm plays a major role in determining the locus of control and corporate priorities of the firm's decision makers.

AT THE START OF GLOBALIZATION

External and internal assessments are conducted before a firm enters global markets. For example, Japanese investors conduct extensive assessments and analyses before selecting a U.S. site for a Japanese-owned firm. They prefer states with strong markets, low unionization rates, and low taxes. In addition, Japanese manufacturing plants prefer counties characterized by manufacturing conglomeration; low unemployment and poverty rates; and concentrations of educated, productive workers.

External assessment involves careful examination of critical features of the global environment, particular attention being paid to the status of the host nations in such areas as economic progress, political control, and nationalism. Expansion of industrial facilities, favorable balances of payments, and improvements in technological capabilities over the past decade are gauges of the host nation's economic progress. Political status can be gauged by the host nation's power in and impact on global affairs.

Global Strategy in Action — Exhibit 5.4

Orientation of a Global Firm

	Orientation of the Firm			
	Ethnocentric	**Polycentric**	**Regiocentric**	**Geocentric**
Mission	Profitability (viability)	Public acceptance (legitimacy)	Profitability and public acceptance (viability and legitimacy)	Same as regiocentric
Governance	Top-down	Bottom-up (each subsidiary decides on local objectives)	Mutually negotiated between region and its subsidiaries	Mutually negotiated at all levels of the corporation
Strategy	Global integration	National responsiveness	Regional integration and national responsiveness	Global integration and national responsiveness
Structure	Hierarchical product divisions	Hierarchical area divisions, with autonomous national units	Product and regional organization tied through a matrix	A network of organizations (including some competitors)
Culture	Home country	Host country	Regional	Global
Technology	Mass production	Batch production	Flexible manufacturing	Flexible manufacturing
Marketing	Product development determined by the needs of home country	Local product development based on local needs	Standardize within region but not across regions	Global product, with local variations
Finance	Repatriation of profits to home country	Retention of profits in host country	Redistribution within region	Redistribution globally
Personnel practices	People of home country developed for key positions in the world	People of local nationality developed for key positions in their own country	Regional people developed for key positions anywhere in the region	Global personnel development and placement

Source: From *Columbia Journal of World Business,* Summer 1985, by B.S. Chukravarthy and Howard V. Perlmuter, "Strategic Planning for a global Business," p. 506.

Understanding the political risk involved is a key element in the decision to do business in a foreign nation. Opportunities for fast growth and attractive profits often arise in countries with suspect political risk. The principal concern of foreign direct investors is whether the foreign government is able to implement its policies during a period of political, social, or economic upheaval. If it can, the country is judged to be stable. Stability provides investors with confidence that the country's regulatory environment will enable it to achieve the economic returns that it deserves.

A second issue that concerns investors is how the stability in a foreign nation is achieved. Strategists often place a country's openness along a simple continuum from closed to open. Closed countries maintain their stability by restricting the flow of money, goods, services, people, and information across their borders. Countries that tend toward this extreme include Cuba, Iran, and North Korea because their isolationist policies prevent their citizens from fully comprehending the conditions and options that are available in other countries.

Global Strategy in Action — Exhibit 5.5

The J-Curve on Country Stability and Openness

The J-curve represents the relationship between stability and openness as shown in the accompanying figure. Each country moves along its own J-curve and the curve itself shifts up and down with fluctuations in the economy. Nations higher on the graph are more stable; those lower are less stable. Nations to the right of the dip in the J are more open; those to the left less open. As a country that is stable because it is closed becomes more open, it slides down the left side of the curve toward the dip in the J, the point of greatest instability. So, for example, if Pakistan, Myanmar, or Cuba held elections next week, political turmoil would likely erupt. If North Koreans had access to South Korea media for a week, Kim Jong Il would have plenty to fear.

The irony is that the energies of globalization and growth in demand for key commodities are driving more businesses to contemplate ventures in politically closed countries, particularly China. But those same energies may destabilize the ground beneath unwary businesses' feet.

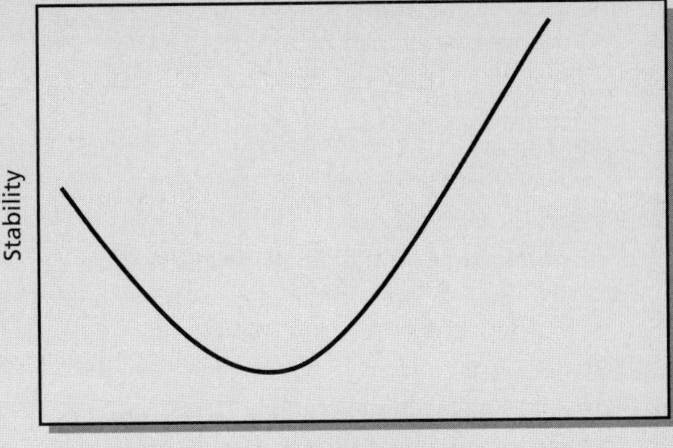

Source: From "Prepare to Lose It all? Read on . . . How to Calculate Political Risk," by Ian Bremmer, *Inc. Magazine.* Copyright © by Mansueto Ventures LLC. Reproduced with permission of Mansueto Ventures LLC via Copyright Clearance Center.

At the other extreme, many nations achieve their stability by allowing and encouraging exchanges among their and business and public institutions, and their citizens and those of other nations. Examples include the countries in Australia, Brazil, the European zone, Japan, and the United States.

Exhibit 5.5, Global Strategy in Action, describes the J-curve, a useful approach for evaluating the relationship between stability and openness and an important element in political risk assessment.

Internal assessment involves identification of the basic strengths of a firm's operations. These strengths are particularly important in global operations, because they are often the characteristics of a firm that the host nation values most and, thus, offer significant bargaining leverage. The firm's resource strengths and global capabilities must be analyzed. The resources that should be analyzed include, in particular, technical and managerial skills, capital, labor, and raw materials. The global capabilities that should be analyzed include the firm's product delivery and financial management systems.

A firm that gives serious consideration to internal and external assessment is Business International Corporation, which recommends that seven broad categories of factors be considered. As shown in Exhibit 5.6, Global Strategy in Action, these categories include economic, political, geographic, labor, tax, capital source, and business factors.

COMPLEXITY OF THE GLOBAL ENVIRONMENT

By 2003, Coke was finally achieving a goal that it had set a decade earlier when it went to India. That goal was to take the market away from Pepsi and local beverage companies. However, when it arrived, Coke found that the Indian market was extremely complex and smaller than it had estimated. Coke also encountered cultural problems, in part because the

Global Strategy in Action — Exhibit 5.6

Checklist of Factors to Consider in Choosing a Foreign Manufacturing Site

The following considerations were drawn from an 88-point checklist developed by Business International Corporation.

Economic Factors:

1. Size of GNP and projected rate of growth
2. Foreign exchange position
3. Size of market for the firm's products; rate of growth

Political Factors:

4. Form and stability of government
5. Attitude toward private and foreign investment by government, customers, and competition
6. Degree of antiforeign discrimination

Geographic Factors:

7. Proximity of site to export markets
8. Availability of local raw materials
9. Availability of power, water, gas

Labor Factors:

10. Availability of managerial, technical, and office personnel able to speak the language of the parent company
11. Degree of skill and discipline at all levels
12. Degree and nature of labor voice in management

Tax Factors:

13. Tax-rate trends
14. Joint tax treaties with home country and others
15. Availability of tariff protection

Capital Source Factors:

16. Cost of local borrowing
17. Modern banking systems
18. Government credit aids to new businesses

Business Factors:

19. State of marketing and distribution system
20. Normal profit margins in the firm's industry
21. Competitive situation in the firm's industry: do cartels exist?

chief of Coke India was an expatriate. The key to overcoming this cultural problem was promoting an Indian to operations chief. Coke also changed its marketing strategy by pushing their "Thums Up" products, a local brand owned by Coke. Then, they began to focus their efforts on creating new products for rural areas and lowering the prices of their existing products to increase sales. Once Coke had new products in the market, they focused on a new advertising campaign to better relate to Indian consumers.

Coke's experience highlights the fact that global strategic planning is more complex than purely domestic planning. There are at least five factors that contribute to this increase in complexity:

1. Globals face multiple political, economic, legal, social, and cultural environments as well as various rates of changes within each of them. Occasionally, foreign governments work in concert with their militaries to advance economic aims even at the expense of human rights. International firms must resist the temptation to benefit financially from such immoral opportunities.

2. Interactions between the national and foreign environments are complex, because of national sovereignty issues and widely differing economic and social conditions.

3. Geographic separation, cultural and national differences, and variations in business practices all tend to make communication and control efforts between headquarters and the overseas affiliates difficult.

4. Globals face extreme competition, because of differences in industry structures within countries.

5. Globals are restricted in their selection of competitive strategies by various regional blocs and economic integrations, such as the European Economic Community, the European Free Trade Area, and the Latin American Free Trade Area.

CONTROL PROBLEMS OF THE GLOBAL FIRM

An inherent complicating factor for many global firms is that their financial policies typically are designed to further the goals of the parent company and pay minimal attention to the goals of the host countries. This built-in bias creates conflict between the different parts of the global firm, between the whole firm and its home and host countries, and between the home country and host country themselves. The conflict is accentuated by the use of various schemes to shift earnings from one country to another in order to avoid taxes, minimize risk, or achieve other objectives.

Moreover, different financial environments make normal standards of company behavior concerning the disposition of earnings, sources of finance, and the structure of capital more problematic. Thus, it becomes increasingly difficult to measure the performance of international divisions.

In addition, important differences in measurement and control systems often exist. Fundamental to the concept of planning is a well-conceived, future-oriented approach to decision making that is based on accepted procedures and methods of analysis. Consistent approaches to planning throughout a firm are needed for effective review and evaluation by corporate headquarters. In the global firm, planning is complicated by differences in national attitudes toward work measurement, and by differences in government requirements about disclosure of information.

Although such problems are an aspect of the global environment, rather than a consequence of poor management, they are often most effectively reduced through increased attention to strategic planning. Such planning will aid in coordinating and integrating the firm's direction, objectives, and policies around the world. It enables the firm to anticipate and prepare for change. It facilitates the creation of programs to deal with worldwide development. Finally, it helps the management of overseas affiliates become more actively involved in setting goals and in developing means to more effectively utilize the firm's total resources.

An example of the need for coordination in global ventures and evidence that firms can successfully plan for global collaboration (e.g., through rationalized production) is the Ford Escort (Europe), the best-selling automobile in the world, which has a component manufacturing network that consists of plants in 15 countries.

GLOBAL STRATEGIC PLANNING

It should be evident from the previous sections that the strategic decisions of a firm competing in the global marketplace become increasingly complex. In such a firm, managers cannot view global operations as a set of independent decisions. These managers are faced with trade-off decisions in which multiple products, country environments, resource sourcing options, corporate and subsidiary capabilities, and strategic options must be considered.

The global growth challenges in the aerospace and defense industries are indicative of conditions often faced by strategic planners in preparing their firms for international competition, as explained in Exhibit 5.7, Global Strategy in Action. Industry experts are important to the United States, but so too are the international supply chain and foreign direct investments. The shift in wealth toward emerging economies is changing the competitive landscape, providing great opportunities for companies that can overcome the challenges of working with economically developing nations.

stakeholder activism
Demands placed on a global firm by the stakeholders in the environments in which it operates.

A recent trend toward increased activism of stakeholders has added to the complexity of strategic planning for the global firm. **Stakeholder activism** refers to demands placed on the global firm by the foreign environments in which it operates, principally by foreign

Global Strategy in Action

Exhibit 5.7

Global Growth Challenges in the Aerospace and Defense Industries

The aerospace and defense industry is the largest exporter in the USA. But exports are only one measure of globalization. When we also consider the international supply chain and foreign direct investments, aerospace and defense ranks in the middle among other industries. The shift in wealth toward emerging economies is changing the competitive landscape, and as aerospace and defense companies expand their global footprints, a race to capitalize on rising opportunities has begun.

The Asia-Pacific region is expected to account for 37% of the value of all new aircraft deliveries over the next 20 years—nearly as much as North America and Europe combined. "Who would have thought 20 years ago that we would be able to sell aero structure products to China and other countries that were closed markets? This has changed the world tremendously," says Gilles Labbé, president and chief executive of Héroux-Devtek.

Since the end of the Cold War, international threats have changed but not diminished. The world faces adversaries who are often unpredictable and difficult to identify. Regional tensions in the Middle East and Asia keep defense equipment in demand. US companies took $38 billion in new defense orders in the most recent fiscal year, and that could increase.

Globalization also offers companies greater access to talent and labor. According to some estimates, India produces about as many engineering graduates as the USA, and China produces significantly more engineering and technology PhDs than the USA or India. Aerospace and defense companies cannot remain competitive by relying solely on traditional sources of talent; companies must recruit the best people from around the world.

"I don't think there's a talent shortage, but I think there are particular societies and economies that focus on different areas of expertise," said Tim Mahoney, president and chief executive of Honeywell Aerospace. "Our strategic plan is to hire the best engineers around the world."

In 2008, foreign direct investment by the top 50 global aerospace and defense companies climbed to a record. While the search for low-cost manufacturing remains an important motivation, research and development investments have increased significantly, including the hiring of talent in engineering and other critical areas. The top five recipients of foreign direct investment in the aerospace and defense industry were India, China, the USA, Russia, and Mexico.

OPPORTUNITIES

As globalization creates opportunities, it introduces challenges that require new management tactics. Industry executives interviewed for a PricewaterhouseCoopers' report identified the following issues as their top challenges: protection of intellectual property; cost and complexity of export regulations; ethics and compliance across cultures; increasing financial risk, particularly currency exchange rate risk; and management of expanding offset requirements.

Intellectual property protection poses perhaps the most significant barrier to globalization—many countries with the highest growth rates have the weakest intellectual property laws and enforcement.

The complexity and limitations of export regulations offer another key challenge. US regulations restrict the export of certain technologies and place regulations on foreign governments such as end-use monitoring requirements. The complexity of regulations creates significant risks and increases compliance costs.

Companies also face challenges in the area of ethics and compliance. They must not only understand local laws and cultures, but also educate their international employees and partners on their own country's regulations and ethical standards.

International customers are demanding more in the way of technology transfer, direct offsets and foreign direct investment. Companies must weigh the competitive and performance risks inherent in these issues, as well as the value of their offset investments. Companies must also manage financial risk related to foreign currencies. This can be particularly challenging because revenue and costs may be in different currencies over a long period, combined with the inherent limitations of the currency hedging markets.

With these issues in mind, companies must conduct thorough due diligence and understand long-term economic, political, cultural, and demographic trends before investing in global markets.

Globalization is driving growth in the aerospace and defense industry. However, the changing landscape creates new competitive threats and complex operational challenges. The race is on. Companies that can best manage these complex challenges will be tomorrow's leaders.

Source: Excerpted from Neil Hampson, "Accelerating Global Growth," *Flight International*, September 20, 2010, 178 (5257), p. 39.

governments. This section provides a basic framework for the analysis of strategic decisions in this complex setting.

Multidomestic Industries and Global Industries

Multidomestic Industries

International industries can be ranked along a continuum that ranges from multidomestic to global.

multidomestic industry
An industry in which competition is segmented from country to country.

A **multidomestic industry** is one in which competition is essentially segmented from country to country. Thus, even if global corporations are in the industry, competition in one country is independent of competition in other countries. Examples of such industries include retailing, insurance, and consumer finance.

In a multidomestic industry, a global corporation's subsidiaries should be managed as distinct entities; that is, each subsidiary should be rather autonomous, having the authority to make independent decisions in response to local market conditions. Thus, the global strategy of such an industry is the sum of the strategies developed by subsidiaries operating in different countries. The primary difference between a domestic firm and a global firm competing in a multidomestic industry is that the latter makes decisions related to the countries in which it competes and to how it conducts business abroad.

Factors that increase the degree to which an industry is multidomestic include[1]

- The need for customized products to meet the tastes or preferences of local customers.
- Fragmentation of the industry, with many competitors in each national market.
- A lack of economies of scale in the functional activities of firms in the industry.
- Distribution channels unique to each country.
- A low technological dependence of subsidiaries on R&D provided by the global firm.

An interesting example of a multidomestic strategy is the one designed by Renault-Nissan for the low-cost automobile industry. Renault's strategy involves designing cars to fit the budgets of buyers in different countries, rather than being restricted to the production of cars that meet the safety and emission standards of countries in western Europe and the United States or by their consumer preferences for technological advancements and stylish appointments.

Global Industries

global industry
An industry in which competition crosses national borders on a worldwide basis.

A **global industry** is one in which competition crosses national borders. In fact, it occurs on a worldwide basis. In a global industry, a firm's strategic moves in one country can be significantly affected by its competitive position in another country. The very rapidly expanding list of global industries includes commercial aircraft, automobiles, mainframe computers, and electronic consumer equipment. Many authorities are convinced that almost all product-oriented industries soon will be global. As a result, strategic management planning must be global for at least six reasons:

1. *The increased scope of the global management task.* Growth in the size and complexity of global firms made management virtually impossible without a coordinated plan of action detailing what is expected of whom during a given period. The common practice of management by exception is impossible without such a plan.

2. *The increased globalization of firms.* Three aspects of global business make global planning necessary: *(a)* differences among the environmental forces in different countries, *(b)* greater distances, and *(c)* the interrelationships of global operations.

[1]Y. Doz and C. K. Prahalad, "Patterns of Strategic Control within Multinational Corporations," *Journal of International Business Studies,* Fall 1984, pp. 55–72.

3. *The information explosion.* It has been estimated that the world's stock of knowledge is doubling every 10 years. Without the aid of a formal plan, executives can no longer know all that they must know to solve the complex problems they face. A global planning process provides an ordered means for assembling, analyzing, and distilling the information required for sound decisions.

4. *The increase in global competition.* Because of the rapid increase in global competition, firms must constantly adjust to changing conditions or lose markets to competitors. The increase in global competition also spurs managements to search for methods of increasing efficiency and economy.

5. *The rapid development of technology.* Rapid technological development has shortened product life cycles. Strategic management planning is necessary to ensure the replacement of products that are moving into the maturity stage, with fewer sales and declining profits. Planning gives management greater control of all aspects of new-product introduction.

6. *Strategic management planning breeds managerial confidence.* Like the motorist with a road map, managers with a plan for reaching their objectives know where they are going. Such a plan breeds confidence, because it spells out every step along the way and assigns responsibility for every task. The plan simplifies the managerial job.

A firm in a global industry must maximize its capabilities through a worldwide strategy. Such a strategy necessitates a high degree of centralized decision making in corporate headquarters so as to permit trade-off decisions across subsidiaries.

Among the factors that make for the creation of a global industry are

- Economies of scale in the functional activities of firms in the industry.
- A high level of R&D expenditures on products that require more than one market to recover development costs.
- The presence in the industry of predominantly global firms that expect consistency of products and services across markets.
- The presence of homogeneous product needs across markets, which reduces the requirement of customizing the product for each market. The presence of a small group of global competitors.
- A low level of trade regulation and of regulation regarding foreign direct investment.[2]

Six factors that drive the success of global companies are listed in Exhibit 5.8, Global Strategy in Action. They address key aspects of globalizing a business's operations and provide a framework within which companies can effectively pursue the global marketplace.

The Global Challenge

Although industries can be characterized as global or multidomestic, few "pure" cases of either type exist. A global firm competing in a global industry must be responsive, to some degree, to local market conditions. Similarly, a global firm competing in a multidomestic industry cannot totally ignore opportunities to utilize intracorporate resources in competitive positioning. Thus, each global firm must decide which of its corporate functional activities should be performed where and what degree of coordination should exist among them.

Location and Coordination of Functional Activities

Typical functional activities of a firm include purchases of input resources, operations, research and development, marketing and sales, and after-sales service. A multinational corporation has a wide range of possible location options for each of these activities and

[2] G. Hamel and C. K. Prahalad, "Managing Strategic Responsibility in the MNC," *Strategic Management Journal,* October–December 1983, pp. 341–51.

Global Strategy in Action — Exhibit 5.8

Factors That Drive Global Companies

1. **Global Management Team**
   Possesses global vision and culture.
   Includes foreign nationals.
   Leaves management of subsidiaries to foreign nationals.
   Frequently travels internationally.
   Has cross-cultural training.

2. **Global Strategy**
   Implement strategy as opposed to independent country strategies.
   Develop significant cross-country alliances.
   Select country targets strategically rather than opportunistically.
   Perform business functions where most efficient—no home-country bias.
   Emphasize participation in the triad—North America, Europe, and Japan.

3. **Global Operations and Products**
   Use common core operating processes worldwide to ensure quantity and uniformity.
   Produce globally to obtain best cost and market advantage.

4. **Global Technology and R&D**
   Design global products but take regional differences into account.
   Manage development work centrally but carry out globally.
   Do not duplicate R&D and product development; gain economies of scale.

5. **Global Financing**
   Finance globally to obtain lowest cost.
   Hedge when necessary to protect currency risk.
   Price in local currencies.
   List shares on foreign exchanges.

6. **Global Marketing**
   Market global products but provide regional discretion if economies of scale are not affected.
   Develop global brands.
   Use core global marketing practices and themes.
   Simultaneously introduce new global products worldwide.

Source: Reprinted from *Business Horizons,* Volume 37, Robert N. Lussier, Robert W. Baeder and Joel Corman, "Measuring Global Practices: Global Strategic Planning Through Company Situational Analysis," p. 57. Copyright 1994, with permission from Elsevier.

must decide which sets of activities will be performed in how many and which locations. A multinational corporation may have each location perform each activity, or it may center an activity in one location to serve the organization worldwide. For example, research and development centered in one facility may serve the entire organization.

A multinational corporation also must determine the degree to which functional activities are to be coordinated across locations. Such coordination can be extremely low, allowing each location to perform each activity autonomously, or extremely high, tightly linking the functional activities of different locations. Coca-Cola tightly links its R&D and marketing functions worldwide to offer a standardized brand name, concentrate formula, market positioning, and advertising theme. However, its operations function is more autonomous, with the artificial sweetener and packaging differing across locations.

Location and Coordination Issues

How a particular firm should address location and coordination issues depends on the nature of its industry and on the type of international strategy that the firm is pursuing. As discussed earlier, an industry can be ranked along a continuum that ranges between multidomestic at one extreme and global at the other. Little coordination of functional activities across countries may be necessary in a multidomestic industry, since competition occurs within each country in such an industry. However, as its industry becomes increasingly global, a firm must begin to coordinate an increasing number of functional activities to effectively compete across countries.

Global Strategy in Action — Exhibit 5.9

Market Requirements and Product Characteristics

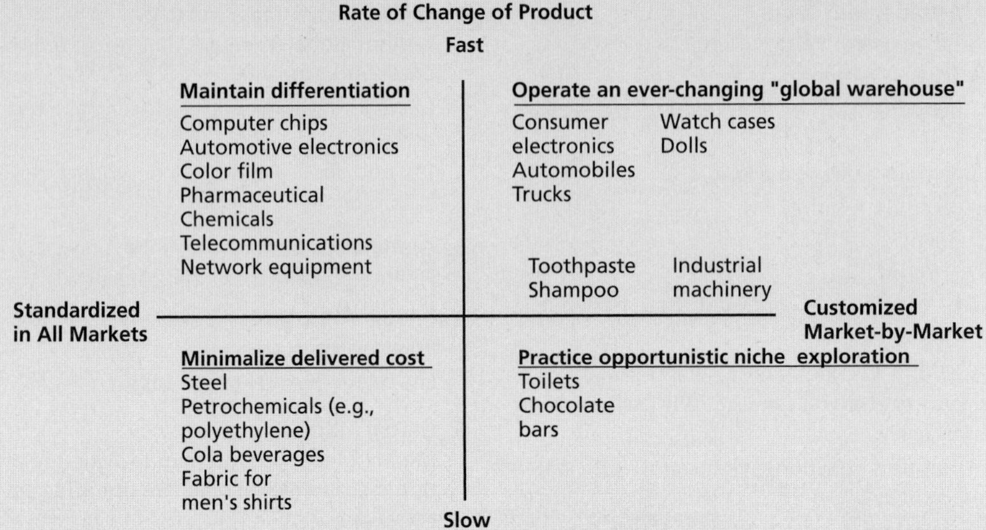

Source: Lawrence H. Wortzel, *1989 International Business Book* (Strategic Direction Publishers, 1989).

Going global impacts every aspect of a company's operations and structure. As firms redefine themselves as global competitors, workforces are becoming increasingly diversified. The most significant challenge for firms, therefore, is the ability to adjust to a workforce of varied cultures and lifestyles and the capacity to incorporate cultural differences to the benefit of the company's mission.

Market Requirements and Product Characteristics

Businesses have discovered that being successful in foreign markets often demands much more than simply shipping their well-received domestic products overseas. Firms must assess two key dimensions of customer demand: customers' acceptance of standardized products and the rate of product innovation desired. As shown in Exhibit 5.9, Global Strategy in Action, all markets can be arrayed along a continuum from markets in which products are standardized to markets in which products must be customized for customers from market to market. Standardized products in all markets include color film and petrochemicals, while dolls and toilets are good examples of customized products.

Similarly, products can be arrayed along a continuum from products that are not subject to frequent product innovations to products that are often upgraded. Products with a fast rate of change include computer chips and industrial machinery, while steel and chocolate bars are products that fit in the slow rate of change category.

Exhibit 5.9 shows that the two dimensions can be combined to enable companies to simultaneously assess both customer need for product standardization and rate of product innovation. The examples listed demonstrate the usefulness of the model in helping firms to determine the degree of customization that they must be willing to accept to become engaged in transnational operations. Starbucks has taken advantage of an industry with a

Global Strategy in Action — Exhibit 5.10

Starbucks' Global Expansion

Starbucks began its international expansion with two stores in Japan in the mid-1980s. By 2000, the company's non-U.S. operations reached 792 stores in 16 countries. Starbucks' global strategy included three key elements:

- Increase market penetration and focus on profitability in existing markets.
- Target long-term store potential of 15,000 locations beyond the United States.
- Focus on emerging markets—especially China, Brazil, and Russia—as a catalyst for long-term revenue and profit growth.

Starbucks was extremely successful with the global strategy. By 2007, Starbucks' 15,012 stores in 44 countries generated net revenues of $9.4 billion for the fiscal year, which was an increase of 21 percent over 2006. Its U.S. revenue grew by 19.4 percent and operating income grew by 12.1 percent. Even more impressive, Starbucks' international segment's revenue growth was 32.1 percent and its operating income grew 27.0 percent, principally because of aggressive expansion into new markets and a refocus on profitability in the large core markets of Canada and the United Kingdom.

In 2008, Starbucks undertook an even more aggressive global strategy. The plan is to accelerate expansion and increase the profitability of Starbucks outside the United States by redeploying a portion of the capital originally earmarked for U.S. store growth to the international business.

Sources: "Starbucks Outlines International Growth Strategy; Focus on Retail Expansion and Profitability," *Business Wire*, October 2004, p. 1; and "Starbucks Announces Strategic Initiatives to Increase Shareholder Value; Chairman Howard Schultz returns as CEO," Starbucks, news release, January 2008, p. 1.

slow rate of change in the product and relatively high standardization in all markets, namely, the retail coffee industry. Exhibit 5.10, Global Strategy in Action, provides some interesting details on how Starbucks' global success is achieved.

COMPETITIVE STRATEGIES FOR FIRMS IN FOREIGN MARKETS

Strategies for firms that are attempting to move toward globalization can be categorized by the degree of complexity of each foreign market being considered and by the diversity in a company's product line (see Exhibit 5.11, Global Strategy in Action). *Complexity* refers to the number of critical success factors that are required to prosper in a given competitive arena. When a firm must consider many such factors, the requirements of success increase in complexity. *Diversity,* the second variable, refers to the breadth of a firm's business lines. When a company offers many product lines, diversity is high.

Together, the complexity and diversity dimensions form a continuum of possible strategic choices. Combining these two dimensions highlights many possible actions.

Niche Market Exporting

The primary niche market approach for the company that wants to export is to modify select product performance or measurement characteristics to meet special foreign demands. Combining product criteria from both the U.S. and the foreign markets can be slow and tedious. There are, however, a number of expansion techniques that provide the U.S. firm with the know-how to exploit opportunities in the new environment. For example, copying product innovations in countries where patent protection is not emphasized and utilizing nonequity contractual arrangements with a foreign partner can assist in rapid product innovation. N. V. Philips and various Japanese competitors, such as Sony

Global Strategy in Action — Exhibit 5.11

Escalating Commitments to International Markets

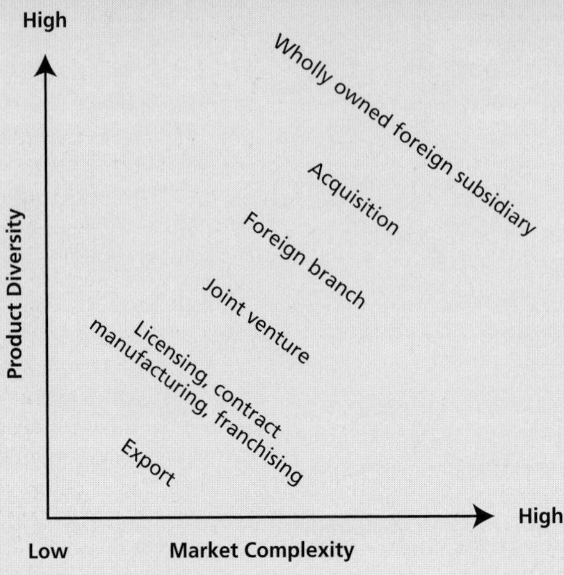

and Matsushita, now are working together for common global product standards within their markets. Siemens, with a centralized R&D in electronics, also has been very successful with this approach.

The Taiwanese company, Gigabyte, researched the U.S. market and found that a sizable number of computer buyers wanted a PC that could complete the basic tasks provided by domestic desktops, but that would be considerably smaller. Gigabyte decided to serve this niche market by exporting their mini-PCs into the United States with a price tag of $200 to $300. This price was considerably less than the closest U.S. manufacturer, Dell, whose minicomputer was still larger and cost $766.

Exporting usually requires minimal capital investment. The organization maintains its quality control standards over production processes and finished goods inventory, and risk to the survival of the firm is typically minimal. Additionally, the U.S. Commerce Department through its Export Now Program and related government agencies lowers the risks to smaller companies by providing export information and marketing advice.

Licensing and Contract Manufacturing

Establishing a contractual arrangement is the next step for U.S. companies that want to venture beyond exporting but are not ready for an equity position on foreign soil. Licensing involves the transfer of some industrial property right from the U.S. licensor to a motivated licensee. Most tend to be patents, trademarks, or technical know-how that are granted to the licensee for a specified time in return for a royalty and for avoiding tariffs or import quotas. Bell South and U.S. West, with various marketing and service competitive advantages valuable to Europe, have extended a number of licenses to create personal computer networks in the United Kingdom.

Another licensing strategy open to U.S. firms is to contract the manufacturing of its product line to a foreign company to exploit local comparative advantages in technology, materials, or labor.

U.S. firms that use either licensing option will benefit from lowering the risk of entry into the foreign markets. Clearly, alliances of this type are not for everyone. They are used best in companies large enough to have a combination of international strategic activities and for firms with standardized products in narrow margin industries.

Two major problems exist with licensing. One is the possibility that the foreign partner will gain the experience and evolve into a major competitor after the contract expires. The experience of some U.S. electronics firms with Japanese companies shows that licensees gain the potential to become powerful rivals. The other potential problem stems from the control that the licensor forfeits on production, marketing, and general distribution of its products. This loss of control minimizes a company's degrees of freedom as it reevaluates its future options.

Franchising

A special form of licensing is franchising, which allows the franchisee to sell a highly publicized product or service, using the parent's brand name or trademark, carefully developed procedures, and marketing strategies. In exchange, the franchisee pays a fee to the parent company, typically based on the volume of sales of the franchisor in its defined market area. The franchise is operated by the local investor who must adhere to the strict policies of the parent.

Franchising is so popular that an estimated 500 U.S. businesses now franchise to more than 50,000 local owners in foreign countries. Among the most active franchisees are Avis, Burger King, Canada Dry, Coca-Cola, Hilton, Kentucky Fried Chicken, Manpower, Marriott, Midas, Muzak, Pepsi, and ServiceMaster. However, the acknowledged global champion of franchising is Subway, which has 34,000 franchisees in 95 nations.

Joint Ventures

As the multinational strategies of U.S. firms mature, most will include some form of joint venture (JV) with a target nation firm. AT&T followed this option in its strategy to produce its own personal computer by entering into several joint ventures with European producers to acquire the required technology and position itself for European expansion. Because JVs begin with a mutually agreeable pooling of capital, production or marketing equipment, patents, trademarks, or management expertise, they offer more permanent cooperative relationships than export or contract manufacturing.

Compared with full ownership of the foreign entity, JVs provide a variety of benefits to each partner. U.S. firms without the managerial or financial assets to make a profitable independent impact on the integrated foreign markets can share management tasks and cash requirements often at exchange rates that favor the dollar. The coordination of manufacturing and marketing allows ready access to new markets, intelligence data, and reciprocal flows of technical information.

For example, Siemens, the German electronics firm, has a wide range of strategic alliances throughout Europe to share technology and research developments. For years, Siemens grew by acquisitions, but now, to support its horizontal expansion objectives, it is engaged in joint ventures with companies like Groupe Bull of France, International Computers of Britain, General Electric Company of Britain, IBM, Intel, Philips, and Rolm. Another example is Airbus Industries, which produces wide-body passenger planes for the world market as a direct result of JVs among many companies in Britain, France, Spain, and Germany.

JVs speed up the efforts of U.S. firms to integrate into the political, corporate, and cultural infrastructure of the foreign environment, often with a lower financial commitment than acquiring a foreign subsidiary. General Electric's (GE) 3 percent share in the

European lighting market was very weak and below expectations. Significant increases in competition throughout many of their American markets by the European giant, Philips Lighting, forced GE to retaliate by expanding in Europe. GE's first strategy was an attempted joint venture with the Siemens lighting subsidiary, Osram, and with the British electronics firm, Thorn EMI. Negotiations failed over control issues. When recent events in eastern Europe opened the opportunity for a JV with the Hungarian lighting manufacturer, Tungsram, which was receiving 70 percent of revenues from the West, GE capitalized on it.

Although joint ventures can address many of the requirements of complex markets and diverse product lines, U.S. firms considering either equity- or non-equity-based JVs face many challenges. For example, making full use of the native firm's comparative advantage may involve managerial relationships where no single authority exists to make strategic decisions or solve conflicts. Additionally, dealing with host-company management requires the disclosure of proprietary information and the potential loss of control over production and marketing quality standards. Addressing such challenges with well-defined covenants agreeable to all parties is difficult. Equally important is the compatibility of partners and their enduring commitments to mutually supportive goals. Without this compatibility and commitment, a joint venture is critically endangered.

Foreign Branching

A foreign branch is an extension of the company in its foreign market—a separately located strategic business unit directly responsible for fulfilling the operational duties assigned to it by corporate management, including sales, customer service, and physical distribution. Host countries may require that the branch be "domesticated," that is, have some local managers in middle and upper-level positions. The branch most likely will be outside any U.S. legal jurisdiction, liabilities may not be restricted to the assets of the given branch, and business licenses for operations may be of short duration, requiring the company to renew them during changing business regulations. Gruma, Mexico's leading flour producer and the world's leading tortillas manufacturer, has manufacturing branches in 89 foreign countries and sales of $4 billion annually.

Acquisition

When one company buys another, the purchase is called an acquisition. The purchase can be achieved either by acquiring the seller's stock or by purchasing its assets. There are many reasons that one company might buy another, such as to grow assets quickly, deploy funds more profitably, improve the company's competitive position, bypass regulations, leverage the acquirer's competitive advantages in a new market, and gain access to cash, patents, technologies, customers, employees, locations or other physical assets, or its recognized brand. In future chapters, we will explore these reasons in greater depth. However, in the context of competitive strategies for foreign markets, it is important to know that buying a company that is already established in the market that you wish to enter may be the most attractive strategic option.

When Irish software giant SAS wanted to expand its law enforcement business, it acquired Memex, a Scottish firm whose software is used to combat crime and terrorism. "The Memex acquisition is a key element of our global initiative to enhance our law enforcement, criminal justice, homeland security and intelligence offerings," SAS co-founder and CEO Jim Goodnight said. Of major importance in the acquisition, Memex's customers include the Delaware, Michigan, New Hampshire and Pennsylvania state police; the Georgia Bureau of Investigation; the Los Angeles and Philadelphia police

Top Strategist
CEO Nooyi Spearheads PepsiCo's International Expansion Strategy

Exhibit 5.12

PepsiCo is one of the largest food and beverages companies in the world. It manufactures, markets, and sells a variety of salty, sweet, and grain-based snacks and carbonated and noncarbonated beverages. Indra Nooyi has been the chairman and chief executive officer of PepsiCo since 2007.

Nooyi wanted to become less reliant on the U.S. market, where sales growth has slowed for some of its flagship sodas and snacks. In 2008, 40 percent of PepsiCo revenue came from international business. About her strategic intention, Nooyi said, "Revitalizing this business is a huge priority for us and investments will be made to expand the company's footprint in fast-growing emerging markets."*

Nooyi planned to strengthen PepsiCo's presence in emerging high-growth markets—including China, India, and Russia, where it has an established market in carbonated beverages and planned to expand with more focus on snack foods and other beverages.

PepsiCo planned to invest $1 billion in China between 2008 and 2011 to build more plants in western and interior areas of China, expand local R&D to develop products tailored to Chinese consumers, and build a larger sales force to expand marketing and distribution.

In an effort to expand its presence in the Russian juice category, PepsiCo bought a 75.53 percent stake in Russia's leading branded juice company, JSC Lebedyansky. PepsiCo also built a potato chip factory in southern Russia.

In 2008, Nooyi announced an investment plan of $500 million aimed at upgrading its manufacturing capacity, infrastructure, and R&D in India. With an established carbonated business, Pepsi India began to launch localized product offerings, such as the drink "nimbu paani."

*B. McKay and A. Cordeiro, "Pepsi Results Send Chills in Beverage, Snack Sector," *The Wall Street Journal,* October 15, 2008, p. B.1.

Source: B. McKay, "Pepsi to Boost China Outlay by $1 Billion," *The Wall Street Journal,* November 4, 2008, p. B. 3.

departments; the Bedfordshire, Surrey and British Transport police departments in the United Kingdom; Belize Police Department; Albania State Police; and the U.N. Office on Drugs and Crime.

Wholly Owned Subsidiaries

Wholly owned foreign subsidiaries are considered by companies that are willing and able to make the highest investment commitment to the foreign market. These companies insist on full ownership for reasons of control and managerial efficiency. Policy decisions about local product lines, expansion, profits, and dividends typically remain with the U.S. senior managers.

Fully owned subsidiaries can be started either from scratch or by acquiring established firms in the host country. U.S. firms can benefit significantly if the acquired company has complementary product lines or an established distribution or service network. For example, in 2007, PepsiCo's CEO Indra Nooyi led her company's large-scale global expansion based on developing wholly owned subsidiaries. The plan builds brands in emerging markets to compensate for the slow growth in the United States, as described in Exhibit 5.12, Top Strategist.

U.S. firms seeking to improve their competitive postures through a foreign subsidiary face a number of risks to their normal mode of operations. First, if the high capital investment is to be rewarded, managers must attain extensive knowledge of the market,

Global Strategy in Action — Exhibit 5.13

For Small Businesses, the Big World Beckons

Husband-and-wife business partners Matt and Rene Greff are on track to open the first out-of-state branch of their Michigan brewpub—in Bangalore, India.

At Peter Frykman's Palo Alto, Calif., irrigation-equipment company, seven of the 20 employees are located outside the United States, in China and India, while Gangesh Ganesan's communications-chip firm, in San Jose, has about a quarter of its staffers in Istanbul, and others in Tokyo and Taipei.

While big companies have been the trailblazers of globalization, a growing number of relatively small businesses are following in their footsteps. Like their larger counterparts, they are drawn by new markets that are often growing much faster than those at home. Their forays abroad are made possible by technologies like file sharing and videoconferencing, which allow managers to communicate easily across continents. Though these technologies are not new, their price has fallen sharply over the past decade, putting them within reach of more companies.

Still, crossing borders does not come easily. Advances in technology have not done away with the need for small-business owners to spend face time with employees and clients in other countries. PharmaSecure Inc., for example, is based in Lebanon, New Hampshire, but Chief Executive and co-founder Nathan Sigworth says he has been spending more time in India, his primary market, than at home.

Venturing abroad also requires small companies to put a lot of care into choosing the employees or local partners who will represent their interests overseas. The task often requires bridging cultural differences and navigating complex and unfamiliar bureaucracies. The Greffs, in Ann Arbor, Michigan, were skeptical when Gaurav Sikka, a former University of Michigan student, approached them about opening a brewpub in Bangalore. Mr. Sikka, a native of India, was a regular at the couple's 200-seat Arbor Brewing Co. The couple had recently opened a small brewery in nearby Ypsilanti, and worried about stretching themselves too thin. "We said no, we don't have any time or money," recalls Mr. Greff. "He said: 'Don't rule it out of hand.'" The Greffs traveled to India, where they came to believe Mr. Sikka's idea was feasible. Now, a group of local investors, led by Mr. Sikka, is supervising arrangements for the Bangalore opening. The Greffs will have a stake in the new brewpub, and will receive consulting and licensing fees.

Though there are no hard figures available, the number of small businesses that have invested directly in overseas operations remains relatively small. But it is growing, says Larry Harding, president of High Street

the host nation's language, and its business culture. Second, the host country expects both a long-term commitment from the U.S. enterprise and a portion of their nationals to be employed in positions of management or operations. Fortunately, hiring or training foreign managers for leadership positions is commonly a good policy, because they are close to both the market and contacts. This is especially important for smaller firms when markets are regional. Third, changing standards mandated by foreign regulations may eliminate a company's protected market niche. Product design and worker protection liabilities also may extend back to the home office.

The strategies shown in Exhibit 5.11 may be undertaken singly or in combination. For example, a firm may engage in any number of joint ventures while maintaining an export business. Additionally, there are a number of other strategies that a firm should consider before deciding on its long-term approach to foreign markets. These will be discussed in detail in Chapter 7 under the topic of grand strategies. However, the strategies discussed in this chapter provide the most popular starting points for planning the globalization of a firm.

While big companies have been the trailblazers of globalization, a growing number of relatively small businesses are achieving success by adopting the strategic models of large firms. As described in Exhibit 5.13, Global Strategy in Action, small businesses based in the United States are locating profitable operations in such far-flung countries as China, Ethiopia, India, Japan, Turkey, and the United Kingdom.

Partners Inc., an Annapolis, Maryland, company that helps small firms set up foreign offices. A year ago, he says, his company was working with about 200 companies; now it's working with more than 300. "There's an explosion of 50- to 100-person companies that are going overseas," he says.

Mr. Frykman, the irrigation-gear executive, helped to develop a method for making drip irrigation systems inexpensively. After testing them in Ethiopia, he formed Driptech Inc. A pilot project in India went well and caught the eye of Chinese officials. In 2009, the company made its first sales, in India and China, and began to seek angel investors. In 2010, it raised $900,000 in funding. Seven of Driptech's employees are now working in its offices in Beijing and outside of Mumbai, and Mr. Frykman expects that half of its workers will soon be overseas. Having offices in three countries is a challenge, he says, but thanks to the revolution in communications technology he is able to hand off work in the evening to his co-workers in Asia, and pick it back up in the morning.

PharmaSecure got its start in 2007 when Mr. Sigworth and a friend came up with a low-cost way to combat counterfeit drugs, a big problem in the developing world. PharmaSecure's system, which combines mobile-software apps and databases, allows customers to send text messages containing the codes printed on drug packages and get a reply indicating whether the code is legitimate. After a year of traveling, the partners decided that India, the source of much of the developing world's drug supply, was the best place to begin. Now, most of the company's 15 employees work out of New Delhi. Mr. Sigworth says the ability to communicate cheaply has been crucial. "We use [Internet telephone service] Skype a lot; we use email a ton," he says, but he adds that just as important has been the company's ease and comfort working across cultures.

To videoconference, chat and work together on projects, Ubicom's offices use technology that would have been too costly for the company a decade ago, says Mr. Ganesan, the CEO. Ubicom Inc., which produces chips for products such as wireless routers, made its first international foray three years ago when it tapped a Turkish employee to start an office in Istanbul. Now about 20 of its 85 employees work there. Ubicom also has offices in Taipei and Tokyo, as well as a group of engineers in the United Kingdom.

Source: Excerpted from Justin Lahart, "For Small Businesses, the Big World Beckons," *Wall Street Journal*, January 27, 2011, p. B.1.

Summary

To understand the strategic planning options available to a corporation, its managers need to recognize that different types of industry-based competition exist. Specifically, they must identify the position of their industry along the global versus multidomestic continuum and then consider the implications of that position for their firm.

The differences between global and multidomestic industries about the location and coordination of functional corporate activities necessitate differences in strategic emphasis. As an industry becomes global, managers of firms within that industry must increase the coordination and concentration of functional activities.

The Appendix at the end of this chapter lists many components of the environment with which global corporations must contend. This list is useful in understanding the issues that confront global corporations and in evaluating the thoroughness of global corporation strategies.

As a starting point for global expansion, the firm's mission statement needs to be reviewed and revised. As global operations fundamentally alter the direction and strategic capabilities of a firm, its mission statement, if originally developed from a domestic perspective, must be globalized.

The globalized mission statement provides the firm with a unity of direction that transcends the divergent perspectives of geographically dispersed managers. It provides a basis for strategic decisions in situations where strategic alternatives may appear to conflict. It promotes corporate values and commitments that extend beyond single cultures and satisfies the demands of the firm's internal and external claimants in different countries. Finally, it ensures the survival of the global corporation by asserting the global corporation's legitimacy with respect to support coalitions in a variety of operating environments.

Movement of a firm toward globalization often follows a systematic pattern of development. Commonly, businesses begin their foreign nation involvements progressively through niche market exporting, license-contract manufacturing, franchising, joint ventures, foreign branching, and foreign subsidiaries.

Key Terms

ethnocentric orientation, *p. 127*
geocentric orientation, *p. 127*
global industry, *p. 133*
globalization, *p. 123*
multidomestic industry, *p. 133*
polycentric orientation, *p. 127*
regiocentric orientation, *p. 127*
stakeholder activism, *p. 131*

Questions for Discussion

1. How does environmental analysis at the domestic level differ from global analysis?
2. Which factors complicate environmental analysis at the global level? Which factors are making such analysis easier?
3. Do you agree with the suggestion that soon all industries will need to evaluate global environments?
4. Which industries operate almost devoid of global competition? Which inherent immunities do they enjoy?
5. Explain when and why it is important for a company to globalize.
6. Describe the four main strategic orientations of global firms.
7. Explain the control problems that are faced by global firms.
8. Describe the differences between multinational and global firms.
9. Describe the market requirements and product characteristics in global competition.
10. Evaluate the competitive strategies for firms in foreign markets:
    a. Niche market exporting
    b. Licensing and contract manufacturing
    c. Franchising
    d. Joint ventures
    e. Foreign branching
    f. Private equity investment
    g. Wholly owned subsidiaries

Chapter 5 Appendix

Components of the Global Environment

Global firms must operate within an environment that has numerous components. These components include the following:

1. Government, laws, regulations, and policies of home country (United States, for example)
   a. Monetary and fiscal policies and their effect on price trends, interest rates, economic growth, and stability
   b. Balance-of-payments policies
   c. Mandatory controls on direct investment
   d. Interest equalization tax and other policies
   e. Commercial policies, especially tariffs, quantitative import restrictions, and voluntary import controls
   f. Export controls and other restrictions on trade
   g. Tax policies and their impact on overseas business
   h. Antitrust regulations, their administration, and their impact on international business
   i. Investment guarantees, investment surveys, and other programs to encourage private investments in less-developed countries
   j. Export-import and government export expansion programs
   k. Other changes in government policy that affect international business
2. Key political and legal parameters in foreign countries and their projection
   a. Type of political and economic system, political philosophy, national ideology
   b. Major political parties, their philosophies, and their policies
   c. Stability of the government
      (1) Changes in political parties
      (2) Changes in governments
   d. Assessment of nationalism and its possible impact on political environment and legislation
   e. Assessment of political vulnerability
      (1) Possibilities of expropriation
      (2) Unfavorable and discriminatory national legislation and tax laws
      (3) Labor laws and problems
   f. Favorable political aspects
      (1) Tax and other concessions to encourage foreign investments
      (2) Credit and other guarantees
   g. Differences in legal system and commercial law
   h. Jurisdiction in legal disputes
   i. Antitrust laws and rules of competition
   j. Arbitration clauses and their enforcement
   k. Protection of patents, trademarks, brand names, and other industrial property rights
3. Key economic parameters and their projection
   a. Population and its distribution by age groups, density, annual percentage increase, percentage of working age, percentage of total in agriculture, and percentage in urban centers
   b. Level of economic development and industrialization
   c. Gross national product, gross domestic product, or national income in real terms and also on a per capita basis in recent years and projections over future planning period
   d. Distribution of personal income
   e. Measures of price stability and inflation, wholesale price index, consumer price index, other price indexes
   f. Supply of labor, wage rates
   g. Balance-of-payments equilibrium or disequilibrium, level of international monetary reserves, and balance-of-payments policies
   h. Trends in exchange rates, currency stability, evaluation of possibility of depreciation of currency
   i. Tariffs, quantitative restrictions, export controls, border taxes, exchange controls, state trading, and other entry barriers to foreign trade
   j. Monetary, fiscal, and tax policies
   k. Exchange controls and other restrictions on capital movements, repatriation of capital, and remission of earnings
4. Business system and structure
   a. Prevailing business philosophy: mixed capitalism, planned economy, state socialism
   b. Major types of industry and economic activities
   c. Numbers, size, and types of firms, including legal forms of business
   d. Organization: proprietorships, partnerships, limited companies, corporations, cooperatives, state enterprises
   e. Local ownership patterns: public and privately held corporations, family-owned enterprises

f. Domestic and foreign patterns of ownership in major industries
g. Business managers available: their education, training, experience, career patterns, attitudes, and reputations
h. Business associations and chambers of commerce and their influence
i. Business codes, both formal and informal
j. Marketing institutions: distributors, agents, wholesalers, retailers, advertising agencies, advertising media, marketing research, and other consultants
k. Financial and other business institutions: commercial and investment banks, other financial institutions, capital markets, money markets, foreign exchange dealers, insurance firms, engineering companies
l. Managerial processes and practices with respect to planning, administration, operations, accounting, budgeting, and control

5. Social and cultural parameters and their projections
   a. Literacy and educational levels
   b. Business, economic, technical, and other specialized education available
   c. Language and cultural characteristics
   d. Class structure and mobility
   e. Religious, racial, and national characteristics
   f. Degree of urbanization and rural-urban shifts
   g. Strength of nationalistic sentiment
   h. Rate of social change
   i. Impact of nationalism on social and institutional change

Internal Analysis

After reading and studying this chapter, you should be able to

1. Understand how to conduct a SWOT analysis, and be able to summarize its limitations.
2. Understand value chain analysis and how to use it to disaggregate a firm's activities and determine which are most critical to generating competitive advantage.
3. Understand the resource-based view of a firm and how to use it to disaggregate a firm's activities and resources to determine which resources are best used to build competitive advantage.
4. Apply four different perspectives for making meaningful comparisons to assess a firm's internal strengths and weaknesses.
5. Refamiliarize yourself with ratio analysis and basic techniques of financial analysis to assist you in doing internal analysis to identify a firm's strengths and weaknesses.

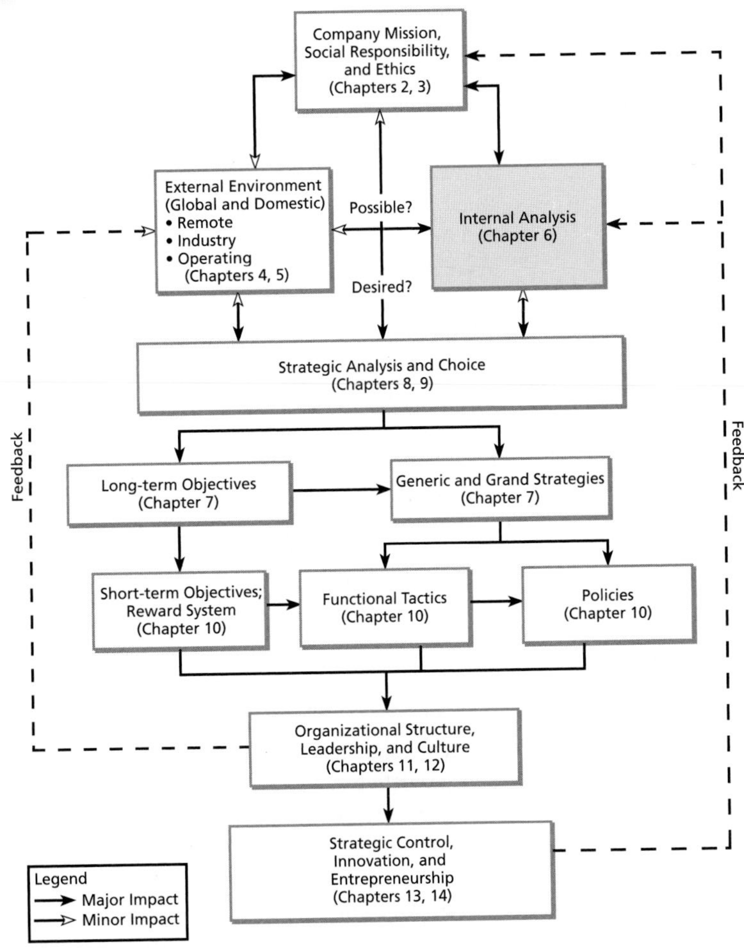

Andrew Mason, 30-year-old former rock band keyboardist turned entrepreneur/CEO and creator of Groupon, was in his hometown, Chicago, as we write this chapter, figuring out how to chart a strategy to guide his highly successful three-year-old digital couponing startup into a rebirth of itself as Groupon Now. The company reached over $4 billion in sales in less than five years. Mason's job was to shape a strategy that addressed massive copycat competition and Facebook competition so as to make Groupon something much more difficult to replicate. Amazingly, Mason turned down a $6 billion offer for Groupon at its second birthday, in part because of the many venture capitalists that felt Groupon could become the fastest growing company of all time. The late R. David Thomas, who could have been Mason's grandfather, had a similar albeit more negative reception when he was ridiculed by many restaurant industry veterans and analysts as he set about building "yet another" hamburger chain, named after his young daughter, Wendy. Okay with the name, these critics questioned Thomas' sanity for entering a North American market saturated with hamburger stores such as Burger King, Hardees, McDonald's, White Castle, Dairy Queen, and others. Interestingly, Wendy's became the fastest growing restaurant chain in the history of the world. Cisco, the global leader in networking equipment and switching devices linking wired and wireless computer systems worldwide, twice entered and tried to dominate the home-networking market. It failed each time, wasting more than $250 million in the process. Finally, Cisco changed its approach and acquired Linksys, the market leader, with the promise it would never try to bring Linksys into the normal Cisco company structure for fear of destroying the extraordinary success Linksys had achieved—not the least of which was vanquishing the much more powerful and wealthy Cisco twice in the last decade. Apple Computer was being written off in the increasingly competitive personal computer industry when it introduced, to a lukewarm reception, its new iTunes music download service to allow customers to buy digital songs legally for use on their computer or MP3 player, most notably Apple's iPod. Questioned by many as another cute Apple fad, that modest innovation revolutionized the global music industry in five short years and led to the iPhone, the iPad, the AppStore—much like Apple's original personal computer did three decades earlier.

Common to each of these diverse settings were insightful managers and business leaders who based their firm's pursuit of market opportunities not only on the existence of external opportunities but also on a very sound awareness of their firm's competitive advantages arising from the firm's internal resources, capabilities, and skills. A *sound, realistic awareness and appreciation of their firm's internally generated advantages* should help Andrew Mason's team chart a strategy that can enable Groupon Now to fulfill its predicted destiny. History suggests doing so helped bring Wendy's, Apple, and Linksys immense success while its absence brought much the opposite to Cisco's home-networking ventures and to the competitors and critics of R. David Thomas and Steve Jobs. This chapter, then, focuses on how managers identify the key resources and capabilities around which to build successful strategies.

Managers often do this subjectively, based on intuition and "gut feel." Years of seasoned industry experience positions managers to make sound subjective judgments. But just as often, or more often, this may not be the case. In fast-changing environments, reliance on past experiences can cause management myopia—or a tendency to accept the status quo and disregard signals that change is needed. And with managers new to strategic decision making, subjective decisions are particularly suspect. A lack of experience is easily replaced by emotion, narrow functional expertise, and the opinions of others, thus creating the foundation on which newer managers build strategic recommendations. So it is that new managers' subjective assessments often come back to haunt them.

John W. Henry broke the most fabled curse in sports when his Boston Red Sox won their first World Championship since 1918. Most sports analysts, sports business managers, and regular fans (if they are honest now) would have bet a small fortune, based on their own subjective assessment, that there was no way the Boston Red Sox, having already lost three games, would win four straight games to beat the New York Yankees and then go on to win the World Series. That subjective assessment or "feel" would have led them to believe there were just too many reasons to bet the Red Sox would fail. At the same time, a seasoned global futures market trader, John W. Henry, relied on applying his systematic global futures market approach to baseball player selection along with selected other resources and capabilities unique to the Boston area and situation in his bet that the Red Sox could win it all. His very systematic approach to internal analysis of the Boston Red Sox sports enterprise and the leveraging of his/their strengths led to the World Series championship and perhaps many more, as described in Exhibit 6.1, Top Strategist.

Managers often start their internal analysis with questions like, How well is the current strategy working? What is our current situation? or What are our strengths and weaknesses? The chapter begins with a review of a long-standing, traditional approach managers have frequently used to answer these questions, SWOT analysis. This approach is a logical framework intended to help managers thoughtfully consider their company's internal capabilities and use the results to shape strategic options. Its value and continued use is found in its simplicity. At the same time, SWOT analysis has limitations that have led strategists to seek more comprehensive frameworks for conducting internal analysis.

Value chain analysis is one such framework. Value chain analysis views a firm as a "chain" or sequential process of value-creating activities. The sum of all of these activities represents the "value" the firm exists to provide its customers. So undertaking an internal analysis that breaks down the firm into these distinct value activities allows for a detailed, interrelated evaluation of a firm's internal strengths and weaknesses that improves upon what strategists can create using only SWOT analysis.

The resource-based view (RBV) of a firm is another important framework for conducting internal analysis. This approach improves upon SWOT analysis by examining a variety of different yet specific types of resources and capabilities any firm possesses and then evaluating the degree to which they become the basis for sustained competitive advantage based on industry and competitive considerations. In so doing, it provides a disciplined approach to internal analysis.

Common to all the approaches to internal analysis is the use of meaningful standards for comparison in internal analysis. We conclude this chapter by examining how managers use past performance, comparison with competitors, or other "benchmarks," industry norms, and traditional financial analysis to make meaningful comparisons.

SWOT ANALYSIS: A TRADITIONAL APPROACH TO INTERNAL ANALYSIS

SWOT analysis
SWOT is an acronym for the internal Strengths and Weaknesses of a firm, and the environmental Opportunities and Threats facing that firm. SWOT analysis is a technique through which managers create a quick overview of a company's strategic situation.

SWOT is an acronym for the internal **S**trengths and **W**eaknesses of a firm and the environmental **O**pportunities and **T**hreats facing that firm. **SWOT analysis** is a historically popular technique through which managers create a quick overview of a company's strategic situation. It is based on the assumption that an effective strategy derives from a sound "fit" between a firm's internal resources (strengths and weaknesses) and its external situation (opportunities and threats). A good fit maximizes a firm's strengths and opportunities and minimizes its weaknesses and threats. Accurately applied, this simple assumption has sound, insightful implications for the design of a successful strategy.

Environmental and industry analysis in Chapters 3 and 4 provides the information needed to identify opportunities and threats in a firm's environment, the first fundamental focus in SWOT analysis.

Top Strategist
John W. Henry, Principal Owner of the Boston Red Sox

Exhibit 6.1

John W. Henry, Principal Owner of the Boston Red Sox, and slugger David "Big Papi" Ortiz

The return of pain and broken hearts for every Boston Red Sox fan with each new professional baseball season was legendary. Not since 1918 had they experienced winning the World Series, yet they had suffered through their arch nemesis, the New York Yankees, doing it 26 times over that lengthy spell. But something happened in the new millennium, and suddenly in 2004 and again in 2007 sports' best-known curse was broken after almost a century of trying—the Boston Red Sox won two World Series titles.

It could not have happened in a more dramatic fashion. The Red Sox were down three games to none in the American League Championship series, once again, to the hated New York Yankees . . . and playing in New York for the deciding Game 4. Somehow, the Red Sox rallied to win that game, and then the next three, allowing them to go to the World Series. They won that too. Since then, the Sox have won another and are now in the championship hunt each year. What happened? John W. Henry became the Principal owner a few years before that initial win, and he took a different approach to charting the Red Sox's future. He may well have achieved immortality, at least in the Red Sox nation.

Henry set about a careful, internal analysis to determine the Red Sox's skills, resources, capabilities, and weaknesses. He set the tone by firing the manager during the 2003 playoff series for what he thought was a critical, poor decision in a decisive game. That set a tone of seriousness—and gained fan support. Henry had previously earned his fortune developing and building a business around his proprietary global futures trading system still widely used today. So he secondly approached internal assessments of the Red Sox player possibilities in a similar manner—he used a system called *sabermetrics* to mine baseball statistics about minor league and other young players, systematically finding undervalued players to bring into the Red Sox organization while also identifying when to avoid long-term contracts with aging stars.*

He further saw other underutilized capabilities, such as generating more revenue from Fenway Park, the oldest stadium in Major League Baseball, by squeezing in more seats and then charging the highest prices for home games. They always sold out. He started high-definition (HD) broadcasts of home games on their 80 percent–owned New England Sports Cable Network, broadening the fan base, increasing advertising revenue, and routinely winning regional prime-time ratings. The Red Sox quickly turned into the second-highest-earning MLB franchise, giving it the financial muscle to compete with the perennial highest payroll Yankees.

New York Times writer George Vecsey once said about the Yankees: "They are becoming the Red Sox of old—25 players and a bunch of separate cabs." The Sox organization, led by Henry, has become a team of players who get along, hang out, and play together. It all started with Henry's objective internal analysis, and he's now aiming for a dynasty.**

* "John Henry: Boston Red Sox," *BusinessWeek*, January 10, 2005.

**Recalling an earlier *New York Times* compliment as the featured writer honored at "The Boston Red Sox & The Great Fenway Park Writers Series," June 2, 2011, Boston, MA.

opportunity
A major favorable situation in a firm's environment.

Opportunities

An **opportunity** is a major favorable situation in a firm's environment. Key trends are one source of opportunities. Identification of a previously overlooked market segment, changes in competitive or regulatory circumstances, technological changes, and improved buyer or supplier relationships could represent opportunities for the firm. Sustained, growing interest in organic foods has created an opportunity that is a critical factor shaping strategic decisions at groceries and restaurants worldwide.

AT&T's decision to attempt to acquire T-Mobile in 2011 created a sudden potential opportunity for Verizon in three ways. Regulatory approval of the deal would take a lot of time and attention on AT&T; and confusion for T-Mobile customers with the future ability to continue the lower cost T-Mobile contracts when they were up for renewal creating a possibility for considerable T-Mobile customer unhappiness. Finally, the deal came just after the Apple iPhone had finally become available through Verizon and not just AT&T, creating a major additional opportunity for Verizon.

Threats

threat
A major unfavorable situation in a firm's environment.

A **threat** is a major unfavorable situation in a firm's environment. Threats are key impediments to the firm's current or desired position. The entrance of new competitors, slow market growth, increased bargaining power of key buyers or suppliers, technological changes, and new or revised regulations could represent threats to a firm's success. Japan's sudden, massive earthquake and the tsunami it unleashed created an unanticipated opportunity for wood and building products companies still trying to emerge from the global "Great Recession." But it was a new, potentially major threat for companies like GE and others with significant new investments anticipating long-term growth in the newly revitalized nuclear energy industry. Literally overnight, as a result of this unprecedented natural disaster and its effect on several Japanese nuclear power plants, hundreds of major global companies faced a serious, unfolding long-term threat to take into account as they each reevaluated their company's capabilities in light of this new environment.

Once managers agree on key opportunities and threats facing their firm, they have a frame of reference or context from which to evaluate their firm's ability to take advantage of opportunities and minimize the effect of key threats. And vice versa: Once managers agree on their firm's core strengths and weaknesses, they can logically move to consider opportunities that best leverage their firm's strengths while minimizing the effect certain weaknesses may present until remedied.

Strengths

strength
A resource advantage relative to competitors and the needs of the markets a firm serves or expects to serve.

A **strength** is a resource or capability controlled by or available to a firm that gives it an advantage relative to its competitors in meeting the needs of the customers it serves. Strengths arise from the resources and competencies available to the firm. Southland Log Homes' southeastern plant locations (Virginia, South Carolina, and Mississippi) provide both transportation and raw material cost advantages along with ideal proximity to the United States' most rapidly growing second-home markets. Southland leveraged these strengths to take advantage of the moderate interest rates and rapidly growing baby-boomer second-home demand trend to become one of the largest log home companies in North America. This strength has continued to sustain Southland even as it navigates the recent economic depression in the U.S. housing market.[1]

Weaknesses

weakness
A limitation or deficiency in one or more resources or competencies relative to competitors that impedes a firm's effective performance.

A **weakness** is a limitation or deficiency in one or more of a firm's resources or capabilities relative to its competitors that create a disadvantage in effectively meeting customer needs. Limited financial capacity was a weakness recognized by Southwest Airlines, which charted a selective route expansion strategy to build the best profit record in a deregulated airline industry.

[1] www.SouthlandLogHomes.com

Using SWOT Analysis in Strategic Analysis

The most common use of SWOT analysis is as a logical framework guiding discussion and reflection about a firm's situation and basic alternatives. This often takes place as a series of managerial group discussions. What one manager sees as an opportunity, another may see as a potential threat. Likewise, a strength to one manager may be a weakness to another. The SWOT framework provides an organized basis for insightful discussion and information sharing, which may improve the quality of choices and decisions managers subsequently make. Consider what initial discussions among Apple Computer's management team might have been that led to the decision to pursue the rapid development and introduction of the iPod. A brief SWOT analysis of their situation might have identified:

Strengths

Sizable miniature storage expertise
User-friendly engineering skill
Reputation and image with youthful consumers
Brand name
Web-savvy organization and people
Jobs's Pixar experience

Weaknesses

Economies of scale versus computer rivals
Maturing computer markets
Limited financial resources
Limited music industry expertise

Opportunities

Confused online music situation
Emerging file-sharing restrictions
Few core computer-related opportunities
Digitalization of movies and music

Threats

Growing global computer companies
Major computer competitors

It is logical to envision Apple managers' discussions evolving to a consensus that the combination of Apple's storage and digitalization strengths along with their strong brand franchise with "sophisticated" consumers, when combined with the opportunity potentially arising out of the need for a simple way to legally buy and download music on the Web, would be the basis for a compelling strategy for Apple to become a first mover in the emerging downloadable music industry.

Exhibit 6.2 illustrates how SWOT analysis might take managerial planning discussions into a slightly more structured approach to aid strategic analysis. The objective is identification of one of four distinct patterns in the match between a firm's internal resources and external situation. Cell 1 is the most favorable situation; the firm faces several environmental opportunities and has numerous strengths that encourage pursuit of those opportunities. This situation suggests growth-oriented strategies to exploit the favorable match. Our example of Apple Computer's intensive market development strategy in the online music services and the iPod is the result of a favorable match of its strong technical expertise,

EXHIBIT 6.2
SWOT Analysis Diagram

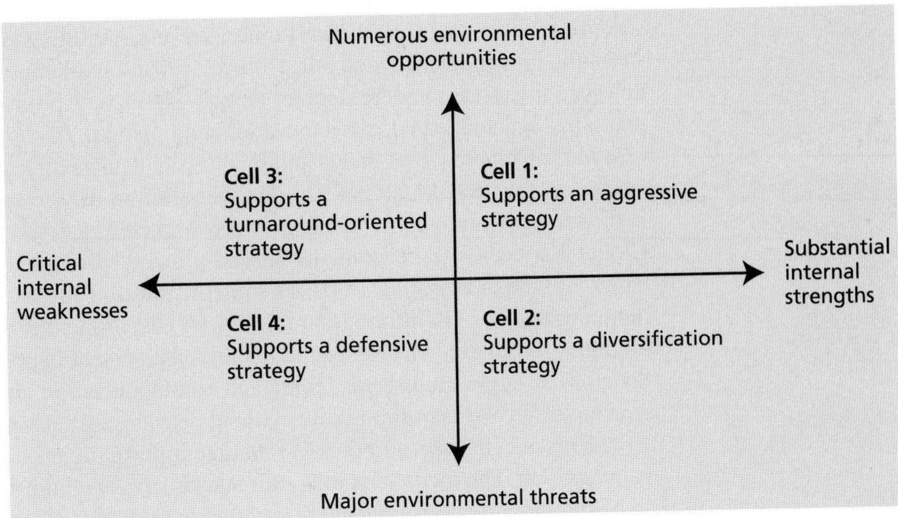

early entry, and reputation resources with an opportunity for impressive market growth as millions of people sought a legally viable, convenient way to obtain, download, store, and use their own customized music choices.

Recent efforts by Kodak to compete in the ink-jet printer market, highlighted later in this chapter in Exhibit 6.13, Strategy in Action (see page 175), offer another example of a firm in cell 1. Kodak views its expertise in ink pigments, and how to display them in an inexpensive yet impressive manner on all types of paper, as a unique strength from its photography roots that give it a basis for a competitive advantage in both costs and quality with traditional printer makers. Furthermore, it sees consumer frustration with the high costs of ink cartridge replacements in all ink-jet printers as a major external opportunity upon which it can capitalize by offering a printer solution that dramatically lowers a user's total printing costs over time.

Cell 4 is the least favorable situation, with the firm facing major environmental threats from a weak resource position. This situation clearly calls for strategies that reduce or redirect involvement in the products or markets examined by means of SWOT analysis. Texas Instruments (TI) offers a good example of a cell 4 firm. It was a sprawling maker of chips, calculators, laptop PCs, military electronics, and engineering software on a sickening slide toward oblivion. Rich Templeton, current chairman and CEO, rose to this position based on his success in helping to define and execute TI's strategy to focus narrowly on semiconductors for signal processing. Templeton convinced his boss at the time, Tom Engibous, to divest TI of most of the products and businesses in which it had become involved in order to rebuild TI around its core semiconductor technology, even during the worst downturn in semiconductor history. These actions ultimately reinvigorated the ailing electronics giant and turned it into one of the hottest players in signal semiconductors by betting the company on an emerging class of chips known as digital signal processors—DSPs. The chips crunch vast streams of data for an array of digital gadgets, phones, and other cellular devices. TI has experienced increasing market share every year since then, and now commands more than 60 percent of the global market for advanced DSPs, becoming the No. 1 chip supplier to the digital wireless phone industry.[2]

In cell 2, a firm that has identified several key strengths faces an unfavorable environment. In this situation, strategies would seek to redeploy those strong resources and competencies to build long-term opportunities in more opportunistic product markets. IBM,

[2] http://www.ti.com/corp/docs/investor/compinfo/CEOPerspective.shtml; and "TI's Next-Gen OMAP5 Chips Are on a Whole 'Nother Level of Crazy.'" GIZMODO.com, February 8, 2011.

a dominant manufacturer of mainframes, servers, and PCs worldwide, has nurtured many strengths in computer-related and software-related markets for many years. Increasingly, however, it has had to address major threats that include product commoditization, pricing pressures, accelerated pace of innovation, and the like. IBM's decision to sell its PC business to the Chinese firm Lenovo and focus instead on continued development of ISSC, better known now as IBM Global Services, has allowed IBM to build a long-term opportunity in the (hopefully) more profitable, growing markets of the next decade. In the past 10 years, Global Services has become the fastest-growing division of the company, its largest employer, and the keystone of IBM's strategic future. The group does everything from running a customer's IT (information technology) department to consulting on legacy system upgrades to building custom supply-chain management applications. As IBM's hardware divisions struggle against price wars and commoditization and its software units fight to gain share beyond mainframes, it is Global Services that drives the company's growth.

A firm in cell 3 faces impressive market opportunity but is constrained by weak internal resources. The focus of strategy for such a firm is eliminating the internal weaknesses so as to more effectively pursue the market opportunity. Microsoft has big problems with computer viruses. Alleviating such problems, or weaknesses, is driving massive changes in how Microsoft writes software—to make it more secure before it reaches the market rather than fix it later with patches. Microsoft is also shaking up the security software industry by acquiring several smaller companies to accelerate its own efforts to create specialized software that detects, finds, and removes malicious code.[3]

Limitations of SWOT Analysis

SWOT analysis has been a framework of choice among many managers for a long time because of its simplicity and its portrayal of the essence of sound strategy formulation—matching a firm's opportunities and threats with its strengths and weaknesses. But SWOT analysis is a broad conceptual approach, making it susceptible to some key limitations.

1. A SWOT analysis can overemphasize internal strengths and downplay external threats. Strategists in every company have to remain vigilant against building strategies around what the firm does well now (its strengths) without due consideration of the external environment's impact on those strengths. Apple's success with the iPod and its iTunes downloadable music Web site provides a good example of strategists who placed a major emphasis on external considerations—the legal requirements for downloading and subsequently using individual songs, what music to make available, and the evolution of the use of the Web to download music—as a guide to shaping Apple's eventual strategy. What would Apple's success have been like if its strategy had been built substantially with a focus on its technology in making the iPod device and offering it in the consumer marketplace—without bothering with the development and creation of iTunes?

2. A SWOT analysis can be static and can risk ignoring changing circumstances. A frequent admonition about the downfall of planning processes says that plans are one-time events to be completed, typed, and relegated to their spot on a manager's shelf while he or she goes about the actual work of the firm. So it is not surprising that critics of SWOT analysis, with good reason, warn that it is a one-time view of a changing, or moving, situation. Major U.S. airlines pursued strategies built around strengths that were suddenly much less important when airline deregulation took place. Likewise, those airlines built huge competitive advantages around "hub and spoke" systems for bringing small-town flyers to key hubs to be redistributed to flights elsewhere and yet allow for centralized maintenance and economies of scale. The change brought about by discount airlines that "cherry-picked"

[3] "Microsoft Has Secretly Acquired 15 Companies in the Last Year," businessinsider.com , Oct. 2, 2010.

key routes, and eventual outsourcing of routine maintenance to Latin America and the Caribbean, did great harm to those strategies. Bottom line: SWOT analysis, along with most planning techniques, must avoid being static and ignoring change.

3. A SWOT analysis can overemphasize a single strength or element of strategy. Dell Computer's long-dominant strength based on a highly automated, Internet, or phone-based direct sales model gave Dell, according to chairman and founder Michael Dell, "a competitive advantage [strength] as wide as the Grand Canyon." He viewed it as being prohibitively expensive for any rival to copy this source of strength. Unfortunately for Dell shareholders, Dell's reliance on that "key" strength proved to be an oversimplified basis around which to sustain the company's strategy for continued dominance and growth in the global PC industry. HP's size alone, with its reemphasis on printing and technical skills, and Lenovo's home base in the fast-growing Asian market have overcome Dell's dominance in the global PC industry.

4. A strength is not necessarily a source of competitive advantage. Cisco Systems Inc. has been a dominant player in providing switching equipment and other key networking infrastructure items around which the global computer communications system has been able to proliferate. It has substantial financial, technological, and branding expertise. Cisco Systems twice attempted to use its vast strengths in these areas as the basis to enter and remain in the market for home computer networks and wireless home-networking devices. It failed both times and lost hundreds of millions of dollars in the process. It possesses several compelling strengths, but none were sources of sustainable competitive advantage in the home-computer-networking industry. After leaving that industry for several years, it recently chose to reenter it by acquiring Linksys, an early pioneer in that industry. Cisco management acknowledged that it was doing so precisely because it did not possess those sources of competitive advantage and that, furthermore, it would avoid any interference with that business lest it disrupt the advantage around which Linksys' success has been built.

In summary, SWOT analysis is a longtime, traditional approach to internal analysis among many strategists. It offers a generalized effort to examine internal capabilities in light of external factors, most notably key opportunities and threats. It has limitations that must be considered if SWOT analysis is to be the basis for any firm's strategic decision-making process. Another approach to internal analysis that emerged, in part, to add more rigor and depth in the identification of competitive advantages around which a firm might build a successful strategy is value chain analysis. We examine it next.

VALUE CHAIN ANALYSIS

value chain
A perspective in which business is seen as a chain of activities that transforms inputs into outputs that customers value.

value chain analysis
An analysis that attempts to understand how a business creates customer value by examining the contributions of different activities within the business to that value.

The term **value chain** describes a way of looking at a business as a chain of activities that transform inputs into outputs that customers value. Customer value derives from three basic sources: activities that differentiate the product, activities that lower its cost, and activities that meet the customer's need quickly. **Value chain analysis** (VCA) attempts to understand how a business creates customer value by examining the contributions of different activities within the business to that value.

VCA takes a process point of view: It divides (sometimes called disaggregates) the business into sets of activities that occur *within the business,* starting with the inputs a firm receives and finishing with the firm's products (or services) and after-sales service to customers. VCA attempts to look at its costs across the series of activities the business performs to determine where low-cost advantages or cost disadvantages exist. It looks at the attributes of each of these different activities to determine in what ways each activity that occurs between purchasing inputs and after-sales service helps differentiate the company's products and services. Proponents of VCA believe it allows managers to better identify their firm's competitive advantages by looking at the business as a process—a chain of activities—of what actually happens in the business rather than simply looking at it based on arbitrary organizational dividing lines or historical accounting protocol.

Exhibit 6.3 shows a typical value chain framework. It divides activities within the firm into two broad categories: primary activities and support activities. **Primary activities**

EXHIBIT 6.3
The Value Chain

Source: Based on Michael Porter. *On Competition,* 1998. Harvard Business School Press.

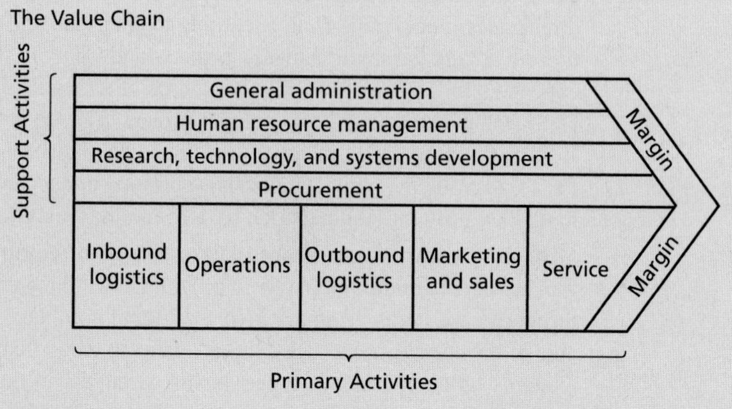

primary activities
The activities in a firm of those involved in the physical creation of the product, marketing and transfer to the buyer, and after-sale support.

Primary Activities

- **Inbound logistics**—Activities, costs, and assets associated with obtaining fuel, energy, raw materials, parts components, merchandise, and consumable items from vendors; receiving, storing, and disseminating inputs from suppliers; inspection; and inventory management.
- **Operations**—Activities, costs, and assets associated with converting inputs into final product form (production, assembly, packaging, equipment maintenance, facilities, operations, quality assurance, environmental protection).
- **Outbound logistics**—Activities, costs, and assets dealing with physically distributing the product to buyers (finished goods warehousing, order processing, order picking and packing, shipping, delivery vehicle operations).
- **Marketing and sales**—Activities, costs, and assets related to sales force efforts, advertising and promotion, market research and planning, and dealer/distributor support.
- **Service**—Activities, costs, and assets associated with providing assistance to buyers, such as installation, spare parts delivery, maintenance and repair, technical assistance, buyer inquiries, and complaints.

Support Activities

- **General administration**—Activities, costs, and assets relating to general management, accounting and finance, legal and regulatory affairs, safety and security, management information systems, and other "overhead" functions.
- **Human resources management**—Activities, costs, and assets associated with the recruitment, hiring, training, development, and compensation of all types of personnel; labor relations activities; development of knowledge-based skills.
- **Research, technology, and systems development**—Activities, costs, and assets relating to product R&D, process R&D, process design improvement, equipment design, computer software development, telecommunications systems, computer-assisted design and engineering, new database capabilities, and development of computerized support systems.
- **Procurement**—Activities, costs, and assets associated with purchasing and providing raw materials, supplies, services, and outsourcing necessary to support the firm and its activities. Sometimes this activity is assigned as part of a firm's inbound logistic purchasing activities.

Global Strategy in Action

Exhibit 6.4

FedEx Uses Value Chain Analysis to Reinvent Itself

Stories of Fred Smith's early years creating Federal Express, like when he went to Las Vegas to gamble in order to [luckily] win $28,000 to use the next day to make payroll, are the stuff of legend. But the analysis and decision to reinvent FedEx into a logistics information company, rather than an overnight transportation company, has created a revolution in how companies around the world do business, allowing FedEx to maximize the value it adds in the process and the value it receives from doing so. FedEx becomes the logistical infrastructure for any client's business, handling everything from the customer order to the delivery, often including assembly and warehousing in the process.

"Moving an item from point A to point B is no longer a big deal," said James Barksdale, an early architect of the FedEx transformation. "Having the information about the item, where it is, what to connect it up with, and the best way to use that info . . . that is the value. The companies that maximize that step in their value chain will be the big winners." Fred Smith bought into that concept, envisioning a time when FedEx's value—long built on large planes and trucks—would be built on information, computers, coordination, and the FedEx brand.

That day has arrived at FedEx. It is now the linchpin of a just-in-time revolution for companies worldwide. Its planes and trucks are mobile warehouses, sometimes stopping at FedEx-operated assembling centers serving clients, all the while significantly cutting costs and increasing productivity for clients worldwide, large and small.

FedEx's value chain has dramatically shrunk the area involved with planes and trucks, while the overall logistical value added now contributes more than 90 percent of FedEx annual revenues. And, this all started with an objective, careful analysis of the FedEx value chain 10 years ago. That was followed by a visionary commitment to build that chain around activities that contribute the most value to a customer, in the process seeking to make them the core competencies upon which FedEx reinvented itself and built its future success.

Source: Various FedEx annual reports and www.fedex.com.

support activities
The activities in a firm that assist the firm as a whole by providing infrastructure or inputs that allow the primary activities to take place on an ongoing basis.

(sometimes called *line functions*) are those involved in the physical creation of the product, marketing and transfer to the buyer, and after-sale support. **Support activities** (sometimes called *staff* or *overhead functions*) assist the firm as a whole by providing infrastructure or inputs that allow the primary activities to take place on an ongoing basis. The value chain includes a profit margin because a markup above the cost of providing a firm's value-adding activities is normally part of the price paid by the buyer—creating value that exceeds cost so as to generate a return for the effort.[4]

Judgment is required across individual firms and different industries because what may be seen as a support activity in one firm or industry may be a primary activity in another. Computer operations might typically be seen as infrastructure support, for example, but may be seen as a primary activity in airlines, newspapers, or banks. Exhibit 6.4, Global Strategy in Action, describes how Federal Express reconceptualized its company using a value chain analysis that ultimately saw its information support become its primary activity and source of customer value.

Conducting a Value Chain Analysis

Identify Activities

The initial step in value chain analysis is to divide a company's operations into specific activities or business processes, usually grouping them similarly to the primary and support activity categories shown earlier in Exhibit 6.3. Within each category, a firm typically performs a number of discrete activities that may be key to the firm's success. Service

[4] Different "value chain" or value activities may become the focus of value chain analysis. For example, companies using Hammer's *Reengineering the Corporation* might use (1) order procurement, (2) order fulfillment, (3) customer service, (4) product design, and (5) strategic planning plus support activities.

activities, for example, may include such discrete activities as installation, repair, parts distribution, and upgrading—any of which could be a major source of competitive advantage or disadvantage. The manager's challenge at this point is to be very detailed attempting to "disaggregate" what actually goes on into numerous distinct, analyzable activities rather than settling for a broad, general categorization.

Allocate Costs

The next step is to attempt to attach costs to each discrete activity. Each activity in the value chain incurs costs and ties up time and assets. Value chain analysis requires managers to assign costs and assets to each activity, thereby providing a very different way of viewing costs than traditional cost accounting methods would produce. Exhibit 6.5 helps illustrate this distinction. Both approaches in Exhibit 6.5 tell us that the purchasing department (procurement activities) cost $320,075. The traditional method lets us see that payroll expenses are 73 percent [($175 + $57.5)/$320] of our costs with "other fixed charges" the second largest cost, 19 percent [$62/$320] of the total procurement costs. VCA proponents would argue that the benefit of this information is limited. Their argument might be the following:

> With this information we could compare our procurement costs to key competitors, budgets, or industry averages and conclude that we are better, worse, or equal. We could then ascertain that our "people" costs and "other fixed charges" cost are advantages, disadvantages, or "in line" with competitors. Managers could then argue to cut people, add people, or debate fixed overhead charges. However, they would get lost in what is really a budgetary debate without ever examining what it is those people do in accomplishing the procurement function, what value that provides, and how cost effective each activity is.

VCA proponents hold that the activity-based VCA approach would provide a more meaningful analysis of the procurement function's costs and consequent value added. The activity-based side of Exhibit 6.5 shows that approximately 21 percent of the procurement cost or value added involves evaluating supplier capabilities. A rather sizable cost, 20 percent, involves internal administration, with an additional 17 percent spent resolving problems and almost 15 percent spent on quality control efforts. VCA advocates see this information as being much more useful than traditional cost accounting information, especially when compared with the cost information of key competitors or other

EXHIBIT 6.5 **The Difference between Traditional Cost Accounting and Activity-Based Cost Accounting**

Traditional Cost Accounting in a Purchasing Department		**Activity-Based Cost Accounting in the Same Purchasing Department for Its "Procurement" Activities**	
Wages and salaries	$175,000	Evaluate supplier capabilities	$ 67,875
Employee benefits	57,500	Process purchase orders	41,050
Supplies	3,250	Expedite supplier deliveries	11,750
Travel	1,200	Expedite internal processing	7,920
Depreciation	8,500	Check quality of items purchased	47,150
Other fixed charges	62,000	Check incoming deliveries against purchase orders	24,225
Miscellaneous operating expenses	12,625	Resolve problems	55,000
	$320,075	Internal administration	65,105
			$320,075

"benchmark" companies. VCA supporters assert the following argument that the benefit of this activity-based information is substantial:

> Rather than analyzing just "people" and "other charges," we are now looking at meaningful categorizations of the work that procurement actually does. We see, for example, that a key value-added activity (and cost) involves "evaluating supplier capabilities." The amount spent on "internal administration" and "resolving problems" seems high and may indicate a weakness or area for improvement if the other activities' costs are in line and outcomes favorable. The bottom line is that this approach lets us look at what we actually "do" in the business—the specific activities—to create customer value, and that in turn allows more specific internal analysis than traditional, accounting-based cost categories.

Recognizing the Difficulty in Activity-Based Cost Accounting

It is important to note that existing financial management and accounting systems in many firms are not set up to easily provide activity-based cost breakdowns. Likewise, in virtually all firms, the information requirements to support activity-based cost accounting can create redundant work because of the financial reporting requirements that may force firms to retain the traditional approach for financial statement purposes. The time and energy to change to an activity-based approach can be formidable and still typically involve arbitrary cost allocation decisions—trying to allocate selected asset or people costs across multiple activities in which they are involved. Challenges dealing with a cost-based use of VCA have not deterred use of the framework to identify sources of differentiation. Indeed, conducting a VCA to analyze competitive advantages that differentiate the firm is compatible with the resource-based view's examination of intangible assets and capabilities as sources of distinctive competence.

Identify the Activities That Differentiate the Firm

Scrutinizing a firm's value chain may not only reveal cost advantages or disadvantages, it may also bring attention to several sources of differentiation advantage relative to competitors. Google considers its Internet-based search algorithms (activities) to be far superior to any competitor's. Google knows it has a cost advantage because of the time and expense replicating this activity would take. But Google considers it an even more important source of value to the customer because of the importance customers place on this activity, which differentiates Google from many would-be competitors. Likewise, Federal Express, as we noted in Exhibit 6.4, considers its information management skills to have become the core competence and essence of the company because of the value these skills allow FedEx to provide its customers and the importance they in turn place on such skills. Exhibit 6.6 suggests some factors for assessing primary and support activities' differentiation and contribution.

Examine the Value Chain

Once the value chain has been documented, managers need to identify the activities that are critical to buyer satisfaction and market success. It is those activities that deserve major scrutiny in an internal analysis. Three considerations are essential at this stage in the value chain analysis. First, the company's basic mission needs to influence managers' choice of activities to be examined in detail. If the company is focused on being a low-cost provider, then management attention to lower costs should be very visible, and missions built around commitment to differentiation should find managers spending more on activities that are differentiation cornerstones. Retailer Walmart focuses intensely on costs related to inbound logistics, advertising, and loyalty to build its competitive advantage, while Nordstrom builds its distinct position in retailing by emphasizing sales and support activities on which they spend twice the retail industry average.

EXHIBIT 6.6 Possible Factors for Assessing Sources of Differentiation in Primary and Support Activities

Support Activities

General Administration

- Capability to identify new-product market opportunities and potential environmental threats
- Quality of the strategic planning system to achieve corporate objectives
- Coordination and integration of all value chain activities among organizational subunits
- Ability to obtain relatively low-cost funds for capital expenditures and working capital
- Level of information systems support in making strategic and routine decisions
- Timely and accurate management information on general and competitive environments
- Relationships with public policymakers and interest groups
- Public image and corporate citizenship

Human Resource Management

- Effectiveness of procedures for recruiting, training, and promoting all levels of employees
- Appropriateness of reward systems for motivating and challenging employees
- A work environment that minimizes absenteeism and keeps turnover at desirable levels
- Relations with trade unions
- Active participation by managers and technical personnel in professional organizations
- Levels of employee motivation and job satisfaction

Technology Development

- Success of research and development activities in leading to product and process innovations
- Quality of working relationships between R&D personnel and other departments
- Timeliness of technology development activities in meeting critical deadlines
- Quality of laboratories and other facilities
- Qualification and experience of laboratory technicians and scientists
- Ability of work environment to encourage creativity and innovation

Procurement

- Development of alternate sources for inputs to minimize dependence on a single supplier
- Procurement of raw materials (1) on a timely basis, (2) at lowest possible cost, (3) at acceptable levels of quality
- Procedures for procurement of plant, machinery, and buildings
- Development of criteria for lease-versus-purchase decisions
- Good, long-term relationships with reliable suppliers

Primary Activities

Inbound Logistics	Operations	Outbound Logistics	Marketing and Sales	Service
■ Soundness of material and inventory control systems ■ Efficiency of raw material warehousing activities	■ Productivity of equipment compared to that of key competitors ■ Appropriate automation of production processes ■ Effectiveness of production control systems to improve quality and reduce costs ■ Efficiency of plant layout and work-flow design	■ Timeliness and efficiency of delivery of finished goods and services ■ Efficiency of finished goods warehousing activities	■ Effectiveness of market research to identify customer segments and needs ■ Innovation in sales promotion and advertising ■ Evaluation of alternate distribution channels ■ Motivation and competence of sales force ■ Development of an image of quality and a favorable reputation ■ Extent of brand loyalty among customers ■ Extent of market dominance within the market segment or overall market	■ Means to solicit customer input for product improvements ■ Promptness of attention to customer complaints ■ Appropriateness of warranty and guarantee policies ■ Quality of customer education and training ■ Ability to provide replacement parts and repair services

Profit Margin

Source: Based on Michael Porter, *On Competition*, 1998, Harvard Business School Press.

Second, the nature of value chains and the relative importance of the activities within them vary by industry. Lodging firms like Marriott have major costs and concerns that involve operational activities—it provides its service instantaneously at each location—and marketing activities, while having minimal concern for outbound logistics. Yet for a distributor, such as the food distributor PYA, inbound and outbound logistics are the most critical area. Major retailers like Walmart have built value advantages focusing on purchasing and inbound logistics, while the most successful personal computer companies have built via sales, outbound logistics, and service through the mail-order process.

Third, the relative importance of value activities can vary by a company's position in a broader value system that includes the value chains of its upstream suppliers and downstream customers or partners involved in providing products or services to end users. A producer of roofing shingles depends heavily on the downstream activities of wholesale distributors and building supply retailers to reach roofing contractors and do-it-yourselfers. Maytag manufactures its own appliances, sells them through independent distributors, and provides warranty service to the buyer. Sears outsources the manufacture of its appliances while it promotes its brand name—Kenmore—and handles all sales and service.

As these examples suggest, it is important that managers take into account their level of vertical integration when comparing their cost structure for activities on their value chain to those of key competitors. Comparing a fully integrated rival with a partially integrated one requires adjusting for the scope of activities performed to achieve meaningful comparison. It also suggests the need for examining costs associated with activities provided by upstream or downstream companies; these activities ultimately determine comparable, final costs to end users. Said another way, one company's comparative cost disadvantage (or advantage) may emanate more from activities undertaken by upstream or downstream "partners" than from activities under the direct control of that company—therefore suggesting less of a relative advantage or disadvantage within the company's direct value chain.

COMPETITIVE ADVANTAGE VIA CUSTOMER VALUE: THREE CIRCLES ANALYSIS

There is considerable appeal and anecdotal evidence that a company must build a distinct value chain–based competitive advantage to grow and be profitable over the long term. However, in using the value chain approach just described or the resource-based approach (described in the next section), it can remain difficult for many strategists to clearly articulate what their company's competitive advantage is and how it differs from those of competitors while in the midst of strategic analysis activities. University of Notre Dame Professors Joel Urbany and James Davis have developed a clever, useful, and simple tool to help in this analysis that can also complement and help articulate the findings from a value chain analysis or the resource-based view.[5] In this section, we use their ideas and examples to describe their "three circle analysis."

three circles analysis
An internal analysis technique wherein strategists examine customers' needs, company offerings, and competitor's offerings to more clearly articulate what their company's competitive advantage is and how it differs from those of competitors.

To begin the **three circles analysis,** the strategizing team of executives should begin their analysis by thinking deeply about what customers of their type of product or service value and why. For example, they might value speedy service because they want to minimize inventory costs with a just-in-time inventory system. Looking at findings from the value chain analysis, or from a resource-based view of the firm, but through the eyes of their key target customers, is a simple but often overlooked perspective from which to evaluate core competencies. It is a central part of this technique and logically hits the core of the reason for the firm's existence in the first place.

[5] Joel E. Urbany and James H. Davis, "Strategic Insight in Three Circles," *Harvard Business Review* 85, no. 11 (2007), pp. 28–30.

EXHIBIT 6.7
Three Circles Analysis

Source: Reprinted by permission of *Harvard Business Review,* Exhibit from "Strategic Insight in Three Circles," by Joel E. Urbany and James H. Davis, November 2007.

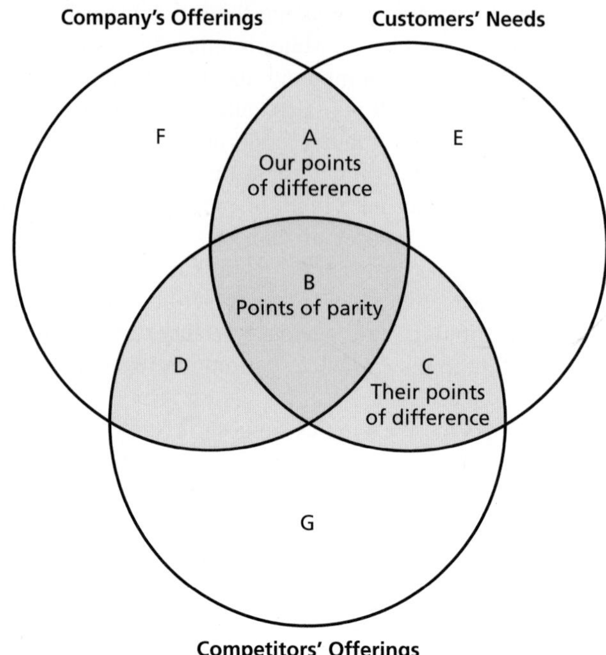

Next, the strategists should draw three circles as shown in Exhibit 6.7. The first circle (seen on the top right) is to represent the team's consensus of what the most important customers or customer segments need or want from the product or service.

Urbany and Davis observe that even in very mature industries, customers do not articulate all their wants in conversations with companies. For example, there was no consumer demand on Procter & Gamble to invent the Swiffer, whose category contributes significantly to the company's recent double-digit sales growth in home care products. Instead, the Swiffer emerged from P&G's careful observation of the challenges of household cleaning. Therefore, in conducting this initial phase of competitive advantage analysis, the consumers' unexpressed needs can often become growth opportunities.

The second circle represents the team's view of how customers perceive the company's offerings (seen on the top left). The extent to which the two circles overlap indicates how well the company's offerings are fulfilling customers' needs.

The third circle represents the strategists' view of how customers perceive the offerings of the company's competitors.

Each area within the circles is important, but areas A, B, and C are critical to identifying and building a real value-based competitive advantage. The planning team should ask questions about each:

- *Circle A:* How big and sustainable are our advantages? Are they based on distinctive capabilities?
- *Circle B:* Are we delivering effectively in the area of parity?
- *Circle C:* How can we counter our competitors' advantages?

As Urbany and Davis explain, the team should form hypotheses about the company's competitive advantages and test them by asking customers. The process can yield surprising insights, such as how much opportunity for growth exists in the white space (E). Another insight might be what value the company or its competitors create that customers do not need (D, F, or G). For example, Zeneca Ag Products discovered that one of its most important distributors would be willing to do more business with the firm only if Zeneca eliminated the time-consuming promotional programs that its managers thought were an essential part of their value proposition.

But the biggest surprise is often that area A, envisioned as huge by the company, turns out to be quite small in the eyes of the customer. One important contribution that the next internal analysis technique, the resource-based view of the firm, can make in this regard is to help provide an in-depth method to more thoroughly identify and examine a firm's existing or potential competitive advantages. Let's examine the resource-based view.

RESOURCE-BASED VIEW OF THE FIRM

Toyota versus Ford is a competitive situation virtually all of us recognize. Stock analysts for the last two decades have concluded that Toyota was the clear leader. They often cited Toyota's superiority in tangible assets (newer factories worldwide, R&D facilities, computerization, cash, etc.) and intangible assets (reputation, brand name awareness, quality-control culture, global business system, etc.). They also felt that Toyota led Ford in several capabilities that made use of those assets effectively—managing distribution globally, influencing labor and supplier relations, managing franchise relations, marketing savvy, and speed of decision making to take quick advantage of changing global conditions are just a few that are frequently mentioned. The combination of capabilities and assets, most analysts concluded, created several competencies that gave Toyota key competitive advantages over Ford that were durable and not easily imitated.

In the last decade, Ford has begun to reverse that view. Capitalizing on an accelerator-sticking series of incidents that uncovered surprising quality-control problems attributed to Toyota's rapid global expansion, Ford found a "glitch" in the Toyota resource base that was a major deficiency. Then Toyota compounded the impact on its quality reputation with its initially poor handling of the PR aspects and response worldwide. That massive series of recalls stymied Toyota for some time, which was happening as the worldwide recession of recent years unfolded, again weakening Toyota's financial strength and Ford's. Fortunately for Ford, that period of time called for a massive turnaround strategy, which saw Ford eliminate outdated production facilities, reduce a bloated organization, sell off or shut down unproductive product lines, and concentrate on identifying several new product offerings that were carefully and methodically conceived, designed, and built to meet valid market concerns about quality, innovative electronics, appearance, and fuel efficiency. The result saw Ford come out of the recession a dramatically changed company, with new tangible assets (manufacturing facilities, improved R&D coordination, financial strength, smaller and stronger dealer networks) and some key, improved intangible assets (reputation, market-driven focus, brand leadership in midrange sedans). Ford executives managed these new assets with considerable skill, taking quick advantage of globally changing conditions to leverage them into a dramatic improvement in Ford's position relative to Toyota by 2012.

resource-based view
A method of analyzing and identifying a firm's strategic advantages based on examining its distinct combination of assets, skills, capabilities, and intangibles as an organization.

The Toyota–Ford situation provides a useful illustration for understanding several concepts central to the **resource-based view** (RBV) of the firm. The RBV is a method of analyzing and identifying a firm's strategic advantages based on examining its distinct combination of assets, skills, capabilities, and intangibles as an organization. The RBV's underlying premise is that firms differ in fundamental ways because each firm possesses a unique "bundle" of resources—tangible and intangible assets and organizational capabilities to make use of those assets. Each firm develops competencies from these resources, and, when developed especially well, these become the source of the firm's competitive advantages. Toyota's decision to enter global markets locally and regularly invest in or build newer factory locations in those global markets gave Toyota a competitive advantage, which it leveraged against Ford and others for over 25 years into the last decade to rise to become the top global car company. Now, after an extended passage of time accompanied by a deterioration in some of Toyota's historical distinctive competencies, Ford was able to build selective resources and capabilities, while it literally sought to survive, in a manner that has made those into several clear core distinctive competencies that may well be sustainable competitive advantages versus Toyota for many years to come.

Core Competencies

core competence
A capability or skill that a firm emphasizes and excels in doing while in pursuit of its overall mission.

Executives charting the strategy of their business have more recently concentrated their thinking on the notion of a "core competence." A **core competence** is a capability or skill that a firm emphasizes and excels in doing while in pursuit of its overall mission. Core competencies that differ from those found in competing firms would be considered *distinctive competencies*. Apple's competencies in pulling together available technologies and others' software and combining this with their own product design skills and new-product introduction prowess result in an innovation competence that is different and distinct from any firm against which Apple competes. Toyota's pervasive organizationwide pursuit of quality; Wendy's systemwide emphasis on and ability to provide fresh meat daily; and the University of Phoenix's ability to provide comprehensive educational options for working adults worldwide are all examples of competencies that are unique to these firms and distinctive when compared to their competitors.

tangible assets
The most easily identified assets, often found on a firm's balance sheet. They include production facilities, raw materials, financial resources, real estate, and computers.

Distinctive competencies that are identified and nurtured throughout the firm, allowing it to execute effectively so as to provide products or services to customers that are superior to competitor's offerings, become the basis for a lasting *competitive advantage*. Executives, enthusiastic about the notion that their job as strategists was to identify and leverage core competencies into distinctive ones that create sustainable competitive advantage, encountered difficulty applying the concept because of the generality of its level of analysis. The RBV emerged as a way to make the core competency notion and thought process more focused and measurable—creating a very important, and more meaningful, tool for internal analysis. Let's look at the basic concepts underlying the RBV.

intangible assets
A firm's assets that you cannot touch or see but that are very often critical in creating competitive advantage: brand names, company reputation, organizational morale, technical knowledge, patents and trademarks, and accumulated experience within an organization.

Three Basic Resources: Tangible Assets, Intangible Assets, and Organizational Capabilities

The RBV's ability to create a more focused, measurable approach to internal analysis starts with its delineation of three basic types of resources, some of which may become the building blocks for distinctive competencies. These resources are defined below and illustrated in Exhibit 6.8.

Tangible assets are the easiest "resources" to identify and are often found on a firm's balance sheet. They include production facilities, raw materials, financial resources, real estate, and computers. Tangible assets are the physical and financial means a company uses to provide value to its customers.

organizational capabilities
Skills (the ability and ways of combining assets, people, and processes) that a company uses to transform inputs into outputs.

Intangible assets are "resources" such as brand names, company reputation, organizational morale, technical knowledge, patents and trademarks, and accumulated experience within an organization. While they are not assets that you can touch or see, they are very often critical in creating competitive advantage.

Organizational capabilities are not specific "inputs" like tangible or intangible assets; rather, they are the skills—the ability and ways of combining assets, people, and processes—that a company uses to transform inputs into outputs. Apple pioneered and has subsequently

EXHIBIT 6.8
Examples of Different "Resources"

Source: From R.M. Grant, *Contemporary Strategy Analysis,* Blackwell Publishing, 2001, p. 140. Reprinted with permission of John Wiley & Sons, Ltd.

Tangible Assets	Intangible Assets	Organizational Capabilities
Hampton Inn's reservation system	Budweiser's brand name	Travelocity's customer service P&G's management training program
Apple's cash reserves	Apple's reputation	Walmart's purchasing and inbound logistics
Georgia Pacific's landholdings	Nike's advertising with LeBron James	Google's product-development processes
FedEx's plane fleet	Brain Williams as NBC's *Evening News* anchor	Coke's global distribution coordination
Coca-Cola's Coke formula	eBay's management team Google's culture	3M's innovation process

Classifying and Assessing the Firm's Resources

Resource	Relevant Characteristics	Key Indicators
Tangible Resources		
Financial resources	The firm's borrowing capacity and its internal funds generation determine its resilience and capacity for investment.	• Debt/equity ratio • Operating cash flow/free cash flow • Credit rating
Physical resources	Physical resources constrain the firm's set of production possibilities and impact its cost position. Key characteristics include • The size, location, technical sophistication, and flexibility of plant and equipment • Location and alternative uses for land and buildings • Reserves of raw materials	• Market values of fixed assets • Vintage of capital equipment • Scale of plants • Flexibility of fixed assets
Intangible Resources		
Technological resources	Intellectual property: patent portfolio, copyright, trade secrets Resources for innovation: research facilities, technical and scientific employees	• Number and significance of patents • Revenue from licensing patents and copyrights • R&D staff as a percent of total employment • Number and location of research facilities
Reputation	Reputation with customers through the ownership of brands and trademarks; established relationships with customers; the reputation of the firm's products and services for quality and reliability. The reputation of the company with suppliers (including component suppliers, banks and financiers, employees and potential employees), with government and government agencies, and with the community.	• Brand recognition • Brand equity • Percent of repeat buying • Objective measures of comparative product performance (e.g., Consumers' Association ratings, J. D. Power ratings) • Surveys of corporate reputation (e.g., *BusinessWeek*)

leveraged its iPod, iTunes, iPhone, iPad, and AppStore successes into major leadership positions in digitalized music, entertainment, and communication on a global basis for individual consumers. Microsoft and others have attempted to copy Apple, but remain far behind Apple's diverse organizational capabilities. Apple has subsequently refined or revolutionized these devices and services to automate and individually customize a whole new level of communication and entertainment capability that combines assets, people, and processes throughout and beyond the Apple organization. Finely developed capabilities, such as Apple's Internet-based, customer-friendly iTunes and AppStore systems, can be a source of sustained competitive advantage. They enable a firm to take the same input factors as rivals (such as Microsoft, HP, Google, or Dell) and convert them into products and services, either with greater efficiency in the process or greater quality in the output, or both.

What Makes a Resource Valuable?

Once managers identify their firm's tangible assets, intangible assets, and organizational capabilities, the RBV applies a set of guidelines to determine which of those resources represent strengths or weaknesses—which resources generate core competencies that are sources of sustained competitive advantage. These RBV guidelines derive from the idea that resources are more valuable when they

1. Are *critical to* being able to *meet a customer's need* better than other alternatives.
2. Are *scarce*—few others if any possess that resource or skill to the degree you do.
3. *Drive* a key portion of overall *profits,* in a manner controlled by your firm.
4. Are *durable* or sustainable over time.

Before proceeding to explain each basis for making resources valuable, we suggest that you keep in mind a simple, useful idea: Resources are most valuable when they meet all four of these guidelines. We return to this point after we explain each guideline more thoroughly.

RBV Guideline 1: Is the resource or skill critical to fulfilling a customer's need better than that of the firm's competitors?

Two restaurants offer similar food, at similar prices, but one has a location much more convenient to downtown offices than the other. The tangible asset, location, helps fulfill daytime workers' lunch-eating needs better than its competitor, resulting in greater profitability and sales volume for the conveniently located restaurant. Walmart redefined discount retailing and outperformed the industry in profitability by 4.5 percent of sales—a 200 percent improvement. Four resources—store locations, brand recognition, employee loyalty, and sophisticated inbound logistics—allowed Walmart to fulfill customer needs much better and more cost effectively than Kmart and other discount retailers. In both of these examples, *it is important to recognize that only resources that contributed to competitive superiority were valuable.* At the same time, other resources such as the restaurant's menu and specific products or parking space at Walmart were essential to doing business but contributed little to competitive advantage because they did not help fulfill customer needs better than those of the firm's key competitors.

RBV Guideline 2: Is the resource scarce? Is it in short supply or not easily substituted for or imitated?

Short Supply When a resource is scarce, it is more valuable. When a firm possesses a resource and few if any others do, and it is central to fulfilling customers' needs, then it can become the basis of a competitive advantage for the firm. Literal physical scarcity is perhaps the most obvious way a resource might meet this guideline. Very limited natural resources, a unique location, skills that are truly rare—all represent obvious types of scarce resource situations.

Availability of Substitutes We discussed the threat of substitute products in Chapter 4 as part of the five forces model for examining industry profitability. This basic idea can be taken further and used to gauge the scarcity-based value of particular resources. Whole Foods has been an exciting growth company for several years, focused exclusively on selling wholesome, organic food. The basic idea was to offer food grown organically, without pesticides or manipulation, in a convenient grocery atmosphere. Investors were excited about this concept because of the processed, nonorganic foods offered by virtually every existing grocery chain. Unfortunately for their more recent investors, substitutes for Whole Foods's offerings are becoming easily available from several grocery chains and regional organic chains. Publix, Harris-Teeter, and even Walmart are easily adapting their grocery operations to offer organic fare. With little change to their existing facilities and operational resources, these companies are quickly creating alternatives to Whole Foods's offerings if not offering some of the same items, cheaper. So some worry about the long-term impact on Whole Foods. Investors have seen the value of their Whole Foods's stock decline as substitute resources and capabilities are readily created by existing and new entrants into the organic grocery sectors.

Imitation A resource that competitors can readily copy can only generate temporary value. It is "scarce" for only a short time. It cannot generate a long-term competitive advantage. When Wendy's first emerged, it was the only major hamburger chain with a drive-through window. This unique organizational capability was part of a "bundle" of resources that allowed Wendy's to provide unique value to its target customers: young adults seeking convenient food service. But once this resource, or organizational capability, proved valuable to fast-food customers, every fast-food chain copied the feature. Then Wendy's continued success was built on other resources that generated other distinctive competencies.

The scarcity that comes with an absence of imitation seldom lasts forever, as the Wendy's example illustrates. Competitors will match or better any resource as soon as they can. It should be obvious, then, that the firm's ability to forestall this eventuality is very important. So how does a firm create resource scarcity by making resources hard to imitate? The RBV identifies four characteristics, called **isolating mechanisms,** that make resources difficult to imitate:

isolating mechanisms
Characteristics that make resources difficult to imitate. In the RBV context these are physically unique resources, path-dependent resources, causal ambiguity, and economic deterrence.

- *Physically unique resources* are virtually impossible to imitate. A one-of-a-kind real estate location, mineral rights, and patents are examples of resources that cannot be imitated. Disney's Mickey Mouse copyright or Winter Park, Colorado's Aspen resort possess physical uniqueness. While many strategists claim that resources are physically unique, this is seldom true. Rather, other characteristics are typically what make most resources difficult to imitate.
- *"Path-dependent" resources* are very difficult to imitate because of the difficult "path" another firm must follow to create the resource. These are resources that cannot be instantaneously acquired but rather must be created over time in a manner that is frequently very expensive and always difficult to accelerate. Google's creation of proprietary search algorithms; interlocking and directly targeted online advertising; very easy to use, and also interwined, e-mail services; and an extraordinary environment to attract and retain the world's top talent have combined to create a combination of path-dependent resources that are very difficult for even the wealthiest software and Internet companies worldwide to easily emulate, acquire, or accelerate. It will take years for any competitor to develop the expertise, infrastructure, reputation, and capabilities to compete effectively with Google. Coca-Cola's brand name, Gerber Baby Food's reputation for quality, and Steinway's expertise in piano manufacture would take competitors many years and millions of dollars to match. Consumers' many years of experience drinking Coke or using Gerber or playing a Steinway would also need to be matched.

EXHIBIT 6.9
Degree to Which Resource Can Be Imitated

Source: © RCTrust LLC, 2010.

	Easily Imitated	Possibly Imitated	Hard to Imitate	Cannot be Imitated
Examples	Utilities	Skilled employees	Image/reputation	Unique location
	Cash	Additional capacity	Customer satisfaction	Patents
	Common raw materials	Economies of scale	Employee attitudes	Unique licenses/assets
Specific example: Google	Electricity Server farms	Smart people Larger server farms	Search leadership Brand image	Patented search algorithms "Google"

- *Causal ambiguity* is a third way resources can be very difficult to imitate. This refers to situations in which it is difficult for competitors to understand exactly how a firm has created the advantage it enjoys. Competitors can't figure out exactly what the uniquely valuable resource is or how resources are combined to create the competitive advantage. Causally ambiguous resources are often organizational capabilities that arise from subtle combinations of tangible and intangible assets and culture, processes, and organizational attributes the firm possesses. Southwest Airlines has regularly faced competition from major and regional airlines, with some like United and Continental eschewing their traditional approach and attempting to compete by using their own version of the Southwest approach—same planes, routes, gate procedures, number of attendants, and so on. They have yet to succeed. The most difficult thing to replicate is Southwest's "personality," or culture of fun, family, and frugal yet focused services and attitude. Just how that works is hard for United and Continental to figure out.
- *Economic deterrence* is a fourth source of inimitability. This usually involves large capital investments in capacity to provide products or services in a given market that are scale sensitive. It occurs when a competitor understands the resources that provide a competitive advantage and may even have the capacity to imitate, but chooses not to because of the limited market size that realistically would not support two players the size of the first mover.

While we may be inclined to think of the ability to imitate a resource as a yes-or-no situation, imitation is more accurately measured on a continuum that reflects difficulty and time. Exhibit 6.9 illustrates such a continuum. Some resources may have multiple imitation deterrents. For example, 3M's reputation for innovativeness may involve path dependencies and causal ambiguity.

RBV Guideline 3: Appropriability: Who actually gets the profit created by a resource?

Warren Buffett is known worldwide as one of the most successful investors of the last 25 years. One of his legendary investments was the Walt Disney Company, which he once said he liked "because the Mouse does not have an agent."[6] What he was really saying was that Disney owned the Mickey Mouse copyright, and all profits from that valuable resource went directly to Disney. Other competitors in the "entertainment" industry generated similar profits from their competing offerings, for example, movies, but they often "captured" substantially less of those profits because of the amounts that had to be paid to well-known actors or directors or other entertainment contributors seen as the real creators of the movie's value.

Disney's eventual acquisition of Pixar illustrates just the opposite situation for the home of the Mouse. Pixar's expertise in digital animation had proven key to the impressive success of several major animation films released by Disney in the past several years. While

[6] *The Harbus,* March 25, 1996, p. 12.

Disney apparently thought its name and distribution clout justified its sizable share of the profits this five-year joint venture generated, Steve Jobs and his Pixar team felt otherwise. Pixar's assessment was that their capabilities were key drivers of the huge profits by *Ants* and *Finding Nemo*, leading them not to renew their Disney partnership. Pixar's unmatched digitalization animation expertise quickly "appropriated" the profits generated by this key competitive advantage, and Disney Studios struggled to catch up. Disney eventually solved the dilemma by acquiring Pixar at a handsome premium. The movie *Cars* soon followed.[7]

Sports teams, investment services, and consulting businesses are other examples of companies that generate sizable profits based on resources (e.g., key people, skills, contacts) that are not inextricably linked to the company and therefore do not allow the company to easily capture the profits. Superstar sports players can move from one team to another or command excessively high salaries, and this circumstance could arise in other personal services business situations. It could also occur when one firm joint ventures with another, sharing resources and capabilities and the profits that result. Sometimes restaurants or lodging facilities that are franchisees of a national organization are frustrated by the fees they pay the franchisor each month and decide to leave the organization and go "independent." They often find, to their dismay, that the business declines significantly. The value of the franchise name, reservation system, and brand recognition is critical in generating the profits of the business.

RBV Guideline 4: Durability: How rapidly will the resource depreciate?

The slower a resource depreciates, the more valuable it is. Tangible assets, such as commodities or capital, can have their depletion measured. Intangible resources, such as brand names or organizational capabilities, present a much more difficult depreciation challenge. The Coca-Cola brand has continued to appreciate, whereas technical know-how in various computer technologies depreciates rapidly. In the increasingly hypercompetitive global economy of the twenty-first century, distinctive competencies and competitive advantages can fade quickly, making the notion of durability a critical test of the value of key resources and capabilities. Some believe that this reality makes well-articulated visions and associated cultures within organizations potentially the most important contributor to long-term survival.[8]

Using the Resource-Based View in Internal Analysis

To use the RBV in internal analysis, a firm must first identify and evaluate its resources to find those that provide the basis for future competitive advantage. This process involves defining the various resources the firm possesses and examining them based on the preceding discussion to gauge which resources truly have strategic value. It is usually helpful in this undertaking to

- *Disaggregate resources*—break them down into more specific competencies—rather than stay with broad categorizations. Saying that Domino's Pizza has better marketing skills than Pizza Hut conveys little information. But dividing that into subcategories such as advertising that, in turn, can be divided into national advertising, local promotions, and coupons allows for a more measurable assessment. Exhibit 6.10 provides a useful illustration of this at the United Kingdom's largest full-service restaurant operator—Whitbread's Restaurant.
- *Utilize a functional perspective.* Looking at different functional areas of the firm, disaggregating tangible and intangible assets as well as organizational capabilities that are present, can begin to uncover important value-building resources and activities that deserve

[7] "Disney Buys Pixar," *Money.CNN.com*, January 1, 2006.

[8] "The Power of One Person . . . And Your Corporate Culture," Scott McKain, January 19, 2011, http://mckainviewpoint.com/2011/01/the-power-of-one-person-and-your-corporate-culture/

EXHIBIT 6.10
Disaggregating Whitbread Restaurant's Customer Service Resource

Source: Andrew Campbell and Kathleen Sommers-Luchs, *Core Competency-Based Strategy* (London: International Thomson, 1997).

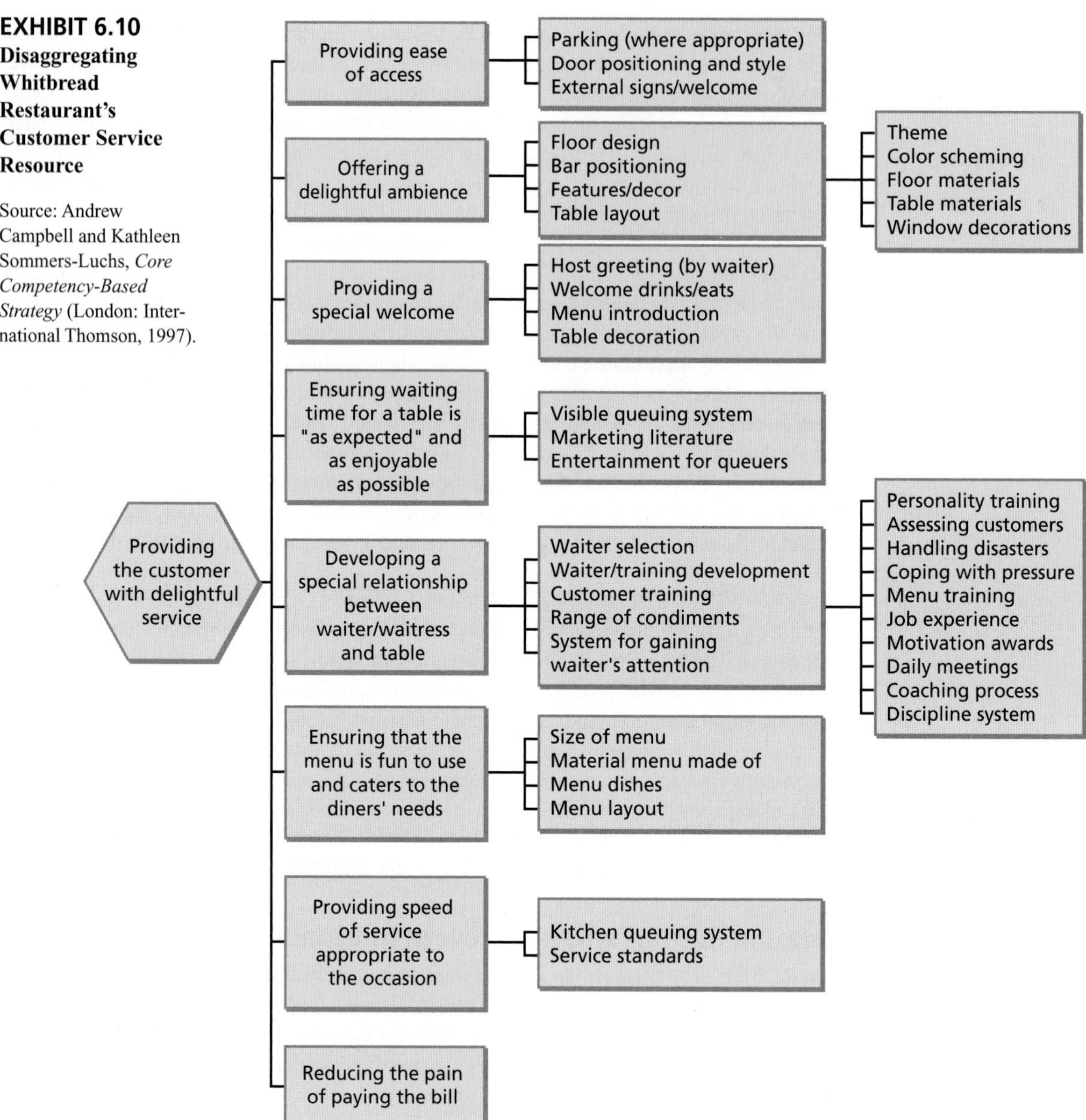

further analysis. Appendix 6A lists a variety of functional area resources and activities that deserve consideration.

- *Look at organizational processes* and combinations of resources and not only at isolated assets or capabilities. While disaggregation is critical, you must also take a creative, gestalt look at what competencies the firm possesses or has the potential to possess that might generate competitive advantage.
- *Use the value chain approach* to uncover organizational capabilities, activities, and processes that are valuable potential sources of competitive advantage.

Once the resources are identified, managers apply the four RBV guidelines for uncovering "valuable" resources. The objective for managers at this point is to identify resources and capabilities that are valuable for most if not all of the reasons our guidelines suggest a resource can be valuable.

If a resource creates the ability to meet a unique customer need, it has value. But if it is not scarce, or if it is easily imitated, it would be unwise to build a firm's strategy on that resource or capability unless that strategy included plans to build scarcity or inimitability into it. If a resource provided the basis for meeting a unique need, was scarce, was not easily imitated, and was easily sustainable over time, managers would be attracted to build a strategy on it more than likely. Our example of Pixar's relationship with Disney earlier in this chapter would seem to suggest this was Pixar's position early in its joint venture with Disney. Yet even with all of those sources confirming a very high value in its digital animation expertise and intellectual property resources, Pixar was not "appropriating" the share of the animation movie profits that were attributable to those resources. Pixar was fortunate: It had the choice not to renew its five-year contract with Disney, and so it did. That eventually led Disney to pay a premium price to acquire Pixar, to regain the strategic value of Pixar's unique resources.

The key point here is that applying RBV analysis should focus on identifying resources that contain all sources of value identified in our four guidelines. Consider the diagram in Exhibit 6.11. Each circle in that diagram represents one way resources have value. The area where all circles intersect or overlap would represent resources that derive value in all four ways. Such resources are the ones managers applying the RBV should seek to identify. They are powerful sources around which to build competitive advantage and craft successful strategies. And resources that possess some but not all sources of value become points of emphasis by a management team able to identify ways to build the missing source of value into that resource over time much like Pixar did in its relationship with Disney.

EXHIBIT 6.11
Applying the Resource-Based View to Identify the Best Sources of Competitive Advantage

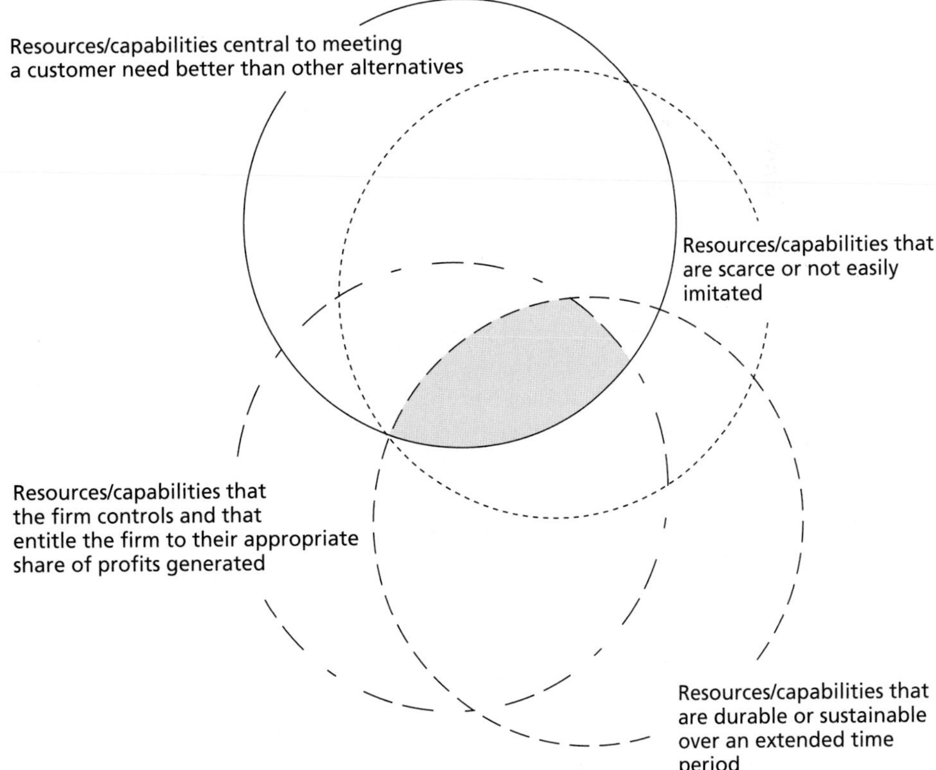

By using RBV, value chain analysis, three circles analysis, and SWOT analysis, firms are virtually certain to improve the quality of internal analysis undertaken to help craft a company's competitive strategy. Central to the success of each technique is the strategists' ability to make meaningful comparisons. The next section examines how meaningful comparisons can be made.

INTERNAL ANALYSIS: MAKING MEANINGFUL COMPARISONS

Managers need objective standards to use when examining internal resources and value-building activities. Whether applying the SWOT approach, VCA, or the RBV, strategists rely on three basic perspectives to evaluate how their firms stack up on internal capabilities. These three perspectives are discussed in this section.

Comparison with Past Performance

Strategists use the firm's historical experience as a basis for evaluating internal factors. Managers are most familiar with the internal capabilities and problems of their firms because they have been immersed in the financial, marketing, production, and R&D activities. Not surprisingly, a manager's assessment of whether a certain internal factor—such as production facilities, sales organization, financial capacity, control systems, or key personnel—is a strength or a weakness will be strongly influenced by his or her experience in connection with that factor. In the capital-intensive package delivery industry, for example, operating margin is a strategic internal factor affecting a firm's flexibility to add capacity. A few years ago, UPS managers viewed its declining operating margins (down from 12 percent to 9 percent by mid-decade) as a troubling weakness, limiting their flexibility to aggressively continue to expand their overnight air fleet. FedEx managers viewed a similar operating margin around the same time as a growing strength because it was a steady improvement and almost double its 5 percent level five years earlier.

Although historical experience can provide a relevant evaluation framework, strategists must avoid tunnel vision in making use of it. NEC, Japan's HP, initially dominated Japan's PC market with a 70 percent market share by using a proprietary hardware system, much higher screen resolution, powerful distribution channels, and a large software library from third-party vendors. Far from worried, Hajime Ikeda, manager of NEC's planning division at the time, was quoted as saying, "We don't hear complaints from our users." Soon, IBM, Apple, and HP filled the shelves in Japan's famous consumer electronics district, Akihabara. Hiroki Kamata, president of a Japanese computer research firm, reported that Japan's PC market, worth more than $50 billion, saw Apple, Dell, IBM, and HP with more market share than NEC because of better technology, software, and the restrictions created by NEC's proprietary technology. As NEC learned, using only historical experience as a basis for identifying strengths and weaknesses can prove dangerously inaccurate.

Benchmarking: Comparison with Competitors

A major focus in determining a firm's resources and competencies is comparison with existing (and potential) competitors. Firms in the same industry often have different marketing skills, financial resources, operating facilities and locations, technical know-how, brand images, levels of integration, managerial talent, and so on. These different internal resources can become relative strengths (or weaknesses) depending on the strategy a firm chooses. In choosing a strategy, managers should compare the firm's key internal capabilities with those of its rivals, thereby isolating its key strengths and weaknesses.

Global Strategy in Action

Exhibit 6.12

Social Couponing Instant Deal Players—2011

	LivingSocial	Groupon	Facebook	Google
Company Founded in . . .	2007	2008	2011	2011
Revenue est. for 2011	$50M per month	$100M per month	$200M per month	$3Bn per month
Est. 2011 Market Value	$3Bn	$6–$15Bn	$80Bn	$200Bn
Co. Takes Part of Deal?	YES	YES, plus revenue from unused purchases	YES, but not from check-in deals	YES
Retailer's Cut—2011	60%	50%	Undecided	Undecided
Membership Base	30M+	80M+	600M+ potentially	100–200M+ potentially
Advertising?	Web and E-mail	Web and E-mail	Facebook Newsfeed Deals Page Sponsored Units Notifications	Web and E-mail, Ad Networks, & Google Reader
Markets?	200+ Worldwide	575+ Worldwide	5 (in 2011) Atlanta, Austin, Dallas, San Diego, & San Francisco	6 (in 2011) Beta in NYC, San Francisco, Oakland, Portland
Minimum Purchase Req'd	NO . . . Deal becomes free if 2 friends buy it	YES!	NO	NO
Apps Available?	iPhone	iPhone, Android, and Blackberry	To be determined	To be determined
Competitive Advantages?	Established "Deal" Brand	Brand Loyalty First-Mover Advantage	Complete Integration with Facebook	Integration w/ All Google Services; Resources; Brand Recognition
Bottom line in 2011	LivingSocial is adjusting to the competition by varying offerings; it estimates surpassing Groupon's revenue by 2012	Competition is heating up; Groupon staying w/ original business model; will aggressive plans be enough to keep Groupon on top?	Facebook's potential reach is limitless, & if their consumers prove that they want good deals to share w/in a social circle, Facebook will be THE FORCE to be reckoned with.	The reach of Google is mighty, though with no truly innovative features, IT LOOKS LIKE GOOGLE has its ROAD CUT OUT for them in this very competitive daily deal market.

Source: From http://www.onlinemba.com

Exhibit 6.12, Global Strategy in Action above shows how some managers might have benchmarked the social couponing daily deals industry in 2011 with LivingSocial and Groupon as active participants and Facebook as well as Google beta testing likely entries into the industry. See if you find the comparison an accurate predictor of what is happening today—the prediction being Facebook would eventually dominate.

In the global tech-services industry, New York–based IBM and India–based Tata Consultancy Services are major rivals. Tata has focused on large American and European companies providing lower-cost information technology (IT) services and business process simplification consulting. IBM has taken a different strategy, focusing in on helping U.S. clients cut costs while helping emerging market customers build out their technology infrastructure. Tata's strength has become its ability to offer low-cost outsourcing options to large U.S. and European firms for their information system operation needs. IBM, with a personnel cost structure that would put it at a disadvantage versus Tata in this regard, has emphasized systems design and optimization of the latest technology infrastructure to make that system perform well—building on its technical skills and computer technology expertise where it maintains a relative strength. Interestingly, this has led to a situation where Tata generates half of its revenue from U.S. clients, while IBM generates 65 percent of its revenue overseas and is the largest seller of tech services in India. Managers in both Tata and IBM have built successful strategies, yet those strategies are fundamentally different. Benchmarking each other, they have identified ways to build on relative strengths while avoiding dependence on capabilities at which the other firm excels.[9]

benchmarking
Evaluating the sustainability of advantages against key competitors. Comparing the way a company performs a specific activity with a competitor or other company doing the same thing.

Benchmarking, or comparing the way "our" company performs a specific activity with a competitor or other company doing the same thing, has become a central concern of managers in quality commitment companies worldwide. Particularly as the value chain framework has taken hold in structuring internal analysis, managers seek to systematically benchmark the costs and results of the smallest value activities against relevant competitors or other useful standards because it has proven to be an effective way to continuously improve that activity.

Exhibit 6.13 shows Kodak highlighting a value chain activity in which it believes it excels, low-cost/high-quality inks, and using it to differentiate its recently introduced printer. Kodak is seeking to not only highlight its internal managerial benchmarking versus other ink-jet printer makers, notably Hewlett-Packard, but it is also taking a page out of benchmarking to touch a long-held raw nerve they believe millions of customers share—the shock and awe they feel every time they go to a store and buy a new printer cartridge for their HP, Canon, or Epson printer. They want to identify with and inform the average consumer looking for a credible alternative when "benchmarking" different solutions to their printer needs.

The ultimate objective in benchmarking is to identify the "best practices" in performing a value chain activity and to learn how lower costs, fewer defects, or other outcomes linked to excellence can be achieved. Companies committed to benchmarking attempt to isolate and identify where their costs or outcomes are out of line with what they identify as the best practices of competitors or other companies or organizations that undertake similar tasks. Once identified and studied, this allows managers to change what they do or how they do these activities to achieve the new best practices "benchmarks." General Electric sends managers to benchmark FedEx's customer service practices, seeking to compare and improve on its own practices within a diverse set of businesses none of which compete directly with FedEx. It earlier did the same thing with Motorola, leading it to embrace Motorola's Six Sigma program for quality control and continuous improvement.

Comparison with Success Factors in the Industry

Industry analysis (see Chapter 4) involves identifying the factors associated with successful participation in a given industry. As was true for the evaluation methods discussed earlier, the key determinants of success in an industry may be used to identify a firm's internal strengths and weaknesses. By scrutinizing industry competitors as well as customer needs, vertical industry structure, channels of distribution, costs, barriers to entry, availability of

[9] "The Future of Enterprise Software," http://blogs.amrresearch.com/enterprisesoftware/2008/05/ibm-vs-tata .html, July 27, 2010.

Strategy in Action

Exhibit 6.13

The Ink Wars: Kodak Takes Benchmarking Public versus Hewlett-Packard

Save more every time you refill your printer with ink.

$9.99 black MSRP $14.99 color MSRP

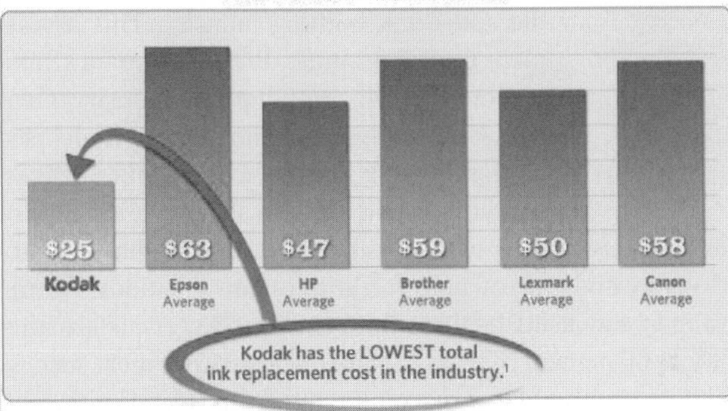

Ink Value Comparison Chart

Kodak's promise to you is that you'll save up to 50% on everything you print compared to similar consumer inkjet printers[10]. View the information below for details on ink yield, as verified by third party test and quality assurance professionals.

What you get for every $5 (USD) spent on ink[6]

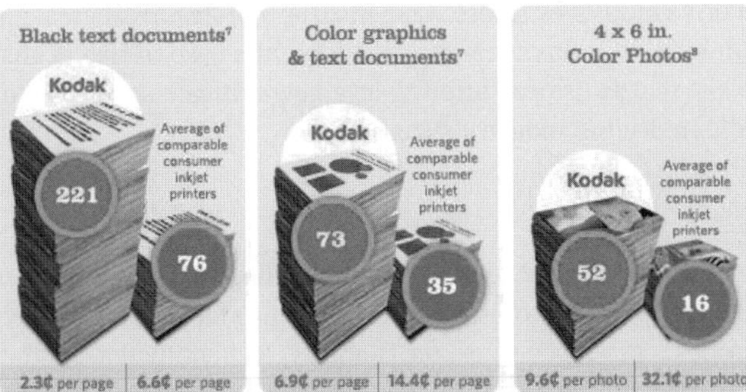

Look how much more you get a year for just $70.[5]

	Kodak	HP Average	Epson Average	Brother Average	Lexmark Average	Canon Average
photos & documents	1500	574	541	782	308	669

Select Printer Models Tested

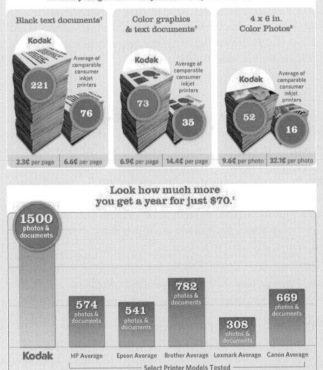

Kodak has long been a world leader in film processing, but it's a new player in the ink-jet printer industry, facing intense competition from entrenched players Hewlett-Packard, Epson, and Canon. Forgoing conventional wisdom based on the Gillette model to "give away" its printer and make money on consumables, the ink cartridges, Kodak seeks to differentiate itself and gain market share by tapping into consumer dissatisfaction with high ink prices by selling its printers for slightly more than the competition while selling its cartridges for less than half the price. Kodak is sharing its benchmarking results, suggesting its EasyShare printers have a lower total cost of ownership than competitors' models and that users will save substantially on consumables over the life of the printer.

Source: Reprinted with permission of Eastman Kodak Company.

substitutes, and suppliers, a strategist seeks to determine whether a firm's current internal capabilities represent strengths or weaknesses in new competitive arenas. The discussion in Chapter 4 provides a useful framework—five industry forces—against which to examine a firm's potential strengths and weaknesses. General Cinema Corporation, the largest

EXHIBIT 6.14
Illustration of the Product Life Cycle

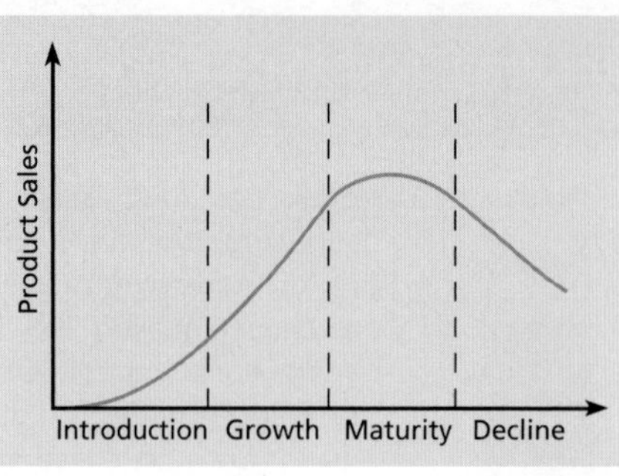

U.S. movie theater operator, determined that its internal skills in marketing, site analysis, creative financing, and management of geographically dispersed operations were key strengths relative to major success factors in the soft-drink bottling industry. This assessment proved accurate. Within 10 years after it entered the soft-drink bottling industry, General Cinema became the largest franchised bottler of soft drinks in the United States, handling Pepsi, 7UP, Dr Pepper, and Sunkist. Or consider large-scale discount retailing, where two key success factors in that industry are same-store sales growth and steady updating of store facilities or new locations. During the last decade, once-mighty Walmart saw itself begin to fall behind its key rivals in same-store sales growth and age/quality of 60 percent of its U.S. stores. These two critical success factors drive and indicate the relative health of large discount retail firms. Firms with solid same-store sales growth indicate wise choices in location, attractiveness of their stores, and the merchandise inside them. Likewise, aging and probably substandard store facilities are typically not as efficient as newer ones, nor are they as inviting to shoppers. So Walmart, Target, and other discount retailers conduct internal analyses in part by comparing themselves on these two (and surely others) critical success factors to interpret their strength or weakness relative to factors that drive industry success. And, in 2012, the steadily increasing impact of Amazon.com on traditional "big box" retailers is adding the ease of use of that traditional retailer's newer Web site–based "store" offering as a new critical success factor now monitored for its critical role in driving industry success.[10]

Product Life Cycle

product life cycle
A concept that describes a product's sales, profitability, and competencies that are key drivers of the success of that product as it moves through a sequence of stages from development, introduction to growth, maturity, decline, and eventual removal from a market.

Product life cycle (PLC) is one way to identify success factors against which executives can evaluate their firm's competencies relative to its key product or products. The **product life cycle** is a concept that describes a product's sales, profitability, and competencies that are key drivers of the success of that product as it moves through a sequence of stages from development, introduction to growth, maturity, decline, and eventual removal from a market. Exhibit 6.14 illustrates the "typical" product life cycle.

Core competencies associated with success are thought to vary across different stages of the product life cycle. Those competencies might include the following.

Introduction Stage

During this stage the firm needs competence in building product awareness and market development along with the resources to support initial losses:

- Ability to create product awareness.
- Good channel relationships in ways to get the product introduced quickly, gaining a first-mover advantage.
- Premium pricing to "skim" profitability if few competitors exist.
- Solid relationships with and access to trendsetting early adopters.
- Financial resources to absorb an initial cash drain and lack of profitability.

[10] "Walmart's Slump Persists," *The Wall Street Journal*, February 23, 2011, B3.

Growth

During this stage market growth accelerates rapidly, with the firm seeking to build brand awareness and establish/increase market share:

- Brand awareness and ability to build brand.
- Advertising skills and resources to back them.
- Product features that differentiate versus increased competitive offerings.
- Establishing and stabilizing market shares.
- Access to multiple distribution channels.
- Ability to add additional features.

Maturity

This stage sees growth in sales slow significantly, along with increased competition and similar product offerings leading the firm to need competencies that allow it to defend its market share while maximizing profit:

- Sustained brand awareness.
- Ability to differentiate products and features.
- Resources to initiate or sustain price wars.
- Operating advantages to improve slimming margins.
- Judgment to know whether to stay in or exit saturated market segments.

Decline

At this point the product and its competitors start to experience declining sales and increased pressure on margins. Competencies needed are:

- Ability to withstand intense price-cutting.
- Brand strength to allow reduced marketing.
- Cost cutting capacity and slack to allow it.
- Good supplier relationships to gain cost concessions.
- Innovation skills to create new products or "re-create" existing ones.

The PLC is an interesting concept or framework against which executives might gauge the strength of relevant competencies. Caution is necessary in its use beyond that purpose, however. In reality, very few products follow exactly the cycle portrayed in the PLC model. The length in each stage can vary, the length and nature of the PLC for any particular product can vary dramatically, and it is not easy to tell exactly what stage a product might be in at any given time. Not all products go through each stage. Some, for example, go from introduction to decline. And movement from one stage to the next can be accelerated by strategies or tactics executives emphasize. For example, price-cutting can accelerate the movement from maturity to decline.

Product life cycles can describe a single product, a category of products, or an industry segment. Applying the basic idea to an industry segment (category of products) rather than a specific product has been a more beneficial adaptation of the PLC concept, providing executives with a conceptual tool to aid them in strategic analysis and choice in the context of the evolution of an industry segment in which their firm competes. So we examine the concept of stages of evolution of an industry segment or category of products as a tool of strategic analysis and choice in Chapter 8.

Summary

This chapter looked at several ways managers achieve greater objectivity and rigor as they analyze their company's internal resources and capabilities. Managers often start their internal analysis with questions like, How well is the current strategy working? What is our current situation? What are our strengths and weaknesses? SWOT analysis is a traditional approach that has been in use for decades to help structure managers' pursuit of answers to these questions. A logical approach still used by many managers today, SWOT analysis has limitations linked to the depth of its analysis and the risk of overlooking key considerations.

Three techniques for internal analysis have emerged that overcome some of the limitations of SWOT analysis, offering more comprehensive approaches that can help managers identify and assess their firm's internal resources and capabilities in a more systematic, objective, and measurable manner. Value chain analysis has managers look at and disaggregate their business as a chain of activities that occur in a sequential manner to create the products or services they sell. The value chain approach breaks down the firm's activities into primary and support categories of activities, then breaks these down further into specific types of activities with the objective to disaggregate activity into as many meaningful subdivisions as possible. Once done, managers attempt to attribute costs to each. Doing this gives managers very distinct ways of isolating the things they do well and not so well, and it isolates activities that are truly key in meeting customer needs—true potential sources of competitive advantage. Three circles analysis provides an additional technique, simple yet insightful, for applying a customer needs perspective that should help improve the quality of a management team's internal analysis in understanding potential value-based sources of competitive advantage at the firm's disposal.

The third approach covered in this chapter was the resource-based view (RBV). RBV is based on the premise that firms build competitive advantage based on the unique resources, skills, and capabilities they control or develop, which can become the basis of unique, sustainable competitive advantages that allow them to craft successful competitive strategies. The RBV provides a useful conceptual frame to first inventory a firm's potential competitive advantages among its tangible assets, intangible assets, and its organizational capabilities. Once inventoried, the RBV provides four fundamental guidelines that managers can use to "value" these resources and capabilities. Those with major value, defined as ones that are valuable for several reasons, become the bases for building strategies linked to sustainable competitive advantages.

Finally, this chapter covered three ways objectivity and realism are enhanced when managers use meaningful standards for comparison regardless of the particular analytical framework they employ in internal analysis. This chapter is followed by two appendixes. The first provides a useful inventory of the types of activities in different functional areas of a firm that can be sources of competitive advantage. The second appendix covers traditional financial analysis to serve as a refresher and reminder about this basic internal analysis tool.

When matched with management's environmental analyses and mission priorities, the process of internal analysis provides the critical foundation for strategy formulation. Armed with an accurate, thorough, and timely internal analysis, managers are in a better position to formulate effective strategies. The next chapter describes basic strategy alternatives that any firm may consider.

Key Terms

benchmarking, *p. 174*
core competence, *p. 164*
intangible assets, *p. 164*
isolating mechanisms, *p. 167*
opportunity, *p. 150*
organizational capabilities, *p. 164*
primary activities, *p. 156*
product life cycle, *p. 176*
resource-based view, *p. 163*
strength, *p. 151*
SWOT analysis, *p. 149*
support activities, *p. 157*
tangible assets, *p. 164*
threat, *p. 151*
three circles analysis, *p. 161*
value chain, *p. 155*
value chain analysis, *p. 155*
weakness, *p. 151*

Questions for Discussion

1. Describe SWOT analysis as a way to guide internal analysis. How does this approach reflect the basic strategic management process?
2. What are potential weaknesses of SWOT analysis?
3. Describe the difference between primary and support activities using value chain analysis.
4. How is VCA different from SWOT analysis?
5. What is three circles analysis, and how might it help doing internal analysis?
6. What is the resource-based view? Give examples of three different types of resources.
7. What are three ways resources become more valuable? Provide an example of each.
8. Explain how you might use VCA, RBV, three circles analysis, and SWOT analysis to get a better sense of what might be a firm's key building blocks for a successful strategy.
9. Attempt to apply SWOT, VCA, RBV, and three circles analysis to yourself and your career aspirations. What are your major strengths and weaknesses? How might you use your knowledge of these strengths and weaknesses to develop your future career plans?

Chapter 6 Appendix A

Key Resources across Functional Areas

MARKETING

Firm's products-services: breadth of product line
Concentration of sales in a few products or to a few customers
Ability to gather needed information about markets
Market share or submarket shares
Product-service mix and expansion potential: life cycle of key products; profit-sales balance in product-service
Channels of distribution: number, coverage, and control
Effective sales organization: knowledge of customer needs
Internet usage; Web presence; e-commerce
Product-service image, reputation, and quality
Imaginativeness, efficiency, and effectiveness of sales promotion and advertising
Pricing strategy and pricing flexibility
Procedures for digesting market feedback and developing new products, services, or markets
After-sale service and follow-up
Goodwill—brand loyalty

FINANCIAL AND ACCOUNTING

Ability to raise short-term capital
Ability to raise long-term capital; debt-equity
Corporate-level resources (multibusiness firm)
Cost of capital relative to that of industry and competitors
Tax considerations
Relations with owners, investors, and stockholders
Leverage position; capacity to utilize alternative financial strategies, such as lease or sale and leaseback
Cost of entry and barriers to entry
Price-earnings ratio
Working capital; flexibility of capital structure
Effective cost control; ability to reduce cost
Financial size
Efficiency and effectiveness of accounting system for cost, budget, and profit planning

PRODUCTION, OPERATIONS, TECHNICAL

Raw materials' cost and availability, supplier relationships
Inventory control systems; inventory turnover
Location of facilities; layout and utilization of facilities
Economies of scale
Technical efficiency of facilities and utilization of capacity
Effectiveness of subcontracting use
Degree of vertical integration; value added and profit margin
Efficiency and cost-benefit of equipment
Effectiveness of operation control procedures: design, scheduling, purchasing, quality control, and efficiency
Costs and technological competencies relative to those of industry and competitors
Research and development—technology—innovation
Patents, trademarks, and similar legal protection

PERSONNEL

Management personnel
Employees' skill and morale
Labor relations costs compared with those of industry and competitors
Efficiency and effectiveness of personnel policies
Effectiveness of incentives used to motivate performance
Ability to level peaks and valleys of employment
Employee turnover and absenteeism
Specialized skills
Experience

QUALITY MANAGEMENT

Relationship with suppliers, customers
Internal practices to enhance quality of products and services
Procedures for monitoring quality

INFORMATION SYSTEMS

Timeliness and accuracy of information about sales, operations, cash, and suppliers
Relevance of information for tactical decisions
Information to manage quality issues: customer service
Ability of people to use the information that is provided
Linkages to suppliers and customers

INTERNET AND WIRELESS CAPABILITIES

Web site quality and functionality
Online sales and marketing
Customer connectivity
Use of social networking
Facebook, Twitter, LinkedIn, etc.
Wireless relevance; apps
Global cultural and language connection via the Web

ORGANIZATION AND GENERAL MANAGEMENT

Organizational structure
Firm's image and prestige
Firm's record in achieving objectives
Organization of communication system
Overall organizational control system (effectiveness and utilization)

Organizational climate; organizational culture
Use of systematic procedures and techniques in decision making

Top-management skill, capabilities, and interest
Strategic planning system
Intraorganizational synergy (multibusiness firms)

Chapter 6 Appendix B

Using Financial Analysis

One of the most important tools for assessing the strength of an organization within its industry is financial analysis. Managers, investors, and creditors all employ some form of this analysis as the beginning point for their financial decision making. Investors use financial analyses in making decisions about whether to buy or sell stock, and creditors use them in deciding whether or not to lend. They provide managers with a measurement of how the company is doing in comparison with its performance in past years and with the performance of competitors in the industry.

Although financial analysis is useful for decision making, some weaknesses should be noted. Any picture that it provides of the company is based on past data. Although trends may be noteworthy, this picture should not automatically be assumed to be applicable to the future. In addition, the analysis is only as good as the accounting procedures that have provided the information. When making comparisons between companies, one should keep in mind the variability of accounting procedures from firm to firm.

There are four basic groups of financial ratios: liquidity, leverage, activity, and profitability.

Depicted in Exhibit 6.B1 are the specific ratios calculated for each of the basic groups. Liquidity and leverage ratios represent an assessment of the risk of the firm. Activity and profitability ratios are measures of the return generated by the assets of the firm. The interaction between certain groups of ratios is indicated by arrows.

Typically, two common financial statements are used in financial analyses: the balance sheet and the income statement. Exhibit 6.B2 is a balance sheet and Exhibit 6.B3 an income statement for the ABC Company. These statements will be used to illustrate the financial analyses.

LIQUIDITY RATIOS

Liquidity ratios are used as indicators of a firm's ability to meet its short-term obligations. These obligations include any current liabilities, including currently maturing long-term debt. Current assets move through a normal cash cycle of inventories—sales—accounts receivable—cash. The firm then uses cash to pay off or reduce its current liabilities. The best-known liquidity ratio is the current ratio: current assets divided by current liabilities. For the ABC Company, the current ratio is calculated as follows:

$$\frac{\text{Current assets}}{\text{Current liabilities}} = \frac{\$4{,}125{,}000}{\$2{,}512{,}500} = 1.64\ (2014)$$

$$= \frac{\$3{,}618{,}000}{\$2{,}242{,}250} = 1.161\ (2013)$$

Most analysts suggest a current ratio of 2 to 3. A large current ratio is not necessarily a good sign; it may mean that an organization is not making the most efficient use of its assets. The optimum current ratio will vary from industry to industry, with the more volatile industries requiring higher ratios.

Because slow-moving or obsolescent inventories could overstate a firm's ability to meet short-term demands, the quick ratio is sometimes preferred to assess a firm's liquidity. The quick ratio is current assets minus inventories, divided by current liabilities. The quick ratio for the ABC Company is calculated as follows:

$$\frac{\text{Current assets} - \text{Inventories}}{\text{Current liabilities}} = \frac{\$1{,}950{,}000}{\$2{,}512{,}500} = 0.78\ (2014)$$

$$= \frac{\$1{,}618{,}000}{\$2{,}242{,}250} = 0.72\ (2013)$$

A quick ratio of approximately 1 would be typical for American industries. Although there is less variability in the quick ratio than in the current ratio, stable industries would be able to operate safely with a lower ratio.

LEVERAGE RATIOS

Leverage ratios identify the source of a firm's capital—owners or outside creditors. The term *leverage* refers to the fact that using capital with a fixed interest charge will "amplify" either profits or losses in relation to the equity of holders of common stock. The most commonly used ratio is total debt divided by total assets. Total debt includes current liabilities and long-term liabilities. This ratio is a measure of the percentage of total funds provided by debt. A total debt–total assets ratio higher than 0.5 is usually considered safe only for firms in stable industries.

$$\frac{\text{Total debt}}{\text{Total assets}} = \frac{\$3{,}862{,}500}{\$7{,}105{,}000} = 0.54\ (2014)$$

$$= \frac{\$3{,}667{,}250}{\$6{,}393{,}000} = 0.57\ (2013)$$

EXHIBIT 6.B1 Financial Ratios

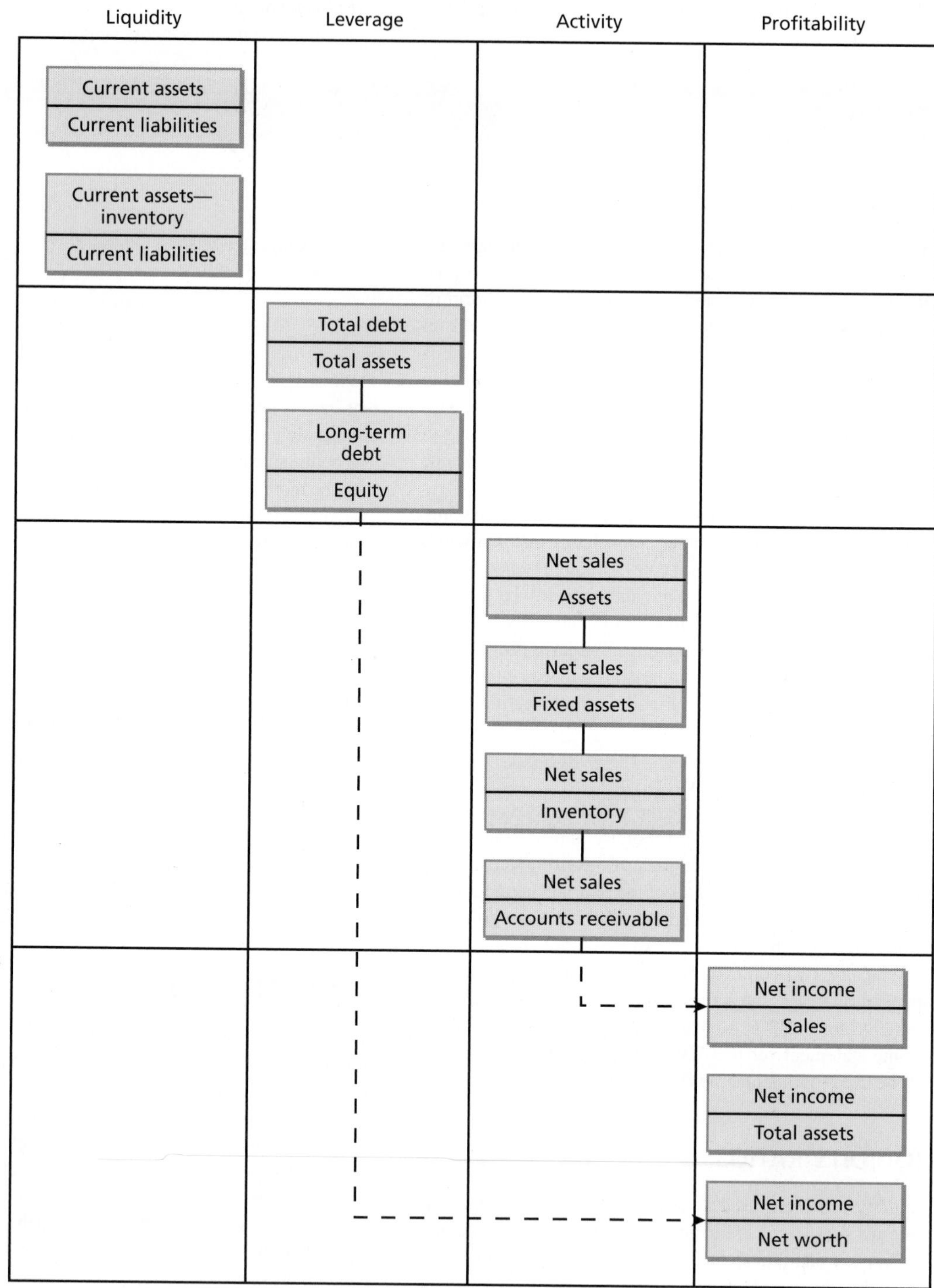

EXHIBIT 6.B2 **ABC Company Balance Sheet as of December 31, 2013 and 2014**

		2014		2013
Assets				
Current assets:				
Cash		$ 140,000		$ 115,000
Accounts receivable		1,760,000		1,440,000
Inventory		2,175,000		2,000,000
Prepaid expenses		50,000		63,000
Total current assets		4,125,000		3,618,000
Fixed assets:				
Long-term receivable		1,255,000		1,090,000
Property and plant	$2,037,000		$2,015,000	
Less: Accumulated depreciation	862,000		860,000	
Net property and plant		1,175,000		1,155,000
Other fixed assets		550,000		530,000
Total fixed assets		2,980,000		2,775,000
Total assets		$7,105,000		$6,393,000
Liabilities and Stockholders' Equity				
Current liabilities:				
Accounts payable		$1,325,000		$1,225,000
Bank loans payable		475,000		550,000
Accrued federal taxes		675,000		425,000
Current maturities (long-term debt)		17,500		26,000
Dividends payable		20,000		16,250
Total current liabilities		2,512,500		2,242,250
Long-term liabilities		1,350,000		1,425,000
Total liabilities		3,862,500		3,667,250
Stockholders' equity:				
Common stock (104,046 shares outstanding in 2014; 101,204 shares outstanding in 2013)		44,500		43,300
Additional paid-in-capital		568,000		372,450
Retained earnings		2,630,000		2,310,000
Total stockholders' equity		3,242,500		2,725,750
Total liabilities and stockholders' equity		$7,105,000		$6,393,000

EXHIBIT 6.B3 **ABC Company Income Statement for the years ending December 31, 2013 and 2014**

		2014		2013
Net sales		$8,250,000		$8,000,000
Cost of goods sold	$5,100,000		$5,000,000	
Administrative expenses	1,750,000		1,680,000	
Other expenses	420,000		390,000	
Total		7,270,000		7,070,000
Earnings before interest and taxes		980,000		930,000
Less: Interest expense		210,000		210,000
Earnings before taxes		770,000		720,000
Less: Federal income taxes		360,000		325,000
Earnings after taxes (net income)		$ 410,000		$ 395,000
Common stock cash dividends		$ 90,000		$ 84,000
Addition to retained earnings		$ 320,000		$ 311,000
Earnings per common share		$ 3.940		$ 3.90
Dividends per common share		$ 0.865		$ 0.83

The ratio of long-term debt to equity is a measure of the extent to which sources of long-term financing are provided by creditors. It is computed by dividing long-term debt by the stockholders' equity:

$$\frac{\text{Long-term debt}}{\text{Equity}} = \frac{\$1{,}350{,}000}{\$3{,}242{,}500} = 0.42\ (2014)$$

$$= \frac{\$1{,}425{,}000}{\$2{,}725{,}750} = 0.52\ (2013)$$

ACTIVITY RATIOS

Activity ratios indicate how effectively a firm is using its resources. By comparing revenues with the resources used to generate them, it is possible to establish an efficiency of operation. The asset turnover ratio indicates how efficiently management is employing total assets. Asset turnover is calculated by dividing sales by total assets. For the ABC Company, asset turnover is calculated as follows:

$$\text{Asset turnover} = \frac{\text{Sales}}{\text{Total assets}} = \frac{\$8{,}250{,}000}{\$7{,}105{,}000} = 1.16\ (2014)$$

$$= \frac{\$8{,}000{,}0000}{\$6{,}393{,}000} = 1.25\ (2013)$$

The ratio of sales to fixed assets is a measure of the turnover on plant and equipment. It is calculated by dividing sales by net fixed assets.

$$\text{Fixed asset turnover} = \frac{\text{Sales}}{\text{Net fixed assets}} = \frac{\$8{,}250{,}000}{\$2{,}980{,}000} = 2.77\ (2014)$$

$$= \frac{\$8{,}000{,}000}{\$2{,}775{,}000} = 2.88\ (2013)$$

Industry figures for asset turnover will vary with capital-intensive industries, and those requiring large inventories will have much smaller ratios.

Another activity ratio is inventory turnover, estimated by dividing sales by average inventory. The norm for U.S. industries is 9, but whether the ratio for a particular firm is higher or lower normally depends on the product sold. Small, inexpensive items usually turn over at a much higher rate than larger, expensive ones. Because inventories normally are carried at cost, it would be more accurate to use the cost of goods sold in place of sales in the numerator of this ratio. Established compilers of industry ratios, such as Dun & Bradstreet, however, use the ratio of sales to inventory.

$$\text{Inventory turnover} = \frac{\text{Sales}}{\text{Inventory}} = \frac{\$8{,}250{,}000}{\$2{,}175{,}000} = 3.79\ (2014)$$

$$= \frac{\$8{,}000{,}000}{\$2{,}000{,}000} = 4.00\ (2013)$$

The accounts receivable turnover is a measure of the average collection period on sales. If the average number of days varies widely from the industry norm, it may be an indication of poor management. A too-low ratio could indicate the loss of sales because of a too-restrictive credit policy. If the ratio is too high, too much capital is being tied up in accounts receivable, and management may be increasing the chance of bad debts. Because of varying industry credit policies, a comparison for the firm over time or within an industry is the only useful analysis. Because information on credit sales for other firms generally is unavailable, total sales must be used. Because not all firms have the same percentage of credit sales, there is only approximate comparability among firms:

$$\text{Accounts receivable turnover} = \frac{\text{Sales}}{\text{Accounts receivable}}$$

$$= \frac{\$8{,}250{,}000}{\$1{,}760{,}000} = 4.69\ (2014)$$

$$= \frac{\$8{,}000{,}000}{\$1{,}440{,}000} = 5.56\ (2013)$$

$$\text{Average collection period} = \frac{360}{\text{Accounts receivable turnover}}$$

$$= \frac{360}{4.69} = 77\text{ days } (2014)$$

$$= \frac{360}{5.56} = 65\text{ days } (2013)$$

PROFITABILITY RATIOS

Profitability is the net result of a large number of policies and decisions chosen by an organization's management. Profitability ratios indicate how effectively the total firm is being managed. The profit margin for a firm is calculated by dividing net earnings by sales. This ratio is often called *return on sales* (ROS). There is wide variation among industries, but the average for U.S. firms is approximately 5 percent.

$$\frac{\text{Net earnings}}{\text{Sales}} = \frac{\$410{,}000}{\$8{,}250{,}000} = 0.0497\ (2014)$$

$$= \frac{\$395{,}000}{\$8{,}000{,}000} = 0.0494\ (2013)$$

A second useful ratio for evaluating profitability is the *return on investment*—or ROI, as it is frequently called—found by dividing net earnings by total assets. The ABC Company's ROI is calculated as follows:

$$\frac{\text{Net earnings}}{\text{Total assets}} = \frac{\$410{,}000}{\$7{,}105{,}000} = 0.0577\ (2014)$$

$$= \frac{\$395{,}000}{\$6{,}393{,}000} = 0.0618\ (2013)$$

The ratio of net earnings to net worth is a measure of the rate of return or profitability of the stockholders' investment. It is calculated by dividing net earnings by net worth, the

EXHIBIT 6.B4 DuPont's Financial Analysis

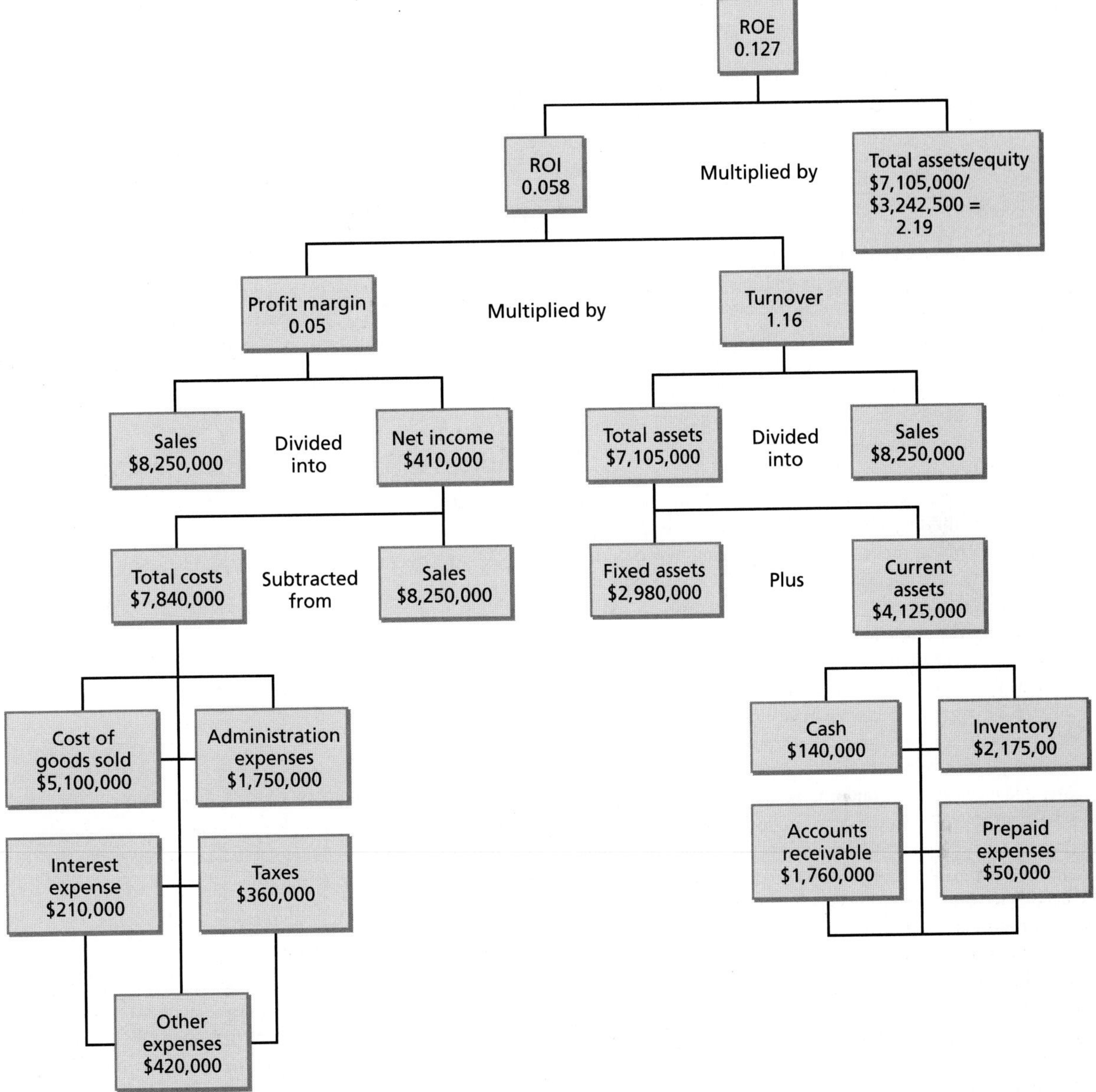

common stock equity and retained earnings account. ABC Company's *return on net worth or return on equity*, also called ROE, is calculated as follows:

$$\frac{\text{Net earnings}}{\text{Net worth}} = \frac{\$410,000}{\$3,242,500} = 0.1264\ (2014)$$

$$= \frac{\$395,000}{\$2,725,750} = 0.1449\ (2013)$$

It is often difficult to determine causes for lack of profitability. The DuPont system of financial analysis provides management with clues to the lack of success of a firm. This financial tool brings together activity, profitability, and leverage measures and shows how these ratios interact to determine the overall profitability of the firm. A depiction of the system is set forth in Exhibit 6.B4.

The right side of the exhibit develops the turnover ratio. This section breaks down total assets into current assets (cash, marketable securities, accounts receivable, and inventories) and fixed assets. Sales divided by these total assets gives the turnover on assets.

The left side of the exhibit develops the profit margin on sales. The individual expense items plus income taxes are subtracted from sales to produce net profits after taxes. Net profits divided by sales gives the profit margin on sales. When the asset turnover ratio on the right side of Exhibit 6.B4 is multiplied by the profit margin on sales developed on the left side of the exhibit, the product is the return on assets (ROI) for the firm. This can be shown by the following formula:

$$\frac{\text{Sales}}{\text{Total assets}} \times \frac{\text{Net earnings}}{\text{Sales}} = \frac{\text{Net earnings}}{\text{Total assets}} = \text{ROI}$$

The last step in the DuPont analysis is to multiply the rate of return on assets (ROI) by the equity multiplier, which is the ratio of assets to common equity, to obtain the rate of return on equity (ROE). This percentage rate of return, of course, could be calculated directly by dividing net income by common equity. However, the DuPont analysis demonstrates how the return on assets and the use of debt interact to determine the return on equity.

The DuPont system can be used to analyze and improve the performance of a firm. On the left, or profit, side of the exhibit, attempts to increase profits and sales could be investigated. The possibilities of raising prices to improve profits (or lowering prices to improve volume) or seeking new products or markets, for example, could be studied. Cost accountants and production engineers could investigate ways to reduce costs. On the right, or turnover, side, financial officers could analyze the effect of reducing investment in various assets as well as the effect of using alternative financial structures.

There are two basic approaches to using financial ratios. One approach is to evaluate the corporation's performance over several years. Financial ratios are computed for different years, and then an assessment is made about whether there has been an improvement or deterioration over time. Financial ratios also can be computed for projected, pro forma, statements and compared with present and past ratios.

The other approach is to evaluate a firm's financial condition and compare it with the financial conditions of similar firms or with industry averages in the same period. Such a comparison gives insight into the firm's relative financial condition and performance. Financial ratios for industries are provided by Robert Morris Associates, Dun & Bradstreet, Prentice Hall, and various trade association publications. (Associations and their addresses are listed in the *Encyclopedia of Associations* and in the *Directory of National Trade Associations.*) Information about individual firms is available through *Moody's Manual,* Standard & Poor's manuals and surveys, annual reports to stockholders, and the major brokerage houses.

To the extent possible, accounting data from different companies must be so standardized that companies can be compared or so a specific company can be compared with an industry average. It is important to read any footnotes of financial statements, because various accounting or management practices can have an effect on the financial picture of the company. For example, firms using sale-leaseback methods may have leverage pictures quite different from what is shown as debts or assets on the balance sheet.

ANALYSIS OF THE SOURCES AND USES OF FUNDS

The purpose of this analysis is to determine how the company is using its financial resources from year to year. By comparing balance sheets from one year to the next, we can determine how funds were obtained and how these funds were employed during the year.

To prepare a statement of the sources and uses of funds, it is necessary to (1) classify balance sheet changes that increase and decrease cash, (2) classify from the income statement those factors that increase or decrease cash, and (3) consolidate this information on a sources and uses of funds statement form.

Sources of Funds That Increase Cash

1. A net decrease in any other asset than a depreciable fixed asset.
2. A gross decrease in a depreciable fixed asset.
3. A net increase in any liability.
4. Proceeds from the sale of stock.
5. The operation of the company (net income, and depreciation if the company is profitable).

Uses of Funds

1. A net increase in any other asset than a depreciable fixed asset.
2. A gross increase in depreciable fixed assets.
3. A net decrease in any liability.
4. A retirement or purchase of stock.
5. Payment of cash dividends.

We compute gross changes to depreciable fixed assets by adding depreciation from the income statement for the period to net fixed assets at the end of the period and then subtracting from the total net fixed assets at the beginning of the period. The residual represents the change in depreciable fixed assets for the period.

For the ABC Company, the following change would be calculated:

Net property and plant (2014)	$1,175,000
Depreciation for 2014	+ 80,000
	$1,255,000
Net property and plant (2013)	−1,155,000
	$ 100,000

To avoid double counting, the change in retained earnings is not shown directly in the funds statement. When

ABC Company Sources and Uses of Funds Statement for 2014

Sources		Uses	
Prepaid expenses	$ 13,000	Cash	$ 25,000
Accounts payable	100,000	Accounts receivable	320,000
Accrued federal taxes	250,000	Inventory	175,000
Dividends payable	3,750	Long-term receivables	165,000
Common stock	1,200	Property and plant	100,000
Additional paid-in capital	195,550	Other fixed assets	20,000
Earnings after taxes (net income)	410,000	Bank loans payable	75,000
Depreciation	80,000	Current maturities of long-term debt	8,500
Total sources	$1,053,500	Long-term liabilities	75,000
		Dividends paid	90,000
		Total uses	$1,053,500

the funds statement is prepared, this account is replaced by the earnings after taxes, or net income, as a source of funds, and dividends paid during the year as a use of funds. The difference between net income and the change in the retained earnings account will equal the amount of dividends paid during the year. The accompanying sources and uses of funds statement was prepared for the ABC Company.

A funds analysis is useful for determining trends in working-capital positions and for demonstrating how the firm has acquired and employed its funds during some period.

Conclusion

It is recommended that you prepare a chart, such as that shown in Exhibit 6.B5, so you can develop a useful portrayal of these financial analyses. The chart allows a display of the ratios over

EXHIBIT 6.B5 **A Summary of the Financial Position of a Firm**

Ratios and Working Capital	2010	2011	2012	2013	2014	Trend	Industry Average	Interpre-tation
Liquidity: Current								
Quick								
Leverage: Debt-assets								
Debt-equity								
Activity: Asset turnover								
Fixed asset ratio								
Inventory turnover								
Accounts receivable turnover								
Average collection period								
Profitability: ROS								
ROI								
ROE								
Working-capital position								

time. The "Trend" column could be used to indicate your evaluation of the ratios over time (e.g., "favorable," "neutral," or "unfavorable"). The "Industry Average" column could include recent industry averages on these ratios or those of key competitors. These would provide information to aid interpretation of the analyses. The "Interpretation" column could be used to describe your interpretation of the ratios for this firm. Overall, this chart gives a basic display of the ratios that provides a convenient format for examining the firm's financial condition.

Finally, Exhibit 6.B6 is included to provide a quick reference summary of the calculations and meanings of the ratios discussed earlier.

EXHIBIT 6.B6 **A Summary of Key Financial Ratios**

Ratio	Calculation	Meaning
Liquidity Ratios:		
Current ratio	Current assets / Current liabilities	The extent to which a firm can meet its short-term obligations.
Quick ratio	Current assets–Inventory / Current liabilities	The extent to which a firm can meet its short-term obligations without relying on the sale of inventories.
Leverage Ratios:		
Debt-to-total-assets ratio	Total debt / Total assets	The percentage of total funds that are provided by creditors.
Debt-to-equity ratio	Total debt / Total stockholders' equity	The percentage of total funds provided by creditors versus the percentage provided by owners.
Long-term-debt-to-equity ratio	Long-term debt / Total stockholders' equity	The balance between debt and equity in a firm's long-term capital structure.
Times-interest-earned ratio	Profits before interest and taxes / Total interest charges	The extent to which earnings can decline without the firm becoming unable to meet its annual interest costs.
Activity Ratios:		
Inventory turnover	Sales / Inventory of finished goods	Whether a firm holds excessive stocks of inventories and whether a firm is selling its inventories slowly compared to the industry average.
Fixed assets turnover	Sales / Fixed assets	Sales productivity and plant equipment utilization.
Total assets turnover	Sales / Total assets	Whether a firm is generating a sufficient volume of business for the size of its assets investment.
Accounts receivable turnover	Annual credit sales / Accounts receivable	In percentage terms, the average length of time it takes a firm to collect on credit sales.
Average collection period	Accounts receivable / Total sales/365 days	In days, the average length of time it takes a firm to collect on credit sales.
Profitability Ratios:		
Gross profit margin	Sales – Cost of goods sold / Sales	The total margin available to cover operating expenses and yield a profit.

EXHIBIT 6.B6 *(continued)*

Ratio	Calculation	Meaning
Operating profit margin	$\frac{\text{Earnings before interest and taxes (EBIT)}}{\text{Sales}}$	Profitability without concern for taxes and interest.
Net profit margin	$\frac{\text{Net income}}{\text{Sales}}$	After-tax profits per dollar of sales.
Return on total assets (ROA)	$\frac{\text{Net income}}{\text{Total assets}}$	After-tax profits per dollar of assets; this ratio is also called *return on investment* (ROI).
Return on stockholders' equity (ROE)	$\frac{\text{Net income}}{\text{Total stockholders' equity}}$	After-tax profits per dollar of stockholders' investment in the firm.
Earnings per share (EPS)	$\frac{\text{Net income}}{\text{Number of shares of common stock outstanding}}$	Earnings available to the owners of common stock.
Growth Ratios:		
Sales	Annual percentage growth in total sales	Firm's growth rate in sales.
Income	Annual percentage growth in profits	Firm's growth rate in profits.
Earnings per share	Annual percentage growth in EPS	Firm's growth rate in EPS.
Dividends per share	Annual percentage growth in dividends per share	Firm's growth rate in dividends per share.
Price-earnings ratio	$\frac{\text{Market price per share}}{\text{Earnings per share}}$	Faster-growing and less risky firms tend to have higher price-earnings ratios.

Chapter Seven

Long-Term Objectives and Strategies

After reading and studying this chapter, you should be able to

1. Discuss seven different topics for long-term corporate objectives.
2. Describe the five qualities of long-term corporate objectives that make them especially useful to strategic managers.
3. Explain the generic strategies of low-cost leadership, differentiation, and focus.
4. Discuss the importance of the value disciplines.
5. List, describe, evaluate, and give examples of the 15 grand strategies that decision makers use as building blocks in forming their company's competitive plan.
6. Understand the creation of sets of long-term objectives and grand strategies options.

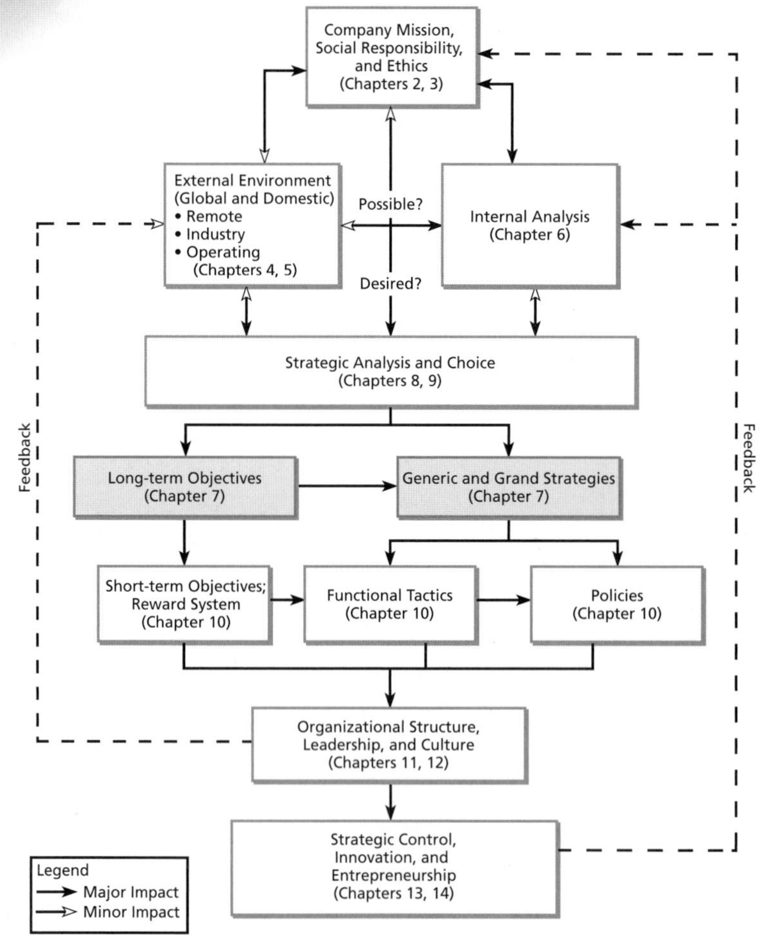

The company mission was described in Chapter 2 as encompassing the broad aims of the firm. The most specific statement of aims presented in that chapter appeared as the goals of the firm. However, these goals, which commonly dealt with profitability, growth, and survival, were stated without specific targets or time frames. They were always to be pursued but could never be fully attained. They gave a general sense of direction but were not intended to provide specific benchmarks for evaluating the firm's progress in achieving its aims. Providing such benchmarks is the function of objectives.[1]

The first part of this chapter will focus on long-term objectives. These are statements of the results a firm seeks to achieve over a specified period, typically three to five years. The second part will focus on the formulation of grand strategies. In combination, these two components of long-term planning provide a comprehensive general approach in guiding major actions designed to accomplish the firm's long-term objectives.

The chapter has two major aims: (1) to discuss in detail the concept of long-term objectives, the topics they cover, and the qualities they should exhibit; and (2) to discuss the concept of grand strategies and to describe the 15 principal grand strategy options that are available to firms singly or in combination, including three newly popularized options that are being used to provide the basis for global competitiveness.

LONG-TERM OBJECTIVES

Strategic managers recognize that short-run profit maximization is rarely the best approach to achieving sustained corporate growth and profitability. An often repeated adage states that if impoverished people are given food, they will eat it and remain impoverished; however, if they are given seeds and tools and shown how to grow crops, they will be able to improve their condition permanently. A parallel choice confronts strategic decision makers:

1. Should they eat the seeds to improve the near-term profit picture and make large dividend payments through cost-saving measures such as laying off workers during periods of slack demand, selling off inventories, or cutting back on research and development?
2. Or should they sow the seeds in the effort to reap long-term rewards by reinvesting profits in growth opportunities, committing resources to employee training, or increasing advertising expenditures?

For most strategic managers, the solution is clear—distribute a small amount of profit now but sow most of it to increase the likelihood of a long-term supply. This is the most frequently used rationale in selecting objectives.

To achieve long-term prosperity, strategic planners commonly establish long-term objectives in seven areas.

Profitability The ability of any firm to operate in the long run depends on attaining an acceptable level of profits. Strategically managed firms characteristically have a profit objective, usually expressed in earnings per share or return on equity.

Productivity Strategic managers constantly try to increase the productivity of their systems. Firms that can improve the input-output relationship normally increase profitability. Thus, firms almost always state an objective for productivity. Commonly used productivity objectives are the number of items produced or the number of services rendered per unit of input. However, productivity objectives sometimes are stated in terms of desired

[1] The terms *goals* and *objectives* are each used to convey a special meaning, with goals being the less specific and more encompassing concept.

cost decreases. For example, objectives may be set for reducing defective items, customer complaints leading to litigation, or overtime. Achieving such objectives increases profitability if unit output is maintained.

Competitive Position One measure of corporate success is relative dominance in the marketplace. Larger firms commonly establish an objective in terms of competitive position, often using total sales or market share as measures of their competitive position. An objective with regard to competitive position may indicate a firm's long-term priorities. For example, Gulf Oil set a five-year objective of moving from third to second place as a producer of high-density polypropylene. Total sales were the measure.

Employee Development Employees value education and training, in part because they lead to increased compensation and job security. Providing such opportunities often increases productivity and decreases turnover. Therefore, strategic decision makers frequently include an employee development objective in their long-range plans. For example, PPG has declared an objective of developing highly skilled and flexible employees and, thus, providing steady employment for a reduced number of workers.

Employee Relations Whether or not they are bound by union contracts, firms actively seek good employee relations. In fact, proactive steps in anticipation of employee needs and expectations are characteristic of strategic managers. Strategic managers believe that productivity is linked to employee loyalty and to appreciation of managers' interest in employee welfare. They, therefore, set objectives to improve employee relations. Among the outgrowths of such objectives are safety programs, worker representation on management committees, and employee stock option plans.

Technological Leadership Firms must decide whether to lead or follow in the marketplace. Either approach can be successful, but each requires a different strategic posture. Therefore, many firms state an objective with regard to technological leadership. For example, Caterpillar Tractor Company established its early reputation and dominant position in its industry by being in the forefront of technological innovation in the manufacture of large earthmovers. E-commerce technology officers will have more of a strategic role in the management hierarchy of the future, demonstrating that the Internet has become an integral aspect of corporate long-term objective setting. In offering an e-technology manager higher-level responsibilities, a firm is pursuing a leadership position in terms of innovation in computer networks and systems. Officers of e-commerce technology at GE and Delta Air Lines have shown their ability to increase profits by driving down transaction-related costs with Web-based technologies that seamlessly integrate their firms' supply chains. These technologies have the potential to "lock in" certain suppliers and customers and heighten competitive position through supply chain efficiency.

Public Responsibility Managers recognize their responsibilities to their customers and to society at large. In fact, many firms seek to exceed government requirements. They work not only to develop reputations for fairly priced products and services but also to establish themselves as responsible corporate citizens. For example, they may establish objectives for charitable and educational contributions, minority training, public or political activity, community welfare, or urban revitalization. In an attempt to exhibit their public responsibility in the United States, Japanese companies, such as Toyota, Hitachi, and Matsushita, contribute more than $500 million annually to American educational projects, charities, and nonprofit organizations.

Qualities of Long-Term Objectives

What distinguishes a good objective from a bad one? What qualities of an objective improve its chances of being attained? These questions are best answered in relation to five criteria that should be used in preparing long-term objectives: flexible, measurable over time, motivating, suitable, and understandable.

Flexible Objectives should be adaptable to unforeseen or extraordinary changes in the firm's competitive or environmental forecasts. Unfortunately, such flexibility usually is increased at the expense of specificity. One way of providing flexibility while minimizing its negative effects is to allow for adjustments in the level, rather than in the nature, of objectives. For example, the personnel department objective of providing managerial development training for 15 supervisors per year over the next five-year period might be adjusted by changing the number of people to be trained.

Measurable Objectives must clearly and concretely state what will be achieved and when it will be achieved. Thus, objectives should be measurable over time. For example, the objective of "substantially improving our return on investment" would be better stated as "increasing the return on investment on our line of paper products by a minimum of 1 percent a year and a total of 5 percent over the next three years." A great example is provided by IAG (Insurance Australia Group), which offers a wide range of commercial and personal insurance products. IAG stated its 2008 financial objective as a return on equity of 1.5 times the weighted average cost of capital.

Motivating People are most productive when objectives are set at a motivating level—one high enough to challenge but not so high as to frustrate or so low as to be easily attained. The problem is that individuals and groups differ in their perceptions of what is high enough. A broad objective that challenges one group frustrates another and minimally interests a third. One valuable recommendation is that objectives be tailored to specific groups. Developing such objectives requires time and effort, but objectives of this kind are more likely to motivate.

Objectives must also be achievable. This is easier said than done. Turbulence in the remote and operating environments affects a firm's internal operations, creating uncertainty and limiting the accuracy of the objectives set by strategic management. To illustrate, the rapidly declining U.S. economy in 2007–2009 made objective setting extremely difficult, particularly in such areas as sales projections.

Motorola provides a good example of well-constructed company objectives. Motorola saw its market share of the mobile telephone market shrink from 26 to 14 percent between 1996 and 2001, while its main rival Nokia captured all of Motorola's lost share and more. As a key part of a plan to recapture its market position, Motorola's CEO challenged his company with the following long-term objectives:

1. Cut sales, marketing, and administrative expenses from $2.4 billion to $1.6 billion within one year.
2. Increase gross margins from 20 to 27 percent within two years.
3. Reduce the number of Motorola telephone styles by 84 percent to 20 and the number of silicon components by 82 percent to 100 within three years.

Suitable Objectives must be suited to the broad aims of the firm, which are expressed in its mission statement. Each objective should be a step toward the attainment of overall goals. In fact, objectives that are inconsistent with the company mission can subvert the firm's aims. For example, if the mission is growth oriented, the objective of reducing the debt-to-equity ratio to 1.00 would probably be unsuitable and counterproductive.

Understandable Strategic managers at all levels must understand what is to be achieved. They also must understand the major criteria by which their performance will be evaluated. Thus, objectives must be so stated that they are as understandable to the recipient as they are to the giver. Consider the misunderstandings that might arise over the objective of "increasing the productivity of the credit card department by 20 percent within two years." What does this objective mean? Increase the number of outstanding cards? Increase the use of outstanding cards? Increase the employee workload? Make productivity gains each year? Or hope that the new computer-assisted system, which should improve productivity, is approved by year 2? As this simple example illustrates, objectives must be clear, meaningful, and unambiguous.

The Balanced Scorecard

balanced scorecard A set of four measures directly linked to a company's strategy: financial performance, customer knowledge, internal business processes, and learning and growth.

The **balanced scorecard** is a set of measures that are directly linked to the company's strategy. It directs a company to link its own long-term strategy with tangible goals and actions. The scorecard allows managers to evaluate the company from four perspectives: financial performance, customer knowledge, internal business processes, and learning and growth.

The balanced scorecard, as shown in Exhibit 7.1, contains a concise definition of the company's vision and strategy. Surrounding the vision and strategy are four additional boxes; each box contains the objectives, measures, targets, and initiatives for one of the four perspectives:

- The box at the top of Exhibit 7.1 represents the financial perspective and answers the question "To succeed financially, how should we appear to our shareholders?"

EXHIBIT 7.1 The Balanced Scorecard

The balanced scorecard provides a framework to translate a strategy into operational terms

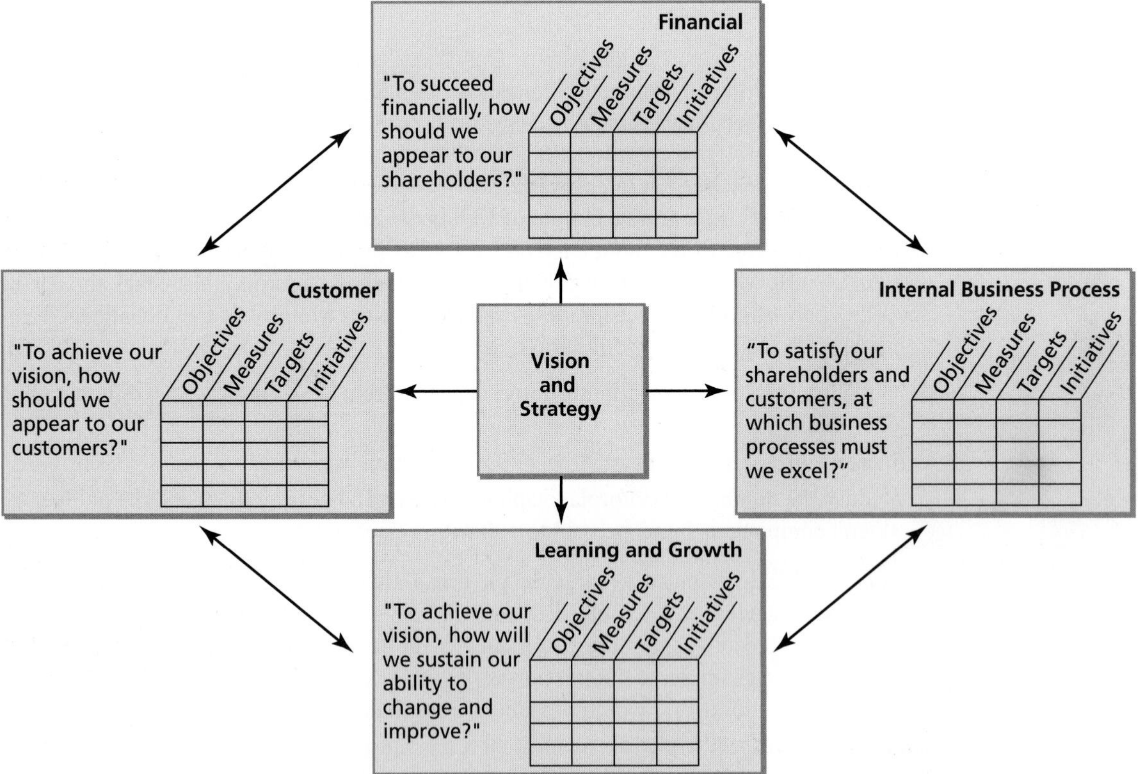

Source: Reprinted by permission of *Harvard Business Review*, Exhibit from "Using the Balanced Scorecard as a Strategic Management System," by Robert S. Kaplan and David P. Norton, February 1996.

- The box to the right represents the internal business process perspective and addresses the question "To satisfy our shareholders and customers, what business processes must we excel at?"
- The learning and growth box at the bottom of Exhibit 7.1 answers the question "To achieve our vision, how will we sustain our ability to change and improve?"
- The box at the left reflects the customer perspective and responds to the question "To achieve our vision, how should we appear to our customers?"

All of the boxes are connected by arrows to illustrate that the objectives and measures of the four perspectives are linked by cause-and-effect relationships that lead to the successful implementation of the strategy. Achieving one perspective's targets should lead to desired improvements in the next perspective, and so on, until the company's performance increases overall.

A properly constructed scorecard is balanced between short- and long-term measures, financial and nonfinancial measures, and internal and external performance perspectives.

The balanced scorecard is a management system that can be used as the central organizing framework for key managerial processes. Chemical Bank, Mobil Corporation's US Marketing and Refining Division, and CIGNA Property and Casualty Insurance have used the balanced scorecard approach to assist in individual and team goal setting, compensation, resource allocation, budgeting and planning, and strategic feedback and learning.

The Balanced Scorecard offers more than a way to think about the priorities of a company; it can also serve as a vehicle to help the company achieve those priorities. Exhibit 7.2, Strategy in Action provides nine steps for strategic managers to follow to succeed in implementing a Balanced Scorecard approach.

GENERIC STRATEGIES

Many planning experts believe that the general philosophy of doing business declared by the firm in the mission statement must be translated into a holistic statement of the firm's strategic orientation before it can be further defined in terms of a specific long-term strategy. In other words, a long-term or grand strategy must be based on a core idea about how the firm can best compete in the marketplace.

generic strategy
A core idea about how a firm can best compete in the marketplace.

The popular term for this core idea is **generic strategy.** From a scheme developed by Michael Porter, many planners believe that any long-term strategy should derive from a firm's attempt to seek a competitive advantage based on one of three generic strategies:

1. Striving for overall *low-cost leadership* in the industry.
2. Striving to create and market unique products for varied customer groups through *differentiation*.
3. Striving to have special appeal to one or more groups of consumer or industrial buyers, *focusing* on their cost or differentiation concerns.

Advocates of generic strategies believe that each of these options can produce above-average returns for a firm in an industry. However, they are successful for very different reasons.

Low-Cost Leadership

Low-cost leaders depend on some fairly unique capabilities to achieve and sustain their low-cost position. Examples of such capabilities are having secured suppliers of scarce raw materials, being in a dominant market share position, or having a high degree of capitalization. Low-cost producers usually excel at cost reductions and efficiencies. They maximize economies of

Strategy in Action — Exhibit 7.2

Implementing a Balanced Scorecard: Nine Steps to Success

1. Assess the organization's mission and vision, challenges, and values. Prepare a change management plan for the organization.
2. Develop elements of the organization's strategy, including strategic results, strategic themes, and perspectives to focus attention on customer needs and the organization's value proposition.
3. Decompose the strategic elements developed in steps one and two into strategic objectives. Objectives should be initiated and categorized on the strategic theme level, categorized by perspective, linked in cause-effect linkages (strategy maps) for each strategic theme, and then later merged to produce one set of strategic objectives for the entire organization.
4. Formalize the cause and effect linkages between the enterprise-wide strategic objectives in an enterprise-wide strategy map.
5. Develop performance measures for each of the enterprise-wide strategic objectives. Identify leading and lagging measures, establish targets, thresholds, and baseline and benchmarking data.
6. Develop strategic initiatives that support the strategic objectives. Build accountability throughout the organization by assigning ownership of performance measures and strategic initiatives to the appropriate staff and documented in data definition tables.
7. Begin the implementation process by applying performance measurement software to get the right performance information to the right people at the right time. Automation adds structure and discipline when implementing the balanced scorecard system, helps transform disparate corporate data into information and knowledge, and helps communicate performance information. In short, automation helps people make better decisions because it offers quick access to actual performance data.
8. Cascade the enterprise-level scorecard down into business and support unit scorecards, meaning the organizational level scorecard (the first tier) is translated into business unit or support unit scorecards (the second tier) and then later to team and individual scorecards (the third tier). Cascading translates high-level strategy into lower level objectives, measures, and operational details and is the key to organization alignment around strategy. Team and individual scorecards link day-to-day work with department goals and corporate vision. Performance measures are developed for all objectives at all organizational levels. As the scorecard management system is cascaded down through the organization, objectives and performance measures become more operational and tactical. Accountability follows the objectives and measures, as ownership is defined at each level. An emphasis on the results and the strategies needed to produce results is communicated throughout the organization.
9. Evaluate the completed scorecard to answer questions such as, "Are our strategies working?", "Are we measuring the right things?", "Has our environment changed?" and "Are we budgeting our money strategically?"

Source: Excerpted from Ashu Sharma, "Implementing Balanced Scorecard for Performance Measurement," *IUP Journal of Business Strategy*, March 2009, 6(1): 7–16.

scale, implement cost-cutting technologies, stress reductions in overhead and in administrative expenses, and use volume sales techniques to propel themselves up the earning curve.

A low-cost leader is able to use its cost advantage to charge lower prices or to enjoy higher profit margins. By so doing, the firm effectively can defend itself in price wars, attack competitors on price to gain market share, or, if already dominant in the industry, simply benefit from exceptional returns. As an extreme case, it has been argued that National Can Company, a corporation in an essentially stagnant industry, is able to generate attractive and improving profits by being the low-cost producer.

In the wake of the tremendous successes of such low-cost leaders as Wal-Mart and Target, only a rare few companies can ignore the mandate to reduce costs. Yet, doing so without compromising the key attributes of a company's products or services is a difficult challenge. One company that has succeeded in its efforts to become a low-cost leader while maintaining quality is IAG. The company's CEO, Michael Wilkins, expresses the principle of the company's focus on low costs in its mission statement by saying: "IAG's large scale allows us to manage costs across our brands through access to volume discounts throughout the supply chain, without sacrificing quality, thereby keeping costs per policy down."

Differentiation

Strategies dependent on differentiation are designed to appeal to customers with a special sensitivity for a particular product attribute. By stressing the attribute above other product qualities, the firm attempts to build customer loyalty. Often such loyalty translates into a firm's ability to charge a premium price for its product. Cross-brand pens, Brooks Brothers suits, Porsche automobiles, and Chivas Regal Scotch whiskey are all examples.

The product attribute also can be the marketing channels through which it is delivered, its image for excellence, the features it includes, and the service network that supports it. As a result of the importance of these attributes, competitors often face "perceptual" barriers to entry when customers of a successfully differentiated firm fail to see largely identical products as being interchangeable. For example, General Motors hopes that customers will accept "only genuine GM replacement parts."

Because advertising plays a major role in a company's development and differentiation of its brand, many strategists use celebrity spokespeople to represent their companies. These spokespeople, most often actors, models, and athletes, help give the company's products and services a popular, successful, trendy, modern cachet.

Focus

A focus strategy, whether anchored in a low-cost base or a differentiation base, attempts to attend to the needs of a particular market segment. Likely segments are those that are ignored by marketing appeals to easily accessible markets, to the "typical" customer, or to customers with common applications for the product. A firm pursuing a focus strategy is willing to service isolated geographic areas; to satisfy the needs of customers with special financing, inventory, or servicing problems; or to tailor the product to the somewhat unique demands of the small- to medium-sized customer. The focusing firms profit from their willingness to serve otherwise ignored or underappreciated customer segments. The classic example is cable television. An entire industry was born because of a willingness of cable firms to serve isolated rural locations that were ignored by traditional television services. Brick producers that typically service a radius of less than 100 miles and commuter airlines that serve regional geographic areas are other examples of industries where a focus strategy frequently yields above-average industry profits.

While each of the generic strategies enables a firm to maximize certain competitive advantages, each one also exposes the firm to a number of competitive risks. For example, a low-cost leader fears a new low-cost technology that is being developed by a competitor; a differentiating firm fears imitators; and a focused firm fears invasion by a firm that largely targets customers.

THE VALUE DISCIPLINES

International management consultants Michael Treacy and Fred Wiersema propose an alternative approach to generic strategy that they call the value disciplines.[2] They believe that strategies must center on delivering superior customer value through one of three value disciplines: operational excellence, customer intimacy, or product leadership.

[2] The ideas and examples in this section are drawn from Michael Treacy and Fred Wiersema, "Customer Intimacy and Other Value Disciplines," *Harvard Business Review* 71, no. 1 (1993), pp. 84–94.

Operational excellence refers to providing customers with convenient and reliable products or services at competitive prices. Customer intimacy involves offerings tailored to match the demands of identified niches. Product leadership, the third discipline, involves offering customers leading-edge products and services that make rivals' goods obsolete.

Companies that specialize in one of these disciplines, while simultaneously meeting industry standards in the other two, gain a sustainable lead in their markets. This lead is derived from the firm's focus on one discipline, aligning all aspects of operations with it. Having decided on the value that must be conveyed to customers, firms understand more clearly what must be done to attain the desired results. After transforming their organizations to focus on one discipline, companies can concentrate on smaller adjustments to produce incremental value. To match this advantage, less focused companies require larger changes than the tweaking that discipline leaders need.

Operational Excellence

Operational excellence is a specific strategic approach to the production and delivery of products and services. A company that follows this strategy attempts to lead its industry in price and convenience by pursuing a focus on lean and efficient operations. Companies that employ operational excellence work to minimize costs by reducing overhead, eliminating intermediate production steps, reducing transaction costs, and optimizing business processes across functional and organizational boundaries. The focus is on delivering products or services to customers at competitive prices with minimal inconvenience.

Operational excellence is also the strategic focus of General Electric's large appliance business. Historically, the distribution strategy for large appliances was based on requiring that dealers maintain large inventories. Price breaks for dealers were based on order quantities. However, as the marketplace became more competitive, principally as a result of competition multibrand dealers like Sears, GE recognized the need to adjust its production and distribution plans.

The GE system addresses the delivery of products. As a step toward organizational excellence, GE created a computer-based logistics system to replace its in-store inventories model. Retailers use this software to access a 24-hour online order processing system that guarantees GE's best price. This system allows dealers to better meet customer needs, with instantaneous access to a warehouse of goods and accurate shipping and production information. GE benefits from the deal as well. Efficiency is increased since manufacturing now occurs in response to customer sales. Additionally, warehousing and distribution systems have been streamlined to create the capability of delivering to 90 percent of destinations in the continental United States within one business day.

Firms that implement the strategy of operational excellence typically restructure their delivery processes to focus on efficiency and reliability, and use state-of-the art information systems that emphasize integration and low-cost transactions.

Customer Intimacy

Companies that implement a strategy of customer intimacy continually tailor and shape products and services to fit an increasingly refined definition of the customer. Companies excelling in customer intimacy combine detailed customer knowledge with operational flexibility. They respond quickly to almost any need, from customizing a product to fulfilling special requests to create customer loyalty.

Customer-intimate companies are willing to spend money now to build customer loyalty for the long term, considering each customer's lifetime value to the company, not the profit of any single transaction. Consequently, employees in customer-intimate companies go to great lengths to ensure customer satisfaction with low regard for initial cost.

Home Depot implements the discipline of customer intimacy. Home Depot clerks spend the necessary time with customers to determine the product that best suits their needs, because the company's business strategy is built around selling information and service in addition to home-repair and improvement items. Consequently, consumers concerned solely with price fall outside Home Depot's core market.

Companies engaged in customer intimacy understand the difference between the profitability of a single transaction and the profitability of a lifetime relationship with a single customer. The company's profitability depends in part on its maintaining a system that differentiates quickly and accurately the degree of service that customers require and the revenues their patronage is likely to generate. Firms using this approach recognize that not every customer is equally profitable. For example, a financial services company installed a telephone-computer system capable of recognizing individual clients by their telephone numbers when they call. The system routes customers with large accounts and frequent transactions to their own senior account representative. Other customers may be routed to a trainee or junior representative. In any case, the customer's file appears on the representative's screen before the phone is answered.

The new system allows the firm to segment its services with great efficiency. If the company has clients who are interested in trading in a particular financial instrument, it can group them under the one account representative who specializes in that instrument. This saves the firm the expense of training every representative in every facet of financial services. Additionally, the company can direct certain value-added services or products to a specific group of clients that would have interest in them.

Businesses that select a customer intimacy strategy have decided to stress flexibility and responsiveness. They collect and analyze data from many sources. Their organizational structure emphasizes empowerment of employees close to customers. Additionally, hiring and training programs stress the creative decision-making skills required to meet individual customer needs. Management systems recognize and utilize such concepts as customer lifetime value, and norms among employees are consistent with a "have it your way" mind set.

Product Leadership

Companies that pursue the discipline of product leadership strive to produce a continuous stream of state-of-the-art products and services. Three challenges must be met to attain that goal. Creativity is the first challenge. Creativity is recognizing and embracing ideas usually originating outside the company. Second, innovative companies must commercialize ideas quickly. Thus, their business and management processes need to be engineered for speed. Product leaders relentlessly pursue new solutions to problems. Finally, firms utilizing this discipline prefer to release their own improvements rather than wait for competitors to enter. Consequently, product leaders do not stop for self-congratulation; they focus on continual improvement.

For example, Johnson & Johnson's organizational design brings good ideas in, develops them quickly, and looks for ways to improve them. In 1983, the president of J&J's Vistakon Inc., a maker of specialty contact lenses, received a tip concerning an ophthalmologist who had conceived of a method to manufacture disposable contact lenses inexpensively. Vistakon's president received this tip from a J&J employee from a different subsidiary whom he had never met. Rather than dismiss the tip, the executives purchased the rights to the technology, assembled a management team to oversee the product's development, and built a state-of-the-art facility in Florida to manufacture disposable contact lenses called Acuvue. Vistakon and its parent, J&J, were willing to incur high manufacturing and inventory costs before a single lens was sold. A high-speed production facility helped give Vistakon a six-month head start over the competition that, taken off guard, never caught up.

Like other product leaders, J&J creates and maintains an environment that encourages employees to share ideas. Additionally, product leaders continually scan the environment for new-product or service possibilities and rush to capitalize them. Product leaders also avoid bureaucracy because it slows commercialization of their ideas. In a product leadership company, a wrong decision often is less damaging than one made late. As a result, managers make decisions quickly, their companies encouraging them to decide today and implement tomorrow. Product leaders continually look for new methods to shorten their cycle times.

The strength of product leaders lies in reacting to situations as they occur. Shorter reaction times serve as an advantage in dealings with the unknown. For example, when competitors challenged the safety of Acuvue lenses, the firm responded quickly and distributed data combating the charges to eye care professionals. This reaction created goodwill in the marketplace.

Product leaders act as their own competition. These firms continually make the products and services they have created obsolete. Product leaders believe that if they do not develop a successor, a competitor will. So, although Acuvue is successful in the marketplace, Vistakon continues to investigate new material that will extend the wearability of contact lenses and technologies that will make current lenses obsolete. J&J and other innovators recognize that the long-run profitability of an existing product or service is less important to the company's future than maintaining its product leadership edge and momentum.

GRAND STRATEGIES

grand strategy
A master long-term plan that provides basic direction for major actions for achieving long-term business objectives.

Grand strategies, sometimes called master or business strategies, provide basic direction for strategic actions. They are the basis of coordinated and sustained efforts directed toward achieving long-term business objectives.

The purpose of this section is twofold: (1) to list, describe, and discuss 15 grand strategies that strategic managers should consider and (2) to present approaches to the selection of an optimal grand strategy from the available alternatives.

Grand strategies indicate the time period over which long-range objectives are to be achieved. Thus, a grand strategy can be defined as a comprehensive general approach that guides a firm's major actions.

The 15 principal grand strategies are concentrated growth, market development, product development, innovation, horizontal acquisition, vertical acquisition, concentric diversification, conglomerate diversification, turnaround, divestiture, liquidation, bankruptcy, joint ventures, strategic alliances, and consortia. Any one of these strategies could serve as the basis for achieving the major long-term objectives of a single firm. But a firm involved with multiple industries, businesses, product lines, or customer groups—as many firms are—usually combines several grand strategies. For clarity, however, each of the principal grand strategies is described independently in this section, with examples to indicate some of its relative strengths and weaknesses.

1. Concentrated Growth

Many of the firms that fell victim to merger mania were once mistakenly convinced that the best way to achieve their objectives was to pursue unrelated diversification in the search for financial opportunity and synergy. By rejecting that "conventional wisdom," such firms as Martin-Marietta, KFC, Compaq, Avon, Hyatt Legal Services, and Tenant have demonstrated the advantages of what is increasingly proving to be sound business strategy.

These firms are just a few of the majority of businesses worldwide firms that pursue a concentrated growth strategy by focusing on a dominant product-and-market combination.

concentrated growth
A grand strategy with which a firm directs its resources to the profitable growth of a single product, in a single market, with a single dominant technology.

Concentrated growth is the strategy of the firm that directs its resources to the profitable growth of a dominant product, in a dominant market, with a dominant technology. The main rationale for this approach, sometimes called a market penetration strategy, is that by thoroughly developing and exploiting its expertise in a narrowly defined competitive arena, the company achieves superiority over competitors that try to master a greater number of product and market combinations.

Rationale for Superior Performance

Concentrated growth strategies lead to enhanced performance. The ability to assess market needs, knowledge of buyer behavior, customer price sensitivity, and effectiveness of promotion are characteristics of a concentrated growth strategy. Such core capabilities are a more important determinant of competitive market success than are the environmental forces faced by the firm. The high success rates of new products also are tied to avoiding situations that require undeveloped skills, such as serving new customers and markets, acquiring new technology, building new channels, developing new promotional abilities, and facing new competition.

A major misconception about the concentrated growth strategy is that the firm practicing it will settle for little or no growth. This is certainly not true for a firm that correctly utilizes the strategy. A firm employing concentrated growth grows by building on its competencies, and it achieves a competitive edge by concentrating in the product-market segment it knows best. A firm employing this strategy is aiming for the growth that results from increased productivity, better coverage of its actual product-market segment, and more efficient use of its technology.

Conditions That Favor Concentrated Growth

Specific conditions in the firm's environment are favorable to the concentrated growth strategy. The first is a condition in which the firm's industry is resistant to major technological advancements. This is usually the case in the late growth and maturity stages of the product life cycle and in product markets where product demand is stable and industry barriers, such as capitalization, are high. Machinery for the paper manufacturing industry, in which the basic technology has not changed for more than a century, is a good example.

An especially favorable condition is one in which the firm's targeted markets are not product saturated. Markets with competitive gaps leave the firm with alternatives for growth, other than taking market share away from competitors. The successful introduction of traveler services by Allstate and Amoco demonstrates that even an organization as entrenched and powerful as the AAA could not build a defensible presence in all segments of the automobile club market.

A third condition that favors concentrated growth exists when the firm's product markets are sufficiently distinctive to dissuade competitors in adjacent product markets from trying to invade the firm's segment. John Deere scrapped its plans for growth in the construction machinery business when mighty Caterpillar threatened to enter Deere's mainstay, the farm machinery business, in retaliation. Rather than risk a costly price war on its own turf, Deere scrapped these plans.

A fourth favorable condition exists when the firm's inputs are stable in price and quantity and are available in the amounts and at the times needed. Maryland-based Giant Foods is able to concentrate in the grocery business largely due to its stable long-term arrangements with suppliers of its private-label products. Most of these suppliers are makers of the national brands that compete against the Giant labels. With a high market share and aggressive retail distribution, Giant controls the access of these brands to the consumer. Consequently, its suppliers have considerable incentive to honor verbal agreements, called bookings, in which they commit themselves for a one-year period with regard to the price, quality, and timing of their shipments to Giant.

The pursuit of concentrated growth also is favored by a stable market—a market without the seasonal or cyclical swings that would encourage a firm to diversify. Night Owl Security, the District of Columbia market leader in home security services, commits its customers to initial four-year contracts. In a city where affluent consumers tend to be quite transient, the length of this relationship is remarkable. Night Owl's concentrated growth strategy has been reinforced by its success in getting subsequent owners of its customers' homes to extend and renew the security service contracts. In a similar way, Lands' End reinforced its growth strategy by asking customers for names and addresses of friends and relatives living overseas who would like to receive Lands' End catalogs.

A firm also can grow while concentrating, if it enjoys competitive advantages based on efficient production or distribution channels. These advantages enable the firm to formulate advantageous pricing policies. More efficient production methods and better handling of distribution also enable the firm to achieve greater economies of scale or, in conjunction with marketing, result in a product that is differentiated in the mind of the consumer. Graniteville Company, a large South Carolina textile manufacturer, enjoyed decades of growth and profitability by adopting a "follower" tactic as part of its concentrated growth strategy. By producing fabrics only after market demand had been well established, and by featuring products that reflected its expertise in adopting manufacturing innovations and in maintaining highly efficient long production runs, Graniteville prospered through concentrated growth.

Finally, the success of market generalists creates conditions favorable to concentrated growth. When generalists succeed by using universal appeals, they avoid making special appeals to particular groups of customers. The net result is that many small pockets are left open in the markets dominated by generalists, and that specialists emerge and thrive in these pockets. For example, hardware store chains, such as Home Depot, focus primarily on routine household repair problems and offer solutions that can be easily sold on a self-service, do-it-yourself basis. This approach leaves gaps at both the "semi-professional" and "neophyte" ends of the market—in terms of the purchaser's skill at household repairs and the extent to which available merchandise matches the requirements of individual homeowners. To learn about the important success of BNSF with a concentrated growth strategy, read about CEO Matthew Rose's grand strategy in the railroad industry in Exhibit 7.3, Top Strategist.

Risk and Rewards of Concentrated Growth

Under stable conditions, concentrated growth poses lower risk than any other grand strategy; but, in a changing environment, a firm committed to concentrated growth faces high risks. The greatest risk is that concentrating in a single product market makes a firm particularly vulnerable to changes in that segment. Slowed growth in the segment would jeopardize the firm because its investment, competitive edge, and technology are deeply entrenched in a specific offering. It is difficult for the firm to attempt sudden changes if its product is threatened by near-term obsolescence, a faltering market, new substitutes, or changes in technology or customer needs. For example, the manufacturers of IBM clones faced such a problem when IBM adopted the OS/2 operating system for its personal computer line. That change made existing clones out of date.

The concentrating firm's entrenchment in a specific industry makes it particularly susceptible to changes in the economic environment of that industry. For example, Mack Truck, the second-largest truck maker in America, lost $20 million as a result of an 18-month slump in the truck industry.

Top Strategist

CEO Matthew Rose Focuses BNSF on Concentrated Growth

Exhibit 7.3

As CEO of BNSF, Matthew Rose's concentrated growth strategy relies on technology to improve operational efficiency in an increasingly congested rail network. Strategic planning in this industry is critical because rail tonnage was expected to increase by 88 percent between 2008 and 2035, and rail capacity was fully utilized in 2008. Missing the opportunity to increase capacity would lead to rail congestion, diminished safety, and an accelerated consumer shift to other channels of freight transportation.

BNSF's concentrated growth strategy required a tightly coordinated effort. A major component involved transferring ownership of railcars to third-party shippers. Divesting railcars improved customer service because third-party shippers were able to manage these assets more efficiently. By shifting focus away from railcar operations, BNSF was able to concentrate on improving its overall network utilization. Evidence of this strategic shift was the investment in a satellite-based computer program that optimized logistics and ensured that all trains are fully utilized. Additionally, BNSF used 10,000-foot trains to increase economies of scale and accommodate the growing West Coast shipping ports.

Maintaining quality through operational efficiency increased customer usage in this highly competitive industry. High-quality service also protected BNSF from pricing pressures and enabled investment in strategic positioning; as CEO Rose explained, "higher returns have allowed us to make the investments required to improve velocity and efficiency and to handle increased demand from our customers and the nation."

Sources: Matthew K. Rose, "Executive Commentary," *The Journal of Commerce,* January 2008, p. 116; and Bill Mongelluzzo, "Long Hauls BNSF Breaks the 10,000-Foot Barrier with Intermodal Trains," *The Journal of Commerce,* October 6, 2008, p. 30.

Entrenchment in a specific product market tends to make a concentrating firm more adept than competitors at detecting new trends. However, any failure of such a firm to properly forecast major changes in its industry can result in extraordinary losses. Numerous makers of inexpensive digital watches were forced to declare bankruptcy because they failed to anticipate the competition posed by Swatch, Guess, and other trendy watches that emerged from the fashion industry.

A firm pursuing a concentrated growth strategy is vulnerable also to the high opportunity costs that result from remaining in a specific product market and ignoring other options that could employ the firm's resources more profitably. Overcommitment to a specific technology and product market can hinder a firm's ability to enter a new or growing product market that offers more attractive cost-benefit trade-offs. Had Apple Computers maintained its policy of making equipment that did not interface with IBM equipment, it would have missed out on what have proved to be its most profitable strategic options.

Concentrated Growth Is Often the Most Viable Option

Examples abound of firms that have enjoyed exceptional returns on the concentrated growth strategy. Such firms as McDonald's, Goodyear, and Apple Computers have used firsthand knowledge and deep involvement with specific product segments to become powerful competitors in their markets. The strategy is associated even more often with successful smaller firms that have steadily and doggedly improved their market position.

The limited additional resources necessary to implement concentrated growth, coupled with the limited risk involved, also make this strategy desirable for a firm with limited funds. For example, through a carefully devised concentrated growth strategy, medium-sized John Deere & Company was able to become a major force in the agricultural machinery business even when competing with such firms as Ford Motor Company. While other firms were trying to exit or diversify from the farm machinery business, Deere spent $2 billion in upgrading its machinery, boosting its efficiency, and engaging in a program to strengthen its dealership system. This concentrated growth strategy enabled it to become the leader in the farm machinery business despite the fact that Ford was more than 10 times its size.

The firm that chooses a concentrated growth strategy directs its resources to the profitable growth of a narrowly defined product and market, focusing on a dominant technology. Firms that remain within their chosen product market are able to extract the most from their technology and market knowledge and, thus, are able to minimize the risk associated with unrelated diversification. The success of a concentration strategy is founded on the firm's use of superior insights into its technology, product, and customer to obtain a sustainable competitive advantage. Superior performance on these aspects of corporate strategy has been shown to have a substantial positive effect on market success.

A grand strategy of concentrated growth allows for a considerable range of action. Broadly speaking, the firm can attempt to capture a larger market share by increasing the usage rates of present customers, by attracting competitors' customers, or by selling to nonusers. In turn, each of these options suggests more specific options, some of which are listed in the top section of Exhibit 7.4.

When strategic managers forecast that their current products and their markets will not provide the basis for achieving the company mission, they have two options that involve moderate costs and risk: market development and product development.

2. Market Development

market development
A grand strategy of marketing present products, often with only cosmetic modification, to customers in related marketing areas.

Market development commonly ranks second only to concentration as the least costly and least risky of the 15 grand strategies. It consists of marketing present products, often with only cosmetic modifications, to customers in related market areas by adding channels of distribution or by changing the content of advertising or promotion. Several specific market development approaches are listed in Exhibit 7.4. Thus, as suggested by the exhibit, firms that open branch offices in new cities, states, or countries are practicing market development. Likewise, firms are practicing market development if they switch from advertising in trade publications to advertising in newspapers or if they add jobbers to supplement their mail-order sales efforts.

Market development allows firms to leverage some of their traditional strengths by identifying new uses for existing products and new demographically, psychographically, or geographically defined markets. Frequently, changes in media selection, promotional appeals, and distribution signal the implementation of this strategy. Du Pont used market development when it found a new application for Kevlar, an organic material that police, security, and military personnel had used primarily for bulletproofing. Kevlar now is being used to refit and maintain wooden-hulled boats, since it is lighter and stronger than glass fibers and has 11 times the strength of steel. Coca-Cola provides another example, as described in Exhibit 7.5, Top Strategist. Under the leadership of CEO Muhtar Kent, Coca-Cola implemented advertising and public relations initiatives to develop its market share among the Hispanic population in North America.

The medical industry provides other examples of new markets for existing products. The National Institutes of Health's report of a study showing that the use of aspirin may lower the

EXHIBIT 7.4
Specific Options under the Grand Strategies of Concentration, Market Development, and Product Development

Source: Adapted from Philip Kotler and Kevin Keller, *Marketing Management*, 14th Edition, 2012. Reprinted by permission of Pearson Education, Upper Saddle River, NJ.

Concentration (increasing use of present products in present markets):

1. Increasing present customers' rate of use:
   a. Increasing the size of purchase.
   b. Increasing the rate of product obsolescence.
   c. Advertising other uses.
   d. Giving price incentives for increased use.
2. Attracting competitors' customers:
   a. Establishing sharper brand differentiation.
   b. Increasing promotional effort.
   c. Initiating price cuts.
3. Attracting nonusers to buy the product:
   a. Inducing trial use through sampling, price incentives, and so on.
   b. Pricing up or down.
   c. Advertising new uses.

Market development (selling present products in new markets):

1. Opening additional geographic markets:
   a. Regional expansion.
   b. National expansion.
   c. International expansion.
2. Attracting other market segments:
   a. Developing product versions to appeal to other segments.
   b. Entering other channels of distribution.
   c. Advertising in other media.

Product development (developing new products for present markets):

1. Developing new-product features:
   a. Adapt (to other ideas, developments).
   b. Modify (change color, motion, sound, odor, form, shape).
   c. Magnify (stronger, longer, thicker, extra value).
   d. Minify (smaller, shorter, lighter).
   e. Substitute (other ingredients, process, power).
   f. Rearrange (other patterns, layout, sequence, components).
   g. Reverse (inside out).
   h. Combine (blend, alloy, assortment, ensemble; combine units, purposes, appeals, ideas).
2. Developing quality variations.
3. Developing additional models and sizes (product proliferation).

incidence of heart attacks was expected to boost sales in the $2.2 billion analgesic market. It was predicted that the expansion of this market would lower the market share of nonaspirin brands, such as industry leaders Tylenol and Advil. Product extensions currently planned include Bayer Calendar Pack, 28-day packaging to fit the once-a-day prescription for the prevention of a second heart attack.

Another example is Chesebrough-Ponds, a major producer of health and beauty aids, which decided several years ago to expand its market by repacking its Vaseline Petroleum Jelly in pocket-size squeeze tubes as Vaseline "Lip Therapy." The corporation decided to place a strategic emphasis on market development, because it knew from market studies that its petroleum-jelly customers already were using the product to prevent chapped lips. Company leaders reasoned that their market could be expanded significantly if the product were repackaged to fit conveniently in consumers' pockets and purses.

Top Strategist
CEO Muhtar Kent Leads Coca-Cola in Its Development of the Hispanic Market

Exhibit 7.5

Coca-Cola Company's CEO, Muhtar Kent, set one of his 2008 priorities as "fixing" sales in the North American market. Success required acknowledging shifting consumer demographics in the United States and undertaking a new market development strategy, specifically targeting the fast-growing Hispanic population, according to assistant vice president of Hispanic marketing, Reinaldo Padua.

Under Kent's leadership, the Hispanic market was developed through advertising and public relations initiatives. On November 11, 2008, the company announced its partnership with Mexican soccer superstar "Memo" Ochoa. As an official Coca-Cola spokesperson, Memo participated in customer appearances, autograph signings, and other marketing and public relations initiatives.

Kent also continued the company's successful Coca-Cola Telenovela Club, which was launched in 2007 and targeted Hispanics. The program allowed My Coke Rewards to personalize prizes so that consumers could earn products and experiences that relate to the telenovela.

Sources: Joe Guy Collier, "Coke Pursues a Fix for North America," *The Atlanta Journal Constitution,* September 14, 2008, p. B1; and Zayda Rivera, "Effective Marketing to Latinos: The Common Thread," *Diversity Inc.*, http://www.diversityinc.com/public/4544.cfm

3. Product Development

product development
A grand strategy that involves the substantial modification of existing products that can be marketed to current customers.

Product development involves the substantial modification of existing products or the creation of new but related products that can be marketed to current customers through established channels. The product development strategy often is adopted either to prolong the life cycle of current products or to take advantage of a favorite reputation or brand name. The idea is to attract satisfied customers to new products as a result of their positive experience with the firm's initial offering. The bottom section in Exhibit 7.4 lists some of the options available to firms undertaking product development. A revised edition of a college textbook, a new car style, and a second formula of shampoo for oily hair are examples of the product development strategy.

Similarly, Pepsi changed its strategy on beverage products by creating new products to follow the industry movement away from mass branding. This new movement was designed to attract a younger, hipper customer segment. Pepsi's new products include a version of Mountain Dew, called Code Red, and new Pepsi brands, called Pepsi Twist and Pepsi Blue.

The product development strategy is based on the penetration of existing markets by incorporating product modifications into existing items or by developing new products with a clear connection to the existing product line. The telecommunications industry provides an example of product extension based on product modification. To increase its estimated 8 to 10 percent share of the $5 to $6 billion corporate user market, MCI Communication Corporation extended its direct-dial service to 146 countries, the same as those serviced by AT&T, at lower average rates than those of AT&T. MCI's addition of 79 countries to its network underscores its belief in this market, which it expects to grow 15 to 20 percent annually. Another example of expansions linked to existing lines is Gerber's decision to engage in general merchandise marketing. Gerber's recent introduction included 52 items that ranged from feeding accessories to toys and children's wear. Likewise, Nabisco Brands seeks competitive advantage by placing its strategic emphasis on product development. With headquarters in Parsippany, New Jersey, the company is one of three operating units of RJR Nabisco. It is the leading producer of biscuits, confections, snacks, shredded cereals, and processed fruits and vegetables. To maintain its position as leader, Nabisco pursues a strategy of developing and introducing new products and expanding its existing product line. Spoon Size Shredded Wheat and Ritz Bits crackers are two examples of new products that are variations on existing products.

4. Innovation

innovation
A grand strategy that seeks to reap the premium margins associated with creation and customer acceptance of a new product or service.

In many industries, it has become increasingly risky not to innovate. Both consumer and industrial markets have come to expect periodic changes and improvements in the products offered. As a result, some firms find it profitable to make **innovation** their grand strategy. They seek to reap the initially high profits associated with customer acceptance of a new or greatly improved product. Then, rather than face stiffening competition as the basis of profitability shifts from innovation to production or marketing competence, they search for other original or novel ideas. The underlying rationale of the grand strategy of innovation is to create a new product life cycle and thereby make similar existing products obsolete. Thus, this strategy differs from the product development strategy of extending an existing product's life cycle. For example, Intel, a leader in the semiconductor industry, pursues expansion through a strategic emphasis on innovation. Companies under pressure to innovate often supplement their own R&D efforts by partnering with other firms in their industry that have complementary needs.

While most growth-oriented firms appreciate the need to be innovative, a few firms use it as their fundamental way of relating to their markets. An outstanding example is Polaroid, which heavily promoted each of its new cameras until competitors were able to match its technological innovation; by then, Polaroid normally was prepared to introduce a dramatically new or improved product. For example, it introduced consumers in quick succession to the Swinger, the SX-70, the One Step, and the Sun Camera 660.

Few innovative ideas prove profitable because the research, development, and premarketing costs of converting a promising idea into a profitable product are extremely high. A study by the Booz Allen Hamilton management research department provides some understanding of the risks. As shown in Exhibit 7.6, Booz Allen found that fewer than 2 percent of the innovative projects initially considered by 51 companies eventually reached the marketplace. Specifically, out of every 58 new product ideas, only 12 pass an initial screening test that finds them compatible with the firm's mission and long-term objectives, only 7 remain after an evaluation of their potential, and only 3 survive development attempts. Of the three survivors, two appear to have profit potential after test marketing and only one is commercially successful.

5. Horizontal Acquisition

horizontal acquisition
A grand strategy based on growth through the acquisition of similar firms operating at the same stage of the production-marketing chain.

When a firm's long-term strategy is based on growth through the acquisition of one or more similar firms operating at the same stage of the production-marketing chain, its grand strategy is called **horizontal acquisition.** Such acquisitions eliminate competitors and provide the acquiring firm with access to new markets. One example is Warner-Lambert's acquisition of Parke Davis, which reduced competition in the ethical drugs field for Chilcott Laboratories, a firm that Warner-Lambert previously had acquired. Another example is the long-range acquisition pattern of White Consolidated Industries, which expanded in the refrigerator and freezer market through a grand strategy of horizontal acquisition, by acquiring Kelvinator

EXHIBIT 7.6
Decay of New Product Ideas

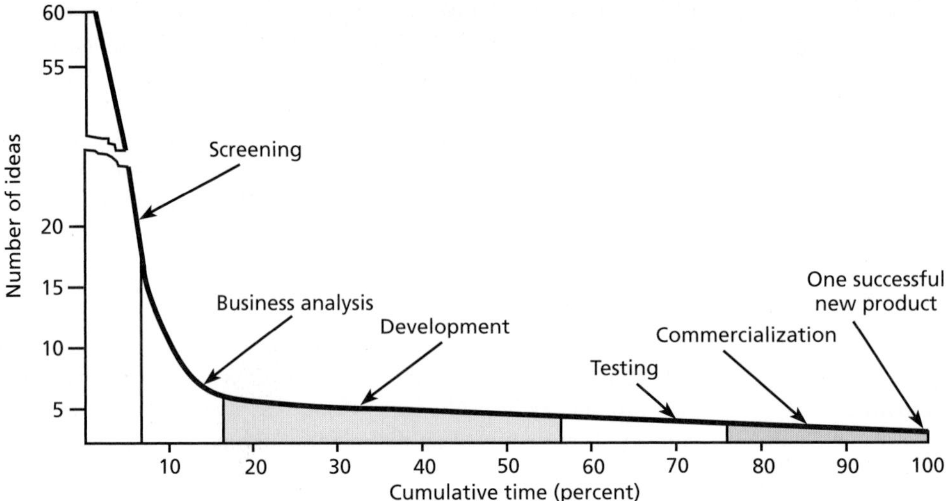

Appliance, the Refrigerator Products Division of Bendix Westinghouse Automotive Air Brake, and Frigidaire Appliance from General Motors. Nike's acquisition in the dress shoes business and N. V. Homes's purchase of Ryan Homes have vividly exemplified the success that horizontal acquisition strategies can bring.

The attractions of a horizontal acquisition strategy are many and varied.[3] However every benefit provides the parent firm with critical resources that it needs to improve overall profitability. For example, the acquiring firm that uses a horizontal acquisition can quickly expand its operations geographically, increase its market share, improve its production capabilities and economies of scale, gain control of knowledge-based resources, broaden its product line, and increase its efficient use of capital. An added attraction of horizontal acquisition is that these benefits are achieved with only moderately increased risk, because the success of the expansion is principally dependent on proven abilities.

A horizontal merger can provide the firm with an opportunity to offer its customers a broader product line. This motivation has sparked a series of acquisitions in the security software industry. Because Entrust purchased Business Signatures, the consolidated company is able to offer banks a full suite of antifraud products. Similarly, Verisign's acquisitions of m-Qube and Snapcentric enabled Verisign to expand its cross-marketing options by offering password-generating software, transaction monitoring software, and identity protection. RSA Security's horizontal acquisitions started with the purchase of PassMark, which reduced competitors in the authentication software space. RSA Security then acquired Cyota to provide its customers with both transaction monitoring and authentication software. As a final example, Symantec bought both Veritas Software and WholeSecurity to provide its customers of storage with additional features, such as antivirus software.

The motivation to gain market share has prompted the financial industry to feature horizontal merger strategies. The acquisition of First Coastal Bank by Citizens Business Bank provided new bases of operation in Los Angeles and Manhattan for Citizens Business Bank. The merger of Raincross Credit Union with Visterra Credit Union enabled these credit unions to achieve the size to justify the expansion of services their customers were demanding.

In a deal that created a dominant supplier of computer disk drives, Western Digital Corp. purchased Hitachi Ltd.'s disk-drive business for $4.3 billion in 2011. The transaction reduced

[3] This section was drawn from John A. Pearce II and D. Keith Robbins, "Strategic Transformation as the Essential Last Step in the Process of Business Turnaround," *Business Horizons* 50, no. 5 (2008).

Global Strategy in Action

Exhibit 7.7

NFI Acquires World Warehouse

NFI, one of the country's most diverse supply chain solutions companies acquired World Warehouse and Distribution in 2011, a third-party logistics and warehouse company headquartered in Champlain, NY, with facilities in Champlain and Albany, NY, and Montreal, Canada. World Warehouse remained a separate entity under the umbrella of NFI's Warehousing and Distribution division. The horizontal acquisition of World Warehouse added nearly one million additional square feet to the warehouse and distribution space managed by NFI, bringing the total warehouse space owned or managed by NFI to over 19 million square feet.

"Acquiring World Warehouse is part of our strategic plan to increase our footprint in Canada. This transaction continues to build upon our previous acquisition of IPD Global—now NFI Canada—expanding our services cross border and within Canada. By the end of 2011, NFI will operate over 1 million square feet of distribution space in four cities in Canada and manage close to $75M in transport-related revenues," said NFI Chief Executive Officer Sidney Brown.

"This acquisition expands NFI's network of third party logistics and warehouse services, and further enhances our cross border capacity and capabilities," Brown continued. "In turn, NFI provides the World Warehouse customer base with access to a vast network of integrated logistics services and supply chain solutions."

World Warehouse provides a wide array of transportation and logistics solutions for a variety of industries, including pharmaceuticals, perishable and nonperishable manufacturers and distributors, beverage manufacturers and sporting goods retailers. "We look forward to being integrated into this powerhouse company, and the ability to better service existing customers and grow our base," said Kevin O'Shea, continuing president of World Warehouse.

With $900 million in gross revenue in 2010 achieved through organic growth and an aggressive acquisition strategy, the purchase of World Warehouse marks the tenth acquisition that NFI has made in as many years. The company's growth strategy has positioned NFI as a nationwide integrated supply chain solutions provider with 5,600 employees, over 19 million square feet of owned or managed warehouse space in the US and Canada, and over 2,000 tractors and more than 6,700 dry trailers and 500 refrigerated trailers.

Source: Excerpted from "NFI Acquires World Warehouse," *Transportation Business Journal*, March 27, 2011, p. 59.

the number of hard drive makers to four giants. Western Digital's share of global shipments after adding Hitachi's operations became nearly 50 percent, compared with about 30 percent for No. 2, Seagate Technology PLC. Because Hitachi was the industry's price aggressor, the merger greatly reduced the cutthroat price cutting that characterized the industry's rivalry.

Some horizontal mergers are motivated by the opportunity to combine resources as a means to improve operational efficiency. In the energy industry, for example, there were eight announced horizontal acquisitions with a combined value of $64 billion between January 2004 and January 2007. In each case, increased operational efficiencies resulted from the elimination of duplicated costs. In 2005, Duke Energy acquired Cinergy Corp. for $14.1 billion. The friendly takeover worked well because Duke Energy's North America division was a great match with Cinergy's energy trading operation and provided economies of scale and scope. The combined company lowered costs by an estimated $400 million per year by using a broad platform to serve both electricity and natural gas customers.[4]

When one of the United States' most diverse supply chain solutions companies acquired a third-party logistics and warehouse company, the strategy was horizontal acquisition. As described in Exhibit 7.7, Global Strategy in Action, NFI's 2011 acquisition of World Warehouse added nearly one million square feet to the warehouse and distribution space managed by NFI and extended its international operations.

[4] G. Terzo,"Duke and Cinergy Spur Utility M&A," *The Investment Dealer's Digest IDD,* January 16, 2006, p. 1.

Global Strategy in Action — Exhibit 7.8

Horizontal Acquisition of Aon and Benfield

In 2008, Aon acquired its top rival Benfield and immediately undertook a full horizontal acquisition. Aon could then deliver new solutions in expanded reinsurance markets under a new brand: Aon Benfield.

Aon and Benfield were ideal candidates for horizontal integration due to their shared focus on service excellence and creating value for clients through thought leadership. The firms also overlapped in their targeted developing markets, including those in Asia, central and eastern Europe, Africa, and Latin America.

Aon Benfield anticipated that once the acquisition was complete, shared services would lead to $122 million in annual cost savings. The acquisition also doubled the new combination's access to key major accounts, allowing Aon Benfield to serve most global insurance and reinsurance carriers. Importantly, Aon gained access to property-catastrophe markets in the southeastern United States, where it can leverage Benfield's unique risk analysis and modeling technologies.

Source: "Aon Completes Acquisition of Benfield Group Limited," *Marketwatch*, November 28, 2008.

A second example of an efficiency-driven merger is one between Constellation and FPL, which saves between $1.5 and $2.1 billion by eliminating overlapping operations.[5] Another example is the acquisition of Green Mountain Power by Gaz Metro, a subsidiary of Northern New England Energy Power for $187 million. The merger was prompted by Green Mountain Power's expiring supplier contracts that threatened it with high costs of going to suppliers who were out of its geographic region—but within the region of Gaz Metro. The horizontal acquisition enabled Green Mountain Power to avail itself of Gaz Metro's suppliers.

Deutsche Telekom's growth strategy was horizontal acquisition. Deutsche Telekom was a dominant player in the European wireless services market, but without a presence in the fast-growing U.S. market in 2000. To correct this limitation, Deutsche Telekom horizontally integrated by purchasing the American firm VoiceStream Wireless, a company that was growing faster than most domestic rivals and that owned spectrum licenses providing access to 220 million potential customers.

Finally, through a horizontal acquisition designed to take advantage of the multiple strengths of the grand strategy, Aon acquired its top rival Benfield. The new company, Aon Benfield, promises to be the world leader in reinsurance brokerage and expects significant cost reductions, increased efficiencies, and stronger presence in the reinsurance market, as discussed in Exhibit 7.8, Global Strategy in Action.

6. Vertical Acquisition

vertical acquisition
A grand strategy based on the acquisition of firms that supply the acquiring firm with inputs or new customers for its outputs.

When a firm's grand strategy is to acquire firms that supply it with inputs (such as raw materials) or are customers for its outputs (such as warehousers for finished products), **vertical acquisition** is involved. To illustrate, if a shirt manufacturer acquires a textile producer—by purchasing its common stock, buying its assets, or exchanging ownership interests—the strategy is vertical acquisition. In this case, it is *backward* vertical integration, because the acquired firm operates at an earlier stage of the production-marketing process. If the shirt manufacturer had merged with a clothing store, it would have been *forward* vertical acquisition—the acquisition of a firm nearer to the ultimate consumer.

Amoco emerged as North America's leader in natural gas reserves and products as a result of its acquisition of Dome Petroleum. This backward acquisition by Amoco was made

[5] J. Fontana,"A New Wave of Consolidation in the Utility Industry," *Electric Light and Power* 84, no. 4 (July/August 2006), pp. 36–38.

Strategy in Action

Exhibit 7.9

Vertical and Horizontal Acquisition

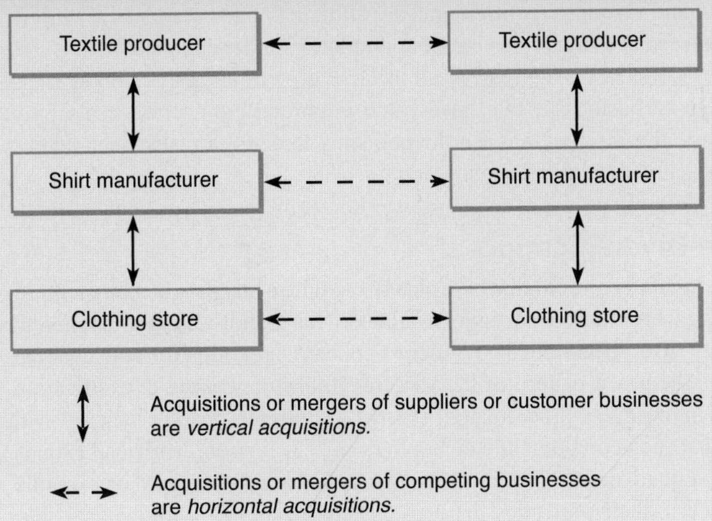
Textile producer
Textile producer
Shirt manufacturer
Shirt manufacturer
Clothing store
Clothing store
Acquisitions or mergers of suppliers or customer businesses are *vertical acquisitions.*
Acquisitions or mergers of competing businesses are *horizontal acquisitions.*

in support of its downstream businesses in refining and in gas stations, whose profits made the acquisition possible.

Exhibit 7.9, Strategy in Action depicts both horizontal and vertical acquisition. The principal attractions of a horizontal acquisition grand strategy are readily apparent. The acquiring firm is able to greatly expand its operations, thereby achieving greater market share, improving economies of scale, and increasing the efficiency of capital use. In addition, these benefits are achieved with only moderately increased risk, because the success of the expansion is principally dependent on proven abilities.

The reasons for choosing a vertical acquisition grand strategy are more varied and sometimes less obvious. The main reason for backward acquisition is the desire to increase the dependability of the supply or quality of the raw materials used as production inputs. That desire is particularly great when the number of suppliers is small and the number of competitors is large. In this situation, the vertically integrating firm can better control its costs and, thereby, improve the profit margin of the expanded production-marketing system. Forward acquisition is a preferred grand strategy if great advantages accrue to stable production. A firm can increase the predictability of demand for its output through forward acquisition; that is, through ownership of the next stage of its production-marketing chain.

Some increased risks are associated with both types of acquisition. For horizontally acquired firms, the risks stem from increased commitment to one type of business. For vertically acquired firms, the risks result from the firm's expansion into areas requiring strategic managers to broaden the base of their competencies and to assume additional responsibilities.

concentric diversification
A grand strategy that involves the operation of a second business that benefits from access to the first firm's core competencies.

7. Concentric Diversification

Concentric diversification involves the acquisition of businesses that are related to the acquiring firm in terms of technology, markets, or products. With this grand strategy, the selected new businesses possess a high degree of compatibility with the firm's current businesses. The ideal concentric diversification occurs when the combined company profits increase the strengths and opportunities and decrease the weaknesses and exposure to risk. Thus, the acquiring firm searches for new businesses whose products, markets, distribution channels, technologies, and resource requirements are similar to but not identical with its own, whose acquisition results in synergies but not complete interdependence.

Abbott Laboratories pursues an aggressive concentric growth strategy. Abbott seeks to acquire a wide range of businesses that have some important connection to its basic business. In recent years, this strategy has led the company to acquire pharmaceuticals, a diagnostic business, and a medical device manufacturer.

8. Conglomerate Diversification

conglomerate diversification
A grand strategy that involves the acquisition of a business because it presents the most promising investment opportunity available.

Occasionally a firm, particularly a very large one, plans to acquire a business because it represents the most promising investment opportunity available. This grand strategy is commonly known as **conglomerate diversification.** The principal concern, and often the sole concern, of the acquiring firm is the profit pattern of the venture. Unlike concentric diversification, conglomerate diversification gives little concern to creating product-market synergy with existing businesses. What such conglomerate diversifiers as ITT, Textron, American Brands, Litton, U.S. Industries, Fuqua, and I. C. Industries seek is financial synergy. For example, they may seek a balance in their portfolios between current businesses with cyclical sales and acquired businesses with countercyclical sales, between high-cash/low-opportunity and low-cash/high-opportunity businesses, or between debt-free and highly leveraged businesses.

The principal difference between the two types of diversification is that concentric diversification emphasizes some commonality in markets, products, or technology, whereas conglomerate diversification is based principally on profit considerations.

Several of the grand strategies discussed above, including concentric and conglomerate diversification and horizontal and vertical acquisition, often involve the purchase or acquisition of one firm by another.

Motivation for Diversification

Grand strategies involving either concentric or conglomerate diversification represent distinctive departures from a firm's existing base of operations, typically the acquisition or internal generation (spin-off) of a separate business with synergistic possibilities counterbalancing the strengths and weaknesses of the two businesses. For example, Head Ski sought to diversify into summer sporting goods and clothing to offset the seasonality of its "snow" business. Additionally, diversifications occasionally are undertaken as unrelated investments, because of their high profit potential and their otherwise minimal resource demands.

Regardless of the approach taken, the motivations of the acquiring firms are the same:

- Increase the firm's stock value. In the past, mergers often have led to increases in the stock price or the price-earnings ratio.
- Increase the growth rate of the firm.
- Make an investment that represents better use of funds than plowing them into internal growth.
- Improve the stability of earnings and sales by acquiring firms whose earnings and sales complement the firm's peaks and valleys.
- Balance or fill out the product line.
- Diversify the product line when the life cycle of current products has peaked.
- Acquire a needed resource quickly (e.g., high-quality technology or highly innovative management).

- Achieve tax savings by purchasing a firm whose tax losses will offset current or future earnings.
- Increase efficiency and profitability, especially if there is synergy between the acquiring firm and the acquired firm.[6]

9. Turnaround

For any one of a large number of reasons, a firm can find itself with declining profits. Among these reasons are economic recessions, production inefficiencies, and innovative breakthroughs by competitors. In many cases, strategic managers believe that such a firm can survive and eventually recover if a concerted effort is made over a period of a few years to fortify its distinctive competencies. This grand strategy is known as **turnaround.** It typically is begun through one of two forms of retrenchment, employed singly or in combination:

turnaround
A grand strategy of cost reduction and asset reduction by a company to survive and recover from declining profits.

1. *Cost reduction*. Examples include decreasing the workforce through employee attrition, leasing rather than purchasing equipment, extending the life of machinery, eliminating elaborate promotional activities, laying off employees, dropping items from a production line, and discontinuing low-margin customers.

   In 2009, electronics giant Sony took major steps to reduce staff and supply chain costs. It reduced its reliance on a high-priced, high-tech approach in favor of more popular low-cost items. Consequently, Sony reduced the number of its suppliers by 50 percent to cut costs, and laid off 8,000 of its 186,000 employees.
2. *Asset reduction*. Examples include the sale of land, buildings, and equipment not essential to the basic activity of the firm and the elimination of "perks," such as the company airplane and executives' cars.

   Alcoa, one of the world's largest aluminum makers, sold several unprofitable business lines in 2009 and stopped all "noncritical" capital investment programs to try to conserve cash in response to the continuing economic downturn that followed the recession of 2007–2009. Alcoa reduced output by 18 percent and cut its head count by 13 percent, or 13,500 employees. Facing a steep decline in demand for its fabricated goods, Alcoa believed that the moves were necessary for the firm to try to conserve cash and reduce costs. Alcoa also froze all hiring and salaries for one year.

Interestingly, the turnaround most commonly associated with this approach is in management positions. In a study of 58 large firms, researchers found that turnaround almost always was associated with changes in top management.[7] Bringing in new managers was believed to introduce needed new perspectives on the firm's situation, to raise employee morale, and to facilitate drastic actions, such as deep budgetary cuts in established programs.

Strategic management research provides evidence that the firms that have used a *turnaround strategy* have successfully confronted decline. The research findings have been assimilated and used as the building blocks for a model of the turnaround process shown in Exhibit 7.10, Strategy in Action.

The model begins with a depiction of external and internal factors as causes of a firm's performance downturn. When these factors continue to detrimentally impact the firm, its financial health is threatened. Unchecked decline places the firm in a turnaround situation.

[6] Godfrey Devlin and Mark Bleackley, "Strategic Alliances—Guidelines for Success," *Long Range Planning,* October 1988, pp. 18–23.

[7] D. Schendel, R. Patton, and J. Riggs, "Corporate Turnaround Strategies: A Study of Profit Decline and Recovery," *Journal of General Management* 3, no. 3 (1976), pp. 3–11.

Strategy in Action Exhibit 7.10

A Model of the Turnaround Process

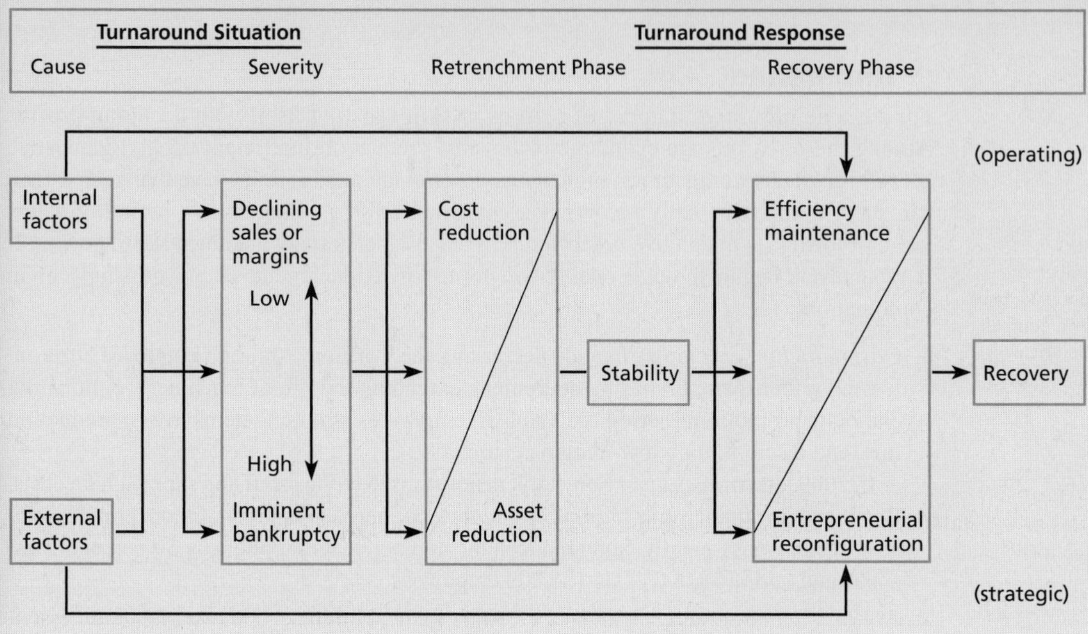

A *turnaround situation* represents absolute and relative-to-industry declining performance of a sufficient magnitude to warrant explicit turnaround actions. Turnaround situations may be the result of years of gradual slowdown or months of sharp decline. In either case, the recovery phase of the turnaround process is likely to be more successful in accomplishing turnaround when it is preceded by planned retrenchment that results in the achievement of near-term financial stabilization. For a declining firm, stabilizing operations and restoring profitability almost always entail strict cost reduction followed by a shrinking back to those segments of the business that have the best prospects of attractive profit margins. The need for retrenchment often arises when companies face an economic recession. The United States has experienced 12 economic recessions since the end of WWII in 1945. During this period, the average business cycle was 70 months or roughly one full cycle every 5.8 years. The average expansion period has been 59 months, and the average recession has been 11 months. However, statistical patterns often fail to provide useful guidance in predicting the specifics of a recession. For example, economists failed to predict the "great recession" of 2007–2009, which resulted in massive layoffs and high levels of unemployment. Roughly 8.5 million jobs were lost during the recession, and it is predicted that these jobs might not fully return until 2018. In addition, from 2007 to 2009 the rate at which new business establishments were started fell 13.3 percent.

During the 2007–2009 recession, pretax corporate profits fell for three consecutive years. In 2006, pretax corporate profits, with inventory valuation and capital consumption adjustments, reached an all-time high of $1.6083 trillion. However, these corporate profits dropped to $1.5106 trillion in 2007, $1.2628 trillion in 2008, and $1.258 trillion in 2009. By the end of 2009, pretax corporate profits were 27 percent lower than the 2006 high.

Strategy in Action — Exhibit 7.11

Cutting Costs to Increase Profits

Because of successful cost-cutting at Gap, which boosted profits despite declining industry sales, shares of Gap increased 27 percent in the first three quarters of 2008, even as sales fell 8 percent for competitors Banana Republic and Old Navy. Gap's survival odds were aided by cost savings achieved through reduced inventory levels and the sell-off of noncore assets such as selected real estate holdings.

Similarly, in the face of sharply declining revenues, Dell undertook cost-cutting in 2008, including massive layoffs that totaled 11,000 employees for the year and an aggressive plan to sell its manufacturing facilities worldwide.

Although many firms find it possible to maintain some level of profit by cost-cutting for as long as one full year, aggressive cost-cutters must eventually find ways to increase their revenues. Circuit City and Radio Shack cut costs and increased profit margins in 2008 but were undone by sharp declines in their revenues. Circuit City filed for bankruptcy in November, the day after it announced that it would close 155 retail stores, and Radio Shack lost 50 percent of its market value for the year of 2008.

Managers need to understand the economic factors that foreshadow an economic downturn. Companies that are able to understand the economic uncertainties facing their industry and make timely adjustments to their company will outperform their competitors.

The immediacy of the resulting threat to company survival posed by the turnaround situation is known as *situation severity*. Severity is the governing factor in estimating the speed with which the retrenchment response will be formulated and activated. When severity is low, a firm has some financial cushion. Stability may be achieved through cost retrenchment alone. When turnaround situation severity is high, a firm must immediately stabilize the decline or bankruptcy is imminent. Cost reductions must be supplemented with more drastic asset reduction measures. Assets targeted for divestiture are those determined to be underproductive. In contrast, more productive resources are protected from cuts and represent critical elements of the future core business plan of the company (i.e., the intended recovery response).

Turnaround responses among successful firms typically include two stages of strategic activities: retrenchment and the recovery response. *Retrenchment* consists of cost-cutting and asset-reducing activities. The primary objective of the retrenchment phase is to stabilize the firm's financial condition. Situation severity has been associated with retrenchment responses among successful turnaround firms. Firms in danger of bankruptcy or failure (i.e., severe situations) attempt to halt decline through cost and asset reductions. Firms in less severe situations have achieved stability merely through cost retrenchment. However, in either case, for firms facing declining financial performance, the key to successful turnaround rests in the effective and efficient management of the retrenchment process.

The primary causes of the turnaround situation have been associated with the second phase of the turnaround process, the *recovery response*. During the first year of the 2007–2009 recession, many firms retrenched sharply to avoid financial failure. For examples of firms that turned losses into profits in 2008 by cost-cutting, read Exhibit 7.11, Strategy in Action. For firms that declined primarily as a result of external problems, turnaround most often has been achieved through creative new entrepreneurial strategies. For firms that declined primarily as a result of internal problems, turnaround has been most frequently achieved through efficiency strategies. *Recovery* is achieved when economic measures indicate that the firm has regained its predownturn levels of performance.

Turnaround strategies can help a corporation to achieve spectacular results. Exhibit 7.12, Global Strategy in Action describes three of the most impressive turnarounds in recent history.

Global Strategy in Action — Exhibit 7.12

Best Corporate Turnarounds

BEST BUY

In one of the more impressive retail turnarounds ever, Best Buy saw a dramatic reversal of its fortunes between 1997 and 1999. This was reflected in a share price that rebounded from less than $2 to nearly $60 over the same time frame. The growing pains started after a rapid growth trajectory in which the corporate culture was decentralized to leave each new store to function relatively on its own.

The company soon began to lose repeat customers because of its inability to deliver a consistent sales experience throughout its stores. Management quickly turned to a more cohesive strategy of delivering a better shopping experience and using inventory controls to more efficiently track and purchase inventory across the entire company. Similar efforts to tie up every aspect of Best Buy's operations saved the company in just a couple of years. Since then the company has grown to dominate the electronics retailing industry in the United States. In 2011 it announced ambitions to replicate this success overseas.

APPLE

Apple's reinvention was even more impressive given it operates in the rapidly changing technology industry. It was one of the first companies to introduce desktop computers and had a large market share in the 1980s. This market share was steadily eroded from the double digits to an estimated 4.6 percent in 1996. The company gained the undesirable status of a has-been in the industry as computers that operated on Windows came to dominate the market.

The introduction of the iPod in 2001 started a stunning reversal of fortune. It took a couple of years, but the stock took off in 2003 from less than $8 per share to a current $340 per share. The iPod and related iTunes store revolutionized the music industry, as has the iPhone in mobile phones and the iPad for tablet computers for an impressive and lasting impact on three different segments of the technology industry.

AIG

A disastrous foray into credit derivatives sent one of the largest insurers in the world to the brink of collapse at the height of the credit crisis. Nearly $200 billion in government bailout funding was required, and the company reported multibillion dollar losses in 2008 and some of the largest quarterly losses in company history.

Since that time, it has been in the process of selling off profitable overseas operations to pay back the government and has become a truly independent entity again. The corporate comeback is reflected in a share price that dipped to $7 per share in March 2009 and then rose to $37 in April 2011.

Source: Excerpted from Ryan C. Fuhrmann, "5 Best Corporate Comebacks," *Investopedia*. http//www.investopedia.com/. Accessed April 6, 2011.

10. Divestiture

divestiture strategy
A grand strategy that involves the sale of a firm or a major unit of a firm as a going concern.

A **divestiture strategy** involves the sale of a firm or a major component of a firm. Sara Lee Corp. provides a good example. It sells everything from Wonderbras and Kiwi shoe polish to Endust furniture polish and Chock Full o'Nuts coffee. The company used a conglomerate diversification strategy to build Sara Lee into a huge portfolio of disparate brands. A new president, C. Steven McMillan, faced stagnant revenues and earnings. So he consolidated, streamlined, and focused the company on its core categories—food, underwear, and household products. He divested 15 businesses, including Coach leather goods, which together equaled more than 20 percent of the company's revenue, and laid off 13,200 employees, nearly 10 percent of the workforce. McMillan used the cash from asset sales to snap up brands that enhanced Sara Lee's clout in key categories, like the $2.8 billion purchase of St. Louis–based breadmaker Earthgrains Co. to quadruple Sara Lee's bakery operations. In another case of divestitures, Kraft Foods found that it could improve its overall operations by selling some of its best-known brands, including Cream of Wheat.

When retrenchment fails to accomplish the desired turnaround, or when a nonintegrated business activity achieves an unusually high market value, strategic managers often decide to sell the firm. However, because the intent is to find a buyer willing to pay a premium above the value of a going concern's fixed assets, the term *marketing for sale* is often more appropriate. Prospective buyers must be convinced that because of their skills and resources or because of the firm's synergy with their existing businesses, they will be able to profit from the acquisition.

The reasons for divestiture vary. They often arise because of partial mismatches between the acquired firm and the parent corporation. Some of the mismatched parts cannot be integrated into the corporation's mainstream activities and, thus, must be spun off. A second reason is corporate financial needs. Sometimes the cash flow or financial stability of the corporation as a whole can be greatly improved if businesses with high market value can be sacrificed. The result can be a balancing of equity with long-term risks or of long-term debt payments to optimize the cost of capital. A third, less frequent reason for divestiture is government antitrust action when a firm is believed to monopolize or unfairly dominate a particular market.

Although examples of the divestiture grand strategy are numerous, CBS Inc. provides an outstanding example. In a two-year period, the once diverse entertainment and publishing giant sold its Records Division to Sony, its magazine publishing business to Diamandis Communications, its book publishing operations to Harcourt Brace Jovanovich, and its music publishing operations to SBK Entertainment World. Other firms that have pursued this type of grand strategy include Esmark, which divested Swift & Company, and White Motors, which divested White Farm.

11. Liquidation

liquidation
A grand strategy that involves the sale of the assets of the business for their salvage value.

When **liquidation** is the grand strategy, the firm typically is sold in parts, only occasionally as a whole—but for its tangible asset value and not as a going concern. In selecting liquidation, the owners and strategic managers of a firm are admitting failure and recognize that this action is likely to result in great hardships to themselves and their employees. For these reasons, liquidation usually is seen as the least attractive of the grand strategies. As a long-term strategy, however, it minimizes the losses of all the firm's stockholders. Faced with bankruptcy, the liquidating firm usually tries to develop a planned and orderly system that will result in the greatest possible return and cash conversion as the firm slowly relinquishes its market share.

Planned liquidation can be worthwhile. For example, Columbia Corporation, a \$130 million diversified firm, liquidated its assets for more cash per share than the market value of its stock. Much more commonly, liquidation goes hand-in-hand with bankruptcy, as shown in the Circuit City experience that is discussed in Exhibit 7.13, Strategy in Action.

More commonly, liquidation is the companion to Chapter 7 bankruptcy. For example, in 2011 the bankrupt Robb & Stucky furniture chain started a court-ordered liquidation sale of all inventory just hours after being bought in court by an investment fund that specializes in winding down bankrupt stores. Like most retail shutdowns, the sale followed the pattern of escalating discounts until all inventory, store fixtures, and equipment were sold. The sale of \$90 million in inventory ended 96 years in business for the Florida-based upscale furniture seller. After the liquidation sale, all 20 Robb & Stucky stores were closed. The corporation filed bankruptcy following a rapid expansion of new stores into Nevada and Texas that suffered some of the worst of a housing downturn, with resulting massive losses for the furniture retailer.

The unfortunate need for liquidations is obviously not limited to problems in a single nation. Liquidation is a global issue. For example, as described in Exhibit 7.14, Global Strategy in Action, South Africa has recently experienced a rash of companies going out of business through liquidation.

Strategy in Action — Exhibit 7.13

The Ultimate Failure of Circuit City

On November 10, 2008, Circuit City filed for Chapter 11 bankruptcy, as a consequence of bad management in an industry where competition for market share is fierce among competitors such as Best Buy and Wal-Mart.

An article in *Time* magazine called the culprit in Circuit City's disastrous performance "good ole fashioned bad management." Specifically, Circuit City's failure is attributed to inconvenient store locations, eliminating appliances from the product line, languishing in the gaming market, utilizing an underpaid and undertrained workforce, and ignoring big-name cross-promotional opportunities. Such missteps suggested an underlying cause: marketplace complacency. In the fiercely competitive retail electronics industry, Circuit City faced, most notably, Best Buy and Wal-Mart and a myriad of lesser firms, including Amazon, Apple, Costco, Dell, Fry's Electronics, and Radio Shack.

Circuit City was the largest electronics retailer in the United States through the mid-1990s. During that time, the company signed leases on cheap, often out-of-the-way real estate, which made for some uninviting shopping experiences in too-big spaces. As sales decreased, Circuit City replaced its higher paid, more experienced workforce with lower paid, less experienced workers, resulting in a deteriorating reputation for bad customer service. In the meantime, competitors secured better real estate deals, offered better services, and adapted more quickly to the competitive marketplace. Circuit City lost its market share lead to Best Buy, which became known as a higher end, customer-centric retailer, as contrasted to Wal-Mart, the low-price provider.

On January 16, 2009, Circuit City announced that it could not resolve its financial problems and would close its remaining 567 U.S. stores (with 34,000 employees) and liquidate the business. It continued to negotiate the sale of its 765 retail stores and dealer outlets in Canada.

Hudson Capital Partners, the liquidator for Circuit City, estimated the retail value of the company's assets at $1.8 billion. These items were placed on sale at a 30 percent discount that increased until the liquidation was complete.

Sources: A. Hamilton, "Why Circuit City Busted, While Best Buy Boomed," *Time Online*, 2008, http://www.time.com/time/business/article/0,8599,1858079,00.html; and S. Rosenbloom, "Electronics Store Files for Bankruptcy," *The New York Times*, 2008, p. B1.

12. Bankruptcy

bankruptcy
When a company is unable to pay its debts as they become due.

Business failures are playing an increasingly important role in the American economy. In an average week, more than 300 companies fail and file for **bankruptcy.** More than 75 percent of these financially desperate firms file for a *liquidation bankruptcy*—they agree to a complete distribution of their assets to creditors, most of whom receive a small fraction of the amount they are owed. Liquidation is what the layperson views as bankruptcy: the business cannot pay its debts, so it must close its doors. Investors lose their money, employees lose their jobs, and managers lose their credibility. In owner-managed firms, company and personal bankruptcy commonly go hand in hand.

The other 25 percent of these firms refuse to surrender until one final option is exhausted. Choosing a strategy to recapture its viability, such a company asks the courts for a *reorganization bankruptcy*. The firm attempts to persuade its creditors to temporarily freeze their claims while it undertakes to reorganize and rebuild the company's operations more profitably. The appeal of a reorganization bankruptcy is based on the company's ability to convince creditors that it can succeed in the marketplace by implementing a new strategic plan, and that when the plan produces profits, the firm will be able to repay its creditors, perhaps in full. In other words, the company offers its creditors a carefully designed alternative to forcing an immediate, but fractional, repayment of its financial obligations. The option of reorganization bankruptcy offers maximum repayment of debt at some specified future time if a new strategic plan is successful.

Global Strategy in Action — Exhibit 7.14

Liquidations in South Africa Soar as Downturn Bites

Liquidations auctions have soared in number and value, according to the country's largest auction group. In 2009, "we saw the volume of auctions shoot through the roof due to the sheer number of distressed homes hitting the auction floor," Auction Alliance CE Rael Levitt said. "Luckily, we have seen lower-value forced sales slow down quite significantly due to lower interest rates, banks assisting defaulting debtors and a stabilisation of house prices. Now the turn has arrived for large liquidations of commercial properties and property developments."

"While we have not seen large-scale liquidations of property portfolios, we certainly have conducted the highest value liquidation sales that SA has seen in years." Mr. Levitt says liquidation auctions peak well after a turnaround. "Liquidation auctions are a typical late-cycle indicator and generally only surge well after the economy has started to improve."

Company and close corporation liquidations rose by 35.7 percent year on year in May 2010, with the three months from March to May posting a 17.7 percent rise. "That said, the overall level of liquidations remains extremely high by historical standards and high-value liquidation auctions are an indicator that there is distress (among property owners) with large bank exposures. Businesses burn through their cash reserves during recessions. Distressed property developers may manage to hold on to their properties for a period, but if the downturn lasts longer than expected, or if post-recession activity is slow, these companies cannot claw back their losses. The longer and deeper the recession, the more damage is inflicted."

Even when the economy starts to improve, businesses are typically highly indebted and have depleted their cash reserves. Property developments that survive the initial property downturn faced another hurdle in securing finance, due to liquidity constraints at banks.

Liquidation auctions are a result of a long period of a soft property market and weak economic activity, rather than the slow pace of recovery. For the next 12 months, "we will see higher-value liquidation auctions than we have ever seen before."

Source: Madden Cole, "Liquidations Soar as Downturn Bites," *Business Day*, August 20, 2010.

The Bankruptcy Situation

Imagine that your firm's financial reports have shown an unabated decline in revenue for seven quarters. Expenses have increased rapidly, and it is becoming difficult, and at times not possible, to pay bills as they become due. Suppliers are concerned about shipping goods without first receiving payment, and some have refused to ship without advanced payment in cash. Customers are requiring assurances that future orders will be delivered and some are beginning to buy from competitors. Employees are listening seriously to rumors of financial problems and a higher than normal number have accepted other employment. What can be done? What strategy can be initiated to protect the company and resolve the financial problems in the short term?

Chapter 7: The Harshest Resolution

If the judgment of the owners of a business is that its decline cannot be reversed, and the business cannot be sold as a going concern, then the alternative that is in the best interest of all may be a liquidation bankruptcy, also known as Chapter 7 of the Bankruptcy Code. The court appoints a trustee, who collects the property of the company, reduces it to cash, and distributes the proceeds proportionally to creditors on a pro rata basis as expeditiously as possible. Because all assets are sold to pay outstanding debt, a liquidation bankruptcy terminates a business. This type of filing is critically important to sole proprietors or partnerships. Their owners are personally liable for all business debts not covered by the sale of the business assets unless they can secure a Chapter 7 bankruptcy, which will allow them to cancel any debt in excess of exempt assets. Although they will be left with little personal property, the liquidated debtor is discharged from paying the remaining debt.

The shareholders of corporations are not liable for corporate debt and any debt existing after corporate assets are liquidated is absorbed by creditors. Corporate shareholders may simply terminate operations and walk away without liability to remaining creditors. However, filing a Chapter 7 proceeding will provide for an orderly and fair distribution of assets to creditors and thereby may reduce the negative impact of the business failure.

Chapter 11: A Conditional Second Chance

A proactive alternative for the endangered company is reorganization bankruptcy. Chosen for the right reasons, and implemented in the right way, reorganization bankruptcy can provide a financially, strategically, and ethically sound basis on which to advance the interests of all of the firm's stakeholders.

A thorough and objective analysis of the company may support the idea of its continuing operations if excessive debt can be reduced and new strategic initiatives can be undertaken. If the realistic possibility of long-term survival exists, a reorganization under Chapter 11 of the Bankruptcy Code can provide the opportunity. Reorganization allows a business debtor to restructure its debts and, with the agreement of creditors and approval of the court, to continue as a viable business. Creditors involved in Chapter 11 actions often receive less than the total debt due to them but far more than would be available from liquidation.

A Chapter 11 bankruptcy can provide time and protection to the debtor firm (which we will call the *Company*) to reorganize and use future earnings to pay creditors. The Company may restructure debts, close unprofitable divisions or stores, renegotiate labor contracts, reduce its workforce, or propose other actions that could create a profitable business. If the plan is accepted by creditors, the Company will be given another chance to avoid liquidation and emerge from the bankruptcy proceedings rehabilitated.

Seeking Protection of the Bankruptcy Court

If creditors file lawsuits or schedule judicial sales to enforce liens, the Company will need to seek the protection of the Bankruptcy Court. Filing a bankruptcy petition will invoke the protection of the court to provide sufficient time to work out a reorganization that was not achievable voluntarily. If reorganization is not possible, a Chapter 7 proceeding will allow for the fair and orderly dissolution of the business.

If a Chapter 11 proceeding is the required course of action, the Company must determine what the reorganized business will look like, if such a structure can be achieved, and how it will be accomplished while maintaining operations during the bankruptcy proceeding. Will sufficient cash be available to pay for the proceedings and reorganization? Will customers continue to do business with the Company or seek other more secure businesses with which to deal? Will key personnel stay on or look for more secure employment? Which operations should be discontinued or reduced?

Emerging from Bankruptcy

Bankruptcy is only the first step toward recovery for a firm. Many questions should be answered: How did the business get to the point at which the extreme action of bankruptcy was necessary? Were warning signs overlooked? Was the competitive environment understood? Did pride or fear prevent objective analysis? Did the business have the people and resources to succeed? Was the strategic plan well designed and implemented? Did financial problems result from unforeseen and unforeseeable problems or from bad management decisions?

Commitments to "try harder," "listen more carefully to the customer," and "be more efficient" are important but insufficient grounds to inspire stakeholder confidence. A recovery strategy must be developed to delineate how the company will compete more successfully in the future.

An assessment of the bankruptcy situation requires executives to consider the causes of the Company's decline and the severity of the problem it now faces. Investors must decide whether the management team that governed the company's operations during the downturn can return the firm to a position of success. Creditors must believe that the company's managers have learned how to prevent a recurrence of the observed and similar problems. Alternatively, they must have faith that the company's competencies can be sufficiently augmented by key substitutions to the management team, with strong support in decision making from a board of directors and consultants, to restore the firm's competitive strength.

The 12 grand strategies just discussed, used singly and much more often in combinations, represent the traditional alternatives used by firms in the United States. Recently, three new additional grand types fit under the broad category of corporate combinations. These grand strategies deserve special attention and consideration—especially by companies that operate in global, dynamic, and technologically driven industries. They are joint ventures, strategic alliances, and consortia.

13. Joint Ventures

Occasionally two or more capable firms lack a necessary component for success in a particular competitive environment. For example, no single petroleum firm controlled sufficient resources to construct the Alaskan pipeline. Nor was any single firm capable of processing and marketing all of the oil that would flow through the pipeline. The solution was a set of **joint ventures,** which are commercial companies (children) created and operated for the benefit of the co-owners (parents). These cooperative arrangements provided both the funds needed to build the pipeline and the processing and marketing capacities needed to profitably handle the oil flow.

joint venture
A grand strategy in which companies create a co-owned business that operates for their mutual benefit.

The particular form of joint ventures discussed above is *joint ownership.* In recent years, it has become increasingly appealing for domestic firms to join foreign firms by means of this form. For example, Diamond-Star Motors was the result of a joint venture between a U.S. company, Chrysler Corporation, and Japan's Mitsubishi Motors Corporation. Located in Normal, Illinois, Diamond-Star was launched because it offered Chrysler and Mitsubishi a chance to expand on their long-standing relationship in which subcompact cars (as well as Mitsubishi engines and other automotive parts) were imported to the United States and sold under the Dodge and Plymouth names.

The joint venture extends the supplier-consumer relationship and has strategic advantages for both partners. For Chrysler, it presented an opportunity to produce a high-quality car using expertise brought to the venture by Mitsubishi. It also gave Chrysler the chance to try new production techniques and to realize efficiencies by using the workforce that was not included under Chrysler's collective bargaining agreement with the United Auto Workers. The agreement offered Mitsubishi the opportunity to produce cars for sale in the United States without being subjected to the tariffs and restrictions placed on Japanese imports.

As a second example, Bethlehem Steel acquired an interest in a Brazilian mining venture to secure a raw material source. The stimulus for this joint ownership venture was grand strategy, but such is not always the case. Certain countries virtually mandate that foreign firms entering their markets do so on a joint ownership basis. India and Mexico are good examples. The rationale of these countries is that joint ventures minimize the threat of foreign domination and enhance the skills, employment, growth, and profits of local firms.

Relatively small firms also see the advantages of joint ventures and cooperative arrangements. The British law firm of Barlow Lyde & Gilbert entertained the options of a merger,

Global Strategy in Action — Exhibit 7.15

Barlows Sets Sights on Global Market with New Growth Plan

Barlow Lyde & Gilbert plans to substantially build up its international practice in the wake of a wide-ranging strategy review, with markets including the US, continental Europe and the Middle East all under discussion. The top 40 UK law firm, which currently has offices in Hong Kong, Sao Paulo, Shanghai, and Singapore, is still exploring its options but expects to gain a presence in at least one new market during 2011.

Options on the table include some form of tie-up with firms in the United States and continental Europe, with Barlows open to a merger, alliance, or the launch of an independent office with partners relocating from London. It is thought the firm is more likely to launch a green field operation in the Middle East.

Barlows' chief executive David Jabbari said: "International expansion is at the forefront of our strategy for 2011. At the close of last year, senior partner Simon Konsta and I presented our strategy to the partners and have been given a mandate to explore international opportunities aggressively."

"We have now very clearly outlined that insurance and dispute resolution is our core focus, and if we did enter into any kind of relationship with another firm, it is likely to be driven by international consolidation of those strengths."

The firm's plan to rapidly globalize its practice is the latest in a series of substantive changes to the insurance leader's business and strategy after a period in which it is regarded as having lagged some of its peer group. The firm overhauled its practice structure as part of a review looking at three areas: core markets, plans for future growth and increasing profitability.

Source: Excerpted from Suzanna Ring, "Barlows Sets Sights on Global Market with New Growth Plan," *Legal Week*, February 10, 2011, 13(5):1.

alliance, or the launch of an independent office with partners relocating from London in its search for ways to explore international opportunities aggressively. For details, read Exhibit 7.15, Global Strategy in Action.

It should be noted that strategic managers understandably are wary of joint ventures. Admittedly, joint ventures present new opportunities with risks that can be shared. On the other hand, joint ventures often limit the discretion, control, and profit potential of partners, while demanding managerial attention and other resources that might be directed toward the firm's mainstream activities. Nevertheless, increasing globalization in many industries may require greater consideration of the joint venture approach, if historically national firms are to remain viable.

Collaborative Growth in China through Joint Ventures[8]

A prime example of the value of joint ventures is seen in their use by foreign businesses that seek to do business in China. Until very recently, China enthusiastically invited foreign investment to help in the development of its economy. However, in the early 2000s, China increased its regulations on foreign investment to moderate its economic growth and to ensure that Chinese businesses would not be at a competitive disadvantage when competing for domestic markets. The new restrictions require local companies to retain control of Chinese trademarks and brands, prevent foreign investors from buying property that is not for their own use, limit the size of foreign-owned retail chains, and restrict foreign investment in selected industries.[9] With these increasing regulations, investment in China through joint ventures with Chinese companies has become a prominent strategy for foreign investors who hope to circumvent some of the limitations on their strategies, therefore more fully capitalizing on China's economic growth.

[8] This section was drawn from Pearce II and Robbins, "Strategic Transformation as the Essential Last Step in the Process of Business Turnaround."

[9] E. Kurtenbach, "China Raising Stakes for Foreign Investment," *Philadelphia Inquirer,* September 24, 2006.

In China, a host country partner can greatly facilitate the acceptance of a foreign investor and help minimize the costs of doing business in an unknown nation. Typically, the foreign partner contributes financing and technology, while the Chinese partner provides the land, physical facilities, workers, local connections, and knowledge of the country.[10] In a wholly owned venture, the foreign company is forced to acquire the land, build the workspace, and hire and train the employees, all of which are especially expensive propositions in a country in which the foreign company lacks *guanxi*.[11] *Guanxi* is a network of relationships a person cultivates through the exchange of gifts and favors to attain mutual benefits. It is based on friendship and affection, and on a reciprocal obligation to respond to requests for assistance. People who share a *guanxi* network are committed to one another by an unwritten code. Disregarding this commitment can destroy a business executive's prestige and social reputation.

For example, *guanxi* networks bind millions of Chinese firms into social and business webs, largely dictating their success. In China, enterprises are built on long-lasting links with political party administrative leaders and executives in other companies. Through connections with people who are empowered to make decisions, Chinese executives obtain vital information and assistance. Many Chinese entrepreneurs rely almost exclusively on their "old friends" to obtain material and financial resources, skilled personnel, and even tax considerations. Because *guanxi* is based on reciprocity, executives implicitly accept an obligation to "return a favor" in the unspecified future whenever they benefit from the *guanxi* network. Thus, developing and expanding *guanxi* is a form of social investment that enriches the executive's current resources and future potential.

Foreign partners in equity joint ventures benefit from speed of entry to the Chinese market, tax incentives, motivational and competitive advantages of a mutual long-term commitment, and access to the resources of its Chinese partner. Two large joint ventures in the media industry were created when Canada's AGA Resources partnered with Beijing Tangde International Film and Culture Co and when the United States' Sequoia Capital formed a joint venture with Hunan Greatdreams Cartoon Media.[12] Joint ventures in China's asset management industry include the partnerships between Italy's Banca Lombarda, the United States' Lord Abbett, and Chinese companies.

Similar opportunities exist for international joint ventures in the construction and operation of oil refineries, in the building of the nation's railroad transportation system, and in the development of specific geographic areas. In special economic zones, foreign firms operate businesses with Chinese joint venture partners. The foreign companies receive tax incentives in the form of rates that are lower than the standard 30 percent corporate tax rate. For example, in the Shanghai Pudong New Area, a 15 percent tax rate applies.[13]

The number of international joint ventures is increasing because of China's admission to the World Trade Organization (WTO). Under the conditions of its membership, China is expanding the list of industries that permit foreign investment.[14] As of 2007, for example, foreign investors that participate with Chinese partners in joint ventures are permitted to hold an increased share of JVs in several major industries: banks (up to

[10] Ying Qui,"Problems of Managing Joint Ventures in China's Interior: Evidence from Shaanxi," *Advanced Management Journal* 70, no. 3 (2005), pp. 46–57.

[11] J. A. Pearce II and R. B. Robinson Jr.,"Cultivating Guanxi as a Corporate Foreign-Investor Strategy," *Business Horizons* 43, no. 1 (2000), pp. 31–38.

[12] Andrew Bagnell,"China Business," *China Business Review* 33, no. 5 (2006), pp. 88–92.

[13] N. P. Chopey, "China Still Beckons Petrochemical Investments," *Chemical Engineering* 133, no. 8 (2006) pp. 19–23.

[14] "China's WTO Scorecard: Selected Year-Three Service Commitments," *The US-China Business Council* (2005), pp. 1–2.

20 percent), investment funds (33 percent), life insurance (50 percent), and telecommunications (25 percent).

14. Strategic Alliances

strategic alliances
Contractual partnerships because the companies involved do not take an equity position in one another

Strategic alliances are distinguishable from joint ventures because the companies involved do not take an equity position in one another. In many instances, strategic alliances are *partnerships* that exist for a defined period during which partners contribute their skills and expertise to a cooperative project. For example, one partner provides manufacturing capabilities while a second partner provides marketing expertise. In other situations, a strategic alliance can enable similar companies to combine their capabilities to counter the threats of a much larger or new type of competitor.

Strategic alliances are sometimes undertaken because the partners want to develop in-house capabilities to supplant the partner when the contractual arrangement between them reaches its termination date. Such relationships are tricky because, in a sense, the partners are attempting to "steal" each other's know-how.

In other instances, strategic alliances are synonymous with *licensing agreements*. Licensing involves the transfer of some industrial property right from the U.S. licensor to a motivated licensee in a foreign country. Most tend to be patents, trademarks, or technical know-how that are granted to the licensee for a specified time in return for a royalty and for avoiding tariffs or import quotas. Bell South and U.S. West, with various marketing and service competitive advantages valuable to Europe, have extended a number of licenses to create personal computers networks in the United Kingdom. Another example of licensing is UTEK Corporation's successful strategy for licensing discoveries resulting from research efforts at universities.

Another licensing strategy is to contract the manufacturing of its product line to a foreign company to exploit local comparative advantages in technology, materials, or labor. MIPS Computer Systems licensed Digital Equipment Corporation, Texas Instruments, Cypress Semiconductor, and Bipolar Integrated Technology in the United States and Fujitsu, NEC, and Kubota in Japan to market computers based on its designs in the partner's country.

Service and franchise-based firms—including Anheuser-Busch, Avis, Coca-Cola, Hilton, Hyatt, Holiday Inns, Kentucky Fried Chicken, McDonald's, and Pepsi—have long engaged in licensing arrangements with foreign distributors as a way to enter new markets with standardized products that can benefit from marketing economies.

Outsourcing is a basic approach to strategic alliances that enables firms to gain a competitive advantage. Significant changes within many segments of American business continue to encourage the use of outsourcing practices. Within the health care arena, an industry survey recorded 67 percent of hospitals using provider outsourcing for at least one department within their organization. Services such as information systems, reimbursement, and risk and physician practice management are outsourced by 51 percent of the hospitals that use outsourcing.

consortia
Large interlocking relationships between businesses of an industry.

keiretsu
A Japanese consortia of businesses that is coordinated by a large trading company to gain a strategic advantage.

chaebol
A Korean consortia financed through government banking groups to gain a strategic advantage.

Another successful application of outsourcing is found in human resources. A survey of human resource executives revealed 85 percent have personal experience leading an outsourcing effort within their organization. In addition, it was found that two-thirds of pension departments have outsourced at least one human resource function. Within customer service and sales departments, outsourcing increases productivity in such areas as product information, sales and order taking, sample fulfillment, and complaint handling.

15. Consortia, *Keiretsus,* and *Chaebols*

Consortia are defined as large interlocking relationships between businesses of an industry. In Japan such consortia are known as ***keiretsus;*** in South Korea as ***chaebols.***

In Europe, consortia projects are increasing in number and in success rates. Examples include the Junior Engineers' and Scientists' Summer Institute, which underwrites cooperative learning and research; the European Strategic Program for Research and Development in Information Technologies, which seeks to enhance European competitiveness in fields related to computer electronics and component manufacturing; and EUREKA, which is a joint program involving scientists and engineers from several European countries to coordinate joint research projects.

A Japanese *keiretsu* is an undertaking involving up to 50 different firms that are joined around a large trading company or bank and are coordinated through interlocking directories and stock exchanges. It is designed to use industry coordination to minimize risks of competition, in part through cost sharing and increased economies of scale. Examples include Sumitomo, Mitsubishi, Mitsui, and Sanwa.

A South Korean *chaebol* resembles a consortium or keiretsu except that it is typically financed through government banking groups and is largely run by professional managers trained by participating firms expressly for the job.

SELECTION OF LONG-TERM OBJECTIVES AND GRAND STRATEGY SETS

At first glance, the strategic management model seems to suggest that strategic choice decision making leads to the sequential selection of long-term objectives and grand strategies. In fact, however, strategic choice is the simultaneous selection of long-range objectives and grand strategies. When strategic planners study their opportunities, they try to determine which are most likely to result in achieving various long-range objectives. Almost simultaneously, they try to forecast whether an available grand strategy can take advantage of preferred opportunities so the tentative objectives can be met. In essence, then, three distinct but highly interdependent choices are being made at one time. Several triads, or sets, of possible decisions are usually considered.

A simplified example of this process is shown in Exhibit 7.16, Strategy in Action. In this example, the firm has determined that six strategic choice options are available. These options stem from three interactive opportunities (e.g., West Coast markets that present little competition). Because each of these interactive opportunities can be approached through different grand strategies—for options 1 and 2, the grand strategies are horizontal acquisition and market development—each offers the potential for achieving long-range objectives to varying degrees. Thus, a firm rarely can make a strategic choice only on the basis of its preferred opportunities, long-range objectives, or grand strategy. Instead, these three elements must be considered simultaneously, because only in combination do they constitute a strategic choice.

In an actual decision situation, the strategic choice would be complicated by a wider variety of interactive opportunities, feasible company objectives, promising grand strategy options, and evaluative criteria. Nevertheless, Exhibit 7.16 does partially reflect the nature and complexity of the process by which long-term objectives and grand strategies are selected.

In the next chapter, the strategic choice process is fully explained. However, knowledge of long-term objectives and grand strategies is essential to understanding that process.

SEQUENCE OF OBJECTIVES AND STRATEGY SELECTION

The selection of long-range objectives and grand strategies involves simultaneous, rather than sequential, decisions. While it is true that objectives are needed to prevent the firm's direction and progress from being determined by random forces, it is equally true that objectives can be achieved only if strategies are implemented. In fact, long-term objectives and grand strategies

Strategy in Action — Exhibit 7.16

A Profile of Strategic Choice Options

	Six Strategic Choice Options					
	1	2	3	4	5	6
Interactive opportunities	West Coast markets present little competition		Current markets sensitive to price competition		Current industry product lines offer too narrow a range of markets	
Appropriate long-range objectives (limited sample):						
Average 5-year ROI.	15%	19%	13%	17%	23%	15%
Company sales by year 5.	+ 50%	+ 40%	+ 20%	+ 0%	+ 35%	+ 25%
Risk of negative profits.	.30	.25	.10	.15	.20	.05
Grand strategies	Horizontal integration	Market development	Concentration	Selective retrenchment	Product development	Concentration

are so interdependent that some business consultants do not distinguish between them. Long-term objectives and grand strategies are still combined under the heading of company strategy in most of the popular business literature and in the thinking of most practicing executives.

However, the distinction has merit. Objectives indicate what strategic managers want but provide few insights about how they will be achieved. Conversely, strategies indicate what types of actions will be taken but do not define what ends will be pursued or what criteria will serve as constraints in refining the strategic plan.

Does it matter whether strategic decisions are made to achieve objectives or to satisfy constraints? No, because constraints are themselves objectives. The constraint of increased inventory capacity is a desire (an objective), not a certainty. Likewise, the constraint of an increase in the sales force does not ensure that the increase will be achieved, given such factors as other company priorities, labor market conditions, and the firm's profit performance.

DESIGNING A PROFITABLE BUSINESS MODEL

business model
A clear understanding of how the firm will generate profits and the strategic actions it must take to succeed over the long term.

The process of combining long-term objectives and grand strategies produces a **business model.** Creating an effective model requires a clear understanding of how the firm will generate profits and the strategic action it must take to succeed over the long term.

Adrian Slywotzky, David Morrison, and Bob Andelman identified 22 business models—designs that generate profits in a unique way.[15] They present these models as examples,

[15] This section is excerpted from A. J. Slywotzky, D. J. Morrison, and B. Andelman, *The Profit Zone; How Strategic Business Design Will Lead You To Tomorrow's Profits* (New York: Times Books, 1997).

believing that others do or can exist. The authors also believe that in some instances profitability depends on the interplay of two or more business models. Their study demonstrates that the mechanisms of profitability can be very different but that a focus on the customer is the key to the effectiveness of each model.

Slywotzky, Morrison, and Andelman suggest that the two most productive questions asked of executives are these:

1. What is our business model?
2. How do we make a profit?

The classic strategy rule suggested: "Gain market share and profits will follow." This approach once worked for some industries. However, because of competitive turbulence caused by globalization and rapid technological advancements, the once-popular belief in a strong correlation between market share and profitability has collapsed in many industries.

How can businesses earn sustainable profits? The answer is found by analyzing the following questions: Where will the firm make a profit in this industry? How should the business model be designed so that the firm will be profitable? Slywotzky, Morrison, and Andelman describe the following profitability business models as ways to answer those questions.

1. *Customer development customer solutions profit model.* Companies that use this business model make money by finding ways to improve their customers' economics and investing in ways for customers to improve their processes.

2. *Product pyramid profit model.* This model is effective in markets where customers have strong preferences for product characteristics, including variety, style, color, and price. By offering a number of variations, companies can build so-called product pyramids. At the base are low-priced, high-volume products, and at the top are high-priced, low-volume products. Profit is concentrated at the top of the pyramid, but the base is the strategic firewall (i.e., a strong, low-priced brand that deters competitor entry), thereby protecting the margins at the top. Consumer goods companies and automobile companies use this model.

3. *Multicomponent system profit model.* Some businesses are characterized by a production/marketing system that consists of components that generate substantially different levels of profitability. In hotels, for example, there is a substantial difference between the profitability of room rentals and that of bar operations. In such instances, it often is useful to maximize the use of the highest-profit components to maximize the profitability of the whole system.

4. *Switchboard profit model.* Some markets function by connecting multiple sellers to multiple buyers. The switchboard profit model creates a high-value intermediary that concentrates these multiple communication pathways through one point or "switchboard" and thereby reduces costs for both parties in exchange for a fee. As volume increases, so too do profits.

5. *Time profit model.* Sometimes, speed is the key to profitability. This business model takes advantage of first-mover advantage. To sustain this model, constant innovation is essential.

6. *Blockbuster profit model.* In some industries, profitability is driven by a few great product successes. This business model is representative of movie studios, pharmaceutical firms, and software companies, which have high R&D and launch costs and finite product cycles. In this type of environment, it pays to concentrate resource investments in a few projects rather than to take positions in a variety of products.

7. *Profit multiplier model.* This business model reaps gains, repeatedly, from the same product, character, trademark capability, or service. Think of the value that Michael Jordan Inc. creates with the image of the great basketball legend. This model can be a powerful engine for businesses with strong consumer brands.

8. *Entrepreneurial profit model.* Small can be beautiful. This business model stresses that diseconomies of scale can exist in companies. They attack companies that have become comfortable with their profit levels with formal, bureaucratic systems that are remote from customers. As their expenses grow and customer relevance declines, such companies are vulnerable to entrepreneurs who are in direct contact with their customers.

9. *Specialization profit model.* This business model stresses growth through sequenced specialization. Consulting companies have used this design successfully.

10. *Installed base profit model.* A company that pursues this model profits because its established user base subsequently buys the company's brand of consumables or follow-on products. Installed base profits provide a protected annuity stream. Examples include razors and blades, software and upgrades, copiers and toner cartridges, and cameras and film.

11. *De facto standard profit model.* A variant of the installed base profit model, this model is appropriate when the installed base model becomes the de facto standard that governs competitive behavior in the industry.

Summary

Before we learn how strategic decisions are made, it is important to understand the two principal components of any strategic choice; namely, long-term objectives and the grand strategy. The purpose of this chapter was to convey that understanding.

Long-term objectives were defined as the results a firm seeks to achieve over a specified period, typically five years. Seven common long-term objectives were discussed: profitability, productivity, competitive position, employee development, employee relations, technological leadership, and public responsibility. These, or any other long-term objectives, should be flexible, measurable over time, motivating, suitable, and understandable.

Grand strategies were defined as comprehensive approaches guiding the major actions designed to achieve long-term objectives. Fifteen grand strategy options were discussed: concentrated growth, market development, product development, innovation, horizontal acquisition, vertical acquisition, concentric diversification, conglomerate diversification, turnaround, divestiture, liquidation, bankruptcy, joint ventures, strategic alliances, and consortia.

Key Terms

balanced scorecard, *p. 194*
bankruptcy, *p. 218*
business model, *p. 226*
chaebol, *p. 224*
concentrated growth, *p. 201*
concentric diversification, *p. 211*
conglomerate diversification, *p. 212*
consortia, *p. 224*
divestiture strategy, *p. 216*
generic strategy, *p. 195*
grand strategy, *p. 200*
horizontal acquisition, *p. 207*
innovation, *p. 207*
joint venture, *p. 221*
keiretsu, *p. 224*
liquidation, *p. 217*
market development, *p. 204*
product development, *p. 206*
strategic alliances, *p. 224*
turnaround, *p. 213*
vertical acquisition, *p. 210*

Questions for Discussion

1. Identify firms in the business community nearest to your college or university that you believe are using each of the 15 grand strategies discussed in this chapter.
2. Identify firms in your business community that appear to rely principally on 1 of the 15 grand strategies. What kind of information did you use to classify the firms?

3. Write a long-term objective for your school of business that exhibits the seven qualities of long-term objectives described in this chapter.
4. Distinguish between the following pairs of grand strategies:

   a. Horizontal and vertical acquisition.
   b. Conglomerate and concentric diversification.
   c. Product development and innovation.
   d. Joint venture and strategic alliance.

5. Rank each of the 15 grand strategy options discussed in this chapter on the following three scales:

High	Low
Cost	
High	**Low**
Risk of failure	
High	**Low**
Potential for exceptional growth	

6. Identify firms that use the eight specific options shown in Exhibit 7.4 under the grand strategies of concentration, market development, and product development.

Business Strategy

After reading and studying this chapter, you should be able to

1. Determine why a business would choose a low-cost, differentiation, or speed-based strategy.
2. Explain the nature and value of a market focus strategy.
3. Illustrate how a firm can pursue both low-cost and differentiation strategies.
4. Identify requirements for business success at different stages of industry evolution.
5. Determine good business strategies in fragmented and global industries.
6. Decide when a business should diversify.

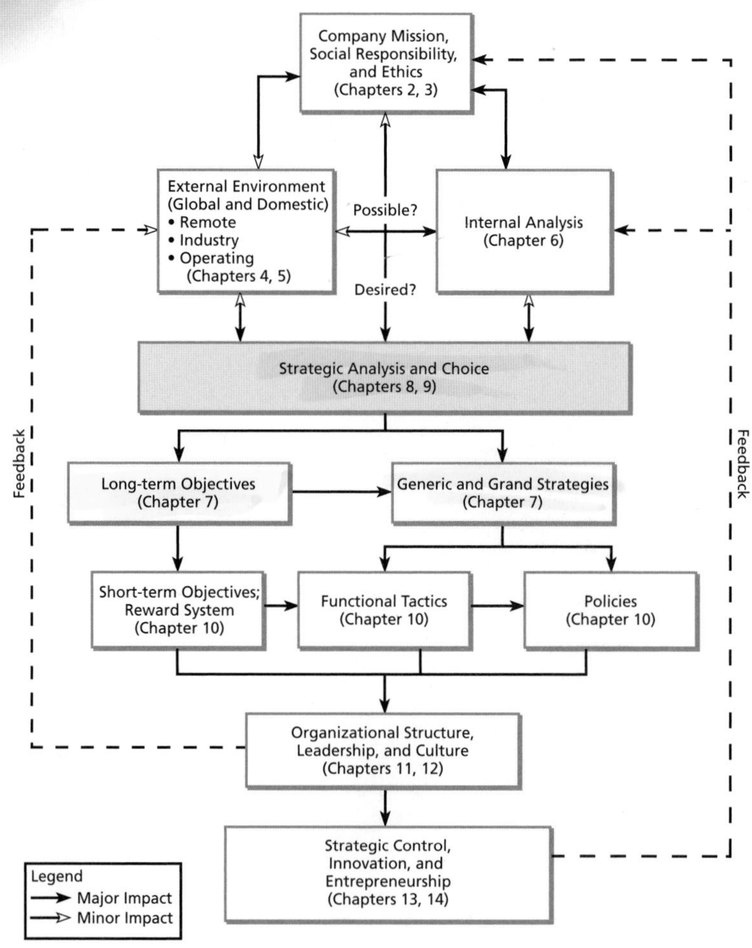

Strategic analysis and choice is the phase of the strategic management process in which business managers examine and choose a business strategy that allows their business to maintain or create a sustainable competitive advantage. Their starting point is to evaluate and determine which competitive advantages provide the basis for distinguishing the firm in the customer's mind from other reasonable alternatives. Businesses with a dominant product or service line must also choose among alternate grand strategies to guide the firm's activities, particularly when they are trying to decide about broadening the scope of the firm's activities beyond its core business. This chapter examines strategic analysis and choice in single- or dominant-product/service businesses by addressing two basic issues:

1. **What strategies are most effective at building sustainable competitive advantages for single business units?** What competitive strategy positions a business most effectively in its industry? For example, Scania, the most productive truck manufacturer in the world, joins its major rival Volvo as two anchors of Sweden's economy. Scania's return on sales of 9.9 percent far exceeds Mercedes (2.6 percent) and Volvo (2.5 percent), a level it has achieved most of the last 60 years. Scania has built a sustainable competitive advantage with a strategy of focusing solely on heavy transport vehicles in three geographic markets—Europe, Latin America, and Asia—by providing vehicles customized to specific tasks yet built using modularized components (20,000 components per vehicle versus 25,000 for Volvo and 40,000 for Mercedes). Scania is a low-cost producer of a differentiated heavy transport vehicle that can be custom-manufactured quickly and sold to a regionally focused market.
2. **Should dominant-product/service businesses diversify to build value and competitive advantage?** For example, Dell and Coca-Cola managers have examined the question of diversification and apparently concluded that continued concentration on their core products and services and development of new markets for those same core products and services are best. IBM and Pepsi examined the same question and concluded that concentric diversification and vertical acquisition were best. Why?

EVALUATING AND CHOOSING BUSINESS STRATEGIES: SEEKING SUSTAINED COMPETITIVE ADVANTAGE

Business managers evaluate and choose strategies that they think will make their business successful. Businesses become successful because they possess some advantage relative to their competitors. The two most prominent sources of competitive advantage can be found in the business's cost structure and its ability to differentiate the business from competitors. DisneyWorld in Orlando offers theme park patrons several unique, distinct features that differentiate it from other entertainment options. Costco offers retail customers the lowest prices on popular consumer items because they have created a low-cost structure that results in a competitive advantage over most competitors.

Businesses that create competitive advantages from one or both of these sources usually experience above-average profitability within their industry. Businesses that lack a cost or differentiation advantage usually experience average or below-average profitability. Two well-recognized studies found that businesses that do not have either form of competitive advantage perform the poorest among their peers, while businesses that possess both forms of competitive advantage enjoy the highest levels of profitability within their industry.[1]

The average return on investment for more than 2,500 businesses across seven industries looked like this:

Differentiation Advantage	Cost Advantage	Overall Average ROI across Seven Industries
High	High	35.0%
Low	High	26.0
High	Low	22.0
Low	Low	9.5

Initially, managers were advised to evaluate and choose strategies that emphasized one type of competitive advantage, often referred to as generic strategies. Firms were encouraged to become either a differentiation-oriented or low-cost-oriented company. In so doing, it was logical that organizational members would develop a clear understanding of company priorities and, as these studies suggest, likely experience profitability superior to competitors without either a differentiation or low-cost orientation.

The studies mentioned here, and the experience of many other businesses, indicate that the highest profitability levels are found in businesses that possess both types of competitive advantage at the same time. In other words, businesses that have one or more resources/capabilities that truly differentiate them from key competitors and also have resources/capabilities that let them operate at a lower cost will consistently outperform their rivals that don't. Southwest Airlines has followed a low-cost strategy by simplifying reservations, eliminating reserved seats, not serving meals, and cutting operating costs by flying only 737 aircraft. It has simultaneously emphasized differentiation by creating a fun experience for customers, unique commercials, baggage flying for free, and an unusual culture that customers can see and "feel." So the challenge for today's business managers is to evaluate and choose business strategies based on core competencies and value chain activities that sustain both types of competitive advantage simultaneously. Exhibit 8.1, Top Global Strategist, describes how Facebook founder Mark Zuckerberg and COO Sheryl Sandberg are charting a Facebook course that is pursuing a strategy that includes both low-cost and differentiation elements, which they strongly feel will help Facebook achieve long-term success and viability in the Web-based business environment of 2030.

Evaluating Cost Leadership Opportunities

Business success built on cost leadership requires the business to be able to provide its product or service at a cost below what its competitors can achieve. And it must be a sustainable

[1] G. G. Dess and G. T. Lumpkin, "Emerging Issues in Strategy Process Research," in *Handbook of Strategic Management,* M. A. Hitt, R. E. Freeman, and J. S. Harrison (eds) (Oxford: Blackwell, 2001), pp. 3–34; R. B. Robinson and J. A. Pearce, "Planned Patterns of Strategic Behavior and Their Relationship to Business Unit Performance," *Strategic Management Journal* 9, no. 1 (1988), pp. 43–60; and V. Phongpetra and L. M. Johri, "Impact of Business Strategies of Automobile Manufacturers in Thailand," *International Journal of Emerging Markets* 6, no. 1 (2011), pp. 17–37; and http://www.openlearningworld.com/olw/courses/books/Business%20Strategies/Business%20Strategy/Integrated%20Cost%20Leadership%20-%20Differentiation%20Strategy.html.

Top Global Strategist

Zuckerberg and Sandberg Choose Differentiation and Long-Term Low Costs to Build Facebook's Long-Term Business Strategy

Exhibit 8.1

Mark Zuckerberg, CEO, Facebook, and Sheryl Sandberg, COO, Facebook

A dramatic emphasis on cutting expenses and forgoing growth took place in 2009—even in Silicon Valley. Not at Facebook. Founder and CEO Mark Zuckerberg, along with COO Sheryl Sandberg, are emphasizing accelerated growth in their worldwide user base to build a site for the next 30 years while also creating a basis to significantly differentiate Facebook from current social networking business models.

LOW-COST LEADERSHIP

Facebook's emphasis on aggressively pursuing sustained user growth, even during a global depression, is—at its heart—a way to build economies of scale years out that will allow Facebook to be a cost leader among social networking sites in the value it can offer advertisers and other customers desiring to get the widest audience exposure per dollar spent within a social networking venue. Rather than being someone in social networking for a fast buck, says Sheryl Sandberg, "We're in this game for 20 to 30 years." So, in the face of a global economic depression, Facebook is not cutting costs, but rather taking developers off ad revenue generation and instead cooking up versions in languages like French Canadian, Tagalog, Xhosa, and Arabic. Says Zuckerberg, "A social networking site that can connect people with friends in Saudi Arabia or the Phillipines or Tonga is simply more valuable than one that can't." So Facebook is also aggressively looking for acquisitions of sites in Brazil, Germany, India, and Japan as "a way for us to acquire a geography or a demographic," says CFO Gideon Yu. Ultimately, if it works, Facebook will have a size advantage that will allow it to offer advertisers an unparalleled cost advantage in reaching social network users on a broad global basis, or in narrower geographic or demographic settings.*

DIFFERENTIATION—FACEBOOK STYLE

Facebook is creating a business model designed to go beyond traditional online advertising. It seeks to have ad business, but also to create interactive ads that are more like digital bulletin boards than traditional banner ads. Called *engagement ads,* such advertising would seek comments on a *Tropic Thunder* movie trailer or thoughts about other advertisers linked to Facebook through individual connections and messages. A second leg of the "new" Facebook expects to differentiate itself by including e-commerce—selling digital items and virtual gifts, which sell for modest amounts like $1 a pop. Sending digital flowers, guitars, and other virtual gifts from one Facebook user to another via Facebook is rapidly growing as a revenue source and, more importantly, a way to differentiate the Facebook social network user experience, which in turn creates a different milieu for commercial advertisers. Third, Facebook has opened itself to software developers/entrepreneurs who can make applications to be used on Facebook with advertisers paying the developers (where relevant) and Facebook taking a cut.

*"Facebook Lures Advertisers at MySpace's Expense," *BusinessWeek*, July 9, 2009; "Zuckerberg on Facebook's Future," *BusinessWeek.com*, March 6, 2008; and "Facebook's Sheryl Sandberg," *BusinessWeek.com*, April 9, 2009.

cost advantage. Through the skills and resources identified in Exhibit 8.2, a business must be able to accomplish one or more activities in its value chain activities—procuring materials, processing them into products, marketing the products, and distributing the products or support activities—in a more cost-effective manner than that of its competitors or it must

EXHIBIT 8.2 Evaluating a Business's Cost Leadership Opportunities

Source: Based on Michael Porter, *On Competition*, 1998, Harvard Business School Press.

A. Skills and Resources That Foster Cost Leadership

Sustained capital investment and access to capital
Process engineering skills
Intense supervision of labor or core technical operations
Products or services designed for ease of manufacture or delivery
Low-cost distribution system

B. Organizational Requirements to Support and Sustain Cost Leadership Activities

Tight cost control
Frequent, detailed control reports
Continuous improvement and benchmarking orientation
Structured organization and responsibilities
Incentives based on meeting strict, usually quantitative targets

C. Examples of Ways Businesses Achieve Competitive Advantage via Cost Leadership

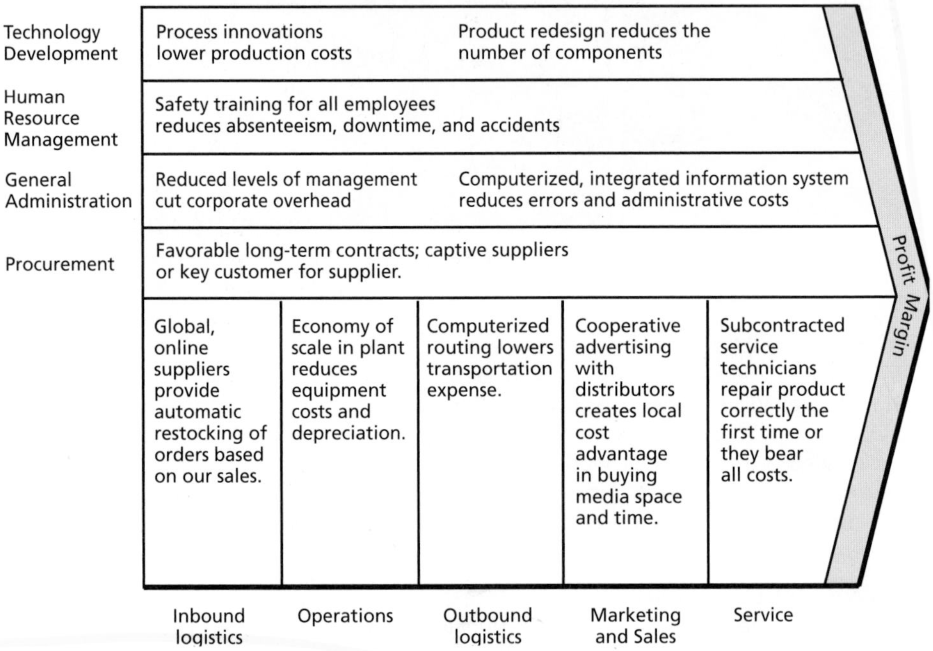

Support Activity		
Technology Development	Process innovations lower production costs	Product redesign reduces the number of components
Human Resource Management	Safety training for all employees reduces absenteeism, downtime, and accidents	
General Administration	Reduced levels of management cut corporate overhead	Computerized, integrated information system reduces errors and administrative costs
Procurement	Favorable long-term contracts; captive suppliers or key customer for supplier.	

Inbound logistics	Operations	Outbound logistics	Marketing and Sales	Service
Global, online suppliers provide automatic restocking of orders based on our sales.	Economy of scale in plant reduces equipment costs and depreciation.	Computerized routing lowers transportation expense.	Cooperative advertising with distributors creates local cost advantage in buying media space and time.	Subcontracted service technicians repair product correctly the first time or they bear all costs.

Profit Margin

be able to reconfigure its value chain so as to achieve a cost advantage. Exhibit 8.2 provides examples of such **low-cost strategies.**

low-cost strategies
Business strategies that seek to establish long-term competitive advantages by emphasizing and perfecting value chain activities that can be achieved at costs substantially below what competitors are able to match on a sustained basis. This allows the firm, in turn, to compete primarily by charging a price lower than competitors can match and still stay in business.

Strategists examining their business's value chain for low-cost leadership advantages evaluate the sustainability of those advantages by benchmarking (refer to Chapter 6 for a discussion of this comparison technique) their business against key competitors and by considering the effect of any cost advantage on the five forces in their business's competitive environment. Low-cost activities that are sustainable and that provide one or more of these advantages relative to key industry forces should become a key basis for the business's competitive strategy:

Low-cost advantages that reduce the likelihood of pricing pressure from buyers When key competitors cannot match prices from the low-cost leader, customers pressuring the leader risk establishing a price level that drives alternate sources out of business.

Truly sustained low-cost advantages may push rivals into other areas, lessening price competition Intense, continued price competition may be ruinous for all rivals, as seen occasionally in the airline industry.

New entrants competing on price must face an entrenched cost leader without the experience to replicate every cost advantage EasyJet, a British start-up with a Southwest Airlines copycat strategy, entered the European airline market with much fanfare and low-priced, city-to-city, no-frills flights.

Analysts have cautioned for some time that British Airways, KLM's no-frills off-shoot (Buzz), and Virgin Express will simply match fares on easyJet's key routes and let high landing fees and flight delays take their toll on the British upstart. Yet first-mover easyJet has survived and solidified its leadership position in the European airline industry's low-cost segment.[2]

Low-cost advantages should lessen the attractiveness of substitute products A serious concern of any business is the threat of a substitute product in which buyers can meet their original need. Low-cost advantages allow the holder to resist this happening because it allows them to remain competitive even against desirable substitutes, and it allows them to lessen concerns about price facing an inferior, lower-priced substitute.

Higher margins allow low-cost producers to withstand supplier cost increases and often gain supplier loyalty over time Sudden, particularly uncontrollable increases in the costs suppliers face can be more easily absorbed by low-cost, higher-margin producers. Severe droughts in California quadrupled the price of lettuce—a key restaurant demand. Some chains absorbed the cost; others had to confuse customers with a "lettuce tax." Furthermore, chains that worked well with produce suppliers gained a loyal, cooperative "partner" for possible assistance in a future, competitive situation.

Once managers identify opportunities to create cost advantage–based strategies, they must consider whether key risks inherent in cost leadership are present in a way that may mediate sustained success. The key risks with which they must be concerned are discussed next.

Many cost-saving activities are easily duplicated Computerizing certain order entry functions among hazardous waste companies gave early adopters lower sales costs and better customer service for a brief time. Rivals quickly adapted, adding similar capabilities with similar effects on their costs.

Exclusive cost leadership can become a trap Firms that emphasize lowest price and can offer it via cost advantages where product differentiation is increasingly not considered must truly be convinced of the sustainability of those advantages. Particularly with commodity-type products, the low-cost leader seeking to sustain a margin superior to lesser rivals may encounter increasing customer pressure for lower prices with great damage to both leader and lesser players.

Obsessive cost cutting can shrink other competitive advantages involving key product attributes Intense cost scrutiny can build margin, but it can reduce opportunities for or investment in innovation, processes, and products. Similarly, such scrutiny can lead to the use of inferior raw materials, processes, or activities that were previously viewed by customers as a key attribute of the original products. Some mail-order computer companies that sought to maintain or enhance cost advantages found reductions in telephone service personnel and automation of that function backfiring with a drop in demand for their products even though their low prices were maintained.

Cost differences often decline over time As products age, competitors learn how to match cost advantages. Absolute volumes sold often decline. Market channels and suppliers

[2] "EasyJet Expands as Profits Soar," *BBC News*, November 14, 2006; and "Demand Boost Cuts easyJet Losses," *BBC News*, May 9, 2007.

mature. Buyers become more knowledgeable. All of these factors present opportunities to lessen the value or presence of earlier cost advantages. Said another way, cost advantages that are not sustainable over a period of time are risky.

Once business managers have evaluated the cost structure of their value chain, determined activities that provide competitive cost advantages, and considered their inherent risks, they start choosing the business's strategy. Those managers concerned with differentiation-based strategies, or those seeking optimum performance incorporating both sources of competitive advantage, move to evaluating their business's sources of differentiation.

Evaluating Differentiation Opportunities

differentiation
A business strategy that seeks to build competitive advantage with its product or service by having it be "different" from other available competitive products based on features, performance, or other factors not directly related to cost and price. The difference would be one that would be hard to create and/or difficult to copy or imitate.

Differentiation requires that the business have sustainable advantages that allow it to provide buyers with something uniquely valuable to them. A successful differentiation strategy allows the business to provide a product or service of perceived higher value to buyers at a "differentiation cost" below the "value premium" to the buyers. In other words, the buyer feels the additional cost to buy the product or service is well below what the product or service is worth compared with other available alternatives.

Differentiation usually arises from one or more activities in the value chain that create a unique value important to buyers. Perrier's control of a carbonated water spring in France, Stouffer's frozen food packaging and sauce technology, Apple's control of iTunes download software that worked solely with iPods, iPhones, and iPads at first, American Greeting Card's automated inventory system for retailers, and Federal Express's customer service capabilities are all examples of sustainable advantages around which successful differentiation strategies have been built. A business can achieve differentiation by performing its existing value activities or reconfiguring in some unique way. And the sustainability of that differentiation will depend on two things: a continuation of its high perceived value to buyers and a lack of imitation by competitors.

Exhibit 8.3 provides examples of the types of key skills and resources on which managers seeking to build differentiation-based strategies would base their underlying, sustainable competitive advantages. Examples of value chain activities that provide a differentiation advantage are also provided.

Strategists examining their business's resources and capabilities for differentiation advantages evaluate the sustainability of those advantages by benchmarking (refer to Chapter 6 for a discussion of this comparison technique) their business against key competitors and by considering the effect of any differentiation advantage on the five forces in their business's competitive environment. Sustainable activities that provide one or more of the following opportunities relative to key industry forces should become the basis for differentiation aspects of the business's competitive strategy:

Rivalry is reduced when a business successfully differentiates itself BMW's Z4, made in Greer, South Carolina, does not compete with Saturns made in central Tennessee. A Harvard education does not compete with an education from a local technical school. Both situations involve the same basic needs—transportation or education. However, one rival has clearly differentiated itself from others in the minds of certain buyers. In so doing, they do not have to respond competitively to that competitor.

Buyers are less sensitive to prices for effectively differentiated products The Highlands Inn in Carmel, California, and the Ventana Inn along the Big Sur charge a minimum of $750 and $1,000, respectively, per night for a room with a kitchen, fireplace, hot tub, and view. Other places are available along this beautiful stretch of California's spectacular coastline, but occupancy rates at these two locations remain over 90 percent. Why? You can't get a

EXHIBIT 8.3
Evaluating a Business's Differentiation Opportunities

Source: Based on Michael Porter, *On Competition*, 1998, Harvard Business School Press.

A. Skills and Resources That Foster Differentiation

Strong marketing abilities
Product engineering
Creative talent and flair
Strong capabilities in basic research
Corporate reputation for quality or technical leadership
Long tradition in an industry or unique combination of skills drawn from other businesses
Strong cooperation from channels
Strong cooperation from suppliers of major components of the product or service

B. Organizational Requirements to Support and Sustain Differentiation Activities
Strong coordination among functions in R&D, product development, and marketing
Subjective measurement and incentives instead of quantitative measures
Amenities to attract highly skilled labor, scientists, and creative people
Tradition of closeness to key customers
Some personnel skilled in sales and operations—technical and marketing

C. Examples of Ways Businesses Achieve Competitive Advantage via Differentiation

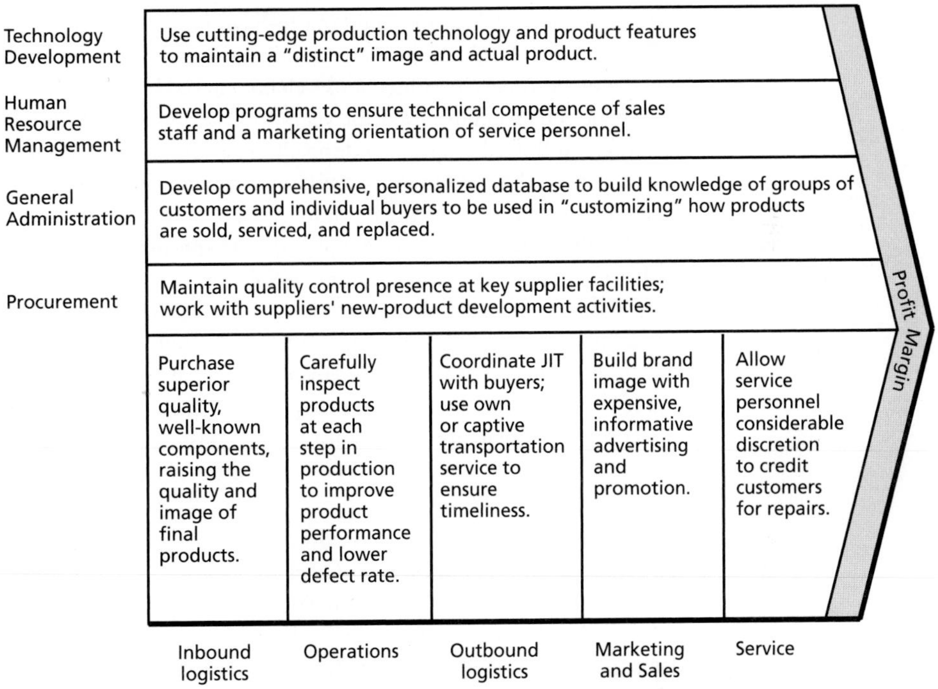

Support activity	
Technology Development	Use cutting-edge production technology and product features to maintain a "distinct" image and actual product.
Human Resource Management	Develop programs to ensure technical competence of sales staff and a marketing orientation of service personnel.
General Administration	Develop comprehensive, personalized database to build knowledge of groups of customers and individual buyers to be used in "customizing" how products are sold, serviced, and replaced.
Procurement	Maintain quality control presence at key supplier facilities; work with suppliers' new-product development activities.

Inbound logistics	Operations	Outbound logistics	Marketing and Sales	Service
Purchase superior quality, well-known components, raising the quality and image of final products.	Carefully inspect products at each step in production to improve product performance and lower defect rate.	Coordinate JIT with buyers; use own or captive transportation service to ensure timeliness.	Build brand image with expensive, informative advertising and promotion.	Allow service personnel considerable discretion to credit customers for repairs.

Profit Margin

better view and a more relaxed, spectacular setting to spend a few days on the Pacific Coast. Similarly, buyers of differentiated products tolerate price increases low-cost-oriented buyers would not accept. The former become very loyal to certain brands. Harley-Davidson motorcycles continue to rise in price, and its buyer base continues to expand worldwide, even though many motorcycle alternatives more reasonably priced are easily available.

Brand loyalty is hard for new entrants to overcome Many new beers are brought to market in the United States, but Budweiser continues to gain market share. Why? Brand loyalty is hard to overcome! And Anheuser-Busch has been clever to extend its brand loyalty from its core brand into newer niches, such as nonalcohol brews, that other potential entrants have pioneered.

Managers examining differentiation-based advantages must take potential risks into account as they commit their business to these advantages. Some of the more common ways risks arise are discussed next.

Imitation narrows perceived differentiation, rendering differentiation meaningless AMC pioneered the Jeep passenger version of a truck 40 years ago. Ford created the Explorer, or luxury utility vehicle, in 1990. It took luxury car features and put them inside a jeep. Ford's payoff was substantial. The Explorer became Ford's most popular domestic vehicle. However, virtually every vehicle manufacturer offered a luxury utility a few years later, resulting in customers beginning to be hard pressed to identify clear distinctions between lead models. Ford's Explorer managers have sought to shape a new business strategy for the next decade that relies both on new sources of differentiation and placing greater emphasis on low-cost components in their value chain.

Technological changes that nullify past investments or learning Consider the strategic decisions of numerous companies committed to differentiation strategies just a few years ago as they also tried to extrapolate the implications of the Internet and social media on how to build competitive advantages that enabled greater differentiation. Blockbuster sought to ensure convenient location and first-to-have new movie releases as key ways to build in differentiation. Borders, the differentiated pioneer of the book superstore business model, and the niche-focused Waldenbooks chain entered bankruptcy in 2011. Numerous regional newspaper chains committed for years to differentiate themselves with excellent regional coverages followed a similar fate in the last few years. Google—the incredible Internet-based story of the last ten years, built on unmatched search algorithms differentiating them from all others as the starting point for most people connecting to the Internet—is suddenly faced with the reality that Facebook's simple sharing of pictures and personal information with friends will revolutionize how people first come to the Internet and as a result how advertisers might best link to their interests. All of these examples are ones where the fundamental underpinnings of companies' differentiation-based advantages—best locations, best selection, unique atmosphere, and even the reason you go onto the Internet—have changed suddenly and dramatically due to a technological change or shift. The result in each case is a company-threatening reality for the business as it is or was operating; with the reality that what had been a stellar and powerful differentiation strategy suddenly is becoming a potential death-trap.

The cost difference between low-cost competitors and the differentiated business becomes too great for differentiation to hold brand loyalty Buyers may begin to choose to sacrifice some of the features, services, or image possessed by the differentiated business for large cost savings. The rising cost of a college education, particularly at several "premier" institutions, has caused many students to opt for lower-cost destinations that offer very similar courses without image, frills, and professors who seldom teach undergraduate students anyway.

Evaluating Speed as a Competitive Advantage

The cool design of the iPod is often cited as prima facie evidence of the product's greatness. But what you hear less about are the scores of little strategic decisions that were equally important in its speed-related tactics that ultimately made it a phenomenon. For instance, Apple licensed key technologies for the gadget's guts to accelerate its readiness for prototype availability; it acquired, rather than wrote, the software that became iTunes for the same reason; and chief executive Steve Jobs set a demanding nine-month time line to get the first version done, which focused internal attention throughout the organization on the device and ensured speed to market. Altogether, those steps systematically "de-risked" the iPod launch by placing a key emphasis on *speed* and enabled the phenomenal success of Apple's $100 million bet.[3]

[3] "Don't Worry, Be Ready," *BusinessWeek,* May 28, 2007.

Global Strategy in Action

Exhibit 8.4

Building Ryanair with an Emphasis on SPEED

In 2010, Michael O'Leary was pushing the idea of a quick, low-cost, international flight service from Europe to America . . . fly across the pond last minute for $55. Vintage O'Leary. Years earlier he drove a World War II tank to England's Luton airport demanding access to "attack" rival easyJet and liberate the public from easyJet's high fares. Behind it all is a strategy built around SPEED.*

SPEED1: Ryanair uses small, secondary airports outside major cities. They allow Ryanair to fly into and out of an area quicker, turn around faster, and get customers on their way with far less time lost compared to regular airlines and airports. These airports also cost less to use, get people close to big city destinations, and get planes back in the air in 25 minutes—half the time competitors experience. This allows Ryanair to provide more frequent flights, adding timesaving convenience for both leisure and business travelers.

SPEED2: Ryanair has made large bulk purchases of Boeing's newest 737 airplanes. These planes require less maintenance and are easy to handle in smaller airports—all leading to speedier operations on a daily basis and quicker in and out maintenance downtimes.

SPEED3: Ryanair sells more than 98 percent of its tickets on Ryanair.com—allowing for quicker, more accessible service for customers seeking simplicity, speed, and convenience. It also sells hotels, car rentals, and various other offerings at the same Web site, further simplifying and saving considerable time [think speed] for customers.

* Felix Gillette, "Ryanair's O'Leary: The Duke of Discomfort," *Bloomberg BusinessWeek*, Sept. 2, 2010.

speed-based strategies
Business strategies built around functional capabilities and activities that allow the company to meet customer needs directly or indirectly more rapidly than its main competitors.

Speed-based strategies, or rapid responses to customer requests or market and technological changes, have become a major source of competitive advantage for numerous firms in today's intensely competitive global economy. Speed is certainly a form of differentiation, but it is more than that. Speed involves the *availability of a rapid response* to a customer by providing current products quicker, accelerating new-product development or improvement, quickly adjusting production processes, and making decisions quickly. While low cost and differentiation may provide important competitive advantages, managers in tomorrow's successful companies will base their strategies on creating speed-based competitive advantages. Facebook is perhaps the perfect example of speed-based strategic choice, becoming the fourth largest "country" in the world, with over 500 million users in three years, and its breakneck continuous introduction of new features, capabilities, even sometimes "borking up the site," as one blogger now making a living covering Facebook's constant new features[4] asserts. And Facebook's acquisition of Snaptu, the Israeli mobile applications for feature phones company, foretells a yet faster pace.[5]

Exhibit 8.4, Global Strategy in Action tells how Irishman Michael O'Leary built Ryanair using a speed-based competitive strategy. Exhibit 8.5 describes and illustrates key skills and organizational requirements that are associated with speed-based competitive advantage. Jack Welch, the now-retired CEO who transformed General Electric from a fading company into one of Wall Street's best performers over the past 25 years, had this to say about speed:

> Speed is really the driving force that everyone is after. Faster products, faster product cycles to market. Better response time to customers. . . . Satisfying customers, getting faster communications, moving with more agility, all these things are easier when one is small. And these are all characteristics one needs in a fast-moving global environment.[6]

[4] Zack Whittaker, "Facebook's New Features, But Borking Up the Site in the Process," *ZDNet.com*, March 20, 2011.
[5] Ben Parr, "Facebook Acquires Snaptu to Bring Social Networking to Feature Phones," *mashable.com*, March 20, 2011.
[6] "Jack Welch: A CEO Who Can't Be Cloned," *BusinessWeek*, September 17, 2001.

EXHIBIT 8.5 Evaluating a Business's Rapid Response (Speed) Opportunities

A. Skills and Resources That Foster Speed

Process engineering skills
Excellent inbound and outbound logistics
Technical people in sales and customer service
High levels of automation
Corporate reputation for quality or technical leadership
Flexible manufacturing capabilities
Strong downstream partners
Strong cooperation from suppliers of major components of the product or service

B. Organizational Requirements to Support and Sustain Rapid Response Activities

Strong coordination among functions in R&D, product development, and marketing.
Major emphasis on customer satisfaction in incentive programs
Strong delegation to operating personnel
Tradition of closeness to key customers
Some personnel skilled in sales and operations—technical and marketing
Empowered customer service personnel

C. Examples of Ways Businesses Achieve Competitive Advantage via Speed

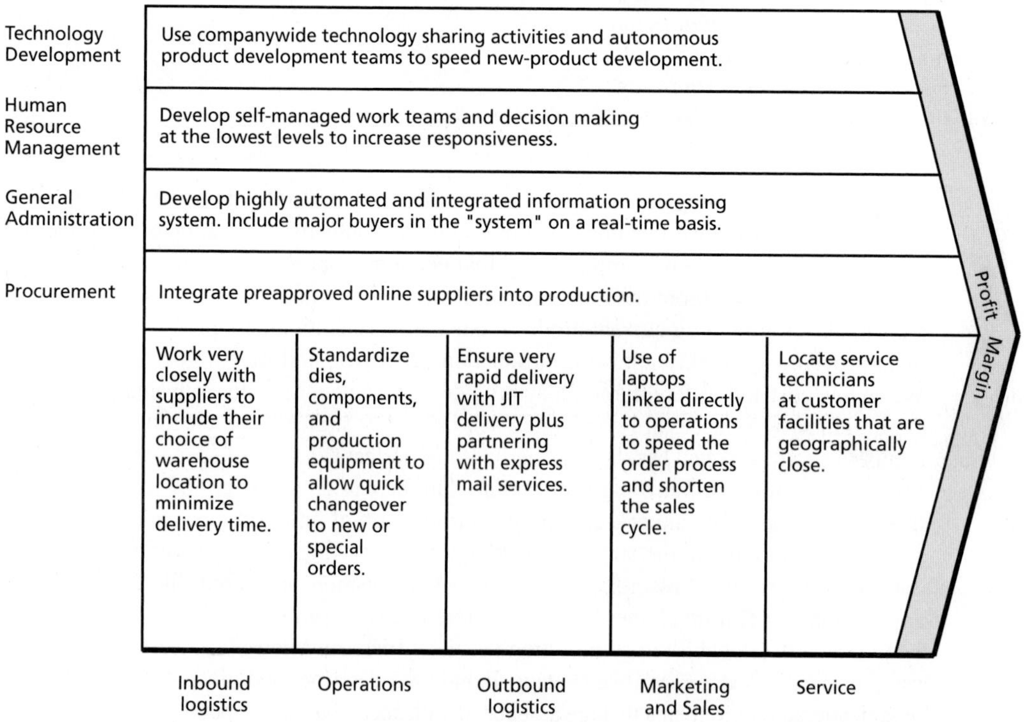

Technology Development	Use companywide technology sharing activities and autonomous product development teams to speed new-product development.				
Human Resource Management	Develop self-managed work teams and decision making at the lowest levels to increase responsiveness.				
General Administration	Develop highly automated and integrated information processing system. Include major buyers in the "system" on a real-time basis.				
Procurement	Integrate preapproved online suppliers into production.				
	Work very closely with suppliers to include their choice of warehouse location to minimize delivery time.	Standardize dies, components, and production equipment to allow quick changeover to new or special orders.	Ensure very rapid delivery with JIT delivery plus partnering with express mail services.	Use of laptops linked directly to operations to speed the order process and shorten the sales cycle.	Locate service technicians at customer facilities that are geographically close.
	Inbound logistics	Operations	Outbound logistics	Marketing and Sales	Service

Profit Margin

Speed-based competitive advantages can be created around several activities:

Customer Responsiveness All consumers have encountered hassles, delays, and frustration dealing with various businesses from time to time. The same holds true when dealing business to business. Quick response with answers, information, and solutions to mistakes can become the basis for competitive advantage—one that builds customer loyalty quickly.

Product Development Cycles Japanese automakers have focused intensely on the time it takes to create a new model because several experienced disappointing sales growth in the last decade in Europe and North America competing against new vehicles like Ford's Explorer and Renault's Megane. VW had recently conceived, prototyped, produced, and marketed a totally new 4-wheel-drive car in Europe within 12 months. Honda, Toyota, and Nissan lowered their product development cycle from 24 months to 9 months from conception to production. This capability is old hat to 3M Corporation, which is so successful at speedy product development that one-fourth of its sales and profits each year are from products that didn't exist five years earlier.

Product or Service Improvements Like development time, companies that can rapidly adapt their products or services and do so in a way that benefits their customers or creates new customers have a major competitive advantage over rivals that cannot do this.

Speed in Delivery or Distribution Firms that can get you what you need when you need it, even when that is tomorrow, realize that buyers have come to expect that level of responsiveness. Federal Express's success reflects the importance customers place on speed in inbound and outbound logistics.

Information Sharing and Technology Speed in sharing information that becomes the basis for decisions, actions, or other important activities taken by a customer, supplier, or partner has become a major source of competitive advantage for many businesses. Telecommunications, the Internet, and networks are but a part of a vast infrastructure that is being used by knowledgeable managers to rebuild or create value in their businesses via information sharing.

These rapid response capabilities create competitive advantages in several ways. They create a way to lessen rivalry because they have *availability* of something that a rival may not have. It can allow the business to charge buyers more, engender loyalty, or otherwise enhance the business's position relative to its buyers. Particularly where impressive customer response is involved, businesses can generate supplier cooperation and concessions because their business ultimately benefits from increased revenue. Finally, substitute products and new entrants find themselves trying to keep up with the rapid changes rather than introducing them.

While the notion of speed-based competitive advantage is exciting, it has risks managers must consider. First, speeding up activities that haven't been conducted in a fashion that prioritizes rapid response should only be done after considerable attention to training, reorganization, and/or reengineering. Second, some industries—stable, mature ones that have very minimal levels of change—may not offer much advantage to the firm that introduces some forms of rapid response. Customers in such settings may prefer the slower pace or the lower costs currently available, or they may have long time frames in purchasing such that speed is not that important to them.

market focus
This is a generic strategy that applies a differentiation strategy approach, or a low-cost strategy approach, or a combination—and does so solely in a narrow (or "focused") market niche rather than trying to do so across the broader market. The narrow focus may be geographically defined or defined by product type features, or target customer type, or some combination of these.

Evaluating Market Focus as a Way to Competitive Advantage

Small companies, at least the better ones, usually thrive because they serve narrow market niches. This is usually called **market focus,** the extent to which a business concentrates on a narrowly defined market. Take the example of Soho Beverages, a business former Pepsi manager Tom Cox bought from Seagram after Seagram had acquired it and was unable to make it thrive. The tiny brand, once a healthy niche product in New York and a few other East Coast locations, languished within Seagrams because its sales force was unused to selling in delis. Cox was able to double sales in one year. He did this on a lean marketing budget that didn't include advertising or database marketing. He hired Korean- and Arabic-speaking college students and had his people walk into practically every deli in Manhattan in order to reacquaint owners with the brand, spot consumption trends, and take orders. He provided rapid stocking services to all Manhattan-area delis, regardless of size. The business has continued sales growth at more than 50 percent per year. Why? Cox says, "It is attributable

Top Global Strategist

Zhang Ruimin, Chairman, Haier Corporation

Exhibit 8.6

Zhang Ruimin has emphasized a focus strategy in first building Haier into a well-known maker of refrigerators in China and now a significant force in the U.S. market and beyond. The result has been a 40 percent annualized growth in sales so far this century.

It all started several years ago in China with a sledgehammer. Appointed to run a marginal state-owned refrigerator factory, Ruimin quickly saw that "the real problem was that workers had no faith in the company and didn't care. Quality didn't even enter into anybody's mind." So after a customer complained, Ruimin lined up 76 defective models on the factory floor. He picked up a sledgehammer and told those responsible to smash them. He included himself in the task. "The message got through that there's no A, B, C, and D quality," said Ruimin, "There's only acceptable and unacceptable."

Fast-forward to taking Haier into the United States. Instead of trying to compete in the market for large, high-end refrigerators as it does in China, Ruimin chose a market focus strategy, introducing a multipurpose mini-refrigerator designed for use in college dormitories and as a small wine cellar. Haier's niche products rapidly gained in popularity.

Combined with its legendary commitment to quality control that all started with sledgehammer-wielding Zhang Ruimin emphasizing the importance of quality to his employees, Ruimin's Haier has leveraged its FOCUS strategy to move into different product lines and grab market share in the United States. By choosing market focus, Haier delivered a clear and unique value proposition to American consumers.

to focusing on a niche market, delis; differentiating the product and its sales force; achieving low costs in promotion and delivery; and making rapid, immediate response to any deli owner request its normal practice."[7]

Two things are important in this example. First, this business focused on a narrow niche market in which to build a strong competitive advantage. But focus alone was not enough to build competitive advantage. Rather, Cox created several capabilities, resources, and value chain activities that achieved differentiation, low-cost, and rapid response competitive advantages within this niche market that would be hard for other firms, particularly mass market—oriented firms, to replicate. Exhibit 8.6, Top Global Strategist, describes how China's Zhang Ruimin used quality and a sledgehammer to evaluate and choose a market focus strategy that Haier subsequently used to enter the U.S. refrigerator market.

Market focus allows some businesses to compete on the basis of low cost, differentiation, and rapid response against much larger businesses with greater resources. Focus lets a business "learn" its target customers—their needs, special considerations they want accommodated—and establish personal relationships in ways that "differentiate" the smaller firm or make it more valuable to the target customer. Low costs can also be achieved, filling niche needs in a buyer's operations that larger rivals either do not want to bother with or cannot do as cost effectively. Cost advantage often centers around the high level of customized service the focused, smaller business can provide. And perhaps the greatest competitive weapon that can arise is

[7] Michael Porter, *On Competition* (Boston: Harvard Business School Press, 1998), p. 57.

rapid response. With enhanced knowledge of its customers and intricacies of their operations, the small, focused company builds up organizational knowledge about timing-sensitive ways to work with a customer. Often the needs of that narrow set of customers represent a large part of the small, focused business's revenues. Exhibit 8.6, Top Global Strategist, illustrates how China's Haier has become the global leader in small refrigerators via the focused application of low cost, differentiation, and quality.

The risk of focus is that you attract major competitors who have waited for your business to "prove" the market. Domino's proved that a huge market for pizza delivery existed and now faces serious challenges. Likewise, publicly traded companies built around focus strategies become takeover targets for large firms seeking to fill out a product portfolio. And perhaps the greatest risk of all is slipping into the illusion that it is focus itself, and not some special form of low cost, differentiation, or rapid response, that is creating the business's success.

Managers evaluating opportunities to build competitive advantage should link strategies to resources, capabilities, and value chain activities that exploit low cost, differentiation, and rapid response competitive advantages. When advantageous, they should consider ways to use focus to leverage these advantages. One way business managers can enhance their likelihood of identifying these opportunities is to consider several different "generic" industry environments from the perspective of the typical value chain activities most often linked to sustained competitive advantages in those unique industry situations. The next section discusses key generic industry environments and the value chain activities most associated with success.

Stages of Industry Evolution and Business Strategy Choices

The requirements for success in industry segments change over time. Strategists can use these changing requirements, which are associated with different stages of industry evolution, as a way to isolate key competitive advantages and shape strategic choices around them. Exhibit 8.7 depicts four stages of industry evolution and the typical functional capabilities that are often associated with business success at each of these stages.

Competitive Advantage and Strategic Choices in Emerging Industries

Emerging industries are newly formed or re-formed industries that typically are created by technological innovation, newly emerging customer needs, or other economic or sociological changes. **Emerging industries** of the last decade have been the Internet social networking, satellite radio, surgical robotics, and online services industries.

emerging industry
An industry that has growing sales across all the companies in the industry based on growing demand for the relatively new products, technologies, and/or services made available by the firms participating in this industry.

From the standpoint of strategy formulation, the essential characteristic of an emerging industry is that there are no "rules of the game." The absence of rules presents both a risk and an opportunity—a wise strategy positions the firm to favorably shape the emerging industry's rules.

Business strategies must be shaped to accommodate the following characteristics of markets in emerging industries:

- Technologies that are mostly proprietary to the pioneering firms and technological uncertainty about how product standardization will unfold.
- Competitor uncertainty because of inadequate information about competitors, buyers, and the timing of demand.
- High initial costs but steep cost declines as the experience curve takes effect.
- Few entry barriers, which often spurs the formation of many new firms.
- First-time buyers requiring initial inducement to purchase and customers confused by the availability of a number of nonstandard products.

EXHIBIT 8.7 Sources of Distinctive Competence at Different Stages of Industry Evolution

Functional Area	Introduction	Growth	Maturity	Decline
Marketing	Resources/skills to create widespread awareness and find acceptance from customers; advantageous access to distribution	Ability to establish brand recognition, find niche, reduce price, solidify strong distribution relations, and develop new channels	Skills in aggressively promoting products to new markets and holding existing markets; pricing flexibility; skills in differentiating products and holding customer loyalty	Cost-effective means of efficient access to selected channels and markets; strong customer loyalty or dependence; strong company image
Production operations	Ability to expand capacity effectively, limit number of designs, develop standards	Ability to add product variants, centralize production, or otherwise lower costs; ability to improve product quality; seasonal subcontracting capacity	Ability to improve product and reduce costs; ability to share or reduce capacity; advantageous supplier relationships; subcontracting	Ability to prune product line; cost advantage in production, location, or distribution; simplified inventory control; subcontracting or long production runs
Finance	Resources to support high net cash overflow and initial losses; ability to use leverage effectively	Ability to finance rapid expansion, to have net cash outflows but increasing profits; resources to support product improvements	Ability to generate and redistribute increasing net cash inflows; effective cost control systems	Ability to reuse or liquidate unneeded equipment; advantage in cost of facilities; control system accuracy; streamlined management control

- Inability to obtain raw materials and components until suppliers gear up to meet the industry's needs.
- Need for high-risk capital because of the industry's uncertainty prospects.

For success in this industry setting, business strategies require one or more of these features:

1. The ability to *shape the industry's structure* based on the timing of entry, reputation, success in related industries or technologies, and role in industry associations.
2. The ability to *rapidly improve product quality* and performance features.

EXHIBIT 8.7 *(continued)*

Functional Area	Introduction	Growth	Maturity	Decline
Personnel	Flexibility in staffing and training new management; existence of employees with key skills in new products or markets	Existence of an ability to add skilled personnel; motivated and loyal workforce	Ability to cost effectively, reduce workforce, increase efficiency	Capacity to reduce and reallocate personnel; cost advantage
Engineering and research and development	Ability to make engineering changes, have technical bugs in product and process resolved	Skill in quality and new feature development; ability to start developing successor product	Ability to reduce costs, develop variants, differentiate products	Ability to support other grown areas or to apply product to unique customer needs
Key functional area and strategy focus	Engineering: market penetration	Sales: consumer loyalty; market share	Production efficiency; successor products	Finance; maximum investment recovery

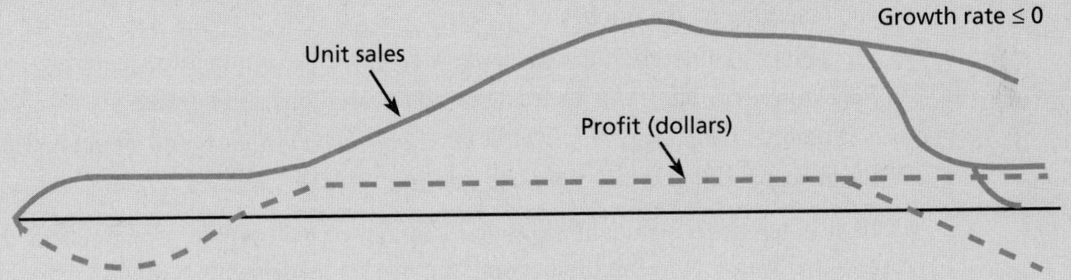

3. *Advantageous relationships* with key suppliers and promising distribution channels.
4. The ability to *establish the firm's technology as the dominant one* before technological uncertainty decreases.
5. The early acquisition of *a core group of loyal customers* and then the expansion of that customer base through model changes, alternative pricing, and advertising.
6. The ability to *forecast future competitors* and the strategies they are likely to employ.

A firm that has had repeated successes with business in emerging industries is 3M Corporation. In each of the past 20 years, more than 25 percent of 3M's annual sales have come from products that did not exist five years earlier. Start-up companies enhance their success by having experienced entrepreneurs at the helm, a knowledgeable management team and board of directors, and patient sources of venture capital. Steven Jobs's dramatic unveiling of Apple's iPod, iPhone, and then iPad came to be seen by many as the catalysts for the emergence of a new personalized digital post-PC world. Jobs and Apple certainly took advantage by building a strategy that shaped the industry's structure, established the firm's technology as a dominant one, endeared themselves to a core group of loyal customers, and rapidly improved each product's quality and wireless, Web-based functionality.

Competitive Advantages and Strategic Choices in Growing Industries

Rapid growth brings new competitors into the industry. Oftentimes, those new entrants are large competitors with substantial resources who have waited for the market to "prove" itself

growth industry strategies
Business strategies that may be more advantageous for firms participating in rapidly growing industries and markets.

before they committed significant resources. At this stage, **growth industry strategies** that emphasize brand recognition, product differentiation, and the financial resources to support both heavy marketing expenses and the effect of price competition on cash flow can be key strengths. Accelerating demand means scaling up production or service capacity to meet the growing demand. Doing so may place a premium on being able to adapt product design and production facilities to meet rapidly increasing demand effectively. Increased investment in plant and equipment, in research and development (R&D), and especially marketing efforts to target specific customer groups along with developing strong distribution capabilities place a demand on the firm's capital resources.

For success in this industry setting, business strategies require one or more of these features:

1. The ability to *establish strong brand recognition* through promotional resources and skills that increase selective demand.
2. The ability and resources to *scale up to meet increasing demand*, which may involve production facilities, service capabilities, and the training and logistics associated with that capacity.
3. *Strong product design skills* to be able to adapt products and services to scaled operations and emerging market niches.
4. The ability to *differentiate the firm's product[s]* from competitors entering the market.
5. *R&D resources and skills* to create product variations and advantages.
6. The ability to *build repeat buying from established customers* and attract new customers.
7. Strong capabilities in *sales and marketing*.

IBM entered the personal computer market—which Apple pioneered in the growth stage—and was able to rapidly become the market leader with a strategy based on its key strengths in brand awareness and possession of the financial resources needed to support consumer advertising. Many large technology companies today prefer exactly this approach: to await proof of an industry or product market and then to acquire small pioneer firms with first-mover advantage as a means to obtain an increasingly known brand, or to acquire technical know-how and experience behind which the firms can put its resources and distribution strength to build brand identify and loyalty. In 2005 as the PC market matured, IBM sold its PC division to China's Lenovo and has exited the personal computer industries.

Competitive Advantages and Strategic Choices in Mature Industry Environments

As an industry evolves, its rate of growth eventually declines. This "transition to maturity" is accompanied by several changes in its competitive environment: Competition for market share becomes more intense as firms in the industry are forced to achieve sales growth at one another's expense. Firms working with the **mature industry strategies** sell increasingly to experienced, repeat buyers who are now making choices among known alternatives. Competition becomes more oriented to cost and service as knowledgeable buyers expect similar price and product features. Industry capacity "tops out" as sales growth ceases to cover up poorly planned expansions. New products and new applications are harder to come by. International competition increases as cost pressures lead to overseas production advantages. Profitability falls, often permanently, as a result of pressure to lower prices and the increased costs of holding or building market share.

mature industry strategies
Strategies used by firms competing in markets where the growth rate of that market from year to year has reached or is close to zero.

These changes necessitate a fundamental strategic reassessment. Strategy elements of successful firms in maturing industries often include the following:

1. *Product line* pruning, or dropping unprofitable product models, sizes, and options from the firm's product mix.
2. *Emphasis on process innovation* that permits low-cost product design, manufacturing methods, and distribution synergy.
3. *Emphasis on cost reduction* through exerting pressure on suppliers for lower prices, switching to cheaper components, introducing operational efficiencies, and lowering administrative and sales overhead.
4. *Careful buyer selection* to focus on buyers who are less aggressive, more closely tied to the firm, and able to buy more from the firm.
5. *Horizontal acquisition* to acquire rival firms whose weaknesses can be used to gain a bargain price and that are correctable by the acquiring firms.
6. *International expansion* to markets where attractive growth and limited competition still exist and the opportunity for lower-cost manufacturing can influence both domestic and international costs.

Milliken, the world's largest private textile company and a chemical company, offers a notable example of a company making solid strategic choices in what are often considered mature industries. Milliken's choice has been to emphasize technology and process innovation, integrate textiles capabilities and chemical capabilities, achieve international expansion, and promote careful buyer selection—thus serving major consumer and industrial industry buyers with significant fabric-related needs. Milliken also includes constant emphasis on cost reduction along with environmental impact reduction. Taken together, these strategic choices regularly result in Milliken being named one of the top global companies in many recognition forums, plus being named one of the world's most ethical companies by Ethisphere.com—all this in two "mature" industries that have seen numerous well-known companies exit or lose out to low-cost competitors in emerging economies. Exhibit 8.8, Global Strategy in Action, illustrates just one strategic choice at Milliken—minimizing its environmental impact while also endeavoring to save costs and limit future waste-related liability.

Business strategists in maturing industries must avoid several pitfalls. First, they must make a clear choice among the three generic strategies and avoid a middle-ground approach, which would confuse both knowledgeable buyers and the firm's personnel. Second, they must avoid sacrificing market share too quickly for short-term profit. Finally, they must avoid waiting too long to respond to price reductions, retaining unneeded excess capacity, engaging in sporadic or irrational efforts to boost sales, and placing their hopes on "new" products, rather than aggressively selling existing products.

Competitive Advantages and Strategic Choices in Declining Industries

declining industry
An industry in which the trend of total sales as an indicator of total demand for an industry's products or services among all the participants in the industry have started to drop from the last several years with the likelihood being that such a trend will continue indefinitely.

Declining industries are those that make products or services for which demand is growing slower than demand in the economy as a whole or is actually declining. This slow growth or decline in demand is caused by technological substitution (such as the substitution of electronic calculators for slide rules), demographic shifts (such as the increase in the number of older people and the decrease in the number of children), and shifts in needs (such as the decreased need for red meat).

Firms in a declining industry should choose strategies that emphasize one or more of the following themes:

1. *Focus* on segments within the industry that offer a chance for higher growth or a higher return.
2. *Emphasize product innovation and quality improvement,* where this can be done cost effectively, to differentiate the firm from rivals and to spur growth.

Global Strategy in Action

Exhibit 8.8

Milliken's Strategic Choice to Reduce Its Environmental Impact

Milliken personnel responsible for cost-control strategic choices related to waste and environmental impact management communicate the essence of those choices in the interesting triangular "Waste Management Pyramid" shown here. The least desirable option for Milliken facilities to handle manufacturing waste is to dispose of it in a secure, legal landfill. Milliken sees this as the most costly option, both directly and in liability terms. Reuse is the most desirable option—least liability and least costly. Shown also are the results Milliken achieved in 2010: a 7 percent reduction in waste over the previous year, with only 0.008 percent of its waste going to landfills, none incinerated, 24 percent converted to energy at Milliken facilities, 60 percent recycled, and 16 percent reused.

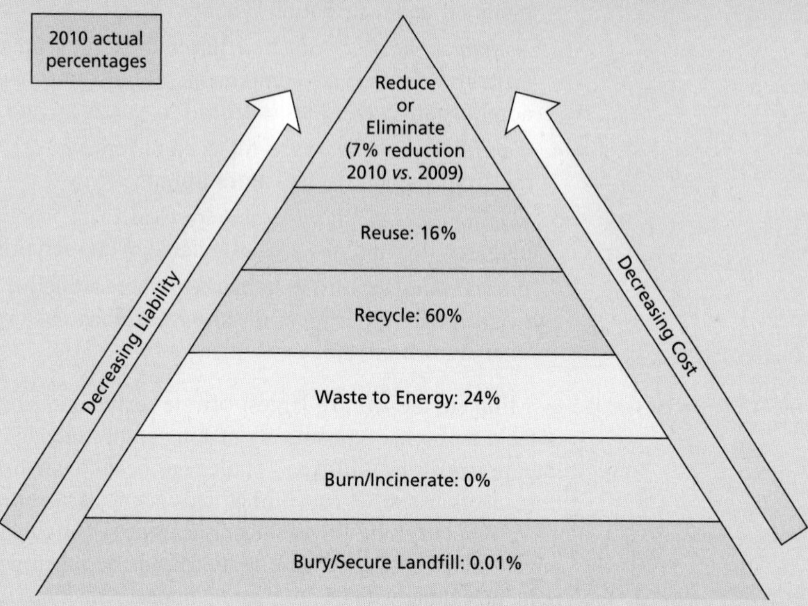

Source: Estimate based on Innoventure Sustainability Forum, Moore School of Business, University of South Carolina, presentation by Miliken Sustainability Team; and Milliken.com.

3. *Emphasize production and distribution efficiency* by streamlining production, closing marginal production facilities and costly distribution outlets, and adding effective new facilities and outlets.
4. *Gradually harvest the business*—generate cash by cutting down on maintenance, reducing models, and shrinking channels and make no new investment.

Strategists who incorporate one or more of these themes into the strategy of their business can anticipate relative success, particularly where the industry's decline is slow and smooth and some profitable niches remain. Penn Tennis, the nation's no. 1 maker of tennis balls, watched industrywide sales steadily decline over the last decade. In response it started marketing tennis balls as "dog toys" in the rapidly growing pet products industry. It secondly made Penn balls the official ball at major tournaments. Third, it created three different quality levels; then, as sales revived, Penn Sports sold its tennis ball business to Head Sports.

fragmented industry
An industry in which there are numerous competitors (providers of the same or similar products or services the industry involves) such that no single firm or small group of firms controls any significant share of the overall industry sales.

Competitive Advantage in Fragmented Industries

Fragmented industries are another setting in which identifiable types of competitive advantages and the strategic choices suggested by those advantages can be identified. A **fragmented industry** is one in which no firm has a significant market share and can strongly influence industry outcomes. Fragmented industries are found in many areas of the economy and are common in such areas as professional services, retailing, distribution, wood and metal fabrication, and agricultural products. The funeral industry is an example of a highly fragmented industry. Business strategists in fragmented industries pursue low-cost or differentiation strategies or focus competitive advantages in one of five ways:

Tightly Managed Decentralization Fragmented industries are characterized by a need for intense local coordination, a local management orientation, high personal service, and local autonomy. Recently, however, successful firms in such industries have introduced a high degree of professionalism into the operations of local managers.

"Formula" Facilities This alternative, related to the previous one, introduces standardized, efficient, low-cost facilities at multiple locations. Thus, the firm gradually builds a low-cost advantage over localized competitors. Fast-food and motel chains have applied this approach with considerable success.

Increased Value Added The products or services of some fragmented industries are difficult to differentiate. In this case, an effective strategy may be to add value by providing more service with the sale or by engaging in some product assembly that is of additional value to the customer.

Specialization Focus strategies that creatively segment the market can enable firms to cope with fragmentation. Specialization can be pursued by

1. *Product type.* The firm builds expertise focusing on a narrow range of products or services.
2. *Customer type.* The firm becomes intimately familiar with and serves the needs of a narrow customer segment.
3. *Type of order.* The firm handles only certain kinds of orders, such as small orders, custom orders, or quick turnaround orders.
4. *Geographic area.* The firm blankets or concentrates on a single area.

Although specialization in one or more of these ways can be the basis for a sound focus strategy in a fragmented industry, each of these types of specialization risks limiting the firm's potential sales volume.

Bare Bones/No Frills Given the intense competition and low margins in fragmented industries, a "bare bones" posture—low overhead, minimum wage employees, tight cost control—may build a sustainable cost advantage in such industries.

Competitive Advantage in Global Industries

global industry
Industry in which competition crosses national borders.

Global industries present a final setting in which success is often associated with identifiable sources of competitive advantage. A **global industry** is one that comprises firms whose competitive positions in major geographic or national markets are fundamentally affected by their overall global competitive positions. To avoid strategic disadvantages, firms in global industries are virtually required to compete on a worldwide basis. Oil, steel, automobiles, apparel, motorcycles, televisions, and computers are examples of global industries.

Global industries have four unique strategy-shaping features:

- Differences in prices and costs from country to country due to currency exchange fluctuations, differences in wage and inflation rates, and other economic factors.
- Differences in buyer needs across different countries.
- Differences in competitors and ways of competing from country to country.
- Differences in trade rules and governmental regulations across different countries.

These unique features and the global competition of global industries require that two fundamental components be addressed in the business strategy: (1) the approach used to gain global market coverage and (2) the generic competitive strategy. Three basic options can be used to pursue global market coverage:

1. *License* foreign firms to produce and distribute the firm's products.
2. *Maintain a domestic production base* and export products to foreign countries.

Global Strategy in Action — Exhibit 8.9

Nineteenth-Century French Steelmaker Crafts a Global Focus Strategy

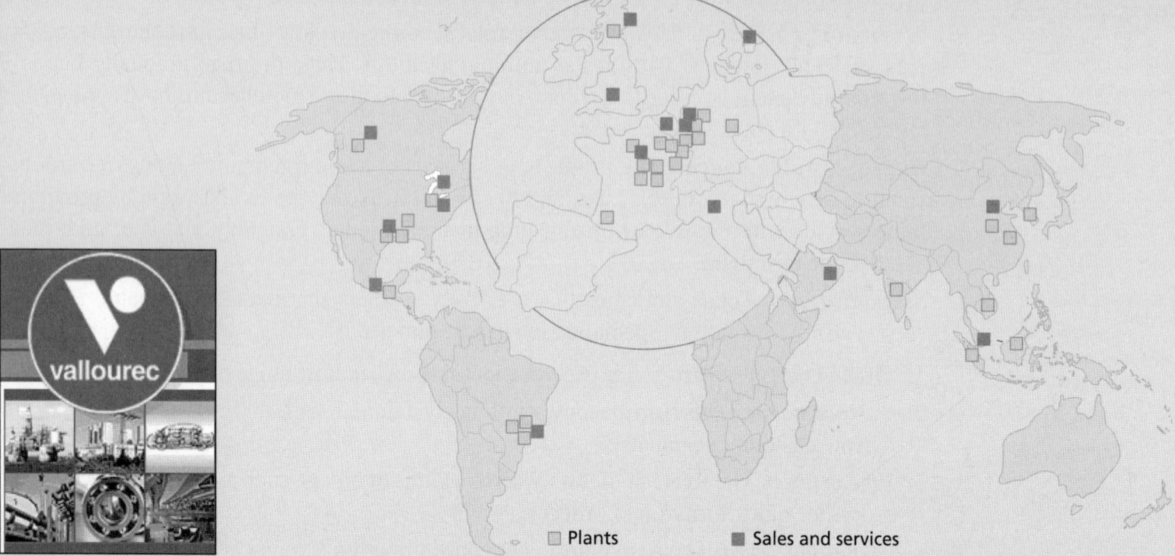

Vallourec's beginnings go back to the late 1800s in northern France with construction, engineering, metallurgy, and steelmaking. Early the next century, it began making welded and eventually seamless tubes (round pipe). As it prepared to enter the twenty-first century, with all of its plants in Europe, its management decided to sell off various parts of its businesses and commit instead to a global focus strategy providing seamless steel pipes, primarily to the oil and gas and electric power industries.

Vallourec acquired MSA in Brazil in 2000, and, by 2011, had moved over half its manufacturing capacity outside Europe, shown in the accompanying world map. It is the world leader in the global seamless steel tube market. Its global focus strategy is reinforced by a decentralized organizational structure, where regional subsidiaries enjoy considerable autonomy to work closely with clients in their target markets. The global focus strategy must be working well, as evidenced in by more than 20,000 employees—more than 74 percent of its workforce—choosing to buy 1.2 million shares of Vallourec stock, in globally recovering equity and oil markets, at the current market price. At the ground level of a global focus strategy, that is a strong vote of confidence.

Source: www.vallourec.com

3. *Establish foreign-based plants and distribution* to compete directly in the markets of one or more foreign countries.

Along with the market coverage decision, strategists must scrutinize the condition of the global industry features identified earlier to choose among four generic global competitive strategies:

1. *Broad-line global competition*—directed at competing worldwide in the full product line of the industry, often with plants in many countries, to achieve differentiation or an overall low-cost position.
2. *Global focus* strategy—targeting a particular segment of the industry for competition on a worldwide basis.

3. *National focus* strategy—taking advantage of differences in national markets that give the firm an edge over global competitors on a nation-by-nation basis.
4. *Protected niche* strategy—seeking out countries in which governmental restraints exclude or inhibit global competitors or allow concessions, or both, that are advantageous to localized firms.

Competing in a global context has become a reality for most businesses in virtually every economy around the world. So most firms must consider among the global competitive strategies identified above. Exhibit 8.9, Global Strategy in Action, describes how an "Old World" French steelmaker did just this to craft a global focus strategy selling steel pipe worldwide and in the process become the world leader in seamless steel tubing.

DOMINANT PRODUCT/SERVICE BUSINESSES: EVALUATING AND CHOOSING TO DIVERSIFY TO BUILD VALUE

McDonald's has frequently looked at numerous opportunities to diversify into related businesses or to acquire key suppliers. Its decision has consistently been to focus on its core business using the grand strategies of concentration, market development, and product development. Rival Yum Brands, on the other hand, has chosen to diversify into related businesses and vertical acquisition as the best grand strategies for it to build long-term value. Both firms experienced unprecedented success during the last 20 years.

Many dominant product businesses face this question as their core business proves successful: What grand strategies are best suited to continue to build value? Under what circumstances should they choose an expanded focus (diversification, vertical acquisition); steady continued focus (concentration, market or product development); or a narrowed focus (turnaround or divestiture)? This section examines two ways you can analyze a dominant product company's situation and choose among 12 of the 15 grand strategies identified in Chapter 7.

grand strategy selection matrix
A four-cell guide to strategies based upon whether the business is (1) operating from a position of strength or weakness and (2) rely on its own resources versus having to acquire resources via merger or acquisition.

vertical acquisition
Acquisition of firms that supply inputs such as raw materials, or customers for its outputs, such as warehouses for finished products.

conglomerate diversification
Acquiring or entering businesses unrelated to a firm's current technologies, markets, or products.

Grand Strategy Selection Matrix

One valuable guide to the selection of a promising grand strategy is the **grand strategy selection matrix** shown in Exhibit 8.10. The basic idea underlying the matrix is that two variables are of central concern in the selection process: (1) the principal purpose of the grand strategy and (2) the choice of an internal or external emphasis for growth or profitability.

In the past, planners were advised to follow certain rules or prescriptions in their choice of strategies. Now, most experts agree that strategy selection is better guided by the conditions of the planning period and by the company strengths and weaknesses. It should be noted, however, that even the early approaches to strategy selection sought to match a concern over internal versus external growth with a desire to overcome weaknesses or maximize strengths.

The same considerations led to the development of the grand strategy selection matrix. A firm in quadrant I, with "all its eggs in one basket," often views itself as overcommitted to a particular business with limited growth opportunities or high risks. One reasonable solution is **vertical acquisition,** which enables the firm to reduce risk by reducing uncertainty about inputs or access to customers. Another is **conglomerate diversification,** which provides a profitable investment alternative with diverting management attention from the original

EXHIBIT 8.10 Grand Strategy Selection Matrix

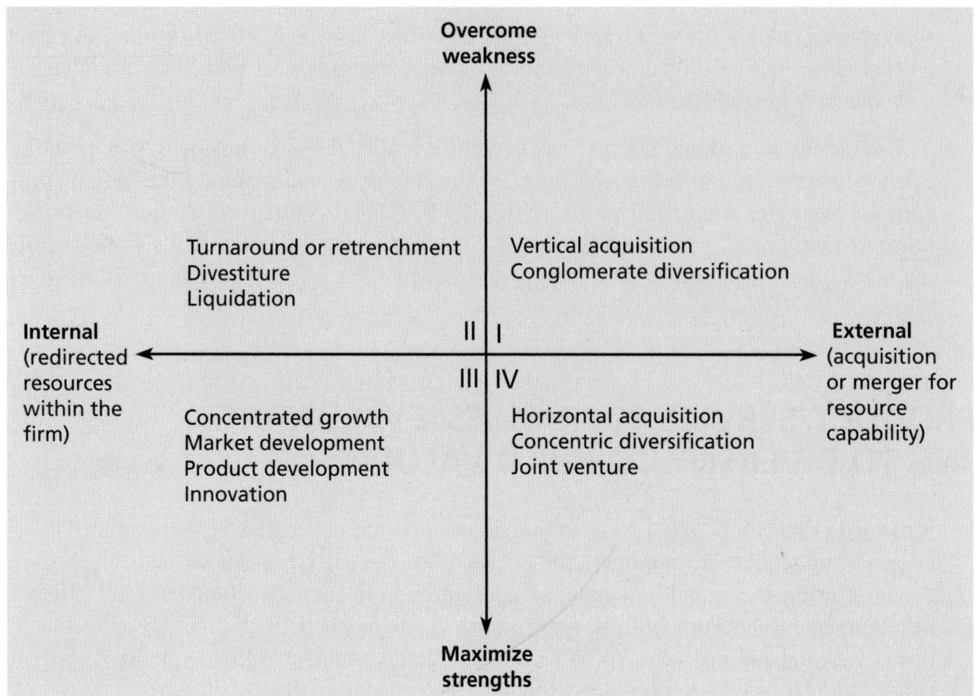

retrenchment
Cutting back on products, markets, operations because the firm's overall competitive and financial situation cannot support commitments needed to sustain or build its operations.

divestiture
The sale of a firm or a major component.

liquidation
Closing down the operations of a business and selling its assets and operations to pay its debts and distribute any gains to stockholders.

concentrated growth
Aggressive market penetration where a firm's strong position and favorable market growth allow it to "control" resources and effort for focused growth.

business. However, the external approaches to overcoming weaknesses usually result in the most costly grand strategies. Acquiring a second business demands large investments of time and sizable financial resources. Thus, strategic managers considering these approaches must guard against exchanging one set of weaknesses for another.

More conservative approaches to overcoming weaknesses are found in quadrant II. Firms often choose to redirect resources from one internal business activity to another. This approach maintains the firm's commitment to its basic mission, rewards success, and enables further development of proven competitive advantages. The least disruptive of the quadrant II strategies is **retrenchment,** pruning the current activities of a business. If the weaknesses of the business arose from inefficiencies, retrenchment can actually serve as a *turnaround* strategy—that is, the business gains new strength from the streamlining of its operations and the elimination of waste. However, if those weaknesses are a major obstruction to success in the industry and the costs of overcoming them are unaffordable or are not justified by a cost-benefit analysis, then eliminating the business must be considered. **Divestiture** offers the best possibility for recouping the firm's investment, but even **liquidation** can be an attractive option if the alternatives are bankruptcy or an unwarranted drain on the firm's resources.

A common business adage states that a firm should build from strength. The premise of this adage is that growth and survival depend on an ability to capture a market share that is large enough for essential economies of scale. If a firm believes that this approach will be profitable and prefers an internal emphasis for maximizing strengths, four grand strategies hold considerable promise. As shown in quadrant III, the most common approach is **concentrated growth,** that is, market penetration. The firm that selects this strategy is strongly committed to its current products and markets. It strives to solidify its position by reinvesting resources to fortify its strengths.

market development
Selling present products, often with only cosmetic modification, to customers in related marketing areas by adding channels of distribution or by changing the content of advertising or promotion.

product development
The substantial modification of existing products or the creation of new but related products that can be marketed to current customers through established channels.

innovation
A strategy that seeks to reap the initially high profits associated with customer acceptance of a new or greatly improved product.

horizontal acquisition
Growth through the acquisition of one or more similar firms operating at the same stage of the production-marketing chain.

concentric diversification
Acquisition of businesses that are related to the acquiring firm in terms of technology, markets, or products.

joint ventures
Commercial companies created and operated for the benefit of the co-owners; usually two or more separate companies that form the venture.

strategic alliances
Partnerships that are distinguished from joint ventures because the companies involved do not take an equity position in one another.

Two alternative approaches are **market development** and **product development.** With these strategies, the firm attempts to broaden its operations. Market development is chosen if the firm's strategic managers feel that its existing products would be well received by new customer groups. Product development is chosen if they feel that the firm's existing customers would be interested in products related to its current lines. Product development also may be based on technological or other competitive advantages. The final alternative for quadrant III firms is **innovation.** When the firm's strengths are in creative product design or unique production technologies, sales can be stimulated by accelerating perceived obsolescence. This is the principle underlying the innovative grand strategy.

Maximizing a firm's strengths by aggressively expanding its base of operations usually requires an external emphasis. The preferred options in such cases are shown in quadrant IV. **Horizontal acquisition** is attractive because it makes possible a quick increase in output capability. Moreover, in horizontal acquisition, the skills of the managers of the original business often are critical in converting newly acquired facilities into profitable contributors to the parent firm; this expands a fundamental competitive advantage of the firm—its management.

Concentric diversification is a good second choice for similar reasons. Because the original and newly acquired businesses are related, the distinctive competencies of the diversifying firm are likely to facilitate a smooth, synergistic, and profitable expansion.

The final alternative for increasing resource capability through external emphasis is a **joint venture** or **strategic alliance.** This alternative allows a firm to extend its strengths into competitive arenas that it would be hesitant to enter alone. A partner's production, technological, financial, or marketing capabilities can reduce the firm's financial investment significantly and increase its probability of success.

Model of Grand Strategy Clusters

A second guide to selecting a promising strategy is the **grand strategy cluster** shown in Exhibit 8.11. The figure is based on the idea that the situation of a business is defined in terms of the growth rate of the general market and the firm's competitive position in that market. When these factors are considered simultaneously, a business can be broadly categorized in one of four quadrants: (I) strong competitive position in a rapidly growing market, (II) weak position in a rapidly growing market, (III) weak position in a slow-growth market, or (IV) strong position in a slow-growth market. Each of these quadrants suggests a set of promising possibilities for the selection of a grand strategy.

Firms in quadrant I are in an excellent strategic position. One obvious grand strategy for such firms is continued concentration on their current business as it is currently defined. Because consumers seem satisfied with the firm's current strategy, shifting notably from it would endanger the firm's established competitive advantages. McDonald's Corporation has followed this approach for 25 years. However, if the firm has resources that exceed the demands of a concentrated growth strategy, it should consider vertical acquisition. Either forward or backward acquisition helps a firm protect its profit margins and market share by ensuring better access to consumers or material inputs. Finally, to diminish the risks associated with a narrow product or service line, a quadrant I firm might be wise to consider concentric diversification; with this strategy, the firm continues to invest heavily in its basic area of proven ability.

Firms in quadrant II must seriously evaluate their present approach to the marketplace. If a firm has competed long enough to accurately assess the merits of its current grand strategy, it must determine (1) why that strategy is ineffectual and (2) whether it is capable of competing effectively. Depending on the answers to these questions, the firm should choose

EXHIBIT 8.11 Model of Grand Strategy Clusters

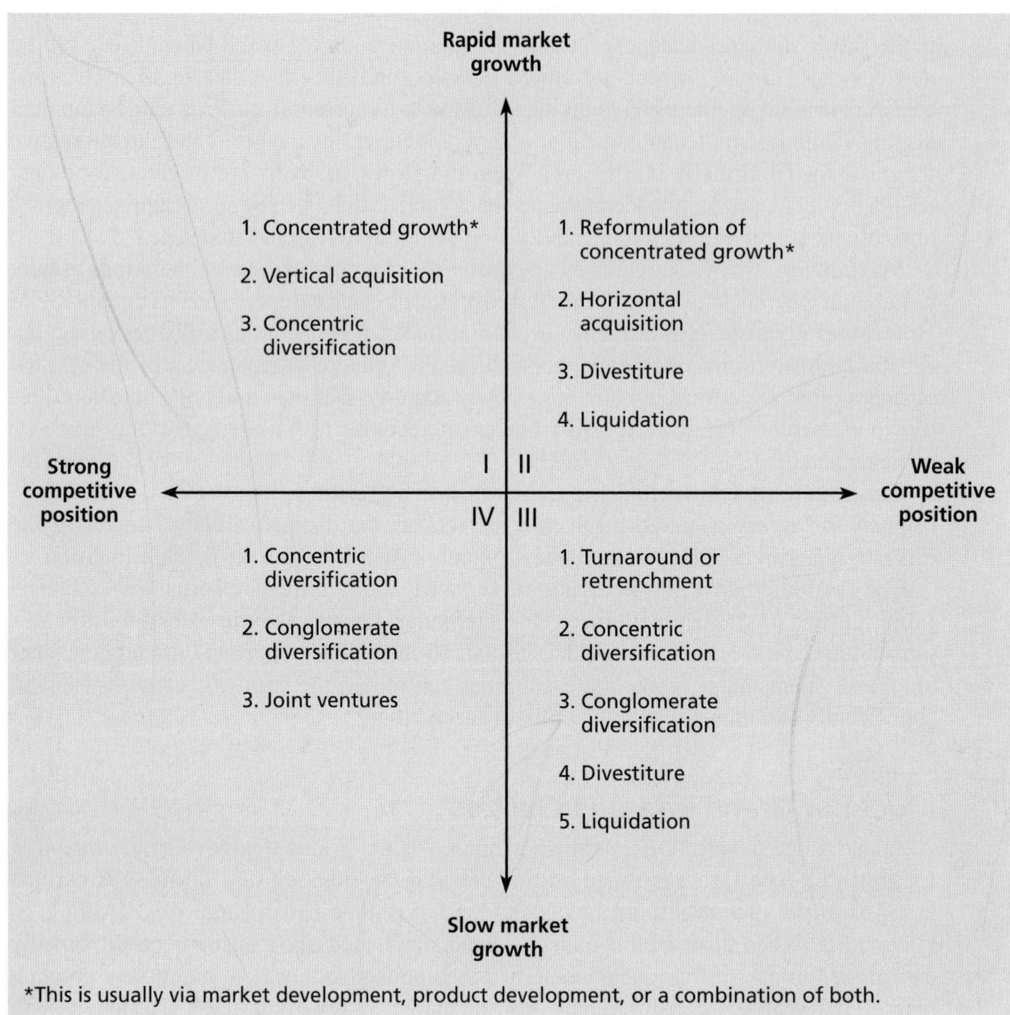

*This is usually via market development, product development, or a combination of both.

grand strategy clusters
Strategies that may be more advantageous for firms to choose under one of four sets of conditions defined by market growth rate and the strength of the firm's competitive position.

one of four grand strategy options: formulation or reformulation of a concentrated growth strategy, horizontal acquisition, divestiture, or liquidation.

In a rapidly growing market, even a small or relatively weak business often is able to find a profitable niche. Thus, formulation or reformulation of a concentrated growth strategy is usually the first option that should be considered. However, if the firm lacks either a critical competitive element or sufficient economies of scale to achieve competitive cost efficiencies, then a grand strategy that directs its efforts toward horizontal acquisition is often a desirable alternative. A final pair of options involves deciding to stop competing in the market or product area of the business. A multiproduct firm may conclude that it is most likely to achieve the goals of its mission if the business is dropped through divestiture. This grand strategy not only eliminates a drain on resources but also may provide funds to promote other business activities. As an option of last resort, a firm may decide to liquidate the business. This means that the business cannot be sold as a going concern and is at best worth only the value of its tangible assets. The decision to liquidate is an undeniable admission of failure by a firm's strategic management and, thus, often is delayed—to the further detriment of the firm.

Strategic managers tend to resist divestiture because it is likely to jeopardize their control of the firm and perhaps even their jobs. Thus, by the time the desirability of divestiture is acknowledged, businesses often deteriorate to the point of failing to attract potential buyers. The consequences of such delays are financially disastrous for firm owners because the value of a going concern is many times greater than the value of its assets.

Strategic managers who have a business in quadrant III and expect a continuation of slow market growth and a relatively weak competitive position will usually attempt to decrease their resource commitment to that business. Minimal withdrawal is accomplished through retrenchment; this strategy has the side benefits of making resources available for other investments and of motivating employees to increase their operating efficiency. An alternative approach is to divert resources for expansion through investment in other businesses. This approach typically involves either concentric or conglomerate diversification because the firm usually wants to enter more promising arenas of competition than acquisition or concentrated growth strategies would allow. The final options for quadrant III businesses are divestiture, if an optimistic buyer can be found, and liquidation.

Quadrant IV businesses (strong competitive position in a slow-growth market) have a basis of strength from which to diversify into more promising growth areas. These businesses have characteristically high cash flow levels and limited internal growth needs. Thus, they are in an excellent position for concentric diversification into ventures that utilize their proven acumen. A previous example in this chapter described how the no. 1 tennis ball maker, Penn Racquet Sports, chose concentric diversification from humans to dogs as their best option. A second option is conglomerate diversification, which spreads investment risk and does not divert managerial attention from the present business. The final option is joint ventures, which are especially attractive to multinational firms. Through joint ventures, a domestic business can gain competitive advantages in promising new fields while exposing itself to limited risks.

Opportunities for Building Value as a Basis for Choosing Diversification or Acquisition

The grand strategy selection matrix and model of grand strategy clusters are useful tools to help dominant product company managers evaluate and narrow their choices among alternative grand strategies. When considering grand strategies that would broaden the scope of their company's business activities through acquisition, diversification, or joint venture strategies, managers must examine whether opportunities to build value are present. Opportunities to build value via diversification, acquisition, or joint venture strategies are usually found in market-related, operating-related, and management activities. Such opportunities center around reducing costs, improving margins, or providing access to new revenue sources more cost effectively than traditional internal growth options via concentration, market development, or product development. Major opportunities for sharing and value building as well as ways to capitalize on core competencies are outlined in the next chapter, which covers strategic analysis and choice in diversified companies.

Dominant product company managers who choose diversification or acquisition eventually create another management challenge. That challenge is charting the future of a company that becomes a collection of several distinct businesses. These distinct businesses often encounter different competitive environments, challenges, and opportunities. The next chapter examines ways managers of such diversified companies attempt to evaluate and choose corporate strategy. Central to their challenge is the continued desire to build value, particularly shareholder value.

Summary

This chapter examined how managers in businesses that have a single or dominant product or service evaluate and choose their company's strategy. Two critical areas deserve their attention: (1) their business's value chain, and (2) the appropriateness of 12 different grand strategies based on matching environmental factors with internal capabilities.

Managers in single-product-line business units examine their business's value chain to identify existing or potential activities around which they can create sustainable competitive advantages. As managers scrutinize their value chain activities, they are looking for three sources of competitive advantage: low cost, differentiation, and rapid response capabilities. They also examine whether focusing on a narrow market niche provides a more effective, sustainable way to build or leverage these three sources of competitive advantage.

Managers in single- or dominant-product/service businesses face two interrelated issues: (1) They must choose which grand strategies make best use of their competitive advantages. (2) They must ultimately decide whether to diversify their business activity. Twelve grand strategies were identified in this chapter along with three frameworks that aid managers in choosing which grand strategies should work best and when diversification or acquisition should be the best strategy for the business. The next chapter expands the coverage of diversification to look at how multibusiness companies evaluate continued diversification and how they construct corporate strategy.

Key Terms

concentrated growth, *p. 252*
concentric diversification, *p. 253*
conglomerate diversification, *p. 251*
declining industry, *p. 247*
differentiation, *p. 236*
divestiture, *p. 252*
emerging industry, *p. 243*
fragmented industry, *p. 248*
global industry, *p. 249*
grand strategy clusters, *p. 254*
grand strategy selection matrix, *p. 250*
growth industry strategies, *p. 246*
horizontal acquisition, *p. 253*
innovation, *p. 253*
joint ventures, *p. 253*
liquidation, *p. 252*
low-cost strategies, *p. 234*
market development, *p. 253*
market focus, *p. 241*
mature industry strategies, *p. 246*
product development, *p. 253*
retrenchment, *p. 252*
speed-based strategies, *p. 239*
strategic alliances, *p. 253*
vertical acquisition, *p. 251*

Questions for Discussion

1. What are three activities or capabilities a firm should possess to support a low-cost leadership strategy? Use Exhibit 8.2 to help you answer this question. Can you give an example of a company that has done this?
2. What are three activities or capabilities a firm should possess to support a differentiation-based strategy? Use Exhibit 8.3 to help you answer this question. Can you give an example of a company that has done this?
3. What are three ways a firm can incorporate the advantage of speed in its business? Use Exhibit 8.5 to help you answer this question. Can you give an example of a company that has done this?
4. Do you think it is better to concentrate on one source of competitive advantage (cost versus differentiation versus speed) or to nurture all three in a firm's operation?
5. How does market focus help a business create competitive advantage? What risks accompany such a posture?
6. Using Exhibits 8.10 and 8.11, describe situations or conditions under which horizontal acquisition and concentric diversification would be preferred strategic choices.

Multibusiness Strategy

After reading and studying this chapter, you should be able to

1. Understand the portfolio approach to strategic analysis and choice in multibusiness companies.
2. Understand and use three different portfolio approaches to conduct strategic analysis and choice in multibusiness companies.
3. Identify the limitations and weaknesses of the various portfolio approaches.
4. Understand the synergy approach to strategic analysis and choice in multibusiness companies.
5. Evaluate the parent company role in strategic analysis and choice to determine whether and how it adds tangible value in a multibusiness company.

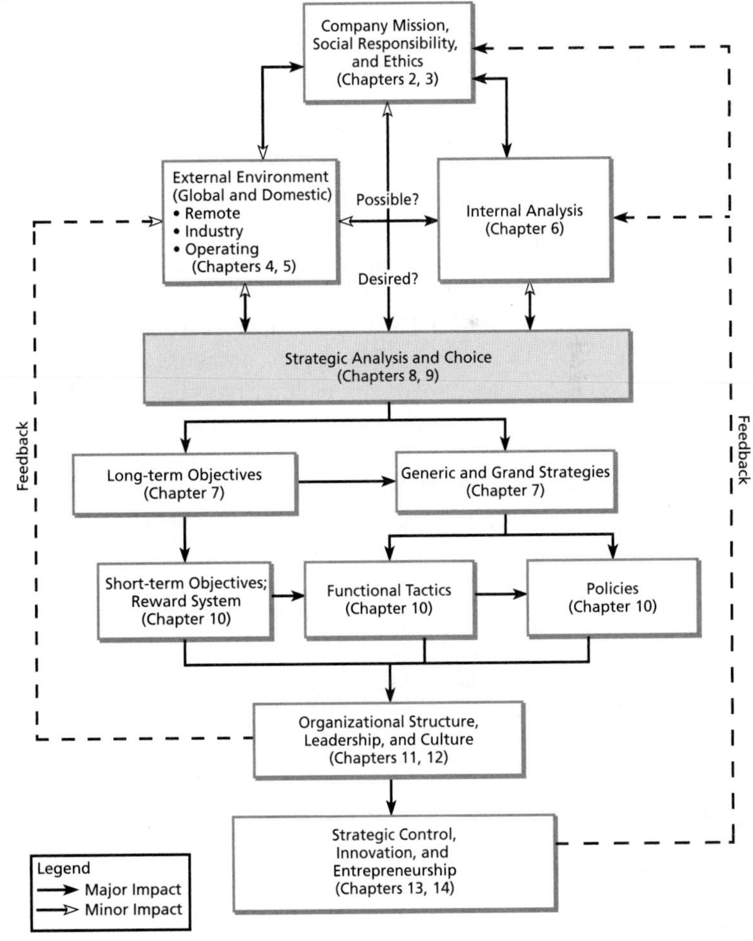

Jeff Immelt has faced two recessions and accelerated global competition in his first decade at General Electric's helm, personally selected for the job by his predecessor, the globally admired Jack Welch. The worst recession since the Great Depression, driven by a swift virtual collapse of the global financial system, made Immelt's challenge even greater as it placed in jeopardy GE Capital, one of five GE business groups and a usual key source of profit to finance its other businesses. GE remains—and has long been—one of the world's most admired companies, a bellwether of the global economy, even in the face of these unprecedented challenges. The job facing Immelt and his executive team, having begun to recover from the "great recession," was to determine what businesses GE should remain in, and which it should exit, to survive and prosper in the twenty-first century. Should it continue with plans to sell its appliance business? Should it grow its energy infrastructure businesses, enter biomedicine, stay in movies and TV? Which businesses should receive the greatest investment of its currently limited resources, and which should it sell or otherwise reduce to generate resources and shift talent?

Japan-based Sony Corporation, once the darling of the consumer electronics world, has proven a major challenge to Welsh-born American CEO Howard Stringer: A sluggish global economy, a rising yen, an organizational culture based on consensus decision making facing swiftly changing conditions—and conglomerate Sony being outfought by more focused, leaner companies: Nintendo in games, Apple in personal communication devices, Canon in cameras, Samsung in TVs, and Microsoft in software. Eight years into his tenure, Stringer is at a crossroads. Facing Sony's second year of operating losses in 14 years, what should he do? Should he emphasize certain businesses? Sell others? Outsource and refocus the nature of each business? Reorganize?

Strategic analysis and choice is complicated for corporate-level managers because they must create a strategy to guide a company that contains numerous businesses. They must examine and choose which businesses to own and which ones to forgo or divest. They must consider business managers' plans to capture and exploit competitive advantage in each business, and then decide how to allocate resources among those businesses. This chapter covers ways managers in multibusiness companies analyze and choose what businesses to be in and how to allocate resources across those businesses.

The portfolio approach was one of the early approaches for charting strategy and allocating resources in multibusiness companies. This approach, with its appealing fundamental logic, was initially popularized by consulting groups like the Boston Consulting Group and McKinsey and Company as they helped corporate clients pursue and "rationalize" diversification strategies. Inevitably, some corporate managers, concerned with possible shortcomings in this type of approach, welcomed new options. Yet, while some companies moved on to other techniques, the portfolio approach remains a useful way of evaluating corporate strategy options. Interestingly, GE pioneered one form of the approach, which was subsequently abandoned under Jack Welch, only to now have successor Jeff Immelt bring it back as part of GE's corporate strategy vocabulary and decision making. Immelt's comments to GE stakeholders during his tenure to date that show this include:

> I would ask investors to think about the progress we have made with our portfolio [of businesses] . . . We have executed a disciplined portfolio strategy to aggressively reshape GE . . . We have exited businesses with revenues of about $50 billion—the equivalent of a *Fortune* 50 company. We have exited all or most of our insurance, materials, equipment services, and slow-growth entertainment and industrial platforms . . . our mortgage origination business and our personal loan business in Japan . . . Over the same time period we acquired $80 billion of new businesses—the equivalent of a *Fortune* 30 company . . . investing in Infrastructure, creating one of the largest renewable-energy businesses in the world . . . diversified our Healthcare and NBC Universal (NBCU) franchises by investing

in fast-growth markets such as life sciences, healthcare IT, and cable programming . . . and created a new high-tech industrial business called Enterprise Solutions. We sold our Plastics business because of rampant inflation in raw material costs . . . used that capital to acquire Vetco Gray, adding a subsea platform in Oil & Gas; we acquired Smiths Aerospace to create an avionics platform; we built global cable content through the acquisition of Oxygen and Sparrowhawk; and we added several industrial service platforms.

I have begun my tenth year as CEO of GE. Looking back, no one could have predicted the volatile events of the last decade: two recessions; the 9/11 tragedy; Hurricane Katrina; the world at war; the rise of the BRICS; the financial crisis; the Gulf oil spill; and the Japanese earthquake and tsunami, just to name a few.

I took over a great company, but one where we had a lot of work to do to position GE to win in the twenty-first century. Despite our high valuation, we were in businesses where we could not sustain a competitive advantage, like plastics and insurance. We made a capital-allocation decision to reduce our exposure to media and invest in infrastructure. And we had to rebuild our Energy business, where most of our earnings in the late 1990s came from a "U.S. power bubble" that created a decade of excess capacity.

Our team rolled up their sleeves. Ultimately, we exited about half of our portfolio. We invested in infrastructure businesses like oil and gas, life sciences, renewable energy, avionics, molecular medicine and water. We restored our manufacturing muscle. And we focused and strengthened GE Capital. As a result of these actions, we have our most competitive portfolio in decades.

We made big bets in technology, globalization and customer service. We doubled our R&D spending over the past 10 years and it now equals 6 percent of Infrastructure revenue. We repositioned leadership and capability to win in global growth markets. We have grown global revenue from 36 percent of GE's revenue to nearly 55 percent in the last decade. We have invested in sales force excellence, marketing and customer support. Services have grown from 30 percent of GE's Infrastructure earnings to 70 percent in the last decade. GE is the world's fifth most valuable brand.

We promoted a culture that demanded financial accountability and long-term thinking. Leaders understand their responsibility to invest in the future of their business. But we still compete hard. Our productivity, measured by revenue per employee, has expanded by 50 percent since 2000. Our Industrial margins and returns exceed other great companies like Honeywell, Siemens and United Technologies.

Despite all these changes, our cumulative earnings and cash flow over the last decade would rank in the top ten of all the companies in the world.[1]

Perhaps history repeats itself, or what goes around comes around in terms of using a portfolio approach. Some see GE and argue, particularly in recent economic times, that it is too big and complicated to achieve success compared to what could be achieved if its various businesses were separated. Others point out that it has produced impressive innovation and growth for most of its 130 years and that its individual businesses benefit from synergies gained across each other as they face common global themes. Both perspectives have legitimate points. Regardless, where managers in a company like GE, with multiple diverse businesses, need to examine and develop corporate-level strategy, the need to look at the "whole" as a porfolio of different businesses appears one way to pursue that task.[2] Exhibit 9.1, Global Strategy in Action shows eBay's view of its business portfolio's evolving in much this way. That portfolio went from a broad collection of Web-based ventures to an attempt to rationalize them into three themes or a "3-legged stool" portfolio—Online

[1] "Letter to Shareholders," 2006–2011 *G.E. Annual Reports*.

[2] "In Grim Times, Hoping for 'Reset,'" *Fortune*, January 28, 2009; Jeff Immelt, "A Blueprint for Keeping America Competitive," *WashingtonPost.com*, Jan. 21, 2011; and Ulrich Pidun, Harald Rubner, Matthias Kruhlerr, and Michael Nippa, "Corporate Portfolio Management: Theory and Practice," *Journal of Applied Corporate Finance* 23, no. 1 (Winter 2011), pp. 63–76.

Global Strategy in Action — Exhibit 9.1

eBay's Business Portfolio—Three Businesses . . . Did Skype Fit?

This "map" from eBay shows the evolution of its "business portfolio" from a collection of about 24 different businesses to what became viewed as its "3-Legged Stool" business portfolio—a division of those 24 businesses based on related aspects of these businesses into Online Commerce, Payments, or Communications. Many analysts, eBay sellers, and increasingly eBay managers questioned the rationale for having Skype in the business mix. They saw Skype as having snookered former CEO Meg Whitman into paying $3.1 billion in 2005 for "synergies" that have never materialized, thus the name "Whitman's Folly." eBay took a $1.4 billion write-down two years later, and Skype's fourth president since the acquisition, Josh Silverman, started trying to increase Skype's financial value to eBay by separating it from eBay as a part of the eBay portfolio; selling a 70 percent interest to an investment group led by Marc Andreessen for $2 billion in cash; and 18 months later in 2011 that group sold it to Microsoft for $8.5 billion in cash. So now the eBay portfolio is a two-legged stool, logically interrelated, and energized by getting approximately $5 billion in cash "back" for its trouble. Now Skype is Microsoft's opportunity, or problem.

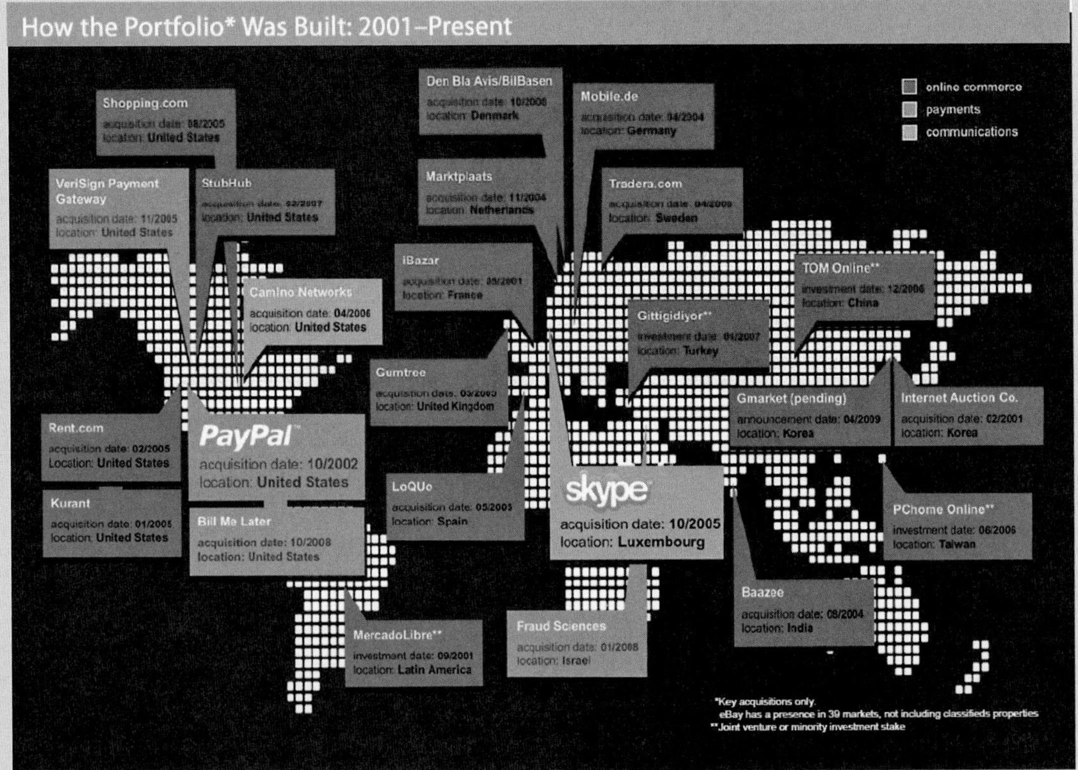

Source: Fair Use per EBay

commerce, Payments, and Communications. That last leg was Skype, for which it paid handsomely and struggled to derive any real payoff. Serious questions about its "fit" into eBay's portfolio followed with an eventual decision to disengage it as an eBay business.

Improvement on the portfolio approach focused on ways to broaden the rationale behind pursuit of diversification strategies. This approach centered on the idea that at the heart of effective diversification is the identification of core competencies in a business or set of businesses to then leverage as the basis for competitive advantage in the growth of those businesses and the entry in or divestiture of other businesses. This notion of leveraging core competencies as a basis for strategic choice in multibusiness companies has been a popular one for the past 20 years.

Recent evolution of strategic analysis and choice in this setting has expanded on the core competency notion to focus on a series of fundamental questions that multibusiness companies should address in order to make diversification work. With both the accelerated rates of change in most global markets and trying economic conditions, multibusiness companies have adapted the fundamental questions into an approach called "patching" to map and remap their business units swiftly against changing market opportunities. Finally, as companies have embraced lean organizational structures, strategic analysis in multibusiness companies has included careful assessment of the corporate parent, its role, and value or lack thereof in contributing to the stand-alone performance of their business units. This chapter will examine each of these approaches to shaping multibusiness corporate strategy.

THE PORTFOLIO APPROACH: A HISTORICAL STARTING POINT

portfolio techniques
An approach pioneered by the Boston Consulting Group that attempted to help managers "balance" the flow of cash resources among their various businesses while also identifying their basic strategic purpose within the overall portfolio.

The past 30 years we have seen a virtual explosion in the extent to which single-business companies seek to acquire other businesses to grow and to diversify. There are many reasons for this emergence of multibusiness companies: Companies can enter businesses with greater growth potential; enter businesses with different cyclical considerations; diversify inherent risks; increase vertical integration, and thereby reduce costs; capture value added; and instantly have a market presence rather than slower internal growth. As businesses jumped on the diversification bandwagon, their managers soon found a challenge in managing the resource needs of diverse businesses and their respective strategic missions, particularly in times of limited resources. Responding to this challenge, the Boston Consulting Group (BCG) pioneered an approach called **portfolio techniques** that attempted to help managers "balance" the flow of cash resources among their various businesses while also identifying their basic strategic purpose within the overall portfolio. Three of these techniques are reviewed here. Once reviewed, we will identify some of the problems with the portfolio approach that you should keep in mind when considering its use.

The BCG Growth-Share Matrix

market growth rate
The projected rate of sales growth for the market being served by a particular business.

relative competitive position
The market share of a business divided by the market share of its largest competitor.

stars
Businesses in rapidly growing markets with large market shares.

Managers using the BCG matrix plotted each of the company's businesses according to market growth rate and relative competitive position. **Market growth rate** is the projected rate of sales growth for the market being served by a particular business. Usually measured as the percentage increase in a market's sales or unit volume over the two most recent years, this rate serves as an indicator of the relative attractiveness of the markets served by each business in the firm's portfolio of businesses. **Relative competitive position** usually is expressed as the market share of a business divided by the market share of its largest competitor. Thus, relative competitive position provides a basis for comparing the relative strengths of the businesses in the firm's portfolio in terms of their positions in their respective markets. Exhibit 9.2 illustrates the growth-share matrix.

The **stars** are businesses in rapidly growing markets with large market shares. These businesses represent the best long-run opportunities (growth and profitability) in the firm's portfolio. They require substantial investment to maintain (and expand) their dominant position in a growing market. This investment requirement is often in excess of the funds that they can generate internally. Therefore, these businesses are often short-term, priority consumers of corporate resources.

EXHIBIT 9.2
The BCG Growth-Share Matrix

Source: The growth-share matrix was originally developed by the Boston Consulting Group.

Description of Dimensions

Market share: Sales relative to those of other competitors in the market (dividing point is usually selected to have only the two to three largest competitors in any market fall into the high market share region)

Growth rate: Industry growth rate in constant dollars (dividing point is typically the GNP's growth rate)

Cash Use (growth rate)	Cash Generation (market share): High	Low
High	★ Star	? Problem Child
Low	$ Cash Cow	X Dog

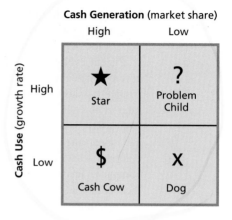

cash cows
Businesses with a high market share in low-growth markets or industries.

Cash cows are businesses with a high market share in low-growth markets or industries. Because of their strong competitive positions and their minimal reinvestment requirements, these businesses often generate cash in excess of their needs. Therefore, they are selectively "milked" as a source of corporate resources for deployment elsewhere (to stars and question marks). Cash cows are yesterday's stars and the current foundation of corporate portfolios. They provide the cash needed to pay corporate overhead and dividends and provide debt capacity. They are managed to maintain their strong market share while generating excess resources for corporatewide use.

dogs
Low market share and low market growth businesses.

Low market share and low market growth businesses are the **dogs** in the firm's portfolio. Facing mature markets with intense competition and low profit margins, they are managed for short-term cash flow (e.g., through ruthless cost cutting) to supplement corporate-level resource needs. According to the original BCG prescription, they are divested or liquidated once this short-term harvesting has been maximized.

question marks
Businesses whose high growth rate gives them considerable appeal but whose low market share makes their profit potential uncertain.

Question marks are businesses whose high growth rate gives them considerable appeal but whose low market share makes their profit potential uncertain. Question marks are cash guzzlers because their rapid growth results in high cash needs, while their small market share results in low cash generation. At the corporate level, the concern is to identify the question marks that would increase their market share and move into the star group if extra corporate resources were devoted to them. Where this long-run shift from question mark to star is unlikely, the BCG matrix suggests divesting the question mark and repositioning its resources more effectively in the remainder of the corporate portfolio.

The Industry Attractiveness–Business Strength Matrix

Corporate strategists found the growth-share matrix's singular axes limiting in their ability to reflect the complexity of a business's situation. Therefore, some companies adopted a matrix with a much broader focus. This matrix, developed by McKinsey & Company at General Electric, is called the industry attractiveness–business strength matrix. This matrix uses multiple factors to assess industry attractiveness and business strength rather than the single measures (market share and market growth, respectively) employed in the BCG matrix. It also has nine cells as opposed to four—replacing the high/low axes with high/medium/low axes to make finer distinctions among business portfolio positions.

The company's businesses are rated on multiple strategic factors within each axis, such as the factors described in Exhibit 9.3. The position of a business is then calculated by "subjectively" quantifying its rating along the two dimensions of the matrix. Depending on

EXHIBIT 9.3
Factors Considered in Constructing an Industry Attractiveness–Business Strength Matrix

Industry Attractiveness	Business Strength
Nature of Competitive Rivalry	**Cost Position**
Number of competitors	Economies of scale
Size of competitors	Manufacturing costs
Strength of competitors' corporate parents	Overhead scrap/waste/rework
Price wars	Experience effects
Competition on multiple dimensions	Labor rates
	Proprietary processes
Bargaining Power of Suppliers/Customers	**Level of Differentiation**
Relative size of typical players	Promotion effectiveness
Numbers of each	Product quality
Importance of purchases from or sales to	Company image
Ability to vertically integrate	Patented products
	Brand awareness
Threat of Substitute Products/New Entrants	**Response Time**
Technological maturity/stability	Manufacturing flexibility
Diversity of the market	Time needed to introduce new products
Barriers to entry	Delivery times
Flexibility of distribution system	Organizational flexibility
Economic Factors	**Financial Strength**
Sales volatility	Solvency
Cyclicality of demand	Liquidity
Market growth	Break-even point
Capital intensity	Cash flows
	Profitability
	Growth in revenues
Financial Norms	**Human Assets**
Average profitability	Turnover
Typical leverage	Skill level
Credit practices	Relative wage/salary
	Morale
	Managerial commitment
	Unionization
Sociopolitical Considerations	**Public Approval**
Government regulation	Goodwill
Community support	Reputation
Ethical standards	Image

the location of a business within the matrix as shown in Exhibit 9.4, one of the following strategic approaches is suggested: (1) invest to grow, (2) invest selectively and manage for earnings, or (3) harvest or divest for resources. The resource allocation decisions remain quite similar to those of the BCG approach.

Although the strategic recommendations generated by the industry attractiveness–business strength matrix are similar to those generated by the BCG matrix, the industry attractiveness–business strength matrix improves on the BCG matrix in three fundamental ways:

1. The terminology associated with the industry attractiveness–business strength matrix is preferable because it is less offensive and more understandable.

EXHIBIT 9.4 **The Industry Attractiveness–Business Strength Matrix**

Industry Attractiveness	Business Strength: Strong	Business Strength: Average	Business Strength: Weak
High	***Premium—invest for growth:*** • Provide maximum investment • Diversify worldwide • Consolidate position • Accept moderate near-term profits • Seek to dominate	***Selective—invest for growth*** • Invest heavily in selected segments • Share ceiling • Seek attractive new segments to apply strengths	***Protect/refocus—selectively invest for earnings:*** • Defend strengths • Refocus to attractive segments • Evaluate industry revitalization • Monitor for harvest or divestment timing • Consider acquisitions
Medium	***Challenge—invest for growth:*** • Build selectively on strengths • Define implications of leadership challenge • Avoid vulnerability—fill weaknesses	***Prime—selectively invest for earnings:*** • Segment market • Make contingency plans for vulnerability	***Restructure—harvest or divest:*** • Provide no unessential commitment • Position for divestment or • Shift to more attractive segment
Low	***Opportunistic—selectively invest for earnings:*** • Ride market and maintain overall position • Seek niches, specialization • Seek opportunity to increase strength (for example through acquisition) • Invest at maintenance levels	***Opportunistic—preserve for harvest:*** • Act to preserve or boost cash flow • Seek opportunistic sale or • Seek opportunistic rationalization to increase strengths • Prune product lines • Minimize investment	***Harvest or divest:*** • Exit from market or prune product line • Determine timing so as to maximize present value • Concentrate on competitor's cash generators

Source: Reprinted by permission of the publisher, from *Strategic Market Planning* by Bernard A. Rausch, AMACOM, division of American Management Association, New York, 1982, www.amanet.org.

2. The multiple measures associated with each dimension of the business strength matrix tap many factors relevant to business strength and market attractiveness besides market share and market growth.
3. In turn, this makes for broader assessment during the planning process, bringing to light considerations of importance in both strategy formulation and strategy implementation.

BCG's Strategic Environments Matrix

BCG's latest matrix offering (see Exhibit 9.5) took a different approach, using the idea that it was the nature of competitive advantage in an industry that determined the strategies available to a company's businesses, which in turn determined the structure of the industry. Their idea was that such a framework could help ensure that individual businesses' strategies were consistent with strategies appropriate to their strategic environment.

EXHIBIT 9.5
BCG's Strategic Environments Matrix

Source: From R.M. Grant, *Contemporary Strategy Analysis,* Blackwell Publishing, 2001, p. 327. Reprinted with permission of Wiley-Blackwell.

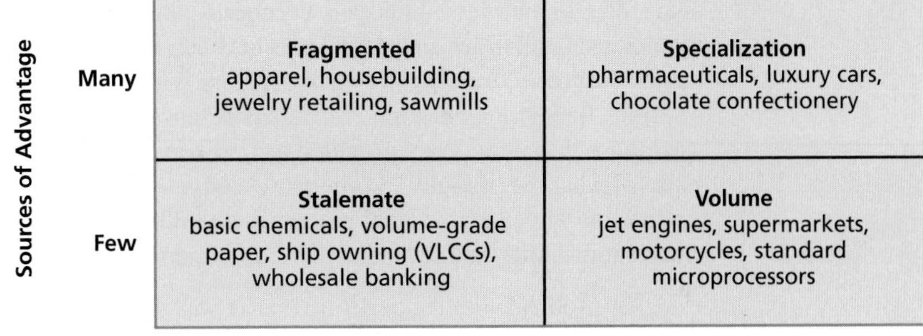

volume businesses
Businesses that have few sources of advantage, but the size is large—typically the result of scale economies.

stalemate businesses
Businesses with few sources of advantage, most of them small. Skills in operational efficiency, low overhead, and cost management are critical to profitability.

fragmented businesses
Businesses with many sources of advantage, but they are all small. They typically involve differentiated products with low brand loyalty, easily replicated technology, and minimal scale economies.

specialization businesses
Businesses with many sources of advantage. Skills in achieving differentiation (product design, branding expertise, innovation, and perhaps scale) characterize winning specialization businesses.

Furthermore, for corporate managers in multiple-business companies, this matrix offered one way to rationalize which businesses they are in—businesses that share core competencies and associated competitive advantages because of similar strategic environments.

The matrix has two dimensions. The number of sources of competitive advantage could be many with complex products and services (e.g., automobiles, financial services) and few with commodities (chemicals, microprocessors). Complex products offer multiple opportunities for differentiation as well as cost, while commodities must seek opportunities for cost advantages to survive.

The second dimension is size of competitive advantage. How big is the advantage available to the industry leader? The two dimensions then define four industry environments as follows:

- **Volume businesses** are those that have few sources of advantage, but the size is large—typically the result of scale economies. Advantages established in one such business may be transferable to another as Honda has done with its scale and expertise with small gasoline engines.
- **Stalemate businesses** have few sources of advantage, with most of those small. This results in very competitive situations. Skills in operational efficiency, low overhead, and cost management are critical to profitability.
- **Fragmented businesses** have many sources of advantage, but they are all small. This typically involves differentiated products with low brand loyalty, easily replicated technology, and minimal scale economies. Skills in focused market segments, typically geographic, the ability to respond quickly to changes, and low costs are critical in this environment.
- **Specialization businesses** have many sources of advantage and find those advantages potentially sizable. Skills in achieving differentiation—product design, branding expertise, innovation, first-mover, and perhaps scale—characterize winners here.

BCG viewed this matrix as providing guidance to multibusiness managers to determine whether they possessed the sources and size of advantage associated with the type of industry facing each business and allowed them a framework to realistically explore the nature of the strategic environments in which they competed or were interested in entering.

Limitations of Portfolio Approaches

Portfolio approaches made several contributions to strategic analysis by corporate managers convinced of their ability to transfer the competitive advantage of professional management across a broad array of businesses. They helped convey large amounts of information about diverse business units and corporate plans in a greatly simplified format. They illuminated similarities and differences between business units and helped convey the logic behind corporate strategies for each business with a common vocabulary. They simplified priorities for sharing corporate resources across diverse business units that generated and used those resources. They provided a simple prescription that gave corporate managers a sense of what they should accomplish—a balanced portfolio of businesses—and a way to control and allocate resources among them. While these approaches offered meaningful contributions, they had several critical limitations and shortcomings:

- A key problem with the portfolio matrix was that it did not address how value was being created across business units—the only relationship between them was cash. Addressing each business unit as a stand-alone entity ignores common core competencies and internal synergies among operating units.
- Truly accurate measurement for matrix classification was not as easy as the matrices portrayed. Identifying individual businesses, or distinct markets, was not often as precise as underlying assumptions required. Comparing business units on only two fundamental dimensions can lead to the conclusion that these are the only factors that really matter and that every unit can be compared fairly on those bases.
- The underlying assumption about the relationship between market share and profitability—the experience curve effect—varied across different industries and market segments. Some have no such link. Some find that firms with low market share can generate superior profitability with differentiation advantages.
- The limited strategic options, intended to describe the flow of resources in a company, came to be seen more as basic strategic missions, which creates a false sense of what each business's strategy actually entails. What do we actually "do" if we're a star? A cash cow? This becomes even more problematic when attempting to use the matrices to conceive strategies for average businesses in average-growth markets.
- The portfolio approach portrayed the notion that firms needed to be self-sufficient in capital. This ignored capital raised in capital markets.
- The portfolio approach typically failed to compare the competitive advantage a business received from being owned by a particular company with the costs of owning it. The 1980s saw many companies build enormous corporate infrastructures that created only small gains at the business level. The reengineering and deconstruction of numerous global conglomerates in the past 10 years reflects this important omission. We will examine this consideration in greater detail later in this chapter.
- Recent research by well-known consulting firm Booz Allen Hamilton suggests that "conventional wisdom is wrong. Corporate managers often rely on accounting metrics [based on past performance] to make business decisions." They go on to argue that "past performance is a poor predictor of the future. When performance is assessed over time, greater shareholder value can be created by improving the operations of the company's worst-performing businesses." "The way to thrive," they say, "is to love your dogs." Their point, backed up by impressive research, is that a corporate manager can learn to identify "value assets," hold and nurture them, and produce superior performance ultimately leading to increased shareholder value more so than can be achieved by acquiring and trying to add value to an overvalued "star."[3]

[3] A comprehensive discussion of these ideas to include their research examining the performance of "falling stars" and "rising dogs" can be found at Harry Quaris, Thomas Pernsteiner, and Kasturi Rangan, "Love your 'Dogs,'" *Strategy+Business Magazine*, Booz Allen Hamilton, www.strategy-business.com/resiliencereport/resilience/rr00030, 2007.

Constructing business portfolio matrices must be undertaken with these limitations in mind. Perhaps it is best to say that they provide one form of input to corporate managers seeking to balance financial resources. While limitations have meant portfolio approaches are seen as mere historical concepts, others appear to find them useful in evaluating strategic options as we saw happening in the chapter introduction example about General Electric's current efforts to manage its diverse business portfolio in the rapidly changing global economy of the twenty-first century. A recent comprehensive study of over 200 large, global companies found that over 90 percent of these firms continue to actively use the corporate portfolio management (CPM) techniques we have been discussing in this chapter. Forty years after the introduction of the BCG growth-share matrix, the study found that corporate portfolio management continues to be a topic that is very relevant and challenging for twenty-first-century corporate leaders. Managing and developing the corporate portfolio was still found to be a top strategic priority in most major firms worldwide. Yet, while acknowledging its importance, the majority of the companies studied were not satisfied with their current CPM approaches and processes. There was a noticeable gap between the effort that many companies put into corporate portfolio management and its impact on corporate-level decisions.[4]

The study identified the following twelve "best practices" thought to address many of the short-comings found in the study and in the academic criticism we noted above regarding traditional corporate portfolio management techniques:[5]

- Analyze the businesses in your corporate portfolio from all relevant perspectives, including the market-based view (market attractiveness and competitive position), the value-based view (current and anticipated financial returns), and the resource-based view (parenting advantage).
- Rather than integrating the different perspectives in a single matrix, keep the various perspectives distinct and let the integration happen in the strategy discussion. In most cases, the process is more important than the final matrix representation. CPM can help you ask the right questions, but it will not give you definitive answers. It supports strategic thinking but should not replace it.
- Do not focus your analysis solely on the individual strategic business units. Portfolio management is about creating a total that is more than the sum of its parts, which can only be assessed at the portfolio level, not at the level of individual SBUs.
- Think like your shareholders and measure the quality of the portfolio against your corporate goals. What is the short-term versus long-term value creation profile of the portfolio? What is its balance along critical dimensions such as risk versus return, cash generation versus cash use, and growth versus profitability?
- Do not apply CPM as a deterministic exercise but rather as a means of facilitating thinking in scenarios and discussing portfolio strategy in terms of risk and uncertainty in the context of alternative portfolio development options.
- Establish corporate portfolio management as a regular process that is clearly driven top-down by the center but also ensures strong SBU involvement both in generating the data and in drawing conclusions. Successful CPM processes tend to be rather formal and standardized, without becoming overly complex and inefficient.

[4] Ulrich Pidun, Harald Rubner, Matthias Kruhlerr, and Michael Nippa, "Corporate Portfolio Management: Theory and Practice," *Journal of Applied Corporate Finance* 23, no. 1 (Winter, 2011), p. 75.
[5] Ibid, pp. 75–76.

- Apply CPM not only as a corporate development instrument (such as for identifying divestiture and acquisition candidates) but also as an instrument for steering the SBUs—setting strategic as well as financial targets and allocating resources such as capital, human resources, and management attention.
- Treat generic portfolio roles with respect: They are a double-edged sword. Many boards still love to classify their businesses into simple roles—such as explore, attack, grow, defend, or harvest—with role-specific strategic goals and financial performance targets. This can be an effective approach for reducing the complexity of a broad portfolio. But beware of oversimplification. Consider corporate portfolio management as a mind set, not a tool. It should be not a one-time or once-a-year exercise but an ongoing process—and ultimately a way of thinking—that is fully integrated into other corporate processes.[6]

This study foretells a continued use of the portfolio approach, recognizing its limitations, to provide a picture of the "balance" of resource generators and users, to test underlying assumptions about these issues and the individual SBUs in more involved corporate planning efforts, and to leverage core competencies to build sustained competitive advantages. Indeed, two key findings in this comprehensive study included the importance of looking at the multibusiness company's corporate strategy from the perspective of leveraging core competencies across a company's portfolio of businesses, and secondly to examine the corporate "parenting" role as a vehicle for doing so. The following two sections of this chapter look at those two considerations. We will first examine the next major approach in multibusiness strategic analysis, leveraging shared capabilities and core competencies.

THE SYNERGY APPROACH: LEVERAGING CORE COMPETENCIES

Opportunities to build value via diversification, integration, or joint venture strategies are usually found in market-related, operations-related, and management activities. Each business's basic value chain activities or infrastructure become a source of potential synergy and competitive advantage for another business in the corporate portfolio. Mars (the M&M company) acquired Wrigley (the gum company) a few years ago based on what both legendary companies saw as multiple opportunities for synergy leveraging core competencies in the global confectionery market. Cadbury Schweppes, the European confectionary global powerhouse, was looking to acquire Wrigley, but Mars achieved the "deal" in part because of what executives from both companies saw as the strongest leveraging capability across key sales, marketing, distribution, and manufacturing synergies between Mars and Wrigley. There were numerous opportunities for shared operating capabilities—sales forces that could immediately add a variety of products to their daily sales calls; the ability to blend marketing events, materials, and promotions again leveraging the gap-filling ability to reach across both product offerings. Management talents in both companies were complementary in many regions and product lines and in functional areas—gaps in one company's talent pool found support from the other company's people strengths. Cost-saving and cost-sharing opportunities were quickly targeted across manufacturing facilities, sometimes location driven and other times based on innovative and/or newer operating equipment and skill. Some of the more common opportunities to share value chain activities and build value are identified in Exhibit 9.6.

[6] Ibid, pp. 75–76.

Strategic analysis is concerned with whether or not the potential competitive advantages expected to arise from each value opportunity have materialized. Where advantage has not materialized, corporate strategists must take care to scrutinize possible impediments to achieving the synergy or competitive advantage. We have identified in Exhibit 9.6 several impediments associated with each opportunity, which strategists are well advised to examine. Good strategists assure themselves that their organization has ways to avoid or minimize the effects of any impediments, or they recommend against further integration or diversification and consider divestiture options.

Two elements are critical in meaningful shared opportunities:

1. The shared opportunities must be a significant portion of the value chain of the businesses involved. Disney acquired Pixar, or it is perhaps better to say Pixar joined Disney, and in so doing acted on two simple shared opportunities that were significant portions of the value chain of both businesses. One critical part of the value chain for movie-related excellence in the twenty-first-century entertainment industry is excellence and innovative talent in digital animation, digital artisan skill, and advanced visualization wizardry. Disney was still a bit "old fashioned," and falling behind the new breed in creating animations for twenty-first-century young audiences. Pixar had that capability "nailed" as perhaps the most innovative animation house in that space. Meanwhile, Disney had a vast distribution and proprietary brand name and entertainment breadth upon which to build new offerings, new niches, a whole spectrum to monetize an animation of existing Disney stars or totally new animated characters through deals with its own theme parks, TV programs, preteen entertainment star factories, and ongoing relationships with every fast-food outlet globally.
2. The businesses involved must truly have shared needs—need for the same activity—or there is no basis for synergy in the first place. Skype is a pioneering success story of the use of the Internet for telephone and video communication between any two computer locations worldwide. eBay acquired Skype, anticipating numerous synergies with its worldwide online auction business—but such synergies failed to emerge. eBay management took quite a lot of criticism for the price it paid and, after three successive Skype CEOs failed to uncover any shared needs common to both businesses leading to any meaningful synergy, a fourth Skype CEO installed by eBay sought to "harvest" Skype. Josh Silverman's first step was to operate Skype as a separate business and sell off 70 percent of eBay's interest in it. Subsequently, in 18 months, he and that investment group succeeded in selling Skype to Microsoft for $8.5 billion (see Exhibit 9.1).[7]

Corporate strategies have repeatedly rushed into diversification only to find perceived opportunities for sharing were nonexistent because the businesses did not really have shared needs.

The most compelling reason companies should diversify can be found in situations where core competencies—key value-building skills—can be leveraged with other products or into markets that are not a part of where they were created. Where this works well, extraordinary value can be built. Managers undertaking diversification strategies should dedicate a significant portion of their strategic analysis to this question.

General Cinema was a company that grew from drive-in theaters to eventually dominate the multicinema, movie exhibition industry. Next, they entered soft-drink bottling and became the largest bottler of soft drinks (Pepsi) in North America. Their stock value rose 2,000 percent

[7] Hermantha Abeywardena, "Sale of Skype: Business Hype and Ground Realities," AsianTribune.com, London, May 14, 2011. http://www.asiantribune.com/news/2011/05/14/sale-skype-business-hype-and-ground-realities

EXHIBIT 9.6 Value Building in Multibusiness Companies

Opportunities to Build Value or Sharing	Potential Competitive Advantage	Impediments to Achieving Enhanced Value
Market-Related Opportunities		
Shared sales force activities, shared sales office, or both	Lower selling costs Better market coverage Stronger technical advice to buyers Enhanced convenience for buyers (can buy from single source) Improved access to buyers (have more products to sell)	• Buyers have different purchasing habits toward the products. • Different salespersons are more effective in representing the product. • Some products get more attention than others. • Buyers prefer to multiple-source rather than single-source their purchases.
Shared after-sale service and repair work	Lower servicing costs Better utilization of service personnel (less idle time) Faster servicing of customer calls	• Different equipment or different labor skills, or both, are needed to handle repairs. • Buyers may do some in-house repairs.
Shared brand name	Stronger brand image and company reputation Increased buyer confidence in the brand	• Company reputation is hurt if quality of one product is lower.
Shared advertising and promotional activities	Lower costs Greater clout in purchasing ads	• Appropriate forms of messages are different. • Appropriate timing of promotions is different.
Common distribution channels	Lower distribution costs Enhanced bargaining power with distributors and retailers to gain shelf space, shelf positioning, stronger push and more dealer attention, and better profit margins	• Dealers resist being dominated by a single supplier and turn to multiple sources and lines. • Heavy use of the shared channel erodes willingness of other channels to carry or push the firm's products.
Shared order processing	Lower order processing costs One-stop shopping for buyer to enhance service and, thus, differentiation	• Differences in ordering cycles disrupt order-processing economies.
Operating Opportunities		
Joint procurement of purchased inputs	Lower input costs Improved input quality Improved service from suppliers	• Input needs are different in terms of quality or other specifications. • Inputs are needed at different plant locations, and centralized purchasing is not responsive to separate needs of each plant.
Shared manufacturing and assembly facilities	Lower manufacturing/assembly costs Better capacity utilization, because peak demand for one product correlates with valley demand for the other Bigger scale of operation to improve access to better technology, resulting in better quality	• Higher changeover costs in shifting from one product to another. • High-cost special tooling or equipment is required to accommodate quality differences or design differences.

EXHIBIT 9.6 *(continued)*

Opportunities to Build Value or Sharing	Potential Competitive Advantage	Impediments to Achieving Enhanced Value
Operating Opportunities (cont.)		
Shared inbound or outbound shipping and materials handling	Lower freight and handling costs Better delivery reliability More frequent deliveries, such that inventory costs are reduced	• Input sources or plant locations, or both, are in different geographic areas. • Needs for frequency and reliability of inbound/outbound delivery differ among the business units.
Shared product and process technologies, technology development, or both	Lower product or process design costs, or both, because of shorter design times and transfers of knowledge from area to area More innovative ability, owing to scale of effort and attraction of better R&D personnel	• Technologies are the same, but the applications in different business units are different enough to prevent much sharing of real value.
Shared administrative support activities	Lower administrative and operating overhead costs	• Support activities are not a large proportion of cost, and sharing has little cost impact (and virtually no differentiation impact).
Management Opportunities		
Shared management know-how, operating skills, and proprietary information	Efficient transfer of a distinctive competence—can create cost savings or enhance differentiation More effective management as concerns strategy formulation, strategy implementation, and understanding of key success factors	• Actual transfer of know-how is costly or stretches the key skill personnel too thinly, or both. • Increased risks that proprietary information will leak out.

Source: Based on Michael Porter, *On Competition*, Harvard Business School Press.

in 10 years. They found that core competencies in movie exhibition—managing many small, localized businesses; dealing with a few large suppliers; applying central marketing skills locally; and acquiring or crafting a "franchise"—were virtually the same in soft-drink bottling. IBM CEO Sam Palmisano and his management team have done an extraordinary job of creating a virtually new IBM by adapting a multibusiness strategy centered around finding, sharing, and leveraging core competencies across a seemingly diverse set of businesses and markets. Not only have they done so with existing competencies, but their organization has proven remarkably adept at leveraging newly found technologies and capabilities within each business across other businesses—enterprise focused business competencies deployed in consumer product offerings and vice versa as described in Exhibit 9.7, Top Global Strategist.

Each Core Competency Should Provide a Relevant Competitive Advantage to the Intended Businesses

The core competency must assist the intended business in creating strength relative to key competition. This could occur at any step in the business's value chain. But it must represent a major source of value to be a basis for competitive advantage—and the core

Top Global Strategist

IBM's Sam Palmisano

Exhibit 9.7

Sam Palmisano, CEO at IBM, sets the stage for explaining IBM's global integrated enterprise product and service offerings by describing "the new global business" as a way of explaining what they can help clients do because they do it for themselves:

> Start with a simple jar of face cream. The jar's pump is a packaging innovation created by an independent inventor in Sweden. The jar itself is manufactured in China—an arrangement made by a global procurement center in Manila. The natural ingredients in the cream are sourced by a wholesaler in Italy. The finished product is assembled in the US. Customer service is provided by a call center in Nova Scotia. And all of these functions integrate seamlessly across a shared, standard global technology infrastructure, allowing the consumer-packaged goods company that owns the face-cream brand to sell its moisturizer in seven different scents and three sizes for $8.00 less than the competitor. Welcome to the Globally Integrated Enterprise.

IBM has spent the past several years becoming, in essence, a social networking organization, allowing it to identify internal expertise, capacity, and availability among its more than 200,000 employees and numerous production or operational facilities in 160 countries around the world. It then pulls needed people/capacity together in, most often, a virtual fashion to get work done for projects and clients worldwide in the most efficient, timely, and cost-effective manner possible. This "experiment" has been an extraordinary path toward identifying and leveraging core competencies both within IBM and then out to all types of businesses and industries from enterprise computing to consumer products.

IBM's internal Facebook, called BeeHive, contains a wide variety of personal and work-related information about every IBMer worldwide. A special search engine, SmallBlue, scans BeeHive, e-mails, reports, instant messages, personal calendars, and everything digital and makes determinations of skills, availability, cost, and proximity (think automated identification and leveraging of core competencies across people, operating units, and locations worldwide) to assemble teaming options to provide solutions, solve problems, and create products efficiently and effectively.

IBM has introduced a commercial beta version, referred to as SmallBlue, and also IBM Atlas, which is an information analytics suite that automatically visualizes social networks, helps an IBMer or a client manage and expand their social capital, enabling them to find specific knowledge, and provides the shortest social paths to reach a person. And, look out 3-D Internet and Second Life. Sam Palmisano's avatar along with many serious IBMers have now spent several years in Second Life seeking to leverage this networked concept in reverse—IBM is learning from the consumer world's computerized virtual space to create new services and products to offer. It has rapidly learned that video gaming is perhaps the best format for managerial development in the globalized twenty-first century, which it is using to train IBM managers, and it will soon sell the ability to do so to other clients globally.

Source: www.ibm.com; and http://smallblue.research.ibm.com

competence must be transferable. Honda of Japan viewed itself as having a core competence in manufacturing small, internal combustion engines. It diversified into small garden tools, perceiving that traditional electric tools would be much more attractive if powered by a lightweight, mobile, gas combustion motor. Their core competency created a major competitive advantage in a market void of gas-driven hand tools. When

Coca-Cola added bottled water to its portfolio of products, it expected its extraordinary core competencies in marketing and distribution to rapidly build value in this business. Ten years later, Coke sold its water assets, concluding that the product did not have enough margin to interest its franchised bottlers and that marketing was not a significant value-building activity among many small suppliers competing primarily on the cost of "producing" and shipping water. In the last few years, however, Coke has reversed its decision and added the Dasani water brand because a rapidly increasing consumer demand has made the value of its extensive distribution network a relevant competitive advantage to the Dasani water product line.

Businesses in the Portfolio Should Be Related in Ways That Make the Company's Core Competencies Beneficial

Related versus unrelated diversification is an important distinction to understand as you evaluate the diversification question. "Related" businesses are those that rely on the same or similar capabilities to be successful and attain competitive advantage in their respective product markets. Earlier, we described General Cinema's spectacular success in both movie exhibition and soft-drink bottling. Seemingly unrelated, they were actually very related businesses in terms of key core competencies that shaped success—managing a network of diverse business locations, localized competition, reliance on a few large suppliers, and centralized marketing advantages. Thus, the products of various businesses do not necessarily have to be similar to leverage core competencies. While their products may not be related, it is essential that some activities in their value chains require similar skills to create competitive advantage if the company is going to leverage its core competence(s) in a value-creating way. Exhibit 9.7 offered an example of IBM's remarkable effectiveness in doing just this the last 10 years. IBM's CEO started with his own avatar in Second Life, joining thousands of other IBMers committed to building a ground-up understanding of ways IBM's core competencies could be related to and leveraged in emerging online virtual worlds and 3-D Internet. IBM is now helping to drive the growth and adoption of the 3-D Internet, helping to "make the 3-D Internet the essential tool for helping people work, live and play to their fullest potential." IBM's focus is on "identifying, delivering, sustaining, protecting and expanding value for IBM and its clients."[8] Translated, it is leveraging the company's core competencies in ways that build value in unfolding markets and technologies yet to be clearly defined.

Situations that involve "unrelated" diversification occur when no real overlapping capabilities or products exist other than financial resources. We refer to this as *conglomerate diversification* in Chapter 7. Recent research indicates that the most profitable firms are those that have diversified around a set of resources and capabilities that are specialized enough to confer a meaningful competitive advantage in an attractive industry, yet adaptable enough to be advantageously applied across several others. The least profitable are broadly diversified firms whose strategies are built around very general resources (e.g., money) that are applied in a wide variety of industries, but that are seldom instrumental to competitive advantage in those settings.[9]

Any Combination of Competencies Must Be Unique or Difficult to Recreate

Skills that corporate strategists expect to transfer from one business to another, or from corporate to various businesses, may be transferable. They may also be easily replicated by

[8] http://www.ibm.com/virtualworlds/.

[9] David J. Collis and Cynthia A. Montgomery, *Corporate Strategy* (New York: McGraw-Hill/Irwin, 2005), p. 88; "Why Mergers Fail," *McKinsey Quarterly Report*, 2001, vol. 4; and "Deals That Create Value," *McKinsey Quarterly Report*, 2001, vol. 1.

competitors. When this is the case, no sustainable competitive advantage is created. Sometimes strategists look for a combination of competencies, a package of various interrelated skills, as another way to create a situation where seemingly easily replicated competencies become unique, sustainable competitive advantages. 3M Corporation has the enviable record of having 25 percent of its earnings always coming from products introduced within the last five years. 3M has been able to "bundle" the skills necessary to accelerate the introduction of new products so that it consistently extracts early life-cycle value from adhesive-related products that hundreds of competitors with similar technical or marketing competencies cannot touch.

All too often companies envision a combination of competencies that make sense conceptually. This vision of synergy develops an energy of its own, leading CEOs to relentlessly push the merger of the firms involved. But what makes sense conceptually and is seen as difficult for competitors to recreate often proves difficult if not impossible to create in the first place.

THE CORPORATE PARENT ROLE: CAN IT ADD TANGIBLE VALUE?

Realizing synergies from shared capabilities and core competencies is a key way value is added in multibusiness companies. Research suggests that figuring out if the synergies are real and, if so, how to capture those synergies is most effectively accomplished by business unit managers, not the corporate parent.[10] How then can the corporate parent add value to its businesses in a multibusiness company? We want to acquaint you with two perspectives to use in attempting to answer this question: the parenting framework and the patching approach.

The Parenting Framework

parenting framework
The perspective that the role of corporate headquarters (the "parent") in multibusiness (the "children") companies is that of a parent sharing wisdom, insight, and guidance to help develop its various businesses to excel.

The **parenting framework** perspective sees multibusiness companies as creating value by influencing—or parenting—the businesses they own. The best parent companies create more value than any of their rivals do or would if they owned the same businesses. To add value, a parent must improve its businesses. Obviously there must be room for improvement. Advocates of this perspective call the potential for improvement within a business "a parenting opportunity." They identify 10 places to look for parenting opportunities, which then become the focus of strategic analysis and choice across multiple businesses and their interface with the parent organization.[11] Let's look at each briefly.

Size and Age

Old, large, successful businesses frequently engender entrenched bureaucracies and overhead structures that are hard to dismantle from inside the business. Doing so may add value,

[10] See most recently Ulrich Pidun, Harald Rubner, Matthias Kruhlerr, and Michael Nippa, "Corporate Portfolio Management: Theory and Practice," *Journal of Applied Corporate Finance* 23, no. 1 (Winter, 2011), pp. 63, 68–69, for a recent study of 200 global companies' parenting approaches; and, as an earlier foundation to this perspective on "parenting" as a framework for understanding the corporate role in multibusiness companies, see Michael Goold, Andrew Campbell, and Marcus Alexander, "The Quest for Parenting Advantage," *Harvard Business Review*, March–April 1995; and Michael Goold, Andrew Campbell, and Marcus Alexander, "How Corporate Parents Add Value to the Stand-Alone Performance of Their Businesses," *Business Strategy Review*, Winter 1994.

[11] These 10 areas of opportunity are taken from an insert entitled "Ten Places to Look for Parenting Opportunities" on page 126 of the *Harvard Business Review* article by Goold, Campbell, Alexander (footnote 10).

and getting it done may be best done by an external catalyst, the parent. Small, young businesses may lack some key functional skills, or outgrow their top managers' capabilities, or lack capital to deal with a temporary downturn or accelerated growth opportunity. Where these are relevant issues within one or more businesses, a parenting opportunity to add value may exist.

Management

Does the business employ managers superior in comparison with its competitors? Is the business's success dependent on attracting and keeping people with specialized skills? Are key managers focused on the right objectives? Ensuring that these issues are addressed and objectively assessed and assisting in any resolution may be a parenting opportunity that could add value.

Business Definition

Business unit managers may have a myopic or erroneous vision of what their business should be, which, in turn, has them targeting a market that is too narrow or broad. They may employ too much vertical integration or not enough. Accelerated trends toward outsourcing and strategic alliances are changing the definitions of many businesses. All of this creates a parenting opportunity to help redefine a business unit in a way that creates greater value.

Predictable Errors

The nature of a business and its unique situation can lead managers to make predictable mistakes. Managers responsible for previous strategic decisions are vested in the success of those decisions, which may prevent openness to new alternatives. Older, mature businesses often accumulate a variety of products and markets, which becomes excessive diversification within a particular business. Cyclical markets can lead to underinvestment during downturns and overinvestment during the upswing. Lengthy product life cycles can lead to overreliance on old products. All of these are predictable errors a parent can monitor and attempt to avoid, creating, in turn, added value.

Linkages

Business units may be able to improve market position or efficiency by linking with other businesses that are not readily apparent to the management of the business unit in question. Whether apparent or not, linkages among business units within or outside the parent company may be complex or difficult to establish without parent company help. In either case, an opportunity to add value may exist.

Common Capabilities

Fundamental to successful diversification, as we have discussed earlier, is the notion of sharing capabilities and competencies needed by multiple business units. Parenting opportunities to add value may arise from time to time through regular scrutiny of opportunities to share capabilities or add shared capabilities that would otherwise go unnoticed by business unit managers closer to daily business operations.

Specialized Expertise

There may be situations in which the parent company possesses specialized or rare expertise that may benefit a business unit and add value in the process. Unique legal, technical, or administrative expertise critical in a particular situation or decision point, which is quickly and easily available, can prove very valuable.

External Relations

Does the business have external stakeholders—governments, regulators, unions, suppliers, shareholders—the parent company could manage more effectively than individual business units? If so, a natural parenting opportunity exists that should add value.

Major Decisions

A business unit may face difficult decisions in areas for which it lacks expertise—for example, making an acquisition, entering China, a major capacity expansion, divesting and outsourcing a major part of the business's operations. Obtaining capital externally to fund a major investment may be much more difficult than doing so through the parent company—GE proved this could be a major parenting advantage in the way it developed GE Capital into a major source of capital for its other business units as well as to finance major capital purchases by customers of its own business units.

Major Changes

Sometimes a business needs to make major changes in ways critical to the business's future success yet which involve areas or considerations in which the business unit's management has little or no experience. A complete revamping of a business unit's information management process, outsourcing all that capability to India, or shifting all of a business unit's production operations to another business unit in another part of the world—these are just a few examples of major changes in which the parent may have extensive experience with what feels like unknown territory to the business's management team.

Overlap in some of these 10 sources of parenting opportunities may exist. For example, specialized expertise in China and a major decision to locate or outsource operations there may be the same source of added value. And that decision would involve a major change. The fact that overlap or redundancy may exist in classifying sources of parenting opportunity is a minor consideration, however, relative to the value of the parenting framework for strategic analysis in multibusiness companies. The portfolio approaches focus on how businesses' cash, profit, and growth potential create a balance within the portfolio. The core competence approach concentrates on how business units are related and can share technical and operating know-how and capacity. The parenting framework adds to these approaches and the strategic analysis in a multibusiness company because it focuses on competencies of the parent organization and on the value created from the relationship between the parent and its businesses. Exhibit 9.8, Top Global Strategist, shows how Xerox's new chairwoman and CEO Ursula Burns went about crafting a corporate parenting role through which she has helped lead a dramatic turnaround in Xerox's business fortunes. She, along with her predecessor Anne Mulcahy, carefully assumed complementary parental corporate leadership roles that stabilized Xerox's rapidly declining prospects for survival at one point; and then, particularly with Ms. Burns's leadership, guided Xerox's businesses into more profitable, strategically critical up-market services tied to its office products and technologies core. Along the way Ms. Burns has begun meaningfully shoring up the "Xerox family" culture. She has emphasized the unique privilege outside managerial candidates can enjoy if they pass her parental test. At the same time she went about negotiating and integrating into Xerox a major acquisition of a business IT outsourcing provider, which instantly and dramatically accelerated Xerox's new integrated services vision with offerings to large global clients in over 160 countries.

Top Global Strategist
Ursula Burns, Chairwoman and CEO, Xerox

Exhibit 9.8

Ursula Burns joined Xerox over 30 years ago in New York as a young mechanical engineer summer intern. Twenty years later she celebrated the dawn of the twenty-first century as Xerox's new V.P. for Global Manufacturing. Xerox, though, was heading into a precipitous decline led by a new, non-Xerox outsider CEO's misguided strategies and eventual related challenges—SEC accounting irregularities, substantial debt, excesive bureaucracy, senior management drama, and echoes of bankruptcy.

Ms. Burns, frustrated with what was happening to Xerox, almost left. A board member convinced her that abandoning Xerox would signal the company was unsalvageable. She stayed. Anne Mulcahy, another Xerox lifer, soon thereafter became CEO, replacing the "outsider." She then went about stabilizing Xerox and rebuilding the maligned, dedicated Xerox family.

Burns became a key part of Mulcahy's executive team, and eventually heir apparent. She and Mulcahy approached the salvaging and rebirth of the Xerox family of businesses as parental siblings, sisters, stabilizing this business "family" and creating for it a better future. They both in effect assumed the roles of corporate parents to Xerox's different businesses and its people. Mulcahy focused on the immediate situation—managing external relations with key stakeholders to help different parts of Xerox stabilize; to identify predictable errors currently affecting Xerox businesses, like overreliance on old products, and fix them; to gain better efficiencies sharing common capabilities; and to balance the precious, precarious capital resources.

Burns took the corporate parenting role focused on the future—foremost being a major companywide bet to move Xerox up-market into more profitable services—business services handling all a large company's document, packaging, work flow, and related business process needs. This major decision required careful buy-in and coordination across operations in 160 countries. It required a carefully handled, $6.4 billion major acquisition of Affiliated Computer Services to credibly position Xerox into outsourcing IT capabilities. And she also decided to put into place a clear hurdle for any outsider being considered for a Xerox management position—they must answer to her satisfaction "What is it that you see in Xerox that you love—that you can love—you can grow to love?"*As a good corporate "parent," the answer lets her protect and carefully rebuild the right "Xerox family."

* Adam Bryant, "Xerox's New Chief Tries to Redefine Its Culture," *The New York Times*, February 21, 2010.

The Patching Approach

patching
The process by which corporate executives routinely "remap" their businesses to match rapidly changing market opportunities—adding, splitting, transferring, exiting, or combining chunks of businesses.

Another approach that focuses on the role and ability of corporate managers to create value in the management of multibusiness companies is called "patching."[12] **Patching** is the process by which corporate executives routinely remap businesses to match rapidly changing

[12] J. A. Martin and K. M. Eisenhardt, "Rewiring: Cross-Business-Unit Collaborations in Multibusiness Organizations," *The Academy of Management Journal* 53, no. 2 (April, 2010), pp. 265–301; K. M. Eisenhardt, "Has Strategy Changed?" *MIT Sloan Management Review* (Winter, 2002), pp. 88–91; K. M. Eisenhardt and S. L. Brown, "Patching: Restitching Business Portfolios in Dynamic Markets," *Harvard Business Review* (May–June, 1999), pp. 72–82; K. M. Eisenhardt and D. N. Sull, "Strategy as Simple Rules," *Harvard Business Review* (January, 2001), pp. 104–112; S. A. Zahra, R. S. Sisodia, and S. R. Das, "Technological Choices within Competitive Strategy Types: A Conceptual Integration," *International Journal of Technoloav Management* 9, no. 2 (May 2009), pp. 172–195; and M. Garbuio, A. W. King, and D. Lovallo, "Looking Inside: Psychological Influences on Structuring a Firm's Portfolio of Resources," *Journal of Management* 37, no. 3 (May, 2011), pp. 651–681.

EXHIBIT 9.9 **Three Approaches to Strategy**

Managers competing in business can choose among three distinct ways to fight. They can build a fortress and defend it; they can nurture and leverage unique resources; or they can flexibly pursue fleeting opportunities within simple rules. Each approach requires different skill sets and works best under different circumstances.

	Position	Resources	Patching [Simple Rules]
Strategic logic	Establish position	Leverage resources	Pursue opportunities
Strategic steps	Identify an attractive market	Establish a vision Build resources	Jump into the confusion Keep moving
	Locate a defensible position	Leverage across markets	Seize opportunities Finish strong
	Fortify and defend		
Strategic question	Where should we be?	What should we be?	How should we proceed?
Source of advantage	Unique, valuable position with tightly integrated activity system	Unique, valuable, inimitable resources	Key processes and unique simple rules
Works best in	Slowly changing, well-structured markets	Moderately changing, well-structured markets	Rapidly changing, ambiguous markets
Duration of advantage	Sustained	Sustained	Unpredictable
Risk	Too difficult to alter position as conditions change	Too slow to build new resources as conditions change	Too tentative in executing promising opportunities
Performance goal	Profitability	Long-term dominance	Growth

Source: Reprinted by permission of *Harvard Business Review.* Exhibit from "Strategy as Simple Rules," by Kathleen M. Eisenhardt and Donald M. Sull, January 2001.

market opportunities. It can take the form of adding, splitting, transferring, exiting, or combining chunks of businesses. Patching is not seen as critical in stable, unchanging markets. When markets are turbulent and rapidly changing, patching is seen as critical to the creation of economic value in a multibusiness company.

Proponents of this perspective on the strategic decision-making function of corporate executives say it is the critical, and arguably only, way corporate executives can add value beyond the sum of the businesses within the company. They view traditional corporate strategy as creating defensible strategic positions for business units by acquiring or building valuable assets, wisely allocating resources to them, and weaving synergies among them. In volatile markets, they argue, this traditional approach results in business units with strategies that are quickly outdated and competitive advantages rarely sustained beyond a few years.[13] As a result, they say, strategic analysis should center on **strategic processes** more than **strategic positioning.** In these volatile markets, patchers' strategic analysis focuses on making quick, small, frequent changes in parts of businesses and organizational processes that enable dynamic strategic repositioning rather than building long-term defensible positions. Exhibit 9.9 compares differences between traditional approaches to shaping corporate strategy with the patching approach.

strategic processes
Decision making, operational activities, and sales activities that are critical business processes.

strategic positioning
The way a business is designed and positioned to serve target markets.

[13] Eisenhardt and Brown, "Patching," p. 76.

EXHIBIT 9.10 Simple Rules, Summarized

In turbulent markets, managers should flexibly seize opportunities—but flexibility must be disciplined. Smart companies focus on key processes and simple rules. Different types of rules help executives manage different aspects of seizing opportunities.

Type	Purpose	Example
How-to rules	Spell out key features of how a process is executed—"What makes our process unique?"	Akami's rules for the customer service process: Staff must consist of technical gurus, every question must be answered on the first call or e-mail, and R&D staff must rotate through customer service.
Boundary rules	Focus on which opportunities can be pursued and which are outside the pale.	Cisco's early acquisitions rule: Companies to be acquired must have no more than 75 employees, 75 percent of whom are engineers.
Priority rules	Help managers rank the accepted opportunities.	Intel's rule for allocating manufacturing capacity: Allocation is based on a product's gross margin.
Timing rules	Synchronize managers with the pace of emerging opportunities and other parts of the company.	Nortel's rules for product development: Project teams must know when a product has to be delivered to the customer to win, and product development time must be less than 18 months.
Exit rules	Help managers decide when to pull out of yesterday's opportunities.	Oticon's rule for pulling the plug on projects in development: If a key team member—manager or not—chooses to leave the project for another within the company, the project is killed.

Source: Reprinted by permission of *Harvard Business Review.* Exhibit from "Strategy as Simple Rules," by Kathleen M. Eisenhardt and Donald M. Sull, January 2001.

To be successful with a patching approach to corporate strategic analysis and choice in turbulent markets, Eisenhardt and Sull suggest that managers should flexibly seize opportunities—as long as that flexibility is disciplined. Effective corporate strategists, they argue, focus on key processes and *simple rules.* The following example at Miramax helps illustrate the notion of strategy as simple rules:

> Miramax—well known for artistically innovative movies such as *The Crying Game, Life is Beautiful,* and *Pulp Fiction*—has boundary rules that guide the all-important movie-picking process: First, every movie must revolve around a central human condition, such as love *(The Crying Game)* or envy *(The Talented Mr. Ripley).* Second, a movie's main character must be appealing but deeply flawed—the hero of *Shakespeare in Love* is gifted and charming but steals ideas from friends and betrays his wife. Third, movies must have a very clear story line with a beginning, middle, and end (although in *Pulp Fiction* the end comes first). Finally, there is a firm cap on production costs. Within the rules, there is flexibility to move quickly when a writer or director shows up with a great script. The result is an enormously creative and even surprising flow of movies and enough discipline to produce superior, consistent financial results. *The English Patient,* for example, cost $27 million to make, grossed more than $200 million, and grabbed nine Oscars.[14]

Different types of rules help managers and strategists manage different aspects of seizing opportunities. Exhibit 9.10 explains and illustrates five such types of rules. These rules are

[14] Ibid., Eisenhardt and Sull, p. 111.

called "simple" rules because they need to be brief, be axiomatic, and convey fundamental guidelines to decisions or actions. They need to provide just enough structure to allow managers to move quickly to capture opportunities with confidence that the judgments and commitments they make are consistent with corporate intent. At the same time, while they set parameters on actions and decisions, they are not thick manuals or rules and policies that managers in turbulent environments may find paralyze any efforts to quickly capitalize on opportunities.

The patching approach then relies on simple rules unique to a particular parent company that exist to guide managers in the corporate organization and its business units in making rapid decisions about quickly reshaping parts of the company and allocating time as well as money to capitalize on rapidly shifting market opportunities. The fundamental argument of this approach is that no one can predict how long a competitive advantage will last, particularly in turbulent, rapidly changing markets. While managers in stable markets may be able to rely on complex strategies built on detailed predictions of future trends, managers in complex, fast-moving markets—where significant growth and wealth creation may occur—face constant unpredictability; hence, strategy must be simple, responsive, and dynamic to encourage success.

Summary

This chapter examined how managers make strategic decisions in multibusiness companies. One of the earliest approaches was to look at the company as a portfolio of businesses. This portfolio was then examined and evaluated based on each business's growth potential, market position, and need for and ability to generate cash. Corporate strategists then allocated resources, divested, and acquired businesses based on the balance across this portfolio of businesses or possible businesses.

The notion of synergy across business units—sharing capabilities and leveraging core competencies—has been another very widely adopted approach to making strategic decisions in multibusiness companies. Sharing capabilities allows for greater efficiencies, enhanced expertise, and competitive advantage. Core competencies that generate competitive advantage can often be leveraged across multiple businesses, thereby expanding the impact and value added from that competitive advantage.

Globalization, rapid change, outsourcing, and other major forces shaping today's economic landscape have ushered in multibusiness strategic decision making that also focuses on the role and value-added contributions, if any, of the parent company itself. Does the parent company add or could it add value beyond the sum of the businesses it owns? Two perspectives that have gained popularity in multibusiness companies' strategic decision making are the parenting framework and the patching approach. The parenting framework focuses on 10 areas of opportunity managers should carefully explore to find ways the parent organization might add value to one or more businesses and the overall company. The patching approach concentrates on multibusiness companies in turbulent markets of the twenty-first century, where managers need to make quick, small shifts and adjustments in processes, markets, and products, and offers five types of "simple rules" that managers use as guidelines to structure quick decisions throughout a multibusiness company on a continuous basis.

Key Terms

businesses, *p. 265*
cash cows, *p. 262*
dogs, *p. 262*
fragmented businesses, *p. 265*
market growth rate, *p. 261*
parenting framework, *p. 274*
patching, *p. 277*
portfolio techniques, *p. 261*
position, *p. 261*
question marks, *p. 262*
relative competitive
specialization
stalemate businesses, *p. 265*
stars, *p. 261*
strategic positioning, *p. 278*
strategic processes, *p. 278*
volume businesses, *p. 265*

Questions for Discussion

1. How does strategic analysis at the corporate level differ from strategic analysis at the business unit level? How are they related?
2. When would multibusiness companies find the portfolio approach to strategic analysis and choice useful?
3. What are three types of opportunities for sharing that form a sound basis for diversification or vertical integration? Give an example of each from companies you have read about.
4. Describe three types of opportunities through which a corporate parent could add value beyond the sum of its separate businesses.
5. What does "patching" refer to? Describe and illustrate two rules that might guide managers to build value in their businesses.

Strategy Implementation, Control, and Innovation

The last section of this book examines what is often called the action phase of the strategic management process: implementation of the chosen strategy. Up to this point, three phases of that process have been covered—strategy formulation, analysis of alternative strategies, and strategic choice. Although important, these phases alone cannot ensure success.

To ensure success, the strategy must be translated into carefully implemented action. This means that

1. The strategy must be translated into guidelines for the daily activities of the firm's members.
2. The strategy and the firm must become one—that is, the strategy must be reflected in
   a. The way the firm organizes its activities.
   b. The key organization leaders.
   c. The culture of the organization.
3. The company's managers must put into place "steering" controls that provide strategic control and the ability to adjust strategies, commitments, and objectives in response to ever-changing future conditions.
4. Increasingly, organizations must make a serious commitment to be innovative and must consider bringing the entrepreneurship process into their company to survive, grow, and prosper in a vastly more competitive and rapidly changing global business arena.

Chapter 10 explains how organizational action is successfully initiated through four interrelated steps:

1. Creation of clear *short-term objectives* and *action plans*.
2. Development of specific *functional tactics*, to include *outsourcing*, that create competitive advantage.
3. Empowerment of operating personnel through *policies* to guide decisions.
4. Implementation of effective *reward systems*.

Short-term objectives and action plans guide implementation by converting long-term objectives into short-term actions and targets. Functional tactics, whether done internally or outsourced to other partners, translate the business strategy into activities that build advantage. Policies empower operating personnel by defining guidelines for making decisions. Reward systems encourage effective results.

Today's competitive environment requires careful analysis in designing the organizational structure most suitable to build and sustain competitive advantage. Chapter 11 examines traditional organizational structures—their pros and cons. It looks at the pervasive trend toward outsourcing, along with outsourcing's pros and cons. It concludes with examination of the latest developments in creating ambidextrous, virtual, boundaryless organizations designed to adapt in a highly interconnected, lightning-speed, global business environment.

There can be no doubt that effective organizational leadership and the consistency of a strong organizational culture reinforcing norms and behaviors best suited to the organization's mission are two central ingredients in enabling successful execution of a firm's strategies and objectives. Chapter 12 examines leadership, the critical things good leaders do, and how to nurture effective operating managers as they become outstanding future organizational leaders. Chapter 12 then examines the organizational culture, how it is shaped, and creative ways of managing the strategy-culture relationship.

Because the firm's strategy is implemented in a changing environment, successful implementation requires strategic control—an ability to "steer" the firm through an extended future time period when premises, sudden events, internal implementation efforts, and general economic and societal developments will be sources of change not anticipated or predicted when the strategy was conceived and initiated. Chapter 13 examines how to set up strategic controls to deal with the important steering function during the implementation process. The chapter also examines operational control functions and the balanced scorecard approach to integrating strategic and operational control.

The overriding concerns in executing strategies and leading a company are survival, growth, and prosperity. In a global economy that allows everyone everywhere instant information and instant connectivity, change often occurs at lightning speed. Thus, leaders are increasingly encouraging their firms to embrace innovation and entrepreneurship as key ways to respond to such overwhelming uncertainty. Chapter 14 examines innovation in general, different types of innovation, and the best ways to bring more innovative activity into a firm. It examines the entrepreneurship process as another way to build innovative responsiveness and opportunity recognition into a firm, both in new-venture settings and in large business organizations.

Implementation is "where the action is." It is the arena that most students enter at the start of their business careers. It is the strategic phase in which staying close to the customer, achieving competitive advantage, and pursuing excellence become realities. These five chapters in Part Three will help you understand how this is done and how to prepare to take your place as a future leader of successful, innovative business organizations.

Implementation

After reading and studying this chapter, you should be able to

1. Understand how short-term objectives are used in strategy implementation.
2. Identify and apply the qualities of good short-term objectives to your own experiences.
3. Illustrate what is meant by functional tactics and understand how they are used in strategy implementation.
4. Gain a general sense of what outsourcing is and how it becomes a choice in functional tactics decisions for strategy implementation.
5. Understand what policies are and how to use policies to empower operating personnel in implementing business strategies and functional tactics.
6. Understand the use of financial reward in executive compensation.
7. Identify different types of executive compensation and when to use each in strategy implementation.

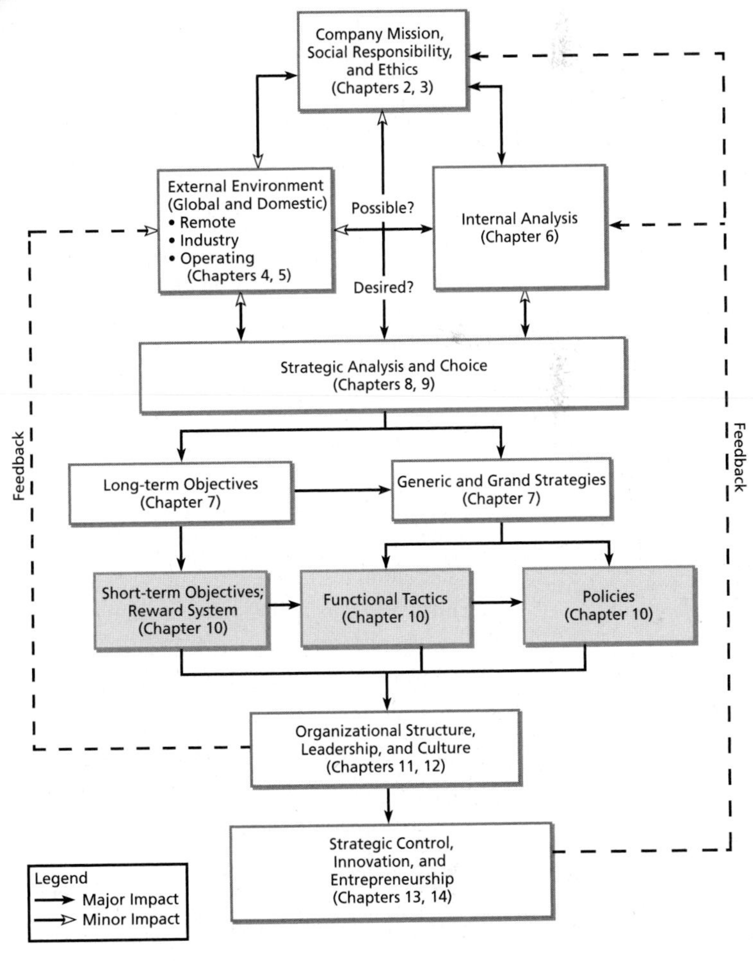

Xerox and Hewlett-Packard faced difficult times during the last decade. For Xerox, bankruptcy was a real possibility given its $14 billion debt and its serious problems with the U.S. Securities and Exchange Commission. Hewlett-Packard was falling behind in the computer business while living solely on profits from its printer division. Anne Mulcahy became Xerox CEO during this time. Carly Fiorina became HP's CEO. Five years later, Anne Mulcahy was celebrated for the success of her strategy at Xerox while Carly Fiorina was dismissed for the failure of the path she chose. Two legendary technology companies and two celebrated CEOs who shattered the "glass ceiling" in being selected to lead two legendary companies back to glory: Why did one succeed and the other fail?

Analysts suggest that the "devil is in the detail." Fiorina's strategy was to acquire Compaq, build the size of HP's PC business, and use profits from HP's venerable printer business to sustain a reorganization of the combined companies. Mark Anderson, an investment analyst who has followed HP for more than 20 years, said this about Carly Fiorina's strategy:

> I would say it stinks, but it isn't even a strategy. A few bullet points don't make a strategy. Such an approach lacks the technical and market understanding necessary to drive HP.[1]

In other words, Carly Fiorina's strategy was a glitzy combination of two large computer companies, but it was less clear exactly what key actions and tactics would bring about a reinvented, "new," profitable HP.

Anne Mulcahy took a different approach, in part reflecting her 28 years inside Xerox. She set about to "reinvent" Xerox as well, but made four functional tactics and their respective short-term objectives very clear building blocks for reinventing Xerox: (1) She prioritized aggressive cost cutting—30 percent—throughout the company to restore profitability. (2) She emphasized a productivity increase in each Xerox division. (3) She quickly settled Xerox's SEC litigation about its accounting practices, and she refinanced Xerox's massive debt. (4) She made a major point of continued heavy R&D funding even as every other part of Xerox suffered through severe cost cutting. This, she felt, sent a message of belief in Xerox's future. It clearly established her priorities.

Mulcahy's articulation of specific tactical efforts, and the short-term objectives they were intended to achieve, turned Xerox around in three short years. As she proudly pointed out:

> Probably one of the hardest things was to continue investing in the future, in growth. One of the most controversial decisions we made was to continue our R&D investment. When you're drastically restructuring in other areas, that's a tough decision. It makes it harder for the other businesses to some extent. But it was important for the Xerox people to believe we were investing in the future. Now two-thirds of our revenue is coming from products and services introduced in the last two years.[2]

The reason Anne Mulcahy succeeded while Carly Fiorina did not, the focus of this chapter, involves translating strategic thought into organizational action. In the words of two well-worn phrases, they move from "planning their work" to "working their plan." Anne Mulcahy successfully made this shift at Xerox when she did these five things well:

1. Identify short-term objectives.
2. Initiate specific functional tactics.
3. Outsource nonessential functions.
4. Communicate policies that empower people in the organization.
5. Design effective rewards.

[1] "The Only HP Way Worth Trying," Viewpoint, *BusinessWeek*, March 9, 2005.

[2] "American Innovation: A Competitive Crisis," speech by Anne M. Mulcahy at The Chief Executive's Club of Boston, June 12, 2008; and "She Put the Bounce Back in Xerox," *BusinessWeek*, January 10, 2005.

Top Global Strategist

John Thompson, retired Chairman of Symantec

Exhibit 10.1

John Thompson became Symantec's chairman in 2010 after a 10-year tenure as CEO, wherein he helped transform Symantec into a leader in security, storage, and systems management IT solutions delivered to a broad base of customers, from individual consumers to the largest enterprises in the world. Symantec's revenues grew from $632 million to $6.2 billion, and its worldwide workforce reached more than 17,500 employees under his leadership.

An important component that drove this impressive success for John Thompson was his belief in the importance of short-term objectives to help managers guide strategy implementation. He viewed these objectives as "vectors" for how you are performing "now" and as indicators of how you will perform in the future.

"I am a little old-fashioned—I don't believe you can manage what you can't measure," Thompson has said. "The importance of objectives becomes more important as the company grows in size and scale. Objectives also serve as an indication for the 'team' about what you are paying attention to. If employees know you are measuring market growth and customer satisfaction, they will pay attention to those considerations and act based on indicators that you, as leader, emphasize within the company. Objectives help teams and focus on what's important for the company to succeed."*

Describing what makes a good objective into an effective management tool, Thompson said "the best objectives are simple to understand, simple to communicate, and relatively easy for everyone to get access to the data that represents the results. If you make your objectives hard to measure, manage, and communicate, they won't be effective. Simplicity is key." Thompson also believes in brevity, saying that "experience has proven to me the importance of picking the few objectives that are most critical for running the business or your unit. Stick with them—and communicate them to both internal and external audiences."**

*"The Key to Success? Go Figure," *BusinessWeek*, July 21, 2003.
**Ibid.; and "Symantec's CEO Takes the Long View," *BusinessWeek*, February 8, 2007.

Short-term objectives translate long-range aspirations into this year's targets for action. If well developed, these objectives provide clarity, a powerful motivator and facilitator of effective strategy implementation. In Exhibit 10.1, Top Global Strategist, John Thompson, retired chairman of the board at Symantec, summarizes how short-term objectives were critical to his success.

Functional tactics translate business strategy into daily activities people need to execute. Functional managers participate in the development of these tactics, and their participation, in turn, helps clarify what their units are expected to do in implementing the business's strategy.

Outsourcing nonessential functions normally performed in-house frees up resources and the time of key people to concentrate on leveraging the functions and activities critical to the core competitive advantages around which the firm's long-range strategy is built.

Policies are empowerment tools that simplify decision making by empowering operating managers and their subordinates. Policies can empower the "doers" in an organization by reducing the time required to decide and act.

Rewards that align manager and employee priorities with organizational objectives and shareholder value provide very effective direction in strategy implementation.

SHORT-TERM OBJECTIVES

short-term objective
Measurable outcomes achievable or intended to be achieved in one year or less.

Chapter 7 described business strategies, grand strategies, and long-term objectives that are critically important in crafting a successful future. To make them become a reality, however, the people in an organization who actually "do the work" of the business need guidance in exactly what they need to do. Short-term objectives help do this. **Short-term objectives** are measurable outcomes achievable or intended to be achieved in one year or less. They are specific, usually quantitative, results operating managers set out to achieve in the immediate future.

Short-term objectives help implement strategy in at least three ways:

1. Short-term objectives "operationalize" long-term objectives. If we commit to a 20 percent gain in revenue over five years, what is our specific target or objective in revenue during the current year, month, or week to indicate we are making appropriate progress?
2. Discussion about and agreement on short-term objectives help raise issues and potential conflicts within an organization that usually require coordination to avoid otherwise dysfunctional consequences. Exhibit 10.2 illustrates how objectives within marketing, manufacturing, and accounting units within the same firm can be very different even when created to pursue the same firm objective (e.g., increased sales, lower costs).
3. Finally, short-term objectives assist strategy implementation by identifying measurable outcomes of action plans or functional activities, which can be used to make feedback, correction, and evaluation more relevant and acceptable.

Short-term objectives are usually accompanied by action plans, which enhance these objectives in three ways. First, action plans usually identify functional tactics and activities that will be undertaken in the next week, month, or quarter as part of the business's effort to build competitive advantage. The important point here is *specificity*—what exactly is to be done. We will examine functional tactics in a subsequent section of this chapter. The

EXHIBIT 10.2
Potential Conflicting Objectives and Priorities

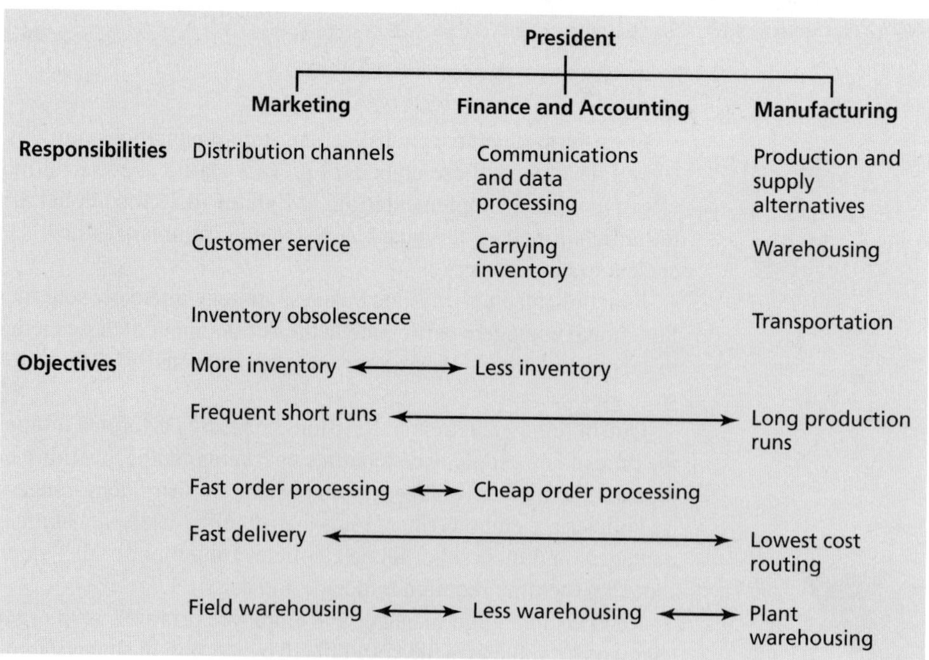

second element of an action plan is a clear *time frame for completion*—when the effort will begin and when its results will be accomplished. A third element action plans contain is identification of *who is responsible* for each action in the plan. This accountability is very important to ensure action plans are acted upon.

Qualities of Effective Short-Term Objectives

Measurable

Short-term objectives are more consistent when they clearly state *what* is to be accomplished, *when* it will be accomplished, and *how* its accomplishment will be *measured*. Such objectives can be used to monitor both the effectiveness of each activity and the collective progress across several interrelated activities. Exhibit 10.3 illustrates several effective and ineffective short-term objectives. Measurable objectives make misunderstanding less likely among interdependent managers who must implement action plans. It is far easier to quantify the objectives of *line* units (e.g., production) than of certain *staff* areas (e.g., personnel). Difficulties in quantifying objectives often can be overcome by initially focusing on *measurable activity* and then identifying *measurable outcomes*.

Priorities

Although all annual objectives are important, some deserve priority because of a timing consideration or their particular impact on a strategy's success. If such priorities are not established, conflicting assumptions about the relative importance of annual objectives may inhibit progress toward strategic effectiveness. Anne Mulcahy's turnaround of Xerox described at the beginning of this chapter emphasized several important short-term objectives. But it was clear throughout Xerox that her highest priority in the first two years was

EXHIBIT 10.3
Creating Measurable Objectives

Examples of Deficient Objectives	Examples of Objectives with Measurable Criteria for Performance
To improve morale in the division (plant, department, etc.)	To reduce turnover (absenteeism, number of rejects, etc.) among sales managers by 10 percent by January 1, 2014. *Assumption:* Morale is related to measurable outcomes (i.e., high and low morale are associated with different results).
To improve support of the sales effort	To reduce the time lapse between order data and delivery by 8 percent (two days) by June 1, 2014. To reduce the cost of goods produced by 6 percent to support a product price decrease of 2 percent by December 1, 2014. To increase the rate of before- or on-schedule delivery by 5 percent by June 1, 2014.
To improve the firm's image	To conduct a public opinion poll using random samples in the five largest U.S. metropolitan markets to determine average scores on 10 dimensions of corporate responsibility by May 15, 2014. To increase our score on those dimensions by an average of 7.5 percent by May 1, 2014.

to dramatically lower overhead and production costs so as to satisfy the difficult challenge of continuing to invest heavily in R&D while also restoring profitability.

Priorities are established in various ways. A simple ranking may be based on discussion and negotiation during the planning process. However, this does not necessarily communicate the real difference in the importance of objectives, so such terms as primary, top, and secondary may be used to indicate priority. Some firms assign weights (e.g., 0 to 100 percent) to establish and communicate the relative priority of objectives. Whatever the method, recognizing priorities is an important dimension in the implementation value of short-term objectives.

Cascading: From Long-Term Objectives to Short-Term Objectives

The link between short-term and long-term objectives should resemble cascades through the firm from basic long-term objectives to specific short-term objectives in key operation areas. The cascading effect has the added advantage of providing a clear reference for communication and negotiation, which may be necessary to integrate and coordinate objectives and activities at the operating level.

Milliken, a U.S.–based global leader and innovator in the global textile industry, provides a good example of cascading objectives. One of Milliken's long-term priorities is sustainability—being an exemplary corporate steward of its global environment. That strategic commitment has been in existence almost 20 years—since Roger Milliken set forth four strategic principles and goals for all of Milliken's plants and facilities:

- Complete regulatory compliance.
- Strive for zero waste generation.
- Conserve natural resources.
- Continuously develop new environmental solutions.

Exhibit 10.4 shows how Milliken's Sustainability Team translates the four long-range goals into cascading and more specific, measurable short-term objectives for one year. This cascading approach gives solid guidance to Milliken "associates" at all its plants and facilities worldwide—cascading downward in specificity and also, ultimately, cascading

EXHIBIT 10.4
Milliken Global Environmental Objectives

Source: "Enhancing Sustainability at Milliken," presentation at SwampFox Sustainability Forum, Moore School of Business, University of South Carolina, Columbia, SC.

Strategic Priority	Functional Tactic	This Year's Objectives
Complete compliance	Zero serious environmental incidents	Number of serious incidents: 0 20% fewer significant incidents
Zero waste to landfill	Reduce solid waste	Zero waste to landfill 5% less solid waste/pound Increase reuse/recycle 75% to 78%
Conserve national resources	Reduce energy use	10% less energy consumed per pound
Conserve national resources	Reduce water use	10% less water consumed per pound
Zero emissions to air	Zero net greenhouse gas emissions	5% reduction greenhouse gas emit per pound
Environmental education	100% plant coverage worldwide	100% plant coverage worldwide
Quality control	ISO-14001 registration	ISO regulations for St. George; Gillespie; Autotex; Brazil; Zhangliangang; China

upward to consolidate and evaluate Miliken's overall improvement in global environmental stewardship.[3]

FUNCTIONAL TACTICS THAT IMPLEMENT BUSINESS STRATEGIES

functional tactics
Detailed statements of the "means" or activities that will be used by a company to achieve short-term objectives and establish competetive advantage.

Functional tactics are the key, routine activities that must be undertaken in each functional area—marketing, finance, production/operations, R&D, and human resource management—to provide the business's products and services. In a sense, functional tactics translate thought (grand strategy) into action designed to accomplish specific short-term objectives. Every value chain activity in a company executes functional tactics that support the business's strategy and help accomplish strategic objectives.

Exhibit 10.5 summarizes key benefits that result from clearly stated functional tactics accompanied by measurable short-term objectives during the implementation process. Exhibit 10.6, Global Strategy in Action, illustrates the difference between functional tactics and business strategy. It also shows that functional tactics are essential to implement business strategy. It explains the situation at the leading U.K. restaurant company, where consultants were brought in to identify specific tactical things employees needed to do or deal with to implement an overall business strategy to differentiate the growing chain from many other restaurant competitors. The business strategy outlined the competitive posture of its operations in the restaurant industry. To increase the likelihood that these strategies would be successful, specific functional tactics were needed for the firm's operating components. These functional tactics clarified the business strategy, giving specific, short-term guidance to operating managers and employees in the areas of marketing, operations, and finance.

Differences between Business Strategies and Functional Tactics

Functional tactics are different from business or corporate strategies in three fundamental ways:

1. Specificity.
2. Time horizon.
3. Participants who develop them.

Specificity

Functional tactics are more specific than business strategies. Business strategies provide general direction. Functional tactics identify the specific activities that are to be undertaken in each functional area and thus allow operating managers to work out *how* their unit is expected to pursue short-term objectives. Exhibit 10.6, Global Strategy in Action,

EXHIBIT 10.5
The Value-Added Benefit of Short-Term Objectives and Specific Functional Tactics

- They give operating personnel a better understanding of their role in the firm's mission.
- The process of developing them becomes a forum for raising and resolving conflicts between strategic intent and operational reality.
- They provide a basis for developing budgets, schedules, trigger points, and other sources of strategic control.
- They can be powerful motivators, especially when connected to the reward system.

[3] "Enhancing Sustainability at Milliken," SwampFox Sustainability Forum, Moore School of Business, University of South Carolina, Columbia, SC.

Global Strategy in Action — Exhibit 10.6

The Nature and Value of Specificity in Functional Tactics versus Business Strategy

A European restaurant business was encountering problems. Although its management had agreed unanimously that it was committed to a business strategy to differentiate itself from other competitors based on concept and customer service rather than price, the multilocation business continued to encounter inconsistencies across different store locations in how well it did this. Consultants indicated that the customer experience varied greatly from store to store. The conclusion was that while the management understood the "business strategy," and the employees did too in general terms, the implementation was inadequate because of a lack of specificity in the functional tactics—what everyone should do every day in the restaurant—to make the vision a reality in terms of the customers' dining experience. The following breakdown of part of their business strategy into specific functional tactics just in the area of customer service helps illustrate the value specificity in functional tactics brings to strategy implementation.

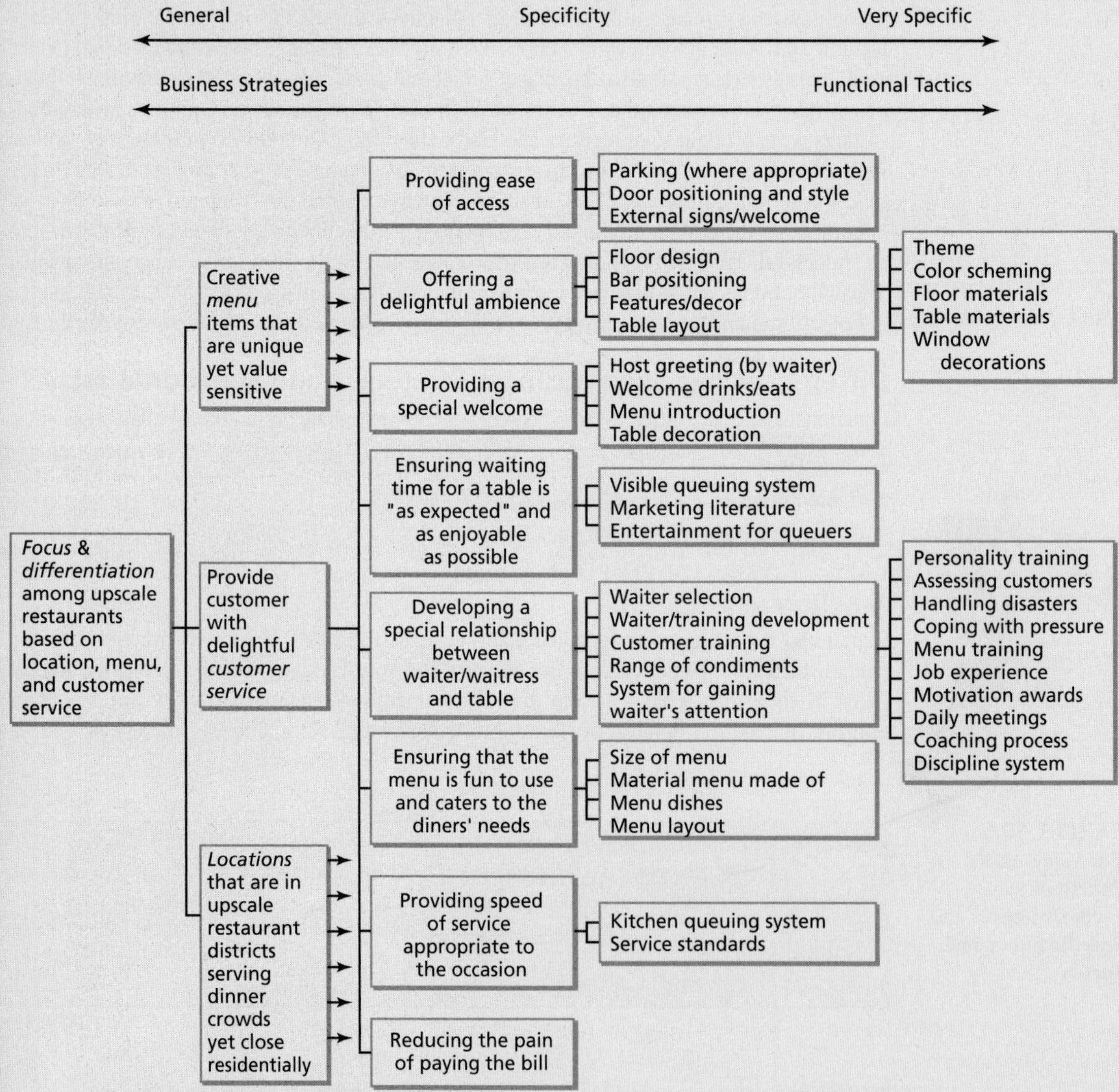

Source: Adapted from A. Campbell and K. Luchs, Eds., *Core Competency – Based Strategy* (London: Thompson, 1997).

Top Global Strategist
Tim Cook, Apple

Exhibit 10.7

Tim Cook, the little-known CEO hand-picked by Steve Jobs to replace Jobs after his death, is an intensely private Auburn University engineering grad (1982) and Apple workaholic passionate about cycling, outdoors, and Auburn football. His operational and tactical genius has been the behind-the-limelight reason for Apple's amazing success. A few examples of his tactics:

- When Apple introduced the Nano, which was revolutionary in its use of flash memory far superior to others on the market, Cook prepaid $1.25 billion to suppliers Samsung and Hynix, effectively cornering the market through 2010 on that specific kind of memory.
- Upon arriving at Apple, Cook closed factories and warehouses and instead established relationships with contract manufacturers, reducing Apple's days in inventory from months to days, equaling Dell's gold standard in computer manufacturing efficiency.

Yet Cook's tactics continually control a diverse supply chain and ensure a seamless orchestration of Apple's product introductions and delivery—unveiling revolutionary products kept completely secret until they magically appear in stores worldwide as promised.

Source: Dan Frommer, "Everything You Need to Know About Tim Cook, Apple's COO," *businessinsider.com*, Jan. 17, 2011.

illustrates the nature and value of specificity in functional tactics versus business strategy at the United Kingdom's leading restaurant chain.

Specificity in functional tactics contributes to successful implementation by

- Helping ensure that functional managers know what needs to be done and can focus on accomplishing results.
- Clarifying for top management how functional managers intend to accomplish the business strategy, which increases top management's confidence in and sense of control over the business strategy.
- Facilitating coordination among operating units within the firm by clarifying areas of interdependence and potential conflict.

Time Horizon

Functional tactics identify activities to be undertaken "now" or in the immediate future. Business strategies focus on the firm's posture three to five years out. Exhibit 10.7, Top Global Strategist, describes how Tim Cook, Apple's rising star, implemented immediate functional tactics to quickly turn around that company's broken manufacturing operations shortly after Steve Jobs brought him on board specifically to help do just that.

The shorter time horizon of functional tactics is critical to the successful implementation of a business strategy for two reasons. First, it focuses the attention of functional managers on what needs to be done *now* to make the business strategy work. Second, it allows functional managers like those at Apple to adjust to changing current conditions.

Participants

Different people participate in strategy development at the functional and business levels. Business strategy is the responsibility of the general manager of a business unit. That manager typically delegates the development of functional tactics to subordinates charged with running the operating areas of the business. The manager of a business unit must establish long-term objectives and a strategy that corporate management feels contributes to corporate-level goals. Similarly, key operating managers must establish short-term objectives and operating strategies that contribute to business-level goals. Just as business strategies and objectives are approved through negotiation between corporate managers and business managers, so, too, are short-term objectives and functional tactics approved through negotiation between business managers and operating managers.

Involving operating managers in the development of functional tactics improves their understanding of what must be done to achieve long-term objectives and, thus, contributes to successful implementation. It also helps ensure that functional tactics reflect the reality of the day-to-day operating situation. And perhaps most important, it can increase the commitment of operating managers to the strategies developed.

OUTSOURCING FUNCTIONAL ACTIVITIES

A generation ago, it was conventional wisdom that a business has a better chance of success if it controls the doing of everything necessary to produce its products or services. Referring back to Chapter 6's value chain approach, the "wise" manager would have sought to maintain control of virtually all the "primary" activities and the "support" activities associated with the firm's work. Not any longer. Starting for most firms with the outsourcing of producing payroll each week, companies worldwide are embracing the idea that the best way to implement their strategies is to retain responsibility for executing some functions while seeking outside people and companies to do key support and key primary activities where they can do so more effectively and more inexpensively. **Outsourcing,** then, is acquiring an activity, service, or product necessary to provide a company's products or services from "outside" the people or operations controlled by that acquiring company.

outsourcing
Obtaining work previously done by employees inside the companies from sources outside the company.

DuPont Co. has always run corporate training and development out of its Wilmington (Delaware) head office. But these days, Boston-based Forum Corp. handles it instead. In Somers, New York, PepsiCo Inc. employees, long used to receiving personal financial planning from their employer, now get that service from KPMG Peat Marwick. Denver's TeleTech Holdings Inc. is taking customer-service calls from AT&T customers and books seat reservations for Continental Airlines.

Relentless cost-cutting was an early driver behind the trend to outsource. When Tim Cook first came to Apple from Compaq Computer, he was a 16-year computer industry veteran with 12 years at IBM. His mandate at Apple was to clean up the atrocious state of Apple's manufacturing, distribution, and supply apparatus. He quickly closed factories and warehouses around the world and instead established relationships with contract manufacturers. By outsourcing almost all of its manufacturing and warehousing, Apple cut its inventory costs by a substantial amount (see Exhibit 10.7, Top Global Strategist, on page 293).

Outsourcing now occurs across every function in a business—marketing, product design, and computer operations are just a few functions other than typical rote functions that have been regularly outsourced by many companies. Infosys, the India–based bastion of early call center outsourcing followed by many types of outsourcing, is itself now outsourcing

EXHIBIT 10.8
Outsourcing Is Increasing

Source: Estimated based on various articles in *BusinessWeek* on outsourcing.

ORDERING OUT... Companies That Say They Outsource Some Functional Activity		
	Yes	**No**
2010	98%	2%
2000	75	25
1995	52	48
1990	23	77

. . . FOR EVERYTHING Functional Activities Most Frequently Outsourced	
Payroll	75%
Manufacturing	72
Maintenance	68
Warehousing/transportation/distribution	62
Information technology	52
Travel	48
Temporary service	48
HR activities (varied)	40
Product design	35
R&D	25
Marketing	22

back to the United States certain software engineering activities—the leading outsourcer outsourcing itself.[4] Exhibit 10.8 shows how rapidly outsourcing has become commonplace in today's global economy.

The embrace of outsourcing's benefits, however, can obscure the potential for numerous problems. Boeing's 787 Dreamliner was three years late before finally being delivered to its early customers because of repeated production and design mistakes as well as problems related to quality and response time from a large number of outsourced partners around the globe. Communication glitches, production delays, and routine design adjustments required in any major production effort can be a real problem when they occur with outsourced partners halfway around the globe, rather than when the project is all done under one roof. Southern Pacific Railroad suffered through numerous computer breakdowns, delays, and scheduling mistakes after outsourcing its internal computer network to IBM.

The important point to recognize at this point is that functional activities long associated with doing the work of any business organization are increasingly subject to be outsourced if they can be done more cost effectively by other providers. So it becomes critical for managers implementing strategic plans to focus company activities on functions deemed central to the company's competitive advantage and to seek others outside the firm's structure to provide the functions that are necessary, but not within the scope of the firm's core competencies. And, increasingly, this decision considers every organizational activity fair game—even marketing, product design, innovation. We will explore this in greater detail in Chapter 11.

[4] A. Giridharadas, "Outsourcing Works, So India Is Exporting Jobs," nytimes.com, September 25, 2007.

EMPOWERING OPERATING PERSONNEL: THE ROLE OF POLICIES

Specific functional tactics provide guidance and initiate action implementing a business's strategy, but more is needed. Supervisors and personnel in the field have been charged in today's competitive environment with being responsible for customer value—for being the "front line" of the company's effort to truly meet customers' needs. Meeting customer needs is a buzzword regularly cited as a key priority by most business organizations. Efforts to do so often fail because employees that are the real contact point between the business and its customers are not empowered to make decisions or act to fulfill customer needs. One solution has been to empower operating personnel by pushing down decision making to their level. General Electric allows appliance repair personnel to decide about warranty credits on the spot, a decision that used to take several days and multiple organizational levels. American Air Lines allows customer service personnel and their supervisors wide range in resolving customer ticket pricing decisions. Federal Express couriers make decisions and handle package routing information that once involved five management levels in the U.S. Postal Service.

empowerment
The act of allowing an individual or team the right and flexibility to make decisions and initiate action.

Empowerment is the act of allowing an individual or team the right and flexibility to make decisions and initiate action. It is being expanded and widely advocated in many organizations today. Training, self-managed work groups, eliminating whole levels of management in organizations, and aggressive use of automation are some of the ways and ramifications of this fundamental change in the way business organizations function. At the heart of the effort is the need to ensure that decision making is consistent with the mission, strategy, and tactics of the business while at the same time allowing considerable latitude to operating personnel. One way operating managers do this is through the use of policies.

policies
Broad, precedent-setting decisions that guide or substitute for repetitive or time-sensitive managerial decision making.

Policies are directives designed to guide the thinking, decisions, and actions of managers and their subordinates in implementing a firm's strategy. Sometimes called *standard operating procedures,* policies increase managerial effectiveness by standardizing many routine decisions and clarifying the discretion managers and subordinates can exercise in implementing functional tactics. Logically, policies should be derived from functional tactics (and, in some instances, from corporate or business strategies) with the key purpose of aiding strategy execution.[5] Exhibit 10.9, Global Strategy in Action, illustrates selected policies of several well-known firms.

Creating Policies That Empower

Policies communicate guidelines to decisions. They are designed to control decisions while defining allowable discretion within which operational personnel can execute business activities. They do this in several ways:

1. *Policies establish indirect control over independent action* by clearly stating how things are to be done *now*. By defining discretion, policies in effect control decisions yet empower employees to conduct activities without direct intervention by top management.

[5] The term *policy* has various definitions in management literature. Some authors and practitioners equate policy with strategy. Others do this inadvertently by using "policy" as a synonym for company mission, purpose, or culture. Still other authors and practitioners differentiate policy in terms of "levels" associated, respectively, with purpose, mission, and strategy. "Our policy is to make a positive contribution to the communities and societies we live in" and "Our policy is not to diversify out of the hamburger business" are two examples of the breadth of what some call policies. This book defines *policy* much more narrowly as specific guides to managerial action and decisions in the implementation of strategy. This definition permits a sharper distinction between the formulation and implementation of functional strategies. And, of even greater importance, it focuses the tangible value of the policy concept where it can be most useful—as a key administrative tool to enhance effective implementation and execution of strategy.

Global Strategy in Action — Exhibit 10.9

Selected Policies That Aid Strategy Implementation

Google has a personnel policy, the ITO **(Innovation Time Out) policy,** which encourages Google employees to spend 80 percent of their time on core projects and roughly 20 percent (or one day per week) on "innovation" activities to examine and develop ideas they have that might lead to something new at Google or related to Google. (This policy helps implement two strategic priorities at Google—creating new product/service offerings or improvements in those that exist; and keeping employees challenged and engaged in ways that aid retention and keep staff learning and growing.)

IBM has an ever-changing set of social computing policies, which they call "social computing guidelines," with one such guideline being that "if you publish content online relevant to IBM in your personal capacity use a disclaimer such as this: 'The postings on this site are my own and don't necessarily represent IBM's positions, strategies or opinions.'" (IBM has a strategic priority that IBMers are encouraged to engage in online social computing as a key way to keep IBM innovative and technology savvy. This guideline is one of many that have emerged to help IBMers individually manage their online social networking in a way that is consistent with IBM's overall strategy.)

Prior to its acquisition by AMC, General Cinema had a financial policy that required annual capital investment in movie theaters not exceed annual depreciation. (This policy supported General Cinema's financial strategy at the time to maximize cash flow for growth area investment, and to increase its valuation. It also helped implement the financial strategy that area managers would use leasing as much as possible.)

Fundamental to Wendy's concept and strategy was to offer fresh meat and produce in its core products, to ensure the best taste possible. It established early-on a policy that gave local managers the authority to buy fresh meat and produce locally, rather than from regionally or nationally designated suppliers like all of its competitors did to reduce costs. (This policy supported the Wendy's product strategy of having fresh, unfrozen, "juicy" hamburgers daily.)

The highly successful West Coast Kelly-Moore Paint Company has had an R&D policy since its founding not to invest financial or people resources in basic paint research. It prefers instead to invest those resources in exceptional service and closeness to its target customer, independent paint contractors. (This policy supported Kelly-Moore's strategy to quickly adapt new paint research findings to continuously improve the quality of its paints, doing so in a way that was consistent with its priority of focusing on the independent painter's need to complete a job cost-effectively with one coat, and then move on to the next job.)

2. *Policies promote uniform handling of similar activities.* This facilitates the coordination of work tasks and helps reduce friction arising from favoritism, discrimination, and the disparate handling of common functions—something that often hampers operating personnel.

innovation time out policy
Innovation Time Out policy refers to what is usually an official company guideline, or policy, establishing an amount of time during each work week an employee, or specific types of employees (e.g. engineers) can at their choice set aside from their regular assignment to work on innovative, new ideas they are thinking about.

3. *Policies ensure quicker decisions* by standardizing answers to previously answered questions that otherwise would recur and be pushed up the management hierarchy again and again—something that requires unnecessary levels of management between senior decision makers and field personnel.

4. *Policies institutionalize basic aspects of organization behavior.* This minimizes conflicting practices and establishes consistent patterns of action in attempts to make the strategy work—again, freeing operating personnel to act.

5. *Policies reduce uncertainty in repetitive and day-to-day decision making*, thereby providing a necessary foundation for coordinated, efficient efforts and freeing operating personnel to act.

6. *Policies counteract resistance to or rejection of chosen strategies by organization members.* When major strategic change is undertaken, unambiguous operating policies clarify what is expected and facilitate acceptance, particularly when operating managers participate in policy development.

Strategy in Action — Exhibit 10.10

Make Sure Policies Aren't Used to Drive Away Customers

Every year *Inc.* magazine sponsors a conference for the 500 fastest growing companies in the United States to share ideas, hear speakers, and network. A conference in Palm Springs, CA, included a talk by Martha Rogers, co-author of *The One to One Future*. Here is an interesting anecdote about policies she used in her talk:

> The story was about a distinguished-looking gentleman in blue jeans who walked into a bank and asked a teller to complete a transaction. The teller said she was sorry, but the person responsible was out for the day. The man would have to come back. He then asked to have his parking receipt validated. Again, she said she was sorry, but under bank policy she could not validate a parking receipt unless the customer completed a transaction. The man pressed her. She did not waver. "That's our policy," she said.
>
> So the man completed a transaction. He withdrew all $1.5 million from his account. It turned out he was John Akers, then chairman of IBM.
>
> The moral: Give employees information about the value of customers, not mindless policies.

7. *Policies offer predetermined answers to routine problems*. This greatly expedites dealing with both ordinary and extraordinary problems—with the former, by referring to these answers; with the latter, by giving operating personnel more time to cope with them.

8. *Policies afford managers a mechanism for avoiding hasty and ill-conceived decisions in changing operations*. Prevailing policy can always be used as a reason for not yielding to emotion-based, expedient, or temporarily valid arguments for altering procedures and practices.

Policies may be written and formal or unwritten and informal. Informal, unwritten policies are usually associated with a strategic need for competitive secrecy. Some policies of this kind, such as promotion from within, are widely known (or expected) by employees and implicitly sanctioned by management. Managers and employees often like the latitude granted by unwritten and informal policies. However, such policies may detract from the long-term success of a strategy. Formal, written policies have at least seven advantages:

1. They require managers to think through the policy's meaning, content, and intended use.
2. They reduce misunderstanding.
3. They make equitable and consistent treatment of problems more likely.
4. They ensure unalterable transmission of policies.
5. They communicate the authorization or sanction of policies more clearly.
6. They supply a convenient and authoritative reference.
7. They systematically enhance indirect control and organizationwide coordination of the key purposes of policies.

The strategic significance of policies can vary. At one extreme are such policies as travel reimbursement procedures, which are really work rules and may not have an obvious link to the implementation of a strategy. Exhibit 10.10, Strategy in Action, provides an interesting example of how the link between a simple policy and strategy implementation regarding customer service can have serious negative consequences when it is neither obvious to operating personnel nor well thought out by bank managers. At the other extreme are organizationwide policies that are virtually functional strategies, such as Wendy's requirement that every location invest 1 percent of its gross revenue in local advertising.

Policies can be externally imposed or internally derived. Policies regarding equal employment practices are often developed in compliance with external (government) requirements, and policies regarding leasing or depreciation may be strongly influenced by current tax regulations.

Regardless of the origin, formality, and nature of policies, the key point to bear in mind is that they can play an important role in strategy implementation. Communicating specific policies will help overcome resistance to strategic change, empower people to act, and foster commitment to successful strategy implementation.

Policies empower people to act. Compensation, at least theoretically, rewards their action. The last decade has seen many firms realize that the link between compensation, particularly executive management compensation, and value-building strategic outcomes within their firms was uncertain. The recognition of this uncertainty has brought about increased recognition of the need to link management compensation with the successful implementation of strategies that build long-term shareholder value. The next section examines this development and major types of executive bonus compensation plans.

BONUS COMPENSATION PLANS[6]

Major Plan Types

Company shareholders typically believe that the goal of a bonus compensation plan is to motivate executives and key employees to achieve maximization of shareholder wealth. Because shareholders are both owners and investors of the firm, they desire a reasonable return on their investment. Because they are absentee landlords, shareholders expect their board of directors to ensure that the decision-making logic of their firm's executives is concurrent with their own primary motivation.

However, the goal of shareholder wealth maximization is not the only goal that executives may pursue. Alternatively, executives may choose actions that increase their personal compensation, power, and control. Therefore, an executive compensation plan that contains a bonus component can be used to orient management's decision making toward the owners' goals. The success of bonus compensation as an incentive hinges on a proper match between an executive bonus plan and the firm's strategic objectives. Recent research suggests that compensation committees that link executive rewards (compensation) to the unique nature of their firm's strategy achieve better outcomes."[7] Exhibit 10.11 summarizes five types of executive compensation plans we will now explore in more detail.

Stock Options

stock options
The right, or "option," to purchase company stock at a fixed price at some future date.

A common measure of shareholder wealth creation is appreciation of company stock price. Therefore, a popular form of bonus compensation is stock options. Stock options have typically represented more than 50 percent of a chief executive officer's average pay package, and remain the most significant component of CEO pay even after the recent Great Recession and the criticism they took from a variety of supposed faults.[8] **Stock options** provide the executive with the right to purchase company stock at a fixed price in the future.

[6] We wish to thank Roy Hossler for his assistance on this section.

[7] Steven Balsam, Guy Fernando, and Arindam Tripathy, "The Impact of Firm Strategy on Performance Measures in Executive Compensation," *Journal of Business Research* 64 (2011), pp. 187–193.

[8] Richard A. Booth, "Why Stock Options Are the Best Form of Executive Compensation," *New York University Journal of Law and Business* 6 (Spring, 2010), p. 281.

EXHIBIT 10.11 Types of Executive Bonus Compensation

Bonus Type	Description	Rationale	Shortcomings
Stock option grants	Right to purchase stock in the future at a price set now. Compensation is determined by "spread" between option price and exercise price.	Provides incentive for executive to create wealth for shareholders as measured by increase in firm's share price.	Movement in share price does not explain all dimensions of managerial performance.
Restricted stock plan	Shares given to executive who is prohibited from selling them for a specific time period. May also include performance restrictions.	Promotes longer executive tenure than other forms of compensation.	No downside risk to executive, who always profits unlike other shareholders.
Golden handcuffs	Bonus income deferred in a series of annual installments. Deferred amounts not yet paid are forfeited with executive resignation.	Offers an incentive for executive to remain with the firm.	May promote risk-averse decision making due to downside risk borne by executive.
Golden parachute	Executives have right to collect the bonus if they lose position due to takeover, firing, retirement, or resignation.	Offers an incentive for executive to remain with the firm.	Compensation is achieved whether or not wealth is created for shareholders. Rewards either success or failure.
Cash based on internal business performance using financial measures	Bonus compensation based on accounting performance measures such as return on equity.	Offsets the limitations of focusing on market-based measures of performance.	Weak correlation between earnings measures and shareholder wealth creation. Annual earnings do not capture future impact of current decisions.

The precise amount of compensation is based on the difference, or "spread," between the option's initial price and its selling, or exercised, price. As a result, the executive receives a bonus only if the firm's share price appreciates. If the share price drops below the option price, the options become worthless.

Stock options were the source of extraordinary wealth creation for executives, managers, and rank-and-file employees in the technology boom of the 1990s. Behind using options as compensation incentives was the notion that they were essentially free. Although they dilute shareholders' equity when they're exercised, taking the cost of stock options as an expense against earnings was not required. That, in turn, helped keep earnings higher than actual costs to the company and its shareholders. The bear market and corporate scandals of the last few years brought increased scrutiny on the use of and accounting for stock options. Recent changes in SEC guidelines have encouraged expensing stock options to more accurately reflect company performance. The following table shows the effect expensing stocks options would have on the net earnings of Standard & Poor's (S&P) 500 firms between 1996 and 2005. "Stock options were a free resource, and because of that, they were used freely," said then BankOne CEO James Dimon, who voluntarily began to expense stock options in 2003. "But now," he said, "when you have to expense options, you start to think, 'Is it an effective cost? Is there a better way?'" Legendary investor Warren Buffet argued for years that many companies enticed executives and managers with lower-than-market salaries because they also offered options. This inflated the companies' profits because of the lower salaries—hence lower expenses on the income statement.

The other side of the argument has been that it is very difficult to value stock options when issued below current values, or when a company is very new. To settle this matter, the Financial Accounting Standards Board issued a ruling in 2004 that required expensing of stock options beginning in 2006. Although challenged in the U.S. Congress, the changes were upheld and companies now expense options.[9]

A Big Hit to Earnings

If options had been expensed between 1996 and 2005, earnings would have been whacked as their popularity grew as shown below:

Options Expense as a Percent of Net Earnings for S&P 500 Companies

1996	1998	2000	2002	2005
2%	5%	8%	23%	22%

Source: *The Analysis Accounting Observer*, R. G. Associates Inc.

Microsoft shocked the business world during this time by announcing it would discontinue stock options, eliminating a form of pay that made thousands of Microsoft employees millionaires and helped define the culture of the tech industry. Starting in September 2003, the company began paying its 54,000 employees with restricted stock, a move that will let employees make money even if the company's share price declines. Like options, the restricted stock will vest gradually over a five-year period, and grants of restricted stock are counted as expenses and charged against earnings. Said CEO Steven Ballmer, "We asked: Is there a smarter way to compensate our people, a way that would make them feel even more excited about their financial deal at Microsoft and at the same time be something that was at least as good for the shareholders as today's compensation package?" At the time of Ballmer's announcement, more than 20,000 employees who had joined Microsoft in the past three years held millions of stock options that were "under water," meaning the market value of Microsoft stock was far below the stock price of their stock options.

Restricted stock has the advantage of offering employees more certainty, even if there is less potential for a big win. It also means shareholders don't have to worry about massive dilution after employees exercise big stock gains, as happened in the 1990s. Another advantage is that grants of restricted stock are much easier to value than options because restricted

[9] U.S. GAAP (generally accepted accounting principles) required expensing of stock options using one of two acceptable valuation methods starting in the first fiscal year after June 15, 2005. (www.wikipedia.org/wiki/employee_stock_options); and Karen Berman and Joe Knight, "Expensing Stock Options: The Controversy," Blogs; HBR.org, *Harvard Business Review*, August 28, 2009.

stock is equivalent to a stock transfer at the market price. That improves the transparency of corporate accounting.[10]

Research suggests that stock option plans lack the benefits of plans that include true stock ownership. Stock option plans provide unlimited upside potential for executives, but limited downside risk because executives incur only opportunity costs. Because of the tremendous advantages to the executive of stock price appreciation, there is an incentive for the executive to take undue risk. Thus, supporters of stock ownership plans argue that direct ownership instills a much stronger behavioral commitment, even when the stock price falls, because it binds executives to their firms more than do options.[11] Additionally, "Executive stock options may be an efficient means to induce management to undertake more risky projects."[12]

Options may have been overused and indeed abused in the last two bull markets,[13] but evidence suggests that the smart use of options and other incentive compensation does boost performance. Companies that spread ownership throughout a large portion of their workforce deliver higher returns than similar companies with more concentrated ownership. If options seemed for a time to be the route that enriched CEOs, employees, and investors alike, it still appears they will be used, although with less emphasis than a mix of options, restricted stock, and cash bonuses. Whatever the exact mix, they are likely to be more closely tied to achieving specific operating goals. The next section examines restricted stock and cash bonuses in greater detail.

Restricted Stock

restricted stock
Stock given to an employee who is prohibited or "restricted" from selling the stock for a certain time period and not at all if they leave the company before that time period.

A **restricted stock** plan is designed to provide benefits of direct executive stock ownership. In a typical restricted stock plan, an executive is given a specific number of company stock shares. The executive is prohibited from selling the shares for a specified time period. Should the executive leave the firm voluntarily before the restricted period ends, the shares are forfeited. Therefore, restricted stock plans are a form of deferred compensation that promotes longer executive tenure than other types of plans.

In addition to being contingent on a vesting period, restricted stock plans may also require the achievement of predetermined performance goals. Price-vesting restricted stock plans tie vesting to the firm's stock price in comparison to an index or to reaching a predetermined goal or annual growth rate. If the executive falls short on some of the restrictions, a certain amount of shares are forfeited. The design of these plans motivates the executive to increase shareholder wealth while promoting a long-term commitment to stay with the firm.

If the restricted stock plan lacks performance goal provisions, the executive needs only to remain employed with the firm over the vesting period to cash in on the stock. Performance

[10] Many argue that stock options are critical to start-up firms as a way to motivate and retain talented employees with the promise of getting rich should the new venture succeed. Among them appear to be recently retired FASB chairman Robert Herz, who favors sentiment to make special exceptions in the expensing of options in pre-IPO firms.

[11] Jeffrey Pfeffer, "Seven Practices of Successful Organizations," *California Management Review*, Winter 1998; John Barron and Glen Waddell, "Work Hard, Not Smart: Stock Options in Executive Compensation," *Journal of Economic Behavior and Organization* 66, no. 3 (June 2008), pp. 767–790; and Yan Wendy Wu, "Optimal Executive Compensation: Stock Options or Restricted Stock," *International Review of Economics & Finance* 32 (January 2011), pp. 45–64.

[12] William Gerard Sanders and Donald C. Hambrick, "Swinging for the Fences: The Effects of CEO Stock Options on Company Risk-Taking and Performance," *Academy of Management Journal* (October–November 2007); and Z. Dong and C. Wong, "Do Executive Stock Options Induce Excessive Risk Taking?" *Journal of Banking and Finance* 34, no. 10 (October 2010), pp. 2518–2529.

[13] Z. Dong and C. Wong, "Do Executive Stock Options Induce Excessive Risk Taking?" *Journal of Banking and Finance* 34, no. 10 (October 2010), pp. 2518–2529. This review of several studies found that over 30 percent of all U.S. publicly traded firms apparently manipulated (backdated) stock option grants to increase the payoff to executives receiving the grants.

provisions make sure executives are not compensated without achieving some level of shareholder wealth creation. Like stock options, restricted stock plans offer no downside risk to executives because the shares were initially gifted to the executive. Unlike options, the stock retains value tied to its market value once ownership is fully vested. Shareholders, on the other hand, do suffer a loss in personal wealth resulting from a share price drop.

Golden Handcuffs

golden handcuffs
A form of executive compensation where compensation is deferred (either a restricted stock plan or bonus income deferred in a series of annual installments).

The rationale behind plans that defer compensation forms the basis for another type of executive compensation called golden handcuffs. **Golden handcuffs** refer to either a restricted stock plan, where the stock compensation is deferred until vesting time provisions are met, or to bonus income deferred in a series of annual installments. This type of plan may also involve compensating an executive a significant amount upon retirement or at some predetermined age. In most cases, compensation is forfeited if the executive voluntarily resigns or is discharged before certain time restrictions.

Many boards consider their executives' skills and talents to be their firm's most valuable assets. These "assets" create and sustain the professional relationships that generate revenue and control expenses for the firm. Research suggests that the departure of key executives is unsettling for companies and often disrupts long-range plans when new key executives adopt a different management strategy.[14] Thus, the golden handcuffs approach to executive compensation is more congruent with long-term strategies than short-term performance plans, which offer little staying-power incentive.

Firms may turn to golden handcuffs if they believe stability of management is critical to sustained growth. Jupiter Asset Management recently tied 10 fund managers to the firm with golden handcuffs. The compensation scheme calls for a cash payment in addition to base salaries if the managers remain at the firm for five years. In the first year of the plan, the firm's pretax profits more than doubled, and their assets under management increased 85 percent. The firm's chairman has also signed a new incentive deal that will keep him at Jupiter for four years.

Deferred compensation is worrisome to some executives. In cases where the compensation is payable when the executives are retired and no longer in control, as when the firm is acquired by another firm or a new management hierarchy is installed, the golden handcuff plans are considerably less attractive to executives.

Golden handcuffs may promote risk averseness in executive decision making due to the huge downside risk borne by executives. This risk averseness could lead to mediocre performance results from executives' decisions. When executives lose deferred compensation if the firm discharges them voluntarily or involuntarily, the executive is less likely to make bold and aggressive decisions. Rather, the executive will choose safe, conservative decisions.

Golden Parachutes

golden parachute
A form of bonus compensation that guarantees a substantial cash payment if the executive quits, is fired, or simply retires.

Golden parachutes are a form of bonus compensation that guarantees a substantial cash payment to an executive if the executive quits, is fired, or simply retires. In addition, the golden parachute may also contain covenants that allow the executive to cash in on noninvested stock compensation.

[14] William E. Hall, Brian J. Lake, Charles T. Morse, and Charles T. Morse Jr., "More Than Golden Handcuffs," *Journal of Accountancy* 184, no. 5 (1997), pp. 37–42; R. L. Heneman, J. W. Tansky, and S. Michael Camp, "Human Resource Strategies of High-Growth Entrepreneurial Firms," in *International Handbook of Entrepreneurship and HRM*, Chapter 8, Edward Elgar Publishing, 2008; and David DeLong and Steve Trautman, *The Executive Guide to High-Impact Talent Management* (New York: McGraw-Hill, 2011).

The popularity of golden parachutes grew with the increased popularity of takeovers, which often led to the ouster of the acquired firm's top executives. In these cases, the golden parachutes encouraged executives to take an objective look at takeover offers. The executives could decide which move was in the best interests of the shareholders, having been personally protected in the event of a merger. The "parachute" helps soften the fall of the ousted executive. It is "golden" because the size of the cash payment often varies from several to tens of millions of dollars.

Golden parachutes caused quite an uproar in the financial services industry during the recent Great Recession. Financial engineering and several highly leveraged, marginally regulated practices associated with several major firms in that setting ended up releasing top executives, which in turn brought attention to their significant golden parachutes. Those exit commitments for ten of the largest financial firms involved in the financial meltdown were:

Million-Dollar Exit Amounts for CEOs in Key Financial Services Firms Dismissed during the Great Recession

Cash, pension, benefits, accelerated stock and options and other compensation for CEOs of financial firms and mortgage lenders:

Company	CEO	Date	Total
Merrill Lynch	Stanley O'Neal	Oct. 28, 2007	$161,000,000
Citigroup	Charles Prince	Nov. 4, 2007	$105,000,000
Washington Mutual	Kerry Killinger	Sept. 8, 2008	$44,000,000
Wachovia	Ken Thompson	June 1, 2008	$42,000,000
Lehman Bros.	Richard Fuld	Sept. 17, 2008	$24,000,000
Washington Mutual	Alan Fishman	Sept. 25, 2008	$19,000,000
Freddie Mac	Richard Syron	Sept. 8, 2008	$16,000,000
Bear Stearns	James Cayne	Jan. 8, 2008	$13,000,000
Merrill Lynch	John Thain	Sept. 14, 2008	$9,000,000
Fannie Mae	Daniel Mudd	Sept. 8, 2008	$8,000,000

Source: "CEO Pay Takes a Hit in Bailout Plan," *USAToday*, Oct. 2, 2008.

Golden parachutes typically pay ousted CEOs three times annual pay, bonuses and pensions and often include perks lasting well into retirement. They similarly cover typical key executives and company officers. Intended originally to attract executive talent, plus protect them in the case of an acquisition or takeover, golden parachutes include making the executives "whole" on restricted stock grants and options that would have been available over the three-year period in question. Should an acquisition or hostile takeover come to fruition, the executives would receive the total value of the restricted stock even if it was not yet vested. The stock options would also become available immediately. Some of the restricted stock was performance restricted. Under normal conditions this stock would not be available without the firm reaching certain performance levels.

Golden parachutes are designed in part to anticipate hostile takeovers. In the event such a situation arises, the executives' position is to lead the firm's board of directors in deciding if the hostile offer is in the long-term interests of shareholders. Because the executives are compensated heavily whether the company is taken over or not, the golden parachute has helped remove the temptation they could have of not acting in the best interests of shareholders.

Cash

Executive bonus compensation plans that focus on accounting measures of performance are designed to offset the limitations of market-based measures of performance. This type of plan is most usually associated with the payment of periodic (quarterly or annual) cash bonuses. Market factors beyond the control of management, such as pending legislation, can keep a firm's share price repressed even though a top executive is exceeding the performance expectations of the board. In this situation, a highly performing executive loses bonus compensation due to the undervalued stock. However, accounting measures of performance correct for this problem by tying executive bonuses to improvements in internally measured performance. Traditional accounting measures, such as net income, earnings per share, return on equity, and return on assets, are used because they are easily understood, are familiar to senior management, and are already tracked by firm data systems.

Critics argue that because of inherent flaws in accounting systems, basing compensation on these figures may not result in an accurate gauge of managerial performance. Return on equity estimates, for example, are skewed by inflation distortions and arbitrary cost allocations. Accounting measures are also subject to manipulation by firm personnel to artificially inflate key performance figures. Firm performance schemes, critics believe, need to be based on a financial measure that has a true link to shareholder value creation. This issue led to the creation of the Balanced Scorecard, which emphasizes not only financial measures, but also such measures as new-product development, market share, and safety as discussed in Chapter 13.

Matching Bonus Plans and Corporate Goals

Exhibit 10.12 matches a company's strategic goal with the most likely compensation plan. On the vertical axis are common strategic goals. The horizontal axis lists the main compensation types that serve as incentives for executives to reach the firm's goals. A rationale is provided to explain the logic behind the connection between the firm's goal and the suggested method of executive compensation.

Researchers emphasize that fundamental to these relationships is the importance of incorporating the level of strategic risk of the firm into the design of the executive's compensation plan. Incorporating an appropriate level of executive risk can create a desired behavioral change commensurate with the risk level of strategies shareholders and their firms want.[15] To help motivate an executive to pursue goals of a certain risk-return level, the compensation plan can quantify that risk-return level and reward the executive accordingly.

The links we show between bonus compensation plans and strategic goals were derived from the results of prior research. The basic principle underlying Exhibit 10.12 is that different types of bonus compensation plans are intended to accomplish different purposes; one element may serve to attract and retain executives; another may serve as an incentive

[15] Carola Frydman and Raven Saks, "Executive Compensation: A New View from a Long-Term Perspective, 1936–2005," *The Review of Financial Studies* 23, no. 5 (2010), pp. 2099–2138.

EXHIBIT 10.12 Compensation Plan Selection Matrix

	Type of Bonus Compensation					
Strategic Goal	**Cash**	**Golden Handcuffs**	**Golden Parachutes**	**Restricted Stock Plans**	**Stock Options**	**Rationale**
Achieve corporate turnaround					X	Executive profits only if turnaround is successful in returning wealth to shareholders.
Create and support growth opportunities					X	Risk associated with growth strategies warrants the use of this high-reward incentive.
Defend against unfriendly takeover			X			Parachute helps takeover remove temptation for executive to evaluate takeover based on personal benefits.
Evaluate suitors objectively			X			Parachute compensates executive if job is lost due to a merger favorable to the firm.
Globalize operations					X	Risk of expanding overseas requires a plan that compensates only for achieved success.
Grow share price incrementally	X					Accounting measures can identify periodic performance benchmarks.
Improve operational efficiency	X					Accounting measures represent observable and agreed-upon measures of performance.
Increase assets under management				X		Executive profits proportionally as asset growth leads to long-term growth in share price.
Reduce executive turnover		X				Handcuffs provide executive tenure incentive.
Restructure organization					X	Risk associated with major change in firm's assets warrants the use of this high-reward incentive.
Streamline operations				X		Rewards long-term focus on efficiency and cost control.

to encourage behavior that accomplishes firm goals.[16] Although every strategy option has probably been linked to each compensation plan at some time, experience shows that there may be scenarios where a plan type best fits a strategy option. Exhibit 10.12 attempts to display the "best matches."

[16] Ibid.

Top Global Strategist

Carol Bartz, former CEO, Yahoo!

Exhibit 10.13

Yahoo! stock was battered for several years, leading up to the crisis-laden replacement of CEO and co-founder Jerry Yang with Carol Bartz. Several poor competitive strategy decisions, compounded by Yang's spurning overtures and offers to buy Yahoo! from Microsoft, led Yahoo!'s board to "encourage" Yang to finally step down in early 2009 to be replaced by Bartz, Autodesk CEO at the time. Her compensation package upon taking the helm at Yahoo! was intended to focus her efforts on rebuilding the Yahoo! stock price. The seven elements of her initial Yahoo! compensation package were:

1. Annual base salary of $1,000,000.
2. Annual bonus with a target of 200% of base salary and a maximum of two times the target, to be determined by the Compensation Committee of the Board of Directors of Yahoo!
3. Stock options for 5,000,000 shares at the price on February 1, 2009.
4. Annual equity grants as generally made to senior executives, including a grant valued at $8 million in February 2009.
5. Health, life, disability insurance, an employee stock purchase plan, a 401k plan, and four weeks vacation per year.
6. $150,000 in advisory fees related to this agreement.
7. An equity grant valued at $10,000,000 to compensate Bartz for forfeiture of the value of equity grants and medical coverage with her previous employer, Autodesk.

Carol Bartz was named the highest paid S&P 500 CEO during her first year at Yahoo's helm with this package being valued at $47.2 million. Within 20 months, she was named as the highest paid of all *overpaid* CEOs by the proxy advisory group Glass, Lewis & Co. in a report on the 25 most overpaid CEOs on the S&P 500. Yahoo's stock price went from approximately $13 per share when she became CEO to $17 per share two years later in early 2011.

What is your evaluation of this "deal?" Does it seem fair and appropriate to Bartz, Yahoo!, and its stockholders? If you want to see what other people thought about the compensation package shortly after Glass, Lewis's rating of overpaid executives, go to http://www.tomsguide.com/us/Carol-Bartz-Glass-Lewis-Most-Overpaid-Executives,news-8289.html. An interesting interview with Carol Bartz around this time where she discusses Yahoo and her leadership of it can be found on YouTube in a 4-minute interview: Carol Bartz was abruptly fired as CEO on Sept. 7, 2011, in a phone call from Yahoo Chairman Roy Bostock. Yahoo's stock rose 6 percent in after hours trading on the news.

Source: http://idea.sec.gov/Archives/edgar/data/1011006/000089161809000005/f51094e8vk.htm; "Yahoo's Carol Bartz Top Paid S&P CEO at $47.2M," *CBSNews.com*, May 10, 2010; and Jay Yarow, "The 25 Most Overpaid CEOs," *businessinsider.com*, Oct. 12, 2010. Yahoo CEO Bartz fired over the phone, rocky run ends, www.reuters.com/article/2011/09/07/us-yahoo-cep-idUSTRE7857R320110907.

Once the firm has identified strategic goals that will best serve shareholders' interests, an executive bonus compensation plan can be structured in such a way as to provide the executive with an incentive to work toward achieving these goals. Exhibit 10.13, Top Global Strategist summarizes the compensation plan Yahoo!'s board gave new CEO Carol Bartz, which sought to match her compensation with one key goal—increasing Yahoo!'s stock price after it had been steadily battered with the way co-founder and CEO Jerry Yang mishandled Microsoft's acquisition overtures and company strategy for several years.

Summary

The first concern in the implementation of business strategy is to translate that strategy into action throughout the organization. This chapter discussed five considerations for accomplishing this.

Short-term objectives are derived from long-term objectives, which are then translated into current actions and targets. They differ from long-term objectives in time frame, specificity, and measurement. To be effective in strategy implementation, they must be integrated and coordinated. They also must be consistent, measurable, and prioritized.

Functional tactics are derived from the business strategy. They identify the specific, immediate actions that must be taken in key functional areas to implement the business strategy.

Outsourcing of selected functional activities has become a central tactical agenda for virtually every business firm in today's global economy. Can we get that activity done more effectively—and more inexpensively—outside our company? This question has become a regular one managers ask as they seek to make their business strategies work.

Employee empowerment through policies provides another means for guiding behavior, decisions, and actions at the firm's operating levels in a manner consistent with its business and functional strategies. Policies empower operating personnel to make decisions and take action quickly.

Compensation rewards action and results. Once the firm has identified strategic objectives that will best serve stockholder interests, there are five bonus compensation plans that can be structured to provide the executive with an incentive to work toward achieving those goals.

Objectives, functional tactics, policies, and compensation represent only the start of the strategy implementation. The strategy must be institutionalized—it must permeate the firm. The next chapter examines this phase of strategy implementation.

Key Terms

empowerment, *p. 296*
functional tactics, *p. 290*
golden handcuffs, *p. 303*
golden parachute, *p. 303*
Innovation Time Out policy, *p. 297*
outsourcing, *p. 294*
policies, *p. 296*
restricted stock, *p. 302*
short-term objective, *p. 288*
social computing, *p. 310*
Social Computing Guidelies, *p. 311*
stock options, *p. 299*

Questions for Discussion

1. How does the concept "translate thought into action" bear on the relationship between business strategy and operating strategy? Between long-term and short-term objectives?
2. How do fun.0ctional tactics differ from corporate and business strategies?
3. What key concerns must functional tactics address in marketing? finance? production/operations management? personnel?
4. What is "outsourcing?" Why has it become a key element in shaping functional tactics within most business firms today?
5. How do policies aid strategy implementation? Illustrate your answer.
6. Use Exhibits 10.11 and 10.12 to explain five executive bonus compensation plans.
7. Illustrate a policy, an objective, and a functional tactic in your personal career strategy.
8. Why are short-term objectives needed when long-term objectives are already available?

Chapter 10 Appendix

Functional Tactics

FUNCTIONAL TACTICS THAT IMPLEMENT BUSINESS STRATEGIES

Functional tactics are the key, routine activities that must be undertaken in each functional area—marketing, finance, production/operations, R&D, and human resource management—to provide the business's products and services. In a sense, functional tactics translate thought (grand strategy) into action designed to accomplish specific short-term objectives. Every value chain activity in a company executes functional tactics that support the business's strategy and help accomplish strategic objectives.

The next several sections will highlight key tactics around which managers can build competitive advantage and add value in each of the various functional areas.

FUNCTIONAL TACTICS IN PRODUCTION/OPERATIONS

Basic Issues

Production/operations management (POM) is the core function of any organization. That function converts inputs (raw materials, supplies, machines, and people) into value-enhanced output. The POM function is most easily associated with manufacturing firms, but it also applies to all other types of businesses (e.g., service and retail firms). POM tactics must guide decisions regarding (1) the basic nature of the firm's POM system, seeking an optimum balance between investment input and production/operations output, and (2) location, facilities design, and process planning on a short-term basis. Exhibit 10.A1 highlights key decision areas in which the POM tactics should provide guidance to functional personnel.

POM facility and equipment tactics involve decisions regarding plant location, size, equipment replacement, and facilities utilization that should be consistent with grand strategy and other operating strategies. In the mobile home industry, for example, the facilities and equipment tactic of Winnebago was to locate one large centralized, highly integrated production center (in Iowa) near its raw materials. On the other extreme, Fleetwood Inc., a California-based competitor, located dispersed, decentralized production facilities near markets and emphasized maximum equipment life and less-integrated, labor-intensive production processes. Both firms are leaders in the mobile home industry, but have taken very different tactical approaches.

The interplay between computers and rapid technological advancement has made flexible manufacturing systems (FMS) a major consideration for today's POM tacticians.

EXHIBIT 10.A1 Key Functional Tactics in POM

Functional Tactic	Typical Questions That the Functional Tactic Should Answer
Facilities and equipment	How centralized should the facilities be? (One big facility or several small facilities?) How integrated should the separate processes be? To what extent should further mechanization or automation be pursued? Should size and capacity be oriented toward peak or normal operating levels?
Sourcing	How many sources are needed? How should suppliers be selected, and how should relationships with suppliers be managed over time? What level of forward buying (hedging) is appropriate?
Operations planning and control	Should work be scheduled to order or to stock? What level of inventory is appropriate? How should inventory be used, controlled, and replenished? What are the key foci for control efforts (quality, labor cost, downtime, product use, other)? Should maintenance efforts be oriented to prevention or to breakdown? What emphasis should be placed on job specialization? Plant safety? The use of standards?

FMS allows managers to automatically and rapidly shift production systems to retool for different products or other steps in a manufacturing process. Changes that previously took hours or days can be done in minutes. The result is decreased labor cost, greater efficiency, and increased quality associated with computer-based precision.

Sourcing has become an increasingly important component in the POM area. Many companies now accord sourcing a separate status like any other functional area. Sourcing tactics provide guidelines about questions such as: Are the cost advantages of using only a few suppliers outweighed by the risk of overdependence? What criteria (e.g., payment requirements) should be used in selecting vendors? Which vendors can provide "just-in-time" inventory, and how can the business provide it to our customers? How can operations be supported by the volume and delivery requirements of purchases?

POM planning and control tactics involve approaches to the management of ongoing production operations and are intended to match production/operations resources with longer-range, overall demand. These tactical decisions usually determine whether production/operations will be demand oriented, inventory oriented, or outsourcing oriented to seek a balance between the two extremes. Tactics in this component also address how issues such as maintenance, safety, and work organization are handled. Quality control procedures are yet another focus of tactical priorities in this area.

Just-in-time (JIT) delivery, outsourcing, and statistical process control (SPC) have become prominent aspects of the way today's POM managers create tactics that build greater value and quality in their POM system. JIT delivery was initially a way to coordinate with suppliers to reduce inventory carrying costs of items needed to make products. It also became a quality control tactic because smaller inventories made quality checking easier on smaller, frequent deliveries. It has become an important aspect of supplier-customer relationships in today's best businesses.

Outsourcing, or the use of a source other than internal capacity to accomplish some task or process, has become a major operational tactic in today's downsizing-oriented firms. Outsourcing is based on the notion that strategies should be built around the core competencies that add the most value in the value chain and that functions or activities that add little value or that cannot be done cost effectively should be done outside the firm—outsourced. When done well, the firm gains a supplier that provides superior quality at lower cost than it could provide itself. JIT and outsourcing have increased the strategic importance of the purchasing function. Outsourcing must include intense quality control by the buyer. ValuJet's tragic 1996 crash in the Everglades was caused by poor quality control over its outsourced maintenance providers.

social computing
Social computing refers to the area of computer science that is concerned with the intersection of social behavior and computation systems. It typically refers to software that contributes to compelling and effective social interactions.

The Internet and e-commerce have begun to revolutionize functional tactics in operations and marketing. How we sell, where we make things, how we logistically coordinate what we do—all of these basic business functions and questions have new perspectives and ways of being addressed because of the technological effect of the globally emerging ways we link together electronically, quickly, and accurately.

FUNCTIONAL TACTICS IN MARKETING

The role of the marketing function is to achieve the firm's objectives by bringing about the profitable sale of the business's products/services in target markets. Marketing tactics should guide sales and marketing managers in determining who will sell what, where, to whom, in what quantity, and how. Marketing tactics at a minimum should address four fundamental areas: products, price, place, and promotion. Exhibit 10.A2 highlights typical questions marketing tactics should address.

In addition to the basic issues raised in Exhibit 10.A2, marketing tactics today must guide managers addressing the effect of the communication revolution and the increased diversity among market niches worldwide. The Internet and the accelerating blend of computers and telecommunications has facilitated instantaneous access to several places around the world. A producer of plastic kayaks in Easley, South Carolina, receives orders from somewhere in the world about every 30 minutes over the Internet without any traditional distribution structure or global advertising. It fills the order within five days without any transportation capability. Speed linked to the ability to communicate instantaneously is causing marketing tacticians to radically rethink what they need to do to remain competitive and maximize value.

Diversity has accelerated because of communication technology, logistical capability worldwide, and advancements in flexible manufacturing systems. The diversity that has resulted is a virtual explosion of market niches—adaptations of products to serve hundreds of distinct and diverse customer segments that would previously have been served with more mass-market, generic products or services. Where firms used to rely on volume associated with mass markets to lower costs, they now encounter smaller niche players carving out subsegments they can serve more timely *and* more cost effectively. These new, smaller players lack the bureaucracy and committee approach that burdens the larger firms. They make decisions, outsource, incorporate product modifications, and make other agile adjustments to niche market needs before their larger competitors get through the first phase of committee-based decision making.

FUNCTIONAL TACTICS IN SOCIAL COMPUTING

The role of **social computing**—blogs, wikis, networks, virtual worlds, and social media—has become a key aspect

EXHIBIT 10.A2 **Key Functional Tactics in Marketing**

Functional Tactic	Typical Questions That the Functional Tactic Should Answer
Product (or service)	Which products do we emphasize? Which products/services contribute most to profitability? What product/service image do we seek to project? What consumer needs does the product/service seek to meet? What changes should be influencing our customer orientation?
Price	Are we competing primarily on price? Can we offer discounts on other pricing modifications? Are our pricing policies standard nationally, or is there regional control? What price segments are we targeting (high, medium, low, and so on)? What is the gross profit margin? Do we emphasize cost/demand or competition-oriented pricing?
Place	What level of market coverage is necessary? Are there priority geographic areas? What are the key channels of distribution? What are the channel objectives, structure, and management? Should the marketing managers change their degree of reliance on distributors, sales reps, and direct selling? What sales organization do we want? Is the sales force organized around territory, market, or product?
Promotion	What are the key promotion priorities and approaches? Which advertising/communication priorities and approaches are linked to different products, markets, and territories? Which media would be most consistent with the total marketing strategy?

of implementing a firm's strategy in today's global economy. Sites like Facebook, MySpace, Twitter, Second Life, and Web-based blogs are part of the daily routine and means of connecting with others in our personal and work environments. So it is important to incorporate this phenomenon in strategy implementation with tactics and guidelines for company personnel to use when working on behalf of and representing the company.

IBM is deeply involved in information technology–based assistance to clients worldwide. In so doing, it has long embraced the rapidly growing Web-based social computing developments as an important arena for organizational and individual development and connection with colleagues, clients, partners, stakeholders, and virtually every part of a company's external environment. So they decided very quickly in the last decade to create tactical guidelines for social computing, which are regularly updated and adapted so as to keep pace with the rapidly developing and ever changing social computer scene on the Web. Twelve Fundamental **Social Computing Guidelines** (or tactics) IBM uses with its people and openly shares for others to consider using are:

Social Computing Guidelines
Social Computing Guidelines are a set of norms and shared rules designed to guide behavior when involved in social computing activities, like blogs, social websites, etc.

1. Know and follow IBM's *Business Conduct Guidelines*.[1]
2. IBMers are personally responsible for the content they publish on-line, whether in a blog, social computing site or any other form of user-generated media. Be mindful that what you publish will be public for a long time—protect your privacy and take care to understand a site's terms of service.
3. Identify yourself—name and, when relevant, role at IBM—when you discuss IBM or IBM-related matters, such as IBM products or services. You must make it clear that you are speaking for yourself and not on behalf of IBM.
4. If you publish content online relevant to IBM in your personal capacity, use a disclaimer such as this: "The postings on this site are my own and don't necessarily represent IBM's positions, strategies or opinions."
5. Respect copyright, fair use, and financial disclosure laws.
6. Don't provide IBM's or another's confidential or other proprietary information and never discuss IBM business performance or other sensitive matters publicly.

[1] See http://www.ibm.com/investor/governance/business-conduct-guidelines.wss for details on IBM's Business Conduct Guidelines. Obviously any company making use of these guidelines would do so in that company's name, not IBM's.

7. Don't cite or reference clients, partners or suppliers without their approval. When you do make a reference, link back to the source. Don't publish anything that might allow inferences to be drawn which could embarrass or damage a client.
8. Respect your audience. Don't use ethnic slurs, personal insults, obscenity, or engage in any conduct that would not be acceptable in IBM's workplace. You should also show proper consideration for others' privacy and for topics that may be considered objectionable or inflammatory—such as politics and religion.
9. Be aware of your association with IBM in online social networks. If you identify yourself as an IBMer, ensure your profile and related content is consistent with how you wish to present yourself with colleagues and clients.
10. Don't pick fights, be the first to correct your own mistakes.
11. Try to add value. Provide worthwhile information and perspective. IBM's brand is best represented by its people and what you publish may reflect on IBM's brand.
12. Don't use IBM logos or trademarks unless approved to do so.

An excellent, detailed discussion of each of these guidelines can be found at IBM Social Computing Guidelines, http://www.ibm.com/blogs/zz/en/guidelines.html. A video slide show from IBM to its employees about social computing guidelines, which IBM shares with clients and organizations interested in what it does and how it communicates doing so with its employees, can be found at http://www.ibm.com/blogs/zz/en/social_computing_guidelines.html.

Tactics in marketing and sales related to social media are particularly important—using Facebook to connect with current and potential customers; to build your brand; using Twitter to maintain frequent connection with key people and partners. For some businesses, particularly locally focused retailers and service providers, using Groupon and other instant digital coupon providers has become another important social media tactic to manage. Using virtual worlds to build global "virtual" teams or train to do so; using B2B sites to develop supply chain relationships worldwide; simple e-mail, texting, video conferencing . . . all are rapidly developing social media–related means to work together and "do business" leveraging what the Web enables. Use of social computing also carries with it greater security responsibilities for your company as your IT system inevitably stores confidential information on employees, customers, clients, and so forth. Breaches in this responsibility can be harmful if not catastrophic to your company and those affected, so tactics and policies to manage this responsibility are an essential part of this new, exciting strategic reality. Overall, in every aspect of social computing, it is critical for a company, in implementing its strategy, to create useful guidelines in the use of these tools that help employees know how to use them effectively as they represent the business and do the things that make its strategies and tactics more successful.

FUNCTIONAL TACTICS IN ACCOUNTING AND FINANCE

While most functional tactics guide implementation in the immediate future, the time frame for functional tactics in the area of finance varies because these tactics direct the use of financial resources in support of the business strategy, long-term goals, and annual objectives. Financial tactics with longer time perspectives guide financial managers in long-term capital investment, debt financing, dividend allocation, and leveraging. Financial tactics designed to manage working capital and short-term assets have a more immediate focus. Exhibit 10.A3 highlights some key questions that financial tactics must answer.

Accounting tactics increasingly emphasize more accurately identifying a meaningful basis from which managers can determine the relative value of different activities undertaken throughout the company contribute to the company's overall success. Traditional cost accounting approaches proved inadequate in doing this, as we discussed in Chapter 6. So, in addition to accounting tactics centered on positioning the company to accurately comply with securities, tax, and regulatory considerations, considerable accounting tactical attention centers on providing value-based accounting of the costs of creating and providing the business' products and services so that managers in different units—as well as company executives—can more truly understand the value of activities undertaken in, between, and among those units. See Exhibit 6.6 in Chapter 6 for a refresher explanation of activity-based versus traditional cost accounting tactics.

FUNCTIONAL TACTICS IN RESEARCH AND DEVELOPMENT

With the increasing rate of technological change in most competitive industries, research and development has assumed a key strategic role in many firms. In the technology-intensive computer and pharmaceutical industries, for example, firms typically spend between 4 and 6 percent, respectively, of their sales dollars on R&D. In other industries, such as the hotel/motel and construction industries, R&D spending is less than 1 percent of sales. Thus, functional R&D tactics may be more critical instruments of the business strategy in some industries than in others.

Exhibit 10.A4 illustrates the types of questions addressed by R&D tactics. First, R&D tactics should clarify whether basic research or product development research will be emphasized. Several major oil companies now have solar energy subsidiaries in which basic research is emphasized,

EXHIBIT 10.A3 Key Functional Tactics in Finance and Accounting

Functional Tactic	Typical Questions That the Functional Tactics Should Answer
Acquiring capital	What is the optimal balance between external and internal funding? What proportion of debt should be long-term versus short-term? How should leasing be used? What levels of common versus preferred equity would be best? What ownership restrictions apply? What is a target cost of capital?
Using/allocating capital	What are priorities for allocating capital across different parts of the business and key projects? What approval processes and what levels should be allowed to make capital allocation decisions? How should competing demands for capital be resolved?
Working capital management	What levels of cash flow are needed? What are maximum/minimum cash flow requirements and balances? What should the credit policies be? How might client-specific changes be determined? What are payment terms, limits on credit, and what collection steps/procedures are needed? What are our payment policies, terms, and timing procedures?
Dividends	Are dividends important in support of the company's overall strategy? What portion of earnings, or range, should be used to set dividend payout levels? When can dividends be raised or lowered? How important is dividend stability? Should dividends be exclusively cash? What other things other than cash are appropriate?
Accounting	How can we best account for the costs of creating and providing our business's products and services? What is the "value" of each activity within different parts of our business versus traditional cost categories?

EXHIBIT 10.A4 Key Functional Tactics in R&D

R&D Decision Area	Typical Questions That the Functional Tactics Should Answer
Basic research versus product and process development	To what extent should innovation and breakthrough research be emphasized? In relation to the emphasis on product development, refinement, and modification? What critical operating processes need R&D attention? What new projects are necessary to support growth?
Time horizon	Is the emphasis short term or long term? Which orientation best supports the business strategy? The marketing and production strategy?
Organizational fit	Should R&D be done in-house or contracted out? Should R&D be centralized or decentralized? What should be the relationship between the R&D units and product managers? Marketing managers? Production managers?
Basic R&D posture	Should the firm maintain an offensive posture, seeking to lead innovation in its industry? Should the firm adopt a defensive posture, responding to the innovations of its competitors?

while the smaller oil companies emphasize product development research.

The choice of emphasis between basic research and product development also involves the time horizon for R&D efforts. Should these efforts be focused on the near term or the long term? The solar energy subsidiaries of the major oil companies have long-term perspectives, while the smaller oil companies focus on creating products now in order to establish a competitive niche in the growing solar industry.

R&D tactics also involve organization of the R&D function. For example, should R&D work be conducted solely within the firm, or should portions of that work be contracted out? A closely related issue is whether R&D should be centralized or decentralized. What emphasis should be placed on process R&D versus product R&D?

Decisions on all of these questions are influenced by the firm's R&D posture, which can be offensive or defensive, or both. If that posture is offensive, as is true for small high-technology firms, the firm will emphasize technological innovation and new-product development as the basis for its future success. This orientation entails high risks (and high payoffs) and demands considerable technological skill, forecasting expertise, and the ability to quickly transform innovations into commercial products.

A defensive R&D posture emphasizes product modification and the ability to copy or acquire new technology. Converse Shoes is a good example of a firm with such an R&D posture. Faced with the massive R&D budgets of Nike and Reebok, Converse placed R&D emphasis on bolstering the product life cycle of its prime products (particularly canvas shoes).

Large companies with some degree of technological leadership often use a combination of offensive and defensive R&D strategy. GE in the electrical industry, IBM in the computer industry, and Du Pont in the chemical industry all have a defensive R&D posture for currently available products *and* an offensive R&D posture in basic, long-term research.

FUNCTIONAL TACTICS IN HUMAN RESOURCE MANAGEMENT

The strategic importance of human resource management (HRM) tactics received widespread endorsement in the 1990s. HRM tactics aid long-term success in the development of managerial talent and competent employees, the creation of systems to manage compensation or regulatory concerns, and guiding the effective utilization of human resources to achieve both the firm's short-term objectives and employees' satisfaction and development. HRM tactics are helpful in the areas shown in Exhibit 10.A5. The recruitment, selection, and orientation should establish the basic parameters for bringing new people into a firm and adapting them to "the way things are done" in the firm. The career development and training component should guide the action that personnel take to meet the future human resources needs of the overall business strategy. Merrill Lynch, a major brokerage firm whose long-term corporate strategy is to become a diversified financial service institution, has moved into such areas as investment

EXHIBIT 10.A5 **Key Functional Tactics in HRM**

Functional Tactic	Typical Questions That HRM Tactics Should Answer
Recruitment, selection, and orientation	What key human resources are needed to support the chosen strategy? How do we recruit these human resources? How sophisticated should our selection process be? How should we introduce new employees to the organization?
Career development and training	What are our future human resource needs? How can we prepare our people to meet these needs? How can we help our people develop?
Compensation	What levels of pay are appropriate for the tasks we require? How can we motivate and retain good people? How should we interpret our payment, incentive, benefit, and seniority policies?
Evaluation, discipline, and control	How often should we evaluate our people? Formally or informally? What disciplinary steps should we take to deal with poor performance or inappropriate behavior? In what ways should we "control" individual and group performance?
Labor relations and equal opportunity requirements	How can we maximize labor-management cooperation? How do our personnel practices affect women/minorities? Should we have hiring policies?

banking, consumer credit, and venture capital. In support of its long-term objectives, it has incorporated extensive early-career training and ongoing career development programs to meet its expanding need for personnel with multiple competencies. Larger organizations need HRM tactics that guide decisions regarding labor relations; Equal Employment Opportunity Commission requirements; and employee compensation, discipline, and control.

Current trends in HRM parallel the reorientation of managerial accounting by looking at their cost structure anew. HRM's "paradigm shift" involves looking at people expense as an investment in human capital. This involves looking at the business's value chain and the "value" of human resource components along the various links in that chain. One of the results of this shift in perspective has been the downsizing and outsourcing phenomena of the last quarter century. While this has been traumatic for millions of employees in companies worldwide, its underlying basis involves an effort to examine the use of "human capital" to create value in ways that maximize the human contribution. This scrutiny continues to challenge the HRM area to include recent major trends to outsource some or all HRM activities not regarded as part of a firm's core competence. The emerging implications for human resource management tactics may be a value-oriented perspective on the role of human resources in a business's value chain as suggested here:

Traditional HRM Ideas	Emerging HRM Ideas
Emphasis solely on physical skills	Emphasis on total contribution to the firm
Expectation of predictable, repetitious behavior	Expectation of innovative and creative behavior
Comfort with stability and conformity	Tolerance of ambiguity and change
Avoidance of responsibility and decision making	Accepting responsibility for making decisions
Training covering only specific tasks	Open-ended commitment; broad continuous development
Emphasis placed on outcomes and results	Emphasis placed on processes and means
High concern for quantity and throughput	High concern for total customer value
Concern for individual efficiency	Concern for overall effectiveness
Functional and subfunctional specialization	Cross-functional integration
Labor force seen as unnecessary expense	Labor force seen as critical investment
Workforce is management's adversary	Management and workforce are partners

Source: From A. Miller and G. Dess, *Strategic Management,* 2002, p. 400. Reprinted with permission of The McGraw-Hill Companies, Inc.

To summarize, functional tactics reflect how each major activity of a firm contributes to the implementation of the business strategy. The specificity of functional tactics and the involvement of operating managers in their development help ensure understanding of and commitment to the chosen strategy. A related step in implementation is the development of policies that empower operating managers and their subordinates to make decisions and to act autonomously.

Organizational Structure

After reading and studying this chapter, you should be able to

1. Identify five traditional organizational structures and the pros and cons of each.
2. Describe the product-team structure and explain why it is a prototype for a more open, agile organizational structure.
3. Explain five ways improvements have been sought in traditional organizational structures.
4. Describe what is meant by agile, virtual organizations.
5. Explain how outsourcing can create agile, virtual organizations, along with its pros and cons.
6. Describe boundaryless organizations and why they are important.
7. Explain why organizations of the future need to be ambidextrous learning organizations.

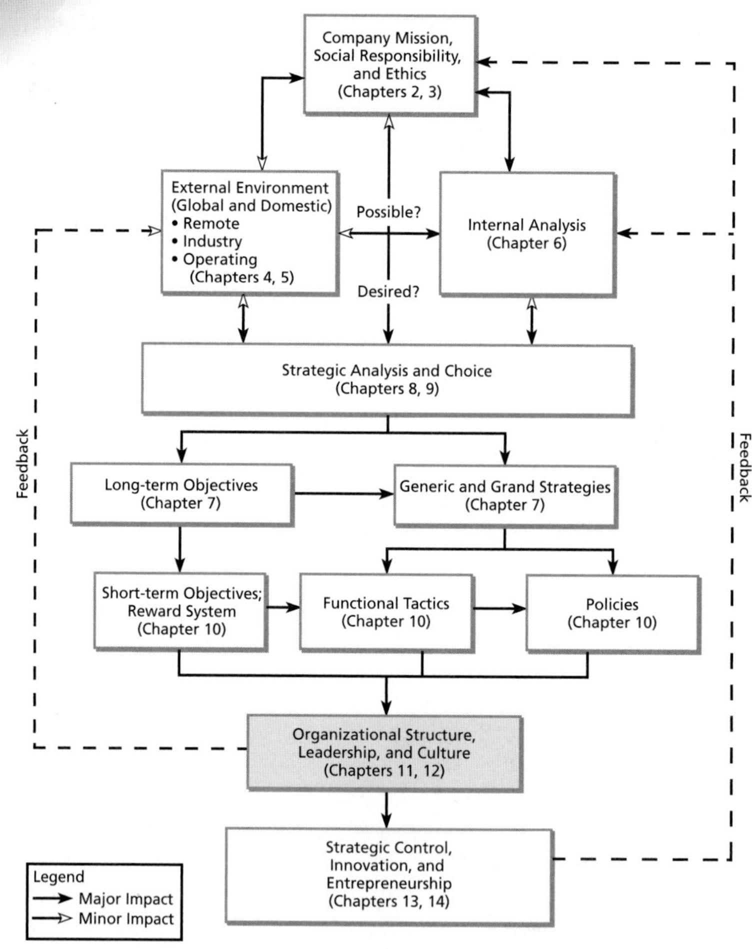

The implementation process is initiated through the creation of action plans detailing tactics and actions to be taken that initiate long-term strategies through the work of the organization. Getting that work done involves a simple but nonetheless serious and sometimes contentious question about the organization's structure—how can we best get the work of the business done efficiently and effectively so as to make the chosen strategy work?

The core question is: What is the best way to organize people, tasks, and resources to execute the strategy most effectively? A simple question, but one that demands other questions as its answer will usually be the key determinant of the effectiveness by which the organization accomplishes its mission. Questions like: What changes in how we are currently organized might improve our success? Should we organize around our product lines, or would doing so geographically make us more responsive to regional or international differences? Is it mission-critical to keep some specific activities "in-house," in one location or at the corporate level? Are there activities better "outsourced," even though we will lose control of the underlying skill set and expertise over time? With the rapid growth we are projecting, how can we design or redesign our organization to ensure better coordination between sales and manufacturing or operations so as to avoid problems arising with new customers unfamiliar with our product or service? Logic says we should combine several product groupings into one division with similar customer characteristics, but that necessitates changing the way several product groups have been organized and done good work for many years. Will that cause serious problems or resistance? How can we reorganize the way in which remote teams communicate with their functional home bases to get quick decisions before team solutions are implemented with the customers they are serving in regions halfway around the world?

These are but the tip of the iceberg of the types of questions arising every day in most organizations as they come to grips with the question of how to organize the work done on behalf of a business on behalf of its customers so as to create profitable, lasting value. Organizational structure can seem a rather boring notion, but it is far from that. It is the setting for enabling the energy of the people and capabilities and excellence a company has available to come together in a meaningful, profitable, exciting manner.

What happened at Hewlett-Packard over the last decade provides an interesting example of just these kinds of questions, issues, and outcomes. Let's look at that story before jumping into the ideas about organizational structures and ways to use them to improve strategy implementation. It gives you a recent history, some of which you may have witnessed or read about, that shows how important organizational structure usually is in helping a strategy succeed or falter.

The last decade began with an exciting development at Hewlett-Packard. In the midst of a global recession, Carly Fiorina left AT&T's Lucent to become HP's new twenty-first-century CEO. The unfortunate reality for her: HP's lumbering organization was losing touch with its global customers. Her team's response as illustrated in Exhibit 11.1, Global Strategy in Action, was to immediately dismantle the decentralized structure honed throughout HP's 64-year history. Pre-Fiorina, HP had been a collection of 83 independently run units, each focused on a product such as scanners or security software. The new structure sought to collapse those 83 units into four sprawling organizations. One so-called "back-end" unit developed and built computers; another focused on printers and imaging equipment. The "back-end" divisions were to hand products off to the two "front-end" sales and marketing groups to sell all HP products—one to consumers, the other to corporations. The theory: the new structure would boost collaboration, giving sales and marketing managers a direct pipeline to engineers so products were developed from the ground up to solve customer problems. This was the first time a company with thousands of product lines and scores of

Global Strategy in Action

Exhibit 11.1

HP's Search for the Best Organizational Structure

When the Fiorina team arrived at HP, the company was a confederation of 83 autonomous product units reporting through four groups. They radically revamped the structure into two "back-end" divisions—one developing printers, scanners, and the like, and the other computers. These report to "front-end" groups that market and sell HP's wares. Here's how the overhaul went:

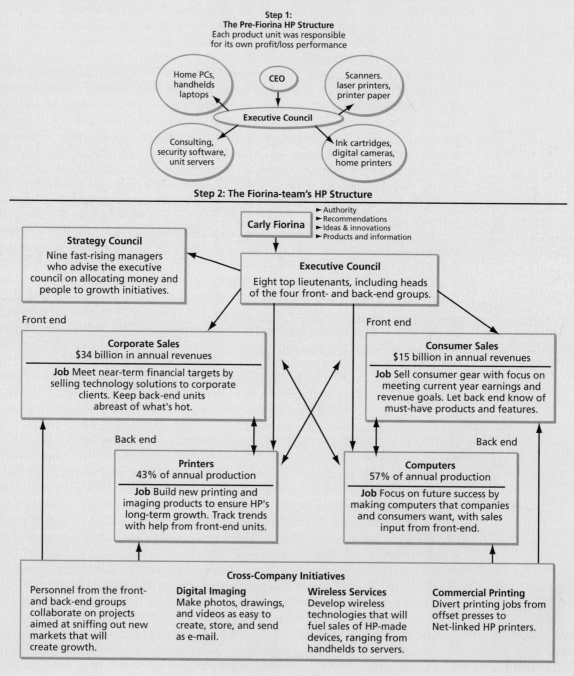

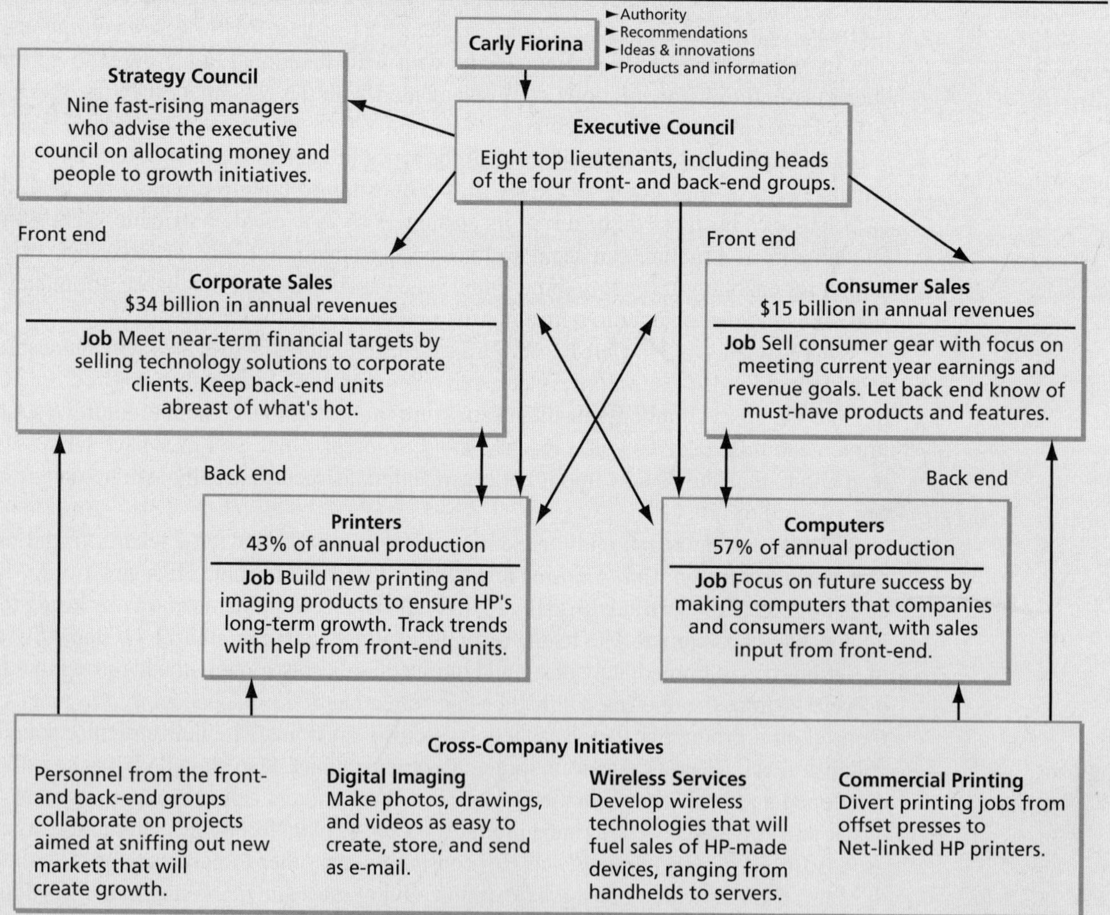

businesses attempted a "front-back" approach, a structure that requires laser focus and superb coordination.

Fiorina's team believed they had little choice lest the company experience a near-death experience like Xerox or, 10 years earlier, IBM. The conundrum: how could HP put the full force of the company behind winning in its immediate fiercely competitive technology business when they must also cook up brand-new megamarkets? It was a riddle Fiorina's team felt could only be solved by sweeping structural change that would allow HP to pursue a strategy focused on the next stage of the twenty-first-century technology revolution—companies latching onto the Internet to transform their operations. At its core lay a conviction that HP must become "ambidextrous and boundaryless," excelling at short-term execution while pursuing long-term visions that created new markets.

Did it work? No. After five years had passed, the chairman of the HP board of directors, Patricia Dunn, said at that time that the board did not intend to change HP's strategy. She indicated that the board was confident in HP's overall strategy even though, she acknowledged, several analysts and stockholders disagreed with the board on this. Confident that the strategy was correct, she indicated that the HP board concluded it had been execution of that strategy, particularly with regard to the "new" HP organizational structure, that the board felt was a major contributor to the lack of success at HP. So, Dunn said, the board wanted to bring on a new CEO and executive team to solve the "execution" problem. Two months later, Mark Hurd, a 25-year veteran of NCR's sprawling portfolio of businesses, became HP's new chief executive.

This new executive team had distinguished itself by turning around NCR over the previous two years by cutting costs and tightening marketing and increasing accountability. Their NCR turnaround produced eight consecutive profitable quarters at NCR. Their organizational structure preference—smaller independently run units, each with a narrow product focus—allowed a clear sense of responsibilities, measurable accountability, tight spending controls, and the ability to execute by controlling their units' production-to-sales activities.

Did it work? Yes. HP's return to smaller, semi-autonomous units led to improved effectiveness in sales growth and profitability over the next five years, culminating in HP becoming the world's largest computer company, among other things. Now, a new executive team, led by Leo Apothelar, is in charge at HP. It appears that choice is in part to add leadership in innovative enterprise software, to increase the software and services side of HP's success with its strategy to be a major IT solutions provider to a global customer base. In so doing, it appears for now this new team has chosen to retain the same decentralized organizational structure. That structure helped HP become the world's largest computer company, or what they now describe as the world's largest "information technology" company, seemingly to imply comparable software leadership in the future too.[1]

The HP story is one we select for you to read about because it shows you a well-known global company dealing with its organizational structure as a key means to implement a very logical long-term strategy built upon proven core competencies. Exhibit 11.2 offers a summary of the reasons and expectations that led the initial Fiorina-led team to pursue the "back-end/front-end" structure and the outcomes that resulted from that structure. It would appear, in their decision to abandon this new structure and return to a structure more closely resembling the earlier structure, that HP's strategy is better implemented by a combination of numerous semi-autonomous units producing and selling to target customers; yet with a greater emphasis on operational efficiency monitored aggressively at the unit and corporate level.

[1] www.hp.com

Global Strategy in Action — Exhibit 11.2

The Outcome with the "New" HP Structure and the Resulting Step #3 HP Structure

The New HP Structure Assumptions/Expectations

Happier Customers Clients should find HP easier to deal with, since they'll work with just one account team.

Sales Boost HP should maximize its selling opportunities because account reps will sell all HP products, not just those from one division.

Real Solutions HP can sell its products in combination as "solutions"—instead of just PCs or printers—to companies facing e-business problems.

Financial Flexibility With all corporate sales under one roof, HP can measure the total value of a customer, allowing reps to discount some products and still maximize profits on the overall contract.

Cross-Functional Team Innovation Teams formed by members of "front-end" and "back-end" functions will pursue projects that will quickly identify new opportunities that will create future growth.

What Actually Happened in the New Structure over the Next Five Years

Overwhelmed with Duties With so many products being made and sold by just four units, HP execs had more on their plates and missed the details that keep products competitive.

Poorer Execution When product managers oversaw everything from manufacturing to sales, they could respond quickly to changes. That was harder with front- and back-end groups synching their plans only every few weeks.

Less Accountability Profit-and-loss responsibility is shared between the front- and back-end groups so no one person is on the hot seat. Finger-pointing and foot-dragging replaced HP's collegial cooperation.

Fewer Spending Controls With powerful division chiefs keeping a tight rein on the purse strings, spending rarely got out of hand in the old HP. In the fourth quarter, expenses soared as those lines of command broke down.

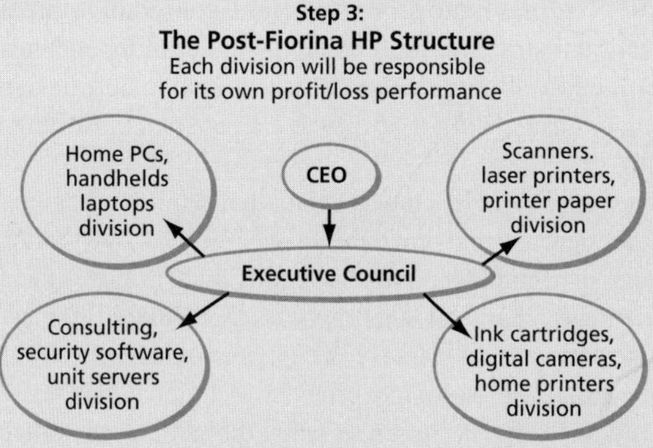

The HP search for the right structure to implement its very appropriate long-term strategy highlights the need for more "openness" in an organizational structure—a "boundaryless" organization as we will discuss in this chapter, but also the importance of coordination and control of the organization's performance and execution of strategy through its structure. In some ways the new structure chosen by the Fiorina executive team better reflected the way twenty-first century organizations are seeking to modernize themselves, while the subsequent structure the HP board approved moving back to was a return to a more traditional organization. This latter approach found success because it combined attributes of traditional organizational structures and those of newer, boundaryless or virtual organization approaches in an effort to balance a need for control, coordination, openness, and innovation in implementing a strategy best suited to HP's situation.

Today's fast-changing, global economy demands ever-increasing productivity, speed, and flexibility from companies that seek to survive, perhaps thrive. To do so, companies must change their organizational structures dramatically, retaining the best of their traditional (hierarchical) structures while embracing radically new structures that leverage the value of the people who generate ideas, collaborate with colleagues and customers, innovate and therein generate future value for the company. So this chapter seeks to familiarize you with both perspectives on organizational structure and the major trends in structuring business organizations today. Let's start by looking at what have been traditional ways to organize, along with the advantages and disadvantages of each organizational structure.

TRADITIONAL ORGANIZATIONAL STRUCTURES AND THEIR STRATEGY-RELATED PROS AND CONS

You may be one of several students who choose to start your own business rather than take a job with an established company when you finish your current degree program. Or perhaps you are currently in a full-time job position but soon plan to leave that job and start your own company. Like millions of others who have done or will soon do the same thing, usually with a few other "partners," your group will be faced with the question of how to organize your work and the activities and tasks necessary to do the work of your new company. What you are looking for is an organizational structure. We do not mean, here, the "legal" structure of your company such as a proprietorship, corporation, limited liability corporation, or limited partnership to mention a few. **Organizational structure** refers to the formalized arrangement of interaction between and responsibility for the tasks, people, and resources in an organization. It is most often seen as a chart, often a pyramidal chart, with positions or titles and roles in cascading fashion. The organizational structure you and your partners would have in this start-up of which you are a part would most likely be a "simple" organization.

organizational structure
Refers to the formalized arrangements of interaction between and responsibility for the tasks, people, and resources in an organization.

Simple Organizational Structure

simple organizational structure
Structure in which there is an owner and a few employees and where the arrangement of tasks, responsibilities, and communication is highly informal and accomplished through direct supervision.

In the smallest business enterprise, a simple structure usually prevails. A **simple organizational structure** is one where there is an owner and, usually, a few employees and where the arrangement of tasks, responsibilities, and communication is highly informal and accomplished through direct supervision. All strategic and operating decisions are made by the owner, or a small owner-partner team. Because the scope of the firm's activities are modest, there is little need to formalize roles, communication, and procedures. With the strategic concern primarily being survival, and the likelihood that one bad decision could seriously threaten continued existence, this structure maximizes the owner's control. It can also allow rapid response to product/market shifts and the ability to accommodate unique customer demands without major coordination difficulties. This is in part because the owner is directly involved with customers on a regular basis. Simple structures encourage employees to multitask, and they are efficacious in businesses that serve a simple, local product/market or narrow niche.

The simple structure can be very demanding on the owner-manager. If it is successful, and starts to grow, this can cause the owner-manager to give increased attention to day-to-day concerns, which may come at the expense of time invested in stepping back and examining strategic questions about the company's future. At the same time, the company's reliance on the owner as the central point for all decisions can limit the development of future managers capable of assuming duties that allow the owner time to be a strategist. And, this structure usually requires a multitalented, resourceful owner, good at producing and selling a product or service—and at controlling scarce funds.

Most businesses in this country and around the world are of this type. Many survive for a period of time, then go out of business because of financial, owner, or market conditions. Some grow, having been built on an idea or capability that taps a great need for what the company does. As they grow, the need to "get organized" is increasingly heard among owners and a growing number of employees in the growing company. That fortunate circumstance historically led to the need for a functional organizational structure.

Functional Organizational Structure

Continuing our example, you and your partners, no doubt being among the successful ones, find increased demand for your product or service. Your sales have grown substantially—and so have the number of people you employ to do the work of your business. Once you reach 15 to 25 people in the organization, you will experience a need to have some people handle sales, some operations, a financial accounting person or two—that is, you will need to have different people focus on different functions within the business to become better organized and efficient, and to achieve control and coordination. A **functional organizational structure** is one in which the tasks, people, and technologies necessary to do the work of the business are divided into separate "functional" groups (such as marketing, operations, finance) with increasingly formal procedures for coordinating and integrating their activities to provide the business's products and services.

functional organizational structure
Structure in which the tasks, people, and technologies necessary to do the work of the business are divided into separate "functional" groups (e.g., marketing, operations, finance) with increasingly formal procedures for coordinating and integrating their activities to provide the business's products and services.

Functional structures predominate in firms with a single or narrow product focus and that have experienced success in their marketplace, leading to increased sales and an increased number of people needed to do the work behind those sales. Such firms require well-defined skills and areas of specialization to build competitive advantages in providing their products or services. Dividing tasks into functional specialties enables the personnel of these firms to concentrate on only one aspect of the necessary work. This allows use of the latest technical skills and develops a high level of efficiency.

Product, customer, or technology considerations determine the identity of the parts in a functional structure. A hotel business might be organized around housekeeping (maids), the front desk, maintenance, restaurant operations, reservations and sales, accounting, and personnel. An equipment manufacturer might be organized around production, engineering/quality control, purchasing, marketing, personnel, and finance/accounting. Two examples of functional organizations are illustrated in Exhibit 11.3.

The strategic challenge presented by the functional structure is effective coordination of the functional units. The narrow technical expertise achieved through specialization can lead to limited perspectives and to differences in the priorities of the functional units. Specialists may see the firm's strategic issues primarily as "marketing" problems or "production" problems. The potential conflict among functional units makes the coordinating role of the chief executive critical. Integrating devices (such as project teams or planning committees) are frequently used in functionally organized firms to enhance coordination and to facilitate understanding across functional areas.

Divisional Structure

When a firm diversifies its product/service lines, covers broad geographic areas, utilizes unrelated market channels, or begins to serve heterogeneous customer groups, a functional structure rapidly becomes inadequate. If a functional structure is retained under these circumstances, production managers may have to oversee the production of numerous and varied products or services, marketing managers may have to create sales programs

EXHIBIT 11.3
Functional Organization Structures

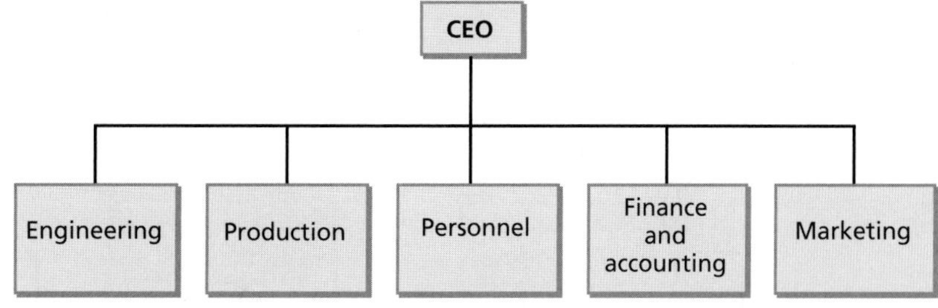

A process-oriented functional structure (an electronics distributor):

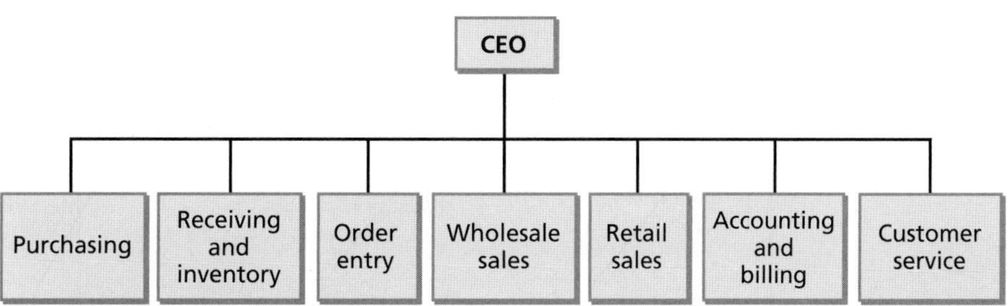

Strategic Advantages	Strategic Disadvantages
1. Achieves efficiency through specialization	1. Promotes narrow specialization and functional rivalry or conflict
2. Develops functional expertise	2. Creates difficulties in functional coordination and interfunctional decision making
3. Differentiates and delegates day-to-day operating decisions	3. Limits development of general managers
4. Retains centralized control of strategic decisions	4. Has a strong potential for interfunctional conflict—priority placed on functional areas, not the entire business
5. Tightly links structure to strategy by designating key activities as separate units	5. May cost more to do a function than it does "outside" the company, unless outsourced

divisional organizational structure
Structure in which a set of relatively autonomous units, or divisions, are governed by a central corporate office but where each operating division has its own functional specialists who provide products or services different from those of other divisions.

for vastly different products or sell through vastly different distribution channels, and top management may be confronted with excessive coordination demands. A new organizational structure is often necessary to meet the increased coordination and decision-making requirements that result from increased diversity and size, and the divisional structure is the form often chosen.

A **divisional organizational structure** is one in which a set of relatively autonomous units, or divisions, are governed by a central corporate office but where each operating division has its own functional specialists who provide products or services different from those of other divisions. For many years, global automobile companies have used divisional structures organized by product groups. Manufacturers often organize sales into divisions based on differences in distribution channels.

A divisional structure allows corporate management to delegate authority for the strategic management of distinct business entities—the division. This expedites decision making

EXHIBIT 11.4
Divisional Organization Structure

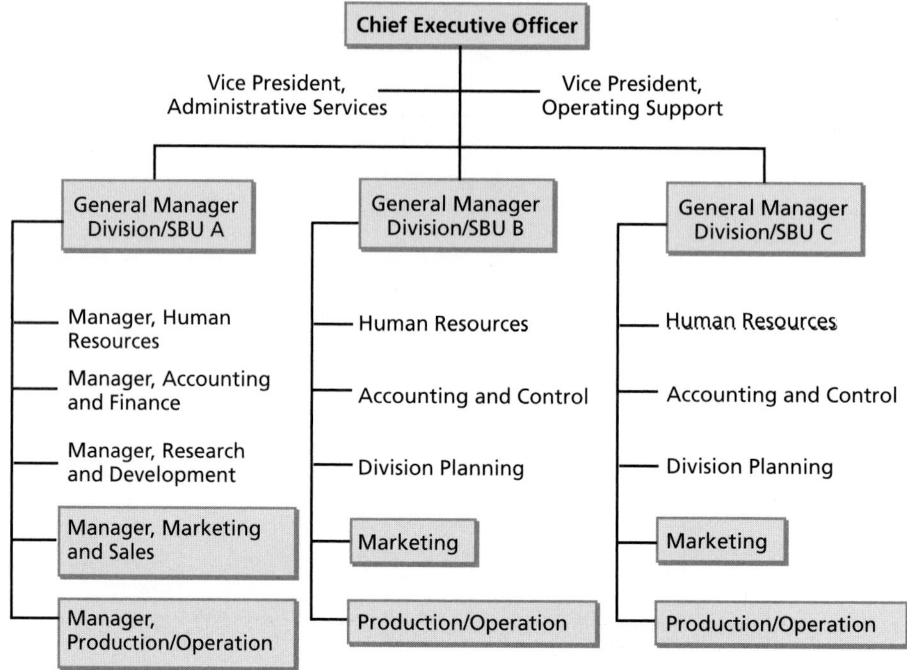

Strategic Advantages	Strategic Disadvantages
1. Forces coordination and necessary authority down to the appropriate level for rapid response	1. Fosters potentially dysfunctional competition for corporate-level resources
2. Places strategy development and implementation in closer proximity to the unique environments of the division	2. Presents the problem of determining how much authority should be given to division managers
3. Frees chief executive officer for broader strategic decision making	3. Creates a potential for policy inconsistencies among divisions
4. Sharply focuses accountability for performance	4. Presents the problem of distributing corporate overhead costs in a way that's acceptable to division managers with profit responsibility
5. Retains functional specialization within each division	5. Increases costs incurred through duplication functions
6. Provides good training ground for strategic managers	6. Creates difficulty maintaining overall corporate image
7. Increases focus on products, markets, and quick response to change	

in response to varied competitive environments and enables corporate management to concentrate on corporate-level strategic decisions. The division usually is given profit responsibility, which facilitates accurate assessment of profit and loss. Exhibit 11.4 illustrates a divisional organizational structure and specifies the strategic advantages and disadvantages of such structures.

Strategic Business Unit

Some firms encounter difficulty in controlling their divisional operations as the diversity, size, and number of these units continues to increase. Corporate management may encounter difficulty in evaluating and controlling its numerous, often multi-industry divisions. Under these conditions, it may become necessary to add another layer of management in order to improve implementation, promote synergy, and gain greater control over the diverse business interests. The **strategic business unit** (SBU) is an adaptation of the divisional structure whereby various divisions or parts of divisions are grouped together based on some common strategic elements, usually linked to distinct product/market differences. General Foods, after originally organizing itself along product lines (which served overlapping markets), created an SBU organization along menu lines with SBUs for breakfast foods, beverages, main meals, desserts, and pet foods. This change allowed General Foods to adapt a vast divisional organization into five strategic business areas with a distinct market focus for each unit and the divisions each contained.

strategic business unit
An adaptation of the divisional structure in which various divisions or parts of divisions are grouped together based on some common strategic elements, usually linked to distinct product/market differences.

The advantages and disadvantages of the SBU form are very similar to those identified for divisional structures in Exhibit 11.4. Added to its potential disadvantages would be the increased costs of coordination with another "pricy" level of management. Exhibit 11.5, Global Strategy in Action, describes how two companies you may recognize made key changes in their divisional structures in order to improve their strategy execution. Dell twice changed from a geographically focused divisional structure to a customer-type divisional structure to be able to improve its sales response. Nortel abandoned a long used matrix organizational structure in favor of a strategic business unit structure so as to maximize the value generated as it implemented a bankruptcy strategy.

Holding Company

A final form of the divisional organization is the **holding company structure,** where the corporate entity is a broad collection of often unrelated businesses and divisions such that it (the corporate entity) acts as financial overseer "holding" the ownership interest in the various parts of the company but has little direct managerial involvement. Berkshire Hathaway owns a wide variety of businesses in full or in part. Essentially, at the corporate level, it provides financial support and manages each of these businesses, or divisions, through financial goals and annual review of performance, investment needs, and so forth. Otherwise, strategic and operating decisions are made in each separate company or division, which operates autonomously. The corporate office acts simply as a holding company.

holding company structure
Structure in which the corporate entity is a broad collection of often unrelated businesses and divisions such that it (the corporate entity) acts as financial overseer "holding" the ownership interest in the various parts of the company, but has little direct managerial involvement.

This approach can provide a cost savings over the more active SBU approach since the additional level of "pricy" management is not that much. The negative, of course, becomes the degree to which the corporate office is dependent on each business unit's management team and the lack of control over the decisions those managers make in terms of being able to make timely adjustments or corrections.

Matrix Organizational Structure

In large companies, increased diversity leads to numerous product and project efforts of major strategic significance. The result is a need for an organizational form that provides skills and resources where and when they are most vital. For example, a product development project needs a market research specialist for two months and a financial analyst one day per week. A customer site application needs a software engineer for one month and a customer service trainer one day per month for six weeks. Each of these situations is an example of a matrix organization that has been used to temporarily put people and resources where they are most

Global Strategy in Action — Exhibit 11.5

Changing Organizational Structures to Better Implement a Company's Strategy

Dell Computer founder and newly returned CEO Michael Dell decided to reorganize the side of Dell that sold to business customers, saying that "customer requirements are increasingly being defined by how they use technology rather than where they use it. That's why we won't let ourselves be limited by geographic boundaries in solving their needs."

So, at that point, Dell changed its structure from three distinct business units focused geographically—Asia, the Americas, and Europe (including Africa and the Middle East)—to a product/service-based organizational structure focused on distinct types of business customers, regardless of their geographic location. Said Dell, "We are in a transition from a global business that's run regionally to distinct business units that are globally organized." That structure had three distinct units—a large enterprise unit, public unit, and small-to-medium-sized business unit.

Three years later, Dell acquired Perot Systems as part of a growing trend in its industry with traditional hardware companies seeking to become IT/system service providers. The result was that Dell announced a revised organizational structure. It integrated Perot Systems into a more robust Dell Services business unit, comprised of over 43,000 employees in 90 countries; it combined Public and Large Enterprises into one globally focused business unit solving hardware and system needs of large businesses and governments; then combined its consumer business with its small-to-medium business focus to comprise a third business unit. Each change was described as an effort to increase efficiency, but more importantly, to improve its focus in implementing a new strategy designed to better focus on targeted customer groups and/or their specific needs.

Nortel, born out of Canadian Alexander G. Bell's invention of the telephone in 1874, was a global innovator in telecommunications for 135 years until it ran into a need for bankruptcy protection in 2009. Its strategy in bankruptcy was to salvage maximum value for creditors and shareholders. Step one in doing so was to reorganize the company so as to create distinct, independently operating units, making them more easily sold to potential acquirers and preserving both value and jobs of the many talented Nortel employees. CEO Mike Zafirovski decided it best to abandon the legacy matrix structure in favor of a strategic business unit structure to best implement that strategy. He said that by having discrete business units and eliminating the complex matrix organization, which Nortel had used for a long time, these independent business units could make quicker decisions, optimize their processes, and adjust technology and market strategy far faster than before. That structure in turn made it much easier, and more valuable, to implement a strategy in bankruptcy of obtaining the greatest value in selling off parts of one of the greatest companies to be born in North America. By 2012, Nortel completed the sale of all its business units, as well as a final stalking horse sale* of its portfolio of over 6,000 patents related to 4G, wireless technologies, and so forth to Google for just less than $1 billion.

* A "stalking horse sale" is an attempt by a bankruptcy *debtor* to test the market in advance of an auction of certain of its assets. The intent is to maximize the value of these *assets* as part of (or before) a *bankruptcy* court–approved *auction* process. See http://en.wikipedia.org/wiki/Stalking_horse_offer.

Source: www.dell.com; "Dell Expands Dell Services, Consolidates Public and Large Enterprise Business Units," Jan. 13, 2011.

matrix organizational structure
The matrix organization is a structure in which functional and staff personnel are assigned to both a basic functional area and to a project or product manager. It provides dual channels of authority, performance responsibility, evaluation, and control.

needed. Siemens, Infosys, Microsoft, IBM, Procter & Gamble (P&G), and Accenture are just a few of many firms that now use some form of matrix organization.

The **matrix organizational structure** is one in which functional and staff personnel are assigned to both a basic functional area and to a project or product manager. It provides dual channels of authority, performance responsibility, evaluation, and control, as shown in Exhibit 11.6. The matrix form is intended to make the best use of talented people within a firm by combining the advantages of functional specialization and product-project specialization.

The matrix structure also increases the number of middle managers who exercise general management responsibilities (through the project manager role) and, thus, broaden their exposure to organizationwide strategic concerns. In this way, the matrix structure overcomes a key deficiency of functional organizations while retaining the advantages of functional specialization.

EXHIBIT 11.6
Matrix Organizational Structure

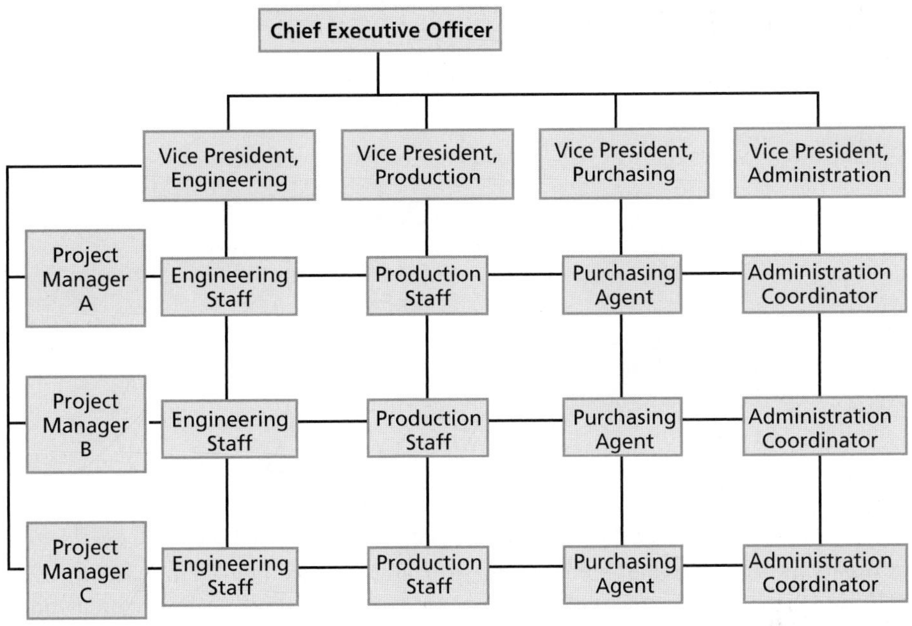

Strategic Advantages	Strategic Disadvantages
1. Accommodates a wide variety of project-oriented business activities	1. May result in confusion and contradictory policies
2. Provides good training ground for strategic managers	2. Necessitates tremendous horizontal and vertical coordination
3. Maximizes efficient use of functional managers	3. Can proliferate information logjams and excess reporting
4. Fosters creativity and multiple sources of diversity	4. Can trigger turf battles and loss of accountability
5. Gives middle management broader exposure to strategic issues	

Although the matrix structure is easy to design, it is difficult to implement. Dual chains of command challenge fundamental organizational orientations. Negotiating shared responsibilities, the use of resources, and priorities can create misunderstanding or confusion among subordinates. These problems are heightened in an international context with the complications introduced by distance, language, time, and culture. Exhibit 11.5, Strategy in Action, also describes how Nortel had to abandon its matrix structure in favor of an SBU approach due to just these kinds of problems as it sought to better implement a bankruptcy strategy that sought to maximize creditor and shareholder value.

Product-Team Structure

To avoid the deficiencies that might arise from a permanent matrix structure, some firms are accomplishing particular strategic tasks, by means of a "temporary" or "flexible" *overlay structure.* This approach, used recently by such firms as Motorola, Matsushita, Philips, and Unilever, is meant to take *temporary* advantage of a matrix-type team while preserving an

EXHIBIT 11.7
The Product-Team Structure

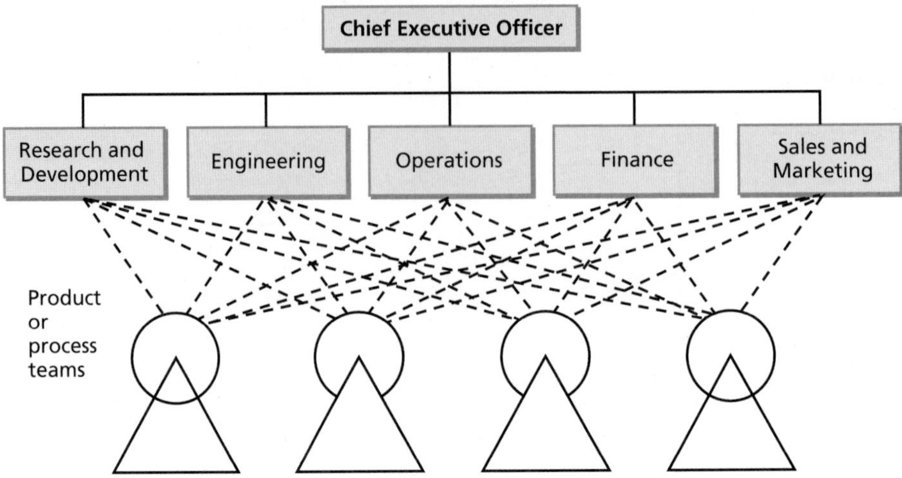

product-team structure
Assigns functional managers and specialists to a new product, project, or process team that is empowered to make major decisions about their product. Team members are assigned permanently in most cases.

underlying divisional structure. This adaptation of the matrix approach has become known as the "product-team structure." The **product-team structure** seeks to simplify and amplify the focus of resources on a narrow but strategically important product, project, market, customer, or innovation. Exhibit 11.7 illustrates how the product-team structure looks.

The product-team structure assigns functional managers and specialists (e.g., engineering, marketing, financial, R&D, operations) to a new product, project, or process team that is empowered to make major decisions about their product. The team is usually created at the inception of the new-product idea, and they stay with it indefinitely if it becomes a viable business. Instead of being assigned on a temporary basis, as in the matrix structure, team members are assigned permanently to that team in most cases. This results in much lower coordination costs and, because every function is represented, usually reduces the number of management levels above the team level needed to approve team decisions.

It appears that product teams formed at the beginning of product-development processes generate cross-functional understanding that irons out early product or process design problems. They also reduce costs associated with design, manufacturing, and marketing, while typically speeding up innovation and customer responsiveness because authority rests with the team allowing decisions to be made more quickly. That ability to make speedier, cost-saving decisions has the added advantage of eliminating the need for one or more management layers above the team level, which would traditionally have been in place to review and control these types of decisions. While seemingly obvious, it has only recently become apparent that those additional management layers were also making these decisions with less firsthand understanding of the issues involved than the cross-functional team members brought to the product or process in the first place. Exhibit 11.8, Global Strategy in Action, gives examples of a product-team approach at two well-known companies and some of the advantages that appear to have accrued.

THE NEW MILLENNIUM

Exhibit 11.9 offers a useful perspective for designing effective organizational structures in today's global economy. In contrasting twentieth- and twenty-first-century corporations on different characteristics, it offers a historical or evolutionary perspective on organizational attributes associated with successful strategy execution today and just a few years ago. Successful organizations once required an internal focus, structured interaction,

Global Strategy in Action — Exhibit 11.8

Cross-Functional Teams Add Value in Implementing a Company's Strategy

Monsanto CEO Hugh Grant took over Monsanto when it was a chemical conglomerate, selling for $10 per share. Five years later, it had become a global leading producer of biotech seeds. Within the first 100 days at Monsanto, Grant's management team made the decision to reduce staff and product lines in its chemicals businesses and redirect resources to the new but still unprofitable biotech seeds business. Furthermore, they decided to abandon wheat and focus on corn, soybeans, and cotton. All were very risky bets.

To help enable this transformation of Monsanto to more high-tech, fast-changing lines of business, Grant introduced the extensive use of cross-functional teams. These teams would draw on people from five or six different functional specialties within Monsanto and focus on a specific problem related to new seeds, markets, or similar issues. That structure accelerated to an ability to commercialize the newest seed technologies, ultimately becoming a strategic advantage at Monsanto Formerly an agriculture chemical company before Hugh Grant and his cross-funtional teams, Monsanto enters 2013 as the world's largest seed company for four years running. Much of that success is attributed to Grant's aggressive strategic bet and the organizational structure of cross-functional teams in implementing it from the beginning.

IBM uses cross-functional teams consisting of hundreds of people to implement its new Smart Planet strategy. These teams are constantly being combined, dismantled and reconfigured to work on anything from the Stockholm traffic system to a smart electric grid for the island of Malta. This constant assembly and disassembly of cross-functional teams is commonplace at IBM. Responding to the complexity of a global economy, IBM has returned to a functional structure and assembles teams to address all dimensions, whether they are products, countries, new businesses, or Smart Planet solutions. IBM can then restructure itself around any dimension.* Bentley College business graduate turned **IBM** Workplace Domain Engineer Sally McSwiney is a prime example of IBM's extensive use of cross-functional teams to become more competitive in a global computer services marketplace. She said this about her role on a cross functional team: "As part of a cross-functional software product development team, I manage product requirements by working with clients, analysts, and experts to adapt the product and strengthen its position. I have regular meetings and discussions with my cross-functional team members located in North Carolina, Massachusetts, and China. And as external communicator for my team, I talk with customers, press, analysts—and provide product demos to audiences worldwide—regularly."**

* Jay Galbraith, "The Multi-Dimensional and Reconfigurable Organization," *Center for Effective Organizations* Working Paper, University of Southern California, May, 2010.
** "Always on the Go at Big Blue," *BusinessWeek*, May 17, 2007.

self-sufficiency, a top-down approach. Today and tomorrow, organizational structure reflects an external focus, flexible interaction, interdependency, and a bottom-up approach, just to mention a few characteristics associated with strategy execution and success. Three fundamental trends are driving decisions about effective organizational structures in the twenty-first century: globalization, the Internet, and speed of decision making.

Globalization

Pulitzer Prize–winning author Thomas Friedman[2] described the first 10 years of the twenty-first century as "Globalization 3.0." This, he says, is a whole new era in which the world is shrinking from a size "small" to a size "tiny" and flattening the global playing field for everyone at the same time. He describes it as follows:

> Globalization 1.0 was countries globalizing;
> Globalization 2.0 was companies globalizing;
> Globalization 3.0 is the newfound power for *individuals*
> To collaborate and compete globally, instantly;

[2] Thomas L. Friedman, *The World Is Flat* (New York: Farrar, Straus and Giroux, 2005).

EXHIBIT 11.9
What a Difference a Century Can Make

Source: From "21st Century Companies," *BusinessWeek*. Reprinted from August 28, 2000 issue of *BusinessWeek* by special permission. Copyright © 2000 by The McGraw-Hill Companies, Inc.

Contrasting Views of the Corporation

Characteristic	20th Century	21st Century
Organization	The pyramid	The Web or network
Focus	Internal	External
Style	Structured	Flexible
Source of strength	Stability	Change
Structure	Self-sufficiency	Interdependencies
Resources	Atoms—physical assets	Bits—information
Operations	Vertical integration	Virtual integration
Products	Mass production	Mass customization
Reach	Domestic	Global
Financials	Quarterly	Real time
Inventories	Months	Hours
Strategy	Top-down	Bottom-up
Leadership	Dogmatic	Inspirational
Workers	Employees	Employees and free agents
Job expectations	Security	Personal growth
Motivation	To compete	To build
Improvements	Incremental	Revolutionary
Quality	Affordable best	No compromise

Individuals from every corner of the flat world are
Being empowered to enter a wide open, global marketplace.[3]

This means that companies in virtually every industry either operate globally (e.g., computers, aerospace) or will soon do so. In the past 20 years, the percentage of sales from outside the home market for these five companies grew dramatically:

	1995	2000	2005	2010	2015 est.
General Electric	16%	35%	41%	55%	75%
Walmart	0	14	22	32	50
McDonald's	46	65	71	75	80
Siemens	53	62	75	85	90
Toyota	44	53	61	75	85

The need for global coordination and innovation is forcing constant experimentation and adjustment to get the right mix of local initiative, information flow, leadership, and corporate culture. At Swedish-based Ericsson, top managers scrutinize compensation schemes to make managers pay attention to global performance and avoid turf battles, while also attending to their local operations. Companies such as Dutch electronics giant Philips regularly move headquarters for different businesses to the hottest regions for new trends—the "high voltage" markets. Its TV and home theater business is now in California; its audio business moved from Europe to Hong Kong.[4]

[3] Ibid, p. 10.

[4] www.philips.com.

Global once meant selling goods in overseas markets. Next was locating operations in numerous countries. Today companies will call on talents and resources wherever they can be found around the globe, just as they now sell worldwide. Such companies may be based in the United States, do their software programming in New Delhi, their engineering in Germany, and their manufacturing in Indonesia. Philips, the Amsterdam-based health care, lighting, and consumer products company, has manufacturing sites in 28 countries and sales outlets in 150 countries and is one of the largest multinationals in China. And that is fast becoming the norm. The ramifications for organizational structures are revolutionary.

The Internet

The Net gives everyone in the organization, or working with it—from the lowest clerk to the CEO to any supplier or customer—the ability to access a vast array of information—instantaneously, from anywhere. Ideas, requests, and instructions zap around the globe in the blink of an eye. The Net allows the global enterprise with different functions, offices, and activities dispersed around the world to be seamlessly connected so that far-flung customers, employees, and suppliers can work together in real time. The result—coordination, communication, and decision-making functions are accomplished quickly and easily, making traditional organizational structures look slow, inefficient, and noncompetitive. Take www.speedtree.com, a South Carolina–based maker of virtual foliage for video games and movies, like the tree-intense movie *Avatar*. Its largest geographic niche market for inserting trees into new video games has become Korea, even though none of its personnel have ever been there. That was all accomplished via the Internet. The ramifications of the Internet for typical business functions and the organizational structures needed to carry them out are, once again, revolutionary.

Speed

Technology, or digitization, means removing human minds and hands from an organization's most routine tasks and replacing them with computers and networks. Digitizing everything from employee benefits to accounts receivable to product design cuts cost, time, and payroll, resulting in cost savings and vast improvements in speed. "Combined with the Internet, the speed of actions, deliberations, and information will increase dramatically," says Intel's Andy Grove. "You are going to see unbelievable speed and efficiencies," says Cisco's John Chambers, "with many companies about to increase productivity 20 percent to 40 percent per year." Leading-edge technologies will enable employees throughout the organization to seize opportunity as it arises. These technologies will allow employees, suppliers, and freelancers anywhere in the world to converse in numerous languages online without need for a translator to develop markets, new products, new processes. Again, the ramifications for organizational structures are revolutionary.

Whether technology assisted or not, globalization of business activity creates a potential velocity of decision making that challenges traditional hierarchical organizational structures. A company like Cisco, for example, may be negotiating 50 to 60 alliances at one time due to the nature of its diverse operations. The speed at which these negotiations must be conducted and decisions made requires a simple and accommodating organizational structure lest the opportunities may be lost.

Faced with these and other major trends, what are managers doing to structure effective organizations? Let's examine this question two ways. First, we will summarize some key ways managers are changing traditional organizational structures to make them more responsive to this new reality. Second, we will examine current ideas for creating agile, virtual organizations.

INITIAL EFFORTS TO IMPROVE THE EFFECTIVENESS OF TRADITIONAL ORGANIZATIONAL STRUCTURES

Major efforts to improve traditional organizational structures seek to reduce unnecessary control and focus on enhancing core competencies, reducing costs, and opening organizations more fully to outside involvement and influence. One key emphasis in large organizations has been corporate headquarters.

Redefine the Role of Corporate Headquarters from Control to Support and Coordination

The role of corporate management in multibusiness and multinational companies increasingly face a common dilemma: how can the resource advantages of a large company be exploited, while ensuring the responsiveness and creativity found in the small companies against which each of their businesses compete? This dilemma constantly presents managers with conflicting priorities or adjustments as corporate managers:[5]

- Rigorous financial controls and reporting enable cost efficiency, resource deployment, and autonomy across different units; flexible controls are conducive to responsiveness, innovation and "boundary spanning."
- Multibusiness companies historically gain advantage by exploiting resources and capabilities across different businesses and markets, yet competitive advantage in the future increasingly depends on the creation of new resources and capabilities.
- Aggressive portfolio management seeking maximum shareholder value is often best achieved through independent businesses; the creation of competitive advantage increasingly requires the management—recognition and coordination—of business interdependencies.

Increasingly, globally engaged, multibusiness companies are changing the role of corporate headquarters from one of control, resource allocation, and performance monitoring to one of coordinator of linkages across multiple businesses, supporter, and enabler of innovation and synergy. One way this has been done is to create an executive council comprised of top managers from each business, usually including four to five of their key managers, with the council then serving as the critical forum for corporate decision, discussions, and analysis. IBM's Sam Palmisano uses this approach today at IBM to cross-fertilize ideas and opportunities across its software, enterprise services, chip design, and now virtual world business activities. These councils replace the traditional corporate staff function of overseeing and evaluating various business units, replacing it instead with a forum to share business unit plans, to discuss problems and issues, to seek assistance and expertise, and to foster cooperation and innovation. Exhibit 11.10, Global Strategy in Action provides an example of the need for trade-offs in control versus coordination between a global corporate headquarters and a regional part of the same company.

John Chambers's experiment at Cisco provides a useful example. He realized that Cisco's hierarchical structure was precluding it from moving quickly into new markets, so he began to group executives like cross-functional teams. Chambers figured that putting together managers in sales and leaders in engineering would break down walls. It then expanded to be a means to replace corporate executives with "councils" or "boards"

[5] Robert M. Grant, *Contemporary Strategy Analysis* (Oxford: Blackwell, 2001), p. 503.

Global Strategy in Action — Exhibit 11.10

Toyota vs. Ford on Reexamining the Need for Control versus Coordination

Toyota's legendary safety challenges and eventual recalls that started with sticking accelerator pedals and went much further caused much pain for the "top quality" automobile global leader. When Jim Lentz, the American head of Toyota Motor Sales in North America, was called before a congressional committee about handling their defective automobiles, he testified under oath that he had no power to order the recall of a vehicle. Stating a longstanding fact of life at Toyota, Lentz had neither the authority nor the information to do so. Executives at other automakers were reportedly stunned. Said one top manager, "Jim Lentz saying the American management team had no say in recalls was the thing that surprised me the most. There was not a lot of cross-divisional communication."*

Toyota, some argue, has basically the same underlying functional organization it had when it first began selling cars in the United States over 50 years ago. None of its operations outside Japan are functionally integrated. Rather, they all—sales, engineering, manufacturing, and purchasing—report independently back to their functional chain of command in Japan. Some observers even reported action was delayed because of a power struggle between the powerful U.S. sales unit and other functional divisions of the global company. Lentz's predecessor, Jim Press, reportedly stepped down in 2007 after sensing he had become a "window worker," a Japanese term for an older employee with no responsibilities, when his requests to Toyota's board asking for the North American operation to be improved by strengthening communication with Toyota Motor Sales, Toyota Engineering and Manufacturing, and company headquarters in Japan were ignored.**

Meanwhile, Ford, long suffering under internal competition among executives across different functional and divisional fiefdoms as the company descended close to failing in the global recession, seemed to do just the opposite. New CEO Alan Mulally initiated weekly meetings, every Thursday, attended by all of his top functional managers, at which they were expected to share information. That way, when problems arose like a sticking accelerator or a dealership sales issue or a product design question, implications across different functions could be relayed and cooperation initiated so that a solution could be found that worked across functions more quickly. That balanced demand for integration while preserving relevant control is cited as a major reason for Ford's rebirth as a significant global automotive company once again.

* Alex Taylor III, "What's Really behind the Toyota Debacle," *Fortune*, April 14, 2010.

** Ibid.

composed of three to seven managers from various Cisco businesses and functional areas to quickly find synergies, opportunities, and expedite decisions.[6]

Balance the Demands for Control/Differentiation with the Need for Coordination/Integration

Specialization of work and effort allows a unit to develop greater expertise, focus, and efficiency. So it is that some organizations adopt functional, or similar, structures. Their strategy depends on dividing different activities within the firm into logical, common groupings—sales, operations, administration, or geography—so that each set of activities can be done most efficiently. Control of sets of activities is at a premium. Dividing activities in this manner, sometimes called "differentiation," is an important structural decision. At the same time, these separate activities, however they are differentiated, need to be coordinated and integrated back together as a whole so the business functions effectively. Demands for control and the coordination needs differ across different types of businesses

[6] "Cisco Systems Layers It On," *Fortune*, December 3, 2008.

and strategic situations. Exhibit 11.10, Global Strategy in Action provides an interesting contrast between how this need for control versus coordination led Toyota into a major, seemingly unnecessary safety-driven setback in North America while its crippled rival, Ford, switched to a more functionally integrative approach that led to its dramatic turnaround coming out of the recent global recession.

The rise of a consumer culture around the world has led brand marketers to realize they need to take a multidomestic approach to be more responsive to local preferences. Coca-Cola, for example, used to control its products rigidly from its Atlanta headquarters. But managers have found in some markets consumers thirst for more than Coke, Diet Coke, and Sprite. So Coke has altered its structure to reduce the need for control in favor of greater coordination/integration in local markets where local managers independently launch new flavored drinks. At the same time, GE, the paragon of new-age organization, had altered its GE Medical Systems organization structure to allow local product managers to handle everything from product design to marketing. This emphasis on local coordination and reduced central control of product design led managers obsessed with local rivalries to design and manufacture similar products for different markets—a costly and wasteful duplication of effort. So GE reintroduced centralized control of product design, with input from a worldwide base of global managers and their customers, resulting in the design of several single global products produced quite cost competitively to sell worldwide. GE's need for control of product design outweighed the coordination needs of locally focused product managers.[7] At the same time, GE obtained input from virtually every customer or potential customer worldwide before finalizing the product design of several initial products, suggesting that it rebalanced in favor of more control, but organizationally coordinated input from global managers and customers so as to ensure a better potential series of medical scanner for hospitals worldwide. Virtually all companies serving global markets face a similar organizational puzzle—how does the company integrate itself with diverse markets yet ensure adequate control and differentiation of internal units so that it executes profitably and effectively? We will examine some ways to do so later in this chapter.

Restructure to Emphasize and Support Strategically Critical Activities

restructuring
Redesigning an organizational structure with the intent of emphasizing and enabling activities most critical to a firm's strategy to function at maximum effectiveness.

Restructuring is redesigning an organizational structure with the intent of emphasizing and enabling activities most critical to the firm's strategy to function at maximum effectiveness. At the heart of the restructuring trend is the notion that some activities within a business's value chain are more critical to the success of the business's strategy than others. Walmart's organizational structure is designed to ensure that its impressive logistics and purchasing competitive advantages operate flawlessly. Coordinating daily logistical and purchasing efficiencies among separate stores lets Walmart lead the industry in profitability yet sell retail for less than many competitors buy the same merchandise at wholesale. Qualcomm's organizational structure is designed to protect and nurture its legendary R&D and new-product development capabilities—spending over twice the industry average in R&D alone each year. Qualcomm's R&D emphasis continually spawns proprietary technologies that support its technology-based competitive advantage. Coca-Cola emphasizes the importance of distribution activities, advertising, and retail support to its bottlers in its organizational structure. All three of these companies emphasize very different parts of the value chain process, but they are extraordinarily successful in part because they have designed their

[7] www.ge.com/ar2010/innovation.

organizational structures to emphasize and support strategically critical activities. Two developments that have become key ways many of these firms have sought to improve their emphasis and support of strategic activities are business process reengineering and downsizing/self-management.

business process reengineering
A customer-centric restructuring approach. It involves fundamental rethinking and radical redesigning of a business process so that a company can best create value for the customer by eliminating barriers that create distance between employees and customers.

Business process reengineering (BPR) was originally advocated by consultants Michael Hammer and James Champy[8] as a "customer-centric" restructuring approach. BPR is intended to place the decision-making authority that is most relevant to the customer closer to the customer, in order to make the firm more responsive to the needs of the customer. This is accomplished through a form of empowerment, facilitated by revamping organizational structure.

Business reengineering reduces fragmentation by crossing traditional departmental lines and reducing overhead to compress formerly separate steps and tasks that are strategically intertwined in the process of meeting customer needs. This "process orientation," rather than a traditional functional orientation, becomes the perspective around which various activities and tasks are then grouped to create the building blocks of the organization's structure. This is usually accomplished by assembling a multifunctional, multilevel team (the product-team approach discussed earlier) that begins by identifying customer needs and how the customer wants to deal with the firm. Customer focus must permeate all phases. Companies that have successfully reengineered their operations around strategically critical business processes have pursued the following steps:[9]

- Develop a flowchart of the total business process, including its interfaces with other value chain activities.
- Try to simplify the process first, eliminating tasks and steps where possible and analyzing how to streamline the performance of what remains.
- Determine which parts of the process can be automated (usually those that are repetitive, time-consuming, and require little thought or decision); consider introducing advanced technologies that can be upgraded to achieve next-generation capability and provide a basis for further productivity gains down the road.
- Evaluate each activity in the process to determine whether it is strategy-critical or not. Strategy-critical activities are candidates for benchmarking to achieve best-in-industry or best-in-world performance status—and ones to emphasize in reengineered organizational structures.
- Weigh the pros and cons of outsourcing activities that are noncritical or that contribute little to organizational capabilities and core competencies.
- Design a structure for performing the activities that remain; reorganize the personnel and groups who perform these activities into the new structure.

IBM provides a good example of reengineering. As globalization started to take hold in the world's economy, IBM was struggling to survive. To do so, it embraced reengineering—with efforts designed to simplify its enormous complexity associated with its highly decentralized organization. Said its CEO at the time, "It's called reengineering. It's called getting competitive. It's called reducing cycle time and cost, flattening organizations, increasing customer responsiveness. All of this requires close collaboration with the customer, with suppliers, and with vendors." That effort helped save IBM from a probably steady, PC-maker-based decline.

[8] Michael Hammer, *The Agenda* (New York: Random House, 2001); and Michael Hammer and James Champy, *Reengineering the Corporation* (New York: HarperBusiness, 1993).

[9] Alexis Leon, *ERP Demystified*, 2nd. ed. (New Delhi, India: Tata McGraw-Hill, 2008), pp. 99–208.

through efforts to create distinct businesses within a business—conceiving a business as a confederation of many "small" businesses, rather than one large, interconnected business. Whatever the terminology, the idea is to push decision making down in the organization by allowing major management decisions to be made at operating levels. The result is often the elimination of up to half the levels of management previously existing in an organizational structure.

CREATING AGILE, VIRTUAL ORGANIZATIONS

virtual organization
A temporary network of independent companies—suppliers, customers, subcontractors, and even competitors—linked primarily by information technology to share skills, access to markets, and costs.

agile organization
A firm that identifies a set of business capabilities central to high-profitability operations and then builds a virtual organization around those capabilities.

outsourcing
Obtaining work previously done by employees inside the companies from sources outside the company.

Corporations today are increasingly seeing their "structure" become an elaborate network of external and internal relationships. This organizational phenomenon has been termed the **virtual organization,** which is defined as a temporary network of independent companies—suppliers, customers, subcontractors, even competitors—linked primarily by information technology to share skills, access to markets, and costs.[11] An **agile organization** is one that identifies a set of business capabilities central to high-profitability operations and then builds a virtual organization around those capabilities, allowing the agile firm to build its business around the core, high-profitability information, services, and products. Creating an agile, virtual organization structure involves outsourcing, strategic alliances, a boundaryless structure, an ambidextrous learning approach, and Web-based organization. Let's examine each of the approaches to creating a virtual organization in more detail.

Outsourcing—Creating a Modular Organization

Outsourcing was an early driving force for the virtual organization trend. Dell does not make PCs. Cisco doesn't make its world renowned routers. Motorola doesn't make cell phones. **Outsourcing** is simply obtaining work previously done by employees inside the companies from sources outside the company. Managers have found that as they attempt to restructure their organizations, particularly if they do so from a business process orientation, numerous activities can often be found in their company that are not "strategically critical activities." This has particularly been the case with numerous staff activities and administrative control processes previously the domain of various middle management levels in an organization. But it can also refer to primary activities that are steps in their business's value chain—purchasing, shipping, manufacturing, and so on. Further scrutiny has led managers to conclude that these activities either add little or no value to the product or services, or that they can be done much more cost effectively (and competently) by other

[11] Early identification of the rise of the "virtual organization" was found in W. H. Davidow and M. S. Malone, *The Virtual Corporation* (New York: Harper, 1992); and Steven Goldman, *Agile Competitors and Virtual Organizations* (New York: Van Nostrand Reinhold, 1995). As virtual organizations have become mainstream, additional coverage of use for further reading can be found in books like Malcolm Warner and Morgen Witzel, *Managing in Virtual Organizations* (London: Thomson, 2008), *The Economist's* "The Virtual Organisation," Nov. 23, 2009; or research like Rene Algesheimer, Utpal M. Dholakia, and Calin Gurau, "Virtual Team Performance in a Highly Competitive Environment," *Group Organization Management* 36, no. 2 (March 15, 2011), pp. 161–190. It is interesting that NSF allocates research attention to evolving virtual organizations with a program called "VOSS: Virtual Organizations as Sociotechnical Systems," allocating $3 million for annual research; see NSF 09 Jan 2013 solicitation from its Office of Cyber Infrastructure; and, finally the focus on virtual organizations has become academic mainstream as evidenced by the University of Phoenix's use of "virtual organizations" as a way to customize business education as can be seen at: http://www.phoenix.edu/students/how-it-works/innovative_education_technology/virtual-organizations.html, 2012.

businesses specializing in these activities. If this is so, then the business can enhance its competitive advantage by outsourcing the activities.

modular organization
An organization structured via outsourcing where the organization's final product or service is based on the combination of several companies' self-contained skills and business capabilities.

Choosing to outsource activities has been likened to creating a "modular" organization. A **modular organization** provides products or services using different, self-contained specialists or companies brought together—outsourced—to contribute their primary or support activity to result in a successful outcome. Dell is a "modular" organization because it uses outsourced manufacturers and assemblers to provide parts and assemble its computers. It also uses outsourced customer service providers in different parts of the world to provide most of its customer service and support activities. These outsourced providers are independent companies, many of which offer similar services to other companies including, in some cases, Dell's competitors. Dell remains the umbrella organization and controlling organization in fact and certainly in the customers' mind, yet it is able to do so based on putting together a variety of "modules" or parts because of its ability to provide computers and related services through extensive dependence on outsourcing.

Many organizations long ago started outsourcing functions like payroll and benefits administration—routine administrative functions more easily and cost effectively done by a firm specializing in that activity. But outsourcing quickly moved into virtually every aspect of what a business does to provide the products and services it exists to provide. Exhibit 11.13, Top Global Strategist, shows the biggest sectors for outsourcing by as early as 2005. Just think, the UK's Virgin Group briefly held 5 percent of the British cola market with just five employees. This was achieved by narrowly focusing on Virgin's core competence—marketing. Everything else, from making the drink to distribution and delivery, was done by other companies.[12] And not only large companies are involved. A New York insurance company was once started from scratch by someone whose overriding aim was to employ no one but himself.[13] Veteran entrepreneur and co-founder of Celestial Seasonings, Wyck Hay, having sold that company to Kraft Foods for $40 million, returned from retirement several years later to build a new company, Kaboom Beverages, in California. What is interesting is that Hay, like many entrepreneurs today, is building a totally modular organization. Every function in Kaboom Beverages is outsourced to a variety of specialists and specialized companies. Indeed, one of the drivers for outsourcing to create a modular organization is to be able to combine world-class talent, wherever it resides, into a company's ability to deliver the best product and service it can.

Boeing opened its own engineering center in Moscow, where it employs 1,100 skilled but relatively inexpensive aerospace engineers to design parts of the 787 Dreamliner. It also has Japanese, Korean, and European companies making various parts of that critical new plane. Chicago-based law firm Baker and Mckenzie has its own English-speaking team in Manila that drafts documents and does market research. Bank of America (BoA) has its own India subsidiary, but also teamed up with InfoSys and Tata Consultancies—BoA estimates that it has saved almost $200 million in IT work in their first two years, while improving product quality at the same time.

business process outsourcing
Having an outside company manage numerous routine business management activities previously done by employees inside the company such as HR, supply procurement, finance and accounting, customer care, supply-chain logistics, engineering, R&D, sales and marketing, facilities management, and management/development.

Business process outsourcing (BPO) is the most rapidly growing segment of the outsourcing services industry worldwide. BPO includes a broad array of administrative functions—HR, supply procurement, finance and accounting, customer care, supply-chain logistics, engineering, research and development, sales and marketing, facilities management and even management training and development. Earlier this decade, IBM strategist Bruce Harreld estimated that the world's companies spend about $19 trillion each year on

[12] "The Virtual Organization," *The Economist*, Nov. 23, 2009.

[13] Ibid.

Top Global Strategist

The Modular Corporation

Exhibit 11.13

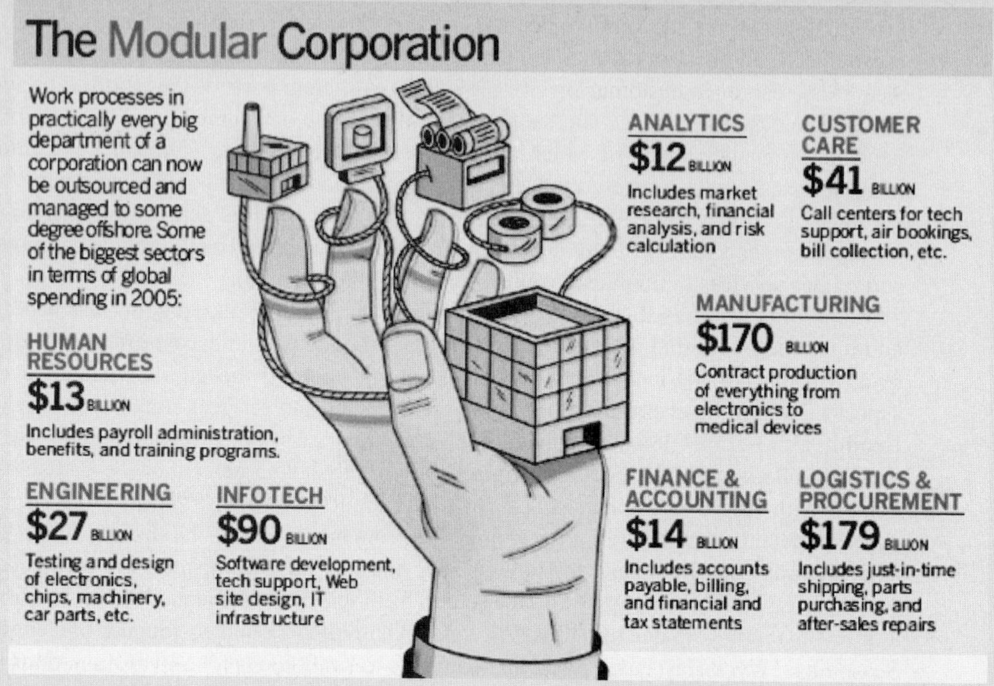

The Modular Corporation
Work processes in practically every big department of a corporation can now be outsourced and managed to some degree offshore. Some of the biggest sectors in terms of global spending in 2005:
HUMAN RESOURCES
$13 BILLION
Includes payroll administration, benefits, and training programs.
ENGINEERING
$27 BILLION
Testing and design of electronics, chips, machinery, car parts, etc.
INFOTECH
$90 BILLION
Software development, tech support, Web site design, IT infrastructure
ANALYTICS
$12 BILLION
Includes market research, financial analysis, and risk calculation
CUSTOMER CARE
$41 BILLION
Call centers for tech support, air bookings, bill collection, etc.
MANUFACTURING
$170 BILLION
Contract production of everything from electronics to medical devices
FINANCE & ACCOUNTING
$14 BILLION
Includes accounts payable, billing, and financial and tax statements
LOGISTICS & PROCUREMENT
$179 BILLION
Includes just-in-time shipping, parts purchasing, and after-sales repairs

Source: From "The Modular Corporation," *BusinessWeek*. Reprinted from January 30, 2006 issue of *BusinessWeek* by special permission. Copyright © 2006 by The McGraw-Hill Companies, Inc.

sales, general, and administrative expenses. Only $14 trillion-worth of this, he estimated, has been outsourced to other firms. He further expected that many of the advantages in scale, wage rates, and productivity found when manufacturing was outsourced will quickly emerge driving a rapid increase in BPO over the next 10 years.[14] Many big companies estimate they could outsource half or more of this work currently done in-house. U.S. banks are outsourcing back-office processing duties at an accelerated rate, suggested to reach almost $70 billion by 2015. And some banks, like Wachovia, are getting into the outsourcing business by selling their expertise and ability to provide banking services on behalf of other banks in an aggressive manner—having your competitor also being your outsource partner in some aspects of your banking business.[15] Yet banking services currently deliver less than 5 percent of their services remotely—a major global outsourcing opportunity.[16]

Perhaps the more controversial outsourcing trends involve product design and even innovation activities. Particularly in consumer electronics markets, companies such as Dell, Motorola, and Philips are buying complete designs of some digital devices from

[14] "A World of Work," *The Economist*, November 11, 2004.

[15] "Banks' Back Office Outsourcing Expected to Reach $67.2 Bn in 2015," *Global Services Media*, Aug. 21, 2010.

[16] Global Services Media, ibid.

Asian developers, tweaking them to their own specifications, and just adding their brand name before selling or having a more effective sales channel sell the product for them. This trend seems to be spreading. Boeing works with an Indian software company to develop its software for landing gear, navigation systems, and cockpit controls in its newest planes. Procter & Gamble, the consummate innovator, targeted and reached half of its new-product ideas by 2010 to come from outside the company—outsourced R&D or innovation—versus 20 percent five years earlier. Eli Lilly has outsourced selected biotech research for new drugs to an Asian biotech research firm. Consider this admonition in a still widely referenced *BusinessWeek* article:

> The result is a rethinking of the structure of the modern corporation. What, specifically, has to be done in-house anymore? At a minimum, most leading Western companies are turning toward a new model of innovation, one that employs global networks of partners. These can include U.S. chipmakers, Taiwanese engineers, Indian software developers, and Chinese factories. IBM is even offering the smarts of its famed research labs and a new global team of 1,200 engineers to help customers develop future products using next-generation technologies. When the whole chain works in sync, there can be a dramatic leap in the speed and efficiency of product development.[17]

Outsourcing as a means to create an agile, virtual organization has many potential advantages:

1. *It can lower costs incurred when the activity outsourced is done in-house.*

An accountant with a masters degree from UGA working for Ernst & Young in Atlanta, Georgia, costs E&Y at least $75,000 annually. Her colleague with the same education, returning to her native Philippines to live, works on a similar E&Y audit team in Southeast Asia and via the Internet in the United States—$7,000 annual salary.

2. *It can reduce the amount of capital a firm must invest in production or service capacity.*

Lenovo will cover the capital expenditure for its new Chinese PC manufacturing facilities; IBM will not. IBM will sell Lenovo its existing PC manufacturing facilities around the world, freeing up that capital for investment in IBM's development of its Global Business Services core competencies, and just buy PCs very cheaply from Lenovo as it needs them. It will include a markup in doing so to pass along to its IT management services clients.

3. *The firm's managers and personnel can concentrate on mission-critical activities.*

As noted in the preceding example, not only does IBM free up capital, but it frees up its people and remaining capital to focus more intensely on its new emphasis on IT systems, BPO, and consulting.

4. *This concentration and focus allow the firm to control and enhance the source of its core competitive advantage.*

Dell outsources the manufacture of its computers. It carefully controls and continuously improves its Web-based direct sales capability so that it increasingly distances itself from the closest competitors. It is able to build such a strong direct sales capability because that is virtually all it concentrates on, even though it is a computer company.

5. *Careful selection of outsourced partners allows the firm to potentially learn and develop its abilities through ideas and capabilities that emerge from the growing expertise and scope of work done by the outsource partner for several firms.*

Outsourced cell phone manufacturers in Korea and Taiwan have become large providers to several large, global cell phone companies. Their product design prototypes and

[17] Pete Engardio and Bruce Einhorn, "Outsourcing Innovation," *BusinessWeek*, March, 2005.

improvements for one client quickly find their way to the attention of other clients. Their improvement in logistics with some firms becomes knowledge incorporated in their dealings with another client.

Outsourcing is not without its "cons," however. There are several:

1. *Outsourcing involves loss of some control and reliance on "outsiders."*

By definition, outsourcing places control of that function or activity "outside" the requesting firm. This loss of control can result in many future problems such as delays, quality issues, customer complaints, and loss of competitor-sensitive information. Recent thefts of personal ID information from U.S.–based bank clients using major information management outsourcing services from Indian companies have caused major problems for the banks obtaining these services.

2. *Outsourcing can create future competitors.*

Companies that supply the firm with basic IT services or software programming assistance or product design services may one day move "up the chain" to undertake the higher level work the firm was attempting to reserve for itself. IBM has outsourced considerable work to Indian companies related to its "value-added" IT system management services—its strategic future. It now is experiencing competition from some of these former suppliers of programming support that have become multi-billion-dollar software and IT service providers in their own right.

3. *Skills important to a product or service are "lost."*

While things a company does may not be considered essential to its core competency, they still may be quite important. And as it continues over time to outsource that activity, it loses any capacity in the firm of being able to do it effectively. That, potentially, leaves the company vulnerable.

4. *Outsourcing may cause negative reaction from the public and investors.*

Outsourcing manufacturing, tech support, and back-office work may make sense to investors, but product design and innovation? Asking what value the company is providing and protecting will be an obvious potential reaction. Publicly, the loss of jobs from home country to low-cost alternative locations represents difficult job losses and transitions for people who bring political heat.

5. *Crafting good legal agreements, especially for services, is difficult.*

When outsourced manufacturers send product, you take delivery, inspect, and pay. When service providers supply a service, it is a continuous process. Bottom line: it takes considerable trust and cross-cultural understanding to work.

6. *The company may get locked into long-term contracts at costs that are no longer competitive.*

Multiyear IT management contracts can be both complex and based on costs that are soon noncompetitive because of other sources providing much more cost-effective solutions.

7. *Cost aren't everything: What if my supplier underbids?*

EDS (Dallas, Texas) has a multiyear contract as an outsource provider to the U.S. Navy to provide IT services and consolidate 70,000 different IT systems. Two years into the contract, in 2005, it was $1.5 billion in the red. It hopes to make that heavy loss up over the life of the contract. But what if it was a smaller company and couldn't afford to carry a loss for a contract it poorly bid?

8. *Outsourcing can lead to increasingly fragmented work cultures where low-paid workers get the work done with little initiative or enthusiasm.*

"A mercenary may shoot a gun the same as a soldier, but he will not create a revolution, build a new society, or die for the homeland," says a Silicon Valley manager who objects to his company's turning to contract workers for services.[18]

9. *Intellectual property development and ownership can be complicated.*

Several manufacturers outsourcing work to some Asian manufacturers have experienced these companies seeking ways to incrementally improve the products and processes by which they make them over time. Who owns those improvements? May the manufacturer also become its own seller of the incrementally improved, yet now "their" own version of and competitor to the original product? And progressive development and protection of intellectual property often comes from the daily processes of making, assembling, and simply figuring out ways to do current activities, processes, and products or services better—incremental innovation. So giving up control of that aspect of a product or services creation can result in lost future value.[19]

Its potential disadvantages not withstanding, outsourcing has become a key, standard means by which agile, virtual organization structures are built. It has become an essential building block; most firms in any market anywhere in the world structure some of their business activities to allow them to remain cost competitive, dynamic, and able to develop their future core competencies. As outsourcing moves from sourcing manufacturing and IT management to all business management processes, careful attention and efforts to build trust and cross-cultural understanding will be important as will effective contractual arrangements to govern multiyear, ongoing relationships.

Strategic Alliances

strategic alliances
Alliances with suppliers, partners, contractors, and other providers that allow partners in the alliance to focus on what they do best, farm out everything else, and quickly provide value to the customer.

Strategic alliances are arrangements between two or more companies in which they both contribute capabilities, resources, or expertise to a joint undertaking, usually with an identity of its own, with each firm giving up overall control in return for the potential to participate in and benefit from the joint venture relationship. They are different from outsourcing relationships because the requesting company usually retains control when outsourcing, whereas strategic alliances involve firms giving up overall control to the joint entity, or alliance, in which they become a partner. Texas-based EDS was awaiting word at the time of this writing on whether the "Atlas Consortium" would be awarded a 10-year, $7.6 billion contract to manage 150,000 computers and networking software for British military personnel. The Atlas Consortium is a strategic alliance, formed by EDS as the "lead" firm with the Dutch firm LogicaCMG and a British subsidiary of the defense company, EADS, as full partners. While EDS is the "lead" member of the alliance, final control of the alliance rests not in EDS but in the governance that all three partners have the right to influence and shape.

This is a good example of a strategic alliance—three different firms all with other major business commitments and activities. They have joined together, investing time, analysis resources, and negotiations so as to be in a position to bid as a team (or alliance) on a major 10-year contract. In a few weeks they will know. If they get the contract, then their alliance will have a lengthy commitment to the British military and their firms to the Atlas Consortium. If they don't, then they may or may not work together to pursue other deals.

[18] "Time to Bring It Back," *The Economist*, March 3, 2005.

[19] Subroto Roy and K. Sivakumar, "Managing Intellectual Property in Global Outsourcing for Innovation Generation," *The Journal of Product Innovation Management* 28, no. 1 (2011).

But this relationship allowed each firm to seek work it could not have otherwise pursued independently because of restrictions imposed by the British government, the limitations of each firm individually, or both. It expanded the exposure of each firm to the other, to selected markets, to the building of relationships that may be usefully leveraged in each company's interests in the future.

Strategic alliances can be for long-term or for very short periods. Engaging in alliances, whether long-term or one time, lets each participant take advantage of fleeting opportunities quickly, usually without tying up vast amounts of capital. Strategic alliances allow companies with world-class capabilities to partner together in a way that combines different core competencies so that within the alliance each can focus on what they do best, but the alliance can pull together what is necessary to quickly provide superior value to the customer. FedEx and the U.S. Postal Service have formed an alliance—FedEx planes carry USPS next-day letters and USPS delivers FedEx ground packages—to allow both to challenge their common rival, UPS.

Strategic alliances have the following pros and cons for firms seeking agile, responsive organizational structures:

Advantages

1. *Leverages several firms' core competencies.*

This allows alliance members to be more competitive in seeking certain project work or input.

2. *Limits capital investment.*

One partner firm does not have to have all the resources necessary to do the work of the alliance.

3. *Is flexible.*

Alliances allow a firm to be involved yet continue to pursue its other, "regular" business opportunities.

4. *Leads to networking and relationship building.*

Alliances get companies together, sometimes even competitors. They allow key players to build relationships that are valuable, even if the present alliance doesn't "pan out." Alliance partners learn more about each others' capabilities and gain advantage or benefit from referrals and other similar behaviors, creating win–win situations.

Disadvantages

1. *Can result in loss of control.*

A firm in an alliance by definition cedes ultimate control to the broader alliance for the undertaking for which the alliance is formed. This can prove problematic if the alliance doesn't work out as planned—or is not well planned.

2. *Can be hard to establish good management control of the project—loss of operational control.*

Where multiple firms have interrelated responsibilities for a sizable joint project, it should not be difficult to imagine problems arising as the players go about implementing a major project as in the example of EDS and its Dutch and British partners in the Atlas Consortium. It requires good up-front planning and use of intercompany project team groups early on in the bidding process.

3. *Can distract a participating company's management and key players.*

One strategic alliance can consume the majority attention of key players essential to the overall success of the "home" company. Whether because of their technical skills, managerial skills, key roles, or all three, the potential for lost focus or time to devote to key responsibilities exists.

4. *Raises issues of control of proprietary information and intellectual property.*

Where technology development is the focus of the alliance, or maybe part of it, firms partnered together may also compete in other circumstances. Or they may have the potential to do so. So partnering together gives each the opportunity to learn much more about the other, their contacts, capabilities, and unique skills or trade secrets.

Strategic alliances have proven a very popular mechanism for many companies seeking to become more agile competitors in today's dynamic global economy. They have proven a major way for small companies to become involved with large players to the benefit of both—allowing the smaller player to grow in a way that builds its future survival possibilities and the larger player to tap expertise and knowledge it can no longer afford to retain or develop in-house.

Toward Boundaryless Structures

Management icon Jack Welch[20] is recognized worldwide for his success as a global executive, his teaching of management and leadership, and his insight into making organizations more effective. When he was leading General Electric, he coined the term **boundaryless organization** to characterize his vision of what he wanted GE to become: to be able to generate knowledge, share knowledge, and get knowledge to the places it could be best used to provide superior value. A key component of this concept was erasing internal divisions so the people in the company could work across functional, business, and geographic boundaries to achieve an integrated diversity—the ability to transfer the best ideas, the most developed knowledge, and the most valuable people quickly, easily, and freely throughout the organization. Here is his description:

boundaryless organization
Organizational structure that allows people to interface with others throughout the organization without need to wait for a hierarchy to regulate that interface across functional, business, and geographic boundaries.

> Boundaryless behavior is the soul of today's GE . . . Simply put, people seem compelled to build layers and walls between themselves and others, and that human tendency tends to be magnified in large, old institutions like ours. These walls cramp people, inhibit creativity, waste time, restrict vision, smother dreams and above all, slow things down . . . Boundaryless behavior shows up in actions of a woman from our Appliances Business in Hong Kong helping NBC with contacts needed to develop satellite television service in Asia . . . And finally, boundaryless behavior means exploiting one of the unmatchable advantages a multibusiness GE has over almost any other company in the world. Boundaryless behavior combines 12 huge global businesses—each number one or number two in its markets—into a vast laboratory whose principal product is new ideas, coupled with a common commitment to spread them throughout the Company.
>
> —*Letter to Shareholders, Jack Welch, chairman, General Electric Company, 1981–2001*

horizontal boundaries
Rules of communication, access, and protocol for dealing with different departments or functions or processes within an organization.

vertical boundaries
Limitations on interaction, contact, and access between operations and management personnel; between different levels of management; and between different organizational parts like corporate versus divisional units.

Boundaries, or borders, arise in four "directions" based on the ways we traditionally structure and run organizations:

1. **Horizontal boundaries**—between different departments or functions in a firm. Salespeople are different from administrative people or operating people or engineering people. One division is separate from another.
2. **Vertical boundaries**—between operations and management, and levels of management; between "corporate" and "division," in virtually every organization.

[20] www.welchway.com.

geographic boundaries Limitations on interaction and contact between people in a company based on being at different physical locations domestically and globally.

external interface boundaries Formal and informal rules, locations, and protocol that separate and/or dictate the interaction between members of an organization and those outside the organization—customers, suppliers, partners, regulators, associations, and even competitors.

3. **Geographic boundaries**—between different physical locations; between different countries or regions of the world (or even within a country) and between cultures.
4. **External interface boundaries**—between a company and its customers, suppliers, partners, regulators, and, indeed, its competitors.

Outsourcing, strategic alliances, product-team structures, reengineering, restructuring—all are ways to move toward boundaryless organization. Culture and shared values across an organization that value boundaryless behavior and cooperation help enable these efforts to work.

As we noted at the beginning of this section, globalization has accelerated many changes in the way organizations are structured, and that is certainly driving the recognition by many organizations of their need to become more boundaryless, to become an agile, virtual organization. Technology, particularly driven by the Internet, has and will be a major driver of the boundaryless organization. Commenting on technology's effect on Cisco, John Chambers observed that with all its outsourcing and strategic alliances, roughly 90 percent of all orders come into Cisco without ever being touched by human hands. "To my customers, it looks like one big virtual plant where my suppliers and inventory systems are directly tied into our virtual organization," he said. "That will be the norm in the future. Everything will be completely connected, both within a company and between companies. We will become boundaryless. The people who get that will have a huge competitive advantage."[21]

The Web's contribution electronically has simultaneously become the best analogy in explaining the future boundaryless organization. And it is not just the Web as in the Internet, but a weblike shape of successful organizational structures in the future. If there are a pair of images that symbolize the vast changes at work, they are the pyramid and the web. The organizational chart of large-scale enterprise had long been defined as a pyramid of ever-shrinking layers leading to an omnipotent CEO at its apex. The twenty-first-century corporation, in contrast, is far more likely to look like a web: a flat, intricately woven form that links partners, employees, external contractors, suppliers, and customers in various collaborations. The players will grow more and more interdependent. Fewer companies will try to master all the disciplines necessary to produce and market their goods but will instead outsource skills—from research and development to manufacturing—to outsiders who can perform those functions with greater efficiency.[22]

Exhibit 11.14 illustrates this evolution in organization structure to what it predicted would become the B-Web, a truly Internet-driven form of organization designed to deliver speedy, customized, service-enhanced products to savvy customers from an integrated boundaryless B-Web organization, pulling together abundant, world-class resources digitally. Take Colgate-Palmolive. The company needed a more efficient method for getting its toothpaste into the tube—a seemingly straightforward problem. When its internal R&D team came up empty-handed, the company posted the specs on InnoCentive, one of many new marketplaces that link problems with problem-solvers. A Canadian engineer named Ed Melcarek proposed putting a positive charge on fluoride powder, then grounding the tube. It was an effective application of elementary physics, but not one that Colgate-Palmolive's team of chemists had ever contemplated. Melcarek was duly rewarded with $25,000 for a few hours' work. Today, some 120,000 scientists like Melcarek have registered with InnoCentive and

[21] Peter Burrows, "Can Cisco Shift into Higher Gear?" *BusinessWeek Online*, October 4, 2004; and http://blogs.cisco.com/collaboration, 2011.

[22] John Byrne, www.C-ChangeMedia.com.

EXHIBIT 11.14
From Traditional Structure to B-Web Structure

Source: Reprinted by permission of Harvard Business School Publishing. Exhibit from *Digital Capital: Harnessing the Power of Business Webs,* by Don Tapscott, David Ticoll and Alex Lowy. Copyright 2000 by the Harvard Business School Publishing Corporation; all rights reserved.

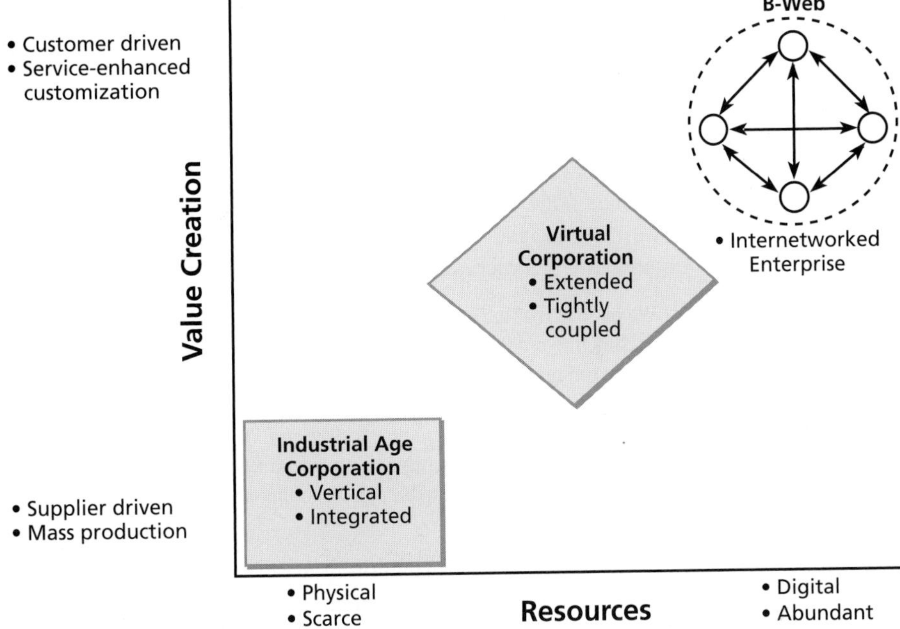

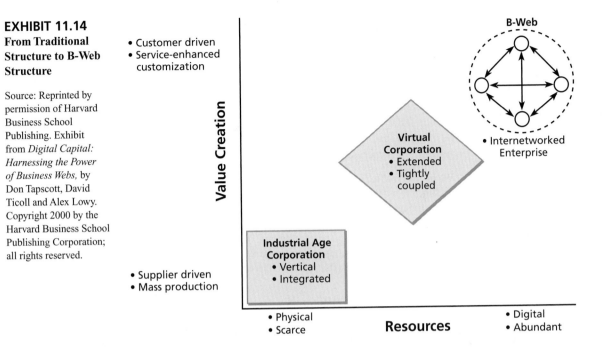

hundreds of companies pay annual fees of roughly $80,000 to tap the talents of a global scientific community. Launched as an e-business venture by U.S. pharmaceutical giant Eli Lilly, the company now provides on-demand solutions to innovation-hungry titans such as Boeing, Dow, DuPont, P&G, and Novartis.[23]

Managing this intricate network of partners, spin-off enterprises, contractors, and free-lancers will be as important as managing internal operations. Indeed, it will be hard to tell the difference. All of these constituents will be directly linked in ways that will make it nearly impossible for outsiders to know where an individual firm begins and where it ends. "Companies will be much more molecular and fluid," predicted futurist Don Tapscott, co-author of *Digital Capital* and more recently, *MacroWikinomics*. "They will be autonomous business units connected not necessarily by a big building but across geographies all based on networks. The boundaries of the firm will be not only fluid or blurred but in some cases hard to define.[24] Just as events in Northern Africa and the Middle East in 2011 amazed the world, they also showed the power for change enabled by social media and Internet connections to bring individual to individual yet simultaneous collective action on a mass scale, instantaneously. Tapscott and Williams suggest that such developments are also images of the nature and speed of collaboration and action and idea exchange enabled by the Web in B-web organizational structures, or what they now call Enterprise 2.0. Rapid sharing of information, ideas, action, and movement in all aspects of an enterprise are taken quickly rather than the plodding dinosaur-like action of their not so old predecessor organizational structures.[25]

[23] www.innocentive.com. See also Don Tapscott, *grown up digital* (New York: McGraw-Hill, 2008); and Don Tapscott and Anthony D. Williams, *MacroWikinomics* (New York: The Penguin Group, 2010).

[24] www.innocentive.com; and Tapscott and Williams, *MacroWikinomics*

[25] Tapscott and Williams, *MacroWikinomics*

Ambidextrous Learning Organizations

The evolution of the virtual organizational structure as an integral mechanism managers use to implement strategy has brought with it recognition of the central role knowledge plays in this process. *Knowledge* may be in terms of operating know-how, relationships with and knowledge of customer networks, technical knowledge upon which products or processes are based or will be, relationships with key people or a certain person that can get things done quickly, and so forth. Consulting firm McKinsey's organizational expert, Lowell Bryan, and co-author Claudia Joyce, describe the role of knowledge in effective organizational structures this way:

> We believe that the centerpiece of corporate strategy for most large companies should become the redesign of their organizations. We believe this for a very simple reason—it's where the money is.
>
> Let us explain. Most companies today were designed for the 20th century. By remaking them to mobilize the mind power of their 21st century workforces, these companies will be able to tap into the presently underutilized talents, knowledge, relationships, and skills of their employees, which will open up to them not only new opportunities but also vast sources of new wealth.[26]

corporate lattice
Corporate lattice is a model of how work, careers and communication get done in 21st century organizations up, down and across organizational levels and positions versus a "corporate ladder" tradition that views work, careers and communication as predominantly hierarchical driven.

lattice
A metaphor used to describe the reality of the nature & structure of work in organizations today—a 3-dimensional structure extending vertically, horizontally, and diagonally whereby people communicate and work with others anywhere, anytime, to provide answers, ideas, form teams, and solve problems.

learning organization
Organization structured around the idea that it should be set up to enable learning, to share knowledge, to seek knowledge, and to create opportunities to create new knowledge. It would move into new markets to learn about those markets rather than simply to bring a brand to it, or find resources to exploit in it.

Bryan and Joyce see this shaping future organizational structure with managers becoming knowledge "nodes" through which intricate networks of personal relationships—inside and outside the formal organization—are constantly coordinated to bring together relevant know-how and successful action. Cathleen Benko and Molly Anderson's book, ***The Corporate Lattice***, takes the notion of "nodes" with knowledge a major step forward, identifying the reality in many organizations that relevant knowledge exists with many organizational members other than just managers. Their book and the research that underlies it help document this phenomenon of networks of relationships as a multidirectional and almost randomly natural latticework, which describes the reality of the nature of work today, and the way a workplace in many organizations large and small really works. Rather than the usual "ladder" metaphor to describe communication and career processes in organizations, they suggest that an organization today is more like a **lattice**—a three-dimensional structure extending infinitely vertically, horizontally, and diagonally. People are less tethered to offices, even to tradition career patterns—with major technological advances, globalization, and different options for where, when and how work gets done. So the work of a lattice-functioning organization gets done in a virtual, dynamic, typically project-based manner resembling nodes on a network, each with the possibility of connecting anywhere and anytime to others to provide answers, ideas, form teams, or communities. With strong horizontal along with diagonal and vertical supports, the visual image of an organization is one far less reliant on or constrained by top-down hierarchy. This broader, sometimes unexpected pattern of participation enables interaction, gets involvement, spreads ideas and knowhow throughout an organization regardless of exact levels and roles in an organizational chart.[27] Exhibit 11.15, Global Strategy in Action provides an example about AT&T from their book to illuminate both the lattice view and the boundaryless, Web-enabled fluid organizations through which strategies are enabled today.

A shift from what Subramanian Rangan called *exploitation to exploration* indicated the growing importance of organizational structures that enable a **learning organization** to

[26] Lowell L. Bryan, and Claudia I. Joyce (McKinsey and Company), *Mobilizing Minds* (New York: McGraw-Hill, 2007), p. 1.

[27] Cathleen Benko and Molly Anderson, *The Corporate Lattice* (Cambridge, Mass: Harvard Business Review Press, 2010), www.threcorporatelattice.com.

Global Strategy in Action

Exhibit 11.15

The Corporate Lattice—A Social Media Organizational Structure at AT&T

John Donovan, AT&T's chief technology officer, was looking for a nonhierarchical approach to harness the rich depth of knowledge and creativity inside the multibillion-dollar firm. Leveraging social media, Donovan created a mass participation approach to innovation that, by design, would not replicate the company's existing functional or hierarchical organizational structure.

This approach features a Web site that allows anyone (and Donovan is quick to underscore anyone) to contribute an idea, become a collaborator on someone else's idea, provide encouragement and critical feedback, assess a concept's marketability, challenge its engineering and affordability, and the like. Each employee can also vote on the caliber of the insights and rate additional postings of suggestions and comments, earning the contributors reputation points. "This is meritocracy at its best—a highly diverse set of people, in every sense of the word, crowd-sourcing and crowd-storming," says Donovan.

By the end of its third quarter, the site had more than 24,000 members, 2,000 ideas, and more than a million page views and was still growing. The first season's winners have been funded and are moving from PowerPoint to prototype.

Source: Cathleen Benko and Molly Anderson, *The Corporate Lattice* (Cambridge, Mass: Harvard Business Review Press, 2010), www.threcorporatelattice.com

ambidextrous organization
Organization structure most notable for its lack of structure wherein knowledge and getting it to the right place quickly are the key reasons for organization. Managers become knowledge "nodes" through which intricate networks of personal relationships—inside and outside the formal organization—are constantly, and often informally, coordinated to bring together relevant know-how and successful action.

allow global companies the chance to build competitive advantage.[28] Rather than going to markets to exploit brands or for inexpensive resources, in Rangan's view, the smart ones were going global to learn. This shift in the intent of the structure, then, is to seek information, to create new competences. Demand in another part of the world could be a new-product trendsetter at home. So a firm's structure needs to be organized to enable learning, to share knowledge, to create opportunities to create it. Others look to companies like 3M or Procter & Gamble that allow slack time, new-product champions, manager mentors—all put in place in the structure to provide resources, support, and advocacy for cross-functional collaboration leading to innovation in new-product development, and the generation and use of new ideas. This perspective is similar to the boundaryless notion—accommodate the speed of change and therefore opportunity by freeing up historical constraints found in traditional organizational approaches. So having structures that emphasize coordination over control, that allow flexibility (are **ambidextrous**), that emphasize the value and importance of informal relationships and interaction over formal systems, techniques, and controls are all characteristics associated with what are seen as effective structures for the twenty-first century.

[28] Subramanian Rangan, *A Prism on Globalization* (Fountainebleau, France: INSEAD, 1999).

Summary

This chapter has examined ways organizations are structured and ways to make those structures most effective. It described five traditional organizational structures–simple organization, functional structure, divisional structure, matrix structure, and product-team structure.

Simple structures are often found in small companies, where tight control is essential to survival. Functional structures take advantage of the specialization of work by structuring the organization into interconnected units like sales, operations, and accounting/finance. This approach generates more efficiency, enhances functional skills over time, and is perhaps the most pervasive organizational structure. Coordination and conflict across functional units are the perpetual challenge in functional structures.

As companies grow they add products, services, and geographic locations, which leads to the need for divisional structures which divide the organization into units along one or more of these three lines. This division of the business into units with common settings increases focus and allows each division to operate more like an independent business itself. That in turn can generate competition for corporate-level resources and potentially loose consistency and image corporatewide. Companies that work intensely with certain clients or projects created the matrix organization structure to temporarily assign functional specialists to those activities while having them remain accountable to their "home" functional unit. The product-team structure has evolved from the matrix approach, where functional specialists' assignments can be for an extended time and usually center around creating a functionally balanced team to take charge of a new-product idea from generation to production, sales, and market expansion. This approach has been found to create special synergy, teamwork, and cooperation because these specialists are together building a new revenue stream from its inception through its success and expansion.

The twenty-first century has seen an accelerating move away from traditional organizational structures toward hybrid adaptations that emphasize an external focus, flexible interaction, interdependency, and a bottom-up approach. Organizations have sought to adapt their traditional structures in this direction by redefining the role of corporate headquarters, rebalancing the need for control versus coordination, adjusting and reengineering the structure to emphasize strategic activities, downsizing, and moving toward self-managing operational activities.

More successful organizations are becoming agile, virtual organizations—temporary networks of independent companies linked by information technology to share skills, markets, and costs. Outsourcing has been a major way organizations have done this. They retain certain functions, while having other companies take full responsibility for accomplishing other functions necessary to provide the product or services of this host organization. Strategic alliances are arrangements between two or more companies who typically contribute resources or skills to a joint undertaking where the joint entity is a separate, distinct organization itself and usually created to seek a particular contract or activities that represent too great an undertaking for any one player in the alliance.

Twenty-first century leaders have increasingly spoken about making their organizations boundaryless, by which they mean the absence of internal and external "boundaries" between units, levels, and locations that lessen their company's ability to generate knowledge, share knowledge, and get knowledge to the places it can be best used to create value. Forward thinkers describe ambidextrous learning organizations as ones that innately share knowledge, enable learning within and across organizations, and nurture informal relationships within and outside organizations to foster opportunities to be at the forefront of creating new knowledge.

Key Terms

agile organization, *p. 338*
ambidextrous organization, *p. 349*
boundaryless organization, *p. 345*
business process outsourcing, *p. 339*
business process reengineering, *p. 335*
corporate lattice, *p. 348*
divisional organizational structure, *p. 323*
downsizing, *p. 336*
external interface boundaries, *p. 346*
functional organizational structure, *p. 322*
geographic boundaries, *p. 346*
holding company structure, *p. 325*
horizontal boundaries, *p. 345*
lattice, *p. 348*
learning organization, *p. 348*
matrix organizational structure, *p. 326*
modular organization, *p. 339*
organizational structure, *p. 321*
outsourcing, *p. 338*
product-team structure, *p. 328*
restructuring, *p. 334*
self-management, *p. 337*
simple organizational structure, *p. 321*
strategic alliances, *p. 343*
strategic business unit, *p. 325*
vertical boundaries, *p. 345*
virtual organization, *p. 338*

Questions for Discussion

1. Explain each traditional organizational structure.
2. Select a company you have worked for or research one in the business press that uses one of these traditional structures. How well suited is the structure to the needs and strategy of the organization? What seems to work well, and what doesn't?
3. What organizations do you think are most likely to use product-team structures? Why?
4. Identify an organization that operated like a twentieth-century organization but has now adopted a structure that manifests twenty-first-century characteristics. Explain how you see or detect the differences.
5. How would you use one or more of the ways to improve traditional structures to improve the company you last worked in? Explain what might result.
6. What organization are you familiar with that you would consider the most agile, virtual organization? Why?
7. What situation have you personally seen outsourcing benefit?
8. What "boundary" would you first eliminate or change in an organization you are familiar with? Explain what you would do to eliminate it or change it and how that should make it more effective.
9. What would be the advantages of a corporate lattice–type organization? Are there disadvantages? How is it similar or different from the "grapevine" notion?

Chapter Twelve

Leadership and Culture

After reading and studying this chapter, you should be able to

1. Describe what good organizational leadership involves.
2. Explain how vision and performance help leaders clarify strategic intent.
3. Explain the value of passion and selection/development of new leaders in shaping an organization's culture.
4. Briefly explain seven sources of power and influence available to every manager.
5. Define and explain what is meant by organizational culture, and how it is created, influenced, and changed.
6. Describe four ways leaders influence culture.
7. Explain four strategy-culture situations.

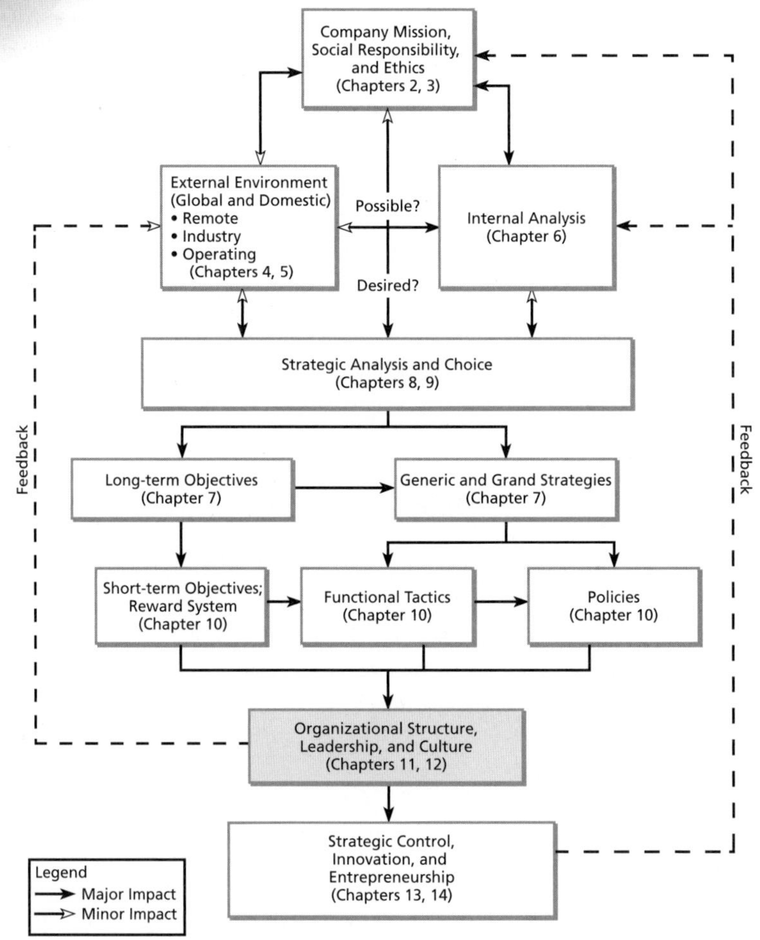

The job of leading a company has never been more demanding, and it will only get more challenging amidst the global dynamism businesses face today. The CEO will retain ultimate authority, but the corporation will depend increasingly on the skills of the CEO and a host of subordinate leaders to lead, coordinate, make decisions, and act quickly. The accelerated pace and complexity of business will continue to force corporations to push authority down through increasingly horizontal, flattened management structures. As we saw in the last chapter, these organizations will also need to be more and more open, agile, and boundaryless. This will require all the more emphasis on able leadership and a strong culture to shape decisions that must be made quickly, even when the stakes are big. In the future, every line manager will have to exercise leadership's prerogatives—and bear its burdens—to an extent unthinkable 20 years ago.[1]

John Kotter, a widely recognized leadership expert, predicted this evolving role of leadership in an organization when he distinguished between management and leadership:

> Management is about coping with complexity. Its practices and procedures are largely a response to one of the most significant developments of the twentieth century: the emergence of large organizations. Without good management, complex enterprises tend to become chaotic in ways that threaten their very existence. Good management brings a degree of order and consistency to key dimensions like the quality and profitability of products.
>
> Leadership, by contrast, is about coping with change. Part of the reason it has become so important in recent years is that the business world has become more competitive and more volatile.... The net result is that doing what was done yesterday, or doing it 5 percent better, is no longer a formula for success. Major changes are more and more necessary to survive and compete effectively in this new environment. More change always demands more leadership.[2]

organizational leadership
The process and practice by key executives of guiding and shepherding people in an organization toward a vision over time and developing that organization's future leadership and organization culture.

Organizational leadership, then, involves action on two fronts. The first is in guiding the organization to deal with constant change. This requires CEOs who embrace change, and who do so by clarifying strategic intent, who build their organization and shape their culture to fit with opportunities and challenges change affords. The second front is in providing the management skill to cope with the ramifications of constant change. This means identifying and supplying the organization with operating managers prepared to provide operational leadership and vision as never before. Thus, organizational leadership is guiding and shepherding toward a vision over time and developing that organization's future leadership and organizational culture.

Consider the challenge currently facing Ford Motor Company CEO Alan Mulally as he seeks to transform Ford's culture and return the company to profitability after years of accelerating decline and a severe economic downturn. He was brought in by CEO Bill Ford, great-grandson of the founder, who finally threw up his arms in frustration and concluded that an insider could no longer fix Ford. Mulally was not Bill Ford's first choice, but Ford concluded Mulally was someone who knows how to shake the company to its foundations.

Mulally inherited virtually all the managers he must work through. Ford was losing from \$3,000 to \$5,000 on most every car it sold. There is a legacy within the company of placing a premium on personal ties to the Ford family, sometimes trumping actual performance in promotion decisions. Mulally had no experience in the automobile industry and was viewed with suspicion as an outsider in a town that places a premium on lifelong association with

[1] Ram Charan, *Leadership in the Era of Economic Uncertainty* (New York: McGraw-Hill, 2008); Larry Bossidy, "What Your Leader Expects of You," *Harvard Business Review*, June 2007; and Anthony Bianco, "The New Leadership," *BusinessWeek*, August 28, 2000.

[2] John P. Kotter, "What Leaders Really Do," *Harvard Business Review* (May–June 1990), p. 104.

the industry. On Mulally's first meeting with his inherited management team, one manager asked early on: "How are you going to tackle something as complex and unfamiliar as the auto business when we are in such tough financial shape?"

Wall Street was skeptical early on. Of 15 analysts surveyed by Bloomberg.com, only two rated it a buy. The other 13's opinion: fixing Ford will require much more than simply whacking expenses and replacing a few key people. The company will have to figure out how to produce more vehicles consumers actually want. And doing that requires addressing the most fundamental problem of all: Ford's dysfunctional, often defeatist, culture. Once a model of efficiency, it has degenerated into a symbol of inefficiency, and its managers seem comfortable with the idea of losing money.

If you were Alan Mulally, how would you lead the dramatic change that appears to be needed at Ford Motor Company? How would you seek to move Ford's 300,000-plus employees and managers in a direction that abandons ingrained, and to some "sacred," cultural and leadership norms, quickly?

Consider another example. Jeff Immelt took the reins of leadership of GE from Jack Welch, recognized worldwide as one of the truly great business leaders of the twentieth century, and faced a leadership and organizational culture challenge quite different in some ways from what Alan Mulally is addressing. GE under Welch built more value for its stockholders than any other company in the history of global commerce. That legacy alone would be pressure enough on a new leader, wouldn't you think?

Fortunately, some would quickly answer, Immelt had trained for many years under and in Welch's shadow. He was Welch's choice as successor. He was deeply schooled in the GE way and the Jack Welch leadership approach, as were all the other 300,000 GE employees over the prior 20 years. That Welch/GE way valued, above all, executives who could cut costs, cut deals, and generate continuous improvement in their business units. They were evaluated personally by Welch on an annual basis, in front of each other at the GE School.

But a storm was brewing. Shortly after Immelt became CEO, the 9/11 tragedy unfolded. A major recession and stock market drop soon followed. The option to continue mega deal making was slowing down with fewer candidates. The ability to generate GE-caliber earnings growth via sales growth combined with relentless efficiency was slowing down. So Immelt concluded that he could not continue with the old strategy. Rather, he would have to embark on virtually a new direction at GE that would dramatically change what he needed GE executives as leaders to prioritize and become. Instead of being experts in deal making and continuous improvement, they needed, in Immelt's vision, to become creative, innovators of internal growth generated by identifying new markets and technologies and needs as yet unknown.

With a slower-growing domestic economy, less tolerance among investors for buying your way to growth, and more global competitors, Immelt, like many of his peers, is being forced to shift the emphasis from deals and cost-cutting to new products, services, and markets. "It's a different world," says Immelt, than the one Welch knew. And so, he inherited one of the world's greatest companies yet faced a situation he concluded required dramatic changes in the way GE would be led, in the nature of the culture it needed, and in the fundamental priorities with which its managers would build GE's future. The dramatic 2008–2010 financial services initiated global economic collapse further underscored the challenge Immelt faced.

If you were Jeff Immelt, how would you lead such a change? How would you seek to move GE's 300,000 people in a direction that abandons "sacred" cultural and leadership norms that were well used and entrenched under Welch's watch to make GE great? How would you quickly and convincingly lead those people to accept massive change throughout this special company and very quickly have that uncertain change produce the growth and profitability investors understandably expect?

The challenges Immelt and Mulally faced were different, but both were nothing short of a revolution. The bottom line is that Immelt and Mulally, as well as all good executives, focus intensely and aggressively on the organizational leadership and organizational culture elements we will now examine.

STRATEGIC LEADERSHIP: EMBRACING CHANGE

The blending of telecommunications, computers, the Internet, and one global marketplace has increased the pace of change exponentially during the past 10 years. All business organizations are affected. Change has become an integral part of what leaders and managers deal with daily. The opening example about Jeff Immelt shows a manager normally able to celebrate 20 years of historically unmatched accomplishment, only to face the need for dramatic change at a GE employees and investors had come to believe was infallible.

The leadership challenge is to galvanize commitment among people within an organization as well as stakeholders outside the organization to embrace change and implement strategies intended to position the organization to succeed in a vastly different future. Leaders galvanize commitment to embrace change through three interrelated activities: clarifying strategic intent, building an organization, and shaping organizational culture.

Clarifying Strategic Intent

strategic intent
Leaders' clear sense of where they want to lead their company and what results they expect to achieve.

Leaders help their company embrace change by setting forth their **strategic intent**—a clear sense of where they want to lead the company and what results they expect to achieve. They do this by concentrating simultaneously and very clearly on two very different issues: vision and performance.

Vision

leader's vision
An articulation of a simple criterion or characterization of what a leader sees the company must become in order to establish and sustain global leadership.

A leader needs to communicate clearly and directly a fundamental vision of what the business needs to become. Traditionally, the concept of vision has been a description or picture of what the company could be that accommodates the needs of all its stakeholders. The intensely competitive, rapidly changing global marketplace has refined this to be targeting a very narrowly defined **leader's vision**—an articulation of a simple criterion or characterization of what the leader sees the company must become to establish and sustain global leadership. Former IBM CEO Lou Gerstner is a good example of a leader in the middle of trying to shape strategic intent when he began to try to change IBM from a computer company to a business solutions management company. He said at the time: "One of the great things about this industry is that every decade or so, you get a chance to redefine the playing field." He further commented, "We're in that phase of redefinition right now, and winners or losers are going to emerge from it. We've got to become the leader in 'network-centric computing.' It's a shift brought about by telecommunications-based change that is changing IBM more than semiconductors did in the last decade." Said Gerstner, "I sensed there were too many people inside IBM who wanted to fight the war we lost," referring to PCs and PC software, so he aggressively instilled network-centric computing as the strategic intent for IBM in the next decade. It is a comment on his sense of vision that his successor, Sam Palmisano, sold IBM's PC business to China's Lenovo, creating the world's third-largest PC company, and is aggressively pushing his IBMers to concentrate on newer IBM businesses in IT services, software, and servers—and seriously examining IBM's future in the online digital world, the 3D Internet.

Keep the Vision Simple Mark Zuckerberg and Facebook have, in a few short years, dramatically changed the paradigm of how people worldwide interface with the Internet.

Instead of search and e-mail as the main reasons individuals log onto the Internet, Zuckerberg's simple vision for Facebook—*Facebook helps you connect and share with the people in your life*—has become the initial connecting point with the Web for over a billion people worldwide. John Donahoe, taking over for the well-known Meg Whitman at eBay, has sold off several prior acquisitions, like Skype, with a vision to reconnect eBay with its roots—*to remain the world's largest online marketplace, where practically anyone can buy and sell practically anything.* In the annals of business leadership, Coca-Cola's legendary former chairman and CEO, Roberto Goizueta, was known for reinvigorating Coke at a key point in its history by articulating a very simple, powerful strategic vision for Coke when he said, "*Our company is a global business system for which we raise capital to make concentrate and sell it at an operating profit. Then we pay the cost of that capital. Shareholders pocket the difference.*" Coke averaged 27 percent annual return on stockholder equity for 18 years under his leadership. Exhibit 12.1, Top Global Strategist, shows how Mayor Michael Bloomberg articulated a radical yet simple vision of New York City that has resonated with New York's famously cynical citizenry, who give him a 75 percent approval rating. All four of these organizations are very different, but their leaders were each effective in shaping and communicating a vision that clarified strategic intent in a way that helped everyone understand, or at least have a sense of, where the organization needed to go and, as a result, created a better sense of the rationale behind any new, and often radically changing, strategy.

Performance

Clarifying strategic intent must also ensure the survival of the enterprise as it pursues a well-articulated vision, and after it reaches the vision. So a key element of good organizational leadership is to make clear the performance expectations a leader has for the organization, and managers in it, as they seek to move toward that vision.

Oftentimes this can create a bit of a paradox, because the vision is a future picture and performance is now and tomorrow and next quarter and this year. Larry Page, Google co-founder, stepped back in to assume the CEO role in mid-2011. A major reason for doing so was his belief, and many others, that Google was at risk to lose its global dominance as a key entry point to the Internet, and therefore eventually ad revenue, to the fast-rising Facebook. He moved immediately to tie vision and performance. His immediate sense of vision was simple—*Google needs to go "social" to compete*. To that end, Page sent out a company-wide memo his first week as CEO alerting all Google employees that 25 percent of their annual bonus would be tied to the success or failure of Google's social strategy that year. Page told employees that were not directly involved in Google's social efforts that they, too, would be held accountable. He wrote that employees must test the products and give feedback; that they should push Google's social products on their "family and friends."[3] So Larry Page was directly clarifying Google's strategic intent by focusing on a simple vision—social—and linking performance immediately and in the near future for *every* Google employee on the success of that vision. Steven Reinemund, dean of the Wake Forest School of Business and Indra Nooyi's predecessor at Pepsico, offers a good characterization of what it would seem Larry Page has attempted at Google: Good leaders know that results count: "*If you can't get the results over the goal line, are you really a leader*?"[4]

[3] Read more: http://www.businessinsider.com/larry-page-just-tied-employee-bonuses-to-the-success-of-the-googles-social-strategy-2011-4#ixzz1IxMq2Sg6

[4] North Carolina CEO Forum, 2010, Raleigh, North Carolina, May 18, 2010.

Top Global Strategist

Mike Bloomberg, New York's CEO Leader

Exhibit 12.1

Michael Bloomberg, classic entrepreneurial success story, has proven to be an extraordinary leader as mayor of New York City. Sworn in as mayor shortly after 9/11, Bloomberg's leadership approach was based on a businesslike view of NYC—NYC is the company; its citizens are its customers; its public servants NYC's talent; and Bloomberg the CEO responsible for results. Here's his leadership approach.

BE BOLD AND TAKE RISKS

Bloomberg's first major decision was to raise property taxes to put NYC in a better financial condition. Overwhelmingly advised this was political suicide, Bloomberg saw only two choices, reduce services or increase taxes. The risk paid off. NYC's finances improved—and economic activity in the city improved in the process. At the same time, he sought to have NYC win the 2012 Winter Olympics. He lost to London. Bloomberg's reaction: "In business, you reward people for taking risks. When it doesn't work out, you promote them because of their willingness to try new things. If people come back and tell me they skied all day and never fell down, I tell them to try a different mountain."

BE OPEN ABOUT PERFORMANCE AND RESULTS

He insisted that employees, and customers, see decision making in action and regularly see results. So he first changed doors on key meeting rooms and offices from wood to glass, so people could look inside the city's administrative activities. Second, he made semi-annual reports in detail about NYC's revenues and expenses, so citizens and others can see in paper and online a detailed financial picture of what each agency of NYC government costs, is doing, and so forth.

COMMUNICATE WITH CUSTOMERS

Bloomberg has long been obsessed with maintaining constant customer contact and feedback. So as mayor, he immediately established a 311 telephone and Web-based system so that any citizen or guest of NYC could call, 24/7, to comment on any- and everything being done in NYC. And, Bloomberg personally reviewed weekly summaries of all calls to get a feeling for key citizen concerns. The number of calls reached 50 million within the first 16 months and has resulted in numerous improvements in services and actions solving problems or complaints. It has also reduced dramatically the number of 911 calls, by more than 1 million annually, meaning critical first-responders are used more for real emergencies, while nonemergency concerns get addressed in a more appropriate manner.

RECRUIT TOP OPERATIONAL TALENT

Most politicians fill top jobs with people owed political patronage. Not Bloomberg. He views as critical to his success as a leader, regardless of whether he is leading a business or a government, the priority of filling key operating positions with the best talent he can get. And he wants that talent to be able to identify targets for their units, and then lead their people in achieving them. He immediately sought to hire Katherine Oliver, a talented executive with Bloomberg—the business operation in London—to join NYC to build first-class film and TV operations in NYC. The targets she set were impressive, and the results have been even more so.

Bloomberg has maintained a very high approval rating in perhaps the world's most cynical city populace. He recently managed to change the rules to be allowed to run for an unprecedented third term as NYC mayor. His impressive, open, dedicated leadership style has won him not only the approval of his citizenry and NYC employees, it has won him admiration worldwide as a proven leader in both business and government settings.

Source: "The CEO Mayor," *BusinessWeek,* June 25, 2007.

Jim McNerney, Boeing CEO and GE alumnus, described how he handled this paradox at Boeing and 3M as a contrast between an encouraging style (visioning) and setting expectations (performance).

> I think the harder you push people, the more you have to encourage them. Some people feel you either have a demanding, command-and-control management style or you have a nurturing, encouraging management style. I believe you have to have both. If you're only demanding, without encouraging, eventually that runs out of gas. And if you're only encouraging, without setting high expectations, you're not getting as much out of people. It's not either/or. You can't have one without the other.[5]

A real challenge for Alan Mulally at Ford was changing managers' mindsets about being profitable. When he was reviewing Ford's product line as the new CEO facing an unprecedented global recession, he was told that Ford loses close to $3,000 every time a customer buys a Focus compact. "Why haven't you figured out a way to make a profit?" he asked. Executives explained that Ford needed the high sales volume to maintain the company's CAFÉ, or corporate average fuel economy, rating and that the plant that made the car was a high-cost UAW factory in Michigan. "That's not what I asked," he shot back. "I want to know why no one figured out a way to build this car at a profit, whether it has to be built in Michigan or China or India, if that's what it takes." Nobody had a good answer.[6]

Building an Organization

The previous chapter examined alternative structures to use in designing the organization necessary to implement strategy. Leaders spend considerable time shaping and refining their organizational structure and making it function effectively to accomplish strategic intent. Because leaders are attempting to embrace change, they are often rebuilding or remaking their organization to align it with the ever-changing environment and needs of a new strategy. And because embracing change often involves overcoming resistance to change, leaders find themselves addressing problems such as the following as they attempt to build or rebuild their organization:

- Ensuring a common understanding about organizational priorities.
- Clarifying responsibilities among managers and organizational units.
- Empowering newer managers and pushing authority lower in the organization.
- Uncovering and remedying problems in coordination and communication across the organization and across boundaries inside and outside the organization.
- Gaining the personal commitment to a shared vision from managers throughout the organization.
- Keeping closely connected with what's going on inside and outside the organization and with its customers.

There are three ways good leaders go about building the organization they want and dealing with problems and issues like those listed: education, perseverance, and principles.

leadership development
The effort to familiarize future leaders with the skills important to the company and to develop exceptional leaders among the managers employed.

Education and **leadership development** is the effort to familiarize future leaders with the skills important to the company and to develop exceptional leaders among the managers you employ. Jack Welch was legendary for the GE education center in Croton-on-Hudson, New York, and its role in allowing the GE leader to educate current and future GE managers on the ways of GE and the vision of its future. It allowed a leader to shape future leaders,

[5] Michael Arndt, "The Hard Work in Leadership," *BusinessWeek Online*, April 12, 2004; and Maria Bartiromo, "Facetime with Boeing's Jim McNerney," *BusinessWeek.com*, May 28, 2008.

[6] David Kiley, "New Heat on Ford," *BusinessWeek*, June 4, 2007.

thereby building an organization. His successor, Jeff Immelt, uses the same facility to interact with and discuss GE's future with a new crop of future leaders.

Leaders do this in many ways. Larry Bossidy, former chairman of Honeywell and coauthor of the best seller, *Execution,* spent 50 percent of his time each year flying to Allied Signal's various operations around the world, meeting with managers and discussing decisions, results, and progress. Bill Gates at Microsoft reportedly spent two hours each day reading and sending e-mail to any of Microsoft's 36,000 employees who wanted to contact him. All managers adapt structures, create teams, implement systems, and otherwise generate ways to coordinate, integrate, and share information about what their organization is doing and might do. Once again, here is what Jim McNerney had to say:

> It comes down to personal engagement. I spend a lot of time out with our people. I probably do 30 major events a year with 100 people or more, where I spend time debating things and pushing my ideas, telling them what I am thinking and soliciting feedback. Most CEOs are smart enough to figure out where to go with a company. The hard work is engaging everyone in doing it. That's the hard work in leadership.[7]

Others create customer advisory groups, supplier partnerships, R&D joint ventures, and other adjustments to build an adaptable, learning organization that buys into the leader's vision and strategic intent and the change driving the future opportunities facing the business. These, in addition to the fundamental structural guidelines described in the previous chapter for restructuring to support strategically critical activities, are key ways leaders constantly attempt to educate and build a supportive organization.

perseverance (of a leader)
The capacity to see a commitment through to completion long after most people would have stopped trying.

Perseverance is the capacity to see a commitment through to completion long after most people would have stopped trying. Exhibit 12.2, Top Global Strategist, describes how Jeff Bezos personifies perseverance in leading Amazon.com. The opening example about Jeff Immelt conjures up images of some people in GE being hesitant to follow him because of their longtime loyalty to Jack Welch and his ways. Immelt will need to have patience and perseverance to deal with these people, to help them gradually shift their loyalty and accept the new. The example also conjures up another image, one of people excited to embrace Immelt's effort to take GE in a new direction—just because of the excitement of the moment along with some sense that a change is needed. But imagine that the first signs are not good, that it is unclear whether the radical new approach will work or not. It is relatively easy to then imagine a significant negative shift in the enthusiasm and faith of this group—again, Immelt must call on considerable perseverance to simply continue to bring them along and build their commitment over the long term.

"When the going gets tough, the tough get going" is a mantra often heard in sports and in U.S. Marine Corps leadership training. The real point in this is perseverance. NYC Mayor Michael Bloomberg's perspective on risk described in Exhibit 12.1 reflects an emphasis on perseverance. The capacity to take a risk, to make a tough decision, to commit to a new vision, and then to stick with that decision even when it doesn't appear "right" early on is a scenario often found in the history of effective leadership that ultimately creates a favorable future. A broad panel of U.S. historians recently rated Abraham Lincoln the best American president—based in large part on his perseverance in preserving the union. Winston Churchill's perseverance was perhaps his most compelling trait as he successfully led England through World War II.

Principles (of a leader)
A leader's fundamental personal standards that guide her sense of honesty, integrity, and ethical behavior.

Principles are your fundamental personal standards that guide your sense of honesty, integrity, and ethical behavior. If you have a clear moral compass guiding your priorities and those you set for the company, you will be a more effective leader. This observation is repeatedly one of the first thing effective leaders interviewed by researchers, business writers, and

[7] Ibid.

Top Global Strategist

Jeff Bezos, Founder and CEO, Amazon.com

Exhibit 12.2

Since starting Amazon.com, Jeff Bezos has often been in Wall Street's doghouse. The main reason is his insistence on building capacity to support new services his team has determined Amazon's customers need, even as their stock price steadily declines or fluctuates wildly. Asked about his seemingly consistent ability to ignore Wall Street's criticism, Bezos offered these thoughts: "We don't claim that our long-term approach is the right approach. We just claim it's ours. Our approach has been to be as clear as we can be about what kind of company we are and let investors choose." To his employees, Bezos repeatedly makes it clear that Amazon's vision is to find ways that make Amazon's operations more efficient and lower its costs so that it can make its customer experience more value-added while also less costly. And, Bezos notes, "I've taken repeated criticism about our stock price, but never about our customer experience." He goes on to describe that he has repeatedly sat with harsh critics discussing fluctuations in Amazon's stock price yet its insistence on innovation investments, and then, he notes, they would end the meeting saying "I am a huge [Amazon] customer."

Bezos also describes how he clarifies this simple vision to his employees—continuously improving on providing what Amazon customers need. "We have three all-hands meetings a year, and I'll tell people that if the stock is up 30%, please don't feel you are 30% smarter. Because when the stock is 30% down, it's not good to feel 30% dumber." The key is to continuously focus on ways to improve the ways we provide customers what they need. "Companies get skills-focused, instead of customer-needs-focused. When they look at growing their business into some new area, the first question is 'why should we do that—we don't have any skills in that area.'" That approach, Bezos believes, leads eventually to a company's decline because the world constantly changes and a company's current skills eventually become less important. So he leads Amazon by focusing on one simple question, "What do our customers need?" From there he urges his managers to determine if Amazon has the skills to meet the needs and, if not, to go out and hire the people that do. Bezos cites Amazon's Kindle, and electronic books, as a clear example of doing just that, hiring people who know how to build hardware devices, creating a whole new book-reading-related competency in the process. His principles and perseverance to stick with that simple question as Amazon's foundation have proven, over time, to provide solid leadership, ultimately allowing Amazon to emerge as a key Internet-based business model.

Sources: "Bezos on Innovation," *BusinessWeek*, April 17, 2008; and Peter Sims, "The Montessouri Mafia," *Wall Street Journal*, April 5, 2011.

students mention when they answer a question about what they think is most important in explaining their success as leaders and the success of leaders they admire. Steven Reinemund, Wake Forest Business School dean, former Pepsico chairman, and member of the board of directors for Walmart, Marriott, American Express, Exxon Mobil, Ocean Park Hotels, and Johnson & Johnson, described the role of principles in leadership this way:

> It starts with basic beliefs and values. It's important to make clear to the people in the organization what those are, so you're transparent. They have to be consistent with the values of the organization, or there will be a problem. If you look at all the issues that have happened in the corporate world of the last few years, . . . it all boils down to a basic lack of a moral compass and checks and balances among leaders. We as leaders have to check each other. We're going to make mistakes. If we don't check each other on them, you get in

Global Strategy in Action

Exhibit 12.3

Test *YOUR* Principles

Just a few years ago, the dean of Duke's Fuqua School of Business announced that 10 percent of its MBA class had been caught cheating on a take-home final exam and would be dismissed. These MBAs were "cream of the crop" students with six years of corporate experience and careers under way in the new "wiki" world of online collaboration and aggregation of others,' knowledge via the Web as an emerging key source of competitive advantage. So they collaborated in crafting answers to the take-home final exam, sharing insights and ideas, and so forth. Their professors saw the similarity in answers, and, looking to evaluate individual performance, found the collaboration unethical, dishonest, lacking integrity, and fundamentally wrong. So they were dismissed for cheating.

Three years later, Centenary College, a small Hackettstown, New Jersey-based institution, ended its MBA program for Chinese-speaking students after finding "evidence of widespread plagiarism," the school said in a statement posted on its Web site. The China MBA program was based in Beijing, Shanghai, and Taiwan. All 400 students were given the choice of accepting a tuition refund—as much as $1,400—or taking a comprehensive exam to earn a degree.*

According to the statement, all but two students decided to take a refund. The college also noted in the statement that students who cheat are ordinarily dismissed from the school, but the China MBA students are being given more leniency "in an effort to afford students every fair possibility."*

A *BusinessWeek* Commentary took issue with the Duke decision—and saw a different interpretation. Their point: the new world order is about teamwork, shared information. Social networking, a new culture of shared information, postmodern learning wiki style. Text messaging, downloading essays, getting questions answered from others, often unknown, via the Web. All of these are the new ways we work today. We function in an interdependent world, where success often hinges on creative collaboration, networking, and "googling" to tap a literal world of information and expertise available at the click of a keyboard or a cell phone.

Others, starting with their Duke professors, viewed these students collaborating on a take-home exam as a conscious effort to break the rules, or at least, gain unauthorized advantage. And maybe, they apparently thought, this was a good situation about which to make an example in order to rein in an increasingly rudderless business culture.

What do you think? Is what these students did ethical, principled leadership? Is it "cheating," or simply collaborative learning?

* Michelle Conlin, "Commentary: Cheating—or Postmodern Learning?" *BusinessWeek*, May 14, 2007; and Geoff Gloeckler, "MBA Program Withdraws from China due to 'Widespread Plagiarism,' Other Issues," Bloomberg-Businessweek, www.businessweek.com, July 26, 2010.

trouble. Most of the companies that got into trouble had a set of stated principles, but the leaders didn't check each other on those principles.[8]

Principle boils down to a personal philosophy we all deal with at an individual level—choices involving honesty, integrity, ethical behavior. Indeed Exhibit 12.3, Global Strategy in Action, gives you the chance to "test" *your* personal principles in comparison with the actions of some of your business school peers at Duke University's MBA program and at Centenary College's China MBA program, along with BusinessWeek's thoughts on the subject too. The key thing to remember as a future leader is that your personal philosophies, or choices, manifest themselves exponentially for you or any key leaders of any organization. The people who do the work of any organization watch their leaders and what their leaders do, sanction, or stand for. So do people outside that organization who deal with it. These people then reflect those principles in what they do or come to believe is the way to do things in or with that organization.

[8] "Diane Brady, "The Six P's of Pepsico's Chief," Businessweek Online, January 10, 2005; and Dean Reinemund discusses "Principled Leadership," Wake Forest University School of Business, September 27, 2010, Worrell Professional Center.

An effective organization is better built—is stronger—when its leaders show by example what they want their people to do and the principles they want their people to operate by on a day-to-day basis and in making decisions shaped by values and principles—a clear sense of right or wrong. "Values," "Lead by example," "Do as I say AND as I do"—these are very basic notions that good leaders find great strength in using. *BusinessWeek*'s "The Ethics Guy" says simply that principles should boil down to "five easy principles," which are:[9]

1. Do no harm.
2. Make things better.
3. Respect others.
4. Be fair.
5. Be compassionate.

The value of that kind of clarity, and transparency, as Wake Forest Dean Reinemund described it, can become a major force by which a leader will shape and move his or her organization.

Shaping Organizational Culture

Leaders know well that the values and beliefs shared throughout their organization will shape how the work of the organization is done. And when attempting to embrace accelerated change, reshaping their organization's culture is an activity that occupies considerable time for most leaders. Elements of good leadership—vision, performance, perseverance, principles, which have just been described—are important ways leaders shape organizational culture as well. Leaders shape organizational culture through their passion for the enterprise and the selection/development of talented managers to be future leaders. We will examine these two ideas and then cover the notion of organizational culture in greater detail.

passion (of a leader)
A highly motivated sense of commitment to what you do and want to do.

Passion, in a leadership sense, is a highly motivated sense of commitment to what you do and want to do. The late Steve Jobs, perhaps more so than most any business leader of the last 25 years, is an excellent example of the role of passion in the recipe of good organizational leadership. What he said when he returned as CEO of Apple after a 12-year absence, the company close to bankruptcy, is very instructive about understanding passion as a leader. Those first few months Apple was being written off by the business media, and employees were unsure too. Mr. Jobs held an informal staff meeting, and what he said is as instructive today as it was then:

> Marketing is about values. This is a very complicated world. It's a very noisy world. We're not going to get a chance for people to remember a lot about us. No company is. So we have to be really clear about what they want them to know about us. Our customers want to know what we stand for. What we're about is not making boxes for people to get their jobs done. Although we do that very well. Apple is about more than that. We believe that people with passion can change the world for the better. That's what we believe.[10]

Over the next decade Steve Jobs not only helped revitalize Apple through the passion ever present in his leadership, he turned Apple into one of the most important brands of our time. Like many other traits of good leaders, passion is best seen through the leader's intermittent behaviors while in the throws of the challenging times of the organizations they lead. They must use special moments to convey a sincere passion for and delight in the work of the company they lead. These observations by and about Ryanair CEO Michael O'Leary

[9] Bruce Weinstein, "Five Easy Principles," *BusinessWeek*, January 10, 2007.

[10] Carmine Gallo, "Steven Jobs: People with Passion Can Change the World," Jan. 17, 2011, http://blogs.forbes.com/carminegallo/2011/01/17/steve-jobs-people-with-passion-can-change-the-world/.

about competing in the increasingly competitive European airline industry and archrival easyJet provide a useful example:

> It was vintage Michael O'Leary. On May 13, the 42-year-old CEO of Dublin-based discount airline Ryanair outfitted his staff in full combat gear, drove an old World War II tank to England's Luton airport, an hour north of London, then demanded access to the base of archrival easyJet Airline Co. With the theme to the old television series *The A-Team* blaring, O'Leary declared he was "liberating the public from easyJet's high fares." When security—surprise!—refused to let the Ryanair armor roll in, O'Leary led the troops in his own rendition of a platoon march song: "I've been told and it's no lie. EasyJet's fares are way too high!" So it is that there are new rivals for O'Leary to conquer. "When we were a much smaller company, we compared ourselves to British Airways. But they are such a mess, most people just feel sorry for them," O'Leary says. "Now we're turning the guns on easyJet."[11]

It was readily apparent to anyone on this scene that O'Leary was passionate about Ryanair, and that example sent a clear message that he wanted an organizational culture that was aggressive, competitive, and somewhat freewheeling in order to take advantage of change in the European airline industry. He did this by passionate example, by expectations felt by his managers, and in the way decision making is approached within Ryanair.

Sam Walton used to lead cheers at every Walmart store he visited each year before and long after Wal-Mart was an overwhelming success. Ursula Burns, the first African-American woman CEO of a Fortune 500 company, has made sure her 30-year colleagues at Xerox sense her passion for the candor she was most known for in Xerox, as a way to build its future, and not all the sudden accolades she is getting for her "first." In building her management team, she set a clear hurdle for anyone Xerox is considering from outside the company. Their skills already vetted, her main question is: "What do you see in this company that you love—that you can love—you can grow to love?"[12] She's looking for underlying passion for Xerox as an essential leadership skill. GE's Jeff Immelt is described by a board member as a natural salesman who still happily recounts the days when he drove around his territory in a Ford Taurus while at GE Plastics. "He knows the world looks to GE as a harbinger of future trends," says Ogilvy & Mather Worldwide CEO Rochelle Lazarus, who sits on the board. "He really feels GE has a responsibility to the world to get out in front and play a leadership role." Immelt, it would seem, is passionate about GE and its future opportunities. Indeed, at a recent gathering of GE's top 650 executives, amidst a situation where GE stock price is down more than 70 percent since he became CEO, Immelt insisted that "there's never been a better day, a better time, or a better place to be," meaning than GE. That's passion.

Leaders also use reward systems, symbols, and structure among other means to shape the organization's culture. Travelers' Insurance Co.'s notable turnaround was accomplished in part by changing its "hidebound" culture through a change in its agent reward system. Employees previously on salary with occasional bonuses were given rewards that involved substantial cash bonuses and stock options. A major Travelers' customer and risk management director at drug-maker Becton Dickinson said: "They're hungrier now. They want to make deals. They're different than the old, hidebound Travelers' culture." Jeff Immelt is doing something similar to reshape the ingrained GE culture—tying executive compensation to their ability to come up with new ideas that show improved customer service, generate cash growth, and boost sales instead of simply meeting bottom-line targets.[13]

As leaders clarify strategic intent, build an organization, and shape their organization's culture, they look to one key element to help—their management team throughout their

[11] "Ryanair Rising," *Businessweek*, June 2, 2003.

[12] Adam Bryant, "Xerox's New Chief Tries to Redefine Its Culture," *The New York Times*, Feb. 21, 2010.

[13] "Jeff Immelt on Pay, His AAA Rating, and Taking the Train," *Businessweek*, February 1, 2009.

organization. As Honeywell's chairman Larry Bossidy candidly observed when asked about how after 42 years at General Electric, Allied Signal, and now Honeywell, with seemingly drab businesses, he could expect exciting growth: "There's no such thing as a mature market. What we need is mature executives who can find ways to grow."[14] Leaders look to managers they need to execute strategy as another source of leadership to accept risk and cope with the complexity that change brings about. So selection and development of key managers become major leadership roles.

Recruiting and Developing Talented Operational Leadership

Fundamental to a leader's responsibility in developing operational talent is to serve as a role model to younger managers. The purpose of doing so is to model behaviors and habits that become instinctive ways those younger managers address issues and make decisions. This has been particularly critical in the dramatic global economic downturn—which virtually every business has been dealing with the past few years. It has required leadership that is lean and focused at every level, and particularly at operating levels of the organization.

Modeling behavior and desired habits is particularly relevant in the depressed economic times most companies have been facing for the past few years and that many still face today. In many cases, their very survival may be at stake. Thus, modeling and ensuring these specific leadership habits can be absolutely critical.

As we noted at the beginning of this section on organizational leadership, the accelerated pace and complexity of business beyond the immediate economic contraction will also increase pressure on corporations to push authority down in their organizations, ultimately meaning that every line manager will have to exercise leadership's prerogatives to an extent unthinkable a generation earlier. We also defined one of the key roles of good organizational leadership as building the organization by educating and developing new leaders. They will each be global managers, change agents, strategists, motivators, strategic decision makers, innovators, and collaborators if the business is to survive and prosper. So we want to examine this more completely by looking at key competencies these future managers need to possess or develop. Exhibit 12.4, Global Strategy in Action provides an interesting interview with IBMer Helen Cheng about her introduction to the *World of Warcraft* online game and how it is now a key way IBM is using online multiplayer games to develop its young managers of global teams into better team leaders and future global leaders for the reality of today's fast-paced, global marketplace.

Today's need for fluid learning organizations capable of rapid response, sharing, and cross-cultural synergy place incredible demands on young managers to bring important competencies to the organization. Exhibit 12.5 describes the needs organizations look to managers to meet and then identifies the corresponding competencies managers would need to do so. Ruth Williams and Joseph Cothrel drew this conclusion in their research about competencies needed from managers in today's fast-changing business environment.

> Today's competitive environment requires a different set of management competencies than we traditionally associate with the role. The balance has clearly shifted from attributes traditionally thought of as masculine (strong decision making, leading the troops, driving strategy, waging competitive battle) to more feminine qualities (listening, relationship-building, and nurturing). The model today is not so much "take it on your shoulders" as it is to "create the environment that will enable others to carry part of the burden." The focus is on unlocking the organization's human asset potential.[15]

[14] Larry Bossidy and Ram Charan, *Execution: The Discipline of Getting Things Done*, as reviewed in http://bookreviewsummaries.wordpress.com/2008/03/30/execution-by-larry-bossidy-ram-charan/.

[15] Ruth Williams and Joseph Cothrel, *Current Trends in Strategic Management* (New York: Blackwell Publishing, 2007).

Global Strategy in Action — Exhibit 12.4

Helen Cheng and MMORPG—IBM's Setting for Twenty-First-Century New Leaders, Skill Development

MMORPGs (massively multiplayer online role-playing games) like *World of Warcraft* are perhaps the most realistic setting for leadership training and development in our new "wiki" world, according to IBM leadership development researchers. "It's not a stretch to think that résumés that include detailed gaming experience will be landing on the desks of *Fortune* 500 executives in the very near future. Those hiring managers would do well to look closely at that experience, and not disregard it as a mere hobby. After all, that gamer may just be your next CEO."* Reading the experience of Helen Cheng helps explain why IBM is moving aggressively into the use of MMORPGs as a basis for leadership selection and development at IBM, as well as at client businesses worldwide. Helen Cheng got her first taste of online gaming three years ago, when a friend got her to join up with *Star Wars Galaxies*™. "I was pretty skeptical," she recalled. "I mean, fighting dragons in a fantasy world? Sounds kinda nerdy." Three days later Cheng was hooked. She soon moved on to *World of Warcraft*™, an online game that counts more than 8 million members. She moved quickly up the ranks and spent six months as a level-60 guild leader, the highest level of leadership in the game. Here are some of her leadership lessons gleaned from the game:

Q: Do you consider yourself a natural leader?

A: I'm pretty quiet. The first time I thought I could be a leader was during a raid that involved 40 people. The raid went bad, and everybody died. The designated raid leader went silent. Everyone was waiting for instruction. I pushed my button to talk and rallied the troops. It was me, a girl, talking to 39 guys. To my surprise, everyone complied, and we got going. That was a defining moment for me, eventually leading to me becoming a guild leader.

Q: What was it about the environment that made it easy for you to try a leader role?

A: The speed at which things happens contributes to that. You don't have a lot of time, and decisions have to be made. Also, there are different forms of communication. You can send instant messages, use a chat channel, speak over VOIP [Voice Over Internet Protocol], even leave messages on the Web site. These different communications mediums affort opportunities to lead.

Q: What is it like managing people you never see in person?

A: Not that different from real life. I've had my share of personality conflicts that I had to mediate. In my last guild, we had a raid officer who was extremely capable. He was great leading 40-man raids in real time. But he was extremely practical and did not care about other guild members' feelings, or guild unity. On the other hand, we had a recuiting officer who was very friendly and gung ho about building relationships. They often went head-to-head on issues. I found it difficult to mediate between them. So eventually I left to go raid with another guild that was more advanced.

Q: Kind of like climbing the corporate ladder?

A: Something like that.

* "Virtual World, Real Leaders: Online Games Put the Future of Business Leadership on Display," IBM Corporation, http://domino.research.ibm.com/comm/www_innovate.nsf/images/gio-gaming/$FILE/ibm_gio_gaming_report.pdf, 2008.

EXHIBIT 12.5
What Competencies Should Managers Possess?

Source: From Ruth L. Williams and Joseph P. Cothrel, "Building Tomorrow's Leaders Today," *Strategy and Leadership* 26, October 1997. Reprinted with permission of Emerald Group Publishing Limited.

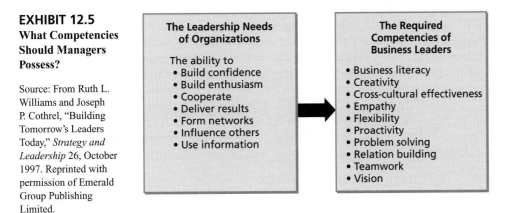

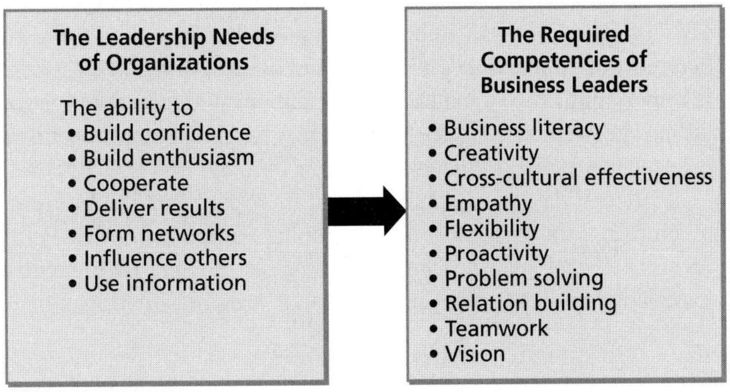

The Leadership Needs of Organizations	→	The Required Competencies of Business Leaders
The ability to • Build confidence • Build enthusiasm • Cooperate • Deliver results • Form networks • Influence others • Use information		• Business literacy • Creativity • Cross-cultural effectiveness • Empathy • Flexibility • Proactivity • Problem solving • Relation building • Teamwork • Vision

Researcher David Goleman addressed the question of what types of personality attributes generate the type of competencies described in Exhibit 12.5. His research suggested that a set of four characteristics commonly referred to as emotional intelligence play a key role in bringing the competencies needed from today's desirable manager:[16]

- *Self-awareness* in terms of the ability to read and understand one's emotions and assess one's strengths and weaknesses, underlain by the confidence that stems from positive self-worth.
- *Self-management* in terms of control, integrity, conscientiousness, initiative, and achievement orientation.
- *Social awareness* in relation to sensing others' emotions (empathy), reading the organization (organizational awareness), and recognizing customers' needs (service orientation).
- *Social skills* in relation to influencing and inspiring others; communicating, collaborating, and building relationships with others; and managing change and conflict.

position power
The ability and right to influence and direct others based on the power associated with your formal position in the organization.

reward power
The ability to influence and direct others that comes from being able to confer rewards in return for desired actions or outcomes.

information power
The ability to influence others based on your access to information and your control of dissemination of information that is important to subordinates and others yet not otherwise easily obtained.

punitive power
Ability to direct and influence others based on your ability to coerce and deliver punishment for mistakes or undesired actions by others, particularly subordinates.

expert influence
The ability to direct and influence others because they defer to you based on your expertise or specialized knowledge that is related to the task, undertaking, or assignment in which they are involved.

A key way these characteristics manifest themselves in a manager's routine activities is found in the way they seek to get the work of their unit or group done over time. How do they use power and influence to get others to get things done? Effective leaders seek to develop managers who understand they have many sources of power and influence, and that relying on the power associated with their position in an organization is often the least effective means to influence people to do what is needed. Managers have available seven sources of power and influence:

Organizational Power	Personal Influence
Position power	Expert influence
Reward power	Referent influence
Information power	Peer influence
Punitive power	

Organizational sources of power are derived from a manager's role in the organization. **Position power** is formally established based on the manager's position in the organization. By virtue of holding that position, certain decision-making authorities and responsibilities are conferred that the manager is entitled to use to get things done. It is the source of power many new managers expect to be able to rely on, but often the least useful. **Reward power** is available when the manager confers rewards in return for desired actions and outcomes. This is often a power source. **Information power** can be particularly effective and is derived from a manager's access to and control over the dissemination of information that is important to subordinates yet not easily available in the organization. **Punitive power** is the power exercised via coercion or fear of punishment for mistakes or undesired actions by a manager's subordinates.

Leaders today increasingly rely on their personal ability to influence others perhaps as much, if not more so, than organizational sources of power. Personal influence, a form of "power," comes mainly from three sources. **Expert influence** is derived from a leader's knowledge and expertise in a particular area or situation. This can be a very important

[16] D. Goleman "What Makes a Leader?" *HBR OnPoint Enhanced Edition, Harvard Business Review* (March 2009), pp. 1–14.

EXHIBIT 12.6
Management Processes and Levels of Management

Source: S. Ghoshal, in R. M. Grant, *Contemporary Strategy Analysis* (Oxford: Blackwell, 2005), p. 501.

	Front-Line Management	Middle Management	Top Management
RENEWAL PROCESS	Attracting resources and capabilities and developing the business	Developing operating managers and supporting their activities; maintaining organizational trust	Providing institutional leadership through shaping and embedding corporate purpose and challenging embedded assumptions
INTEGRATION PROCESS	Managing operational interdependencies and personal networks	Linking skills, knowledge, and resources across units; reconciling short-term performance and long-term ambition	Creating corporate direction; developing and nurturing organizational values
ENTREPRENEURIAL PROCESS	Creating and pursuing opportunities; managing continuous performance improvement	Reviewing, developing, and supporting initiatives	Establishing performance standards

referent influence
The ability to influence others derived from their strong desire to be associated with you, usually because they admire you, gain prestige or a sense of purpose by that association, or believe in your motivations.

peer influence
The ability to influence individual behavior among members of a group based on group norms, a group sense of what is the right thing or right way to do things, and the need to be valued and accepted by the group.

source of power in influencing others. **Referent influence** comes from having others want to identify with the leader. We have all seen or worked for leaders who have major influence over others based simply on their charisma, personality, empathy, and other personal attributes. And finally, **peer influence** can be a very effective way for leaders to influence the behavior of others. Most people in organizations and across an organization find themselves put in groups to solve problems, serve customers, develop innovations, and perform a host of other tasks. Leaders can use the assignment of team members and the charge to the team as a way to enable peer-based influence to work on key managers and the outcomes they produce.

Effective leaders make use of all seven sources of power and influence, very often in combination, to deal with the myriad situations they face and need others to handle. The exact best source(s) of power and influence are often shaped by the nature of the task, project, urgency of an assignment, or the unique characteristics of specific personnel, among myriad factors. Organizational leaders such as Jeff Immelt at GE draw on all these sources and, equally important, seek to develop their organizations around subordinate leaders and managers who insightfully and effectively make use of all their sources of power and influence.

One final perspective on the role of organizational leadership and management selection is found in the work of Bartlett and Ghoshal. Their study of several of the most successful global companies in the 1990s suggests that combining flexible responsiveness with integration and innovation requires rethinking the management role and the distribution of management roles within a twenty-first-century company. They see three critical management roles: the *entrepreneurial process* (decisions about opportunities to pursue and resource deployment), the *integration process* (building and deploying organizational capabilities), and the *renewal process* (shaping organizational purpose and enabling change). Traditionally viewed as the domain of top management, their research suggests that these functions need to be shared and distributed across three management levels as suggested in Exhibit 12.6.[17]

[17] R. M. Grant, *Contemporary Strategic Management* (Oxford: Blackwell, 2005), p. 500.

Strategy in Action — Exhibit 12.7

What Is Your Workplace Culture Most Like?

BusinessWeek

THE BIG PICTURE

THINK YOUR WORKPLACE is like a sitcom? In an online survey, Staffing.org, a performance research firm, asked 300 people to describe their company's culture using one of four fictional touchstones. The results:

"A lot like *The Office*"	"More like *Dilbert* than I'd like to admit"	"*M*A*S*H*, on a good day"	"Like *Leave It to Beaver*"
57%	24%	14%	5%

Source: From "The Big Picture," *BusinessWeek*. Reprinted from May 25, 2007 issue of *BusinessWeek* by special permission.

ORGANIZATIONAL CULTURE

organizational culture
The set of important assumptions and beliefs (often unstated) that members of an organization share in common.

Organizational culture is the set of important assumptions (often unstated) that members of an organization share in common. Every organization has its own culture. An organization's culture is similar to an individual's personality—an intangible yet ever-present theme that provides meaning, direction, and the basis for action. In much the same way as personality influences the behavior of an individual, the shared assumptions (beliefs and values) among a firm's members influence opinions and actions within that firm. Exhibit 12.7, Strategy in Action, shows the results of a *BusinessWeek* survey conducted by Staffing.org to identify how employees view their company's culture in the context of various TV shows or cartoon characters.

A member of an organization can simply be aware of the organization's beliefs and values without sharing them in a personally significant way. Those beliefs and values have more personal meaning if the member views them as a guide to appropriate behavior in the organization and, therefore, complies with them. The member becomes fundamentally committed to the beliefs and values when he or she internalizes them; that is, comes to hold them as personal beliefs and values. In this case, the corresponding behavior is *intrinsically rewarding* for the member—the member derives personal satisfaction from his or her actions in the organization because those actions are congruent with corresponding personal beliefs and values. *Assumptions become shared assumptions through internalization among an organization's individual members.* And those shared, internalized beliefs and values shape the content and account for the strength of an organization's culture.[18]

[18] Edgar H. Shein, *Organizational Culture and Leadership* 4th ed. (San Francisco: Jossey-Bass), 2010.

The Role of the Organizational Leader in Organizational Culture

The previous section of this chapter covered organizational leadership in detail. Part of that coverage discussed the role of the organizational leader in shaping organizational culture. Several points in that discussion apply here. We will not repeat them, but it is important to emphasize that the leader and the culture of the organization she or he leads are inextricably intertwined. The leader is the standard bearer, the personification, the ongoing embodiment of the culture (Mark Zuckerberg at Facebook; Indra Nooyi at Pepsico), or the new example of a desired new culture (Alan Mulally at Ford; Stephen Elop at Nokia) for long existing and well-known companies. As such, several of the aspects of what a leader does or should do represent influences on the organization's culture, either to reinforce it or to exemplify the standards and nature of what it needs to become. How the leader behaves and emphasizes those aspects of being a leader become what all the organization sees are "the important things to do and value."

Build Time in the Organization

Some leaders have been with the organization for a long time. If they have been in the leader role for an extended time, then their association with the organization is usually strongly entrenched. They continue to reinforce the current culture, are empowered by it, and understandably go to considerable lengths to reinforce it as a key element in sustaining continued success. The problematic long-time leaders are those who have built a successful enterprise that also sustains a culture that appears unethical or worse. Either type of long-time leader is often a widely known figure in today's media-intense business world. And in their setting, while the culture may be exceptionally strong, their role in creating it usually means they seemingly hold sway over the culture rather than the other way around.

Many leaders in recent years, and inevitably in any organization, are new to the top post of the organization. Their relationship with the organization's culture is perhaps more complex. Those who built a management career within that culture—Jeff Immelt at GE, Ursula Burns at Xerox, Tim Cook at Apple—have the benefit of knowledge of the culture and credibility as an "initiated" member of that culture. This may be quite useful in helping engender confidence as they take on the task of leader of that culture or, perhaps more difficult (as with these three), as change agent for parts of that culture as the company moves forward.

In the other situation, a new leader who is not an "initiated" member of the culture or tribe faces a much more challenging task. Quite logically, they must earn credibility with the "tribe," which is usually somewhat resistant to change. And, very often, they are being brought in with a board of directors desiring change in the strategy, company, and usually culture. That becomes a substantial challenge for these new leaders to face. Some make it happen, others find the strength of the organization's culture far more powerful than their ability to change it.

"Cultural awareness is one of the most neglected and yet most powerful predictors of executive success and it's also one of the things [incoming new] executives know the least about," says Kenneth Siegel, a managerial psychologist with Beverly Hills–based Impact Group, who works with boards and executive teams to improve performance.[19] And just because an executive worked in a high-performance company does not necessarily mean they are the right person to lead somewhere else. Siegel suggests that board members and others engaged in hiring senior management ask themselves a simple question before hiring

[19] "Culture Club," *BusinessWeek*, March 3, 2008.

their next executive: "Will this person enhance the culture we have here or be devoured by it?"[20] Why? Because a cultural mismatch could disrupt organizational performance for years to come as well as have a major impact on that executive's future career options. That makes the decision of bringing in an outsider, as a new leader, as important to the executive as it is to the hiring organization.[21]

Exhibit 12.8, Strategy in Action, provides an interesting example of these two perspectives as viewed through the experience of the same founder/CEO of successful companies with two very different cultures. It explains how Netflix founder and CEO Reed Hastings sought to dramatically change the culture and way of doing things at Netflix, his second company, after his experience with the nature of the culture that his first start-up, Pure Software, grew into as it became a part of IBM through a series of acquisitions and mergers. Hastings said of Pure, "We got more bureaucratic as we grew," and that it went from being a place that was fast-paced and the "where-everybody-wanted-to-be" place to a "dronish, when-does-the-day-end" software factory. After leaving Pure, Hastings spent about two years thinking about how to build a culture in his next start-up that would not have "big company creep."

At Netflix, Hastings has instilled a very unique "freedom and responsibility" culture that seeks to revolutionize both the way people rent movies and, perhaps more important to Hastings, how his managers work. Facing Blockbuster, Wal-Mart, Amazon, the cable companies, and Apple, Hastings created a culture so unique at Netflix that it is an "A" talent magnet, ensuring the best players in the business line up to help Netflix outsmart these very sizable competitors. And in doing so, Hastings is a "new" leader of a new company with a different business model that is trying to outlast and outcompete other, well established, major players in selling movie rentals. Blockbuster became Netflix's first victim, recently filing for bankruptcy and languishing over a year before finally being bought out of bankruptcy very cheaply. It would appear that Hastings, and his unique Netflix culture, is building a lasting presence based on his experiences and inclinations as a successful entrepreneur and innovator in similarly competitive, large, firmly competitor-entrenched industry niches.

When "new" leaders come into a company with a mandate to consider adjusting / changing its culture, another important approach is through an infusion of "outsiders." The basic underpinning is that shared assumptions can be changed by changing the dominant groups or coalitions within an organization. Obviously such a key group would be composed of the key executives leading the company. And so it is often the case that a new CEO will bring in his or her "own people" to replace existing executives, even and often particularly those with long tenure in the organization. This creates the perception of replacing those representing the old and seemingly ineffective way of doing things, starting the process of new culture formation.[22] Interestingly, referring back to Reed Hastings and Netflix in Exhibit 12.8, Hastings persuaded two key executives, Neil Hunt and Patty McCord, to leave the first company he was a part of building to join him in building Netflix, with a particular emphasis on doing so with a unique culture.[23]

ethical standards
A person's basis for differentiating right from wrong.

Ethical standards are a person's basis for differentiating right from wrong. An earlier section of this chapter emphasized the importance of "principles" in defining what a leader needs to incorporate in his or her recipe to become an effective leader. We need not repeat those points in the context of being a leader, but it is critical to recognize that the

[20] Ibid.

[21] Ibid.

[22] Edgar H. Schein, *Organizational Culture and Leadership* (San Francisco: Josey-Bass), 2010, p. 287.

[23] Michael Copeland, "Reed Hastings: Leader of the Pack," *Fortune*, November 18, 2010.

Global Strategy in Action

Exhibit 12.8

Reed Hastings Builds a Unique, Revolutionary Culture at Netflix

"I had the great fortune of doing a mediocre job at my first company," said Netflix founder Reed Hastings. He was talking about his software startup, Pure Software, which was a very successful debugging software maker acquired by Rational Software for $750 million, which was later acquired by IBM. Hastings had two observations on that time: "We got more bureaucratic as we grew," but "it was so different how they [Rational Software] operated—the level of trust and the quality of interaction between them was impressive, . . . something I wanted to grow toward."*

Hastings cashed out and spent the next two years thinking about his next start-up and the type of culture he wanted that company to embrace. A $40 late fee on a DVD movie rental and the subsequent hassle germinated the next venture, Netflix. Then it was on to figure out, in creating Netflix, how to create a culture that would revolutionize the way managers and employees worked as well as the way people rent movies. His initial step was to convince two key colleagues from his Pure days to leave Rational/IBM and join him—Neil Hunt and Patty McCord. Today, Neil Hunt remains chief product officer and Patty McCord chief talent officer. They joined Hastings in crafting from the very start a dramatically different culture, even for Silicon Valley standards.

Priority one from day one—make Netflix a place Hastings, Hunt, and McCord enjoyed coming to every day, with people who pushed them intellectually, and in a company they were proud of. They carefully added to the executive team, and that team has now been with the company since its beginning, with the trust and quality of interaction they have with each other a key to Netflix's success, a key foundation to its culture, and an accomplishment Reed set for his future when he observed the Rational Software core team in his first venture.

The Netflix culture they created is like no other. It was called from the beginning the "Freedom and Responsibility Culture." Hastings believed understanding it in detail is so important that he created a 128-slide PowerPoint presentation to help new employees understand it in detail. In 2009 he even made it public on the Web, with entrepreneurs and managers worldwide immediately absorbing its every detail. (You can too . . . go to http://www.slideshare.net/reed2001/culture-1798664 or http://blog.summation.net/2009/08/reed-hastings-on-corp-culture.html). Fundamental to the Netflix culture is the belief shared by Hastings, Hunt, and McCord, which McCord dedicatedly oversees, that Netflix requires "talent density" to survive and thrive. That in turn means that Netflix wants only "A" talent, not average. And its approach to do this, its culture, and the policies that drive it, all seek to enable this talent-dense "A" team approach to work masterfully.

At Netflix, there is no vacation policy, or as Hastings would say, "no policy on vacation." Employees take what they need as long as they get their job done. Compensation is flexible, there are no strict compensation rules. Salaries are typically higher than Silicon Valley standards; "we're unafraid to pay high," said Hastings.** Employees typically choose their stock-to-cash compensation ratios. Pay increase is not tied to performance reviews, or a raise pool, but rather to the job market.

Formal titles are few. Perks are minimal. "If you are looking for perks, this the wrong place. The fun we have here is all about building products," offered McCord.† "We hire a lot of seasoned people but we don't have all the perks—cubes, not offices, very few assistants, small staffs, no traditional HR support," said Hastings in a recent interview.‡ Formal titles are few. Parties are few—there are no Friday afternoon bands or beer bashes.

There is also the concept that "We're not a family, we're a professional sports team. Therefore, we're going to try to have the best players at every position, and that means that folks who are B-players are going to be working elsewhere."§ Translated, Netflix seeks to have the best team possible, and get their players placed in the role that best leverages their talents and potential. Said Hastings, "It's an honest and candid environment, and as a result, most employees that don't work out say thank you when they leave. And severances are generous."§§

Finally, Hastings sees Netflix managers' role as a leader being to educate people on what they're trying to do, giving context, and not guiding every specific action. In his mind that "context" includes finding a talented person who would come up with the right decision in most situations. So poor performance to Hastings mostly reflects back on the Netflix manager/leader. What context did they fail to set that led to a poor hire? In the Netflix culture, that might just lead to a major bonus for one manager, and maybe a generous severance for both another manager and the poorly performing employee they hired. Why such generous severances? Because Hastings is of the opinion that otherwise managers might feel too guilty to let someone go.§§§

* "Netflix Flees to the Max," *BusinessWeek*, September 24, 2007; and Michael Copeland, "Reed Hastings: Leader of the pack," *Fortune*, November 18, 2010.

** Ibid, "Netflix Flees . . ." † Ibid, Copeland.

‡ Hastings, http://www.businessinsider.com/netflix-ceo-reed-hastings-interview-2011-4?page=5.

§ Ibid, Hastings. §§ Ibid, Hastings. §§§ Ibid, "Netflix Flees."

culture of an organization, and particularly the link between the leader and the culture's very nature, is inextricably tied to the ethical standards of behavior, actions, decisions, and norms that leader personifies. Enron, Merrill Lynch, WorldCom, Bear Sterns, Madoff, are companies, people, and situations we discussed in Chapter 3—they are all imprinted in each of our minds. They speak volumes about this very point: leaders, and their key associates, play a key role in shaping and defining the ethical standards that become absorbed into and shape the culture of the organizations they lead. Those ethical standards then become powerful, informal guidelines for the behaviors, decisions, and dealings of members of that culture or tribe.

Leaders use every means available to them as an organizational leader to influence an organization's culture and their relationship with it. It bears repeating in this regard that reward systems, assignment of new managers from within versus outside the organization, composition of the firm's board of directors, reporting relationships, and organizational structure—each of these fundamental elements of executing a company's vision and strategy are also a leader's key "levers" for attempting to shape organizational culture in a direction she or he sees it needing to go. Because we have already discussed these levers, we move on to other ways leaders have sought to shape and reinforce their organization's culture.

Emphasize Key Themes or Dominant Values

Businesses build strategies around distinct competitive advantages they possess or seek. Quality, differentiation, cost advantages, and speed are four key sources of competitive advantage. Insightful leaders nurture key themes or dominant values within their organization that reinforce competitive advantages they seek to maintain or build. Key themes or dominant values may center around wording in an advertisement. They are often found in internal company communications. They are most often found as a new vocabulary used by company personnel to explain "who we are." At Xerox, the key themes include respect for the individual and services to the customer. At Procter & Gamble (P&G), the overarching value is product quality; McDonald's uncompromising emphasis on QSCV—quality, service, cleanliness, and value—through meticulous attention to detail is legendary; Southwest Airlines is driven by the "family feeling" theme, which builds a team spirit and nurtures each employee's cooperative attitude toward others, cheerful outlook toward life, and pride in a job well done. Du Pont's safety orientation—a report of every accident must be on the chairman's desk within 24 hours—has resulted in a safety record that was 27 times better than the chemical industry average and 68 times better than the all-manufacturing average.

Encourage Dissemination of Stories and Legends about Core Values

Companies with strong cultures are enthusiastic collectors and tellers of stories, anecdotes, and legends in support of basic beliefs. Frito-Lay's zealous emphasis on customer service is reflected in frequent stories about potato chip route salespeople who have slogged through sleet, mud, hail, snow, and rain to uphold the 99.5 percent service level to customers in which the entire company takes great pride. Milliken (a textile leader) holds "sharing" rallies once every quarter at which teams from all over the company swap success stories and ideas. Typically, more than 100 teams make five-minute presentations over a two-day period. Every rally is designed around a major theme, such as quality, cost reduction, or customer service. No criticisms are allowed, and awards are given to reinforce this institutionalized approach to storytelling. L.L.Bean tells customer service stories; 3M tells innovation stories; P&G, Johnson & Johnson, IBM, and Maytag tell quality and innovation stories. These stories are very important in developing an organizational culture, because organization members identify strongly with them and come to share the beliefs and values they support.

Institutionalize Practices That Systematically Reinforce Desired Beliefs and Values

Companies with strong cultures are clear on what their beliefs and values need to be and take the process of shaping those beliefs and values very seriously. Most important, the values espoused by these companies underlay the strategies they employ. For example, McDonald's has a yearly contest to determine the best hamburger cooker in its chain. First, there is a competition to determine the best hamburger cooker in each store; next, the store winners compete in regional championships; finally, the regional winners compete in the "All-American" contest. The winners, who are widely publicized throughout the company, get trophies and All-American patches to wear on their McDonald's uniforms. As noted earlier in Exhibit 12.8, Netflix's founder Reed Hastings created a 128-slide PowerPoint presentation shared with all Netflix employees and aspirants to explain Netflix beliefs and values that drive its culture in simple, clear, unambiguous terms. He has also made it available to anyone via the Web, further institutionalizing and reinforcing the culture he views as essential to Netflix's future success.

Adapt Some Very Common Themes in Their Own Unique Ways

The most typical beliefs that shape organizational culture include (1) a belief in being the best (or, as at GE, "better than the best"); (2) a belief in superior quality and service; (3) a belief in the importance of people as individuals and a faith in their ability to make a strong contribution; (4) a belief in the importance of the details of execution, the nuts and bolts of doing the job well; (5) a belief that customers should reign supreme; (6) a belief in inspiring people to do their best, whatever their ability; (7) a belief in the importance of informal communication; and (8) a belief that growth and profits are essential to a company's well-being. Every company implements these beliefs differently (to fit its particular situation), and every company's values are the handiwork of one or two legendary figures in leadership positions. Accordingly, every company has a distinct culture that it believes no other company can copy successfully. And in companies with strong cultures, managers and workers either accept the norms of the culture or opt out from the culture and leave the company.

The stronger a company's culture and the more that culture is directed toward customers and markets, the less the company uses policy manuals, organization charts, and detailed rules and procedures to enforce discipline and norms. The reason is that the guiding values inherent in the culture convey in crystal-clear fashion what everybody is supposed to do in most situations. Poorly performing companies often have strong cultures. However, their cultures are dysfunctional, being focused on internal politics or operating by the numbers as opposed to emphasizing customers and the people who make and sell the product.

Manage Organizational Culture in a Global Organization[24]

The reality of today's global organizations is that organizational culture must recognize cultural diversity. *Social norms* create differences across national boundaries that influence how people interact, read personal cues, and otherwise interrelate socially. *Values* and

[24] Differing backgrounds, often referred to as *cultural diversity*, is something that most managers will certainly see more of, both because of the growing cultural diversity domestically and the obvious diversification of cultural backgrounds that result from global acquisitions and mergers. For example, Harold Epps, manager of a computer keyboard plant in Boston, manages 350 employees representing 44 countries of origin and 19 languages.

attitudes about similar circumstances also vary from country to country. Where individualism is central to a North American's value structure, the needs of the group dominate the value structure of their Japanese counterparts. *Religion* is yet another source of cultural differences. Holidays, practices, and belief structures differ in very fundamental ways that must be taken into account as one attempts to shape organizational culture in a global setting. Finally, *education,* or ways people are accustomed to learning, differs across national borders. Formal classroom learning in the United States may teach things that are only learned via apprenticeship in other cultures. Because the process of shaping an organizational culture often involves considerable "education," leaders should be sensitive to global differences in approaches to education to make sure their cultural education efforts are effective. Henning Kagermann, former CEO of German-based global software company SAP, spoke to this issue when he said: "If you are a big company, you need to tap into the global talent pool. It's foolish to believe the smartest people are in one nation. In Germany, we now have this big public debate about there being a shortage of engineers in the country. Well, I don't care, or at least not as CEO of SAP. We are a collection of talented engineers in Germany, India, China, the U.S., Israel, Brazil, and the diversity therein represented enriches the culture, creativity, and market responsiveness of SAP."[25] Kagermann was seeking significant representation of cultures and communities worldwide so that SAP truly reflected the vast global settings in which it does business.

Manage the Strategy-Culture Relationship

Managers find it difficult to think through the relationship between a firm's culture and the critical factors on which strategy depends. They quickly recognize, however, that key components of the firm—structure, staff, systems, people, style—influence the ways in which key managerial tasks are executed and how critical management relationships are formed. And implementation of a new strategy is largely concerned with adjustments in these components to accommodate the perceived needs of the strategy. Consequently, managing the strategy-culture relationship requires sensitivity to the interaction between the changes necessary to implement the new strategy and the compatibility or "fit" between those changes and the firm's culture. Exhibit 12.9 provides a simple framework for managing the strategy-culture relationship by identifying four basic situations a firm might face.

EXHIBIT 12.9
Managing the Strategy-Culture Relationship

Changes in key organizational factors that are necessary to implement the new strategy	High (Potential compatibility of changes with existing culture)	Low (Potential compatibility of changes with existing culture)
Many	1 Link changes to basic mission and fundamental organizational values	4 Reformulate strategy or prepare carefully for long-term, difficult cultural change
Few	2 Synergistic—focus on reinforcing culture	3 Manage around the culture

[25] "Tapping Global Talent in Software," *BusinessWeek*, June 9, 2007.

Link to Core Values

A firm in cell 1 is faced with a situation in which implementing a new strategy requires several changes in structure, systems, managerial assignments, operating procedures, or other fundamental aspects of the firm. However, most of the changes are potentially compatible with the existing organizational culture. Firms in this situation usually have a tradition of effective performance and are either seeking to take advantage of a major opportunity or are attempting to redirect major product-market operations consistent with proven core capabilities. Such firms are in a very promising position: they can pursue a strategy requiring major changes but still benefit from the power of cultural reinforcement.

Four basic considerations should be emphasized by firms seeking to manage a strategy-culture relationship in this context:

1. *Key changes should be visibly linked to the basic company mission.* Because the company mission provides a broad official foundation for the organizational culture, top executives should use all available internal and external forums to reinforce the message that the changes are inextricably linked to it.

2. *Emphasis should be placed on the use of existing personnel* where possible to fill positions created to implement the new strategy. Existing personnel embody the shared values and norms that help ensure cultural compatibility as major changes are implemented.

3. *Care should be taken if adjustments in the reward system are needed.* These adjustments should be consistent with the current reward system. If, for example, a new product-market thrust requires significant changes in the way sales are made, and, therefore, in incentive compensation, common themes (e.g., incentive oriented) should be emphasized. In this way, current and future reward approaches are related, and the changes in the reward system are justified (encourage development of less familiar markets).

4. *Key attention should be paid to the changes that are least compatible with the current culture,* so current norms are not disrupted. For example, a firm may choose to subcontract an important step in a production process because that step would be incompatible with the current culture.

P&G's shift to open innovation under Alan Lafley, described in Exhibit 12.10, Global Strategy in Action, offers an example of a company in this situation. P&G's long-standing Core value as a consumer products company had been one of innovative product design and development. Alan Lafley was very careful to push for a more open culture in terms of who would help P&G innovate more effectively, but he was also emphatic about linking these new efforts at changing how the "great innovator" innovated with the core notion that P&G people, and P&G's 170-year-old tradition or mission was still *THE* global consumer products innovator. He linked changes to the basic P&G values. Lafley next emphasized speaking positively about P&G people and getting them to buy in to the changes he sought. He placed emphasis on existing personnel. Third, he included new rewards to encourage acceptance of the different way of doing things. And fourth, he made sure on changes that were "stretching people too much" to use what he called an accelerator and a throttle approach. He identified himself as the accelerator, pushing aggressively for change. And he assigned his managers as his throttle, to regularly meet and discuss and perhaps alter the pace of change, depending on their assessment of whether the changes were taking or whether people were being pushed to change too quickly. So in this way Lafley made sure to monitor changes least compatible with P&G's current culture.

Global Strategy in Action — Exhibit 12.10

Rebirthing P&G as the Company Its 170-Year-Old Values Intended

For most of the first decade of the twenty-first century, Alan Lafley was CEO of P&G. An insider, he nonetheless dramatically changed the culture at P&G by interpreting the organization's 170-year-old values in light of the dramatically changing twenty-first-century consumer and competitive landscape. Lafley followed Dirk Jager, an aggressive outside change agent who launched new brands, openly criticized P&G's "internally focused culture," and sought to change that culture. P&G was built on a culture that emphasized internally focused, "invented here" innovation; incremental innovation; and intense loyalty to its core brands—Tide, Crest, and Pampers. Poor earnings and employee resistance to change resulted in Jager's departure. Lafley, a comfortable insider, nonetheless agreed with Jager's assessment. He just took a different approach. Said Lafley, "At P&G we're purpose driven and values led. Focusing first on what would *not* change—the company's core purpose and values—made it easier to ask the organization to take on what I knew would be fairly dramatic changes elsewhere. The challenge was to understand and embrace the values that had guided P&G over generations—trust, integrity, ownership, leadership and a passion for winning—while reorienting them toward the outside and translating them for current and future relevance."

Before he retired, Lafley had opened up P&G far beyond what anyone expected. He has made innovation from folks outside P&G a key priority, started new product lines, and outsourced key functions like IT and soap manufacturing. He has made major acquisitions and moved P&G into the beauty care business. He personally spent considerable time with everyday consumers around the globe to understand their basic cleaning product needs and processes.

Lafley described his perspective in an interview with Jay Greene of *BusinessWeek* early in his reign:

Q: When you started, you weren't perceived as a forceful change agent like your predecessor. Yet you're making more dramatic changes. Can you discuss that?

A: Durk and I had believed very strongly that the company had to change and make fundamental changes in a lot of the same directions. There are two simple differences: One is I'm very externally focused. I expressed the change in the context of how we're going to serve consumers better, how we're going to win with the retailer, and how we're going to defeat the competitor in the marketplace.

The most important thing—I didn't attack. I avoided saying P&G people are bad. I thought that was a big mistake [on Jager's part]. The difference is, I preserved the core of the culture and pulled people where I wanted to go. I enrolled them in change. I didn't tell them.

Q: Why did you both see a need for change?

A: We were looking at slow growth. An inability to move quickly, to commercialize on innovation and get full advantage out of it. We were looking at new technologies that were changing competition in our industry, retailers, and the supply base. We were looking at a world that all of a sudden was going to go 24/7, and we weren't ready for that kind of world.

Q: Are you concerned about the [trying to change P&G too fast]?

A: I'm worried that I will ask the organization to change ahead of its understanding, capability, and commitment, because that's a problem.

I have been a catalyst of change and encourager of change and a coach of change management.

And I've tried not to drive change for the sake of change.

Q: How do you pace change?

A: I have tremendous trust in my management team. I let them be the brake. I am the accelerator. I help with direction and let them make the business strategic choices.

Q: Did the fact that P&G was in crisis when you came in help you implement change?

A: It was easier. I was lucky. When you have a mess, you have a chance to make more changes.

Source: Jay Greene and Mike France, "P&G: New & Improved," *BusinessWeek*, July 7, 2003; and Alan Lafley, "What Only the CEO Can Do," *Harvard Business Review*, May 2009.

Maximize Synergy

A firm in cell 2 needs only a few organizational changes to implement its new strategy, and those changes are potentially quite compatible with its current culture. A firm in this situation should emphasize two broad themes:

1. *Take advantage of the situation to reinforce and solidify the current culture.*
2. *Use this time of relative stability to remove organizational roadblocks to the desired culture.*

3M's efforts to reacquire its culture of innovation illustrates this situation. Earlier this decade, James McNerney became the first outsider to lead 3M in its 100-year history. He had barely stepped off the plane before he announced he would change the DNA of the place. His playbook was classic pursuit of efficiency: he axed 8,000 workers (about 11 percent of the workforce), intensified the performance-review process, tightened the purse strings, and implemented a Six Sigma program to decrease production defects and increase efficiency. Five years later, McNerney abruptly left for a bigger opportunity—Boeing. His successor, George Buckley, faced a challenging question: whether the relentless emphasis on efficiency had made 3M a less creative company. That's a vitally important issue for a company whose very identity is built on innovation—the company that has always prided itself on drawing at least one-third of sales from products released in the past five years; today that fraction has slipped to only one-quarter.

Those results are not coincidental. Efficiency programs such as Six Sigma are designed to identify problems in work processes—and then use rigorous measurement to reduce variation and eliminate defects. When these types of initiatives become ingrained in a company's culture, as they did at 3M, creativity can easily get squelched. After all, a breakthrough innovation is something that challenges existing procedures and norms. "Invention is by its very nature a disorderly process," says CEO Buckley, who has dialed down some key McNerney initiatives as he attempts to return 3M to its roots and its culture of innovation. "You can't put a Six Sigma process into that area and say, well, I'm getting behind on invention, so I'm going to schedule myself for three good ideas on Wednesday and two on Friday. That's not how creativity works." While process excellence demands precision, consistency, and repetition, innovation calls for variation, failure, and serendipity.[26] Buckley is taking advantage of this difficult situation to reinforce and solidify 3M's "re"-embrace of its former, innovation culture by bringing back flexible funding for innovative ideas among other traditions. At the same time, he is using the general embrace of a return to its old culture to make some key changes in manufacturing practices and plant locations outside the United States to make 3M more cost effective and competitive in a global economy. Indeed, 3M's innovation revival under Buckley's leadership—3M's even in the iPhone 5—is a popular business press topic the last few years.[27]

Manage around the Culture

A firm in cell 3 must make a few major organizational changes to implement its new strategy, but these changes are potentially inconsistent with the firm's current organizational culture. The critical question for a firm in this situation is whether it can make the changes with a reasonable chance of success.

A firm can manage around the culture in various ways: create a separate firm or division; use task forces, teams, or program coordinators; subcontract; bring in an outsider; or sell out. These are a few of the available options, but the key idea is to create a method of achieving the change desired that avoids confronting the incompatible cultural norms. As cultural resistance diminishes, the change may be absorbed into the firm.

[26] "At 3M, a Struggle Between Efficiency and Creativity," *BusinessWeek*, June 11, 2007; and Marc Gunther, "3M's Innovation Revival," *Fortune*, September 24, 2010.

[27] Marc Genther, "3M's Innovation Revival," *Fortune*, Sept. 24, 2010; "Popular Consumer Electronics Utilize 3M Innovation Without Being Seen," www.businesswire.com, January 12, 2011; and "3M Wins Silver and Bronze in Product Innovation Awards," *Barron's*, April 6, 2011.

IBM's sale of its PC business to China's Lenovo, creating the third-largest global PC firm behind Dell and HP, was a strategic decision it took three years to conclude. IBM management became increasingly concerned with the problem that the PC business, and the culture surrounding it, were incompatible with the culture and direction IBM's core business had been taking for some time. The conflict, and the inability to reconcile different cultural needs, led IBM executives to explore the sale of the PC division to Lenovo. At the time IBM's PC division was in disarray and losing $400 million annually. Lenovo's reaction was to send IBM packing out of China with a sense they had tried to take Lenovo's executives for fools who would buy a "pig in a poke." But IBM executives, still desperately concerned about the fundamental and cultural difference between the PC business and the rest of IBM set about an intense 18-month effort to wring costs out of the PC's supply chain, bring it back to profitability, and then go to call on Lenovo again. They achieved both in 18 months and, in their next business, found a more receptive Lenovo management team—ultimately concluding the deal a few months later. In so doing, IBM worked feverishly even to include creating a profitable global PC business only to then sell it quickly and cheaply so that it could "manage around a culture" in the sense of allowing IBM to unify around a different business model and remove the business it was most known for, the IBM-PC business, from its organization along with the cultural incompatibility it represented.

Reformulate the Strategy or Culture

A firm in cell 4 faces the most difficult challenge in managing the strategy-culture relationship. To implement its new strategy, such a firm must make organizational changes that are incompatible with its current, usually entrenched, values and norms. A firm in this situation faces the complex, expensive, and often long-term challenge of changing its culture; it is a challenge that borders on impossible.

When a strategy requires massive organizational change and engenders cultural resistance, a firm should determine whether reformulation of the strategy is appropriate. Are all of the organizational changes really necessary? Is there any real expectation that the changes will be acceptable and successful? If these answers are yes, then massive changes are often necessary. Alan Mulally's actions at Ford over the last few years saw him making major changes in an attempt to change Ford's culture to suit its new strategy: bringing outsiders in as top execs, changing long-standing executive compensation programs, emphasizing sales and marketing over the traditional, patronage-based culture as, sadly, Ford's most "prized" cultural element. These are elements through which Ford, under Mulally, is undergoing massive change as he tries to build a different culture compatible with a new vision and strategy.

The John Deere company faced a growing challenge in a globally competitive farm equipment industry as it moved into the twenty-first century. Its financial performance was marginal, and it retained a "family" culture borne out of its century-long roots in the land and farm setting it served. New CEO at the time Bob Lane first developed a new strategy that placed straightforward emphasis on improving Deere's efficient use of its assets and clear profitability targets. Pursuing this strategy required several organizational changes at Deere, which were received relatively easily in a tradition-laden company. But Lane quickly found that a greater challenge needed confronting—and that was Deere's "family" culture, which manifests itself in what he called a "best efforts mentality." That mentality drove the culture that had many Deere managers often satisfied with making earnest efforts and doing "pretty good." Lane had to change that culture, or change his new results-driven strategy. He chose to change the culture, which meant moving from the commonly heard expression of "the John Deere family" to one that prioritized high-performance teams. As Lane described it, "We're changing from being a family to being a high-performance team. To use an American football analogy, some people prefer to play intramurals. That's okay, but they are no longer a good fit for John Deere. It was as if you could always count on Deere to move the ball at least six or seven yards. And when we got to that point, we could say 'good work, good enough'—even though we hadn't reached the first-down marker." Now, Deere people are expected to have exhausted every legitimate effort to move the ball farther and meet the goal, and then move the ball farther again. The management team, decided to stick with the strategy and reformulate Deere's culture.[28] The cultural changes and emphasis on profitability from high-performance teams appears to have taken hold. Lane's replacement, Sam Allen, recently announced the "John Deere Strategy 2018" as a continuation of the transformative strategy that propelled the company's performance in the last 10 years under former Chief Executive Robert Lane, emphasizing a "Shareholder Value-Added" operating model focusing the company on generating cash by driving out waste and inefficiency from Deere's operations, aligning equipment production to retail demand to avoid inventory overhangs, and increasing the company's global focus. "By all accounts, it worked exceeding well," Allen said. "Now it's time to build on that strong foundation of achievement."[29]

[28] "Leading Change," *McKinsey on Organization*, McKinsey and Company, December 2006.

[29] http://www.foxbusiness.com/industries/2011/02/23/deere-wants-nearly-double-sales-50-billion-2018/.

Summary

This chapter has examined organizational leadership and organization culture—two factors essential to the successful implementation and execution of a company's strategic plan. Organizational leadership is guiding and shepherding an organization over time and developing that organization's future leadership and its organization culture.

We saw that good organizational leadership involves three considerations: clarifying strategic intent, building an organization, and shaping the organization's culture. Strategic intent is clarified through the leader's vision, a broad picture of where he or she is leading the firm, and candid attention to and clear expectations about performance.

Leaders use education, principles, and perseverance to build their organization. Education involves familiarizing managers and future leaders with an effective understanding of the business and the skills they need to develop. Perseverance, the ability to stick to the challenge when most others falter, is an unquestionable tool for leaders to instill faith in the vision they seek when times are hard. Principles are the leader's personal standards that guide her or his sense of honesty, integrity and ethical behavior. They are more essential than ever in today's world as key building blocks for the type of organization for which a leader's principles reflect and are watched with great interest by every manager, employee, customer, and supplier of the organization.

Leaders start to shape organizational culture by the passion they bring to their role, and their choice and development of young managers and future leaders. Passion, a highly motivated sense of commitment to what you do and want to do, is a force that permeates attitudes throughout an organization and helps them buy into your cultural aspirations. Combining those with the skills, aspirations, and inclinations you seek to make the vision a reality—and then helping them develop—is a key way to build a culture over the long term. One of the key skills of these rising leaders is to learn how to motivate, lead, and get others to do what they need.

Understanding seven sources of power and influence, rather than just the power of position and punishment, is a critical skill for effective future leaders to grasp.

Organizational culture is the set of important assumptions, values, beliefs, and norms that members of an organization share in common. The organizational leader plays a critical role in developing, sustaining, and changing organizational culture. Ethical standards, the leader's basis for differentiating right from wrong, quickly spread as a centerpiece between the leader and the organization's culture. Leaders use many means to reinforce and develop their organization's culture—from rewards and appointments to storytelling and rituals. Managing the strategy-culture relationship requires different approaches, depending on the match between the demands of the new strategy and the compatibility of the culture with that strategy. This chapter examined four different scenarios.

Key Terms

ethical standards, *p. 370*
expert influence, *p. 367*
information power, *p. 366*
leadership development, *p. 358*
leader's vision, *p. 355*
organizational culture, *p. 368*
organizational leadership, *p. 353*
passion (of a leader), *p. 362*
peer influence, *p. 367*
perseverance (of a leader), *p. 359*
position power, *p. 366*
principles (of a leader), *p. 359*
punitive power, *p. 366*
referent influence, *p. 367*
reward power, *p. 366*
strategic intent, *p. 355*

Questions for Discussion

1. Think about any two leaders you have known, preferably one good and one weak. They can be businesspersons, coaches, someone you work(ed) with, and so forth. Make a list of five traits, practices, or characteristics that cause you to consider one good and the other weak. Compare the things you chose with the seven factors used to differentiate effective organizational leadership in the first half of this chapter.
2. This chapter describes seven attributes that enable good leadership—vision, performance, principles, education of subordinates, perseverance, passion, and leader selection/development. Which one have you found to be the most meaningful to you in the leaders you respond to the best?
3. Consider the following situation and determine whether the VC group is engaging in something that would violate your principles, or be totally acceptable to you. Explain why.

   Who likes those ubiquitous online pop-up ads planted by intrusive spyware? Technology Crossover Ventures is betting few do. The Silicon Valley venture-capital firm helped to finance the anti-spyware company Webroot Software. But it appears to hedge that bet with a sizable investment in Claria, a company vilified for spreading spyware.

   More than 40 million Web surfers viewed Claria ads. TCV pumped at least $13 million into Claria, but it has removed the company from a list of investments on its Web site.

   Critics wonder why TCV would make dual investments. "Users are rubbed the wrong way by even the suggestion that the same companies that made this mess are now profiting from helping to clean it up," says Harvard University researcher and spyware expert Ben Edelman. TCV declined to comment. There is a similar element in both ventures: the potential to make money.

4. Read Exhibit 12.3. What would you do if you were asked to serve as an Ethics Review Arbitrator and render a decision on what should happen to the Duke MBA students? The Centenary College Chinese MBA program? Summarize the key reasons supporting your ruling.
5. Do you think Alan Lafley was a good organizational leader? What was his most important contribution to his organizational culture in your opinion?
6. What is your opinion of the Netflix organizational culture crafted by Reed Hastings? What pros and cons do you detect?
7. What three sources of power and influence are best suited to you as a manager?
8. Describe two organizations you have been a part of based on differences in their organizational cultures.
9. What key things is Alan Mulally doing at Ford as an organizational leader to shape Ford's organizational culture? Do you think he will succeed? Why?

Strategic Control

After reading and studying this chapter, you should be able to

1. Describe and illustrate four types of strategic control.
2. Summarize the balanced scorecard approach and how it integrates strategic and operational control.
3. Illustrate the use of controls to guide and monitor strategy implementation.

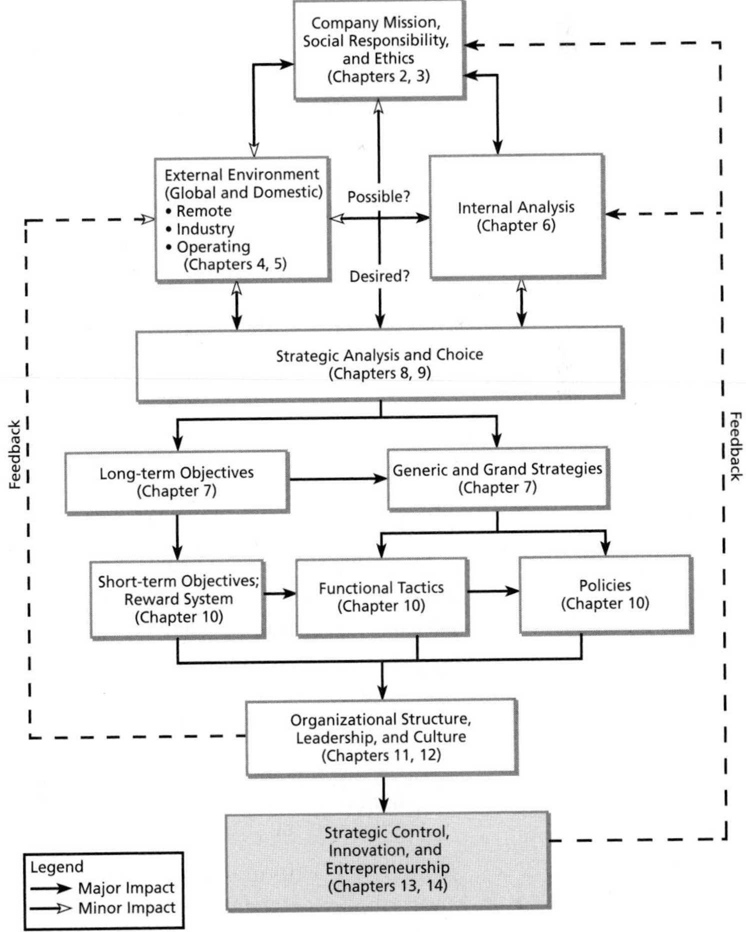

STRATEGIC CONTROL

Strategies are forward looking, designed to be accomplished several years into the future. They are based on management assumptions about numerous events that have not yet occurred. How should executives "control" a strategy, and its execution?

Consider the experiences over the last decade of Motorola and Dell Computer. Motorola and its CEO at the time, Ed Zander, were rolling with a strategy centered on technology-edgy products like the Razr phone, which had Motorola number two in the world for cell phone sales. Those sales were delivered via a well-orchestrated, widely dispersed supply chain worldwide, and a strong belief in the sustained popularity of the technology underlying the Razr. The year was 2007. Within a year, Motorola would drop from number two to number six, seeing its Razr-led sales and stock price drop 50 percent in one year. By 2009, Motorola's cell phone sales were falling by over 50 percent the last two years. Once responsible for half of cell phone sales worldwide, its share was now 6 percent. Motorola was being clobbered with a price war, dramatically lowering margins, made worse by a mostly outsourced manufacturing process and supply chain. Meanwhile, competitors were introducing numerous flashier, sleeker, and more functional smartphones. Within no time, Zander was out as CEO and Motorola was splitting the company in two to reposition and survive.

Meanwhile, Dell Computer had been enjoying renewed success after its rival Hewlett-Packard had struggled with a difficult acquisition of Compaq followed by a confusing reorganization and new strategy under Carly Fiorina's leadership. IBM sold its PC business to China's Lenovo, exiting the PC industry, and Dell was adding more printers and electronic devices to its PC-outsourced pipeline. Then, within two years, HP's new CEO Mark Hurd had HP much more focused, and it soon eclipsed Dell as the world's largest seller of PCs. Lenovo was gaining strength in the Asia-Pacific area. And Apple's renewal was putting pressure on, too, as more people saw the Mac as a viable and desirable option to PCs. Dell found itself continuing to lose market share—experiencing declining profitability, excess inventory, and major problems with outsourced customer service. Founder Michael Dell returned as CEO to replace his handpicked successor Ken Rollins, who had worked as CEO more than five years but had yet to make major headway rebuilding Dell and any newly successful strategy.

So we see two great companies with seemingly solid strategies that deteriorated very quickly. What could they have done or done better? How could Motorola and Dell have adjusted their strategies and actions when key premises, technology, competitors, or sudden events changed everything for them? How could they have established better "strategic control" and reduced the impact of negative events or taken advantage of new opportunities?

strategic control
Management efforts to track a strategy as it is being implemented, detect problems or changes in its underlying premises, and make necessary adjustments.

Strategic control is concerned with tracking a strategy as it is being implemented, detecting problems or changes in its underlying premises, and making necessary adjustments. In contrast to postaction control, strategic control is concerned with guiding action on behalf of the strategy as that action is taking place and when the end result is still several years off. Managers responsible for the success of a strategy typically are concerned with two sets of questions:

1. Are we moving in the proper direction? Are key things falling into place? Are our assumptions about major trends and changes correct? Are we doing the critical things that need to be done? Should we adjust or abort the strategy?
2. How are we performing? Are objectives and schedules being met? Are costs, revenues, and cash flows matching projections? Do we need to make operational changes?

The rapidly accelerating level of change in the global marketplace has made the need for strategic control key in managing a company. This chapter examines strategic control.

ESTABLISHING STRATEGIC CONTROLS

The control of strategy can be characterized as a form of "steering control." As time elapses between the initial implementation of a strategy and achievement of its intended results, investments are made and numerous projects and actions are undertaken to implement the strategy. Also, during that time, changes are taking place in both the environmental situation and the firm's internal situation. Strategic controls are necessary to steer the firm through these events. They must provide the basis for adapting the firm's strategic actions and directions in response to these developments and changes. The four basic types of strategic control summarized in Exhibit 13.1 are

1. Premise control.
2. Strategic surveillance.
3. Special alert control.
4. Implementation control.

Premise Control

premise control
Management process of systematically and continuously checking to determine whether premises upon which the strategy is based are still valid.

Every strategy is based on certain planning premises—assumptions or predictions. **Premise control** is the systematic recognition and analysis of assumptions upon which a strategic plan is based, to determine if those assumptions remain valid in changing circumstances and in light of new information. If a vital premise is no longer valid, the strategy may have to be changed. The sooner an invalid premise can be recognized and rejected, the better are the chances that an acceptable shift in the strategy can be devised. Planning premises are primarily concerned with environmental and industry factors.

Environmental Factors

Although a firm has little or no control over environmental factors, these factors exercise considerable influence over the success of its strategy, and strategies usually are based on key premises about them. Inflation, technology, interest rates, regulation, and demographic/social changes are examples of such factors.

The third-generation Internet, Web 3.0, with cloud computing, virtualization, and ultra mobility, is spawning an instantaneously connected global youth culture that presents both a challenge to the old ways of doing business and an opportunity to gain tremendous leverage via the right goods and services. "Flying blind" is how some executives describe their effort to adapt to it: the tens of millions of digital elite who are the vanguard of a fast-emerging global culture based on smartphones, blogs, text messaging, social networks, YouTube, Twitter, Facebook, iPhone apps, to mention a few. These highly influential young people are sharing ideas and information across borders that will drive products, employment, services, food, fashion, and ideas—rapidly. Savvy companies are recognizing this phenomenon as perhaps the most critical environmental factor/phenomenon they need to monitor and understand.[1]

Industry Factors

The performance of the firms in a given industry is affected by industry factors. Competitors, suppliers, product substitutes, and barriers to entry are a few of the industry factors about which strategic assumptions are made.

Motorola, the introductory example in this chapter, entered American consciousness 75 years ago with the first commercially successful car radios. From that beginning it

[1] Steve Hamm, "Children of the Web," *BusinessWeek*, July 2, 2007.

EXHIBIT 13.1
Four Types of Strategic Control

Source: From *Academy of Management Review* by G. Schreyogg and H. Steinmann. Copyright © 1987 by Academy of Management. Reproduced with permission of Academy of Management via Copyright Clearance Center.

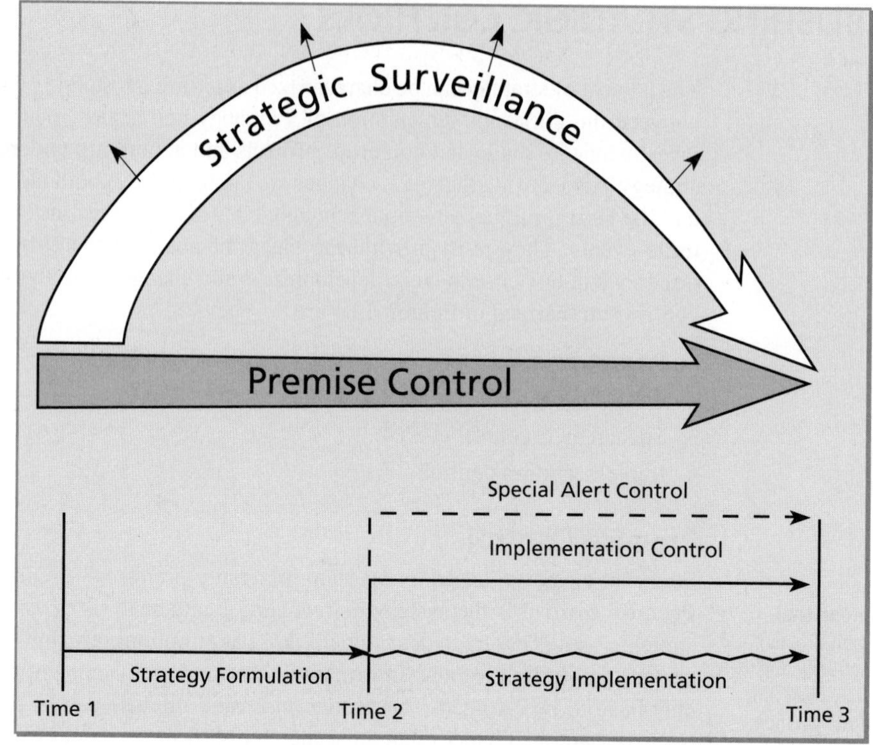

Characteristics of the Four Types of Strategic Control

	Types of Strategic Control			
Basic Characteristics	**Premise Control**	**Implementation Control**	**Strategic Surveillance**	**Special Alert Control**
Objects of control	Planning premises and projections	Key strategic thrusts and milestones	Potential threats and opportunities related to the strategy	Occurrence of recognizable but unlikely events
Degree of focusing	High	High	Low	High
Data acquisition:				
Formalization	Medium	High	Low	High
Centralization	Low	Medium	Low	High
Use with:				
Environmental factors	Yes	Seldom	Yes	Yes
Industry factors	Yes	Seldom	Yes	Yes
Strategy-specific factors	No	Yes	Seldom	Yes
Company-specific factors	No	Yes	Seldom	Seldom

Source: From *Academy of Management Review* by G. Schreyogg and H. Steinmann. Copyright © 1987 by Academy of Management. Reproduced with permission of Academy of Management via Copyright Clearance Center.

became a global leader in cell phones with its stylish Razr phones. Throughout that run, its strategies were based on a premise that technology excellence and continuity would drive continued market receptivity to its steadily unfolding product offerings. As globalization and outsourcing unfolded, it added the value to be found in a supply chain that reduced its investment in manufacturing facilities with the added premise that driving costs down by reducing its level of backward vertical integration could let it bargain with suppliers on price to capture incremental value. Its final premise was the value inherent in the Motorola brand, which led to a premise that consumer loyalty, particularly in cell phones, would be a strong asset for Motorola and its Razr cell phone line as long as it continued to add technological advances in that product line.

Those industry-related premises served Motorola well for the early part of the last decade. But, as it continued those beliefs, a few things started to change that took Motorola a year or more to recognize, with that recognition driven by serious pain in consumer reaction to Motorola's offerings. Contradicting Motorola's premise about the strength of its technological advantage driving consumer reaction to its offerings, more nimble competitors lured away consumers with flashier, sleeker, and more functional smartphones. The efficiencies found in its outsourced supply chain started to disappear when Motorola needed to press suppliers to innovate and reduce prices so as to net a competitive response by Motorola to the rapid competitive offerings from other smartphone players. Motorola's premise about those interdependent supply chain relationships being able to rapidly respond to competitive pressures proved questionable.

Ultimately, Motorola adjusted both sets of premises as it implemented dramatic responses to its new reality. It split itself into two companies, with Motorola Mobility being the smartphone and tablet-type consumer product company, whereas Motorola Services served corporate and government customers. Motorola Mobility moved forward on the premise that it would need to identify with an outside operating system, wherein it also premised that the Android operating system from Google would be the basis of any smartphone or tablet offering. Secondly, it also has the premise that it needs to continue the tradition of technology prowess in offering the newest and best, but doing so under the premise that this is a trendy consumer-driven market, not a technology-powerhouse-driven market it once thought it owned. These two premises appear to be positive bases for Motorola's comeback, perhaps particularly its decision to, in effect, be the first global smartphone player to standardize on the Android platform.

Sanjay Jha, Motorola's co-chief executive, said Motorola shipped 2.3 million smartphones in the quarter and that the company expected to ship 12 million to 14 million handsets by the end of 2010. Analysts and industry experts say the company's efforts now appear to be paying off. Mr. Jha said Motorola's early adoption of Android, Google's operating system for mobile devices, helped the company streamline its efforts, which contributed to its comeback. Motorola has released or announced Android-powered smartphones with each of the major carriers in the United States. The company delivered more than 20 by the end of 2012.[2]

Strategies are often based on numerous premises, some major and some minor, about environmental and industry variables. Tracking all of these premises is unnecessarily expensive and time consuming. Managers must select premises whose change (1) is likely and (2) would have a major impact on the firm and its strategy.

[2] Two YouTube videos from Motorola that speak to these premise changes and the future Motorola focus include http://www.youtube.com/watch?v=CWoD4q_2q5c, where Motorola CEO Sanjay Jha speaks about the new focus for Motorola leveraging Android; and http://dealbook.nytimes.com/2011/01/04/a-new-era-for-motorola/?ref=motorolainc, which, after a 13-second ad by Virginia's governor, provides Sanjay Jha's discussion on Motorola's new approach.

Top Global Strategist
Alan Lafley, Former CEO, P&G

Exhibit 13.2

Alan Lafley turned P&G into a global juggernaut. Some 4 billion people, more than half the world's population, use a P&G product each day. Lafley's philosophy on how to do that is very simple: observe people going about their daily lives, identify their unmet needs, and come up with new products that meet them.

He tells the story of how he had managers in Mexico study the daily washing rituals of low-income women to help kick start P&G sales in that country. He once described another time doing this himself: "I have sat with my legs in the water of a rural village in China talking with an interpreter to an older woman and her daughter doing her laundry in the river. I have probably done laundry in 25 countries. It is like being a social anthropologist." He went on to say it is really "commercial" rather than social or academic anthropology, but clarifying that in saying, "We are observing because we believe that if we don't do anything to improve the life then we don't do anything to deserve to reap the commercial rewards."

Lafley's insistence on strategic surveillance, or commercial anthropology, takes place in many forums. P&G managers in Europe noticed the accelerated growth of private-label consumer products due to the rapid growth of discount retailers like Germany's Aldi and France's Leader Price. While other leading brands were hurt, P&G's manager had been following articles in European publications looking at consumer lifestyles. "We have studied this trend for some time, and concluded that discounters can be a real opportunity." Good strategic surveillance, or commercial anthropology? Lafley was no doubt very proud.

Source: Elizabeth Rigby, "I Normally Have Lunch in 10 Minutes," *Financial Times*, December 6, 2008, Life and Arts, p. 3. See an excellent extended YouTube video discussion by Lafley, which includes a few examples of commercial anthropology early in the video, at http://www.youtube.com/watch?v=Stz9HkKdRS8.

Strategic Surveillance

strategic surveillance
Management efforts to monitor a broad range of events inside and more often outside the firm that are likely to affect the course of its strategy over time.

By their nature, premise controls are focused controls; strategic surveillance, however, is unfocused. **Strategic surveillance** is designed to monitor a broad range of events inside and outside the firm that are likely to affect the course of its strategy.[3] The basic idea behind strategic surveillance is that important yet unanticipated information may be uncovered by a general monitoring of multiple information sources.

Strategic surveillance must be kept as unfocused as possible. It should be a loose "environmental scanning" activity. Trade magazines, *The Wall Street Journal*, trade conferences, conversations, and intended and unintended observations are all subjects of strategic surveillance. Despite its looseness, strategic surveillance provides an ongoing, broad-based vigilance in all daily operations that may uncover information relevant to the firm's strategy. P&G's widely admired former CEO Alan Lafley used "commercial anthropology," his way of describing strategic surveillance, to identify and monitor developments that were central to the success of its ongoing innovation strategy to provide products that meet basic needs better and do so repeatedly. In Exhibit 13.2, Top Global Strategist, Lafley talks about watching women wash clothes in rivers in China, watching others doing laundry in Mexico, and

[3] G. Schreyogg and H. Steinmann, "Strategic Control: A New Perspective," *Academy of Management Review* 12, no. 1 (1987), p. 101.

having European managers study consumer preferences in buying diapers from German and French discount retailers—all examples of strategic surveillance, Alan Lafley style.

Special Alert Control

special alert control
Management actions undertaken to thoroughly, and often very rapidly, reconsider a firm's strategy because of a sudden, unexpected event.

Another type of strategic control, really a subset of the other three, is special alert control. A **special alert control** is the thorough, and often rapid, reconsideration of the firm's strategy because of a sudden, unexpected event. The tragic events following the sudden 2011 earthquake and tsunami in Japan; an outside firm's sudden acquisition of a leading competitor; an unexpected product difficulty, like the fingertip in a bowl of Wendy's chili—events of these kinds can drastically alter the firm's strategy.

Such an event should trigger an immediate and intense reassessment of the firm's strategy and its current strategic situation. In many firms, crisis teams handle the firm's initial response to unforeseen events that may have an immediate effect on its strategy. IBM's shock at the precipitous decline in the sales growth and profitability of its core IT services business resulted in a special alert and ongoing focus on this business's strategy to allow it to immediately adjust by cutting staff or changing services frequently each quarter.

The sudden 2011 media drama involving Charlie Sheen, star of CBS TV's most profitable sitcom, *Two and a Half Men*, dominated Web-based, cable, and traditional TV for many months. CBS chose to cancel the series and fire Mr. Sheen, and Sheen chose to take on CBS and societal convention, dominating celebrity TV and Web-based coverage for most of 2011. That series was the most profitable and popular sitcom for CBS, which in turn caused a lengthy special alert control for CBS. A few years earlier, the sudden release of a photo of Olympic gold medalist Michael Phelps at a South Carolina fraternity house party using a special pipe often associated with smoking marijuana caused an instant crisis for several companies paying Phelps as a celebrity sports endorser of their products after his unprecedented eight gold medals in the Olympics held months earlier in China. Kellogg chose to cancel his contract with their cereals, while Speedo chose to continue their association with Phelps. While others pondered what to do, it showed vividly why a process of special alert controls has become a key for companies using celebrity endorsers as described in Exhibit 13.3, Global Strategy in Action.

implementation control
Management efforts designed to assess whether the overall strategy should be changed in light of results associated with the incremental actions that implement the overall strategy. These are usually associated with specific strategic thrusts or projects and with predetermined milestone reviews.

Implementation Control

Strategy implementation takes place as a series of steps, programs, investments, and moves that occur over an extended time. Special programs are undertaken. Functional areas initiate strategy-related activities. Key people are added or reassigned. Resources are mobilized. In other words, managers implement strategy by converting broad plans into the concrete, incremental actions and results of specific units and individuals.

Implementation control is the type of strategic control that must be exercised as those events unfold. **Implementation control** is designed to assess whether the overall strategy should be changed in light of the results associated with the incremental actions that implement the overall strategy. The two basic types of implementation control are (1) monitoring strategic thrusts and (2) milestone reviews.

strategic thrusts or projects
Special efforts that are early steps in executing a broader strategy, usually involving significant resource commitments yet where predetermined feedback will help management determine whether continuing to pursue the strategy is appropriate or whether it needs adjustment or major change.

Monitoring Strategic Thrusts or Projects

As a means of implementing broad strategies, narrow strategic projects often are undertaken—projects that represent part of what needs to be done if the overall strategy is to be accomplished. These **strategic thrusts** provide managers with information that helps them determine whether the overall strategy is progressing as planned or needs to be adjusted.

Global Strategy in Action — Exhibit 13.3

Examples of Strategic Control

PREMISE CONTROL AT NEWSCRED.COM

NewsCred.com is a Web site–based business that seeks to build advertising and content success around global obsession with news coverage. As we sit here writing this chapter, NewsCred.com is a very cool news site with a variety of applications that will become more interesting and powerful as more people visit the site and participate in its applications.

The premise underlying NewsCred.com's strategy is that people around the world will visit its site to rank the credibility of a whole host of news sources, from mainstream to bloggers, with the result being that the most credible—accurate, believable, and honest—will rise to the top of the community rankings. Some observers argue that in a politically polarized society and world, some people will trash the publications they disagree with. So, for example, *The Wall Street Journal* or *The New York Times* will be relegated to mediocre status, while media outlets and blogs barely known will rise to the top. So NewsCred.com will have to carefully monitor and control its premise, or it may just lose out on what seems an interesting Net-based business opportunity.

IMPLEMENTATION CONTROL

Boeing was scheduled to be delivering its first 787 Dreamliners in 2008. It did not until 2011. Boeing was forced to delay the 787 program four times due to problems with a shortage of parts, the need to redesign parts of the aircraft, and incomplete work by suppliers. For example, Boeing found out in early 2009 that tens of thousands of fasteners on several aircraft had apparently been incorrectly installed after mechanics at Boeing's Seattle plant misunderstood installation instructions. Boeing's ambitious worldwide outsourcing strategy—combined with the 787 being the largest, lightest, biggest plane in history—clearly necessitated careful, coordinated implementation planning and control to meet the milestones and deadline Boeing promised its many customers.

Virgin Atlantic is one typical example. Virgin committed to buy 15 of the new aircraft, at prices approaching $200 million each. This necessitated deposits of notable sums, plus plans and commitments on Virgin's part in working these planes into its fleet, its schedules, its decisions about existing aircraft and routes. Expecting delivery in April 2011, but with Boeing still "testing" the planes in mid-2011, Virgin is "guessing" it will be mid-2013 at the earliest.

The consolation that Boeing will pay them some compensation for the impact of these delays offers Virgin little solace. What they want from Boeing is better control of the implementation of its Dreamliner strategy. That, and a safe aircraft, seem like reasonable expectations for a $200 million price tag each.

Although the utility of strategic thrusts seems readily apparent, it is not always easy to use them for control purposes. It may be difficult to interpret early experience or to evaluate the overall strategy in light of such experience. One approach is to agree early in the planning process on which thrusts or which phases of thrusts are critical factors in the success of the strategy. Managers responsible for these implementation controls will single them out from other activities and observe them frequently. Another approach is to use stop/go assessments that are linked to a series of meaningful thresholds (time, costs, research and development, success, and so forth) associated with particular thrusts. Exhibit 13.3 describes Boeing's challenge to do this as it coordinates globally diverse outsourcing partners' production of various parts of the revolutionary new 787 Dreamliner fuselage and its components.

milestone reviews
Points in time, or at the completion of major parts of a bigger strategy, where managers have predetermined they will undertake a go–no go type of review regarding the underlying strategy associated with the bigger strategy.

Milestone Reviews

Managers often attempt to identify significant milestones that will be reached during strategy implementation. These milestones may be critical events, major resource allocations, or simply the passage of a certain amount of time. The **milestone reviews** that then take place usually involve a full-scale reassessment of the strategy and of the advisability of continuing or refocusing the firm's direction.

STRATEGIC SURVEILLANCE AT WELLS FARGO

Wells Fargo, and most other banks large and small via the American Bankers Association, aggressively fought and lobbied against Walmart's application for a bank charter. They didn't like the idea of losing credit card processing fees. They won the lobbying battle and Walmart withdrew its application to open a bank in the United States.

According to Walmart's management at the time of their application, their primary motivation was to reduce the cost of allowing customers to buy on credit every time they used a Discover, MasterCard, or Visa branded charge card. Every time a customer uses one of these cards, Walmart pays a small processing fee to the bank that processes the payment. And so, from Walmart's perspective, why should they give that fee to Wells Fargo or others when they could just as easily handle the processing through their own bank? They could then pass that fee back to their customer, thereby saving them money.

Wells Fargo is now carefully engaging in strategic surveillance of Walmart's activities related to banking because of this situation—and because Walmart now has banking operations in 38 Mexican Walmarts with plans to increase that number 10-fold with new "banking booths" over the next few years. Walmart has filed an application in Canada seeking to open a pocket bank for its Canadian subsidiary. So is Walmart going to enter the U.S. bank market from its new foreign bases? You can bet Wells Fargo and others have ongoing strategic surveillance of Walmart's Mexican and Canadian banking activities so as to be ready to act.

SPECIAL ALERT CONTROL FOR CELEBRITY ENDORSEMENT COMPANIES

Critical to the strategies, and the success of many companies is the use of celebrity endorsements to promote their products and the perception of that product in the buyer's mind. Tiger Woods was almost always believable as a user of everything he endorses. Nike and Michael Jordan, Bill Cosby and Jell-O, Dan Marino and NutriSystem. But Paris Hilton's ads for Carl's Jr. and Hardees? Peyton Manning for Oreo Cookies? Catherine Zeta Jones for T-Mobile? Jason Alexander for KFC? Or, Michael Phelps for Frosted Flakes? Or even Tiger Woods for Buick (recently dropped) or Tag Heuer?

Bottom line: any company that uses the celebrity endorsement approach to build its brand and image has committed to a part of "borrowed equity," meaning they define their product by borrowing the equity, image, and reputation of the celebrity as a user/endorser. In so doing, they are well advised to maintain a careful special alert control for changes that might immediately or gradually erode the connection with that celebrity.

A useful example of implementation control based on milestone review is offered by an earlier Boeing's product-development strategy of entering the supersonic transport (SST) airplane market. Boeing had invested millions of dollars and years of scarce engineering talent during the first phase of its SST venture, and competition from the British/French Concorde effort was intense. Because the next phase represented a billion-dollar decision, Boeing's management established the initiation of the phase as a milestone. The milestone reviews greatly increased the estimates of production costs; predicted relatively few passengers and rising fuel costs, thus raising the estimated operating costs; and noted that the Concorde, unlike Boeing, had the benefit of massive government subsidies. These factors led Boeing's management to scrap its SST strategy in spite of high sunk costs, pride, and patriotism. Only an objective, full-scale strategy reassessment could have led to such a decision. A similar decision by Boeing regarding its strategic "bet" on the new 787 Dreamliner is very unlikely as it nears final assembly and initial test flights of this revolutionary, next-generation, composite airplane (see Exhibit 13.3).

In the SST example, a milestone review occurred at a major resource allocation decision point. Milestone reviews may also occur concurrently when a major step in a strategy's implementation is being taken or when a key uncertainty is resolved. Managers even may set an arbitrary period, say, two years, as a milestone review point. Whatever the basis for selecting that point, the critical purpose of a milestone review is to thoroughly scrutinize the firm's strategy so as to control the strategy's future.

Implementation control is also enabled through operational control systems like budgets, schedules, and key success factors. While strategic controls attempt to steer the company over an extended period (usually five years or more), operational controls provide postaction evaluation and control over short periods—usually from one month to one year. To be effective, operational control systems must take four steps common to all postaction controls:

1. Set standards of performance.
2. Measure actual performance.
3. Identify deviations from standards set.
4. Initiate corrective action.

Exhibit 13.4 illustrates a typical operational control system. These indicators represent progress after two years of a five-year strategy intended to differentiate the firm as a customer-service–oriented provider of high-quality products. Management's concern is to compare *progress to date* with *expected progress.* The *current deviation* is of particular interest because it provides a basis for examining *suggested actions* (usually suggested by subordinate managers) and for finalizing decisions on changes or adjustments in the firm's operations.

From Exhibit 13.4, it appears that the firm is maintaining control of its cost structure. Indeed, it is ahead of schedule on reducing overhead. The firm is well ahead of its delivery cycle target, while slightly below its target service-to-sales personnel ratio. Its product returns look OK, although product performance versus specification is below standard. Sales per employee and expansion of the product line are ahead of schedule. The absenteeism rate in the service area is on target, but the turnover rate is higher than that targeted. Competitors appear to be introducing products more rapidly than expected.

After deviations and their causes have been identified, the implications of the deviations for the ultimate success of the strategy must be considered. For example, the rapid product-line expansion indicated in Exhibit 13.4 may have been a response to the increased rate of competitors' product expansion. At the same time, product performance is still low, and, while the installation cycle is slightly above standard (improving customer service), the ratio of service to sales personnel is below the targeted ratio. Contributing to this substandard ratio (and perhaps reflecting a lack of organizational commitment to customer service) is the exceptionally high turnover in customer service personnel. The rapid reduction in indirect overhead costs might mean that administrative integration of customer service and product development requirements have been cut back too quickly.

This information presents operations managers with several options. They may attribute the deviations primarily to internal discrepancies. In that case, they can scale priorities up or down. For example, they might place more emphasis on retaining customer service personnel and less emphasis on overhead reduction and new-product development. On the other hand, they might decide to continue as planned in the face of increasing competition and to accept or gradually improve the customer service situation. Another possibility is reformulating the strategy or a component of the strategy in the face of rapidly increasing competition. For example, the firm might decide to emphasize more standardized or lower-priced products to overcome customer service problems and take advantage of an apparently ambitious salesforce.

This is but one of many possible interpretations of Exhibit 13.4. The important point here is the critical need to monitor progress against standards and to give serious in-depth attention to both the causes of observed deviations and the most appropriate responses to

EXHIBIT 13.4 Monitoring and Evaluating Performance Deviations

Key Success Factors	Objective, Assumption, or Budget	Forecast Performance at This Time	Current Performance	Current Deviation	Analysis
Cost control: Ratio of indirect overhead cost to direct field and labor costs	10%	15%	12%	+3 (ahead)	Are we moving too fast, or is there more unnecessary overhead than was originally thought?
Gross profit	39%	40%	40%	0%	
Customer service:					
Installation cycle in days	2.5 days	3.2 days	2.7 days	+0.5 (ahead)	Can this progress be maintained?
Ratio of service to sales personnel	3.2	2.7	2.1	–0.6 (behind)	Why are we behind here? How can we maintain the installation-cycle progress?
Product quality: Percentage of products returned	1.0%	2.0%	2.1%	–0.1% (behind)	Why are we behind here? What are the ramifications for other operations?
Product performance versus specification	100%	92%	80%	–12% (behind)	
Marketing: Monthly sales per employee	$12,500	$11,500	$12,100	+$600 (ahead)	Good progress. Is it creating any problems to support?
Expansion of product line	6	3	5	+2 products (ahead)	Are the products ready? Are the perfect standards met?
Employee morale in service area:					
Absenteeism rate	2.5%	3.0%	3.0%	(on target)	Looks like a problem!
Turnover rate	5%	10%	15%	–8% (behind)	Why are we so far behind?
Competition: New-product introductions (average number)	6	3	6	–3 (behind)	Did we underestimate timing? What are the implications for our basic assumptions?

balanced scorecard A management control system that enables companies to clarify their strategies, translate them into action, and provide quantitative feedback as to whether the strategy is creating value, leveraging core competencies, satisfying the company's customers, and generating a financial reward to its shareholders.

them. After the deviations have been evaluated, slight adjustments may be made to keep progress, expenditure, or other factors in line with the strategy's programmed needs. In the unusual event of extreme deviations—generally because of unforeseen changes—management is alerted to the possible need for revising the budget, reconsidering certain functional plans related to budgeted expenditures, or examining the units concerned and the effectiveness of their managers.

The Balanced Scorecard Methodology

An alternative approach linking operational and strategic control, developed by Harvard Business School professors Robert Kaplan and David Norton, is a system they named the **balanced scorecard.** Recognizing some of the weaknesses and vagueness of previous implementation and control approaches, the balanced scorecard approach was intended to provide a clear prescription as to what companies should measure in order to "balance" the financial perspective in implementation and control of strategic plans.[4] The global consulting firm Bain and Company estimates that more than 60 percent of all large global companies are using the balanced scorecard.[5]

The balanced scorecard is a management system (not only a measurement system) that enables companies to clarify their strategies, translate them into action, and provide meaningful feedback. It provides feedback around both the internal business processes and external outcomes in order to continuously improve strategic performance and results. When fully deployed, the balanced scorecard is intended to transform strategic planning from a separate top management exercise into the nerve center of an enterprise. Kaplan and Norton describe the innovation of the balanced scorecard as follows:

> The balanced scorecard retains traditional financial measures. But financial measures tell the story of past events, an adequate story for industrial age companies for which investments in long-term capabilities and customer relationships were not critical for success. These financial measures are inadequate, however, for guiding and evaluating the journey that information age companies must make to create future value through investment in customers, suppliers, employees, processes, technology, and innovation.[6]

The balanced scorecard methodology adapts the total quality management (TQM) ideas of customer-defined quality, continuous improvement, employee empowerment, and measurement-based management/feedback into an expanded methodology that includes traditional financial data and results. The balanced scorecard incorporates feedback around internal business process *outputs,* as in TQM, but also adds a feedback loop around the *outcomes* of business strategies. This creates a "double-loop feedback" process in the balanced scorecard. In doing so, it links together two areas of concern in strategy execution—quality operations and financial outcomes—that are typically addressed separately yet are obviously critically intertwined as any company executes its strategy. A system that links shareholder interests in return on capital with a system of performance management that is linked to ongoing, operational activities and processes within the company is what the balanced scorecard attempts to achieve.

Exhibit 13.5 illustrates the balanced scorecard approach drawing on the traditional Du Pont formula discussed in Chapter 6 and historically used to examine drivers of stockholder-related financial performance across different company activities. The balanced scorecard seeks to "balance" shareholder goals with customer goals and operational performance goals, and Exhibit 13.5 shows that they are interconnected: shareholder value creation is linked to divisional concerns for return on capital employed, which, in turn, is driven by functional outcomes in sales, inventory, capacity utilization, that, in turn, come about through the results

[4] This methodology is covered in great detail in a number of books and articles by R. S. Kaplan and D. P. Norton. It is also the subject of frequent special publications by the *Harvard Business Review,* providing updated treatment of uses and improvements in the balanced scorecard methodology. See, for example, "Harvard Business Review Balanced Scorecard Report," *Harvard Business Review,* monthly, 2002 to present; Robert S. Kaplan, and David P. Norton, "The Balanced Scorecard: Measures That Drive Performance," *Harvard Business Review,* July 2005, pp. 71–79; Robert S. Kaplan, and David P. Norton, *Alignment: Using the Balanced Scorecard to Create Corporate Synergies* (Boston: Harvard Business School Press, 2008); Paul R. Niven, *Balanced Scorecard Step-by-Step: Maximizing Performance and Maintaining Results,* 2nd ed. (New York: John Wiley & Sons, 2006). Numerous Web sites also exist such as www.bscol.com and www.balancedscorecard.org.

[5] Darrell Rigby, "Management Tools 2008: An Executive's Guide," Bain and Company, 2009.

[6] Another useful treatment of various aspects of the balanced scoreboard that includes further learning opportunities you may wish to explore, especially with regard to the use of this approach with governmental organizations, may be found at www.balancedscorecard.org. Chapter 7 in this book describes how the balanced scorecard approach is used to help create measurable objectives linked directly to the company's strategy.

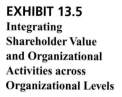

EXHIBIT 13.5
Integrating Shareholder Value and Organizational Activities across Organizational Levels

Source: From R.M. Grant, *Contemporary Strategy Analysis,* Blackwell Publishing, 2001, p. 56. Reprinted with permission of Wiley-Blackwell.

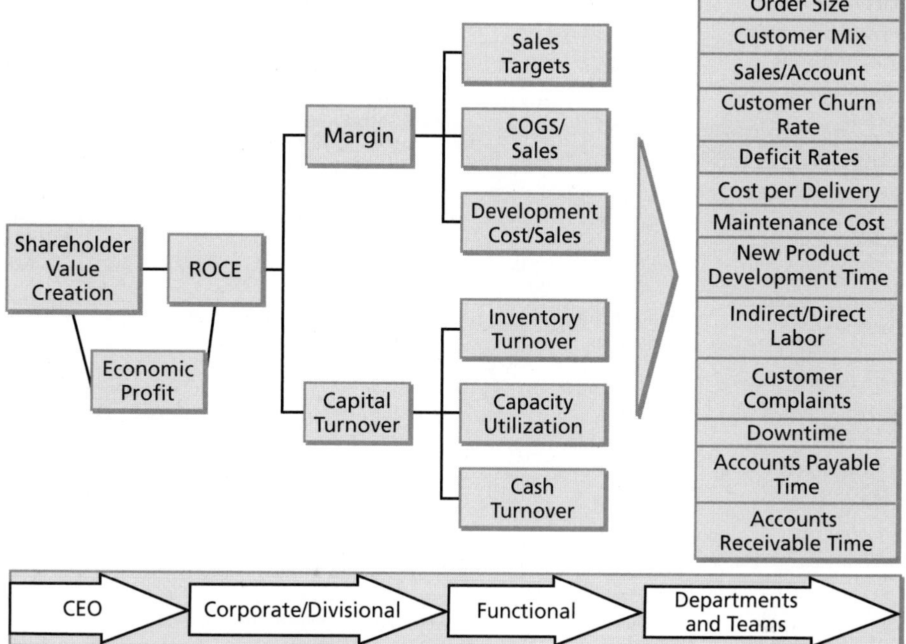

of departments' and teams' daily activities throughout the company. The balanced scorecard suggests that we view the organization from four perspectives and to develop metrics, collect data, and analyze it relative to each of these perspectives:

1. *The learning and growth perspective: How well are we continuously improving and creating value?* The scorecard insists on measures related to innovation and organizational learning to gauge performance on this dimension—technological leadership, product development cycle times, operational process improvement, and so on.
2. *The business process perspective: What are our core competencies and areas of operational excellence?* Internal business processes and their effective execution as measured by productivity, cycle time, quality measures, downtime, and various cost measures, among others, provide scorecard input here.
3. *The customer perspective: How satisfied are our customers?* A customer satisfaction perspective typically adds measures related to defect levels, on-time delivery, warranty support and product development, among others, that come from direct customer input and are linked to specific company activities.
4. *The financial perspective: How are we doing for our shareholders?* A financial perspective typically uses measures like cash flow, return on equity, sales, and income growth.

Through the integration of goals from each of these four perspectives, the balanced scorecard approach enables the strategy of the business to be linked with shareholder value creation while providing several measurable short-term outcomes that guide and monitor strategy implementation. The integrating power of the balanced scorecard can be seen at ExxonMobil Corporation's North American Marketing and Refining business (NAM&R). NAM&R's scorecard is shown in Exhibit 13.6. Assisted by Kaplan and Norton, an unprofitable NAM&R adopted the scorecard methodology to better link its strategy with financial objectives and to translate these into operating performance targets tailored to outcomes in each business unit, functional departments, and operating process within them. They

EXHIBIT 13.6
Balanced Scorecard for ExxonMobil Corporation's NAM&R

Source: Reprinted by permission of Harvard Business School Publishing. Exhibit from *The Strategy Focused Organization,* by Robert Kaplan and David Norton. Copyright by the Harvard Business School Publishing Corporation; all rights reserved.

		Strategic Objectives	Strategic Measures
Financially Strong	Financial	F1 Return on Capital Employed F2 Cash Flow F3 Profitability F4 Lowest Cost F5 Profitable Growth F6 Manage Risk	• ROCE • Cash Flow • Net Margin • Full cost per gallon delivered to customer • Volume growth rate vs. industry • Risk index
Delight the Consumer	Customer	C1 Continually delight the targeted consumer	• Share of segment in key markets • Mystery shopper rating
Win–Win Relationship	Customer	C2 Improve dealer/distributor profitability	• Dealer/distributor margin on gasoline • Dealer/distributor survey
Safe and Reliable	Internal	I1 Marketing 1. Innovative products and services 2. Dealer/distributor quality	• Non-gasoline revenue and margin per square foot • Dealer/distributor acceptance rate of new programs • Dealer/distributor quality ratings
	Internal	I2 Manufacturing 1. Lower manufacturing costs 2. Improve hardware and performance	• ROCE on refinery • Total expenses (per gallon) vs. competition • Profitability index • Yield index
Competitive Supplier	Internal	I3 Supply, Trading, Logistics 1. Reducing delivered cost 2. Trading organization 3. Inventory management	Delivered cost per gallon vs. competitors • Trading margin • Inventory level compared to plan and to output rate
Good Neighbor	Internal	I4 Improve health, safety, and environmental performance	• Number of incidents • Days away from work
On Spec On Time	Internal	I5 Quality	• Quality index
Motivated and Prepared	Learning and growth	L1 Organization involvement L2 Core competencies and skills L3 Access to strategic information	• Employee survey • Strategic competitive availability • Strategic information availability

included measures developed with key customers from their perspective. The result was an integrated system in which scorecards provided measurable outcomes through which the performance of each department and operating unit, team, or activity within NAM&R was monitored, adjusted, and used to determine performance-related pay bonuses.[7]

[7] "How ExxonMobil Became a Strategy-Focused Organization," Chapter 2 in R. Kaplan and D. Norton, *The Strategy-Focused Organization* (Boston: Harvard Business School Press, 2001). For an online version of the ExxonMobil NAM&R case study, see www.bscol.com.

Top Global Strategists
Using a Dashboard for Strategic Control

Exhibit 13.7

IVAN SEIDENBERG, VERIZON

Seidenberg and others can choose from more than 300 metrics to put on their dashboards, from broadband sales to wireless defections. Managers pick the metrics they want to track, and the dashboard flips the pages 24 hours a day.

LARRY ELLISON, ORACLE

A fan of dashboards, Ellison uses them to track sales activity at the end of a quarter, the ratio of sales divided by customer service requests, and the number of hours that technicians spend on the phone solving customer problems.

JAMES P. CAMPBELL, GE

James Campbell was an early user of dashboard technology when he led GE's Consumer & Industrial Division at the time. He would typically look at it first thing each morning to get a quick global view of sales and service levels across this division. Campbell described his dashboard as "a key strategic control tool in the Consumer & Industrial Division business." Fellow GE executives reportedly used dashboards to follow the production of everything from lightbulbs to jet engines, facilitating strategic control of the production and sale of millions of items at GE throughout the year.

JEFF RAIKES MICROSOFT AND, NOW, GATES FOUNDATION

Jeff Raikes, while president of Microsoft's Office Division, said that more than half of Microsoft Division's employees use dashboards. "Every time I go to see Balmer, or now Gates, it was an expectation that I bring my dashboard." Ballmer, he says, reviews the dashboards of his seven business heads in one-on-one meetings to focus on sales, customer satisfaction, and the status of key product development.

dashboard
A user interface that organizes and presents information from multiple digital sources simultaneously in a user-designed format on the computer screen.

Executives and CEOs are increasingly monitoring specific measurable outcomes related to the execution of their strategies. Now, thanks to the Internet and new Web-based software tools known as **dashboards,** accessing this type of specific information is as easy as clicking a mouse. Exhibit 13.7, Top Global Strategists shows how a few well-known CEOs embrace the dashboard as a key management tool for timely strategic and operational control. So, for example, an executive at ExxonMobil Corporation might now use a dashboard to monitor updated information on where the company stands on some of the key measures generated through their balanced scorecard process as shown in Exhibit 13.6. The opportunity to react, take action, ask questions, and so forth approaches real time with the advent of the dashboard software options. That is, of course, when there is a high level of confidence in the reliability of the data that appear—both for the CEO and the managers who might expect a question or expression of concern. The variety of ways the four executives in Exhibit 13.7 report they use their dashboards gives an interesting look at the different ways they might use them, and the different types of information they would choose as key indicators about the unfolding success of their strategies.[8]

Strategic controls and comprehensive control programs like the balanced scorecard bring the entire management task into focus. Organizational leaders can adjust or radically change their firm's strategy based on feedback from a balanced scorecard approach as well as other strategic controls. Other, similar approaches like Six Sigma, which is described in Chapter 14, can also be sources of information and specific measurable outcomes useful in strategic and operational control efforts. The overriding goal is to enable the survival and long-term success of the business. In addition to using controls, leaders are increasingly embracing innovation and entrepreneurship as a way to accomplish this overriding goal in rapidly changing environments. They look to young business graduates, like you, to bring a fresh sense of innovativeness and entrepreneurship with you as you join their companies. We will examine innovation and entrepreneurship in the next chapter.

[8] Some examples of dashboards can be found on the Web and on YouTube.com, typically provided by software vendors offering customizable dashboard solutions. For example, the company idashboards offers examples of screen shots of different dashboard solutions at http://www.idashboards.com/ and http://examples2.idashboards.com/idashboards/?guestuser=wpsc1. Another example can be found from Klipfolio at http://www.klipfolio.com/products/default. The large company SAP offers an explanation of its dashboard offerings via YouTube at: http://www.youtube.com/watch?v=11EWvGwaD2Q.

Summary

Strategies are forward looking, usually designed to be accomplished over several years into the future. They are often based in part on management assumptions about numerous events and factors that have not yet occurred. Strategic controls are intended to steer a company toward its long-term strategic goals under uncertain, often changing, circumstances.

Premise controls, strategic surveillance, special alert controls, and implementation controls are four types of strategic controls. All four types are designed to meet top management's needs to track a strategy as it is being implemented; to detect underlying problems, circumstances, or assumptions surrounding that strategy; and to make necessary adjustments. These strategic controls are linked to environmental assumptions and the key operating requirements necessary for successful strategy implementation. Ever-present forces of change fuel the need for and focus of strategic control.

Operational control systems require systematic evaluation of performance against predetermined standards and targets. A critical concern here is identification and evaluation of performance deviations, with careful attention paid to determining the underlying reasons for and strategic implications of observed deviations before management reacts. Approaches like the balanced scorecard and Six Sigma (discussed in the next chapter) have emerged as comprehensive control systems that integrate strategic goals, operating outcomes, customer satisfaction, and continuous improvement into an ongoing strategic management system.

The emergence of the Internet has led to innovative software that further assists executives in more closely and carefully monitoring outcomes in real time as a strategy is being implemented. This allows executives and managers to have *dashboards* on their computers, laptops, or mobile devices that further enhance their ability to control and adjust strategies as they are being executed.

A central goal with any strategy is the survival, growth, and improved competitive position of the company in the face of ever-accelerating rates of change. Executives, as they seek to control the execution of their strategy, are also increasingly aware of the need for innovation and entrepreneurial thinking as a companion to their emphasis on control as a means to accomplish these key goals in the face of rapid global change. The next chapter will examine innovation and entrepreneurship.

Key Terms

balanced scorecard, *p. 391*
dashboard, *p. 395*
implementation control, *p. 387*
milestone reviews, *p. 388*
premise control, *p. 383*
special alert control, *p. 387*
strategic control, *p. 382*
strategic surveillance, *p. 386*
strategic thrusts or projects, *p. 387*

Questions for Discussion

1. Distinguish between strategic control and operating control. Give an example of each.
2. Select a business whose strategy is familiar to you. Identify what you think are the key premises of the strategy. Then select the key indicators that you would use to monitor each of these premises.
3. Explain the differences between implementation controls, strategic surveillance, and special alert controls. Give an example of each.
4. Why are budgets, schedules, and key success factors essential to operations control and evaluation?
5. What are the key considerations in monitoring deviations from performance standards?
6. How is the balanced scorecard related to strategic and operational control?
7. What is a dashboard?

Innovation and Entrepreneurship

After reading and studying this chapter, you should be able to

1. Summarize the difference between incremental and breakthrough innovation.
2. Explain what is meant by continuous improvement and how it contributes to incremental innovation.
3. Summarize the risks associated with an incremental versus a breakthrough approach to innovation.
4. Describe the three key elements of the entrepreneurship process.
5. Explain intrapreneurship and how to enable it to thrive.

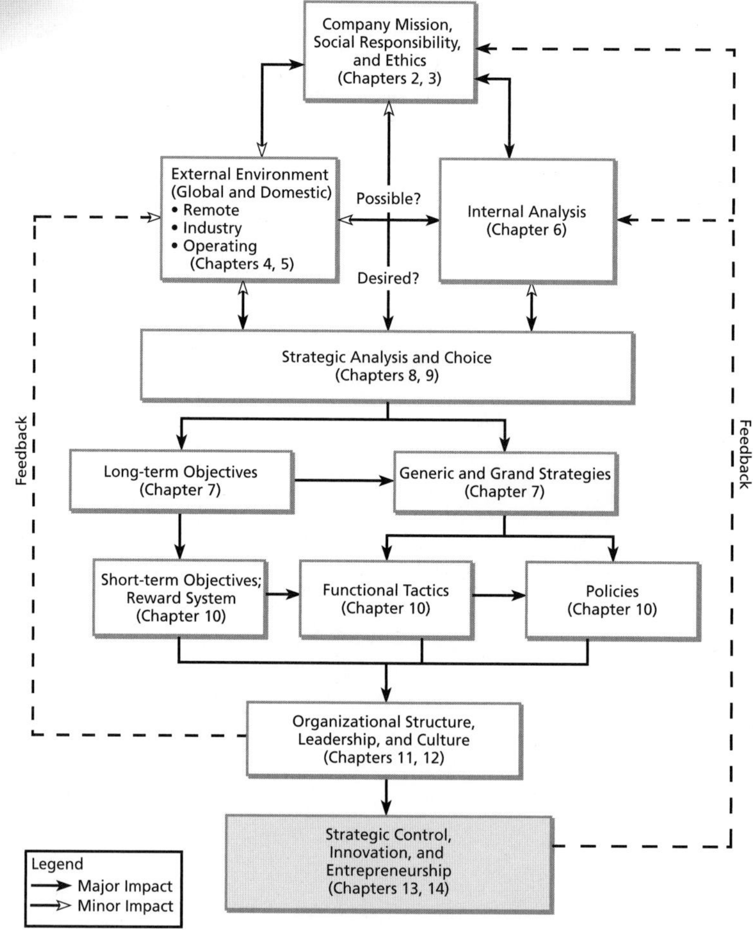

Survival and long-term success in a business enterprise eventually come down to two outcomes: sales growth or lower costs, and hopefully both. Rapid change, globalization, and connectivity in the global economy have led to impressive growth across many sectors of the global economy. Most companies have spent the last decade or two putting continuous pressure on their organizations to drive out excessive costs and inefficiencies so as to compete in this increasingly price sensitive global arena. Increasingly, executives in these same companies see growth, particularly growth via innovation, as the key priority to their firm's long-term survival and prosperity.

Recent studies by four prominent consulting organizations have documented the critical importance of innovation for CEOs of companies large and small around the globe as these CEOs seek to chart the destinies of their companies into the next decade. IBM's study of almost 800 CEOs found innovation in three ways to be the central focus among today's CEOs:—product/service/market innovation, business model innovation, and operational innovation.[1] Accenture and the Center for Strategy Research surveyed executives in the *Fortune* 1000 companies and found innovation to be very important to 95 percent of the firms represented, with innovation being most important when it results in improvements to existing products or services, decreases in costs, or improvements in meeting customer needs.[2] McKinsey and Company interviewed 2,000 executives and found accelerated embrace of innovation—and, specifically, open innovation—was deemed essential to the future growth and success of their companies. They report increasing use of customers, suppliers, independent inventors, and universities as active participants in their innovation efforts as the new-age approach to innovation.[3]

While executives logically embrace innovation, a Boston Consulting Group survey of senior executives in 500 companies headquartered across 47 countries found that fewer than half of these executives were satisfied with the returns on their investments to date in innovation. "Unless companies improve their approach to innovation," BCG Senior Vice President Jim Andrew said, "increased investment may in fact lead to increased disappointment." These executives indicated their three biggest problems with innovation were

1. Moving quickly from the idea generation to initial sales.
2. Leveraging suppliers for new ideas.
3. Appropriately balancing risks, time frames, and returns.

Yet these executives, like those in other similar studies, were anxious to become more innovative. Typically identifying Apple, 3M, GE, Microsoft, and Sony as the innovators they most admire—the "most innovative" companies worldwide, the majority of executives in several of these studies indicate they anticipate spending more time and money resources on innovation in each of the next five years.[4]

WHAT IS INNOVATION?

Common to the vocabulary of most business executives is a distinction between *invention* and *innovation*. We define the two using this common perspective:

invention
The creation of new products or processes through the development of new knowledge or from new combinations of knowledge.

Invention is the creation of new products or processes through the development of new knowledge or from new combinations of existing knowledge. The jet engine was patented

[1] *IBM Global CEO Study,* IBM Global Business Services, www-935.ibm.com/services/us/gbs/thoughtleadership/, 2010.

[2] http://www.accenture-blogpodium.nl/category/innovation/, 2011.

[3] Jacques R. Bughin, Michael Chui, and Brad Johnson, "The Next Step in Open Innovation," *The McKinsey Quarterly* 4, (June 2008), pp. 113–23.

[4] Nicholas J. Webb, *The Innovation Playbook* (John Wiley and Sons, Inc., Hoboken, New Jersey: Lassen Scientific, Inc., 2011).

in 1930, yet the first commercial jet airplane did not fly until 1957. Computers were based on three different sets of knowledge created decades before the first computer.

innovation
The initial commercialization of invention by producing and selling a new product, service, or process.

Innovation is the initial commercialization of invention by producing and selling a new product, service, or process. As executives across each of the surveys summarized earlier typically put it, "Innovation is turning ideas into profits."[5]

Apple's iPod, iPhone, and then iPad were three successive *product innovations* that applied, among other things, Apple's chip storage technology with sleek device styling to create three blockbuster products within a short time frame in each instance. After creating the iPod, Steven Jobs then worked intensely for almost two years negotiating digital music rights with a recalcitrant music industry, culminating in the launching of iTunes in 2003—a music download *service innovation* with an initial 200,000 digital songs to choose from for your iPod and subsequently your iPhone. In five short years, that became 3 million songs and more than $5 billion in annual revenue added to the business, allowing Apple in the process to replace Walmart as the world's largest music retailer. Starbucks added the simple service of wireless access free to its customers at most of its 8,000 stores in what turned out to be a highly successful *service innovation* that resulted in customers using the service staying nine times longer than regular customers, and doing so during off-peak hours.

While these two leading innovators are creating profitable product and service innovations, Toyota is a widely acknowledged and studied business *process innovator* worldwide due to its meticulous attention to business and operating processes. Several years ago, Toyota made one change to its production lines, using a single brace to hold auto frames together instead of the 50 it previously took. While a minute part of Toyota's overall production process, this "global body line" system slashed 75 percent off the cost of refitting a production line. It is the reason behind Toyota's ability to make different models on a single production line, estimated to save Toyota more than $3 billion annually.

To some business managers, "innovation seems as predictable as a rainbow and as manageable as a butterfly. Penicillin, Teflon, Post-it-notes—they sprang from such accidents as moldy Petri dishes, a failed coolant, and a mediocre glue." Not surprisingly, many managers forgo trying to harness innovation systematically. "Our approach has always been very simple, which is to try not to manage innovation," says Michael Moritz, a partner with world-renowned venture capital firm Sequoia Capital. "We prefer to just let the market manage it."[6] For those managers who try to manage innovation, it is important to distinguish two types of innovations: incremental innovation and breakthrough innovation.

Incremental Innovation

incremental innovation
Simple changes or adjustments in existing products, services, or processes.

continuous improvement
The process of relentlessly trying to find ways to improve and enhance a company's products and processes from design through assembly, sales, and service. It is called *kaizen* in Japanese. It is usually associated with incremental innovation.

Incremental innovation refers to simple changes or adjustments in existing products, services, or processes. There is growing evidence that companies seeking to increase the payoff from innovation investments best do so by focusing on incremental innovations. We will examine the payoff research more completely in a subsequent section on risks associated with innovation. First, however, we need to examine how companies are seeking incremental innovation. A major driver of incremental innovation in many companies the last several years has come from programs aimed at continuous improvement, cost reduction, and quality management.

Continuous improvement, what in Japanese is called *kaizen,* is the process of relentlessly trying to find ways to improve and enhance a company's products and processes

[5] "Global Firms Will Increase Their Spending on Innovation," *PRNewswire*, December 8, 2004.

[6] Robert Hof, Steve Hamm, Diane Brady, and Ian Rowley, "Building an Idea Factory," *BusinessWeek,* October 11, 2004.

Top Global Strategist

Taiichi Ohno . . . Father of the Toyota Production System

Exhibit 14.1

All we are doing is looking at the time line, from the moment the customer gives us an order to the point when we collect the cash. And we are reducing the time line by reducing the non-value-adding wastes.

—*Taiichi Ohno*

Why not make the work easier and more interesting so that people do not have to sweat? The Toyota style is not to create results by working hard. It is a system that says there is no limit to people's creativity. People don't go to Toyota to "work," they go there to "think."

—*Taiichi Ohno*

Every 20-year-old factory worker, or designer, and every Toyota executive reveres the heritage bestowed upon them by Taiichi Ohno. Sixty years ago, after observing Henry Ford's work, and American grocery stores, he set about creating in-house precepts at Toyota's production facilities to eliminate waste while improving efficiency, which became JIT; continuous improvement (*kaizen*); mistake proofing (*pokayoke*); and regular brainstorming sessions among suppliers, designers, engineering, and sales personnel. The result has revolutionized car manufacturing.

Toyota's plants are high-tech marvels, building multiple car models on the same production line with parts descending on time from above and below via numerous conveyor belts like a manufacturing ballet. While sophisticated, Ohno's spirit is ever present, seeking creative frugality—reducing the use of PowerPoint handouts in meetings to save on ink costs, or lessening heating during working hours at company dormitories, or pushing suppliers to reduce the number of side-view mirror sizes from 50 to 3 for all Toyota cars. All these actions and many, many more reflect Ohno's passion for continuous, simple innovation borne out of the minds of Toyota's employees going about their daily work, building the best cars and trucks in the world.

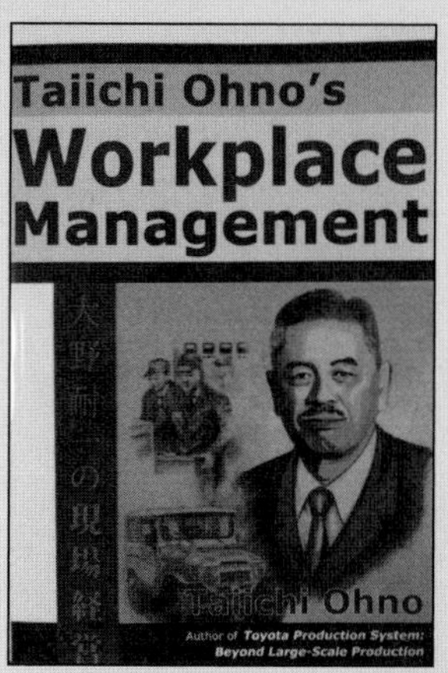

Source: http://www.kellogg.northwestern.edu/course/opns430/modules/lean_operations/ohno-tps.pdf; and quotes courtesy of www.matthrivnak.com

from design through assembly, sales, and service. This approach, or really an operating philosophy, seeks to always find slight improvements or refinements in every aspect of what a company does so that it will result in lower costs, higher quality and speed, or more rapid response to customer needs.[7]

A few years ago Toyota responded to incidents of potentially defective accelerator systems with a companywide, humble reaffirmation of the philosophy of the father of its long-famous production system, Taiichi Ohno. That system, credited with leading Toyota to become one of if not the world's leading automobile companies, is one good example of a cost-oriented continuous improvement effort (see Exhibit 14.1, Top Global Strategist). Called **CCC21** (Construction of Cost Competitiveness for the 21st Century), Toyota embarked on this intense scrutiny of every product it purchases or builds to include in the assembly of its automobiles in response to growing concern about the relative cost advantage to be derived from a surge in global automobile company mergers starting with Daimler-Chrysler. The result: a stunning $20 billion in cost savings over the last decade in the parts it buys, while also improving quality significantly. Taking the Japanese perspective, 1001 small innovations or improvements together have become something

CCC21
A world-famous, cost-oriented continuous improvement program at Toyota (Construction of Cost Competitiveness for the 21st Century).

[7] TQM, total quality management, is the initial continuous improvement philosophy used worldwide to focus managers and employees on customer defined quality since starting in Japan in the 1970s.

transformative. A good example would be Toyota engineers disassembling the horns made by a Japanese supplier and finding ways to eliminate 6 of 28 horn components, saving 40 percent in costs and improving quality. Or, interior assist grips above each door—once there were 35 different grips but now, across 90 different Toyota models, there are only 3. Toyota engineers call this process *kawaita zokin wo shiboru,* or "wringing drops from a dry towel," which means an excruciating, unending process essential to Toyota's continuous improvement success.

Six Sigma
A continuous improvement program adopted by many companies in the last two decades that takes a very rigorous and analytical approach to quality and continuous improvement with an objective to improve profits through defect reduction, yield improvement, improved customer satisfaction, and best-in-class performance.

Six Sigma is another continuous improvement approach widely used by many companies worldwide to spur incremental innovation in their businesses. Six Sigma is a rigorous and analytical approach to quality and continuous improvement with an objective to improve profits through defect reduction, yield improvement, improved consumer satisfaction, and best-in-class performance. Six Sigma complements TQM philosophies such as management leadership, continuous education, and customer focus while deploying a disciplined and structured approach of hard-nosed statistics.[8]

Companies such as Honeywell, Motorola, BMW, GE, SAP, IBM, and Texas Instruments have adopted the Six Sigma discipline as a major business initiative. Many of these companies invested heavily in and pursued this model initially to create products and services that were of equal and higher quality than those of its competitors and to improve relationships with customers. A Six Sigma program at many organizations simply means a measure of quality that strives for near perfection in every facet of the business including every product, process, and transaction:

How the Six Sigma Statistical Concept Works

Six Sigma means a failure rate of 3.4 parts per million or 99.9997 percent. At the sixth standard deviation from the mean under a normal distribution, 99.9996 percent of the population is under the curve with not more than 3.4 parts per million defective. The higher the sigma value, the less likely a process will produce defects as excellence is approached.

If you played 100 rounds of golf per year and played at:

2 Sigma: You'd miss 6 putts per round.
3 Sigma: You'd miss 1 putt per round.
4 Sigma: You'd miss 1 putt every 9 rounds.
5 Sigma: You'd miss 1 putt every 2.33 years.
6 Sigma: You'd miss 1 putt every 163 years!

Source: From John Petty, "When Near Enough Is Not Good Enough," *Australian CPA,* May 2000, pp. 34–35. Reprinted with permission of the author.

Many frameworks, management philosophies, and specific statistical tools exist for implementing the Six Sigma methodology and its objective to create a near-perfect process or service. One such method for improving a system for existing processes falling below specification while looking for incremental improvement is the DMAIC process (define, measure, analyze, improve, control) shown in Exhibit 14.2.

Incremental innovation via continuous improvement programs is viewed by most proponents as virtually a new organizational culture and way of thinking. It is built around an intense focus on customer satisfaction; on accurate measurement of every critical variable in a business's operation; on continuous improvement of products, services, and processes; and on work relationships based on trust and teamwork. One useful explanation of the

[8] ISO certification, from the International Standards Organization, is another widely used means of encouraging rigorous and analytically based assessment and confirmation of meeting quality and building continuous improvement into the way the organization functions.

EXHIBIT 14.2 The DMAIC Six Sigma Approach

Define

- Project definition
- Project charter
- Gathering voice of the customer
- Translating customer needs into specific requirements

Measure

- Process mapping (as-is process)
- Data attributes (continuous vs. discrete)
- Measurement system analysis
- Gauge repeatability and reproducibility
- Measuring process capability
- Calculating process sigma level
- Visually displaying baseline performance

Analyze

- Visually displaying data (histogram, run chart, Pareto chart, scatter diagram)
- Value-added analysis
- Cause-and-effect analysis (a.k.a. Fishbone, Ishikawa)
- Verification of root causes
- Determining opportunity (defects and financial) for improvement
- Project charter review and revision

Improve

- Brainstorming
- Quality function deployment (house of quality)
- Failure modes and effects analysis (FMEA)
- Piloting your solution
- Implementation planning
- Culture modification planning for your organization

Control

- Statistical process control (SPC) overview
- Developing a process control plan
- Documenting the process

continuous improvement philosophy suggests 10 essential elements that lead to meaningful incremental innovation:

1. *Define quality and customer value.* Rather than be left to individual interpretation, company personnel should have a clear definition of what *quality* means in the job, department, and throughout the company. It should be developed from your customer's perspective and communicated as a written policy. Thinking in terms of customer value broadens the definition of *quality* to include efficiency and responsiveness. Said another way, quality to your customer often means that the product performs well; that it is priced competitively (efficiency); and that you provide it quickly and adapt it when needed (responsiveness). Customer value is found in the combination of all three—quality, price, and speed.

2. *Develop a customer orientation.* Customer value is what the customer says it is. Don't rely on secondary information—talk to your customers directly. Also recognize your "internal" customers. Usually less than 20 percent of company employees come into contact with external customers, while the other 80 percent serve internal customers—other units with real performance expectations—in a process that looks like this:

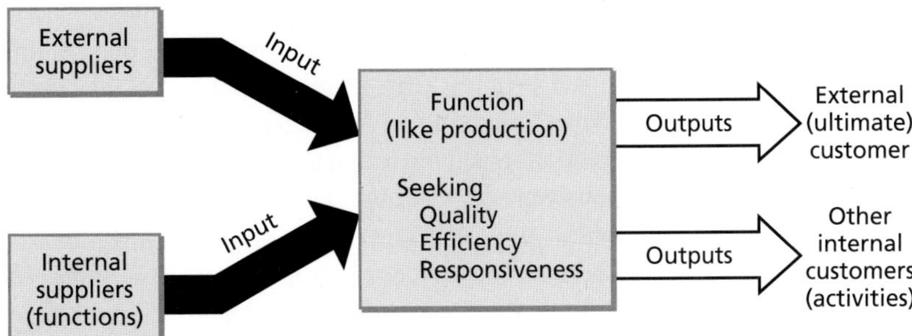

3. *Focus on the company's business processes.* Break down every minute step in the process of providing the company's product or service, and look at ways to improve it, rather

than focusing simply on the finished product or service. Each process contributes value in some way, which can be improved or adapted to help other processes (internal customers) improve. Here are several examples of ways customer value is enhanced across business processes in several functions:

	Quality	Efficiency	Responsiveness
Marketing	Provides accurate assessment of customer's product preferences to R&D	Targets advertising campaign at customers, using cost-effective medium	Quickly uncovers and reacts to changing market trends
Operations	Consistently produces goods matching engineering design	Minimizes scrap and rework through high-production yield	Quickly adapts to latest demands with production flexibility
Research and development	Designs products that combine customer demand and production capabilities	Uses computers to test feasibility of idea before going to more expensive full-scale prototype	Carries out parallel product/process designs to speed up overall innovation
Accounting	Provides the information that managers in other functions need to make decisions	Simplifies and computerizes to decrease the cost of gathering information	Provides information in "real time" (as the events described are still happening)
Purchasing	Selects vendors for their ability to join in an effective "partnership"	Given the required vendor quality, negotiates prices to provide good value	Schedules inbound deliveries efficiently, avoiding both extensive inventories and stock-outs
Personnel	Trains workforce to perform required tasks	Minimizes employee turnover, reducing hiring and training expenses	In response to strong growth in sales, finds large numbers of employees and quickly teaches needed skills

4. *Develop customer and supplier partnerships.* Organizations have a destructive tendency to view suppliers and even customers adversarily. It is better to understand the horizontal flow of a business—outside suppliers to internal suppliers/customers (a company's various departments) to external customers. This view suggests suppliers are partners in meeting customer needs, and customers are partners by providing input so the company and suppliers can meet and exceed those expectations.

Ford Motor Company's Dearborn, Michigan, plant is linked electronically with supplier Allied Signal's Kansas City, Missouri, plant. A Ford computer recently sent the design for a car's connecting rod to an Allied Signal factory computer, which transformed the design into instructions that it fed to a machine tool on the shop floor. The result: quality, efficiency, and responsiveness.

5. *Take a preventive approach.* Many organizations reward "fire fighters" not "fire preventers" and identify errors after the work is done. Management, instead, should be rewarded for being prevention oriented and seeking to eliminate non-value-added work as CCC21 does quite well at Toyota.

6. *Adopt an error-free attitude.* Instill an attitude that "good enough" is not good enough anymore. "Error free" should become each individual's performance standard, with

managers taking every opportunity to demonstrate and communicate the importance of this Six Sigma–type imperative.

7. *Get the facts first.* Continuous improvement–oriented companies make decisions based on facts, not on opinions. Accurate measurement, often using readily available statistical techniques, of every critical variable in a business's operation—and using those measurements to trace problems to their roots and eliminate their causes—is a better way.

8. *Encourage every manager and employee to participate.* Employee participation, empowerment, participative decision making, and extensive training in quality techniques, statistical techniques, and measurement tools are the ingredients continuous improvement companies employ to support and instill a commitment to customer value.

9. *Create an atmosphere of total involvement.* Quality management cannot be the job of a few managers or of one department. Maximum customer value cannot be achieved unless all areas of the organization apply quality concepts simultaneously.

10. *Strive for continuous improvement.* Stephen Yearout, director of Ernst & Young's Quality Management Center, recently observed that "Historically, meeting your customers' expectations would distinguish you from your competitors. The twenty-first century will require that you anticipate customer expectations and deliver quality service faster than the competition."

Quality, efficiency, and responsiveness are not one-time programs of competitive response because they create a new standard to measure up to. Organizations quickly find that continually improving quality, efficiency, and responsiveness in their processes, products, and services is not just good business; it's an excellent means to identify incremental innovations that become foundations for long-term survival.

Disciplines like Six Sigma are systematic ways to improve customer service and quality; the added benefit that emerged has been its effectiveness in cutting costs and improving profitability. That has made it a powerful tool, but the notion that Six Sigma is a survival cure-all is subsiding. Once a company has created incremental innovations that maximize profitability, some argue that "kick-starting the top line" becomes paramount, which in turn means acquisition or dramatic, revenue-generating product or service innovations. And that, they argue, calls less for Six Sigma's "define, measure, analyze, improve, control" regimen and more for a "fuzzier" front-end, creative-idea-generation type of orientation.[9] That calls for a more disruptive form of innovation, which we call *breakthrough innovation.*

Breakthrough Innovation

Clayton Christensen of Harvard Business School makes the distinction between "sustaining" technologies, which are incremental innovations that improve product or process performance, and "disruptive" technologies, which revolutionize industries and create new ones.[10] Rather than an innovation that reduces the cost of a mirror on a car by 40 percent, Christensen is focusing when speaking of disruptive technologies on the product idea that works 10 times better than existing ones or costs less than half what the existing ones do to make—a breakthrough innovation. A **breakthrough innovation,** then, is an innovation in a product, process, technology, or the cost associated with it that represents a quantum leap forward in one or more of these ways.

breakthrough innovation
An innovation in a product, process, technology, or the cost associated with it that represents a quantum leap forward in one or more of these ways.

Apple's innovation with iPod and iTunes is a breakthrough innovation. It was not an incremental improvement in Apple's computer offerings. It was an application of the microprocessor technology associated with Apple's computers, applied in a totally different industry. Apple, which only has a 2 percent market share in the personal computer industry,

[9] Brian Hindo and Brian Grow, "Six Sigma: So Yesterday?" *BusinessWeek*, June 11, 2007.

[10] Clayton M. Christensen, *The Innovator's Dilemma* (New York: HarperCollins, 2003).

EXHIBIT 14.3
From Idea to Profitable Reality

Source: Industrial Research Institute, Washington, D.C.

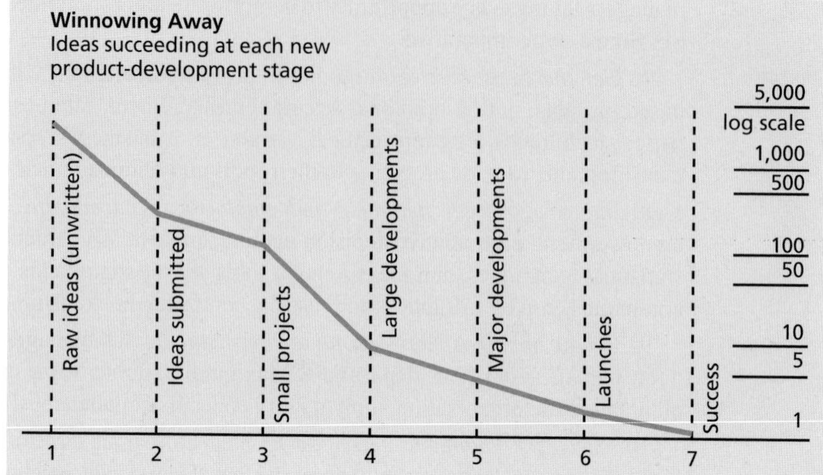

now has positioned itself as a dominant force in the emerging digital music and entertainment industries based on this breakthrough innovation, becoming the top music retailer worldwide in five short years after it introduced iTunes.

Breakthrough innovations, which Christensen calls "disruptive," often shake up the industries with which they are associated, even though many times they may come from totally different origins or industry settings than the industry to start with. Apple seems to make a habit of creating new industries; Apple's original innovation 20 years earlier in Jobs's and Wozniak's garage that created the first Apple computer was viewed as a toy by most players in the computer industry at the time, but it quickly tore the mainstream computer industry apart and almost brought down the mighty IBM. Texas Instrument's digital watch resulted in the virtual destruction of the dominant Swiss watch industry. Breakthrough innovations can also be appreciated by some fringe (often new) customer group for features such as being cheap, simple, easy to use, or smaller, which is seen as underperforming the mainstream products. San Disk's memory stick, Walmart's discount retailing, and Groupon Now's instant digital coupons are all examples of breakthrough innovations that ultimately caused the demise of or significant reduction in key industry participants. Former Digital Equipment Company CEO Ken Olsen, a leading industry figure and a leading computer manufacturer at the time, said of Apple and the idea of a personal computer in your home when the early Apple computers were being sold: "I can think of no reason why an individual should wish to have a computer in his own home."[11]

Breakthrough approaches to innovation are inherently more risky than incremental innovation approaches. The reason can be seen in Exhibit 14.3, which is provided by the Industrial Research Institute in Washington, D.C. Their conclusion is that firms committed to breakthrough innovation must first have the ability to explain clearly to all employees, at every level, just how critical the breakthrough project is to the company's future. The second is to set next-to-impossible goals for those involved. The third is to target only "rich domains"—areas of investigation where plenty of answers are still waiting to be found. The fourth, and maybe the most important, is to move people regularly between laboratories and business units, to ensure that researchers fully understand the needs of the marketplace. These thoughts, of course, apply more to larger firms and particularly ones where breakthrough efforts are concentrated in laboratories and other separate R&D units.

Smaller firms are often sources for breakthrough innovation because they have less invested in serving a large, established customer base and gradually improving on the

[11] Robert M. Grant, *Contemporary Strategic Analysis* (Oxford: Blackwell, 2002), p. 330.

products, services, or processes used to serve them. We will explore these differences more completely in the section on entrepreneurship. Regardless of the size of a firm, it is important to consider risks associated with incremental versus breakthrough innovation.

Risks Associated with Innovation[12]

Innovation involves creating something that doesn't now exist. It may be a minor creation or something monumental. In either case, there is risk associated with it. Exhibit 14.3 shows the conclusions of the Industrial Research Institute's examination of breakthrough innovation outcomes, which suggests that you need to start with 3,000 "bright" ideas, which are winnowed down to four product launches, then one major success emerges. Long odds for sure.

A study reported in *The Economist* of 197 product innovations, 111 of which were successes and 86 failures, sought to compare the two groups in order to see what might explain differences between innovation success and innovation failure. They first sought to examine what was common to successful innovations and what was common to failing innovations First, they found that successful innovations had some, or all, of the following five characteristics:[13]

- Moderately new to the marketplace.
- Based on tried and tested technology.
- Saved money for users of the innovation.
- Reportedly met customer needs.
- Supported existing practices.

In contrast, product innovations that failed were based on cutting-edge or untested technology, followed a "me-too" approach, or were created with no clearly defined problem or solution in mind.

The second set of findings from this study emerged from the researchers' examination of what they called "idea factors." Idea factors were concerned with how the idea for the innovation originated. They identified six idea factors:

- *Need spotting*—actively looking for an answer to a known problem.
- *Solution spotting*—finding a new way of using an existing technology.
- *Mental inventions*—things dreamed up in the head with little reference to the outside world.
- *Random events*—serendipitous moments when innovators stumbled on something they were not looking for but immediately recognized its significance.

[12] See Morten Hansen and Julian Birkinshaw, "The Innovation Value Chain," *Harvard Business Review,* June 2007, for an interesting use of a value chain "breakdown" of innovation to use in assessing risks and sources of problems in innovation efforts. See the more recent, interesting study by CPA Global Limited called "Closing the Innovation Value Gap," wherein it examined in detail the risk/reward differences across 11 global industries, which executives need to take into account as they address the process of taking ideas from intellectual property into commercially viable products and services quickly. www.cpaglobal.com, 2011.

[13] "Expect the Unexpected," *The Economist*, September 4, 2004. Similar and more recent findings were found in a study reported by McKinsey and Company that surveyed 300 employees at 28 companies across North America and Europe working on a variety of new product innovation projects over time. Their findings support what is reported above in the *Economist* study, with particular emphasis on the importance of maintaining close contact with customers through a project's duration, nurturing a strong project culture in their workplace, and having clear project goals early on. Divided into successful vs. unsuccessful project outcomes, product innovation teams McKinsey studied that embraced these three aspects were 17 times more likely to have projects come in on time, five times more likely to be on budget, and twice as likely to meet the company's ROI targets. Read more at Mike Gordon, Chris Musso, Eric Rebentisch, and Nisheeth Gupta, "The Path to Successful New Products,"*McKinsey Quarterly*, January, 2010.

- *Market research*—traditional market research techniques to find ideas.
- *Trend following*—following demographic and other broad trends and trying to develop ideas that may be relevant and useful.

The researchers then compared the "success-to-failure" ratio of these six idea factors to see which idea factors were more often associated with success or failure of the related innovation. The two most failure-prone idea factors were trend following and mental inventions, both producing three times as many failures as successes. Need spotting produced twice as many successes as failures. Market research produced four times as many, and solution spotting seven times more successes than failures. Taking advantage of random events was the clear winner, generating 13 times more successes than failures. Their conclusion: focus on eliminating bad ideas early in the process, emphasize market research and technology application/solution spotting efforts, while being open to serendipitous outcomes in the process.

Inherent in their analysis is the presence of two key risks associated with innovation—market risks and technology risks. Market risks come from uncertainty with regard to the presence of a market, its size, and its growth rate for the product or service in question: do customers exist and will they buy it? Technology risks derive from uncertainty about how the technology will evolve and the complexity through which technical standards and dominant designs or approaches emerge: will it work?

Research by Michael Treacy of GEN3 Partners reported in the *Harvard Business Review* suggests that incremental innovation is far more effective than breakthrough innovation in managing the market and technology risk associated with innovation. Exhibit 14.4 provides a visual portrayal of his research.[14] In it he suggests that technology risk is primary and marketplace risk secondary in product innovations; the reverse is true for business model or process innovations.

The point that emerges from this graph is that breakthrough innovation, while glamourous and exciting, is very risky compared with incremental innovation. Breakthrough innovations, according to Treacy's examination of much of the research to date on innovation, usually get beaten down or outperformed by the slow and steady approach of incremental innovation. He makes several useful points about managing the resulting risks:

- Remember, *the point of innovation is growth*. So ask the question, Can I increase revenue without innovation? Retain existing customers and improve targeted coverage of existing and similar new customers, where innovation isn't necessary to keep existing customers.
- *Get the most out of minimum innovation*. Tweaking a business process doesn't incur much technology risk. Incremental product or service innovation does not incur nearly the market risk that a radical one would. So emphasize an incremental approach to most innovation efforts.
- Incremental product innovations can be particularly good at *locking in existing customers*. Every saved customer is an additional source of revenue.
- Incremental business process innovations can *generate more revenue gain or cost savings with less risk* than radical ones. The earlier example about Toyota's single brace to hold auto frames is a dramatic example of the payoff—$2.6 billion annually—from one simple, incremental business process innovation.

[14] Michael Treacy, "Innovation As a Last Resort," *Harvard Business Review,* July 1, 2004. See also http://www.youtube.com/user/treacyandcompany#p/a/u/0/a7D25Ub95yc, and http://www.youtube.com/watch?v=bRTQRS1rJaQ, to have Dr. Michael Treacy explain his perspective on *Growth Through Innovation*. And you can visit his Web site, http://treacyandco.com/aboutus/our-leadership/michael-treacy/, and explore his new book, *Growth Through Innovation*, 2012.

EXHIBIT 14.4 Risks Associated with Innovation

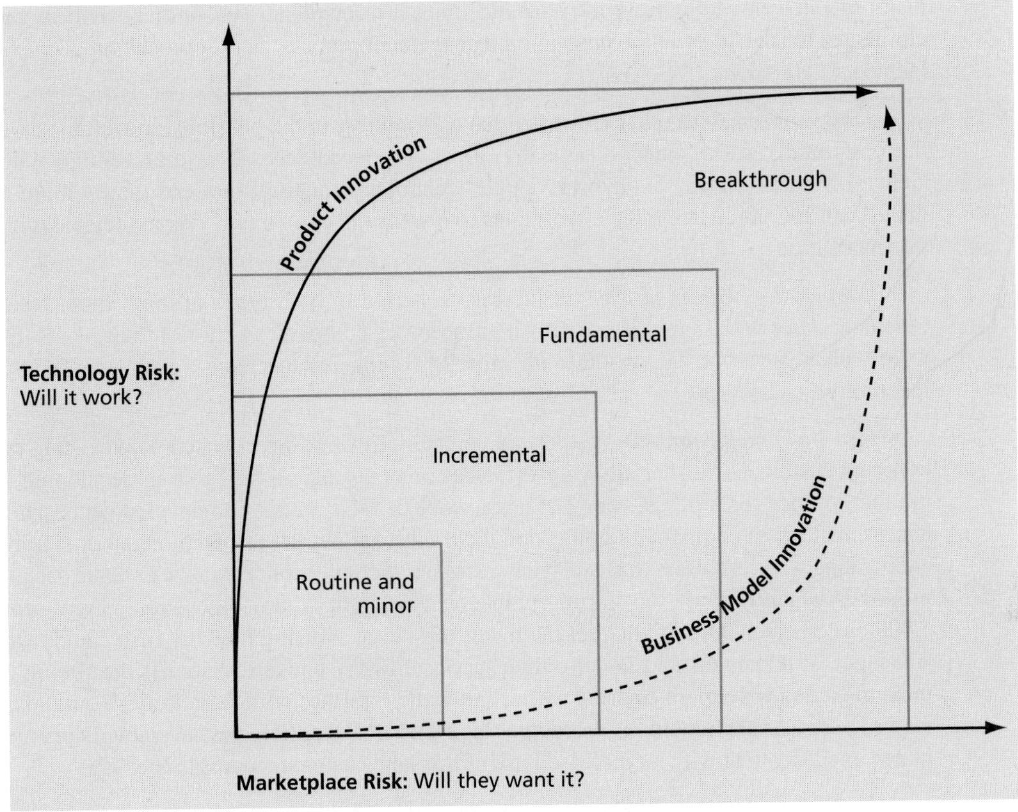

Source: Reprinted by permission of *Harvard Business Review.* Exhibit from "Innovation as a Last Resort," by Michael Treacy, July 1, 2004. Copyright 2004 by the Harvard Business School Publishing Corporation; all rights reserved.

- Radical innovations are often *too radical for existing markets,* and customers will balk at paying for that new approach, product, process, or technology. So it will fail with existing customers.
- The time to launch breakthrough innovations is not when they are necessary, important, or of interest to your business, but *when they are essential to the marketplace.* And that usually takes time, like the 10 years it has taken for car buyers to become interested in the electric/hybrid vehicles that have been available for more than 10 years.

disruptive innovation
A term to characterize breakthrough innovation popularized by Harvard Professor Clayton Christensen; usually shakes up or revolutionizes industries with which they are associated even though they often come from totally different origins or industry settings than the industry they "disrupt."

The case for incremental innovation as a less risky approach than breakthrough innovation is widely advocated. Clayton Christensen offers a word of caution in this regard, arguing that as important as incremental improvements are, steady improvements to a company's product do not conquer new markets. Nor do they guarantee survival. He argues that while **disruptive** (breakthrough) **innovations** may underperform established products in mainstream markets, they often offer features or capabilities appreciated by some fringe (usually new) customer group—like being easier to use, cheaper, smaller, or more versatile. Often, his research suggests, those fringe customers swell in numbers to become the mainstream market, absorbing the newly informed old mainstream in the process. And in so doing, they "disrupt" or bring about the downfall of leading existing industry players.

Not surprisingly, many companies are experimenting with new ways to lower risks and improve chances for failure regardless of the innovation approach they use. For years the idea of product teams and cross-functional groups within the company has played a major role in trying to improve the odds that innovations will succeed, or that bad ideas are eliminated much earlier in the innovation management process. This approach broadens to include several more:

• *Joint ventures* with other firms that have an interest in the possible innovation share the costs and risks associated with the effort. Toyota undertook a joint venture with General Motors to share its hybrid vehicle technology for the Prius and jointly build a manufacturing facility in the United States to lower both companies' risk associated with this innovation.

• *Cooperation with lead users* is increasingly used in both types of innovation. Nike tests new shoes with inner-city street gangs; software companies beta-test their new software with loyal users; GE works with railroad companies to create a new, ecofriendly locomotive.

• *"Do it yourself"* innovation allows a company to work directly with key existing or expected customers, further allowing these customers to play a lead role in developing a product, service, or process—not just get a sense of their reaction to developments. This approach allows a company to go beyond the traditional market research model or simply cooperating with lead users. Instead, it has customers actually conceptualize or make design proposals which become the starting point for developing a new innovation. BMW sent 1,000 customers a "toolkit" that let them develop ideas, showing how the firm could take advantage of telematics and in-car online services. BMW chose 15 submissions, brought them to Germany from all over the world, and worked further with them to flesh out those ideas. Four ideas are now in the prototype stage, and BMW anticipates several will emerge in new models along with an increased use of this new customer-innovation effort.

• *Acquiring innovation* has become a major way larger companies bring innovation into their firm while mitigating the risk/reward trade-off in the process. Cisco has built itself into a dominant player in the computer and networking equipment industries in large part by buying smaller companies that had developed and tentatively proven new market niches but who needed capital and distribution to rapidly exploit the new technological advantage. Cisco acquired these companies for a premium using stock, but it invested little or nothing in the early development of the technology. Thus, the smaller firm bore all the early risk of failure, and those that succeeded were rewarded in the price of the sale of their company, but Cisco got to avoid the losses associated with the majority of the innovations attempted but not successful. Exhibit 14.5, Global Strategy in Action, describes how Google does something similar in acquiring innovation and how the results are not always to the liking of the entrepreneur company founders they acquire in the process.

• *Outsourcing innovation,* particularly product design, has become a major part of the "modular" organizational structure of today's global technology companies. Nokia, Samsung, and Motorola—cell phone giants—get proposed new-product design prototypes from HTC, Flextronics, and Cellon—unknown global, billion-dollar-plus companies that create new designs and sell them to cell phone and other electronics brand-name companies annually at the biggest trade shows around the world. To Nokia and its competitors, this shifts the risk of product design innovation to these emerging technology outsourcing powerhouses.

Procter & Gamble, under Alan Lafley, radically changed that company's culture so that it accepts as a matter of corporate strategy that 50 percent of its consumer product innovations will come from outside P&G. The resulting growth and profitability due to new-product

Global Strategy in Action

Exhibit 14.5

Google Acquires Dodgeball to Innovate, Then Has the Latitude to Drop the Ball

Dodgeball started life as a Manhattan company providing a cell phone service aimed at young barhoppers wanting to let their friends know where they were hanging out. Founders Dennis Crowley and Alex Rainert sold it to Google in 2005, providing a good payday for them and a potential basis for a social networking niche innovation for Google. Within two years, Crowley and Rainert left Google, frustrated by what they reported as minimal support from Google.* Crowley stayed in New York City to run the operation, but had trouble competing for the attention of other Google engineers to expand the service. "If you're a product manager, you have to recruit people from their '20 percent time,'" said Crowley,† who then started building a new location-based service called FourSquare.

Google, for its part, found the concepts behind Dodgeball interesting and adapted those concepts to create *Latitude,* a more sophisticated add-on to Google Maps that lets people share their location with friends and family automatically, while including different privacy and communication options. Said Google's senior engineering vice president, "Maybe it worked in Manhattan. It didn't fly in Chicago, or St. Louis, or Denver, or the rest of the world."‡ Still, Google appears to have found innovations worth adapting, as its new Latitude service seems to indicate.

* See their Flickr departure posting at http://www.flickr.com/photos/dpstyles/460987802/.

† Vindu Goel, "How Google Decides to Pull the Plug," *The New York Times,* February 15, 2009.

‡ Ibid.

innovations at P&G over the last five years of Lafley's tenure made it the new model of open source product/service/market innovation worldwide.[15]

ideagoras
Web-enabled, virtual marketplaces which connect people with unique ideas, talents, resources, or capabilities with companies seeking to address problems or potential innovations in a quick, competent manner.

Ideagoras, defined as places where millions of ideas and solutions change hands in something akin to an eBay for innovation, reflects one of the newest approaches to open innovation, which leverages the value of the Internet to access talent worldwide, instantly. Also referred to as "crowdsourcing" and "open innovation," companies seeking solutions to seemingly insoluble problems can tap the insights of hundreds of thousands of enterprising scientists without having to employ any of them full time. Take, for example, Colgate-Palmolive, which needed a more efficient method for getting its toothpaste into the tube—a seemingly straightforward problem. When its internal R&D team came up empty-handed, the company posted the specs on InnoCentive, one of many ideagoras or marketplaces that link problems with problem solvers. A Canadian engineer named Ed Melcarek proposed putting a positive charge on fluoride powder, then grounding the tube. It was an effective solution, an application of elementary physics, but not one that Colgate-Palmolive's team of chemists had ever contemplated.[16] Melcarek earned $25,000 for a few hours' work, and a timely innovation from outside the company accrued to another client company.

[15] "Lafley Leaves Big Shoes to Fill at P&G," Bloomberg-BusinessWeek, June 8, 2009; http://www.businessweek.com/bwdaily/dnflash/content/jun2009/db2009068_155480.htm. An excellent 3-minute video with Alan Lafley a year after he retired talking about his approach to open innovation at P&G can be found on YouTube at http://www.youtube.com/watch?v=_7mMToRlAxs. Another, longer YouTube video (14 minutes) with Lafley describes in more detail the P&G approach to innovation, particularly their customer or end consumer–focused innovation driver. This 14-minute video was done during the last year of Lafley's leadership at P&G prior to retiring: http://www.youtube.com/watch?v=xvIUSxXrffc&feature=related. It covers more specifics of how they make innovation happen.

[16] Don Tapscott and Anthony D. Williams, "Ideagora, a Marketplace for Minds," *BusinessWeek*, February 15, 2007; a quick video to explain InnoCentive that won the 2010 InnoCentive Idea competition: http://www.youtube.com/user/innocentiveinc#p/c/A81E23D5AC6511C3/2/cac-XdXL-Qk; an explanation of The Power of Open Innovation and Crowdsourcing by Dwayne Spradlin, CEO, InnoCentive, in 2010 at Columbia Business School: http://www.youtube.com/watch?v=phA_NSApxrQ. Another excellent example of the value of crowdsourcing, or an ideagora, is the well-known story of Goldcorp's use of crowdsourcing to turn a $1 million investment into a $6+ billion payoff for Goldcorp: http://www.youtube.com/watch?v=EQca_xH3BVI&feature=relmfu; it is very good for seeing the value of youthful input into corporate innovation decision making.

Today more than 160,000 scientists like Melcarek have registered with InnoCentive, and hundreds of companies pay annual fees of roughly $80,000 to tap the talents of this global scientific community. Launched as an e-business by Eli Lilly in 2001, InnoCentive was spun off in 2005, enabling it to expand its offerings and serve clients in a variety of industries. The company now provides solutions to some of the world's most well-known and innovation-hungry companies. The reason? Mature companies cannot keep up with the speed of innovation nor the demands for growth by relying on internal capabilities alone. This approach creates a much more flexible, free-market mechanism; secondly, it taps a vastly changing global landscape where the talent to generate disruptive or path-breaking innovation will increasingly reside in China, India, Brazil, Eastern Europe, or Russia. P&G figures that for every one of its 9,000 top-notch scientists, there are another 200 outside who are just as good. That's a total of 1.8 million talented people it could potentially tap, using ideagoras to seek out ideas, innovations, and uniquely qualified minds on a global scale quickly, efficiently, and productively.[17]

Such openness in seeking new, key innovations that determine a company's future survival and growth—as opposed to doing innovation on a closely guarded, internal basis—is viewed with skepticism and as a risk that cuts at the very core of what a company essentially exists to do. Product design, major innovations, even incremental innovations, have long been viewed as key, secret core competencies and competitive advantages that generate the long-term success of the company that possesses them. Outsourcing these activities, or doing so via ideagoras, puts the whole firm at risk in the minds of observers opposed to this open type of innovation. That said, the impressive progress Dwayne Spratlin has engineered at InnoCentive, described in Exhibit 14.6, Top Global Strategist, seems to be reflective of a broadening embrace of Web-enabled, wide-open collaboration in breakthrough innovation.

Another way of looking at the notion of innovation, and an organization's ability to manage it effectively, is found in the argument that innovation is associated with entrepreneurial behavior. And so, to be more innovative, a firm has to become more entrepreneurial.

The examples of Cisco and Google, as they used the "acquiring innovation" approach illustrate the useful ways some companies deal with the reality that breakthrough innovation occurs very often in the smallest of firms, where focus, intensity, and total survival depend on that innovation succeeding. Advocates of this perspective make the point that many industry-creating and paradigm-changing breakthrough innovations (e.g., personal computers; digital file sharing), as well as seemingly obvious incremental innovations ignored by large industry players (e.g., Paychex serving small businesses), came from start-up or small companies—entrepreneurs—that have since become major industry leaders.

Taking this perspective has led some other forward-thinking large companies to seek ways to make themselves more entrepreneurial and to enable their "entrepreneurs within" to emerge and succeed in building new businesses around innovative ideas. Such people, termed "intrapreneurs" in the business and academic press, have proven to be effective champions of innovation-based growth in many companies that have sincerely encouraged their emergence. But whether it is through the entrepreneurs within, or becoming or teaming with independent entrepreneurs, ensuring the presence of entrepreneurship in an organization is central to innovation, long-term survival, and renewal.

[17] Ibid. See also www.innovate-ideagora.ning.com; "Innovation in the Age of Mass Collaboration," *BusinessWeek,* February 1, 2007; "The New Science of Sharing," *BusinessWeek*, March 2, 2007; *Wikinomics*, by Don Tapscott and Anthony Williams; and Satish Nambisan and M. Sawhney, "A Buyer's Guide to the Innovation Bazaar," *Harvard Business Review*, June 2007, p. 109.

Top Global Strategist

Dwayne Spradlin, President and CEO, InnoCentive, www.innocentive.com

Exhibit 14.6

InnoCentive is an open-innovation marketplace in the world, where corporations and nonprofits ("seekers") post their toughest research problems and a global network of 160,000 "solvers" takes a crack at solving them for cash rewards. Dwayne Spradlin was a co-founder of InnoCentive, based on his passionate belief that crowdsourcing—allowing experts around the world to help solve problems and create innovation—would easily become a powerful tool for more efficient and speedy problem solving, allowing clients to develop new commercial solutions and allowing many opportunities for more effectively doing good. Spradlin says of this approach, "In this prize-based world, companies and organizations [those pursuing a crowdsourcing approach] are paying predominantly for success. Most innovation efforts fail. With the monolithic view of R&D and innovation, one of the main reasons it's insufficient is that you're paying for failure. In this [crowdsourcing, open-innovation] InnoCentive model, you're paying only for the winning solutions."

He offers a few recent examples: Oil Spill Recovery Institute out of Cordova, Alaska, needed to find a new and novel way to get oil off the bottom of Prince William Sound from the Exxon Valdez spill. For 15 years, that oil has been sitting down there at the bottom of the ocean. They could get the oil off the bottom and onto the barges, but the surface temperature drops so dramatically that the oil almost solidifies and they can't pump it through the barge system.

The solver ended up being an engineer out of the Midwest, and he recognized a way to solve that problem using technology that is fairly common in the construction industry. He recognized that was very similar to the problem of keeping cement liquid when pouring a foundation. They used commercial-grade vibrating equipment on the barges to keep the oil fluid enough so they could process it through the system.

Prize4Life, which is focused on ALS, also known as Lou Gehrig's disease, wanted to find a biomarker to help identify and treat Lou Gehrig's disease patients. They decided to run the challenge in multiple phases. The first phase was a prize to anyone on Earth who can come up with a new and novel way of identifying where a promising biomarker might be.

What's amazing about this was that solutions were coming not necessarily from the medical field—computer scientists; experts in bioinformatics, who were suggesting algorithmic approaches; and machine manufacturers, who knew enough about the disease to say the following kind of approach might provide a highly predictive model of who might be susceptible to this disease were all participating. They were getting solutions from outside the establishment that ended up generating some of the most innovative thinking in that field in recent years.

Crowdsourcing works in other settings too. Toronto-based Goldcorp, a gold mining company heavily in debt, facing labor strikes and high costs, was about to fold. In desperation, CEO Rob McEwen published all their proprietary geological data, a usually carefully guarded company secret in the mining industry, on the Web—400 megabytes of data about 55,000 acres. McEwen made $575,000 in prize money available to anyone who could propose the best methods of finding gold and estimating the likely find.

Within weeks, submissions came from around the world, ultimately resulting in several awards and, for Goldcorp, totally new ways to prospect. The company has now reached more than $6 billion in gold sales by applying the solutions "problem-solvers" from around the world helped them find: $100 invested in Goldcorp in 1993 is worth more than $6,000 today.

Swiss drugmaker Novartis has done something similar, again unheard of in the world of large pharmaceuticals. It decided to share online, after investing millions in secret proprietary research, all of its raw data regarding its efforts to unlock the genetic basis for type 2 diabetes. Among the most challenging and potentially lucrative areas of broad public health needs, Novartis and its partners at MIT decided that the problem is still sufficiently complex that Novartis hopes to leverage the talents and training of a global scientific community to speed the development of gene-related interventions to help solve the type 2 diabetes challenge.

Source: www.innocentive.com. A short video of Rob McEwen on his use of crowdsourcing at Goldcorp can be found at: http://www.youtube.com/watch?v=EQca_xH3BVI&feature=relmfu.

EXHIBIT 14.7
Who Is the Entrepreneur?

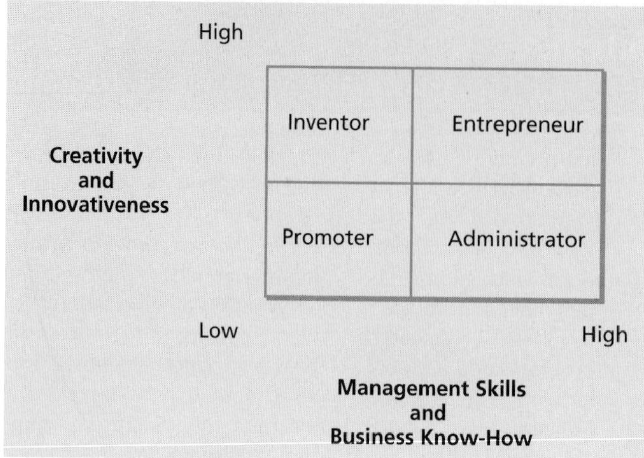

WHAT IS ENTREPRENEURSHIP?

The Global Entrepreneurship Monitor estimates that 15 percent of all working adults are self-employed, a number they project is steadily growing.[18] New entrepreneurial ventures are recognized globally as key drivers of economic development, job creation, and innovation. So what is entrepreneurship? What does it involve?

entrepreneurship
The process of bringing together the creative and innovative ideas and actions with the management and organizational skills necessary to mobilize the appropriate people, money, and operating resources to meet an identifiable need and create wealth in the process.

Entrepreneurship is the process of bringing together creative and innovative ideas and actions with the management and organizational skills necessary to mobilize the appropriate people, money, and operating resources to meet an identifiable need and create wealth in the process. Whether the process is undertaken by a single individual or a team of individuals, there is mounting evidence that growth-minded entrepreneurs possess not only a creative and innovative flair but also solid management skills and business know-how—or they ensure the presence of both in the fledgling organizations they start. Exhibit 14.7 illustrates the fundamental skills associated with being entrepreneurial versus those suitable for promoters, managers, and inventors.

Inventors are exceptional for their technical talents, insights, and creativity. But their creations and inventions often are unsuccessful in becoming commercial or organizational realities because their interests and skills are lacking in terms of reading a market and bringing products or services to creation and then marketing and selling them effectively. *Promoters* are in some way just the opposite—clever at devising schemes or programs to push a product or service, but aimed more at a quick payoff than a profitable, business-building endeavor for the longer term.

Administrators, the good ones, develop strong management skills, specific business know-how, and the ability to organize people. They usually take pride in overseeing the smooth, efficient functioning of operations largely as they are. Their administrative talents are focused on creating and maintaining efficient routines and organization—creative and innovative behavior may actually be counterproductive within the organizations they operate.

[18] The Global Entrepreneurship Monitor is a not-for-profit research consortium that is the largest single study of entrepreneurial activity in the world. Initiated in 1999 by Babson College and London Business School, it now involves research teams at universities and other organizations worldwide. It provides annual and quarterly GEM updates at www.gemconsortium.org.

Global Strategy in Action

Exhibit 14.8

Fred. W. Smith: Entrepreneur Extraordinaire

Frederick W. Smith, a Yale economics major, first laid out his idea for an express delivery service in what is now the most infamous term paper in business school settings. Legend has it he received a low C, though Smith is rather vague on that folklore. Whatever the professorial critique, he was undeterred. After a stint with the Marines in Vietnam, he returned to hawk the idea to venture capitalists, ultimately getting a significant investment to which he added his family's holdings. He purchased a used aircraft company in Little Rock, Arkansas, and used it to start Federal Express in Memphis, Tennessee.*

Smith apparently had transportation in his blood. His grandfather was a steamboat captain; his father built a regional bus service from scratch, ultimately selling it to Greyhound Bus System. Smith learned to fly on weekends as a charter pilot while attending Yale. FedEx's first night's run involved just seven packages.

The postal monopoly was a big headache early in the effort to start FedEx. Smith became so desparate for cash at one point that he flew to Las Vegas, played blackjack, and won $27,000—which he wired back to Memphis to use to make payroll at one critical point in the company's survival. But by the late 1970s, FedEx started to take off as America came to rely on its overnight delivery. Merrill Lynch excutives came to find that employees even used it to deliver documents overnight between floors of its Manhattan headquarters because it was more reliable and faster than interoffice mail.†

Today, FedEx is a global supply chain linchpin for global companies worldwide. It carries more than 8 million shipments in 240 countries every day. All because a young college student first sensed a need for overnight delivery others couldn't or didn't see.

* "Frederick W. Smith: No Overnite Success," *BusinessWeek*, September 20, 2004.

† Ibid.

The ideal *entrepreneur* has that unusual combination of talent: strength in both creativity and management. In a new venture, these strengths enable the entrepreneur to conceive and launch a new business as well as make it grow and succeed. In a large organization, these talents enable strong players to emerge and build new ideas into impressive new revenue streams and profitability for a larger company. Because these strengths so rarely coexist in one individual, entrepreneurship is increasingly found to involve teams of people that combine their strengths to build the business they envision. Exhibit 14.8, Global Strategy in Action, tells the story of just such a rare entrepreneur, Fred Smith, founder and chairman of Federal Express.

New ventures and small, growth-oriented business entrepreneurs are able to achieve success from effectively managing three elements central to the entrepreneurial process in creating and sustaining new ventures. Those three elements are opportunity, the entrepreneurial team, and resources:

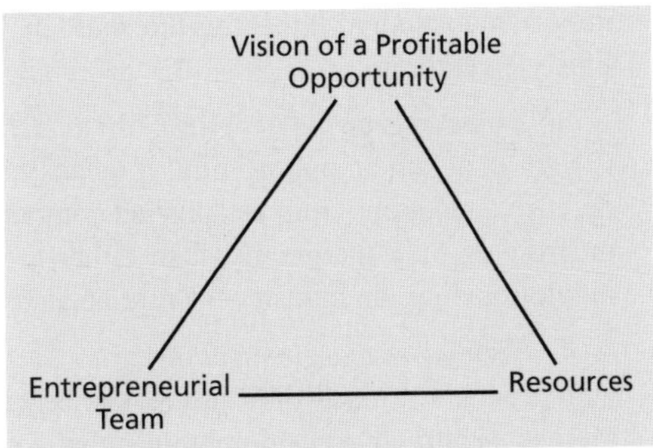

Source: RCTrust, LLC, © 2010.

Opportunity

The most frequent cause of failure of new ventures, as reported by Dun & Bradstreet (D&B) in its yearly failure record, is lack of sales; the second is competitive weakness. Both causes stem from the lack of appreciation of the necessity for a market orientation as the basis of any new venture. In other words, failure among new ventures is heavily linked to ventures started because someone had the idea for such a business but did not identify a concrete market opportunity.

Entrepreneurs doomed to learn from their all too frequent failure conceive an idea for a product or service and immediately become enamored of it. They invest time, money, and energy in developing the idea into a commercial reality. And, tragically, they make only a minimum investment in identifying the customers, the customers' needs, and their willingness to buy the product or service as an answer to those needs. Such entrepreneurs are focused inward, perhaps satisfying their own personal ego needs. The result is often a product or service that few customers will buy. The customers are seeking to buy benefits, and the ineffective entrepreneur is consumed with selling his or her product.

The effective entrepreneur is more likely to assume a marketing orientation and look outward at a target market to identify or confirm the presence of a specific need or desired solution. Here the entrepreneur is focused on potential customers and on seeking to understand their need. The effective entrepreneur seeks to confirm an opportunity defined by what the customer wants and is willing to pay. It is interesting that the most effective approach in the way firms seek to innovate is to bring customers into the innovation process to help shape the solution they seek. In essence, customers define what they want. The design of an effective entrepreneur's product or service comes in response to an opportunity, not the other way around.

Another way to determine if an entrepreneur is focused on simply an idea or a good opportunity is to apply the same criteria venture capitalists use to evaluate new venture investment opportunities. It is important to recognize that these criteria are applied by investors interested primarily in high-growth ventures. The criteria for smaller ventures would be less demanding in scope (e.g., a minimum $250 million market) but similar in the types of concerns that should be addressed in an effort to determine whether the opportunity is a good one. Let's look at each criterion individually:

1. *The venture team can clearly identify its customers and the market segment(s) it plans to capture.* Exactly who are the target customers? Who makes the buying decision? Does the entrepreneur have evidence that these customers are enthusiastic about the product or service and will act favorably (e.g., pay in advance) on that enthusiasm? Firm purchase orders or other tangible purchase commitments help confirm the timing is right.

2. *A minimum market as large as $250 million.* A market this size suggests that the firms can achieve significant sales without having to attain a dominant share of its market. That, in turn, means the new venture can grow without attracting much competitive reaction. It is important to recognize that this threshold pertains to high-growth opportunities, not smaller, lifestyle ventures.

3. *A market growing at a rate of 30 to 50 percent.* This is another indicator that the timing is right to act on an opportunity; it means new entrants can enter the fray without evoking defensive reactions from established competitors. On the other hand, if the market is static or growing only marginally, then either the opportunity must offer a realistic chance of revolutionizing the industry—a rare occurrence—or the timing is bad.

4. *High gross margins (selling price less direct, variable costs) that are durable.* When entrepreneurs can sell their product or service at gross margins in the 50+ percent range, there is an attractive cushion built in that covers the mistakes they are likely to make while developing a new enterprise. When margins are small, the margin for error is too.

5. *There is no dominant competitor in the market segments representing the venture opportunity.* A market share of 40 to 60 percent usually translates into significant power over suppliers, customers, pricing, and costs. The absence of such a competitor means more room for the newcomer to maneuver, without fear of serious retaliation.

6. *A significant response time, or lead time, in terms of technical superiority, proprietary protection, distribution, or capacity.* When a new venture possesses this type of legitimate "unfair advantage," the new firm should be able to create barriers to entry or expansion by others who are aware of the profitable opportunity. When an entrepreneur can take advantage of this sort of proprietary edge, and the edge will last, the timing is right.

7. *An experienced entrepreneur or team capable of enthusiastically and professionally building a company to exploit the profitable opportunity.* Venture capitalists universally identify this as an essential ingredient for the timing to be right to invest in a proposed venture. Aspiring entrepreneurs should likewise use it as a criterion for whether it is wise to pursue the new venture opportunity they are considering. Let's examine this last point more fully.

Entrepreneurial Teams

Successful entrepreneurs and entrepreneurial teams bring several competencies and characteristics to their new ventures. Let's examine both.

- *Technical competence.* The entrepreneur or team must possess the knowledge and skill necessary to create the products or services the new venture will provide. It may be that some of those competencies exist outside the entrepreneur or team, in which case meaningful arrangements to outsource them become part of the technical competence equation. But know-how and capability are essential to success.
- *Business management skills.* The survival and growth of a technically viable new venture depend on the ability of the entrepreneur to understand and manage the economics of the business. Financial and accounting know-how in areas of cash flow, liquidity, costs and contributions, record keeping, pricing, structuring debt, and asset acquisition are essential. People management skills, marketing, organizational skills, sales, computer literacy, and planning skills are just some of those essential to success.

Technical and business skills being critical, they alone are not enough. Observers identify several behavioral and psychological characteristics that are usually associated with successful entrepreneurs:

- *Endless commitment and determination.* Ask any number of entrepreneurs the secret of their success, and they inevitably cite this one. Entrepreneurs' level of commitment can usually be gauged by their willingness to jeopardize personal economic well-being, to tolerate a lower standard of living than they would otherwise enjoy early in the enterprise, and even to sacrifice time with their family.
- *A strong desire to achieve.* Need to achieve is a strong entrepreneurial motivator. Money is a way to keep score, but outdoing their own expectations is an almost universal driver.
- *Orientation toward opportunities and goals.* Good entrepreneurs always like to talk about their customers and their customers' needs. They can readily respond when asked what their goals are for this week, month, and year.
- *An internal locus of control.* Successful entrepreneurs are self-confident. They believe they control their own destiny. To use a sports analogy, they want the ball for the critical last-second shot.

- *Tolerance for ambiguity and stress.* Start-up entrepreneurs face the need to meet payroll when revenue has yet to be received, jobs are constantly changing, customers are ever new, and setbacks and surprises are inevitable.
- *Skills in taking calculated risks.* Entrepreneurs are like pilots: they take calculated risks. They do everything possible to reduce or share risks. They prepare or anticipate problems; confirm the opportunity and what is necessary for success; create ways to share risk with suppliers, investors, customers, and partners; and are typically obsessed with controlling key roles in the execution of the firm's operations.
- *Little need for status and power.* Power accrues to good entrepreneurs, but their focus is on opportunities, customers, markets, and competition. They may use that power in these settings, but they do not often seek status for the sake of having it.
- *Problem solvers.* Good entrepreneurs seek out problems that may affect their success and methodically go about overcoming them. Not intimidated by difficult situations, they are usually decisive and capable of enormous patience.
- *A high need for feedback.* "How are we doing?" The question is ever-present in an entrepreneur's mind. They seek feedback. They nurture mentors to learn from and expand their network of contacts.
- *Ability to deal with failure.* Entrepreneurs love to win, but they accept failure and aggressively learn from it as a way to better manage their next venture.
- *Boundless energy, good health, and emotional stability.* Their challenges are many, so good entrepreneurs seem to embrace their arena and pursue good health to build their stamina and emotional well-being.
- *Creativity and innovativeness.* New ways of looking at things, tinkering, staying late to talk with a customer or employee—all these are typical of entrepreneurs' obsession with doing things better, more efficiently, and so forth. They see an opportunity instead of a problem, a solution instead of a dilemma.
- *High intelligence and conceptual ability.* Good entrepreneurs have "street smarts," a special sense for business, and the ability to see the big picture. They are good strategic thinkers.
- *Vision and the capacity to inspire.* The capacity to shape and communicate a vision in a way that inspires others is a valuable skill entrepreneurs need in themselves or from someone in their core team.

Resources

The third element in new venture entrepreneurship involves *resources*—money and time. Let's summarize money first. A vital ingredient for any business venture is the capital necessary to acquire equipment, facilities, people, and capabilities to pursue the targeted opportunity. New ventures do this in two ways. **Debt financing** is money provided to the venture that must be repaid at some point in time. The obligation to pay is usually secured by property or equipment bought by the business, or by the entrepreneur's personal assets. **Equity financing** is money provided to the venture that entitles the provider to rights or ownership in the venture and which is not expected to be repaid. It entitles the source to some form of ownership in the venture, for which the source usually expects some future return or gain on that investment.

debt financing
Money "loaned" to an entrepreneur or business venture that must be repaid at some point in time.

equity financing
Money provided to a business venture that entitles the provider to rights or ownership in the venture and which is not expected to be repaid.

Debt financing is generally obtained from a commercial bank to pay for property, equipment, and maybe provide working capital—all available only after there is proven revenue coming into the business. Family and friends are debt sources, as are leasing companies, suppliers, and companies that lend against accounts receivable. Entrepreneurs benefit when using debt capital because they retain ownership and increase the return on their investment if things go as planned. If not, debt financing can be a real problem for new ventures because rapid growth requires steady cash flow (to pay salaries, bills, interest), which creates a real dilemma if interest rates rise and sales slow down. Most new ventures find early debt capital hard to get anyway, so gradually nurturing a relationship with a commercial lender, letting them get to know the entrepreneur and the business, is a wise approach for the new entrepreneur.

Equity financing is usually obtained from one or more of three sources: friendly sources, informal venture investors, or professional venture capitalists. In each case, it is often referred to as "patient money," meaning it does not have to be paid back immediately or on any particular schedule. *Friendly sources* are prevalent early in many new ventures— friends, family, wealthy individuals who know the entrepreneur. *Informal venture investors,* usually wealthy individuals, or what are now called "angel" investors (for obvious reasons), are increasingly active and accessible as possible equity investors. *Professional venture capitalists* seek investment in the truly high-growth potential ventures. They have stringent criteria as we have seen, and expect a return of five times their money in three to five years! A fourth source of equity capital, *public stock offerings,* is available for a very select few new ventures. They are usually firms that have gone through the other three sources first.

Regardless of the source, equity capital is money that does not have to be repaid on an immediate, regular basis as debt capital requires. So when a firm is rapidly growing and needs to use all its cash flow to grow, not having to repay makes equity more attractive than debt. The unattractive aspect of equity financing for some people is that it constitutes selling part of the ownership of the business and, with it, a say in the decisions directing the venture.

The other resource is time—time of the entrepreneur(s) and key players in the business venture's chance for success. The entrepreneur is the catalyst, the glue that holds the fledgling business together and oftentimes the critical source of energy to make success happen. As we noted earlier, determination is a key characteristic of entrepreneurs. And time is the most critical resource, combined with determination, to virtually "will" the new venture's success at numerous junctures in its early development.

intrapreneurship
A term associated with entrepreneurship in large, established companies; the process of attempting to identify, encourage, enable, and assist entrepreneurship within a large, established company so as to create new products, processes, services, or improvements that become major new revenue streams and/or sources of cost savings for the company.

Successful entrepreneurs are impressive growth and value building innovators. Their success often comes at the expense of large firms with which they compete, do business, obtain supplies, and such. Their success in commercializing new ideas has drawn the attention of many larger companies leading to the question, Can a big firm be more entrepreneurial? The conclusion has been a tentative yes, that larger firms can increase their level of innovation and subsequent commercialization success if they encourage entrepreneurship and entrepreneurs within their organizations. Understanding and encouraging entrepreneurship in large organizations to improve future survival and growth has become a major agenda in thousands of large companies today. The ideas behind these efforts, which have been called *intrapreneurship,* are examined in the next section.

Intrapreneurship

intrapreneurship freedom factors
Ten characteristics identified by Dr. Gorden Pinchot and elaborated upon by others that need to be present in large companies seeking to encourage and increase the level of intrapreneurship within their company.

Intrapreneurship, or entrepreneurship in large companies, is the process of attempting to identify, encourage, enable, and assist entrepreneurship within a large, established company so as to create new products, processes, or services that become major new revenue streams and sources of cost savings for the company. Gordon Pinchot, founder of a school for intrapreneurs and creator of the phrase itself, suggests 10 **freedom factors** that need to be present in large companies seeking to encourage intrapreneurship:

1. *Self-selection.* Companies should give innovators the opportunity to bring forth their ideas, rather than making the generation of new ideas the designated responsibility of a few individuals or groups.

2. *No hand-offs.* Once ideas surface, managers should allow the person generating the idea to pursue it rather than instructing him or her to turn it over ("hand it off") to someone else.

3. *The doer decides.* Giving the originator of an idea some freedom to make decisions about its further development and implementation, rather than relying on multiple levels of approval for even the most minor decision, enhances intrapreneurship.

4. *Corporate "slack."* Firms that set aside money and time ("slack") facilitate innovation.

5. *End the "home run" philosophy.* Some company cultures foster an interest in innovative ideas only when they represent major breakthroughs. Intrapreneurship is restricted in that type of culture.

6. *Tolerance of risk, failure, and mistakes.* Where risks and failure are damaging to their careers, managers carefully avoid them. But innovations inherently involve risks, so calculated risks and some failures should be tolerated and chalked up to experience.

7. *Patient money.* The pressure for quarterly profits in many U.S. companies stifles innovative behavior. Investment in intrapreneurial activity may take time to bear fruit.

8. *Freedom from turfness.* In any organization, people stake out turf. Boundaries go up. Intrapreneurship is stifled by this phenomenon because cross-fertilization is often central to innovation and successful entrepreneurial teams.

9. *Cross-functional teams.* Organizations inhibit cross-functional interaction by insisting that communication flow upward. That inhibits sales from learning from operations and company people from interacting with relevant outsiders.

10. *Multiple options.* When an individual with an idea has only one person to consult or one channel to inquire into for developing the idea, innovation can be stifled. Intrapreneurship is encouraged when people have many options for discussing or pursuing innovative ideas.

When you read Pinchot's 10 freedom factors, they sound very much like characteristics associated with entrepreneurs or the nature of the types of resources—money and time—that we identified as being central to the entrepreneurship process. And that, obviously, is exactly what intrapreneurship is trying to do—replicate the presence of entrepreneurs (small undertakings) inside a large enterprise that offers the potential advantage of easier money, expertise, facilities, distribution, and so forth. Exhibit 14.9, Global Strategy in Action describes a variety of intrapreneurial successes with companies you should readily recognize. Nine specific ways companies are attempting to enable intrapreneurs and intrapreneurship to flourish in their companies are given here:[19]

• *Designate intrapreneurship "sponsors."* Formally identify several people with credibility and influence in the company to serve as facilitators of new ideas. These "sponsors" usually have discretionary funds to allocate on the spot to help innovators develop their ideas.

• *Allow innovation time.* 3M was know for its "15 percent rule," which means that members of its engineering group can spend 15 percent of their time tinkering with whatever idea they think has market potential. Google gives employees one day a week to work on their own projects.

[19] For elaboration on these and other ideas, see "Lessons from Apple," *The Economist*, June 7, 2007; "Remember to Forget, Borrow, and Learn," *BusinessWeek*, March 28, 2007; "Clayton Christensen's Innovation Brain," *BusinessWeek*, June 15, 2007; and www.Businessweek.com/innovation.

Global Strategy in Action

Exhibit 14.9

Intrapreneurs—They Are Everywhere! Just Give Them Time to Blossom

Google encourages all its employees to spend 20 percent of their time on ideas that they would like to develop or feel passionate about. This is the reason Google is constantly introducing new products such as Gmail, Google Earth, and Google Apps. Google Adsense and Adwords were created by an employee who was paid $10 million for his internal-entrepreneurial effort.

Arthur Fry, 53, a 3M chemical engineer, used to get annoyed at how pieces of paper that marked his church hymnal always fell out when he stood up to sing. He knew that Spencer Silver, a scientist at 3M, had accidentally discovered an adhesive that had very low sticking power. Normally that would be bad, but for Fry it was good. He figured that markers made with the adhesive might stick lightly to something and would come off easily. Since 3M allows employees to spend 15 percent of their office time on independent projects, he began working on the idea. Fry made samples and then distributed the small yellow pads to company secretaries. They were delighted. 3M eventually began selling it under the name **Post-it.** Sales last year were more than **$100 million.**

Ken Kutaragi was working in Sony's sound labs when he bought his daughter a Nintendo game console. Watching her play, he was dismayed by the system's primitive sound effects. With Sony's blessing, Kutaragi worked with Nintendo to develop a CD-ROM–based Nintendo. But Nintendo decided not to go forward with it, so Kutaragi helped Sony develop its own gaming system, which became the PlayStation. The first PlayStation made Sony a major player in the games market, but the PlayStation 2 did even better, becoming the best-selling game console of all time. Kutaragi founded Sony Computer Entertainment, one of the Sony's most profitable divisions.

W.L. Gore, known primarily as the maker of Gore-Tex rain gear, encourages employees to develop new ideas through its "dabble time" policy: 10 percent of a workday can be devoted to personal projects. A few years ago, the company was experimenting with ePTFE, a chemical cousin to Teflon, to coat push-pull cables for use in animatronics. Dave Myers, an associate in the company's medical unit, thought the coating might be good for guitar strings and recruited both marketing and manufacturing personnel to work on the project. Myers's team originally believed that the coating's appeal would be in making strings more comfortable to use. But extensive market research, piloted by John Spencer, and more than 15,000 guitar-player field tests led the team to realize their real selling point: better sound. The coated strings were only nominally more comfortable than noncoated strings, but they kept their tone longer than conventional guitar strings. W.L. Gore launched them under the brand name ELIXIR Strings, now the No. 1 seller of acoustic guitar strings and the overall No. 2 seller in the guitar string market.

There's an engineer in Dallas whose "wasteful" tinkering with a flow problem he had to deal with every day almost got him fired. Now his oil delivery spout invention is used by almost every major oil company in the world.

Caterpillar took its own internal logistics problem and created Caterpillar Logistics, which now spans 25 countries and six continents.

Alicia Ledlie, co-manager at a Walmart store in Long Island, New York, attended a conference at the company's Arkansas headquarters and heard about a possible new venture: in-store health clinics. It was Ledlie's idea to include drug-testing services for Walmart job applicants in the clinics' scope of services. Ledlie knew that all new hires had to have a drug test within 24 hours of receiving a job offer. "Working in the stores, I'd seen how this requirement created a challenge for recruits who relied on public transportation," she says. "Adding this service to the clinics' roster was a quick win. Store managers raved about the effect it had on helping them keep new recruits." Walmart has added over 2,000 sites in the last three years.

Jim Lynch's big idea came out of the most ordinary of activities—cleaning the gutters on his suburban Massachusetts home. "It occurred to me that this was a perfect job for a robot," Lynch says, "because it fit into our company's three criteria: dumb, dirty, and dangerous." A senior electrical engineer at Burlington, Massachusetts–based iRobot, Lynch began tinkering with different models and built a prototype using a spaghetti ladle and an electric screwdriver. His chance to present it came when the company held its first-ever "idea bake-off," where employees got 10 minutes each to pitch an idea for a new product. Lynch's project was green-lighted by the company brass, and the new gutter-cleaning robot, named "Looj" (after the Olympic sport), launched on schedule last year.

Source: www.bnet.com/2403-1313070_23-196888.htm, and 23-196890.htm.

• *Accommodate intrapreneurial teams.* 3M calls it "tin cupping." American Cement calls it "innovation volunteers." P&G sets up teams across product divisions to intentionally cross-pollinate new business. The idea is for companies to give managers interdepartmental or unit flexibility to let informal idea-development teams (a marketing person, an engineer, and an operations person) interact about promising ideas and develop them as though they were an independent business.

• *Provide intrapreneurial forums.* Owens Corning calls them "skunkworks, innovation boards, and innovation fairs." 3M has "technical forums," annual "technical review fairs," and "sales clubs." P&G, eBay, and Amazon bring in outsiders, customers especially, to help form the basis for interaction about new ideas where ones that gain traction can quickly move to more serious pursuit using other specific ways described here.

• *Use intrapreneurial controls.* Quarterly profit contribution does not work with intrapreneurial ventures at their early stages. Milestone reviews like we discussed earlier in this chapter—key timetables, resource requirements—provide a type of control more suited to early, innovative activity.

• *Provide intrapreneurial rewards.* Recognition for success, financial bonuses if successful, and most importantly the opportunity to "do it again," with even greater freedom in developing and implementing the next idea are extremely important to this type of venture.

• *Articulate specific innovation objectives.* Clearly setting forth organizational objectives that legitimize and indeed call for intrapreneurship and innovation helps encourage an organizational culture to support this activity. 3M is the "granddaddy" of this approach, having long held to a corporate objective, which they have hit every year since 1970, that "25 percent of annual sales each year will come from products introduced within the last five years." P&G has a corporate goal that 50 percent of its innovations originate outside the company to encourage collaborative, "open," innovative behavior.

• *Create a culture of intrapreneurship.* Jeff Bezos of Amazon.com calls it a "culture of divine discontent," in which everyone itches to improve things. P&G calls it letting outsiders into P&G to innovate, and, prior to his retirement, CEO Lafley established the P&G norm that more than half of P&G new products will come from outsiders teamed with inside intrapreneurs. GE's Immelt hires successful intrapreneurs from other companies to become leaders in a usually insider-promoted organization, both to get the intrapreneur involved and even more importantly to send a message of fundamental cultural change toward intrapreneurship. Other firms create internal "banks" to invest in new internal start-ups. Intel has its own venture capital arm investing aggressively in entrepreneurial ventures inside and outside the company, often spinning them off.

• *Encourage innovation from without as well as within.* Apple is widely assumed to be an innovator "within." In fact, its real skill lies in stitching together its own ideas with technologies from outside and then wrapping the results in elegant software and simple, stylish designs.

Innovation and entrepreneurship are intertwined phenomena and processes. Organizations seeking to control their destiny, which most all seek to do, increasingly "get it" that even having a destiny may be the issue. And to have that opportunity or chance, organizations need leaders who embrace the importance of being innovative and entrepreneurial to give their companies the chance to find ways to adapt, be relevant, to position themselves in a future that, to use a trite phrase, has but one real constant—change.

Summary

A central goal with any strategy is the survival, growth, and improved competitive position of the company in the future. Executives seek ways to make their organizations innovative and entrepreneurial because these are increasingly seen as essential capabilities for survival, growth, and relevance. Incremental innovation—where companies increasingly, in concert with their customers, seek to steadily refine and improve their products, services, and processes—has proven to be a very effective approach to innovation. The continuous improvement philosophy, and programs such as CCC21 and Six Sigma, are key ways firms make incremental innovation a central part of their organization's ongoing work activities.

Breakthrough innovation involves far more risk than the incremental approach yet brings high reward when successful. Firms with this approach need a total commitment and are often going against mainstream markets in the process. Large, well-known global companies are increasingly embracing "open" approaches to innovation, including breakthrough innovation, in ways that would have been unthinkable 20 years ago. They have embraced the outsourcing of much product design innovation in recent years and are rapidly adopting Web-enabled forums for tapping expertise located around the globe to gain assistance and collaboration in generating breakthrough innovation. They also increasingly look to innovate by acquiring small, entrepreneurial firms that often generate breakthrough innovations because they have a narrow focus, tolerate risks, have a passion for what they are doing, and benefit greatly if they succeed.

Entrepreneurship is central to making businesses innovative and fresh. New-venture entrepreneurship is the source of much innovation, and it is really a process involving opportunity, resources, and key people. Opportunity is focusing intensely on solving problems and benefits to customers rather than product or service ideas someone just dreams up. Resources involve money and time. Key people, the entrepreneurial team, need to bring technical skill, business skill, and key characteristics to the new venture endeavor for it to succeed.

Intrapreneurship is entrepreneurship in large organizations. Many firms now claim that they seek to encourage intrapreneurship. For intrapreneurship to work, individual intrapreneurs need freedom and support to pursue perceived opportunities, be allowed to fail, and do more of the same more easily if they succeed.

Key Terms

breakthrough innovation, *p. 405*
CCC21, *p. 401*
continuous improvement, *p. 400*
debt financing, *p. 418*
disruptive innovation, *p. 409*
entrepreneurship, *p. 414*
equity financing, *p. 418*
ideagoras, *p. 411*
incremental innovation, *p. 400*
innovation, *p. 400*
intrapreneurship, *p. 419*
intrapreneurship freedom factors, *p. 419*
invention, *p. 399*
Six Sigma, *p. 402*

Questions for Discussion

1. What is the difference between incremental and breakthrough innovation? What risks are associated with each approach?
2. Why is continuous improvement, and programs such as CCC21 and Six Sigma, a good way to develop incremental innovation?
3. What is an ideagora?
4. How are big, global companies looking "outward" to accelerate their innovativeness and breakthrough innovations?
5. Why do most breakthrough innovations occur in smaller firms?
6. What are the three key elements in the entrepreneurship process in new ventures?
7. What is intrapreneurship, and how is it best enabled?

Part **Four**

Cases

Guide to Strategic Management Case Analysis

Guide to Strategic Management Case Analysis

THE CASE METHOD

Case analysis is a proven educational method that is especially effective in a strategic management course. The case method complements and enhances the text material and your professor's lectures by focusing attention on what a firm has done or should do in an actual business situation. Use of the case method in a strategic management course offers you an opportunity to develop and refine analytical skills. It also can provide exciting experience by allowing you to assume the role of the key decision maker for the organizations you will study.

When assuming the role of the general manager of the organization being studied, you will need to consider all aspects of the business. In addition to drawing on your knowledge of marketing, finance, management, production, and economics, you will be applying the strategic management concepts taught in this course.

The cases in this book are accounts of real business situations involving a variety of firms in a variety of industries. To make these opportunities as realistic as possible, the cases include a variety of quantitative and qualitative information in both the presentation of the situation and the exhibits. As the key decision maker, you will need to determine which information is important, given the circumstances described in the case. Keep in mind that the results of analyzing one firm will not necessarily be appropriate for another since every firm is faced with a different set of circumstances.

PREPARING FOR CASE DISCUSSION

The case method requires an approach to class preparation that differs from the typical lecture course. In the typical lecture course, you can still benefit from each class session, even if you did not prepare, by listening carefully to the professor's lecture. This approach will not work in a course using the case method. For a case course, proper preparation is essential.

Suggestions for Effective Preparation

1. *Allow adequate time in preparing a case.* Many of the cases in this text involve complex issues that are often not apparent without careful reading and purposeful reflection on the information in the cases.

2. *Read each case twice.* Because many of these cases involve complex decision making, you should read each case at least twice. Your first reading should give you an overview of the firm's unique circumstances and the issues confronting the firm. Your second reading allows you to concentrate on what you feel are the most critical issues and to understand what information in the case is most important. Make limited notes identifying key points during your first reading. During your second reading, you can add details to your original notes and revise them as necessary.

3. *Focus on the key strategic issue in each case.* Each time you read a case you should concentrate on identifying the key issue. In some cases, the key issue will be identified by the case writer in the introduction. In other cases, you might not grasp the key strategic issue until you have read the case several times. (Remember that not every piece of information in a case is equally important.)

4. *Do not overlook exhibits.* The exhibits in these cases should be considered an integral part of the information for the case. They are not just "window dressing." In fact, for many cases you will need to analyze financial statements, evaluate organizational charts, and understand the firm's products, all of which are presented in the form of exhibits.

5. *Adopt the appropriate time frame.* It is critical that you assume the appropriate time frame for each case you read. If the case ends in 2009, that year should become the present for you as you work on that case. Making a decision for a case that ends in 2009 by using data you could not have had until 2011 defeats the purpose of the case method. For the same reason, although it is recommended that you do outside reading on each firm and industry, you should not read material written after the case ended unless your professor instructs you to do so.

6. *Draw on all of your knowledge of business.* As the key decision maker for the organization being studied, you will need to consider all aspects of the business and industry. Do not confine yourself to strategic management concepts presented in this course. You will need to determine if the key strategic issue revolves around a theory you have learned in a functional area, such as marketing, production, finance, or economics, or in the strategic management course.

USING THE INTERNET IN CASE RESEARCH

The proliferation of information available on the Internet has direct implications for business research. The Internet has become a viable source of company and industry data to assist those involved in case study analysis. Principal sources of useful data include company Web sites, U.S. government Web sites, search engines, investment research sites, and online data services. This section will describe the principal Internet sources of case study data and offer means of retrieving that data.

Company Web Sites

Virtually every public and private firm has a Web site that any Internet user can visit. Accessing a firm's Web site is easy. Many firms advertise their Web address through both TV and print advertisements. To access a site when the address is known, enter the address into the address line on any Internet service provider's homepage. When the address is not known, use of a search engine will be necessary. The use of a search engine will be described later. Often, but not always, a firm's Web address is identical to its name, or is at least an abbreviated form of its name.

Company Web sites contain data that are helpful in case study analysis. A firm's Web site may contain descriptions of company products and services, recent company accomplishments and press releases, financial and stock performance highlights, and an overview of a firm's history and strategic objectives. A company's Web site may also contain links to relevant industry Web sites that contain industry statistics as well as current and future industry trends. The breadth of data available on a particular firm's Web site will vary but in general larger, global corporations tend to have more complete and sophisticated Web sites than do smaller, regional firms.

U.S. Government Web Sites

The U.S. government allows the public to access virtually all of the information that it collects. Most of this information is available online to Internet users. The government collects a great range of data types, from firm-specific data the government mandates all publicly traded firms to supply to highly regarded economic indicators. The usefulness of many U.S. government Web sites depends on the fit between the case you are studying and the data located on the Web site. For example, a study of an accounting firm may be supplemented with data supplied by the Internal Revenue Service Web site, but not the Environmental Protection Agency Web site. A sampling of prominent government Web sites and their addresses is shown here:

Environmental Protection Agency: www.epa.gov
General Printing Office: www.gpo.gov
Internal Revenue Service: www.irs.ustreas.gov
Libraries of Congress: www.loc.gov
National Aeronautics and Space Administration: www.hq.nasa.gov
SEC's Edgar Database: www.sec.gov/edgarhp.htm
Small Business Administration: www.sba.gov
STAT-USA: www.stat-usa.gov
U.S. Department of Commerce: www.doc.gov
U.S. Patent and Trademark Office: uspto.gov
U.S. Department of Treasury: www.ustreas.gov

One of the most useful sites for company case study analysis is the Securities and Exchange Commission's EDGAR database. The EDGAR database contains the documents that the government mandates all publicly traded firms to file including 10-Ks and 8-Ks. A Form 10-K is the annual report that provides a comprehensive overview of a firm's financials in addition to discussions regarding industry and product background. Form 8-K reports the occurrence of any material events or corporate changes that may be of importance to investors. Examples of reported occurrences include key management personnel changes, corporate restructures, and new debt or equity issuance. This site is very user friendly and requires the researcher to provide only the company name in order to produce a listing of all available reports.

Search Engines

Search engines allow a researcher to locate information on a company or industry without prior knowledge of a specific Internet address. Generally, to execute a search the search engine requires the entering of a keyword, for example, a company name. However, each search engine differs slightly in its search capabilities. For example, to narrow a search on one search engine may be accomplished differently than narrowing a search on another.

The information retrieved by search engines typically includes articles and other information that contain the entered keyword or words. Because the search engine has retrieved data that contain keywords does not necessarily mean that the information is useful. Internet data are unfiltered, meaning they may not be checked for accuracy before the data are posted online. However, data copyrighted or published by a reputable source may greatly increase the chance that the data are indeed accurate. Popular search options like google.com, bing.com, yahoo.com, and ask.com should work just fine to allow you to do basic research on the companies and industries discussed in the cases.

Investment Research Sites

Investment research sites provide company stock performance data including key financial ratios, competitor identification, industry data, and links to research reports and SEC filings. These sites provide support for the financial analysis portion of a case study, but only for publicly traded businesses. Most investment research sites also contain macro market data that may not be company specific, but may still affect many investors of equities.

Investment research sites usually contain a search mechanism if a desired stock's ticker symbol is not known. In this case, the company name is entered to enable the site to find the corresponding equity. Because these sites are geared toward traders who want recent stock prices and data, searching for data relevant to a case may require more elaborate investigations at multiple sites. The following list includes many popular investment research sites:

American Stock Exchange: www.amex.com
CBS Market Watch: cbsmarketwatch.com
CNN FinancialNews: money.cnn.com
DBC Online: www.esignal.com
Hoover's Online: www.hoovers.com
InvestorGuide: www.investorguide.com
Wall Street Research Net: www.wsrn.com
Market Guide: www.marketguide.com
Money Search: www.moneysearch.com
MSN Money: moneycentral.msn.com
NASDAQ: www.nasdaq.com
New York Stock Exchange: www.nyse.com
PC Financial Network: www.csfbdirect.com
Quote.Com: finance.lycos.com
Stock Smart: www.stocksmart.com
Yahoo.com/finance
Wright Investors' Service on the World Wide Web: www.wisi.com
The Wall Street Journal Online: online.wsj.com/public/us
Zacks Investment Research: my.zacks.com

One site that conveniently contains firm, industry, and competitor data is Hoover's Online. Hoover's also provides financials, stock charts, current and archived news stories, and links to research reports and SEC filings. Yahoo!'s "Finance" option is another excellent resource for company-related research. Some of these data, most notably the lengthy research reports produced by analysts, are fee-based and must be ordered.

Online Data Sources

Online data sources provide wide access to a huge volume of business reference material. Information retrieved from these sites typically includes descriptive profiles, stock price performance, SEC filings, and newspaper, magazine, and journal articles related to a particular company, industry, or product. Online data services are popular with educational and financial institutions. While some services are free to all users, to utilize the entire array of these sites' services, a fee-based subscription is usually necessary.

Accessing these sites requires only the source's address, or the use of a search engine to find the address. The source's homepage will clearly indicate the nature of the information available and describe how to search for and access the data. Most sites have help screens to assist in locating the desired information.

One of the most useful online sources for business research is the Lexis-Nexis Universe. This source provides a wide array of news, business, legal, and reference information. The information is categorized into dozens of topics including general news; company and industry news; company financials that include SEC filings; government and political news; accounting, auditing, and tax data; and legal research. One particularly impressive service is a search mechanism that allows a user to locate a particular article when the specific citation is known. A list of several notable online data sources is shown here:

ABI/Inform (Proquest Direct): www.il.proquest.com/proquest
American Express: americanexpress.com
Bloomberg Financial News Services: www.bloomberg.com
BusinessWeek Online: businessweek.com
Dow Jones News Retrieval: http://bis.dowjones.com
EconLit: www.econlit.org
Lexis-Nexis Universe: www.lexis-nexis.com

PARTICIPATING IN CLASS

Because the strategic management course uses the case method, the success and value of the course depend on class discussion. The success and value of the class discussion, in turn, rely on the roles both you and your professor perform. Following are aspects of your role and your professor's that, if kept in mind, will enhance the value and excitement of this course.

Students as Active Learners

The case method requires your active participation. This means your role is no longer one of sitting and listening.

1. *Attend class regularly.* Not only is your grade likely to depend on your involvement in class discussions, but the benefit you derive from this course is directly related to your involvement in and understanding of the discussions.

2. *Be prepared for class.* The need for adequate preparation already has been discussed. You will benefit more from the discussions, will understand and participate in the exchange of ideas, and will avoid the embarrassment of being called on when not prepared. By all means, bring your book to class. Not only is there a good chance you will need to refer to a

specific exhibit or passage from the case, you may need to refresh your memory of the case (particularly if you made notes in the margins while reading).

3. *Participate in the discussion.* Attending class and being prepared are not enough; you need to express your views in class. You can participate in a number of ways: by addressing a question asked by your professor, by disagreeing with your professor or your classmates (by all means, be tactful), by building on an idea expressed by a classmate, or by simply asking a relevant question.

4. *Participate wisely.* Although you do not want to be one of those students who never raises his or her hand, you also should be sensitive to the fact that others in your class will want to express themselves. You have probably already had experience with a student who attempts to dominate each class discussion. A student who invariably tries to dominate the class discussion breeds resentment.

5. *Keep a broad perspective.* By definition, the strategic management course deals with the issues facing general managers or business owners. As already mentioned, you need to consider all aspects of the business, not just one particular functional area.

6. *Pay attention to the topic being discussed.* Focus your attention on the topic being discussed. When a new topic is introduced, do not attempt to immediately introduce another topic for discussion. Do not feel you have to have something to say on every topic covered.

Your Professor as Discussion Leader

Your professor is a discussion leader. As such, he or she will attempt to stimulate the class as a whole to share insights, observations, and thoughts about the case. Your professor will not necessarily respond to every comment you or your classmates make. Part of the value of the case method is to get you and your classmates to assume this role as the course progresses.

The professor in a strategic management case course performs several roles:

1. *Maintaining focus.* Because multiple complex issues need to be explored, your professor may want to maintain the focus of the class discussion on one issue at a time. He or she may ask you to hold your comment on another issue until a previous issue is exhausted. Do not interpret this response to mean your point is unimportant; your professor is simply indicating there will be a more appropriate time to pursue that particular comment.

2. *Getting students involved.* Do not be surprised if your professor asks for input from volunteers and nonvolunteers alike. The value of the class discussion increases as more people share their comments.

3. *Facilitating comprehension of strategic management concepts.* Some professors prefer to lecture on strategic management concepts on a "need-to-know" basis. In this scenario, a lecture on a particular topic will be followed by an assignment to work on a case that deals with that particular topic. Other professors will have the class work through a case or two before lecturing on a topic to give the class a feel for the value of the topic being covered and for the type of information needed to work on cases. Still other professors prefer to cover all of the theory in the beginning of the course, thereby allowing uninterrupted case discussion in the remaining weeks of the term. All three of these approaches are valued.

4. *Playing devil's advocate.* At times your professor may appear to be contradicting many of the comments or observations being made. At other times your professor may adopt a position that does not immediately make sense, given the circumstances of the case. At other times your professor may seem to be equivocating. These are all examples

of how your professor might be playing devil's advocate. Sometimes the professor's goal is to expose alternative viewpoints. Sometimes he or she may be testing your resolve on a particular point. Be prepared to support your position with evidence from the case.

ASSIGNMENTS

Written Assignments

Written analyses are a critical part of most strategic management courses. Each professor has a preferred format for these written analyses, but a number of general guidelines will prove helpful to you in your written assignments.

1. *Analyze.* Avoid merely repeating the facts presented in the case. Analyze the issues involved in the case and build logically toward your recommendations.
2. *Use headings or labels.* Using headings or labels throughout your written analysis will help your reader follow your analysis and recommendations. For example, when you are analyzing the weaknesses of the firm in the case, include the heading Weaknesses. Note the headings in the cases that follow.
3. *Discuss alternatives.* Follow the proper strategic management sequence by *(a)* identifying alternatives, *(b)* evaluating each alternative, and *(c)* recommending the alternative you think is best.
4. *Use topic sentences.* You can help your reader more easily evaluate your analysis by putting the topic sentence first in each paragraph and following with statements directly supporting the topic sentence.
5. *Be specific in your recommendations.* Develop specific recommendations logically and be sure your recommendations are well defended by your analysis. Avoid using generalizations, clichés, and ambiguous statements. Remember that any number of answers are possible and so your professor is most concerned about how your reasoning led to your recommendations and how well you develop and support your ideas.
6. *Do not overlook implementation.* Many good analyses receive poor evaluations because they do not include a discussion of implementation. Your analysis will be much stronger when you discuss how your recommendation can be implemented. Include some of the specific actions needed to achieve the objectives you are proposing.
7. *Specifically state your assumptions.* Cases, like all real business situations, involve incomplete information. Therefore, it is important that you clearly state any assumptions you make in your analysis. Do not assume your professor will be able to fill in the missing points.

Oral Presentations

Your professor is likely to ask you and your classmates to make oral presentations on a particular case. Oral presentations usually are done by groups of students. In these groups, each member will typically be responsible for one aspect of the overall case. Keep the following suggestions in mind when you are faced with an oral presentation:

1. *Use your own words.* Avoid memorizing a presentation. The best approach is to prepare an outline of the key points you want to cover. Do not be afraid to have the outline in front of you during your presentation, but do not just read the outline.
2. *Rehearse your presentation.* Do not assume you can simply read the outline you have prepared or that the right words will come to you when you are in front of the class making

your presentation. Take the time to practice your speech, and be sure to rehearse the entire presentation with your group.

3. *Use visual aids.* The adage "a picture is worth a thousand words" contains quite a bit of truth. The people in your audience will more quickly and thoroughly understand your key points—and will retain them longer—if you use visual aids. Think of ways you and your team members can use the blackboard in the classroom; a graph, chart, or exhibit on a large posterboard; or, if you will have a number of these visual aids, a flip chart.

4. *Be prepared to handle questions.* You probably will be asked questions by your classmates. If questions are asked during your presentation, try to address those that require clarification. Tactfully postpone more elaborate questions until you have completed the formal phase of your presentation. During your rehearsal, try to anticipate the types of questions that you might be asked.

Working as a Team Member

Many professors assign students to groups or teams for analyzing cases. This adds more realism to the course, since most strategic decisions in business are addressed by a group of key managers. If you are a member of a group assigned to analyze a case, keep in mind that your performance is tied to the performance of the other group members, and vice versa. The following are some suggestions to help you be an effective team member:

1. *Be sure the division of labor is equitable.* It is not always easy to decide how the workload can be divided equitably, since it is not always obvious how much work needs to be done. Try breaking down the case into the distinct parts that need to be analyzed to determine if having a different person assume responsibility for each part is equitable. All team members should read and analyze the entire case, but different team members can be assigned primary responsibility for each major aspect of the analysis. Each team member with primary responsibility for a major aspect of the analysis also will be the logical choice to write that portion of the written analysis or to present it orally in class.

2. *Communicate with other team members.* This is particularly important if you encounter problems with your portion of the analysis. Because, by definition, the team members are dependent on each other, it is critical that you communicate openly and honestly with each other. Therefore, it is essential that your team members discuss problems, such as some members not doing their fair share of work or members insisting that their point of view dominate the team's report.

3. *Work as a team.* A group's output should reflect a combined effort, so the whole group should be involved in each part of the analysis, even if different individuals assume primary responsibility for different parts of the analysis. Avoid having the marketing major do the marketing portion of the analysis, the production major handle the production issues, and so forth. This will both hamper the group's aggregate analysis and do all of the team members a disservice by not giving each member exposure to decision making involving the other functional areas. The strategic management course provides an opportunity to look at all aspects of the business situation, to develop the ability to see the big picture, and to integrate the various functional areas.

4. *Plan and structure team meetings.* When you are working with a group on case analysis, it is impossible to achieve the team's goals and objectives without meeting outside of class. As soon as the team is formed, establish mutually convenient times for regular meetings, and be sure to keep this time available each week. Be punctual in going to the meetings, and manage the meetings so they end at a predetermined time. Plan several

shorter meetings, as opposed to one longer session right before the case is due. (This, by the way, is another way realism is introduced in the strategic management course. Planning and managing your time is essential in business, and working with others to achieve a common set of goals is a critical part of life in the business world.)

SUMMARY

The strategic management course is your opportunity to assume the role of a key decision maker in a business organization. The case method is an excellent way to add excitement and realism to the course. To get the most out of the course and the case method, you need to be an active participant in the entire process.

The case method offers you the opportunity to develop your analytical skills and to understand the interrelationships of the various functional areas of business; it also enables you to develop valuable skills in time management, group problem solving, creativity, organization of thoughts and ideas, and human interaction.

Case 1

American Public Education, Inc.

Richard B. Robinson

PART 1: 2001–2009 . . . AN IMPRESSIVE STORY![1]

1 For active duty soldiers, the price can't be beat. American Public Education's courses are free to military personnel, thanks to government tuition benefits. But the government doesn't pay that much, just $750 per three-credit course. That forced the for-profit educator to keep its expenses low.

2 But those low prices, often half what some competitors charge, could give APE a leg up on the civilian side. "Convenience and cost, that's what working adults are looking for," said Harry T. Wilkens, APE's executive vice president and chief financial officer. The school saw revenue climb 55% in 2008. It has grown by double-digits in each quarter since APE went public in 2007. Enrollment jumped 50% in 2008 to 45,200 students.

CIVILIAN SURGE

3 More than two-thirds of them are military personnel. But the civilian side is growing fast. Wilkens thinks teachers, police officers and other civilians could make up half or more of the student body in three or four years. The recession that started in 2008 has given the entire for-profit education sector a boost as workers scramble to update their skills and burnish resumes.

4 But the military side has legs, too. It grew faster than expected in the fourth quarter of 2008 in part due to an expanded partnership with the U.S. Navy. The number of active duty and reserve personnel in the U.S. services has held relatively constant for decades at a little above 2.1 million. But there's a churn of about 300,000 new soldiers a year replacing retiring ones.

5 The DoD's [Department of Defense's] tuition program has become a key Pentagon recruiting and retention tool. More soldiers are applying that tuition credit to online schools, APE thinks. It calculates that it now has about 12% of the military education market, up from 10% a year earlier. Wilkens says the school is committed to keeping the course free to military personnel.

6 A typical three-credit undergraduate course costs about $750. A graduate-level course costs $850. The company throws in the books to make sure there are no out-of-pocket expenses for military personnel. But with its DNA firmly rooted in that military cost structure, it can deliver that same cheap education to the civilian sector.

[1] Source: Part 1 of this case is developed from "Commercial Online School Keeps Costs Low for Military Personnel," *Investor's Business Daily*, March 24, 2009. © Investor's Business Daily, Inc. 2009. Reprinted with permission of *Investor's Business Daily*.

7 A full four-year degree totals about $30,000, far less than a brick-and-mortar university. And a masters in business administration costs about $10,000 total, vs. $20,000 to $25,000 at other online institutions, such as Capella Education, Apollo Group's University of Phoenix, and Strayer Education.

8 Those institutions instead push the quality of their education, support programs they offer, and their longer histories. "But in the end of the day, if consumers are unwilling to take on more debt looking for a post-secondary education, then American Public wins," Barrington Research's Alexander Paris Jr. said. Barrington has done banking business with APE.

9 West Virginia-based American Public was formed in 1991 by retired Marine Corps Major Jim Etter. He had taught at the Corps' Amphibious Warfare School and wanted to help service personnel continue their educations. The school, then known as American Military University, enrolled its first students in January 1993. Over the years, it built up its course offerings and earned the accreditations necessary to grant degrees.

10 In 2002, it formed a second university, American Public University, to better appeal to the civilian market. It created American Public Education as the parent over the two institutions. With shared faculty and administration, the two universities have a combined 74 degree and 51 certificate programs in areas such as national security, military studies, criminal justice, technology, business administration, education, and liberal arts. American Public Education, Inc., went public in 2005 [symbol APEI].

11 Now, it's actively reaching out to police, teachers and other civilian-sector groups, where education can bolster careers, but costs are still a concern. The programs became eligible for federal Title IV loans in late 2006, opening the doors wider to the civilian students.

12 But to keep costs under the DoD reimbursement rate, American Public Education has had to watch costs. It pays its professors based on the number of students enrolling, for instance. So if enrollment dips, so do expenses.

WORD OF MOUTH

13 APE is also very modest in its market expenses. It relies instead on word-of-mouth marketing. About 55% of students heard about the school from another student, which analysts say is tops in the industry. One "strategic" challenge will be keeping that cost of acquiring students down as it expands beyond the civilian market. So far, APE has been able to do so. And, the DoD hasn't raised its tuition reimbursement rate in years. Should it do so, which should happen with the new GI bill, that would allow APE to raise tuitions.

PROFITABILITY

14 APE [earnings] per share [was] 86 cents in 2008, up from 64 cents in 2007. The company projected 2009 EPS to come in between $1.16 and $1.20. Stock market analysts were even more optimistic, expecting a minimum of $1.21 per share.

15 American Public's low-cost model could give it traction against its civilian-focused competitors, analysts think. "It's pretty interesting and potentially disruptive in that marketplace," said Trace Urdan, an analyst with Signal Hill. "But we haven't really seen it take off yet. I guess it's still in the category of promising."

Learn—That's an Order

American Public Education has grown by providing online education to U.S. military personnel. But its ability to live within the government's tuition reimbursement rates means it can offer those same degrees to civilians at less cost than competitiors.

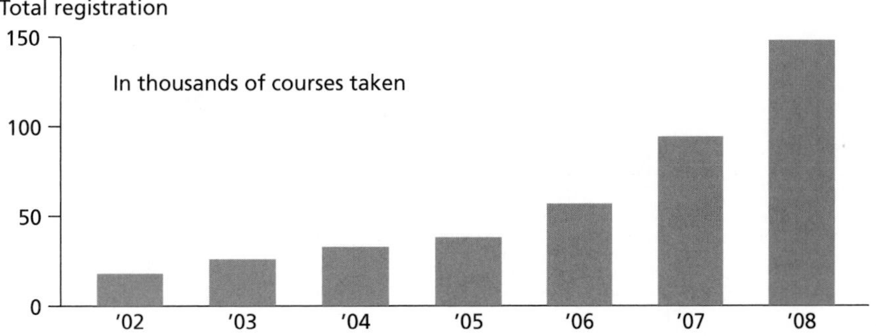

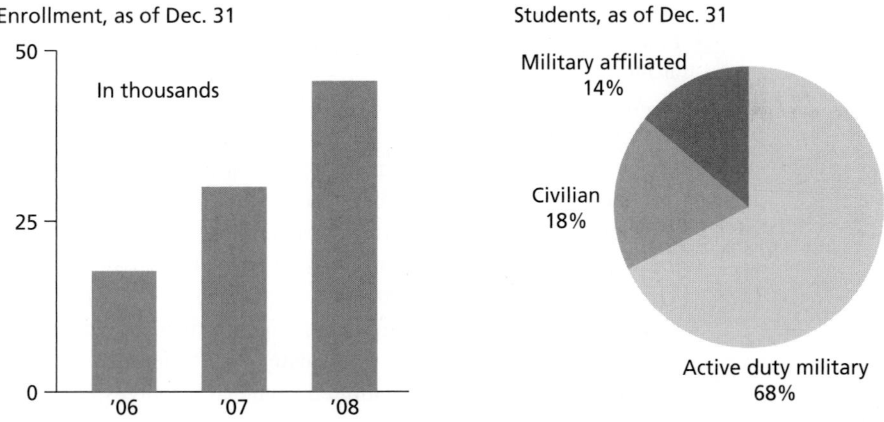

PART 2: THREE YEARS LATER . . .[2]

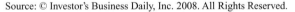

16 The last three years may have traumatized most companies facing the global "Great Recession," but not, it would seem, APEI. Instead, APEI has experienced continued growth. Net course registrations, tuition revenue, and income before taxes have virtually doubled since 2008. Total revenue increased from $107.1M to $198.2M, which represents a compounded annual growth rate (CAGR) of 36 percent. Net course registrations increased 41 percent and 31 percent in 2009 and 2010, respectively, over the prior periods. Earnings before interest and taxes increased 95 percent and net income improved to $29.9 million in 2010 from net income of $16.2 million in 2008.

17 By 2011, APEI was serving around 85,000 adult students, most holding full-time employment. They are living in all 50 states and the District of Columbia and are enrolled

[2] ©2012. Developed based on publicly available information and APEI Annual Reports and 10-Ks.

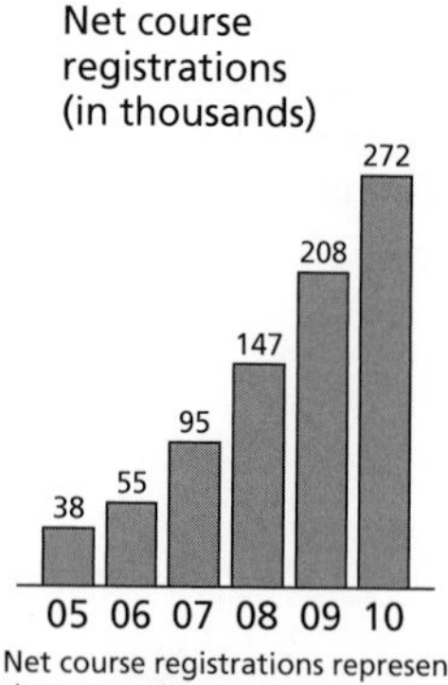

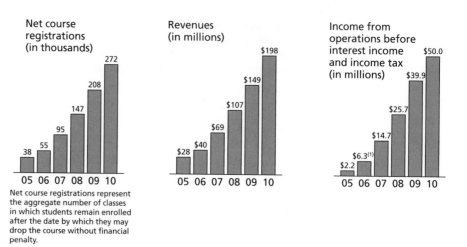

Net course registrations represent the aggregate number of classes in which students remain enrolled after the date by which they may drop the course without financial penalty.

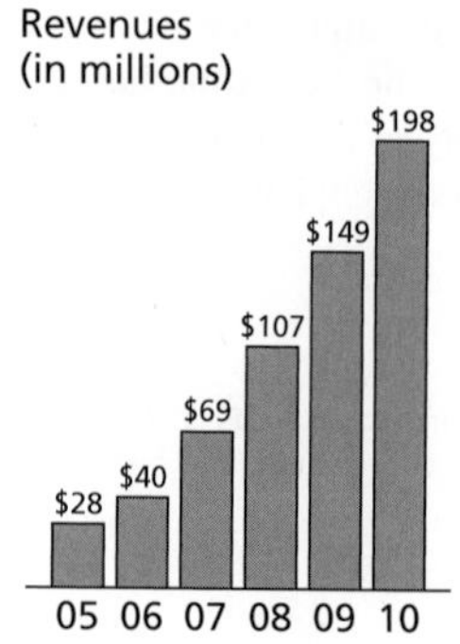

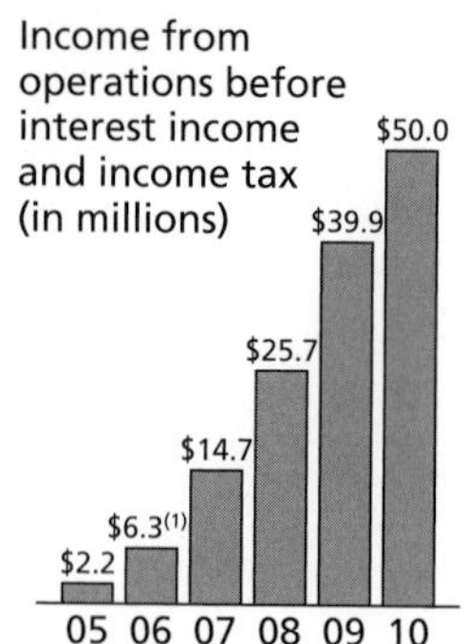

Source: APEI 2010 Annual Report

in 79 different degree programs taught by 1,250 adjunct faculty and 250 full-time faculty members considered top professionals in their respective fields teaching from locations around the world.

18 Approximately 62 percent of APEI students serve in the United States military on active duty. The remainder of their student population is generally civilians with careers in public service, such as federal, national, and local law enforcement personnel or other first responders, or they are civilians who are military-affiliated professionals, such as veterans, reservists, or National Guard members. APEI's programs are primarily designed to help these and other students advance in their current professions or prepare for their next career. Their exclusively online method of instruction is well suited to these particular students, many of whom serve in positions requiring extended and irregular schedules, are on-call for rapid response missions, participate in extended deployments and exercises, travel or relocate frequently, and have limited financial resources.

APEI'S STRATEGIC ASSESSMENT AND GROWTH STRATEGIES TOWARD 2020

19 ***Core Competencies.*** The APEI executive team believed they had the following core competencies and competitive strengths in 2012 upon which to build a successful strategy:

- ***Exclusively Online Education***—All of the courses and programs at APEI's two schools, American Military University and American Public University, have been specifically designed via a proprietary system for online delivery, and APEI recruits and trains faculty exclusively for online instruction. Since their students are located around the globe, APEI has focused on asynchronous, interactive instruction that provides students the flexibility to study and interact during the hours of the day or days of the week that suit their situation and schedules.
- ***Emphasis on Military and Public Services Communities***—Since its founding, APEI's culture has reflected its devotion to its mission of *Educating Those Who Serve*™. They have designed every one of their academic programs, policies, marketing strategies, and tuition specifically to meet the needs of the military and public service communities.

- ***Affordable Tuition***—AMU and APU tuition is generally consistent with less expensive in-state tuition at state universities and is established at a competitive rate whereby DoD tuition assistance programs fully cover the cost of undergraduate course tuition and over 75 percent of the cost of graduate course tuition. APEI's two universities have not increased their undergraduate tuition of $250 per credit hour since 2000 and have no current intention to do so.
- ***Commitment to Academic Excellence***—APEI academic programs are overseen by their Board of Trustees, which counts as members two former college presidents, active accreditation peer evaluators, a former commandant of the Marine Corps, and a former Department of the Army inspector general. APEI claims an exceptional commitment to continuously improving its academic programs and services, as evidenced by the level of attention and resources they apply to instruction and educational support. That includes intermittent, national standardized competency tests, which they have administered during and after related classes to help "JIT" monitor learning outcomes and teaching effectiveness. It also includes continuous monitoring of employers of APEI graduates to see if they would hire another APEI student. The recent results of this survey as reported in their recent annual report were as follows: Ninety-nine percent of APUS alumni employers surveyed would hire another graduate from APUS.[3]
- ***Proprietary Information Systems and Processes***—APEI's proprietary PAD—"Partnership At a Distance" system provides students 24/7 access to APEI services, such as admission, orientation, course registrations, tuition payments, book requests, grades, transcripts and degree progress, and various other inquiries. APEI has also created management tools based on the data from the PAD system that help them in their efforts to continuously improve APEI academic quality, student support services, and marketing efficiency. A key benefit they find with these proprietary systems and processes is that they allow APEI to seamlessly manage the complexities involved in starting over 1,740 classes in over 920 unique courses starting the first Monday of each month in either 8- or 16-week formats; adapted also to semester and academic year formats to assist students using Title IV programs meet eligibility requirements. APEI's proprietary systems and processes will allow them to support a much larger student body at minimal incremental costs, which in turn they believe provides them with important future competitive and cost advantages. They obtained patent protection on their PAD system in 2010.
- ***Highly Scalable and Profitable Business Model***—APEI executives believe that their exclusively online education model, their proprietary management information systems, their relatively low student acquisition costs, and their variable faculty cost model have enabled them to expand APEI operating margins. Related, they often note that their narrow market focus (and quality offerings) created a satisfied tightly-knit base of students that has been a significant source of referrals over time, which they believe has led to lower marketing costs, particularly among the military and police/first responder groups of their student populations.

20 **Growth Strategies.** APEI believes these six core competencies, along with (1) high student satisfaction and referral rates; (2) regional accreditation; (3) increasing acceptance of distance learning within their targeted markets; and (4) variety and affordability

[3] APEI 2010 Annual Report.

of APEI programs will lead to considerably higher growth to 2020 and beyond. APEI's executive has identified four primary strategies to grow APEI that build on these core competencies:

- ***Expand in APEI's Core Military Market***—APEI has focused on the needs of the military community since its founding, and this community has been responsible for the vast majority of APEI growth to date. The combination of their online model, focused curriculum and outreach to the military has enabled APEI to gain share from more established schools that have served this market for longer periods, many of which are traditional brick and mortar schools.
- ***Broaden APEI's Acceptance in the Public Service and Civilian Markets***—APEI believes its curriculum is directly relevant to federal, state, and local law enforcement, first responders, and other public service professionals. Historically this market was limited because, outside the federal government, only a few agencies or departments have the tuition reimbursement plans critical to fund continuing adult education. APEI students can now obtain Title IV grants or low-cost student loans, so APEI will increase its focus on these markets. APEI believes that the affordability and diversity of its academic program offerings, including its liberal arts degrees, attracts civilian students.
- ***Pursue and Expand Strategic Partnerships***—APEI believes that articulation agreements and partnerships with institutions of higher learning, corporations, professional associations, and other organizations are important to APEI enrollment growth and to expanding access to higher education.
- ***Add New Degree Programs***—APEI will expand its degree offerings to meet students' needs. In 2010, APEI received approval from the Higher Learning Commission to offer three new degree programs in information technology, psychology, and nursing.

COMPETITION

21 More than 4,000 U.S. colleges and universities serve traditional college-age students and adult students. Competition is highly fragmented and varies by geography, program offerings, delivery method, ownership, quality level, and selectivity of admissions. No one institution has a significant share of the total postsecondary market. Within APEI's primary military market, there are more than 1,000 institutions that serve military students and receive tuition assistance funds.

22 APEI executives believe for-profit (proprietary) schools, particularly the publicly traded ones, may increasingly be seeking to attract military students. One major reason, they surmise, is that these schools, such as the University of Phoenix, may well see increasing their number of active military personnel as students can be helpful in their efforts to comply with the "90/10 rule." The 90/10 rule[4] says that a proprietary university will not be able to receive Title IV funds (federal student loan funds or loan funds guaranteed by the

[4] Under the Higher Education Opportunity Act, a proprietary institution is prohibited from deriving from Title IV funds, on a cash accounting basis (except for certain institutional loans) for any fiscal year, more than 90 percent of its revenues. Under the terms of HEOA, a proprietary institution that violates the 90/10 rule for any fiscal year will be placed on provisional status for two fiscal years. Proprietary institutions of higher education that violate the 90/10 rule for two consecutive fiscal years will become ineligible to participate in Title IV programs for at least two fiscal years and will be required to demonstrate compliance with Title IV eligibility and certification requirements for at least two fiscal years prior to resuming Title IV program participation. (Read the "Adult Education Market" section provided in Case 3 on the Apollo Group to understand the 90/10 rule in more detail.)

federal government) if more than 90 percent of its tuition revenue comes from such funds. Currently Dept. of Defense tuition assistance and veterans education benefits do not count towards the 90 percent limit. So that, in turn, can become attractive to companies like the UOP, whose large adult student population using Title IV funding has put the UOP at approximately 88 percent in 2011 and, UOP executives project, will potentially exceed the 90 percent limit by 2012 or 2013 given the heavy borrowing levels of recent years.

23 Whatever the cause, something was happening with APEI's growth rate among active duty military students as APEI managers examined their enrollment data starting in late 2010. Said one executive:

> Beginning with registrations for the 3rd quarter of 2010, we observed that the growth of our net course registrations from active duty military students slowed more than we expected. We do not know all of the factors that caused this to occur, and we cannot determine whether over time net course registrations from active duty military students will return to our previous expectations, continue to grow more slowly than expected, remain flat or decline. We believe that the changes in net course registrations from active duty military students were in part due to increased operations activity and overseas deployments across all branches of the US military, particularly the level of activity in the United States Marine Corps.

24 Another manager pointed to numerous pictures of military personnel in uniform prominently displayed on Web sites and promotional material from key competitors as evidence it might be competitors enrolling more active duty military students, and at an increasing rate of growth. At the same time, APEI's overall participation in federal student aid programs under Title IV constituted 23.9 percent of its net registrations in 2010. They expect that the ability to participate in these programs is important to APEI's growth, and also have a signification margin relative to the 90/10 rule compared to other proprietary institutions.

25 ***Student Loan Defaults*** have become another significant financial factor shaping the competitive landscape among proprietary universities. Under the recent Higher Education Act, a proprietary educational institution may lose its eligibility to participate in some or all of the Title IV programs if, for three consecutive federal fiscal years, 25 percent or more of its students who were required to begin repaying their student loans in the relevant federal fiscal year default on their payment by the end of the next federal fiscal year. For each federal fiscal year, a rate of student defaults (known as a "cohort default rate") is calculated for each institution with 30 or more borrowers entering repayment in a given federal fiscal year by determining the rate at which borrowers who become subject to their repayment obligation in that federal fiscal year default by the end of the next federal fiscal year. If the Department of Education notifies an institution that its cohort default rates for each of the three most recent federal fiscal years are 25 percent or greater, the institution's participation in all Title IV and Pell Grant programs ends 30 days after the notification. An institution whose participation ends under these provisions may not participate in the relevant programs for the remainder of the fiscal year in which the institution receives the notification, as well as for the next two fiscal years.

26 This will certainly increase competition among proprietary schools to enroll students that have or will have solid capacity to repay Title IV loans they incur to pay for attending that school. APEI executives express some concern, given that the majority of APEI's students and target students are typically fully employed and often have company/employer tuition reimbursement assistance, which in turn makes them better credit risks that competitors will aggressively seek to enroll.

27 Prior to 2006, APEI did not even participate in Title IV programs. But with its opening of American Public University to be its civilian counterpart to its American Military University, APEI has increased its population of Title IV–using students. Still, in carefully

monitoring its cohort default rate, APEI reports that its rates for federal fiscal years 2007 and 2008 are 0.0 percent and 5.2 percent, respectively. These rates are considerably better than those of its major competitors, although some APEI executives report expecting the rate to rise as more civilian students are added to its student body. At the same time, competitors will inevitably see adding military and public service students able to take advantage of tuition reimbursement benefits as a way to ultimately drive down their cohort default rates. Students at proprietary colleges represent 12 percent of higher education enrollment, yet they take out 26 percent of all student loans and represent 46 percent of all student-loan dollars in default in 2011.

28 ***Gainful Employment*** has become a third significant financial factor shaping the competitive landscape among proprietary universities. The U.S. Department of Education will soon publish final regulations defining "gainful employment" to take effect on July 1, 2012. Those regulations will set a third financial hurdle facing proprietary colleges and universities that is intended to make sure the jobs their graduates can get provide the earning capacity sufficient to allow the student to repay the loans taken to pay the cost of attending that school. Currently, the gainful employment regulation will deny federal aid to programs that fail three "tests" of gainful employment three times in a four-year span:

- Are at least 35 percent of former students actively paying down their loans? In other words, roughly a third of ex-students must make payments that lower the loan balance by at least a dollar in a given year.
- Are graduates spending 30 percent or less of their discretionary income on loan payments? This test seeks to ensure that loan payments are not eating up too much of the money left after graduates pay for basic needs.
- Are graduates spending 12 percent or less of their total income on loan payments? This standard, related to the previous test, establishes that loan bills should not consume more than about an eighth of total earnings.

29 Programs that pass any of the three tests would retain eligibility to participate in federal aid initiatives, enabling qualified students to secure federal grants or loans. And, with recent intense lobbying by proprietary school proponents, a three-year grace period until 2015 has been tentatively incorporated instead of an immediate enforcement should a school not meet these three tests.

30 Again, APEI executives evidence little concern about this impacting its two universities in the near future. At the same time, concern among some of those executives about the impact it will have driving other powerful proprietary university competitors into its target market is rising.

31 **Lead Generation and Student Recruitment** is the lifeblood of proprietary schools, which in turn makes it a driver influencing the competitive landscape. APEI has historically focused mainly on a relationship-based marketing strategy, striving to build long-term, mutually beneficial relationships with organizations and individuals in the military and public service communities. APEI's assumption is that people working in these fields tend to be tightly knit affinity groups, which greatly facilitates personal referrals from influential members as well as from current students and alumni to prospective students. They believe this approach enables APEI universities to achieve student acquisition costs that are substantially less than the industry average. APEI also supplement this approach with multifaceted interactive marketing campaigns (organic search; pay-per-click and banner advertising; participation in online social communities) to help build brand awareness and drive inquiries. APEI has recently experienced increases in student acquisition costs, which they primarily attribute to APEI's APU expansion in nonmilitary markets. As a result, APEI

executives have alerted stockholders that, as it continues to grow in size and diversity, its student acquisition costs may continue to increase. An APEI marketing executive recently made this observation:

> To continue to grow our enrollment, we expect to continue to increase the amounts that we spend on marketing and advertising as our traditional approach to marketing and advertising may not be able to sustain meaningful growth rates. However, because we are smaller than most of our competitors and because our tuition is generally lower, we have fewer dollars available to spend on marketing and advertising than they do. Accordingly, we may find it increasingly difficult to continue to compete and grow our enrollments.[5]

32 The UOP spent $1.2 billion in selling and promo expenditures—6 times APEI's total revenue, 24 times APEI's PBTax, and 35 times APEI's selling and promotional expenditures last year.

33 ***Incentive Payment Rules.*** As part of an institution's program participation agreement with the Department of Education and in accordance with the Higher Education Act, an institution may not provide any commission, bonus, or other incentive payment to any person or entity engaged in any student recruitment, admissions, or financial aid awarding activity based directly or indirectly on success in securing enrollments or financial aid. Failure to comply with the incentive payment rule could result in termination of participation in Title IV programs, limitation on participation in Title IV programs, or financial penalties.

34 The wave of DOE Title IV-related regulatory attention sweeping Washington has not ignored proprietary colleges' lead generation and student recruitment practices either. The immediate focus in all of this attention, indeed, the practice that ignited the flame of attention, was undercover scrutiny of "enrollment counseling" and recruitment practices undertaken by the Department of Education. The results were damaging to the industry, particularly the large public proprietary schools, even those including APEI that weren't targeted or indicted relative to their practices. Most actions were settled before extended litigation, with the most meaningful change being the implementation of a regulation that barred proprietary college or university students from receiving Title IV funding if that school paid bonuses or financial incentives to recruiters or enrollment counselors. That, in turn, has caused a fundamental change in how key large proprietary colleges and universities go about their lead generation and recruitment efforts. That has caused some significant organization and compensation adjustments for the biggest APEI competitors, which APEI has not had to do.

35 **Tuition, Books, and Fees.** APEI's ability to provide affordable programs is one of its competitive strengths. As noted earlier, APEI has maintained its undergraduate tuition costs in line with public, in-state rates and within the DoD tuition ceilings—$250 per semester credit hour, or $750 per three-credit course, DoD's maximum tuition assistance levels per semester credit hour. Since 2000, APEI has not raised undergraduate tuition rates per semester credit hour, and they anticipate no tuition increase for undergraduate students for the foreseeable future. A full 121-semester hour undergraduate degree may be earned for $30,250.

36 Eligible undergraduate students also receive their textbooks at no cost to them through APEI's book grant program, which represents a potential average student savings over the course of a degree of approximately $4,500 when compared to four-year colleges according to The College Board Study, Annual Survey of Colleges report. Most students transfer in a significant amount of prior credit earned, which also reduces the cost and time of earning their degree.

[5] APEI 2010 10-K.

37 Graduate tuition was increased to $325 per semester hour, or $975 per three-credit hour course. For military students, the service branch pays $750 of the tuition costs per three-semester credit hour course, and students have the option of paying the remainder out of pocket or applying their GI Bill entitlements to cover the cost above $750. At these tuition rates, including the planned tuition increase, students may earn a graduate degree for less than $12,000 in tuition costs.

38 Despite being an open enrollment institution, APEI does not charge an admission fee, nor does it charge fees for services such as registration, technology, course drops, and similar events that trigger fees at many institutions. In addition, as a total distance learning institution, there are no resident fees, such as for parking, food service, student union, and recreation. While APEI charges a fee for transfer credit evaluation for non–active duty military students, unlike transfer credit fees at many institutions, the fee is a one-time fee that does not increase as more credits are transferred.

THE FUTURE FOR APEI

39 Dr. Wallace Boston, a certified public Accountant and certified management accountant who earned an AB degree in history from Duke University, an MBA in marketing and accounting from Tulane University's Freeman School of Business Administration, and a doctorate in higher education management from the University of Pennsylvania's Graduate School of Education, had these thoughts to share looking toward APEI's future as its president and CEO:

> American Public Education, Inc. two universities are built on certain fundamental principles. In 1991, Jim Etter, recently retired as a USMC colonel, launched what would become one of the first 100% online universities. AMU was established to serve the unique needs of a mobile military by offering affordable, accessible, quality academic programs—and to prepare students for service and leadership in a diverse, global society. We serve an increasingly diverse body of students. In 2001, AMU expanded into the American public university system and established American Public University, to serve civilian students, with an emphasis on public service professionals and others dedicated to fulfilling critical needs. All of our students face enormous responsibilities. Many are actively engaged in defending our country abroad and protecting our local communities. Whatever their career path and academic goals, each one faces the challenge of an increasingly complex world. APUS faculty and staff are committed to preparing our students for the challenges that lie ahead. As we celebrate our 20th year as an institution of higher education in 2011, we continue to recognize and embrace the original vision of our founder. We are leading the way in higher education, by offering an affordable, high-quality education to military and civilian students in a collaborative online classroom led by faculty who are themselves leaders in their fields.
>
> Letter to APEI Shareholders in the 2010 Annual Report.

	YEAR ENDED DECEMBER 31				
(In thousands, except per share and net registration data)	**2006**	**2007**	**2008**	**2009**	**2010**
Statement of Operations Data:					
Reserves	$40,045	$69,095	$107,147	$148,998	$198,172
Costs and expenses:					
Instructional costs and services	17,959	29,479	43,561	58,383	75,309
Selling and promotional	4,895	6,765	12,361	20,479	34,206
General and administrative	9,150	15,335	21,302	25,039	32,045

(continued)

(In thousands, except per share and net registration data)	YEAR ENDED DECEMBER 31				
	2006	**2007**	**2008**	**2009**	**2010**
Write-off of software development project	3,148	—	—	—	—
Depreciation and amortization	1,953	2,825	4,235	5,231	6,502
Total costs and expenses	37,105	54,404	81,459	109,132	148,152
Income from continuing operations before interest Income and income taxes	2,940	14,691	25,688	39,866	50,022
Interest income, net	289	888	706	94	111
Income from continuing operations before income taxes	3,229	15,579	26,394	39,960	50,133
Income tax expense	771	6,829	10,207	16,017	20,265
Income from continuing operations attributable to common stockholders	2,458	8,750	16,157	23,943	29,868
Loss from discontinued operations net of income tax benefit	(660)	—	—	—	—
Net income attributable to common stockholders	$ 1,798	$ 8,750	$ 16,187	$ 23,943	$ 29,868

Percent of Sales Analysis	2006	2007	2008	2009	2010
REVENUES	100.0%	100.0%	100.0%	100.0%	100.0%
Costs and Expenses					
Instructional costs & services	44.8%	42.6%	40.7%	39.2%	38.0%
Selling and Promotional	12.2%	9.8%	11.5%	13.7%	17.3%
General and administrative	22.8%	22.2%	19.9%	16.8%	16.2%
Write-off software development	7.9%				
Depreciation and amortiz.	4.9%		3.9%	3.5%	3.3%
Total Costs and Expenses	92.6%	74.6%	76.0%	73.2%	74.8%
Income from oprns before II & txs	7.3%	25.4%	24.0%	26.8%	25.2%
Interest Income, net	0.7%		0.6%	0.1%	0.1%
Income from operations bef. taxes	8.1%	25.4%	24.6%	26.9%	25.3%
Income tax expense	1.9%		9.5%	10.7%	10.2%
Income from continuing operations	6.1%	25.4%	15.1%	16.2%	15.1%
Loss from discontinued operations	–1.6%				
NET INCOME	4.5%	25.4%	15.1%	16.2%	15.1%

APEI CONSOLIDATED BALANCE SHEET [in thousands]

	2006	2007	2008	2009	2010
ASSETS					
Current Assets					
Cash and cash equivalents	$ 11,678	$ 26,951	$ 47,714	$ 74,866	$ 81,352
Accounts receivable, net	$ 5,448	$ 4,896	$ 6,188	$ 8,664	10,269
Prepaid expenses	$ 856	$ 1,596	$ 2,156	$ 2,990	$ 4,233
Income tax receivable	$ 679	$ 1,089	$ 1,306	$ 863	$ 780
Deferred income taxes	$ 299	$ 309	$ 640	$ 999	$ 1,369
Total current assets	$ 18,960	$ 34,841	$ 58,004	$ 88,382	$ 98,003
Property and equipment, net	$ 9,363	$ 13,364	$ 19,662	$ 25,294	$ 42,415
Other assets	$ 427	$ 775	$ 1,187	$ 2,077	$ 1,421
Total assets	$ 28,750	$ 48,980	$ 78,853	$ 115,753	$ 141,839
LIABILITIES & STOCKHOLDER EQUITY					
Current Liabilities					
Accounts payable	$ 1,502	$ 2,471	$ 4,946	$ 6,756	$ 9,422
Accrued liabilities	$ 3,165	$ 2,770	$ 5,250	$ 8,003	$ 9,349
Accrued bonuses		$ 1,553	$ 1,825		
Deferred rev. & student deposits	$ 3,852	$ 6,614	$ 9,626	$ 14,204	$ 18,815
Current portion of L-term debt	$ 29				
Total current liabilities	$ 8,548	$ 13,408	$ 21,647	$ 28,963	$ 37,586
Deferred taxes	$ 1,437	$ 2,065	$ 3,691	$ 4,772	$ 6,953
Long-term debt	$ 1,944				
Total Liabilities	$ 11,929	$ 15,473	$ 25,338	$ 33,735	$ 44,539
Commitments & Contingencies					
Stockholder equity	$ 118	$ 177	$ 180	$ 183	$ 186
Additional paid-in capital	$ 26,378	$ 128,005	$ 132,078	$ 136,380	$ 141,757
Less share repurchase			$ (295)		$ (19,966)
Accumulated deficit	$ (9,675)	$ (94,675)	$ (78,488)	$ (54,545)	$ (24,677)
Total stockholders' equity	$ 16,821	$ 33,507	$ 53,475	$ 82,018	$ 97,300
Total Liabilities & Stockholders' equity	$ 28,750	$ 48,980	$ 78,813	$ 115,753	$ 141,839

Case 2

Ann Taylor: *Survival in Specialty Retail*

Pauline Assenza *Manhattanville College*
Alan B. Eisner *Lubin School of Business, Pace University*
Jerome C. Kuperman *Minnesota State University Moorhead*

1 In the summer of 2008, headlines announced that the declining economy was generating a "wave of retail closures" among many well-known companies, including Home Depot, Pier 1 Imports, Zales, Gap, Talbots, Lane Bryant, and Ann Taylor. The Chief Executive of J.C. Penney's called the 2008 situation "the most unpredictable environment in his 39-year retail career".[1] One industry group forecasted that nearly 6,000 retail stores would close in 2008, a 25 percent increase from the previous year. A representative from the National Retail Federation (NRF) suggested that these businesses should "look at where they're underperforming and how can they change their operations so that they have a little bit more power in another area, or a little bit more growth potential."[2] Kay Krill, President and CEO of Ann Taylor Stores Corporation (ANN), was already considering this advice.

2 Krill had been appointed President of ANN in late 2004, and succeeded to President/CEO in late 2005 when J. Patrick Spainhour retired after eight years as CEO. At that time, there had been concern among commentators and customers that the Ann Taylor look was getting "stodgy", and the question was how to "reestablish Ann Taylor as the preeminent brand for beautiful, elegant, and sophisticated occasion dressing".[3] In order to reestablish the brand, Kay Krill had acknowledged the importance of the consumer, since for Ann Taylor to succeed long term, "enough women still need to dress up for work".[4]

3 Krill's challenge was based in the ANN legacy as a women's specialty clothing retailer. Since 1954, Ann Taylor had been the wardrobe source for busy socially upscale women, and the classic basic black dress and woman's power suit with pearls were Ann Taylor staples. The Ann Taylor client base consisted of fashion conscious women from the ages of 25 to 55. The overall Ann Taylor concept was designed to appeal to professional women who had limited time to shop and who were attracted to Ann Taylor Stores by its total wardrobing strategy, personalized client service, efficient store layouts and continual flow of new merchandise.

4 ANN had two divisions focused on different segments of this customer base:

- Ann Taylor (AT), the company's original brand, provided sophisticated, versatile and high quality updated classics.

Source: *The CASE Journal* 5, no. 2 (Spring 2009). TCJ 050202. This case is intended to be used as the basis for class discussion rather than to illustrate either effective or ineffective handling of a management situation.

[1] Maestri, N. "Retailers try to thrive in tumultuous climate", *Reuters.com*, 6/16/2008, from http://www.reuters.com/article/email/idUKN1332245620080616

[2] Adams, T. 2008. "Economy generating 'wave' of retail closures", *Columbus Ledger-Enquirer, McClatchy Tribune Business News*, 6/14/2008.

[3] Krill, K. As quoted in "Q3 2005 Ann Taylor Stores Earnings Conference Call—Final", *Fair Disclosure Wire*, 12/2/2005.

[4] Merrick, A. 2005. "Parent Trap: Once a bellwether, Ann Taylor fights its stodgy image", *Wall Street Journal (Eastern Edition)*, 7/12/2005, p. A.1.

- Ann Taylor LOFT (LOFT) was a concept that appealed to women with a more relaxed lifestyle and work environment and who appreciated the more casual LOFT style and compelling value. Certain clients of Ann Taylor and Ann Taylor LOFT cross-shopped both brands.

5 Ann Taylor Factory was the company's newest division. The merchandise in these stores was specifically designed to carry the Ann Taylor Factory label. The stores were located in outlet malls where customers expected to find these and other major label bargains.

6 ANN had regularly appeared in the Women's Wear Daily "Top 10" list of firms selling dresses, suits and eveningwear and the "Top 20" list of publicly traded women's specialty retailers. The listings recognized the total company, i.e., the result of the impact of all three divisions. Financial data from 2004–2008 shows the performance of LOFT compared to AT (See Exhibit 1: AT vs. LOFT Financial Performance 2004–2008.)

7 In October of 2004, for the first time, the LOFT division outsold the flagship Ann Taylor (AT) division stores.[5] In the second quarter of 2004 LOFT had opened its 300th store, passing the Ann Taylor division in total square footage. Since its emergence as a distinctly competitive division, LOFT had been such a success for the company that some analysts credited the division for "keeping the entire ANN corporation afloat".[6]

8 In the company's 2007 Annual Report Krill acknowledged the ongoing challenge:

> To be successful in meeting the changing needs of our clients, we must continually evolve and elevate our brands to ensure they remain compelling—from our product, to our marketing, to our in-store environment.[7]

9 Although Krill believed that the overall Ann Taylor brand still had its historic appeal, the question remained whether that appeal could be sustained indefinitely in such a risky and uncertain specialty retail environment where success was so dependent on the "ability to predict accurately client fashion preferences."[8]

10 Krill was evaluating the company and its growth prospects. Macroeconomic conditions had worsened, and the retailing environment was being threatened by slowing consumer demand. As one analyst put it,

> More mature female shoppers are probably more likely to be very careful how they spend their money in this economy. They are not your footloose-and-fancy-free teen shoppers. These consumers are far more likely to open their pocketbooks only if the merchandise is right (and now, probably only if the price is right, too).[9]

11 Within the company, Krill was contemplating how to revitalize the flagship AT store brand, and what effect that would have on the recent growth of LOFT. In addition, ANN had recently launched a beauty business as a department within the AT and LOFT stores, had expanded the high end fashion offerings in AT as a separate *Collections* line, announced the opening of LOFT Outlet stores to complement Ann Taylor Factory, and was considering a

[5] ANN representatives noted that there was no apparent cause and effect relationship between AT sales decline and the growth of LOFT. Personal communication, Beth Warner, Director, Corporate Communications, Ann Taylor Stores Corporation, July 2007.

[6] Tucker, R. 2004. "LOFT Continues to Pace Ann Taylor", *Women's Wear Daily*, 8/12/2004, Vol. 188, Iss. 21, p. 12.

[7] Letter to Shareholders, ANN 2007 Annual Report, at http://investor.anntaylor.com/phoenix.zhtml?c=78167&p=irol-reportsAnnual

[8] Q1 2008 AnnTaylor Stores Earnings Conference Call, 5/22/2008, available at http://seekingalpha.com/article/78473-ann-taylor-stores-corp-q1-2008-earnings-call-transcript

[9] Lomax, A, "More fickle fashion", *Motley Fool,* 5/23/2008, at http://www.fool.com/investing/general/2008/05/23/more-fickle-fashion.aspx?terms=ann&vstest=search_042607_linkdefault

EXHIBIT 1 **AT vs. LOFT Financial Performance 2004–2008**

(Net sales in millions)

	February 2, 2008	February 3, 2007	January 28, 2006	January 29, 2005	January 31, 2004
Total Company	$2,396.5	$2,343.0	$2,073.1	$1,853.6	$1,587.7
Ann Taylor	866.6	912.8	873.9	854.9	867.9
Ann Taylor LOFT	1,174.4	1,146.5	991.9	826.6	588.8
Other*	355.6	283.7	207.3	172.2	131.1

*Includes Ann Taylor Factory stores and Internet business

Comparable Store Sales Percentage Increase (decrease)

Total Company	(3.3)%	2.8%	0.1%	3.6%	5.3%
Ann Taylor	(3.7%)	3.1%	0.6%	(2.7%)	3.2%
Ann Taylor LOFT	(5.4%)	1.9%	(0.3)%	12.8%	9.4%

The following table provides consolidated income statement data expressed as a percentage of net sales. All fiscal years presented contain 52 weeks, except for the fiscal year ended February 3, 2007, which contains 53 weeks:

	February 2, 2008	February 3, 2007	January 28, 2006
Net sales	100%	100%	100%
Cost of sales	47.8	46.3	49.1
Gross margin	52.2	53.7	50.9
Selling, general & admin expenses	44.4	44.1	44.6
Restructuring & asset impairment	1.3	—	—
Operating income	6.5	9.6	6.3
Interest income	0.3	0.7	0.4
Interest expense	0.1	0.1	0.1
Income before income taxes	6.7	10.2	6.6
Income tax provision	2.6	4.1	2.7
Net income	4.1%	6.1%	3.9%

% Change From Prior Period	**2/2/08**	**2/3/07**	**1/28/06**	**1/29/05**
Net Sales	2.3%	13.0%	11.8%	16.7%
Operating Income	(30.6%)	70.8%	24.8%	(38.7%)
Net Income	(32.0%)	74.6%	29.4%	(37.2%)

Source: Company financials at http://investor.anntaylor.com/

new concept store specifically targeting the "older" segment of women ages 55–64. Krill was firmly committed to long-term growth, and felt that she could pursue that growth agenda even as the economy had worsened. However, she was confronted with significant questions. For example, was her agenda too aggressive? Were the actions she had undertaken the kinds of moves needed to unleash what she believed was the firm's "significant untapped potential"?[10]

ANN TAYLOR BACKGROUND

12 Ann Taylor was founded in 1954 as a wardrobe source for busy socially upscale women. Starting out in New Haven, CT, Ann Taylor founder Robert Liebeskind established a standalone clothing store. When Liebeskind's father, Richard Liebeskind, Sr., a designer himself, as a good luck gesture gave his son exclusive rights to one of his best selling dresses, "Ann Taylor", the company name was established. Ann Taylor was never a real person, but her persona lived on in the profile of the consumer.

13 Ann Taylor went public on the New York Stock Exchange in 1991 under the symbol ANN. In 1994 the company added a mail catalog business, a fragrance line, and free standing shoe stores positioned to supplement the Ann Taylor (AT) stores. The mail order catalog attempt ended in 1995, and the lower-priced apparel concept, Ann Taylor LOFT, was launched. LOFT was meant to appeal to a younger more casual and cost-conscious but still professional consumer. CEO Sally Kazaks incorporated more casual clothing, petite sizes, and accessories in an attempt to create a one-stop shopping environment, to "widen market appeal and fuel growth".[11]

14 Following losses in fiscal 1996 that could be attributed to a fashion misstep—cropped T-shirts didn't fit in with the workplace attire—Kasaks left the company. New ANN CEO Patrick Spainhour, who had been Chief Financial Officer at Donna Karan and had also had previous experience at Gap, shelved the fragrance line, and closed the shoe stores in 1997.

15 Originally the LOFT stores were found only in outlet centers, but later expanded to other kinds of locations. In 1998 the LOFT stores in the discount outlet malls were moved to a third division, Ann Taylor Factory (Factory). The Factory carried clothes from the Ann Taylor (AT) line. The concept offered customers direct access to the AT designer items "off the rack" without elaborate promotion, and with prices regularly 25–30 percent less than at the high end Ann Taylor (AT) stores. The LOFT concept was revamped and stores were opened in more prestigious regional malls and shopping centers. By 1999 LOFT clothes were a distinct line of "more casual, yet business tailored, fun, and feminine", and were about 30 percent less expensive than the merchandise at the flagship Ann Taylor (AT) division's stores.[12] At that time, the LOFT was under the direction of Kay Krill, who had been promoted to the position as Executive Vice President of the LOFT division.

16 Ann Taylor attempted a cosmetic line in 2000, which it discontinued in 2001. In 2000, the Online Store at www.anntaylor.com was launched, only to be cut back in late 2001 when projected cash flow goals were not met. In early 2001 Spainhour restructured management reporting relationships, creating new President positions for both Ann Taylor (AT) and Ann

[10] Letter to Shareholders, ANN 2007 Annual Report, at http://investor.anntaylor.com/phoenix.zhtml?c=78167&p=irol-reportsAnnual

[11] Wilson, M. 1995. "Reinventing Ann Taylor", *Chain Store Age Executive with Shopping Center Age*, New York, January, 1995, Vol. 71, Iss. 1, p. 26.

[12] Summers, M. 1999. "New Outfit", *Forbes*, 12/27/1999, Vol. 164, Iss. 15, p. 88.

Taylor LOFT divisions. Kay Krill was promoted from executive vice-president to president of LOFT. Spainhour commented that,

> Kay has been instrumental in developing the strategy for the Ann Taylor Loft concept since its inception. Her in-depth understanding of the Ann Taylor Loft client, and strong grounding in the Ann Taylor brand, combined with her proven ability in driving the development of this division, make her an ideal choice for the new President position.[13]

17 Kay Krill was made president of the entire ANN corporation in 2004, bringing both Ann Taylor and LOFT under her control. In February of 2005 Kay Krill announced that LOFT had reached $1 billion dollars in sales, stating,

> This is an important milestone for our Company. In an intensely competitive and fragmented apparel market, Ann Taylor LOFT has been one of the industry's most successful and fastest-growing apparel retail concepts since its launch in 1998. . . . LOFT's success reaffirms the importance of maintaining a strong connection with our client and evolving with her wardrobe needs over time.[14]

18 In June 2005 ANN completed a move to new headquarters in Times Square Tower in New York City.[15] In the fall of 2005, Chairman and CEO J. Patrick Spainhour retired and President Kay Krill was elevated to the CEO position. In a conference call following her promotion, Krill stated her goals as "improving profitability while enhancing both brands", "restoring performance at the Ann Taylor division and restoring the momentum at LOFT".[16]

19 Krill felt the outlook for fiscal year 2006 was cautiously positive, and announced continued plans for expansion and related capital expenditure. The stock responded with new highs, moving to a peak of over $40 in late 2006. At that time, analysts were mainly supportive citing "confidence in the retailer's strong management team, improving store products, and conservative inventory management".[17] ANN's stock price subsequently retreated in 2007, along with the rest of the retailing sector. (See Exhibit 2: ANN Stock Price 1992–2008; Exhibit 3: Stores Operational Data. For full financials and operating statistics for 2004–2008, see Exhibits 4–6.)

20 Challenges in the macroeconomic climate prompted Krill to announce a restructuring plan in 2008. In the 2007 Annual Report letter to shareholders Krill said,

> We understand that the economy invariably goes through cycles. We firmly believe that the manner in which we approach growth and manage our business through these cycles will differentiate us and determine our success in the market over the long term. In this regard, we have planned fiscal 2008 cautiously and realistically, focusing on three key areas—the evolution of our brands and channels, the reduction of our overall cost structure, and the continued pursuit of growth.[18]

[13] "Krill promoted to President of the Ann Taylor Loft Division of Ann Taylor, Inc.", 5/3/2001, http://investor.anntaylor.com/news/20010503-40453.cfm?t=n

[14] "Ann Taylor Announces LOFT Division Reaches $1 Billion in Sales", 2/12/2005, from http://investor.anntaylor.com/news/20060213-187405.cfm?t=n

[15] Curan, C. 2001. "Ann Taylor LOFTs expansion plans right into a storm", *Crain's New York Business*, 4/30/2001, Vol. 17, Iss. 18, P. 4.

[16] Krill, K. 2005, op. cit.

[17] "Ann Taylor Stores Jumps on Strong Earnings", *Associated Press,* 3/10/2006, from http://news.moneycentral.msn.com/ticker/article.asp?Feed=AP&Date=20060310&ID=5570346&Symbol=US:ANN

[18] Letter to Shareholders, ANN 2007 Annual Report, at http://investor.anntaylor.com/phoenix.zhtml?c=78167&p=irol-reportsAnnual

EXHIBIT 2 **ANN Stock Price 1992–2008**

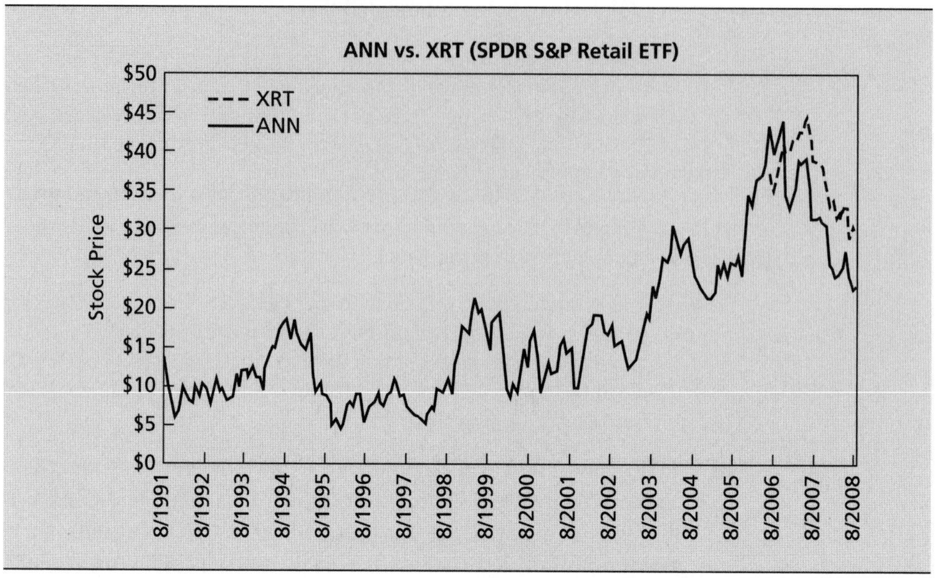

ANN vs. XRT (SPDR S&P Retail ETF)

--- XRT
—— ANN

Stock Price: $50, $45, $40, $35, $30, $25, $20, $15, $10, $5, $0

8/1991, 8/1992, 8/1993, 8/1994, 8/1995, 8/1996, 8/1997, 8/1998, 8/1999, 8/2000, 8/2001, 8/2002, 8/2003, 8/2004, 8/2005, 8/2006, 8/2007, 8/2008

For comparison purposes, the adjusted close stock price of the Exchange Traded Fund (ETF) S&P Retail SPDR is included. This fund began trading on 6/22/2006. The top ten holdings (22.48% of total assets as of 8/2008) in this fund (in alphabetical order) consist of Aeropostale Inc., AnnTaylor Stores Corp., Brown Shoe Co., Inc., Charming Shoppes, FootLocker, Inc., Genesco Inc., Limited Brands Inc., Ross Stores Inc., Supervalu Inc., and Tiffany & Co.

Derived from: http://finance.yahoo.com/q/bc?s=ANN&t=my&l=on&z=l&q=l&c=

EXHIBIT 3 **Stores Operational Data**

	FY2007	FY2006	FY2005	FY2004	FY2003
Employees, Total	18,400	17,700	16,900	14,900	13,000
Inventory Turns*	4.7	5.0	4.7	4.5	4.1
Net Sales/sq ft	$ 457	$ 474	$ 461	$ 471	$ 456
Net Sales (Revenue)/ Employee	$130,603	$130,227	$123,008	$124,743	$122,467
Average sq ft/Store					
Ann Taylor	5,300				
Ann Taylor LOFT	5,700				
Ann Taylor Factory	6,700				

*Inventory turns can be calculated differently, depending on whether yearly average or year end inventory values are used. These numbers are from ANN's 10K filing.

EXHIBIT 3 (*Continued*)

Specific Store Detail

Fiscal Year	Total Stores Open at Beginning of Fiscal Year	No. Stores Opened During Fiscal Year			No. Stores Closed During Fiscal Year	No. Stores Open at End of Fiscal Year				No. Stores Expanded During Fiscal Year
		ATS	ATL	ATF		ATS	ATL	ATF	Total	
2003	584	8	61	1	6	354	268	26	648	8
2004	648	10	77	8	5	359	343	36	738	6
2005	738	9	73	15	11	357	416	51	824	12
2006	824	11	52	7	25	348	464	57	869	16
2007	869	14	52	11	17	349	512	68	929	14

Source: Company Reports at http://investor.anntaylor.com/

EXHIBIT 4 **Income Statements**

AnnTaylor Stores Corp. Annual Income Statement (In Millions of US$)					
	Jan08	Jan07	Jan06	Jan05	Jan04
Sales	2,396.510	2,342.907	2,073.146	1,853.583	1,587.708
Cost of Goods Sold	1,028.442	980.007	923.336	827.378	669.638
Gross Profit	1,368.068	1,362.900	1,149.810	1,026.205	918.070
Selling, General, & Administrative Expense	1,063.623	1,033.173	908.966	842.590	694.590
Depreciation, Depletion & Amortization	116.804	105.890	93.786	78.657	51.825
Operating Profit	187.641	223.837	147.058	104.958	171.655
Interest Expense	2.172	2.230	2.083	3.641	6.665
Non-Operating Income/Expense	7.826	17.174	9.318	5.037	3.298
Special Items	(32.255)	0.000	(16.032)	0.000	0.000
Pretax Income	161.040	238.781	138.261	106.354	168.288
Total Income Taxes	63.805	95.799	56.389	43.078	67.346
Net Income	97.235	142.982	81.872	63.276	100.942

Source: Standard & Poor's

THE APPAREL RETAIL INDUSTRY

21 **History** Prior to the development of a retailing industry, the only option for upper-class wealthy women who desired to be fashionable was to hire local dressmakers to create one-of-a-kind personalized garments. Women with more limited resources had few options until

EXHIBIT 5 Balance Sheets

AnnTaylor Stores Corp. Annual Balance Sheet (In Millions of US$)					
ASSETS	**Jan08**	**Jan07**	**Jan06**	**Jan05**	**Jan04**
Cash and Equivalents	134.025	360.560	380.654	62.412	337.087
Short-Term Investments	9.110	0.000	0.000	192.400	0.000
Total Receivables	16.944	16.489	17.091	12.573	12.476
Inventories	250.697	233.606	204.503	229.218	172.058
Current Assets—Other	97.115	79.950	73.964	90.711	55.747
Total Current Assets	507.891	690.605	676.212	587.314	577.368
Gross Plant, Property & Equipment	1,148.003	1,105.240	995.897	853.770	542.449
Accumulated Depreciation	586.733	541.132	483.132	419.442	276.880
Net Plant, Property & Equipment	561.270	564.108	512.765	434.328	265.569
Intangibles	286.579	286.579	286.579	286.579	286.579
Deferred Charges	0.288	0.652	1.017	1.382	4.886
Other Assets	37.727	26.559	16.333	17.735	17.471
TOTAL ASSETS	1,393.755	1,568.503	1,492.906	1,327.338	1,151.873
LIABILITIES					
Accounts Payable	125.388	106.519	97.398	88.340	52.170
Accrued Expenses	132.924	139.910	114.272	116.514	77.330
Other Current Liabilities	54.564	52.989	45.916	38.892	32.120
Total Current Liabilities	312.876	299.418	257.586	243.746	161.620
Long Term Debt	0.000	0.000	0.000	0.000	125.152
Deferred Taxes	1.960	—	—	—	—
Other Liabilities	239.435	219.174	200.838	156.848	34.465
TOTAL LIABILITIES	554.271	518.592	458.424	400.594	321.237
EQUITY					
Total Preferred Stock	0.000	0.000	0.000	0.000	0.000
Common Stock	0.560	0.559	0.558	0.545	0.336
Capital Surplus	781.048	753.030	711.224	657.382	510.676
Retained Earnings	762.948	664.934	527.325	445.410	393.926
Less: Treasury Stock	705.072	368.612	204.625	176.593	74.302
Common Equity	839.484	1,049.911	1,034.482	926.744	830.636
TOTAL EQUITY	839.484	1,049.911	1,034.482	926.744	830.636
TOTAL LIAB & COMMON EQUITY	1,393.755	1,568.503	1,492.906	1,327.338	1,151.873
Common Shares Outstanding	60.880	69.373	72.491	70.632	68.067

Source: Standard & Poor's

EXHIBIT 6 **Statement of Annual Cash Flows**

AnnTaylor Stores Corp. Annual Statement of Cash Flows (In Millions of US$)					
INDIRECT OPERATING ACTIVITIES	**Jan08**	**Jan07**	**Jan06**	**Jan05**	**Jan04**
Net Income	97.235	142.982	81.872	63.276	100.942
Depreciation and Amortization	116.804	105.890	93.786	78.657	51.825
Deferred Taxes	(9.361)	(10.809)	(15.421)	(5.022)	3.771
Funds from Operations—Other	58.850	41.290	28.022	23.163	13.133
Receivables—Decrease (Increase)	(0.455)	0.602	(5.024)	0.056	(1.909)
Inventory—Decrease (Increase)	(17.091)	(29.103)	24.715	(57.159)	10.926
Accounts Payable and Accrued Liabilities—Inc (Dec)	0.550	37.580	28.185	62.196	12.725
Other Assets and Liabilities—Net Change	10.665	7.499	75.188	4.092	(1.795)
Operating Activities—Net Cash Flow	257.197	295.931	311.323	169.259	189.618
INVESTING ACTIVITIES					
Short-Term Investments—Change	(16.422)	0.000	192.400	117.975	0.000
Capital Expenditures	139.998	165.926	187.613	152.483	71.364
Investing Activities—Net Cash Flow	(156.420)	(165.926)	4.787	(34.508)	(71.364)
FINANCING ACTIVITIES					
Sale of Common and Preferred Stock	17.935	30.038	50.285	22.822	20.329
Purchase of Common and Preferred Stock	(347.575)	(185.129)	(48.153)	(121.698)	(12.781)
Excess Tax Benefit from Stock Options	2.328	4.992	0.000	—	—
Financing Activities—Other	0.000	0.000	0.000	(0.022)	(1.536)
Financing Activities—Net Cash Flow	(327.312)	(150.099)	2.132	(98.898)	6.012
Cash and Equivalents—Change	(226.535)	(20.094)	318.242	35.853	124.266
Interest Paid—Net	1.723	1.769	1.293	1.770	2.202
Income Taxes Paid	77.355	94.723	47.030	58.226	56.147

Source: Standard & Poor's

the 1800s. Enterprising seamstresses began mass-producing dresses at that time, utilizing the increased availability of textiles and the invention of the sewing machine. The increasing availability of diverse products led to the creation of the variety store, the precursor of the current department store. At the same time, entrepreneurial seamstresses previously working as personalized dressmakers began to open specialty stores for fashionable women's clothing. Thus came the origins of modern retailing, with both department stores and specialty retailers co-existing in many downtown locations.

22 The movement of the U.S. population into the suburbs, along with an increasing use of automobiles, led to the development in the 1930s and 1940s of planned shopping centers and highway strips of unified shopping stores. This expansion included the first free-standing stores with on-site parking, as run by Sears Roebuck & Co. The shopping mall concept expanded further in the 1950s. Usually "anchored" by either supermarkets or department stores, these shopping centers also allowed specialty and department retailers to co-exist in the same physical location.

23 By the 1980s, there were 16,000 retail shopping centers in the U.S.[19] However, as customers showed their increased interest in more convenient and quicker service, alternatives to traditional 'brick and mortar' shopping centers appeared. They included non-store direct mail order, infomercial and shopping channel TV venues, and online options. Many retailers also made a strategic decision to create specialty clothing departments and focus on items such as sports wear, or appeal to specific niches such as either large-sized or petite women.[20] In addition, response to the threat of discounter department stores like Target and Wal-Mart prompted some established specialty firms to create separate divisions focused on lower priced fashions.[21]

24 **Industry Sectors** Practically speaking, industry watchers tended to recognize three separate categories of clothing retailers. Industry publications such as the Daily News Record (DNR—reporting on men's fashions news and business strategies), Women's Wear Daily (WWD—reporting on women's fashions and apparel business), and industry associations such as the National Retail Federation (NRF) reported data within the clothing sector broken out by:

- Discount mass merchandisers like Target, Wal-Mart, TJX (TJ Maxx, Marshall's, A.J. Wright, Bob's Stores), and Costco.
- Multi-tier department stores (those offering a large variety of goods, including clothing, like Macy's and J.C. Penney's, and the more luxury-goods focused stores like Nordstrom's and Neiman Marcus).
- Specialty store chains (those catering to a certain type of customer or type of goods, e.g. Abercrombie & Fitch for casual apparel).

25 More specifically in the case of specialty retail, many broadly recognized primary categories existed such as women's, men's, and children's clothing stores (e.g., Victoria's Secret for women's undergarments[22], Men's Wearhouse for men's suits, Abercrombie Kids for children aged 7–14[23]). Women's specialty stores were "establishments primarily engaged in retailing a specialized line of women's, juniors' and misses' clothing."[24]

[19] 2000. "A brief history of shopping centers", *International Council of Shopping Centers,* June 2000, from http://www.icsc.org/srch/about/impactofshoppingcenters/briefhistory.html

[20] The "large-sized woman" market is best represented nation wide in shopping malls by Lane Bryant stores and catalog sales, Fashion Bug Plus, and Catherine's stores, all divisions of Charming Shoppes; and by Avenue stores, a division of United Retail Group. Charming Shoppes also targets the petite woman, 5'4" and shorter, with its Petite Sophisticate Outlet.

[21] As an example, Gap, Inc. created the Old Navy division in 1994 to offer lower priced casual clothing. An apparel retail industry overview by *Encyclopedia of American Industries* Online Edition. Thomson Gale, 2006, reported that in 2002 nearly 35 percent of Target's sales came from the clothing department.

[22] Victoria's Secret is a division of Limited Brands, which also operates Pink (a sub-brand of Victoria's Secret focused on sleepwear & intimate apparel for high school & college students), Bath & Body Works and C.O. Bigelow (personal beauty, body & hair products), The White Barn Candle Co. (candles & home fragrances), Henri Bendel (high fashion women's clothing), and La Senza (lingerie sold in Canada & worldwide).

[23] Abercrombie & Fitch, as of 2008, had four brand divisions in addition to the flagship Abercrombie & Fitch stores: abercrombie (the brand name is purposely lowercase) for kids ages 7–14; Hollister Co. for southern California surf lifestyle teens; RUEHL No. 925 for ages 22–35; and Gilly Hicks: Sydney, launched in 2008, specializing in women's intimate apparel.

[24] http://www.census.gov/svsd/www/artsnaics.html, op cit.

26 A unique form of organization that sometimes appeared as competition in the specialty retail category was the clothing designer. Originally an evolution of the custom seamstress, for one-of-a-kind garments, fashion design houses such as Liz Claiborne and Ralph Lauren could also produce their creations in bulk, as ready-to-wear clothing. These firms were generally considered apparel wholesalers, with their items normally for sale to the clothing retailers, such as Macy's, but well-established designers could also build their own specialty stores to sell directly to the consumer.

SPECIALTY RETAILER GROWTH: BRANDING CHALLENGES

27 Unlike department stores that sold many different types of products for many types of customers, specialty retailers focused on one type of product item, and offered many varieties of that item. However, this single product focus increased risk, as lost sales in one area could not be recouped by a shift of interest to another entirely different product area. Therefore, many specialty retailers constantly sought out new market segments (i.e., niches) that they could serve. However, this strategy created potential problems for branding[25]. A participant at the 2007 NRF convention commented,

> Brand building, acquisition, and tiering is hotter than ever in retail and consumer products—so much so they may be contributing to shorter life spans for some brands and perhaps diluting the value of all. In any event, the massive proliferation of brands in recent years—some out of thin air, others even reborn from the grave—brings with it a minefield of potential dangers.[26]

28 Gap, Inc. was an example of a specialty retailer that had added several brand extensions to appeal to different customer segments. In addition to the original Gap line of casual clothing, the company offered the following: Old Navy with casual fashions at low prices, Banana Republic for more high-end casual items, and Piperlime as an online shoe store. However, in 2005 Gap had also spent $40 million to open a chain for upscale women's clothing called Forth & Towne, which closed after only 18 months. The store was supposed to appeal to upscale women over 35—the "baby boomer" segment—but, instead, the designers seemed "too focused on reproducing youthful fashions with a more generous cut" instead of finding an "interesting, affordable way" for middle-aged women to "dress like themselves."[27]

29 Chico's FAS, Inc. was another specialty retailer who tried brand expansions. Chico's focused on private-label, casual-to-dressy clothing to women 35 years old and up, with relaxed, figure-flattering styles constructed out of easy-care fabrics. An outgrowth of a Mexican folk art boutique, Chico's was originally a stand-alone brand. Starting in late 2003, Chico's FAS decided to promote two new brands: White House/Black Market (WH/BM), and Soma by Chico's (Soma).

30 Chico's WH/BM brand was based on the acquisition of an existing store chain, and focused on women 25 years old and up, offering fashion and merchandise in black and white and related shades. Soma was a newly developed brand offering intimate apparel, sleepwear and active wear. Each brand had its own storefront, mainly in shopping malls, and was augmented by both mail order catalog and Internet sales. The idea was that the loyal

[25] According to the American Marketing Association (AMA), a brand is a "name, term, sign, symbol or design, or a combination of them intended to identify the goods and services of one seller or group of sellers and to differentiate them from those of other sellers. . . . branding is not about getting your target market to choose you over the competition, but it is about getting your prospects to see you as the only one that provides a solution to their problem." A good brand will communicate this message clearly and with credibility, motivating the buyer by eliciting some emotion that inspires future loyalty. From http://marketing.about.com/cs/brandmktg/a/whatisbranding.htm

[26] Felgner, B. 2007. "New challenges in branding", *Home Textiles Today,* 2/5/2007, Vol. 28, No. 5, p. 1.

[27] Turner, J. 2007. "Go forth and go out of business", *Slate*, 2/26/2007, at http://www.slate.com/id/2160668/

Chico's customer would be drawn to shop at these other concept stores, expecting the same level of quality, service, and targeted offerings that had pleased her in the past.

31 Although Chico's had been a solid performer during the decade, surpassing most other women's clothing retailers in sales growth, a downturn in 2006 caused Chico's shares to fall more than 50 percent when the company reported sales and earnings below analysts' expectations. Chico's had seen increasing competition for its baby boomer customers, and said it had lost momentum during 2006, partly because of "fashion missteps" and lack of sufficiently new product designs. The company's response was to create brand presidents for the three divisions to hopefully create more "excitement and differentiation."[28]

32 In an attempt to better manage the proliferation of brands, many firms, similar to Chico's, created an organizational structure where brands had their own dedicated managers, with titles such as executive vice president (EVP)/general merchandise manager, chief merchandising officer, or outright "brand president."[29] Since each brand was supposedly unique, companies felt the person responsible for a brand's creative vision should be unique as well.

33 An alternative to brand extension was the divestiture of brands. In 1988 Limited Brands[30] acquired Abercrombie and Fitch (A&F) and rebuilt A&F to represent the "preppy" lifestyle of teenagers and college students aged 18–22. In 1996 Limited Brands spun A&F off as a separate public company. Limited Brands continued divesting brands: teenage clothing and accessories brand The Limited TOO in 1999, plus-size women's clothing brand Lane Bryant in 2001, professional women's clothing brand Lerner New York in 2002, and in 2007 the casual women's clothing brands Express and The Limited. Paring down in order to focus mostly on key brands Victoria's Secret and Bath & Body Works, the corporation had made it clear as of 2007 that it was still not done reconfiguring itself.[31]

WOMEN'S SPECIALTY RETAIL—COMPETITORS AND THE "OLDER WOMEN" SEGMENT

34 The National Retail Federation, a Washington, D.C.-based trade group, reported that the retail niches showing the greatest growth in 2006 were department stores, stores catering to the teenage children of baby boomers, and those apparel chains aimed at women over 35.[32] The four major women's specialty retailers who were trying to target older upscale shoppers were Ann Taylor, Chicos FAS, Coldwater Creek and Talbots. Ann Taylor was the only one of these with a significant brand extension for the younger professional, but all four were promising a shopping environment and merchandise clearly focused on women over 35. (See Exhibit 7: Selected Retail Performers.)

35 Talbot's CEO Trudy Sullivan noted,

> Nobody is clearly winning in the 35+ consumer space right now . . . we need to absolutely wow her with this irresistible product and none of us have done that.[33]

[28] Lee, G. 2007. "Chico's outlines plan to improve on results", *Women's Wear Daily*, 3/8/2007, Vol. 193, Iss. 50, p. 5.

[29] The responsibilities of these positions include "creative vision" for the brand: marketing materials, store design, and overall merchandising (developing product, ensuring production efficiency, monitoring store inventory turnover, and adjusting price points as needed).

[30] In 2007, Limited Brands owned the brands Victoria's Secret (including Pink, a Victoria's Secret sub-brand), Bath & Body Works (the 2 major brands), and C.O. Bigelow, Henri Bendel, White Barn Candle, and La Senza.

[31] "Limited Brands cutting 530 jobs", Columbus Business First, 6/22/2007, at http://columbus.bizjournals.com/columbus/stories/2007/06/18/daily26.html

[32] Jones, Sandra M. 2007. "Sweetest Spots in Retail", *Knight Ridder Tribune Business News,* 7/31/2007, pg. 1.

[33] Sarkar, Pia. 2007. "Talbots still can't find its way", 10/24/2007, http://www.thestreet.com/newsanalysis/retail/10386340.html

EXHIBIT 7 **Selected Retail Performers, end of 2007**

Company/ Ticker Symbol	2007 Revenue (millions)	Comparable Stores Sales Increase (Decrease)		# of Stores	Locations Served	Merchandise Market Served	Comments
		2006	2005				
Ann Taylor/ ANN	$ 2,396.5	(3.3%)	2.8%	929	46 states plus Puerto Rico	Specialty Women's—private label "total ward-robing strategy" to achieve the "AnnTaylor look" in suits, separates, footwear & accessories	Brands are Ann Taylor for updated professional classics, Ann Taylor LOFT for lower priced more casual wear, AnnTaylor Factory for outlet priced garments developed specifically for this market
Talbots/ TLB	$ 2,289.3	(5.7%)*	1.3%*	1,421	47 states plus Canada, United Kingdom	Specialty—women's apparel, shoes, accessories via store, catalog, Internet	Brands are Talbots, modern classics for women; J.Jill for casual women. Brands target high income, college educated professionals 35 years old & up. Talbots Kids, Talbots Mens were closed in 2007.
Chico's FAS/ CHS	$ 1,714.3	(8.1%)	2.1%	1,070	47 states plus U.S. Virgin Islands & Puerto Rico	Specialty Women's—Privately branded clothing, intimate garments & gifts for fashion-conscious women with moderate-high income	Brands are Chico's for women 35+, White House/Black Market for women 25+, Soma intimates
Coldwater Creek, Inc./ CWTR	$ 1,151.5	(7.9%) averages	8.5%	336	48 states	Specialty Women's—apparel, accessories, jewelry, gifts via instore, catalog, Internet, also Spa locations	Offers Coldwater Creek brand of cosmetics, personal care products to women over 35 with incomes in excess of $75K. Socially responsible.

* Does not include J. Jill Data Source: 10K filings, plus data from "Top 100 Retailers", *Stores: A magazine of the NFR,* July 2008, downloadable by link at http://www.nrf.com/modules.php?name=News&op=viewlive&sp_id=543

(continued)

EXHIBIT 7 (*Continued*)

Selected Retail Performers, 2008 Financial Data

Company Name	Total Revenue*	Net Income*	Inventory Turnover	Revenue $ per Employee
Abercrombie & Fitch Co.	$ 3,749.8	$475.7	9.89	$ 37,981
AnnTaylor Stores Corp.	$ 2,396.5	$ 97.3	9.92	$ 130,603
Charming Shoppes, Inc.	$ 3,010.0	($ 83.4)	7.35	$ 99,941
Chico's FAS Inc.	$ 1,714.3	$ 88.9	13.48	$ 120,212
Coldwater Creek Inc.	$ 1,151.5	($ 2.5)	8.65	$ 87,665
Limited Brands Inc.	$10,134.0	$718.0	6.73	$ 57,869
Talbots, Inc.	$ 2,289.3	($188.8)	6.73	$ 138,288
The Gap, Inc.	$15,763.0	$833.0	9.38	$ 105,375

Company Name	Selling Gen & Admin % Tot Rev	Gross Margin %	Operating Margin %	Net Profit Margin %
Abercrombie & Fitch Co.	47.54	66.97	19.75	12.69
AnnTaylor Stores Corp.	44.38	52.21	6.48	4.06
Charming Shoppes, Inc.	25.83	26.95	–2.62	–2.77
Chico's FAS Inc	49.44	56.53	7.08	5.18
Coldwater Creek Inc.	40.02	39.1	–0.93	–0.22
Limited Brands Inc.	26.27	34.95	10.95	7.09
Talbots, Inc.	33.1	32.12	–8.14	–8.25
The Gap, Inc.	N/A	36.11	8.34	5.28

Data from Mergent Online, as of 2008, *dollars in millions

36 This group of women, born between 1946 and 1964, was part of the "baby boomer" demographic, and the purchasing power of these women had not gone unnoticed.[34] Accounting for nearly half of the $102.7 billion in women's clothing purchases in 2007, these women were very diverse, ranging from "traditional types who prefer flat shoes and ankle-length skirts to women who resemble characters from *Desperate Housewives*."[35]

37 To respond to this diversity in the marketplace, woman's specialty retailer Talbot's Inc. acquired catalog and mail order company J.Jill Group in 2006. J.Jill was a woman's clothing specialty retailer offering quality casual fashion through multi-channel mail order, Internet, and in-store venues. J.Jill targeted women ages 35–55, while Talbot's focused on the 45–65 age group. The acquisition positioned Talbot's as "the leading apparel retailer for the highly

[34] See, for instance, the website http://www.aginghipsters.com/, a "source for trends, research, comment and discussion" about this group.

[35] Agins, Teri. 2007. "The Boomer Balancing Act: Retailers say new looks for middle-age women are both youthful and mature", *Wall Street Journal (Eastern Edition)*, 11/3/2007, pg. W3.

coveted age 35+ female population," and allowed the company to "protect the distinct identity of each brand, while maximizing the synergies" in its business model.[36]

38 Coldwater Creek, with its large jewelry, accessory, and gift assortment in addition to apparel, targeted women over 35 with incomes in access of $75K by appealing with a Northwest/Southwest lifestyle approach that included a group of Spa locations. Coldwater's customer was not considered "trendy" by any means: "She's never going to be a fashion leader . . . but she wants to look modern."[37] Coldwater Creek created a common brand identity for its three distribution channels: catalog, Internet, and in-store shopping. This distinct brand image yielded the best shareholder return in the group (Coldwater Creek, Chico's FAS, Ann Taylor, and Talbot's) since 2002, with a 33.8% revenue growth in fiscal year 2006.[38]

39 Chico's FAS was one of the first to introduce the concept of apparel designed for the lifestyle of dynamic mature women who were at the higher age end of the boomer demographic.[39] Chico's, along with Coldwater Creek, was one of the recipients of the 50+Fabulous Company award in 2007, an award that promoted positive images of women who were in their 50's or older. The founder of 50+Fabulous had established this award to promote "the value of 50+ women in the workplace and beyond", noting, "companies have been slow to recognize the vast potential" of this demographic.[40]

40 In August of 2007 Kay Krill announced ANN would be creating a new chain of stores expected to launch sometime in 2008 or 2009, targeting this "older women" segment, stating,

> While there are a number of companies that currently play in the broader boomer market, we believe that this particular segment has been the most significantly underserved and a huge opportunity for us.[41]

41 Some analysts wondered about this move into an overlooked but risky market that "has tripped up several competitors like Gap." They pointed out that although ANN's clothes were expected to be more fashionable, the company still faced stiff competition, made even tougher given the uneven performance of AT and LOFT.[42] In 2008, as a result of the overall economic conditions, Krill announced that this new concept offering would have to be delayed at least until 2009.[43]

ANN OPERATIONAL INFORMATION[44]

42 At the end of fiscal year 2007, ANN had 929 stores in 46 states, the District of Columbia and Puerto Rico, with flagship locations in New York, San Francisco, and Chicago.

[36] 2006. "Talbots completes the acquisition of the J.Jill Group; combined company creates leading brand portfolio for the age 35+ female market; key executives promoted to maximize growth", *Business Wire,* 5/3/2006, from The Talbot's Inc. http://phx.corporate-ir.net/phoenix.zhtml?c=65681&p=irol-newsArticle&ID=851481&highlight=

[37] Edelson, Sharon. 2007. "Coldwater Creek brings natural vibe to Manhattan", *Women's Wear Daily,* 8/13/2007, Vol. 194, Iss. 32, pg. 4.

[38] See, for instance, the graph at Coldwater Creek, Inc. 2006 Annual Report, http://www.coldwatercreek.com/InvRel/. Doing a comparative analysis using any stock reporting tool shows both Coldwater Creek and Chico's beating Ann Taylor during the period from 2004–mid 2007. Talbots trails them all.

[39] Some marketers believe the boomers are a bifurcated demographic: although the boomer market encompasses those born between 1946–1964, boomers born between 1946–1954 have slightly different life experiences than those born between 1955–1964.

[40] "50+Fabulous Awards Companies that Promote Positive Images of 50+ Women", *Business Wire,* 01/30/2007.

[41] Kingsbury, Kevin & Moore, Angela. 2007. "Ann Taylor tires for a better fit", *Wall Street Journal (Eastern Edition),* 8/25/2007, p. B6.

[42] Barbaro, Michael. 2007. "Ann Taylor said to plan boomer unit", *The New York Times,* 8/13/2007, p. C3.

[43] ANN 2007 Annual Report, at http://investor.anntaylor.com/phoenix.zhtml?c=78167&p=irol-reportsAnnual

[44] Information in this section comes from ANN 10K filing as of FY2007.

(See Exhibit 3: Stores Operational Data for specifics.) The company had also had an online presence since 2000, and transacted sales at www.anntaylor.com and www.anntaylorLOFT.com. This "very profitable" Internet channel was considered "a meaningful and effective marketing vehicle for both brands", representing 10 percent of AT sales, less than that for LOFT, and was a way for ANN to reach out to the international market.[45]

43 Substantially all merchandise offered in ANN's stores was exclusively developed for the company by its in-house product design and development teams. ANN sourced merchandise from approximately 231 manufacturers and vendors, none of whom accounted for more than 4 percent of the company's merchandise purchases in Fiscal 2007. Merchandise was manufactured in over 15 countries, including China, the Philippines, Indonesia, Hong Kong and Thailand.

44 ANN's planning departments analyzed each store's size, location, demographics, sales, and inventory history to determine the quantity of merchandise to be purchased for and then allocated to the stores. The company used a centralized distribution system with a single warehouse in Louisville, Kentucky. At the store level, merchandise was typically sold at its original marked price for several weeks. After that, markdowns were used if inventory did not sell. Store planners recognized that the lack of inventory turnover could have been because of poor merchandise design, seasonal adaptation or changes in client preference, or that the original price points had been set incorrectly.

45 Recent ANN initiatives had focused on improving supply chain speed, flexibility and efficiency. Reduced floor inventory levels combined with the use of new "quick-sourcing" software were meant to help create quicker inventory turns. Faster turns would lead to continual updating of floor merchandise and a greater emphasis on "full-price selling".[46] As a result, ANN was hoping to see fewer markdowns and higher margins. The new "quick-sourcing" software was just one example of continued efforts to improve the company's information systems.

46 ANN had initiated a real estate reinvestment program focused on enhancing the look and feel of 43 stores in 2005, in a move toward the "store of the future".[47] In addition, the firm had begun a real estate expansion program designed to reach new clients either by opening new stores, relocating stores, or expanding the size of existing stores. Store locations were determined on the basis of various factors including

- Geographic location
- Demographic studies
- Anchor tenants in a mall location
- Other specialty stores in a mall or specialty center location or in the vicinity of a village location
- The proximity to professional offices in a downtown or village location

47 Two potential concerns were emerging for ANN as a result of its recent investments in store expansion and remodeling. First, the increasing sales volume threatened to put stress on the company's internal distribution system. The distribution center in Louisville had been investing in incremental improvements through automation and software integration. However the distribution center had only sufficient capacity to supply 1,050 stores. After that, ANN's logistical experts cautioned that the building footprint would have to be expanded.[48]

[45] Q1 2008 AnnTaylor Stores Earnings Conference Call, 5/22/2008, available at http://seekingalpha.com/article/78473-ann-taylor-stores-corp-q1-2008-earnings-call-transcript

[46] O'Donnell, J. 2006. "Retailers try to train shoppers to buy now; Limited supplies, fewer sales could get consumers to stop waiting for discounts", *USA TODAY*, 9/26/2006, p. B3.

[47] ANN 2005 Annual Report at http://investor.anntaylor.com/downloads/2005AnnualReport.pdf

[48] "Ann Taylor: Upgrade with style", *Modern Material Handling (Warehousing Management Edition)*, March 2006, Vol. 61, Iss. 3, p. 38.

48 A second concern was whether projected earnings, given economic weakness, would actually be able to cover the projected long-term lease obligations that were being added. One analyst had warned,

> Store expansion is a risk for all apparel retailers. Gap Inc., for example, spent massively to add stores in the 1990s and . . . the stores became a big cost overhead once Gap's clothes stopped selling well.[49]

ANN TAYLOR'S BRAND IDENTITY

49 When ANN went public in 1991, the Ann Taylor brand, with its historically loyal following, was a candidate for brand extension. At one point in its history, the company had five separate store concepts: Ann Taylor (AT), Ann Taylor's Studio Shoes, Ann Taylor LOFT, Ann Taylor Petites (clothing for women 5'4" and under), and Ann Taylor Factory. In addition, ANN's management had experimented with a make-up line and children's clothes. By 2005, the company had closed the shoe stores, reduced the accessories inventory that stores carried, and eliminated the make-up line. However, ANN was still offering petites, as a separate section in the AT and LOFT stores, and experimenting with children's clothes and sleepwear through the LOFT division. A separate maternity section in selected LOFT stores was also undergoing a trial period.

50 Since 1999 analysts had warned that ANN needed to be wary of cannibalization within the brands. The analysts speculated that customers might turn away from Ann Taylor (AT) in order to buy at LOFT. ANN had always tried to respond to the customer with "wardrobing", a philosophy of "outfitting from head to toe", combining relaxed everyday wear with more dressy pieces.[50] Since LOFT sold more relaxed but still tailored items at a lower price than AT, it was possible that some of AT's customers shopped at LOFT for things that they previously would have bought at AT.

51 The industry was used to brand extensions such as Gap's Old Navy chain. In contrast to Gap, LOFT used "Ann Taylor" in its name, reinforcing the perception of customers that they could get the same brand for less. As one analyst put it,

> It's not clear that the Ann Taylor customer will continue paying $88 for a silk cardigan sweater when she knows she can pick up a similar cardigan for $39 . . . a few blocks away at LOFT.[51]

52 As new CEO in the fall of 2005, one of Krill's first actions was to recruit Laura Weil to a new position as Corporate Operations Officer (COO). Weil came from American Eagle Outfitters where she had focused on financial issues involving real estate, pricing, sourcing, and logistics. In addition, Weil handled the divestiture of underperforming assets. In her role as COO at ANN she would be expected to "focus on inventory management and merchandise planning, information systems and supply chain operations".[52]

53 The appointment of Weil and four other staff changes reconfigured ANN's top management structure. Krill created three positions that reported directly to her—COO, Executive

[49] Jones, S.D. 2006. "Moving the Market—Tracking the Numbers/Outside Audit: Ann Taylor's Data Draw a Big Critic; Research Firm Questions Retailer's Earnings Quality Amid High Costs of Capital", *Wall Street Journal (Eastern Edition),* 7/17/2006, p. C3.

[50] Kennedy, K. 2000. "This is not your momma's clothing store—not by a longshot", *Apparel Industry Magazine,* Altanta, December 2000, Vol. 61, Iss. 12, p. 22–25.

[51] Curan, C. 1999. "Ann Taylor aims for LOFT-y goal with new stores", *Crain's New York Business,* 3/29/1999, Vol. 15, Iss. 13, p. 1.

[52] Derby, M. 2005. "Wall Street bullish on Ann Taylor's Weil", *Women's Wear Daily,* 10/3/2005, Vol. 190, Iss. 71, p. 20.

Vice President (EVP) of planning and allocation, and EVP/chief marketing officer. The three additional positions provided specific expertise while still allowing Krill to "lead both divisions [AT & LOFT] in a more hands-on-way". Krill then focused on merchandising and marketing, especially brand differentiation.[53] AT and LOFT continued to have separate EVP's for merchandising and design, and Senior Vice Presidents for divisional marketing, design, sourcing and store direction.

54 Krill had asked her staff to spend time with ANN customers and develop "brand books" or profiles of the typical Ann Taylor (AT) and LOFT clients.[54] The "Ann" (AT) marketing profile was of a married 36 year-old working mother with two children and a household income of $150K. She would lead a busy, sophisticated life. When giving a presentation to a client, she'd wear a formal suit with a blouse, not a camisole, underneath, and her idea of dressing down at work might be a velvet jacket with jeans.

55 In contrast, the typical LOFT client was married, in her 30's with children, worked in a laid-back less corporate environment, and had a household income between $75K and $100K. She would call her style "casual chic" and might wear pants and a floral top with ruffled sleeves to work, while on the weekend she would wear a printed shoulder-baring halter top with cropped jeans. Krill had always felt that both AT and LOFT were recognizably different from one another. In 2005, Krill stated that there was "a pretty clear differentiation", with "special occasion and work primarily being the focus" at AT, and "more relaxed, separates and fashion" at LOFT.[55]

56 In support of the AT brand, the company also expanded its focus on special events with the introduction of its *Celebrations* collection. The company introduced *Celebrations* into the AT stores as a line of classic, elegant dresses and coordinating accessories for special occasion, such as weddings and engagement parties. Of particular interest to long-term ANN customers was the introduction of dye-to-match sashes and accessories for bridesmaids, with fully coordinated jewelry and shoe styles, offered in petites as well as regular sizes (petites being women shorter than 5'4" in height). The expansion of the selection in petite sizes, especially online, was seen as a "great opportunity", since some department stores had reduced their petite offerings.[56]

TOP MANAGEMENT TEAM TURNOVER

57 As Krill was working to resolve branding issues between divisions, improve efficiencies and find ways to grow the company, she also had to deal with a variety of top management team resignations. In the spring of 2006 COO Laura Weil left abruptly after only a few months. Weil's many responsibilities at ANN included merchandise planning; information systems; all supply chain operations including sourcing, logistics and distribution; real estate; construction and facilities, and purchasing; as well as finance, accounting and investor relations.[57] Krill decided not to replace Weil and eliminated the position on the organizational chart. Krill assumed leadership of LOFT again, playing a dual role while searching for a new divisional president.

[53] Moin, D. 2005. "Ann Taylor stores taps two to fill out executive ranks", *Women's Wear Daily,* 3/3/2005, Vol. 189, Iss. 45.

[54] Merrick, A. 2006. "Boss Talk: Asking 'What Would Ann Do?'; In Turning Around Ann Taylor, CEO Kay Krill Got to Know Her Customers, 'Ann' and 'Loft'", *Wall Street Journal (Eastern Edition),* 9/15/2006, p. B1.

[55] "Q3 2005 Ann Taylor Stores earnings conference call—final", *Fair Disclosure Wire,* 12/2/2005.

[56] "Ann Taylor and Ann Taylor Loft—The Specialty Resource for Petites", 8/23/2006, from http://investor.anntaylor.com/news/20060823-208165.cfm?t=n

[57] Moin, D. 2006. "Laura Weil exits Ann Taylor", *Women's Wear Daily,* 5/5/2006, Vol. 191, Iss. 97, p. 2.

58 Krill commented, "I believe that building a winning team is critical to fully realizing our company's full potential".[58] However, it appeared that creating that "winning team" was taking longer than anticipated. One source wondered about the pressure on Krill, especially since she didn't have a "strong operating partner" to help with merchandising and other creative decisions.[59]

59 Even though Krill had made differentiation between AT and LOFT a top priority, analysts continued to challenge Krill's efforts, noting that it had been hard to get both divisions moving forward simultaneously. As one analyst said "it just seems like it's a struggle to get both of these divisions firing on all cylinders at the same time".[60] Krill responded to the comment that consistency had been a problem:

> The notion that Ann Taylor got soft because I was supporting the LOFT team is really a completely inaccurate comment. As CEO of the company I have to spend my time on many things, and if one of our businesses is softening in any way I will focus extra time on it.[61]

60 In August 2007, long-time CFO James Smith and Chief Marketing Officer Elaine Boltz both resigned, and then in July 2008 long-time Chief Supply Chain Officer Anthony Romano also left to "pursue other interests"[62]. Although she had hired a new CFO and Chief Marketing Officer in late 2007, these departures left Krill once again without a lot of depth at the top.[63] However, Krill had had experience with management turnover as she had had to deal with seven resignations, seven new hires, and two promotions in her upper management team over two years' time. As of the end of 2008 she had finally filled the AT and LOFT Divisional President positions. (See Exhibit 8: Summary of Personnel Changes at ANN.)

FUTURE PLANS AND INITIATIVES

61 As part of a multi-year restructuring program begun in 2008, ANN was focused on reducing excess costs, and planned to do so by closing underperforming stores, downsizing ANN's corporate and divisional staff by eliminating approximately 260 positions, reducing executive compensation bonus payout as a result of higher performance goals, and consolidating "all purchasing activities under a centralized strategic procurement organization to leverage scale".[64] The restructuring program included a suspension of the share repurchase plan and a scale back of capital spending, and was expected to result in ongoing annualized savings of approximately \$80 to \$90 million.[65] The pre-tax costs of this restructuring were forecasted to be \$65 to \$70 million over the period from 2008 to 2010, but Krill felt

[58] ANN 2005 Annual Report, at http://investor.anntaylor.com/annual.cfm

[59] Moin, D. 2006. "Rebound at Ann Taylor: CEO Kay Krill Fashions Retailer's New Career", *Woman's Wear Daily,* 6/26/2006, Vol. 191, Iss. 134, p. 1.

[60] Q4 2007 AnnTaylor Stores Earnings Conference Call, 03/14/2008, available at http://seekingalpha.com/article/68606-ann-taylor-stores-corporation-q4-2007-earnings-call-transcript?page=8

[61] Q1 2008 AnnTaylor Stores Earnings Conference Call, 5/22/2008, available at http://seekingalpha.com/article/78473-ann-taylor-stores-corp-q1-2008-earnings-call-transcript

[62] "Ann Taylor Announces Executive Management Changes", 7/15/2008, from http://investor.anntaylor.com/phoenix.zhtml?c=78167&p=irol-newsArticle&ID=1174968&highlight=

[63] Poggi, Jeanine. 2007. "Specialty Retailers see High Exec Turnover", *Women's Wear Daily,* 8/20/2007, Vol. 194, Iss. 37, pg. 2-2.

[64] "Ann Taylor launches strategic restructuring program to enhance profitability; Multi-year program expected to generate \$50 million in ongoing annualized pre-tax savings; Company takes a conservative approach to new store growth for fiscal 2008", *PR Newswire,* 1/30/2008.

[65] "Ann Taylor Expands Strategic Restructuring Program", 11/6/2008, from http://investor.anntaylor.com/phoenix.zhtml?c=78167&p=irol-newsArticle&ID=1223638&highlight=.

EXHIBIT 8 **Summary of Personnel Changes at ANN Mid-2006 to End-2008**

Note: These personnel changes represent seven resignations, seven new hires, and two promotions in Kay Krill's upper management team over two years' time.

11/3/2008 New hire Gary Muto, President, Ann Taylor LOFT, came from Gap, Inc., most recently as President of Gap Adult/Gap Body, had also been President of Forth & Towne

9/8/08 New hire Paula J. Zusi, EVP, Chief Supply Chain Officer, from Liz Claiborne

8/12/08 New hire Christine M. Beauchamp, President Ann Taylor Stores, came from Limited Brands, most recently was President & CEO of Victoria's Secret Beauty

8/12/08 Resignation Adrienne Lazarus, President Ann Taylor Stores, after 17 years

7/15/08 Resignation Anthony Romano, Chief Supply Officer, after 11 years at ANN

9/17/07 New hire Michael J. Nicholson, EVP, CFO, additional responsibility for Information Technology and Global Procurement, came from Limited Brands

8/24/07 New hire Robert Luzzi, Chief Marketing Officer, from New York & Company

8/20/07 Resignation Elaine Boltz, Chief Marketing Officer, after three years at ANN

8/13/07 New hire Mark Mendelson, President New "Boomer" Concept, from Jones Apparel, was at ANN in the early 1990s as General Merchandise Manager

8/10/07 Resignation CFO James Smith, after 14 years at ANN

7/10/07 Brian Lynch promoted from EVP to President AT Factory, will lead new LOFT Factory concept as well, with launch planned in summer 2008. Given additional responsibility for E-Commerce, and Corporate Real Estate and Construction, as President of Corporate Operations, added on 7/15/2008

6/6/07 New hire Diane Holtz, EVP Merchandising & Design, LOFT, from The Limited, was at ANN in late 1990s as General Merchandise Manager

1/22/07 Resignation Donna Noce, President LOFT, Krill to take over temporarily

6/6/2006 Adrienne Lazarus promoted to President Ann Taylor Stores from EVP Merchandise & Design Ann Taylor Stores

5/4/2006 Resignation Laura Weil, COO, after eight months (hired 9/1/2005)

5/3/2006 Resignation Muriel Gonzalez, Chief Marketing Officer, after a little over a year

the company was "well positioned to support our brands and focus on strengthening our underlying business" due to the "debt-free balance sheet and approximately $295 million in available liquidity".[66]

62 The company planned to open fewer stores in 2008 than in previous years. The shift of emphasis was planned to "aggressively invest in factory channel expansion" for both the existing Ann Taylor Factory Stores and a new Ann Taylor LOFT factory outlet concept.[67] These stores offered merchandise 25 to 30 percent less than at the AT or LOFT regular stores. The outlet or factory business had delivered "strong gross margin" previously, and was considered "an important growth driver" even though "the general economic softness" was "having some impact on this price sensitive consumer".[68]

63 Krill had also announced that the *Collections* line, an augmentation of the *Celebrations* bridal and special occasion wear line introduced in late 2006, would have its own department within the Ann Taylor (AT) stores. With offerings 40 percent more expensive than regular AT merchandise, it would be an effort to "grab more affluent working women who

[66] Ibid.

[67] Ann Taylor launches strategic restructuring program. Op cit.

[68] Q1 2008 AnnTaylor Stores Earnings Conference Call, 5/22/2008, available at http://seekingalpha.com/article/78473-ann-taylor-stores-corp-q1-2008-earnings-call-transcript

weren't feeling pinched in the pocketbook," and would be built around the suits and dresses that created Ann Taylor's reputation. The plan was to introduce this upscale, expensive product in some of the top-selling Ann Taylor locations around the country, where AT was already "sitting next to Neiman's, Prada, Gucci," since, "we know there's a client there who has an appetite for more upscale, expensive product."[69]

64 Krill also announced that ANN would be developing an exclusive beauty business. The company introduced Ann Taylor label fragrance and bath and body products as a separate department within AT stores for the 2007 holiday season, and scheduled the launch of beauty products in the LOFT division during 2008. Krill believed that specialty stores with only a 10 percent share of the beauty products market were in a position to add to that share. Responding to comments about ANN's previous foray into the cosmetic business, Krill said, "in the past, we've dipped our baby toes in, and have not done it justice. Now we are trying to find meaningful ways to grow the business".[70]

65 Krill planned to eventually expand the beauty collection into every ANN brand. Analysts predicted this introduction could generate up to $15 million in sales in its first year, since it represented a high-margin category that traditionally drew greater repeat traffic than apparel. It could also be an important gift business, especially around the holidays. First quarter results in 2008 showed that although the fragrance line had done well, the body care component had not. The line of maternity clothes in selected LOFT stores was also still undergoing a test of this product's viability.[71]

66 Regarding ANN's new initiatives, one brand consultant commented,

> Tweaking a few elements of a product line doesn't work. Branding is far more than just product. It is about the entire entity and the perception that entity (in all of its components) has created in the consumer's mind . . . The most successful brands in any category never fail to cater to and reward their core customers all the time. [And, responding specifically to the announcement of the upscale *Collections* line,] . . . trying to be too many things to a diverse audience under one roof is a losing business strategy for an established brand.[72]

67 Krill responded,

> The Company remains firmly committed to long-term growth, and we believe we have significant untapped potential ahead of us. . . . For fiscal 2008, we are relentlessly focused on strengthening our business, improving our gross margins with tight inventory management, executing our restructuring program with excellence, and pursuing growth in a measured and prudent manner. Beyond 2008, we are confident that we have positioned the Company for long-term growth and success.[73]

68 Krill appeared to be confident in her strategies for the future. However, the retail environment was increasingly unpredictable. Had Krill's new strategies been well considered, given the ongoing challenges of AT and LOFT, and the difficult specialty retail environment in 2008? What else could Krill have done to create growth? Should ANN have focused on improving its current businesses, or on developing new initiatives?

[69] Merrick, Amy. 2007. "Ann Taylor's Loftier Goal: A more upscale shopper", *Wall Street Journal,* 9/14/2007, http://online.wsj.com/public/article/SB118972474680527004.html

[70] Moin, David. 2007. "New in beauty: Ann Taylor taps Robin Burns to develop collection", *Women's Wear Daily,* 03/16/2007, Vol. 193, Iss. 57, pg. 1.

[71] Q1 2008 AnnTaylor Stores Earnings Conference Call, 5/22/2008, available at http://seekingalpha.com/article/78473-ann-taylor-stores-corp-q1-2008-earnings-call-transcript

[72] Eli, 2007. "Another mid-priced retail brand, Ann Taylor, trying to go upscale," 9/14/2007, from http://theportnoygroup.typepad.com/my_weblog/2007/09/another-mid-pri.html

[73] Letter to Shareholders, ANN 2007 Annual Report, at http://investor.anntaylor.com/phoenix.zhtml?c=78167&p=irol-reportsAnnual

Case 3

The Apollo Group, Inc. [University of Phoenix]

Richard B. Robinson

1 A 55-year-old college professor at San Jose State University with a PhD from Cambridge University and previous teaching jobs at Maryland, Ohio State, and Northern Illinois, John Sperling was a surprise entrepreneur when he started the Apollo Group, parent company of the University of Phoenix, in 1976. Ambitious, his goal was to revolutionize conventional higher education. Most people would say that Sperling, recently celebrating his 91st birthday, has done just that.

2 Rather than catering to 18- to 22-year-olds looking to find themselves, Sperling focused on the then-neglected market of working adults. And he recruited working professionals as teachers, rather than tenured professors. UOP (on-campus and online) has more than 33,000 faculty members with less than 5 percent being full-time. Most radical of all, while nearly all other universities are nonprofits, Sperling ran his university to make money. Those ideas sparked overwhelming resistance from the education establishment, which branded UOP a "diploma mill." The result? "We faced failure every day for the first 10 years," said founder Sperling, who turned 91 in 2012.

3 From an IPO adjusted price of $0.76 to a mid-2005 high of $98, Apollo's stock reflected a company *BusinessWeek* considered among the top 50 performing companies on Wall Street. The Phoenix-based company, whose day-to-day operations were still generating average annual revenue growth exceeding 30 percent over that time, saw its revenues reach $5 billion in 2010 with net income exceeding $550 million. It has also joined the S&P 500.

4 Tuition at Apollo averages only $18,000 a year, 60 percent of what a typical private college charges. A key factor, says Sperling, is that universities for the young require student unions, sports teams, student societies, and so on. The average age of a UOP student is 35, so UOP doesn't have those expenses. It also saves by holding classes in leased office spaces around the country, and online, By 2010, over 75 percent of UOP students studied at University of Phoenix Online.

5 By 2010, the UOP had become the dominant player in the online education market that still has lots of potential for growth. The bricks-and-mortar University of Phoenix was one of the first institutions to identify and serve the burgeoning market for educating working adults. In the late 1980s, long before the Web debuted, the school began to experiment with offering its classes online. It got off to a slow start, "and we lost money for a number of years," recalled Brian Mueller, Apollo's former president.

6 As a result of this head start, however, UOP's online option was ready to capitalize on an online-education market that began exploding in the mid-1990s. Today, it is estimated that over 10 percent of the U.S. students earning a degree via the Net are enrolled through the UOP's online option. UOP's online option also garners an outsize share of the industry's revenues—about one-third of the total. That's because as the market leader, it can charge higher tuition than most rivals. Undergraduates pay a little more than $18,000 a year at UOP, while students seeking a master's degree pay nearly $25,000. "They're by far the giant in this industry," says Eduventure market analyst Sean Gallagher.

Source: ©2012. This case was developed based on publicly available information from the Apollo Group, Inc., the University of Phoenix, interviews with UOP students and professors, and selected reports as cited.

7 Online education is rapidly growing, but it is still just getting started. "There are 70 million working adults in this country who don't have a college degree," says Gallagher. Increasingly, they realize that they need a degree to get ahead. But because they often have a family as well as a job, studying online is the most convenient solution. Howard Block, an analyst at Banc of America Securities, predicts "dramatic enrollment growth" for UOP's online option. He expects that half of the students in postsecondary education will one day make at least some use of the Internet to earn their degrees.

GLOBAL OUTREACH

8 UOP began to seriously tap the international market with its online option in 2005, initially "bringing in about 500 students a month," said Mueller. "But that's just the tip of the iceberg." Though the UOP started offering online classes only in English, it has begun to offer courses in Spanish and plans to introduce Mandarin soon as well. Ironically, UOP has done all this with plain-vanilla technology. While other companies charged into online education with dazzling digital content, UOP has historically offered primarily a text-heavy format that can easily be accessed with dial-up modems.

9 This might sound like a recipe for failure. But UOP realized that interaction with humans—the professor and other students in the class—was far more important to success than interaction with the digital content. Thus, UOP keeps its classes small, averaging just 12 students. And to combat the Achilles heel of distance education—a high dropout rate—it offers its students plenty of hand-holding, including round-the-clock tech support. The result: 65 percent of its students go on to graduate.

10 Some see plain technology as a potential negative for the virtual college. "At some point, UOP online will need to upgrade the sophistication of its platform," warned Trace Urdan, an analyst with ThinkEquity Partners, a boutique investment bank. That will require more spending on research and development and information technology, he warns, which could crimp margins. Still, any extra spending could be easily offset if UOP bumped up its class size to 15 students, argueed Block. Even with today's small classes, operating profit margins now top 20 percent. As if listening to them, the UOP now has an excellent, visual explanation of how this type of multifaceted online educational approach works.[1]

THE ONLINE TREND

11 The dot-com bubble may have burst in the world of commerce, but the promise of harnessing the Internet for paradigm-changing growth—and even profits—still thrives in the halls of academia.

12 A decade after the dot-com fizzle began, e-learning has emerged from the wreckage as one of the Internet's most useful applications. Nearly 90 percent of the 4,000 major colleges and universities in the United States now offer classes over the Internet or use the Web to enhance campus classes, according to market researcher International Data Corp. About 7 million students took online classes from U.S. higher-ed institutions in 2010 according to John G. Flores, head of the U.S. Distance Learning Assn., a nonprofit trade group outside Boston. And it's not just a U.S. phenomenon: students from developing countries are jumping online, too.

13 These classes continue to open new horizons for the fastest-growing segment of higher education: working adults, who often find it difficult to juggle conventional classes with jobs and families. Adults over 25 now represent nearly half of higher-ed students; most are employed and want more education to advance their careers.

[1] www.phoenix.edu/students/how-it-works.html.

14 E-learning is an influence in the traditional college class as well. Online classes won't replace the college experience for most 18- to 24-year-olds. But from the Massachusetts Institute of Technology to Wake Forest University in North Carolina, colleges are using the Web in on-campus classes to augment textbooks and boost communication. And students, far more technology savvy than many of their professors or administrators, are using Web-based tools, social media, and many other approaches to morph Web-based capabilities into their academic experience with or without their university following along, or even approving.

MASS MARKET?

15 Quality is a problem, which is a key reason why many online students drop out. That will force a further shakeout, eliminating mediocre players. Many colleges grapple with such issues as how much time their faculty should devote to e-teaching. And long-established rules make it difficult for online students to get financial aid. Even as these problems are resolved, "online learning will never be as good as face-to-face instruction," argues Andy DiPaolo, director of the Stanford Center for Professional Development, which offers online graduate classes to engineers.

16 Ultimately, the greatest e-learning market may lie in the developing world, where the population of college-age students is exploding. Just as cell phones leapfrogged land-based telephones in many developing countries, so may e-learning help to educate the masses in countries that lack the colleges to meet demand—and can't afford to build them.

COST-EFFECTIVE

17 E-learning is a good fit with the military, where frequent transfers complicate pursuing a degree. The U.S. Army awarded PWC Consulting a $453 million, five-year contract to create an electronic university that allows soldiers to be anywhere and study at Kansas State University or any of the 24 colleges involved in the program.

18 eArmyU already has changed the perspective of soldiers like Sergeant Jeremy Dellinger, 22, who had been planning to leave the Army to go back to school when his basic enlistment ends. Then he enrolled in eArmyU to earn his bachelor's degree from Troy State University in Alabama. "Now I can get my degree and still do the work I love" as a supply sergeant, says the Fort Benning (Ga.)-based soldier. Like Dellinger, about 15 percent of those who have signed up so far have reenlisted or extended their commitment. By cutting turnover, "eArmyU could almost pay for itself," says program director Lee Harvey, since it costs nearly $70,000 to train green recruits.

19 Corporations, too, see e-learning as a cost-effective way to get better-educated employees. Indeed, corporate spending on e-learning is expected to more than quadruple by 2015, to $35 billion, estimates IDC. At IBM, some 500,000 employees received education or training online last year, and 75 percent of the company's Basic Blue class for new managers is online. The move cut IBM's training bill by $750 million last year, because online classes don't require travel.

CAUTIOUS ELITES

20 Phoenix Online aside, the big e-learning winners so far are the traditional nonprofit universities. They initially captured nearly 95 percent of online enrollments, figures A. Frank Mayadas, head of e-learning grants at the Alfred P. Sloan Foundation. Most active are state

and community colleges that started with strong brand names, a faculty, and accreditation, says Mayadas, as well as a tradition of extension programs.

21 By contrast, many elite universities have been far more cautious about diluting the value of their name. Harvard Business School believes it would be impossible to replicate its classroom education online. "We will never offer a Harvard MBA online," vows professor W. Earl Sasser, chairman of HBS Interactive, which instead develops e-learning programs for companies. MIT faculty nixed teaching classes online, fearing "it would detract from the residential experience," says former faculty chair Steven Lerman.

22 That didn't stop MIT from embracing the Internet in a different way. Over the next five years, MIT plans to post lecture notes and reading assignments for most of its 2,000 classes on the Web for free, calling the effort "OpenClassWare." Lerman says "it's a service to the world," but he says it's no substitute for actual teaching, so faculty aren't worried about a threat to classroom learning.

23 A few other top schools see profit-making opportunities. Since 1996, Duke University's Fuqua School of Business has been offering MBAs for working executives. In these blended programs, some 65 percent of the work is done online and just 35 percent in classes held during required residencies that consume 9 to 11 weeks over two years. Duke charges well over $95,000 for these programs—vs. $75,000 for its traditional residential MBA. Yet they have been so popular that by next year, "we'll have more students in nontraditional programs than the daytime program," according to Fuqua's dean. The extra revenues are helping Fuqua to double its faculty.

The Adult Education Market

24 The adult education market is a significant and growing component of the postsecondary education market, which is estimated by the U.S. Department of Education to be a more than $450 billion industry. According to the U.S. Department of Education, over 7 million, or 45 percent of all students enrolled in higher education programs are over the age of 24. This number is projected to reach 6.7 million in 2011. The market for adult education in the United States is expected to increase as working adults seek additional education and training to update and improve their skills, to enhance their earnings potential, and to keep pace with the rapidly expanding knowledge-based economy.

25 Many working adults are seeking accredited degree programs that provide flexibility to accommodate the fixed schedules and time commitments associated with their professional and personal obligations. President Obama, with the United States trying to gain traction coming out of the "Great Recession," said in his 2011 State of the Union address that having no degree is really no longer an option:

> Many people watching tonight can probably remember a time when finding a good job meant showing up at a nearby factory or a business downtown. You didn't always need a degree, and your competition was pretty much limited to your neighbors. If you worked hard, chances are you'd have a job for life, with a decent paycheck, good benefits, and the occasional promotion. Maybe you'd even have the pride of seeing your kids work at the same company. That world has changed. And for many, the change has been painful. I've seen it in the shuttered windows of once booming factories, and the vacant storefronts of once busy Main Streets. I've heard it in the frustrations of Americans who've seen their paychecks dwindle or their jobs disappear—proud men and women who feel like the rules have been changed in the middle of the game.

26 His point: the rules of the game have changed. And, it would seem, the for-profit (industry participants prefer "proprietary") collegiate education sector has grown to reflect the new reality that access to a higher education is no longer the province of the privileged few, but a prerequisite to "owning our future" as individuals, or as he sees it, a country.

27 The need for more options in higher education to ensure more people gain the education necessary in a knowledge-based economy is greater today than ever before. Demographics, and a changing global economy, say it is a need that will only grow.

28 Dr. Bruce Chaloux, president of the Sloan Consortium, estimates that there are more than 50 *million* working-age adults with some college credit but no degree, or who have a high school diploma but never entered college. Chaloux says that many of these adults would like to get their college degrees, but only if they're given practical "adult-friendly" alternatives to traditional, campus-based programs. He identified eight key factors that influence an adult learner's decision to attend college:[2]

- Convenient time and place for classes
- Flexible pacing for completing the program
- Ability to transfer credits
- Reputation of institution as being adult friendly
- Need the degree for current or future job
- Receive credit for life/work experiences
- Financial aid or employer assistance
- Child care

29 The Southern Regional Education Board in turn offers four guiding principles it finds essential to meeting the needs of adult college students:[3]

- Online or blended delivery
- Accelerated (or compressed) terms
- Adult-friendly policies
- Supportive credit transfer and prior learning assessment

30 Traditional colleges and universities have been slow to address the unique requirements of working adult students. First John Sperling, and now a global chorus of observers, has cited the following attributes of traditional, not-proprietary education institutions:

- Traditional universities and colleges were designed to fulfill the educational needs of conventional, full-time students aged 18 to 24, who remain the primary focus of these universities and colleges.
- This focus has resulted in a capital-intensive teaching/learning model in typical state and private colleges and universities that may be characterized by:
    - a high percentage of full-time tenured faculty with doctoral degrees;
    - fully configured library facilities and related full-time staff;
    - dormitories, student unions, and other significant plant assets to support the needs of younger students;
    - often major investment in and commitment to comprehensive sports programs;
    - major administrative overhead for all the various university functions;
    - politically-based funding;

[2] http://sloanconsortium.org.

[3] http://sreb.org.

- major resistance to change in any academic programs, even in the face of rapid global change across disciplines and professions;
- an emphasis on research and the related staff and facilities; and
- faculty with PhDs and a research focus but limited practical experience, even in key programs like business and other working-related professions.

- The majority of accredited colleges and universities continue to provide the bulk of their educational programming from September to mid-December and from mid-January to May. As a result, most full-time faculty members only teach during that limited period of time.
- While this structure serves the needs of the full-time 18- to 24-year-old student, it limits the educational opportunity for working adults who must delay their education for up to five months during these spring, summer, and winter breaks.
- Traditional universities and colleges are also limited in their ability to market to or provide the necessary customer service for working adult students because it requires the development of additional administrative and enrollment infrastructure.

31 Traditional colleges and universities, born out of a centuries old academic model and tradition, have seen adult and continuing education as awkward institutional fits for their mission—ancillary, less rigorous, yet subtly necessary activities to serve their state or local population needs but not rooted in the institution's core academic tradition.

32 The UOP's format since its inception has focused on working adult students by providing an accredited collegiate education that enables them to attend classes and complete classwork in a schedule and manner more convenient to the constraints their work life imposes on their ability to obtain a college or advanced degree. It may well be that proprietary schools such as the UOP have proved more adaptable, if not more creative, in responding to this 21st century, knowledge-economy adult student reality.

THE PROPRIETARY (FOR-PROFIT) COLLEGE AND UNIVERSITY SECTOR

33 Undergraduate enrollments in the United States increased by more than a third to 17.6 million in the first decade of the 21st century, with the most dramatic growth occurring at proprietary colleges. It was the fastest decade of growth since the 1970s. Proprietary colleges enrolled 10 percent of all undergraduates in 2010, up from 3 percent in 2000. Proprietary enrollments increased fivefold to 1.2 million at four-year colleges, and nearly doubled to 385,000 at two-year institutions, according to Jack Buckley, Commissioner, National Center for Education Statistics. The *Chronicle of Higher Education* says it is even higher—10 percent of all students enrolled full-time in degree-granting institutions, and rising by an average rate of 9 percent annually over the last 30 years. "We are seeing a shift" that has "created additional opportunities . . . (and) brought to light differences in how students pursue and pay for that education," Buckley said, adding that higher education "may look quite different" in 2020, when enrollments are projected to reach 20 million.[4]

34 Thirty-five years ago, approximately 90,000 students attended proprietary colleges and universities. The sector was populated primarily by small, privately owned businesses; "mom and pop" enterprises that looked little like their traditional, four-year counterparts. The colleges—most started primarily in east coast cities like New York, Philadelphia, and Boston—taught skills for front-line jobs in high-demand fields, including business, health care, cosmetology, food, and secretarial services. They enrolled people that traditional higher

[4] Susan Aud, William Hussar, and Grace Kena, *The Condition of Education 2011*, http://nces.ed.gov, May, 2011.

education tended to ignore: working-class adults with children of their own who needed more skills to get better-paying jobs but couldn't take time out to attend a traditional campus.[5]

35 Proprietary institutions maintain much of the same mission today, amid a market that has seen sweeping changes, now populated by over 3,000 proprietary institutions. Forty percent are owned by one of 13 large, publicly traded companies. Half of those institutions offer associate, bachelor, or professional degrees today, versus less than 10 percent having done so in 1990. Over 90 percent of students at proprietary institutions are now enrolled in degree programs. Interestingly, only about 30 percent attend part-time. As the sector expands, it is attracting students who might otherwise have attended community colleges or even four-year institutions. "They are clearly a threat for both public and private schools," says Jim Scannell, president of the higher-education consulting group Scannell & Kurz, "especially for adult students returning to get a B.A. or going part time to get a master's."[6]

36 The NCES study entitled *The Condition of Education 2011,* offered these summary observations:[7]

- Enrollments and the number of degrees conferred by proprietary institutions increased faster than in the nonprofit sector, which includes public and private universities. Proprietary institutions awarded 5 percent of all bachelor's degrees in 2008–2009, and 10 percent of all master's degrees.
- For-profit colleges were more likely to enroll full-time students 25 and older, and to enroll students in distance education such as online courses. Nearly one in five students (19 percent) attending proprietary four-year colleges were enrolled entirely in distance education.
- The average price of attendance, including tuition, books, and living costs, for students enrolled full-time for a full year was highest at proprietary colleges after average grants were factored in. Students at proprietary colleges paid $30,900 on average in 2007–2008, compared with $26,600 at private, nonprofit colleges and $15,600 at public institutions.
- Proprietary institutions spent an average $2,659 on instruction per student in 2008–2009, compared with $9,418 at public colleges and $15,289 at private nonprofits. They spent more per student ($9,101) than public institutions ($6,647) but less than privates ($14,118) on student services and other types of support, including administrative and marketing salaries.
- Among four-year colleges, retention and graduation rates were lower at proprietary schools, which enroll about 1.2 million students compared with their nonprofit counterparts, which enroll about 8.9 million students.
- Among two-year colleges, retention and graduation rates were higher at proprietary colleges, which enrolled 385,000 students, than at public community colleges, where enrollments reached 7.1 million.
- Students at proprietary colleges were more likely to take out larger loans and to default on them. The average annual loan amount for all students was $7,000; the average was $9,800 at four-year proprietary institutions and $7,800 at two-year proprietary institutions.

37 Many small schools, particularly private liberal-arts colleges, are seeing drops in enrollment. After initially trying tuition increases as a solution, which has only driven students away in many cases, some of these schools are attempting to make up tuition revenue by

[5] Robin Wilson, "For-Profit Colleges Change Higher Education's Landscape," *Chronicle of Higher Education,* Feb. 7, 2010.

[6] Ibid.

[7] Aud et al., 2011.

increasing their adult student enrollment. In so doing, they are competing directly with proprietary colleges; and a recent trend has been for some of those colleges to be acquired by larger proprietary education companies as a way to enter certain geographic areas, or rebrand the small college, or leverage its brand across multiple locations. And public colleges feel the heat too. Students who have been rejected by budget-strapped public colleges, and others who find the public university bureaucracy often too much of a hassle to deal with, are being aggressively recruited by the proprietary sector. It's not clear whether this shift of students from public institutions to proprietary universities will be permanent, industry analysts say, but it continues to increase the size and legitimacy of the proprietary sector.[8]

38 Amazingly, even while facing constant budget cuts, layoffs, dwindling state support, and turning students away, most professors and administrators at traditional public colleges and universities remain dismissive of proprietary colleges. Some see proprietary institutions as a second-class education; others as too costly, or consuming too much of federal student aid; and some even arrogantly see them as trivial wannabe sideshows amid the real business of research-based education. Increasingly though, thoughtful observers of traditional universities see folly in their leaders' loyalty to a 200+ year-old model of higher education that has changed little, creating blinders for leaders of the typical public college or university. They point to the typical pattern where a two-year community college often evolves to seek accreditation as a four-year degree granting institution; and eventually, with proper political support, seeks to become an advanced degree-granting university institution with a larger "research" mission for the new faculty it starts to hire, and with appropriately credentialed expensive, additional in-state presidents, provosts, and chancellors, among other administrative layers.

39 Critics often point out to the observation that at these traditional college and university campuses, the focus is foremost on the faculty members. Tenure, seniority, obsessive reliance on faculty committee-based decision-making, lengthy deliberation to alter a curriculum, or even whether or not a class typically offered on "Tu-Th" at 10 am could be offered on other days, or a Saturday, become serious, administratively intense issues. The application process, and time to a decision, can take months. It often is a tedious affair to talk with someone in the admissions process. Availability of classes, timing of required subjects, and accessibility of professors and/or advisors is often a concern cited by students at many traditional colleges and universities.

40 Leading proprietary institutions tend to point out with pride that they take a different approach on some of these issues, which their advocates argue is born out of a core focus on "the student" as their customer, and what that student needs/seeks to accomplish in attending that school. Faculty members are not tenured, but rather are hired based on expertise, experience, and qualifications. They are retained based on student demand. Course timing is oriented toward accommodating the special scheduling needs of the student. Some proprietary institutions use block times and concentrate courses in those blocks. So, for example, where a traditional college student might have a class at 9 am, another at noon, and a third at 4 pm or 10 am the next day, the proprietary would set course offerings in four-hour blocks so students could get all classwork done in efficient timing sequences compatible with their work life. Others, following an approach pioneered by the University of Phoenix, let students concentrate on one or two courses maximum at a time. They last 5–6 weeks, include online or on-campus options, and allow students to concentrate their topical focus as well as the efficient use of their time. And it is not unusual to have early Saturday classes at several of these schools, because it is

[8] Wilson, 2010.

a convenient time for their student populations. Plus, classes start anew every month at most proprietary institutions, making availability and planning or sequencing courses very different from a traditional college or university.

41 In admissions, the timetable at a proprietary is entirely different from its traditional counterpart. Expression of interest is quickly followed up, with that person to work with you to complete an application, figure out what program makes sense for you, and take you through the application process. Part of this activity has received considerable regulatory scrutiny in recent years as a pressure sales process. That sales process and the pressure to sign up new students versus the patient accuracy of the information provided by the "counselor" to the prospective student, to include financial aid information, has come under intense federal regulatory scrutiny in recent years. Nonetheless, the speed of attention to the inquiry from prospective students, and the effort to explain what is offered and the nature of the education process at a proprietary is typically in marked contrast to that process in a traditional college or university.

CHALLENGES FACING THE PROPRIETARY EDUCATION PROVIDERS

42 Speaking in a 2011 conference call with reporters, U.S. Secretary of Education Arne Duncan said of the proprietary education industry, "The quality here has been very uneven. There have been some absolute superstars. And there have been some players whose intentions, quite frankly, we doubt." So other notable employers, such as Intel, have recently adopted policies in recruitment that eliminate employment consideration for graduates of most of the better known proprietary schools. Harkening back to the 50 percent rule in the early 1990s,[9] recent regulatory changes have sought to address widespread growing concerns with this "quality" issue as well as others' concern with the proprietary industry's disproportionate reliance on federal student loans as a source of revenue used by its students to pay for their education at proprietary schools. Two regulations created by federal law have been put into place seeking, according to their supporters, to address these concerns—the gainful employment rule and the 90/10 rule.

43 **The Gainful Employment Rule.** Set to take effect in July 2012, this rule will deny federal aid to programs that fail three "tests" of gainful employment three times in a four-year span:

- *Are at least 35 percent of former students actively paying down their loans?* The test: Do a third of ex-students make payments that lower their student loan balance by at least a dollar in a given year?
- *Are graduates spending 30 percent or less of their discretionary income on loan payments?* The test: Student loan payments are not costing too much of the money left after graduates pay for basic needs. (In other words, the proprietary's education leads to a job paying sufficiently well so as to justify the costs to the students for which they took out student loans arranged by the school.)
- *Are graduates spending 12 percent or less of their total income on loan payments?* This test, related to the previous test, is another way based on total income which establishes that loan bills should not consume more than an amount regulators believe is the appropriate level of student loan costs after graduation—about an eighth of total earnings.

[9] The 50 percent rule (federal law) mandated that students at universities providing more than 50 percent of their courses online couldn't qualify for Title IV Higher Education Act financial assistance as a means to address what they considered false advertising by "diploma mills" from online and correspondence schools. It was repealed in 2006.

44 Programs that pass any of the three tests would retain eligibility to participate in federal aid initiatives, enabling qualified students to secure federal grants or loans. The rule effectively would shut down proprietary programs that repeatedly fail to show, through measures associated with these three rules, that graduates are earning enough to pay down the loans taken out to attend those programs. Advocates say it addresses the chief complaint against proprietary schools that students emerge from them with too much debt and too little earning power. Proprietary defenders have aggressively opposed the measure, with lobbyists alleging the Education Department was unjustly swayed by short-sellers with a financial interest in seeing the publicly traded school operators suffer. They also say the rule will limit access to higher education, particularly for minorities. And, they argue it regulates them based on behavior and actions over which they have no control. A handful of lawsuits were quickly filed by numerous parties on issues related to the rule.

45 **The 90/10 Rule.** This is a Higher Education Act rule that makes a proprietary institution of higher education ineligible to participate in Title IV (student loan) programs if for any two consecutive fiscal years it derives more than 90 percent of its cash basis revenue from Title IV programs. An institution that derives more than 90 percent of its revenue from Title IV programs for any single fiscal year will be automatically placed on provisional certification for two fiscal years and will be subject to possible additional sanctions determined to be appropriate under the circumstances by the U.S. Department of Education in the exercise of its broad discretion. An institution that derives more than 90 percent of its revenue from Title IV programs for two consecutive fiscal years will be ineligible to participate in Title IV programs for at least two fiscal years.

46 Proponents of the 90/10 rule see it as a way to ensure quality and discourage fraud at proprietary colleges by requiring students to invest some of their own money in tuition, just as homebuyers make down payments on their mortgages. Opponents argue that it penalizes low-income recipients that do not have the savings or family income to pay educational costs without receiving a full loan. Traditional universities increasingly argue that proprietary institutions are taking a disproportionate share of the student loan funds.

47 Proprietary colleges as a whole were approaching the 90 percent cap in 2012 as the Education Department has increased the availability of student loans and Pell Grants, according to Harris Miller, president of the Association of Private Sector Colleges & Universities, a Washington-based trade group. He argued that Congress needs to act so the schools can continue to operate and students can stay in class. Industry leader University of Phoenix sent out an e-mail saying it "believes 90/10 is not a good measure of quality, which is better assessed through graduation rates, default rates, compliance audits, financial ratios, etc." The UOP reported that federal student grants and loans made up almost 88 percent of the college's revenue in its 2011 fiscal year.

48 **Student Loan Defaults—Student Loan Cohort Default Rate Rule.** To remain eligible to participate in Title IV programs, educational institutions must maintain student loan cohort default rates below specified levels. Each cohort is the group of students who first enter into student loan repayment during a federal fiscal year (ending September 30). Under the Higher Education Act, as reauthorized, the currently applicable cohort default rate for each cohort is the percentage of the students in the cohort who default on their student loans prior to the end of the following two federal fiscal years, which represents a three-year measuring period.

49 Beginning with the 2011 three-year cohort default rate published in September 2014, the three-year rates will be applied for purposes of measuring compliance with the requirements as follows:

- *Annual test.* If the 2011 three-year cohort default rate exceeds 40 percent, the institution will cease to be eligible to participate in Title IV programs; and

- *Three consecutive years test.* If the institution's three-year cohort default rate exceeds 30 percent for three consecutive years, beginning with the 2009 cohort, the institution will cease to be eligible to participate in Title IV programs.

50 **A Pending Student Loan Crisis?** A growing concern that "echoes" as background with these rules is the dramatically increasing level of student debt in the United States. Entering 2011, total student loan debt, at $830 billion, exceeded total U.S. credit card debt, itself bloated to what some call a bubble level of $827 billion. Student loan debt was estimated to be growing at the rate of $90 billion a year. The younger generation appears to have begun to mortgage its future earnings in the form of student loan debt. And student loans are not dischargeable in bankruptcy—meaning future wages, tax refunds, and so forth can be garnished to recoup these obligations. Only 40 percent of that student debt is actively being repaid. The rest is in default, or in deferment (when a student requests temporary postponement of payment because of economic hardship), which means payments and interest are halted, or in forbearance. Interest on government loans is suspended during deferment, but continues to accrue on private loans. As tuitions increase, loan amounts increase; private loan interest rates reached highs of 20 percent in 2011. Among the top private lenders: Citigroup, Wells Fargo, and JPMorgan Chase.[10] Recent statistics indicate that student debt was held by 62 percent of students from public universities, 72 percent from private nonprofit schools, and a whopping 96 percent from private proprietary schools.

51 **It Is, After All, "Proprietary."** Whatever one's opinion of the proprietary university model, "it's been a tremendous growth story," says Jeffrey M. Silber, a stock analyst and managing director of BMO Capital Markets, which figures the proprietary sector brought in $30 billion in 2011. Most of that was earned by 13 large publicly traded companies that now dominate the market.

52 The biggest player among those is the Apollo Group. Its flagship University of Phoenix has morphed from an institution with 25,100 students in 1995 to one with over 550,000 today. That means that 25 years ago Phoenix was about the same size as George Washington University. Now it is larger than the entire undergraduate enrollment of the Big Ten.[11] Phoenix's enrollment dwarfs that of each of the other 12 publicly traded companies, including Education Management Corporation, with over 160,000 students; American Public Education, Inc. with over 130,000 students; Career Education Corporation, with about 118,000 students; and DeVry Inc., with 116,000 students. While Kaplan Higher Education is one of the country's largest proprietary companies, with approximately 110,000 students, it is owned by the Washington Post Company and so is not one of the 13 large publicly traded proprietary universities. The proprietary sector is not only more robust than the rest of higher education, it is helping to force some changes in the way traditional colleges do business. Yet while some traditional colleges are reaching out to adult students, starting online programs, and saving money by rejecting tenure in favor of hiring professors by the class, traditional higher education characteristically remains far from being nimble and quick to change. It has been operating in roughly the same way for hundreds of years, so by its very nature it may continue to be ill-suited to respond to competition from the proprietary sector. The Apollo Group's leadership put it this way in 2011 amidst the growing scrutiny of the proprietary sector's offerings, value, and reliance on student loans:[12]

> These factors—a greater number of individuals now wanting to pursue a college degree and students having a higher number of risk factors—are placing burdens on a higher education

[10] Alan Nasseu and Kelly Norman, "The Student Loan Debt Bubble," www.globalresearch.ca, June 5, 2011.

[11] The "Big Ten" conference name remains, even though there are actually 11 universities in the Big Ten—Illinois, Indiana, Iowa, Michigan, Michigan State, Minnesota, Northwestern, Ohio State, Penn State, Purdue, and Wisconsin.

[12] The Apollo Group, Inc., 2010 Annual Report, p. 4.

> system that was not built to accommodate the needs of nontraditional students. The higher education system must significantly expand capacity to reach greater numbers of students and provide a higher level of academic and student support services in order to successfully educate nontraditional students.
>
> These burdens come at a time when public funding for higher education is under pressure and budgets and capacity are being cut at traditional schools. Delivering quality education at traditional institutions generally relies upon a high fixed-cost, ground-based system of learning, and whether by design, or due to resource constraints, the traditional higher education system is rigid and inflexible. As such, the economics underlying the traditional university system's asset-intensive, high cost structure have been essentially unchanged over time.

THE APOLLO GROUP, INC.

53 Apollo Group, Inc. is one of the world's largest private education providers and has been in the education business for almost 40 years. Echoing a president's speech and the role it views itself as playing as an innovator for nontraditional students (73 percent of all U.S. college student candidates, it believes) in today's global economy, the Apollo Group's Annual Report released in 2011 had this interesting statement toward the front of the document:

> Traditional colleges and universities are the backbone of the U.S. higher education system, but they alone cannot meet the country's needs. This system, which is exclusive by design, was built to meet the needs of a different era when only a small portion of the nation's workforce needed a college degree. Today's globally competitive, knowledge-based economy requires a more broadly educated society. We believe innovation and new alternatives are required to adapt to our rapidly changing world. Accredited, degree-granting proprietary [meaning "proprietary"] institutions play a critical role in the future of education. . . . Apollo Group is committed to leading the way in meeting the evolving needs of millions of nontraditional learners and producing graduates necessary to achieve the world's collective educational goals.

54 The Apollo Groups schools, led by the University of Phoenix (UOP), served a student enrollment exceeding 550,000 in 2011. Apollo Group provides educational programs and services both online and on-campus at the undergraduate, master, and doctoral levels through wholly-owned subsidiaries:

- **The University of Phoenix, Inc. (UOP)**—the largest private university in the United States, and source of over 91 percent of the Apollo Group's revenue.
- **Institute for Professional Development**—provides adult education program development, administration, and management consulting services to private U.S. colleges and universities.
- **The College for Financial Planning Institutes**—one of the nation's leading providers of financial services education and certification for individuals and corporations in the financial services industry.
- **Meritus University**—offers degree programs online to working learners throughout Canada.

55 In addition, Apollo Group formed a joint venture with The Carlyle Group in late 2007 called Apollo Global, Inc., to pursue investments in the international education services industry. Apollo Group owns 86 percent of Apollo Global; Carlyle owns the remaining 14 percent. Consolidated into the Apollo Group's financial statements, Apollo Global currently operates the following educational institutions:

- **BPP Holdings** in the United Kingdom.
- **Western International** University in the China, India, and the Netherlands.

- **Universidad de Artes**, Ciencias y Comunicación in Chile.
- **Universidad Latinoamericana** in Mexico.

56 Revenue at the Apollo Group doubled during the last five fiscal years as follows:

	Revenue [$$ in millions]				
Source of the Revenue	**2010**	**2009**	**2008**	**2007**	**2006**
University of Phoenix	$4,498.3	$3,766.6	$2,987.7	$2,537.8	$2,074.4
Apollo Global:					
BPP	$ 251.7	13.1	—	—	—
Other	$ 78.3	76.1	42.3		
Total Apollo Global	$ 330.0	89.0	42.3	—	—
Other Schools	95.7	95.0	93.6	182.6	402.1
Corporate	1.8	2.8	9.8	1.4	1.0
Net Revenue	$4,925.8	$3,953.6	$3,133.4	$2,723.8	$2,477.5

57 Apollo Group executives gave a hint of a global focus when they said in a recent letter to shareholders:

> We are committed to strengthening and capitalizing on Apollo Group's position as a leading provider of high quality, accessible education for individuals around the world. This means putting the student first as we focus on academic quality and the student experience. To that end, we are intensely focused on leveraging our core capabilities and expertise—developed over our 35-plus year history—to, first and foremost, maximize the long-term value of University of Phoenix, which is our top investment priority for Apollo Group, and then, to expand intelligently beyond University of Phoenix.

58 It would appear that, over time, Apollo Global will become the organizational mechanism to take all that is known and learned from the University of Phoenix truly global, in due time. For the University of Phoenix, Apollo executives translated this vision into three priorities:

1. ***Growing the UOP the right way*** by identifying and attracting students who are willing to put in the effort to succeed and who UOP believes can benefit from UOP programs.
2. ***Delivering a high-value, energizing and compelling learning experience*** for UOP students through quality, convenience, relevant academic programs, innovative content delivery, engaging instruction, and student-centric services and protections.
3. ***Increasing the efficiency of UOP operations*** via scalability and process innovation.

59 They add that the fundamental Apollo Group strategic plan emphasizes two core themes:

1. Maximize the value of the core UOP business, and
2. Expand intelligently beyond the UOP.

THE UNIVERSITY OF PHOENIX STRATEGY

60 The UOP's 2007 strategic plan prioritized six core "strategies." UOP's plan heading into 2012 is noticeably different in the core strategies it emphasizes in its 10-K and other key documents.

61 The 2007 plan highlighted six key elements in order of priority:

1. **Establish New UOP Campuses and Learning Centers**—be in every state and every major U.S. metro area.
2. **International Expansion**—accommodate working adults abroad that want a U.S. education without the hassle of coming to the United States.
3. **Enhance Existing Educational Programs**—add more accredited degree programs, increase pedagogical/instructional excellence, and keep tuition down.
4. **Expand the Types of Educational Programs**—master's and doctoral programs.
5. **Serve a Broader Student Age Group**—by targeting the 18–23-year-old group.
6. **Market Aggressively**—spend over 20 percent of revenue [~$600,000] on intensive marketing to build enrollments to in turn build revenue growth.[13]

62 The results from that strategic plan were impressive. UOP revenues grew 150 percent from just over $2B in 2006 to virtually $5B in 2010. And that included the Great Recession of 2008–2009.

63 The UOP's 2011 strategic plan for the next five years was remarkably different in order of priority and emphasis. Key elements of that strategic plan in presumed order of priority as outlined in 2011 were, all echoing a UOP theme of "transitioning the UOP to more effectively support our students and improve their educational outcomes":

1. **Student Education Financing Decisions**—Adopt new tools to better support students' educational financing decisions in enrolling and staying at the UOP. Emphasize the new UOP's Responsible Borrowing Calculator, and help prospective and current students use it to help them calculate the amount of student borrowing necessary to achieve their educational objectives; and to not incur unnecessary student loan debt.
2. **Responsible Target Marketing**—Transition the UOP marketing approaches to more effectively identify students who have the ability to succeed in UOP educational programs, including reduced emphasis on the use of third parties for lead generation.
3. **Improved New Student Orientation**—Require all students who enroll in UOP with fewer than 24 incoming credits to first attend a free, three-week University Orientation program designed to help the inexperienced prospective student understand the rigors of higher education prior to enrollment.
4. **Prioritize Student Success over Financial Incentives in Employees' Compensation**—Better align UOP enrollment, admissions, and other employees to UOP students' success by redefining roles and responsibilities, resetting individual objectives and measures, and implementing new compensation structures, including eliminating factors in UOP admissions personnel compensation structures.

[13] Apollo Group agreed to pay a fine of $9.8 million to the U.S. Education Dept. in 2005 to close an investigation of aggressive recruiting practices in which its UOP was depicted as a high-pressure sales culture that resembled a telemarketing boiler room more than a university admissions office. "Phoenix recruiters soon find out that UOP bases their salaries solely on the number of students they recruit," the report charged. That's prohibited by federal law. One recruiter who started at $28,000, for instance, was bumped to $85,000 after recruiting 151 students in six months. But another who started at the same level got just a $4,000 raise after signing up 79 students. Ultimately, such violations could have led the government to bar Phoenix from the federal student loan program, crippling the university. Apollo's CEO called the report "very misleading and full of inaccuracies." But he says he decided to settle rather than wage a protracted fight. Apollo agreed to change its compensation system and pay a $9.8 million fine without admitting guilt. Still, Apollo's defenders note that the point of the law is to prevent for-profits from luring unqualified students. If Phoenix is doing that, it hadn't showed up in student-loan default rates, which were a low 6% at the time.

5. **Upgrading UOP Learning and Data Platforms**—Continue to improve online learning platforms and e-pedagogies; and ensure state-of-the-art computer equipment and operational software to continuously enhance the student experience online and on-campus. All class materials are delivered electronically, making both its online and on-campus consistent, easy to use, and up-to-date electronic educational services.

64 Commenting in 2011 on these five somewhat new, key elements of the UOP's 2015 strategy, Apollo executives offered the following:

> We believe that the changes in our marketing approaches and the University Orientation pilot program implemented during FY 2010 contributed to the 9.8% reduction in University of Phoenix New Degreed Enrollment in the fourth quarter of FY 2010 compared to the fourth quarter of the previous year. We expect that the continuing changes in our marketing approaches and the implementation of the additional initiatives described above will significantly reduce fiscal year 2011 University of Phoenix New Degreed Enrollment and will adversely impact our net revenue, operating income and cash flow. However, we believe that these efforts are in the best interests of our students and, over the long-term, will improve student persistence and completion rates, reduce bad debt expense, reduce the risks to our business associated with our regulatory environment, and position us for more stable long-term growth in the future.[14]

65 Other elements of UOP's previous strategy remain a part of its strategic agenda toward 2015. The difference would seem to be in emphasis, focus, and/or scope.

6. **Selectively Establish New Locations and/or Learning Centers**—UOP is now in 40 states and virtually all major U.S. metro areas. It is within 10 miles of 87 million Americans. So UOP's need for aggressively seeking new locations has passed. Plus, it is now an online leader, with a proprietary online learning system, small online classes, mandatory participation requirements for faculty and students, and flexibility to attend both online and on-campus class sessions. Its aggressive growth and purchasing of new locations in areas targeted for growth is no longer critical to its growth, or survival.
7. **International Expansion**—UOP will play an eventual essential role in partnership with the new Apollo Global developing the capabilities to take the UOP-proven approaches to comprehensive postsecondary education global. This strategic element appears to be emerging as the key vector for the Apollo Group's long-term growth. Executives had this comment about international expansion, which they appear to be approaching cautiously, and with an appreciation for local market considerations and customs:

> We believe we can capitalize on opportunities to utilize our core expertise and organizational capabilities to grow in areas outside of UOP's current markets, both domestically and internationally. In particular, we have observed a growing demand for high quality postsecondary and other education services outside of the U.S., including in Europe, Latin America and Asia, and we believe that we have the capabilities and expertise to provide these services beyond our current reach. We intend to actively pursue quality opportunities to partner with or acquire existing institutions of higher learning where we believe we can achieve attractive long-term growth and value creation.[15]

66 UOP has as the assumption guiding its increased emphasis on preparing for global expansion that proprietary education is playing an important role in advancing the development

[14] Apollo Group 2010 Annual Report.

[15] Ibid.

of education, specifically higher education and lifelong learning, in many countries around the world. While primary and secondary education outside the United States are still funded mainly through government expenditures, postsecondary education outside the United States is experiencing governmental funding constraints that create opportunities for a broader proprietary sector role. UOP and Apollo executives cite several trends driving their international market optimism:

- Unmet demand for education.
- Insufficient public funding to meet demand for education.
- Shortcomings in the quality of higher education offerings, resulting in the rise of supplemental training to meet industry demands in the developing world.
- Worldwide appreciation of the importance that knowledge plays in economic progress.
- Globalization of education.
- Increased availability and role of technology in education, broadening the accessibility and reach of education.

8. **Make UOP a Comprehensive University Based on Accredited Degrees Offered**—The quality and comprehensiveness of UOP's degree offerings are critical to further establishing it as the "gold standard" among proprietary universities, and all universities, in order to allow it to deal with and separate itself from perceived low-quality and "lite" offerings that plague the industry. UOP now offers degrees in the follow program areas, all accredited:

Associate's	Bachelor's	Master's	Doctoral
• Arts and Sciences • Business and Management • Criminal Justice and Security • Education • Health Care • Human Services • Psychology • Technology	• Arts and Sciences • Business and Management • Criminal Justice and Security • Education • Health Care • Human Services • Nursing • Psychology • Technology	• Business and Management • Counseling • Criminal Justice and Security • Education • Health Care • Nursing • Psychology • Technology	• Business and Management • Education • Health Care • Nursing • Psychology • Technology

67 This breadth of accredited offerings makes the UOP, degree-wise, the equal of virtually any traditional comprehensive public or private, nonprofit university.

9. **Emphasize Input from Employers of UOP Students**—The UOP has long placed an emphasis on maintaining a close relationship with employers of its students. They are solicited for curriculum input; for project-type issues and problems, which can be used to have coursework in appropriate classes include student teams working on current, relevant applications of topics and course content they are covering. These relationships with major global employers have led to pedagogical innovations, like UOP's "Virtual Organizations." Created by subject matter experts and relevant professionals, six composite businesses, schools, health care, and government organizations provide virtual settings that allow students and their instructors to immerse themselves inside virtual real-world settings. These settings provide a more realistic form of

experiential learning, UOP claims, than case studies and simulations while also fostering critical thinking and resourcefulness skills.

68 Employer closeness also helps financially, since over 60 percent of UOP's working students have historically had some level of tuition assistance from their employers. And it typically helps manage course timing and scheduling issues.

UNIVERSITY OF PHOENIX STUDENT DEMOGRAPHICS

69 As noted previously, a majority of UOP's students have been working adults employed full-time, and having been on the job at least six years. Some characteristics of UOP's student population over the last five years are shown below:

UOP Student Demographics:	**2010**	**2009**	**2008**	**2007**	**2006**
Gender					
Female	67.7%	66.0%	66.0%	63.0%	54.0%
Male	32.3%	34.0%	34.0%	37.0%	46.0%
	100.0%	100.0%	100.0%	100.0%	100.0%
Age (1)					
22 and under	12.1%	14.9%	14.0%	9.7%	9.5%
23 to 29	32.6%	34.3%	34.0%	32.8%	32.0%
30 to 39	32.7%	31.0%	31.0%	33.8%	33.5%
40 to 49	16.2%	14.5%	15.0%	17.2%	18.0%
50 & over	6.4%	5.3%	6.0%	6.5%	7.0%
	100.0%	100.0%	100.0%	100.0%	100.0%
Race/Ethnicity (1)					
African-American	28.1%	27.7%	25.0%	26.3%	26.1%
Asian/Pacific Islander	3.3%	3.6%	4.1%	4.0%	4.1%
Caucasian	51.9%	52.2%	53.8%	52.9%	53.1%
Hispanic	11.6%	11.6%	12.0%	11.5%	11.6%
Native Amr./Alaskan	1.2%	1.3%	1.3%	1.5%	1.6%
Other/Unknown	3.9%	3.6%	3.8%	3.8%	3.5%
	100.0%	100.0%	100.0%	100.0%	100.0%

(1) Based on New Degreed Enrollment students

Degreed Enrollment:					
Associates	200,800	201200	146500	104500	74000
Bachelors	193,600	163600	141800	138700	140700
Masters	68,700	71200	67700	65300	63400
Doctoral	7,700	7000	6100	5200	4200
	470,800	443,000	362,100	313,700	282,300

(continued)

Degreed Enrollment as % of total:					
Associates	42.7%	45.4%	40.5%	33.3%	26.2%
Bachelors	41.1%	36.9%	39.2%	44.2%	49.8%
Masters	14.6%	16.1%	18.7%	20.8%	22.5%
Doctoral	1.6%	1.6%	1.7%	1.7%	1.5%
	100.0%	100.0%	100.0%	100.0%	100.0%

FINANCIAL PICTURE FOR THE APOLLO GROUP AND THE UNIVERSITY OF PHOENIX

70 A consolidated summary of the Apollo Group's business for the last five years is as follows:

	As of August 31,				
	2010	**2009**	**2008**	**2007**	**2006**
($ in thousands)					
Consolidated Balance Sheets Data:					
Cash and cash equivalents and marketable securities	$1,299,943	$ 987,825	$ 511,459	$ 392,681	$ 408,728
Restricted cash and cash equivalents	$ 444,132	$ 432,304	$ 384,155	$ 296,469	$ 238,267
Long-term restricted cash and cash equivalents	$ 126,615	$ —	$ —	$ —	$ —
Total assets	$3,601,451	$3,263,377	$1,860,412	$1,449,863	$1,283,005
Current liabilities	$1,793,511	$1,755,278	$ 865,609	$ 743,835	$ 595,756
Long-term debt	168,039	127,701	15,428	—	—
Long-term liabilities	251,161	155,785	133,210	72,188	82,876
Total equity	1,388,740	1,224,613	846,165	633,840	604,373
Total liabilities and shareholders' equity	$3,601,451	$3,263,377	$1,860,412	$1,449,863	$1,283,005

	Year Ended August 31,				
	2010	**2009**	**2008**	**2007**	**2006**
(In thousands, except per share data)					
Consolidated Statements of Income Data:					
Net revenue	$4,925,819	$3,953,566	$3,133,436	$2,721,812	$2,477,533
Cost and expenses:					
Instructional costs and services	2,125,082	1,567,754	1,349,879	1,230,253	1,109,584
Selling and promotional	1,112,666	952,884	800,989	658,012	544,706
General and administrative	314,795	286,493	215,192	201,546	153,004
Goodwill and other intangibles impairment	184,570	—	—	—	20,205
Estimated litigation loss	177,982	80,500	—	—	—
Total costs and expenses	3,915,095	2,887,631	2,366,060	2,089,811	1,827,499
Operating Income	1,010,724	1,065,935	767,376	632,001	650,034
Interest income	2,920	12,591	30,078	31,172	18,465

Interest expense	(11,891)	(4,448)	(3,450)	(232)	(326)
Other, net	(685)	(7,151)	6,772	672	(85)
Income from continuing operations before income taxes	1,001,068	1,066,927	800,776	663,613	668,088
Provision for income taxes	(464,063)	(456,720)	(314,025)	(250,961)	(253,255)
Income from continuing operations	537,005	610,207	486,751	412,652	414,833
Loss from discontinued operations, net of tax	(15,424)	(16,377)	(10,824)	(3,842)	—
Net income	521,581	593,830	475,927	408,810	414,833
Net loss attributable to noncontrolling interests	31,421	4,489	598	—	—
Net income attributable to Apollo	$ 553,002	$ 598,319	$ 476,525	$ 408,810	$ 414,833

71 Components of Net Revenue were as follows over those five years and in FY2005:

	Year Ended August 31,					
	2010		2009		2008	
($ in millions)						
Tuition and educational services revenue	$4,757.9	97%	$3,815.0	96%	$2,988.6	96%
Educational materials revenue	324.9	6%	226.4	6%	184.4	6%
Services revenue	84.2	2%	83.2	2%	77.7	2%
Other revenue	22.4	—	28.3	1%	43.9	1%
Gross Revenue	5,189.4	105%	4,152.9	105%	3,294.6	105%
Less: Discounts	(263.6)	(5)%	(199.3)	(5)%	(161.2)	(5)%
Net revenue	$4,925.8	100%	$3,953.6	100%	$3,133.4	100%

	Year Ended August 31,					
	2007		2006		2005	
($ in thousands						
Tuition revenue	$2,553,075	94%	$2,304,288	93%	$2,114,082	94%
IPD services revenue	73,577	2%	74,442	3%	69,564	3%
Application and related fees	27,596	1%	33,795	1%	36,381	2%
Online course material revenue	160,973	6%	138,661	6%	104,528	5%
Other revenue	21,018	1%	31,728	1%	33,786	1%
Tuition and other revenue, gross	2,836,239	104%	2,582,914	104%	2,358,341	105%
Less: Discounts	(112,446)	(4)%	(105,381)	(4)%	(107,227)	(5)%
Tuition and other revenue, net	$2,723,793	100%	$2,477,533	100%	$2,251,114	100%

72 Total revenues from Title IV funding were as follows over the 2005–2007 time period:

	2007	2006	2005
($ in thousands)			
Total Title IV funding received	$1,765,642	$1,536,616	$1,345,405
Total tuition and other revenues, net	2,723,793	2,477,533	2,251,114
Total Title IV funding as a percentage of total revenue	64.8%	62.0%	59.8%

73 While a similar table was not provided in their most recent annual report, the Apollo Group noted in their FY2010 Annual Report the following information regarding the percentage of revenue coming from Title IV and Pell Grant programs as a percent of total tuition revenue:

> The 90/10 Rule percentage for University of Phoenix [meaning Title IV funding as a percentage of total revenue] has increased materially over the past several fiscal years and UOP leaders expect further increases in the near term. These increases are primarily attributable to the following factors:
>
> - *Increased student loan limits.* The Student Loans Act of 2008 increased the annual loan limits on federal unsubsidized student loans by $2,000 for the majority of our students enrolled in associate's and bachelor's degree programs, and also increased the aggregate loan limits (over the course of a student's education) on total federal student loans for certain students. This in-turn increased the amount of Title IV program funds used by our students to pay tuition, fees and other costs; which has increased the proportion of our revenue from Title IV programs.
> - *Increase in Pell Grants.* The eligibility for and maximum amount of Pell Grants have increased in each of the past three years. These changes further increase the Title IV funds available used by our students to pay tuition, fees and other costs, which, in turn, has further increased the proportion of our revenue deemed to be from Title IV programs.
>
> The Higher Education Opportunity Act provides temporary relief from the impact of the loan limit increases by excluding from the 90/10 Rule calculation any amounts received between July 1, 2008 and June 30, 2011 that are attributable to the increased annual loan limits. The UOP refers to this as the "LLI relief." The following table details the 90/10 Rule percentages for University of Phoenix and Western International University, as well as the percentages for University of Phoenix with the LLI relief, for fiscal years 2010 and 2009:

	90/10 Rule Percentages for Fiscal Years Ended August 31,			
	2010		2009	
	Including LLI Relief	Excluding LLI Relief	Including LLI Relief	Excluding LLI Relief
University of Phoenix	85%	88%	83%	86%
Western International University (1)		62%		57%

(1) We have not calculated the 90/10 Rule percentages for Western International University with the LLI Relief because of its relatively low 90/10 Rule percentages.

74 Looking toward 2011 and beyond, they further said:

> Based on currently available information, we expect that the 90/10 Rule percentage for University of Phoenix, net of the LLI relief, will approach 90% for fiscal year 2011 . . . we believe that, absent a change in recent trends or the implementation of additional effective measures to reduce the percentage, the 90/10 Rule percentage for University of Phoenix is likely to exceed 90% in fiscal year 2012 due to the expiration of the LLI relief in July 2011.[16]

75 The other way this student loan derived revenue creates a potential problem involves loan defaults as was discussed earlier in this case, called the "cohort default rate." If an institution's two year cohort default rate exceeds 25% for three consecutive years, it will

[16] Ibid.

become ineligible to participate in Title IV programs. Apollo's two-year cohort default rates as of FY2010 were:

	Two-Year Cohort Default Rates for Cohort Years Ended September 30,		
	2008	2007	2006
University of Phoenix (1)	12.9%	9.3%	7.2%
Western International University (1)	10.7%	18.5%	27.4%
All proprietary postsecondary institution (1)	11.6%	11.0%	9.7%

(1) Based on information published by the U.S. Department of Education.

76 Apollo Group said in this regard:

> The University of Phoenix cohort default rates have been increasing over the past several years. We expect this upward trend to intensify due to the current challenging economic climate and the continuing effect of the historical growth in our associate's degree student population. Consistent with this, the available preliminary data for the University of Phoenix 2009 cohort reflect a substantially higher default rate than the 2008 cohort, although we do not expect the rate to exceed 25%.[17]

77 Related, the FY2010 Annual Report has this footnote to its balance sheet about allowances for doubtful accounts receivable:

Note 6. Accounts Receivable, Net

Accounts receivable, net consist of the following as of August 31:

($ in thousands)	2010	2009
Student accounts receivable	$ 419,714	$ 380,226
Less allowance for doubtful accounts	(192,857)	(110,420)
Net student accounts receivable	226,857	269,806
Other receivables	37,520	28,464
Total accounts receivable, net	$ 264,377	$ 298,270

Accounts receivable, net consist of the following as of August 31:

($ in thousands)	2008	2007
Student accounts receivable	$ 279,841	$ 281,834
Less allowance for doubtful accounts	(78,362)	(99,818)
Net student accounts receivable	201,479	182,016
Other receivables	20,440	8,896
Total accounts receivable, net	$ 221,919	$ 190,912

Student accounts receivable is composed primarily of amounts due related to tuition.

[17] Ibid.

78 These numbers identify a large, and growing doubtful amount of tuition revenue will be collected for services provided in FY2009 and FY2010. That situation appears to be common across the Title IV loan program, which in turn is drawing regulatory attention to it. Fears of another credit bubble have been raised. A generation that has grown up adding this debt to their financial picture just as they begin their adult life is acutely aware of the seriousness of the obligation to repay those loans, especially when they start working and begin paying their loan payments. The feature of these loans that has them excluded from bankruptcy protection further reinforces that burden. And interest rates on delinquent and/or unmade payments, particularly from private loan providers, can rival the levels on higher interest credit cards. All of this makes the issue of defaults and the regulatory CDRs or cohort default rates a major issue industry-wide and for the country as a whole.

79 Apollo/UOP's costs as a percent of revenue were as follows over the last six years:

				% of Revenues			% Change	
	Year Ended August 31,			Year Ended August 31,			2007 vs.	2006 vs.
	2007	2006	2005	2007	2006	2005	2006	2005
($ in millions)								
Revenues:								
Tuition and other, net	$2,723.8	$2,477.5	$2,251.1	100.0%	100.0%	100.0%	9.9%	10.1%
Costs and expenses:								
Instructional costs and services	1,237.5	1,109.6	952.5	45.4%	44.8%	42.3%	11.5%	16.5%
Selling and promotional	659.1	544.7	485.5	24.2%	22.0%	21.6%	21.0%	12.2%
General and administrative	201.5	153.0	98.6	7.4%	6.2%	4.4%	31.7%	55.2%
Goodwill impairment	—	20.2	—	—	0.8%	—		
Share-based compensation (1)	—	—	16.9	—	—	0.7%		
	2,098.1	1,827.5	1,553,5	77.0%	73.8%	69.0%	14.8%	17.6%
Income from operations	625.7	650.0	697.6	23.0%	26.2%	31.0%	(3.7)%	(6.8)%
Interest income and other, net	31.6	18.1	16.8	1.1%	0.7%	0.7%	74.6%	7.7%
Income before income taxes	657.3	668.1	714.4	24.1%	26.9%	31.7%	(1.6)%	(6.5)%
Provision for income taxes	248.5	253.3	286.5	9.1%	10.2%	12.7%	(1.9)%	(11.6)%
Net Income	$ 408.8	$ 414.8	$ 427.9	15.0%	16.7%	19.0%	(1.4)%	(3.1)%

Fiscal Year 2009 Compared to Fiscal Year 2008
Analysis of Consolidated Statements of Income

			% of Net Revenue		
	Year Ended August 31,		Year Ended August 31,		
	2009	2008	2009	2008	% Change
($ in millions)					
Net revenue	$ 3,953.6	$ 3,133.4	100.0%	100.0%	26.2%
Costs and expenses:					
Instructional costs and services	1,567.8	1,349.9	39.7%	43.1%	16.1%
Selling and promotional	952.9	801.0	24.1%	25.6%	19.0%

General and administrative	286.5	215.1	7.2%	6.8%	33.2%
Estimated litigation loss	80.5	—	2.0%	—	*
Total costs and expenses	2,887.7	2,366.0	73.0%	75.5%	22.0%
Operating income	1,065.9	767.4	27.0%	24.5%	38.9%
Interest income	12.6	30.1	0.3%	1.0%	(58.1)%
Interest expense	(4.4)	(3.5)	(0.1)%	(0.1)%	(25.7)%
Other, net	(7.2)	6.7	(0.2)%	0.2%	*
Income from continuing operations before income taxes	1,066.9	800.7	27.0%	25.6%	33.2%
Provision for income taxes	(456.7)	(314.0)	(11.6)%	(10.1)%	(45.4)%
Income from continuing operations	610.2	486.7	15.4%	15.5%	25.4%
Loss from discontinued operations, net of tax	(16.4)	(10.8)	(0.4)%	(0.3)%	(51.9)%
Net income	593.8	475.9	15.0%	15.2%	24.8%
Net loss attributable to noncontrolling interests	4.5	0.6	0.1%	—	*
Net income attributable to Apollo	$ 598.3	$ 476.5	15.1%	15.2%	25.6%

* not meaningful

	Year Ended August 31,		% of Net Revenue Year Ended August 31,		
	2010	**2009**	**2010**	**2009**	**% Change**
($ in millions)					
Net revenue	$ 4,925.8	$3,953.6	100.0%	100.0%	24.6%
Costs and expenses:					
Instructional costs and services	2,125.1	1,567.8	43.1%	39.7%	35.5%
Selling and promotional	1,112.6	952.9	22.6%	24.1%	16.8%
General and administrative	314.8	286.5	6.4%	7.2%	9.9%
Goodwill and other intangibles impairment	184.6	—	3.8%	—	*
Estimated litigation loss	178.0	80.5	3.6%	2.0%	*
Total costs and expenses	3,915.1	2,887.7	79.5%	73.0%	35.6%
Operating income	1,010.7	1,065.9	20.5%	27.0%	(5.2)%
Interest income	2.9	12.6	0.1%	0.3%	(77.0)%
Interest expense	(11.9)	(4.4)	(0.3)%	(0.1)%	(170.5)%
Other, net	(0.6)	(7.2)	0.0%	(0.2)%	91.7%
Income from continuing operations before income taxes	1,001.1	1,066.9	20.3%	27.0%	(6.2)%
Provision for income taxes	(464.1)	(456.7)	(9.4)%	(11.6)%	(1.6)%
Income from continuing operations	537.0	610.2	10.9%	15.4%	(12.0)%
Loss from discontinued operations, net of tax	(15.4)	(16.4)	(0.3)%	(0.4)%	6.1%
Net income	521.6	593.8	10.6%	15.0%	(12.2)%

Net loss attributable to noncontrolling interests	31.4	4.5	0.6%	0.1%	*
Net income attributable to Apollo	$ 553.0	$ 598.3	11.2%	15.1%	(7.6)%

* not meaningful

80 Further breakdown of the Apollo Group's "Selling and Promotional" expenses for the last five years offered in their 10-K's were as follows:

	Year Ended August 31,			% of Net Revenues			% Change	
				Year Ended August 31,			2008 vs.	2007 vs.
	2008	2007	2006	2008	2007	2006	2007	2006
($ in millions)								
Enrollment counselors compensation and related expenses	$ 385.8	$ 320.3	$ 254.3	12.3%	11.8%	10.3%	20.4%	26.0%
Advertising	322.5	277.7	231.6	10.3%	10.2%	9.3%	16.1%	19.9%
Other selling and promotional expenses	93.5	58.0	56.5	2.9%	2.1%	2.3%	61.2%	2.7%
Share-based compensation	3.6	3.1	2.3	0.1%	0.1%	0.1%	16.1%	34.8%
Selling and promotional	$ 805.4	$ 659.1	$ 544.7	25.6%	24.2%	22.0%	22.2%	21.0%

81 Interestingly, the Apollo Group 2010 10-K chose not to break out expenses in this same manner and instead provided this summary referring to FY2009 and FY2008, with no breakdown of the $1.1B+ selling and promotional expenditures in 2010:

Selling and Promotional

Selling and promotional expenses increased $151.9 million, or 19.0% in fiscal year 2009 compared to fiscal year 2008 representing a 150 basis point decrease as a percentage of net revenue. The decrease as a percentage of net revenue is primarily due to University of Phoenix improved admissions personnel effectiveness. Additionally, investments we made in our corporate marketing function resulted in more effective advertising.

82 The Apollo Group/University of Phoenix offered an impressive white paper called "Higher Education at the Crossroads" in August 2010, which examined issues related to higher education and the knowledge-economy needs envisioned by educational goals set forth by the Obama administration.[18] The research in that report demonstrated the significant challenge of goals like every American having at least one year of college education equivalence and the reality of how critical the "proprietary" university sector will be to that challenge. They quoted U.S. Education Secretary Arne Duncan to emphasize the point:

Let me be crystal clear: proprietary institutions play a vital role in training young people and adults for jobs. They are critical to helping America meet the President's 2020 goal. They are helping us meet the explosive demand for skills that public institutions cannot always meet.

—*Secretary of Education Arne Duncan, May 11, 2010*

[18] You can read the whole report at http://www.apollogrp.edu/Investor/Reports/Higher%20Education%20at%20a%20Crossroad%20FINAL%20v3.pdf.

83 And the Apollo white paper offers some interesting challenges by comparing the University of Phoenix to more tradition (and all) colleges and universities on three central issues:

1. Marketing and promotion expenditures. UOP is not excessive in its marketing and enrollment expenditures; and like other colleges and universities it has a duty to inform.

Average Marketing Spend per New Enrollment

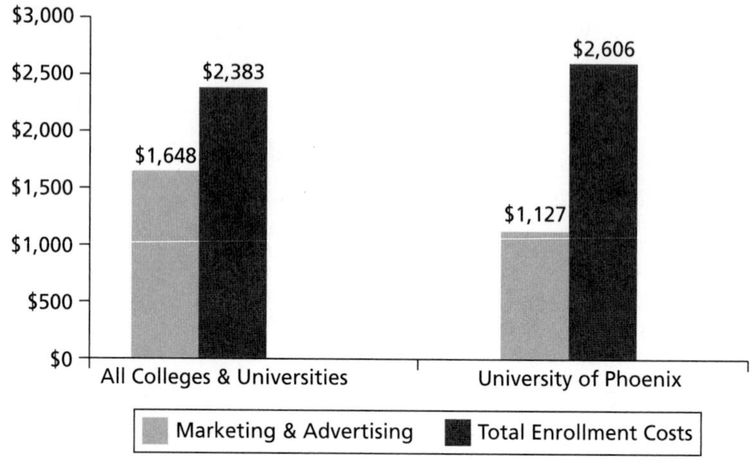

Source: National Association for College Admission Counseling, 2009 State of College Admission, and Apollo Group SEC filings and internal data.

2. Quality of education based on evaluation of learning outcomes.

Percentage Improvement in MAPP Scores: Freshmen to Seniors

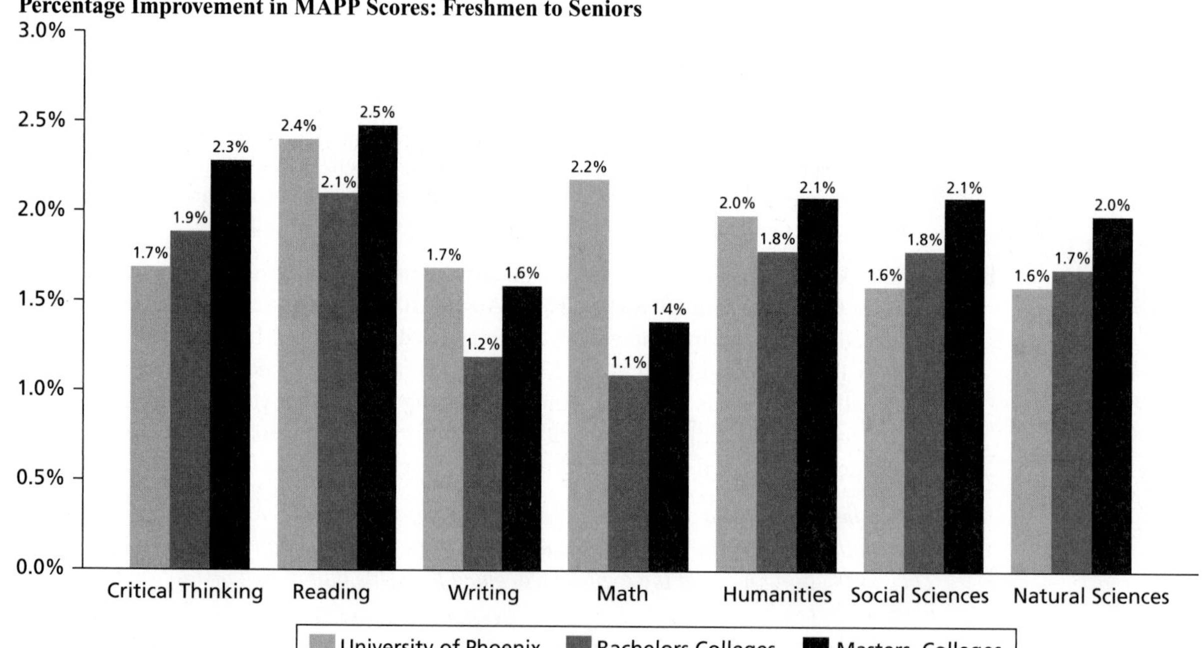

Source: Educational Testing Service (ETS), Measure of Proficiency and Progress (MAPP).
Note: Master's Universities reference institutions that offer baccalaureate through graduate degrees.

3. To meet U.S. educational goals, the U.S. higher education system will have to educate nontraditional students. But their demographic characteristics make them more at risk for graduation/completion rates (although UOP has a higher graduation rate than its most appropriate comparison, community colleges).

   Student demographics by institution types show that proprietary institutions have more 25+ year-old students that financially are more dependent upon themselves to pay for college without parental assistance and are more likely to be a minority—African American or Hispanic.

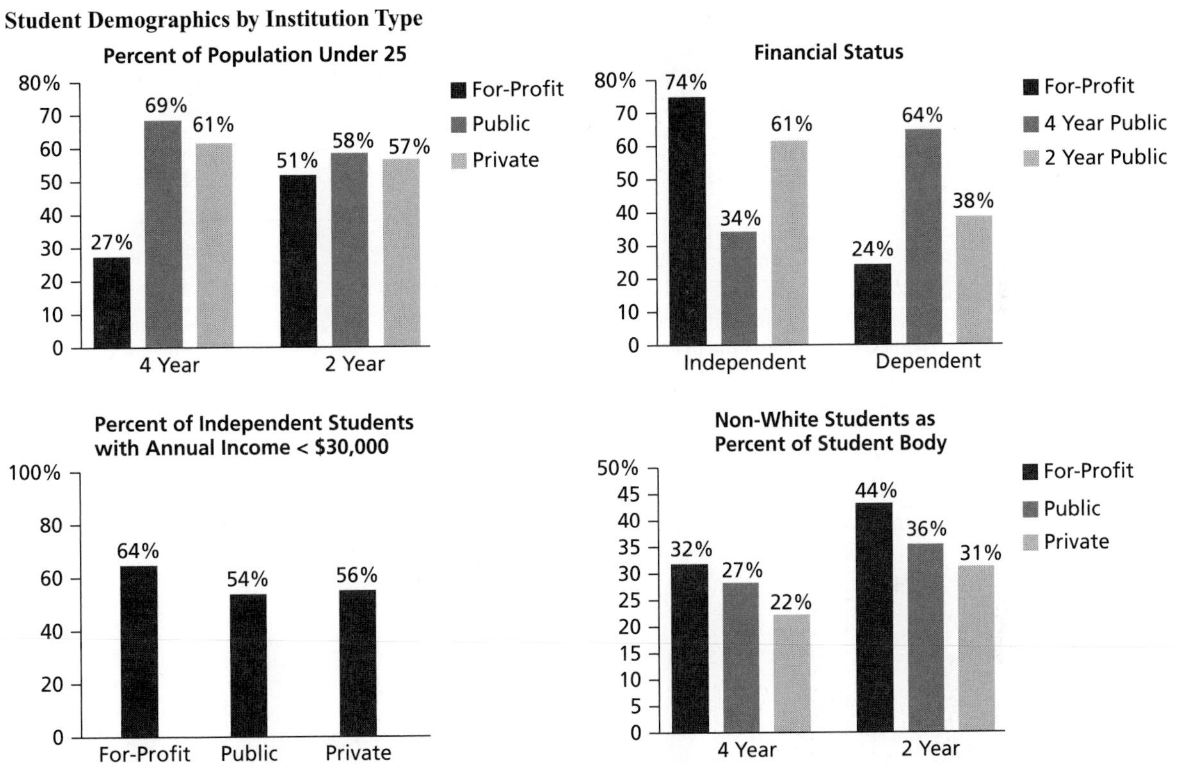

Source: U.S. Department of education, National Center of Education Statistics.

Financial independence (aka the lack of parental financial support) among nontraditional students leads to higher borrowing needs among proprietary institutions' students. Yet they still borrow less, on average, than students at independent private institutions.

This financial independence, and borrowing, among nontraditional students means they rely solely on their earning capacity and resourcefulness. Juggling all that this implies, especially for the average nontraditional student, means they are more likely to move intermittently in and out of their academic programs while managing life's realities. That in turn affects the graduation/completion rates and timing as a population.

Average Student Debt Levels by Institution Type

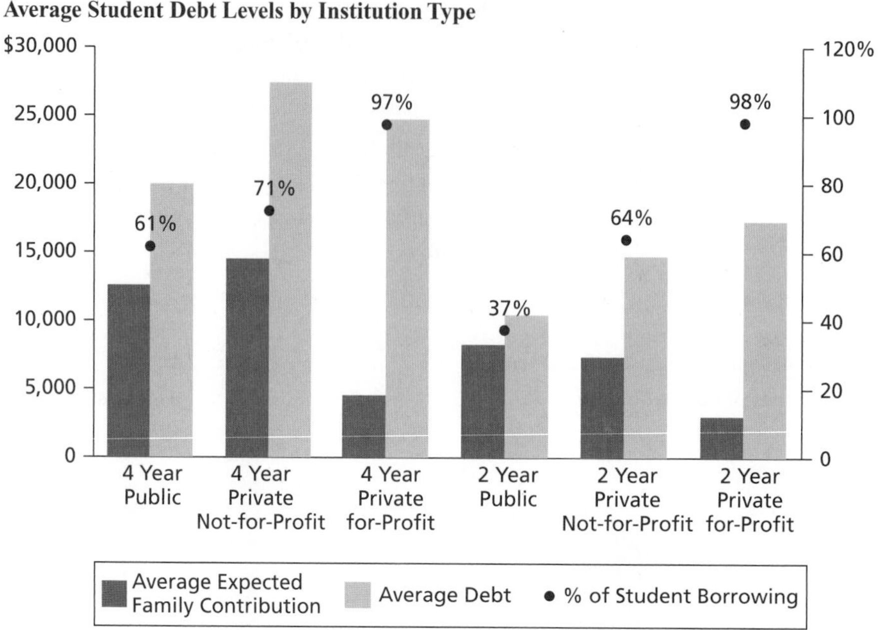

Source: U.S. Department of Education, National Center for Education Statistics, 2007–2008 National Postsecondary Student Aid Study (NPSAS: 08).

Completion Rates by Various Demographic Characteristics

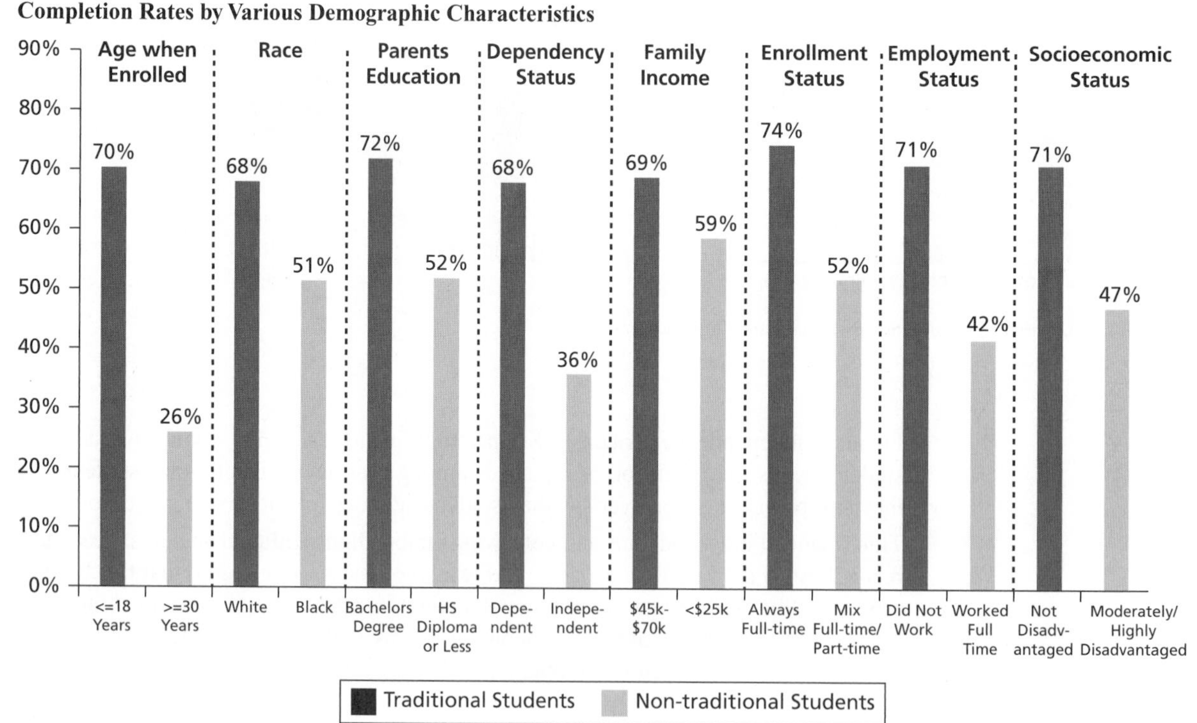

Source: U.S. Department of Education, National Center for Education Statistics.

4. And those factors then affect potential to default on loans, or as an aggregate student pool, make for higher "cohort default rates," also referred to by the acronym "CDR."

University of Phoenix Default Rates (2-Year)

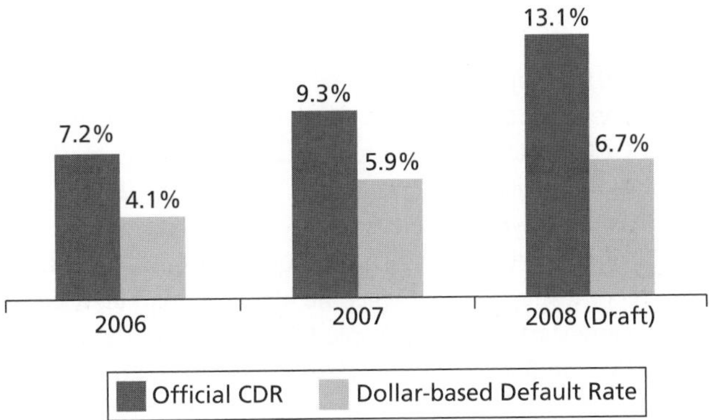

Source: U.S. Department of Education, Apollo Group internal analysis.

This last analysis shows a potentially important argument related to the regulatory environment and manner in which student loan default is monitored/regulated. UOP's point:

> The official CDR metric is a measure of default incidence, not a measure of dollar default. Students who drop out drive CDRs and drop-outs have lower debt levels as individuals who drop tend to do so early in their programs. As a result, two additional data points are worth noting. First, if you only look at students who have graduated with a University of Phoenix degree, UPO managers estimate that the UOP's cumulative default rate is *less than 1%* (using the official 2005, 2006 and 2007 cohort files). Second, the dollar value default percentage (the true economic impact of defaults) is about half of the incidence percentage. UOP officials estimate that the 2-year default rate on student loans for students at University of Phoenix in the 2008 cohort was just 6.7% on a dollar-basis calculation, despite one of the worst economic recessions in modern history.

What is the conclusion this white paper reaches? It is one that speaks to the role well-managed proprietary colleges and universities need to play in educating an essential student, the nontraditional student, if states, nations, and the world are to rise to the challenge of a global knowledge-based world. Here is how they say it:

> By providing an accessible, high quality education, University of Phoenix is producing successful outcomes–graduates who are better positioned to enjoy the professional, financial and personal benefits that a degree brings, as well as a more educated, competitive society as a whole. . . .
>
> Through a framework of thoughtful and consistent regulation, well managed proprietary colleges and universities—those that are committed to responsible, ethical practices and regulatory compliance—play a vital role in the future of America's higher education system, helping it to rise to the challenge of meeting the needs of the millions of non-traditional learners and producing the graduates necessary to achieve the nation's shared educational and economic goals. Apollo Group is committed to leading the nation towards this future.

Case 4

Apple Inc. in 2010

David B. Yoffie
Renee Kim

1 On April 4, 2010, Apple Inc. launched its eagerly anticipated iPad amid great hype. The multimedia computer tablet was the third major innovation that Apple had released over the last decade. CEO Steve Jobs had argued that the iPad was another revolutionary product that could emulate the smashing success of the iPod and the iPhone. Expectations ran high. Even *The Economist* displayed the release of the iPad on its magazine cover with Jobs illustrated as a biblical figure, noting that, "The enthusiasm of the Apple faithful may be overdone, but Mr. Jobs's recor d suggests that when he blesses a market, it takes off."[1]

2 The company started off as "Apple Computer," best known for its Macintosh personal computers (PCs) in the 1980's and 1990's. Despite a strong brand, rapid growth, and high profits in the late 1980s, Apple almost went bankrupt in 1996. Then Jobs went to work, transforming "Apple Computer" into "Apple Inc." with innovative non-PC products starting in the early 2000's. In fact, by 2010, the company viewed itself as a "mobile device company."[2] In the 2009 fiscal year, sales related to the iPhone and the iPod represented nearly 60% of Apple's total sales of $43 billion.[3] Even in the midst of a severe economic recession, revenues and net income both soared (see **Exhibits 1a** through **1c**). Meanwhile, Apple's stock was making history of its own. The share price had risen more than 15-fold since 2003 (See **Exhibit 2**).

3 By almost any measure, Apple's turnaround was a spectacular accomplishment. Yet Steve Jobs knew that no company in the technology industry could relax. Challenges abounded. In 2009, for example, iPod sales were falling. At the same time, Microsoft introduced Window 7, which led to a resurgence in PC sales. Even though Macintosh sales had grown faster than the industry in recent years, Apple's share of the worldwide PC market had remained below 5% since 1997 (see **Exhibit 3**). In addition, there was great uncertainty about the iconic CEO's health. Jobs had taken medical leave for a liver transplant in 2009, following treatment for pancreatic cancer a few years earlier. Many wondered—would Jobs remain at Apple and could the company thrive without him? Finally, would the iPhone continue its march to dominate smartphones in the face of growing competition from Google, RIM, and Nokia? And would Apple's newest creation, the iPad, take the company to the next level?

Source: Professor David B. Yoffie and Research Associate Renee Kim prepared this case. This case derives from earlier cases, including "Apple Inc., 2008," HBS No. 708-480, by Professor David B. Yoffie and Research Associate Michael Slind, and "Apple Computer, 2006," HBS No. 706-496 by Professor David B. Yoffie and Research Associate Michael Slind. This case was developed from published sources. HBS cases are developed solely as the basis for class discussion. Cases are not intended to serve as endorsements, sources of primary data, or illustrations of effective or ineffective management.

[1] "The Book of Jobs," *The Economist*, January 30, 2010, p. 11.

[2] Kevin McLaughin, "Apple COO: We're a Mobile Device Company," ChannelWeb, February 23, 2010, http://www.crn.com/mobile/223100456;jsessionid=WIF2WELKTJAT5QE1GHRSKH4ATMY32JVN, accessed March 15, 2010.

[3] Sales included music and iPhone related products and services, such as: the iTunes Store sales, carrier agreements, and Apple-branded and third-party accessories for both products.

EXHIBIT 1a **Apple Inc., Selected Financial Information, 1981–2009 (in millions of dollars, except for number of employees and stock-related data)[a]**

	1981	1986	1991	1996	1998	2000	2002	2004	2006	2008	2009
Net sales	334	1,902	6,309	9,833	5,941	7,983	5,742	8,279	19,315	37,491	42,905
Cost of sales	170	891	3,314	8,865	4,462	5,817	4,139	6,022	13,717	24,294	25,683
Research and development	21	128	583	604	303	380	446	491	712	1,109	1,333
Selling, general, and administrative	77	610	1,740	1,568	908	1,256	1,109	1,430	2,433	3,761	4,149
Operating income (loss)	66	274	447	−1,204	268	530	48	336	2,453	8,327	11,740
Net income (loss)	39	154	310	−816	309	786	65	266	1,989	6,119	8,235
Total cash and ST investments	73	576	893	1,745	2,300	4,027	4,337	5,464	10,110	22,111	23,464
Accounts receivable, net	42	263	907	1,496	955	953	707	1,050	2,845	4,704	5,057
Inventories	104	109	672	662	78	33	45	101	270	509	455
Net property, plant, and equipment	31	222	448	598	348	419	621	707	1,281	2,455	2,954
Total assets	255	1,160	3,494	5,364	4,289	6,803	6,298	8,050	17,205	36,171	47,501
Total liabilities	77	466	1,727	3,306	2,647	2,696	2,203	2,974	7,221	13,874	15,861
Total shareholders' equity	177	694	1,767	2,058	1,642	4,107	4,095	5,076	9,984	22,297	31,640
Cash dividends paid			57	14							
Number of employees	2,456	5,600	14,432	10,896	9,663	8,568	10,211	11,695	17,787	35100	36,800
International sales/sales	27%	26%	45%	52%	45%	46%	43%	41%	41%	44%	48%
Gross margin	49%	53%	47%	10%	25%	27%	28%	27%	29%	35%	40%
R&D/sales	6%	7%	9%	6%	5%	5%	8%	6%	4%	3%	3%
SG&A/sales	23%	32%	28%	16%	15%	16%	19%	17%	13%	10%	10%
Return on sales	12%	8%	5%	NA	5%	10%	1%	3%	10%	16%	19%
Return on assets	24%	15%	10%	NA	7%	12%	1%	3%	12%	17%	17%
Return on equity	38%	25%	19%	NA	22%	22%	2%	6%	23%	33%	31%
Stock price low	$1.78	$2.75	$10.28	$4.22	$3.28	$7.00	$6.80	$10.64	$50.57	$82.58	$82.33
Stock price high	$4.31	$5.47	$18.19	$8.75	$10.75	$36.05	$13.06	$34.22	$91.63	$188.75	$204.45
P/E ratio at year-end	27.7	16.8	21.9	18.8	17.5	6.1	79.6	90.7	37.4	15.9	33.5
Market value at year-end	1,223.7	2,578.3	6,649.9	2,598.5	5,539.7	4,996.2	5,146.4	25,892.5	72,900.8	75,870.6	189,917.0[b]

Source: Compiled from Capital IQ data and Thomson-Reuters Datastream, accessed March 2010.

[a]All data based on Apple's fiscal year that ends in September, except for share price data which reflect calendar-year results.

[b]Apple's market capitalization on April 12, 2010 was $219.25 billion, according to Capital IQ.

EXHIBIT 1b **Apple's Net Sales by Product Category, 2002–2009 (in millions of dollars)**

	2002	2004	2006	2007	2008	2009
Power Macintosh[a]	1,380	1,419	NA	NA	NA	NA
iMac[b]	1,448	954	NA	NA	NA	NA
Desktops[c]	NA	NA	3,319	4,023	5,622	4,324
PowerBook	831	1,589	NA	NA	NA	NA
iBook	875	961	NA	NA	NA	NA
Portables[d]	NA	NA	4,056	6,313	8,732	9,535
Total Macintosh Net Sales	4,534	4,923	7,375	10,336	14,354	13,859
iPod	143	1,306	7,676	8,305	9,153	8,091
Other music products[e]	4	278	1,885	2,496	3,340	4,036
iPhone, related products and services[f]	NA	NA	NA	630	6,742	13,033
Peripherals and other hardware[g]	527	951	1,100	1,303	1,694	1,475
Software	307	502	NA	NA	NA	NA
Service and other net sales	227	319	NA	NA	NA	NA
Software, service, and other sales[h]	NA	NA	1,279	1,508	2,208	2,411
Total Net Sales	**5,742**	**8,279**	**19,315**	**24,578**	**37,491**	**42,905**

Source: Apple's financial statements; casewriter calculations.

Note: All data based on fiscal-year results ending September.

NA = Not Available or Not Applicable.

[a]Includes Xserve product line.

[b]Includes eMac product line.

[c]Includes iMac, Mac Mini, Mac Pro, and Xserve product lines.

[d]Includes MacBook, MacBook Air, and MacBook Pro product lines.

[e]Represents iTunes Store sales, iPod services, and Apple-branded and third-party iPod accessories.

[f]Represents handset sales, carrier agreements, and Apple-branded and third-party iPhone accessories.

[g]Includes sales of displays, wireless connectivity and networking solutions, and other hardware accessories.

[h]Includes sales of Apple-branded operating system, application software, third-party software, AppleCar and Internet services.

EXHIBIT 1c **Apple's Unit Sales by Product Category, 2004–2009 (in thousands of units)**

	2004	2005	2006	2007	2008	2009
Desktops[a]	1,625	2,520	2,434	2,714	3,712	3,182
Portables[b]	1,665	2,014	2,869	4,337	6,003	7,214
Total Macintosh Unit Sales	3,290	4,534	5,303	7,051	9,715	12,396
Net Sales per Unit Sold	*$1,496*	*$1,384*	*$1,391*	*$1,466*	*$1,478*	*$1,333*
iPods	4,416	22,497	39,409	51,630	54,828	54,132
Net Sales per Unit Sold	*$296*	*$202*	*$195*	*$161*	*$167*	*149*
iPhone unit sold	NA	NA	NA	1,389	11,627	20,731

Source: Apple's financial statements; casewriter calculations.

Note: All data based on fiscal-year results ending September.

NA = Not Available or Not Applicable.

[a]Includes iMac, Mac Mini, Mac Pro, and Xserve product lines.

[b]Includes MacBook, MacBook Air, and MacBook Pro product lines.

EXHIBIT 2 **Apple's Share Price vs. S&P 500 Index (December 31, 1980 = 100)**

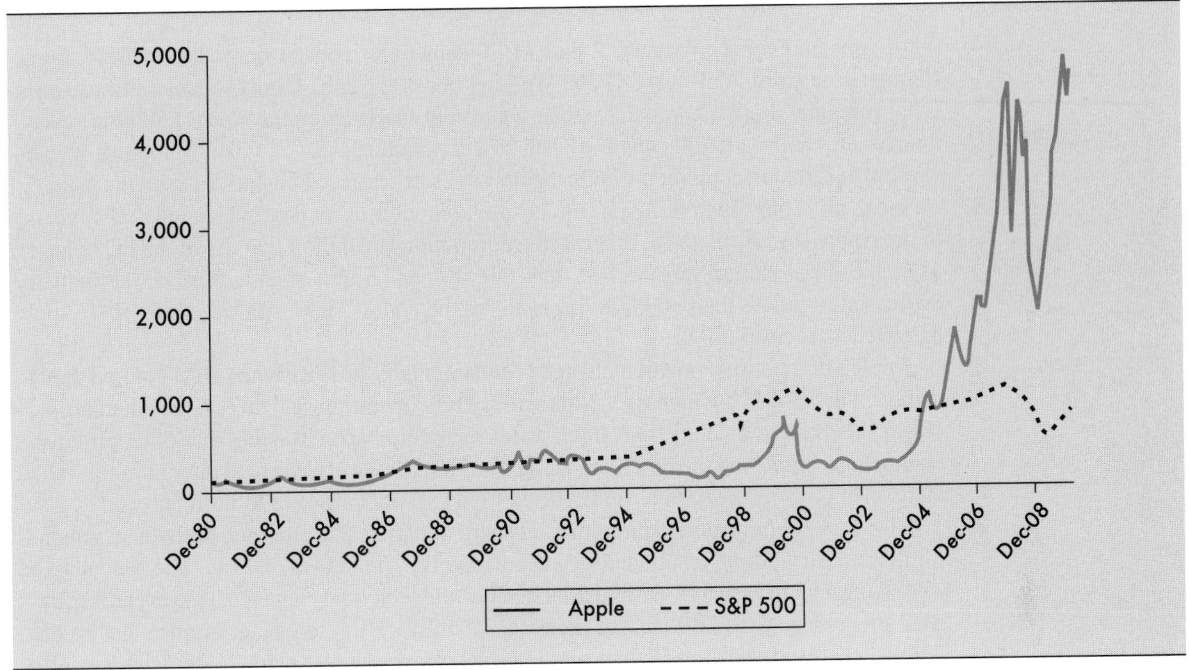

Source: Created by casewriter using data from Thomson-Reuters ONE Banker, accessed March 2010.

EXHIBIT 3 **Apple's Worldwide PC Market Share, 1980–2009**

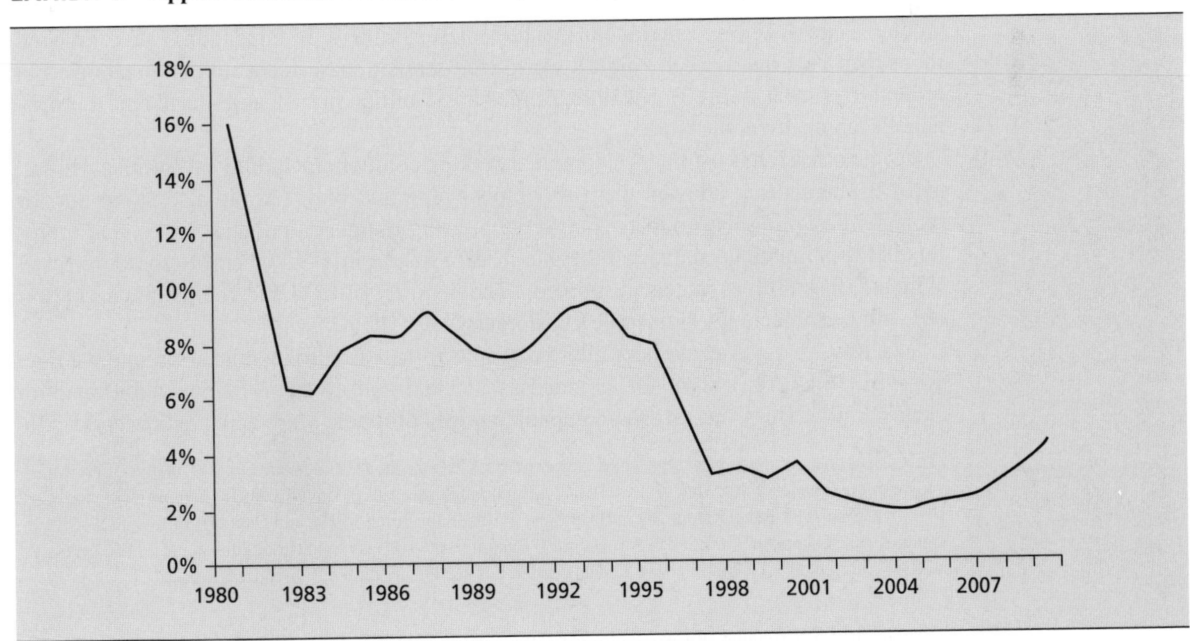

Source: Adapted from InfoCorp., International Data Corp., Gartner Dataquest, and Merrill Lynch Data.

APPLE'S HISTORY

4 Steve Jobs and Steve Wozniak, a pair of 20-something college dropouts, founded Apple Computer on April Fool's Day, 1976.[4] Working out of the Jobs family's garage in Los Altos, California, they built a computer circuit board that they named the Apple I. Within several months, they had made 200 units and taken on a new partner—A.C. "Mike" Markkula, Jr., who was instrumental in attracting venture capital as the experienced businessman on the team.

5 Jobs's mission was to bring an easy-to-use computer to market, which led to the release of the Apple II in April 1978. It sparked a computing revolution that drove the PC industry to $1 billion in annual sales in less than three years.[5] Apple quickly became the industry leader, selling more than 100,000 Apple IIs by the end of 1980. In December 1980, Apple launched a successful IPO.

6 Apple's competitive position changed fundamentally in 1981 when IBM entered the PC market. The IBM PC, which used Microsoft's DOS operating system (OS) and a microprocessor (also called a CPU) from Intel, was a relatively "open" system that other producers could clone. Apple, on the other hand, practiced horizontal and vertical integration. It relied on its own proprietary designs and refused to license its hardware to third parties.

7 IBM PCs not only gained more market share, but they also emerged as the new standard for the industry. Apple responded by introducing the Macintosh in 1984. The Mac marked a breakthrough in ease of use, industrial design, and technical elegance. However, the Mac's slow processor speed and lack of compatible software limited sales. Apple's net income fell 62% between 1981 and 1984, sending the company into a crisis. Jobs, who was often referred to as the "soul" of the company, was forced out in 1985.[6] The boardroom coup left John Sculley, the executive whom Jobs had actively recruited from Pepsi-Cola for his marketing skills, alone at the helm.

The Sculley Years, 1985–1993

8 Sculley pushed the Mac into new markets, most notably in desktop publishing and education. Apple's desktop market was driven by its superior software, such as Aldus (later Adobe) PageMaker, and peripherals, such as laser printers. In education, Apple grabbed more than half the market. Apple's worldwide market share recovered and stabilized at around 8% (see **Exhibit 3**). By 1990, Apple had $1 billion in cash and was the most profitable PC company in the world.

9 Apple offered its customers a complete desktop solution, including hardware, software, and peripherals that allowed them to simply "plug and play." Apple also stood out for typically designing its products from scratch, using unique chips, disk drives, and monitors. IBM-compatibles narrowed the gap in ease of use in 1990 when Microsoft released Windows 3.0. Still, as one analyst noted, "The majority of IBM and compatible users 'put up' with their machines, but Apple's customers 'love' their Macs."[7]

10 Macintosh's loyal customers allowed Apple to sell its products at a premium price. Top-of-the-line Macs went for as much as $10,000 and gross profit hovered around an enviable 50%. However, as IBM-compatible prices dropped, Macs appeared overpriced by

[4] This discussion of Apple's history is based largely on Jim Carlton, *Apple: The Inside Story of Intrigue, Egomania, and Business Blunders* (New York: Times Business/Random House, 1997); David B. Yoffie, "Apple Computer 1992," HBS No. 792-081 (Boston: Harvard Business School Publishing, 1992); and David B. Yoffie and Yusi Wang, "Apple Computer 2002," HBS No. 702-469 (Boston: Harvard Business School Publishing, 2002). Unless otherwise attributed, all quotations and all data cited in this section are drawn from those two cases.

[5] Carlton, *Apple,* p. 10.

[6] "Steve Jobs Takes Another Bite at Apple," *The Independent,* January 6, 1997.

[7] Yoffie, "Apple Computer 1992."

comparison. As the volume leader, IBM compatibles were also attracting the vast majority of new applications. Moreover, Apple's cost structure was high: Apple devoted 9% of sales to research and development (R&D), compared with 5% at Compaq, and only 1% at many other IBM-clone manufacturers. After adding on the Chief Technology Officer title in 1990, Sculley tried to move Apple into the mainstream by becoming a low-cost producer of computers with mass-market appeal. For instance, the Mac Classic, a $999 computer, was designed to compete head-to-head with low-priced IBM clones.

11 Sculley also chose to forge an alliance with Apple's foremost rival, IBM. They worked on two joint ventures; Taligent was set up to create a new OS and Kaleida aimed to write multimedia applications. Apple undertook another cooperative project involving Novell and Intel to rework the Mac OS to run on Intel chips that boasted faster processing speed. These projects, coupled with an ambition to bring out new "hit" products every 6 to 12 months, led to a full-scale assault on the PC industry. Yet Apple's gross margin dropped to 34%, 14 points below the company's 10-year average. In June 1993, Sculley was replaced by Michael Spindler, the company's president.

The Spindler and Amelio Years, 1993–1997

12 Spindler killed the plan to put the Mac OS on Intel chips and announced that Apple would license a handful of companies to make Mac clones. He tried to slash costs, which included cutting 16% of Apple's workforce, and pushed for international growth. In 1992, 45% of Apple's sales came from outside the United States. Yet despite these efforts, Apple lost momentum: A 1995 *Computerworld* survey found that none of the Windows users would consider buying a Mac, while more than half the Apple users expected to buy an Intel-based PC[8] (see **Exhibit 4**). Spindler, like his predecessor, had high hopes for a revolutionary OS

EXHIBIT 4 **Shipments and Installed Base of PC Microprocessor (in millions of units)**

Total Shipments	1992	1994	1996	1998	2000	2002	2004	2006	2007	2008	2009
Intel Technologies											
PC units shipped	30.6	47.8	76	105	156	126	170	230	261	287	294
PC installed base	122.2	211.4	347.5	542.5	839	1,111	1,433	1,863	2,124	2,411	2,705
Mac units shipped	NA	NA	NA	NA	NA	NA	NA	5.7	7.7	9.9	11.2
Intel-Mac installed base	NA	NA	NA	NA	NA	NA	NA	5.7	13.4	23.3	34.5
Motorola (680X0)											
Units shipped	3.9	3.9	0.8	0.2	NA	NA	NA	NA	NA	NA	NA
Installed base	16.5	24.9	26.8	27.5	NA	NA	NA	NA	NA	NA	NA
PowerPC											
Units shipped	0	0.8	4	3.5	4.7	3.1	3.5	NA	NA	NA	NA
Installed base	0	0.8	7.8	14.1	22.2	29.4	36.2	NA	NA	NA	NA

Source: Adapted from Gartner Dataquest, InfoCorp., IDC, Merrill Lynch, and Credit Suisse data.

Notes: Between 5% and 10% of total microprocessor shipments go into non-PC end products. In any given year, as much as 60% of microprocessors in the total installed base involve older technologies that were probably no longer in use. The figures for PowerPC shipments included microprocessors destined for Sony PlayStation and Xbox 360 machines. Figures for "Mac units shipped" over Macintosh calendar year sales.

NA = Not Available or Not Applicable.

[8] David B. Yoffie, "Apple Computer 1996," HBS No. 796-126 (Boston: Harvard Business School Publishing, 1996).

that would turn around the company's fate. But at the end of 1995, Apple and IBM parted ways on Taligent and Kaleida. After spending more than $500 million, neither side wanted to switch to a new technology.[9] Following a $69 million loss in Apple's first fiscal quarter of 1996, the company appointed another new CEO, Gilbert Amelio, an Apple director.[10]

13 Amelio proclaimed that Apple would return to its premium-price differentiation strategy. Yet Macintosh sales fell amid Apple's failure to produce a new OS that would keep it ahead of Microsoft's Windows 95. Amelio ended up turning to Steve Jobs. In December 1996, Amelio announced the acquisition of NeXT Software (founded by Jobs after he left Apple) and plans to develop a new OS based on work done by NeXT. Jobs also returned to Apple as a part-time adviser. Despite more job cuts and restructuring efforts, Apple lost $1.6 billion under Amelio and its worldwide market share tumbled to around 3% (see **Exhibit 3**). In September 1997, Steve Jobs became the company's interim CEO.

Steve Jobs and the Apple Turnaround

14 Steve Jobs moved quickly to reshape Apple. In August 1997, Apple announced that Microsoft would invest $150 million in Apple and make a five-year commitment to develop core products, such as Microsoft Office, for the Mac. Jobs abruptly halted the Macintosh licensing program. Almost 99% of customers who had bought clones were existing Mac users, cannibalizing Apple's profits.[11] Jobs also refused to license the latest Mac OS. Apple's 15 product lines were slashed to just four categories—desktop and portable Macintoshes, for consumers and professionals. Other restructuring efforts involved hiring Taiwanese contract assemblers to manufacture Mac products and revamping Apple's distribution system from smaller outlets to national chains. In addition, in 1997, Apple launched a website to set up direct sales for the first time. Internally, Jobs focused on reinvigorating innovation. Apple pared down its inventory significantly and increased its spending on R&D (see **Exhibit 5**).

15 Jobs's first real coup came with the iMac in August 1998. The $1,299 all-in-one computer featured colorful translucent cases with a distinct eggshell design. The iMac also supported "plug-and-play" peripherals, such as printers, that were designed for Windows-based

EXHIBIT 5 **PC Manufacturers' Key Operating Measures, 1997–2009**

	1997	2000	2003	2006	2008	2009
Gross margins (%)						
Apple	21%	28%	29%	30%	35%	40%
Dell	23%	21%	19%	18%	18%	18%
Hewlett-Packard	38%	31%	29%	26%	24%	24%
R&D/Sales (%)						
Apple	12%	5%	8%	4%	3%	3%
Dell	1%	2%	1%	1%	1%	1%
Hewlett-Packard	7%	5%	5%	4%	3%	2%

Source: Compiled from Capital IQ, accessed March 2010.

Note: All information is on a fiscal-year basis. Apple's fiscal year ends in September, HP in October, and Dell in January.

[9] Charles McCoy, "Apple, IBM Kill Kaleida Labs Venture," *The Wall Street Journal,* November 20, 1995.

[10] Louise Kehoe, "Apple Shares Drop Sharply," *The Financial Times,* January 19, 1996.

[11] David Kirkpatrick, "The Second Coming of Apple," *Fortune,* November 9, 1998.

machines for the first time. Thanks to the iMac, Apple's sales outpaced the industry's average for the first time in years. Following Jobs's return, Apple posted a $309 million profit in its 1998 fiscal year, reversing the previous year's $1 billion loss.

16 Another priority for Jobs was to break away from Apple's tired, tarnished image. Jobs wanted Apple to be a cultural force. Not coincidentally, perhaps, Jobs retained his position as CEO of Pixar, an animation studio that he had bought in 1986. (Jobs later sold Pixar to Walt Disney for $7.4 billion in 2006.) Through multi-million dollar marketing campaigns such as the successful "Think Different" ads and catchy slogans ("The ultimate all-in-one design", "It just works"), Apple promoted itself as a hip alternative to other computer brands. Apple ads were placed in popular and fashion magazines as well, venturing out from general computer publications. Later on, Apple highlighted its computers as the world's "greenest lineup of notebooks" that were energy efficient and used recyclable materials.[12] The goal was to differentiate the Macintosh amid intense competition in the PC industry.

THE PERSONAL COMPUTER INDUSTRY

17 While Apple pioneered the first usable "personal" computing devices, it was IBM that brought PCs into the mainstream in the 1980's. But by the early 1990's, a new standard known as "Wintel" (the Windows OS combined with an Intel processor) dominated the industry. Thousands of manufacturers—ranging from Dell Computer to no-name clone makers—built PCs around standard building blocks from Microsoft and Intel. Growth was driven by lower prices and expanding capabilities. The overall industry continued to boom through the early 2000's, propelled by Internet-demand and emerging markets such as China and the Middle East. By 2010, more than one billion PCs were in use around the world.

18 Revenue growth, however, failed to keep pace with volume growth. Despite PCs that were faster, with more memory and storage, average selling prices (ASPs) declined by a compound annual rate of 8% per year between 1999 and 2005.[13] Prices for key components (CPUs, memory, and hard disk drives) dropped even faster, by an average annual rate of 30%.[14] As a result, most PC manufacturers' average profit margin fell below 5%.[15] The standardization of components also led PC makers to cut spending on research and development. By the early 2000's, Dell—then the industry leader—devoted about 1% of revenue to R&D. Contract manufacturing in Taiwan and China became popular and took over more complex areas, such as design and testing.

19 New PC products emerged as well. More expensive laptop computers gained traction starting in the late 1980's. Two decades later, portable PCs represented 57% of worldwide PC shipments and were expected to reach 70% by 2012.[16] Like desktops, lower prices led to higher sales volume; the ASP for a laptop was around $544 towards the end of 2009, nearly half of the ASP in 2007.[17] Meanwhile, a new sub-product category of netbooks took

[12] http://www.apple.com/macbookair/environment.html, accessed March 2010.

[13] IDC (International Data Corp.) data, as cited in Graham-Hackett, "Computers: Hardware," Standard & Poor's Industry Surveys, December 8, 2005, p. 7.

[14] Bill Shope and Elizabeth Borbolla, "IT Hardware: Top Issue for 2006 and Industry Primer" (analysts' report), JP Morgan, January 30, 2006, pp. 28–29.

[15] Michelle Kessler, "Computer Industry Sits at Critical Crossroads," *USA Today,* March 5, 2007, p. B1, accessed via Factiva.

[16] "PC Market Rebound Will Drive Double-Digit Growth Through 2014, According to IDC," IDC Press Release (Framingham, MA, March 15, 2010).

[17] David Wong, Amit Chandra, and Lindsey Matherne, "Chip/Computer/Cellphone Data," (research report), Wachovia Capital Markets LLC, December 10, 2007, pp. 33–34; "November Computer Technology U.S. Retail Sales Revenue Positive for First Time in 2009, According to NPD," NPD Press Release (Port Washington, NY, December 17, 2009).

off during the global economic downturn in 2009. These light-weight mini notebooks had limited storage capacity and were optimized for the Web. Price-sensitive buyers loved the price; a netbook usually sold for around $400.[18]

Buyers and Distribution

20 PC buyers fell into five categories: Home, small- and medium-sized business (SMB), corporate, education, and government. Home consumers represented the biggest segment, accounting for nearly half of worldwide PC shipments.[19] While all buyers cared deeply about price, home consumers also valued design, mobility, and wireless connectivity, business consumers balanced price with service and support, and education buyers depended on software availability.

21 In distribution, a significant shift occurred in the early 1990's when more knowledgeable PC customers moved away from full-service dealers that primarily sold established brands to business managers. Instead, larger enterprises bought directly from the manufacturer, while home and SMB customers started to buy PCs through superstores (Wal-Mart, Costco), electronics retailers (Best Buy, Circuit City), and Web-based retailers. At the same time, the so-called "white box" channel—which featured generic machines assembled by local entrepreneurs—represented a large channel for PC sales, especially in key emerging markets. "White-box" PCs reportedly represented about 30% of the overall market in 2009, and were most frequently sold into the small office and home office markets.[20]

PC Manufacturers

22 The four top PC vendors—Hewlett-Packard, Dell, Acer, and Lenovo—accounted for 55% of worldwide shipments (see **Exhibit 6**). Industry leader Hewlett-Packard (HP) had staged an impressive comeback following a rough period with the acquisition of Compaq Computer in 2002. HP was also the world's largest technology company, diversifying into services, servers, and storage. Around two thirds of HP's PCs were sold outside the U.S. HP also had a strong retail presence through 110,000 worldwide outlets. Dell on the other hand, stumbled (see **Exhibit 7**). Its distinct combination of direct sales and build-to-order manufacturing was a hit in the corporate market. Yet Dell was late to catch the consumer boom. Founder Michael Dell returned as CEO in January 2007 and emphasized consumer-friendly products, re-entered retail distribution, and pushed for international expansion. Still, Dell struggled with cost controls and poor margins. In 2009, Dell was the only top four PC vendor to lose its worldwide market share.

23 Acer and Lenovo, active in emerging markets, both benefited from acquisitions of high-profile U.S. PC brands. In 2007, Taiwan-based Acer bought Gateway, a leading U.S. PC brand, and became the third-largest PC vendor in the world. Acer also acquired Packard-Bell, a PC maker with a strong presence in Europe (where Acer also was a leading brand). The company's worldwide PC shipments grew 22% in 2009, the fastest among its competitors, thanks to Acer's strength in notebooks and netbooks.[21] China-based Lenovo vaulted into the front ranks of PC vendors in 2005 when it acquired IBM's money-losing PC business for $1.75 billion. Lenovo's greatest strength was its dominant position in China, where it commanded a third of the market.

[18] Thomas W. Smith, "Computers: Hardware," Standard & Poor's Industry Surveys, October 22, 2009, p. 3.

[19] Ibid, p. 27.

[20] "Why Buy a Generic PC?" PC Generic, April 30, 2009, http://www.pcgeneric.com/articles/5131/Whybuy-a-generic-PC, accessed March 2010.

[21] "Global PC market Leaps Back to Double-Digit Growth in the Fourth Quarter, Led by a Record Quarter in the U.S., According to IDC," IDC Press Release (Framingham, MA, January 13, 2010).

EXHIBIT 6 **PC Manufacturers: Worldwide Market Shares, 2000–2009**

	2000	2002	2004	2006	2007	2008	2009
Hewlett-Packard[a]	7.8%	16.0%	15.8%	16.5%	18.8%	18.9%	20.3%
Dell	11.4%	15.1%	17.9%	16.6%	14.9%	14.7%	13.1%
Acer			3.6%	5.8%	7.9%	10.9%	13.0%
Lenovo[b]			2.3%	7.1%	7.5%	7.6%	8.5%
Toshiba	3.0%	3.2%	3.6%	3.9%	4.1%	4.8%	5.4%
Fujitsu Siemens	5.1%	4.2%	4.0%				
IBM[b]	7.1%	5.9%	5.9%				
Compaq[a]	13.0%						
Packard Bell NEC	4.5%	3.3%					
Apple	3.5%	2.3%	1.9%	2.3%	2.6%	3.4%	4.2%
Total shipments (in millions)	128.5	136.9	177.5	235.4	269.1	287.6	294.2

Source: "PC Market Still Strong in Q4 With Solid Growth Across Regions, According to IDC" (press release), IDC Press Release, January 16, 2008; IDC data, as cited in Scott H. Kessler, "Computers: Hardware" (industry survey), Standard & Poor's, April 26, 2007, p. 7, and in previous editions of that survey; Apple Inc. annual financial reports; and casewriter estimates. Data for 2009 based on preliminary figures reported in "Global PC Market Leaps Back to Double-Digit Growth in the Fourth Quarter, Led by a Record Quarter in the U.S., According to IDC," IDC Press Release, January 13, 2010.

Note: Market share data for Apple are derived from Macintosh unit sales, as reported in the company's annual reports. The sampling of market shares for other companies comes mainly from annual listings of the top five PC makers, as measured by IDC. Absence of a figure indicates that a company placed below the top five in a given year.

[a]Hewlett-Packard acquired Compaq in mid-2002. The 2002 market share figure for HP incorporates Compaq sales for the first part of that year.

[b]Lenovo acquired IBM's PC business in mid-2005. The 2005 market share figure for Lenovo incorporates IBM sales for the first part of that year.

EXHIBIT 7 **Apple's Competitors: Selected Financial Information, 2000–2009 (in millions of dollars)**

	2000	2002	2004	2006	2008	2009
Hewlett-Packard						
Total revenues	48,870	56,588	79,905	91,658	118,364	114,552
Cost of sales	34,813	41,457	60,621	69,178	89,370	87,198
R&D	2,627	3,368	3,563	3,591	3,543	2,819
SG&A	6,984	8,763	10,496	11,266	13,326	11,613
Net income	3,697	-903	3,497	6,198	8,329	7,660
Total assets	34,009	70,710	76,138	81,981	113,331	114,799
Total liabilities	19,800	34,448	38,574	43,837	74,389	74,282
Total shareholders' equity	14,209	36,262	37,564	38,144	38,942	40,517
Gross margin	28.3%	26.4%	23.9%	24.3%	24.2%	23.6%
R&D/sales	5.4%	6.0%	4.5%	3.9%	3.0%	2.5%
SG&A/sales	14.3%	15.5%	13.1%	12.3%	11.3%	10.1%
Return on sales	7.6%	-1.6%	4.4%	6.8%	7.0%	6.7%
Market capitalization[a]	66,896	57,764	58,405	110,546	85,461	119,532

[a]Market capitalization figures for each company is based on the date the earnings were filed with the SEC.

(Continued)

EXHIBIT 7 *(Continued)*

	2000	2002	2004	2006	2008	2009
Dell						
Total revenues	25,265	41,444	55,788	61,133	61,101	52,902
Cost of sales	20,047	33,892	45,897	49,462	49,998	43,404
R&D	374	464	458	610	663	624
SG&A	2,387	3,544	4,968	7,446	6,966	6,465
Net income	1,666	2,645	3,602	2,947	2,478	1,433
Total assets	11,471	19,311	23,252	27,561	26,500	33,652
Total liabilities	6,163	13,031	19,205	23,826	22,229	28,011
Total shareholders' equity	5,308	6,280	4,047	3,735	4,271	5,641
Gross margin	20.7%	18.2%	17.7%	19.1%	18.2%	18.0%
R&D/sales	1.5%	1.1%	0.8%	1.0%	1.1%	1.2%
SG&A/sales	9.4%	8.6%	8.9%	12.2%	11.4%	12.2%
Return on sales	6.6%	6.4%	6.5%	4.8%	4.1%	2.7%
Market capitalization[b]	123,194	90,572	68,195	44,640	20,193	28,485
Intel						
Total revenues	33,726	26,764	34,209	35,382	37,586	35,127
Cost of sales	12,650	13,340	14,301	17,164	16,742	15,566
R&D	3,897	4,034	4,778	5,873	5,722	5,653
SG&A	5,089	4,334	4,659	6,138	5,452	5,234
Net income	10,535	3,117	7,516	5,044	5,292	4,369
Total assets	47,945	44,224	48,143	48,368	50,472	53,095
Total liabilities	10,623	8,756	9,564	11,616	10,926	11,391
Total shareholders' equity	37,322	35,468	38,579	36,752	39,546	41,704
Gross margin	62%	50%	58%	51%	55%	56%
R&D/sales	12%	15%	14%	17%	15%	16%
SG&A/sales	15%	16%	14%	17%	15%	15%
Return on sales	31%	12%	22%	14%	14%	12%
Market capitalization	197,341	105,418	147,954	120,242	67,189	115,286
Microsoft						
Total revenues	22,956	28,365	36,835	44,282	60,420	58,437
Cost of sales	3,002	5,699	6,596	7,650	11,598	12,155
R&D	3,772	6,299	7,735	6,584	8,105	9,010
SG&A	5,176	8,095	10,640	12,276	16,587	16,296
Net income	9,421	5,355	8,168	12,599	17,681	14,569
Total assets	52,150	67,646	94,368	69,597	72,793	77,888
Total liabilities	10,782	15,466	19,543	29,493	36,507	38,330

[b]Dell's market capitalization figure for 2009 is from March 18, 2010 rather than the filing date.

EXHIBIT 7 (*Continued*)

	2000	2002	2004	2006	2008	2009
Total shareholders' equity	41,368	52,180	74,825	40,104	36,286	39,558
Gross margin	87%	80%	82%	83%	81%	79%
R&D/sales	16%	22%	21%	15%	13%	15%
SG&A/sales	23%	29%	29%	28%	27%	28%
Return on sales	41%	19%	22%	28%	29%	25%
Market capitalization	322,651	258,967	295,667	257,724	235,364	212,163
Nokia (in million Euros)						
Total revenues	30,376	30,016	29,371	41,121	50,710	40,984
Cost of sales	19,072	18,278	18,179	27,742	32,935	27,569
R&D	2,584	3,052	3,661	3,897	5,922	5,879
SG&A	2,804	3,239	3,175	3,980	5,515	4,963
Net income	3,938	3,381	3,192	4,306	3,988	891
Total assets	19,890	23,327	22,669	22,617	39,582	35,738
Total liabilities	9,082	9,046	8,438	10,649	25,374	22,650
Total shareholders' equity	10,808	14,281	14,231	11,968	14,208	13,088
Gross margin	37%	39%	38%	33%	35%	33%
R&D/sales	9%	10%	12%	9%	12%	14%
SG&A/sales	9%	11%	11%	10%	11%	12%
Return on sales	13%	11%	11%	10%	8%	2%
Market capitalization	119,702	60,935	54,271	65,157	27,107	40,055
RIM						
Total revenues	85	294	595	2,066	6,009	11,065
Cost of sales	49	210	320	926	2,929	5,968
R&D	8	37	63	159	360	685
SG&A	14	94	108	314	881	1,496
Net income	10	(28)	52	375	1,294	1,893
Total assets	337	948	1,937	2,314	5,511	8,101
Total liabilities	26	71	215	319	1,578	2,227
Total shareholders' equity	311	877	1,722	1,995	3,934	5,874
Gross margin	43%	29%	46%	55%	51%	46%
R&D/sales	9%	13%	11%	8%	6%	6%
SG&A/sales	16%	32%	18%	15%	15%	14%
Return on sales	12%	-10%	9%	18%	22%	17%
Market capitalization	3,057	2,203	12,295	13,625	66,461	33,899

Source: Created by casewriter using data from Capital IQ, March 2010.

Note: All information is on a fiscal-year basis, unless noted otherwise. HP's fiscal year ends in October, Dell in January, Intel and Nokia in December, Microsoft in June, and RIM in February.

Suppliers, Complements, and Substitutes

24 Suppliers to the PC industry fell into two categories: Those that made products (such as memory chips, disk drives, and keyboards) with many sources; and those that made products—notably microprocessors and operating systems—that had just a few sources. Products in the first category were widely available at highly competitive prices. Products in the second category were supplied chiefly by two firms: Intel and Microsoft.

25 **Microprocessors** Microprocessors, or CPUs, were the hardware "brains" of a PC. Intel commanded roughly 80% of the PC CPU market. Competition emerged in the 1990s from companies like Advanced Micro Devices and more recently, VIA Technologies. Still, Intel remained the market leader with leading-edge technology, manufacturing scale, and a powerful brand. Since 1970, CPU prices (adjusted for changes in computing power) had dropped by an average of 30% per year.[22]

26 **Operating system** An OS was *the* software that managed a PC's resources and supported its applications. Microsoft had dominated this market since the IBM PC in the 1980's. More than 90% of all PCs in the world ran on some version of Windows. Microsoft's big hit in the last decade was Windows XP. Introduced in October 2001, XP sold 17 million copies in its first eight weeks of sales. Developed at a cost of $1 billion, XP initially garnered Microsoft between $45 and $60 in revenue per copy.[23] Vista, the next version introduced in 2007, did not fare as well. Consumers complained about its sluggish performance and were reluctant to upgrade to Vista. Two years later, Windows 7 was released to strong reviews. Analysts estimated that Microsoft spent $1.5 billion to develop Windows 7 and another $1 billion in marketing. Microsoft shipped over 60 million units of the new OS in its first quarter of sales in the fall of 2009, generating almost $7 billion in revenue. Windows 7 was the fastest selling OS in history.[24]

27 **Application software, content, and complementary products** The value of a computer corresponded directly to the complementary software, content, and hardware that were available on that platform. Key application software included word processing, presentation graphics, desktop publishing, and Internet browsing. Since the early 1990's, the number of applications available on PCs exploded, while ASPs for PC software collapsed. Microsoft was the largest vendor of software for Wintel PCs and, aside from Apple itself, for Macs as well.[25] Firms such as Google even offered productivity software (Google Apps) for free. PCs also benefited from a wide selection of content, and a vast array of complementary hardware, ranging from printers to multimedia devices.

28 **Alternative technologies** Since the early 2000s, consumer electronics (CE) products, ranging from cell phones and PDAs to TV set-top boxes to game consoles, started to encroach on functionality that was once the sole purview of the PC. For example, advanced game devices like Sony PlayStation3 allowed consumers to watch DVDs, surf the Web, and play games directly online in addition to play traditional video games. At the same time, smartphones increasingly functioned as handheld computers, allowing users to do email, visit websites, and manage their online lives. While several industry insiders worried about the impact of digital devices on the PC industry, Jobs had a different view—positioning the Macintosh at the heart of his business strategy for Apple.

[22] Clyde Montevirgen and Karan Kawaguchi, "Semiconductors," Standard & Poor's Industry Surveys, May 31, 2007, p. 25.

[23] David B. Yoffie, Dharmesh M. Mehta, and Rudina I. Suseri, "Microsoft in 2005," HBS Case No. 705-505, (Boston: Harvard Business School Publishing, 2006).

[24] "Microsoft Reports Record Second Quarter Results," Microsoft Press Release (Redmond, WA, January 28, 2010).

[25] Arik Hesseldahl, "What's Behind Apple's iWork?" BusinessWeek Online, August 10, 2007, via Factiva, accessed April 2010.

THE MACINTOSH AND APPLE'S "DIGITAL HUB" STRATEGY

29 In 2001, marking Apple's 25th anniversary, Jobs presented his vision for the Macintosh in what he called the "digital hub." He believed that the Macintosh had a real advantage for consumers who were becoming entrenched in a digital lifestyle, using digital cameras, portable music players, and digital camcorders, not to mention mobile phones. The Mac could be the preferred "hub" to control, integrate, and add value to these devices. Jobs viewed Apple's control of both hardware and software, one of the very few remaining in the PC industry, as a unique strength.

30 Apple subsequently revamped its product line to offer machines that could deliver a cutting-edge, tightly integrated user experience. Although the company remained committed to the education market, new PC products focused on home consumers' lifestyle. Thanks to several technological innovations and a new retail strategy, Apple became the fourth-largest PC vendor in the U.S. market with an 8% share by the end of 2009.[26] The company's greatest strength lay in the premium-priced PC category; 91% of PCs priced $1,000 and above in the U.S. market were sold by Apple.[27]

31 **Shift to Intel CPUs** Apple introduced the first Mac computer to run on an Intel chip in 2006. By the next year, the entire Macintosh line ran on Intel chips that were better for laptops as well as for higher performance desktops and servers.[28] Critical to the Mac's resurgence, Intel's chips enabled Apple to build laptops that were both faster and less power-hungry.[29] By the 2009 fiscal year, notebooks accounted for 69% of all Macintosh sales compared to 38% seven years ago. With "Intel inside," the Mac also became a machine that could natively run a Windows OS along with Windows applications. This capability potentially offset a long-standing disadvantage to choosing a Mac—the relative lack of Macintosh software.

32 **Operating system** Apple introduced a new OS in 2001, the first fully overhauled platform released since 1984. The Mac OS X was based on UNIX, a more stable, industrial-strength OS favored by computer professionals. Analysts estimated that OS X cost Apple roughly $1 billion to develop. Apple issued upgrades every 12 to 18 months, in greater frequency than what Microsoft had done with Windows. The sixth version, named Leopard, was released in October 2007 and sold two million copies in its opening weekend.[30] Leopard ran on more than half of all Mac computers by January 2010.[31] Early sales of the following Snow Leopard version indicated high adoption rates as well. According to one market survey, 81% of Leopard users were "very satisfied" with the OS compared to 53% of Windows XP users.[32]

[26] "Global PC market Leaps Back to Double-Digit Growth in the Fourth Quarter, Led by a Record Quarter in the U.S., According to IDC," IDC Press Release (Framingham, MA, January 13, 2010).

[27] "Windows 7 Release May Test Apple's Winning Streak," Reuters News, October 14, 2009, via Factiva, accessed March 2010.

[28] Nick Turner and Patrick Seitz, "Apple's Intel Machines Ahead of Schedule," *Investor's Business Daily,* January 11, 2006, p. A4; Thomas Clayburn and Darrell Dunn, "Apple Bets Its Chips," *InformationWeek,* "January 16, 2006, p. 26; Daniel Drew Turner, "Apple Shows New Intel Notebooks, Software," *eWeek*, January 10, 2006; "Apple, Inc.," Hoover's, Inc., www.hoovers.com, accessed January 2008.

[29] Stephen Fenech, "Apple's New Core: New Macs with Intel Dual Processors Revealed," *Daily Telegraph* (London), January 18, 2006, p. 11.

[30] Robert Semple, "Apple Inc., Leopard's Lickin' Its Chops," (research report) Credit Suisse North America, October 30, 2007, p. 1.

[31] "Mac OS X Market Share Up 29%, Leopard Still Most Common," AppleInsider blog, February 27, 2010, http://www.appleinsider.com/print/10/02/27/mac_os_x_market_share_up_29_leopard_still_most_common.html, accessed March 2010.

[32] "Apple's Mac OS X Snow Leopard Sales Double Previous Records," AppleInsider blog, October 19, 2009, http://www.appleinsider.com/articles/09/10/19/apples_mac_os_x_snow_leopard_sales_double_previous_rec ordords.html, accessed March 2010.

33 **Applications** Proprietary, Apple-developed applications made up a growing segment of the company's efforts to support the Macintosh line. Building programs such as those in the iLife suite (iPhoto, iTunes, iWeb) required Apple to assume significant development costs.[33] At the same time, the company continued to depend on the cooperation of key independent software vendors—especially Microsoft. In 2003, after Apple developed its Web browser Safari, Microsoft said it would no longer develop Internet Explorer for the Mac. However, Microsoft did continue to develop its Office suite for Macintosh. Full interoperability with Office products was critical to Macintosh's viability. Microsoft benefitted from this arrangement as well. By one estimate, it sold close to $1 billion of Office software to Mac users. Jobs still hedged his bets by developing iWork productivity applications, including Pages, Keynote, and Numbers.[34]

34 **Distribution** The first Apple retail store opened in McLean, Virginia, in 2001. Apple not only wanted consumers to look at the eye-catching Macintosh designs, it also wanted people to directly use and experience Apple's software. The Apple retail experience gave many consumers their first exposure to the Macintosh product line. By 2009, the company estimated that half of all retail Mac sales were to "new to Mac" customers.[35] The retail division—with more than 280 stores in 10 countries—grew to account for 16% of Apple's total revenue.[36] Observers viewed Apple's retail strategy as a huge success: One analyst said that the company had become "the Nordstrom of technology."[37] Other retail revenues were explored as well, such as entering a partnership with Best Buy, the world's largest electronics retailer. Yet a key factor in bringing people into the stores, most analysts believed, was the popularity of the iPod.

MOVING BEYOND THE MACINTOSH

35 Apple's shift towards a digital hub strategy was initiated by the debut of the iPod in 2001, followed by the iPhone in 2007, then the iPad in 2010. These product lines set Apple on a path toward becoming a full-fledged digital convergence company. The change in the company's name from 'Apple Computer' to "Apple Inc." in 2007 marked the official repositioning of the company.

The iPod Sensation

36 While the prospects for the Macintosh business had improved, it was the iPod that set Apple on its explosive growth path. The iPod was initially one of many portable digital music players based on the MP3 standard. Thanks to its sleek design, simple user interface, and large storage, it soon became "an icon of the Digital Age," in the words of one writer.[38] While early MP3 players only stored an hour of music, the first iPod stored up to 1,000 songs and retailed for $399. Over the next five years, Apple delivered one new innovative

[33] Brent Schlender, "How Big Can Apple Get?" *Fortune,* February 21, 2005, p. 66.

[34] Hesseldahl, "What's Behind Apple's iWork?"; Walter S. Mossberg, "New Office for Mac Speeds Up Programs, Integrates Formats," *The Wall Street Journal,* January 3, 2008, p. B1, via Factiva, accessed January 2008.

[35] "Store Financials Blaze Despite Down Economy," Ifoapplestores.com, October 19, 2009, http://www.ifoapplestore.com/the_stores.html, accessed April 2010.

[36] Apple Inc. 10-K/A, January 25, 2010 (Cupertino, CA, 2010), p. 11 and p. 14.

[37] Katie Hafner, "Inside Apple Stores, a Certain Aura Enchants the Faithful," *The New York Times,* December 27, 2007, p. C1, via Factiva, accessed December 2007.

[38] Peter Burrows and Ronald Glover, with Heather Green, "Steve Jobs' Magic Kingdom," *BusinessWeek,* February 6, 2006, p. 62.

design after another. By 2010, Apple reportedly held more than 70% of the MP3 market in the United States.[39]

37 The economics of the iPod were stellar by CE industry standards. The iPod nano, for example, had gross margins of around 40% in 2007.[40] The biggest cost component for the nano was flash memory, which could account for more than half of the bill of materials. Recognizing the importance of flash memory, Apple set out to insure that it got the best prices. In November 2005, for example, Apple agreed to pay $500 million up-front to Intel and Micron to secure "a substantial portion" of their memory output.[41] Similar deals were made with Hynix, Samsung, and Toshiba. Apple subsequently became one of the largest purchasers of flash memory in the world.

38 Apple's approach to developing and marketing the iPod was more open than its strategy for the Macintosh. The iPod could sync with Windows as well as a Mac. Apple also built an ecosystem with the iPod accessory market that ranged from fashionable cases to docking stations. For every $3 dollars spent on an iPod, according to one analyst, consumers spent another $1 on iPod add-on products.[42] Apple, through a program that licensed its "Made for iPod" logo, earned an estimated 5% of the retail price of such items.[43] Many analysts also believed that the iPod's "halo effect" had benefitted Apple's Mac business.[44]

39 Within the iPod product line, the Touch was Apple's premier device. Released in 2007, the Touch was the first iPod that had built-in WiFi, a 3.5 inch screen, and a multi-touch graphical interface. Popular handheld game players such as the Nintendo DS and Sony PSP suddenly found themselves competing with the Touch. Some 35 million iPod Touch devices had been sold by April 2010.[45]

40 While iPods were available in all price segments, iPod ASPs generally ran $50 to $100 higher than the competition.[46] Rivals in the MP3 player market included SanDisk, Creative, and Samsung; each had a market share below 10%. Microsoft also introduced its Zune line of music players in 2006. At the hardware level, most players were roughly comparable to iPod models. Yet competitors found themselves at a major disadvantage with the emergence of Apple's iTunes store.

[39] Yinka Adegoke, "Apple Seen Having Upper Hand in Music Negotiations," Reuters News, April 20, 2007, accessed via Factiva; Ben Cherny and Roger Cheng, "Pressure from IPhone, Rivals Weighs on Latest IPod Debut," Dow Jones Newswires, September 4, 2007, accessed via Factiva; Ricki Morell, "MP3 Options, From Apple to Zune," *The Boston Globe,* June 8, 2008, p. G2, accessed via Factiva; Chris Sorensen, "A Pod-Forsaken Future?" *Toronto Star,* June 14, 2008, p. B1, accessed via Factiva.

[40] Thomas Ricker, "iSuppli: New iPod Nano Costs Apple Less than $83 in Components," September 19, 2007, http://www.engadget.com/2007/09/19/isuppli-new-ipod-nanos-cost-apple-just-59-and-83-in-component/, accessed March 2010.

[41] Arik Hesseldahl, "Unpeeling Apple's Nano," BusinessWeek Online, September 22, 2007, via Factiva, accessed September 2007.

[42] Damon Darlin, "The iPod Ecosystem," *New York Times,* February 3, 2006.

[43] Damon Darlin, "Add-Ons Have Become a Billion-Dollar Bonanza," *The New York Times*, February 3, 2006, p. C1, accessed via Factiva; Nick Wingfield and Don Clark, "Apple Goes Hi-Fi," *The Wall Street Journal,* March 1, 2006, p. B1, accessed via Factiva; Peter Burrows, "Welcome to Planet Apple," *BusinessWeek,* July 9, 2007 p. 88, accessed via Factiva.

[44] Chris Whitmore, Sherri Scribner, and Joakim Mahlberg, "Beyond iPod" (analysts' report), Deutsche Bank, September 21, 2005, p. 31; Megan Graham-Hackett, "Computers: Hardware" (industry survey), Standard & Poor's, December 8, 2005, p. 8; Arik Hesseldahl, "Apple's Growing Army of Converts," BusinessWeek Online, November 10, 2005, via Factiva.

[45] Jason Kincaid, "Apple Has Sold 450,000 iPads, 50,000 Million iPhones to Date," TechCrunch, April 8, 2010, http://techcrunch.com/2010/04/08/apple-has-sold-450000-ipads-50-million-iphones-to-date/, accessed April 2010.

[46] Robert Semple, Stephanie Sun, and Thompson Wu, "Apple Computer Inc." (analysts' report), Credit Suisse, June 5, 2007, p. 6.

41 **iTunes** Two features which dramatically differentiated Apple's iPods were its iTunes desktop software, which synchronized iPods with computers; and its iTunes Music Store, which opened in April 2003. The two, in combination, completed Apple's vision of an entertainment hub.[47] The iTunes store was the first legal site that allowed music downloads on a pay-per-song basis. Visitors could pay 99 cents per song for a title offered by all five major record labels and by thousands of independent music labels. The downloaded songs could be played on the user's computer, burned onto a CD, or transferred to an iPod. Within three days of launching the service, PC owners had downloaded one million copies of free iTunes software and had paid for one million songs.[48] Customers loved the vast music selections and ease of use, transforming the iTunes store into the number one music store in the world.[49] By February 2010, it had sold 10 billion songs and featured the world's largest music catalog. Offerings expanded to audiobooks and TV shows, including the latest episodes of popular shows such as "American Idol." Over 8,000 movies titles could be rented or downloaded to "own" as well, catering to iPod Touch owners.

42 The launch of the iTunes store had a galvanic impact on iPod sales. Before the advent of iTunes, Apple sold an average of 113,000 iPods per quarter. After iTunes' launch, iPod sales shot up to 733,000 units, and exploded thereafter.[50] The direct impact of iTunes on Apple's profitability was far less impressive. Of the 99 cents that Apple collected per song, as much as 70 cents went to the music label that owned it, and about 20 cents went toward the cost of credit card processing. That left Apple with only about a dime of revenue per track, from which Apple had to pay for its website, along with other direct and indirect costs.[51] In essence, Jobs had created a razor-and-blade business, only in reverse: Here, the variable element served as a loss leader for a profit-driving durable good.[52]

43 Central to the initial iTunes model was a set of standards that guarded both the music labels' intellectual property and the proprietary technology inside the iPod. An Apple-exclusive "digital rights management" (DRM) system called FairPlay protected iTunes songs against piracy by limiting the number of computers that could play a downloaded song to five. FairPlay enabled Jobs to coax music executives into supporting the initial iTunes venture. No competing MP3 player could play FairPlay-protected songs.[53] Observers called iTunes a "Trojan horse" that allowed iPod-specific standards to invade users' music libraries and, in effect, to lock out other music players.[54] The iPod, meanwhile, could play content recorded in most standard formats.

44 Despite the success of iTunes, Apple had a tense relationship with content companies. They balked at its dominance of the digital music market and objected, in particular, to its fixed pricing structure. Music labels also saw their higher-priced CD sales pushed aside in favor of 99 cent a-lacarte downloads. Then, in a revised agreement announced in 2009, music labels gave up the DRM in exchange for flexible pricing, allowing them to charge more for new or popular songs. In addition, the removal of DRM allowed people to move the songs they bought on iTunes among different computers, phones, and other devices.

45 **Competition** Online music stores such as Amazon.com, Napster, and Walmart.com offered individual song downloads at competitive or discounted prices to iTunes. To put

[47] iTunes was available from 2001 with the original iPod but the functionality as a store did not come until 2003.

[48] Chris Taylor, "The 99¢ Solution," *Time,* November 17, 2003, p. 66, via Factiva, accessed November 2007.

[49] "iTunes Store Tops 10 Billion Songs Sold," Apple Inc. Press Release (Cupertino, CA, February 25, 2010).

[50] Ibid, p. 7.

[51] Shope, et al., "Apple Computer: iPod Economics II," p. 26; Ronald Grover and Peter Burrows, "Universal Music Takes on iTunes," *BusinessWeek,* October 22, 2007, p. 30, via Factiva, accessed October 2007.

[52] Ibid, pp. 8–10.

[53] Ibid, pp. 10–13.

[54] Taylor, "The 99¢ Solution"; Walker, "The Guts of the New Machine."

more pressure on Apple, music labels had allowed some of these stores to sell DRM-free music for more than a year before signing the new agreement with Apple. Some had subscription plans that allowed unlimited listening, starting at $5 per month. Social networking service MySpace—where millions of music artists maintained profile pages to promote their music—formed a partnership with three major music labels to unveil its own music service in 2008. Most of these competitors offered songs to play on various devices, including the iPod.

46 In addition to music streaming services from social networks, Apple and other MP3 players had to consider other challenges as well. Internet radio sites, such as Pandora and Last.fm, offered free streaming music. Spotify, Europe's largest legal online music jukebox that was partially owned by major music labels, allowed users to create their own playlists, share them, and stream free music like a virtual MP3 player. Although Spotify was not yet available in the U.S., in markets where service was available, some music labels were making more money from Spotify than iTunes.[55] Even mobile handset manufacturers such as Nokia started to bundle unlimited music services with their phones.

47 Jobs had two responses to these threats: In 2009, he bought Lala.com, a music streaming service. The deal raised speculations that Apple could be exploring an alternative model to store and play digital music, bypassing downloads on a media player all together. And of course, in June of 2007, he introduced the iPhone.

The iPhone

48 Hailed as *Time* magazine's "Invention of the Year," the iPhone represented Apple's bid to "reinvent the phone."[56] Two and a half years of development efforts had been devoted to the phone, guarded under intense secrecy, even within the company's own employees. The estimated development cost was around $150 million.

49 Entry into mobile phones might have been a risky move for Apple. The industry was dominated by Nokia, Motorola, and Samsung, with roughly 60% market share. In addition, products were characterized by short product life cycles (averaging six to nine months) and sophisticated technology, including radio technology, where Apple had little experience. In distribution, Apple faced powerful cellular carriers such as NTT DoCoMo and Vodafone, which controlled the networks and often the phones used on those networks. In the U.S., the top two carriers—Verizon Wireless and AT&T—collectively controlled more than 60% of the market and their networks were 'locked': An AT&T phone would only work on AT&T's network. Especially in the U.S., a handset manufacturer was usually dependent on the operator to provide a subsidy, which could lower the consumer's purchase price of a popular new handset by as much as $150 or more. In return, most consumers signed a two-year service contract with the carrier. Operators also maintained "walled gardens," which required consumers to access content only from their own networks. Price competition was especially intense in emerging markets like China and India, where, like the PC market, manufacturers had to compete with "white-box" phones.

50 In the early days when a mobile phone's foremost purpose was to make calls, consumers selected a handset based on its appearance and service provider. Starting in the mid-1990's, the industry's preference shifted towards feature phones that offered more attractive hardware designs and user-friendly interfaces, which was pioneered by Nokia, the world's largest mobile phone manufacturer. Multimedia functions, such as a camera, were added as well. Then smartphones rose to prominence in the next decade. These

[55] Michael Arrington, "Spotify Closing New Financing at €200 Million Valuation, Music Labels Already Shareholders," TechCrunch, August 9, 2009, http://techcrunch.com/2009/08/04/spotify-closing-new-financing-at-e200-million-valuation-music-labels-already-shareholders/, accessed April 2010.

[56] Donna Fuscaldo and Mark Boslet, "Jobs Says Apple to Rename Itself Apple Inc," Dow Jones News Service, January 9, 2007, via Factiva, accessed March 2010.

high-end phones brought multiple functions together in the palm of one's hand, serving as a mobile phone, Internet browser, PDA device (such as managing schedules and address book), and media player.

51 The iPhone, however, changed the rules in the industry. A revolutionary 3.5 inch touch-screen interface placed commands at the touch of users' fingertips without a physical keyboard. The iPhone's entire system ran on a specially adapted version of Apple's OS X platform. Above all, users found it intuitive to use. The first model was priced at $499 for an 8GB model. At that time, handsets that cost more than $300 accounted for only 5% of worldwide mobile phone sales.[57] AT&T, the exclusive U.S. operator for the iPhone, did not provide a subsidy. Instead, AT&T agreed to an unprecedented revenue sharing agreement with Apple, which gave Apple control over distribution, pricing, and branding.

52 The first generation iPhone sold about six million units over five quarters. However, more than a million had been sold in the "grey market," in which consumers bought iPhones from unauthorized resellers and used them on unsanctioned mobile networks. Apple's demand for a share of service revenue had led to only a few markets in the world with legal iPhone distribution. One estimate suggested that Apple could lose $1 billion over three years from the loss of service-share revenue.[58]

53 The second iPhone model was released in 2008. This version ran on a faster 3G network. More importantly, Apple had revamped the pricing model under a new agreement with AT&T. The carrier provided a subsidy on the phone in exchange for dropping the revenue sharing agreement. Consumers could buy an 8GB iPhone with a two-year contract for $199. An unsubsidized iPhone could cost $599 for the same version. With the 3G model, iPhone revenues exploded to $13 billion by the end of the 2009 fiscal year (see **Exhibit 1b**). A third version, the iPhone 3GS, went on sale in June 2009. With its release, the subsidized price of the 8GB iPhone dropped down to $99.

54 Analysts estimated that Apple generated an ASP of $562 from its iPhones, while competitors' ASP on similar handsets ranged between $300 and $400.[59] Falling component costs and design improvements helped to reduce the iPhone's cost structure. According to one analysis, the bill of materials for the latest 16GB model was just under $180.[60] The first iPhone with half of that storage capacity cost around $220 to build.[61] Lower prices and wider international distribution (94 countries) fueled sales. AT&T also benefitted from being the exclusive carrier for the iPhone in the U.S. The carrier generated an average revenue per user (ARPU) of $95 with the iPhone. The top three U.S. carrier's ARPU, in contrast, was around $50.[62]

[57] Nick Wingfield and Li Yuan, "Apple's iPhone: Is It Worth It?" *The Wall Street Journal,* January 10, 2007.

[58] Kharif and Burrows, "On the Trail of the Missing iPhones"; Peter Burrows, "Inside the iPhone Gray Market," BusinessWeek.com, February 13, 2008, accessed via Factiva; David Barboza, "Iphone on Gray Market Merry-Go-Round," *The International Herald Tribune,* February 19, 2008, p. 11, accessed via Factiva; Arik Hesseldahl and Jennifer L. Schenker, "iPhone 2.0 Takes on the World," BusinessWeek.com, June 9, 2008, accessed via Factiva; Jeremiah Marquez, "Asia Underground Market Awaits iPhone," Associated Press Newswires, July 11, 2008, accessed via Factiva; Maria Kiselyova and Sophie Taylor, "Apple in No Rush to Bring iPhone to Russia, China," Reuters News, July 17, 2008, accessed via Factiva; Paul Sonne, "iPhones Hot Even in Places Apple Has Yet to Reach," Associated Press Newswires, July 18, 2008, accessed via Factiva.

[59] "Apple Inc." (analyst report) Credit Suisse, February 4, 2010, p. 3; Om Malik, "U.S. Mobile Market: Highly Competitive and the iPhone Still Rocks," Gigaom, March 4, 2010, http://gigaom.com/2010/03/04/u-s-mobile-market-highly-competitive-and-the-iphone-still-rocks/, accessed April 2010.

[60] Arik Hesseldahl, "Tearing Down the iPhone 3GS," BusinessWeek.com, June 23, 2009, via Factiva, accessed April 2010.

[61] Ibid.

[62] Om Malik, "U.S. Mobile Market: Highly Competitive and the iPhone Still Rocks," Gigaom, March 4, 2010, http://gigaom.com/2010/03/04/u-s-mobile-market-highly-competitive-and-the-iphone-still-rocks/, accessed April 2010.

EXHIBIT 8 Worldwide Smartphone Sales to End User by Operating System, 2006–2009 (% of Total Market Share)

	2006	2007	2008	2009
Symbian	62.4%	63.5%	52.4%	46.9%
RIM	6.9%	9.6%	16.6%	19.9%
Microsoft	9.8%	12.0%	11.8%	8.7%
Mac OS X	NA	2.7%	8.2%	14.4%
Linux	17.6%	9.6%	7.6%	4.7%
Android[a]	NA	NA	0.5%	3.9%
Palm's WebOS[b]	NA	NA	NA	0.7%
Others	1.3%	1.1%	2.9%	0.6%

Source: Adapted from Gartner Smartphone Sales quarterly press releases between 2007 and 2009; "Gartner Says Worldwide Mobile Phone Sales to End Users Grew 8 Per Cent in Fourth Quarter 2009; Market Remained Flat in 2009," Gartner Press Release (Egham, UK, February 23, 2010).

[a]Android was introduced in 2008; data prior to that year is not applicable.

[b]Palm's WebOs was introduced in 2009; data prior to that year is not applicable.

55 Within two years, the iPhone went from zero to 30% of Apple's total revenue. In terms of global smartphones sales, the iPhone was the biggest growth story, capturing more than 14% of the market (see **Exhibit 8**). Like the iTunes store, a key factor behind the iPhone sensation was the extension of the iPhone's ecosystem with the launch of the Apple App Store in 2008.

56 **App Store** Software applications for PDAs and smartphones had been around for years. Palm Inc., the PDA market leader in the 1990's, was known for its wealth of third party-developed applications. Microsoft similarly had more than 20,000 apps written for its mobile OS. These applications could be downloaded through multiple outlets with an average price of $10 or more. But Apple's App Store was the first outlet that made it easy to distribute, access, and download applications directly onto the mobile phone. Customers could downloaded apps onto their iPhones over the network or download them to their PC. Many apps were free; even paid apps usually started at 99 cents. The App Store was introduced as part of iTunes, which consumers were already familiar with through the iPod. Third party developers also welcomed the App Store because Apple made it easier to reach consumers. Apple reserved the right to approve all applications before they went on sale, and kept a 30% cut of the developer's app sales.

57 The popularity of the App Store was stunning. In about 18 months, four billion applications had been downloaded by iPhone and iPod Touch users worldwide.[63] More than 185,000 applications were offered in some 20 categories, ranging from games to health to business productivity programs. Walt Mossberg, the well-known technology columnist for the *Wall Street Journal*, even claimed that, "The App Store is what makes your device worth the price."[64] Mobile apps had turned into a nice side business for Apple as well. Around $4 billion was spent on mobile phone applications in 2009, the bulk of which was spent on iPhone apps.[65] Excluding developers' share, that still left Apple with about $1 billion dollars in app sales.[66] Apple's blockbuster hit sent competitors rushing to offer their own application stores and touchscreen devices as well.

[63] Kincaid, "Apple Has Sold 450,000 iPads, 50,000 Million iPhones to Date."

[64] Walter S. Mossberg, "Apps that Make the iPhone Worth the Price," *The Wall Street Journal,* March 26, 2009.

[65] Kevin J. O'Brian, "A Conference Keen on Finding Open Communication," *The New York Times,* February 16, 2010.

[66] Ibid.

58 **Competitors** Apple's competitors fell into two large categories, based on their business models. Research In Motion (RIM), Palm, and to a lesser extent, Nokia, took a similar approach to Apple by controlling both hardware and software. RIM's BlackBerry smartphones delivered one of the best mobile e-mail experiences and was a popular choice among corporate consumers. BlackBerrys were offered through approximately 550 carriers in 175 countries.[67] By far, RIM and Apple were the most profitable smartphone companies in the world: According to the *Wall Street Journal*, RIM and Apple accounted for roughly 5% of the total unit value of the cellphone industry but 60% of total operating profits in 2009.[68] Palm, on the other hand, was struggling to survive. Over the prior decade, a series of break-ups and mergers left Palm in disarray. Despite new phones with good reviews, Palm continued to suffer. In March 2010, Palm reported its 11th consecutive quarterly loss.

59 The leader in smartphones was Nokia. Its Symbian OS held 47% of worldwide smartphone sales (see **Exhibit 8**). The company's strength lay in Europe and emerging markets such as India and China. However, Nokia's smartphone market share had slipped dramatically. Nokia had a weak presence in the U.S., a key market for smartphones, and struggled to find U.S. carriers to subsidize its handsets. In 2010, Nokia announced that it would abandon Symbian for its high-end smartphones, opting for a new OS developed jointly with Intel. Rejecting Apple's closed system, the new Nokia OS, named MeeGo, would become a free, open platform. One of the main goals was to attract more software developers to write programs and applications for its app store, named Ovi.

60 Meanwhile, manufacturers such as HTC, Samsung Electronics, LG Electronics, and Motorola were taking a different approach. These firms mostly licensed their operating systems from Microsoft or used Google's free Android OS.[69] Microsoft was one of the few leading platforms that still charged a license fee. It was banking on regaining its lost market share with a next generation Windows Phone 7 platform, which was aiming to start shipping around the 2010 holiday season. Android, on the other hand, was an open platform that allowed mobile operators and handset makers to use it for free with few restrictions. By 2010, there were about 50 Android-based smartphone models in the market and Android had gained a 4% market share.

61 Moreover, Android Marketplace, Google's competitive app store to iTunes, was gaining momentum (see **Exhibit 9**). A survey of developers in the spring of 2010 suggested that 87% were very interested in developing iPhone apps; 81% for Android apps, with Blackberry and Microsoft a distant third and fourth, at 43% and 34% respectively.[70] Competition between Apple and Google was expected to intensify with iAd, Apple's own ad system, introduced in April 2010. iAd would allow App Store developers to include ads in their software while Apple tried to tap its App Store customer base to reach out to the evolving mobile ad market. One study indicated that an iPhone user had an average of 37 applications on the device compared to Android's average of 22 apps.[71]

62 **Limitations of the iPhone** Despite enormous momentum, the iPhone had its critics. In several markets around the world, Apple's decision to restrict the iPhone to a single network operator was unpopular. In the U.S., AT&T's network had spotty data access and dropped

[67] RIM Annual Information Form, April 1, 2010, p. 6, http://www.rim.com/investors/documents/, accessed April 2010.

[68] Sara Silver, "Apple, RIM Outsmart Phone Market," *The Wall Street Journal,* July 20, 2009.

[69] Android was officially part of the Open Handset Alliance, a consortium of more than 45 technology and mobile phone companies, including Google, HTC, Samsung, Intel, Texas Instruments, and Sprint Nextel.

[70] Dave Rosenberg, "Apple and Google Race for Mobile Dominence," CNET, March 31, 2010, http://news.cnet.com/8301-13846_3-10471786-62.html, accessed April 2010.

[71] "Nielson New App Playbook Debunks Mobile App Store Myth," Nielson Wire, March 24, 2010, http://blog.nielsen.com/nielsenwire/consumer/nielsen%E2%80%99s-new-app-playbook-debunks-mobile-app-store-myth/, accessed April 2010.

EXHIBIT 9 **Overview of Smartphone Operating Systems and App Stores (as of March 2010)**

Operating System	Owner	Major Handset Vendors	Licensing Fee	App Store	Approximate Number of Available Apps
Symbian	Nokia	Nokia, Sony Ericsson, and Samsung	No	Ovi Store	NA
Mac OS X	Apple	Apple	Proprietary	App Store	185,000
Blackberry	RIM	RIM	Proprietary	BlackBerry App World	6,000
Windows Mobile	Microsoft	HTC, Samsung, LG. Sony Ericsson	Yes	Windows Marketplace for Mobile	700
Android	Open Handset Alliance	HTC, Motorola, Samsung	No	Android Marketplace	30,000
Palm Web OS	Palm	Palm	Proprietary	Palm	2,100
MeeGo	Nokia, Intel	Nokia	No	Ovi Store	NA

Source: Created by case writer based on various public sources.

Note: NA = Not Available or Not Applicable.

calls, especially in New York City and San Francisco. Some even opted to stick with a more reliable carrier such as Verizon Wireless and purchase the iPod Touch instead. Other complaints included the lack of a physical QWERTY keyboard, especially among high-volume e-mail users. The battery life, although improved, was relatively weak, and users could not replace the iPhone battery or add memory. The iPhone did not support Flash technology, which meant that the device could not play embedded video featured on many websites or view shows through Hulu, a popular website that provided streamed video and movies.

The iPad

63 The launch of the iPad in 2010 was yet another bold move by Jobs to redefine an industry. Positioned between a smartphone and a laptop computer, the iPad was priced from $499 to $829. The computer tablet featured a 9.7 inch LED screen for reading books, watching movies, and some business productivity applications. In fact, several reviews referred to the iPad as a "giant iPod Touch" with almost identical hardware and interface. The iPad could either connect to the Internet via WiFi, or consumers could buy a premium iPad and then spend another $30 per month for AT&T's unlimited 3G service. The device could run, with some limitations, almost all iPhone apps. To offset those limitations, software developers had already released over 1,000 applications specifically developed for the iPad at the time of its launch.

64 Apple took a somewhat different approach to the iPad compared to the iPod and the iPhone. Going back to his roots, Jobs decided to take more control over the components. Between 2008 and 2010, Jobs bought two microprocessor design companies for about $400 million.[72] The iPad became the first Apple product to run on its own branded chip, the A4. Like Intel's Atom or Qualcomm's Snapdragon CPUs, the A4 was specifically designed for next generation mobile devices that required low-power and fast processing speed. Apple claimed that the A4 enabled the iPad to deliver 10 hours of battery life.

65 More than 450,000 iPads were sold during its first week on the market. Jobs commented that, "It feels great to have the iPad launched into the world—it's going to be a game changer."[73]

[72] Erika Brown, Elizabeth Corcoran, and Brian Caulfield, "Apple Buys Chip Designer," Forbes.com, April 23, 2008, via Factiva, accessed April 2010, and Ashlee Vance and Brad Stone, "Apples Buys Intrinsity, a Maker of Fast Chips," *The New York Times,* April 27, 2010.

[73] "Apple Sells over 300,000 iPads First Day," Apple Inc. Press Release (Cupertino, CA, April 5, 2010).

Yet the jury was out for the device. Computer tablets, prior to the iPad's launch, accounted for less than one percent of the PC market.[74] The iPad still lacked a physical QWERTY keyboard to the frustration of many business consumers. It could not take advantage of Flash video or animation on the Web. A top complaint was the lack of multi-tasking to run different apps in the background. In April 2010, Jobs announced that the new iPhone OS 4 would enable multi-tasking, and analysts expected the new OS to be available for iPads later in the year.

66 Perhaps the biggest debate about the iPad was its usage model. One possibility was that the iPad would replace the Kindle, Amazon.com's hugely successful e-reader. But Job had bigger ambitions. He argued that the iPad would be a netbook killer and drive new consumer behavior. Others thought that the iPad could not replace a laptop, questioning whether consumers would really spend as much as $829 to carry around a third device.

67 Another controversy for the iPad was its relationship with publishers. For content on the iPod and iPhone, Jobs had insisted on low prices (99 cents for songs, and free or low priced apps). But in trying to woo book and magazine publishers to the iPad, Jobs took a more flexible strategy. Industry leader, Amazon, held an estimated 90% of the small but growing e-book market. Prior to the iPad, Amazon had insisted that electronic books for its Kindle could not be priced higher than $9.99. When Apple entered the market, it chose to let publishers set their own prices, usually ranging from $12 to $15 for an e-book, and took a 30% cut from the sales. After the announcement of the iPad, Amazon was forced to allow some publishers to set their own prices on Kindle books.

68 The hype over the iPad had produced an immediate competitive response: At least a dozen companies announced plans to ship tablets in 2010, ranging from HP, which said it would make a Wintel-based tablet, while Dell planned to ship an Android-based tablet.

The Occasional Failures

69 While almost everything that Steve Jobs had touched in the first decade of the 21st century had turned to gold, his record was not unblemished. Apple had two notable products that failed to live up to expectations. One was the Mac Mini. As Apple's entry-level desktop, the $599 price tag did not come with a keyboard or a mouse. The Mac Mini had limited memory and few expansion options. Consumers could get a similar Windows desktop with more functions and faster performance at a lower price. The other disappointment was Apple TV. Introduced in 2007, the set-top-box was Apple's attempt to bring digital video content directly into consumers' living rooms. Users could stream movies and TV shows to a TV set after downloading content from iTunes. However, Apple TV sales were paltry compared to Apple's other products. Nearly three years after its release, the company's management continued to refer to Apple TV as a "hobby."

APPLE INC. IN THE NEXT DECADE?

70 Few, if any, could disagree that Apple's evolution from a PC manufacturer to a mobile device company had been a spectacular success. Most of the credit went to Steve Jobs, the man who had "changed the rules" for the company and the industry, again and again. As Apple's market capitalization approached $220 billion in the spring of 2010, surpassing IBM, HP, Cisco, Intel, and the rest of the tech world except Microsoft, one couldn't help but wonder—could anything derail Apple's momentum? The history of technology companies was littered with speeding rockets headed to the sky, only to fall back to earth with a crash. Steve Jobs had to think: Was his second act with Apple going to be the exception?

[74] Connie Guglielmo, "Apple iPad's Debut-Weekend Sales May be Surpassing Estimates," BusinessWeek.com, April 4, 2010, http://www.businessweek.com/news/2010-04-04/apple-ipad-s-debut-weekend-sales-may-be-surpassing-estimates.html, accessed April 2010.

Case 5

Best Buy Co., Inc.: *Sustainable Customer Centricity Model?*

Dr. Alan N. Hoffman
Bentley University and Rotterdam School of Management, Erasmus University

SYNOPSIS

1 Best Buy is the largest consumer electronics retailer in the United States, accounting for 19% of the market. Globally, it operates around 4,000 stores in the United States, Canada, Mexico, China, and Turkey. Its subsidiaries include Geek Squad, Magnolia Audio Video, Pacific Sales, and Future Shop.

2 Best Buy distinguishes itself from competitors by deploying a differentiation strategy rather than a low price strategy. In order to become a service-oriented firm, it changed the compensation structure for sales associates and applied a customer-centric operating model to provide end-to-end services. It also heavily invested in the training of sales professionals so they can better understand products and better assist customers. As a result, the company is widely recognized for its superior service.

3 Best Buy still faces competition, however, from large brick and mortar stores like Wal-Mart, as well as e-commerce stores like Amazon. The economic downturn and technological advances (the frequent introduction of new products) have also put stress on its financial strength and the quality of its customer service. The key challenge for Best Buy is to determine the correct path to improve its differentiation strategy. The main question is: How can Best Buy continue to have innovative products, top-notch employees, and superior customer service while facing increased competition, operational costs, and financial stress?

BEST BUY CO., INC.: SUSTAINABLE CUSTOMER CENTRICITY MODEL?

4 Best Buy, headquartered in Richfield, Minnesota, is a specialty retailer of consumer electronics. It operates over 1,100 stores in the United States, accounting for 19% of the market. With approximately 155,000 employees, it also operates over 2,800 stores in Canada, Mexico, China, and Turkey. The company's subsidiaries include Geek Squad, Magnolia Audio Video, Pacific Sales, and in Canada, it operates under both the Best Buy and Future Shop labels.

5 Best Buy's mission is to make technology deliver on its promises to customers. To accomplish this, it helps customers realize the benefits of technology and technological changes so they can enrich their lives in a variety of ways through connectivity: "To make life fun and easy,"[1] as Best Buy puts it. This is what drives the company to continually

Source: The author would like to thank Kevin Clark, Leonard D'Andrea, Amanda Genesky, Geoff Merritt, Chris Mudarri, and Dan Fowler for their research. Please address all correspondence to Dr. Alan N. Hoffman, Bentley University, Dept. of Management, 175 Forest Street, Waltham, MA USA 02452; ahoffman@bentley.edu. Printed by permission of Dr. Alan N. Hoffman.

RSM Case Development Centre prepared this case to provide material for class discussion rather than to illustrate either effective or ineffective handling of a management situation.

[1] Best Buy Co., Inc. (2009, February 28). Form 10-K. Securities and Exchange Commission.

increase the tools to support customers in the hope of providing end-to-end technology solutions.

6 As a public company, Best Buy's top objectives are sustained growth and earnings. This is accomplished in part by constantly reviewing its business model to ensure that it is satisfying customer needs and desires as effectively and completely as possible. The company strives to have not only extensive product offerings but also highly trained employees with extensive product knowledge. The company encourages its employees to go out of their way to help customers understand what these products can do and how customers can get the most out of the products they purchase. Employees must recognize that each customer is unique and thus determine the best method to help that customer achieve maximum enjoyment from the product(s) purchased.

7 From a strategic standpoint, Best Buy moved from being a discount retailer (a low price strategy) to a service-oriented firm that relies on a differentiation strategy. In 1989, it changed the compensation structure for sales associates from commission based to non-commissioned based, which resulted in consumers having more control over the purchasing process and in cost savings for the company (the number of sales associates was reduced). In 2005, Best Buy took customer service a step further by moving from peddling gadgets, to a customer-centric operating model. It is now gearing up for another change to focus on store design and providing products and services in line with customers' desire for constant connectivity.

COMPANY HISTORY[2]

From Sound of Music to Best Buy

8 Best Buy was originally known as Sound of Music. Incorporated in 1966, the company started as a retailer of audio components and expanded to retailing video products in the early 1980s with the introduction of the videocassette recorder to its product line. In 1983, the company changed its name to Best Buy Co, Inc. (Best Buy). Shortly thereafter, it began operating its existing stores under a "superstore" concept by expanding product offerings and using mass marketing techniques to promote those products.

9 Best Buy dramatically altered the function of its sales staff in 1989. Previously, the sales staff worked on a commission basis and was more proactive in assisting customers coming into the stores as a result. Since 1989, however, the commission structure was terminated and sales associates developed into educators that assist customers in learning about the products offered in the stores. The customer, to a large extent, took charge of the purchasing process. The sales staff's mission was to answer customer questions so that the customer could decide which product(s) fit their needs. This differed greatly from their former mission of simply generating sales.

10 In 2000, the company launched its online retail store: BestBuy.com. This allowed customers a choice between visiting a physical store and purchasing products online, thus expanding Best Buy's reach among consumers.

Expansion through Acquisitions

11 Since 2000, Best Buy has begun a series of acquisitions to expand their offerings and enter international markets:

2000—Best Buy acquired Magnolia Hi-Fi, Inc., a high-end retailer of audio and video products and services, which became Magnolia Audio Video in 2004. This acquisition allowed Best Buy access to a set of upscale customers.

[2] Ibid.

2001—Best Buy entered the international market with the acquisition of Future Shop Ltd, a leading consumer electronics retailer in Canada. This helped Best Buy increase revenues, gain market share and leverage operational expertise. The same year, it also opened its first Canadian store. In the same year, the company purchased Musicland, a mall-centered music retailer throughout the United States (divested in 2003).

2002—Best Buy acquired Geek Squad, a computer repair service provider, to help develop a technological support system for customers. The retailer began by incorporating in-store Geek Squad centers in its 28 Minnesota stores and expanding nationally and then internationally in subsequent years.

2005—Best Buy opened the first Magnolia Home Theater "store-within-a-store" (located within the Best Buy complex).

2006—Best Buy acquired Pacific Sales Kitchen and Bath Centers Inc. to develop a new customer base: builders and remodelers. The same year, it also acquired a 75% stake in Jiangsu Five Star Appliance Co., Ltd, a China-based appliance and consumer electronics retailer. This enabled the company to access the Chinese retail market and led to the opening of the first Best Buy China store on January 26, 2007.

2007—Best Buy acquired Speakeasy, Inc., a provider of broadband, voice, data and information technology services, to further its offering of technological solutions for customers.

2008—Through a strategic alliance with the Carphone Warehouse Group, a UK-based provider of mobile phones, accessories and related services, Best Buy Mobile was developed. After acquiring a 50% share in Best Buy Europe (with 2414 stores) from the Carphone Warehouse, Best Buy intends to open small-store formats across Europe in 2011.[3] Best Buy also acquired Napster, a digital downloads provider, through a merger, to counter the falling sales of compact discs.

The first Best Buy Mexico store was opened.

2009—Best Buy acquired the remaining 25% of Jiangsu Five Star. Best Buy Mobile moved into Canada.

INDUSTRY ENVIRONMENT

Industry Overview

12 Despite the negative impact the financial crisis has had on economies worldwide, in 2008 the consumer electronics industry managed to grow to a record high of US$694 billion in sales—a nearly 14% increase over 2007. In years immediately prior, the growth rate was similar: 14% in 2007 and 17% in 2006. This momentum, however, did not last. Sales dropped 2% in 2009, the first decline in 20 years for the electronics giant.

13 A few product segments, including televisions, gaming, mobile phone and Blu-ray players, drive sales for the company. Television sales, specifically LCD units, which account for 77% of total television sales, were the main driver for Best Buy, as this segment alone accounts for 15% of total industry revenues. The gaming segment continues to be a bright spot for the industry as well, as sales are expected to have tremendous room for growth. Smartphones are another electronics industry segment predicted to have a high growth impact on the entire industry.

[3] Ibid.

14 The consumer electronics industry has significant potential for expansion into the global marketplace. There are many untapped markets, especially newly developing countries. These markets are experiencing the fastest economic growth while having the lowest ownership rate for gadgets.[4] Despite the recent economic downturn, the future for this industry is optimistic. A consumer electronics analyst for the European Market Research Institute predicts that the largest growth will be seen in China (22%), the Middle East (20%), Russia (20%), and South America (17%).[5]

Barriers to Entry

15 As globalization spreads and use of the Internet grows, barriers to entering the consumer electronics industry are diminished. When the industry was dominated by brick and mortar companies, obtaining the large capital resources needed for entry into the market was a barrier for those looking to gain any significant market share. Expanding a business meant purchasing or leasing large stores that incurred high initial and overhead costs. However, the Internet has significantly reduced the capital requirements needed to enter the industry. Companies like Amazon.com and Dell have utilized the Internet to their advantage and gained valuable market share.

16 The shift towards Internet purchasing has also negated another once strong barrier to entry—customer loyalty. The trend today is that consumers will research products online to determine which one they intend to purchase and then shop around on the Internet for the lowest possible price.

17 Even though overall barriers are diminished, there are still a few left, which a company like Best Buy can use to their advantage. The first, and most significant, is economies of scale. With over 1,000 locations, Best Buy can use their scale to obtain cost advantages from suppliers due to high quantity of orders. Another advantage is in advertising. Large firms have the ability to increase advertising budgets to deter new entrants into the market. Smaller companies generally do not have the marketing budgets for massive television campaigns, which are still one of the most effective marketing strategies available to retailers. Although Internet sales are growing, the industry is still dominated by brick and mortar stores. Most consumers looking for electronics—especially major electronics—feel a need to actually see their prospective purchases in person. Having the ability to spend heavily on advertising will help increase foot traffic to these stores.

INTERNAL ENVIRONMENT

Finance

18 While Best Buy's increase in revenue is encouraging (see **Exhibit 1**), recent growth has been fueled largely by acquisition, especially Best Buy's 2009 revenue growth. At the same time, net income and operating margins have been declining (see **Exhibit 2** and **Exhibit 3**). Although this could be a function of increased costs, it is more likely due to pricing pressure. Given the current adverse economic conditions, prices of many consumer electronic products have been forced down by economic and competitive pressures. These lower prices have caused margins to decline, negatively affecting net income and operating margins.

[4] Keller, Greg. (2009, May 18). Threat grows by Ipod and laptop. *The Columbus Dispatch.* Retrieved July 10, 2009 from: http://www.dispatch.com/live/content/business/stories/2009/05/18/greener_gadgets.ART_ART_05-18-09_A9_TMDSJR8.html

[5] Magid, Larry. (2008, May 2). Consumer electronics: The future looks bright. *CBSNews.com.* Retrieved July 10, 2009 from: http://www.cbsnews.com/stories/2008/05/02/scitech/pcanswer/main4067008.shtml

EXHIBIT 1 **Quarterly Sales**

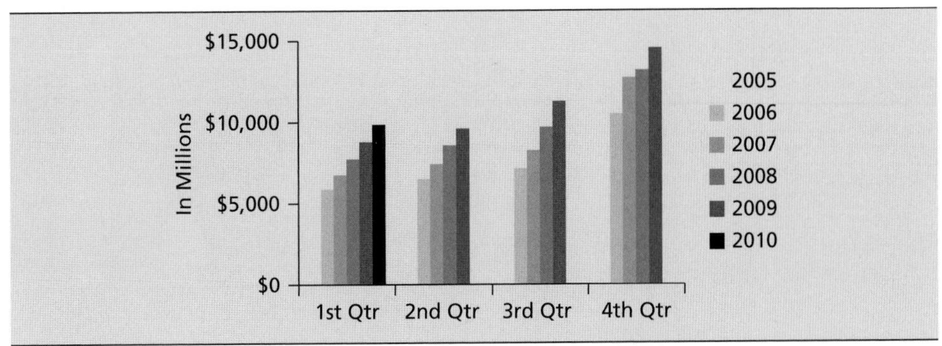

Fiscal Year	1st Qtr	2nd Qtr	3rd Qtr	4th Qtr
2005	$ 5,479	$6,080	$ 6,647	$ 9,227
2006	$ 6,118	$6,702	$ 7,335	$10,693
2007	$ 6,959	$7,603	$ 8,473	$12,899
2008	$ 7,927	$8,750	$ 9,928	$13,418
2009	$ 8,990	$9,801	$11,500	$14,724
2010	$10,095			

EXHIBIT 2 **Quarterly Net Income**

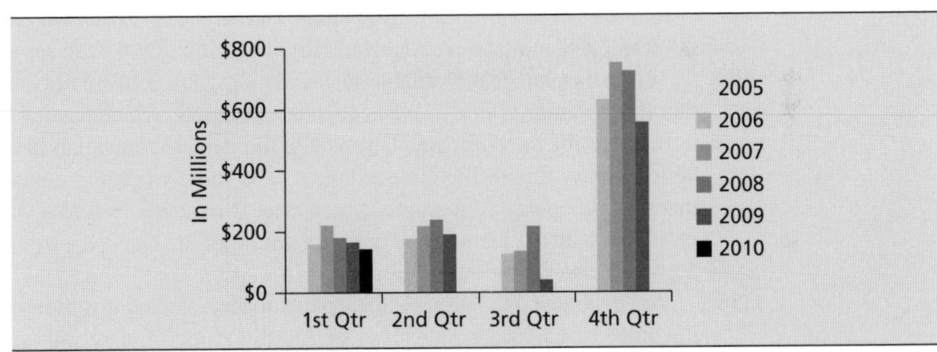

Fiscal Year	1st Qtr	2nd Qtr	3rd Qtr	4th Qtr
2005	$114	$150	$148	$572
2006	$170	$188	$138	$644
2007	$234	$230	$150	$763
2008	$192	$250	$228	$737
2009	$179	$202	$ 52	$570
2010	$153			

EXHIBIT 3 Operating Margin

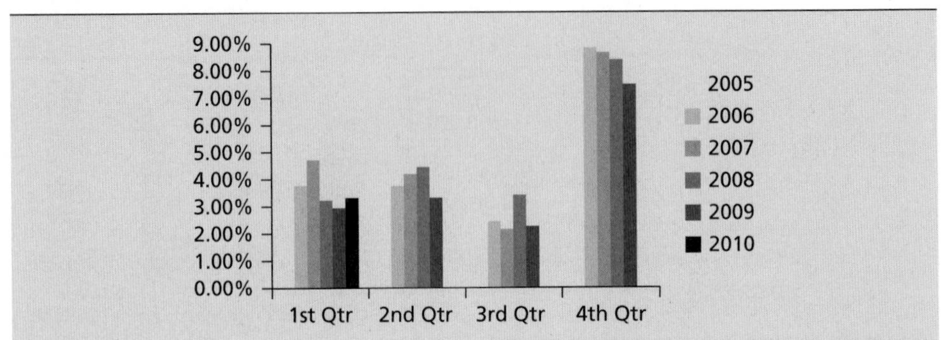

Fiscal Year	1st Qtr	2nd Qtr	3rd Qtr	4th Qtr
2005	3.36%	3.98%	3.51%	8.49%
2006	3.91%	3.89%	2.58%	8.97%
2007	4.84%	4.34%	2.31%	8.81%
2008	3.36%	4.58%	3.54%	8.52%
2009	3.08%	3.46%	2.38%	7.63%
2010	3.45%			

19 Best Buy's long-term debt increased substantially from 2008 to 2009 (see **Exhibit 4**), which is primarily due to the acquisition of Napster and Best Buy Europe. The trend in available cash has been a mirror image of long-term debt. Available cash increased from 2005 to 2008 and then was substantially lower in 2009 for the same reason.

20 While the change in available cash and long-term debt are not desirable, the bright side is that this situation is due to the acquisition of assets, which has led to a significant increase in revenue for the company. Ultimately, the decreased availability of cash would seem to be temporary due to the circumstances. The more troubling concern is the decline in net income and operating margins, which Best Buy needs to find a way to turn around. If the problems with net income and operating margins are fixed, the trends in cash and long-term debt will also begin to turn around.

21 At first blush, the increase in accounts receivable and inventory is not necessarily alarming since revenues are increasing during this same time period (see **Exhibit 5**). However, closer inspection reveals a 1% increase in inventory from 2008 to 2009 and a 12.5% increase in revenue accompanied by a 240% increase in accounts receivable. This creates a potential risk for losses due to bad debts.

Marketing

22 Best Buy's marketing objectives are four-fold: a) to market various products based on the customer centricity operating model, b) to address the needs of customer lifestyle groups, c) to be at the forefront of technological advances, and d) to meet customer needs with end-to-end solutions.

23 Best Buy prides itself on customer centricity that caters to specific customer needs and behaviors. Over the years, the retailer has created a portfolio of products and services that

EXHIBIT 4 **Long-Term Debt and Cash**

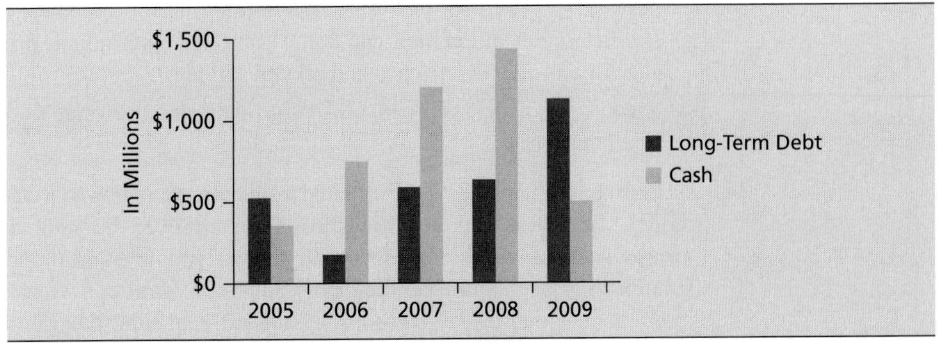

Fiscal Year	2005	2006	2007	2008	2009
Long-Term Debt	$528	$178	$ 590	$ 627	$1,126
Cash	$354	$748	$1,205	$1,438	$ 498
LTD/Equity	0.12	0.03	0.10	0.14	0.24
LTD/Total Assets	0.05	0.02	0.04	0.05	0.07

EXHIBIT 5 **Accounts Receivable and Inventory**

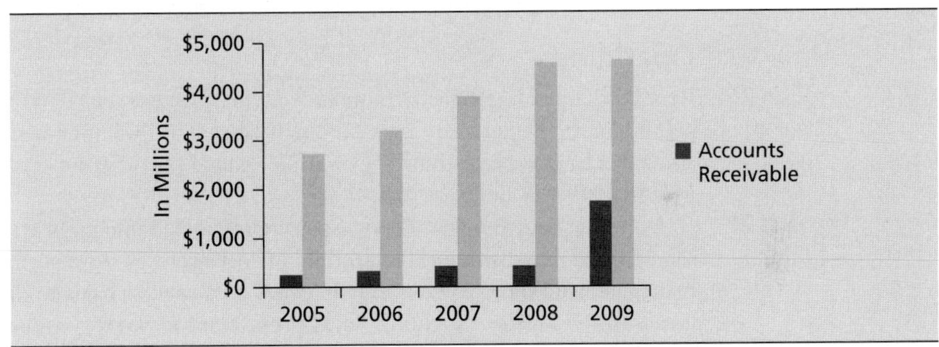

Fiscal Year	2005	2006	2007	2008	2009
Inventory	$2,851	$3,338	$4,028	$4,708	$4,753
Accounts Receivable	$ 375	$ 449	$ 548	$ 549	$1,868

complement one another and have added to the success of the business. These products include seven distinct brands domestically, as well as other brands and stores internationally:

Best Buy—offers a wide variety of consumer electronics, home office products, entertainment software, appliances, and related services.

Best Buy Mobile—stand-alone stores offer a wide selection of mobile phones, accessories, and related eservices in a small-format stores.

Geek Squad—provides residential and commercial product repair, support, and installation services both in-store and on-site.

Magnolia Audio Video—offers high-end audio and video products and related services.

Napster—an online provider of digital music.

Pacific Sales—offers high-end home improvement products primarily including appliances, consumer electronics and related services.

Speakeasy—provides broadband, voice, data, and information technology services to small businesses.

24 Starting in 2005, Best Buy initiated a strategic transition to a customer-centric operating model, which was completed in 2007. Prior to 2005, the company focused on customer groups such as affluent professional males, young entertainment enthusiasts, upscale suburban mothers, and technologically advanced families.[6] After the transition, it focused more on customer lifestyle groups such as affluent suburban families, trend-setting urban dwellers, and the closely knit families of Middle America.[7] To target these various segments, Best Buy acquired firms with aligned strategies, which could be used as a competitive advantage against its strongest competition, such as Circuit City and Wal-Mart. The acquisitions of Pacific Sales, Speakeasy, and Napster, along with the development of Best Buy Mobile, created more product offerings, which led to more profits.

25 To market all these different types of products and services is a difficult task. That is why Best Buy's employees have more training than competitors. This knowledge service is a value-added competitive advantage. Since the sales employees no longer operate on a commission-based pay structure, consumers can obtain knowledge from sales people without being subjected to high-pressure sales techniques. This is generally seen to enhance customer shopping satisfaction.

Operations

26 Best Buy's operating objectives include increasing revenues by growing its customer base, gaining more market share internationally, successfully implementing marketing and sales strategies in Europe, and having multiple brands for different customer lifestyles through M&A.

27 Domestic Best Buy store operations are organized into eight territories, with each territory divided into districts. A retail field officer oversees store performance through district managers, who meet with store employees on a regular basis to discuss operations strategies such as loyalty programs, sales promotion, and new product introductions.[8] Along with domestic operations, Best Buy has an international operation segment, originally established in connection with the acquisition of Canada-based Future Shop.[9]

28 In 2009, Best buy opened up 285 new stores in addition to the European acquisition of 2,414 Best Buy Europe stores, relocated 34 stores, and closed 67 stores.

Human Resources

29 The objectives of Best Buy's human resources department are to provide consumers with the right knowledge of products and services, to portray the company's vision and strategy on an everyday basis, and to educate employees on the ins and outs of new products and services.

[6] Best Buy Co., Inc. (2009). Form 10-K.

[7] Ibid.

[8] Ibid.

[9] Ibid.

30 Best Buy employees are required to be ethical and knowledgeable. This principle starts within the top management structure and filters down from the retail field officer through district managers, and through store managers to the employees on the floor. Every employee must have the company's vision embedded in their service and attitude.

31 Despite Best Buy's efforts to train an ethical and knowledgeable employee force, there have been some allegations and controversy over Best Buy employees, which has given the company a bad black eye in the public mind. One lawsuit claimed that Best Buy employees had misrepresented the manufacturer's warranty in order to sell its own product service and replacement plan. It accused Best Buy of "entering into a corporate-wide scheme to institute high-pressure sales techniques involving the extended warranties" and "using artificial barriers to discourage consumers who purchased the 'complete extended warranties' from making legitimate claims."[10]

32 In a more recent case (March 2009), the U.S. District Court granted Class Action certification to allow plaintiffs to sue Best Buy for violating its "Price Match" policy. According to the ruling, the plaintiffs allege that Best Buy employees would aggressively deny consumers the ability to apply the company's "price match guarantee."[11] The suit also alleges that Best Buy has an undisclosed "Anti-Price Matching Policy," where it tells its employees not to allow price matches and gives financial bonuses to employees who do this.

COMPETITION

Brick and Mortar Competitors

33 *Wal-Mart Stores Inc.,* the world's largest retailer with revenues over US$405 billion, has operations worldwide and offers a diverse product mix with a focus on being a low-cost provider. In recent years, Wal-Mart has increased its focus on grabbing market share in the consumer electronics industry. In the wake of Circuit City's liquidation,[12] it is stepping up efforts by striking deals with Nintendo and Apple that will allow each company to have their own in-store displays. Wal-Mart has also considered using smart phones and laptop computers to drive growth.[13] It is refreshing 3,500 of its electronics departments and will begin to offer a wider and higher range of electronic products. These efforts will help Wal-Mart appeal to the customer segment looking for high quality at the lowest possible price[14].

34 *GameStop Corp.* is the leading video game retailer with sales of almost US$9 billion as of January 2009, in a forecasted US$22 billion industry. It operates over 6,000 stores throughout the United States, Canada, Australia, and Europe, as a retailer of both new and used video game products including hardware, software and gaming accessories.[15]

[10] Manhattan Institute for Policy Research. (2001). They're making a federal case out of it . . . in state court. *Civil Justice Report 3.* Retrieved from: http://www.manhattan-institute.org/html/cjr_3_part2.htm

[11] Best Buy Bombshell. (2009, March 21). HD Guru. Retrieved from: http://hdguru.com/best-buy-bombshell/400/

[12] Circuit City Stores, Inc. was an American retailer in brand-name consumer electronics, personal computers, entertainment software, and (until 2000) large appliances. The company opened its first store in 1949 and liquidated its final American retail stores in 2009 following a bankruptcy filing and subsequent failure to find a buyer. At the time of liquidation, Circuit City was the second largest U.S. electronics retailer, after Best Buy.

[13] Bissonnette, Z. (2009, May 18). Wal-Mart looks to expand electronics business. Bloggingstocks.com. Retrieved from: http://www.bloggingstocks.com/2009/05/18/wal-mart-looks-to-expand-electronics-business/

[14] Maestrie, N. (2009, May 19). Wal-Mart steps up consumer electronics push. *Reuters.* Retrieved from: http://www.reuters.com/article/technologyNews/idUSTRE54I4TR20090519

[15] Capital IQ. (2009). GameStop Corp. Corporate Tearsheet. *Capital IQ.*

35 The advantage GameStop has over Best Buy is the number of locations: 6,207 GameStop locations compared to 1,023 Best Buy locations. However, Best Buy seems to have what it takes to overcome this advantage—deep pockets. With significantly higher net income, Best Buy can afford to take a hit to their margins and undercut GameStop prices.[16]

36 *RadioShack Corp.* is a retailer of consumer electronic goods and services including flat panel televisions, telephones, computers, and consumer electronic accessories. Although the company grosses revenues of over US$4 billion from 4,453 locations, RadioShack has consistently lost market share to Best Buy. Consumers have a preference for RadioShack for audio and video components, yet prefer Best Buy for their big box purchases.[17]

37 *Second tier competitors* are rapidly increasing. Wholesale shopping units are becoming more popular, and companies such as Costco and BJ's have increased their piece of the consumer electronics pie over the past few years. After Circuit City's bankruptcy, mid-level electronics retailers like HH Gregg and Ultimate Electronics are scrambling to grab Circuit City's lost market share. Ultimate Electronics, owned by Mark Wattles, who was a major investor in Circuit City, has a leg up on his competitors. Wattles was on Circuit City's board of executives and had firsthand access to profitable Circuit City stores. Ultimate Electronics has plans to expand its operations by at least 20 stores in the near future.

Online Competitors

38 *Amazon.com, Inc.* has, since 1994, grown into the United States' largest online retailer with revenues of over US$19 billion in 2008 by providing just about any product imaginable through its popular website. Begun as an online bookstore, Amazon soon ventured out into various consumer electronic product categories including computers, televisions, software, video games and much more.[18]

39 Amazon.com gains an advantage over its supercenter competitors as it is able to maintain a lower cost structure compared to brink and mortar companies such as Best Buy. It is able to push those savings through to their product pricing and selection/diversification. With an increasing trend in the consumer electronic industry to shop online, Amazon.com is positioned perfectly to maintain strong market growth and potentially steal some market share away from Best Buy.

40 *Netflix, Inc.* is an online video rental service, offering selections of DVDs and Blu-ray discs. Since its establishment in 1997, it has grown into a US$1.4 billion company. With over 100,000 titles in its collection, it ships for free to approximately 10 million subscribers. It has also begun offering streaming downloads through their website, which eliminates the need to wait for a DVD to arrive.

41 Netflix is quickly changing the DVD market, which has dramatically impacted brick and mortar stores such as Blockbuster and Hollywood Video and retailers who offer DVDs for sale. In a responsive move, Best Buy has partnered with CinemaNow to enter the digital movie distribution market and counter Netflix and other video rental providers.[19]

[16] Sherman, E. (2009, June 24). GameStop faces pain from Best Buy, downloading. *BNET Technology.* Retrieved from: http://industry.bnet.com/technology/10002329/gamestop-faces-pain-from-best-buy-downloading/

[17] Van Riper, T. (2006, February 17). RadioShack Gets Slammed. *Forebes.com.* Retrieved from: http://www.forbes.com/2006/02/17/radioshack-edmondson-retail_cx_tr_0217radioshack.html

[18] Capital IQ. (2009). Amazon.com Corporate Tearsheet. *Capital IQ.*

[19] Kee, T. (2009, June 5). Netflix beware: Best Buy adds digital downloads with CinemaNow deal. *paidContent.org.* Retrieved from: http://paidcontent.org/article/419-best-buy-adds-digital-movie-downloads-with-cinemanow-deal/

CORE COMPETENCIES

Customer Centricity Model

42 Most players in the consumer electronics industry focus on delivering products at the lowest cost (Wal-Mart—brick and mortar, Amazon—Web-based). Best Buy, however, has taken a different approach by providing customers with highly trained sales associates who are available to educate customers regarding product features. This allows customers to make informed buying decisions on big-ticket items. In addition, with the Geek Squad, Best Buy is able to offer and provide installation services, product repair and on-going support. In short, it can provide an end-to-end solution for its customers.

43 Best Buy has used their customer centricity model, which is built around a significant database of customer information, to construct a diversified portfolio of product offerings. This allows the company to offer different products in different stores in a manner that matches customer needs. This in turn helps keep costs lower by shipping the correct inventory to the correct locations. Since Best Buy's costs are increased by the high level of training needed for sales associates and service professionals, it has been important that the company remain vigilant in keeping costs down wherever they can without sacrificing customer experience.

44 The tremendous breadth of products and services Best Buy is able to provide allows customers to purchase all components for a particular need within the Best Buy family. For example, if a customer wants to set up a first-rate audio-visual room at home, he or she can go to the Magnolia Home Theater store-within-a-store at any Best Buy location and use the knowledge of the Magnolia or Best Buy associate in the television and audio areas to determine which television and surround sound theater system best fits their needs. The customer can then employ a Geek Squad employee to install and set up the television and home theater system. None of Best Buy's competitors offer this extensive level of service.

Successful Acquisitions

45 Through its series of acquisitions, Best Buy has gained valuable experience in the process of integrating companies under the Best Buy family. The ability to effectively determine where to expand has been and will be key to the company's ability to differentiate itself in the marketplace. Additionally, Best Buy has also been successfully integrating employees from acquired companies. Due to the importance of high-level employees to company strategy and success, retaining this knowledge base is invaluable. Best Buy now has a significant global presence, which is important because of the maturing domestic market. This global presence has provided the company with insights into worldwide trends in the consumer electronics industry and afforded access to newly developing markets. Best Buy uses this insight to test products in different markets in its constant effort to meet and anticipate customer needs.

Retaining Talent

46 Analyzing Circuit City's demise, many experts have concluded one of the major reasons for the company's downfall is that Circuit City let go of their most senior and well-trained sales staff in order to cut costs. Best Buy, on the other hand, has a reputation for retaining their talent and is widely recognized for its superior service. Highly trained sales professionals have become a unique resource in the consumer electronics industry, where technology is changing at an unprecedented rate, and can be a significant source of competitive advantage.

CHALLENGES AHEAD

Economic Downturn

47 Electronics retailers like Best Buy sell products that can be described as "discretionary items, rather than necessities."[20] During economic recessions, however, consumers have less disposable income to spend. While there has been recent optimism about a possible economic turnaround, if the economy continues to stumble, this presents a real threat to sellers of discretionary products.

48 In order to increase sales revenues, many retailers, including Best Buy, offer customers low interest financing through their private-label credit cards. These promotions have been tremendously successfully for Best Buy. From 2007 to 2009, these private-label credit card purchases accounted for 16% to 18% of Best Buy's domestic revenue. Due to the current credit crisis, however, the Federal Reserve has issued new regulations that could restrict companies from offering deferred interest financing to customers. If Best Buy and other retailers are unable to extend these credit lines, it could have a tremendous negative impact on future revenues.[21]

Pricing and Debt Management

49 The current economic conditions, technological advances, and increased competition have put a tremendous amount of pricing pressure on many consumer electronics products. This is a concern for all companies in this industry. The fact that Best Buy does not compete strictly on price structure alone makes this an even bigger concern. Given the higher costs that Best Buy incurs training employees, any pricing pressure that decreases margins puts stress on Best Buy's financial strength. In addition, the recent acquisition of Napster and the 50% stake in Best Buy Europe have significantly increased Best Buy's debt and reduced available cash. Even in prosperous times, debt management is a key factor in any company's success, and it becomes even more concerning during economic downturn.

Products and Service

50 As technology improves, product life cycles, as well as prices, decrease and as a result, margins therefore decrease. Under Best Buy's service model, shorter product life cycles increase training costs. Employees are forced to learn new products with higher frequency. This is not only costly but also increases the likelihood that employees will make mistakes, thereby tarnishing Best Buy's service record and potentially damaging one of its most important, if not the most important, differentiators. In addition, more resources must be directed at research of new products to make sure Best Buy continues to offer the products consumers desire.

51 One social threat to the retail industry is the growing popularity of the online marketplace. Internet shoppers can browse sites searching for the best deals on specific products. This technology has allowed consumers to become more educated about their purchases, while creating increased downward price pressure. Ambitious consumers can play the role of a Best Buy associate themselves by doing product comparisons and information gathering without a trip to the store. This emerging trend creates a direct threat to companies like Best Buy, which has 1,023 stores in its domestic market alone. One way Best Buy has tried to continue the demand for brick and mortar locations and counter the threat of Internet-based competition is by providing value-added services in stores. Customer service, repairs, and interactive product displays are just a few examples of these services.[22]

[20] Best Buy Co., Inc. (2009). Form 10-K.

[21] Ibid.

[22] Ibid.

Leadership

52 The two former CEOs of Best Buy, Richard Shultze and Brad Anderson, were extremely successful at making the correct strategic moves at the appropriate times. With Brad Anderson stepping aside in June 2009, Brian Dunn replaced him as the new CEO. Although Dunn has worked for the company for 24 years and held the key positions of COO and President during his tenure, the position of CEO brings him to a whole new level and presents new challenges, especially during the current economic downturn. He is charged with leading Best Buy into the world of increased connectivity. This requires a revamping of products and store setups to serve customers in realizing their connectivity needs. This is a daunting task for an experienced CEO, let alone a new CEO who has never held the position.

Wal-Mart

53 Best Buy saw its largest rival, Circuit City, go down for good. A new archrival, Wal-Mart, however, is expanding into consumer electronics and stepping up competition in a price war it hopes to win. Best Buy needs to face the competition not by lowering prices, but by coming up with something really different. It has to determine the correct path to improve its ability to differentiate itself from competitors, which is increasingly difficult given an adverse economic climate and the company's financial stress. How Best Buy can maintain innovative products, top-notch employees, and superior customer service while facing increased competition and operational costs is an open question.

Case 6

Ceja Vineyards: *Marketing to the Hispanic Wine Consumer?*

Armand Gilinsky Jr. *Sonoma State University*
Linda I. Nowak *Sonoma State University*
Cristina Santini *University of Florence*
Ricardo Villarreal deSilva *University of San Francisco*

We are the product of farm labor families. Wouldn't it be wonderful if what we have accomplished could be a spark for others who've come from poverty, who also have goals of achieving the American dream?[1]

—Pedro Ceja

There are a number of people who helped us and we have to thank them. But let's be frank—we got to this point by 99 percent perspiration and 1 percent inspiration. We also realize our community needs leadership. We only hope we can be part of it.[2]

—Armando Ceja

One thing we have in common with most people in this country is that we are all immigrants. We attract everybody from across demographic groups. Why? Because we do not have the sense of arrogance that others in the wine industry possess. We don't hire anyone who is not bilingual in English and Spanish. We live in a global community. We are nice to everybody. And that appeals to everyone.[3]

—Amelia Morán Ceja

1 "Amelia, please, my brother Armando and I want distribution, distribution, distribution!" argued Pedro Ceja to his wife, Amelia Morán Ceja, in September 2007, during what she recalled as one of many "not-so-friendly discussions" that year about marketing Ceja's small production of branded wines to Hispanic consumers.

2 Targeting the emerging and potentially vast U.S. Hispanic consumer segment could require extensive repositioning of Ceja Vinyeards' premium varietal wine brands, entailing across-the-board price decreases. Repositioning its wines in the marketplace could also

Source: Reprinted by permission from the *Case Research Journal*.

This case study was prepared by Armand Gilinsky Jr., professor of business at Sonoma State University; Linda I. Nowak, professor of marketing at Sonoma State University; Cristina Santini, doctoral researcher at the University of Florence; and Ricardo Villarreal deSilva, professor of marketing at the University of San Francisco as a basis for class discussion rather than to illustrate either effective or ineffective handling of an administrative situation. All characters and events are real. The authors wish to thank the owners of Ceja Vineyards for written permission to use this case for classroom purposes and the editor and reviewers of the Case Research Journal for their helpful comments on the drafts. An earlier version of the case was presented at the 2010 North American Case Research Association conference in Santa Cruz, California.

[1] Quoted in L. P. Carson, "The Ceja Family Celebrates a Winemaking Journey," *Napa Valley Register* (May 1, 2002).

[2] Ibid.

[3] All subsequent quotations with the owners are from interviews by the case writers conducted at Ceja Vineyards in March and September 2007.

result in termination of the company's relationships with boutique distributors that cater exclusively to small premium wine producers like Ceja. Marketing to U.S. Hispanic consumers via mass-market distribution channels would divert attention from Ceja's rapidly growing direct sales channel—its wine buying club—and would involve substantial incremental promotional expenses. In addition, the Hispanic wine consumer living outside the U.S. represented another market opportunity with great potential for Ceja.

3 At the company's conference table, which also served as the family dinner table, Amelia replied, "You say you want more distribution, but well, you know, we have no new business plan, no new marketing plan, and I do not want to try to sell 90 percent of our wines through an unfriendly distribution system. We need to sell direct to the consumer through our tasting room and wine club. Only if we do these things, only if we use e-mail and the Internet, only if we can convince people that it is OK to drink Cabernet Sauvignon with rice and beans, can we appeal to Hispanic consumers."

4 Amelia was known in the wine industry as fearless, and more often than not had the final word in family discussions. A local journalist wrote, "Amelia Morán Ceja, a five-foot tall colossus of wit, strength, enthusiasm and intelligence, possessed in her diminutive body enough energy to power the electric grid of the entire Napa Valley."[4]

5 "Do you believe Hispanic consumers have enough discretionary income to buy our wine?" her brother-in-law Armando countered.

6 "Well," Amelia said, with her customary exuberance, "we all know there are now nearly 40 million plus Hispanics in the U.S., which accounts for nearly a country within a country. Twenty percent of that population earns above $100,000 per year. Why wouldn't we target that population?"

• • •

7 Having celebrated their nineteenth harvest and seventh year as California producers and marketers of branded premium wines, the Mexican-born owners of Ceja Vineyards were hotly debating whether or not to make a concerted effort to directly target U.S. Hispanic consumers, or to leave it up to distributors and retailers to make that decision. Distributors and retailers were vital trade intermediates in what was known in the alcoholic beverages industry as the "three-tier system," which moved wines from producer to distributor to retailer. (See **Appendix 1** for an overview of the U.S. wine industry in 2006–2007 and more detail on the three-tier system.) The company was completely family owned, with equal shares and decision-making powers distributed among its four founders: Amelia Morán Ceja (president), her husband Pedro Ceja (artistic director), his brother Armando Ceja (winemaker and vineyard manager), and Armando's wife Martha Ceja, herself a daughter of Mexican immigrants to the U.S.

8 By 2007, Ceja consisted of two legal entities. The first produced 10,000 cases of wine under the Ceja Vineyards brand, and the second was a separate wine-growing company, Viña del Sol, that sold 85 percent of its grape production to other producers who, in turn, sold the wine made from those grapes under their own brand labels. The Ceja family believed strongly in staying diversified between producing their own branded wines and growing grapes for other producers. Business for both entities had remained steady due to increasing demand and increasing prices for high quality wine grapes grown in Sonoma and Napa.[5] Ceja Vineyards had recently been

[4] A. Goldfarb, "A Conversation with Amelia Morán Ceja," *St. Helena Star* (July 14, 2005). Accessed March 21, 2010. http://www.cejavineyards.com/Saint-Helena-Star-Mexican-American-Winery.

[5] In 2007, grapes produced in District 4 (Napa County) received the highest average price of $3,251.05 per ton, up 7 percent from 2006. District 3 (Sonoma and Marin counties) received the second highest return of $2,081.27 per ton, up 5 percent from 2006, according to the U.S. Department of Agriculture, National Agricultural Statistics Service (NASS), Final 2007 Grape Crush Report for California, accessible at: http://www.nass.usda.gov/Statistics_by_State/California/ Publications/Grape_Crush/index.asp, accessed February 28, 2009.

notified that it was to be honored by Cyril Penn, an influential wine industry observer and editor of *Wine Business Monthly,* as one of the top ten hottest wine brands in 2007 (see **Exhibit 1**).

9 The Ceja Vineyards brand competed locally with some very large and well-known northern California wine producers. Wine output ranged from 142,000 to 18 million cases for the top twenty-five wineries and from 20,000–100,000 cases for the twenty-five major independent wineries (see **Exhibits 2** and **3**). Although Ceja grew sufficient grapes to produce upwards of 65,000 cases of wine each year, management had made a conscious decision that annual branded wine production would not exceed 20,000–25,000 cases by 2012.

EXHIBIT 1 ***Wine Business Monthly's*** **Hottest New Small Brands (U.S. Wineries Producing under 150,000 Cases per Year in 2007)**

2007 Rank	Company	Appellation	Location	Key Brand(s)
1	Willamette Valley VIneyards	Willamette Valley	Oregon	2006 Pinot Noir
2	Ceja Vineyards	Carneros	California	2004 Carneros Merlot
3	Tangent Winery	Central Coast	California	2006 Albariño
4	Clos du Val	Napa Valley	California	2004 Cabernet Sauvignon
5	Kutch Wines	Russian River Valley	California	2006 Pinot Noir
6	Coro Mendocino	Mendocino	California	2004 Proprietary Blends
7	J.R. Storey	Central Coast	California	2006 Arroyo Grande Grenache
8	L'Ecole No 41	Walla Walla Valley	Washington	2006 Columbia Valley Semillon
9	King Family Vineyards		Virginia	2006 "Michael Shaps" Viognier
10	Gruet Winery		New Mexico	Gruet Brut NV New Mexico

Source: Penn, C. Review of the industry: Hottest small brands of 2007. *Wine Business Monthly* February 15, 2008.

EXHIBIT 2 **Top Twenty-Five Northern California Wineries, Ranked by Estimated Cases Produced, 2007–2008**

	Company (location)	Local Case Production (estimated)	Key Brands
1	Foster's Wine Estates (Napa)	18,000,000	Cellar 8, Souverain, Beringer
2	Trinchero Family Estates (Napa)	12,000,000	Sutter Home, Trinchero, Napa Valley, Napa Cellars, Folie à Deux
3	Diageo Chateau & Estate Wines (Napa)	5,700,000	Acacia Vineyard, Beaulieu Vineyard, Dynamite, Hewitt, Moon Mountain, Provenance, Sterling
4	Kendall-Jackson Wine Estates (Sonoma)	5,000,000	Kendall-Jackson, Hartford, Dog House, Legacy, Ray's Station
5	Brown-Forman Wines (Mendocino)	4,500,000	Bel Arbor, Bonterra, Fetzer, Five Rivers, Jekel, Little Black Dress, Sanctuary, Sonoma-Cutrer, Virgin Vines
6	Gallo Family Vineyards (Sonoma)	3,200,000	Gallo Family Vineyards Sonoma, Two Rock, Laguna, Single Vineyard, Estate, Frei Brothers Reserve, Indigo Hills, Louis M. Martini, MacMurray Ranch, Rancho, Zabaco

EXHIBIT 2 *(Continued)*

	Company (location)	Local Case Production (estimated)	Key Brands
7	Don Sebastiani & Sons (Sonoma)	1,800,000	Aquinas, Hey Mambo, Leese-Fitch, Mia's Playground, Pepperwood Grove, Plungerhead, Smoking Loon
8	Icon Estates (Napa)	1,700,000	Franciscan, Mt. Veeder Winery, Robert Mondavi, Simi, Estancia
9	Korbel (Sonoma)	1,600,000	Korbel Champagne and Brandy, Kenwood
10	C. Mondavi & Sons (Napa)	1,500,000	Charles Krug, CK Mondavi, CR Cellars
11	Ascentia Wine Estates (Sonoma)	1,000,000	Atlas Peak, Buena Vista, Gary Farrell, Geyser Park
12	The Coppola Companies (Napa)	900,000	Rubicon, FC Reserve, Director's Cut, Diamond Collection, Encyclopedia, Rosso & Bianco, Sofia, Votre Sante
13	Rodney Strong Wine Estates (Sonoma)	886,454	Rodney Strong Vineyards, Davis Bynum, Sonoma Vineyards
14	The Hess Collection (Napa)	598,000	Hess
15	Purple Wine Company (Sonoma)	515,000	Avalon, Bex, Blue Jean, Capolan, Mark West Winery, Rock Rabbit
16	Foley Family Wines (Sonoma)	500,000	Firestone, Foley, Kuleto, Lincourt, Merus, Sebastiani, Three Rivers
17	Adler Fels Winery (Sonoma)	432,000	Adler Fels, Big Ass, Leaping Lizard, Coyote Creek, Coastline
18	Domaine Chandon (Napa)	404,000	Chandon, étoile, Domaine Chandon
19	Rutherford Wine Co. (Napa)	380,000	Rutherford Ranch, Round Hill, Scott Family Estate, Lander Jenkins
20	Langtry Estate & Vineyards (Napa)	294,000	Langry, Guenoc
21	Mumm Napa (Napa)	250,000	Mumm Cuvée Napa
22	St. Francis Wine Co.	240,000	St. Francis
23	Gloria Ferrer/Freixenet USA (Sonoma)	177,587	Gloria Ferrer
24	Benziger Winery (Sonoma)	150,000	Benziger, Signaterra, Estate, Tribute
25	Alexander Valley VIneyards (Sonoma)	142,000	Alexander Valley, CYRUS, Estate, New Gewurz, Redemption Zin, Sin Zin, Temptation Zin, Two Barrel, Wicked Weekend

Source: Loceff, J. *North Bay Business Journal* June 29, 2009.

10 The Ceja family reached a crossroads in late 2007 regarding its marketing strategy. In deciding whether and how to target the Hispanic consumer, and which channel to use, the Cejas needed to avoid a common mistake of marketers who identified Hispanics as a monolithic market segment: not all Hispanics were used to the same recipes and flavors, because they came from different areas and cultures. (See **Appendix 2** for demographic information about U.S. wine consumers.)

EXHIBIT 3 **Twenty-Five Largest Independently-Owned Wineries in Northern California, Ranked by Estimated Cases Produced, 2007–2008**

Winery	Location	Est. Cases Produced	Sales (millions)	Cultivated Acres Owned	Labels
Dry Creek Vineyard	Sonoma	100,000	$10.2	218	Dry Creek Vineyards
St. Supery Vineyards and Winery	Napa	98,000		500	St. Supery
Jordan Vineyard and Winery	Sonoma	90,000	24.7	300	Jordan
Frey Vineyards	Mendocino	80,000	5.6	110	Frey Organic Wines, Frey Biodynamic Wines
Silver Oak Cellars	Sonoma	74,000		350	Silver Oak Cellars
Seghesio Family Vineyards	Sonomoa	70,000		400	Seghesio Family Vineyards
Steele Wines	Lake	70,000		68	Steele, Shooting Star, Writer's Block, Stymie
Clos du Val	Napa	70,000	16.7	283	Clos du Val
Trefethen Family Vineyards	Napa	61,000		450	Trefethen Family Vineyards, Double T, HaLo
Cuvaison Estate Wines	Napa	60,000		330	Cuvaison
Grgich Hills Estate	Napa	60,000		366	Grgich Hills Estate
Groth Vineyards	Napa	60,000		140	Groth
Schramsberg Vineyards	Napa	60,000		90	Schramsberg, J. Schram, J. Davies
Joseph Phelps Vineyards	Napa	60,000		475	Joseph Phelps, Insignia, Backus
Saintsbury	Napa	60,000		34	Saintsbury
Chalk Hill Estate Vineyards & Winery	Sonoma	55,000		350	Chalk Hill Estate, Imagine, Furth
Pedroncelli Winery	Sonoma	50,000	3.5	15	Perdoncelli
Foppiano Vineyards	Sonoma	50,000		115	Foppiano, Lot 96
Schug Carneros Estate Winery	Sonoma	50,000		42	Schug, L'Etage
Silverado Vineyards	Napa	50,000		400	Silverado
Whitehall Lane Winery	Napa	50,000		120	Whitehall Lane
J Vineyards & Winery	Sonoma	40,000		250	J, J Vineyard
Vinovation	Sonoma	30,000	0.4		Winesmith, Penny-furthing, Cheapskate
Iron Horse VIneyards	Sonoma	24,000	6.6	200	Iron Horse
Kirkland Ranch Winery	Napa	20,000	5.0	145	Jameison Canyon, Kirkland Ranch

CEJA'S STORY

11 Ceja was founded in 1983, growing grapes on contract for other branded wineries in nearby Napa Valley and Sonoma County, and introduced its own branded label wines in 2001 (see **Exhibit 4** for milestones in Ceja's history). Ceja was founded by immigrant children of farm workers, so it had a unique history among the forty-two vintners in its Carneros region and among the 3,000 California-based producers of premium branded wines, according to the California Association of Wine Growers (CAWG) in 2007.

12 Amelia and Pedro were both born in Mexico. Amelia's father immigrated to Napa Valley in the 1950s and worked as a foreman for a company that managed famed wine-makers Robert Mondavi and Charles Krug's vineyards. Pedro's father came to Napa Valley in the 1960s to work in the *Bracero program*.[6] Pedro and Amelia met working in the vineyards, enjoyed working in the vineyards, and even returned home to work in the vineyards during the summers while they were in college.

13 As president of the Union of Farm Workers in the Napa Valley Management Vineyard Company, Amelia's father had helped César Chavéz organize the United Farm Workers union in the late 1960s. Amelia reflected,

> My father, who became a vineyard foreman for Oakville Vineyard Management Company, knew that his children couldn't grow up in a small Mexican village and enjoy the same opportunities they could get in the U.S. I have worked in the same vineyards where my dad worked, and it makes me cry thinking that my parents could not go to school.

EXHIBIT 4 **Milestones in Ceja Vineyard's History**

1947	Felipe Morán (Amelia's father) first comes to the U.S.
1967	Morán family relocates to Napa Valley; Amelia was twelve years old.
1983	Amelia, Pedro, and Armando Ceja purchase fifteen acres in Carneros, with Pablo Ceja and his wife.
1986	First grapes planted in Carneros—15,000 vines.
1988	First harvest.
1999	Amelia Morán Ceja named president of Ceja Vineyards.
2001	Initial production of Ceja branded wines.
2002	Named "Winery of the Year" by a panel of ninety wine writers.
2004	Amelia Morán Ceja named *Inc. Magazine* "Entrepreneur of the Year."
2005	Amelia Morán Ceja named "Woman of the Year" by the California Legislature.

[6] The Bracero program (from the Spanish word brazo, meaning arm) was a temporary legal contract labor program initiated by an August 1942 exchange of diplomatic notes between the United States and Mexico. Conditions for the poor and unemployed within Mexico after World War II became so dire that illegal employment was attractive enough to motivate many to leave in search of work within the United States illegally, even if that directly competed with the legal workers within the Bracero program. Competition from lower wage illegal immigrants led to the discontinuation of the Bracero program. The end of the Bracero program in 1964 was followed by the formation of the United Farm Workers, and the subsequent transformation of American migrant labor under the leadership of César Chávez.

14 Amelia returned to Mexico to finish high school at *Instituto La Paz* in Aguascalientes, and later attended the University of California San Diego, where she studied history and literature. While in college, she worked part time as a server in local San Diego restaurants, but on her days off Amelia cooked her grandmother's recipes for her roommates, accompanied by wines her father sent to her from the Napa vineyards.

15 The Ceja Family entered the wine business when they purchased fifteen acres in the Carneros region in 1983—a risky proposition, as Carneros had neither received formal status as a California wine appellation nor achieved the reputation for quality wines that it subsequently attained. Amelia recounted the early years:

> Pedro and I were married in 1980. We had great college degrees, good jobs even, but no money. We worked in the vineyards even after we learned English as children, by choice, because we wanted to learn everything about wine production.

16 Carneros is located between the southern end of Napa Valley and the eastern end of the Sonoma wine-growing region (see map in **Exhibit 5**). Land suitable for growing grapes in this designated appellation of the California wine region was expensive: in late 2007 and early 2008, vineyard land prices ranged from $115,000–150,000 per acre, compared to prime vineyard land prices in Napa, $225,000–300,000 per acre, and in Sonoma County,

EXHIBIT 5 **Map of Carneros American Viticultural Area**

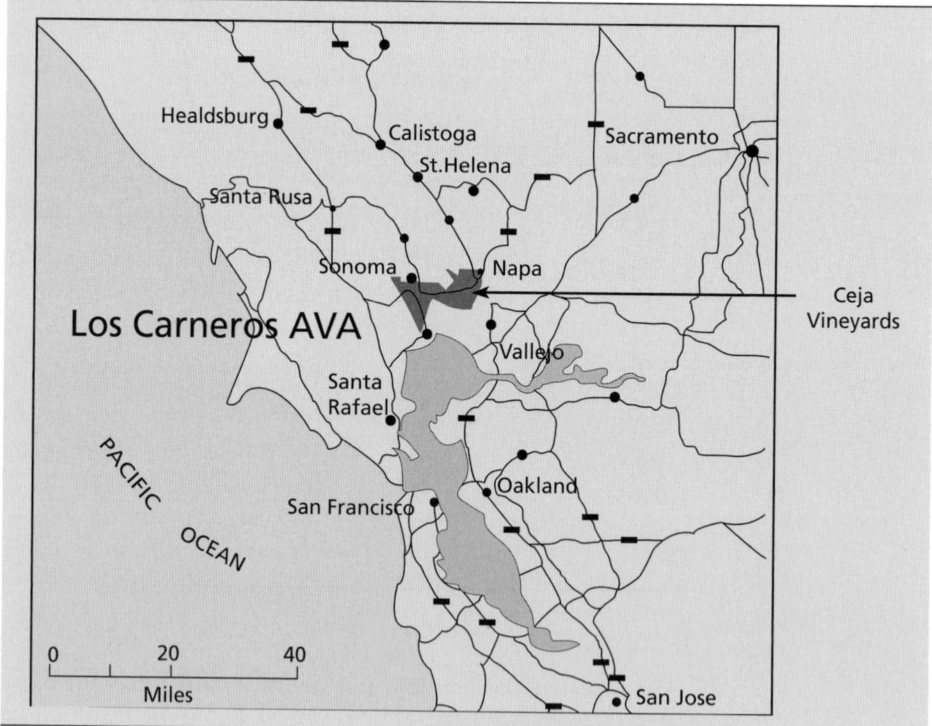

Influenced by the cooling effect of the Pacific Ocean and a combination of summer fog, warm days, and a long growing season, the Carneros wine region is an independent Americal Viticultural Area (AVA). Carneros was the first wine region based on climate rather than political boundaries. It received its designation is 1983.

Source: Carneros Wine Alliance, http://www.carneros.com/appellation.html.

$90,000–125,000 per acre.[7] The family's original vineyard on Las Amigas Road in Carneros remained home to Pedro and Armando's parents Pablo and Juanita Ceja, as well as to Pedro and Amelia and their three children. Their Carneros vineyard consisted of fifteen acres of Pinot Noir vines. Amelia recalled:

> When we first arrived in Carneros, cows and orchards of plums, walnuts, and apples inhabited this land. We purchased fifteen acres with the help of our parents and a bank loan in 1983. This is the bravest thing we ever did. Imagine being in your early twenties and stuck with a $340,000 loan!
>
> We had to use all of our wages to make the balloon monthly payment. Our parents, meanwhile, lost their jobs. We actually put this place up for sale in 1984–1985, but luckily after being on the market for one year, no one bought it. We had to move here. Pedro kept his job and commuted to Silicon Valley ninety miles each way. We lived in a one-room studio for a while with our three small children, so we know a lot about making sacrifices.

17 The family then purchased another eight acres on Ramal Road, about five miles southwest, and planted Pinot Noir vines. In 1989, they purchased another five acres adjacent to the original fifteen acres on Las Amigas Road and planted it with Chardonnay vines. In 1996, they purchased twenty acres on Arnold Drive, closer to the town of Sonoma, about twelve miles to the northwest, and also planted it with Chardonnay. Armando and Martha and their three children moved there in 2000. The Cejas grew eight acres of Merlot on an adjacent leased parcel. The fourth family-owned tract, sixty-five acres, was purchased in 2000, and subsequently planted with five grape varieties (Pinot Noir, Chardonnay, Merlot, Syrah, and a little-known Italian varietal from Piedmont called *Arneis*). This vineyard was located on Adobe Road, five miles northwest, not far from the village of Penngrove and the city of Petaluma, California. Taken together, these vineyard land purchases represented a sizable capital investment for a small winery like Ceja.

18 Ceja planted its first Pinot Noir vineyard in 1986 and enjoyed its first harvest in 1988. Ceja's first customer was Domaine Chandon, a premium Napa producer of sparkling wines. For its first fifteen years Ceja focused solely on growing grapes to be sold to other wineries, including Acacia and Rombauer, the latter producing the best selling Chardonnay brand in fine restaurants. In 2001, Ceja started producing its own wines. Although its grapes were estate-grown in Carneros, a designated American Viticultural Area (AVA), the Cejas contracted with other wine producers to use their facilities for wine production.

19 By 2007, Ceja produced 10,000 cases of wine per year. Its wines included white varietals such as Sauvignon Blanc and Chardonnay, and red varietals such as Pinot Noir, Merlot, Cabernet Sauvignon, and Syrah. Ceja also produced two "Viños de Casa"—a red wine blend and a white wine blend. Prices ranged from $20 to $75 per bottle. Plans were being made to open the Ceja Vineyards Wine Tasting Salon in downtown Napa in 2008. They planned on continuing using only 15 percent of their grapes for their own wine production and selling the balance to other wineries.

20 Amelia recounted:

> These local producers have been loyal to us since the beginning, so we are loyal to them. We have five other wineries on our waiting list to purchase fruit. If we produced and sold all of our grapes under our own label we'd make about 65,000 cases, but we do not ever want to be such a big producer.

[7] P. Franson, "Demand Soft for California vineyards," *Napa Valley Updates* (2009). Accessed November 30, 2009. http://jeffwarren.com/napa_valley_updates/2009/ 05/this-article-is-quasi-accurate.html.

Mission, Values, and Culture

21 While working part-time at the Rutherford Hill winery in the early 1990s, in order to learn how to build Ceja's branded wine business, Amelia enrolled in viticulture and enology as well as wine sales and marketing classes at the nearby Napa Valley Community College. There, she learned the importance of personal selling to convey the value of the brand and began travelling the country to meet with wine distributors, restaurant owners, and wine retailers. She came to consider herself the company's "marketing and sales expert." Amelia summarized Ceja's core purpose and values:

> Diversity is the secret to our success. Our mantra or philosophy is to make wine a part of everyday life. Robert Mondavi made the wine industry pretty much what it is today. We are carrying on his tradition of making wine more accessible to everyone, regardless of who you are, what you like, or where you come from.

22 Amelia's husband, Pedro, was a talented engineer and artist who designed Ceja's Carneros tasting room and offices as well as a new downtown Napa tasting room, scheduled to open in mid-2008. Armando, Pedro's brother, was in charge of grape growing and wine making. Armando often pressed the other partners to increase production, but Amelia remained "cautious about increasing supply when the demand was not yet proven." According to Amelia:

> We are a family business. We all have the same vision, the same goal. I come from a matriarchal family; my partners, however, all come from a patriarchal culture. So, we may disagree, but what makes the most business sense usually wins. We may disagree on how to get there, but eventually we do. We all have equal voting rights—it's a democracy—but we also know that we are all really great at a lot of things. That's why we are so successful.

23 The Spanish word *ceja* literally translates into "eyebrow" or "gentle rolling hills." *Ceja* perfectly described the gently rolling hills of the Carneros region. Prominently displayed at the entrance to the Carneros winery was a brass replica of a Spanish mission bell of the 1800s; an artist's rendering of that bell was prominently featured on Ceja's Web site and labels. Amelia and Pedro's eldest son Ariel graduated from Occidental College with a degree in film production, and worked on developing Ceja's Web site and social media sites.

Winemaking and Quality Control

24 Both Pedro and Armando Ceja considered Napa and Sonoma to be among the most consistent wine growing regions in the world. Walking together through the Carneros vineyards, Armando said: "Anyone can make wine here, but not every wine tells a story. Not all people who come here—lawyers, doctors, high techies—know wine growing as deeply as we do, because we started growing wine grapes as children."

25 Amelia reflected further:

> We've pretty much increased our production by 100 percent per year. We started out at 750 cases—then 1,500—then 3,000. We've also seen what other winemakers have done—and seen other wineries go bankrupt—because they simply grew too fast. We do not need to be in every market. We just want to be in the best markets. It's all about relationships, and friendships, we are just nice people.
>
> Wine growing, after all, is a long-term investment. You have nothing to sell for 3–5 years. Just the real estate cost alone is monumental. Land costs are prohibitive here: to purchase fifteen acres for $25 million in Napa is not unheard of.

26 Back at the winery, Amelia summed up the family's view of winemaking:

> You might say that there are a lot of egos in this business. There are very wealthy investors who are here for the lifestyle—but this business has always been about the family. Yes, we

want to make money, true. But we mainly want to create an environment where everyone on our team will benefit. It's just a different philosophy.

27 According to Pedro, Ceja had avoided "many headaches by being in control of every aspect of wine growing and production."

> From the very beginning we've done quality control over every aspect, from growing to the cork that goes into the bottle. If we receive planning permission to build it, our proposed new fully integrated wine-making facility will be able to increase case production, sure, but we will never buy someone else's fruit to make wine, because we are primarily growers. There are very few wineries like us that make all of their wines from estate-grown grapes. The winery has to be located in the same place where the grapes are grown and you have to own the vineyards in order to qualify as estate-grown. Otherwise, you are out of compliance.

28 Amelia maintained that compliance with regulations was necessary:

> Some other winery owners have been caught and had to go through a costly process of re-labeling all of their wines by hand, meaning taking off the misleading labels and pasting on accurate labels. Alcohol content is another area scrutinized by the Bureau of Alcohol, Tobacco, and Firearms (BATF). We never say our wine has more or less alcohol by volume than it really has because it will raise your excise taxes. So, that's why it is important to build the infrastructure where you can control everything. Being out of compliance can lead to financial distress.

29 Armando, Pedro, and Amelia agreed that just because they were farming on what they considered to be the ideal site in California for Pinot Noir and Chardonnay grapes (due to the dense, clay soil of Carneros), and even though they paid obsessive attention to quality unlike many U.S. winery owners in a rapidly growing industry, they would *never* make more wine than they could sell.

FUTURE CHALLENGES

30 Although she had written a business and marketing plan for the Ceja brand in 1990 as an assignment for one of her night classes at Napa Valley Community College, by mid-2007, Amelia remained unsure how to expand the Ceja brand both inside and outside of California. Her business and marketing plan had not been updated since her days as a student. Expanding distribution via traditional channels would be very difficult due to the barriers posed by the three-tier distribution system, as noted earlier and explained in greater detail in Appendix 1. That system posed a distinct disadvantage to small producers like Ceja.

31 Fortunately for smaller producers, like Ceja, that desired to remain small, the early 2000s had been characterized by an increase in smaller boutique distributors whose portfolios consisted exclusively of boutique or small-scale wine producers. Boutique distributors enabled Ceja to sell its wine to the very top restaurants in various states throughout the U.S., such as the French Laundry in Napa. As a result, some distributors viewed Ceja as an entrée into high-end accounts like those Michelin three-star restaurants.[8] However, boutique distributors were not able to operate in every U.S. state, unlike the largest distributors,

[8] Michelin, the French tire company, had for over a century developed a business of evaluating and recommending restaurants and hotels in a publication known as the Michelin Guide. Michelin employed full-time professional inspectors who anonymously visited restaurants and hotels, and evaluated them on a range of criteria—one star denoted "a very good restaurant in its category," two stars, "excellent cooking and worth a detour," and three stars "exceptional cuisine and worth the journey." The published guides and their ratings were solely produced for European countries until 2007, when Michelin introduced its first guides to U.S. restaurants in New York and the San Francisco Bay Area and Wine Country. Only five U.S. restaurants (of the 59 in the world, nearly all in Europe) received the coveted three stars in 2007.

Young's Market or Southern Wine & Spirits, which were known to be on the hunt to acquire most of the boutique distributors in order to maintain control of this important emerging tier of the wine sales chain.

32 According to Amelia, another challenge for Ceja was how to manage the growth of its wine club:

> Currently, our wine club members are keeping us in business, purchasing 25 percent of the wine, plus about 10 percent more from quarterly shipments to members. It's a great business. It's the answer to small wineries to increase demand across the country and build our "extended family." It's almost viral marketing now. All members bring their friends and family to events that we hold here each quarter and occasionally around the country.

33 Amelia recounted that Ceja had held a wine-tasting event in Los Angeles the previous week and had to turn people away because the wine shop owner's permit allowed only a certain capacity at his store. At the end of 2006, Ceja had about 1,000 wine club members, of which about half self-identified as Hispanics. Ceja's goal for 2007 was 1,500 wine club members (see **Exhibit 6** for 2006 wine club, cased wine production, and price point data). Ceja planned to increase membership to 2,000 in 2008, and 3,000 by 2012. Amelia hoped to sell about 50 percent of any eventual case production to Ceja's wine club members and about 20 to 30 percent of production via tasting rooms. Her goal was to sell 80 percent of production direct to consumers.

34 If Ceja were to sell half of all production—that is, 10,000 cases—to its wine club members, Amelia felt certain that Ceja would need to produce around 20,000 cases of wine each year:

> We already have a sense of being patient and understanding that our wine business is a long-term investment—at least twelve years. In the future we will be building a fully integrated, bonded winery. Hopefully we'll get the necessary permits and begin crushing in 2010. Maybe we'll get to 20,000+ cases in five more years. But even then we'll still be a "boutique" winery. You don't get to mid-sized until you reach over 50,000 cases, and once you get to 100,000 you are considered large.

35 The Ceja brand had been continuously and increasingly profitable since its introduction to the market in 2001, and the company remained largely debt-free (see **Exhibits 7** and **8** for Ceja's financial statements for 2004–2006). Any decision with respect to changing Ceja's marketing strategy would have to take into account the likely impact on profitability in order to preserve the company for the next generation of Cejas. Attaining wine club membership, production, and profitability goals would enable Ceja to capitalize on its heritage as one of the first Hispanic-owned and operated wine businesses in America, but how to attain these goals was no easy decision.

• • •

36 Visitors' tours at Ceja typically ended in the kitchen at the Carneros wine tasting facility, adjacent to the dining room, where the partners were holding their September 2007 conference. The smell of food interrupted the family meeting. Juanita Ceja, Armando and Pedro's mother, offered everyone a spoonful of *molé poblano* that she had been preparing for that afternoon's Ceja wine club members' party.[9] At these events, wine club members

[9] Mole poblano, whose name comes from the Mexican state of Puebla, is a popular sauce in Mexican cuisine and is the mole that most people in English-speaking countries think of when they think of mole. Mole poblano is prepared with dried chili peppers, ground nuts and/or seeds, spices, Mexican chocolate, salt, and a variety of other ingredients including charred avocado leaves, onions, banana, and garlic. Dried seasonings such as ground oregano are also used. In order to provide a rich thickness to the sauce, crushed toasted tortillas, breadcrumbs, or crackers are added to the mix.

EXHIBIT 6 **Ceja Vineyards' Wine Club Memberships and Cased Wine Production, 2001–2006**

Year	Wine Club Members	Production (cases)
2001		750
2002		1,500
2003	Launched	3,000
2004	150	4,500
2005	300	6,000
2006	1,000	7,775*
2007 (estimated)	1,200	8,500

*See table below for breakdown of 2006 case production by varietal wine type and suggested retail price point.

	Cases Produced	Retail Sales Price per Bottle	Retail Sales Price per 12 Bottle × 750 ml Case
2005 Carneros Pinot Noir	450	$40	$480
2005 Sonoma Coast Pinor Noir	450	$50	$600
2005 Sonoma Carneros Merlot	400	$34	$408
2006 Vino de Casa White Blend	600	$20	$240
2005 Vino de Casa Red Blend	2,000	$20	$240
2005 Sonoma Coast Syrah	575	$34	$408
2006 Napa Carneros Chardonnay	650	$34	$408
2006 Sonoma Coast Sauvignon Blanc	2,000	$22	$264
2004 Napa Valley Cabernet Sauvignon	350	$50	$600
2006 Napa Valley Dulce Beso (Sweet Kiss)	300	$55	$660

Sources: Interview with Amelia Ceja, September 2007; and Ceja Vineyards' Web site, accessed September 2007. Ceja's initial Web site was launched in 2000 and its first tasting room at Carneros opened in 2005.

would socialize, eat Mexican cuisine paired with Ceja wines, and pick up pre-ordered cases of wines at the members' discounted price, which ranged from 5–20 percent discounts per case.

37 Armando, unconvinced that direct marketing to Hispanic consumers was the best option for the family, said, in between bites,

> Targeting the U.S. Hispanic consumer segment will require reallocation of our marketing and promotion budgets away from our boutique distributors. There are also, as we all know, a vast number of Hispanic wine consumers living outside the U.S. that could become another high potential market opportunity for us, but we will need larger distributors that have export sales capabilities to reach those customers.

EXHIBIT 7 **Ceja Vineyards Statements of Income, 2004–2006 (unaudited)**

For the year ending December 31	2004	2005	2006
Cased Goods Sales, Net	$508,776	$742,386	$1,227,666
Special Events & Tastings	6,768	21,674	48,098
Other	12,996	23,913	43,804
Total Revenues	$528,540	$787,973	$1,319,568
Cost of Goods Sold	234,893	340,211	528,200
Gross Profit	$293,647	$447,763	$791,368
Operating Expenses—Gen. and Admin.			
Advertising	$385	$12,201	$2,873
Auto Expenses	2,229	3,255	8,497
Bad Debt		286	1,548
Bank Charges	3,825	10,786	3,893
Cash Donations	650	2,654	1,044
Commissions	6,181	5,221	
Computer Supplies	304	1,206	754
Credit Card Discount			17,992
Depreciation and Amortization	1,788	5,409	22,882
Dues	3,571	4,084	6,779
Education and Training	273	632	379
Employee Benefits		982	2,374
Fees and Licenses	3,194	3,605	2,819
Insurance	12,069	14,959	4,328
Legal and Professional	33,993	8,722	19.428
Meals and Entertainment	16,953	17,669	24,513
Outside Services		405	7,010
Payroll Expenses		6,483	24,545
Postage	868	966	2,076
Promotional	992	769	3,145
Repairs and Maintenance	25	35	10,614
Sales and Marketing	655	3,583	
Samples and Billbacks	1,454	6,479	6,863
Subscriptions	187	511	528
Supplies	2,522	10,273	16,773
Tastings and Competitions	5,084	2,820	3,735
Telephone	1,614	5,075	8,459
Travel Expenses	14,525	14,005	16,585
Utilities	67	3,160	6,554
Wages		57,306	267,840
Web Site	655	754	8,715
Other	−15		
Total Expenses	$114,050	$204,297	$503,546
Operating Profit	179,597	243,466	287,822
Interest	171	68	1,062
Other income/expense	541	4,749	12,385
Income Before Taxes	$179,968	$248,146	$299,146
Taxes	1,550	1,225	12,055
Profit After Tax	$178,418	$246,922	$287,090

Source: Ceja Vineyards.

EXHIBIT 8 Ceja Vineyards Balance Sheets, 2004–2006 (unaudited)

At December 31	2004	2005	2006
Assets			
Current Assets			
Cash	$309,374	$563,182	$883,363
Accounts Receivable	59,709	70,858	101,186
Inventory			
Wine in Process	380,081	606,917	590,087
Finished Goods	458,339	476,807	545,398
Other Current Assets	200	200	200
Total Current Assets	$1,207,703	$1,717,964	$2,120,234
Fixed Assets, Net	56,002	118,768	136,119
Total Assets	$1,263,705	$1,836,731	$2,256,353
Liabiliities and Owners' Equity			
Current Liabilities			
Accounts Payable	$282,841	$597,697	$795,218
Sales Tax Collected	4,948	9,421	13,610
Payroll Withholdings		4,277	950
Total Current Liabilities	$287,790	$611,394	$809,778
Long-Term Liabilities			
Note Payable—Viña del Sol	46,088	46,088	46,088
Equity			
Owners Capital Accounts			
Amelia Ceja Capital Account	$87,233	$89,933	$89,933
Pedro Ceja Capital Account	145,500	145,500	145,500
Armando Ceja Capital Account	399,244	399,044	333,192
Martha Ceja Capital Account	25,250	25,250	25,250
Retained Earnings	272,601	519,522	806,613
Total Equity	$929,828	1,179,249	1,400,487
Total Liabilities & Equity	$1,217,617	$1,790,643	$2,210,265

Source: Ceja Vineyards.

38 Meanwhile, Pedro, worrying about cash flow, sampled Juanita's *chimichangas*.[10] He said, "Our current price points may just be too high for the Hispanic consumer, even the high-end Hispanic consumer. We should not reposition our premium wine brands at lower price points or undercut prices via discounted direct sales to Hispanics."

[10] The chimichanga is a deep-fried burrito that is popular in Southwestern cuisine, Tex-Mex cuisine, and the Mexican states of Sinaloa and Sonora. The dish is typically prepared by filling a flour tortilla with a wide range of ingredients, most commonly beans, rice, cheese, ground beef, shredded beef, carne adobada, or shredded chicken, and folding it into a rectangular package. It is then deep-fried and can be accompanied with salsa, guacamole, sour cream and/or cheese.

39 Before Armando and Pedro could get another bite of food or another word in, Amelia interrupted them:

> So, how should we do things differently, to demystify and sell our wine to customers regardless of gender or ethnic or price segment? We know that if we sell direct to consumers, we can make a higher profit margin than by selling to distributors at 50 percent of retail. But direct selling is labor-intensive and not guaranteed to reach Hispanic consumers. Armando, you are the wine maker, and Pedro, you are not ready to quit your day job as an engineer. We need to make the decision.

APPENDIX 1: THE U.S. WINE INDUSTRY IN 2007

40 In 2007, the U.S. wine industry consisted of 6,000 producers in all fifty states plus the District of Columbia. That figure included 4,850 bonded grape wineries and 1,150 "virtual," or non-bonded, wineries. Virtual wineries were those that branded and sold wines made solely by other producers, but had no capital tied up in vineyards, barrels, fermentation tanks, bottling lines, or other tangible assets. The number of U.S. wineries grew 26 percent from 2004–2007. While a majority of the nation's wineries were located outside California, California accounted for 49 percent of the total (2,951, of which 2,098 were bonded and 853 non-bonded). It was highly unlikely that any individual state could overtake California's dominance in wine making in the near future; the five other states with the largest population of wineries were Washington State (519, of which two were owned and founded by Hispanic-Americans), Oregon (393), New York (252), and Texas (154).

41 Three companies—Gallo, The Wine Group, and Constellation Brands—shipped 60 percent of all wines produced in the U.S., and the top ten wine companies in the U.S. controlled 82 percent of all shipments. The largest companies grew their product portfolios via brand extensions, acquisitions of proven brands, or outright purchases of smaller wine producers. Most large firms diversified grape sourcing to lower-cost and counter-seasonal regions outside the U.S., primarily in the southern hemisphere, such as South America, Australia, South Africa, and New Zealand. Those moves left the remaining 5,590 wineries to fend for themselves in a fiercely competitive market that had seen the introduction of 12,000 new brands in 2006–2007.

42 Most wine in the U.S. was sold in supermarkets and warehouse stores, which accounted for just over 80 percent of retail sales. The retail sector witnessed considerable consolidation in the early 2000s, due to mergers of both supermarkets and liquor store chains, which resulted in fewer key buyers. The major national supermarket chains included Kroger's, Lucky, Safeway, Trader Joe's, Whole Foods, Vons and Costco, and Wal-Mart's Sam's Clubs. The retail wine industry in the U.S. was driven by aggressive price promotion based on multi-buy deals and money-off deals. Wine producers and distributors were commonly required to pay supermarkets in order to have their wines included in a promotion, a practice known as "slotting fees," and to accept lower prices. Industry insiders estimated that up to 80 percent of annual volume sales were "on promotion."

43 **Regulatory environment.** The U.S. wine market was very complex and heavily regulated. The Bureau of Alcohol, Tobacco, and Firearms (BATF) regulated the sale and movements of all alcoholic beverages in the U.S. The BATF administered the Code of Federal Regulations, including the labeling and packaging of wine. The Food and Drug Administration (FDA) administered regulations including the Fair Packaging and Labeling Act and

the Bioterrorism Act, both of which impacted the importation and distribution of wine. Advertising of wine was permitted in the U.S. with some restrictions. The industry had taken pre-emptive measures in running "drinking in moderation" advertising campaigns due to perceived government opposition to the binge drinking culture in the U.S., particularly among college and university students.

44 In addition to federal regulators, the fifty individual U.S. states and the District of Columbia administered and levied their own excise, sales, and other taxes, and regulated the distribution and sale of alcohol through a "three-tier system," i.e., from producer to distributor to retailer. State excise taxes per gallon of wine ranged from $0.11 in Louisiana to $2.50 in Alaska; the national median in 2007 was $0.69. Most states also levied additional taxes for sparkling wines and wines with alcohol concentrations by volume exceeding 14 percent.

45 **Competitive environment.** Several major forces operating in concert were said to be driving the U.S. wine industry in 2007, and were expected to be sustained, if not grow stronger, until 2015. Among these forces were: (1) globalization of scope; (2) producer consolidation; (3) distributor consolidation; (4) retailer consolidation; (5) wine market liberalization; and (6) the emergence of Web 2.0 as an Internet marketing medium, spawning new niches, networks, and the emergence of non-mainstream wine consumers in marketing channels.[11] The convergence of these forces resulted in a bifurcation of the U.S. wine industry into two tiers: the top tier included large multibillion-dollar wine and beverage conglomerates, and the second tier included small privately held wine businesses. Each tier operated differently and achieved different profit margins and returns on investment.[12]

46 A widening chasm was appearing between large mass merchandisers that pursued broad or mass markets and small to mid-size producers that pursued focused target markets via differentiated products, i.e., a niche strategy. Successful small to mid-size winer-ies—i.e., under $60 million in revenue—were said by industry analysts to be learning and applying industry best practices, such as improving management team knowledge of consumer branding in regional, national, and export markets. Nevertheless, large distributors, which typically purchased branded wines from wineries at 50 percent of retail prices, increasingly managed all wine at retail and restaurants.

47 In 2006, the "Big Five" U.S. distributors (Southern Wine & Spirits, Charmer, Republic/NDC, Glazer's, and Young's Market) held an estimated 52 percent share of the U.S. wine distribution market, rising nearly 14 percent over the previous five years, and their collective market share was expected to increase substantially over the course of the next decade. This limited the opportunity for a small, 1,000–20,000 case (12,000–240,000 bottles) producer, because a couple of good placements at restaurants would exhaust that inventory before the restaurant even had time to reprint the wine list to feature the wines. The days when business models were conducted on the premise that 80 percent of sales came from 20 percent of the products available were rapidly becoming numbered.

48 Despite the dramatic increase in domestic wineries, imports into the U.S. also grew from 2005 to 2007, at about 9 percent by volume and 14 percent by value, despite the falling U.S. dollar. Imports at supermarkets comprised about 20 percent of retail store sales by volume and 25 percent by value. In 2006–2007, imports accounted for about 31 percent of

[11] R. Macmillan, "2008–2009 State of the Wine Industry," *Silicon Valley Bank* (May 2008), 1–21. See also D. Steinthal and J. Hinman, "The Perfect Storm, Revisited," *Wine Business Monthly* (December 2007), 88–93.

[12] J. Quackenbush, "Consolidation Changing the Wine Business, Industry Experts Say," *North Bay Business Journal* (May 23, 2006).

the overall wine market by value at specialist wine merchants and in on-premises sales in the hotel, restaurant, and café (HORECA) segments. Imports priced below $10 accounted for 91 percent of the sales volume, whereas imports priced above $10 grew at the fastest rate—44 percent annually from 2005–2007. New producers selling small lots of domestically sourced or imported wines faced increasing difficulties gaining traction in the U.S. market for premium wines.[13]

49 **Niche markets.** One way for small producers to gain traction in the U.S. market was to consider direct sales to niche markets consisting of non-mainstream wine consumers. In 2007, wineries began using wine clubs, e-mail newsletters, Web sites, and Internet blogs as vehicles to enhance public relations. Some observers expected that these new marketing communications vehicles would present opportunities for smaller boutique wine producers to introduce niche value-priced brands, although doing so would require greater facility with and use of Internet technologies.[14] Among the most representative of those Internet technologies were:

- *New Media Marketing:* A term to describe the building and managing of social networks and online or virtual communities, such as MySpace, LinkedIn, Twitter, and Facebook, and extending the reach of marketing to the low frequency, low-intensity consumer in a cost-effective way.
- *Buzz Marketing:* The strategic use of word of mouth (the transmission of commercial information from person to person in an online or real-world environment) which works most effectively via inward tourism promotion, blogs, and product reviews.
- *Viral Marketing:* The intentional spreading of marketing messages using preexisting social networks, such as the arts, sports, Internet blog (e.g. Stormboek), and diplomatic communities, with an emphasis on the casual, unintentional, and low cost.

50 According to wine industry researchers, the Gen Y/Millennial consumer, already predisposed to using Internet media such as Web sites, blogs, live chat, and Web 2.0 as social networking tools, was emerging as the target demographic most willing to experiment with new brands, regardless of region, state, or country of origin. This consumer segment was also becoming more sophisticated in choosing beverages that had lower alcohol content and higher perceived health benefits as substitute beverages for distilled spirits. Price sensitivity remained the key driver of consumer wine purchase behavior in this segment. Country of origin, while remaining an influential consumer choice variable at specialist wine merchant outlets, was said by industry researchers to have lesser impact on consumer decision making than price for purchases made at mass-market merchants.[15]

APPENDIX 2: DEMOGRAPHICS OF U.S. WINE CONSUMERS

51 In 2007, the Baby Boomer demographic (those born between 1946 and 1964, or entering 44–62 years of age) represented the largest consuming segment by value and by volume of wine sold. Of the 303 million Americans in 2007 that had reached drinking age (21+), about 12.5 percent comprised about 86 percent of total wine consumption. Major drivers of increasing consumption included the growing sophistication of the 70 million Generation

[13] Ibid.

[14] See blog post November 26, 2006 on goodgrape.com, "Rethinking Wine in a 'Long Tail' World," http://goodgrape.com/index.php/articles/comments/rethinking_wine_in_a_long_tail_world/.

[15] M. Hussain, S. Cholette, and R. Castaldi, "Determinants of Wine Consumption in the U.S.: An Econometric Analysis," *International Journal of Wine Business Research* 19(1): 29–62.

Y/Millennial consumers (born after 1976), of which about half had reached drinking age by 2007. In 2007, Constellation Brands Wines, North America, identified six key psychographic consumer segments shaping consumer behavior for wine purchases in the U.S. These demographic categories are shown in **Table 1**.

52 Beyond psychographic segments, a 2006 Wine Market Council (WMC) study made note of a recent emergence of the Hispanic wine consumer segment, which had traditionally favored drinking beverages such as beer and tequila over wine, and which was said to be in excess of 50 million potential consumers. According to the WMC survey, 31 percent of Hispanics claimed that they drank more wine now than they had during the past few years (as opposed to 11 percent of Caucasians).[16] Sandra Gonzalez, a Sacramento, California, based wine consultant, opined that:

> The wine industry needs to first understand that not all Latinos are the same. Latinos who are born outside U.S., and are largely Spanish-language dependent, are "relatively un-acculturated" and account for about 25 percent of the Latino population. Latinos who are born in the U.S., or have been here over a decade, and are bilingual are the "partially acculturated" and represent the largest segment at 66 percent. American-born and English-dependent Latinos, whose values and traditions are still tied to Latin culture, are the "mostly acculturated" and make up only 9 percent of the population. "Mostly acculturated" Latinos are highly educated, and have both money and an established interest in wine. Sometimes dubbed "Affluentino's," these Hispanic wine consumers are 96 percent more likely to spend $20 or more a bottle than non-Hispanics.[17]

53 Hispanic consumers were an untapped market for wine, as 69 percent of Hispanic adults (aged 21+) had not purchased any wine during the first three months of 2007.[18] Scarborough Wine Research estimated that as many as 10 percent of all U.S. wine consumers were Hispanic.[19] According to Scarborough Wine Research, adult Hispanic consumers were 96 percent more likely than the average American wine consumer to spend $20 or more on a bottle of wine. Imported wines, sourced mostly from Chile and Argentina, accounted for 33 percent of total wines consumed by U.S. Hispanics. Cabernet Sauvignon, Merlot, Malbec, Chardonnay, and Sauvignon Blanc were the most popular Chilean and Argentine wines consumed.[20] There were now 39.9 million Hispanics in the U.S., according to the most recent (2000) census, and 11 million more were expected to arrive by the end of the first decade of the new millennium, and wine-makers were beginning to pay more attention to this customer segment, which had an estimated disposable income—$653 billion by 2003—larger than the gross national product of Spain or Mexico.[21] See **Tables 2A** and **2B** for 2006 demographic data about U.S. Hispanics, and **Figure 1** for the 2006 U.S. census data providing the geographical distribution of U.S. Hispanics or Latinos by country of origin.

[16] U.S. Wine Market Council, "Wine Posts Unprecedented Gains with Hispanic Consumers," (April 10, 2006). Accessed February 26, 2010. http://www.wineanswers.com/Uploads/PressReleases/2006/Hispanicpercent20Trend percent20Release percent20- percent20ENGLISH.pdf. See also, T. Fish and D. Sax, "Wineries Reach Out to Hispanics," *Wine Spectator* 29(10): 12–13.

[17] R. Moreno, "Latino Marketing," *Beverage Media Group* (September 2005). Accessed February 28, 2009. http://www.bevnetwork.com/monthly_issue_article.asp?ID=129.

[18] H. Landi, "Hispanic Tastes," *Beverage World* 126(11): 58.

[19] There were 46.9 million people identified as Hispanic-Americans as of July 2008, according to the U.S. Census, http://www.census.gov/Presselease/www/releases/ archives/facts_for_features_special_editions/013984.html).

[20] Agriculture and Agri-Food, Canada, "Hispanic Consumer Profile: Tri-State Area," (October 2007). Accessed November 30, 2009. http://www.ats-sea.agr.gc.ca/ amr/4372_e.htm.

[21] B. Ebenkamp, "Out of the Box: Not-So-White Wine," *Brandweek* (March 31, 2003).

TABLE 1 Six Psychographic Wine Consumer Segments in North America

Segment	Key Identifiers	Percent of U.S. Wine Consumers	Percent of all U.S. Wine Purchases	Primary Price Point(s)	Preferred Format or Varietal	Considerations for Smaller Wine Producers
ENTHUSIASTS	• Knowledgeable and passionate about wine experience • Wine a global experience—drink from around the world • Appreciate information and wine education • Heaviest consumers of wine by volume of purchases	12 percent	25 percent	> $6 account for 98 percent of wines sold to this segment	47 percent purchase wine in 1.5L bottles	Most reachable target segment or niche
IMAGE SEEKERS	• Average age of 35, still learning about wine • Use Internet to obtain/share information via Web 2.0 • Embrace new packaging and closures • Eager to try new brands/wines	20 percent	24 percent		Merlot most popular; Pinot Noir least popular	Question mark—could be targeted via "cause-related" marketing approaches
SAVVY SHOPPERS	• Enjoy shopping for wine • Seek out the best deals and promotions • View purchase as adventure, process of self-discovery	15 percent	15 percent			Second most reachable target segment or niche
TRADITIONAL-ISTS	• Value things that have a history or tradition • Tend to prefer established wineries with legacy brands • Tend to be repeat purchasers of the same brand	16 percent	15 percent	> $8 accound for 25 percent of volume sold to this segment		Probably not likely to seek out an purchase specific brands
SATISFIED SIPPERS	• Not very knowledgeable about wine • Tend to buy the same, usually domestic, brand • Do not enjoy experience of buying wine • Wine is a part of everyday life • Heavy warehouse store shoppers • Ignore shelf talkers/signs and disinclined to learn more	14 percent	8 percent			Not a realistic segment or niche to target at this time
OVER-WHELMED	• Purchase wine infrequently, once every other month • Confused by hundreds of brands available to purchase • Enjoy wine and seeking knowledge • Biggest opportunity to convert to frequent wine drinkers via market research and brand-building	23 percent	13 percent		80 percent buy white wine (43 percent of volume); 77 percent buy red wine (26 percent); 36 percent buy blush wines (31 percent)	Probably not attain-able target segment or niche in medium term, but could be a long-term "stretch" target
TOTAL		**100 percent**	**100 percent**			

Source: Constellation Brand Wines, North America.

TABLE 2A **Demographic Profiles of U.S. Hispanics, 2005 …**

Country of Origin	Population in U.S.	Foreign-born %	Median Age (Years)	H.S. Diploma Only %	Bachelor's Degree or More %	English Proficient %	U.S. Citizens %	Median h/h Income $	Living in Poverty %	Without Health Insurance %	Home-owners %
Columbia	882,000	66.5	36	26.9	30.3	57.5	65.9	49,901	11.0	26.4	53.0
Cuba	1,631,000	60.1	41	27.6	25.1	58.3	74.9	43,587	13.2	22.7	59.7
Dominican Republic	1,334,000	57.3	29	25.7	15.6	53.4	69.9	35,644	23.2	23.4	28.3
El Salvador	1,560,000	64.7	29	23.4	8.4	44.2	54.2	43,791	15.4	38.9	46.0
Ecuador	591,000	66.4	32	29.0	18.2	49.1	53.3	49,932	13.5	34.7	40.3
Guatemala	986,000	69.4	28	22.1	8.8	39.1	47.1	41,754	20.6	47.9	35.6
Honduras	608,000	68.6	28	22.3	10.3	39.7	46.4	36,662	21.5	49.3	33.9
Mexico	30,746,000	37.0	25	25.5	9.1	61.6	71.1	40,736	22.3	34.8	50.5
Peru	519,000	69.3	35	29.7	29.8	55.1	60.0	51,734	9.5	30.2	50.1
Puerto Rico	4,151,000	1.1	29	28.8	16.0	80.5	99.4	40,736	22.6	15.6	40.3

TABLE 2B **… and Where U.S. Hispanics Lived**

Rank by Hispanic/Latino Population, 2005	2005	2000	Change 2000–2005	Percent Change, 2000–2005	Rank by % Change, 2000–2005	2005	2000	Percent Change, 2000–2005
California	12,534,628	10,741,711	1,792,917	16.7%	North Dakota	11,380	7,020	62.1%
Texas	7,882,254	6,530,459	1,351,795	20.7%	Arkansas	130,328	82,155	58.6%
Florida	3,433,355	2,623,787	809,568	30.9%	South Carolina	136,616	90,263	51.4%
New York	3,026,286	2,782,504	243,782	8.8%	Tennessee	171,690	113,610	51.1%
Illinois	1,807,908	1,509,763	298,145	19.7%	North Carolina	544,470	367,390	48.2%
Arizona	1,679,116	1,267,777	411,339	32.4%	Georgia	625,382	425,305	47.0%
New Jersey	1,312,326	1,098,209	214,117	19.5%	Nevada	557,370	389,336	43.2%
Colorado	895,176	718,956	176,220	24.5%	Mississippi	48,795	34,543	41.3%
New Mexico	827,940	746,555	81,385	10.9%	Alabama	98,624	70,305	40.3%
Georgia	625,382	425,305	200,077	47.0%	Idaho	135,733	97,765	38.8%

Source: Pew Hispanic Research Center, *A Statistical Portrait of HIspanics at Mid-Decade,* http://pewhispanic.org/reports/middecade/. Based on data from the U.S. Census Bureau's 2005 American Community Survey (released August 29, 2006). Accessed June 30, 2010.

FIGURE 1 **Geographic Distribution of Hispanic or Latino Population in the U.S., 2006**

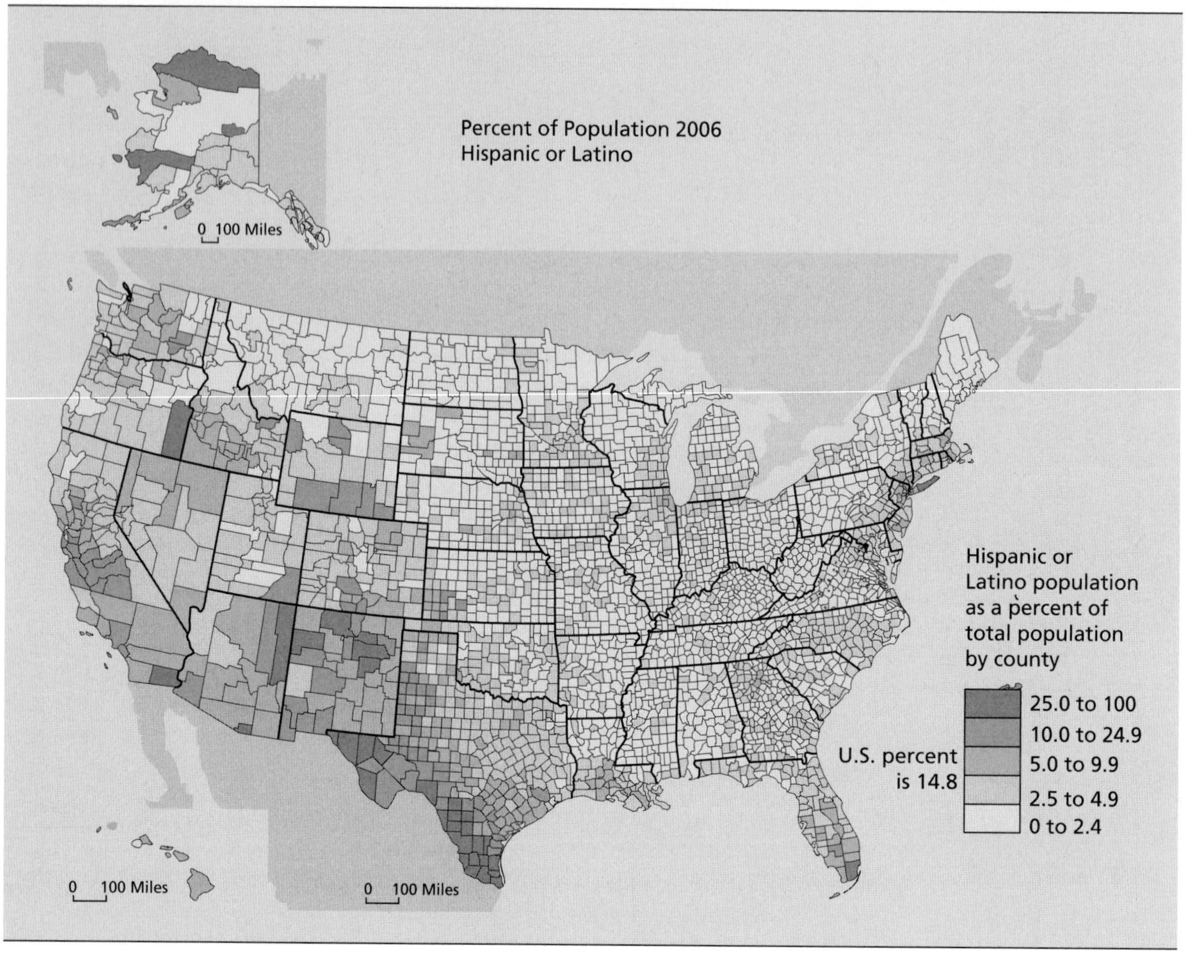

Source: U.S. Census Bureau, Population Estimates, July 1, 2006.

54 Round Hill Vineyards & Cellars, located in St. Helena in the heart of the Napa Valley, was one U.S winery that had successfully targeted the U.S. Hispanic wine consumer, attributing a nearly 400 percent increase in its total case sales from 2005 to 2006 to a surge in sales to Hispanic and Asian-American consumers as the result of its 2004 ethnic outreach program.[22] In 2005, Round Hill launched a Spanish language section on its Web site dedicated to providing information about wine, wine making, and wine and food pairings.

55 **Demographic forecasts.** Three major demographic trends were expected to shape consumer markets in the approach to the second and third decade of the new millennium, according to *American Demographics* editor, Alison Stein Wellner.[23]

[22] C. Jung, "Hispanic Market New Toast of Wine Industry," *San Jose Mercury News* (April 27, 2005). Accessed November 20, 2009, from http://www.isabelvaldes. com/articles/hispanic_business_4-27-2005.htm.

[23] A. S. Wellner, "The Next Twenty-Five Years (Demographic Forecasts)," *American Demographics* (April 1, 2003).

56 First, the U.S. population was expected to increase by 25 percent, or to 350 million by 2025. As the U.S. population grew exponentially, vital resources such as food, water, and power could face shortages. Land prices would be at a premium. Consumers would be aware of these trends and businesses would be scrutinized more closely for their environmental impact, their carbon footprint, and use of precious commodities. Forecasters anticipated rising U.S demand for organically and sustainably grown foods.

57 Second, people 65 and older were forecasted to comprise the highest growing demographic segment. By 2025 the number of seniors was expected to double, to include over 70 million people. If forecasts were accurate, there might be twice as many seniors in 2025 as there were African Americans in 2003, according to Wellner.

58 Another marketing expert, Maddy Dychtwald, predicted that while marketing to younger consumers would remain important, this demographic segment might not be the dominant segment in the future.[24] Instead, according to Dychtwald, the increase in nonwhite consumers represented a third and equally powerful demographic trend predicted for 2025. By then, the Hispanic population in the U.S. was expected to nearly double to almost 68 million. The number of Asians in the U.S. was also forecasted to double, to 24 million. Non-Hispanic whites in the U.S. were forecasted to decrease to 211 million, and black non-Hispanics, to 46 million. Dychtwald opined that producers and marketers who focused solely on white U.S. consumer segments could be making a costly mistake.

[24] M. Dychtwald, *Cycles: How We Will Live, Work, and Play*. (New York: The Free Press, 2003).

Case 7

Chi Mei Optoelectronics

Willy Shih
Chintay Shih
Jyun-Cheng Wang
Howard H. Yu

> *The pressure from running such a large business is intense. We have responsibility for more than 30,000 employees in Taiwan and China. Any misstep in our strategy can cause a lot of damage. The first tier of liquid crystal display (LCD) manufacturers, Samsung, LG Display, AU Optronics [AUO] . . . they all have just under 20% global market share. We are number four at 15%. Samsung has built a Generation 8 fabrication facility [fab] already, LG Display will ramp one up next year, AUO is building one this year as well. We are building one this year too, but the investment is huge. It's like we're in a tournament: you start out with a lot of players, but now we are down to the final four.*
>
> —*Jau-Yang Ho, president of Chi Mei Optoelectronics*

1 In 2008, Jau-Yang Ho, president of Taiwan-based Chi Mei Optoelectronics (CMO), and Biing-Seng Wu, executive vice president and one of Ho's key lieutenants, pondered their investment strategy. Under their leadership, the company had grown from a start-up in 1998 to become the fourth-largest LCD panel manufacturer in the world. LCD panels were the key component in numerous electronic display applications, ranging from notebook computers to desktop computer monitors to flat-panel televisions. The panels were manufactured on large sheets of glass 0.5–0.7 millimeters (mm) thick with circuitry printed on them; subsequently, two sheets were placed together in a sandwich with a gel of chemicals between them. For efficiency, factories manufactured multiple panels simultaneously on large sheets of glass. Progressive generations of fabs could handle larger and larger sheets of glass. Thus, a Gen 5 fab could hold 12 17-inch display panels simultaneously on a single sheet of glass, while a Gen 8 fab could hold 18 individual 32-inch TV screens on a sheet of glass that was roughly 2,200 mm by 2,500 mm (7.22 by 8.20 feet), or larger than a king-sized bed. (**Exhibit 1** shows the relative sizes of different generations of glass. An introduction to the technology of LCDs appears in the **Appendix**.)

2 Out of necessity, the latest factories were highly automated, as human beings could not handle the large glass sheets without breaking them. The factories were enormous in scale and scope, and required as much as a year or more to build and equip, even at the breakneck pace of construction that was the norm in Taiwan. The typical construction and equipment

Source: Senior Lecturer Willy Shih, Professors Chintay Shih and Jyun-Cheng Wang of National Tsinghua University, and Doctoral Candidate Howard H. Yu prepared this case. HBS cases are developed solely as the basis for class discussion. Cases are not intended to serve as endorsements, sources of primary data, or illustrations of effective or ineffective management.

EXHIBIT 1 **LCD Glass Generation Sizes**

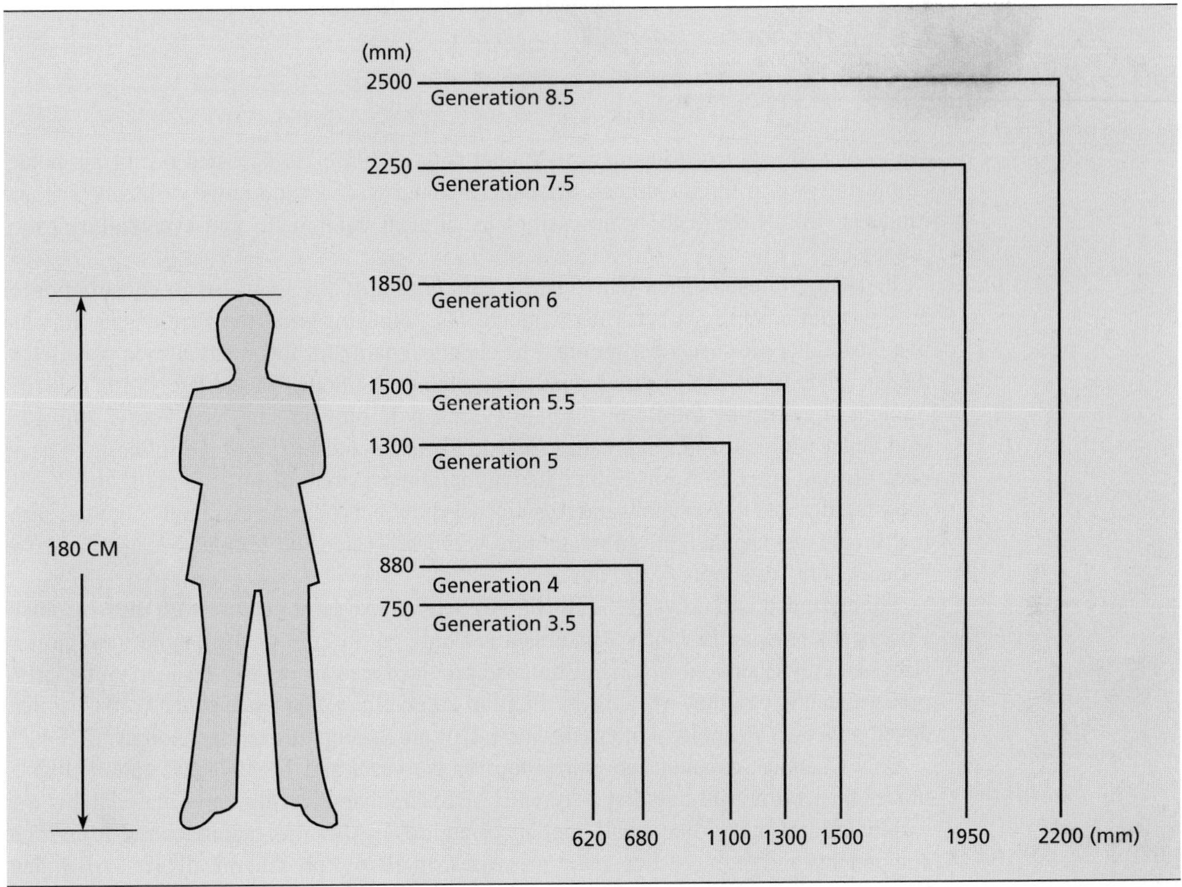

Source: Chi Mei Optoelectronics.

cost for the latest-generation fab was in excess of NT$130 billion (US$4 billion), making barriers to entry very high.

3 The LCD panel business had witnessed explosive growth over the previous 15 years, driven by the wide and expanding range of applications for flat-panel electronic displays. The industry had also experienced extraordinary cyclicality over this time, with periods of rapid growth fueled by capital investment in capacity expansion, which then created large supply-demand imbalances. These up-cycles were followed by harsh downturns during which excess capacity was absorbed. The downturns created opportunities for new entrants, and most new firms that went on to be successful had entered the market during one of these periods.[1]

4 Chi Mei's latest big bet was Fab 8, a Gen 8.5 facility that would be the largest the company had ever built. However, both Ho and Wu had serious reservations about its construction. Ho reflected on the start-and-stop pace of construction: "We actually started clearing the land and building the fab, and then we stopped for almost a year. We stopped because of the industry down cycle and also for financial reasons. In the downturn, we weren't as profitable as we expected, and the pressure on financing of the capital expenditures was intense."

[1] See J. A. Matthews, "The Crystal Cycle," *California Management Review* 47 (Winter 2005) for an excellent analysis of the TFTLCD industry cycle.

5 Ultimately, the decision to proceed was a gamble: Ho and Wu were betting on the growth of the marketplace and Chi Mei's strategy to win in the "tournament."

THE HISTORY OF CHI MEI

6 Wen-Long Shi started a business in Tainan City in 1953. He operated out of his home, employing two to three workers. Shi experimented with a wide range of businesses and products, from toys to daily necessities to surgical equipment, and eventually plastics processing.

7 In 1960, Shi established the Chi Mei Corporation (CMC) and began construction of an industrial complex at Yen Chen, Tainan. The following year, the firm began shipping two tons of acrylic sheets per month. The chemical name for this material was polymethyl methacrylate (PMMA). It was a synthetic polymer developed in the late 1920s and first brought to market by the Rohm & Haas Company in the United States. Forms of it were sold under well-known brand names such as Plexiglas and Lucite. It was often used as an alternative to glass, as it was lighter, had higher impact strength, and did not shatter. CMC grew rapidly, and its Acrypoly and Acryrex acrylic sheets became extremely popular, earning Shi the nickname, "Taiwan's Father of Acrylics." Inside Chi Mei, he became known as "Founder Shi" or simply "My Founder."

8 Shi expanded into polystyrene in 1968 by setting up a joint venture with the Mitsubishi Chemical Company of Japan. Mitsubishi not only put in 20% of the capital into the new firm, the Poly Chemical Company, but also provided free access to a basic manufacturing process technology that was still in the pilot stage. Shi was adamant that Poly Chemical develop its own technology internally instead of purchasing turnkey technology.

9 Poly Chemical expanded its portfolio over the years and, by 1974, was attempting to move into acrylonitrile-butadiene-styrene (ABS) copolymer, an attractive material that was widely used in things like small appliances and toys. ABS was manufactured from three components and required four main processes. In 1976, Poly Chemical's first ABS plant had a monthly production of 200 tons. Rapid expansion every year allowed it to produce 800 tons of ABS per month by 1980.

10 After Ho earned a degree in chemical engineering, he then joined CMC's research and development center after his two years of mandatory military service. More than half of Ho's classmates chose to continue their education overseas. Though CMC was not a big company at the time, Ho knew that the goal of CMC's newly established R&D center was to develop chemical-related products for the future, so there were good growth prospects. The chemical R&D team was responsible for developing and manufacturing many products, including medicines, polyesters, acrylic emulsions, water-based paints, and PVAC adhesives. Ho was directly involved in several of the products in different roles, ranging from entry-level engineer to manager.

11 By 1980, the market for ABS had grown tremendously, and demand was extremely strong. However, Poly Chemical was still experiencing many production and quality problems. In 1981, it was the first purchaser of a new type of production machine from a well-known Japanese equipment manufacturer that pioneered a safer and larger-scale approach to one of the main production processes—mechanical dewatering. Poly Chemical engineers worked closely with the equipment manufacturer for over a year, yet they were unable to get the new process to work. Shi believed strongly in the market potential of ABS and also believed in "consolidating all his firepower" behind a single objective. So he made a company-defining decision in 1982: he shut down all of the chemical-related projects at CMC and transferred key personnel from the R&D center, including Ho, to Poly Chemical to focus all available

resources on developing ABS products. As Shi poured more resources into ABS, product quality improved and volumes increased steadily.

12 Not long after Ho was assigned, the technical team made a breakthrough and got the machine up and running. They were able to ramp up within the next two months, generating acceptable yields and improved product quality. "The existing Poly Chemical technical team had worked very hard on developing this process for over a year. Since I was a newcomer, I assumed that the machine was a total loss and mentally wrote it down to zero. Then I could proceed with an open mind," Ho commented. He convinced his team to change the direction of R&D and redesign the entire process. The technical team, who by now had become very familiar with the machine, was able to make the adjustments very quickly and come up with a new ABS product that caught up with the rapid rise in demand.

13 Improvements were also happening in other processes; the new low-cost Polylac ABS copolymer had the ability to hold colorants well and became extremely popular with manufacturers of a host of consumer products, like small appliances. In June 1983, Poly Chemical produced 2,000 tons per month. CMC continued to expand quickly and by 1994 became the largest ABS producer in the world. With low-cost-efficient manufacturing, it was able to earn very high margins and rapidly grow its global market share, riding a tide of insatiable demand in the growing Southeast Asian economies of the 1980s and 1990s.[2]

14 By 1985, ABS had become the dominant product, and Shi merged CMC and Poly Chemical, keeping the CMC name. In 1994, when the president of CMC retired at the company-mandated 60 years of age, Ho was promoted to president. "Everybody was quite surprised," Ho recalled, including himself. The new role put Ho in the key operating position in the company.

DIVERSIFYING INTO LCD DISPLAYS

15 In the late 1980s, Ho started to think that the future for petrochemicals in Taiwan was not very bright. He viewed Taiwan's geographic location as not well suited to the market, from the standpoint of proximity to feed stocks, the cost of land, and increasing environmental concerns. At that time, he made his first visit to the nascent Hsinchu Science-Based Park. The government of Taiwan had established the park in 1980 to encourage the formation of high-technology businesses. Recalled Ho: "In the north at that time I found that everybody in the Hsinchu Science Park was doing pretty well. So I thought, 'We need to invest in high tech.' In 1997, I invited my founder to Hsinchu. For the first time in a long time, my founder saw something very, very exciting. At that time I suggested that we invest in high tech. We didn't have a particular technology in mind; we just needed something to diversify into."

16 Ho's good friend Biing-Seng Wu was then the vice president of the high-tech company, Prime View International, and was widely viewed as one of *the* Taiwanese experts on the thin-film transistors (TFTs) used in the flat-panel display industry. Wu had been the principal investigator on the first TFT-LCD research project at the Electronics Research Service Organization (ERSO), part of the Industrial Technology Research Institute (ITRI).[3]

[2] In 1999, CMC's ABS+AS capacity was over 1 million metric tons per year. In comparison, the combined capacity of the top 10 Japanese producers of ABS was 800,000 metric tons per year, and the combined capacity of GE Plastics, Monsanto, and Dow Chemical in the United States was 900,000 metric tons per year.

[3] The Industrial Technology Research Institute (ITRI) was a nonprofit R&D organization engaging in applied research and technical service. It was founded in 1973 by the Ministry of Economic Affairs (MOEA) to attend to the technological needs of Taiwan's industrial development.

ITRI was at the heart of Taiwan's technology research infrastructure and spawned countless start-ups in the adjacent Hsinchu Science-Based Park. ITRI had been responsible for the original technology transfer of RCA's CMOS semiconductor process from New Jersey to Taiwan. It set up a four-inch CMOS manufacturing line and spun this off as Taiwan Semiconductor Manufacturing Corporation (TSMC), an event that would have a tremendous impact on the establishment and growth of Taiwan's semiconductor industry.

17 Under Wu, ITRI had begun an investigation of small TFT-LCDs in 1989 and had moved on to three- to six-inch technology in 1990. By 1994, it had set up a line and begun test production of 10.4-inch panels, which were in great demand by the notebook computer industry. But unlike what happened with TSMC, the Taiwanese government suddenly cut the budget, leaving ITRI without enough capital to complete the plant's construction. Instead, the project became part of a technology transfer to Prime View International, and in October 1994, Prime View built the first TFT-LCD production plant in Taiwan.

18 Wu suggested to Ho and Shi that manufacturing color filter arrays for LCD flat panels would be a very good move for Chi Mei, but Shi disagreed. As Ho recalled, "In 1996, my friend Dr. Wu suggested that we should invest in color filters. My founder said no. He said, 'When a horse is running, it must wear blinders and not look around. . . . We must run ABS only, with no distractions!'"

19 But in 1997, the petrochemical industry suffered a severe contraction due to the Asian economic crisis. Ho and Shi visited Mitsubishi Chemical, one of Chi Mei's major shareholders and partners, and found that Mitsubishi was investing with its partner Asahi Glass to build a color filter plant in Kyushu, Japan. "We asked Mitsubishi, they said color filter is good," recounted Ho. Later on, because Mitsubishi and Asahi Glass could not do a joint venture with Chi Mei in Taiwan, Shi went back to Ho and said, "Okay, tell your friend to come back." Ho described the circumstances: "So Dr. Wu stayed outside for almost one and a half years. In the fourth week of June 1997, Dr. Wu again came in to give a presentation. The next day, my founder decided and told me, 'Go.' That Sunday night, at about 11:00 p.m., I telephoned Dr. Wu and told him we've got the okay and decided to go."

20 In fact, Chi Mei had been tracking the TFT-LCD industry since 1996, as many of the key ingredients used in fabricating TFT-LCD panels were based on materials derived from petrochemicals and were therefore closely related to CMC's core products.[4] For example, one of the key materials used in making the color filters, photo resist, shared many of the same ingredients with acrylic plastics. But Shi was skeptical of direct investment because he was not sure whether his company could get a grasp on the core technologies. Chi Mei liked to control its own technology, and the company did not see such an opportunity until Wu came into the picture.

21 Shi soon recognized TFT-LCD as a "once in 100-year opportunity for Taiwan." The semiconductor industry included 18 countries with major participants, and Taiwan could account for only about 10% of overall global production. But the TFT-LCD industry counted only Japan, Korea, and Taiwan as major producers, and most of the demand at the time was coming from Taiwanese notebook computer manufacturers.

22 Color filters were a key enabler of color flat-panel displays, and the color purity, brightness, and optical characteristics were important to display manufacturers. Japanese manufacturers supplied most of the color filters; it was a lucrative business. Color filters were Chi Mei's first step into high-tech, quickly followed by another. Ho explained that by moving to become a full-line TFT-LCD producer, the company would be able to address a

[4] TFT stood for thin film transistor and described an active transistor matrix printed on the glass used to make an LCD display. TFT-LCDs were the highest performance LCD displays on the market.

much larger market: "When we made the decision to invest in color filters, the investment was about NT$3 billion. But when we looked further, we realized that the main market for color filters was TFT-LCDs and that's actually where the future growth for the industry was going to be. So within two months of when we started investing in color filters, we started investing in TFT-LCDs."

23 Another consideration in the decision to enter the TFT-LCD industry was that TFT process technologies were not entirely new territory for CMC. TFT processing involved chemical, mechanical, and electronic technologies. CMC already possessed many chemical processing and mechanical technologies. Wu elaborated on the strategy for finding the missing pieces:

> We would examine the missing pieces in our technology map and find suitable people to fit in. In fact, we didn't really need to purchase technologies. When CMO bought equipment, we tended to have vendors share valuable information. They might reveal who else owned the same equipment, who were the materials providers, and things like that. CMC hired many retired "masters" to be our consultants and purchased several unprofitable companies for their patents.

24 Although CMC was privately held, profitability from its petrochemicals operations made it cash-rich, with almost all of its credit lines unused. At the time, CMC had a strong desire to fund the TFTLCD investment internally. But Ho and Wu realized the importance of being a public company in order to attract the right talent, and they were able to convince Shi. The share offering marked the transition into a publicly traded entity called CMO, partially controlled by CMC. CMO's 2006 Annual Report detailed a long line of fund-raising activities to finance what subsequently turned into a huge string of investments. (See **Exhibit 2** for a list of key fund-raising transactions.)

FOUNDER SHI'S MANAGEMENT PHILOSOPHY

25 Shi espoused three credos as his guiding principles: (1) business was a way to pursue fulfillment, (2) people-oriented management was important, and (3) harmonious relationships were valuable. These credos set a very powerful tone within the company. (See **Exhibit 3** for a profile of Shi and his philanthropic and artistic interests.)

26 A highly decentralized decision-making model enhanced this management philosophy. While Shi would sometimes be involved in major capital investment decisions, he tended to take a very hands-off approach to operational decision making, preferring to empower his key managers. This made the company a very attractive place to work, allowing it to draw personnel from many quarters of Taiwanese industry when new initiatives were launched. Shi described his philosophy:

> I think we've created an environment where people with good ideas come to us, whether internally or externally. One of the strengths of Chi Mei's culture is the entrepreneurship and flexibility. So we encourage our people, and we also constantly try to improve. Going from the chemical business into the TFT-LCD business, many outsiders said it was too big a change. But we didn't look at it that way; we've gone through many changes, and this was a huge opportunity. So that's just part of the old trick of being very flexible and very welcoming of these new opportunities.

27 The power to attract talent would later turn out to be a key enabler, as the company expanded into areas that required specialized technical expertise. When more and more teams moved to CMO, Shi felt a little pressured. He fended off criticism by saying that Chi Mei didn't lure people away from other companies, it just built a good environment and

EXHIBIT 2 Chi Mei Optoelectronics Key Fund-Raising Transactions

Year and Month	Price (NT$)	Authorized Shares (000)		Paid-in Capital (000)		Remarks (all quantities in thousands)	
		Shares	Amount	Shares	Amount	Sources of Capitalization	Capital Increase by Assets Other Than Cash
1998.08	10	300,000	3,000,000	75,000	750,000	Founded 735,312.5	Shares for Acquiring Technology 14,687.5
1999.05	10	600,000	6,000,000	375,000	3,750,000	Cash Offering 2,941,250	Shares for Acquiring Technology 58,750
1999.1	10	600,000	6,000,000	600,000	6,000,000	Cash Offering 2,205,937.5	Shares for Acquiring Technology 44,062.5
1999.05	10	1,700,000	17,000,000	1,070,000	10,700,000	Merge Offering 4,624,800	Shares for Acquiring Technology 75,200
1999.09	20	1,700,000	17,000,000	1,620,000	16,200,000	Cash Offering 5,500,000	
2001.01	42	1,700,000	17,000,000	1,698,187	16,981,870	Cash Offering (Preferred Shares) 781,870	
2003.01	33.5	3,000,000	30,000,000	1,878,187	18,781,870	Private Placement 1,800,000	
2003.05	31.611*	3,000,000	30,000,000	2,098,035	20,980,351	ECB-1 Conversion 2,198,481	
2003.07	10	3,000,000	30,000,000	2,356,934	23,569,339	Dividend Shares 2,588,988	
2003.08	19	3,000,000	30,000,000	2,856,934	28,569,339	Cash Offering 5,000,000	
2003.11	GDR:43.2, ECB1:26.67, ECB2:43.52*	3,750,000	37,500,000	3,372,234	33,722,343	Cash Offering GDR:4,500,000 ECB-1:651,422 ECB-2:1,581	
2004.06	43.52	3,750,000	37,500,000	3,445,510	34,455,103	ECB-2 Conversion 732,760 ECB-2 Conversion: 267,498	
2004.08	ECB2:43.52	5,000,000	50,000,000	3,896,044	38,960,442	Dividend Shares: 3,632,151 Employee Stock Bonus: 605,690	
2004.11	43.52, 38.356**	5,000,000	50,000,000	3,896,601	38,966,008	ECB-2 Conversion 5,566	

2005.04	38.356	5,000,000	50,000,000	3,958,639	39,586,386	ECB-2 Conversion 620,377
2005.06	10	7,500,000	75,000,000	5,458,639	54,538,386	Cash Offering Preferred Shares through Private Placement: 15,000,000
2005.07	GDR:47, ECB2:38.356	7,500,000	75,000,000	5,976,737	59,767,372	Cash Offering GDR:5,000,000 ECB-2 Conversion: 180,986 Dividend Shares: 6,208,722
2005.09	10	7,500,000	75,000,000	6,699,594	66,665,944	Employee Stock Bonus: 689,850
2005.12	38.356, 32.969†	7,500,000	75,000,000	6,699,897	66,998,970	ECB-2 Conversion: 333,026 Cash Offering Common shares through Private Placement:3,500,000
2006.05	47.7	7,500,000	75,000,000	7,049,897	70,498,970	Dividend Shares: 2,626,421
2006.08	10	8,600,000	86,000,000	7,359,383	73,593,831	Employee Stock Bonus: 468,440
2006.12	31.6	8,600,000	86,000,000	8,064,383	80,643,531	Cash Offering Common shares through Private placement: 7,050,000
2007.01	48	8,600,000	86,000,000	7,986,196	79,861,961	Series A Preferred Shares Were Redeemed:-781,870

*CMO's first Euro Convertible Bond issue was fully converted into 284,990,314 common shares in 2003. Also, CMO's second Euro Convertible Bond issue was fully converted into 214,179,538 shares in 2005.

**Due to shared dividends declared from 2003 earnings that were paid in 2004, the conversion price of our ECB-2 was adjusted from NT$43.52 to NT$38.356. Of the ECB-2 that were delivered for conversion, 19,707 shares were converted at NT$ 43.52 and 358,920 shares were converted at NT$38.356.

†Due to shared dividends declared from 2004 earnings that were paid in 2005, the conversion price of our ECB-2 was adjusted from NT$38.356 to NT$32.969. Of the ECB-2 that were delivered for conversion, 9,318,494 shares were converted at NT$38.356 and 23,984,059 shares were converted at NT$32.969

Source: Compiled by casewriter from Chi Mei Optoelectronics 2006 Annual Report, http://www.cmo.com.tw, accessed April 15, 2008.

EXHIBIT 3 The Chi Mei Museum and Chi Mei Founder W. L. Shi

The Chi Mei Meseum

Wen-Long Shi started his first business venture when he was 18 years old. As founder, he is the driving force behind the Chi Mei Group, the largest ABS producer in the world and an industry-leading TFT-LCD panel manufacturer. He is also the power behind one of the most prestigious private museums in the world, as well as one of Taiwan's largest nonprofit medical centers. Shi has dedicated his life to promoting the advancement of society and the cultural enrichment of the community. He has said, "CMC or CMO may not be around 500 years from now, but Chi Mei Medical Center and Chi Mei Museum could still be alive and well."

Birth Date	February 1928		Leadership Roles
Birthplace	Tainan City, Taiwan		
Education	Tainan Industrial Vocational High School, Taiwan		
Career		1953–1959	Cofounder, Chi Mei Plastics Main product: plastic toys and daily necessities
		1960–2004	Founder/Chairman, Chi Mei Corporation Main product: cast acrylic sheets, ABS, AS, PS, TPE, LBR, PMMA resins
		1997–2004	Founder/Chairman, Chi Mei Optoelectronics Corp. Main product: thin-film transistor liquid crystal displays
		1997–2001	Founder/Chairman, Pro Atch Technology, Inc. Main product: computer monitors
Social Activities			
		1970–Present	Adviser, Tainan Fishing Association
		1976–1978	Adviser, Tainan Youth Symphony Orchestra
		1977–Present	Founder/Executive Director/Chairman, Chi Mei Cultural Foundation
		1986–1988	Founder/Executive Director, Tainan Operatic Symphony Orchestra
		1987–Present	Chairman, Chi Mei Medical Center (nonprofit)
		1996–2000	Adviser to the President of the Republic of China (Taiwan)
		2000–2006	Senior Adviser to the President of Republic of China (Taiwan)
Other			The 4th Nikkei Asia Prize Winner for Economic Growth, 1999 Nihon Keizai Shimbun, Inc.

Source: Chi Mei Optoelectronics.

set up "stages" for people to develop businesses. People would just "jump on the stage" to perform. In fact, when people praised Shi for making yet another big strategic move, he invariably said that there were no people behind the scenes making the decisions. All CMO did was build a good environment and everything else followed.

28 During his years at ITRI, Wu had developed a strong network that brought access to a primary source of talent in the field. The rapidly growing cluster around ITRI and the Hsinchu Science-Based Park also become a deep reservoir. And CMC's increasing participation as a supplier of plastics for backlights and other components helped as well.

29 There were other sources of engineers. Japanese manufacturers had set up manufacturing plants for less-advanced LCD displays (so called TN and STN LCDs) in the 1980s. Hitachi had established an STN LCD module facility in Kaohsiung in 1983, and Sharp also produced LCD modules in Kaohsiung starting in 1986 to feed the pocket calculator and other industries in Taiwan. These firms were a training ground for many Taiwanese engineers, who jumped to firms like CMO for their lucrative stock grants. Some LCD firms, particularly AUO, also drew heavily from the semiconductor industry, where the manufacturing process technology and industrial engineering challenges were similar. Taiwanese universities were also rich sources of talent.

THE GROWTH OF CHI MEI OPTOELECTRONICS

30 Though CMO grew out of CMC, the character of the business was quite different from its parent. As Wu explained, "The alignment of these two businesses is really quite different. In CMO, we need the high pressure of the market. We need engineers in Taiwan to manage the ones in China. Not everyone from Taiwan likes to work over there and they would often quit."

31 Ho realized that CMO would be playing a very different game than CMC, and that he would need a correspondingly different organizational structure with different resources, processes, and priorities. He opted for a separate subsidiary, with an independent structure and compensation model as well. He quickly redesigned the pay structure by enlarging the compensation differential across various rankings and put in a larger performance bonus component. Ho recalled proudly, "It only took one board meeting to have it approved!"

32 Ho, Wu, and Shi all recognized the importance of attracting key talent and the value such talent placed on an autonomous unit structure with decentralized management and the flexibility to act quickly. Reflected Ho, "Our founder really played a key role for CMC to move from the petrochemical industry into the high-tech sector. He understands the fundamental differences between the two businesses and is willing to let go of part of the old traditions."

Building Fab 1

33 As CMO began construction of its Fab 1, a Gen 3.5 facility, it licensed the basic TFT-LCD technology from ITRI and also licensed multidomain vertical alignment (MVA) technology, which enabled wide viewing angles, from Fujitsu of Japan. Wu elaborated:

> From the start, CMO's strategy was different from other Taiwanese panel makers. We licensed the basic technology from ERSO, and then modified the licensed TFT structure

> and developed a new structure in Fujitsu's fab. Since this new TFT structure was our own design, we could modify the process by ourselves as needed. Other Taiwanese panel makers transferred the entire TFT-LCD technology—they didn't develop their own processes, they essentially copied the processes from the Japanese panel makers. There was a huge difference in these two strategies. Transferring technology did not have any risks in the beginning; however, not only do we need to pay an initial technology transfer fee, but if we needed to change the process flow, we would also need to get approval from the original technology licensor.[5]

34 CMO was able to take advantage of one of the industry downturn cycles to enter the industry. Japanese firms were more willing to license technology to Taiwanese partners during this period to help fend off competition from Samsung, LG Philips LCD, and other Korean manufacturers, which other Taiwanese competitors took advantage of as well.[6] The pioneering Japanese manufacturers were thus able to extend their window of profitability on older Gen 3 technology by generating licensing income, as they invested in their own next-generation plants.[7] AUO, which had started out by modifying a 4-inch semiconductor wafer line to build its first TFT-LCD line, was able to ink a technology transfer deal with Mitsubishi of Japan and IBM Japan. Chunghwa Picture Tube (CPT) signed a similar technology transfer deal with Mitsubishi for a Gen 3 facility and was able to leverage this into the first larger-sized TFT-LCD facility in Taiwan. (**Exhibit 4** describes some of the core manufacturing technologies for TFT-LCDs and where Taiwanese industry learning came from.)

35 CMO was able to test out some new, experimental cell structure designs using Fujitsu's equipment and develop its internal processes as it was building its own first factory, Fab 1. Recounted Wu,

> We paid a lot of money for two runs, two tests. We also asked them to take a look at our new structures. We sent our engineers to Japan to test for three weeks. . . . We had no way to develop these new ideas otherwise. We found our new electrode structure would cause a production bottleneck that we needed to overcome. The capacity of Fab 1 was 50,000 mother glasses per month, but in the first phase we actually only did 6,000 pieces because we didn't have the confidence yet that we had the right equipment to do this structure.

36 CMO also agreed to work as a Fujitsu supplier for LCD panels. As Chi Mei built Fab 1, Fujitsu sent in people to validate CMO's production methods. Wu explained: "As we wanted to move into the larger sized TV panels, we needed that kind of specific knowledge. In essence, we exchanged our production capacity for Fujitsu's technical support. Not only did we get an 'instant' customer that way, we also had someone from Fujitsu come into our fab and make sure we did it the right way."

37 Fab 1 was a Gen 3.5 facility and could handle glass that was 620 mm by 750 mm. As in other fabs, the need for precision alignment meant the building structure had to

[5] The fee was paid for the initial transfer; subsequent changes or adjustments required separate approvals.

[6] LG Philips LCD was a joint venture between LG of Korea and Philips of the Netherlands. Philips eventually sold much of its share position, and the company was renamed LG Display in 2007.

[7] For an excellent discussion of this history, see T. Murtha, S. Lenway, and J. Hart, *Managing New Industry Creation* (Stanford, CA: Stanford University Press, 2001).

EXHIBIT 4 **TFT-LCD Key Process Technologies**

Process Step	Challenges	Sources of Talent and Experience
TFT array manufacturing	Large-scale patterning of substrates, deposition of Si layers on glass	Similar to the semiconductor industry, but glass instead of silicon wafers. Clean-room practice, industrial engineering similar to semiconductors. Engineers from the semiconductor industry a deep talent pool
LCD cell fabrication	Critical technology with a very steep learning curve. Key determinant of yield	Japan, through licensing or technology transfer
Assembly	Assembly skills and labor management	Extensive Taiwan industry experience, from Japanese TN/STN LCD facilities in Kaohsiung, and Taiwanese tech manufacturing

Source: Casewriter.

be extremely rigid. Fabs employed enormous quantities of steel in their construction and were usually multilevel buildings to facilitate equipment floors sandwiched between levels that provided air handling and utilities. The actual manufacturing took place in a clean-room environment, as dust and particle contamination caused tiny defects that interfered with the operation of an LCD. If a finished LCD had such a defect, it generally had to be thrown away, decreasing the factory's yield. The booming semiconductor manufacturing industry in Taiwan provided a deep pool of knowledge and skills in clean-room operations and fab construction, as the challenges were similar. CMC's experience in petrochemical plant production also provided homegrown construction management expertise. (**Exhibit 5** shows the exterior and interior of Fab 1.)

38 Ho talked about the start-up of Fab 1:

> One of the benefits of our relationship with Fujitsu is that very early on, when we first entered the industry and built our fab and manufactured our product, we had no one to sell to because we were brand new and no one knew the quality of the panels that we were making. With Fujitsu, we brought their team into our fab, here. We had the relationship with them, and that allowed them to validate our quality. Because they brought their people in and checked our processes, they had confidence in our quality and bought our products.

39 In the end, the total investment in Fab 1 was NT$30 billion. Reflecting on this emergent investment strategy, Ho commented, "The NT$3 billion quickly turned into NT$30 billion." And that was only the beginning. (**Exhibit 6** shows a time line of CMO's major milestones and additional fab investments.)

EXHIBIT 5 **Chi Mei Optoelectronics Fab 1**

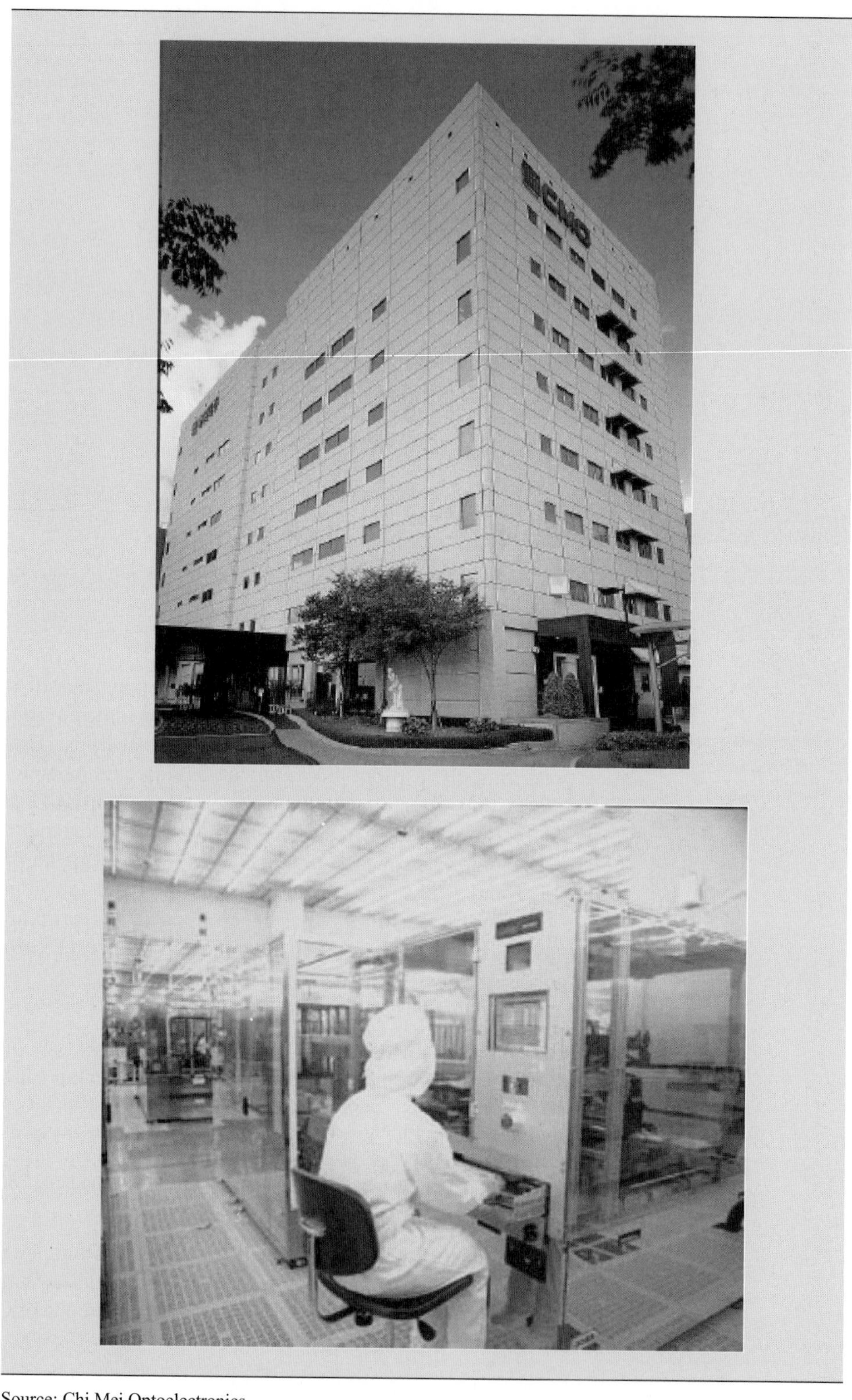

Source: Chi Mei Optoelectronics.

EXHIBIT 6 **Chi Mei Optoelectronics Time Line**

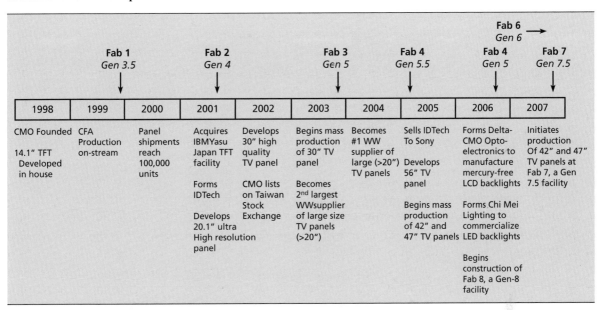

Year	Fab	Events
1998		CMO Founded 14.1" TFT Developed in house
1999	**Fab 1** *Gen 3.5*	CFA Production on-stream
2000		Panel shipments reach 100,000 units
2001	**Fab 2** *Gen 4*	Acquires IBMYasu Japan TFT facility Forms IDTech Develops 20.1" ultra High resolution panel
2002		Develops 30" high quality TV panel CMO lists on Taiwan Stock Exchange
2003	**Fab 3** *Gen 5*	Begins mass production of 30" TV panel Becomes 2nd largest WWsupplier of large size TV panels (>20")
2004		Becomes #1 WW supplier of large (>20") TV panels
2005	**Fab 4** *Gen 5.5*	Sells IDTech To Sony Develops 56" TV panel Begins mass production of 42" and 47" TV panels
2006	**Fab 6** *Gen 6* → **Fab 4** *Gen 5*	Forms Delta-CMO Opto-electronics to manufacture mercury-free LCD backlights Forms Chi Mei Lighting to commercialize LED backlights Begins construction of Fab 8, a Gen-8 facility
2007	**Fab 7** *Gen 7.5*	Initiates production Of 42" and 47" TV panels at Fab 7, a Gen 7.5 facility

Source: Compiled by casewriter from company annual reports.

BUILDING AN INTELLECTUAL PROPERTY BASE

40 During his years at ITRI, Wu became the one person who amassed the most TFT-LCD patents in Taiwan. ITRI was also the source of CMO's initial TFT-LCD technology, which it licensed in mid-1998. CMO then set about developing a new cell structure in-house, which it tested by "renting" Fujitsu's equipment for two test runs, as described earlier. By early 1999, CMO had already started filing for its own TFT-LCD patents. As Wu explained:

> One of the key philosophies that we have is we don't outright purchase a complete technology package. We try to develop what we need to and we may put in some basic technology or hire an outside consultant to develop our proprietary, internal technology. What that allows us to do is to understand that technology much better and it's much quicker for us also to improve that technology. That also gives us a basis to cross-license with other companies. We have some valuable patents that some other companies would like to use and we can enter into cross-licensing agreements.

41 In mid-1999, CMO took another step to strengthen its technology base: in addition to becoming a foundry supplier to Fujitsu, CMO also licensed Fujitsu's MVA technology, which enabled wide viewing angles for large-size TV panels. CMO believed that only by implementing solutions firsthand could it understand the technology intimately enough to come up with its own proprietary innovations. CMO's R&D team subsequently achieved several breakthroughs while working with the original MVA technology, developing its own proprietary "Omniview Color," which significantly reduced the color shift of skin tones when viewing the panel from wide angles.

42 CMO also acquired access to most of IBM's LCD-related intellectual property (IP) when it purchased IBM's LCD business and Gen 3 TFT-LCD fab in 2001, providing CMO with an IP umbrella that shielded it from some of the other IP-related problems within the industry. (See **Exhibit 7** for a list of Chi Mei's key agreements.) In 2002, along with other Taiwanese LCD peers, CMO licensed a set of common TFT-LCD patents from the ERSO unit of ITRI.

EXHIBIT 7 **Chi Mei Optoelectronics' Key Agreements**

Agreement	Contracting Party	Term of Agreement	Summary	Remarks
Technology cooperation agreement	ITRI	May 1, 2002~April 30, 2009	Cross-license arrangements	
	IBM	Effective as of September 24, 2001; may be terminated as provided in the agreement	Flat-panel display-related technology patent licensing	
	Dai Nippon Printing	Effective as of March 11, 2002; may be terminated as provided in the agreement	DNP provides know-how and consulting on color filter manufacturing process	
Technology transfer agreement	Kyocera	December 26, 2006	Sold OLED technology and equipment	
	Vestel	February 17, 2006	Technology transfer and cooperation of TFT-LCD modules	
Cross-license agreement	Sharp	Jan 1, 2006~Dec 31, 2010	CMO and Sharp may use each other's patents relating to LCD technology	
	Hitachi	Jun 1, 2005~Dec 31, 2009	CMO and Hitachi may use each other's patents relating to LCD technology	
License, settlement, and release agreement	Guardian	Jun 1, 2005~Dec 31, 2009	CMO settled certain outstanding disputes with Guardian and entered into certain cross-licensing arrangements.	
	Thomson	Jan 1, 2005~Dec 31, 2009	CMO and controlled subsidiaries received a license to produce complete LCD display monitor units.	
Sale and purchase/ OEM agreement	Sony	Feb 1, 2004~Mar 31, 2007	Sale and purchase of LCD	Nonrenewal option
	Philips	Jul 1, 2006~Jul 1, 2007	Sale of LCD	Nonrenewal option (one year)
	Sharp	Jun 1, 2005~Jun 1, 2006	OA OEM	Nonrenewal option
Procurement agreement	Corning	Jul 21, 2004~Dec 31, 2009	Glass substrate supply	

Source: Compiled by casewriter from Chi Mei Optoelectronics 2006 Annual Report, http://www.cmo.com.tw, accessed April 15, 2008.

THE ONE-DROP FILLING DECISION

43 As CMO developed its capabilities, it sometimes took some major technological risks. One of the best examples was the decision to implement one-drop filling in Fab 2. While Fab 1 was still under construction, Shi realized that the accelerating rate of competition in the LCD industry necessitated bold investment decisions, so he approved the construction of Fab 2, a Gen 4 facility. (See **Exhibit 8** for photos of Fab 2.) This in itself was a risky decision, as the team under Ho had not yet established any history or much of a learning base with Fab 1.

44 By this time, Ho and Wu had become convinced that the key to the market was going to be flat-panel televisions, which meant larger panel sizes (32 inch, for example) than were used in notebook computers and computer monitors. This brought a different set of technical challenges. A Gen 4 mother glass could be conveniently cut into two 30-inch panels, but the process of filling them with liquid crystal material was going to be lengthy because of the sheer size. The established technology, known as "vacuum fill," meant putting the sandwich in a vacuum chamber and allowing the liquid crystal material to get sucked into the evacuated space. But the large panel size meant that it could take as long as three days to fill, and the slowly advancing liquid crystal slurry would carry a band of impurities at the front of the wave as it moved from the edges inward.

45 At that time, Fujitsu VLSI (subsequently acquired by the Japanese equipment maker Ulvac) was developing an experimental technology called one-drop fill (ODF), in which many, many micropipette dispensers would each place a single drop of liquid crystal material between the two pieces of glass before they were sandwiched.[8] This meant that precisely the right amount had to be metered, with no gaps from underfilling or excess from overfilling. CMO had sent a senior R&D team to evaluate the ODF equipment; he came back extremely impressed by the potential of the new technology. Implementing a completely new technology like this in production entailed enormous risks. If the technology failed, it could take a year and a half to switch back to the conventional process. The upside, if it was successful, was also very high because of the improved productivity that would become possible. It would reduce the process time for filling larger panels from three to five days to five minutes. But no one in the industry had the appetite for the implementation risk it entailed.

46 To mitigate the risk, Ho decided to divide Fab 2 in half and implement half the capacity with the older technology and gamble half the capacity on ODF. Wu recounted: "I suggested to President Ho that he report the decision to the chairman since we were risking 50% of the capability on our new fab. That could really potentially bankrupt our company if anything went wrong. But I remember Mr. Ho saying, 'No, people at the board level don't have the technical expertise to make the decision for us.'"

47 Ho was very careful in making that decision. The technical team members were highly confident they could make it work. But, as Ho recalled: "Of course, if that turned out the wrong way, I'd get killed! But we really didn't have much of a choice. Our existing technology back then wasn't superior to our competitor's. We desperately needed a breakthrough. But once that decision was made [investing in ODF], our team became very focused and made it work."

48 Ultimately, the gamble paid off, and CMO not only became an industry pioneer in using ODF but also filed many ODF-related patents. Coming from CMC where process

[8] H. Kamiya et al., "Development of One Drop Fill Technology for AM-LCDs," *SID Symposium Digest of Technical Papers* 32 (June 2001): pp. 1354–1357.

EXHIBIT 8 **CMO Fab 2**

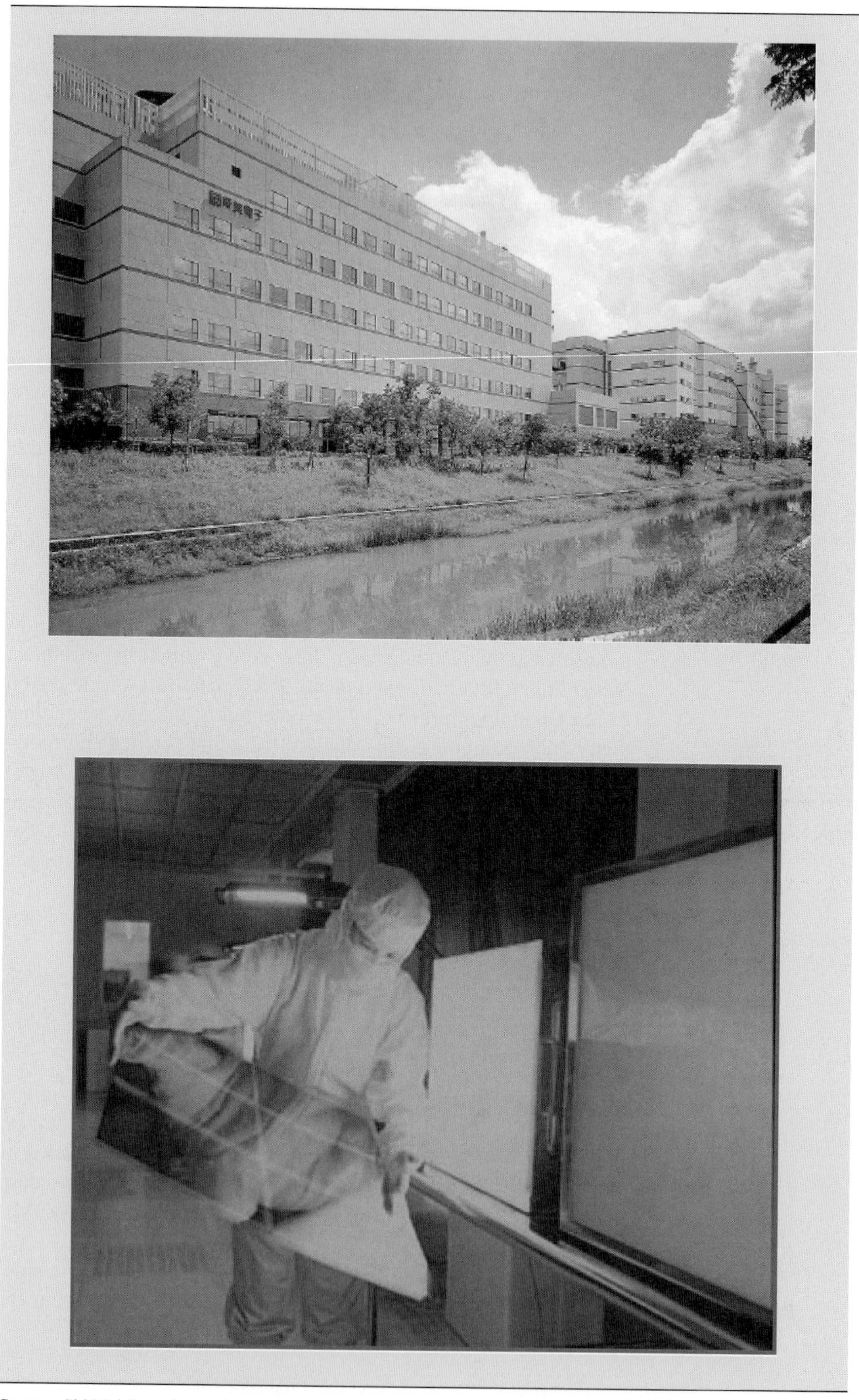

Source: Chi Mei Optoelectronics.

EXHIBIT 9 Differences between the LCD Industry and the Plastics Industry

Attribute	CMO	CMC
Size of capital investment	10X	1X
Market size	10X	1X
Product diversity, product category, product application	10X	1X
Product life cycle	1X	10X
Number of customers	1X	10X
Type of customers	Big customers	Mom and pop
Size of customers	10x	1X
Product target	Consumer market	Industrial market
Inventory value	Always goes down	Fluctuates
Speed of technological change	10X	
Risk	10X to 100X	1X
Dependency on human talent	10X	1X
Salary differentials	Big	Small
Compensation gap	5X to 10X	1X
Importance of staff's tenure	Less important	More important
Need to go public	Is a must	Not necessary

Source: Compiled by casewriter from interviews.

technology was far more mature and predictable, Ho pointed out that the size and risk associated with the process technology bets were in a whole different league: "In my life, I have taken so many gambles. Back in those days, there were several critical environmental issues for us. In Fab 2, our technology was inferior; we had to come up with a breakthrough. Second, we knew we needed to focus on LCD TV because that was going to be hot, we thought."

49 Ho reflected on some of the differences he had experienced in running CMC compared to CMO: "At CMO, the size of capital investment is 10 times CMC, the market size is 10 times, product diversity is 10 times, but product life cycle is one-tenth, the number of customers is one-tenth; speed of technological change is 10 times, risk is 10 to 100 times." (**Exhibit 9** is a summary of Ho's comparison.)

INTEGRATING VERTICALLY

50 Though Chi Mei had originally intended to make only color filters, it had quickly moved into making the TFT-LCD sandwich. This became a highly competitive segment as Samsung, LG Philips LCD, AUO, CPT, Hannstar, and others piled on capacity. From 2003 to 2004 alone, as many as 15 Gen 5 fabs came onstream across Asia, driving finished panel pricing

down. The capacity-driven boom-and-bust cycle put intense cost pressure on the panel manufacturers, which had to source many expensive components to assemble finished displays.

51 In the early part of the decade, display drivers (driver ICs) could make up 15% to 20% of the overall production cost of an LCD display. At that time, there were very few suppliers producing this critical component in the market. CMO relied exclusively on Texas Instruments (TI) for its supply. Severe shortages in the market drove CMO to assemble a team of engineers and start exploring the feasibility of manufacturing driver ICs in-house. Strategically, CMO management felt that to be successful over the longer term, the IC design team needed to have exposure to a more balanced customer portfolio, instead of supplying CMO exclusively. Therefore, management decided to spin off the team into a separate entity, Himax, so that it could engage other customers without conflict. Starting with more than 70% ownership when it first established Himax, CMO deliberately let its equity stake be diluted during subsequent fund-raising rounds to a 14% ownership. With the support of CMO as its first customer, Himax ultimately was quite successful generating revenues of almost US$1 billion in 2007. Although CMO maintained a competitive bidding process between Himax and other IC vendors, it sourced the majority of its driver ICs from Himax, while CMO accounted for around 60% of Himax's revenues.

52 CMO was able to move into photomasks, polarizer films, and many other key components by simply leveraging its expertise in chemical manufacturing. The company was also able to leverage CMC's capabilities in plastics to supply PMMA light guide plates for the LCD backlights (120,000 tons-per-year capacity) and polycarbonate for light diffusion films on top of the backlights. With the Himax model as a successful first step in upstream integration, over the years CMO formed a web of tightly linked subsidiaries across its supply chain. (See **Exhibit 10** for CMO's affiliates.) Although the Chi Mei Group did not necessarily own these subsidiaries 100%, the company often had a large enough equity holding to maintain influence over various strategic issues. These efforts at vertical integration helped alleviate some of the concerns about the availability of critical components.

53 All these efforts made CMO one of the most vertically integrated of Taiwan's TFT-LCD manufacturers. Although the move toward vertical integration seemed natural in retrospect, CMO was really a pioneer at a time when most competing Taiwanese TFT-LCD manufacturers thought outsourcing of components was the way to go. This desire for vertical integration had its roots in the history of CMC when people took pride in their own technical capabilities and manufacturing competence. They gained confidence from their past experiences in successfully integrating advanced technologies with their own manufacturing skills. They realized that the component costs accounted for 60% of the total cost of an LCD panel, so vertical integration allowed them to be far more competitive. Ho commented on how some of the capabilities came to CMO: "The TFT industry is unique in its cluster effect, so in the science park we have a lot of suppliers come in and tell us ideas. . . . I think we've created an environment that people come to us, whether internally or externally. We can make better offers to acquire the expertise."

DIFFERENTIATION IN A COMMODITY BUSINESS

54 Considering the degree of technical difficulty and the enormous capital investments required, it was ironic that standardization of TFT-LCD panel sizes and interfaces made them a pseudo-commodity with spot market pricing fluctuating according to supply and demand. In this environment, each of the manufacturers competed primarily on price, therefore focusing ruthlessly on costs. Some attempted to differentiate their offerings with

EXHIBIT 10 **Chi Mei Optoelectronics Affiliated Companies**

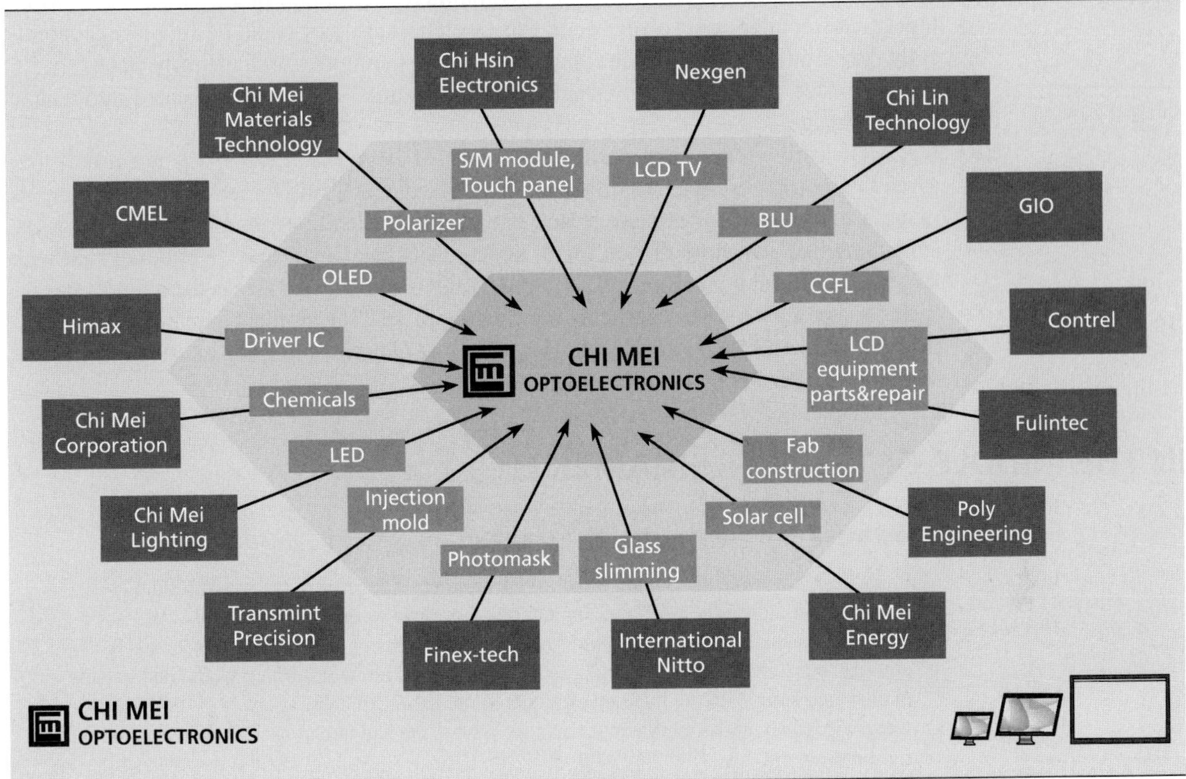

Source: Company presentation.

different driving schemes or color filters, backlighting schemes, frequency response for better television signals, and low motion blur. But in the end, supply and demand were the principal drivers of pricing.

55 From Fabs 1 and 2, CMO followed quickly with its first Gen 5 fab onstream in the fourth quarter of 2003, a Gen 5.5 fab in the first quarter of 2005, a second Gen 5 in September 2006, a Gen 7.5 in May 2007, and a Gen 6 ramp-up in the first half of 2008. This enormous growth outpaced industry capacity growth, but revealed a different view of the optimal product in the marketplace.

56 Though many analysts focused on the generation of a factory that a firm chose to build as a reflection of aggressiveness about technology, CMO focused on its view of product mix that each fab could efficiently produce. Wu explained:

> When you look at a fab generation, it is not a brand-new technology. The generation purely reflects the size of the glass. So when we talk about Gen 3.5 versus Gen 5.5, it is just the size of the glass. Of course there is certain handling technology that needs to be included when dealing with larger size glass, but the actual TFT design rules do not change from generation to generation. So what we look at in terms of what generation to build, for us, we think in terms of technology, product, and customer. When we look at the size of a substrate, we think about how we will cut it in order to minimize the glass wastage and produce the product that people want. That is actually the main focus of our decision on which generation to build.

57 CMO was the only firm in the industry to build a Gen 5.5 fab because it felt there would be strong demand for 32-inch televisions, and Gen 5.5 glass could be cut more economically than Gen 6 glass. And the smaller Gen 5.5 equipment was less expensive than Gen 6. But after fab construction had already been committed, they found that 22-inch-wide-format (16:10) PC monitors were a very good fit as well because they could be cut quite economically. A Gen 5 fab could produce eight 22-inch-wide monitors simultaneously, but a Gen 5.5 could produce 12 at a relatively small increase in capital cost. That translated into a huge cost advantage.

58 CMO's early recognition of the importance of large panel sizes was not a surprise, given the industry consensus at the time. But the company was forced to rapidly refine its manufacturing process technology and practices to generate economically viable yields, something that was more difficult with large panels than small ones. Not being first with fabs of a particular generation also allowed CMO to observe and assess the industry capacity landscape and then place its bets according to where it saw product demand. Smart, well-placed bets like Fab 4 (Gen 5.5) and Fab 5 (second Gen 5) and tight operational discipline then allowed the company to thrive.

IN THE MIDDLE OF THE "TOURNAMENT"

59 Wu reflected on the impending Fab 8 decision:

> In the past, know-how was a big issue. Even when we did Gen 5.5, we were afraid our fundamental knowledge wasn't strong enough. Later we were not confident that the equipment makers could deliver. Now we have very high confidence in our technical abilities, but we worry about market demand. We didn't know if 42-inch would become the mainstream size. With the huge investments in the Fab 7—it costs about NT$100 billion—we were worried about the market and financial issues. We had to choose the right size and the right timing.

60 The TFT-LCD industry had gone through a number of up-and-down cycles since CMO entered it. CMO took advantage of some of the cycles to acquire key technologies and assets. During the down cycles when CMO lost a lot of money, people at the management level took a lot of heat. The scale of losses was not something they had ever experienced in petrochemicals.

61 As the U.S. economy hit a major slowdown in the fourth quarter of 2007 driven by a credit squeeze, the question Ho and Wu faced was whether to maintain the pace of investment in new fabs. Consumer discretionary spending had slowed dramatically in the key U.S. market, though flat-panel television sales seemed to be holding up well. Lead brand producers suggested that they were not seeing problematic build-up in inventory channels, but consumer discretionary spending could be fickle. Now the challenge was, would they get it "right"?

62 The Fab 8 decision had been pending for a long time. The enormous capital needs and the cyclicality of the LCD business were beginning to look similar to the violently cyclical DRAM business. But Wu highlighted some major differences:

> The business of LCDs is very different; it's actually not a commodity. The depreciation cost [in the manufacture of an LCD panel] is actually quite low, 5% to 10% of the total cost, but for DRAM chips it is about 70%. If you look at the cost of producing an LCD panel, materials are around 60% to 70% of total cost, so in a down season, we can stop production. We don't buy materials, and we can stop production. But with DRAM, nobody can afford to stop their production in the slow season.

63 Fab 8 was planned to be a Gen 8.5 facility, the largest that CMO had ever built. In the market for large-size televisions, LCD technology clearly would win over plasma displays,

so the team was becoming more confident. But Ho felt that as a professional manager, he had to take into account the enormous financial risk. As Ho and Wu pondered the decision to restart, Shi reminded them, "As long as the market is still growing . . ."

APPENDIX: TFT-LCD TECHNOLOGY

64 TFT-LCD displays made use of some very unusual properties of a chemical substance known as liquid crystals. While there were three very familiar states of matter—solid, liquid, and gas—liquid crystals were a phase of matter somewhere between solid and liquid. They might actually flow like a liquid, but their molecules had a solid crystallike quality. Nematic liquid crystals were a particular type of liquid crystal that had what was called an orientational order. That meant that while the molecules might seem to be distributed randomly, they were all lined up in the same direction.

65 Each red, green, or blue pixel or picture element of an LCD display had a pair of transparent electrodes, usually a thin layer of indium tin oxide (which was transparent despite its conductivity) that had been patterned on glass and a layer of polarizer on the top and bottom that were aligned perpendicularly. If there was no filler, light passing through from the bottom polarizer would be blocked by the top one. The surfaces of the two opposing electrodes were then treated so that they would align the liquid crystal in a particular direction, and the gap between the electrodes was filled with a twisted nematic liquid crystal.[9] Since the electrodes had been treated to align the liquid crystal in perpendicular directions, the liquid crystal molecules arranged themselves in a helical structure. The liquid crystal material was bi-refringent, meaning that it rotated the light coming from the bottom and passed it through the polarizer at the top (left red pixel in drawing below).

66 If a voltage was applied across the electrodes, the liquid crystal molecules would line up with the electric field and untwist. This prevented the transmission of the polarized light, rendering the cell gray or black (right green pixel below). Hence, the green pixel in this example appears dark:

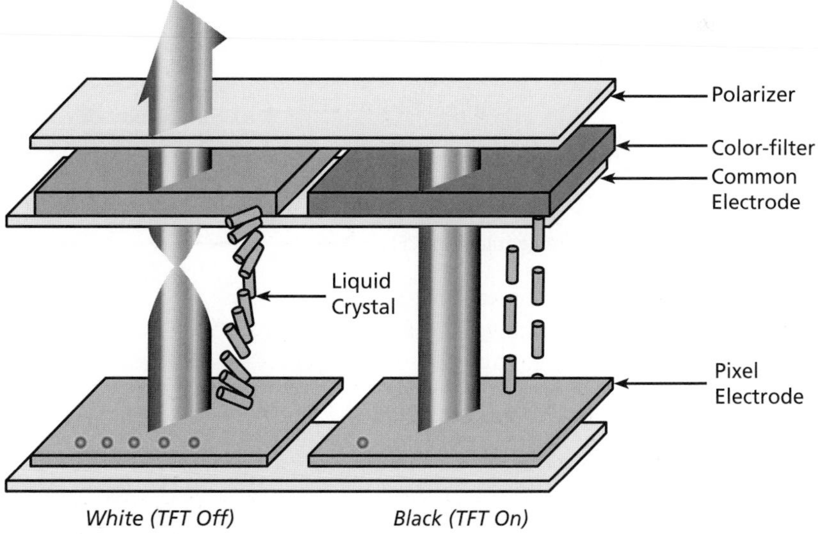

Source: Chi Mei Optoelectronics.

[9] Twisted nematic liquid crystals were the most common form used, but other forms were used as well, depending on the design of the particular cell.

67 The LCD sandwich thus acted as millions of tiny "light valves" that turned on or off depending on whether voltage was applied. In order to turn this array of light valves into a display, a uniform white backlight had to be placed underneath the LCD sandwich. In practice, this was usually done with a cold cathode fluorescent lamp that was optically coupled to a plastic light guide. The light guide spread the light over the lower surface of the LCD sandwich, but intervening layers of brightness enhancement films (usually textured polycarbonate sheets) were interposed to even out the light distribution before the light made it to the lower polarizer. Thus, the entire stack of materials was necessary to make a functioning TFT-LCD panel (see below).

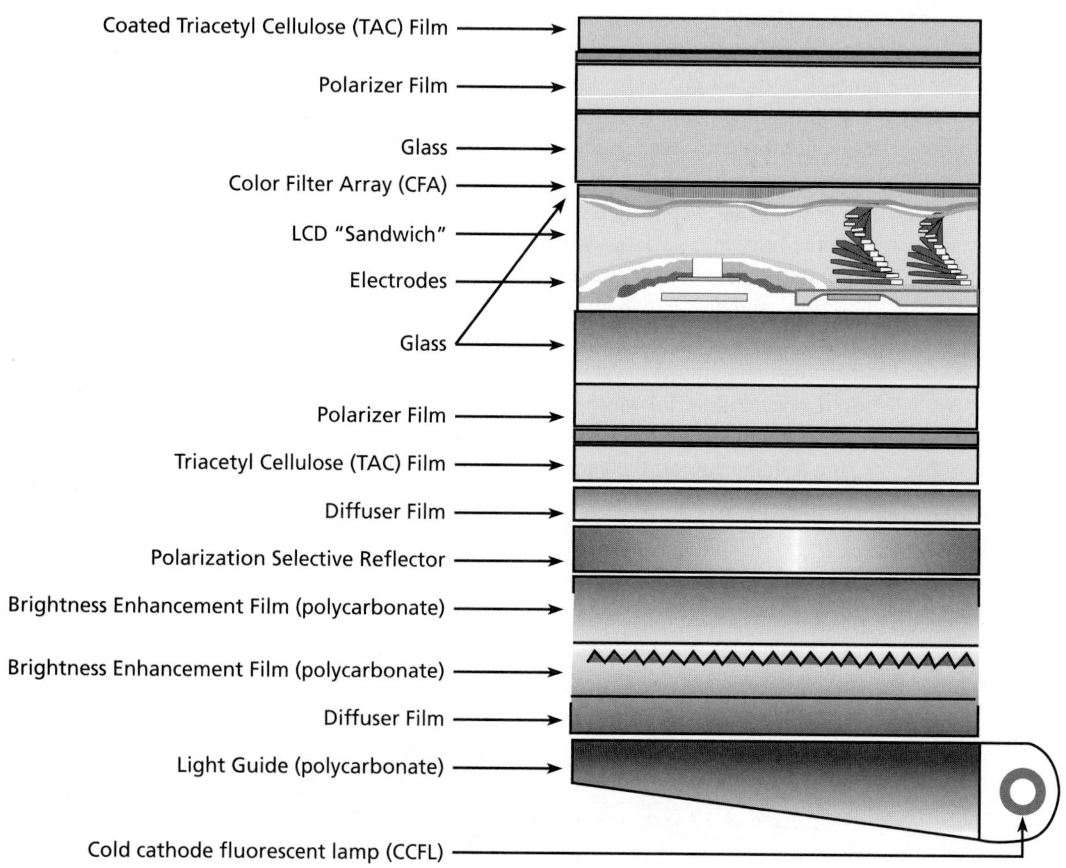

Source: Casewriter.

Case 8

Competing for New York's Best Lobster Roll: *Failed Trade Protection*

David E. Desplaces
College of Charleston

Roxane M. Delaurell
College of Charleston

Laquita C. Blockson
College of Charleston

1 Pearl Oyster Bar owner Rebecca Charles walked out of her attorney's office in Manhattan confused about what could be happening to her business. Even though Rebecca was visiting her attorney tow right a wrong she believed had happened to her, she actually began wondering if what she had done was in fact wrong. She had worked so hard to establish herself in New York over the previous ten years as the best lobster roll restaurant, yet it appeared that she could lose both the recognition and her restaurant's identity to a copy cat. How could this happen? Could she have done things differently?

REBECCA CHARLES AND PEARL OYSTER BAR

2 Pearl Oyster Bar, founded in 1997, established a reputation in Manhattan for serving one of the best lobster rolls on the Island of Manhattan in New York City. Owner Rebecca Charles built this reputation by creating a unique atmosphere with such specialty menu items as "The Pearl Lobster Roll with Shoestring Fries." Rebecca claimed she built recognition and her reputation through various endeavors going back to 1972. Such activities included working at top rated restaurants in Maine and New York and writing a cookbook entitled "Lobster Rolls & Blue Berry Pies" with co-author Deborah DiClementi.[1]

3 As she worked to build Pearl Oyster Bar's reputation, Rebecca hired Ed McFarland in 2003 as a line cook. Ed was a good employee and was promoted to *sous chef* within his first two months of employment. Ed was then in a position of trust and confidence with access to all confidential and propriety information about the restaurant, its cuisine and its operations till his departure in 2007.[2]

THE RESTAURANT INDUSTRY IN NEW YORK CITY

4 According to both the National Restaurant[3] and the New York State Restaurant Associations' data,[4] there were 24,600 restaurant and food service establishments in New York City in 2006. These establishments employed over 225,000 individuals in the Big Apple

Source: *The CASE Journal* 6, no. 2 (Spring 2010). ©2010 by the author and *The CASE Journal.* Contact the author at desplacesd@cofc.edu. This case is intended to be used as the basis for class discussion rather than to illustrate either effective or ineffective handling of a management situation. The case was compiled from public domain information about the legal case including news media coverage of the lawsuit.

[1] *Pearl Oyster Bar vs. Ed McFarland and Ed's Lobster Bar, 2007.* 07-cv-06036 (2007).

[2] *Pearl Oyster Bar vs. Ed McFarland and Ed's Lobster Bar, 2007.* 07-cv-06036 (2007).

[3] National Restaurant Association (n.d.).

[4] Hunt, E. C. (n.d.).

generating gross annual sales of $12 billion. Although this translated into 3.3 restaurants per 1000 residents, the restaurant industry historically had been plagued by a 60 percent failure rate within the first five years[5] especially where competition was most fierce in lower Manhattan. Owners and chefs alike had to compete on price, talent, location, quality of product, and many other important factors to gain competitive advantage and increase their chances of survival. How far would these business people be willing to go to compete or mirror the competition?

COMPETITION OR COPY CAT?

5 Rebecca's attorney filed suit in Federal District Court in the Southern District of New York against Ed McFarland for opening a competing restaurant Ed's Lobster Bar using her trade dress, her recipes and her good reputation.

6 With the restaurants located only nine blocks apart (see Exhibit A), Rebecca alleged that Ed had infringed on her restaurant identity by copying her business' overall look, and claimed that then *sous chef* Ed violated his fiduciary obligation to keep the secrets of her business including the recipes and identity of her restaurant. Rebecca charged that Ed copied "each and every element" of Pearl Oyster Bar.

7 Rebecca alleged that Ed had requested permission several times to reproduce Pearl's success on the upper east side of Manhattan, something Rebecca said she refused categorically. Rebecca claimed that Ed owed her a fiduciary duty of undivided loyalty, good faith and fidelity. Furthermore, Rebecca alleged that Ed purposely deceived her when asked upon announcing his departure from Pearl Oyster Bar, if he would open a "Pearl Knock-off" and he denied having such plans. Furthermore, she alleged that "each and every element" of Pearl Oyster Bar was ripped off, including the bar, the furniture, the paint job (see Exhibit B), and even the Caesar salad dressing (see copies of the menus in Exhibit C). Rebecca was not proud of the fact that Ed never signed any documents upon gaining employment with her.

8 Ed did not defend against any of the allegations made by Rebecca at a press conference he held in his restaurant, which according to local news media, was "deeply reminiscent

EXHIBIT A Restaurant Locations

You can view the distance between the two restaurants using Google maps.

1 Open a browser and type http://maps.google.com
2 Select "Get directions"
3 Type in A: Pearl's Oyster Bar, New York, NY
4 Type in B: Ed's Lobster Bar, New York, NY
5 Click "Get Directions"

Or you can type in the following URL into a web browser:

http://www.google.com/maps?f=d&source=s_d&saddr=pearl's+oyster+bar,+new+york,+ny&daddr=Ed's+Lobster+bar,+new+york,+ny&hl=en&geocode=FUaDbQldstGWyGRV12DLY3-0SkhmGjHk1nCiTGdsjMmw5pRLw%3BFcFebQldieKW-yGhwcc6WzHv0ymXuNXXiFnCiTE1912NsVDjMw&mra=ls&sll=37.0625,-95.677068&sspn=37.136668,53.349609&ie=UTF8&z=15

[5] Parsa, H. G., Self, J. T., Njite, D., & King, T. (2005), p. 304–322.

of Pearl Oyster Bar".[6] He did acknowledge that the restaurants were similar, but would not say that his was a copy,[7] Furthermore, Ed's lawyer scoffed "I didn't know Caesar salads and lobsters are protected under the intellectual-property laws".[8] The questions remained: Were they? What was protected? What could have been protected?

EXHIBIT B Restaurant Interiors

You can view pictures of the inside of each of the restaurants by viewing pictures available on the web using the following instructions:

1. Type in the following url into your web browser: http://ny.eater.com/archives/2007/06/pearl_v_eds.php
2. Review each of the pictures, compare and identify any similarities (if any) by putting pictures side by side.

EXHIBIT C Pearl Oyster and Ed's Lobster Bar Menus[9]

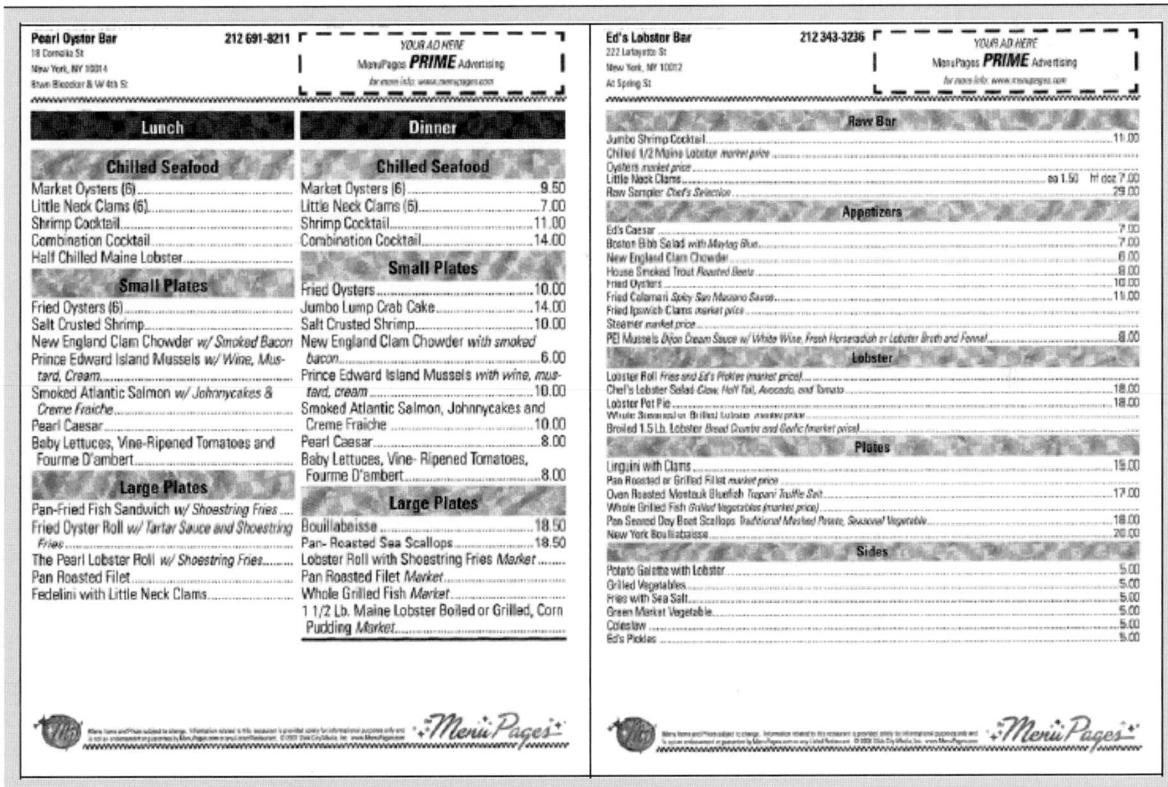

Pearl Oyster Bar 212 691-8211
18 Cornelia St
New York, NY 10014
Btwn Bleecker & W 4th St

YOUR AD HERE
MenuPages **PRIME** Advertising
for more info: www.menupages.com

Lunch

Chilled Seafood

Market Oysters (6)
Little Neck Clams (6)
Shrimp Cocktail
Combination Cocktail
Half Chilled Maine Lobster

Small Plates

Fried Oysters (6)
Salt Crusted Shrimp
New England Clam Chowder *w/ Smoked Bacon*
Prince Edward Island Mussels *w/ Wine, Mustard, Cream*
Smoked Atlantic Salmon *w/ Johnnycakes & Creme Fraiche*
Pearl Caesar
Baby Lettuces, Vine-Ripened Tomatoes and Fourme D'ambert

Large Plates

Pan-Fried Fish Sandwich *w/ Shoestring Fries*
Fried Oyster Roll *w/ Tartar Sauce and Shoestring Fries*
The Pearl Lobster Roll *w/ Shoestring Fries*
Pan Roasted Filet
Fedelini with Little Neck Clams

Dinner

Chilled Seafood

Market Oysters (6) ... 9.50
Little Neck Clams (6) ... 7.00
Shrimp Cocktail ... 11.00
Combination Cocktail ... 14.00

Small Plates

Fried Oysters ... 10.00
Jumbo Lump Crab Cake ... 14.00
Salt Crusted Shrimp ... 10.00
New England Clam Chowder *with smoked bacon* ... 6.00
Prince Edward Island Mussels *with wine, mustard, cream* ... 10.00
Smoked Atlantic Salmon, Johnnycakes and Creme Fraiche ... 10.00
Pearl Caesar ... 8.00
Baby Lettuces, Vine- Ripened Tomatoes, Fourme D'ambert ... 8.00

Large Plates

Bouillabeisse ... 18.50
Pan- Roasted Sea Scallops ... 18.50
Lobster Roll with Shoestring Fries *Market*
Pan Roasted Filet *Market*
Whole Grilled Fish *Market*
1 1/2 Lb. Maine Lobster Boiled or Grilled, Corn Pudding *Market*

Ed's Lobster Bar 212 343-3236
222 Lafayette St
New York, NY 10012
At Spring St

YOUR AD HERE
MenuPages **PRIME** Advertising
for more info: www.menupages.com

Raw Bar

Jumbo Shrimp Cocktail ... 11.00
Chilled 1/2 Maine Lobster *market price*
Oysters *market price*
Little Neck Clams ... ea 1.50 hf doz 7.00
Raw Sampler *Chef's Selection* ... 29.00

Appetizers

Ed's Caesar ... 7.00
Boston Bibb Salad *with Maytag Blue* ... 7.00
New England Clam Chowder ... 6.00
House Smoked Trout *Roasted Beets* ... 8.00
Fried Oysters ... 10.00
Fried Calamari *Spicy San Marzano Sauce* ... 11.00
Fried Ipswich Clams *market price*
Steamer *market price*
PEI Mussels *Dijon Cream Sauce w/ White Wine, Fresh Horseradish or Lobster Broth and Fennel* ... 8.00

Lobster

Lobster Roll *Fries and Ed's Pickles (market price)*
Chef's Lobster Salad *Claw, Half Tail, Avocado, and Tomato* ... 18.00
Lobster Pot Pie ... 18.00
Whole Steamed or Grilled Lobster *market price*
Broiled 1.5 Lb. Lobster *Bread Crumbs and Garlic (market price)*

Plates

Linguini with Clams ... 15.00
Pan Roasted or Grilled Fillet *market price*
Oven Roasted Montauk Bluefish *Trapani Truffle Salt* ... 17.00
Whole Grilled Fish *Grilled Vegetables (market price)*
Pan Seared Day Boat Scallops *Traditional Mashed Potato, Seasonal Vegetable* ... 18.00
New York Bouillabaisse ... 20.00

Sides

Potato Galette with Lobster ... 5.00
Grilled Vegetables ... 5.00
Fries with Sea Salt ... 5.00
Green Market Vegetable ... 5.00
Coleslaw ... 5.00
Ed's Pickles ... 5.00

MenuPages

[6] Grub Street New York (n.d).

[7] Wells, P. (2007).

[8] Grub Street New York (n.d.).

[9] Menu Pages (n.d.).

REFERENCES

Grub Street New York (n.d). Ed's Lobster Bar to Pearl Oyster Bar: Step Off!. Retrieved on November 4, 2009, http://newyork.grubstreet.com/2007/06/eds_lobster_bar_calls_a_press.html

Hunt, E. C. (n.d.) Tips for opening & running a restaurant in New York City. New York State Restaurant Association. Retrieved on February 4, 2010, http://legacy.www.nypl.org/research/sibl/smallbiz/qt6/OpeningRestrInNYC.ppt

Menu Pages (n.d.). Retrieved November 17, 2007 on http://www.menupages.com

National Restaurant Association (n.d.). New York Restaurant Industry at a glance. Retrieved on February 4, 2010: Url: http://www.restaurant.org/pdfs/research/state/newyork.pdf

Parsa, H. G., Self, J. T., Njite, D., & King, T. (2005) Why Restaurant Fail. Quarterly Cornell Hotel and Restaurant Administration, 46 (3): 304–322.

Pearl Oyster Bar vs. Ed McFarland and Ed's Lobster Bar, 2007. 07-cv-06036 (2007). Retrieved on February 4, 2010. http://docs.justia.com/cases/federal/districtcourts/new-york/nysdce/1:2007cv06036/309166/11/0.pdf

Wells, P. (2007). Chef Sues Over Intellectual Property (the Menu). Retrieved on November 17, 2009, http://www.nytimes.com/2007/06/27/nyregion/27pearl.html?_r=1&scp=1&sq=PETE+WELLS+2007+june&st=nyt

Case 9

Defender Direct, Inc.: *A Business of Growing Leaders*

Gosia Glinska
Edward D. Hess

1 Defender Direct, Inc. (Defender), headquartered in Indianapolis, Indiana, was a privately held company that sold and installed ADT security systems and Dish Network Satellite TV to homeowners in the United States. President and CEO Dave Lindsey started the business out of his home in 1998, making the transition to entrepreneur from new-product development at Medeco Security Locks, Inc. He used $30,000 of his and his wife's personal savings to fund the start-up, which he called Defender Security Co.

2 From its humble beginnings in the Lindseys' spare bedroom, Defender became one of the largest security and satellite dealers in the Midwest, experiencing an average annual growth rate of 60% over 10 years. In 2008, Defender generated $150 million in revenues and ranked 387th on the *Inc.* 500 list of America's Fastest-Growing Companies. With 1,500 employees, the company had a national footprint of 120 offices in 40 states.

3 Defender's stellar growth was fueled by an aggressive direct-marketing focus and national expansion, but Lindsey, who was fond of saying that "businesses don't grow—people do," credited the Defender culture, which fostered continuous employee development. He elaborated:

> Defender has grown faster than its peers not because we are better at selling and installing security systems but because our people have grown. Our sales have doubled because the capacity and talents of our leaders have doubled. A few years ago, we stopped trying to double our business and realized the way to grow was to double our team members' enthusiasm, optimism, and skills. Send people to seminars, leadership conferences, and self-help programs. Build a culture on purpose, not by accident.[1]

THE FOUNDER

4 Lindsey was born in 1969 and grew up in the Midwest. He graduated with honors from Indiana University with a BS degree in Business Finance and an MBA in Marketing and Finance. After graduation, he worked for various companies in the lock and door hardware industry and became interested in security systems. A turning point for Lindsey came when he was passed over for a promotion while working for Medeco Security Locks, Inc., in Salem, Virginia. "We're going to start a business," he said to his wife, "because I don't want to ever be in this spot again, where it's office politics controlling my career."

5 At Medeco, Lindsey had been involved in a program called Medeco Business Advantage—a 2X Strategy to Grow Your Business, a set of business processes inspired by Michael Gerber's best-selling book *The E-Myth: Why Most Businesses Don't Work and*

Source: This case was prepared by Senior Researcher Gosia Glinska and Edward D. Hess, Professor and Batten Executive-in-Residence. It was written as a basis for class discussion rather than to illustrate effective or ineffective handling of an administrative situation.

[1] "Defender Security Co." *Indianapolis Business Journal,* September 15, 2003.

What to Do About It. According to Lindsey, "It was a way for a mostly traditional type of locksmith to double their business, using the 2X process and then up-selling. We would teach it to our locksmith dealers, and I saw it work and decided, 'I've always wanted to own my own business, why not buy a locksmith shop, double it, and create value?'"

OPPORTUNITY KNOCKS

6 Lindsey and his wife started looking for a locksmith business to buy, but after finding none at a price they were willing to pay, they moved to Indianapolis. "That's where my family was and my support structure, and where I really wanted to be permanently," said Lindsey. He reflected on his days as a freelance locksmith:

> I began changing locks and installing deadbolts, which was pretty horrible because every psychological test I've ever taken says that me and a power drill should stay as far apart as possible. I have some great stories about taking out my friends' locks and not being able to put them back on. . . . So that's how I began, pretty ugly, and my intention was to never do installation, because I'm not technical. But I had to get out and learn.

7 While his wife took over the role of a family breadwinner, Lindsey researched the security industry. "I was, like, if someone needs a lock, maybe they want an alarm system? And in the mid-'90s the alarm industry really exploded." Lindsey jumped at the opportunity when ADT Security Systems and other brands began offering $99 start-up packages for homeowners, making home-security systems more affordable to a wide group of consumers. "We wrote a business plan, got ADT to take a chance on us, and began as an ADT Authorized Dealer. We never looked back. I never did another lock job once we signed our ADT contract."

LEARNING THE ROPES

8 For his first three months as an ADT Authorized Dealer, Lindsey focused on meeting the sales quota. Failure to sell 15 systems per month not only could lead to problems for the business but also could result in a financial penalty, which would have swallowed much of the Lindseys' start-up capital. A devotee of the principles Gerber laid out in *The E-Myth,* Lindsey said he "was looking for that Gerber-type of repeatable system, something that could be 'McDonaldized.'"

9 Lindsey took advantage of a sales-training program offered by ADT. "The Dealer Program I came into was 90% door-to-door sales," he said. "ADT was teaching us to knock on doors. They threw me in a van with a bunch of other guys and put me on the street, and I'd sell ADT systems door-to-door."

10 The day that Lindsey, who had never sold an ADT system before, made his first sale within a couple of hours, he "saw it work." He immediately called his wife to tell her he was going to buy a 15-passenger van. He recalled:

> I had seen a repeatable process, which involved a van; when you go door-to-door you have to have that team environment—when you drive together in one car, you've got to pick the people up so they can't leave, until they get a sale. When everybody drives individually, they end up getting back in their cars and leaving.

11 During the first month of knocking on doors, Lindsey sold six security systems and fifteen during the second month, with the help of a friend. It was cause for celebration because they had met ADT's monthly quota. The third month was even better; with first hires onboard, Lindsey and his team sold 30 systems.

THE ADT SALES CONTEST

12 By September 1998, Lindsey had assembled a team of 10 salespeople. "I really wanted to start the team out with a bang," he said. "I needed a catalyst, a point of focus." ADT's sales contest with its $15,000 prize was exactly what Lindsey needed to fire up his team. "Each dealer's quota was based on the previous three months' sales," he said. "I believed we had a great opportunity to win since our previous three months' quota would be only 17 units." The team launched a sales blitzkrieg. As Lindsey recalled:

> My living room was converted into our Sales Meeting War Room. My artwork was covered up with a makeshift sales board, and my entertainment center became an employee mailbox system. Administrative paperwork was handled from my back bedroom, complete with a board stretched out on the bed to form a desk, a computer, and a borrowed fax machine. Side meetings and training sessions were held on the front lawn. We were entrepreneurs, making the rules up as we went. We had no fear and knew we had a great product and wanted to meet as many people as possible. We went out together each day, feeding off each other's energy.[2]

13 One day in mid-September, while his sales team was gathered in his living room, Lindsey went to the back bedroom to call ADT's headquarters to find out how his team ranked among other ADT Authorized Dealers. His surprise turned to shock when he learned that, as a new ADT Authorized Dealer, Defender had its sales quota increased from 17 to 45. Shaken, Lindsey weighed his options.

14 What happened next was what Lindsey referred to as "an inflection point in the company" and "the moment of truth" for him as a leader. He took a few minutes to compose himself and went back to the living room to face his sales team. He candidly related the news about the quota and then spent a few minutes rallying his troops. "We're going to blow through this," he said.

15 With 45 sales already under its belt and two more weeks to go, Defender still had a shot at winning the contest. "We took it up a notch or two during those last two weeks and worked long hard days," Lindsey said. Defender's installation crew tripled its capacity to make sure every system Defender sold got installed the next day. By the end of September, with 142 systems sold and installed, Lindsey's sales team was 316% above its quota and 835% above its three-month historical average.[3]

16 In snatching the top prize in the sales contest, the upstart company had defeated hundreds of other ADT Authorized Dealers from across the United States. "September was crazy," Lindsey said. "After four months of knocking on doors, we had a system, and we knew what we were doing. Soon after, we sold 200, 300 systems, and we ran pretty quickly to the 600-range a month. And it kind of skyrocketed from there."

THE ENTREPRENEURIAL MINDSET

17 During its first few months of operation, Defender subcontracted all systems' installations. "You know the old adage, nothing happens until a sale happens," Lindsey said. "So we focused on creating demand." In September, when sales numbered 142 systems, however, Lindsey hired his first installation technician. At the beginning, Defender hired technicians with minimal industry experience, who were able to handle a wireless alarm system that was relatively easy to install.

[2] Excerpted from Defender Direct Web site.

[3] Defender Direct Web site.

18 At approximately the same time, Lindsey hired his first sales manager, who took over driving the van with the sales team, freeing up Lindsey to "get the paperwork done to support this," as he put it. "I was able to stop and go back and put some processes in place." He reflected on the early building of the business:

> We kept in mind Gerber's three roles in a business: the entrepreneur's job is to create the process, the manager's job is to assure the process is used, and the technician's job is to follow the process and use it. And that has dominated my thoughts for the past 10 years. Every time we're trying to grow something, we are very clear about who is playing these roles, and we make sure somebody's doing each of these. In the beginning, I played all those different roles, but I was conscious that I was ultimately the entrepreneur, and for the first three or four years all I did was build processes.

THINKING BIG—WITH A CLEAR FOCUS

19 In November 1998, Defender opened a second office and sold 125 systems the first month. Lindsey's sales team pledged to open a new office every 90 days, and Defender ended its first year of operation with four offices. As Lindsey said, "We lived, and still do, by Gerber's tenet—'big business is just a small business that thought big.' And we wanted to be much bigger. In those days we'd always remind ourselves that it's not okay to put a mom-and-pop system in place, because that's just going to keep us small forever."

20 Looking for ways to grow his business, Lindsey considered expanding into the commercial security market, but after some thought, he decided that the residential market would be Defender's staple. "We weren't so much a security company as a home market and installation company," Lindsey said. "We found another product that could be marketed in a mass way and be installed in homes." That product was satellite TV, which Defender added to its offerings in 2001 and with it quickly became one of the top Dish Network dealers.[4]

21 Since making the decision to concentrate on the residential market, Lindsey stayed on course and steered his company away from potential distractions. "We have a saying posted all over our offices—Focus Equals Growth." He elaborated:

> Today we still only have 13 part numbers in our inventory room, the same 13 we had 10 years ago. We have not added things. We keep doing more of the same better, trying to McDonaldize it. We understood focus as the goal early on, constantly using an ABC format to prioritize. I coach all of our new leaders, "We don't pay you to get everything done—we pay you to get the most important things done."

Defender's "Hedgehog" Statement

22 For help in knowing what to focus on each day, Defender employees turned to what the company called its hedgehog statement—"We are best in the world at customer acquisition for top brand-name products and services that target homeowners."[5] The hedgehog concept was one of the principles of greatness outlined in Jim Collins's 2001 best seller *Good to Great*.[6] As Collins's research indicated, great companies refused to do anything that did not fit with their hedgehog concept, and they made as much use of stop-doing lists as to-do lists.

[4] Terri Greenwell, "*IBJ*'s Fastest Growing Companies," *Indianapolis Business Journal,* September 17, 2007.

[5] Defender Direct Web site.

[6] Jim Collins, *Good to Great: Why Some Companies Make the Leap . . . and Others Don't* (New York: HarperBusiness, 2001).

EXHIBIT 1 Defender Direct, Inc.: A Business of Growing Leaders

Defender's Circle of Life

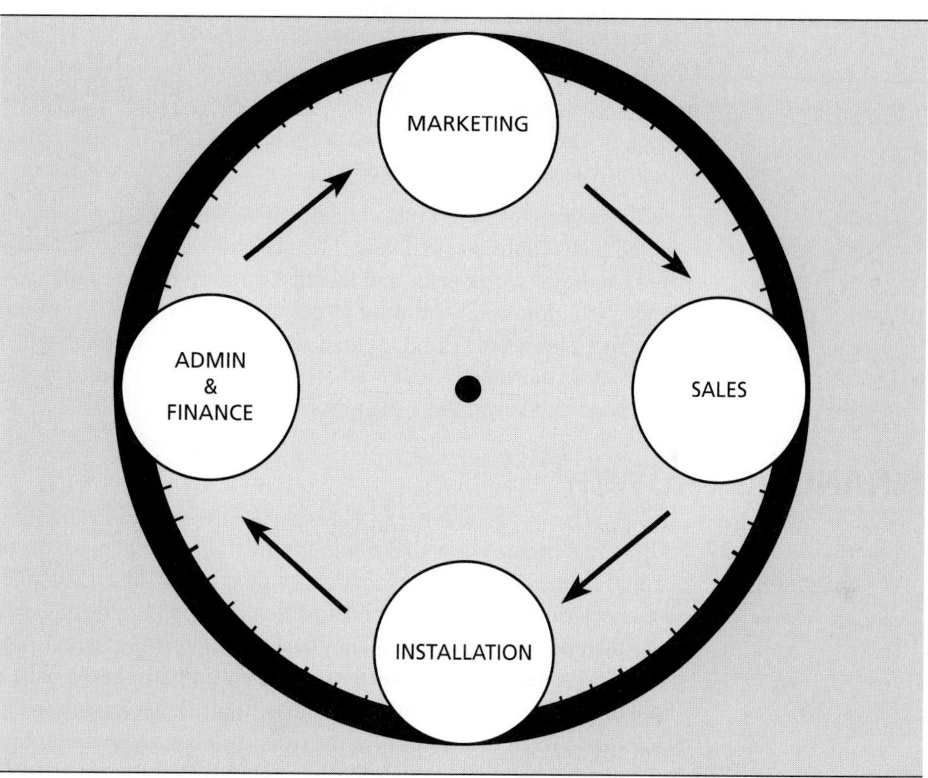

Source: Courtesy of Defender Direct.

23 Lindsey cited Collins as one of his biggest influences and made his employees read his book; they even read whole chapters out loud in the office. Having spent five years discovering its hedgehog concept, Defender leadership used it as a frame of reference for all its decisions. As Lindsey said, "We really pride ourselves not on our to-do list but on our not-to-do list. And we have found that the more we say 'no' to things, the more we grow."

Defender's "Circle of Life"

24 Another practical tool, which Lindsey and his leadership team used on a weekly basis, was the so-called circle of life (**Exhibit 1**). It was a visual representation of their understanding of how the business worked. "Imagine a clock face," Lindsey said. "Twelve o'clock is marketing, three o'clock is sales, six o'clock is installation, and nine o'clock is admin and finance. It used to be just sales, door-to-door, but it all starts with marketing. So I spent my energy on really ramping it up over the last five years."

25 Whenever Lindsey noticed a bottleneck in any of the four areas of the circle of life, he would focus his full attention on that particular spot to alleviate the bottleneck. He elaborated:

> First, I'd work with marketing until we had enough leads. But we didn't have enough salespeople, so I'd jump over to sales, and make sure we close all the leads until we didn't have enough technicians. Then, I'd go down to installation and make sure we're getting all the systems installed, and it would flow back up, and then we'd have a paperwork backup, so I'd make sure ADT was paying us. And then as soon as that is all released, we say that the money

> flows around that. Marketing takes a dollar and starts at 12 o'clock, and you hope that two dollars come up when you spin around the circle. So then I'd go back to marketing and say, "Okay, we've got some more marketing programs: let's go. And I just kept running around that circle. The faster you spin the circle, the faster we grow.
>
> I've had my direct reports say to me, "You're focusing on my part of the circle right now. You've been to my office every day this week," and I'm, "Yeah, I'm going to be in your part of the circle until our install rate or our backlog is down." Today, I'm backing up from that a little bit as I'm changing my role.

26 To keep a close eye on his business's financial performance, Lindsey used a scorecard, which he had introduced a year after starting Defender. "It's a concise Excel spreadsheet," said Lindsey, "with weeks' and months' worth of history and then this week's numbers, like, what's the close rate? We want to get that scorecard more automated, and we want that to be a live dashboard." Lindsey held weekly Friday meetings with his direct reports, during which they thoroughly reviewed all metrics on the scorecard. The meetings started in the afternoon and lasted more than four hours.

FINANCING GROWTH

27 All entrepreneurs know that funding growth is an expensive proposition and that access to capital is one of the biggest challenges facing start-ups. Defender had an advantage in that area because of its business model, which involved acquiring new customers and then "selling" them to ADT and Dish. "They cash us out upfront," said Lindsey. "We sell the contract, which is a three-year agreement that has a value, just like a bank sells a loan. It has always kept us cash rich, and we've been able to fund all this growth without any debt." In addition, Defender pulled in regular revenue from installation and monthly monitoring services.

28 But the company experienced its share of bumps in the road. About a year into his entrepreneurial journey, Lindsey struggled to make payroll. At a family dinner, he wanted to forget about work but could not stop thinking about it. "I remember my dad and I made eye contact," Lindsey said. "I just broke down crying, telling him how stressed out I was. So that's early on, just cash flow and understanding. You've got all these people believing in you, and you're trying to have that initial confidence just to get the ball to roll." Lindsey elaborated:

> It got really ugly, and that led us to getting into Dish Network Satellite TV in addition to ADT. So, luckily, things righted there. But that was huge; we had one year of negative growth in 10 years, and that was that year. It was really just about holding things together. I remember I had everybody in the company on speakerphones, giving them a speech, "We're going to get through this, and these are the three or four things we're going to do." That was probably the biggest time I felt like a general of an army.

THE EVOLUTION OF THE BUSINESS MODEL

29 For the first three years, Defender's sales force consisted of "full-commission door-knockers," as Lindsey put it. "It was a great way to start, because there's no marketing, and you're only paying someone when the sale is made. Then we realized we could set appointments instead of knocking on doors, and we became 100% telemarketing-based."

30 Around the time Defender was transitioning to telemarketing, an acquaintance of Lindsey's introduced him to Marcia Raab, owner of a small call center in Indiana. Defender soon became Raab's exclusive customer. "She did a great job, was such a servant to our

business—she really did it at an exchange rate with us," said Lindsey. "Terrific marketing and sales person. She grew the 20-person call center to 200 people in two centers, and she owned that."

31 Defender eventually bought Raab's call centers, and Raab became Defender's vice president of sales and marketing. "She was an absolute dynamo," said Lindsey. "She started coming to our staff meetings, when she was our outsource partner with her own call centers, which she ran like a division of ours. And then we formalized it and put her in the VP spot."

32 The telemarketing operation had to be scrapped in 2001, with the introduction of the "no-call list hit," as Lindsey named it, which allowed consumers to put a stop to unwanted telemarketing pitches. "So, we reinvented the business for the third time," Lindsey said. "Now it's 100% direct mail and the Internet, so our call centers handle only incoming calls."

33 Defender's call center kept growing, reaching more than 400 sales and customer-service agents in five contact centers located in Indiana and Ohio. The sales agents handled inbound calls from potential customers, who responded to Defender's newspaper ads, pitches on the Internet, or direct-mail offers, while customer-service agents handled the calls from existing customers seeking support. "The inbound agents who are taking calls from prospective customers are paid minimum wage plus heavy commission," said Lindsey. "And with those people we have a fairly high turnover. You have to hire four or five to get one who's good."

LINDSEY'S BIGGEST CHALLENGES

34 From the time Lindsey launched his own business, he had been challenged to continually evolve his relationship with the company, transforming himself from a door-to-door salesman to sales manager to controller to regional manager to president and CEO in 10 years. As he reflected on his changing role,

> My biggest struggle has been constantly reinventing my relationship to the business. You go from a business that's in an extra bedroom to 200 employees nationwide, $150 million in sales, and that is a huge challenge in itself, both in terms of process, skill, and psychologically. Every year I say to my wife that I have to reinvent my relationship to the business. It started with hiring the first sales manager to go take these guys to knock on doors for me, to then jumping to be an admin lead and putting someone else in my place. I feel like I kept filling a hole and then leaving somebody behind. Then taking it from being in Indianapolis to being a regional presence and all the skills it takes. And today I'm evolving even more into being—I think of it as a chairman, a shareholder, investor, as well as business strategy and new products.

Managing People

35 As Lindsey's relationship to his business evolved, so did his management philosophy. At first, he found it hard to delegate. "It was hard to release control," he admitted. "At one time I thought I could do it better than anybody else. All it took was to hire a couple of people and understand they could do it better than me."

36 After six months of driving a van with his door-to-door sales team, Lindsey found a sales manager he trusted who eventually became the number one ADT sales rep in the country and rose through the ranks to become vice president of sales. Similarly, the first installation technician Lindsey hired grew to become Defender's vice president of installation. When Defender was generating $20 million in revenue, he was in charge of installation for the whole company. "When the job started to outstrip him, he was put into a regional role, which was still almost a $10 million region," said Lindsey. "I always say to people whose jobs outstrip them, 'You still have the same level of responsibility or more.'"

37 As a manager who never had much tolerance for mistakes, Lindsey described himself as a proponent of tough love. "I kind of manage with a Bobby Knight–type[7] of mentality with my direct reports," Lindsey said. "I've always said I need people with thick skin who themselves do not tolerate mistakes."

38 By 2008, Lindsey had four direct reports: chief operations officer (COO), chief marketing officer (CMO), chief information officer (CIO), and chief financial officer (CFO).

39 COO John Corliss, whom Lindsey had met at Medeco, came onboard in January 2006 as Defender's CFO, a position he held for a year. As the COO, Corliss was responsible for the company's customer service, human resources, and installations departments. Installations included all field installation technicians, who were full-time Defender employees working in 120 installation locations around the country. In 2008, Lindsey made him a partner in the business.

40 Marcia Raab, a Defender employee since 2001, was promoted from vice president of sales and marketing to CMO and in 2008 became a partner. She was responsible for managing the planning and purchasing of all Defender marketing programs as well as overseeing the operations of Defender call centers. Lindsey said, "Marcia is the drumbeat of the organization, and as fast as she beats that drum, the rest of us dance."

41 Bart Shroyer, the CFO, came onboard in 2007. He was responsible for all accounting, funding, and financial management for Defender. Shroyer, who had a breakout year in 2008, was made a partner in 2009.

42 Gregg Albacete, the CIO, joined Defender in 2007. He was responsible for building and maintaining systems, databases, and the IT infrastructure that supported and extended Defender's business model.

Finding the Right CFO

43 Among the many challenges Lindsey faced while growing his business, one of the toughest was filling the CFO position. At first, Lindsey "gave a box of receipts to an accountant," as he described it, but nine months into his contract with ADT, Lindsey's wife took over the accounting function of the business. A few months later, with the help of QuickBooks accounting software, Lindsey said, "She came on full-blown," and continued in the CFO role for five years, until the arrival of the Lindseys' third child when she became a full-time stay-at-home mom. Then, her assistant, who "grew up in the business," took over.

44 Lindsey admitted that he has had "four to five people" in the CFO position since he started Defender. "It was the hardest job to fill," he said. He elaborated:

> Our average growth rate was 60% a year for the last 10 years. So you hire a bookkeeper, then you need an accountant, and then you need a controller. I didn't shoot far enough ahead. The problem was, when I tried to shoot ahead, I got real schmoheads. CFOs are all by nature pretty conservative people. They are sharp guys, not looking for a $10 million business to work in. The only person who wants to be CFO in a $10 million business says, "Well, I'll just start my own business. I'm not going to work for this guy, take on his risk." So I got a couple of screwballs, who didn't seem that way when I interviewed them. Once we got to $50 million plus, it was a lot easier to attract people.

DEFENDER'S CULTURE

45 Lindsey attributed Defender's success to its culture, which he built around each employee's personal growth. Describing it further, he said, "Another word is 'terrific.' We talk about being terrific every day, and we choose to be that way."

[7] Bobby Knight, the coach with the most career wins in men's collegiate basketball history, led the Indiana University men's basketball team to three NCAA championships between 1971 and 2000.

46 Lindsey was continuously learning and growing, and he encouraged his employees to do the same, sending them to various self-improvement seminars, such as Dale Carnegie Training and Ed Foreman's Successful Life Course. "We coined a saying, 'Businesses don't grow—people do,'" said Lindsey. "I don't want this to become a cliché around Defender because it's been our secret sauce. All of us had to grow. We've accomplished this reinvention through good books and good tapes and networking with good people" (**Exhibit 2**).

47 Over the course of 10 years, Lindsey reinvented Defender's business model three times, reinvented himself and his role, but, most important, he redefined the purpose of his business, which had evolved from making money to growing people. "Our growth plan

EXHIBIT 2 **Defender Direct, Inc.: A Business of Growing Leades**

Defender's Culture

At Defender Direct, we are about being the best! We have founded ourselves on the principle that we can be the best in the world at customer acquisition for top brand-name products and services that target homeowners. It doesn't stop there. It has infiltrated throughout our entire company.

We have the best employees! We have the kind of employees that are constantly working on themselves and building themselves into leaders. At Defender Direct, you will find people that are always striving to set and meet new goals. That is why we are always promoting people from within. Our four passions act as a roadmap for making our people the best they can be, and they really take it to heart.

We work with the best products! As a Dish Network dealer, we are one of the top-five dealers in the country. For ADT, we are also a top dealer. How do we do that? By working with the best products in the industry and products we believe in. Our employees are some of our best customers! At Defender Direct, customers will find that we do our best so we can be the best! We strive for excellence and that is what customers get each time.

Defender Direct is the best in the world at customer acquisition for top brand-name products and services that target homeowners.

Rewards and Recognition

- Annual Superstar Celebration. Every year we celebrate our employees' accomplishments by taking them on an annual trip. For 2008, we took 278 employees and their guests to Cancun, Mexico. Past trips have included trips to Jamaica and the Bahamas. Our superstars are what make us what we are, and we want to celebrate that with a trip that lets them know how much we appreciate their dedication and commitment to achieving their goals.
- Defender Family Day. Each Labor Day, we invite our employees and their families to spend time with us for some fun and sun, our treat! Past events have taken us to Indiana Beach and Six Flags Kentucky Kingdom. It's a great way to celebrate the last hurray of summer.
- Sales Contests. We understand that our sales team is a key driver for our success. We have weekly contests and awards for our sales team to keep them working on hitting and breaking new records. This year we even gave away a car!
- This is just a small list of the many things we do to reward and recognize our employees' dedication and hard work. We are always coming up with new ways to reward them for all they contribute. We put this as a high priority on our to-do list.

(continued)

EXHIBIT 2 *(Continued)*

Training

- Every technician we hire attends Defender University, a complete training program that gets them ready to be successful in the field. We have had some of the top techs in the industry come out of Defender University, and we continue to expand the size of our classes every month.
- We are always looking for opportunities to send our employees to training and seminars, so that they are continuously developing and working on themselves. Programs include the Dale Carnegie Training Program, Ed Foreman's Successful Life Course and much more. We believe in self-improvement, and we are always looking for ways to help employees do just that.

Additional Perks

- Extensive library with books from great authors such as John Maxwell, Jim Collins and Jack Welch.
- Corporate-sponsored Weight Watchers program to help employees achieve personal weight-loss goals.
- Corporate chaplains.
- Much More!

Source: Adapted by case writer from the company Web site.

is that you have to reinvent yourself this year," Lindsey told 1,500 Defender employees at its annual Self-Improvement Day, held in April in Indianapolis. This companywide commitment to personal growth and continuous reinvention was the linchpin of Defender's corporate culture, and Self-Improvement Day provided an opportunity for reaffirmation every year.

48 Lindsey was particularly proud of Defender Advantage, the company's four-year initiation program into the Defender culture, during which employees received leadership training, participated in the company's book club, and traveled with their families on mission trips abroad to work as volunteers.[8] In addition, newly hired installation technicians attended Defender University, a complete training program that prepared them to be successful in the field. Part of the Defender University's curriculum was Corporate Culture Day, during which all new hires listened to Defender's senior managers, including Lindsey, via satellite. The main purpose of Culture Day was to drive the following message: "We are asking you to work harder on yourself than on your job." On Culture Day all new hires were also given the Defender Leadership Advantage Board, which charted the path of their growth (**Exhibit 3**).

49 Besides focus and drive, Lindsey listed forgiveness as one of his greatest strengths as a leader. As he told his staff, he believed that their "ability to forgive each other really built a culture around here. It's the glue that allows us to stay at this breakneck speed." Lindsey, who described himself as a "student of leadership," stressed that his "basic belief in forgiveness comes from [his] Faith and having learned from Jesus, who was a servant leader." Still, when reflecting on his entrepreneurial journey, Lindsey always emphasized the lesson of continuous employee development:

> It's been a humbling learning [experience] for me as a business owner. It's not about having a better plan or a widget. It's about helping your employees, because every time they grow,

[8] *Inc.* 500/5000 Fastest-Growing Private Companies in America, 2008, Defender Direct, Inc.

I grow. And that's what keeps me going, that's my calling in life—to build and develop leaders. . . . We don't want to be in the business of buying and selling businesses. We want to be in the business of growing and developing leaders. We have a platform to do that. So that's what my goal is.

EXHIBIT 3 Defender Direct, Inc.: A Business of Growing Leades

Defender's Leadership Advantage Board

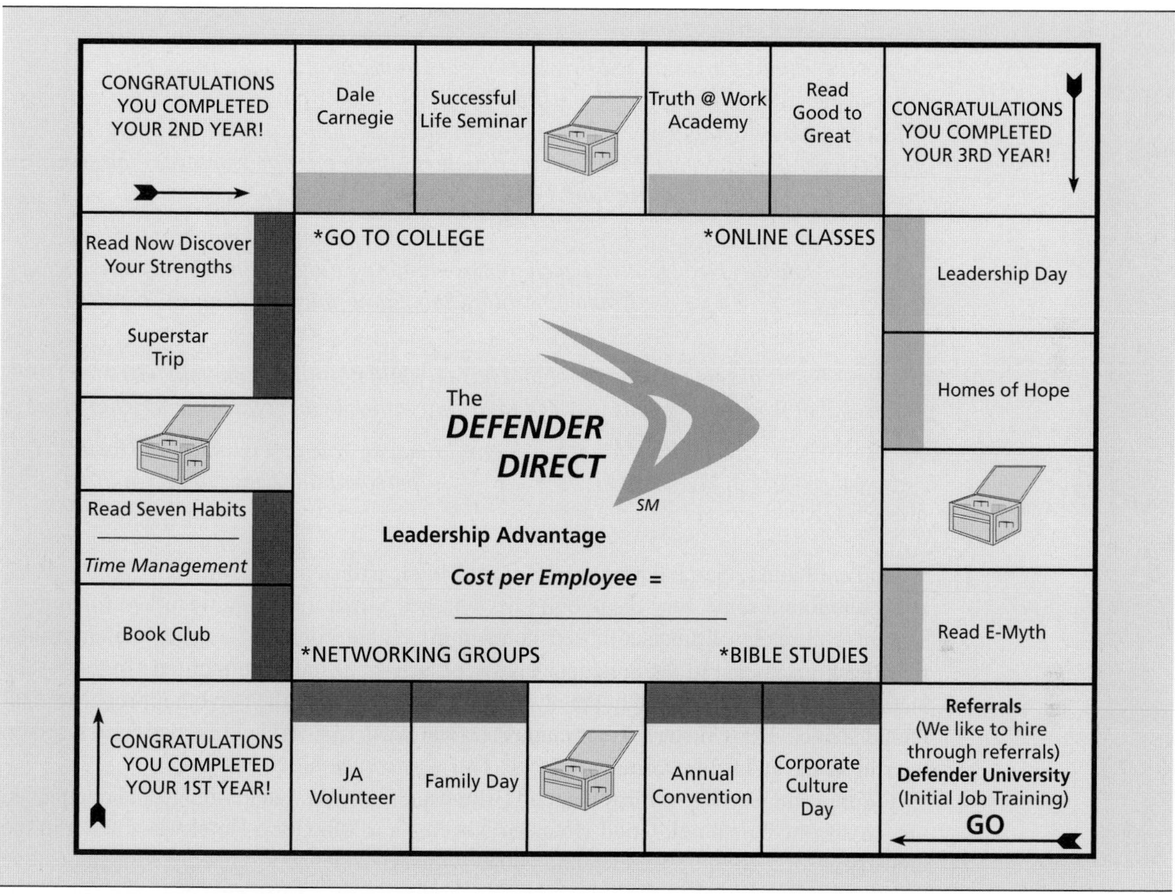

Source: Courtesy of Defender Direct.

Case 10

Good Hotel: *Doing Good, Doing Well?*

Armand Gilinsky, Jr.
Sonoma State University

S. Noorein Inamdar
San José State University

Employees who feel transformed by what they are doing are far more likely to be enthusiastic about their jobs. The hotel industry has become far more expert in retaining its hangers than its employees. The turnover in the hotel business is 70–100 percent; ours is closer to 30 percent. Shouldn't a company want to offer its employees the same opportunities for self-actualization? I call this 'karmic capitalism.'

—Chip Conley, founder and CEO, Joie de Vivre Hotels, speech to Association of Fundraising Professionals, Commonwealth Club, San Francisco, January 22, 2010

All of our hotels are nonconventional and have a philanthropic community vision. This is one of the main reasons why I plan to stay with Joie de Vivre for a very long time.

—Pam Janusz, General Manager, Joie de Vivre SOMA Hotels, personal interview, March 5, 2010

1 When Pam Janusz, General Manager of Good Hotel, arrived at work on Thursday, April 15, 2010, she found some very disquieting news in her e-mail inbox. Pam worked for Joie de Vivre (JdV), a San Francisco-based hotel management company. Earlier that morning, Ingrid Summerfield, JdV's President, had sent an e-mail message marked "urgent". The message confirmed rumors that the owners of Good Hotel and the two other properties that Pam managed, Best Western Americania and Best Western Carriage Inn, had foreclosed on their holdings and sold all three properties to a new ownership group.

2 JdV had renovated Best Western Hotel Britton and Best Western Flamingo and relaunched the two as one new hotel, Good Hotel, in November 2008. Good Hotel was known in the industry as the first to be branded as a "hotel with a conscience"—encompassing a positive attitude, environmental sensitivity, and philanthropy. **Exhibit 1** presents marketing information about Good Hotel. Pam had managed Good Hotel, Best Western Americania and Best Western Carriage Inn, three of JdV's 16 San Francisco properties, since November 2009. A new ownership group planned to run all three hotels in JdV's SOMA ("South of Market Street") group themselves and terminate JdV's management contract at the end of May 2010, barring any unforeseen issues related to the sale. Meanwhile, Pam would be reassigned to another, as yet unknown position at JdV. The remainder of the e-mail message was a request to evaluate the performance of Good Hotel to prepare for its transition to new ownership.

Source: Professor Armand Gilinsky, Jr. of Sonoma State University and S. Noorein Inamdar of San José State University developed this case for class discussion rather than to illustrate either effective or ineffective handling of the situation. The host organization has provided written permission to disseminate this case for academic purposes. The host organization has signed a release letter for this case. Draft dated June 14, 2010.

EXHIBIT 1 **The Good Hotel**

Philosophy and Customer Experience

The Good Hotel is intended to be the first hotel with a conscience. Our philanthropic and positive approach is designed to inspire the "good in us all."

The Good Hotel is a hip San Francisco hotel that practices philanthropy and believes in doing good for the planet. The eco-friendly hotel décor features reclaimed and recycled construction materials.

Vending machines in the lobby are stocked with wallets made from FedEx envelopes and are one example of our inventive ideas to promote a good lifestyle.

We are also as fun as we are inventive. You'll find humorous touches like "Be Good" written on walls of your room.

What does "good" mean to you? For some, the word may inspire visions of helping a homeless person find shelter for a night. Others may think of global warming and chant the mantra, "reduce, re-use, recycle." Or, maybe your mission isn't to save the world, and it simply connotes a positive fun attitude.

Joie de Vivre Hotels' identity as a socially conscious company inspired us to design this SOMA hotel with all these good intentions. From beds and headboards made from locally reclaimed wood to glow in the dark messages, our guests will discover that we are good with a lighthearted twist.

Hotel Services

- Parking available at $20 per night (plus tax). Hybrid cars receive complimentary parking
- *Good Pizza* serving artisan-style pizzas using only fresh and local ingredients is located adjacent to the hotel lobby
- Business stations located in the lobby
- High-speed internet access
- Pet friendly hotel offering complimentary treats and water/food bowls upon check-in (additional $25/pet fee applies)
- Access to outdoor, heated pool located across the street
- Bicycles available on loan when you stay with us

Guestroom Amenities

- "Good" Amenities: bed frame made of 100% reclaimed wood, light fixture made of glass water bottles and toilet top sink
- 26-inch flat screen TV
- iPod docking station
- Hairdryer
- Iron & ironing board
- Coffee/tea maker
- High-speed wireless internet access
- Fold-down writing desk
- Curved shower rod

Source: The Good Hotel, guest brochure.

3 "Wow!" Pam exclaimed,

> I've been trying to get to know our staff, guests, and neighborhood over the last six months. We have a great staff in place. We were able to beat our financial forecasts for the first quarter of 2010. Our guest service has been steadily rising over the last few months. There have not been any major surprises until today.

4 Pam thought about her and Good Hotel's accomplishments during the past six months and her priorities for the remaining six weeks. She wondered what she would say about the change in ownership and possible future direction of Good Hotel to her 130 part- and full-time staff that serviced 308 rooms among the three properties, including 117 rooms at Good Hotel. Hotel staff was to remain with the three properties under new ownership.

5 Pam had spent a good deal of her time training the management team in an effort to increase the standards of service at the hotel and in turn guest loyalty. Employee satisfaction was on the rise. Online reviews of the hotel were increasingly frequent and positive. While she anticipated the new owners would maintain Good Hotel as a theme-based property, she needed to prepare her evaluation and recommendation as to whether to continue, expand, or discontinue the Good Hotel concept to the new ownership group, in the next six weeks.

THE U.S. LODGING INDUSTRY

6 Large, branded hotel chains dominated the U.S. lodging industry. Twelve leading hotel chains and their brands are profiled in **Exhibit 2**. The lodging business was cyclical: hoteliers tended to begin building capacity during the upturns, which came on line just in time for the downturns, according to Standard & Poor's. As a result, the industry suffered from chronic

EXHIBIT 2 **Operating Statistics of Twelve Major Hotel Chains, 2007–2009**

Company Name	Ticker symbol	# Properties (*boutique hotels*)	# Rooms	# Emp.	Key brands
Accor SA	ACRF:Y	4,000	500,000	158,162	Sofitel, Novotel, Mercure, Suitehotel, Motel 6
Best Western	[*private*]	4,000	303,827	1,059	Best Western
Choice Hotels International	CHH	6,021	487,410	1,560	Comfort Inn, Quality Inn, Econo Lodge, Clarion, Rodeway Inn, Sleep Inn
Four Seasons Hotels	[*private*]	80		33,185	Four Seasons, Regent
Hilton Worldwide*	[*private*]	3,500	545,000	130,000	Hilton, Conrad, Doubletree, Embassy Suites, Hampton
Hyatt Hotels Corp	H	431	119,857	45,000	Hyatt Regency, Grand Hyatt, Park Hyatt, Hyatt Place, Hyatt Summerfield Suites, Hyatt Resorts, Andaz
InterContinental Hotel Group	IHG	4,438	646,679	7,556	InterContinental, Holiday Inn Express, Crowne Plaza, Indigo, Staybridge Suites, Candlewood Suites
Kimpton Hotel Group	[*private*]	40 (*all*)	9,322	6,000	Monaco, Palomar
Marriott International	MAR	3,420	595,461	137,000	Marriott, Courtyard, Fairfield Inn, Ritz-Carlton
Red Lions Hotels	RLH	47	8,910	2,860	Red Lion
Starwood Hotels & Resorts Worldwide	HOT	979 (*30*)	292,000	145,000	Four Points, Sheraton, Westin, St. Regis, Luxury Collection, W Hotels, Le Méridien, Aloft, Element
Wyndham Worldwide	WYN	7,000	588,000	24,600	Days Inn, Howard Johnson, Ramada, Super 8

EXHIBIT 2 (*Continued*)

FYE 12/31, U.S. $ million	2009		2008		2007	
Company Name	**Total Revenue**	**Net Income**	**Total Revenue**	**Net Income**	**Total Revenue**	**Net Income**
Accor SA	$10,726.3	$864.0	$11,812.0	$1,342.4	$9,938.3	$567.3
Best Western						
Choice Hotels International	4,140.0	98.3	4,936.0	100.2	4,692.0	111.3
Four Seasons Hotels	21.0					
Hilton Worldwide*			7,770.0		8,162.0	572.0
Hyatt Hotels Corp	3,332.0	(43.6)	3,837.0	168.0	3,738.0	270.0
InterContinental Hotel Group	1,538.0	214.0	1,854.0	262.0	883.0	231.0
Kimpton Hotel Group	600.0					
Marriott International	10,908.0	(346.0)	12,879.0	362.0	12,990.0	696.0
Red Lions Hotels Corp	165.4	(6.6)	187.6	(1.7)	186.9	6.1
Starwood Hotels & Resorts Worldwide	4,712.0	71.0	5,907.0	329.0	6,153.0	542.0
Wyndham Worldwide Corp	3,750.0	293.0	4,281.0	(1,074.0)	4,360.0	403.0

* Acquired by the Blackstone Group in September 2007.

Sources: Mergent OnLine and Hoovers/Dun & Bradstreet (ProQuest), and individual company Web sites, accessed April 24 and 25, 2010.

overcapacity: as of October 2009, the U.S. lodging industry comprised approximately 4.8 million rooms at more than 50,000 properties—about one hotel room for every 64 US residents.

7 *Recent performance.* Beginning in the second half of 2008 and continuing through the first quarter of 2010, the lodging industry experienced one of its longest downturns since industry data first became available in the late 1960s. Headline unemployment, declining business and conference travel, relatively unchanged real GDP, and rampant foreclosures were lead contributors to low occupancy rates of 2008 and 2009. Standard & Poor's projected that 2010 would represent a further decline in hotel industry performance. The prolonged industry downturn was expected to drop occupancy levels between 55 percent and 56 percent, representing the worst rate since the Great Depression, according to Standard & Poor's. In December 2009, Smith Travel Research estimated that U.S. hotel rates for the year had declined 8.9 percent, and would fall another 3.4 percent in 2010. Hotel occupancy had declined 8.8 percent in 2009, and was forecasted to drop a further 0.2 percent in 2010. After ending 2009 down 6 percent, demand was forecasted to grow 1.6 percent in 2010, mostly driven by recovering demand in the second half of the year.

8 A key industry statistic, Revenue Per Available Room or RevPAR, declined 17 percent in 2009, and was forecasted to drop a further 3.6 percent in 2010, according to Smith Travel Research. RevPAR was a ratio commonly used to measure financial performance in the hospitality industry. The metric, which was a function of both room rates and occupancy, was one of the most important gauges of health among hotel operators. There were two ways to calculate RevPAR. The first formula was: Total Room Revenue in a Given Period, Net of Discounts, Sales Tax, and Meals divided by number of Available Rooms in the Same Period. Alternatively, RevPAR could be calculated as: Average Daily Room Rate times

Occupancy Rate. RevPAR was arguably the most important of all ratios used in the hotel industry. Because the measure incorporated both room rates and occupancy, it provided a convenient snapshot of a how well a company was filling its rooms, as well as how much it was able to charge. RevPAR, by definition, was calculated on a per-room basis. Therefore, one company might have a higher RevPAR than another, but still have lower total revenues if the second firm managed more rooms.

9 In a lodging industry review of 2009 and preview for 2010, Jeri Clausing of *Travel Weekly,* a popular trade publication, noted:

> Meetings and business travel will be a big factor in the recovery. Already stung by the slowdown in travel that accompanies any recession, hoteliers were hit with a double whammy in 2009 when luxury and meetings became dirty words. Toward the end of 2009, hotel executives said they were starting to see signs of life again in these markets. The bad news for hoteliers is that most of the corporate rates have already been negotiated, so even if travel picks up more than expected next year, it probably won't show in rates and RevPAR until 2011.

10 *Greening of the hotel industry*. The growing interest in and investments made to support sustainability in the hospitality industry had, by late 2009, moved beyond hotel recycling programs and energy-efficient lighting. According to an 2009 article appearing in *Hotels* magazine, hotels seeking new customers and growth in these difficult economic times could benefit over the long term with investments in sustainability initiatives, including retrofitting existing properties to achieve Leadership in Energy and Environmental Design (LEED) certification and building new properties to LEED standards. A late 2008 Travel Industry Association Study reported that nearly half of U.S. leisure travelers expressed a willingness to pay higher rates for services provided by environmentally friendly travel providers, and of those willing to pay more for "green" lodging, 60 percent said they would pay up to a 9 percent premium. A Deloitte survey from 2008 reported that 28 percent of U.S. business travelers were willing to pay a 10 percent premium to stay in a green lodging facility.

11 *Emerging demographic segment*. A major driver of the growing demand for green lodging came from an emerging demographic segment that consisted of consumers identified as "Cultural Creatives" by American sociologist Paul Ray, and also known as LOHAS (Lifestyles of Health and Sustainability). This segment sought a better world for themselves and their children. They were savvy, sophisticated, ecologically and economically aware customers who believed that society had reached a watershed moment in history owing to increasing public scrutiny of corporations' environmental and ethical practices. The LOHAS consumer focused on health and fitness, the environment, personal development, sustainable living and social justice. This segment was estimated by the Natural Marketing Institute (NMI) to consist of about 38 million people, or 17 percent of the U.S. adult population, with spending power of $209 billion annually. Among all ages of consumers, younger consumers, aged 14–24, were reported to be most concerned about issues such as climate change and environmental protection, and were the major drivers of growth in the LOHAS segment. See **Exhibit 3** for a profile of the LOHAS demographic.

12 Of that segment, the NMI identified a sub-segment of tourists comprising five percent of the overall U.S. travel and tourism market and representing a $77-billion market. Major hotel companies like Ritz Carlton and Starwood were known to be creating eco-branded properties. Hospitality designers and architects increasingly were being asked to "green" facilities across the board, from budget properties to high-end resorts.

13 *San Francisco tourism and lodging patterns*. Of the estimated 15.4 million visitors to San Francisco city and county in 2009, more than 4.5 million overnight visitors stayed in commercial accommodations, comprising 32,976 hotel rooms and 215 hotels. Visitors paid a 14 percent occupancy tax that generated about $210 million for San Francisco city and

EXHIBIT 3 The Green Consumer

	All consumers	"Green" consumers
Average age	44	40
Gender		
Female	51%	54%
Male	49%	46%
Ethnicity		
Caucasian/other	75%	62%
Hispanic	13%	21%
African-American	11%	16%
College educated	25%	31%
Median household income	$58,700	$65,700

Source: Brooks, S. (2009). The green consumer, *Restaurant Business,* September, pp. 20–21.

county services, including schools, police, affordable housing, and arts programs. Most tourists in San Francisco took day trips beyond city limits or extended their visit throughout Northern California by taking side trips to other area locales and attractions, such as the Napa/Sonoma wine country (23 percent), Sausalito (14 percent), and the Monterey peninsula (about 10 percent). **Exhibit 4** presents San Francisco tourism data and **Exhibit 5** shows comparative statistics on the San Francisco hospitality industry for the periods ending March 31, 2008, 2009, and 2010.

14 The San Francisco Convention and Visitors Bureau forecasted that room supply would remain relatively unchanged out to 2015, while demand for rooms would remain flat, in stark contrast to 2004–2008, which represented five consecutive years of growth in both room supply and tourism demand. The Bureau also projected that hotel occupancy rates, average daily rates (ADR) and RevPAR would not begin to recover until 2011–12. One major factor was that the Moscone Convention Center, San Francisco's largest convention and meetings site, was expected to have a weak convention year in 2010 compared to five of the prior six years. Convention center bookings—at places such as the Moscone Center—greatly influenced hotel projections. Nearly 20,000 hotel rooms were in walking distance of the Moscone Center (including Good Hotel, which was five blocks away), and convention travel represented 35 percent of the annual demand for hotel rooms, according to the Convention and Visitor's Bureau. Although eight new hotels were on the drawing board, those new properties were unlikely to alter local room supply in the near-term.

JOIE DE VIVRE

15 Since JdV's founding in 1987, the company had grown to manage 36 boutique hotel properties in California. By 2010, JdV was the second largest U.S. boutique hotel operator after the Kimpton Hotel & Restaurant Group, which had pioneered the boutique concept in San Francisco in 1981.

16 *Boutique hotels.* Boutique hotels differentiated themselves from larger chain branded hotels and motels by providing personalized accommodation and services and facilities. Sometimes known as "design hotels" or "lifestyle hotels", boutique hotels began appearing in the 1980s in major cities like London, New York, and San Francisco. Boutique hotels

EXHIBIT 4 **San Francisco Hotel Guest Profile in 2009**

Average annual household income:	$93,900
Average spending in SF (per-person, per-day):	$244.33
First-time San Francisco visitors:	17.5%
Traveling with children:	8.7%
Gender:	Male = 53.5% Female = 46.5%
Average age:	46 years old
Average nights in SF hotels:	3.6 nights
Average total length of current trip:	4.6 nights
People per room:	1.77
Used Internet in planning trip:	53.9%
Rental car in San Francisco:	25.8%
Arrived by air:	80.2%
Top five feeder markets of hotel guests [by Designated Market Areas (DMAs)]	Los Angeles – v12.7% San Francisco-Oakland-San Jose – 7.7% Sacramento-Stockton-Modesto – 7% New York City – 5.7% Washington, DC – 3.5%
Primary reason for visit (% of all hotel guests):	39.7% Leisure 35.3% Convention 22.1% Transient business 2.9% Other

Source: http://www.sfcvb.org/research/, accessed April 28, 2010.

EXHIBIT 5 **San Francisco Hospitality Statistics, 2008–2010**

Avg. Daily Room Rate ($)			
	March 2008	**March 2009**	**March 2010**
Civic Center/Van Ness	$114.16	$ 92.45	$ 90.67
Financial District	230.21	189.47	181.93
Fisherman's Wharf	155.52	116.61	111.48
Union Square/Nob Hill/Moscone Center	200.00	176.57	161.99
Occupancy Rate (%)			
	March 2008	**March 2009**	**March 2010**
Civic Center/Van Ness	79.6%	69.4%	74.3%
Financial District	76.7	69.0	77.0
Fisherman's Wharf	84.0	74.5	86.0
Union Square/Nob Hill/Moscone Center	73.6	66.8	75.2

Sources: http://www.sfcvb.org/research/, accessed April 28, 2010. Hospitality statistics from PKF Consulting.

were furnished in a themed, stylish and/or aspirational manner. Boutique hotels typically were unique properties operated by individuals or companies with a small collection. Their successes in time prompted several multi-national hotel companies to try to establish their own brands in order to capture a market share. The most notable example was Starwood's W Hotels, ranging from large boutique hotels, such as the W Times Square in New York City, to the W 'boutique resorts' in the Maldives, to true luxury boutique hotel collections, such as the Bulgari collection, SLS Hotels, Thompson Hotels, The Keating Hotel, and the O Hotel, among others.

17 *Strategy*. According to Chip Conley, JdV's founder and CEO,

> I went into hospitality because I enjoyed commercial real estate but hated the transactional part. If you get it right and your customer sees the product as an extension of themselves, you're refreshed the identity of the customers because they feel that by using the product they're becoming more of that aspirational self, according to Abraham Maslow's 'Hierarchy of Needs'.[1]

18 In 2007, Conley related JdV's branding strategy to *Travel Weekly*:

> We know California better than anybody else. We are the largest hotelier in the state. About 40 percent of our customers come from within the state. We went through a whole branding process, and what we heard from our customers was that they loved the fact that we create original hotels. We come up with a personality for the hotel by thinking of magazines. It is sort of like a good touchstone for personality. Each [hotel] is its own unique product. You can be geographically diverse, but that means you have to be product-line focused. Or you can be geographically focused and the product line diverse. Holiday Inn is geographically diverse and product-line focused. We are the opposite of Holiday Inn.[2]

19 Among JdV's most recently opened San Francisco Bay Area properties, the Tomo in Japantown was based on two Japanese pop culture magazines, *Lucky* (a popular women's magazine in Japan) and *Giant Robot* (a Japanese magazine devoted to anime and manga and technology-based art). Other properties included the Vitale (*Dwell* + *Real Simple*), Galleria Park (*Vanity Fair* + *BusinessWeek*), Kabuki (*Travel & Leisure*), and downtown Berkeley's Durant (*Sports Illustrated* + *Economist*). The Good Hotel concept was based on two magazines *Ode* + *Readymade,* and according to Pam, embodied five key words: "Hip, Happy, Humble, Conscious, and Inventive."

20 *Marketing.* JdV spent very little on marketing, preferring to rely mostly on word-of-mouth and social media promotion on the Internet to attract guests to its hotels. According to industry analysts, social media use among travelers continued to grow faster than the travel industry itself.

21 Unique monthly visitors to social travel websites such as TripAdvisor.com and Yelp!.com rose 34 percent between the first half of 2008 and the last half of 2009, to 15.9 million, representing year-over-year growth of more than 30 percent in the first half of 2009 and 45 percent in the second half of 2009. By comparison, U.S. travel gross bookings had declined 16 percent in 2009.[3]

22 *JdV's green programs*. In 2009, JdV's senior vice president of operations and green committee chair, Karlene Holloman, launched the company's Green Dreams portal, a dedicated

[1] Speech to Association of Fundraising Professionals, Commonwealth Club, San Francisco, January 22, 2010. See also Chip Conley's 2007 book on the subject of applying Maslow's Hierarchy of Needs to business, *Peak: How Great Companies Get Their Mojo from Maslow*. San Francisco: Jossey-Bass.

[2] Milligan, M. (2007). Joie de Vivre finds inspiration for properties in pop culture. *Travel Weekly,* May 1, http://www.travelweekly.com/article3_ektid92480.aspx?terms=*joie+de+vivre*, accessed May 1, 2010.

[3] PhoCusWright (2010) *Social Media in Travel: Traffic & Activity,* April.

EXHIBIT 6 LEED Certified Hotels in Northern California

LEED was an acronym for Leadership in Energy and Environmental Design. Buildings attained LEED certification from the U.S. Green Business Council by earning points in six categories: sustainable sites, water efficiency, energy and atmosphere, materials and resources, indoor environmental air quality, and innovation/design process. Based on the total number of points, a business would then receive a silver, gold or platinum designation. Lower operation costs were typically associated with a LEED building: approximately 30 to 40 percent less energy use and 40 percent less water. Application for LEED certification of an existing property could cost upwards of $10,000, depending upon the size of the property, the number of rooms, and the level of certification sought. Most hotels tried for certification of new construction, which was much easier and potentially less costly to earn than from retrofitting an existing building.

As of March 2010, there were 12 LEED-certified hotels in America, of which four were in San Francisco [Hotel Carlton (Gold), Orchard, Orchard Garden, and W Hotel (Silver)], with more than 100 proposals in the works. See table below. Other reputable certifications by Green Seal and the Green Tourism Business Scheme in the United Kingdom have led to confusion, with no universal stamp of approval available.

Hotel Name and Location	LEED Rating System and Certification Level*	Building Type
SAN FRANCISCO		
Hotel Carlton	LEED EBOM **Gold**	Commercial
Orchard Garden Hotel	LEED NC Certified (v2.1)	Commercial
Orchard Hotel	LEED EB Certified (v2.0)	Commercial
W Hotel	LEED EBOM Silver	Commercial
OUTSIDE SAN FRANCISCO		
Gaia Napa Valley Hotel, American Canyon	LEED NC **Gold** (v2.1)	Commercial
Gaia Shasta Hotel, Anderson	LEED NC Silver (v2.1)	Commercial

* Rating Systems
LEED CI = LEED for Commercial Interiors
LEED CS = LEED for Core & Shell
LEED EB = LEED for Existing Buildings
LEED EBOM = LEED for Existing Buildings: Operations & Maintenance
LEED H = LEED for Homes
LEED NC = LEED for New Construction (and Major Renovations)
LEED ND = LEED for Neighborhood Development

LEED Certification Levels:
Certified, Silver, Gold, Platinum

Sources: http://www.mlandman.com/gbuildinginfo/leedbuildings.shtml (updated every 8 weeks, accessed 4/25/2010), and http://www.executivetravelmagazine.com/page/What+is+an+LEED+hotel+--+and+where+are+they%3F, accessed 4/25/2010.

page on its Web site (http://www.jdvhotels.com/greendreams/), where consumers could track the company's ongoing efforts to preserve the environment. Holloman said at the time:

> We want to be transparent and share the progress we've made and the efforts that continue as we strive to have all our hotels green-certified in the near term. In essence, our guests can be green cheerleaders, watching from the sidelines as more of our hotels reach their goals. We hope Joie de Vivre Green Dreams will become a useful tool and resource for our guests and any consumer evaluating green travel programs.[4]

23 To demonstrate its ongoing commitment to the environment, JdV's hotels had a goal of becoming certified green by their local city or county while using the San Francisco Green

[4] In Gale, D. (2009). The green guests are coming. *Hotels,* 43, January, p. 33.

Business Certification standards, as these were the most stringent in the state. Some hotels, like Hotel Carlton, went beyond this goal by investing in solar power and achieving LEED certification, making it San Francisco's first hotel to be awarded a Leadership in Energy and Environmental Design (LEED) Gold certification. **Exhibit 6** presents a definition of LEED and a listing of Northern California hotel properties carrying this certification as of April 2010.

24 *Financial performance*. In 2009, JdV's hotels, restaurants and spas generated an estimated $250 million in revenues, at properties ranging from the high-end Ventana Inn in Big Sur, California, with rooms at $700 per night, to Good Hotel, at $70 per night. JdV's room revenues dropped 18–20 percent in 2008–09, but appeared to be rising at about the same rate in the first quarter of 2010, according to Conley. JdV was privately held and did not release information regarding individual hotel revenues or profits. Nevertheless, Conley publicly stated that JdV had remained profitable throughout the downturn. According to an April 9, 2010 report in the *San Francisco Business Times,* Conley was actively seeking a strategic capital partner for JdV, a partner that could provide an investment of $150 million or more to expand the number of properties under JdV's management.

GOOD HOTEL

25 *Operations*. Formerly managed by JdV as a Best Western motel and an adjacent property, the Hotel Britton, the Good Hotel was refurbished in 2008 and reopened in November of that year. It was located at the corner of Mission and Seventh Streets—a gritty but slowly revitalizing corner of SoMa, as the area south of Market Street in San Francisco was known. In the immediate vicinity were single-room-occupancy housing, the futuristic-looking San Francisco Federal Building and a sleek plaza lined with cafés. Mass transit, including bus, light rail, cable car and subway, was all within walking distance.

26 Good Hotel's lobby showcased many environmentally and socially conscious features including a bench made of recycled felt blankets, a vending machine branded by *Ready-Made* magazine that dispensed wallets fashioned out of FedEx envelopes ($15) and other goodies; wall art by developmentally disabled artists; and an orange phone that connected to a "philanthropy concierge" who arranged volunteer stints through One Brick, a local non-profit. There was also a photo booth in the lobby ($3 for two prints); the hotel encouraged visitors to add to the photo collage of guests prominently displayed in the lobby. The hotel's 38 motel-style rooms opened onto a courtyard parking lot, and the remaining 79 rooms were located in a five-story brick building.

27 In the rooms, which had the feel of a slightly upscale youth hostel, platform beds made of reclaimed pine were draped with fleece blankets made of recycled soda bottles. The pillows were made from old bedspreads salvaged from the previous hotel, a Best Western. Each room had a chandelier made of empty Voss water bottles, a recycling bin, a fold-down metal desk just big enough for a laptop and, overhead, a secret message from the hotel that glowed in the dark. Bathrooms featured a Japanese-style toilet-top sink: the gray water from the sink was collected in the toilet tank, saving water. Rooms provided free Wi-Fi, an iPod docking station and 26-inch flat-screen televisions. A spacious fitness center and outdoor heated pool were available across the street, at the recently renovated Best Western Americania. At checkout, guests donated $1.50 per day to One Brick (donations were automatically added to each room night stay), offset their carbon footprint through Carbonfund.org, or went on-line on one of the iMacs in the small business center with an option to give a $200 computer through One Laptop per Child.

28 Writing in the *San Francisco Chronicle* in December 2008, just after the hotel opened, John Flinn described his experience: "San Francisco's new Good Hotel doesn't miss many tricks in its bid to be the greenest, do-goodingest, most politically correct hotel in America. But even Hummer drivers and spotted owl stranglers will appreciate the gratifyingly low room rates, which start at $67 a night."

29 *Leadership.* Pam received an MBA from the University of Texas at Austin in 2004. She initially was responsible for management of three of JdV's smallest boutique hotels. In 2006, she served as the General Manager of Special Projects relating to transitional hotels, a role in which she was responsible for assisting new JdV hotels and restaurants in acclimating to the culture, processes, and operational standards of the company.

30 In 2007 Pam was promoted to the General Manager role at Hotel Carlton, a certified green business by the city of San Francisco. In this role she became involved in many JdV-wide initiatives including the Safety Task Force, Green Committee and Advisory Panel. Pam led the process at Hotel Carlton to install solar panels that provided 9 percent of the energy used on property, and spearheaded the hotel's application process to become certified by the U.S. Green Building Council at the Gold Level for LEED-EB (existing building). As a member of the JdV Green Committee, Pam also contributed greatly to the new JdV Green Dreams Web site, which outlined and rated the company's environmental initiatives in four main focus areas: recycling and waste reduction, energy conservation, water conservation and pollution prevention.

31 While conducting a tour of Good Hotel in March 2010, Pam remarked that part of her job entailed educating staff members to ensure they were aware of JdV's safety and green programs and could explain them to guests and answer guests' questions. Nearly all guests at Good Hotel were leisure travelers or tourists on a budget. She said,

> Recently, we find travelers are more last minute when reserving their hotel accommodations. We see a lot of walk-in and Internet 'on the day of' reservations which drive occupancy. There is a fine line when setting room rates so we are competitively priced but not too low so we attract clientele that we do not want at our hotels. We've also had to focus a lot on service and safety training due to the fact that this neighborhood is still transitional. Our Green Dreams Web site and personal contact together provide the most effective means of attracting and keeping guests who are concerned about the environment. I was hoping that we could convince the owners of the Good Hotel to apply for LEED certification, like we did at the Hotel Carlton, but they were not in a position to immediately move forward on new investments when I arrived at the hotel.

32 *Financial performance.* Smith Travel Research collected monthly operating statistics for hotels. Statistics for the Hotel Britton (the previous property) and the Good Hotel from March 2008 to the end of March 2010 are shown in **Exhibit 7**, providing comparisons of occupancy rates, average daily rate, and RevPAR with five selected peer group competitors in its neighborhood, size, and class. **Exhibit 8** provides monthly operating data for The Good Hotel from its opening in November 2008 to the end of March 2010.

EXHIBIT 7 **Operating Statistics: Good Hotel vs. San Francisco Peer Group, March 2008–March 2010**

March 31, 2008	Occupancy (%)		ADR ($)		RevPAR ($)	
	Hotel Britton*	Comp Set**	Hotel Britton*	Comp Set**	Hotel Britton*	Comp Set**
Current Month	45.4	67.9	79.38	83.68	36.07	56.79
Year-to-Date	39.3	59.2	73.61	76.76	28.92	45.46
Running 3 Month	39.3	59.2	73.61	76.76	28.92	45.46
Running 12 Month	63.3	69.0	80.23	86.02	50.82	59.38

EXHIBIT 7 (*Continued*)

March 2008 vs. 2007 Percent Change (%)						
	Occupancy		ADR		RevPAR	
	Hotel Britton*	Comp Set**	Hotel Britton*	Comp Set**	Hotel Britton*	Comp Set**
Current Month	–18.5	–1.1	28.2	26.9	2.8	25.6
Year-to-Date	0.3	2.9	9.4	14.7	9.7	18.0
Running 3 Month	0.3	2.9	9.4	14.7	9.7	18.0
Running 12 Month	1.1	8.4	6.8	7.8	8.0	16.9
March 31, 2009* **						
	Occupancy (%)		ADR ($)		RevPAR ($)	
	Good Hotel	Comp Set**	Good Hotel	Comp Set**	Good Hotel	Comp Set**
Current Month	70.3	59.3	65.82	66.51	46.85	39.90
Year-to-Date	55.3	53.4	62.95	63.88	34.36	34.25
Running 3 Month	55.3	53.4	62.95	63.88	34.36	34.25
Running 12 Month	29.7	67.9	85.23	90.22	31.49	60.10
March 2009 vs. 2008 Percent Change (%)* **						
	Occupancy		ADR		RevPAR	
	Good Hotel	Comp Set**	Good Hotel	Comp Set**	Good Hotel	Comp Set**
Current Month	54.9	–12.7	–17.1	–20.5	29.9	–29.7
Year-to-Date	40.6	–9.8	–14.5	–16.8	18.8	–24.7
Running 3 Month	40.6	–9.8	–14.5	–16.8	18.8	–24.7
Running 12 Month	–53.1	–1.6	6.2	4.9	–38.0	1.2
March 31, 2010						
	Occupancy (%)		ADR ($)		RevPAR ($)	
	Good Hotel	Comp Set**	Good Hotel	Comp Set**	Good Hotel	Comp Set**
Current Month	66.2	56.1	73.30	73.66	48.50	41.30
Year-to-Date	57.8	51.7	71.94	67.74	41.60	35.02
Running 3 Month	57.8	51.7	71.94	67.74	41.60	35.02
Running 12 Month	76.7	61.8	78.55	80.27	60.21	49.63
March 2010 vs. 2009 Percent Change (%)						
	Occupancy		ADR		RevPAR	
	Good Hotel	Comp Set**	Good Hotel	Comp Set**	Good Hotel	Comp Set**
Current Month	–6.2	–5.7	10.2	9.7	3.4	3.4
Year-to-Date	4.4	–3.3	12.5	5.7	17.4	2.2
Running 3 Month	4.4	–3.3	12.5	5.7	17.4	2.2
Running 12 Month	61.3	–9.9	–8.5	–12.4	47.7	–21.1

Notes

*JdV's Hotel Britton was refurbished and reopened as the Good Hotel in November 2008.

**Comp set was defined as a peer group of competitive hotels selected by hotel management to benchmark the subject property's performance. The competitive set consisted of five San Francisco hotels near Market Street, with a total of 602 rooms, and included: Knights Inn Downtown San Francisco (68 rooms), The Opal Hotel (164 rooms), Hotel Metropolis (105 rooms), Renoir Hotel (130 rooms), and The Powell Hotel (135 rooms).

*** Good Hotel was closed for a few months in 2008 during renovation. This closure affects the running 12 month averages from the 2009 reports.

Source: Smith Travel Research, March 2008 and March 2010.

EXHIBIT 8 Monthly Operating Statistics: Good Hotel, November 2008–March 2010

	2008	
	Nov	Dec
Number of Rooms	117	117
Occupancy (%)	26.87	55.53
RevPAR ($)	20.53	48.93
TOTAL REVENUE	$2,402	$5,725

	2009											
	Jan	Feb	Mar	Apr	May	Jun	Jul	Aug	Sep	Oct	Nov	Dec
Number of Rooms	117	117	117	117	117	117	117	117	117	117	117	117
Occupancy (%)	40.14	55.49	70.53	77.35	78.22	87.46	91.98	95.01	92.25	90.65	62.28	69.78
RevPAR ($)	26.57	32.50	46.91	56.29	68.65	68.72	77.01	79.63	80.02	83.33	43.48	39.06
TOTAL REVENUE	$3,109	$3,802	$5,488	$6,586	$8,033	$8,040	$9,011	$9,317	$9,362	$9,750	$5,087	$4,570

	2010		
	Jan	Feb	Mar
Number of Rooms	117	117	117
Occupancy (%)	56.96	49.54	66.17
RevPAR ($)	40.31	35.39	48.50
TOTAL REVENUE	$4,716	$4,141	$5,675

Source: Smith Travel Research, March 2010.

MAKING THE TRANSITION

33 As Pam went through her in-box, another message, marked "urgent", had been sent by the organizer of a Norwegian tour group requesting immediate cancellation of 100 rooms booked at The Good Hotel for the week of April 18th. Disruption of all air travel and indefinite closure of nearly all airports in Europe had forced cancellation of the tour, due to the huge plume of ash generated by the unexpected eruption of the *Eyjafjallajökull* volcano in Iceland. Loss of the Norwegian tour group's business meant that many of the 117 rooms would be empty unless last-minute or walk-in bookings showed up. This came at a time when the hotel industry in general was counting on a recovery from the long economic recession in 2008 and 2009, not to mention the normally soft travel bookings during the winter months.

34 In addition to the cancelled bookings, Pam wondered about how to inform and transition the current Good Hotel staff to the new ownership group. She pondered how her recommendation would impact their commitment to the original intent of Good Hotel.

35 Pam's number one task was how best to prepare Good Hotel and its current staff for the transition to new ownership in six weeks' time. She had several weeks remaining to work with her staff to complete a review of Good Hotel, containing her evaluation of the Good Hotel concept.

BIBLIOGRAPHY

_______ (2010). Perspectives: green. *Hospitality Design, 32*(2), March, p. 44.

_______ (2005). Joie de Vivre looks to grow by growing up. *Hotels, 39*(3), March, p. 18.

_______ (2009). Chip Conley, *Marketing News, 43*(3), p. 62.

_______ (2010). San Francisco Convention and Visitor's Bureau Web site, http://www.sfcvb.org/research/

Barrett, S. (2008). Operations key in green effort. *Hotel and Motel Management, 223*(5), p. 1.

Brooks, S. (2009). The green consumer, *Restaurant Business,* September, pp. 20–21.

Chan, W.W. (2009). Environmental measures for hotels' environmental management systems. *International Journal for Contemporary Hospitality Management, 21*(5), pp. 542–560.

Clark, R.A., Hartline, M.D., & Jones, K.C. (2009). Effects of leadership style on hotel employees' commitment to service quality. *Cornell Hospitality Quarterly, 50*(2), March, pp. 209–231.

Clausing, J. (2009). Preview 2010: The supply side: hotels. *Travel Weekly,* December 29, http://www.travelweekly.com/article3_ektid208196.aspx?terms=*clausing*&page=6, accessed May 1, 2010.

Clausing, J. (2010). Hotels struggle to harness the power of social media. *Travel Weekly,* April 21, http://www.travelweekly.com/article3_ektid213392.aspx?terms=*clausing*, accessed May 1, 2010.

Conley, C. (2007). *Peak: How Great Companies Get Their Mojo from Maslow*. San Francisco: Jossey-Bass.

Dahle, C. (2004). Weathering the perfect storm. *Fast Company,* 84, p. 29.

Duxbury, S. (2010, April 9). Joie de Vivre Hospitality seeking $150M, new investor. *San Francisco Business Times,* http://www.bizjournals.com/sanfrancisco/stories/2010/04/05/story4.html?b=1270440000%5E3130821&s=industry&i=travel, accessed May 1, 2010.

Flinn, J. (2008, December 18). The Good Hotel. *San Francisco Chronicle,* G-33. http://www.sfgate.com/cgi-bin/article.cgi?f=/c/a/2008/12/18/NS1R14IARP.DTL#ixzz0mmgSnBY8, accessed May 1, 2010.

Gale, D. (2009). The green guests are coming. *Hotels,* 43, January, p. 33.

Henning, M. (2008, March 11). Success comes from developed leadership. *Hotel & Motel Management, 223*(2), p. 12.

Milligan, M. (2007). Joie de Vivre finds inspiration for properties in pop culture. *Travel Weekly,* May 1, http://www.travelweekly.com/article3_ektid92480.aspx?terms=*joie+de+vivre*, accessed May 1, 2010

Mount, I. (2005). Open-book survival. *Fortune Small Business, 15*(5), June, p. 29.

PhoCusWright (2010) *Social Media in Travel: Traffic & Activity,* April.

Speer, J. (2009, June). Reaching the top of the pyramid. *Apparel Magazine,* p. 2.

Standard & Poor's, (2009). Current environment: lodging & gaming. *Standard & Poor's Industry Surveys,* November 19, pp. 1–23.

Weinstein, J. (2006). Brands vs. independents. *Hotels,* 40, July, p. 7.

Woodward, M. (2010). Average growth rate leads cities out of recession. *Hotel & Motel Management, 225*(2), February 1, p. 14.

Woodworth, R.M. and Walls, A. (2009). Thoughts while waiting for RevPar to grow. *Cornell Hospitality Quarterly, 50*(3), August, pp. 289–291.

Case 11

InBev and Anheuser-Busch

Andrew Inkpen

1 In early June 2008, Belgian-based InBev NV launched an unsolicited $46.4 billion bid to acquire Anheuser-Busch Co., owner of the 132-year-old Budweiser brand. The combination would create the world's largest brewer, with sales of about $36 billion annually. Carlos Brito, CEO of InBev, said that the deal "will create a stronger, more competitive, sustainable global company which will benefit all stakeholders."[1] The initial response from Anheuser was noncommittal, stating that the company "will pursue the course of action that is in the best interests of Anheuser-Busch's stockholders." On June 26, Anheuser's board formally rejected InBev's original proposal of $65 a share, saying it substantially undervalued the company. The board indicated that it would be open to a higher price.

2 In mid-July, InBev raised its offer to $70 a share, and the Anheuser board voted to accept the deal, recognizing that a better offer was unlikely. The $70 price represented a substantial premium for Anheuser shareholders. InBev management would now have to prove to their shareholders that the premium was justified.

THE BREWING INDUSTRY

3 The basic beer brewing process is quite straightforward. Malted barley (malt) is the primary ingredient, although other grains such as unmalted barley, corn, rice, or wheat can also be used. Yeast, hops, and water are the other main ingredients. The most challenging aspects of industrial-scale brewing are maintaining quality control across large volumes, multiple products, and different production sites, and ensuring that costs are closely managed.

Products

4 A common characteristic of global beer markets is the segmentation of products on the basis of quality and price. Premium brands are at the top of the market, with the very top of the market represented by the super-premium segment. Mainstream or core brands are in the middle of the market; value or discount brands at the lower end of the market. For example, in the United States, Michelob would be considered super premium, Budweiser premium, Miller High Life core, and Busch value. Heineken and other imports generally compete against super-premium beers and are priced similarly. Craft beers from small brewers, such as Samuel Adams Boston Lager and Sierra Nevada Pale Ale, were an important growth segment.

5 In the developed countries, most beer consumption was in the mainstream and premium segments. In the United States, the top five brands were all in the premium segment: Bud Light, Miller Lite, Budweiser, Coors Light, and Corona (import). In countries where consumers have lower disposable income, the value and discount segments were more important. Trading up to more expensive products was a more common trend than trading down. Once beer drinkers moved up a segment, they rarely traded down.

[1] D. Kesmodel, and M. Karnitschnig, "InBev Uncorks Anheuser Takeover Bid; Belgian-Brazilian Giant Offers $46.4 Billion for U.S. Icon; Would Create No. 1 Brewer," *Wall Street Journal*, June 12, 2008, A1.

6 Globally, the largest selling brand names by volume were Snow (China; brewed by a joint venture between SABMiller and China Resources Enterprises), Bud Light, Budweiser, Skol (Brazil), Corona, Heineken (Netherlands), Brahma (Brazil), Coors Light, Tsingtao (China), and Miller Lite. (Note: The Snow brand had about 25 extensions. Bud Light was the highest volume single product.)

Markets

7 China was the largest market by volume, followed by the United States, Germany, Brazil, Russia, Japan, U.K., Mexico, South Africa, and Spain. In the developed markets, growth was flat. For example, in the United States, overall growth was slightly more than 1%. However, in the U.S. craft segment, growth was 11%, putting pressure on the large national brewers. Growth in emerging markets was much higher than in the developed countries. The China market was growing about 10% annually, although beer prices were much lower than those in Europe and North America.

8 The distribution of beer varied from country to country and from region to region. The nature of distribution reflected consumption patterns and market structure, geographic density of customers, local regulation, and the existence of third-party wholesalers or distributors. In some markets, brewers distributed directly to customers (e.g., Belgium and France), while in other markets, wholesalers were used, for legal reasons (e.g., United States and South Korea), or because of historical market practice (e.g., Russia and Argentina).

9 The U.S. brewing industry was dominated by a small number of firms. For the major brewers, the entire country represented one huge market with only minor regulatory differences between the states. The major brewers concentrated on establishing a limited number of national brands that generated substantial production and marketing efficiencies. Beer was distributed to wholesalers, who were then free to distribute to retail selling points, which in most states were grocery stores, convenience stores, and drugstores. Prices were controlled only to the extent of taxation.

Consolidation

10 Consolidation among the largest brewers (**Exhibit 1**) was an important industry characteristic of the last decade. In 2002, SAB (South Africa) acquired Miller Brewing Company (#2 in the United States), creating SABMiller. In 2005, SABMiller acquired a majority interest

EXHIBIT 1 **The Largest Brewers**

Company	Millions of hectoliters
SABMiller	230.9
InBev	227.0
Heineken	167.4
Anheuser-Busch	150.6
Carlsberg	121.0
MolsonCoors	58.0
Modelo	50.9
Tsingtao Group	50.5
Beijing Yanjing	40.7
FEMSA	39.9

in Bavaria S.A., South America's second largest brewer, and in 2008, acquired Grolsch, the second largest brewery in the Netherlands. In 2005, Coors (United States) and Molson (Canada) merged, creating the fifth largest global brewer. In 2007, Heineken (Netherlands) became the second largest brewer after partnering with Carlsberg (Denmark) to acquire Scottish and Newcastle (U.K). Also in 2007, SABMiller and Molson Coors agreed to merge their U.S. operations. The large Danish brewer, Carlsberg, made a number of regional acquisitions that strengthened its position in the Baltic States and Russia.

INTERBREW

11 Interbrew was formed in 1987 when two Belgian families merged their private brewing interests. Interbrew's 1995 acquisition of the largest Canadian brewer, John Labatt, moved the company into the top tier of global brewers. In addition to many small acquisitions, the company was involved in two additional major deals: the 2000 acquisitions of U.K. brewers Bass and Whitbread, and the 2003 acquisition of Germany's Beck's. Interbrew went public in 2000.

12 Interbrew's strategy was significantly different than that of companies such as Heineken and Carlsberg. Interbrew had a stable of national and regional products, and did not have what could be called true global brands. With the acquisition of Beck's and increased international marketing emphasis on its Belgian brand, Stella Artois, the company was moving more aggressively to establish a global presence. Also, because the company had grown through many acquisitions, there were many different organizational cultures in the various parts of the company.

AMBEV

13 AmBev's three controlling shareholders were Jorge Paulo Lemann, Marcel Herrmann Telles, and Carlos Alberto Sicupira. The three were among the richest Brazilians (although Lemann was based in Switzerland after a foiled attempt to kidnap his children in Brazil), and were founders of the Brazilian investment bank Banco Garantia (subsequently acquired by Credit Suisse First Boston). In 1989, they purchased Companhia Cervejaria Brahma. AmBev (Companhia de Bebidas das Américas) was created in 2000 with the merger of Brahma and another Brazilian company, Companhia Antarctica Paulista. Almost immediately, the new company began doing acquisitions, buying brewers in Uruguay, Ecuador, Paraguay, and acquiring a significant stake in an Argentine company.

14 Although the three AmBev shareholders had never taken an active role in managing their brewing investments, they were considered shrewd businessmen with a disciplined approach to operations and a strong emphasis on cost cutting. Jorge Paulo Lemann, in particular, was known for his fierce competitive streak, having once played top-level competitive tennis. Before Gillette was acquired by Procter & Gamble, Lemann was a Gillette board member, along with Warren Buffett.

INBEV NV

15 In 2004, a complex deal resulted in a merger between Interbrew and AmBev. (Note: Reports of the deal used various terms to describe it, including alliance and merger. Interbrew announced the deal as a "combination"— see **Exhibit 2**.) At the time of the merger, Interbrew was the world's third largest brewer, with strong positions in Europe and North

EXHIBIT 2 InterBrew and AmBev Deal—Excerpts from Interbrew's Press Release

Combination positions InBev as the world's premier brewer

InBev and Companhia de Bebidas das Américas (AmBev) have today closed the transaction announced on March 3, 2004, to combine Interbrew and AmBev, creating InBev, the world's premier brewer.

InBev's Chief Executive Officer, John Brock said, "We are excited to have formed the world's premier brewer. The companies' full range of international beers means we are well positioned to build on our combined track record of success. We can now focus on delivering value to customers, consumers, employees, and shareholders. I truly look forward to leading a unified world-class management team, building on the best from both companies. As the only true global brewer, we are already the biggest. We aim to be the best."

The transaction consisted of several steps:

- InBev issued 141.712 million new shares in exchange for 100% of Tinsel Investments S.A., which indirectly holds, as of June 2004, approximately 22.5% economic interest and 52.8% voting interest in AmBev. Tinsel Investments S.A. holds the AmBev shares through two subsidiaries, Braco and ECAP.
- InBev transferred Labatt (comprising C$1.3 billion of third-party net debt) to AmBev in exchange for approximately 7.9 billion new AmBev common shares and 11.4 billion new AmBev preferred shares.
- Following the closing of the deal, and in accordance with Brazilian law, InBev will initiate a Mandatory Tender Offer (MTO) for the remaining common shares of AmBev.
- The Fundação Antonio e Helena Zerrenner (a Brazilian charitable foundation providing health benefits to AmBev employees) will remain a common shareholder of AmBev, and has renewed its shareholder agreement with Braco and ECAP until 2019.

As a result of this combination, and assuming full participation by the public float of AmBev in the MTO, InBev will own approximately 31.1 billion AmBev shares (19.7 billion voting and 11.4 billion nonvoting), representing approximately, as of June 2004, a 55.6% economic interest and an 83.9% voting interest.

America and sales in 120 countries. AmBev, with sales primarily in Latin American, was the world's fifth largest brewer

16 The original purpose of the AmBev-Interbrew merger was to give Interbrew a larger foothold in the fast-growing Latin American market and to give AmBev better access to Europe and North America, especially for its Brahma brand. The newly created company was named InBev. Both Interbrew and AmBev believed that the merged company would be at the "forefront of the industry, and consequently would be better positioned than its global competitors to take advantage of any future developments in the sector." InBev would have revenue of almost $12 billion (based on 2003 sales) and 14% of the global brewing industry market share. The company would have a No. 1 or No. 2 position in 20 key markets, more than any other brewer.

17 Despite the substantial premium paid to AmBev's controlling shareholders, the stock market reaction to the deal was positive. The combined annual synergies from the deal were estimated to be around 280 million through a combination of cost savings and commercial synergies. Some industry insiders speculated that one of the reasons for the deal was to transfer AmBev's operational and financial knowhow to Interbrew's sprawling and largely unconnected international businesses. The headquarters for InBev were to be in Leuven, Belgium, with AmBev's Americas headquarters based in Sao Paulo, Brazil.

InBev Products

18 The new company had more than 200 brands, segmented into three categories:

1. Global brands: Beck's and Stella Artois; Beck's was distributed in 100 countries and Stella Artois in 80 countries.
2. Multicountry brands, included Brahma (30 countries), Leffe (60 countries), Staropramen (30 countries), and Hoegaarden (30 countries).
3. Local brands included Keith's and Labatt Blue (Canada); Bohemia, Antarctica, and Skol (Brazil); Quilmes (Argentina); Jupiler (Belgium); Siberian Crown (Russia); and Cass (South Korea).

19 InBev described itself as "predominantly a local brewer with local production based on consumer insights." The company was organized along seven business zones: North America (4.8% of the company's consolidated volume; 10.7% of sales revenue), Latin America North and Latin America South (47.2%; 41.0%), Western Europe (12.8%; 22.5%), Central and Eastern Europe (18.4%; 16.0%), Asia Pacific (14.8%; 6.9%), and Global Export & Holding Companies making up the balance.

20 On an individual country basis, InBev's ten largest markets by volume were Brazil, China, Argentina, Russia, Ukraine, the United Kingdom, Canada, Germany, South Korea, and Belgium. InBev had a minor position in the United States. U.S. sales represented less than 2% of the company's worldwide beer sales.

21 In each country, InBev had a "Grow/Defend/Maintain/Cash" matrix approach to guide its marketing and sales investments. The matrix helped identify brand/country priorities, commonly referred to as the "Contract Brands." Contract Brands accounted for a substantial share of InBev's expected profitable growth and for approximately 60% of InBev's global commercial investment. The "Grow" part of the matrix identified brands that could be future leaders. For grow brands, the objective was to maximize growth, profit, and investment. "Defend" brands were today's leading brands, and the objective was to hold market share, maximize profit, and optimize investment. For "Maintain" brands, the objective was to maintain profit and minimize investment. For "Cash" brands, the objective was to maximize profit and reduce investment.

Leadership and Management Structure of InBev

22 After the Interbrew/AmBev merger, John Brock became the CEO of InBev. Brock was previously the CEO of Interbrew, but had only joined the company six months before the merger. Brock had spent nearly 25 years in consumer products before joining Interbrew, first with Procter & Gamble and then with Cadbury Schweppes. Board seats were split equally between appointees from Interbrew and AmBev.

23 At the end of 2005, Brock left InBev and was replaced as CEO by Carlos Brito. Brito was CEO of AmBev when the merger was done and was a Brazilian citizen with an MBA from Stanford. Brito joined Brahma in 1989 and, before his appointment as InBev CEO, Brito was InBev Zone President for North America. In addition to Brito, most of the other top positions at InBev were occupied by Brazilians.

24 A *Wall Street Journal* article described Brito as follows:

> Carlos Brito, chief executive of brewing giant InBev NV, summarized his business philosophy in a talk at Stanford's business school, his alma mater. "To dream big or dream small takes the same amount of energy," he said. "So why not stretch a little bit?"
>
> Mr. Brito, 48 years old, is the right-hand man of Jorge Paulo Lemann, the hypercompetitive Brazilian investment banker and former tennis champion who built InBev into a global brewing giant. The key to InBev's success—and one explanation

for the occasional controversies it has found itself in—is a meritocratic culture in which performance incentives and cost cutting are given prime importance.

Mr. Brito likes to point out that InBev doesn't have corporate jets—and he himself doesn't even have his own office. Mr. Brito works at a table, set up like a brokerage trading desk, surrounded by his vice presidents. "I sit with my marketing guy on my left, my sales guy on my right, my finance guy in front of me," he told the Stanford audience. As a result, he says, the company can make decisions very quickly—and save money that other companies spend on the unnecessary trappings of corporate power.

"We always say the leaner the business, the more money we'll have at the end of the year to share," he added, referring to the generous InBev bonus system. Part of the Brazilian way is creating a competitive atmosphere with bonuses and promotions based on performance rather than seniority. "In our company, we think that to be fair with people is to treat different people in different ways," Mr. Brito said at Stanford. "Most companies would not be able to say that." Mr. Brito told the Stanford audience that out of InBev's 85,000 employees, only 200 to 250 "are really the ones who make a difference." He said InBev is unapologetic about giving special treatment to the difference makers.[2]

Changes at InBev

25 The new management at InBev followed a merger integration approach that had been successful in previous AmBev deals: cut travel budgets, eliminate executive dining rooms, set up more open-plan offices, use zero-based budgeting—a system where budgets are written from scratch every year—and expand variable compensation tied to performance.[3] InBev management focused on modernizing production and streamlining the extensive product line. In Western Europe, where beer consumption was falling, there was an urgent need to lower costs. In 2006, the company announced it would cut around 300 jobs in Western Europe. InBev also tried to entice younger drinkers to drink more beer. The company launched apple/pear and apple/cherry-flavored beers and a lemon-flavored version of its wheat beer, Hoegaarden.

26 In 2006, InBev became embroiled in a controversy over Hoegaarden. The company announced that it was closing its Hoegaarden brewery, and moving production to the Jupille brewery about 35 miles away where it brewed the Jupiler brand. Hoegaarden had a long history in Belgium, and its origins dated back more than 500 years. The current brewery had operated since the mid-1960s. The planned closure provoked a series of strikes from workers and protests from connoisseurs who feared that the multinational, one of the world's largest beer brewers by volume, was turning its back on tradition by reducing choice at local pubs, "dumbing down" the taste of its brews and focusing on just a few global brands. It was seen as the "McDonaldization" of beer—"all the widely known international beers are of the same type."[4] Making matters worse, Hoegaarden is a Dutch-speaking area, whereas Jupille is French-speaking.

27 In 2007, after the move to Jupille, InBev reversed course and announced that it would shift Hoegaarden production back to the town of Hoegaarden, citing a shortage of capacity as a result of greater-than-expected international sales of the brand. The company also announced that it would invest in making Hoegaarden a dedicated white beer brewery.

Operations and Performance

28 InBev employed around 94,000 people, with operations in 30 countries or more across the Americas, Europe, and Asia Pacific. The company operated 112 plants worldwide. Avoiding unnecessary costs was a core component of InBev's culture. InBev generated an

[2] M. Moffett, "InBev's Chief Built Competitive Culture," *Wall Street Journal*, June 13, 2008, p. B6.

[3] J. W. Miller, "Big Beer Gets Belgian Emotion Flowing," *Wall Street Journal*, Feb. 23, 2010, p. B1.

[4] C. Henson, "InBev Beer Cutbacks Brew Discontent," *Wall Street Journal*, Sept. 27, 2006. p. B5B.

EXHIBIT 3 **InBev Financial Highlights**

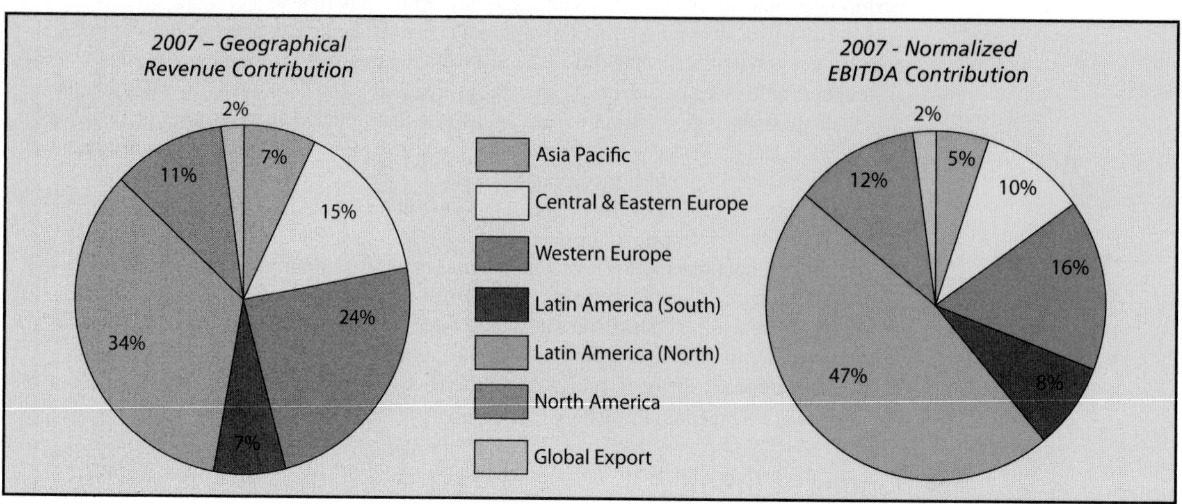

EBITDA margin of 34.6%, which it believed was significantly higher than that of its major competitors. Regional EBITDA contributions are shown in **Exhibit 3**. The 2007 income statement is shown in **Exhibit 4**.

Culture at InBev

At InBev, a work atmosphere reminiscent of an athletic locker room is a key ingredient in a culture that also includes ferocious cost cutting and lucrative incentive-based compensation programs. The work ethic is largely the design of Jorge Paulo Lemann, a former Brazilian

EXHIBIT 4 **Summary Financial Information for InBev**

	2007	**2006**
Year ended 31 Dec (in Million €)		
Revenue	**14,430**	**13,308**
Cost of Sales	5,936	5477
Gross Profit	**8,494**	**7,831**
Distribution Expenses	1,713	1,551
Sales and marketing expenses	2,134	2,115
Administrative expenses	990	1,075
Other income	263	133
Profit from Operations before non-recurring items	**3,920**	**3,223**
Non-recurring items	374	–94
Profit from Operations	**4,294**	**3,129**
Finance cost	598	473
Share of results of associates	1	1
Profit before tax	3,697	2,657
Income tax expense	649	531
Profit	3,048	2,126

tennis champion who is one of InBev's chief shareholders. The Harvard-educated Mr. Lemann, 68 years old, has borrowed management techniques from such corporations as Goldman Sachs Group Inc., Wal-Mart Stores Inc., and PepsiCo Inc., while adding a dash of Brazilian verve and flexibility.[5]

ANHEUSER-BUSCH

29 The roots of Anheuser-Busch reached back some 150 years to 1860 when Eberhard Anheuser bought a struggling St. Louis brewery. He brought on Adolphus Busch, his son-in-law, as a partner in 1869. The current CEO was August Busch IV, the great-great-grandson of Adolphus Busch and the fifth generation of Busch family members to lead the company. The Busch family owned 3.5% of the company.

30 Budweiser Lager was introduced in 1874 and was named after the Bohemian town of Budweis, which Adolphus Busch had visited. With its Budweiser family of brands, including Budweiser, Bud Light, and Bud Select, Anheuser-Busch was the dominant U.S. brewer with almost 50% of the market. The company operated 12 breweries in the United States. Anheuser-Busch also operated five theme parks in the United States that contributed about 6% of net profit. Financial statements are shown in **Exhibits 5** and **6**. Barclays Global Investors was the largest Anheuser-Busch investor with 5-7%. Berkshire Hathaway was Anheuser-Busch's second largest shareholder with a stake of 4.9%. Anheuser-Busch had around 31,000 full-time employees, of which 8,100 were represented by the Teamsters Union. The company considered its employee relationships to be good.

Products

31 The Budweiser family of beers, along with Michelob Golden Draft and Michelob Golden Draft Light, competed primarily in the premium segment. The Busch and Natural Light of beers competed with value-priced beers. Anheuser-Busch's malt liquor products competed against other brands in the malt liquor segment. The company had a broad range of products (some brewed under license) competing in the above-premium-priced beer segment: Michelob, Michelob Light, Michelob AmberBock, Michelob Honey Lager, Michelob ULTRA, Michelob ULTRA Amber, Michelob Marzen, Michelob Pale Ale, Kirin Light, Kirin Ichiban, Tequiza, ZiegenBock Amber, the Bacardi Silver products, American Red, Bare Knuckle Stout, Bud Extra, Land Shark Lager, Redbridge, Stone Mill Pale Ale, Tilt, Rolling Rock, Wild Blue, Redhook, and Widmer. Anheuser-Busch also marketed a range of imports, including several of the InBev brands: Stella Artois, Beck's, Bass Ale, Hoegaarden, and Leffe.

32 Anheuser-Busch owned interests in several craft brewers: 33.1% in Seattle-based Redhook Ale Brewery, and 39.6% interest in Portland-based Widmer Brothers Brewing.

International Strategy

33 Based on volume, Anheuser-Busch was the world's fourth largest brewer, but only about 8% of its sales were outside the United States. The company publicly stated that international expansion and growth were priorities, but August Busch III, chairman of the Board of Directors from 1977-2006, was thought to be uninterested in major international expansion.

[5] M. Moffett, "At InBev, a Gung-Ho Culture Rules; American Icon Anheuser, a Potential Target, Faces Prospect of Big Changes," *Wall Street Journal*, May 28, 2008, p. B1.

EXHIBIT 5 **Anheuser-Busch Income Statement**

	2007	2006	% change
Year ended 31 Dec (in Million $, except where noted)			
Barrels of beer sold			
U.S.	104.4	102.3	2.1%
International	24	22.7	5.7%
Worldwide Anheuser-Busch brands	128.4	125	2.7%
Equity partner brands	33.2	31.6	5.1%
Total brands	161.6	156.6	3.2%
Gross sales	$18,988.70	$17,957.80	5.7%
Excise taxes	$ 2,303.00	$ 2,240.70	2.8%
Net sales	$16,685.70	$15,717.10	6.2%
Gross Profit	$ 5,849.60	$ 5,552.10	5.4%
As a % of sales	35.06%	35.33%	(0.2) pts
Operating income	$ 2,894.00	$ 2,719.60	6.4%
As a % of sales	17.30%	17.30%	(0.0) pts
Equity income net of taxes	$ 662.40	$ 588.60	12.5%
Net income	$ 2,115.30	$ 1,965.20	7.6%
Diluted earnings per share	$ 2.79	$ 2.53	10.3%
Diluted weighted average shares outstanding	757.1	777	–2.6%
Operating cash flow before the change in working capital	$ 2,963.10	$ 2,502.60	18.4%
Common dividend paid	$ 932.40	$ 871.60	7.0%
Per share	$ 1.25	$ 1.13	10.6%
Earnings before interest, income taxes, depreciation and amortization (EBITDA)	$ 4,989.90	$ 4,672.50	6.8%
Return on shareholders' equity	59.70%	51.60%	(8.1) pts
Return on capital employed	16.60%	15.60%	(1.0) pts
Total assets	$17,155.00	$ 6,377.00	4.8%
Debt	$ 9,140.30	$ 7,653.50	19.4%
Capital expenditures	$ 870.00	$ 812.50	7.1%
Depreciation and amortization	$ 996.20	$ 988.70	0.8%
No. of full time employees	30849	30183	2.2%
No. of registered common shareholders	49732	51888	–4.2%
Closing stock price	$ 52.34	$ 49.20	6.4%

EXHIBIT 6 **Anheuser-Busch Balance Sheet**

	2007	2006
Year ended 31 Dec (in Million $, except per share)		
Assets	$ 283.20	$ 219.20
Current Assets	805.2	720.2
Accounts receivable	723.5	694.9
Inventories	212.6	195.2
Other current assets	$ 2,024.50	$ 1,829.50
Total current assets	4019.5	3680.3
Investments in affiliated companies	8833.5	8916.1
Plant & equipment, net	1547.9	1367.2
Intangible assets, including goodwill of $1134.6 & 1077.8, respectively	729.6	584.1
Other assets	$ 17,155.00	$ 16,377.20
Total Assets		
Liabilities and shareholders' equity	$ 1,464.50	$ 1,426.30
Current liability	$ 374.30	$ 342.80
Accounts payable	$ 106.20	$ 133.90
Accrued salaries, wages and benefits	$ 136.40	$ 124.20
Accrued taxes	$ 222.40	$ 218.90
Accrued interest	$ 2,303.80	$ 2,246.10
Total Current liability	$ 1,002.50	$ 1,191.50
Retirement benefits	$ 9,140.30	$ 7,653.50
Debt	$ 1,314.60	$ 1,194.50
Deferred income taxes	$ 242.20	$ 152.90
Other long term liabilities		
Shareholders' Equity	$ 1,482.50	$ 1,473.70
Common stock, $1 par value, authorized 1.6 billion shares	$ 3,382.10	$ 2,962.50
Capital in excess of par value	$ 17,923.90	$ 16,741.00
Retained earnings	$(18,714.70)	$(16,007.70)
Treasury stock, at cost	$ (922.20)	$ (1,230.80)
Accumulated non-owner changes in shareholder equity	$ 3,151.60	$ 3,938.70
Total shareholders' equity	—	—
Commitments and contingencies	$ 17,155.00	$ 16,377.20
Total liabilities and shareholders' equity		

34 The company's international strategy had two main elements: expansion of the Budweiser brand and alliances with other major brewers. Anheuser-Busch was among the first foreign companies to enter China, with the establishment of its Wuhan brewery in 1995. The company owned 100% of Harbin Brewery Group, which had 13 breweries in northeast China. Anheuser-Busch also had a 27% share in Chinese brewer Tsingtao. In 1998, Anheuser-Busch created a strategic alliance with Brazil's Antarctica.[6]

35 Anheuser-Busch had a 50% share in Grupo Modelo, Mexico's leading brewer, producer of Corona, and exclusive importer of Budweiser and Bud Light in Mexico. The company also had a 50% equity interest in a joint venture that owned and operated a brewery in Hyderabad, India, and owned the Stag Brewery near London, England. In a few markets, such as Mexico, Canada, and the U.K., Budweiser had achieved a strong market position in the premium segment. In the U.K., Budweiser had the top position in premium-packaged lager in bars, pubs, clubs, and restaurants. In China, Budweiser was distributed nationally, and was positioned in the super-premium beer segment.

36 Most of the Budweiser sold internationally was brewed under license. In Canada, Budweiser, Bud Light, Busch, and Busch Light were brewed and sold through a license agreement with Labatt (owned by InBev). In Japan, Budweiser was brewed and sold under license with Kirin, with Guinness in Ireland, Oriental in Korea, and Heineken in Italy, Panama, and Russia.

Corporate Culture

37 Anheuser-Busch was regularly ranked as one of America's "Most Admired Companies" by *Fortune* magazine. The company won numerous awards for its philanthropy, diversity, community involvement, and for being an employer of choice. The company was known for luxurious executive offices and lots of perks, with six planes and two helicopters to transport its employees (the fleet was known as Air Bud).

38 As stated below, in St. Louis, Anheuser-Busch was an institution:

> *The Busch clan, which was at the helm of the brewery for six generations, worked as a sort of local patriarch, donating tens of millions of dollars to charity and financing artistic events. Youths dreamed of working at the "brewery," as Anheuser-Busch is called in the city. The salaries were above average, and the company pampered its employees with free cases of beer, tickets to baseball games at Busch Stadium, and to the Busch Gardens theme parks (as you can see, the family name is everywhere).*[7]

Advertising

39 Anheuser-Busch had a reputation as an astute and innovative marketer. Its iconic advertising for Budweiser, using Clydesdale horses, frogs, dogs, and catchy slogans, was a staple of Americana. The company had a huge marketing and advertising budget, with $500 million for ad time in the United States annually. Each year, the company bought about ten ads for the Super Bowl, the priciest TV time in the United States, at a cost of around $20 million. InBev was not as reliant on advertising as Anheuser-Busch.

> *Anheuser's marketing budget has long been the envy of its rivals, and the company has outspent other major brewers by hundreds of millions of dollars for decades . . . Anheuser, one of the largest sports marketers in the world, spent about $300 million last year for sports sponsorships, up 11% from the year earlier, according to IEG, a Chicago-based research unit of WPP Group that tracks sponsorships. Anheuser is affiliated with dozens of sports, from*

[6] "Company Profile—Anheuser Busch," *Datamonitor*, May 24, 2007. www.datamonitor.com.

[7] "American Management by Brazilians," Exame, 2010. http://thebrazilianeconomy.com/american_management_by_ brazilians.php.

> *baseball to equestrian competitions. It sponsors sports leagues, big and small, including Major League Baseball, the National Basketball Association, and Major League Lacrosse, and even the U.S. polo team. This summer, the company is one of the official beers of the Beijing Olympic Games.*[8]

40 The Clydesdale horses became part of Budweiser's history on April 7, 1933, when a team of Clydesdales carried the first beer delivery after the repeal of prohibition. In 2008, the company owned 230 Clydesdales.

THE INBEV OFFER

41 On June 12, 2008, InBev NV made an offer to acquire Anheuser-Busch for $46.4 billion in a cash deal. The combination would create the world's largest brewer with estimated annual net sales of about $36 billion. A few days after the offer, Adolphus Busch IV, an uncle to August Busch IV, said in a statement: "Mr. Buffett, who holds a 5% stake in Anheuser-Busch Inc., has a notable reputation for assisting in matters where family ownership is at stake. His participation in the recent merger of Wrigley and Mars Inc. is evidence of his integrity. Should Mr. Buffett see this merger as a positive action for all shareholders involved, the likelihood of a deal will increase enormously."[9] Warren Buffett did not make any public statements about the deal. On June 25, Carlos Brito outlined the offer in a letter to August Busch IV (**Exhibit 7**).

Anheuser-Busch Board Rejects the Offer

42 On June 26, Anheuser-Busch rejected the unsolicited proposal, stating that "the proposal was greatly undervalued, and that the $65 price per share was financially inadequate and did not match the best interests of the company's shareholders." In a letter to the management of InBev, Anheuser-Busch said:

> *We have noted that your letter is expressly not an offer, but only a nonbinding proposal. Notwithstanding the nonbinding nature of your proposal, the Anheuser-Busch board carefully and thoroughly examined all aspects of your proposal with the assistance of independent advisers.*
>
> *The board unanimously concluded your proposal is inadequate and not in the best interests of Anheuser-Busch shareholders. In reaching this conclusion, the board considered the advice of its independent financial advisers.*
>
> *As you state in your letter, there is limited overlap in our respective businesses. Many of the suggested synergies seem not to be synergies at all, but are instead profit enhancements. We believe that we can deliver similar enhancements to our shareholders independent of a transaction, and have included these enhancements in our accelerated earnings growth plan.*
>
> *From your standpoint, we see that now could be opportunistic timing for you to make this acquisition, given the weak U.S. dollar and sluggish U.S. stock market, but from the standpoint of the Anheuser-Busch shareholder, however, a transaction with InBev at this time would mean foregoing the greater value obtainable from Anheuser-Busch's strategic growth plan.*
>
> *While Anheuser-Busch pursues its plan, its board will continue to consider any strategic alternative that would be in the best interests of Anheuser-Busch shareholders. The board is open to consider any proposal that would provide full and certain value to Anheuser-Busch shareholders.*

[8] S. Vrannica, and S. Kang, "InBev May Water Down Bud's Marketing; Suitor Doesn't Depend as Much on Advertising; Threat to Sports Arena," *Wall Street Journal*, June 13, 2008, p. B6.

[9] www.bizjournals.com/jacksonville/stories/2008/06/16/daily14.html.

EXHIBIT 7 **Letter from Carlos Brito**

June 25, 2008

Mr. August A. Busch IV
President and Chief Executive Officer
Anheuser-Busch Companies, Inc.
One Busch Place
St. Louis, Missouri
63118 USA

Proposal for Combination Creating the World's Leading Beer Company

Dear August,

We are writing to confirm that InBev remains committed to our proposal to combine with Anheuser-Busch by means of acquiring all of the outstanding shares of Anheuser-Busch for $65 per share in cash. Our proposed price would deliver an immediate cash premium to your shareholders of 35% over the 30-day average share price prior to recent market speculation, and 18% above the previous all-time high achieved for your shares in October 2002. The market reaction to our proposal has been extremely positive. We believe this confirms our view that our proposal is the best way to achieve this transformational combination for all constituents.

In my June 11 letter, I indicated that InBev had received the strong support of a group of leading financial institutions with respect to providing all of the financing required for the combination of our two great companies. To demonstrate our conviction in this combination, we have executed commitment letters for the financing and have paid approximately $50 million in commitment fees to a lending group comprised of Banco Santander, Bank of Tokyo-Mitsubishi, Barclays Capital, BNP Paribas, Deutsche Bank, Fortis, ING Bank, JP Morgan, Mizuho Corporate Bank, and Royal Bank of Scotland.

Beyond the immediate financial benefit to your shareholders, our proposal also provides significant benefits to all key stakeholders. The fundamental elements of our proposal include:

- A combination that brings together two companies with centuries of brewing tradition to create the global leader in the beer industry
- A stronger, more competitive global company that will benefit our respective consumers, wholesalers, employees, and business partners
- Budweiser to be expanded globally
- St. Louis to be the North American headquarters and global home of the flagship Budweiser brand
- The heritage of Anheuser-Busch to be evoked in the name of the new combined company
- All U.S. breweries to remain open
- Full support for Anheuser-Busch wholesalers and the three-tier distribution system
- Strong commitment to the communities in which Anheuser-Busch operates
- Members of Anheuser-Busch management to be retained at all levels of seniority
- Members of the Anheuser-Busch Board to be invited to join the Board of the combined company
- A combination that will create one of the world's five largest consumer-goods companies

This firm proposal is subject only to the negotiation of mutually satisfactory definitive agreements and the completion of confirmatory due diligence, all of which could be progressed and finalized without delay.

As we have indicated previously, we are committed to entering into a constructive dialogue with you to achieve a friendly combination. We remain available to discuss our proposal with you, including the fundamental elements enumerated above, but we believe that time is of the essence.

It is clear that the combination of Anheuser-Busch and InBev would be an industry-transforming event, creating an unparalleled opportunity for our stakeholders. Our Board, our majority shareholder, and our management team remain committed to making this happen.

Very truly yours,

Carlos Brito

cc: Board of Directors of Anheuser-Busch

Anheuser-Busch Accepts a Higher Offer

43 In mid-July, InBev raised its offer to $70 a share, and the Anheuser board voted to accept the deal. At $70 a share, the total payment to Anheuser-Busch shareholders would be $52.5 billion. Another $2.4 billion would be required for transaction costs, making the total outlay $54.8 billion. When reports of a possible deal first surfaced in May 2008, Anheuser-Busch shares were trading at about $52.50. The $70 offer represented a 35% percent premium over Anheuser-Busch's 30-day average share price prior to market speculation about the deal.

44 The Board of Directors of the combined company would comprise the existing directors of the InBev Board, Anheuser-Busch President and CEO August Busch IV, and one other current or former director from the Anheuser-Busch Board. The management team would draw from key members of both InBev's and Anheuser-Busch's current leadership.

45 According to the Teamsters union, InBev promised that it would not close any of Anheuser-Busch's 12 U.S. breweries, and would not make significant job cuts. Cash would be generated to help finance the purchase from better supply chain management and selling off "non-core" assets.

Case 12

LEGO Group: *An Outsourcing Journey*

Marcus Møller Larsen
Torben Pedersen
Dmitrij Slepniov

PROLOGUE

1 The last five years' rather adventurous journey from 2004 to 2009 had taught the fifth-largest toy-maker in the world—the LEGO Group—the importance of managing the global supply chain effectively. In order to survive the largest internal financial crisis in the company's roughly 70 years of existence, resulting in a deficit of DKK1.8 billion in 2004, the management had, among many initiatives, decided to offshore and outsource a major chunk of LEGO's production to Flextronics, a large Singaporean electronics manufacturing services (EMS) provider. In this pursuit of rapid cost-cutting sourcing advantages, the LEGO Group planned to license out as much as 80 per cent of its production, besides closing down major parts of the production in high-cost countries. Confident with the prospects of the new partnership, the company signed a long-term contract with Flextronics. "It has been important for us to find the right partner," argued Niels Duedahl, a LEGO vice-president, when announcing the outsourcing collaboration, "and Flextronics is a very professional player in the market with industry-leading plastics capabilities, the right capacity and resources in terms of molding, assembly, packaging and distribution. We know this from looking at the work Flextronics does for other global companies."[1]

2 This decision would eventually prove to have been too hasty, however. Merely three years after the contracts were signed, LEGO management announced that it would phase out the entire sourcing collaboration with Flextronics. In July 2008, the executive vice-president for the global supply chain, Iqbal Padda, proclaimed in an official press release, "We have had an intensive and very valuable cooperation with Flextronics on the relocation of major parts of our production. As expected, this transition has been complicated, but throughout the process we have maintained our high quality level. Jointly we have now come to the conclusion that it is more optimal for the LEGO Group to manage the global manufacturing setup ourselves. With this decision the LEGO supply chain will be developed faster through going for the best, leanest and highest quality solution at all times."[2]

[1] LEGO press release, December 21, 2005.

[2] LEGO press release, June 1, 2008.

3 This sudden change in its sourcing strategy posed LEGO management with a number of caveats. Despite the bright forecasts, the collaboration did not fulfill the initial expectations, and the company needed to understand why this had happened. Secondly, what could LEGO management have done differently? Arguably, with little prior experience in outsourcing this large amount of production, the LEGO Group had had a limited knowledge base to draw on to manage a collaboration like this. Yet, with Flextronics' size and experience with original equipment manufacturers (OEMs), this, in theory, should not have been a problem. Lastly, one could ponder whether the unsuccessful collaboration with Flextronics had been a necessary evil for the LEGO Group. LEGO management's ability to handle its global production network after the Flextronics collaboration had surely changed, and aspects like standardization and documentation had to a much larger extent become valued.

INTRODUCING THE LEGO GROUP: ONLY THE BEST IS GOOD ENOUGH

4 The LEGO Group's vision was to "inspire children to explore and challenge their own creative potential." Its motto, "Only the Best is Good Enough," had stuck with the company since 1932 when Ole Kirk Christiansen, a Danish carpenter, established the company in the small town of Billund in Jutland, Denmark, to manufacture his wooden toy designs. As the company itself said, "It is LEGO philosophy that 'good play' enriches a child's life—and its subsequent adulthood. With this in mind, the LEGO Group has developed and marketed a wide range of products, all founded on the same basic philosophy of learning and developing—through play."[3] With this simple idea, the company, through its history, had grown into a major multinational corporation, and, by 2009, was the world's fifth-largest manufacturer of toys in terms of sales. The same year, the LEGO Group earned DKK11.7 billion in revenues and DKK2.2 billion in profits, and had a workforce of approximately 7,000 employees around the world (see **Exhibit 1**). Its corporate management consisted, besides the chief executive officer and the chief financial officer, of four executive vice-presidents with respective business areas (markets and products; community, education and direct; corporate centre; and global supply chain) (see **Exhibit 2**).

Products and Markets

5 The LEGO brick was the company's main product (see **Exhibit 3**). The iconic brick with the unique principle of interlocking tubes offering unlimited building possibilities was first introduced in 1958 and had basically remained unchanged ever since. The underlying philosophy of the brick was that it would stimulate creative and structured problem-solving, curiosity and imagination. In the company's own words: "In the hands of children, the products inspire the unique form of LEGO play that is fun, creative, engaging, challenging—all at the same time . . . . We strive to accomplish this by offering a range of high quality and fun products centred around our building systems."[4] The simple yet multi-functional and combinational structure of the brick (there were as many as 915 million possible combinations to choose from with six eight-stud LEGO bricks of the same color) had therefore been core to the company's history and success. In fact, the LEGO brick had been rewarded the "Toy of the Century" designation by both Fortune Magazine and the British Association of Toy Retailers.

[3] LEGO Annual Report, 2009.

[4] Ibid.

EXHIBIT 1 The LEGO Group Financial Figures

mDKK	2009	2008	2007	2006	2005
HIGHLIGHTS					
Income statement					
Revenue	11,661	9,526	8,027	7,798	7,027
Expenses	(8,659)	(7,522)	(6,556)	(6,393)	(6,605)
Operating profit	3,002	2,002	1,471	1,405	423
Financial income and expenses	(15)	(248)	(35)	(44)	(51)
Profit before tax	2,887	1,852	1,414	1,281	329
Net profit for the year	2,204	1,352	1,028	1,290	214
Balance sheet					
Total assets	7,788	6,496	6,009	6,907	7,058
Equity	3,291	2,066	1,679	1,191	563
Liabilities	4,497	4,430	4,330	5,716	6,495
Cash flow statement					
Cash flow from operating activities	2,655	1,954	1,033	1,157	587
Investment in activities, plans and equipment	1,042	368	399	316	237
Investment in intangible assets	216	75	34	–	–
Cash flow from financing activities	(906)	(1,682)	(467)	597	(656)
Total cash flow	501	128	592	1,925	1,570
Employees					
Average number of employees	7,058	5,388	4,199	4,908	5,302
RATIO					
Financial ratios (in %)					
Gross margin	70.3	66.8	65.0	64.9	58.0
Operating margin (ROS)	24.9	22.0	18.1	17.0	5.4
Net profit margin	18.9	14.2	12.8	16.5	3.0
Return on equity (ROE)	82.3	72.2	71.6	147.1	44.2
Equity rate	42.3	31.8	27.9	17.2	8.0

Source: The LEGO Group Annual Report, 2009.

6 To segment the products, however, a number of categories had been created: First, "preschool products" comprised products for the youngest children, who had yet to start school. The LEGO DUPLO products were examples of this category. Second, the "creative building" category targeted sets or buckets of traditional LEGO bricks without building instructions. Third, "play themes" products were the products that had a particular story as their

EXHIBIT 2 **The LEGO Group Structure**

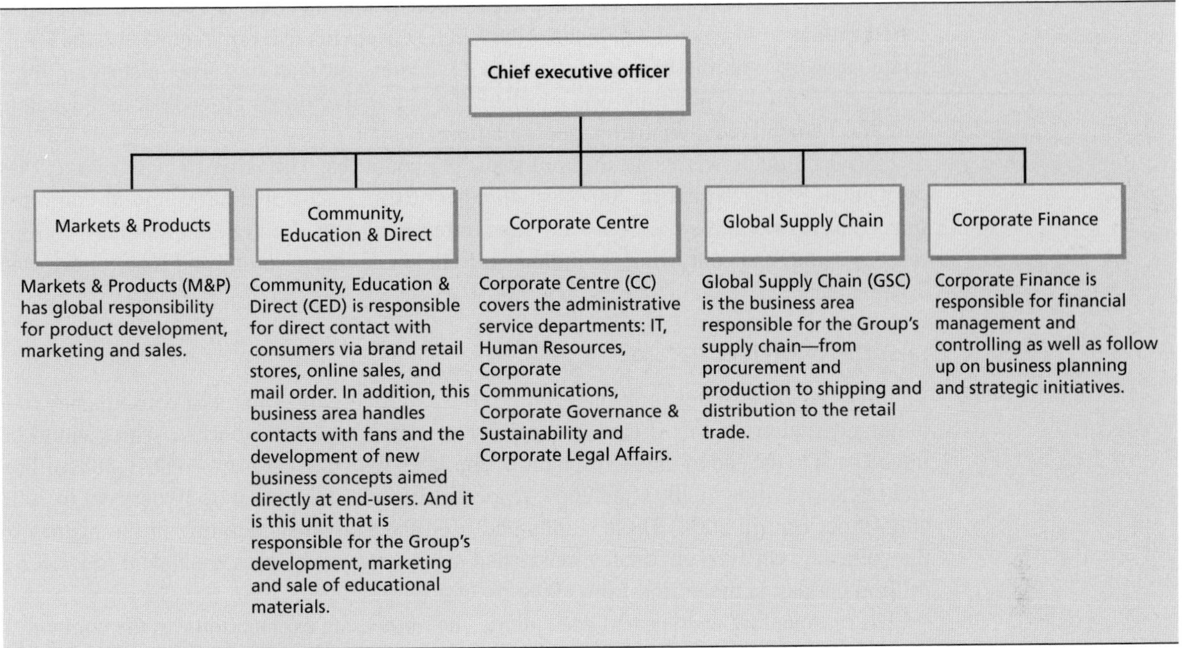

Chief executive officer
Markets & Products
Community, Education & Direct
Corporate Centre
Global Supply Chain
Corporate Finance
Markets & Products (M&P) has global responsibility for product development, marketing and sales.
Community, Education & Direct (CED) is responsible for direct contact with consumers via brand retail stores, online sales, and mail order. In addition, this business area handles contacts with fans and the development of new business concepts aimed directly at end-users. And it is this unit that is responsible for the Group's development, marketing and sale of educational materials.
Corporate Centre (CC) covers the administrative service departments: IT, Human Resources, Corporate Communications, Corporate Governance & Sustainability and Corporate Legal Affairs.
Global Supply Chain (GSC) is the business area responsible for the Group's supply chain—from procurement and production to shipping and distribution to the retail trade.
Corporate Finance is responsible for financial management and controlling as well as follow up on business planning and strategic initiatives.

Source: The LEGO Group Annual Report, 2009.

EXHIBIT 3 **The LEGO Brick**

Source: www.lego.com.

basis. This could be themes such as airports, hospitals and racing tracks. The classic LEGO City line and futuristic BIONICLE theme products were examples of this category. Fourth, and related to the play themes, were the "licensed products," which were built up around movies or books that the LEGO Group had acquired the rights for, such as Harry Potter, Star Wars and Indiana Jones. Fifth, "MINDSTORM NXT" was a programmable robot kit, where consumers could construct and program robots to perform different tasks and operations. Sixth, "LEGO Education" comprised products that had been specifically developed for educational purposes. Last, in 2009 the LEGO Group made its first move into the board game category with the launch of the "LEGO Games" product line. The underlying logic of the entire product portfolio was to reflect the fact that children grow older and develop, and thus demand more challenging stimulation.

7 LEGO products were sold in more than 130 countries. The largest single market was the United States, which in 2007 accounted for 30 per cent of the revenue in combination with Australia, New Zealand and the United Kingdom. Central and Southern Europe represented 27 per cent, while Scandinavia, Benelux, Eastern Europe and Asia represented 26.5 per cent.

Dealing with a Crisis

8 In 2004, radical changes took place within the LEGO organization as a consequence of a major internal crisis that drew the company near bankruptcy. The crisis, which could be traced back to the end of the 1990s, had accumulated with net losses worth DKK888 million and DKK1.8 billion in 2003 and 2004, respectively. Sales had fallen by 30 per cent in 2003 and 40 per cent in 2004. These results had been the most disappointing in the history of the company. On average, the toy maker had made economic losses equivalent to DKK2.2 million per day in the period from 1998 to 2004.

9 The reasons for the crisis had been many. The immediate explanation was the company's general loss of confidence in its core product—the LEGO brick. With an initiative to create new engines of growth and to address a decline in the traditional toy market, LEGO had sought over the last decade to broaden its portfolio into new, rather discrete areas, including computer games, television and clothing. This act of diversification had resulted in vast complexity and inefficiencies, as well as highly confused customers and employees. For instance, with the surge of licensed products like Harry Potter and Star Wars, the LEGO Group produced a range of unique bricks for each single new product. The LEGO Group had at the time roughly 11,000 suppliers—a number almost twice what Boeing used for its planes. Unfavorable developments in the global toy market as well as in the exchange rates of key currencies of important markets had not made matters easier. As former chief executive officer Kjeld Kirk Kristiansen argued, "We have been pursuing a strategy which was based on growth, increase in market shares and growth by focusing on totally new products. This strategy did not give the expected results."[5] Moreover, he noted that "we shifted the focus from our actual core product, which at the same time faced difficulties in a more competitive and dynamic market."[6]

10 In October 2004, Jørgen Vig Knudstorp was appointed as Kristiansen's successor. Kristiansen, who was the grandson of the founder, Ole Kirk Christiansen, had been the president and CEO of the LEGO Group since 1979. Knudstorp was only the second person outside the founding family who held the position of CEO, and his primary task was to steer the company back on track. "I don't have any miracle cure," he explained as to how he would put an end to the financial turmoil. "LEGO shall first and foremost drop its arrogance. We have been too sacred with our own virtues, not open enough, and not willing to listen to what other people say. We shall now listen to customers and consumers; simply drop the sacredness. We must be aggressive in the market; work closely with retailers;

[5] LEGO press release, January 8, 2004.

[6] LEGO Life, September 2007.

and manage LEGO very tightly, also financially."[7] Accordingly, a strategy titled "Shared Vision" was soon implemented, and was defined around three core principles:

- "Be the best at creating value for our customers and sales channels."
- "Refocus on the value we offer our customers."
- "Increase operational excellence."

11 After divesting its theme parks and receiving an extraordinary loan from the founding family of 800 million DKK, the LEGO Group embarked on the comprehensive strategy of right-sizing its activities, its cost base and its many assets. In particular, careful scrutiny of the organization made the LEGO Group aware of the fact that its ineffective and inflexible supply chain was a key problem for the creation of a sound business platform. The degree of organizational complexity on multiple levels had basically undermined an otherwise sound business platform. According to Knudstorp: "From my perspective, the supply chain is a company's circulation system. You have to fix it to keep the blood flowing."[8]

LEARNING FROM OFFSHORE OUTSOURCING: A STORY IN THREE PARTS

1. Preparing for Outsourcing

12 A key revelation of the comprehensive analysis that was initiated in 2004 was that urgent transformations in all major areas of the supply chain were needed. In the development function, the main focus was to simplify the LEGO sets, which over the years had grown highly elaborate. One LEGO senior director noted, "This excessive complexity of shapes and colors of LEGO elements that was coming from the development was badly hitting the supply chain."[9] A major challenge was to ensure that the right components were constantly in stock. Significant forecast errors and seasonal demand fluctuations coupled with customers' expectations of short delivery times resulted in large stocks of many different components. The high numbers of components also required heavy investment in molds. The decision was therefore made to limit the growth in the number of product components and then to gradually reduce it. This was not only supposed to drive costs out of the supply chain, but was also to prepare the company for the new scenarios of the outsourced production set-up.

13 In the area of distribution, the analysis uncovered the need for major changes in how the company approached its retailers. Describing the situation, a senior director was quoted as saying, "It was impossible to be efficient and manage the supply chain with the level of flexibility we had towards all retailers, including the smallest outlets. We clearly needed to put certain rules here."[10] To manage this, clearly defined service policies were established. The new policies distinguished explicitly between different approaches to the retailers and helped the company to focus more on the large retail chains that were increasingly gaining dominance in the toy market. This immediately helped to drive down the cost of distribution, provided a more reliable overview of demand and, along with reducing complexity, took some pressure away from the supply chain. Moreover, the company's five European

[7] *Politiken,* October 23, 2004.

[8] s+b, Autumn 2007.

[9] Interview with LEGO manager, August 27, 2007.

[10] Ibid.

EXHIBIT 4 **Production Value Chain**

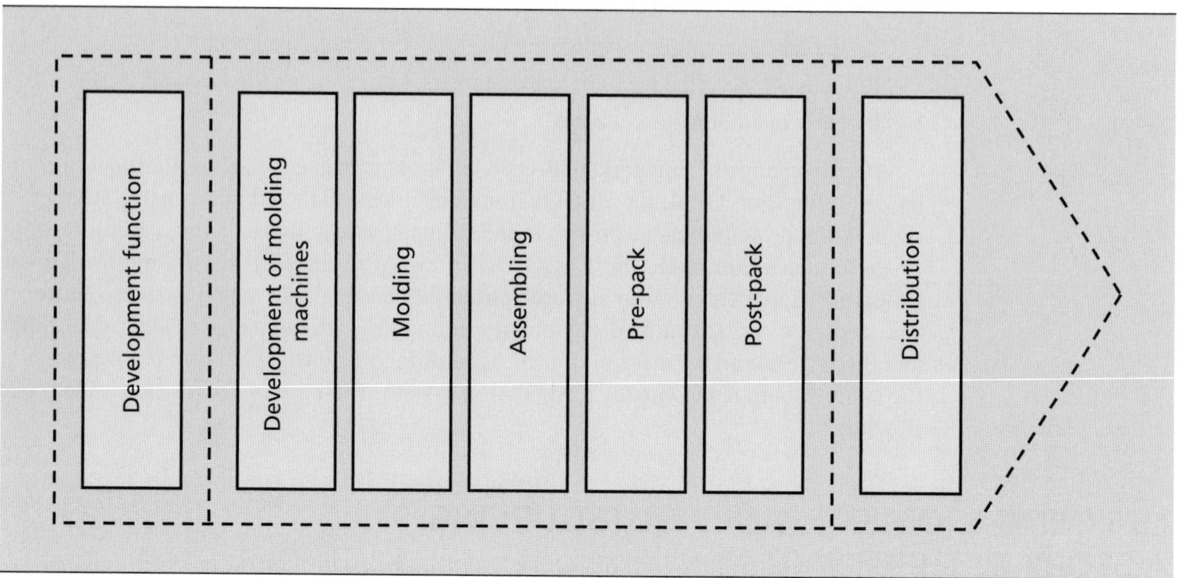

Source: Authors' own creation.

distribution facilities (Flensburg and Hohenwestedt in Germany, Billund in Denmark, and Lyon and Dunkerque in France) were all centralized in Jirny, 10 kilometres east of Prague, Czech Republic. Occupying 51,000 square metres, the new European distribution centre was in full operation at the beginning of 2007 and handled customers in Europe and distribution centres throughout the world (except North America). The operation was outsourced to DHL Solutions. In addition, the distribution of LEGO products in the United States and Canada was outsourced to Exel Inc., a contract logistics provider operating in Alliance, Texas.

14 However, no matter how significant the problems were in product development and distribution, sub-optimizing only those areas without improving various aspects of the actual production could hardly bring the company back on track. The LEGO Group's production value chain was divided into the following steps: the development of the molding machine, molding, assembling, pre-packing and post-packing (see **Exhibit 4**). Assembling and post-packing were the most cost-intensive parts of the value chain. Prior to the crisis, the company owned and operated production plants in Denmark, the United States, Switzerland, the Czech Republic and South Korea. Allocation of roles and responsibilities to most of these factories followed a branding strategy in which one of the Swiss factories only produced DUPLO toys and another produced Technic products. Furthermore, the Danish factory only manufactured LEGO System products, while the U.S. facility predominately served American demands. The vast majority of the production took place in the Danish and U.S. sites, while roughly five to 10 per cent of the LEGO Group's total production was outsourced to Chinese contract manufacturers.

15 With the new strategic direction of achieving a lighter production portfolio, however, the company started to look for external partners to carry out a larger bulk of its production. There were two main strategic rationales for this. First of all, there was the

cost-saving rationale. With the majority of the production in high-cost countries, the management saw major potential for cutting costs by relocating production to low-cost countries. "We were basically turning the 50 year old idea that Denmark and Switzerland were good countries for automatic production upside down," recalled Duedahl, a LEGO vice-president. "The new mantra was: aggressive outsourcing to low-cost countries."[11]

16 In spite of the fact that up to 95 per cent of global toy production was located in China, the LEGO Group decided to avoid relocating production facilities to Asia and instead emphasized proximity to its main markets in Europe and the United States. Based on the fact that the European market accounted for approximately 60 per cent of the company's sales, the Czech Republic and Hungary, two low-cost Eastern European countries, fulfilled both the market proximity and cost-saving criteria. These countries were supposed to accommodate most of the capacity transferred from Denmark and Switzerland. In addition, the decision was made to move the company's U.S. plant in Enfield to Mexico in order to supply the North American market, which constituted approximately 30 per cent of the LEGO Group's sales.

17 Secondly, with a production of approximately 24 billion bricks per year, the LEGO Group rationalized sourcing through potential economies of scale as well as the opportunity to drastically reduce production complexity by targeting large subcontractors. Thus, besides scaling down production in Denmark and closing sites in Switzerland and Korea, it was decided that production should be outsourced to a number of partners. These included Sonoco (a global manufacturer of consumer and industrial packaging products and provider of packaging services); Greiner (a global manufacturer of consumer and industrial packaging products); Weldenhammer (packaging products and services); 2B Pack (packaging products and services); and Flextronics (an electronics manufacturing services company). While the Technic and Bionicle product lines, to a large extent, were to be retained in-house, the Duplo and System lines (characterized by their high-volume production) were predominantly outsourced to Flextronics.

18 Flextronics, a leading multinational electronics manufacturing services (EMS) provider based in Singapore, had a long history of offering services to original equipment manufacturers (OEMs), and was going to be the LEGO Group's largest partner in terms of production undertaken. Flextronics was actually founded in 1969 in Silicon Valley, California, and became in 1981 the first U.S. manufacturer to formally start offshoring production by establishing a manufacturing facility in Singapore. In 1990, however, the company moved its headquarters to Singapore, and had since succeeded in building a network of manufacturing facilities in 30 countries on four different continents. By 2009, Flextronics' net sales were US$31 billion, and it had a workforce of approximately 160,000 employees (see **Exhibit 5**). Flextronics' major clients included large multinational companies like Cisco Systems (consumer electronics products), Hewlett-Packard Company (inkjet printers and storage devices), Microsoft Corporation (computer peripherals and consumer electronics gaming products) and Sony-Ericsson (cellular phones). The company had focused its segments into six core areas—automotive, computing, industrial, infrastructure, medical, and mobile and consumer—and it operated with five business units that consisted of "strategic technologies and augmented services that are leveraged across all segments and customer product categories to create scalability and to add flexibility and speed to our segments."[12] The five business units were Multek

[11] *Ingenøren,* October 24, 2008.

[12] Flextronics Annual Report, 2009.

EXHIBIT 5 **Flextronics in Brief**

- $31 billion in annual sales
- 160,000+ employees worldwide
- 120,000 employees in Asia (90,000 in China)
- Operating in 30 countries
- 27 million square feet of capacity (nine industrial parks)
- Large customers: Casio, Cisco Systems, Dell, Eastman Kodak, Ericsson, Hewlett-Packard, Microsoft, Motorola, Research in Motion, Sony, Sony-Ericsson, Sun Microsystems, and Xerox.

Flextronics' Market Segment Portfolio, 2007

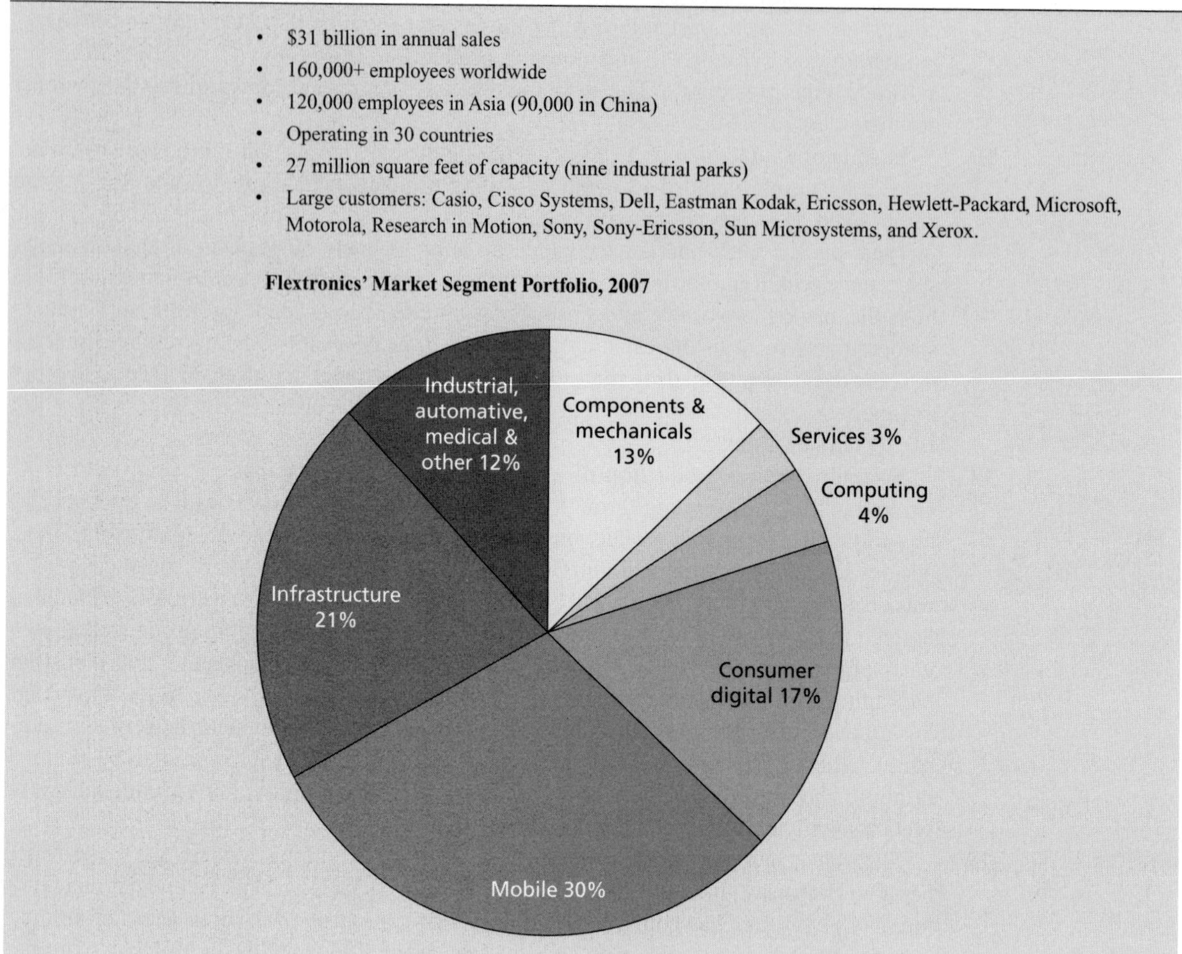

Source: www.flextronics.com.

(multi-layer printed and flexible circuit boards, interconnected technologies and complex display technologies); Vista Point Technologies (unique product solutions for camera modules); Global Services (logistics, reverse logistics and repair operations); FlexPower (design and manufacturing of semi-custom and custom power supplies and battery chargers); and Retail Technological Services (competitive and flexible field services for customer operations) (see **Exhibit 6** for Flextronics' service model).

2. A Troubled Marriage

19 Following the decision to outsource major parts of production to Flextronics, a contract with Flextronics was finalized in June 2006. This was, according to the Danish company, a "brilliant idea," as it locked the prices over a long period and thus eliminated the risk of production price fluctuations. In the period from 2004 to 2006, the following were outsourced to Flextronics: parts of the production facilities' capacity in Denmark and

EXHIBIT 6 Flextronics' Service Model

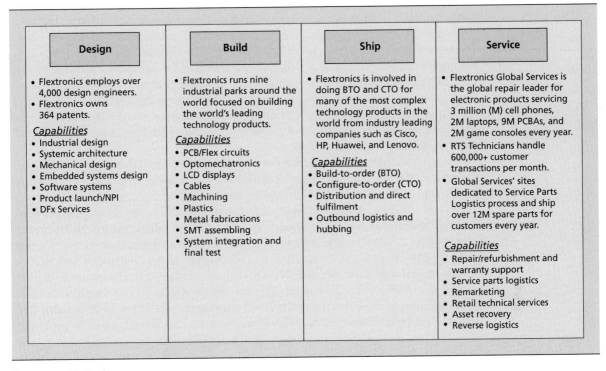

Design

- Flextronics employs over 4,000 design engineers.
- Flextronics owns 364 patents.

Capabilities

- Industrial design
- Systemic architecture
- Mechanical design
- Embedded systems design
- Software systems
- Product launch/NPI
- DFx Services

Build

- Flextronics runs nine industrial parks around the world focused on building the world's leading technology products.

Capabilities

- PCB/Flex circuits
- Optomechatronics
- LCD displays
- Cables
- Machining
- Plastics
- Metal fabrications
- SMT assembling
- System integration and final test

Ship

- Flextronics is involved in doing BTO and CTO for many of the most complex technology products in the world from industry leading companies such as Cisco, HP, Huawei, and Lenovo.

Capabilities

- Build-to-order (BTO)
- Configure-to-order (CTO)
- Distribution and direct fulfilment
- Outbound logistics and hubbing

Service

- Flextronics Global Services is the global repair leader for electronic products servicing 3 million (M) cell phones, 2M laptops, 9M PCBAs, and 2M game consoles every year.
- RTS Technicians handle 600,000+ customer transactions per month.
- Global Services' sites dedicated to Service Parts Logistics process and ship over 12M spare parts for customers every year.

Capabilities

- Repair/refurbishment and warranty support
- Service parts logistics
- Remarketing
- Retail technical services
- Asset recovery
- Reverse logistics

Source: www.flextronics.com

Switzerland were relocated to Flextronics' plants in Nyíregyháza and Sarvar, Hungary; the operating control of the LEGO Group's Kladno site in the Czech Republic was handed over to Flextronics; and the Enfield plant in the United States was closed in favour of using Flextronics' newly opened site in Juárez, Mexico. Throughout the transition phase, the LEGO Group was working intensely towards reducing its in-house production capacity from 90 to 95 per cent to the set target of approximately 20 per cent. Actually, the 20 per cent target had never been a strategic goal in itself. "It is very difficult to give such an estimate," a LEGO vice-president explained. "Right from the beginning, the 80/20 per cent [outsourcing/in-house] ratio was more a communication way. What we have decided is that there are two competences that we need to keep in-house in Billund; that is, molding and packing competences. Whether it is 20 or 10 per cent of production it doesn't matter; what matters is that in the future we will still be able to do what we are doing from the production point of view."[13]

20 Flextronics had indeed been the LEGO Group's preferred partner to undertake this task. Because of Flextronics' long history and vast experience in standardizing and documenting work routines and processes to move business activities from site to site, LEGO management was convinced that Flextronics would excel in reducing the complexity of the LEGO production and organization in general. Knudtrup commented after ramping up the collaboration: "We have come to know Flextronics as a very professional partner in connection with the outsourcing of our DUPLO products, which has taken place over

[13] Interview with LEGO manager, August 27, 2004.

the past year. They understand and appreciate the unique values that LEGO products represent, not least the importance of quality and safety which are fundamental to the good play experience."[14] In an equal manner, Matt Ryan, executive vice-president of Flextronics' worldwide operations, stated that the relationship "is characterized by intense supply chain collaboration that provides strategic and efficient cost-savings to help improve the company's competitive market positioning. We are excited to expand our partnership with the LEGO Group as this allows Flextronics further market diversification and enhanced plastic molding capabilities in low-cost regions."[15] A large part of Flextronics' motivation for getting into business with the LEGO Group had thus been its interest in getting more competencies and knowledge about plastics, which constituted an important part of its electronics manufacturing activities.

21 However, the collaboration did not last for long. Despite LEGO's goal of optimizing its global supply chain, the outsourcing collaboration was cancelled after merely three years. As became evident, the result of attempting to manage and overcome the complexity of the production network by outsourcing it to external providers was actually only a more complex global manufacturing footprint. In particular, the collaboration with Flextronics presented the LEGO Group with some rather daunting and unexpected challenges. Considering the extreme pace of the transition, it eventually turned out problematic for LEGO to coordinate and control the increasingly global and complex network of production facilities as well as to ensure a reliable and seamless transfer of production knowledge between the two. For example, there was the challenge of aligning the LEGO products' seasonal fluctuations and unpredictable demand with Flextronics' business model. About 60 per cent of the LEGO production was made in the second half of the year, the product had an average lifespan of 16 to 18 months, and the demand uncertainty fluctuated with plus or minus 30 per cent. The LEGO Group's need for flexible and market-responsive business solutions presented a strategic misfit with Flextronics' more stable and predictable operations in which economies of scale was a key phrase. Divergence and misalignments between the two had therefore become the outcome.

3. A Bounded New Start

22 In 2008, as the LEGO Group announced that it would phase out the cooperation with Flextronics, the process of sourcing back the production was initiated. This was embarked on by the LEGO Group taking over the control of the Kladno factory in the Czech Republic in February 2008. Flextronics was still in charge of molding LEGO products at two sites in Hungary (Sarvar and Nyíregyháza) and one site in Mexico (Juárez) until July 2008, when LEGO management affirmed that these would follow suit with the site in the Czech Republic. In Hungary, LEGO concentrated its activities at the Nyíregyháza facility by taking over the plant and its workforce. During the first quarter of 2009, the Juárez production moved to a new site fully owned by the LEGO Group in Monterrey in northeast Mexico, and the site was up and running in the second quarter of 2009.

23 "We are not satisfied with the effectiveness in the outsourced facilities," commented Knudstorp briefly after the decision to end the cooperation was made. "It takes more time to educate people than we had expected, and that means that we are still more effective in Billund."[16] Duedahl, however, argued that it might just as well have been the LEGO Group that had not been correct for Flextronics as the other way around: "All in all, we had to

[14] LEGO press release, June 20, 2006.

[15] Ibid.

[16] *JydskeVestkysten,* July 1, 2008.

realize that our contract also made it difficult for Flextronics to carry out the responsibilities of the collaboration with LEGO in a sound manner. The supplier, like us, has the same need for a profitable business model."[17]

24 Looking back, the attempt to cut costs and reduce complexity quickly had, in fact, complicated matters for the worse, and thus hindered a conducive foundation for creating profitable synergies. At a glance, the Flextronics adventure therefore looked like a failure. "We have learned that even though everything points at outsourcing, it might still not be the best solution," said Duedahl.[18] Still, however, the collaboration had brought along a number of positive externalities. The engagement had first of all helped LEGO to expand its global operations footprint despite its difficult financial situation. Prior to Flextronics, it was hardly possible to establish the new and needed operating bases in Mexico and Hungary. Flextronics had thus provided the Danish company with the necessary impetus for altering its global production network to serve important markets while saving costs.

25 Perhaps more importantly, the collaboration had given the LEGO Group an indispensable lesson in understanding its own processes and structures. As Duedahl explained, "We have learned that we are more special than we expected to be."[19] In addition, Flextronics possessed valuable experience and knowledge in relation to the documentation and standardization of the production. Previously, the LEGO Group, to a large extent, had carried out its production processes without paying too much attention to the documentation of it. "We had had the pleasure of being in Billund for 40 years with many loyal colleagues," said Thomas Nielsen, a LEGO manufacturing vice-president. "The downside to this, however, is that you become rather lazy on the documentation side as everybody with many years of experience knows exactly what to do."[20]

26 As the LEGO Group went from producing the absolute majority in-house to becoming highly dependent on external partners, changes were unavoidable. With the Flextronics collaboration, LEGO management came to realize not only the need, but also the value, of documenting work processes, communication lines and interfaces between activities and tasks in the production. "Production in another country—even within the same company—requires ten times more documentation than in the company that it is moved from," rationalized Michael Vaag, a LEGO supply chain manager.[21] The increased employment of process documentation had given the LEGO Group transparency and control, and thus ample room to manage challenges of complexity and to identify the stronger and weaker parts and links of the production network. In this respect, LEGO management had introduced in 2005 a deliberate sales and operations planning (S&OP) process to monitor and coordinate the different production facilities' roles, capacities and responsibilities in relation to the supply. This approach had stuck with the company also after the break-up with Flextronics and was considered "a strong fundament for the process." Before being introduced in 2005 as a global process covering all LEGO in-house and outsourced sites, S&OP ran for a year at the company's site in Enfield, United States, resulting in significant operations performance improvements. Michael Kehlet, a LEGO flow planning director, described S&OP as "a process gluing all operations' work flows together."[22] The

[17] *Ingenøren,* October 24, 2008.

[18] *Ibid.*

[19] *Ibid.*

[20] Interview with Thomas Nielsen, October 7, 2009.

[21] *Ingenøren,* March 14, 2008.

[22] Interview with Michael Kehlet, September 13, 2008.

global S&OP process at LEGO was organized around three key areas: sales, production and product development. Monitoring and coordinating these areas took place through a multi-stage cycle, which started with data consolidation at the site level and concluded at a global executive S&OP meeting. The S&OP cycle took place every month, providing LEGO with a reliable and constantly updated overview of global operations for the following 12 months. Gradually, the S&OP process evolved into a rather critical tool for creating transparency and supporting management efforts in a relatively fragmented and globally distributed operations set-up, which involved numerous capacity groups and outsourcing partners.

27 Along with its surge in documenting business processes, the LEGO Group, through Flextronics, had also recognized the strength of standardizing its processes. Actually, standardizing the business processes had always been an integral part of the LEGO Group's approach to production. With the production of around 24 billion bricks per year, a high degree of standardization was obviously imperative for the extreme accuracy required. The collaboration with Flextronics, however, had illuminated LEGO management's perception of how standardization could be used more strategically in the firm. Chresten Bruun, a senior production director, explained how the virtues of standardization had been taken to new frontiers within the company. "We are standardizing on three levels," he said, "the upper level: that is our way of thinking, our mindset, values, attitudes; on the mid level: how we operate our planning processes, follow-up processes, etc.; and the lower level: that is more the hardware part, the machines, lines and the layout in the production."[23] The total number of component portfolios had accordingly decreased from approximately 12,000 in 2004 to roughly half that number in 2008 (reaching levels that existed before 1996), with the final target being 5,500 for the year 2011. The LEGO mini figure policeman, for instance, was reduced from 16 different versions to only four. The standardization had implications throughout the whole value chain starting with the design of new products—as every new product should contain at least 70 per cent "evergreen" bricks—i.e., bricks that could be used in more products. Reducing the more unique and product-specific bricks to only 30 per cent of all bricks allowed for a more flexible and smooth supply chain.

28 Its international network of production facilities had also changed from mainly branding factories, where each facility had been responsible for one single product, to facilities that were more standardized, with their main purpose being to serve their respective markets. This gave the company considerable room to benchmark the factories, and thus optimize the total cost advantage of the production facilities in which the reaction time to market was a decisive parameter. In the aftermath of Flextronics, Michael Vaag, supply chain manager, summarized his success criteria for global production in four ways: "1) It is easy to move technology—it takes more time to build competences; 2) a clear plan for training and education shall be present; 3) there shall be local leaders who know the working culture in the country; and 4) there shall be a clear key figure structure which ensures actual benchmarks/KPI between the factories."[24]

29 In sum, the LEGO Group read the collaboration with Flextronics in three different stages—before, during and after—each stage with different challenges and opportunities (see **Exhibit 7**). What seemed to be the recurring theme throughout the entire process, however, was how LEGO management continuously increased its stock of knowledge concerning how to optimize its processes and organization to overcome and manage the multitude of complex issues deriving from having a global network of production.

[23] Interview Chresten Bruun, January 8, 2010.

[24] *Ingeniøren,* March 14, 2008.

EXHIBIT 7 **The Three Stages of the LEGO Group's Offshore Outsourcing**

Pre-Flextronics	Flextronics	Post-Flextronics
2003 2004	2005 2006 2007	2008 2009
▪ Tight control of all elements of the value chain **Challenges:** ▪ Cost of production located in predominantly high-cost countries ▪ Over-diversified and complex products portfolio ▪ Underperforming in-house supply chain ▪ Negative financial results ▪ High capital investment requirements ▪ High fixed costs	▪ Plan to outsource up to 80% of production capacity to external partners **Challenges:** ▪ Fast pace of transition ▪ Production know-how transfer to external partners ▪ Brand vulnerability and dependency on partners ▪ Supply uncertainty ▪ Developing new capabilities ▪ Maintaining knowledge about production ▪ Management of new relationships ▪ Increasing complexity of production footprint	▪ Backsourcing of the plants operated by the strategic external partner Flextronics ▪ LEGO maintains relationships with a number of smaller external suppliers **Challenges:** ▪ Stabilizing and optimizing the operations after another stage of transition ▪ Balancing predominately internal supply capacity with market demands.

Source: Authors' own assessment.

EPILOGUE

30 The LEGO Group's recent financial record showed that Knudstorp and his executive management had indeed been successful with the turnaround strategy: the profits for 2008 and 2009 of DKK1.85 billion and DKK2.2 billion, respectively, were the largest in the Group's history. Commenting on this, Knudstorp said, "Our results for 2008 have been extraordinarily good. And this applies not only to the financial results. During 2008, we also took over two factories in the Czech Republic and Hungary, and we began the construction of a factory in Mexico. The successful change to [more in-house] production, combined with strong sales increases, is attributable to the impressive performance by all our employees."[25] The back-sourcing from Flextronics had played an inevitable part in achieving this. The new dominantly in-house production network consisting of factories in Denmark, Hungary, the Czech Republic and Mexico seemingly gave the LEGO Group enough controllable flexibility to balance market demands with its network of offshoring activities. However, the LEGO executive management knew not to rest on its laurels. Although looking promising, the new production network was, in fact, a mere result of avoiding the emerging unexpected costs from having outsourced the production. A central question was therefore: What had the LEGO Group learned from the Flextronics collaboration and how could it use this knowledge constructively in the future?

[25] LEGO press release, February 23, 2009.

Case 13

Lennar Corporation's Joint Venture Investments

Graeme Rankine

Amid our negative sector stance, we are upgrading our relative rating on LEN to Overweight from Neutral, as our new price target represents lower downside potential on the stock vs. its peers. Importantly, in addition to LEN's relative underperformance and below-average valuation, our outlook for below-average book value contraction by 2009-end is a key factor behind our relative ratings change. Specifically, over the last 12 months, LEN has underperformed, down 33% vs. the group's 23% decline (S&P: -36%), we believe largely driven by concerns regarding its above-average JV exposure. This performance, in turn, has in part led to a 35% valuation discount to its peers on a P/B basis, currently at 0.50x vs. its larger-cap peers' 0.77x average. However, while we believe this valuation discount could narrow, given LEN's continued reduction in JV exposure, our outlook for below-average book value contraction is the key driver for LEN's lower downside risk, in our view.

—JP Morgan, Lennar, January 8, 2009.

1 On January 8, 2009, Anna Amphlett reflected on JP Morgan's report that Lennar Corporation's stock price had been negatively impacted by the recent U.S. housing crisis more than other firms in the housing industry, and, therefore, the investment risk was less than that of its peers (see **Exhibit 1** for the company's recent stock price performance). Amphlett, a newly recruited financial analyst at Southern Cross Investments LLC, had been asked to prepare a report on Lennar's joint ventures and how the company accounted for these investments. She knew that she would be questioned by her boss about JP Morgan's concern over Lennar's "above-average JV exposure," since she had learned in her MBA program that joint ventures were a practical way for a company to diversify risk and gain access to the expertise of joint venture partners. But she knew as well that joint ventures were also a method some companies used to finance investments "off-balance sheet." She wondered if the stock might even stage a comeback in the near future. JP Morgan set a price target for Lennar's stock of $8.50 per share, less than the share's trading range of around $11. Lennar had grown considerably through 2006, but in the last two years, revenues had suffered a sizeable reversal (see **Exhibit 2** for historical financial information).

2 On returning from a two-week vacation, Amphlett was shocked to learn that on January 9, Barry Minkow's Fraud Discovery Institute (FDI) had raised questions on a Web site about Lennar's off-balance-sheet debt and a large personal loan taken out by a top company executive (see **Exhibit 3** for details of the allegations).[1] On the day of the announcement, the company's stock price plunged and trading volume increased dramatically (see **Exhibit 4** for information about the stock price reaction to the Minkow claims). Amphlett's completed research report recommended that Southern Cross acquire Lennar's shares, but she now realized it was imperative that she understand the nature and purpose of Lennar's joint ventures before submitting the report.

[1] *The Wall Street Journal*, January 9, 2009.

EXHIBIT 1 **Lennar's Recent Stock Price Performance—Class A Stock (Relative to the S&P 500)**

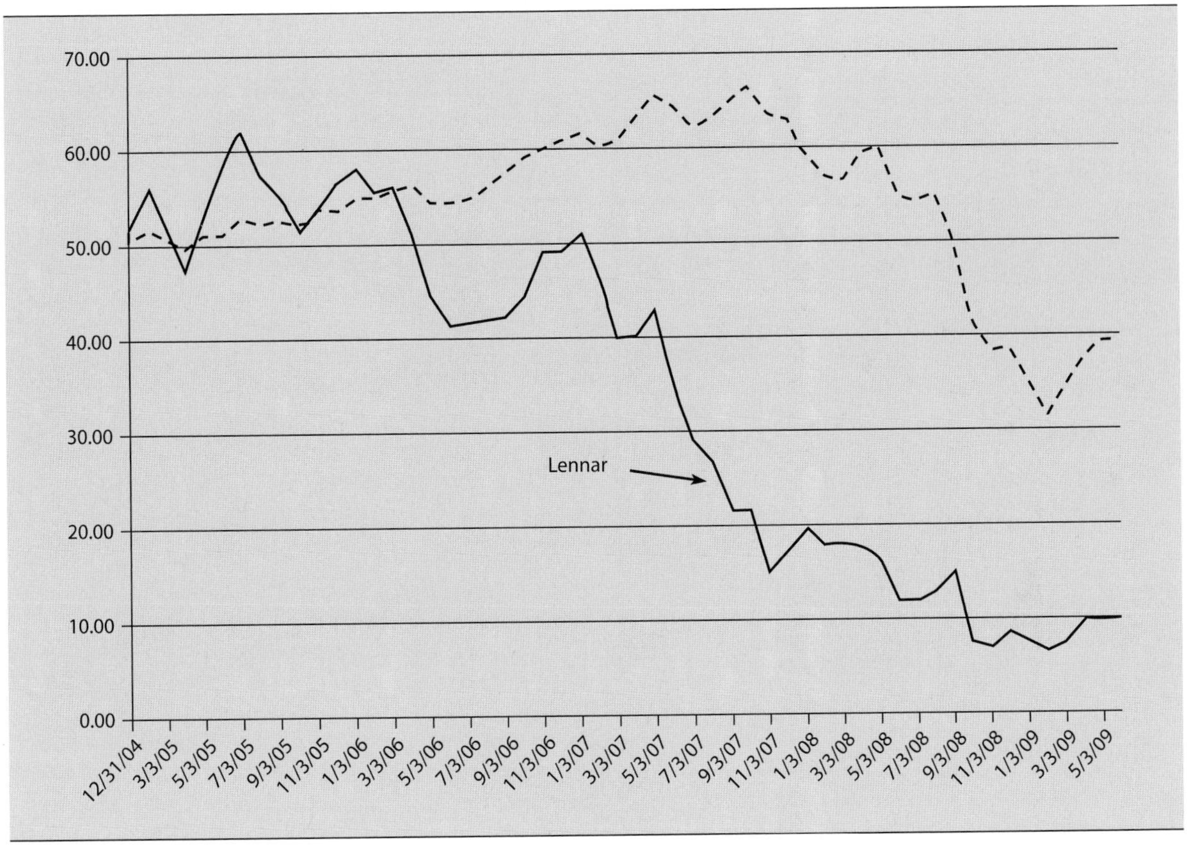

COMPANY BACKGROUND

3 By early 2009, Lennar Corporation was one of the nation's largest homebuilders and a provider of financial services. The company's homebuilding operations included the construction and sale of single-family attached and detached homes, and multilevel residential buildings, in communities targeted to first-time, move-up, and active adult homebuyers. The company was also involved in the purchase, development, and sale of residential land, and in all phases of planning and building in residential communities, including land acquisition, site planning, preparation and improvement of land, and design, construction, and marketing of homes. The company operated in Florida, Maryland, New Jersey, Virginia, Arizona, Colorado, Texas, California, Nevada, Illinois, Minnesota, New York, and both North and South Carolina. The company's financial services business provided mortgage financing, title insurance, closing services, and other ancillary services (including high-speed Internet and cable television) for both buyers and sellers. Substantially all of the loans that the company originated were sold in the secondary mortgage market on a servicing released, nonrecourse basis. The average sales price of a Lennar home was $270,000 in fiscal 2008, compared to $297,000 in fiscal 2007.

4 Lennar was founded as a local Miami homebuilder in 1954. The company completed an initial public offering in 1971, and listed its common stock on the New York Stock Exchange in 1972. During the 1980s and 1990s, the company entered and expanded operations in

EXHIBIT 2 **Historical Financial Information for Lennar**

FISCAL YEAR ENDING (In thousands)	11/30/08	11/30/07	11/30/06	11/30/05	11/30/04	11/30/03	11/30/02	11/30/01	11/30/00	11/30/99
Net sales	4,575,417	10,186,781	16,266,662	13,866,971	10,500,968	8,907,619	7,235,520	6,002,250	4,706,968	3,118,514
Cost of goods sold	4,754,893	12,435,786	14,930,318	11,448,257	8,856,750	7,551,577	6,349,817	4,581,340	4,182,577	2,746,615
Gross profit	(179,476)	(2,249,005)	1,336,344	2,418,714	1,644,218	1,356,042	885,703	1,420,910	524,391	371,899
Net income	(1,109,085)	(1,941,081)	593,869	1,355,155	945,619	751,391	545,129	417,845	229,137	172,714
Outstanding shares	160,558	159,887	158,156	157,560	156,230	78,918	64,913	64,015	62,731	57,917
Cash	1,234,227	830,623	803,115	1,082,024	1,427,941	1,270,872	731,163	824,013	287,627	83,256
Receivables	18,518	147,814	121,570	100,856	77,489	54,706	41,520	24,345	42,270	11,162
Inventories	4,500,090	4,500,403	7,831,483	7,863,531	5,142,070	3,656,101	3,237,577	2,416,541	2,301,584	1,274,551
Investment & advances to subs.	785,891	995,789	1,506,749	1,314,832	887,996	390,334	285,594	300,064	257,639	173,310
Total assets	7,424,898	9,102,747	12,408,266	12,541,225	9,165,280	6,775,432	5,755,633	4,714,426	3,777,914	2,057,647
Long-term debt	2,402,541	2,625,626	3,533,862	2,143,695	2,506,834	1,202,629	1,086,687	1,310,016	NA	NA
Shareholder's equity	2,623,007	3,822,119	5,701,372	5,251,411	4,052,972	3,263,774	2,229,157	1,659,262	1,228,580	881,499
Net Cash Provided (Used) by Operations	1,100,834	444,513	552,535	322,975	420,192	580,799	204,568	59,196	479,399	121,290
Net Cash Provided (Used) by Investing	(265,703)	306,983	(404,354)	(1,003,573)	(534,107)	(118,197)	(365,677)	1,863	(186,716)	(28,522)
Net Cash Provided (Used) by Financing	(426,903)	(734,621)	(429,205)	324,126	304,082	31,111	60,994	482,338	(76,973)	(36,178)

EXHIBIT 3 Fraud Discovery Institute Press Release

Fraud Discovery Institute, Inc. Launches Top 10 Red Flags for Fraud at Lennar Corporation (NYSE:LEN)

Subtitle: Consumer group launches new Web site, www.Lenn-ron.com; Alleges Lennar Corporation (NYSE:LEN) operates a "Ponzi Scheme" through their multiple joint ventures

For Immediate Release, San Diego, California, Friday, January 9, 2009

The Fraud Discovery Institute, Inc. released today the Top 10 Red Flags for Fraud at Lennar Corporation, the country's second largest homebuilder. Through the release of a 30-page report, a YouTube video, and a Web site with a catchy URL (www.Lenn-ron.com), the consumer advocate group is drawing attention to multiple alleged fraudulent activities that have become a pattern of behavior.

According to cofounder Barry Minkow, "You can sum up just how outrageous the fraud and abuse are at Lennar Corporation by simply listening to company President and CEO Stuart Miller who, on a recent conference call, said that Lennar Corporation had improved their cash reserves to $1.1 billion, up from $642 million a year before. What Mr. Miller conveniently left out was how the company obtained the $1.1 billion cash. It came from the June 2008 NewHall/LandSource bankruptcy that has created 5,000 victims. Although Lennar Corporation ended up with hundreds of millions of cash through the debacle, the public must ask how many people, companies, and communities were destroyed in the process of improving Lennar's balance sheet."

A preview of some of the red flags includes:

- How Lennar Corporation tried to "bury" the Forest Lawn Mortuary.
- How Lennar Corporation treats their joint ventures exactly like a Ponzi scheme—pledging their older joint venture interests to leverage themselves into newer joint venture relationships (despite operating agreements that prohibit this unauthorized movement of money).
- How Lennar Chief Operating Officer Jon Jaffe received a $5,000,000 third trust deed loan in late 2007 that literally overencumbers his home. This loan came from a lender who appears to be an undisclosed related party to Lennar Corporation and their joint venture partner in Kern County, California.
- How Lennar Corporation continues to provide vague and less-than-transparent responses to the SEC inquiries about off-balance sheet, joint venture debt.
- How Lennar has exhibited a pattern of behavior over a sustained period of time of deceptive business practices, ranging from building homes using Chinese drywall to cut costs, to causing CALPERS (the California Public Retirement Fund) to lose approximately $1 billion.

The Fraud Discovery Institute, Inc. also refers to multiple lawsuits filed against Lennar Corporation for claims of breach of contract and fraud. FDI became involved with Lennar on behalf of one of their joint venture partners who was involved in the construction of "The Bridges" in Rancho Santa Fe, one of San Diego's most successful residential communities. The joint venture partner is alleging in a lawsuit that Lennar violated the operating agreement. "We began this case with sincere doubts that a public company listed on the New York Stock Exchange, with internal controls that include an audit committee, would allow the exploitation of not just our client, but hundreds and thousands of others as evidenced by the public record. We were shocked and felt compelled to further investigate and educate law enforcement to the 'below the surface' happenings at this company."

some of its current major homebuilding markets including California, Florida, and Texas through both organic growth and acquisitions such as Pacific Greystone Corporation in 1997, among others. In 1997, the company completed the spin-off of its commercial real estate business to LNR Property Corporation. In 2000, Lennar acquired U.S. Home Corporation, which expanded the company's operations into New Jersey, Maryland, Virginia,

EXHIBIT 4 Lennar's Daily Class A Stock Returns around Minkow's Allegations

Date	Open	High	Low	Close	Lennar Return	S&P 500 Return	Market Adjusted Return	Volume
12/24/08	8.91	8.91	8.27	8.32	−4.0%	0.6%	−4.6%	1,256,400
12/26/08	8.61	8.68	8.29	8.58	3.1%	0.5%	2.6%	1,198,500
12/29/08	8.61	8.61	8.02	8.36	−2.6%	−0.4%	−2.2%	3,324,800
12/30/08	8.43	8.66	7.96	8.66	3.6%	2.4%	1.1%	4,134,500
12/31/08	8.56	8.82	8.26	8.67	0.1%	1.4%	−1.3%	5,170,600
1/2/09	8.60	9.33	8.44	9.18	5.9%	3.2%	2.7%	3,412,500
1/5/09	9.09	10.55	8.86	10.20	11.1%	−0.5%	11.6%	8,437,800
1/6/09	10.37	11.27	10.31	11.17	9.5%	0.8%	8.7%	8,743,400
1/7/09	10.86	10.97	10.38	10.57	−5.4%	−3.0%	−2.4%	6,502,500
1/8/09	11.00	11.56	10.41	11.42	8.0%	0.3%	7.7%	7,809,600
1/9/09	**11.28**	**11.28**	**8.23**	**9.15**	**−19.9%**	**−2.1%**	**−17.7%**	**58,290,200**
1/12/09	9.47	9.50	8.24	8.35	−8.7%	−2.3%	−6.5%	17,102,700
1/13/09	8.30	8.79	8.08	8.66	3.7%	0.2%	3.5%	9,429,800
1/14/09	8.50	8.56	7.81	7.90	−8.8%	−3.3%	−5.4%	7,943,700
1/15/09	7.96	8.09	7.02	7.57	−4.2%	0.1%	−4.3%	10,418,600
1/16/09	7.87	8.07	7.09	7.85	3.7%	0.8%	2.9%	7,663,800
1/20/09	7.53	7.90	6.71	6.78	−13.6%	−5.3%	−8.3%	6,147,700
1/21/09	6.94	7.12	6.16	7.08	4.4%	4.3%	0.1%	7,557,900
1/22/09	6.73	7.03	6.47	6.55	−7.5%	−1.5%	−6.0%	6,652,200
1/23/09	6.39	7.13	6.17	6.84	4.4%	0.5%	3.9%	5,436,600
1/26/09	7.55	8.74	7.17	7.82	14.3%	0.6%	13.8%	14,122,800

Minnesota, and Colorado, and strengthened its position in other states. During 2002 and 2003, the company acquired several regional homebuilders, which brought the company into new markets and strengthened its position in several existing markets.[2]

5 The company balanced a local operating structure with centralized corporate level management. Decisions related to the overall strategy, acquisitions of land and businesses, risk management, financing, cash management, and information systems were centralized at the corporate level. The local operating structure consisted of divisions, which were managed by individuals who had significant experience in the homebuilding industry and, in most instances, in their particular markets. They were responsible for operating decisions regarding land identification, entitlement and development, the management of inventory levels for the current volume levels, community development, home design, construction, and marketing homes.

[2] See Lennar Corporation's 2008 10-K filing on the company's Web site.

6 During 2008, Lennar significantly reduced its property acquisitions. The company acquired land for development and for the construction of homes that were sold to homebuyers. At November 30, 2008, Lennar owned 74,681 home sites and had access through option contracts to an additional 38,589 home sites, of which 12,718 were through option contracts with third parties, and 25,871 were through option contracts with unconsolidated entities in which Lennar had investments. At November 30, 2007, the company owned 62,801 home sites and had access through option contracts to an additional 85,870 home sites, of which 22,877 were through option contracts with third parties, and 62,993 were through option contracts with unconsolidated entities.

7 Lennar supervised and controlled the development of land and the design and building of its residential communities with a relatively small labor force. The company hired subcontractors for site improvements and virtually all of the work involved in the construction of homes. Generally, arrangements with subcontractors provided that the company's subcontractors completed specified work in accordance with price schedules and applicable building codes and laws. The price schedules were subject to change to meet changes in labor and material costs or for other reasons. Lennar did not own heavy construction equipment. The company financed construction and land development activities, primarily with cash generated from operations and public debt issuances, as well as cash borrowed under its revolving credit facility.

8 The company employed sales associates who were paid salaries, commissions, or both, to complete on-site sales of homes. Lennar also sold homes through independent brokers. Lennar worked continuously to improve homeowner customer satisfaction throughout the presale, sale, construction, closing, and post-closing periods. Through the participation of sales associates, on-site construction supervisors, and customer care associates, Lennar created a quality home buying experience for its customers, which led to enhanced customer retention and referrals. The company delivered 15,735, 33,283, and 49,568 homes during 2008, 2007, and 2006, respectively.

LENNAR'S JOINT VENTURES

9 At November 30, 2008, Lennar had equity investments in 116 unconsolidated entities, compared to 214 un-consolidated entities at November 30, 2007. Due to market conditions at the time, the company focused on reducing the number of unconsolidated entities in which it had investments. The company's investments in unconsolidated entities by type of venture were as follows:

	November 30,	
	2008	2007
	(In thousands)	
Land development	$633,652	738,481
Homebuilding	133,100	195,790
Total investment	$766,752	934,271

10 Lennar invested in unconsolidated entities that acquired and developed land (1) for its homebuilding operations or for sale to third parties; or, (2) for the construction of homes for sale to third-party homebuyers. Through these entities, Lennar primarily sought to reduce and share risk by limiting the amount of its capital invested in land, while obtaining access to potential future home sites and allowing the company to participate in strategic ventures. The use of these entities also, in some instances, enabled the company to acquire land to which it could not otherwise obtain access, or could not obtain access on as-favorable terms, without the participation of a strategic partner. Participants in these joint ventures were landowners/developers, other homebuilders, and financial or strategic partners. Joint ventures with landowners/developers gave the company access to home sites owned or controlled by a partner. Joint ventures with other homebuilders provided the company with the ability to bid jointly with the partner for large land parcels. Joint ventures with financial partners allowed Lennar to combine its homebuilding expertise with access to its partners' capital. Joint ventures with strategic partners allowed the company to combine its homebuilding expertise with the specific expertise (e.g., commercial or infill experience) of its partner.

11 Although the strategic purposes of its joint ventures and the nature of its joint venture partners varied, the joint ventures were generally designed to acquire, develop, and/or sell specific assets during a limited lifetime. The joint ventures were typically structured through noncorporate entities in which control was shared with its venture partners. Each joint venture was unique in terms of its funding requirements and liquidity needs. Lennar and the other joint venture participants typically made pro-rata cash contributions to the joint venture. In many cases, Lennar's risk was limited to its equity contribution and potential future capital contributions. The capital contributions usually coincided in time with the acquisition of properties by the joint venture. Additionally, most joint ventures obtained third-party debt to fund a portion of the acquisition, development, and construction costs of their communities. The joint venture agreements usually permitted, but did not require, the joint ventures to make additional capital calls in the future. However, capital calls relating to the repayment of joint venture debt, under payment or maintenance guarantees, generally were required. See **Exhibits 5** and **6** for selected financial statement information about Lennar Corporation.

SHARING ARRANGEMENTS

12 Alliances, partnering, mergers and acquisitions, and joint ventures are sharing arrangements that enable parties to collaborate for mutual gain that would not otherwise be available from working alone. Each party may enter the relationship to obtain access to physical resources, financing, risk-sharing opportunities, specific skills and technologies, and new products and markets. Joint ventures usually involve creating a separate organization established through equity participation by the joint venture partners, and under their mutual shared control. Mergers and acquisitions involve the acquisition and control of one entity by another, or the creation of a third entity owned by each of the merger parties. Alliances usually involve contractual agreements to work together in specific ways and for specific periods, and share any resulting revenues, or profits, but do not involve equity participation by the parties.

13 One study found that joint venture announcements in the period 1972-1979 resulted in a statistically significant two-day increase in shareholder wealth of 0.74%, suggesting that investors perceive joint ventures as enhancing shareholder wealth.[3] Another study reported that the NUMMI joint venture established in 1983 between General Motors (GM) and Toyota in an idle GM plant was a major factor in the improvement in manufacturing quality and productivity at GM. At the outset, the cooperation provided an opportunity for each party to gain more from working together than working alone—Toyota wanted to learn about managing an American workforce, while GM wanted to learn about building small

[3] John McConnell and Tim Nantell, "Common Stock Returns and Corporate Combinations: The Case of Joint Ventures," *Journal of Finance*, 40: 519-536 (1985).

EXHIBIT 5 **Lennar's 2008 Financial Statements**

CONSOLIDATED BALANCE SHEETS **November 30, 2008 and 2007**		
ASSETS **Homebuilding:**	**2008**	**2007**
Cash and cash equivalents	1,091,468	642,467
Restricted cash	8,828	35,429
Receivables, net	94,520	207,691
Income tax receivables	255,460	881,525
Inventories:		
Finished homes and construction in progress	2,080,345	2,180,670
Land under development	1,741,407	1,500,075
Consolidated inventory not owned	678,338	819,658
Total inventories	4,500,090	4,500,403
Investments in unconsolidated entities	766,752	934,271
Other assets	99,802	863,152
	6,816,920	8,064,938
Financial services	607,978	1,037,809
Total assets	7,424,898	9,102,747
LIABILITIES AND STOCKHOLDERS' EQUITY		
Homebuilding:		
Accounts payable	246,727	376,134
Liabilities related to consolidated inventory not owned	592,777	719,081
Senior notes and other debts payable	2,544,935	2,295,436
Other liabilities	834,873	1,129,791
	4,219,312	4,520,442
Financial services	416,833	731,658
Total liabilities	4,636,145	5,252,100
Minority interest	165,746	28,528
Stockholders' equity:		
Preferred stock	—	—
Class A common stock of $0.10 par value per share Authorized: 2008 and 2007—300,000 shares Issued: 2008—140,503 shares; 2007—139,309 shares	14,050	13,931
Class B common stock of $0.10 par value per share Authorized: 2008 and 2007—90,000 shares Issued: 2008—32,964 shares; 2007—32,962 shares	3,296	3,296
Additional paid-in capital	1,944,626	1,920,386
Retained earnings	1,273,159	2,496,933
Deferred compensation plan; 2007—36 Class A common shares and 4 Class B common shares	—	(332)
Deferred compensation liability	—	332
Treasury stock, at cost; 2008—11,229 Class A common shares and 1,680 Class B common shares; 2007—10,705 Class A common shares and 1,679 Class B common shares	(612,124)	(610,366)
Accumulated other comprehensive loss	—	(2,061)
Total stockholders' equity	2,623,007	3,822,119
Total liabilities and stockholders' equity	7,424,898	9,102,747

(Continued)

EXHIBIT 6 (*Continued*)

The Company's partners generally are unrelated homebuilders, landowners/developers, and financial or other strategic partners. The unconsolidated entities follow accounting principles that are in all material respects the same as those used by the Company. The Company shares in the profits and losses of these unconsolidated entities, generally in accordance with its ownership interests. In many instances, the Company is appointed as the day-to-day manager of the unconsolidated entities and receives management fees and/or reimbursement of expenses for performing this function. During the years ended November 30, 2008, 2007, and 2006, the Company received management fees and reimbursement of expenses from the unconsolidated entities totaling $33.3 million, $52.1 million, and $72.8 million, respectively.

The Company and/or its partners sometimes obtain options or enter into other arrangements under which the Company can purchase portions of the land held by the unconsolidated entities. Option prices are generally negotiated prices that approximate fair value when the Company receives the options. During the years ended November 30, 2008, 2007, and 2006, $416.2 million, $977.5 million, and $742.5 million, respectively, of the unconsolidated entities' revenues were from land sales to the Company. The Company does not include in its equity in earnings (loss) from unconsolidated entities its pro rata share of unconsolidated entities' earnings resulting from land sales to its homebuilding divisions. Instead, the Company accounts for those earnings as a reduction of the cost of purchasing the land from the unconsolidated entities. This in effect defers recognition of the Company's share of the unconsolidated entities' earnings related to these sales until the Company delivers a home, and title passes to a third-party homebuyer.

The unconsolidated entities in which the Company has investments usually finance their activities with a combination of partner equity and debt financing. In some instances, the Company and its partners have guaranteed debt of certain unconsolidated entities.

In November 2007, the Company sold a portfolio of land consisting of approximately 11,000 home sites in 32 communities located throughout the country to a strategic land investment venture with Morgan Stanley Real Estate Fund II, L.P., an affiliate of Morgan Stanley & Co., Inc., in which the Company has a 20% ownership interest and 50% voting rights. The Company also manages the land investment venture's operations and receives fees for its services. As part of the transaction, the Company entered into option agreements and obtained rights of first offer, providing the Company the opportunity to purchase certain finished home sites. The Company has no obligation to exercise the options, and cannot acquire a majority of the entity's assets. Due to the Company's continuing involvement, the transaction did not qualify as a sale by the Company under GAAP; thus, the inventory has remained on the Company's consolidated balance sheet in consolidated inventory not owned. In 2007, the Company recorded a SFAS 144 valuation adjustment of $740.4 million on the inventory sold to the investment venture. As a result of the transaction, the land investment venture recorded the purchase of the portfolio of land as inventory. As of November 30, 2008, the portfolio of land (including land development costs) of $538.4 million is reflected as inventory in the summarized condensed financial information related to unconsolidated entities in which the Company has investments.

The summary of the Company's net recourse exposure related to the unconsolidated entities in which the Company has investments was as follows:

	November 30, 2008	November 30, 2007
	(In thousands)	
Several recourse debt—repayment	78,547	123,022
Several recourse debt—maintenance	167,941	355,513
Joint and several recourse debt—repayment	138,169	263,364
Joint and several recourse debt—maintenance	123,051	291,727
Land seller debt recourse exposure	12,170	—
The Company's maximum recourse exposure	519,878	1,033,626
Less joint and several reimbursement agreements with the Company's partners	(127,428)	(238,692)
The Company's net recourse exposure	392,450	794,934

EXHIBIT 6 *(Continued)*

The recourse debt exposure in the table above represents the Company's maximum recourse exposure to loss from guarantees and does not take into account the underlying value of the collateral. During the year ended November 30, 2008, the Company reduced its maximum recourse exposure related to unconsolidated joint ventures by $513.7 million.

The Company's Credit Facility requires the Company to effect quarterly reductions of its maximum recourse exposure related to joint ventures in which it has investments by a total of $200 million by November 30, 2009, of which the Company has already made significant progress. The Company must also effect quarterly reductions during its 2010 fiscal year totaling $180 million, and during the first six months of its 2011 fiscal year totaling $80 million. By May 31, 2011, the Company's maximum recourse exposure related to joint ventures in which it has investments cannot exceed $275 million (see Note 7).

Although the Company, in some instances, guarantees the indebtedness of unconsolidated entities in which it has an investment, the Company's unconsolidated entities that have recourse debt have significant amount of assets and equity. The summarized balance sheets of the Company's unconsolidated entities with recourse debt were as follows:

	November 30,	
	2008	2007
	(In thousands)	
Assets	2,846,819	3,220,695
Liabilities	1,565,148	2,311,216
Equity	1,281,671	909,479

In addition, the Company and/or its partners sometimes guarantee the obligations of an unconsolidated entity in order to help secure a loan to that entity. When the Company and/or its partners provide guarantees, the unconsolidated entity generally receives more favorable terms from its lenders than would otherwise be available to it. In a repayment guarantee, the Company and its venture partners guarantee repayment of a portion or all of the debt in the event of a default before the lender would have to exercise its rights against the collateral. The maintenance guarantees only apply if the value or the collateral (generally land and improvements) is less than a specified percentage of the loan balance. If the Company is required to make a payment under a maintenance guarantee to bring the value of the collateral above the specified percentage of the loan balance, the payment would constitute a capital contribution or loan to the unconsolidated entity and increase the Company's share of any funds the unconsolidated entity distributes. During the years ended November 30, 2008 and 2007, amounts paid under the Company's maintenance guarantees were $74.0 million and $84.1 million, respectively. In accordance with FASB Interpretation No. 45, Guarantor's Accounting and Disclosure Requirements for Guarantees, Including Indirect Guarantees of Indebtedness of Others, as of November 30, 2008, the fair values of the maintenance guarantees and repayment guarantees were not material. The Company believes that as of November 30, 2008, in the event it becomes legally obligated to perform under a guarantee of the obligation of an unconsolidated entity due to a triggering event under a guarantee, most of the time the collateral should be sufficient to repay at least a significant portion of the obligation, or the Company and its partners would contribute additional capital into the venture.

In many of the loans to unconsolidated entities, the Company and another entity or entities generally related to the Company's subsidiary's joint venture partner(s) have been required to give guarantees of completion to the lenders. Those completion guarantees may require that the guarantors complete the construction of the improvements for which the financing was obtained. If the construction was to be done in phases, very often the guarantee is to complete only the phases as to which construction has already commenced and for which loan proceeds were used. Under many of the completion guarantees, the guarantors are permitted, under certain circumstances, to use undisbursed loan proceeds to satisfy the completion obligations, and in many of those cases, the guarantors pay interest only on those funds, with no repayment of the principal of such funds required.

(Continued)

EXHIBIT 6 *(Continued)*

Indebtedness of an unconsolidated entity is secured by its own assets. There is no cross collateralization of debt to different unconsolidated entities; however, some unconsolidated entities own multiple properties and other assets. In connection with a loan to an unconsolidated entity, the Company and its partners often guarantee to a lender either jointly and severally or on a several basis, any, or all of the following: (i) the completion of the development, in whole or in part, (ii) indemnification of the lender from environmental issues, (iii) indemnification of the lender from "bad boy acts" of the unconsolidated entity (or full recourse liability in the event of unauthorized transfer or bankruptcy), and (iv) that the loan to value and/or loan to cost will not exceed a certain percentage (maintenance or remargining guarantee) or that a percentage of the outstanding loan will be repaid (repayment guarantee).

In connection with loans to an unconsolidated entity where there is a joint and several guarantee, the Company generally has a reimbursement agreement with its partner. The reimbursement agreement provides that neither party is responsible for more than its proportionate share of the guarantee. However, if the Company's joint venture partner does not have adequate financial resources to meet its obligations under the reimbursement agreement, the Company may be liable for more than its proportionate share, up to its maximum recourse exposure, which is the full amount covered by the joint and several guarantee.

In certain instances, the Company has placed performance letters of credit and surety bonds with municipalities for its joint ventures.

The total debt of the unconsolidated entities in which the Company has investments was as follows:

	November 30,	
	2008	2007
	(In thousands)	
The Company's net recourse exposure	392,450	794,934
Reimbursement agreements from partners	127,428	238,692
Partner several recourse	285,519	465,641
Non-recourse land seller debt or other debt	90,519	202,048
Non-recourse debt with completion guarantee	820,435	1,432,880
Non-recourse debt without completion guarantee	2,345,707	1,982,475
Total debt	4,062,058	5,116,670

cars using lean manufacturing methods, and to utilize an idle plant.[4] A third study noted that joint venture formations reached a peak in 1995, but have declined in popularity because executives have been concerned about three key issues: lack of control, lack of trust, and uncertainty about exiting from the arrangement.[5]

14 Evidence suggests that strategic alliances also create shareholder value. One study of strategic alliances formed during the period 1983-1992 found that there were significant positive announcement returns of 0.64% surrounding the announcement.[6] A study of alliances in the movie industry found that movie studios financed their least risky projects internally, and that cofinanced projects through alliances were relatively riskier and more likely to be

[4] See Andrew C. Inkpen, "Knowledge Transfer and International Joint Ventures: The Case of NUMMI and General Motors, *Strategic Management Journal*, 29: 447–453 (2008).

[5] Dieter Turowski, "The Decline and Fall of Joint Ventures: How JVs Became Unpopular and What That Could Change," *Journal of Applied Corporate Finance*, 17 (2): 82–86 (2005).

[6] Su Han Chan, John W. Kensinger, and Arthur J. Keown, "When Do Strategic Alliances Create Shareholder Value," *Journal of Applied Corporate Finance*, 11 (4): 82–87 (1999).

undertaken by studios that were more financially constrained.[7] The authors argued that the results were consistent with the notion that a studio might improve the incentive of managers of a riskier project by deploying the project outside the firm in an alliance in which the enforceable contract between the two parties guaranteed a "baseline level of financing."[8]

15 Another form of joint venture is a financial joint venture, also known as project financing. Under project financing, two or more equity partners combine their capital with funds provided by lenders to invest in a specific project. Finnerty (1996) defines project finance as: "The raising of funds to finance an economically separable capital investment project in which the providers of funds look primarily to the cash flows from the project as the source of funds to service their loans and provide a return of and a return on their equity invested in the project."[9] Some have suggested that the primary purpose of project financing is to enable equity partners to engage in off-balance sheet financing. For example, if each equity partner owned 50% of the total equity, accounting rules in many countries would enable the partners to avoid consolidating the financial statements of the joint venture, and thereby avoid reporting the joint venture debt on their own books, as permitted under the equity method of accounting. Brealey, Cooper, and Habib suggest that project financing enables equity partners to obtain debt financing on more favorable terms by reducing transaction costs incurred by lenders in assessing the creditworthiness of the specific project assets. If the equity partners borrowed debt funds directly, a lender would be required to assess the creditworthiness of the entire asset portfolio.[10]

COMPETITION

16 The residential homebuilding industry is a very competitive business. Participants compete vigorously for homebuyers in each of the major market regions. Efforts by lenders to sell foreclosed homes were an increasingly competitive factor in the deep recession in the U.S. that began in 2008. Lennar competed for homebuyers on the basis of location, price, reputation, amenities, design, quality, and financing. Lennar also competed with other homebuilders for desirable properties, raw materials, reliable and skilled labor, and with third parties in selling land to homebuilders and others. There were several large geographically diversified homebuilders in the U.S., including D.R. Horton, Inc., KB Home, and Pulte Homes, Inc., vying in the same markets as Lennar. See **Exhibits 7** and **8** for selected financial information about Lennar's competitors in the homebuilding industry.

17 ***D.R. Horton, Inc.*** was the largest homebuilding company in the United States, based on homes closed during the 12 months ended September 30, 2008. The company constructed and sold high-quality homes through its operating divisions in 27 states and 77 metropolitan markets of the United States, primarily under the name of D.R. Horton, America's Builder. The company's homes ranged in size from 1,000 to 5,000 square feet, and in price from $90,000 to $900,000. The downturn in the industry resulted in a decrease in the size of the company's operations during fiscal 2007 and 2008. For the year ended September 30, 2008, Horton closed 26,396 homes with an average closing sales price of approximately $233,500. Through the company's financial services operations, it provided mortgage financing and title agency services to homebuyers in many of its homebuilding markets. DHI Mortgage,

[7] Darius Palia, S. Abraham Ravid, and Natalia Riesel, "Choosing to Cofinance: Analysis of Project-Specific Alliances in the Movie Industry," *Review of Financial Studies,* 21 (2): 483–511 (2008).

[8] Ibid.

[9] John D. Finnerty, *Project Financing*, John Wiley & Sons: New York (1996).

[10] Richard A. Brealey, Ian A. Cooper, and Michel A. Habib, "Using Project Finance to Fund Infrastructure Investments," *Journal of Applied Corporate Finance*, Vol. 9 (3): 25–39 (1996).

EXHIBIT 7 Selected Financial Data for Peer Companies

	DR Horton			KB Home			Pulte Homes		
Selected Financial Items	**Sept 2008**	**Sept 2007**	**Sept 2006**	**Nov 2008**	**Nov 2007**	**Nov 2006**	**Dec 2008**	**Dec 2007**	**Dec 2006**
Cash and Equivalents	1,387.3	269.6	587.6	1,141.5	1,343.7	654.6	1,655.3	1,060.3	551.3
Inventories	5,035.3	9,867.0	12,366.0	2,106.7	3,312.4	6,455.0	4,835.1	7,748.0	10,755.1
Investments at Equity	0.0	0.0	0.0	222.4	320.2	423.0	134.9	105.5	150.7
Total Assets	7,709.6	11,556.3	14,820.7	4,044.3	5,706.0	9,014.5	7,708.5	10,225.7	13,176.9
Long Term Debt Due in One Year	577.4	243.4	26.1	279.5	1.9	98.4	29.2	4.1	19.8
Notes Payable	203.5	387.8	1,191.7	0.0	0.0	0.0	237.6	440.6	814.7
Long Term Debt	2,967.5	3,745.6	4,860.8	1,662.0	2,159.9	3,027.4	3,142.8	3,483.5	3,545.1
Stockholders' Equity	2,834.3	5,586.9	6,452.9	830.6	1,850.7	2,922.7	2,835.7	4,320.2	6,577.4
Common Shares Outstanding	316.7	314.9	313.2	77.7	77.3	77.0	258.2	257.1	255.3
Sales	6,646.1	11,296.5	15,051.3	3,033.9	6,416.5	11,003.8	6,263.1	9,256.5	14,269.8
Cost of Goods Sold	8,228.6	10,420.7	11,361.8	3,305.5	6,809.1	8,833.3	7,037.1	10,001.8	11,837.7
Gross Profit	(1,582.5)	875.8	3,689.5	(271.6)	(392.6)	2,170.5	(774.0)	(745.3)	2,432.1
Operating Profit	(2,527.6)	(483.9)	1,974.2	(786.4)	(1,239.3)	770.1	(1,596.6)	(1,890.0)	1,212.4
Adjusted Net Income	(2,633.6)	(712.5)	1,233.3	(976.1)	(929.4)	482.4	(1,473.1)	(2,255.8)	687.5
Operating Activities—Net Cash Flow	1,879.9	1,355.5	(1,190.8)	341.3	1,194.3	715.7	1,220.4	1,218.3	(267.5)
Investing Activities—Net Cash Flow	(6.6)	(39.8)	(83.3)	(168.0)	486.8	(201.4)	(55.9)	(221.4)	(86.9)
Financing Activities—Net Cash Flow	(755.6)	(1,633.7)	711.9	(375.6)	(1,141.5)	(13.7)	(567.7)	(487.6)	(96.2)

EXHIBIT 8 Selected Financial Ratios for Peer Companies

	DR Horton			KB Home			Pulte Homes		
Liquidity:	**Sept 2008**	**Sept 2007**	**Sept 2006**	**Nov 2008**	**Nov 2007**	**Nov 2006**	**Dec 2008**	**Dec 2007**	**Dec 2006**
Acid Test Ratio	1.9	0.2	0.4	1.9	2.3	1.1	2.3	1.1	0.4
Current ratio	6.7	8.3	5.8	4.5	6.9	6.5	7.7	8.9	7.7
Asset Management:									
Day's Receivable	0.0	0.0	0.0	17.8	17.0	22.0	6.8	0.0	0.0
Day's Inventory	223.4	345.6	397.3	232.6	177.6	266.7	250.8	282.8	331.6
Day's Payable	30.2	27.2	–	95.7	71.4	–	19.3	21.8	–
Asset Turnover	0.9	1.0	1.0	0.8	1.1	1.2	0.8	0.9	1.1
Financial Leverage:									
Long-term Debt to Total Assets	0.5	0.3	0.3	0.5	0.4	0.3	0.4	0.3	0.3
Long-term Debt to Stockholders' Equity	1.3	0.7	0.8	2.3	1.2	1.1	1.1	0.8	0.5
Interest Coverage Ratio	−10.5	−1.5	5.4	−5.4	−6.2	3.1	−7.0	−7.3	4.2
Profitability:									
Gross Profit Margin Ratio	−23.8%	7.8%	24.5%	−9.0%	−6.1%	19.7%	−12.4%	−8.1%	17.0%
Return on Sales (ROS)	−39.6%	−6.3%	8.2%	−32.2%	−14.5%	4.4%	−23.5%	−24.4%	4.8%
Return on Assets (ROA)	−34.2%	−6.2%	8.3%	−24.1%	−16.3%	5.4%	−19.1%	−22.1%	5.2%
Return on (ending) Equity (ROE)	−92.9%	−12.8%	19.1%	−117.5%	−50.2%	16.5%	−51.9%	−52.2%	10.5%
Dupont Analysis:									
Return on (ending) Equity (ROE)									
ROE =	−92.9%	−12.8%	19.1%	−117.5%	−50.2%	16.5%	−51.9%	−52.2%	10.5%
Return on sales	−39.6%	−6.3%	8.2%	−32.2%	−14.5%	4.4%	−23.5%	−24.4%	4.8%
* Asset turnover	0.9	1.0	1.0	0.8	1.1	1.2	0.8	0.9	1.1
* Leverage	2.7	2.1	2.3	4.9	3.1	3.1	2.7	2.4	2.0

the company's wholly owned subsidiary, provided mortgage financing services principally to purchasers of homes built by the company. Horton generally did not retain or service the mortgages it originated but, rather, sold the mortgages and related servicing rights to investors. A subsidiary title company served as title insurance agents by providing title insurance policies, examination, and closing services, primarily to the purchasers of its homes.

18 ***KB Home***, one of the nation's largest homebuilders, was a Fortune 500 company listed on the New York Stock Exchange under the ticker symbol "KBH." The company's four homebuilding segments offered a variety of homes designed primarily for first-time, first move-up, and active adult buyers, including attached and detached single-family homes, townhomes, and condominiums. KB offered homes in development communities, at urban in-fill locations, and as part of mixed-use projects. The company delivered 12,438 homes in 2008 and 23,743 homes in 2007. In 2008, the average selling price of $236,400 decreased from $261,600 in 2007.

19 ***Pulte Homes, Inc.*** was a publicly held holding company whose subsidiaries engaged in the homebuilding and financial services businesses. Homebuilding, the company's core business, was engaged in the acquisition and development of land primarily for residential purposes within the continental United States, and the construction of housing on such land targeted for first-time, first and second move-up, and active adult home buyers.

LENNAR'S FUTURE

20 Amphlett knew that understanding Lennar's business and charting the company's future would be a difficult task. In addition to financial statement information, she gathered capital markets data (see **Exhibit 9**). The recent two-week vacation seemed a long while ago, even though she had been back at work only three days. She wondered whether Lennar's management would become distracted by efforts to control the damage caused by the Fraud Discovery Institute claims, and exacerbate the company's problems caused by the financial crisis, mortgage defaults, and a dramatic fall in house prices across the country, and particularly in Arizona, Florida, and Nevada, markets where Lennar was active.

EXHIBIT 9 Selected Capital Markets Information

Lennar's equity beta (from *Value Line*, July 3, 2009)	1.95
Equity market risk premium (from Dimson, Marsh, and Staunton)	5–6% per year
Lennar's Class A common stock price per share (June 30, 2009)	$9.69
Lennar's Class B common stock price per share (June 30, 2009)	$7.60
Shares outstanding (November 30, 2008):	
Class A	129,251,272
Class B	31,284,003
Lennar's debt rating	B3
Yield to maturity on A-rated debt	6.2%
Yield to maturity on Baa-rated debt	7.30%
Yield to maturity on 10-year Treasury Bond (June 30, 2009)	3.64%
Value Line (July 3, 2009) estimated sales, net income (in thousands), and EPS in 2009	$3,325,000 –$350,000 –$2.10
Value Line (July 3, 2009) estimated sales, net income (in thousands), and EPS in 2010	$3,200,000 –$37,000 –$0.20

Case 14

Louis Vuitton in Japan[1]

Justin Paul
Charlotte Feroul

1 In Japan, whether you are in Tokyo, Osaka or Nagoya, just turn your head and Louis Vuitton is everywhere. The celebration of the 30th anniversary of the presence of the illustrious, glittering French multinational in Japan took place in Aoyama, one of Tokyo's fashionable districts. A unique vision of luxury took shape when Louis Vuitton opened yet another new store inside Comme des Garçons on September 4, 2008, in the heart of Japan's capital. The pop-up store situated on the prestigious Omotesando Street was an illustration of Louis Vuitton's attachment to the Japanese luxury market.

2 Yves Carcelle, chairman and CEO of Louis Vuitton, said, "This project not only brings a new meaning to luxury, but also speaks volumes about how the know-how and heritage of Louis Vuitton have always been perceived in Japan, including by its foremost designers. We are very proud to have been able to help Rei Kawakubo[2] relive her memories in such an original and creative way."[3] The Omotesando guerrilla marketing event reflected Louis Vuitton's success in Japan. Louis Vuitton had been following an aggressive marketing strategy in the country, opening extravagant stores such as those in Ginza or Roppongi. Take a walk on Ginza's main street, Chuo Dori, the centre of a paradise for shoppers, with long-established department stores, such as Mitsukoshi, Takashimaya and Matsuzakaya. Continue through the high-end fashion street Namiki-dori. Stop. There it is. You have reached the massive flagship Louis Vuitton store.

3 When Louis Vuitton, the world's biggest luxury-goods firm, inaugurated its huge shop in 2002 in the district of Omotesando, Tokyo, hundreds of people were queued outside. During the first few days, sales exceeded the initial estimations by ¥1 million.[4] In the last decade, Japan had been Louis Vuitton's most profitable market, representing almost half of its profits, but it seemed that with the 2008–2009 economic crisis, there might be the start of a decline in sales.

[1] This case has been written on the basis of published sources only. Consequently, the interpretation and perspectives presented in this case are not necessarily those of Louis Vuitton or any of its employees.

[2] Rei Kawakubo was a famous Japanese fashion designer. She founded the fashion house Comme des Garçons Co. Ltd in 1973. The designer, known for her anti-fashion, austere and conceptual universe, was the guest designer of Louis Vuitton for one of its collections in 2008.

[3] Lesley Scott, "Louis Vuitton at Comme des Garcons in Tokyo," http://fashiontribes.typepad.com. Accessed July 11, 2008.

[4] "Japan's luxury-goods market—Losing its shine," *The Economist,* September 18, 2008, www.economist.com. US$1 was equivalent to approximately ¥150 (yen) in 2002.

4 Facing a weak economy and a shift in consumer preferences, Louis Vuitton started adapting its strategy in the Japanese market. The days of charging a high price for products with a proprietary logo seemed to be gone in Japan. The company had to launch relatively low-priced collections to boost sales. The firm had also been taking steps to open stores in other mid-size cities where the LV brand was not well known.

5 Louis Vuitton might be French, but Japan had become the land of Louis Vuitton lovers. Over the years, Japanese consumers had demonstrated fascination and passion for the iconic brand. What would be the key to Louis Vuitton's continuing success in the Japanese market?

LOUIS VUITTON —THE HISTORY

The Foundation

6 Louis Vuitton Malletier, often referred to as Louis Vuitton, was an international, well-established brand mostly famous for its craftwork leather bags and trunks. The firm was established in France in 1854 by Louis Vuitton and became known as one of the oldest French luxury fashion houses.

7 Louis Vuitton, the company's founder, was born in 1821 in Anchay, Jura, France. He became a Layetier in Paris and earned a reputation while working for the Empress Eugénie de Montijo, wife of Napoleon III. Learning from his work for the French aristocracy, he acquired personal "savoir-faire"[5] about leather luggage. In 1854, he founded the firm, "Louis Vuitton: Malletier à Paris."[6] The flat-bottom trunks of Louis Vuitton with trianon canvases represented a real revolution for travelling in those days as they combined lightness and storage capacity. In 1885, the firm opened its first overseas store in London, England, on Oxford Street. In 1888, Louis Vuitton developed the Canvas Damier Pattern in order to make the Louis Vuitton experience unique and recognizable by anybody. The logo "marque Louis Vuitton deposée," meaning "mark Louis Vuitton deposited," was also created.

8 Following the death of Louis Vuitton in 1892, his son, Georges Vuitton, took over the leadership of the firm. He was ambitious about taking Louis Vuitton to the next step—building a global brand and setting up a multinational corporation.[7] He participated in the Chicago World Fair in 1893, presenting the company's product, and travelled all around the United States to promote the brand. In 1896, Georges Vuitton created the Monogram Canvas and attained worldwide trademarks on it to limit counterfeiting. The LV monogram was inspired by the Japanese and Oriental designs of the Victorian age. By 1914, the company opened the Louis Vuitton Building of the Champs-Elysées, now a symbol of the success and prestige of the company. Though World War I had begun, the firm initiated its global expansion strategy by opening stores in New York, Bombay, Washington, London, Alexandria and Buenos Aires. In 1936, Gaston-Louis Vuitton took over the direction of the company when his father, Georges Vuitton, passed away.

The Modern Age of Louis Vuitton

9 Gaston-Louis Vuitton guided the brand into its modern age. The company expanded its product line by applying the craftwork and design of its leather to small leather goods, such as purses and wallets, and to its whole luggage line. As a consequence, the Monogram Canvas was redesigned in 1959 to fit the new range of products. The brand started its first advertising strategy by handing bags to Hollywood celebrity actresses. Audrey Hepburn carried a Louis Vuitton bag in 1963 in the film *Charade,* directed by Stanley Donan.

[5] "Know-how."

[6] "Louis Vuitton: Luggage maker in Paris."

[7] Official Louis Vuitton MySpace, www.myspace.com/louisvuittonmyspace, accessed June 25, 2010.

10 In the mid 1970s, Louis Vuitton had become the world's biggest luxury brand in terms of market share. The Vuitton-Racamier family,[8] owner of the brand, had focused mainly on building a Japanese clientele. By 1977, the company owned two stores in Japan with annual profits of US$10 million. It further tapped into the Asian market in 1983, in Taipei, Taiwan and, in 1984, in Seoul, South Korea. The creation of Louis Vuitton Moët-Hennessy (LVMH) in 1987 established the largest luxury-goods conglomerate in the world. Moët et Chandon and Hennessy were the leading manufacturers of champagne and brandy. The merger resulted in an increase in profits for Louis Vuitton of 49 per cent in 1988 compared to 1987. By 1989, Louis Vuitton had entered into 130 countries across the world.[9]

11 In 1990, Yves Carcelles was nominated for president of Louis Vuitton. He carried on with an international expansion strategy, inaugurating the first Chinese store in the Palace Hotel in Beijing. The Monogram Canvas centennial was celebrated in 1996. Seven cities across the world held extravagant parties at stores and Louis Vuitton asked seven prestigious designers to imagine new products featuring the LV monogram. Azzedine Alaia, Manolo Blahnik, Romeo Gigli, Helmut Lang, Isaac Mizrahi, Syvilla and Vivienne Westwood created seven original and functional objects in a limited edition series.[10]

Louis Vuitton in the 21st Century

12 In 1998, the American designer Marc Jacobs was appointed as Louis Vuitton's art director. Jacobs was already a highly successful international designer, who became distinguished as the youngest fashion designer ever to be awarded the industry's highest tribute, the Council of Fashion Designers of America (CFDA) award for New Fashion Talent. The challenge was huge, as Jacobs had to guide Vuitton's first shoes and ready-to-wear collections. With this nomination, Louis Vuitton aimed at establishing the brand as a consistent trendsetter in high fashion.

13 Since the late 1990s, creating limited-edition collections had become Louis Vuitton's marketing strategy to capture consumers' attention and reinvigorate the brand's identity while boosting the bottom line. In 2001, Stephen Sprouse and Jacobs collaborated to design a limited edition series of Louis Vuitton bags. Sprouse was already a highly popular artist, as he had collaborated with the extravagant Andy Warhol and with contemporary artists and musicians such as Debbie Harry and Duran Duran. In line with what *The New York Times* called Sprouse's mix of "uptown sophistication in clothing with a downtown punk and pop sensibility," the collaboration with Jacobs resulted in a limited edition that featured green and white graffiti written over the monogram pattern. All bags were made for Louis Vuitton's VIP list and were meant to be collector's items. In 2001, following the success of the Louis Vuitton limited edition, Jacobs designed Louis Vuitton's first jewelry piece. In 2002, the Tambour watch collection was introduced.

14 Pursuing its globalization strategy in the 21st century, Louis Vuitton opened one of its most famous stores on Fifth Avenue in New York City, then opened more stores in Sao Paulo, Brazil, Johannesburg, South Africa, and Shanghai, China. The brand reopened its store on the Champs-Elysées, which became the largest Louis Vuitton store in the world. Louis Vuitton celebrated world wide its 150th anniversary in 2004. It had taken more than a century starting with a family house to build a timeless image of class, luxury and elegance.

[8] Henri Racamier married a descendant of Louis Vuitton. He was asked at the age of 65 by the family of his wife, Odile Vuitton, the great-granddaughter of Louis Vuitton, to run the family's leather goods business.

[9] Official Louis Vuitton MySpace, www.myspace.com/louisvuittonmyspace, accessed June 25, 2010.

[10] Diana Prince, "Louis Vuitton: The history behind the purse," www.associatedcontent.com, accessed July 26, 2008.

EXHIBIT 6 **The Leading Luxury Brands in the World in 2008**

Rank	Brand	2008 Brand Value in USD (m.)	2008 Brand Value in Euros (m.)	Country of Origin
1	Louis Vuitton	21,602	16,718	France
2	Gucci	8,254	6,388	Italy
3	Chanel	6,355	4,918	France
4	Rolex	4,956	3,836	Switzerland
5	Hermès	4,575	3,541	France
6	Cartier	4,236	3,278	France
7	Tiffany & Co.	4,208	3,257	United States
8	Prada	3,585	2,775	Italy
9	Ferrari	3,527	2,730	Italy
10	Bulgari	3,330	2,577	Italy
11	Burberry	3,285	2,542	United Kingdom
12	Dior	2,038	1,578	France
13	Patek Philippe	1,105	855	Switzerland
14	Zegna	818	633	Italy
15	Ferragamo	722	559	Italy

Source: "2008 Leading Luxury Brands," Interbrand, 2008, www.interbrand.com, accessed July 5, 2008.

earnings in 2003 due to a record operating margin at 45 per cent. The standard average margin in the luxury accessories business was 25 per cent.[12]

Efficient Management Practices

18 Through the years, Louis Vuitton had established a strictly controlled distribution network thanks to an efficient structuring of the company that relied on continuously increasing productivity in design and manufacturing. Louis Vuitton owed much to its executives. Emmanuel Mathieu, who had headed Louis Vuitton's industrial operations since 2000, had contributed to the boost in manufacturing productivity by five per cent a year, with more productivity, efficiency and teamwork. In 1999, the firm took 12 months to launch a new product; in 2004, the time was reduced to about six months. This continuous improvement had been the theme of Louis Vuitton's industrial operations and was facilitated by manufacturing methods from auto makers and other industries that had been adopted to boost productivity.

19 Managers such as Emmanuel Mathieu had helped transform the brand from a family business to a 21st-century business.[13] The manufacturing of Louis Vuitton products was still a labour-intensive process. Each team of 24 workers was responsible for producing about 120 handbags a day. Over a period of time, the brand seemed to have achieved perfect equilibrium between machines and labour.

[12] Carol Matlack, "The Vuitton Money Machine," *Business Week,* www.businessweek.com, accessed March 22, 2004.

[13] Ibid.

Quality Products

20 Louis Vuitton focused on constant improvement of quality and offered lifetime repair guarantees for its customers. The brand had been striving to increase both fidelity and endless desire in its consumers. Louis Vuitton based its strategy on the loyalty of its consumers and strove to attract more consumers to buy bags ranging from classic tan-and-brown monogrammed bags to newer lines, such as the Murakami line, which was priced at $1,000, and Suhali, a line of goatskin bags priced at more than $2,000. As they bought Louis Vuitton items, loyal shoppers stepped into the dream of the brand. The more the prices were raised, the more they would come back.

21 When Jacobs joined Louis Vuitton, the New York designer had a challenge—attracting young buyers. However, Jacobs happened to be the perfect match as the two product lines that he had launched (ready-to-wear and shoe lines) tapped into a market of younger consumers, even if those lines accounted for less than 15 per cent of the brand's sales. The younger buyers were attracted by brand image and older clients by quality and lifetime free repairs.

Production and Quality Control

22 The efficiency of the manufacturing facilities and employees helped Louis Vuitton compensate for its decision to keep most manufacturing plants in France, one of the most expensive labour markets in the world. Eleven out of 13 factories that made Louis Vuitton bags were in France. The brand had never planned to manufacture its products in a location where labour was less expensive as the quality control standards in France were very high and customers expected "un savoir-faire à la Française," meaning the famous refined French know-how.

23 Quality control was conducted in the brand's test laboratories. The leather raw material came from the hides of Northern European cattle. They were known for relatively few blemishes from insect bites. Despite high-quality leather, the quality of the bags was tested with mechanical arm hoists. The bags, loaded with weights, were lifted and dropped, again and again, as part of quality checking. Then, ultraviolet rays were projected on the handbags in order to determine their resistance to fading. Eventually, zippers were opened and shut 5,000 times. For other pieces, such as jewelry and bracelets, mechanized mannequin hands were strongly shaken to make sure none of the charms would fall off.

24 In all Louis Vuitton factories, employees worked in teams of 20 to 30. Each team was responsible for one product at a time and were encouraged to suggest improvements in manufacturing. They were also briefed about the products, such as their price and how they were selling. The aim was to have autonomous and multi-skilled employees.

25 The Boulogne Multicolor shoulder bag provided and example of how the whole production process worked. With the success of the Murakami line in 2003,[14] the marketing executives thought that this line could be a source of further revenue. They questioned store managers and found out that customers wanted a Murakami shoulder bag. A prototype of this new Boulogne Multicolor bag went directly from the marketing department to top executives. Straight away, they approved it. The prototype went to the factory in Ducey on the Normandy coast of France. The teamwork efficiency of Louis Vuitton's factory paid off. When some workers were asked to test it, they discovered that decorative studs were causing the zipper to bunch up. Following this discovery, managers were informed right away and technicians managed to place the studs a few millimetres away from the zipper in less than one or two days. The problem was solved.[15]

[14] In 2003, Takashi Murakami, in collaboration with Marc Jacobs, created the Monogram Multicolor canvas range of handbags and accessories. First designed for the Japanese market, the line was a worldwide success.

[15] Carol Matlack, "The Vuitton Money Machine," *Business Week*, www.businessweek.com, accessed March 22, 2004.

Advertising

26 As Louis Vuitton had been going global, it had been able to develop a successful advertising strategy in line with its global expansion strategy. The advertising strategy of the company remained based on the idea that productivity would not sustain growth. Rather than cutting its ad budget like most luxury groups, the company increased ad spending by 20 per cent in 2003. This figure might have seemed very high but in fact it only represented five per cent of revenues, half the industry average.[16]

27 The company meticulously cultivated a celebrity culture and employed famous models and actresses, such as Jennifer Lopez and more recently Madonna, in its advertisement campaigns. However, in 2007 the firm implemented a change in its strategy and announced that former Soviet leader Mikhail Gorbachev would feature in an advertisement campaign with sports stars Steffi Graf, Andre Agassi and Catherine Deneuve.[17] The firm wanted a shift from hiring traditional top models.

28 Louis Vuitton frequently used print ads in magazines and billboards in large cosmopolitan cities. The campaigns often involved famous stars like Gisele Bündchen, Eva Herzigova, Sean Connery and Francis and Sofia Ford Coppola. Lot of customers were attracted to the mind-boggling 90-second commercial advertisement on television with the catchy question, "Where will life take you?" Translated into 13 different languages, it helped LV to build brand. The media (communication) department was strategic in choosing the newspapers and magazines to reach out to the higher income group.

Future Challenges

29 The most serious issue that would remain for years to come was the question of whether Louis Vuitton had reached its growth potential or not. One of its challenges would consist in reducing its risky dependence on the Japanese market. In 2004, 55 per cent of revenues came from Japanese consumers. To reduce dependence on this market, the brand aspired to continue building its sales in the United States as well as tapping new emerging markets, mainly China and India.

30 The second challenge would be to fight against worldwide counterfeiting. This was important because Louis Vuitton had been itself synonymous with status, convincing customers that they belonged to a privileged club.

31 In the future, Louis Vuitton would have to face a shift that all fashion houses feared, the possible departure of Jacobs. Yet, Jacobs had signed a contract as Louis Vuitton's artistic director until 2018 and Marc Jacobs's label[18] was one of the rising stars in LVMH's portfolio.

32 However, the biggest challenge was in keeping control of the multinational business. As brands went global, the temptation for many was to immediately find new outlets and new channels of distribution and to decide on the price in different countries. However, Louis Vuitton was highly disciplined and focused on quality.

JAPAN —A KEY MARKET

Overview of the Japanese Luxury Market

33 Over the past few years, Japan had become the capital of luxury and a mass market paradise for luxury brands. According to an estimate by HSBC in February 2009, it was the final destination of 45 per cent of luxury goods sold worldwide.[19] According to some luxury

[16] Carol Matlack, "The Vuitton Money Machine," *Business Week*, www.businessweek.com, accessed March 22, 2004.

[17] Official Louis Vuitton MySpace, www.myspace.com/louisvuittonmyspace, accessed June 25, 2010.

[18] Marc Jacob created his own label, Marc Jacobs Co. Ltd, in 1994. The company was part of LVMH.

[19] Glenn Smith, "Luxury sector loses its recession-proof status," Media, February 12, 2009, p. 19.

EXHIBIT 7 **Top Multinational Luxury Fashion Brands—Percentage of Overall Revenue from Japan in Total World Wide Sales (2005)**

Baccarat	35%
Bulgari	26%
Burberry	36%
Coach	22%
Hermes	25%
Gucci Group	27%
LVMH Group	15%
Louis Vuitton (Fashion & Leather Goods)	30%
Salvatore Ferragamo	27%
Tiffany & Co.	20%
Van Cleef and Arpels	33%

Source: "Japan is the world's most concentrated source of revenue for luxury brands," Japan External Trade Organization, May 2006, www.jetro.org/content/361 15, accessed February 18, 2008.

analysts, the statistics were exaggerated. Indeed, Japan was considered the world's largest market for luxury brands but statistics said that Japan represented between 12 and 40 per cent of worldwide sales. The rate would vary according to the definition of the market.

34 Claudia D'Arpizio upheld that, "Japan is the world's largest market, and has the highest per capita spending for luxury goods." She added, "Much of that volume is from Japanese purchases while on trips to Hawaii, the US or Asia."[20]

Competition

35 Japan was the world's most concentrated source of revenue for luxury brands. It represented the mass market and consequently the first source of profit for many international luxury brands. Exhibit 7 shows the percentages of several companies' overall revenues generated in Japan.

36 The CEO of Bulgari, Francesco Trapani, revealed, "Accounting for 26 per cent of total revenues, Japan is for Bulgari the first and most important market." In 2006, Japan represented the biggest market for other luxury brands such as Baccarat, Burberry, the Gucci Group, Louis Vuitton and Salvatore Ferragamo. In addition, Japan was the second biggest market for Coach and Tiffany & Co.[21]

37 Comparing Japan's geography to the U.S. geography, the former was equivalent in size to the region of Montana. Within its tiny territory, Japan was sprinkled with 34 Bulgari stores, 37 Chanel stores, 115 Coach stores, 49 Gucci stores, 64 Salvatore Ferragamo boutiques, 50 Tiffany & Co. boutiques and 252 stores of the LVMH group, including leading brands

[20] Ibid.

[21] "Japan is the world's most concentrated source of revenue for luxury brands," Japan External Trade Organization, www.jetro.org, accessed May 8, 2006.

The Entry into the Japanese Market

49 Louis Vuitton was the first multinational luxury house to open its own shop-in-shops in Japan, without the help of a Japanese distributor. This strategy had become an efficient economic and commercial business model in the luxury market. In the 1970s and 1980s, foreign firms had manufactured and distributed their products by licensing. When Louis Vuitton decided to opt for a controversial strategy and to establish its own subsidiary, the company turned out to be a pioneer. It decided to export products from France to Japan.

50 Kyojiro Hata had been the CEO of Louis Vuitton Japan for 28 years. Louis Vuitton's headquarters' management style meant strict control of the selective retail store network across the globe. Each subsidiary was, to a certain extent, extremely autonomous. The French headquarters had been relying on the Japanese business savoir-faire, believing Japanese managers to be more likely to make efficient market-driven decisions as they understood the local people.

51 Louis Vuitton entered into the Japanese market at first through department stores with a single brand of its portfolio. The company offered its Japanese partners, like Seibu or Mitsukoshi, an interior design comparable to that found in its flagship stores in Paris. The purpose remained making a French luxury purchasing experience and controlling entirely the shop-in-shops (prices, products, sales teams, etc.).

52 A few years later, in 1981, Louis Vuitton opened its first retail store in Namiki Dori, Ginza, in Tokyo. The company followed its expansion strategy and, by 2007, controlled 54 stores through a directly owned shop network in Japan.[30] LVMH as a group had more than 250 stores in Japan. Some of them were stores opened as franchisees during the last decade. New generations of shops opened in Nagoya, Osaka, Sapporo, Tokyo and elsewhere, revolutionizing the whole purchasing experience of luxury goods. The architecture of the stores had become part of the brand's identity. A perfect illustration of this was the architecture of the Louis Vuitton building in Omotesando, Tokyo, built by Jun Aoki, which looked as if several trunks were piled up. Louis Vuitton had shifted towards a new approach in which the experience in a store would accord with the emotion brought out by the products.

53 Louis Vuitton took advantage of the Japanese demand for high fashion. Japan had been and remained a source of creative ideas and trends. In a sense, Japan represented a fantastic laboratory to test new selling methods and to inaugurate innovative Louis Vuitton stores. Contrary to Europe, there were few rules and standards to follow in terms of urbanization and architecture. This enabled Louis Vuitton to design audacious and amazing stores like the ones in Ginza, Ometesando and Roppongi in Tokyo, or even one of the latest stores inaugurated in February 2007 in Nagoya's Midland Square, just below the Toyota headquarters. The Japanese clientele were receptive to Louis Vuitton, as they were truly avid for new products and very demanding of the quality of products they bought.

Strategic Approach

54 Louis Vuitton had always been a trend-setting brand strategist in Japan, a country that revolved around tradition and culture. Since the designation of Jacobs as the artistic director of the brand, Louis Vuitton had successfully entered the Japanese ready-to-wear market. Jacobs had strived to combine his own artistic universe with the tradition and heritage of the brand. The designer had created a new energy and enthusiasm for each ready-to-wear runway collection, mixing tradition and innovation.

[30] Ibid.

55 Since 1995, the worldwide luxury market had been growing by 10 per cent each year.[31] In 2002, the global economy faced a slowdown due to the recession caused by the September 11, 2001 terrorist attacks in the United States. The direct consequence was a decrease in sales, such as luxury shopping in duty free zones in international airports and prestigious luxury destinations like Tokyo's Ginza Namiki Dori, the Place Vendôme in Paris and Madison Avenue in New York. The September 11th attacks had caused a major decline in tourist flows and in the luxury market. In Europe, foreign tourists accounted for 60 per cent of customers of luxury items.[32] Louis Vuitton in Japan had to redefine its strategy because the sluggishness in the United States had an adverse impact on the purchasing power of the Japanese consumers as Japan was relying on export income from the United States. At that time, Louis Vuitton realized that it had to focus on local consumers rather than tourists. Luxury started to go local.[33]

56 Louis Vuitton reacted early to proceed with this major shift in strategy. The brand realized that for the past years it had been setting the trend as a brand leader but that the guarantee of future growth would depend on adapting to and understanding local customers. To do so, the company tried to adjust its approach and products to reach local customers. A revelation came from the Japanese market.

Limited Editions: A New Marketing Strategy

57 After Jacobs had seen an exhibition at the Fondation Cartier pour l'art contemporain in Paris by Takashi Murakami, Louis Vuitton decided to collaborate with the Japanese artist for its 2003 spring/summer collection. Takashi Murakami, who was known as the "Japanese Andy Warhol," re-created a colourful pop version of Louis Vuitton's monogram in 33 colours on a black and white background. In stores, Louis Vuitton's handbags with smiling blossom designs became huge sellers in Japan. The strategy appeared to be a huge success for the leading luxury conglomerate LVMH, as the Murakami line increased Louis Vuitton's profits by 10 per cent.[34] The success was not only in the Japanese market but also in the European and American markets, which showed true admiration for Japanese culture.

58 Following the massive success of the line, in 2003 and 2005 collaborations between Murakami and Jacobs resulted in the Monogram Cherry Blossom line, featuring a trendy motif inspired by the fruit of the cherry blossom—Japanese art wedded to Louis Vuitton's perfection—and the Monogram Cerise line, with a new pattern that gave freshness and cheerfulness to the monogram.

59 While announcing the exclusive Louis Vuitton store at the Murakami Exhibition in the Brooklyn Museum in April 2008, Jacobs had commented on their collaboration. "Our collaboration has produced a lot of work, and has been a huge influence and inspiration to many. It has been and continues to be a monumental marriage of art and commerce. The ultimate cross-over, one for both the fashion and art history books."[35] He had it spot on—it was indeed "commerce" and strategy, as Takashi Murakami had been the starting point of Louis Vuitton's success in Japan.

[31] Claudia D'Arpizio, "Luxury goes local," *The Wall Street Journal Europe,* www.bain.com/bainweb/home.asp, accessed May 1, 2004.

[32] Ibid.

[33] Ibid.

[34] Ibid.

[35] Sally Williams and Mona Sharf, "The Brooklyn Museum announces the inclusion of an exclusive Louis Vuitton store within the retrospective of Japanese artist Takashi Murakami," www.brooklynmuseum.org, accessed March 21, 2008.

The Limits of Limited Editions

60 For the past years, Louis Vuitton had boosted its sales with continuous limited editions in the Japanese market. Once again, in June 2008, Louis Vuitton had launched a major new accessory line called Monogram Ouflage, which combined the iconic brand's monogram canvas with a new camouflage print designed by Takashi Murakami and Jacobs. It was unveiled at the pop-up Louis Vuitton shop opened at the Brooklyn Museum of Art. However, limited editions were under threat. The company had used them to market several lines of bags. In the end, the flood of mass-market interest would end up robbing the brand of some of its cachet and overdoing the profitable "limited edition" strategy would confuse consumers as they would no longer be able to differentiate between a real limited edition and a marketing ploy. Democratized luxury for all was good, but with precautions.

Market Dilution: A Luxury Brand is Dead, a Fashion Brand is Born

61 How did the brand that had been synonymous with luxury and exclusivity grow while retaining its cachet? Though Louis Vuitton had been an enduring status symbol in Japan, it had to face a major challenge: brand dilution as it moved into offering new product lines. As a leader of the sector, the challenge was to continue growing in the Japanese market and still preserve the exclusivity and great quality the brand had always offered.

62 There were two stages in luxury culture—the "show off" stage and the "fit in" stage—and Japan had already passed the two stages. The "fit in" stage was represented by Louis Vuitton. As an example, more than three-quarters of women in Tokyo of about twenty years of age possessed an item of the brand. This phenomenon was considered normal as luxury goods symbolized membership of the "acceptable" group of society. Accordingly, mass expansion and mass distribution had become a real issue.

63 In 2007, in the sulphurous book "Deluxe: How Luxury Lost Its Luster," journalist Dana Thomas reported that 40 per cent of all Japanese owned a Louis Vuitton-monogrammed item. She compared Louis Vuitton's expansive growth over the past decade to that of McDonald's, suggesting that the "LV" logo had become almost as ubiquitous as the Golden Arches.[36] These declarations damaged Louis Vuitton's image. In addition, constant questioning over the origins of Louis Vuitton's products and the repetition of limited editions over the past years had marked a new era for Louis Vuitton—an era characterized by disposable "it" bags with shelf lives of two fashion seasons at most. This climate seemed to be contrary to what was the essence of Louis Vuitton: tradition and longevity.

Counterfeiting

64 The LV branded bags were priced high in Japan (see Exhibit 8) as in other countries. Therefore, the firm had to face challenges from fake bags. Louis Vuitton had been trying to battle against issues such as the falsification of the logo and market dilution. Since the end of the 1990s and the Asian Financial Crisis, there had been a flood of fake Louis Vuitton products coming from Seoul, Hong Kong, Tokyo and Los Angeles. Though China was the largest producer of Louis Vuitton counterfeited bags, South Korea was the largest producer in terms of high-quality bags. Most South Korean Louis Vuitton counterfeits were exported to Japan.

65 Louis Vuitton had been fighting this issue and remained optimistic. In 2001, at an International Herald Tribune conference in Paris, Christophe Girard, director of fashion strategy at LVMH, declared that when the economy is bad, consumers still wish to turn

[36] Dana Thomas, *Deluxe: How Luxury Lost Its Luster,* The Penguin Press, 2007.

EXHIBIT 8 **Louis Vuitton Bestselling Handbags in Japan**

Keepall 55	Speedy 35	The Alma Normande
The world's most famous travel bag that dates back to the 1930s. Price: $1,270.00	The LV Speedy is one of the most classic and easily recognizable LV bags. Price: $725.00	Inspired by a shape invented by Gaston Vuitton in the 1930s, Alma is now a classic. Price: $1,290.00
Keepall 55 Roses	**Multicolore Speedy**	**Multicolore Tote**
Artist: Stephen Sprouse Year of Release: 2001 Price: $2,000.00	Artist: Takashi Murakami Year of Release: 2003 Price: $2,240.00	Artist: Takashi Murakami Year of Release: 2008 Price $1,200.00

Source: Nagoya franchisee of Louis Vuitton. Price has been converted at an exchange rate of ¥100 = US$1.

to luxury products as their value is reliable and long-lasting. He added that "the quest for pleasure" did not fade away and "it even happens in war. People want to enjoy themselves."[37] This statement appeared to be accurate in Japan, which had been suffering from the Asian Financial Crisis and facing 10 years of economic slowdown, but in which women still had a "cult" for luxury brands. In 2000, Louis Vuitton sales in Japan had increased by 16 per cent, reaching ¥100 billion for the first time in the company's history.[38]

66 However, Japanese consumers had been eager to buy Louis Vuitton bags at inexpensive prices. According to Hidehiko Sekizawa, the executive director of the Hakuhodo Institute of Life and Living in Tokyo, "Japanese shoppers have always been very fussy about quality. Now that the counterfeits are hard to distinguish from authentic products, they no longer mind buying fakes, even though they probably own a couple of authentic bags. They save the genuine articles for formal events like weddings and parties, and dinners and dates, and use counterfeits on rainy days, or to go to the supermarket for milk."[39]

67 The Japanese laws regarding intellectual property had been modified in 1985 and had become similar to Western laws. These rules did not really diminish counterfeiting, which remained a gigantic issue in the following years.

68 In 2008, a scandal went public. It was alleged that more than 90 per cent of the Louis Vuitton branded products sold on the Japanese "Super Girls Auction" website (Girl-Oku) were counterfeit.[40] The website, which targeted mobile phone users, was an auction site of Media Matrix Inc, a member company of the XAVEL group. Louis Vuitton reacted through the Union des Fabricants Tokyo (UDFT). A federal inspection was led in order to prove that the auction site had indeed broken the law. Following the investigation, there was a noticeable decline in sales due to Girl-Oku's countermeasures, but the issue remained unsolved.

Louis Vuitton's Further Growth in Japan—Change in Management

69 Even though there were doubts about future opportunities for Louis Vuitton in Japan, Kiyotaka Fujii, the new chief executive officer (CEO) of Louis Vuitton Japan, announced

[37] Velisarios Kattoulas, "Counterfeiting bags of trouble," *Far Eastern Economic Review,* March 21, 2002.

[38] Ibid.

[39] Ibid.

[40] Kenji Toda, "Mobile-phone auction sites flooded with fake brand products," *Nikkei Business,* August 20, 2008.

that this was not the case in December 2006. The designation of Fujii as the new CEO appeared to be the first change in the Japanese management team of the firm.[41]

70 Fujii, a 49-year-old businessman, had previous work experience in consulting and information technology. He had served as the director and an executive committee member of Quintiles Transnational Japan K.K., a leading pharmaceutical services organization providing professional services and information and partnering solutions to the pharmaceutical, biotechnology and healthcare industries. He had also worked at McKinsey & Co. at the New York headquarters. He had graduated from Tokyo University and had obtained an MBA from the Harvard Business School.

71 His vision was to steer the Japanese subsidiary of Louis Vuitton to the next level, relying on the company's long-term vision and high-quality business. When Yves Carcelles had revealed the appointment of the new CEO, he had pointed out that the person who was chosen as CEO had had to necessarily be Japanese with a clear vision of Japanese culture. Fujii's term of office was an absolute success. Among his remarkable acts, the creative collaboration with the Japanese architect Jun Aoki and the artist Takashi Murakami had resulted in smash hits, boosting Louis Vuitton's sales in the market. He had also introduced Kabuki, or Japanese dance-drama, in Paris. Through the years, one of the strengths of the firm's global strategy had been to take the best practices from certain cultures and implement them in selected markets. To continue to do so, Fujii would have to face the challenge of exporting the originality of Japanese artists and best practices internationally.

Next Steps for Further Growth

72 After his designation as CEO of Louis Vuitton in Japan, Fujii announced that the priorities for the brand would be establishing an Internet business and expanding the range of Louis Vuitton's products for children. Sales of smaller leather goods and other products, such as jewelry and eyewear, had outstripped initial sales objectives. Fujii said that, "Ready-to-wear is another category to grow, and this communicates the message from Louis Vuitton to consumers and increases the brand value of Louis Vuitton. Business on the web is another possible approach to consumers."[42]

73 The marketing strategy had been one of the key points of Louis Vuitton's success in Japan. The brand was now expanding its strategy towards mid-size and smaller cities. By 2006, Louis Vuitton already had 52 stores and 40 shops-in-shops and was reconsidering its strategy in terms of adapting to Japanese demographic changes and rethinking the range of products offered.

74 Despite changes in Japanese society, Louis Vuitton was still confident about its future. In 2006, an analyst from Mitsubishi UFJ Securities' research division assessed that, "The Japanese market is not considered saturated yet; the strength of Louis Vuitton is its high recognition among people of wide generations, so opening more shops in middle-size cities makes sense. That's the integrated power of the brand that includes product development and image management."[43] Louis Vuitton's power was not about to fade away.

CONCLUSION

75 The after-shocks of the global recession were a threat to Louis Vuitton's luxury business in Japan since its products were priced very high. There were signs that young Japanese women did not have the same vision as the previous generation. They were no longer eager

[41] Koji Hirano, "Vuitton Sees Further Growth in Japan," *Women's Wear Daily,* December 6, 2006.

[42] Koji Hirano, "Vuitton Sees Further Growth in Japan," *Women's Wear Daily,* December 6, 2006.

[43] Ibid.

to buy Louis Vuitton products. This represented a real change in the Japanese mindset and Louis Vuitton was already suffering the consequences.

76 Japan had always been the luxury mass market symbol of Louis Vuitton's golden age. Over the years, Louis Vuitton had been building its global strategy thanks to the experiences and lessons learned from Japan. In a gloomy economic context, the market was tending towards saturation, sales were declining, and competition was fiercer than ever. How could Louis Vuitton reinvent itself and regain what used to be its well-attested fame in Japan?

Case 15

Milagrol Ltda.

Marc Lipson

1 In June of 2010, Peterson Valve Company was in the final stages of making an offer to purchase Milagrol Ltda., a Brazilian manufacturer of faucets, showers, and other bathroom fittings including a line of high-quality automated fixtures designed to conserve water. Discussions of a merger had proceeded smoothly. Both companies believed there were advantages to combining efforts. Milagrol needed capital to support research and development efforts. Peterson was interested in diversifying its operations globally and in gaining access to manufacturing processes that would be costly to develop.

2 The remaining substantive challenge Peterson faced was determining a reasonable initial offer. Peterson's management was not looking for a bargain price and would be satisfied with capturing only the value created from the synergies arising from information transfer. Peterson therefore wished to offer Milagrol a price consistent with the expected value of the company given its operations in Brazil and exports to neighboring countries. At the time, Milagrol had a 20% share of the Brazilian market. Both companies were privately held.

MILAGROL HISTORY AND STRATEGY

3 Milagrol was founded in 1962 in the Brazilian state of Santa Catarina. It began as a manufacturer of well points for collecting water from wells. To assist with the introduction of polyvinyl chloride (PVC) pipes into Brazil, the company developed shut-off valves that would not generate the sudden water shocks that damaged PVC pipes. This innovation was essential to the newly developing market and launched Milagrol as a pioneering company that would eventually accomplish a string of firsts in Brazil, including the first foot-operated flow control system, first vandal-proof faucets, and first ceramic cartridge valve systems. Engineering innovations were soon matched with design capabilities, and Milagrol expanded into high-quality bathroom fittings featuring world-class designs. The company also developed a line of water-conserving valves that became well known in Brazil.

4 By the end of 2009, Milagrol was the leading manufacturer of the automatic faucets used in airports, shopping centers, and other public locations in South America. In fact, two out of every five major public projects in Brazil used Milagrol products, and the company also exported to Colombia, Ecuador, Mexico, Paraguay, and some Central American countries. Milagrol had been one of the featured firms in a recent Brazilian manufacturing exposition and had won numerous awards. There were few competitors that offered the same capabilities. Although the Milagrol product lines were relatively expensive, the focus on technological innovations that benefit both society and customers was key to its success. All told, Milagrol had lived up to the company's mission statement: "We generate value for our investors and opportunities for our employees by developing technical and design

solutions in water products that improve the lives of our customers and the quality of our environment."

5 Sales growth in the years leading up to 2009 had averaged 15% a year. More growth was anticipated in the near term as interest in water-saving faucets increased and as a result of favorable publicity regarding the firm's product lines. Research and development costs were expected to be high in the near term as the firm took advantage of this opportunity.

6 The water-saving technology Milagrol used was not predominantly proprietary, and much of the technology was well understood. The challenge an entrant faced was developing efficient manufacturing systems that would enable the valves to be profitably manufactured and sold. Furthermore, given their complex design, these valves were highly susceptible to quality problems, and the Milagrol manufacturing processes ensured a consistently high manufacturing quality. Essentially, Peterson was interested in obtaining the manufacturing technology for use in its own U.S. operations and also in the ongoing refining of these processes for Peterson's water-saving devices, which was Milagrol's research focus.

VALUATION CHALLENGES

7 Complicating any analysis was the uncertain economic situation in Brazil. On the one hand, the economy had continued to sizzle despite the global recession—retail sales had continued the steady growth seen over the previous five years, and industrial production had added momentum in the past year. The favorable retail environment was one of the things that was attractive to Peterson. On the other hand, as the economy continued to pick up steam, concerns about inflation began to rise. The central bank had responded with an increase in a key interest rate to 10.25% from 9.50% just one week previously to "assure the convergence of inflation with the trajectory of targets."[1] This was the first increase since September of 2008. Expectations varied, but many predicted continued interest rate increases, with rates likely to reach as high as 11.75%.[2] While the widely anticipated interest rate increase was expected to attenuate inflationary pressures, few believed at the time that the government would be able to keep inflation at its 4.5% target. At the time of the interest rate action, inflation was running at about 5.22%. Many observers anticipated inflation could run a few percent higher than the target over the next two years despite the government's aggressive stance.[3]

8 Uncertainty surrounding the Brazilian real was, under these conditions, quite pronounced. Given the relative health of the economy, there had been a surge of capital flowing into the country and the government had put in place additional controls on those capital flows to mitigate upward pressure on the real. Furthermore, increasing interest rates could generate substantial demand for the real once global financial markets stabilized.[4] But any rise in inflation would put significant downward pressure on the currency over the long run.

9 Forecasting the operating cash flows of Milagrol was a relatively easy task. The cost structure was predictable, and investments in working capital and manufacturing capacity (plant and equipment) were easily determined. Forecasts accounting for unit sales increases

[1] The central bank increased its overnight interest rate, known as the SELIC (Sistema Especial de Liquidação e de Custódia) rate.

[2] "Brazil Lifts Interest Rates by 75 Basis Points to Slow Roaring Economy," Dow Jones Newswires, April 29, 2010.

[3] Central Bank President Henrique Meirelles had recently stated that Brazil's economy risked overheating and that "we certainly won't allow that to happen" and the bank was "ready to take the necessary measures." (Bloomberg, April 26, 2010).

[4] "Brazil Real Fluctuates as Rate Outlook Offsets European Crisis," *Bloomberg Business Week,* May 24, 2010.

and price increases not related to inflation could be developed from demographic data in combination with assumptions about the growing demand for sustainable technologies. Given the uncertainty regarding inflation, Peterson had obtained a forecast of inflation for the coming five years from Econo-Metrics, a reputable international economic forecasting group. That group expected Brazilian inflation of 6% and then 7% over the next two years, before falling gradually toward the government target rate. In contrast, they expected U.S. inflation to be essentially zero for 2011 and then rising by half a percent each year back to a typical 2% level. The resulting forecast is presented in **Exhibit 1; **all cash flows are denominated in Brazilian reais.[5]

EXHIBIT 1 **Milagrol Ltda.**
Free Cash Flow Forecast (numbers in thousands of Brazilian reais)

	2010	2011	2012	2013	2014	2015
Financial Ratios				**Projected**		
Real Sales Growth (%)		15.00%	15.00%	10.00%	10.00%	5.00%
Inflation (%)		6.00%	7.00%	6.00%	5.50%	5.00%
Cost of Goods Sold to Sales (%)		57.00%	57.00%	57.00%	57.00%	57.00%
Selling, Admin., and Research to Sales (%)		16.00%	16.00%	14.00%	12.00%	12.00%
Net Working Capital to Sales (%)		15%	15%	15%	15%	15%
Property, Plant, and Equipment Turnover		2.25	2.25	2.25	2.25	2.25
Free Cash Flow						
Sales	185,467	226,084	278,197	324,377	376,440	415,025
Cost of Goods Sold	104,574	128,868	158,572	184,895	214,571	236,564
Administrative and Research	31,224	36,173	44,511	45,413	45,173	49,803
EBIT	49,669	61,043	75,113	94,069	116,696	128,658
Tax (30%)		18,313	22,534	28,221	35,009	38,597
Net Operating Profit after Tax		42,730	52,579	65,849	81,687	90,060
Less: Change in Net Working Capital		5,647	7,817	6,927	7,809	5,788
Less: Change in Net PPE		16,938	23,161	20,525	23,139	17,149
Free Cash Flow		20,144	21,601	38,397	50,739	67,124
Schedule of Assets						
Net Working Capital	28,265	33,913	41,730	48,657	56,466	62,254
Net Property, Plant, and Equipment	83,544	100,482	123,643	144,168	167,307	184,456

Source: Created by case writer.

[5] Sales to neighboring countries were a modest part of Milagrol's sales and were often denominated in Brazilian reais (the plural of *real,* which is the singular term for the Brazilian currency). Even those sales denominated in other currencies were subject, from Milagrol's point of view, to very little exchange risk because the currencies in the region were highly correlated. For this reason, Peterson was comfortable assuming all sales were in reais.

10 Regarding an estimation of a terminal value for any valuation of Milagrol as a company, an EBIT multiple (enterprise value to EBIT) of five would be appropriate for U.S. companies in this industry. This multiple could also be applied to the Milagrol purchase.

11 One challenge Peterson faced was establishing a discount rate for the analysis. Following standard practice at Peterson, the appropriate discount rate was the average cost of capital of a sample of firms in the same industry as the project or acquisition being evaluated. Such a set had been identified for the Milagrol acquisition, and the cost of capital in dollars was determined to be 12%. What concerned Peterson was whether this rate needed some further adjustment to reflect the additional risks related to a Brazilian investment. A common practice in this regard was to use the spread between the yield on a dollar-denominated U.S. government security and the yield on a dollar-denominated (not real-denominated) Brazilian government security. This "sovereign spread" would be added to any discount rate to reflect risks unique to Brazilian investments.[6] **Exhibit 2** presents information on interest rates and currency rates as of June 19, 2010—the sovereign spread for Brazil at the time was 1.28%.

EXHIBIT 2 **Milagrol Ltda. Market Information and Currency Forecast (in U.S. dollars [USD] and Brazilian reais [BRL])**

Selected Market Information (June 19, 2010)		
Spot Exchange Rate (USD/BRL)	0.549	
Yield on BZ—10-year gov't. USD-denominated	4.85%	
Brazilian Target Inflation	4.50%	
Yields by maturity denominated in the given currency	USD	BRL
3 mo	0.09%	10.80%
6 mo	0.16%	11.30%
1 yr	0.26%	12.00%
3 yr	1.20%	12.38%
5 yr	2.01%	12.37%
7 yr	2.68%	12.32%
10 yr	3.22%	12.44%
Econo-Metrics Exchange Rate Forecast (December of the Year Indicated)		
2011	0.560	
2012	0.540	
2013	0.480	
2014	0.430	
2015	0.390	
2016	0.380	

Data sources: http://www.bloomberg.com/markets/rates/brazil.htm (accessed June 19, 2010); http://www.tradingeconomics.com/Economics/Government-Bond-Yield.aspx?Symbol=BRL (accessed June 19, 2010); expectations generated by case writer.

[6] An alternative to adjusting the discount rate, also employed in practice, was simply to adjust the cash flows to reflect the specific effects of government action that were anticipated. A probability-weighted valuation would then be produced where weights would be associated with the likelihood of each possible outcome.

12 Another challenge was how to handle exchange rates. Clearly, any valuation would have to result in a U.S.-dollar-denominated valuation even though operating cash flows were denominated in Brazilian reais. There were two ways Peterson could have handled the valuation. First, Peterson could have converted future real-denominated cash flows into dollar cash flows at an estimated future exchange rate and then applied an appropriate dollar discount rate to those cash flows to obtain a dollar valuation. Alternatively, Peterson could have converted the appropriate dollar discount rate to an equivalent real discount rate and discounted the real-denominated cash flows and then converted the real valuation to a dollar valuation at the current spot rate. In general, the first method was preferred (**Exhibit 3** provides a more detailed discussion of these approaches).

EXHIBIT 3 Milagrol Ltda.
Valuation Approaches for Projects Denominated in Foreign Currencies

Valuation of international cash flows does not present any particular analytical challenges. There are essentially two standard approaches:

- Forecast future spot exchange rates, convert future cash flows denominated in a foreign currency to dollars at those rates, and use a U.S. discount rate to value the cash flows.
- Find an appropriate local currency discount rate or convert a U.S. discount rate to a foreign currency discount rate based on interest differentials, use this foreign currency discount rate to discount foreign currency cash flows, and convert the resulting foreign currency value to dollars at the current spot rate.

As a practical matter, there are reasons to prefer the first approach. For example, there is a great deal of information that may be used to predict future exchange rates that cannot be readily incorporated into the second approach. Such information includes changing inflation expectations over time, the effect of government regulation and policy, and variation in cash flow magnitudes over time. Another reason is that the first approach is quite explicit about assumptions for exchange rates, and these are often a subject of discussion, further analysis, and concern.

Forecast Exchange Rates

In the absence of a more detailed forecast and assuming that exchange rates adjust to reflect differences in the purchasing power of currencies, one can predict future exchange rates given inflation expectations using the following formula:

$$e_1 = e_0 \frac{1 + i_{domestic}}{1 + i_{foreign}}$$

where $i_{domestic}$ is the domestic currency inflation rate, $i_{foreign}$ is the foreign currency inflation rate, e_0 is the spot exchange rate (expressed as the cost of foreign currency in terms of domestic currency), and e_1 is the exchange rate one year later. To find a series of exchange rate forecasts, one simply repeats the calculation (which can therefore, if necessary, handle changing inflation rates). In other words, the predicted exchange rate for the second year, given inflation rates for the second year (which may or may not be the same as those for the first year), would be

$$e_2 = e_1 \frac{1 + i_{domestic}}{1 + i_{foreign}}$$

A similar approach can be used to generate forecasts from interest rates.*

Consider the following hypothetical project. Assume cash flows in Norwegian krone (NOK) are NOK500,000 a year for the next three years. Assume further that the current spot rate

* Since interest rates are given as yields to maturity, when using those rates one would not calculate a subsequent year exchange rate from the prior year but would compound the rate effect from the initial time period:

$$e_t = e_0 \left(\frac{1 + r_{domestic}}{1 + r_{foreign}} \right)^t$$

EXHIBIT 3 *(Continued)*

is 0.2000USD/NOK and inflation expectations are 3.00% and 5.00% for the United States and Norway, respectively. Finally, assume the appropriate U.S. discount rate is 10.00%. An analysis of the value of these cash flows is show below:

	1	2	3
Future Krone Cash Flows	500,000	500,000	500,000
Forecast Exchange Rate Approach:			
Forecast Rate (dollars to krone)	0.19619 (a)	0.19245 (b)	0.18879 (c)
Cash Flows Converted to dollars	98,095	96,227	94,394
NPV of Dollar Cash Flows (at 10%)	239,623		

(a) 0.20 × (1 + 0.03) ÷ (1 + 0.05)
(b) 0.19619 × (1 + 0.03) ÷ (1 + 0.05)
(c) 0.19245 × (1 + 0.03) ÷ (1 + 0.05)

Convert the Discount Rate

One can use the following formula to convert one discount rate to another:

$$k_{foreign} = (1 + k_{domestic})\frac{1 + r_{foreign}}{1 + r_{domestic}} - 1$$

where $k_{domestic}$ is the domestic discount rate, $k_{foreign}$ is the foreign discount rate, $r_{domestic}$ is the domestic currency interest rate, and $r_{foreign}$ is the foreign currency interest rate. Consider once again the Norwegian project. Assume that the U.S. and Norwegian interest rates are 5.06% and 7.10%, respectively.** An analysis of the value of these cash flows is show below:

	1	2	3
Future Krone Cash Flows	500,000	500,000	500,000
Discount Rate Converted to krone	12.14% (a)		
NPV of krone Cash Flows (at Converted Rate)	1,198,116		
Krone NPV Converted to dollars at Spot Rate	239,623		

(a) (1 + 0.10) × (1 + 0.0710) (1 + 0.0506) – 1

Note that in both cases, the net value of the cash flows in U.S. dollars is equal to USD239,623. This need not be the case. It is true in this example because all the data are consistent with parity in international markets.† In reality, cash flows are complex, and the data used are not always consistent in the manner predicted by parity.

One interesting issue that arises in the context of enterprise-level valuation is what to assume regarding long-term growth rates when a terminal value is calculated from a perpetual growth model. When one assumes parity holds as outlined above, one can convert the growth rate in one country to that of another country using the same approach that would be used to convert discount rates. Similarly, under these same conditions, a valuation multiple can be used across countries.

** These interest rates and inflation rates are consistent with a 2% global real rate of return.

† In particular, the analysis assumes interest rates are consistent with inflation rates (that the Fischer Effect holds across countries, which means all rates reflect the same real rate of return and risk premium) and that exchange rates evolve with inflation rates (that purchasing power parity holds, which means exchange rates evolve to offset changes in local currency prices).

Source: Created by case writer.

13 While an exchange rate forecast could have been obtained from inflation rates or interest rates as outlined in **Exhibit 3,** such forecasts were notoriously inaccurate over the short run. While inflation would affect exchange rates eventually, government actions in response to inflation would have a much greater impact. In general, local government policies and global events generated dramatic currency swings that could persist for a number of years. Of particular concern for Peterson were those scenarios leading to a substantial devaluation of the real, which would attenuate the value of Milagrol to Peterson. Precipitating this concern was the fact that the real had steadily appreciated since 2003 (the recent global turmoil had had only a fleeting effect) and was, therefore, arguably overvalued relative to an inflation-based prediction. **Exhibit 4** graphs the value of the real over the last decade (from when the real first started to float freely), including a prediction of the rate based on inflation over that same time period. Given the uncertainty regarding exchange rates, Peterson had obtained an exchange-rate forecast from Econo-Metrics along with the inflation forecast (the forecast is presented with market information in **Exhibit 2**).

EXHIBIT 4 **Milagrol Ltda.**
Value of Brazilian Real

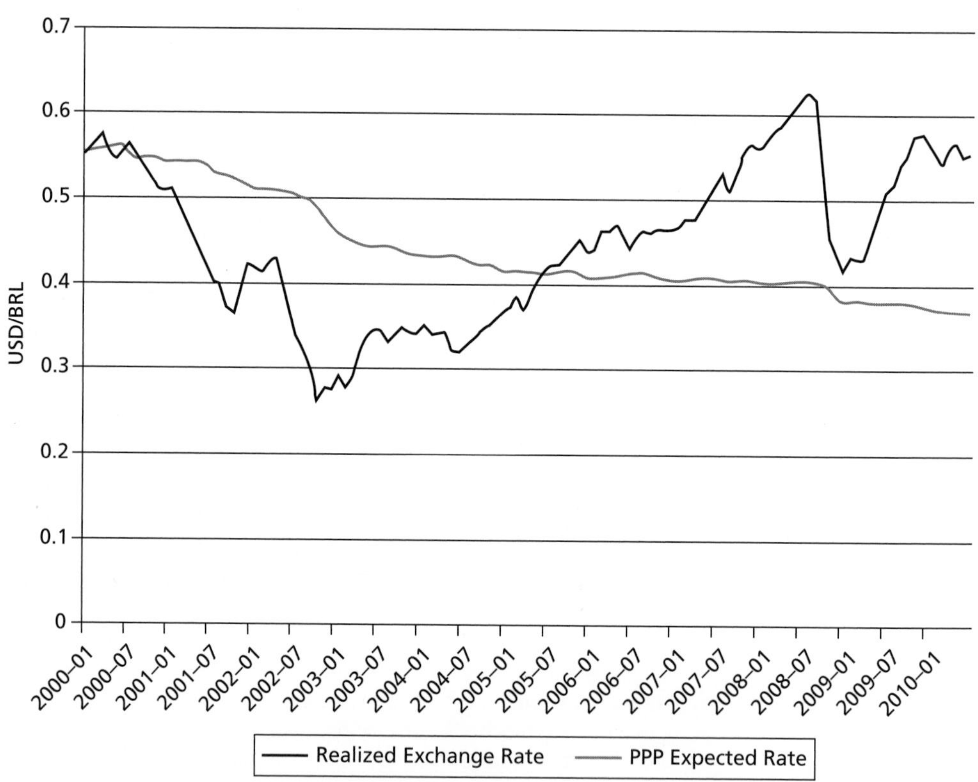

Data source: International Financial Statistics; expected exchange rate from inflation data generated by case writer.

Case 16

The Movie Exhibition Industry: *2011*

Steve Gove,
Virginia Tech

Brett P. Matherne,
Loyola University of New Orleans

David Thornblad
Virginia Tech

1 If the motion picture industry's performance were a feature presentation, the marquee for January 2011 would read "Massive Box Office: A Historic Gross!" At $10.56 billion, the industry box office narrowly missed another record year for revenues, just behind 2009's highest ever gross of $10.59 billion.[1] An astonishing 1.33 billion tickets were sold. But beyond the headlines, the industry is a study in contradictions:

- While 2009 revenues were a full 10 percent above 2008's, revenues for 2010 were down three-tenths of a percent.
- The number of theaters is declining, but the number of screens is near a historical high (**Exhibit 5** & **6**).
- Revenues are near historic highs, but the attendance trend is negative, declining 5 percent in one year; down 15 percent from 2002.
- Ticket sales fell to their lowest level since 1996 and a fraction of the 4 billion sold in 1946. Then the average person attended 28 films a year, today it is 6.5 (**Exhibits 1** & **2**).
- The U.S. population is increasing, but the size of the market in the core demographic group is growing more slowly (**Exhibit 3**).
- Americans spend more time than ever on entertainment—3,500 hours annually—but only 12 are spent at the movies.[2] The average person spends as much time watching TV every 3 days.

2 Movies remain as popular as ever, but opportunities for viewing outside the theater have greatly increased. While motion picture studios increased revenues through product licensing, DVD sales, and international expansion, the exhibitors—movie theaters—have seen their business decline. Movie content is more available than ever, but fewer are venturing to the theater to see it. Many theaters have ceased operation, driven from the market by consolidation and as patrons stayed away. Will the local theater soon disappear? How has this come to be? What can exhibitors do to respond?

THE MOTION PICTURE INDUSTRY VALUE CHAIN

3 The motion picture industry value chain consists of three stages: studio production, distribution, and exhibition—the theaters that show the films. All stages of the value chain are undergoing consolidation.

4 *Studio Production* The studios produce the lifeblood of the industry, they create content. Films from just the top six studios produce just 20 percent of films, but these are

[1] Motion Picture Association of America (MPAA) 2009 Entertainment Industry Market Statistics.

[2] Mintel Report, Movie Theaters—US—February 2008.

EXHIBIT 1 Domestic Tickets Sold & Box Office Gross 1980–2010

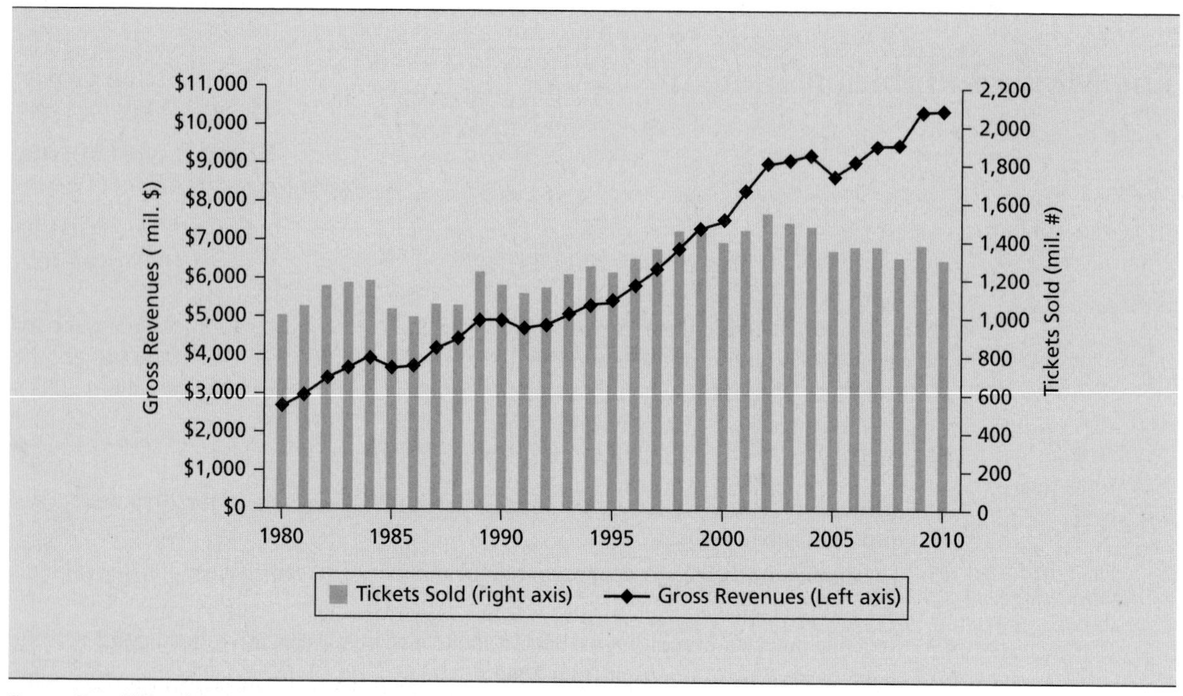

Source: Boxofficemojo.com

EXHIBIT 2 Average Movie Ticket Price, 1980–2010

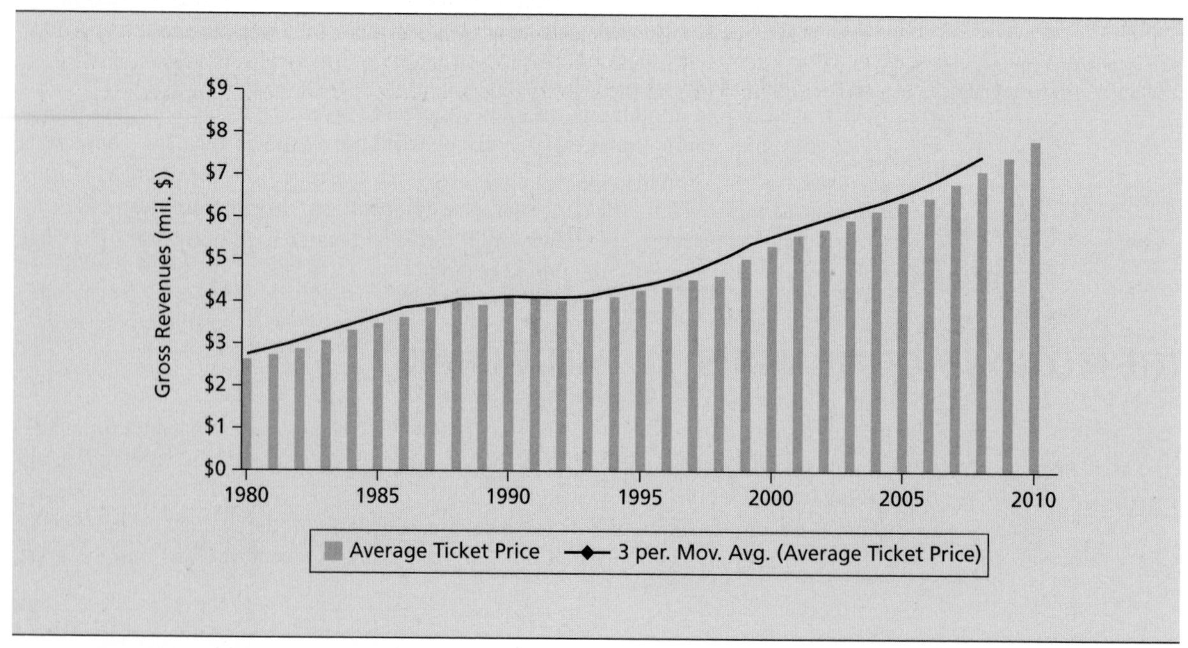

Source: Boxofficemojo.com

EXHIBIT 3 Population Trend Among 14–17 and 18–24 Age Groups (millions)

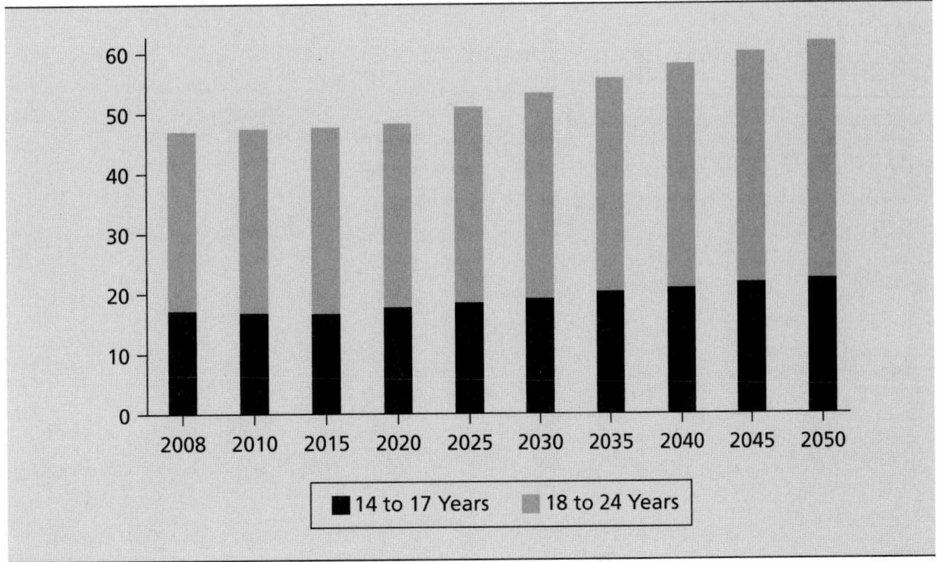

Source: U.S. Census.

responsible for over 80 percent of domestic box office receipts (**Exhibit 4**). Studios are increasingly part of larger corporations, managed as any other profit center. Management is a challenge as investments are large and a success formula elusive. Profitability swings wildly. The cost of bringing a typical feature to market exceeds $100 million, up 25 percent in 5 years.[3] Typically a third of costs are marketing expenses.

5 Studios know their core audience: 12–24 year-olds. This group purchases nearly 40 percent of theater tickets. Half are "frequent moviegoers" attending at least one movie per month. Profits are driven by the studios' ability to satisfy this fickle audience. In 2008, two films targeting the core market and based on two successful comic book characters met with widely different fates.[4] Paramount's successful *Iron Man* was produced for $140 and grossed $318 million at the domestic box office. Warner Bros. *Speed Racer,* produced for $20 million less and released the following weekend was a flop, grossing just $44 million.

6 Demographic trends are not favorable either. The U.S. population will increase 17 percent by 2025, an increase of 54 million people. But the number of 12–24 year olds is expected to increase only 9 percent, just 4 million more potential viewers. Based current theaters and screens, this is an increase of under 700 additional viewers per theater, roughly 100 per screen.

7 *Distribution* Distributors are the intermediaries between the studios and exhibitors. Distribution entails all steps following a film's artistic completion including marketing, logistics, and administration. Exhibitors negotiate a percentage of gross by the studio or purchase rights to films and profit from the box office receipts. Distributors select and market films to exhibitors, seeking to maximize potential attendees. Distributors coordinate the manufacture and distribution of the film to exhibitors. They also handle collections, audits of attendees, and other administrative tasks. There are over 300 active distributors,

[3] MPAA 2007 Entertainment Industry Market Statistics.

[4] All data on these two films from www.BoxOfficeMojo.com.

EXHIBIT 4 **Market Share of Film Production 2000–2010**

Distributor	2010				2005				2000			
	Rank	Market Share	Total Gross	# Movies	Rank	Market Share	Total Gross	# Movies	Rank	Market Share	Total Gross	# Movies
Warner Bros.	1	18.2%	$ 1,924	27	1	15.6%	$1,377	19	3	11.9%	$ 905	22
Paramount	2	16.2%	$ 1,715	15	6	9.4%	$ 832	12	4	10.4%	$ 791	12
20th Century Fox	3	14.0%	$ 1,482	17	2	15.3%	$1,354	18	6	9.5%	$ 723	13
Disney / Buena Vista	4	13.8%	$ 1,456	14	4	10.4%	$ 922	17	1	15.5%	$1,176	21
Sony / Columbia	5	12.1%	$ 1,283	18	5	10.4%	$ 918	24	7	9.0%	$ 682	29
Universal	6	8.3%	$ 882	15	3	11.4%	$1,010	19	2	14.1%	$1,069	13
Total for leading 6		82.6%	$ 8,742	106		72.5%	$6,413	109		70.4%	$5,346	110
Industry Total			$10,565	529			$8,840	547			$7,661	478
As % of Industry			82.7%	20.0%			72.5%	19.9%			69.8%	23.0%

Source: Adapted from Boxofficemojo.com

EXHIBIT 5 **Number of Theaters by Complex Size**

	2000	2005	2010	Change 2000 to 2005	Change 2005 to 2010	Change 2000 to 2010
Single Screens	2,368	1,723	1,610	−27%	−7%	−32%
Miniplexes (2–7 Screens)	3,170	2,381	1,884	−25%	−21%	−41%
Multiplexes (8–15 Screens)	1,478	1,599	1,683	8%	5%	14%
Megaplexes (16+ Screens)	405	558	645	38%	16%	59%
Total	7,421	6,260	5,817	−16%	−7%	−22%

Sources: Author estimates based on data from Entertainment Industry, 2007 & 2009 Report Motion Picture Association of America, and Mintel Report "Movie Theaters—US—February 2008."

EXHIBIT 6 **Exhibition Market Leaders: 2009**

Company	Theater Brands	# U.S. Theater Locations	# U.S. Screens	Avg. Screens per Theater
Regal	Regal, United Artists, Edwards	548	6,768	12.4
AMC	AMC, Loews	297	4,513	15.2
Cinemark	Cinemark, Century	294	3,830	13.0
Carmike	Carmike	244	2,277	9.3
	Total for leading four	1,383	17,388	12.6
	Industry total	6,039	39,717	6.6

Source: SEC Filings & Author estimates

but much is done by a few major firms, including divisions of studios. Pixar, for example, co-produced *Finding Nemo* with Disney and distribution was done by Disney's Buena Vista.

8 *Exhibition* Studios have historically sought full vertical integration through theater ownership, allowing greater control over audiences and capturing exhibition profits. A common practice was for the studios to use their theater ownership to reduce competition by not showing pictures produced by rivals. This ended in 1948 with the Supreme Court's ruling against the studios in *United States v. Paramount Pictures*. Theaters were soon divested, leaving studios and exhibitors to negotiate film access and rental.

9 Theaters are classified according to the number of screens at one location (**Exhibit 5**). Single screen theaters were the standard from the introduction of film through the 1980s. They have since rapidly declined in number, replaced by theater complexes. These include miniplexes (2–7 screens), multiplexes (8–15 screens), and megaplexes (16 or more screens). The number of theaters decreased more than 20 percent between 2000 and 2010, but the number of screens increased due to growth in megaplexes. Over 10 percent of the theaters are now megaplexes and the number of screens is at historically high levels of 39,717.[5]

[5] Developed by author from: Entertainment Industry, 2009 Report Motion Picture Association of America.

Many analysts argue the industry has overbuilt and too many theaters and screens exist to make the business profitable.

THE LEAD ACTORS

10 Declining ticket sales and the increased costs associated with developing megaplexes began a wave of consolidation among exhibitors. Four companies now dominate: Regal, AMC, Cinemark, and Carmike. These companies, operating 1,383 theaters in the country (just 23 percent), control 43 percent of screens. This market share provides these exhibitors with negotiating power for access to films, prices for films and concessions, and greater access to revenues from national advertisers.

11 There is little differentiation in the offerings of the major theater exhibitors—prices within markets differ little, the same movies are shown at the same times, and the food and services are nearly identical. Competition between theaters often comes down to distance from home, convenience of parking, and proximity to restaurants. Innovations by one theater chain are quickly adopted by others. The chains serve different geographic markets and do so in different ways.[6] Regal focuses on mid-size markets using multiplexes and megaplexes. In 2009, Regal's average ticket price of $8.15 is the highest among the leaders. AMC concentrates on urban areas with megaplexes and concentrates on the large population centers such as those in California, Florida, and Texas. Cinemark serves smaller markets, operating as the sole theater chain in over 80 percent of its markets. Cinemark's average ticket price of $5.46 was the lowest of the majors. Carmike concentrates on small to midsized markets, targeting populations of less than 100,000 that have few other entertainment options. Carmike's average ticket price in 2009 was $6.56 but at $3.21, their average concession revenue per patron is the highest among the majors.

12 The different approach of the companies is reflected in the cost of fixed assets per screens. These costs result from decisions made on how to serve customers, such as the level of technology and finish of the theater—digital projection and marble floors cost more than traditional projectors and a carpeted lobby.[7] Despite multi- and megaplex facilities, Regal's cost per screen is the highest, $430,000. Carmike's, the rural operator, is the lower at just $206,000. Cinemark is in the middle at $367,000. Costs for AMC are expected to be near or exceed that of Regal.

THE BUSINESS OF EXHIBITION

13 There are three primary sources of revenue for exhibitors: concessions, advertising, and box office receipts. Managers have low discretion; their ability to influence revenues and expenses is limited. Operating margins among exhibitors average a slim 10 percent. This is before significant expenses such as facility and labor costs. The result is marginal or negative net income. Overall, the business of exhibitors is best described as loss leadership on movies: the firms make money selling concessions and selling ads that are shown to patrons who are drawn by the movie.

14 *Concessions* Movie goers frequently lament the high prices for concessions. In 2009 concessions averaged 30 percent of exhibitor revenues. Direct costs are less than 15 percent of selling price making concessions the largest source of exhibitor profit. These are influenced by the three factors: attendance, pricing, and material costs. The most important is attendance: more attendees = more concession sales. Per patron sales are influenced by

[6] Data on the firms, screen sizes, location, from web sites and SEC filings.

[7] All data is from SEC filings, based on net property, plant and equipment reported in 2007 balance sheet and the number of screens.

prices—a common moviegoer complaint is high concession prices. The $3.75 price point for the large soda is not by accident, but the result of market research and profit maximization calculation. Costs are influenced by purchase volume with larger chains able to negotiation better prices on everything from popcorn and soda pop to cups and napkins.

15 *Advertising* Exhibitors also generate revenue through pre-show advertising. Though this constitutes just 5 percent of revenues, it is highly profitable. Mintel reports that advertising revenues among exhibitors is expected to increase at an annual rate of 10 percent over the coming decade despite audiences' disapproval.[8] Balancing the revenues from ads with audience tolerance is an ongoing struggle for exhibitors, though not a new one. In the early 1970's one industry executive argued: "It is not a policy of our corporation to use commercial advertising for income on our screen. We are selling the public one item—a particular motion picture—and to use the screen for other purposes detracts from this item."[9]

16 *Box Office Revenues* Ticket sales constitute two thirds of exhibition business revenues but yield little or no profit. Historically, the power imbalance between studios and exhibitors yielded rental contracts returning as much as 90 percent of box office revenue to the studios during the initial weeks of a film's release. The split is now closer to 55/45 for large chains. Still, it is common for an exhibitor's portion of ticket revenues to not fully cover the operational costs. The record setting revenues at the box office have been the result of increases in ticket prices that have flowed back to the studios and help cover exhibitors' facilities and debt load.

17 From 2005 to 2009 ticket price increases average 3.8% per year (Exhibit 9).[5] While these increases set records, an even greater opportunity materialized for 3D. Prior to 2009, a $1 to $2 "surcharge" was installed to cover glasses, license fees paid 3D equipment providers, and to studios in higher rental rates. Following the success of "Avatar," exhibitors saw an opportunity to use the surcharge as an alternative to ticket price increases. The 3D premium now reaches $3 to $5; for IMAX it is $4 to $7. Price increases in March 2010 by AMC, Regal and Cinemark averaged 8.3% nationally on 3D movies, rising from $13.60 to $14.73.[10] In some markets, 3D prices jumped 20%.[11]

18 Recent increases in exhibitor revenues are attributed almost entirely to 3D. In 2005 the box office for 3D was just $40 million. In 2009 it was $1.14 billion, 11% of all revenues. From 2008 to 2009, 3D receipts grew 375 percent while revenues for non-3D grew under one percent.[12] This may actually under represent the actual demand for 3D as rapid expansion in the number of 3D films produced created a bottleneck for the 3D screen space.[13] Longer runs on 3D screens will likely increase the proportion of revenues from 3D. However, Paul Dergarabedian of Hollywood.com cautions that the ticket price increases are not sustainable. "It's what we call a recession-resistant business. Times get tough and people go to the movies because it's the one thing they see as a relative bargain. The minute they cease to see it that way, it's not good for the industry."[14]

[8] Mintel, Movie Theaters—US—February 2008—Segment Performance—Cinema Advertising.

[9] Durwood, S. H. (2002). The Exhibitors (1972). In G. A. Waller (Ed.), *Moviegoing in America: A Sourcebook in the History of Film Exhibition* (pp. 279–281). Malden, MA: Blackwell Publishers Ltd.

[10] Reuters. (2010, April 6, 2010). U.S. movie ticket sales strong despite price hike. *Reuters News*. Retrieved from Factiva.

[11] Schuker, L. A. E., & Smith, E. (2010, March 25, 2010). Higher prices make box-office debut. *Wall Street Journal,* pp. B1, B5.

[12] Motion Picture Association of America. (2009). *Theatrical Market Statistics: 2009*: Motion Picture Association of America.

[13] Motion Picture Association of America. (2009). *Theatrical Market Statistics: 2009*: Motion Picture Association of America.

[14] Muther, C. (2010, March 27, 2010). Prices for 3-D movies flyaway with 'Dragon'. *Boston Globe,* p. B1.

19 AMC may have, intentionally or not, stumbled onto a price cap when several of their New York theaters hit $20 per ticket for "Shrek" in IMAX 3D at several locations. Amidst a public outcry and unwanted media attention, the chain apologized, citing a pricing error and reduced prices to $17 and $19. This situation suggests there is indeed a cap on the willingness to pay for even this most extreme viewing experience. The backlash may make it difficult to raise prices in the near future; any cap on ticket prices is a serious cause for concern for exhibitors as it has been the primary way to increase revenues.

20 The evidence is mixed that 3D is having a positive impact on exhibitors' bottom lines. This suggests either that the benefits are yet to accrue to exhibitors or are being appropriated by studios. The National Association of Theater Owners (NATO) estimates the savings of digital over film as $1 billion annually[15] from lower production costs, master reels and prints, elimination of shipping, etc. They argue these cost savings will largely accrue to distributors.

21 By all accounts, revenues per admission have increased, but these are split with studios. At Regal, for example, film rental and advertising costs as a percent of revenues dropped slightly, to 53.3% from 54.2% for the second quarter 2010 compared to the same period 2009. Similarly, Carmike's exhibition costs declined slightly as a percent of revenue, from 57.6% to 56.8%, but other theater operating costs grew from 59.6% to 62.9% of admissions revenue. In each of these cases the data reflects substantial increases in ticket prices and 3D surcharges begun in spring 2010. This suggests studios are appropriating a large portion of the revenue increases.

22 At Regal, this holds true for operating profits, as a percent of revenues, which decreased from 12.2% in the second quarter 2009 to 9.0% 2010. For Carmike, the net effect was operating income declining significantly, from 8.8% of total revenue to 4.1%. The overall picture appears similar for Cinemark. Operating income as a percentage of revenues for second quarter 2010 declined from same period 2009 levels, dropping from 14.6% to 14.4%. While limited to just the first comparative quarter when most price increases and surcharges went into effect, these trends suggest that, despite substantial investments in digital and 3D, exhibitors may not be able to capitalize on them.

23 Overall, the exhibitor has limited control over both revenues and profits. Box office receipts are the bulk of revenues, but yields few profits. Attendance allows for profitable sales of concessions and advertisements, but there are significant caps on the volume of concession sales per person and selling prices seem to have reached a maximum. Advertising remains an attractive avenue for revenues and profits, but audiences loathe it.

THE PROCESS OF EXHIBITION

24 The fundamentals of film exhibition changed little between the introduction of motion pictures until the late 1990s. Historically, each theater received a shipment of physical canisters containing a "release print" from the distributor. Making these prints requires $20,000–$30,000 in up-front costs and $1,000–$1,500 for each print. Thus a modern major motion picture opening on 2,500 screens simultaneously requires $2.50–$3.75 million in print costs. This is borne by the studios, but paid for by movie attendees. Each release print is actually several reels of 35 mm film which are manually loaded onto projector reels, sequenced, and queued for display by a projector operator. The film passes through the projector which shines intense light through the film, projecting the image through a lens

[15] National Association of Theater Owners (2010). Talking Points: Digital Cinema. www.natoonline.org.

which focuses the image on the screen. A typical projection system costs $50,000 with one needed for each screen.

25 The late 1990's saw an industry conversion to digital distribution. Digital cinema is becoming economically viable. Digital cinema involves a high resolution (4096×2160) digitized image projected onto the screen. The cost of a digital projection system is considerable, averaging $75,000 per screen. 3D capability can add an additional $25,000. The costs for digital "release prints" are far lower than traditional film, but these costs savings most directly benefit the studio whereas costs to convert theaters are the exhibitors'. The number of digital theaters is expanding rapidly. In 2004, there were fewer than 100 in the United States. At the end of 2007, 4,702 digital screens were installed, and by 2009 there were 7,736.

26 Financing these investments was a significant issue for exhibitors due to the total costs and their weak balance sheets. Two financing avenues were taken by the major theater chains. Forming an agreement with Christie Digital Systems, Carmike went solo with a lease-service approach. Under the ten year agreement, digital and digital 3-D systems are installed with an upfront cost of $800 per screen. Christie provides equipment service and maintenance amounting to $2,340 per screen annually. This arrangement effectively puts both the risk and upside with Carmike as fixed costs are increased. Revenues beyond these fixed costs benefit Carmike. Alternately, AMC, Cinemark, and Regal financed the transition through the DCIP partnership, securing $660 million in financing to convert nearly 14,000 screens, over 90 percent, of their screens. Each company pays a $5,000 to $10,000 per screen conversion charge and subsequent royalty fees of approximately $0.50 per admission. Conversion of screens ranges from 1,000 screens for Regal to 1,500 for Cinemark.

27 By the end of 2009, 1,000 screens were being converted to digital every six months. Carmike had converted over 90 percent of its screens to digital. The DCIP firms had, on average, converted approximately 25 percent of their screens. Plans are in place for near complete conversion to digital among the leading four exhibitors.

28 To the audience, the most visible aspect of the digital transition is 3D, which went mainstream in 2010. In 2005 just 192 digital 3D capable screens were installed. By 2007 that number climbed to 600, reaching 3,378 by the end of 2009. Twenty-two percent of Carmike's screens are 3D capable. The DCIP partners have on average 10 percent of their screens as 3D capable with plans to achieve approximately 25 percent. In 2010, these 3D screens were responsible for approximately one third of all box office admissions, generating roughly 40–50 percent of all revenues. A study by the International 3D Society reports 3D is responsible for the majority of opening weekend revenues.[16] Of "Avatar's" $77 million opening weekend, 82 percent was from 3D; for "Alice in Wonderland" it was 70 percent.

29 Still, some argue that 3D may be a novelty. The appeal of 3D varies by film, with action and animated as the leading genres. The long-term trend appears to be downward, toward what threshold is unknown (**Exhibit 7**). "Because the pricing of 3-D tickets is now so high, people are becoming more selective about what they see in 3-D," said Rich Greenfield, media analyst for BTIG.[17] A focus on 3D may result in more action movies and fewer comedies and dramas, further alienating the non-core audience for movies.[18]

[16] International 3D Society (2010). *3D Movie Fans Expand Box Office Says International 3D Society Study.*

[17] Schuker, L. A. E. (2010, July 6, 2010). A 2-D 'Eclipse' Stakes Its Claim in 3-D World. *Wall Street Journal,* pp. B1, B2.

[18] The Economist (2010, May 6, 2010). The box office strikes back *The Economist*, from Factiva.

EXHIBIT 7 Percent of Opening Weekend Sales from 3D

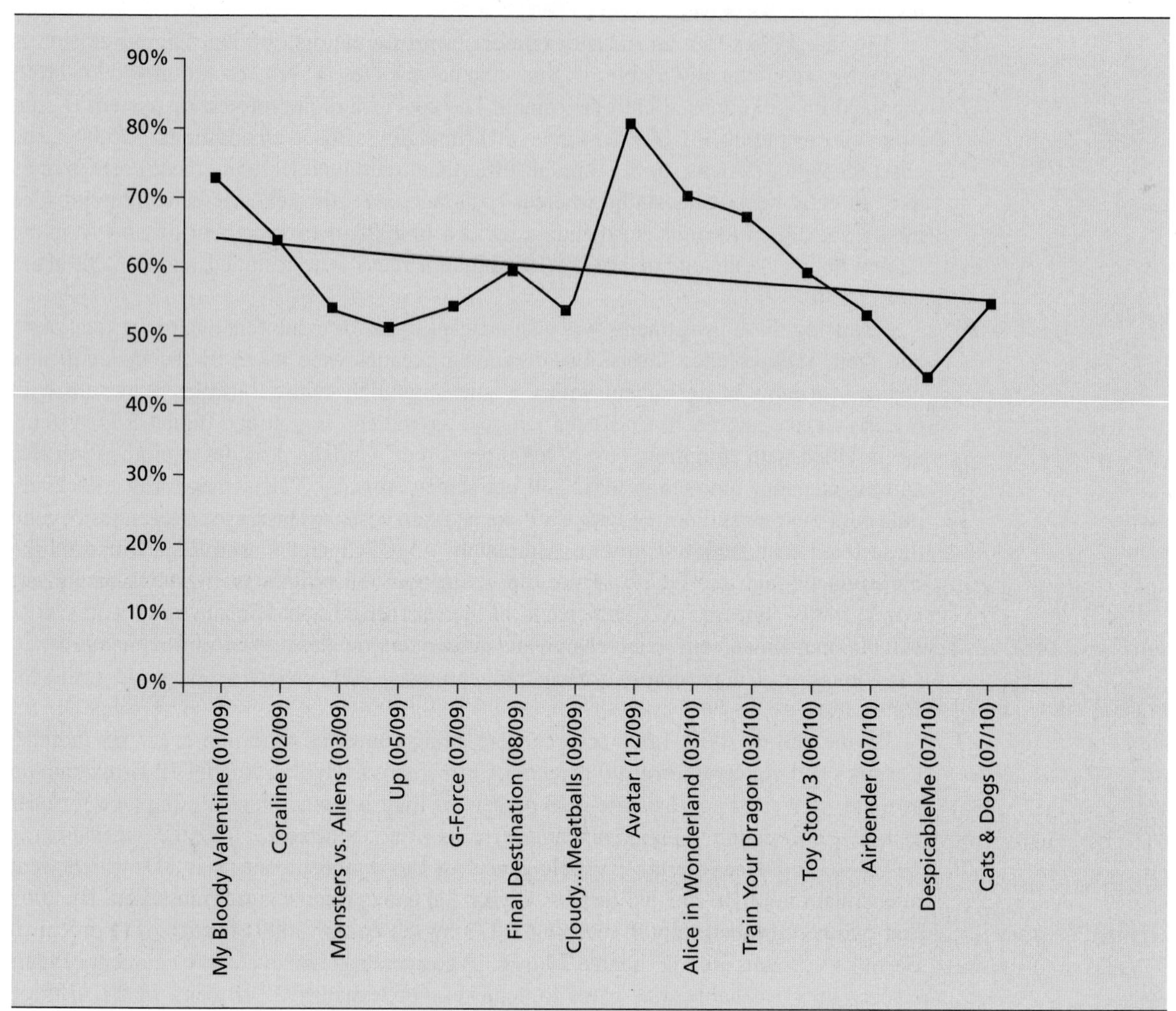

THE THEATER EXPERIENCE

30 While the industry touts the ongoing transition to digital projection and the latest 3D as the draw for the box office, the allure may be more fundamental. Moviegoers describe the attraction of going to the theater as an "experience" based on: (1) the giant theater screen, (2) the opportunity to be out of the house, (3) not having to wait to see a particular movie on home video, (4) the experience of watching movies with a theatrical sound system, and (5) as a location option for dating.[19]

31 The ability of theaters to provide these benefits above what audiences can achieve at home appears to be diminishing. Of the reasons why people go to the movies, only the place aspect, the theater as a place to be out of house and as a place for dating, seem immune from substitution. Few teenagers want movie and popcorn with their date at home with mom and dad.

[19] Mintel Report, Movie Theaters—US—February 2008—Reasons to go to Movies over Watching a DVD.

32 The overall "experience" currently offered by theaters falls short for many. Marketing research firm Mintel reports the reasons for not attending theaters more frequently are largely the result of the declining experience. Specific factors include: the overall cost, at home viewing options, interruptions such as cell phones in the theater, rude patrons, the overall hassle, and ads prior to the show.[20] Patrons report general dismay with the theater experience. A recent *Wall Street Journal* article reported on interruptions ranging from the intrusion of soundtracks in adjacent theaters to cell phones. "The interruptions capped a night of movie going already marred by out-of-order ticketing kiosks and a parade of preshow ads so long that, upon seeing the Coca-Cola polar bears on screen, one customer grumbled: 'This is obscene.'"[21]

33 Recounting bad experiences is a lively topic for bloggers. A typical comment: "I say it has gotten worse. I hate paying $9.00 for a ticket and the movie is 90–100 minutes long, people talking on the cell phone, the people who work at the theaters look like they are bored, and when you ask them a question, the answer is very rude. I worked as an usher in the late 60's and we had to wear uniforms and white gloves on Friday and Saturday nights, those days are long gone."[22]

34 A trip to the local cinemaplex can be eye opening even for industry insiders. In 2005, Toby Emmerich, New Line Cinema's head of production faced a not-so-common choice: attending "War of the Worlds" in a theater or in a screening room at actor Jim Carrey's house. Said Emmerich in an *LA Times* article, "I love seeing a movie with a big crowd, but I had no idea how many obnoxious ads I'd have to endure—it really drove me crazy. After sitting through about 15 minutes of ads, I turned to my wife and said, 'Maybe we should've gone to Jim Carrey's house after all.'"[23]

35 The unique value proposition offered by movie theaters' large screens, the long wait for DVD release, and advantages of theatrical sound systems also appear to be fading. Increasingly larger television sets, DVD content, and the adoption of high definition technology are all eroding these advantages. One blogger posts, "Whereas the electronics industry has been innovating to create immersive experiences from the comfort of our own home, the US theater industry has been dragging their feet."[24]

36 *Home Viewing Technology* Home television sets are increasingly large, high definition sets coupled with inexpensive yet impressive audio systems. In 1997, the screen size of the average television was just 23 inches. Currently almost all LCD televisions sold have screens 36 inches or larger.[25] Because set size is measured as the diagonal screen size, increases in viewable area are greater than the measurement suggests. The viewing area of sets doubled from 250 inches^2 to 550 inches.^{2}

37 The FCC requirement that all broadcasters convert to digital broadcasts by 2009 is widely credited with starting a consumer movement to upgrade televisions. Since the 1950's, television transmissions were formatted as 480 interlaced vertical lines (480i) of resolution. The

[20] Mintel Report, Movie Theaters—US—February 2008—Reasons why Attendance is not Higher.

[21] Kate Kelly, Bruce Orwall, and Peter Sanders, 2005, The Multiplex Under Siege, *Wall Street Journal,* December 24, 2005; Page P1.

[22] blog comment on Cinema Treasures | Over the past ten years, the movie theater experience has . . . ; URL: http://cinematreasures.org/polls/22/, accessed:12/11/2008.

[23] Incident reported in Patrick Goldstein, 2005, Now playing: A glut of ads, *Los Angeles Times,* July 12, 2005 in print edition E-1; URL: http://articles.latimes.com/2005/jul/12/entertainment/et-goldstein12; accessed December 5, 2008.

[24] Designs of the Week: The Movie Theater Experience, Sunday, November 23, 2008, URL: http://www.sramanamitra.com/2008/11/23/designs-of-the-week-the-movie-theater-experience/, Accessed: 20081211.

[25] DuBravac, 2007.

new digital format is high definition (HD), providing up to 1080 vertical lines of resolution (1080p).[26] Three quarters of all televisions sold since 2006 are HD capable.

38 As LCD technology became the standard for both computer and television screens, manufacturing costs declined. Wholesale prices for televisions fell 65 percent from the late 1990's.[27] In 2006, the average television retailed for $29 per diagonal inch of set size. This is expected to decrease to $22 within 5 years.[28] Consumers, however, are actually spending more on every television, consistently electing to purchase larger sets to achieve a better viewing experience. Sharp, a leading manufacturer of televisions, predicts that by 2015 the average screen will reach 60 inches.[29]

39 Large screen televisions, DVD players, and audio and speaker components are commonly packaged as low cost home theaters. The average DVD player now costs just $72[30] and high definition DVD players are beginning to penetrate the market. Retail price wars during the 2008 Christmas season led to HD Blu-Ray players dropping below $200. These home theater systems offer a movie experience that rivals many theaters, all for $1,000—$2,000. Says Mike Gabriel, Sharp's head of marketing and communications, "People can now expect a home cinema experience from their TV. Technology that was once associated with the rich and famous is now accessible to homes across the country."[31]

40 *Content Expansion* Sales of DVDs have aided the expansion of home theaters and profited the studios. DVD sales have been a primary source of studio profits for more than a decade, but fell precipitously, down 13.3 percent in 2009 on top of an 8.4 percent decline in 2008.[32] At $8.5 billion, 2009's DVD sales equaled 2001 levels; total revenues from DVD sales dropped below that of box office receipts in the U.S. for the first time since 2000.[33] This decline in DVD sales is due in part to the expanded availability of rentals and pay-per-view, and at least partially attributable to the studios.

41 Rentals also serve this market. Netflix grew revenues 85 percent from 2006 to 2009 and it is actively expanding into online-streaming. Coinstar's Redbox had over 12,000 rental kiosks offering $1/night rentals through partnerships with McDonalds (which is also an investor in the company), Walmart, Walgreen's, and other retailers even *before* adding kiosks to half of 7-Eleven's national locations.[34]

42 Studios are responding by trying to spur DVD and pay-per-view fees through shorter release windows, actions seemingly incompatible and inconsistent with the drive to increase theater attendance. In 2000, the average window between theatrical release and DVD sales was 5 months, 16 days. In 2009, it was 4 months, 11 days, a 20 percent reduction.[35] Studios are eager to accelerate DVD revenue streams and capitalize on initial marketing

[26] DuBravac, 2007.

[27] DuBravac, 2007.

[28] Bob Keefe, "Prices on flat-screen TVs expected to keep falling" (2008), The Atlanta Journal-Constitution, published on 03/15/08.

[29] Source: Average TV size up to 60-inch by 2015 says Sharp, TechDigest, URL: http://www.techdigest.tv/2008/01/average_tv_size.html; Accessed: 2008/12/11.

[30] MPAA 2007 Entertainment Industry Market Statistics.

[31] Source: Average TV size up to 60-inch by 2015 says Sharp, TechDigest, URL: http://www.techdigest.tv/2008/01/average_tv_size.html; Accessed: 2008/12/11.

[32] National Association of Theater Owners (2009). ShoWest 2010 Talking Points. www.natoonline.org

[33] Shuker, L. A. E., & Smith, E. (2010, May 22, 2010). Hollywood Eyes Shortcut to TV. *Wall Street Journal*, from Factiva.

[34] Business Wire. (2009, January 5, 2009). Convenient Entertainment; 7-Eleven Rolls Out Redbox® $1 per Night New Release DVD Rentals *Business Wire*. Retrieved from Factiva.

[35] National Association of Theater Owners. (2010). *Average Video Announcement and Video Release Windows*: National Association of Theater Owners.

expenditures. Arguing in favor of a reduced window, Bob Iger, CEO of Disney said, "The problem with waiting these days is that we're dealing with a much more competitive marketplace than ever before—there are more choices that people have."[36] Theaters may fear complete disintermediation.

43 The accelerated DVD release of "Alice in Wonderland" in the U.S. (just 88 days after opening and while the film remained in theaters) created great concern among film exhibitors. Exhibitors fear shorter windows deter attendance (Exhibit 8). U.S. theater owners and major Hollywood studios reached an agreement wherein the studios will be able to release one or two movies each year on an accelerated schedule, cutting a month off of the traditional 4 month DVD release window.[37] The *Wall Street Journal* reports, "Theaters have benefited recently from a boom in box-office receipts, even as studios have suffered from a steep decline in DVD sales. Adjusting the windows is an attempt to maintain the health of both camps, which depend on one another."[38]

44 Hollywood is also seeking to expand direct-to-viewer delivery, avoiding the DVD and capturing revenues directly. Studios won regulatory approval to temporarily block analog outputs on viewers' electronics during pay-per-view movies. While controls for digital outputs are features that are built into modern electronics, viewers with analog equipment could record pay-per-view movies if the regulatory block failed. Studios considered this loophole a security issue. Allowing temporary blockage paves the way for studios to pursue short release windows, offering "premium" pay-per-view opportunities prior to DVD release.

45 Overall, studios are increasingly seeking to overcome their own lost profits through increased DVD sales and alternative channels to serve the home audience directly. Both are detrimental to exhibitors.

46 *Recession Effects* Beyond the previous attendance drivers mentioned, there is a more ominous one: recession. There has been a longstanding effect between economic recession and depression and movie attendance: as the economy declines, attendance increases. As early as 1911 one observer described movies as a "door of escape, for a few cents, from the realities of life."[39] During the depression of the 1930's, movie theaters were described as "an acre of seats in a garden of dreams."[40] The recession of 2008 saw rapid increases in gas prices, the stock market decline, and significant layoffs. One summer movie patron commented, "There's not a whole lot you can do for $10 anymore."[41]

47 The recession of 2008 saw attendance increase 10–15 percent over 2007. The air conditioned comfort of a dark theater and the latest Hollywood release offered a break not just

[36] Smith, E., & Schuker, L. A. E. (2010, Februray 12, 2010). Studios Unlock DVD Release Dates. *Wall Street Journal*, from Factiva.

[37] Smith, E., & Schuker, L. A. E. (2010, Februray 12, 2010). Studios Unlock DVD Release Dates. *Wall Street Journal*, from Factiva.

[38] Smith, E., & Schuker, L. A. E. (2010, February 12, 2010). Studios Unlock DVD Release Dates. *Wall Street Journal*, from Factiva.

[39] Vorse, M. H. (2002). Some Picture Show Audiences (1911). In G. A. Waller (Ed.), *Moviegoing in America: A Sourcebook in the History of Film Exhibition* (pp. 50–53). Malden, MA: Blackwell Publishers Ltd.

[40] Fuller, K. H. (2002). "You Can Have the Strand in Your Own Town": The Struggle Between Urban and Small-Town Exhibition in the Picture Palace Era In G. A. Waller (Ed.), *Moviegoing in America: A Sourcebook in the History of Film Exhibition* (pp. 88–98). Malden, MA: Blackwell Publishers Ltd.

[41] John Woestendiek and Chris Kaltenbach, July 8, 2008, $10 is small price for a big escape: Movie box office figures are flourishing despite, or because of, economic worries, The Baltimore Sun; accessed on Factival, December 5, 2008.

EXHIBIT 8 Alice in Wonderland: Weekly Domestic Box Office Gross

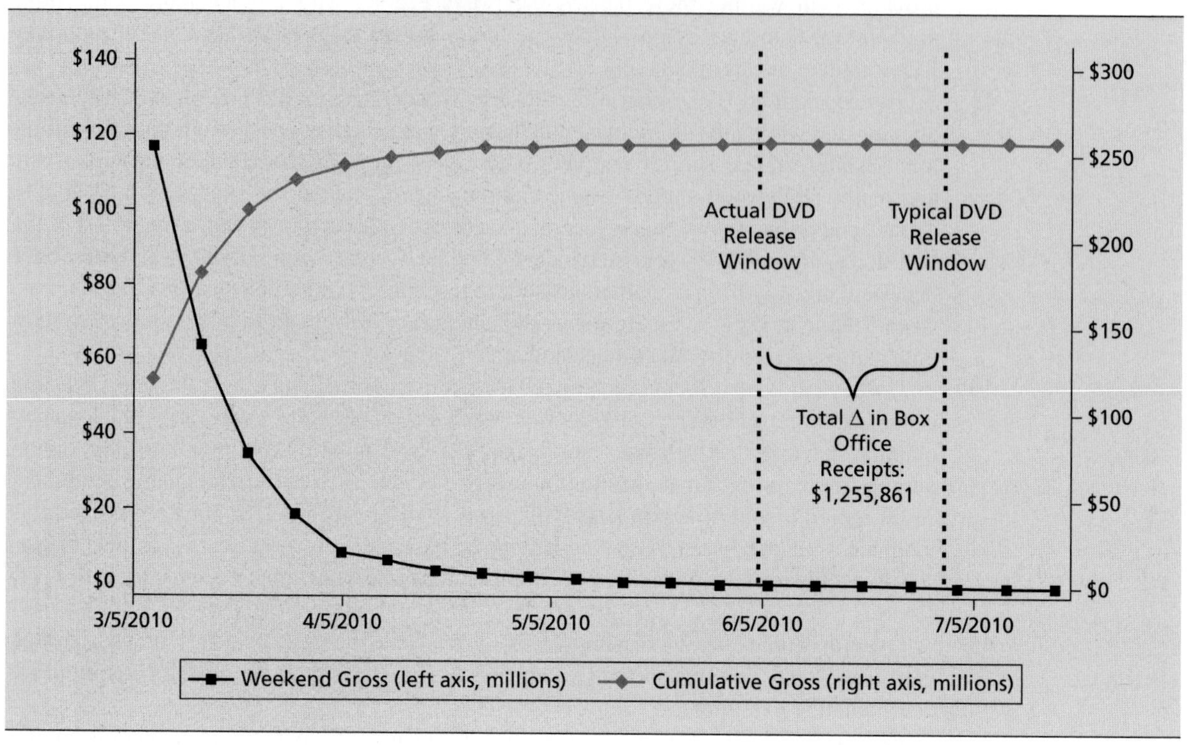

EXHIBIT 9 Change in Average Ticket Price, 1980–2010

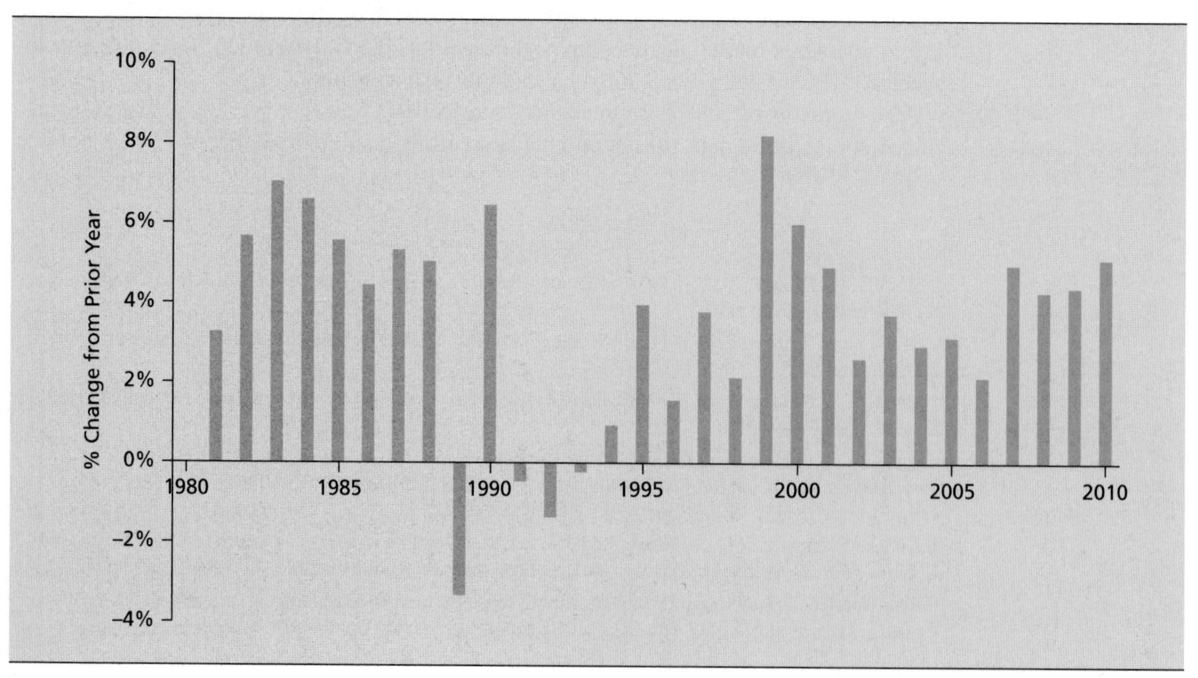

from the summer heat but from reality. "It's escapism, absolutely. It's probably a subconscious thing, and people don't realize it. But there's just so much going on, with people trying to pay their mortgages and get by. It's an escape for a couple of hours."[42] However, attendance for 2008 overall was down 4.1%. The MPAA routinely touts movies as bargain entertainment. Four tickets to a movie costs under $27 compared to $141 for an amusement park or $261for a pro football game.[43] This comparison, however, may no longer be relevant as the true substitute may be a home theater and an existing cable subscription.

POSSIBLE ALTERNATIVE BUSINESS MODELS

48 Under a studio-based film exhibition model, unchanged since the 1930s, exhibitors have just two alternative revenue streams: advertising and concessions. Both appear limited in opportunities for increasing revenues and profits.

49 Advertising, while increasing, threatens to alienate customers. While a 2007 Arbitron survey indicated 63% of those 12 and older report they "do not mind the ads they put on before the movie begins,"[44] other viewers loathe them. Even the industry struggles with the issue. Bob Pisano, President of the MPAA calls increased advertising or higher concession prices "mutually assured destruction" for both exhibitors and the studios. They "try moviegoers' patience" he argues, "leading them to stay home and rent or, worse, illegally download a film."[45]

50 While ticket prices quadrupled, per-capita spending on concessions just doubled since the 1970's.[46] Theater chains have expanded food offerings, some to the point of rivaling mall food courts. The National Association of Theater Owners (NATO) estimates that over 400 theaters now have on-site restaurant or bar service. These theaters appear at odds with the primary demographic market for movies. While the average moviegoer is the teen to twenty-something, these theaters seek 35–50 year olds. AMC is experimenting with an in-theater food model to serve this market. Gold Class Cinemas adds a service approach with 40 seat theaters more akin to club lounges than auditoriums, and offers full food and wine service. Tickets, $20–$25 per person, are purchased not from a ticket booth but from a concierge. Food sales average near $20 per person. Some also offer valet parking and child care to lure customers.[47] Rob Goldberg, Gold Classes COO, explains this is part of the appeal. "We don't get the teenage crowd," he said.[48]

51 Keeping patrons coming to the theater and increased profitability may require a dramatic change for exhibitors. The investment in digital distribution and projection increase both visual quality and operational flexibility, serving as a classic "enabling technology"

[42] John Woestendiek and Chris Kaltenbach, July 8, 2008, $10 is small price for a big escape: Movie box office figures are flourishing despite, or because of, economic worries, The Baltimore Sun; accessed on Factiva, December 5, 2008.

[43] MPAA 2007 Entertainment Industry Market Statistics.

[44] Brodesser-Akner, C. (2008, May 19, 2008). What Popcorn Prices Mean for Movies; Ethanol and rising costs of paper eat into sales that subsidize tickets *Advertising Age*. Retrieved from Factiva.

[45] Ibid.

[46] Ibid.

[47] Russell, J. (2009, November 2, 2009). Winning Ticket? Cinemas hope high-end services pack 'em in. *Los Angeles Business Journal*. Retrieved from Factiva.

[48] Ruggless, R. (2009). Dinner and a movie: One hot ticket for operators. *Nation's Restaurant News, 43*(41).

opening the door for alternative content. New York Metropolitan Opera's *Live in HD* is an alternative content leader, now entering its fifth season. The series offers opera to audiences where it may not be available locally. Featuring 12 performances on Saturday afternoons, the series is broadcast to more than 500 HD equipped theaters. Exhibitors continue to experiment with alternative content, mostly for individual sporting events where exhibitors must compete directly with home viewing. Says Jeremy Devine, marketing VP for a Dallas-based theater chain showing the NBA All-Star game: "I don't care how good your buddy's system is, this is a 52-foot screen. And it's in 3D."[49]

52 Despite the potential for alternative content, virtually all admissions continue to be for studio movies. The evidence suggests continued problems with profitability under this studio-dominated model. The surge in revenues from 3D does not appear to be increasing profitability.

53 While exhibitors are, with the exception of Cinemark, predominantly U.S.-based, studios are increasingly focusing their attention on the international market where growth is highest. While U.S. revenues grew 20 percent from 2005 to 2009, international revenues grew 35 percent.[50] Internationally both attendance and receipts are growing.[51] Studios' proportional revenues are also further shifting toward international. In 2005, box office receipts totaled $23 billion with $14 billion (60 percent) from international. By 2009, that increased to two-thirds on $30 billion total.[52] There appear to be opportunities to increase revenues from increased attendance and ticket price increases. In India, for example, last year's 3.3 billion attendees paid an average of just $0.50.[53] In just that market at current growth rates, the annual volume increase in attendance equals total current U.S. annual admissions.[54] Among leading U.S. exhibitors, Cinemark has the largest international presence with 130 theaters (1,066 screens) in Mexico and seven central and South American countries.

RAISING THE EXHIBITION CURTAIN IN 2011 AND BEYOND

54 Despite a continuing recession, the end of 2010 season saw an alarming statistic: summer admissions declined 3 percent from 2009 levels, resulting in a decline in both admissions and revenues. The increased costs of going to the theater may be causing audiences to be more selective in the movies they see at the theater. Perhaps the escapism of the movies is bumping into a reality of empty wallets. Higher prices are "a very dangerous situation for the movie industry," says Paul Dergarabedian, box-office analyst for Hollywood.com. "When is too much too much? The demand has been huge, but theater owners should not just think that they can charge whatever they want, because there is a point when people will literally just stop coming because they can't afford it."[55] Others explain the decline as a lack of content. Even with expectedly high revenues from big budget movies, no sleeper hits emerged.

[49] Moore, M. T. (2009, Februrary 9, 2009). Moving beyond movies. *USA Today,* p. 3A.

[50] Motion Picture Association of America. (2009). *Theatrical Market Statistics: 2009*: Motion Picture Association of America.

[51] The Economist (2010, May 6, 2010). The box office strikes back *The Economist*, from Factiva.

[52] Ibid.

[53] Thakur, A. (2009, July 29, 2009). India dominates world of films. *The Times of India*. Retrieved from Factiva.

[54] Ibid.

[55] Wood, D. B., & Goodale, G. (2010, March 26, 2010). Want to see a 3D movie? Ticket prices go up 20 percent. *The Christian Science Monitor*. Retrieved from Factiva.

55 Fitch Ratings summarized the long-term situation: "[R]evenues and profitability of movie theatres could be increasingly challenged by factors that are largely out of managements' control . . . [T]he significant degree of operating leverage means that cash flow can be meaningfully affected by moderate top-line declines. These factors and financial policy decisions will remain the main drivers of credit quality over the longer term."[56]

56 What can exhibitors do to improve their performance? To reverse the downward trends in attendance? To improve their profitability at a time when the studios, relying on the box office more than ever, are increasingly looking internationally?

[56] Business Wire. (2009, January 27, 2009). Fitch: High Debt Levels Reduce Flexibility for U.S. Movie Exhibitors in 2009. *Business Wire*. Retrieved from Factiva.

Case 17

NII Holdings, Inc.

Alan N. Hoffman
Bentley University and Rotterdam School of Management, Erasmus University

SYNOPSIS

1 US-based NII Holdings provides integrated mobile communication services in Latin America. Using the iDEN (Integrated Digital Enhanced Network) technology developed by Motorola, it is the first in the region to provide two-way radio with push-to-talk (PTT) functions. It focuses on the mid- to high-usage customer segment, typically postpaid corporate white- and blue-collar workers, offering specialized services while its main competitors serve multiple prepaid customer segments.

2 Having high ARPU levels, low churn rates, and a strong balance sheet, NII Holdings is able to expand its PTT operations aggressively in Latin America, especially Brazil. It also begins to deploy 3G networks in Peru and Chile to complement its iDEN network. This growth pattern, however, is becoming difficult to sustain in the face of increased competition from both global telecom giants and local Latin American rivals. The company needs to find a way to continue differentiating itself from competitors while increasing its market share in its key markets—Mexico, Brazil, Peru, Chile, and Argentina.

NII HOLDINGS, INC.

3 US-based NII Holdings provides integrated mobile communication services in Latin America. Using the iDEN (Integrated Digital Enhanced Network) technology developed by Motorola, it is the first in the region to provide two-way radio with push-to-talk (PTT) functions. It focuses on the mid- to high-usage customer segment, typically postpaid corporate white- and blue-collar workers, offering specialized services while its main competitors serve multiple prepaid customer segments.

4 Initially a subsidiary of Nextel Communications, one of the first PTT system providers in the US, NII Holdings operates under Nextel TM brand in the major urban and suburban centers of Mexico, Brazil, Argentina, Peru, and Chile. It has successfully leveraged the use of the Nextel brand to develop relationships with corporate customers, and has obtained high ARPU (average revenue per user) rates and low monthly churn rates. Consequently, the company can realize its profitable growth strategy.

5 A strong balance sheet enables NII Holdings to continue expanding its network infrastructure in key growth markets like Brazil and Peru. The RIMM BlackBerry handset supported by the iDEN technology is the company's most recent development. Given the corporate world's preference for RIMM phones (second to Apple, see **Exhibit 7**), this new device could become a significant sales driver for NII Holdings.

Source: The author would like to thank Jaime Cobian Garrigosa, Aman Rastogi, Patrick Uyesaka, and Jesus Zubillaga for their research. Please address all correspondence to Dr. Alan N. Hoffman, Bentley University, Dept. of Management, 175 Forest Street, Waltham, MA USA 02452; ahoffman@bentley.edu. Printed by permission of Dr. Alan N. Hoffman.

COMPANY HISTORY

Parent company

6 NII Holdings began as a wholly owned subsidiary of Nextel Communications in 1996. The parent company, founded in 1987 in New Jersey, was originally known as Fleet Call. It changed its name to Nextel Communications in 1993, a year after Fleet Call's IPO in the NASDAQ. Nextel Communications aimed to acquire licenses for cellular-like services using frequencies once confined to taxi and truck fleets, instead of purchasing traditional and expensive cellular licenses (Andrews, 1993). This business model along with strategic collaboration with Motorola, Matsushita Electric, Nippon Telegraph and Communications, and Northern Telecom enabled Nextel Communications to "stitch together its national network" (Helm, 1993) and provide handsets with cellular phone, two-way radio, pager, and electronic mail services combined.

Nextel International

7 Originally called McCaw International Ltd, NII Holdings had its name changed to Nextel International Incorporated in 1997. The CEO of Nextel International, Keith Grinstein, said: "The purpose of the name change is to further consolidate our global presence under the Nextel flag and to highlight our strategy of making iDEN a worldwide standard. Now we can better coordinate roaming, customer care, sales, and branding under the Nextel International logos" (Banta, 1997).

8 Nextel International provided wireless communication services through its subsidiaries in 5 of the largest cities in Latin America, 3 of the largest cities in Asia, primarily in the Philippines, and in some European and Canadian cities. It grew mostly through acquisitions in international markets where it held SMR (Specialized Mobile Radio) channel or iDEN-based operations.

9 In January 2002, Nextel International considered filing for chapter 11 bankruptcy after its Argentina subsidiary missed an US$8.3 million principal payment to banks and defaulted on a payment to Motorola (Bloomberg News, 2002). In May 2002, it filed for bankruptcy court protection with a proposed reorganization plan to reduce the company's debt load (Calgary Herald, 2002). The plan was approved in October 2002 with support from Motorola and Nextel Communications, its largest equity holder, which allowed the company to reemerge under its current name, NII Holdings Incorporated.

NII Holdings

10 NII Holdings saw shares owned by Nextel Communications drop from 95% to 37% and increased control of the company by MacKay Shields, a New York investment firm, and Merrill Lynch. Its Chairman and CEO, Steve Shindler, regarded the company's reemergence as a success: "We completed a successful restructuring with overwhelming support from our creditors that reduced the company's long-term debt from US$2.8 billion to about US$430 million. In addition, the ownership structure of the company changed from a private substantially wholly owned subsidiary of Nextel Communications to an independent publicly traded company with the financial wherewithal to fully fund its business plan without the need for any additional external financing" (Business Wire, 2003).

11 The company prides itself on how it "became a top performing wireless company in Latin America by providing the right customers with the right products in the right places, all supported by the right service" (NII Holdings Inc., 2009). Its quarterly reports show one specific constant related to its growth numbers—quality customer-oriented service. The company has high ARPU levels (US$46) and low churn rates (1.93% versus 2.0%).

The single most important reason for these impressive figures may be that NII Holdings serves the niche high-margin postpaid market while its competitors concentrate in the much larger low-margin prepaid market.

12 NII Holdings continues to expand throughout Latin American by leveraging its iDEN technology to provide its Nextel Direct Connect, International Direct Connect, and other services. It is also rolling out 3G networks in Peru and Chile. During the third quarter of 2009, the company reported a total subscriber base of 7 million. Expecting the postpaid market to have huge potential, it has signed a long-term agreement with Motorola, which will provide iDEN devices and continue developing innovative handsets in exchange for NII Holding's order commitments until December 31, 2011. Although 80% of mobile customers in Latin America have prepaid plans (see **Exhibit 6**), some prepaid subscribers are migrating to postpaid plans because the latter offer a superior airtime option. Postpaid subscribers in Peru, for example, are expected to grow significantly over the next 3 years (Business News Americas, 2009). NII Holdings believes its commitment to iDEN technology will give it an operating strength if this trend continues.

INTERNAL OPERATION

Financial Operations

13 NII Holding's financial objectives are to provide shareholders with an attractive return through accelerating profitable growth and to achieve financial and operational milestones in the following categories:

- Operating revenues
- Operating income
- Market capitalization
- Average service revenue per unit
- Average revenue per subscriber
- Average monthly churn rate

Revenue and Operating Income

14 ***Exhibit 1*** shows that NII Holdings' revenue since bankruptcy reorganization in 2002 has grown at stable and impressive year-to-year rates of 29.7% between 2003 and 2006, 39% in 2007, and 29.5% in 2008. Even though there was a significant drop in revenue growth during 2008, the numbers still look consistently solid thanks to subscriber growth in Mexico and Brazil. The 2002 numbers largely reflect debt and equity restructuring gains from bankruptcy reorganization that led to liability withdrawals and asset selling.

Long Term Debt and Cash

15 ***Exhibit 5*** shows that NII Holdings has a sizable debt liability of about US$2.5 billion, which should limit its opportunity for expansion. But most of the debt will come due between 2011 and 2012, which provides a cushion to continue profitable growth in key markets.

16 The company also has large cash holdings of about US$2.0 billion. Although it has a relatively high LTD/cash ratio of about 1.25, its cash holdings should still be sufficient to internally finance expansion. It has generated a consistent operating cash flow growth of 28% year to year.

17 ***Exhibit 5*** also shows that during the first quarter of 2009 (VERIFY), the LTD/Equity ratio was around 0.96, much improved from 2008's 1.23. Although the ratio is not alarming,

EXHIBIT 1 **Revenue and Net Income from 1998–2008 in Mil$**

	1999	2000	2001	2002	2003	2004	2005	2006	2007	2008	TTM
Revenue	104.5	330.2	679.6	780.4	938.7	1,279.9	1,745.8	2,371.3	3,296.3	4,269.4	4,152.1
O. Income	270.9	293.7	2,081.3	77.6	160.7	250.4	354.6	459.8	619.1	767.9	659.5
N. Income	520.2	478.5	2,497.3	1,997.6	173.0	57.3	174.8	294.5	378.4	369.1	351.0

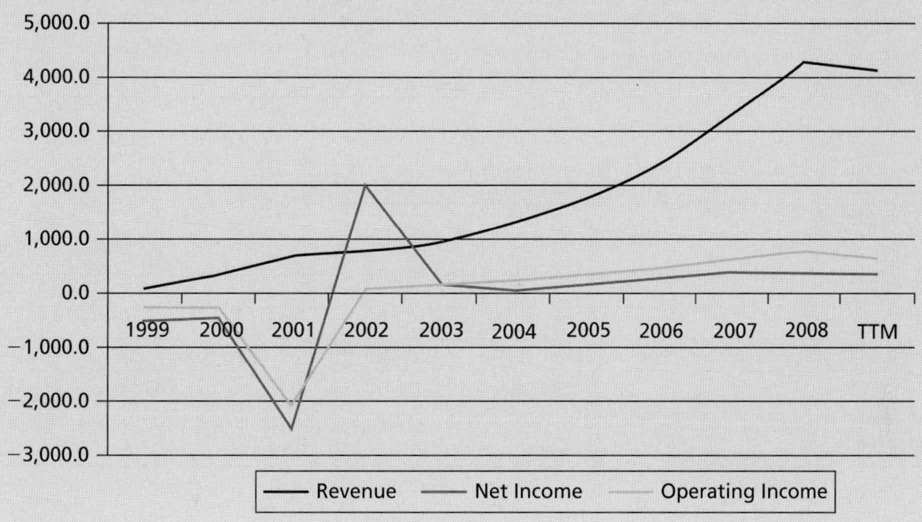

Source: Morningstar Inc.

EXHIBIT 2 **Competitor Market Caps**

Close Competitors	TTM Sales $Mil	Market Cap $Mil
NII Holdings, Inc.	**4,152**	**5,144**
*America Movil S.A.B. de C.V.	25,767	78,906
*Telefonica, S.A.	76,682	136,241
*Telecom Italia SPA	42,340	21,903
*Tele Norte Leste Holding Company	10,409	8,507
*Brasil Telecom Participacoes SA	6,190	4,420

*Morningstar Analyst Report Available
Data as of 03-31-09

the company should recall that it went bankrupt in 2002 mainly because of its inability to cover creditor payments. Any significant increase in LTD ratios should therefore be closely monitored. Additionally, the company and investors should closely monitor the inherent volatility of currencies in the countries where NII Holdings operates, which has a significant effect on both equity and debt positions the company held.

EXHIBIT 3 NII Holdings 3 Year Stock Performance

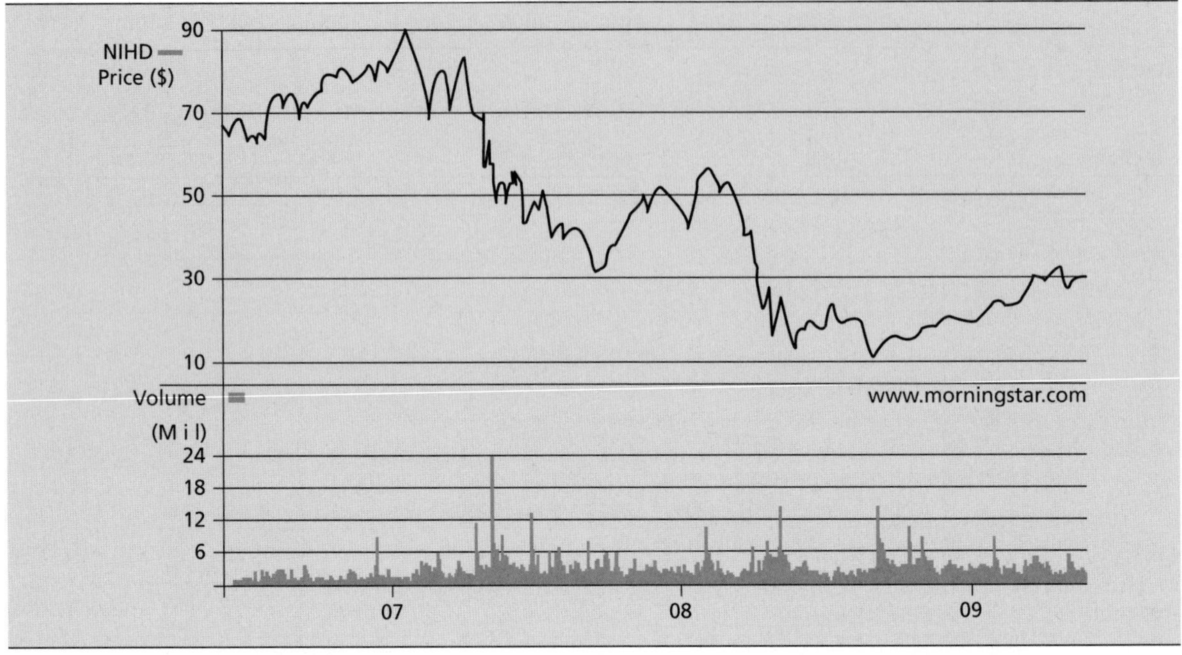

EXHIBIT 4 NII Holdings 10 Year Balance Sheet

	1999	2000	2001	2002	2003	2004	2005	2006	2007	2008	TTM
Cash	100	473.9	250.3	231.2	405.4	331	877.5	708.6	1,370.2	1,243.3	2,001.2
Accts Rec.	23	73.2	116.8	101	120.6	160.7	220.5	298.5	438.4	454.8	591.1
Inventory	16.2	26.7	24.5	18	21.1	32	54.2	70.3	107.3	139.3	199.1
Total Assts	1,681.8	3,193.2	1,244.4	848.9	1,234.4	1491.3	2,621	3,297.7	5,436.7	5,088.1	6,737.2

Source: Morningstar Inc.

Marketing

18 NII Holdings' marketing objectives are to obtain the highest ARPU levels in the regions where it operates, to attract postpaid corporate customers through strong relationships, and to maintain strong brand reputation among high- to mid-usage customers.

Price

19 Since 2002 NII Holdings has been the unquestioned leader in ARPU in the 5 countries where it operates—Mexico, Brazil, Argentina, Peru, and Chile. It will continue to charge the highest tariffs in Brazil and expects its monthly ARPU to remain slightly above BRL 124 from 2009 to 2012. This number has no significance in itself, but compared with the

EXHIBIT 5 **NII Holdings 10-year Balance Sheet**

10-Yr Balance Sheet ASSETS $Mil								
	2002	**2003**	**2004**	**2005**	**2006**	**2007**	**2008**	**2009 1st Qtr**
Cash and Equiv	**231.2**	**405.4**	**331**	**877.5**	**708.6**	**1,370.20**	**1,243.30**	**2,001.20**
Accts Rec.	101	120.6	160.7	220.5	298.5	438.4	454.8	591.1
Inventory	18	21.1	32	54.2	70.3	107.3	139.3	199.1
Other Current Assets	45.5	61	70.6	122.6	131.8	232.3	264.3	299.4
Total Current Assets	**395.6**	**608.1**	**632.7**	**1,282.20**	**1,209.10**	**2,389.80**	**2,183.60**	**3,127.20**
Other Long-Term Assets	23	63.8	232.4	321.2	330.2	783.4	699.4	874.5
Total Assets	**848.9**	**1,234.40**	**1,491.30**	**2,621.00**	**3,297.70**	**5,436.70**	**5,088.10**	**6,737.20**
LIABILITIES and SH Equity								
	2002	**2003**	**2004**	**2005**	**2006**	**2007**	**2008**	**2009 1st Qtr**
Accts Payable	27.7	36.5	87.4	82.3	107.7	125	136.4	143.3
Short-Term Debt	0	1.5	2.1	24.1	23.3	70.5	99.1	577.7
Accrued Liabilities	151.7	164	233.4	323.1	354.2	449.1	459.4	552.3
Other Short-Term Liabilities	72.9	45.5	45.8	59.6	84	109.6	116.3	129.1
Total Current Liabilities	252.3	247.5	368.7	489	569.1	754.3	811.2	1,402.40
Long-Term Debt	**432.2**	**535.3**	**596.2**	**1,148.90**	**1,134.40**	**2,196.10**	**2,193.20**	**2,465.30**
Other Long-Term Liabilities	73.1	122.2	104.5	171.7	247.7	318	296.8	301.7
Total Liabilities	757.5	905	1,069.30	1,809.60	1,951.20	3,268.40	3,301.20	4,169.40
Total Equity	**91.4**	**329.5**	**422**	**811.4**	**1,346.50**	**2,168.40**	**1,786.90**	**2,567.80**
Total Liabilities & Equity	848.9	1,234.40	1,491.30	2,621.00	3,297.70	5,436.70	5,088.10	6,737.20

Source: Morningstar Inc.

expected industry average monthly ARPU of BRL 24-BRL 27, it shows that NII Holdings has carved out a specific niche in Brazil's high-end corporate market.

20 The company's overall churn rate stands at 1.9%, which is low compared with its competitors in Latin American (Morningstar Equity Analysts, 2009). This means customers see the higher value offered by NII Holdings and accept the higher prices to obtain it.

Product

21 NII Holdings' offers consist of business-oriented Nextel wireless communication devices with data services, wireless Internet access, Next Direct Connect, and International Direct Connect. It also offers services that differentiate it from its competitors. One such service is free Suite Multimedia that enables NII subscribers to transfer music, image, and video files to and from their favorite Motorola device, and to easily browse, organize, and manage their multimedia library on their PC. Other services include vehicle and delivery tracking, order entry processing, and workforce monitoring applications.

EXHIBIT 6 **Prepaid Wireless Growth by Region**

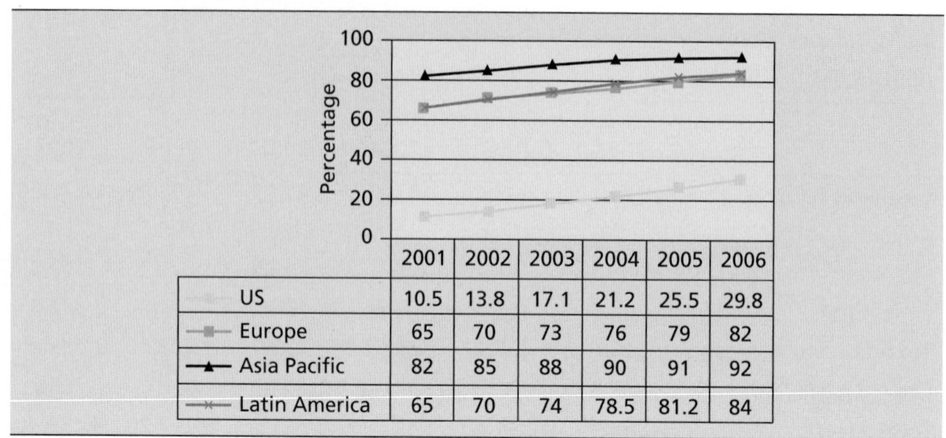

	2001	2002	2003	2004	2005	2006
US	10.5	13.8	17.1	21.2	25.5	29.8
Europe	65	70	73	76	79	82
Asia Pacific	82	85	88	90	91	92
Latin America	65	70	74	78.5	81.2	84

EXHIBIT 7 **J.D. Power and Associates 2008 Business Wireless Smartphone Customer Satisfaction Study℠**
Overall Smartphone Index Rankings (Based on a 1,000-point scale)
JDPower.com Power Circle Ratings™ for consumers:

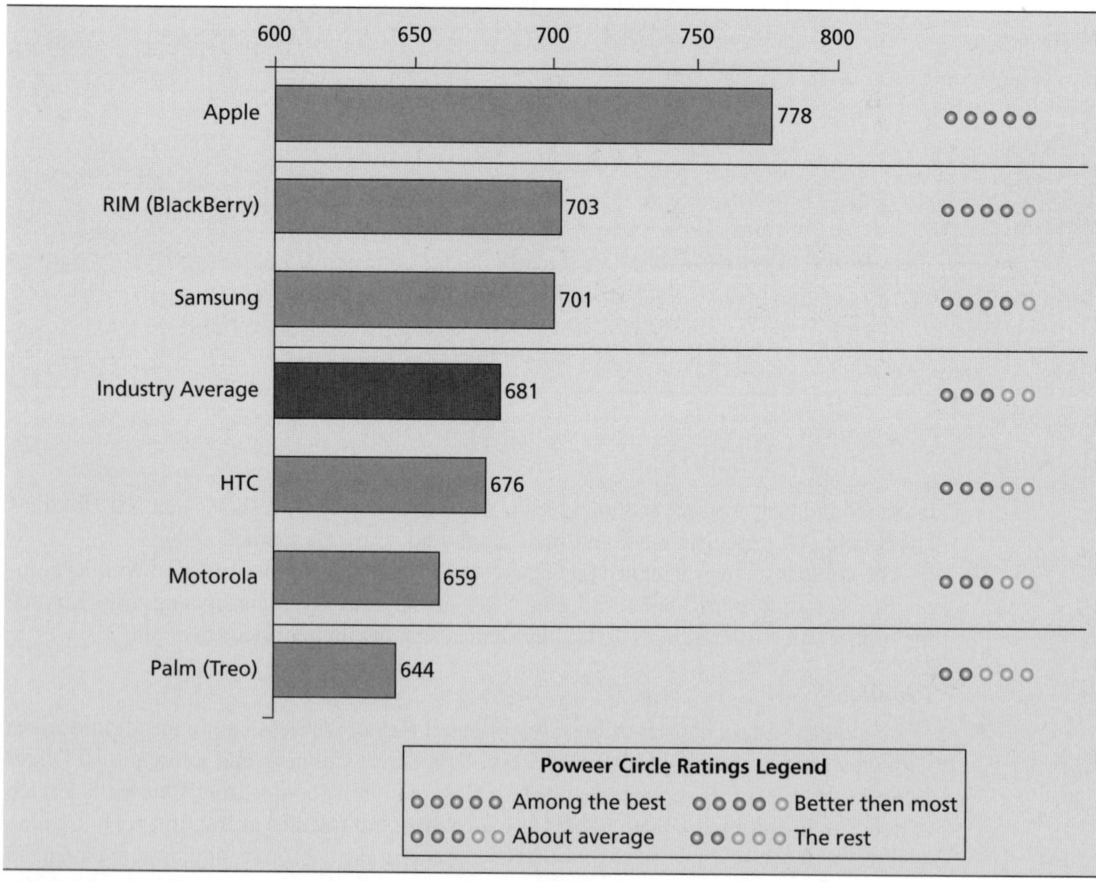

600 650 700 750 800

Apple	778
RIM (BlackBerry)	703
Samsung	701
Industry Average	681
HTC	676
Motorola	659
Palm (Treo)	644

Poweer Circle Ratings Legend

Among the best — Better then most

About average — The rest

Source: J.D. Power and Associates 2008 Business Wireless Smartphone Customer Satisfaction Study℠

Rankings are based on numerical scores and not necessarily on statistical significance. JDPower.com Power Circle Ratings™ are derived from consumer ratings in J.D. Power studies. For more information on Power Circle Ratings, visit jdpower.com/faqs.

EXHIBIT 8 **Fixed Broadband and 3G Subscriptions in Chile, 2005–2014**

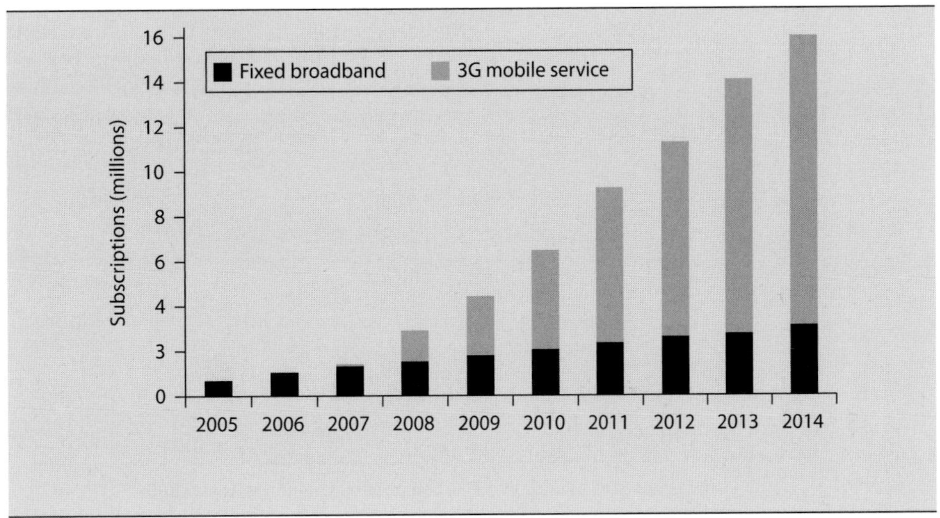

EXHIBIT 9 **Worldwide Coverage**

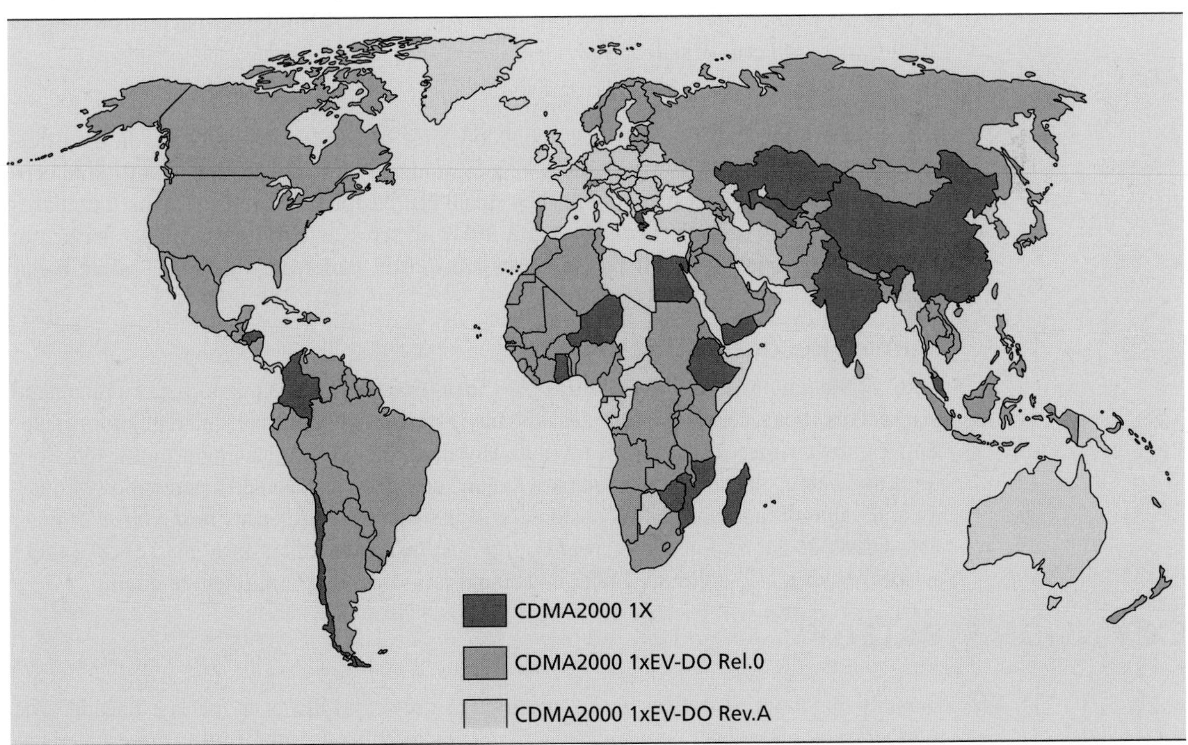

EXHIBIT 10 **US Market: Top-10 Best-Selling Smartphones, 2009**

Ranking	Maker/Vendor	Model
1	RIM	BlackBerry Curve-series
2	Apple	iPhone 3GS
3	RIM	BlackBerry Pearl-series
4	Apple	iPhone 3G
5	RIM	BlackBerry Bold
6	RIM	BlackBerry Storm
7	HTC	T-Mobile G1
8	Palm	Pre
9	HTC	Touch Pro
10	HTC	Touch Diamond

Source: IDC as cited by EDN, compiled by Digitimes, August 2009

22 Most NII products are Motorola devices, including the MOTOROKR and Vi9 cell phones. A new product, the BlackBerry Curve 8350i Smartphone, is the first BlackBerry Smartphone in Latin America to offer a combination of PTT function and premium phone features, leading email and messaging capabilities, web access, productivity applications, and rich multimedia capabilities.

23 All NII products are based on Motorola's iDEN technology, which runs on a 2G (second generation) network on the GSM standard. In response to its competitors' ramping efforts to offer 3G network devices throughout Latin America, NII Holdings also plans to deploy 3G networks in Peru, Brazil, and Mexico between 2010 and 2012.

Promotion

24 NII Holdings does not base advertisements on price or handset diversity but on its differentiated services that enable customers to communicate more quickly, efficiently, and economically (NII Holdings Inc, 2009). The typical NII customer is a business that purchases multiple handsets (usually between 3 and 30) with the Nextel Direct Connect service to facilitate daily operation. NII commercials are mostly targeted at blue- and white-collar workers of those corporations.

Human Resources

25 With 12,000 employees, NII Holdings uses local management teams to better understand market conditions, seize opportunities, and navigate cultural, political, and regulatory issues so it can better meet customer needs (NII Holdings Inc, 2007). Having a motivated work force and being a leader in customer service, the company has created a perception of quality and value in the minds of its customers. It has received numerous *Best Places to Work For* awards, social responsibility awards, and *Best Image* awards in local markets. All these awards enhance NII Holdings' brand image and reinforce its commitment to quality.

EXPANSION STRATEGY

26 Demand for mobile services in Latin America grew steadily over the last decade. The number of mobile subscribers reached 455 million in 2008. As subscription prices decrease because of competition, the number of people who can pay for mobile services will further increase. By 2015, for example, mobile services are expected to account for 61% of Mexico's total telecom market revenue.

27 This business environment gives a company like NII Holdings the opportunity to establish a strong brand name and presence in fast-growing markets where over 50% of the population still do not use mobile services (like Brazil, Mexico, Argentina, and Peru). Positive growth in these markets will enhance the company's customer base and consequently its revenue.

28 The company will continue expanding by penetrating new areas in the countries where it already operates with the current iDEN-based network. Above all, it plans to further invest in Brazil where it has only 1.8 million customers—between 1 and 2% of all wireless subscribers. There it must either purchase existing spectrum rights or enter newly available spectrum license auctions.

29 NII Holdings also considers deploying 3G networks that will enable it to offer higher quality and value added services. The 35 MHz spectrum license obtained in Peru, the spectrum blocks acquired in Chile, and the spectrum modification obtained in Mexico are all preparations for launching 3G networks. Then the company will be able to offer both its successful iDEN network products along with enhanced 3G network products to compete with rival operators.

30 To attract traveling business customers, NII Holdings also plans to reach agreements with local providers for roaming services in countries where it does not operate.

COMPETITION

Global Competitors

America Movil

31 Founded in September 2000 as a spin-off from Telmex, America Movil is Latin America's largest wireless company, serving approximately 190 million customers in 16 countries throughout Latin America and the Caribbean. The family of Mexican billionaire Carlos Slim Helu currently owns 47% of the company; AT&T owns about 25%.

32 When America Movil was founded, it served about 10 million customers in Mexico, Guatemala, Ecuador, and the US. It expanded quickly thereafter via organic growth throughout Central America and acquisitions throughout Latin America, increasing its market share from just over 20% in 2000 to over 42% in the fourth quarter of 2008.

33 In 2008, America Movil generated almost 60% of its total US$31 billion sales in Mexico (±40%) and Brazil (±20%), with year-to-year revenue growth of 9%. Its 2008 overall operating income was US$8.5 billion, a 10% increase from the previous year, with a net income of US$5.3 billion. The company also has a healthy debt-to-equity ratio, with 2008 long-term debt holdings of US$8 billion and total equity of US$10.5 billion. In the second quarter of 2009, it reported year-to-year revenue growth of 17%, beating most predictions and adding 4 million customers. Its ARPU levels, however, were down 2% in Mexico and 10% in Brazil (Zhang, 2009).

34 America Movil manages relatively low cash levels (US$1.5 billion) year to year but generates increasing amounts of cash from operations (US$8 billion), which enables it to expand throughout Latin America. Currently, its Telcel unit is the number one cellular company in Mexico with over 55 million customers, representing over 72% of the mobile market. It has also recently re-branded its operations (under the new Claro brand) in Argentina, Paraguay, and Uruguay to improve its image, particularly in Argentina, the third biggest market in Latin America.

Telefonica

35 A Spain-based company founded in 1923, Telefonica currently serves 25 countries around the world – its Latin American operations account for 40% of total revenues. It has major operations in the 3 biggest Latin American markets—Brazil, Mexico, and Argentina—as well as in Chile, Colombia, Venezuela, and Peru. It also controls the largest cellular operator in Brazil, Vivo, with 45 million subscribers, in partnership with Portugal Telecom.

36 Telefonica began its international expansion in 1971. Since the 1990s, it has consistently increased its presence in Latin America through acquisitions. It signed a deal in 1994 with the Peruvian government that gave it monopolistic power in Peru's telecom industry. The same year, it acquired a large stake in Multicanal (Argentina's number one cable company) and in 1997, it won the Telesp (Telecomunicacoes de Sao Paulo) spectrum auction. By 2000, Telefonica had complete ownership of Telefonica de Argentina, Telefonica del Peru, and Telesp.

37 In 2008, Telefonica earned US$83.1 billion in revenues, a 5% decrease from 2007. Its 2008 net Income was US$10.5 billion, almost 20% down from the previous year, due largely to its European operations (Telefonica S.A., 2008).

Telecom Italia

38 Telecom Italia is a Milan-based company, founded in 1994 through state-owned telecom mergers, and privatized in 1997. From its foundation until 1997, it belonged to the Italian government. Following the privatization of the telecom industry, it began its international expansion in Europe and Latin America. That same year, it took stakes in foreign telecom companies, including Mobilkom Austria, which became Telekom Austria a year later. It entered the Latin American market when it acquired a controlling stake in Digitel (Venezuela) in 2000. The following year, it launched a phone service in Peru and entered the Brazilian market by purchasing two licenses, one in Sao Paulo. Latin America now accounts for 18% of Telecom Italia's total sales, the Brazilian mobile market alone for 17% in 2008.

39 In 2008, Telecom Italia generated US$44.5 billion in revenue, a 4% decrease from 2007. Its net income was US$3.2 billion, a 3% decrease from 2007. Currently, the company has a large debt and slow growth in its domestic Italian market, which significantly hurts its top line and bottom line numbers.

Local Competitors

40 Besides these global competitors, some local Latin American companies also have established a presence in key markets. Moreover, they are better prepared than multinationals to meet customers' specific and immediate needs. These smaller competitors include Iusacell (the number 3 mobile operator in Mexico), Entel (a Chilean mobile phone operator), Telecom Argentina (a major local telephone company covering a big part of Buenos Aires), Telemar Norte Leste (northern Brazil), Tele Norte Celular (the Amazon area), and Telemig Celular (central Brazil), among others.

KEY WEAKNESSES

Postpaid Segment

41 NII Holdings succeeds as a telecom service provider to high- and mid-usage postpaid customers partly because there is little intense competition in this segment within Latin America. As the telecom giants put more resources into the lucrative postpaid segment,

however, it will become harder and harder for NII Holdings to differentiate itself enough to maintain its high ARPU levels.

42 Telefonica announced the deployment of PTT networks throughout Latin America in November 2009, after testing in Ecuador and Peru. Analysts predict it will become the largest PTT provider in Latin America (Cellular-News, 2009). In response to Telefonica's move, America Movil announced that it would replace or upgrade its PTT platform (Nixon, 2009). Competitors' increased encroachment into NII Holdings' niche market may start putting pressure on the company's revenue, especially in Mexico. Currently, NII Holdings derives 40 to 70% of its sales and profits from Mexico. With America Movil's control of almost 80% of the mobile market in Mexico and the rollout of its PTT platform, price pressure in this single market will directly affect NII Holdings' overall revenue.

3G Network

43 NII Holdings started to deploy its 3G networks later than its competitors and may be hard-pressed to deliver service capabilities that Telefonica and America Movil already offer and have lead-time to perfect them. Through the Claro brand, America Movil's 3G network in Brazil now covers about 55% of Brazil's population.

Scale

44 NII Holdings needs to expand its coverage to better use the International Direct Connect service through its PTT platform. It has been unable to do so, however, because of its smaller balance sheet compared with its global competitors. The latter offer much better international plans, such as lower roaming charges, due to their geographic spread across Latin America.

45 While striving for scale, NII Holdings must not forget its service level. Until recently, it has managed to guarantee a high level of service, which may not be sustainable as the company aggressively expands.

Dependence

46 NII Holdings' continued profitable growth will largely depend on subscriber base growth in Brazil and on new 3G networks in Peru and Chile. Heavy investment in Brazil may be risky since the company is putting a bet on the resilience of the Brazilian economy. To deploy 3G networks the company also depends on local Latin American governments to make spectrums available for auction.

47 NII Holdings' long-term commitment to Motorola's iDEN equipment makes it vulnerable to market trends. If the trend from prepaid to postpaid plans does not pick up as predicted, both current customers and potential customers may migrate to more scalable 3G networks offered by competitors. Moreover, the company is highly dependent on Motorola to develop innovative new products to compete with rivals.

THE PATH AHEAD

48 NII Holdings seems to have learned an important lesson about growth and growth finance from the 2002 bankruptcy. Having understood the ramifications of overextended growth in countries with unstable currencies and economies, it now commits only to key markets and has developed a stable growth pattern that enables it to maintain high service levels, large cash positions, balanced debt positions, and consistent profit margins. Expansion is financed primarily internally by operating cash flow. Long-term debt is also managed more efficiently.

49 Since bankruptcy reemergence, the company has achieved a remarkable turnaround with consistently high double-digit top-line and bottom-line growth, coupled with a consolidation strategy in Latin American markets. The question remains whether it can retain its developed niche market and concurrently add new customers in emerging markets to achieve profitable growth. Facing competition from heavy weight rivals with deeper pockets, how can NII Holdings continue to differentiate itself? Should it stick to the postpaid model or move into the prepaid consumer segment with fierce competition and lower margins?

REFERENCES

1. Andrews, E. L. (1993, September 27). In Auctioning the Air Waves, Who'll Risk What? *New York Times,* p. D1.
2. Anonymous. (2009). *IE Market Research Corporation: Brazil will have 205.6 million mobile subscribers in 2013 with Vivo's taking a 30.0% market share, according to new market research report by IEMR.* Coventry: M2 Presswire.
3. Anonymous. (2009). NII Holdings Launches the BlackBerry Curve 8350i, the Most Powerful Push-to-Talk Smartphone with Wi-Fi Capabilities, in Latin America. *PR Newswire.*
4. Anonymous. (2009). NII Holdings Selects Smith Micro Software for Its Premier Mobility Multimedia Suite Offering. *PR Newswire.*
5. Banta, B. (1997, September 4). Nextel's Wholly Owned Subsidiary Changes Name to Nextel International, Inc. *PR Newswire,* p. 1.
6. Bloomberg News. (2002, February 5). Business Briefs. *Seattle Times,* p. C2.
7. Business News Americas Staff Reporters. (2009). *Mobile penetration could reach 85% by year-end—Claro.* Lima: Business News Americas.
8. Business Wire. (2003, February 12). NII Holdings Announces Strong Results for 2002. New York , New York, United States of America.
9. Calgary Herald. (2002, May 25). Nextel's International Unit Files for Bankruptcy. *Calgary Herald,* p. D6.
10. CDMA Development Group. (2009). *CDMA2000 Offers TDMA Operators a Fast Track to 3G.* Retrieved December 4, 2009, from CDMA Development Group Web Site: www.cdg.org/…/images/promises_made_del_01.gif
11. Cellular-News. (2009, November 10). *Cellular-News.* Retrieved 12 4, 2009, from Telefonica to Offer Push to Talk in Latin America: http://www.cellular-news.com/story/40571.php
12. Clark, S. (2009, September 19). *Near Field Communications World.* Retrieved December 03, 2009, from Visa launches NFC trial in Brazil: http://www.nearfieldcommunicationsworld.com/2009/09/15/31686/visa-launches-nfc-trial-in-brazil/
13. Frecuencia, A. (2008, July 24). *You Tube.* Retrieved December 03, 2009, from Fabio Maeda, From Vivo: http://www.youtube.com/watch?v=hxo2Y6T5x2M
14. Helm, L. (1993, December 4). Nextel Key Player in Creation of Largest Wireless Network. *Austin American Statesman,* p. E7.
15. Morningstar Equity Analysts. (2009). *NII Holdings, Inc. NIHD Analyst Report.* Morningstar.
16. NII Holdings . (2007, February 27). *NII Holdings Inc. Q4 2007 Earnings Call Transcript.* Retrieved December 06, 2009, from Seeking Alpha Web Site: http://seekingalpha.com/article/66362-nii-holdings-inc-q4-2007-earnings-call-transcript?source=bnet&page=1
17. NII Holdings Inc. (2007). *Annual Report 2006.* Reston.
18. NII Holdings Inc. (2009). *Form 10-K.* Yahoo Finance.
19. NII Holdings, Inc. (2009). *NII Holdings, Inc.* Retrieved November 19, 2009, from NII Holdings—About Us: http://www.nii.com/about_us.html

20. Nixon, P. (2009, November 23). *Business News Americas*. Retrieved December 3, 2009, from America Movil Studying Upgrade to PTT Platform: http://member.bnamericas.com/story.jsp?sector=2&idioma=I¬icia=499176
21. Nixon, P. (2009, September 17). *Business News Americas: Telecomunications/Perspectives.* Retrieved December 06, 2009, from Business News Americas Web Site: http://member.bnamericas.com/perspectives_qa.jsp?sector=2&idioma=I&documento=925252
22. Telefonica S.A. (2008). *Annual Report 2008.*
23. Wireless Federation. (2008, April 08). *Wireless Federation.* Retrieved December 03, 2009, from Argentina's Mobile Market: http://wirelessfederation.com/news/tag/nfc/
24. Zhang, J. (2009, October 22). *Morningstar* . Retrieved December 04, 2009, from NII Reports 3Q Results: http://quicktake.morningstar.com/StockNet/san.aspx?id=312739&pgid=rss
25. ADDITIONAL WORKS CITED
26. America Movil website: http://www.americamovil.com/index_eng.htm
27. Telefonica website: http://www.telefonica.com
28. Telecom Italia website: http://www.tim.it
29. Hoover Company Profiles: http://www.hoovers.com
30. Yahoo! Finance: http://finance.yahoo.com/
31. Datamonitor: NII Holdings, Inc. Company Profile, 08/28/2009.
32. Funding Universe: http://www.fundinguniverse.com/company-histories

Case 18

Philosopher's Wool Co.: *SME Sustainable Supply Chain Management in the Global Economy*

Miriam F. Weismann,
Suffolk University

PHILOSOPHER'S DILEMMA: FINDING A PROFITABLE SMALL TO MEDIUM ENTERPRISE (SME) SUPPLY CHAIN MODEL IN THE GLOBAL ECONOMY

1 In 1975, Eugene and Ann Bourgeois literally built their home and farm in Inverhuron, Ontario, Canada from the ground up using their own labor and help from friends and neighbors.[1] The farm produced, among other agricultural commodities, wool fleece obtained from shearing their own sheep herd. The business decision to enter into the woolen trade came after the couple learned the ancient Fair Isle two-handed knitting technique during a trip to Great Britain. They decided to use their design talents and commitment to hard work to begin the Philosopher's Wool Company ("Philosopher's") in 1984. The mission of the company was to "support sustainable agriculture . . . We have always been a fair trade company, producing wool yarn that is as natural and organic as possible." To accomplish its mission, Philosopher's designed a business plan using a social entrepreneurship model. It would produce, for wholesale distribution to global markets, natural organic woolen products using a sustainable vertical supply chain which included partnering with other local fleece producers and craftsmen. At that time, Ontario quality fleece production was at a virtual standstill because of government pricing policies that stifled market growth.

2 Another significant component of Philosopher's business plan was to achieve a profitable market entry strategy into global markets through partnering with foreign distributors. However, given its small size and limited operational capacity as an SME (small to medium enterprise), it was difficult to attract foreign distributors. The problem of achieving a competitive advantage became even more complicated when the U.S. government added border tariffs on exportation. This increased delivery and distribution costs. So, Philosopher's was forced to abandon its original plan of wholesale distribution and instead, became a retail distribution operation. That meant that Eugene and Ann had to leave the farm operations for several months at a time and travel across the United States and Canada to sell their products direct to consumers at knitting and craft shows. In their 70's and with no business successor in sight, Eugene and Ann realized that their days of direct retail distribution were numbered given their age and the competing needs of the farm. A return to the original and more costly wholesale distribution model, which included the need to partner with U.S. distributors, seemed inevitable. But, the challenge of how

[1] This account of the transformation of the Philosopher's enterprise from idea to reality barely reflects the real excitement behind the story. Philosopher's Wool published a knitting book that includes a lengthy description of the history and development of the business that really should not be missed by any student of entrepreneurial models. See, Bourgeois, Eugene and Ann Bourgeois, *Fair Isle Sweaters Simplified* (2000). Washington, Martingale & Company, pp. 4–25.

Source: *The CASE Journal* 6, no. 2 (Spring 2010). Contact the author at mweismann@suffolk.edu. This case is intended to be used as the basis for class discussion rather than to illustrate either effective or ineffective handling of a management situation. The case was compiled from published sources.

a SME could successfully compete for foreign distributors where it had little financial leverage in the marketplace remained unresolved. Still unable to close a final deal with a U.S. distributor, Philosopher's continued to search for a solution and remain a viable concern.

INDUSTRY BACKGROUND: CANADIAN WOOL MARKETS

Canada's Wool to Market

3 The Canadian Co-operative Wool Growers Limited (CCWG) was established in 1918 by the sheep industry as a national system of collecting and marketing its member's production through a co-operative system (co-op). The co-op collected, graded, measured, and marketed the producers' wool, and after deducting its costs, returned the difference to the producers as their price. Wool prices in Canada had been historically low for several years.[2] Generally, prices paid to wool producers were insufficient to cover the costs of shearing. Thus, wool production had generally not been the primary reason for raising sheep in Canada. The Canadian co-op system had done nothing to create end use value for fleece production. Other than acting as a conduit through which product was sold in the marketplace, it offered no economic development assistance to local farmers. Whatever collective market power or economic advantage was expected to flow from integrating SME fleece producers in the Canadian market, neither came to fruition. There was a substantial consumer demand for finished woolen products and loose yarn supplies locally but it was being satisfied through importation rather than developing competitive local production and distribution channels.

4 The CCWG co-op graded and marketed approximately three million pounds of raw wool each year with most of this production coming from Quebec, Ontario, and Alberta. China was the major buyer of Canadian wool. In total, 90 percent of Canada's production was shipped to Britain, France, Germany, Spain, Japan, United States, China and India. Canadian wool had a niche in the marketplace because of its high elasticity or springiness that helped it to keep its original shape. (Global market comparisons are provided in **Exhibit 1**.)

Ontario Market

5 Philosopher's was located in Inverhuron, Ontario. With approximately 4200 farms, Ontario had approximately 25–30 percent of the sheep population in Canada. The cost to shear and transport the fleece for sale to the CCWG was \$.50 to \$.70 per pound (in U.S. dollars). In the ten years between 1975 and 1985, the price paid by the co-op to sheep farmers had ranged on average between \$.32 and \$.50 per pound, well below the production cost. Up until this point, shearing sheep and disposing of fleece was seen more as a necessary cost of doing business. Delivery of fleece to the co-op was basically an exercise in waste disposal of an unwanted by-product. Philosopher's managed to turn by-product cost into profit for itself and other sheep farmers in Ontario under these depressed pricing circumstances.

PHILOSOPHER'S SUSTAINABLE SUPPLY CHAIN MODEL

Corporate structure

6 In 1975, Eugene was a doctoral student in philosophy (ergo, the name, "Philosopher's Wool") and Ann, a teacher. Motivated to become entrepreneurs, they started a farming business producing lamb, chickens, eggs, hay, vegetables, fruit, and wool fleece. Upon entering into the

[2] Ontario Sheep Marketing Agency, *Introduction to Sheep Production in Ontario* (2006) at http://www.ontariosheep.org/Intropercent20topercent20Sheeppercent20Production/Introduction.pdf. The Ontario Sheep Marketing Agency (OSMA) is funded by the sheep and lamb producers in Ontario. It was formed in 1985 under the Ontario Farm Products Marketing Act and all sheep, lamb and wool producers must register with the agency.

EXHIBIT 1 **Global Market Comparisons**

Only 5.4 percent of all farms in Canada reported raising sheep in a recent 2001 census (see **Exhibit 2**). In 2003 that translated to approximately 993,000 head of sheep raised nationally with an average flock size of 74 head per farm. The sheep population varied considerably on an annual basis. To put this in perspective using statistics from World Sheep Inventories, China led the world in national flock size at 1,034,007,000 head of sheep. No other nation was even a close second. The next largest national flock was located in Australia with 113,000,000 head. The United States remained ahead of Canada with a national flock size of 6,685,000.

Profits from sheep production included meat from slaughter, sales of sheep, and revenues from wool production. Canada produced 1500 metric tons of wool in 2002, approximately 3.3 million pounds, which represented only one percent of the $102.5 million in farm-gate total revenues from combined sheep production during the same period.

According to the Wool Market & Business Update Fall 2008 Report prepared by the Canadian Co-operative Wool Growers Limited (CCWG), China still remained the major source of global wool production through its own production or through outsourcing of wool processing to China by foreign growers.[3] Italy remained the second largest wool processor and manufacturer in the world but continued to face intense competitive pressure from China and other low cost countries. Canadian wool production represented a mere fraction of the world market production figures. The report further indicated that current financial world turmoil had created volatility in the commodity markets which was not a positive signal for the global wool markets. Analysts did not predict any improvement in depressed wool prices until global financial problems in the world commodity markets became more stabilized.

wool trade in 1984, their plan was to use their flock of sheep to produce both meat product and fleece. Their supply chain business model required growing hay for feed, sheep shearing to produce fleece, processing the fleece into finished wool, dying the yarn, and producing knitting kits based on original designs for customers to make sweaters, shawls, gloves, hats and other woolen articles using the Fair Isle knitting method. The model was designed for the vertical integration or organization of each step of production and distribution of woolen products, from shearing to selling. The idea was to follow a true stakeholder approach aimed at providing an increased economic benefit to each local shearer, farmer and crafts person who added value to the product as it progressed along the supply chain to the end user or consumer. Ann also decided to teach classes to consumers in the Fair Isle knitting technique.

7 Along with the farming partnership, Eugene formed a sole proprietorship called "Philosopher's Stone." Philosopher's Stone was built as a shop connected to the farm house. The shop sold yarns, pottery, finished sweaters, knitting accessories, kits, stained glass and some foodstuffs. Shortly thereafter, in 1985, they incorporated the wool business partnership which became known as The Philosopher's Wool Co., Ltd., a Canadian corporation. Philosopher's was staffed by Eugene and Ann as its first two employees. Family members came in and out of the business and provided temporary help at times but showed no interest in business succession. Later, a bookkeeper/office helper was added to the small staff. When needed, Eugene hired temporary seasonal farm help or received assistance from other friends and nearby farmers.

The Sustainable Vertical Supply Chain: Resources, Production, Distribution

8 Philosopher's grew hay as a source of food for the sheep. As part of this operation, Eugene partnered with local farmers to make round hale bales for feed and then gave a portion of

[3] Wool Market & Business Update Fall 2008 Report at http://www.seregonmap.com/SCM/index.htm

EXHIBIT 2 **Canadian Sheep Industry Table: The Canadian Sheep Federation**

Canadian Sheep Industry

Canadian Sheep Statistics

- 13,232 (5.4%) of all farms in Canada reported sheep on farm in 2001Census
- 975,600 sheep & lambs on farm January 1, 2003
- National Average flock size of 74 head
- 80% of lambs born January to July

NATIONAL REPRESENT ATION:

THE CANADIAN SHEEP FEDERATION

FEDERATION CANADIENNE DU MOUTON

1-888-684-7739
www.cansheep.ca
cansheep@cansheep.ca

Canadian Sheep Breeders Association

Francis Winger, Secretary/Treasurer
R.R. #4
Mount Forest, Ont. N0G 2L0
519-323-0360, Fax: 519-323-0468
email: fwinger@log.on.ca
www.sheepbreeders.ca

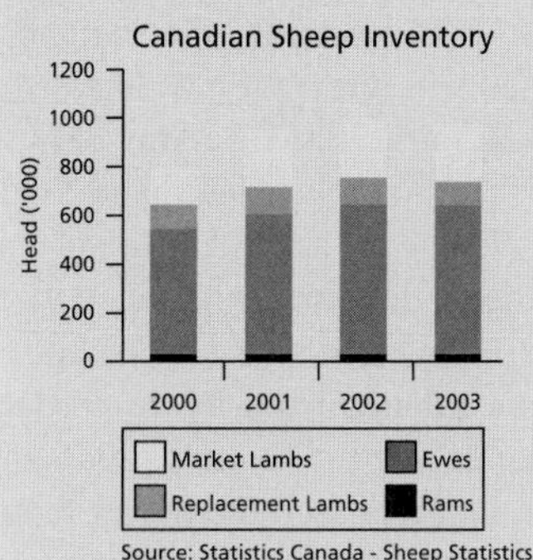

Source: Statistics Canada - Sheep Statistics

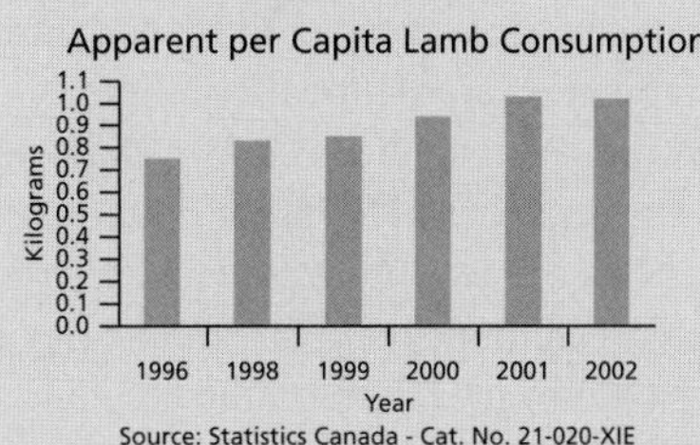

Source: Statistics Canada - Cat. No. 21-020-XIE

Canadian Purebred Sheep:

- Approximately 70,000 head of registered purebred sheep on 1000 farms representing 48 different breeds

- 0464, 726 Sheep and Lambs processed in Canada in 2002
- 34% were processed by 21 Federally Inspected plants
- 66% were processed by hundreds of Provincial plants
- Wool Production: 1500 Metric Tonnes in 2002
- $102.5 million in farm-gate sales

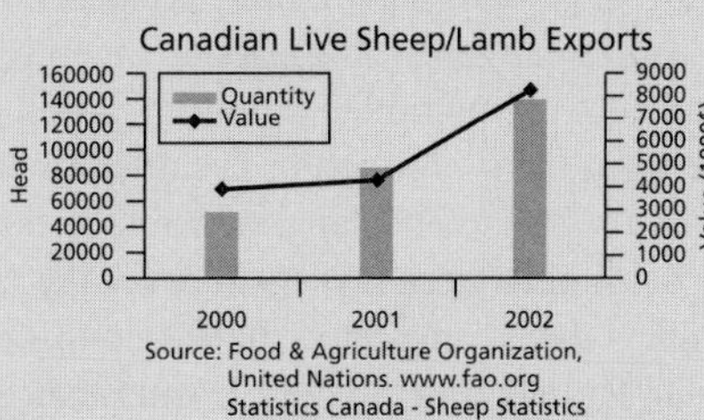

Source: Food & Agriculture Organization, United Nations. www.fao.org
Statistics Canada - Sheep Statistics

Lamb as a percentage of Red Meat Consumption 2002

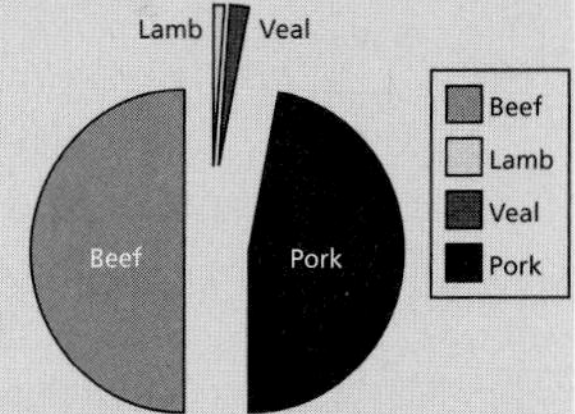

Source: Statistics Canada - Cat. No. 21-020-XIE

Canada's Sheep Industry: $102 Million in Farm-Gate Receipts

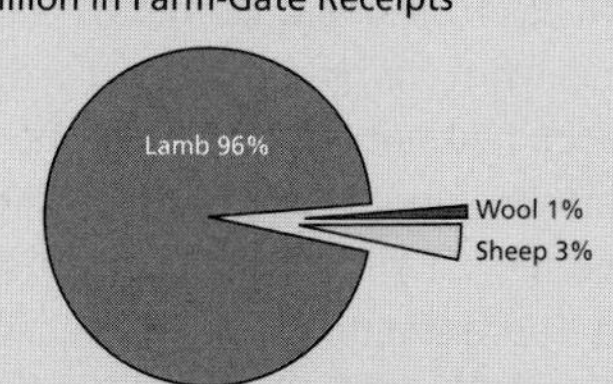

Source: Statistics Canada, Catalogue No. 21-011-XIE, Statistical Services, Policy and Programs Branch, OMAF

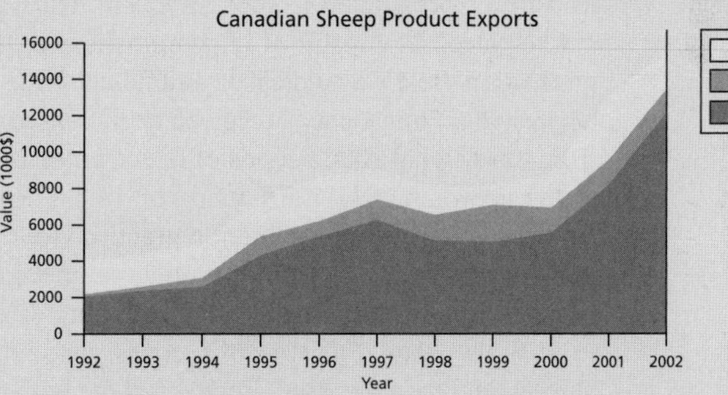

Source: Food & Agriculture Organization, United Nations. www.fao.org

World Sheep Inventories (Thousand Head)

WORLD	1,034,007
China	136,972
Australia	113,000
India	58,800
Iran	53,000
Sudan	47,043
New Zealand	43,141
United Kingdom	35,832
United States	6,685
Canada	993

Source: Food and Agriculture Organization, United Nations. www.fao.org

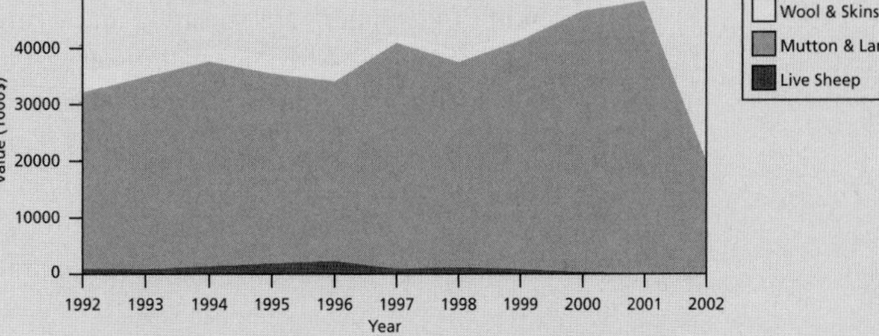

Source: Food & Agriculture Organization, United Nations. www.fao.org

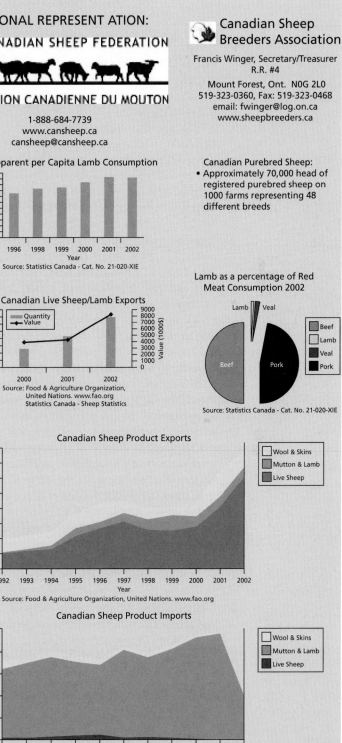

his hay production to other local residents in need. Each year, fleece grew on the sheep and Philosopher's hired a local sheep shearer to assist in the shearing process. Leg wool and belly wool was carted away as trash, called "tags," and sold as "felting wool" after being processed. Philosopher's sold the tags to the co-op for approximately $.50 to $.70 cents per pound through a local farming agent who also charged a small commission.

9 The remaining quality grade fleece was stored in six foot bags each weighing approximately 180 pounds. Other local farmers were contacted directly or through the shearer and invited to supply, sell, and deliver their fleece to Philosopher's as an alternative to supplying the co-op. Unlike large manufacturers, SMEs like Philosopher's operated less formally. There was no formal supplier selection, no supplier certification process, no long-term contractual agreements, no shared technology or demand data. Instead, partnering with other fanners as fleece suppliers was essentially determined by local geography. Selection simply depended upon the person who lived and farmed next door and whether that neighbor had a good reputation in the local community. Through the local integration of like-sized SME farmers into Philosopher's supply chain partnership, the farmers received not only an increased initial payment of $.75 per pound but an additional amount was later paid to the farmer after the fleece was processed and weighed. On the average the second payment was approximately $1.20 per pound, in some cases even more depending on the finished wool yields. Yields could vary based on the cleaning processes used by each individual supplier. As a result of these higher prices paid for fleece, farmers expanded wool fleece production, changing the model from a mere by-product cost of engaging in the meat producing business to a revenue generating part of sheep production. Farmers used the newly found profits from fleece production to defray costs of hay production and for cleaning their barns. The income from meat production became almost pure profit. Another case in point was the local Ewenity Dairy. The dairy was able to develop a cheese and yogurt manufacturing business by using the fleece profits to cover the farming costs.

10 Philosopher's then transported the fleece to several washing mill facilities in Texas and Pennsylvania. The need to integrate American SME washing mills in the supply chain, as opposed to local washing mills, arose because the Canadian co-op system marginalized fleece production to such an extent that washing mills were unable to survive in the marketplace. As a result of improved sheep rearing and fleece cleaning procedures, wool production yield was increased and much waste was eliminated in the production process. On average, Philosopher's received an increased yield of approximately 530 pounds of yarn from the original 1000 pounds of fleece purchased directly from local farmers as compared to the approximately 400 pounds of yarn yield if the wool came from the co-op where improved cleaning and sanitation practices for the fleece had not been implemented. Also, in conformity with its organic production mission, Philosopher's washing process required only one wash cycle instead of two and thereby reduced the use of detergent chemicals used to wash the wool. This washing process also retained approximately 50–60 percent of the natural lanolin in the wool. Because of the high retention of lanolin, there was also no need to put chemical moisturizers in the wool. The process reduced allergic reaction to the wool and produced a softer and more competitive brand quality. After washing, the wool was then returned to Philosopher's for spinning and dying in mills in the United States and Canada.

11 To further integrate SME production as part of the supply chain, Philosopher's hired local knitters from Inverhuron and other adjoining local communities to knit finished product sweaters and other woolen clothing articles. Knitters were hired as independent contractors and paid by the piece, usually $110 to $170 per sweater depending on the complexity of the pattern. The finished sweaters were sold at retail for $400 to $700. Made from some of the finest wool, the finished product was designed to last a lifetime under normal wear and tear conditions. As an added financial benefit, Philosopher's offered its knitters a dollar-for-dollar

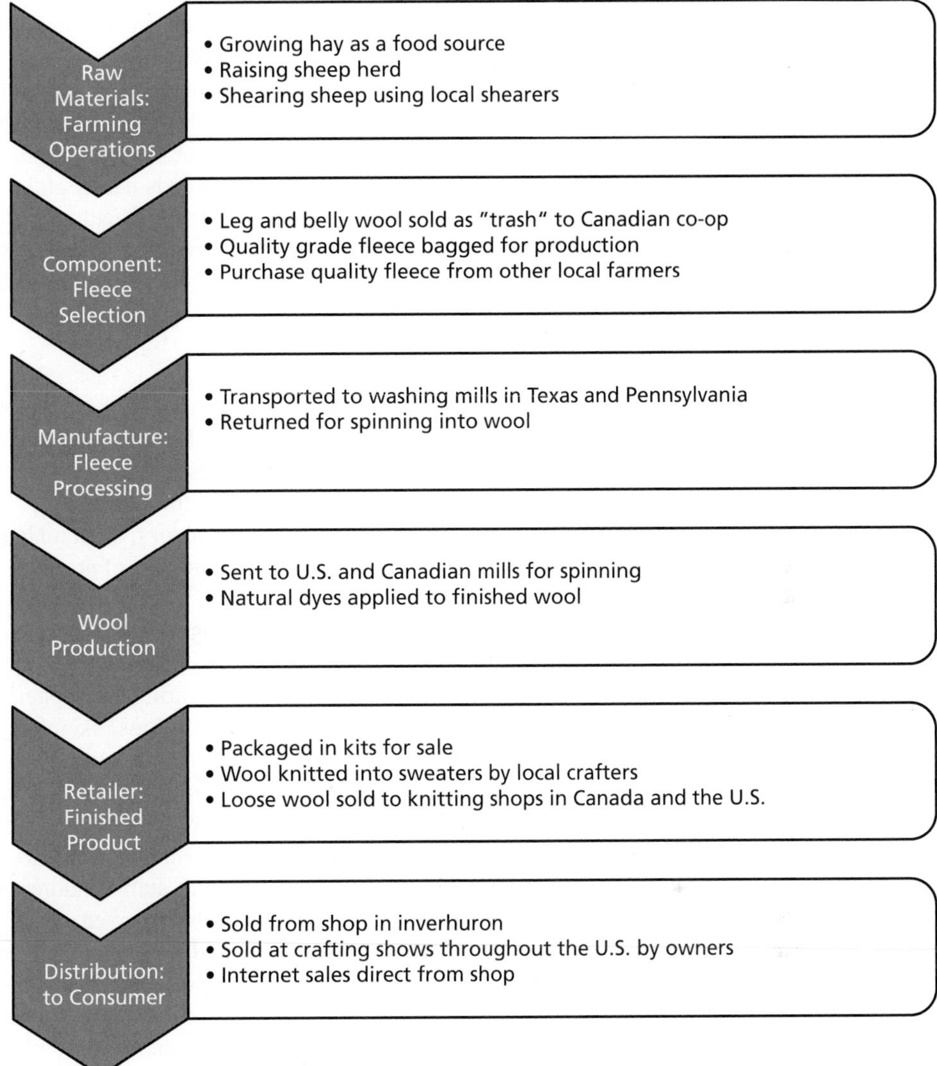
PHILOSOPHER'S VERTICAL SUPPLY CHAIN MODEL
Raw Materials: Farming Operations
• Growing hay as a food source
• Raising sheep herd
• Shearing sheep using local shearers
Component: Fleece Selection
• Leg and belly wool sold as "trash" to Canadian co-op
• Quality grade fleece bagged for production
• Purchase quality fleece from other local farmers
Manufacture: Fleece Processing
• Transported to washing mills in Texas and Pennsylvania
• Returned for spinning into wool
Wool Production
• Sent to U.S. and Canadian mills for spinning
• Natural dyes applied to finished wool
Retailer: Finished Product
• Packaged in kits for sale
• Wool knitted into sweaters by local crafters
• Loose wool sold to knitting shops in Canada and the U.S.
Distribution: to Consumer
• Sold from shop in inverhuron
• Sold at crafting shows throughout the U.S. by owners
• Internet sales direct from shop

matching tuition program up to $2000 for each child of the family attending college. Knitters also received an annual bonus on a pro rata basis for completed pieces during the year which was between $100 and $1000. The company did not outsource globally: its financial commitment was to rebuild the local community in which it conducted its business.

12 Additionally, Philosopher's SCM (supply chain management) philosophy focused on integrating other SMEs to create employment opportunities in local markets and return profits into the community. Shearers, farmers, knitters, and woolen mills were part of the local supply chain partnership which benefitted from Philosopher's goal of sustainable pricing and sharing profits.

13 According to Philosopher's co-owner, Eugene Bourgeois, "it's all about being recognized as a responsible brand." He explained that responsibility meant many things to Philosopher's.

14 The stated goals of the company included fairness in price to other suppliers and creating meaningful partnerships in the supply chain enterprise to induce higher product quality

at competitive prices. "The major difference between my approach to Philosopher's and a large global company approach concerns profits and notions about profits. We took a very long-term approach to profits, demanding first that truly sustainable prices would be paid to farmers [other wool producers] for the commodity produced. If we couldn't develop Philosopher's in such a way that these payments to farmers were achievable, then there was no benefit to operating Philosopher's and it would fail. I readily admit that this is a radical approach to the topic but I genuinely believed that it would be possible to pay farmers and develop a viable business. The reason for doing so is hardly philanthropic alone, although my attitudes about society played a major role. It is difficult to achieve a consistent supply of quality feedstock.[4] Were we able to do so, through pricing structures, we would build a reliable supply chain whose members know the alternative and so have a direct and vested interest in our success. That, in turn, is what has happened."

Products

15 Philosopher's manufactured three principal products: finished woolen goods, knitting kits, and loose wool skeins. Sales of sweaters and finished goods accounted for about one percent of its combined show and shop retail annual sales. The kits accounted for approximately 30 percent of total sales with loose yarn accounting for 70 percent of total sales. Sixty percent of the total revenues were earned at retail show venues; the remainder was generated by the shop and through internet sales. On average, 95 percent of profits were earned in the United States. Once again, Philosopher's followed its own model for sustainable SCM practices involving the consumer. For example, the average sweater cardigan kit cost $130. For this price, Philosopher's included the yarn, patterns, and buttons to complete a sweater. Typically, a sweater required seven to nine skeins of yarn. Philosopher's included eleven skeins to ensure completion and offered to buy back, at its loose skein price, any unused skeins. It also replaced any color in the pattern at the customer's request. Philosopher's assured supply chain continuity in product lines by not discontinuing dye lot colors used in the kits.

16 Philosopher's also created a website where it provided free knitting patterns and knitting instruction. The kit package listed a phone number that was personally answered by Ann Bourgeois or other members of Philosopher's staff to address knitters' questions. The goal was to protect consumer trust. Customers also received a free canvas knitting bag with purchase, personalized help and instruction, and were made to feel part of a special community that knits in an ancient tradition. Knitting training and customer assistance were also available on-line at http://www.philosopherswool.com/Pages/Twohandedvideo.htm.

17 Philosopher's published several knitting books, including several co-authored with other knitters engaged in creative pattern design. They also sold a knitting DVD that demonstrated the Fair Isle technique.

Methods of Distribution

18 The increase in export costs to foreign distributors, as a result of heavier border tariffs, transformed the business from a wholesale operation to a retail operation. Eugene and Ann changed their distribution strategy and began to travel throughout the United States and Canada to attend knitting shows where they sold the kits, provided instruction, and personally met with local yarn distributors who carried their loose wool in knitting specialty stores.

Philosopher's Decisions: Past, Present, and Future

19 At first, Eugene and Ann did their own shearing, kept back some fleece for Ann to card and spin, but sold the bulk of their production to the co-op. They sold the fleece with high

[4] Quality feedstock or sheep from which the fleece is harvested for wool production is critical to the overall quality of the wool used to manufacture end user woolen goods such as clothing. The idea is to increase prices paid to sheep farmers to enable them to improve the overall quality of the feedstock in the supply chain.

PHILOSOPHER'S SUPPLY CHAIN: A Coalition of SMEs Using Cost to Create Value

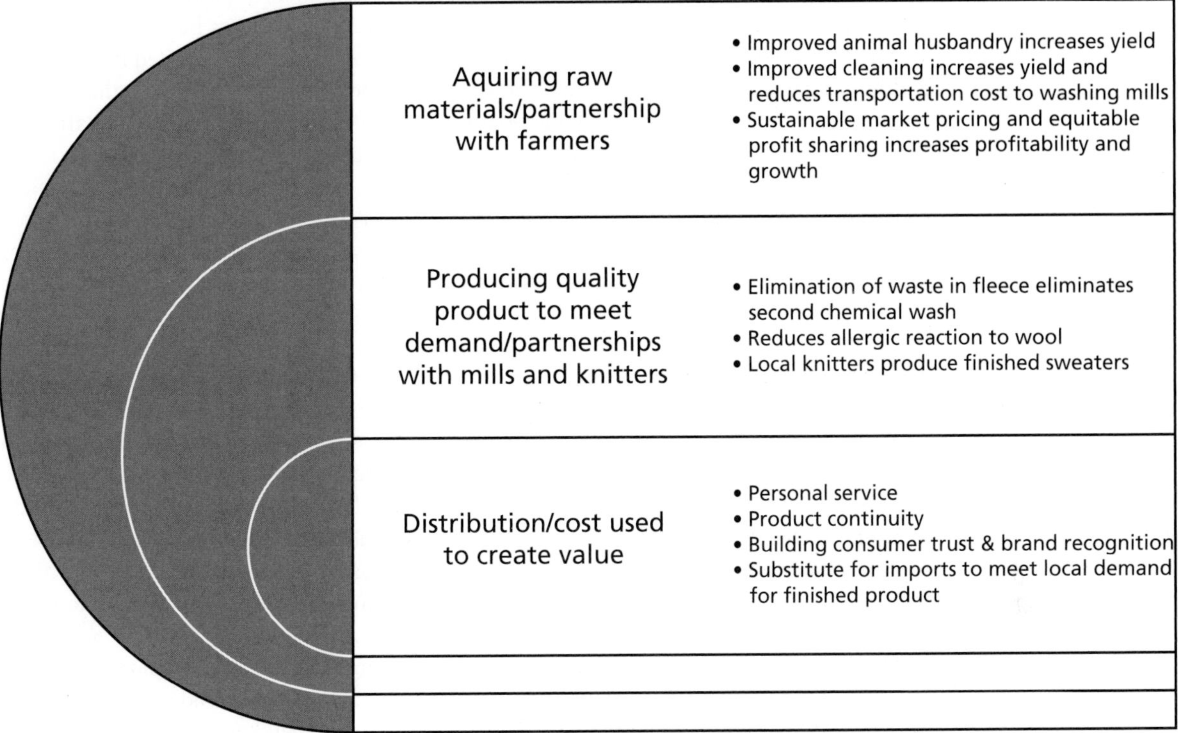

expectations because they had produced the finest quality based on the care and feeding of their livestock. Five months later a check arrived from the co-op paying them $.32 per pound. It had cost them $.70 to sheer and transport the fleece. After discussions with the co-op they expected to do better the next year but the next production returned $.50 per pound from the co-op. Eugene's confusion increased when he visited a local yarn shop (that later sold Philosopher's loose yarn) which offered a 20 percent discount on a yarn purchase of $200 or more. He bought the yarn and quickly realized that he had just spent $22 for a pound of yarn, on sale, compared to the $.32 per pound that Philosopher's had just received for its fleece.

Aquiring raw materials/partnership with farmers
• Improved animal husbandry increases yield
• Improved cleaning increases yield and reduces transportation cost to washing mills
• Sustainable market pricing and equitable profit sharing increases profitability and growth
Producing quality product to meet demand/partnerships with mills and knitters
• Elimination of waste in fleece eliminates second chemical wash
• Reduces allergic reaction to wool
• Local knitters produce finished sweaters
Distribution/cost used to create value
• Personal service
• Product continuity
• Building consumer trust & brand recognition
• Substitute for imports to meet local demand for finished product

20 Eugene was determined to increase his profits. His experience convinced him that farmers could improve fleece prices if they participated directly in marketing the product. The key was to convince other local farmers to clean their fleece to reduce mill processing costs and weight transportation costs. The process also contributed to improving local animal husbandry because farmers were required to engage in better care of their livestock to produce cleaner fleece.

21 Eugene also reviewed a local provincial study that showed Canada had imported the equivalent of eighty five million pounds of finished woolen goods to satisfy a domestic demand of over forty times the amount of wool being produced in Canada. If Canadians were to sell every scrap of wool produced domestically in finished product, it would amount to less than 3 percent of the documented consumer demand. Convinced that a market existed, Eugene devised a plan to buy fleece from other local farmers. If they could deliver dry, clean, and high yielding fleece, he would reward them with a higher price than the co-op. He based the price on the weight of the finished wool that their shipment yielded after it dried. If Philosopher's could earn $2.65 a pound by selling finished yarn after expenses, it was committed to paying local farmers $2.00 a pound and investing the other

$.65 in the company's future operations. Eugene's plan worked. It created a new supply chain partnership between Philosopher's and other local farmers and achieved his original goal of paying sustainable commodity prices to local fleece producers in Ontario.

22 The payment of higher prices to the fanners for cleaner fleece also resulted in less waste and higher yields giving Philosopher's an economic competitive advantage in the marketplace. Fleece sold by the co-op yielded between 48–50 percent of wool product after the fleece was washed. Spinning depleted fleece yield by another 10–13 percent. Because farmers were motivated by increased price to produce cleaner wool, which also had the effect of reducing processing and transportation costs, Philosopher's found that it had received an increased yield of approximately 530 pounds of yarn from the original 1000 pounds of fleece purchased directly from local farmers as compared to the approximately 400 pounds of yarn yield if the wool came from the co-op where improved cleaning and sanitation practices for the fleece had not been implemented. According to Eugene, "Sustainable SCM resulted in higher yields, decreased costs, and less waste, all of which increased Philosopher's bottom line."

23 Philosopher's sustainable business practices in SCM were well-regarded by the Canadian co-op. Eric Bjergso, General Manager of the CCWG stated in a recent 2008 interview: "By sharing the value added revenue with the primary producer, Philosopher's Wool has paid premium prices to some producers of select well prepared wool clips. I do not know how many producers or the amount of wool that they purchase on an annual basis for this niche market. I do commend them for their efforts in developing this specialty market and then forming a partnership with the producer."

24 Eugene and Ann were concerned about the future. In their 70's, the couple was tired of travelling long distances by car throughout the United States and Canada for months at a time only to return to their farm and face neglected duties. They knew that they needed to find U.S. distributors for their kits and loose wool products but it proved difficult to compete in an already well established retail market. Their target customers had been specialty knitters looking for unique kits and woolen products in the craft show markets. Changing to the craft superstore environment and to specialty yarn stores proved to be difficult Philosopher's was known for its unique Fair Isle designs, difficult for the average knitter. Also, hand dyed wools sold at a premium, and that meant less competitive pricing than the established domestic wool manufacturers.

25 In order to become profitable in a wholesale market, Philosopher's was faced with the need either to raise prices or to cut costs. Raising price in an already tight market was not an attractive solution, so they decided to cut costs. However, cutting costs meant changes in their sustainable supply chain model in several respects. First, they stopped purchasing and warehousing local fleece production. Rather than dropping the price paid to farmers as the co-op had done, they simply cut back on annual purchasing. Second, they produced fewer handmade sweaters and reduced their finished inventory supply which meant that they employed fewer local knitters. Finally, they began meeting with larger U.S. wool product distributors in an effort to promote their products for U.S. markets. Eugene and Ann were unhappy with this result. They felt that the cutbacks impeded their efforts to build local economies in their community. The large manufacturing plants that sustained whole communities in the area had long ago closed their doors. Philosopher's had attempted to rebuild the local economies by expanding the woolen trade using the SME supply chain model.

26 In 2009, both Eugene and Ann suffered illnesses that prevented them from continuing to travel to knitting shows. Without any success in establishing a partnering arrangement with a foreign distributor, they confined their retail operations to the shop and Internet sales.

Case 19

Salmones Puyuhuapi (A)

Rafael Echeverria
Phillip E. Pfeifer

1 Osvaldo Correa, CEO of Salmones Puyuhuapi (SP), was in a tense meeting with bank officials negotiating the terms of his firm's line of credit when he received a text on his BlackBerry. The news was not good. Correa tried to remain calm in front of the bankers as he read the terse message about a suspected outbreak of the infectious salmon anemia (ISA) virus in a competitor's salmon farm. Correa knew that if the virus were to spread to his firm's Jacaf Fjord site in northern Patagonia, Chile, it could wipe out his nearly one million salmon two months before they were to be harvested. That would have a devastating impact on his firm's cash flows. Excusing himself to go to "the services" (the only excuse he could come up with), Correa e-mailed his assistant to set up a meeting later that day with Jorge Richards, his operations manager, and Sergio Rivas, the company's veterinarian.

SALMON FARMING IN CHILE

2 Chile was a relatively small country of nearly 16 million inhabitants whose economy was driven principally by mining, agribusiness, forestry, and aquaculture. In particular, the salmon industry, although relatively new, had been wildly successful. The industry was established in the early 1980s to take advantage of natural conditions in the south of the country (moderate sea temperatures, sheltered sites, and ideal salinity levels). It achieved nearly 20 years of 42% annualized growth, allowing it to join Norway as the world's largest salmon producers. In 2006, these two countries shared 78% of global production. Salmon farms, which thrived in the southern regions of Chile, dominated the local economies and led to high rates of employment.

3 In April 2007, however, the industry was changed forever when it was discovered that high fish mortality rates at a few Chilean sites owned and operated by Marine Harvest, a large Norwegian company, were due to the ISA virus. This virus was well known in the aquaculture industry because of the catastrophic effects it had had on the salmon industries of Canada, Great Britain, and Norway. ISA outbreaks sometimes wiped out entire million-fish farms in a matter of months. For smaller firms, the cash flow consequences of these outbreaks were particularly devastating because a significant portion of revenues from one harvest were used to start or continue the 30-month cycles at other sites.

4 To make matters worse, Marine Harvest had initially hid information about the presence of the virus. This lack of warning to other companies allowed the disease to spread to other

Source: This case was prepared by Rafael Echeverria (MBA '11) and Phillip E. Pfeifer, Richard S. Reynolds Professor of Business Administration. It was written as a basis for class discussion rather than to illustrate effective or ineffective handling of an administrative situation. It is based on general experience and should not be used as a source of primary research. All names have been disguised.

farming sites and production zones[1] because the uninformed companies took no precautions. In early 2007, the virus was spread inadvertently by third parties contracted to provide feed and harvesting services. Once the industry learned the ISA virus had made its way to Chile, a host of process changes were immediately implemented to prevent its spread. In addition, Chilean authorities quickly banned the transfer of nondiseased salmon from infected zones out of concern that transferring apparently healthy salmon could actually help spread the disease to healthy zones. Although this policy helped slow down the spread of the virus across zones, it was at the increased risk of infecting all sites in an infected zone.

5 After the 2007 outbreak had run its course, the improved processes and regulations reduced the spread among zones; however, the threat was not eliminated and occasional outbreaks did occur. The last such outbreak had been six months earlier.

ATLANTIC SALMON PRODUCTION CYCLE

6 In the wild, adult Atlantic salmon spawned in natural freshwater streams, where their eggs hatched and juveniles grew through several distinct stages. Eggs quickly hatched into "alevins" that remained in the breeding ground and fed from the remaining nutrients in their yolks. After an alevin absorbed its yolk sack, it became a "fry." In this stage, the fish was an active swimmer and soon left its breeding ground in search of food. In its final freshwater stage, when it became physiologically ready to travel to seawater, a fry became a "smolt." In the wild, the duration of these freshwater phases varied between one and five years.

7 During the seawater phase, which took another one to four years, salmon acclimatized to salinity and grew to adulthood in the open ocean. With continued time and growth, adult salmon became "grilse." At the grilse phase, they were ready to return to their natal streams. (Salmon were well known for swimming upstream to spawn at their birthplace.) The grilse ceased eating altogether prior to spawning, which helped cause their meat to be undesirable. After the grilse spawned, almost all died.

8 In salmon aquaculture, companies tried to replicate the natural cycle of Atlantic salmon with techniques that shortened the total cycle to less than three years. The freshwater phase was replicated in hatcheries with artificial spawning in buckets from genetically selected spawners (adults). Changes in water temperature and amount of light helped the salmon progress quickly through the freshwater stages in eight to twelve months. During this time, water quality and vaccination were the most important factors for future growth and survival. Near the end of the freshwater stage, smolts were moved into estuary sites to improve their ability to adapt to the salinity of their future seawater homes. In the wild, it was estimated that only 15% of fry survived the freshwater stage (less than 1% from egg to smolt)—compared with a 90% survival rate in captivity.

9 The improvement in survival was even more pronounced during the seawater stage. Whereas only about 35% of wild Atlantic salmon survived four years in the open ocean to reach maturity, careful care and feeding in commercial salmon farms led to commercial size in about 18 to 24 months, with 85% survival rates.

10 The SP Jacaf Fjord farming site was typical of the approximately 800 sites that were operating in Chile. It maintained 24 rectangular cages grouped into two rectangular sets of 12 cages containing 900,000 salmon, a floating house for workers, and a floating/movable platform carrying feed silos and blowing machines. Each cage was a floating wharf with walkways along the net boundaries from which a cube-shaped net was suspended

[1] Zones included several sites at which salmon were raised in cages; 10 to 50 cages typically comprised a single farming site, and several sites occupied a single region or zone.

FIGURE 1 **Typical Salmon Cage**

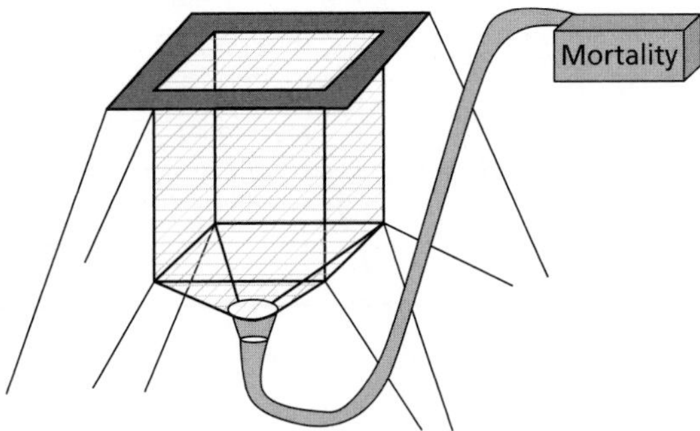

Source: Created by case writer.

and anchored to the sea floor (see **Figure 1**). At the bottom of the net, a specially designed cone allowed dead fish to be easily removed and counted upon sinking to the bottom of the net.

11 A crew tended the site around the clock; the crew's main duties were to feed and protect the fish. Fish were fed a mixture of fish oil, fish meal, and other components twice a day and were allowed to eat as much as they wanted. When conditions were right, the fish ate more and grew faster.

12 The harvest was one of the most critical operations in the process because it dramatically affected the quality of the finished product. Harvesting at the Jacaf site was conducted by Ace Services using boats with special pumps and a percussive-stun harvest system that killed the fish instantly with a blow to the head from a pneumatic piston. The harvest crew (Ace employees with assistance from SP crews) then bled the fish by cutting the gill arches and placed them in ice water for transport to the SP processing plant in Puerto Aisén, Chile. This single processing plant served all five of SP's sites across three zones. (SP had only one site in the Jacaf Fjord zone.)

13 Harvested salmon were used in the production of three different products in fresh or frozen formats. The production mix was determined based on the weight distribution of the harvested fish. Smaller salmon were sold *entero* (whole), midsize salmon were sold as "value-added" *porciones* (portions), and the largest were sold as *filetes* (filets). The fresh versus frozen mix was decided based on prevailing prices and market demand. SP's policy (simplified for the purposes of this case) was to freeze 70% of the entero and filetes production and freeze 100% of porciones.

14 Upon the salmons' arrival at the processing plant, an automatic grader gutted and sorted them by weight. (See **Exhibit 1** for a diagram of the processing plant's operations and **Exhibit 2** for photos.) At the next station, workers removed heads and tails (depending on the product), after which an automatic fileting machine split each fish in two, and another machine removed spines, bones, and skin. At a subsequent workstation, any remaining bones were removed manually. Finally, highly skilled workers trimmed the filetes according to customer requirements. Filetes destined for portioning were put on a portioning machine that scanned and optimized the cuts, converting each filete into four or five porciones.

15 Fresh products were then packed and shipped the same day. Frozen products passed through a tunnel freezer prior to packaging and were stored for later shipment. Each box of the finished product was printed with codes that identified every aspect of the production of the product in that box.

EXHIBIT 1 **Salmones Puyuhuapi (A)**
Processing Plant Diagram

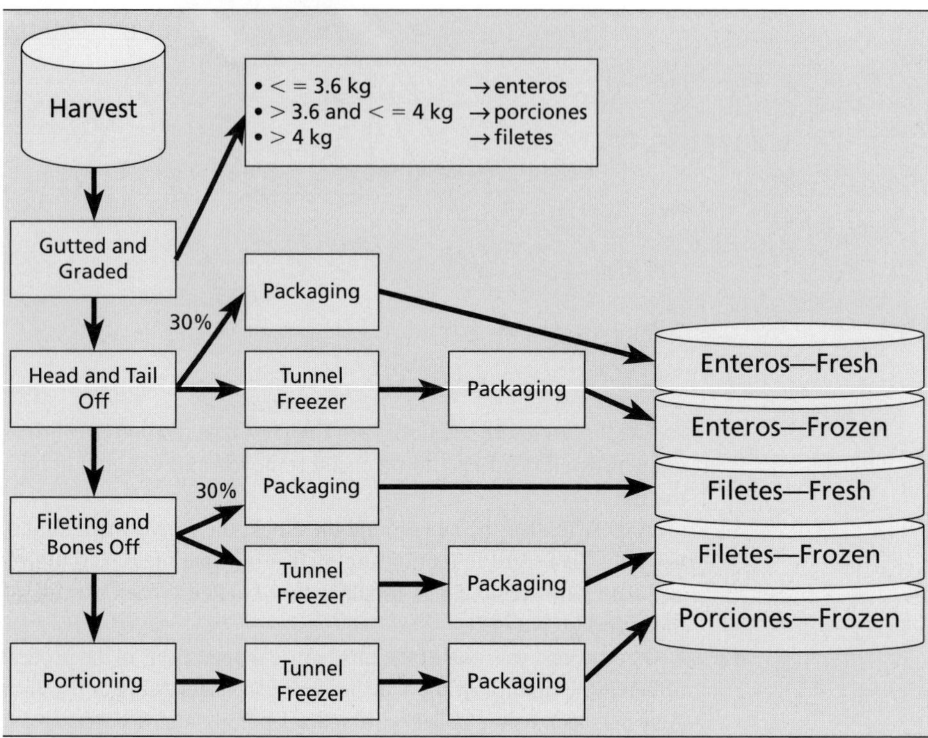

Source: Created by case writer.

SALMONES PUYUHUAPI

16 SP was a relatively small company, with annual sales of $40 million entirely from salmon sold in one of the three product forms mentioned. (The company did its accounting in U.S. dollars because most sales were to the United States.)

17 **Table 1** lists the current prices and processing costs for each of the three products. A complicating feature of aquaculture economics was the distinction between live and finished product weight. The ratio of the weight of the finished product (after processing) to the weight of the live fish before processing was called the yield. Each product had a separate yield factor that was remarkably consistent across fish and companies. This meant that those in the industry were very comfortable talking in terms of either live or finished weights—and easily interchanging between the two. For example, salmon between 3.6 and 4.0 kilograms were processed as porciones and received (on average) $3.71 per kilogram live weight, or (given the 45% yield) $8.25 per finished kilogram.

18 Fish weighing less than 3.6 kilograms at harvest were sold as enteros. The finished weight of a fish sold whole was 89% of its live weight. Fish weighing between 3.6 and 4.0 kilograms at harvest were sold as porciones that, although facing a 45% yield, brought the highest price per finished kilogram of $8.25. (Note that the accounting here is done per fish. A fish produced two filetes, or eight to ten porciones.) Finally, the largest fish at harvest were processed as filetes with finished weights 61% of the live weight.

EXHIBIT 2 **Salmones Puyuhuapi (A)**
Selected Photos of Salmon Production*

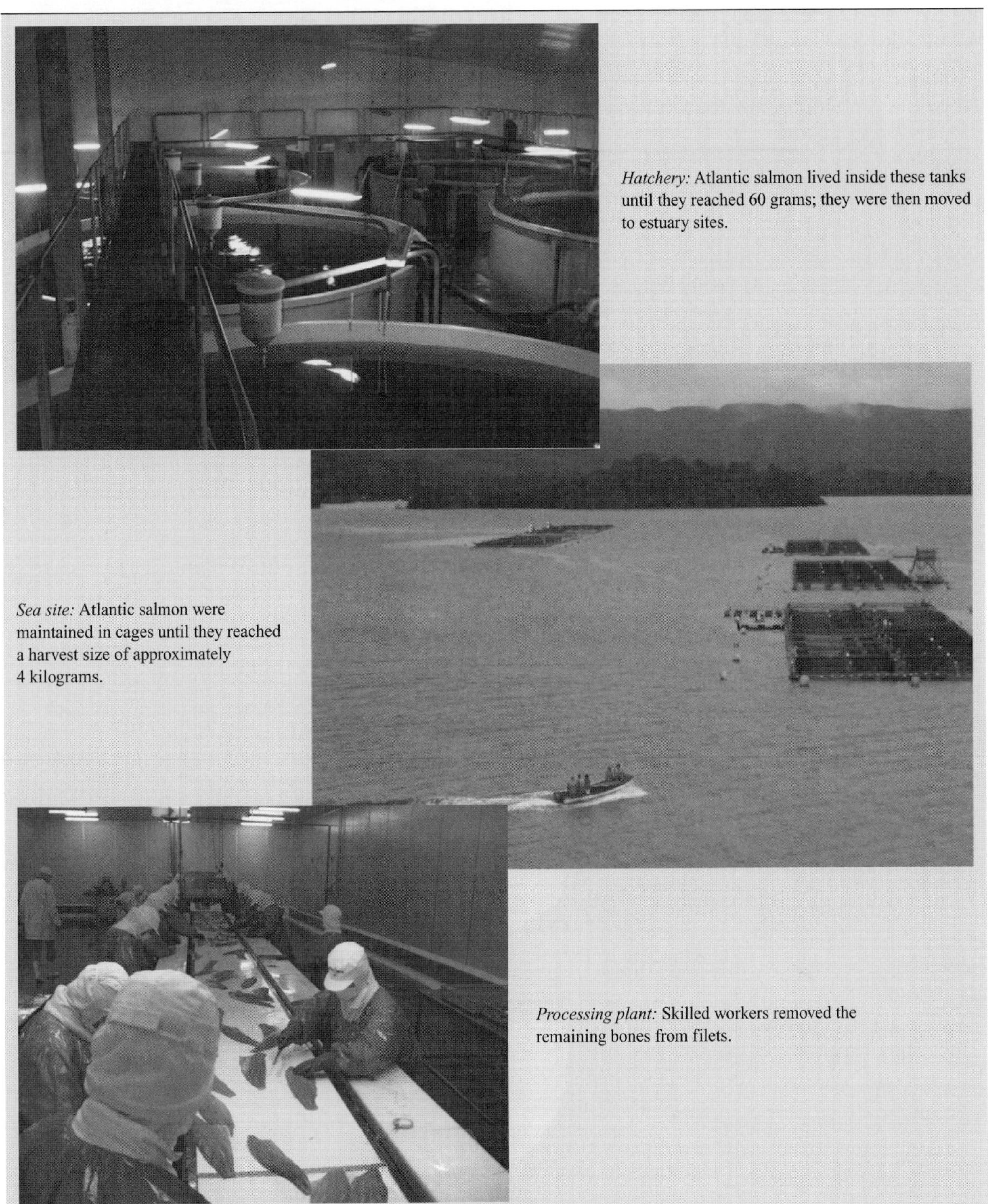

Hatchery: Atlantic salmon lived inside these tanks until they reached 60 grams; they were then moved to estuary sites.

Sea site: Atlantic salmon were maintained in cages until they reached a harvest size of approximately 4 kilograms.

Processing plant: Skilled workers removed the remaining bones from filets.

* All photos were taken by Miguel Angel Leiva and are used with permission.

(Continued)

EXHIBIT 2 *(Continued)*

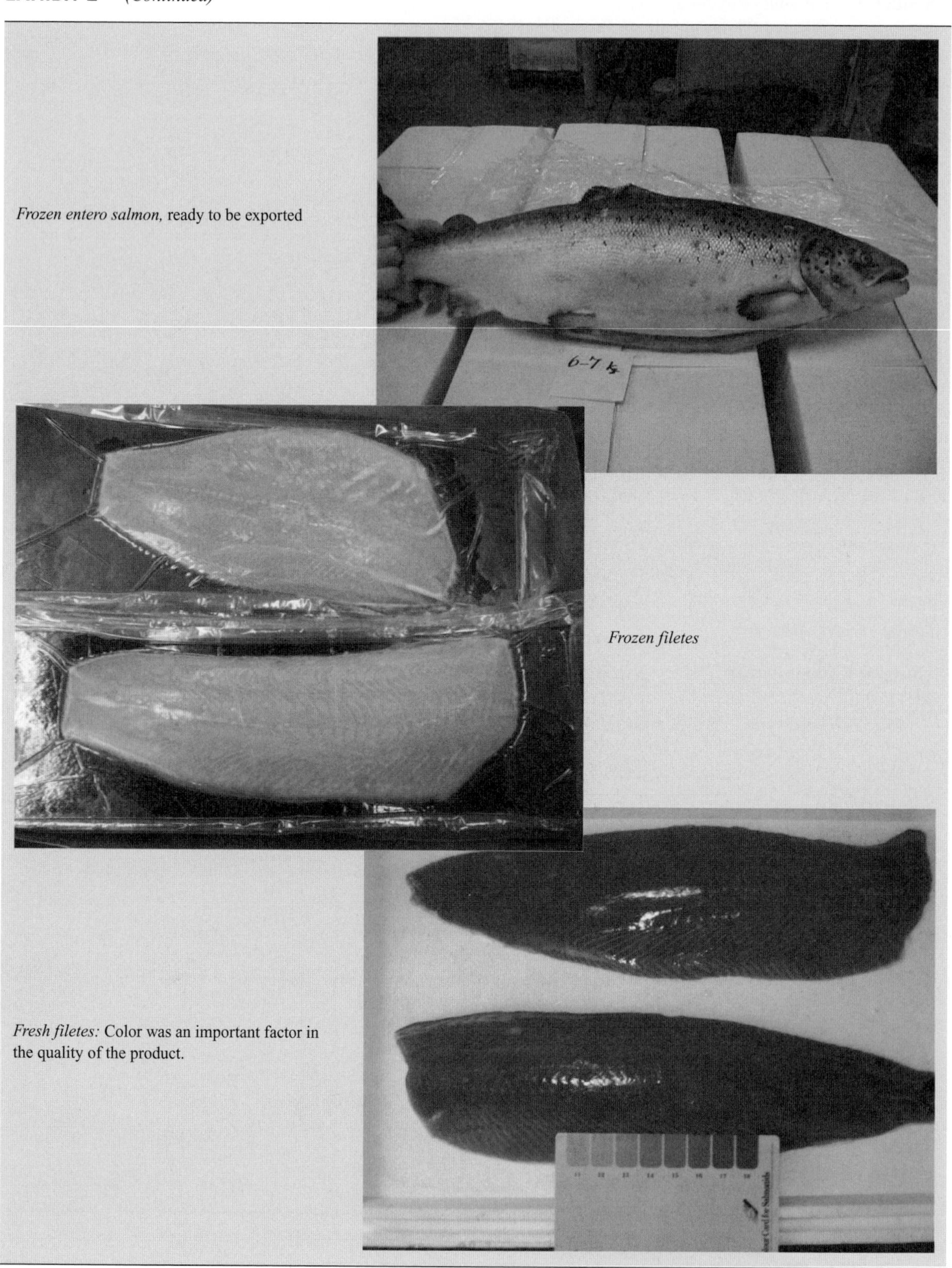

Frozen entero salmon, ready to be exported

Frozen filetes

Fresh filetes: Color was an important factor in the quality of the product.

TABLE 1 **Production Economics**

Product	Live Weight Policy	Yield	Target Weight (kg)	Price at Target (per kg)	Price Change Rate	Processing Cost (per finished kg)
enteros, fresh	< 3.6 kg	0.89	3.20	$3.25	$2.00	$0.45
enteros, frozen	< 3.6 kg	0.89	3.20	$3.20	$2.00	$0.35
porciones, frozen	3.6 to 4 kg	0.45	1.71	$8.25	$1.00	$1.70
filetes, fresh	> 4 kg	0.61	2.75	$5.45	$2.00	$0.70
filetes, frozen	> 4 kg	0.61	2.75	$5.40	$2.00	$0.60

19 Of course, not all finished fish weighed exactly the same. The prices listed in **Table 1** were for finished products averaging the target weight. Departures (up or down) from that target average weight received prices adjusted at the rate of $2.00 per kilogram (for enteros and filetes) and $1.00 per kilogram (for porciones). Thus if a shipment of fresh whole salmon averaged 3.1 kilograms per fish (0.1 kilograms under the target), SP would receive $3.05 per kilogram. (The actual pricing of salmon products was more complicated because finished product was sold in predefined-size "buckets" with a specified price per kilogram of product meeting the weight standards of each bucket. Richards used the simplified pricing model in **Table 1** for projecting revenues.)

20 The Jacaf Fjord farming site had monthly fixed costs of $50,000 ($20,000 of which were for the crews), and the salmon at this point were eating 1.3 kilograms of feed for each kilogram of weight gained. Feed prices were extremely volatile, with a price of $1,200 per ton (1,000 kilograms). Harvest costs (Ace Services) were approximately $0.2 per live kilogram.

THE MEETING

21 Correa closed the door to his office so that he and Richards and Rivas could speak privately about how to respond to the potential crisis. With his laptop open, Richards did not wait for permission to speak. (**Exhibit 3** contains the English translations of their conversation.)

Jorge Richards (operations manager)

Creo que no debiésemos perder tiempo y cosechar la totalidad del centro ahora. Tenemos 900,000 salmones en Jacaf con un peso promedio de 2.77 kilos. ¡Recién hable con el gerente general de Ace Services y estamos con suerte! Un servicio que tenían contratado con otra empresa fue cancelado a último minuto, por lo que tienen tres barcazas con su personal disponible para nosotros. Somos afortunados considerando que ellos generalmente no tienen esta flexibilidad y los servicios se contratan con al menos seis meses de anticipación. Me da terror correr el riesgo de que nos agarre el ISA. El retiro y apropiada disposición de la mortalidad del ISA cuesta casi lo mismo que cosechar y procesar. Los peces están a un peso suficiente para cosechar, procesar y exportar. Puse todos los números en un Excel (**Exhibit 4**) con mis proyecciones en la actual situación si cosecháramos. Usando una desviación estándar de 0.4 kilos podríamos obtener ingresos por casi $4 millones. Nos cuesta $500 mil cosechar y aproximadamente $1 millón procesar. La contribución seria $2.5 millones—$2,567,376 para ser precisos. Tomemos el servicio de Ace Services ahora, antes que alguien más lo haga o sea demasiado tarde. Por supuesto mi plan solo funciona si logramos convencer a los operarios de la planta trabajar un par de semanas más antes de cerrar la planta por fin de temporada. Estoy seguro de poder hacerlo.

Osvaldo Correa (CEO)

Tranquilo Jorge. No nos apresuremos demasiado. Justamente Sergio me sugería que, por estar en el lado opuesto del centro infectado en el fiordo, hay una probabilidad razonable que podamos salvarnos del virus. Por supuesto estoy considerando las medidas extraordinarias tomadas desde el 2007. Sergio reviso las corrientes, temperaturas y las condiciones del fiordo. El riesgo está latente pero no es 100% seguro que nos infectemos. Incluso, siendo atacados por el virus no necesariamente perderemos todos los salmones del centro. Claramente en el peor escenario perderíamos todos, pero también existe un escenario en que al virus solo mataría al 30% de los salmones. También podemos considerar un escenario intermedio donde solo perdemos al 60%. Y esto aplica si y solo si el centro es infectado por el virus y espero que eso no pase.

Recuerda que en los últimos dos meses previos a la cosecha es cuando el salmón crece más rápido (25% mensual). Y ese 25% en peso promedio y desviación estándar se traduce en un aumento aun mayor en ingresos y utilidades. Por lo mismo, porque no aprovechamos tu planilla y vemos cuanto es lo que estamos dejando en la mesa si decidimos cosechar ahora.

Finalmente veo que tus $2.5 millones es contribución. ¿Cómo puedes ignorar los $4.2 millones que ya hemos gastado en el centro en términos de 16 meses de costos fijos, costo de smolts y alimento a la fecha? ¿Tus $2.5 millones son en realidad una pérdida de $1.7 millones, cierto?

Sergio Rivas (veterinarian)

En el escenario donde nos salvamos del virus, Jorge, por favor considera el 2% de mortalidad habitual de los últimos dos meses. Además recuerda que si el virus nos ataca, los salmones sobrevivientes verán afectados su crecimiento desde un 25% a 20% mensual. La mortalidad del virus tiene que ser retirado por un servicio especial que nos cobra $1 por cada salmón.

La otra opción que podemos ver es la de vacunar los 900,000 salmones inmediatamente. Sé que es bastante costosa la vacuna pero lo podemos hacer de inmediato. Ayer mismo hablaba con el representante de la empresa y tiene vacunas en stock. Incluso Ace Services nos podría ayudar con sus barcazas, plataformas y tripulantes. Con ayuda de una red movemos los peces a un lado de la jaula, los bombeamos, vacunamos y devolvemos al otro lado de la red en la misma jaula. Una vez vacunados no habrá posibilidad de que sean infectados con el virus. Ace Services podrá volver en dos meses y realizar la cosecha previamente programada de salmones con un peso de 4.33 kilos. Jorge, por favor incorpora eso en tu planilla y evalúalo.

22 The meeting ended with Rivas's agreeing to collect more information about the outbreak and the likelihood it would spread to SP's site. Richards agreed to contact Ace Services to get an idea of the feasibility and cost of Rivas's vaccination plan. Correa volunteered to alert the processing plant there might be another couple of weeks' worth of work before shutting down for the off-season. He also set about the task of running some numbers to get some understanding of the tradeoffs involved. He was well aware that the ISA virus harmed fish but not humans. Fish that died or were sick were disposed of properly, but fish harvested live (even from an infected cage) could be processed, inspected, and sold without a problem. He also realized that whatever action he took with the current 900,000 fish would have little impact on when SP would be able to start a new cycle at Jacaf Fjord. That would depend mostly on the severity of the outbreak in the zone as a whole. Early harvest or vaccination of his fish would mean very little.

EXHIBIT 3 **Salmones Puyuhuapi (A)**
English Translation of the Meeting*

Jorge Richards (Operations Manager)
I don't think we should waste time and harvest the entire center now. We have 900,000 salmon in Jacaf that weigh 2.77 kilos on average. I recently spoke with the general manager at Ace Services, and we're in luck! An order that had already been contracted with another firm was canceled at the last minute, and as a result, they have three barges and their personnel available to harvest us. We're lucky considering that they don't usually have this much flexibility and these services are booked at least six months in advance. It terrifies me to run the risk that ISA is going to catch us. Proper disposal of the refuse due to ISA costs almost as much as harvesting and processing. The fish weigh enough now to harvest, process, and export. I created an Excel file with my projections if we harvest now under this situation. Using a standard deviation of 0.4 kilograms, we can generate almost $4 million in revenue. It costs us $500,000 to harvest and approximately $1 million to process. The contribution would be $2.5 million—$2,567,376 to be precise. We should grab Ace Services now before someone else does it or it becomes too late. For my plan to work, I'll have to convince our plant workers to stay for a couple more weeks of emergency work before shutting down for the off-season. But I can do that.

Osvaldo Correa (CEO)
Take it easy, Jorge. Let's not rush ourselves too much. Sergio tells me there is a reasonable probability that we can avoid the virus because the infected area is on the opposite side of the fjord. It goes without saying that I am considering the extraordinary measures taken since 2007. Sergio checked the currents, temperatures, and conditions in the fjord. There is some latent risk, but the chance of being infected is not 100%. In addition, being attacked by the virus does not necessarily mean we would lose all the salmon in the center. Clearly, in the worst-case scenario, we would lose them all. But there is also a scenario in which the virus would only kill 30% of the salmon. We can also consider an intermediate scenario in which we would only lose 60%. And this applies if and only if the virus infects the center, which I'm hoping doesn't happen.

Recall that the salmon grow fastest (25% monthly) during the last two months prior to harvest. And that 25% in average weight and standard deviation translate into an even bigger gain in revenue and profit. Nonetheless, why don't we take advantage of your analysis and see how much we're leaving on the table if we decide to harvest now?

Finally, I see that your $2.5 million is contribution. How can you ignore the $4.2 million that we've already invested in the center in terms of 16 months of fixed costs, cost of smolts, and food to date? Your $2.5 million is actually a loss of $1.7 million, right?

Sergio Rivas (Veterinarian)
Under the scenario in which we avoid the virus, Jorge, you have to consider the usual 2% mortality rate of the last two months. In addition, recall that if the virus attacks us, the salmon that survive will see their growth affected by 25% to 20% monthly. Mortality due to the virus has to be removed by a special service that charges us $1 per salmon.

The other option that we have is to immediately vaccinate the 900,000 salmon. I realize that the vaccine costs a lot, but we can do it right away. Just yesterday I spoke with the representative from the company, and he has vaccine in stock. Also, Ace Services can help us with their barges, platforms, and crew. Using a net, we'll move the fish to one side of the pen; we'll pump them, vaccinate them, and we'll return them to the other side of the net in the same pen. Once vaccinated, there would be no chance that they become infected with the virus. Ace Services can return in two months and have the previously planned salmon harvest with a weight of 4.33 kilograms. Jorge, please include that in your analysis and evaluate it forthwith.

* Translation was by Raul O. Chao, Assistant Professor, Darden Graduate School of Business Administration.

EXHIBIT 4 **Salmones Puyuhuapi (A)**
Immediate Harvest Financial Projections (weight in kilograms)

INPUT ASSUMPTIONS

Number of fish	900,000
Average live weight	2.77
Standard deviation	0.4

Harvest cost per live kg	$ 0.20
Feed cost per ton	$ 1,200
Feed efficiency	1.3

Product	Yield	Target Weight	Price at Target	Price Change Rate	Process Cost (per finished kg)
enteros, fresh	0.89	3.20	$3.25	$2.00	$0.45
enteros, frozen	0.89	3.20	$3.20	$2.00	$0.35
porciones, frozen	0.45	1.71	$8.25	$1.00	$1.70
filetes, fresh	0.61	2.75	$5.45	$2.00	$0.70
filetes, frozen	0.61	2.75	$5.40	$2.00	$0.60

MATERIAL FLOW

Live Weight	Number of Fish	Average Live Weight	Total Live Weight	Average Finished Weight	Total Finished Weight
< 3.6-enteros	882,906	2.75	2,428,967	2.45	2,161,781
3.6 to 4-porciones	16,147	3.72	60,138	1.68	27,062
> 4-filetes	947	4.11	3,894	2.51	2,376
Total	900,000		2,493,000		2,191,219

PRODUCT FLOW

Product	Number	Average Finished Weight	Price	Revenue	Process Cost
30% enteros, fresh	264,872	2.45	$1.75	$1,132,968	$291,840
enteros, frozen	618,034	2.45	$1.70	$2,567,930	$529,636
porciones, frozen	16,147	1.68	$8.22	$ 222,344	$ 46,006
30% filetes, fresh	284	2.51	$4.97	$ 3,539	$ 499
filetes, frozen	663	2.51	$4.92	$ 8,174	$ 998
Total	900,000			$3,934,955	$868,979

FINANCIALS

Total revenue	$3,934,955
Feed cost	$ -
Harvest cost	$ 498,600
Processing cost	$ 868,979
Contribution	**$2,567,376**

Source: Created by case writer.

Case 20

Smart Union Group (Holdings) Limited—A (Short) Toy Story

Graeme Rankine

1 Andrew Ferris, a financial analyst with Guo Investments LLC, gathered information about Smart Union Group (Holdings) Limited, a company whose shares Guo was considering short-selling as part of its Shorts portfolio. Ferris graduated from Northwestern University's Kellogg School of Management with an MBA in accounting and finance, and had interned with Guo during the previous summer. The company's shares had increased from its initial public offering (IPO) price in September 2006 of around HK$1.10 per share, to an all-time high of over HK$2.50 in July 2007. Ferris found that Smart Union had grown rapidly during the last five years, but the company's growth had been financed recently by short-term bank debt. Ferris had been asked by the partners at Guo Investments to prepare a financial report on Smart Union, outlining the company's financing options for the bank debt that was due within 12 months. The partners wanted to consider the implications of the re-financing plans for shorting the company's shares, and thereby generating substantial profits from a decline in the company's stock price.

COMPANY BACKGROUND

2 Smart Union Group (Holdings) Limited was engaged in the manufacturing and trading of recreational and educational toys and equipment for OEMs, such as Mattel, Hasbro, and Megablocks.[1] The company's revenues had increased from HK$479 million in 2003 to over HK$953 million in 2007, a cumulative average growth rate (CAGR) of 19% per year. Over the same period, profits fell from HK$26 million to less than HK$6 million (see **Exhibit 1**). The company's major product line was hard and electronic toys, followed by educational and recreational products (see **Exhibit 2**). In 2005, the company's sales revenues were HK$710 million, of which HK$537 million originated in the U.S., where its principal customers were located.[2]

3 The company's manufacturing plants were located in Guangdong province, where other toy manufacturers were also located. In 2005, it was estimated that Guangdong province was expected to face a shortage of one million low-skilled workers, with 70% of enterprises in the Pearl River Delta reporting that they had difficulty hiring labor.[3] Tony Wu, an executive director of Smart Union, reported that the company increased salaries by more than 10% during the year in an effort to lure labor to the company's plants.[4] Wu noted that "the company had failed to fill 20% of vacancies during the peak season between May and October at its production plant in Dongguan" . . . and that the firm would "increase incentives and improve the working environment to retain workers in the short term, but would push ahead with automation to improve efficiency in the near future to cope with the labour

[1] *China Knowledge Press,* September 1, 2006.

[2] Ibid.

[3] *South China Morning Post,* February 2, 2005.

[4] Ibid.

EXHIBIT 1 **Selected Historical Information for Smart Union**

	Year ended 31st December				
	2007	**2006**	**2005**	**2004**	**2003**
	HK$'000	**HK$'000**	**HK$'000**	**HK$'000**	**HK$'000**
Sales	953,623	727,225	709,566	550,696	479,481
Cost of sales	(839,734)	(604,952)	(603,444)	(471,278)	(399,333)
Gross profit	113,889	122,273	106,122	79,418	80,148
Other income	12,320	1,906	5,265	812	2,500
Other (losses)/gains, net	(1,893)	1,804	–	–	–
Administrative expenses	(96,704)	(78,973)	(63,572)	(56,277)	(48,931)
Operating profit	27,612	47,010	47,815	23,953	33,717
Finance costs	(19,035)	(11,242)	(5,773)	(1,839)	(1,827)
Profit before tax	8,577	35,768	42,042	22,114	31,890
Income tax expense	(3,134)	(5,136)	(5,370)	(3,075)	(5,423)
Profit for the year	5,443	30,632	36,672	19,039	26,467
Attributable to:					
Equity holders of the Company	4.680	30,025	36,672	19,167	26,740
Minority interest	763	607		(128)	(273)
	5,443	30,632	36,672	19,039	26,467
Non-current assets	88,576	53,923	36,456	17,994	16,703
Current assets	711,977	429,341	264,771	242,437	149,684
Current liabilities	(481,088)	(313,504)	(202,140)	(186,942)	(109,726)
Non-current liabilities	(1,305)	(2,749)	(6,013)	(4,334)	(1,345)
Minority Interest	(1,370)	(607)	—	—	(128)
Capital and reserves attributable to the company's equity holders	316,790	166,404	93,074	69,155	55,188

shortage."[5] Smart Union was also considering relocating part of its manufacturing facilities to northern Guangdong, perhaps in Qingyuan.[6]

4 With crude oil prices increasing from $47 per barrel in January 2005 to over $74 per barrel in July 2007, profits at China-based manufacturers that used oil-derivative products, such as plastics, were adversely affected. The toy industry was particularly hard hit by the rapid rise in crude oil prices, since a significant portion of costs were derived from plastic resins made from oil derivatives.[7] Executive Director Tony Wu estimated that the average net profit margins of Hong Kong toymakers with factories in Guangdong would drop from 6% to 4% due to the rise in the cost of plastics used in toy manufacturing.[8]

[5] Ibid.

[6] Ibid.

[7] *South China Morning Post,* August 9, 2005.

[8] Ibid.

EXHIBIT 2 **Line of Business Information for Smart Union**

	2007	2006	2005	2004	2003
Hard and electronic toys	60%	54%	57%	61%	50%
Educational and recreational products	17%	21%	19%	23%	26%
Soft toys	9%	9%	9%	9%	19%
Sports products	12%	15%	10%	1%	0%
Others	2%	1%	5%	6%	5%
	100%	100%	100%	100%	100%

5 In March 2006, the company was incorporated in the Cayman Islands, and the company's shares were listed on the main board of The Stock Exchange of Hong Kong Limited on September 29, 2006. The company's Hong Kong initial public offering (IPO) was 42 times oversubscribed, as was the international tranche. Based on the final offer price of HK$1.10, the net proceeds from the share offer amounted to HK$55 million.[9] Proceeds from the IPO were to increase the company's capital base, providing funds to pursue the company's business strategy and future expansion plans.[10] Most of the proceeds, or approximately HK$25 million, were intended to be used for the expansion of production facilities in Qing Yuan, China. HK$13 million would be directed to the repayment of bank borrowings, including bank overdrafts and bank revolving loans; HK$5 million were to be used for the development of the company's ODM business; and HK$5 million would go to enhance production capacity, standard, and environment.[11]

6 In 2006, Smart Union reached an exclusive agreement for three years to produce and sell railway and remote-controlled car toys for Artin International (Holdings) Ltd., worth HK$150 million the following year. The new products were anticipated to have a gross profit margin of between 10%–20%. Smart Union Group and Artin International (Holdings) planned to lower costs through joint purchasing of raw material. Smart Union Group would use Artin International's factory in Dongguan for production.[12]

7 In December 2006, Smart Union Chairman Wu Kam-bun acquired 1.2 million shares in the company at an average price of HK$0.69, increasing his holdings to 169.2 million shares, or 70.5% of the company's outstanding shares.[13]

8 In 2007, Smart Union announced that it had entered into a stake acquisition agreement with the China Mining Corp. through its wholly owned subsidiary Queen Glory Ltd., in order to gain access to a silver mine in Fujian Province. According to the agreement, Queen Glory Ltd. would acquire a 45.51% stake in the China Mining Corp., worth a total of HK$269 million ($34.71 million), and purchase convertible bonds issued by the China Mining Corp. amounting to HK$40 million ($5.16 million), in order to increase its final stake in the mining company to 48.96% and gain access to the Da'an Silver Mine situated in Shouning county, under the jurisdiction of Ningde City in southeastern China's Fujian

[9] *AFX Asia,* September 28, 2006.

[10] *China Knowledge Press,* September 1, 2006.

[11] Ibid.

[12] *NewsTrak Daily,* December 1, 2006.

[13] *South China Morning Post,* December 18, 2006.

Province. Smart Union planned to use the stake acquisition to extend its operational scope because of the recent high demand for precious metals, including silver, which it used extensively in its manufacturing process.[14] The silver mine was estimated to contain 50.8 billion tonnes of silver and metal, valued at over HK$700 million.[15]

9 In addition to the impact of oil and labor costs, Smart Union was affected by currency exchange rate changes. During the period 2005–2007, the HK$/US$ exchange rate moved from 7.778 to 7.805, while the HK$/RMB exchange rate changed from 1.0642 to 0.935. The HK$/Euro relationship shifted from 10.481 to 11.388.

STRENGTHS AND COMPETITIVE ADVANTAGES

10 Smart Union's directors cited the group's principal strengths and competitive advantages as follows:[16]

1. Experienced management in toy industry. Most of the executive directors have extensive experience in the toy industry and solid engineering knowledge.
2. Long-term relationship with customers.
3. Vertically and horizontally integrated operation which offers one-stop production capabilities encompassing design, model fabrication, tooling, different processes of manufacturing, assembly, and packaging.
4. Effective cost management through monitoring of overheads.
5. Committed and proactive teamwork.
6. Solid production capability and engineering support.
7. Quality products and services.
8. Diversified product classes including hard and electronic toys, soft toys, educational and recreational products, and sports products.

TOY MARKET

11 The toy market is heavily influenced by the purchasing habits of young children. In 2008, there were 36 million children between 3–11 years of age in the U.S., and this population was expected to grow 4% per year by 2012.[17] In 2008, these children had an estimated income of $19.1 billion from allowances, gifts from parents, income from chores, and other jobs, which was expected to increase to $22 billion in 2012. Purchases by children were likely to be influenced by technology. In 2008, 35% of 8–12-year-olds owned a mobile phone, and 20% regularly used text messaging. Playing online games was the most popular online pursuit of children of all ages.[18] In 2008, 25% of girls and 20% of boys in the 9–12 age range had a computer in their bedroom. Although children devoted a significant amount of time and attention to computer and video games, they still owned a wide variety of traditional toys, such as cars, trucks, crayons, building sets, and arts and crafts.

[14] *China Metals & Mining Newswire,* October 30, 2007.

[15] *NewsTrak Daily,* July 17, 2007.

[16] Smart Union's corporate Web site.

[17] *Packaged Facts, The Kids and Tweens Market in the U.S.,* 9th Ed., August 2008.

[18] Mattel's 2007 Annual Report.

COMPETITION

12 ***Nintendo Co. Ltd.*** was one of the largest videogame console and handheld device makers, with products such as Nintendo's Game Boy, GameCube, and Wii systems, which competed with Microsoft's Xbox and Sony's PlayStation for the hearts and dollars of devoted gamers. Nintendo, loosely translated, means "leave luck to heaven." The company sold more than 5.8 million units of Wii hardware within the first five months after its launch. Wii software, such as "The Legend of Zelda: Twilight Princess" and "Wii Sports," are seeing brisk sales. The company recently broadened its focus on children and concentrated its efforts on its games, unlike competitors Sony and Microsoft, which developed increasingly complex multimedia systems. Nintendo owned a majority stake in the Seattle Mariners baseball team, which it purchased for $125 million in 1992.[19]

13 ***Mattel, Inc.*** designed, manufactured, and marketed a broad variety of toy products worldwide through sales to its customers and directly to consumers. Mattel's products were among the most widely recognized toy products in the world. Mattel's portfolio of brands and products consisted of Mattel Girls & Boys Brands—including Barbie fashion dolls and accessories, Polly Pocket, Little Mommy, Disney Classics, Pixel Chix, High School Musical, Hot Wheels, Matchbox, Tyco R/C vehicles and playsets, CARS, Radica products, and games and puzzles; Fisher-Price Brands—including Fisher-Price, Little People, BabyGear, View-Master, Sesame Street, Dora the Explorer, Winnie the Pooh, Go-Diego-Go!, See N Say, Power Wheels; and American Girl Brands—including Just Like You, the historical collection, and Bitty Baby.[20]

14 ***Hasbro, Inc.*** was a worldwide leader in children's and family leisure time and entertainment products and services, including the design, manufacture, and marketing of games and toys. The company's core brands included Playskool, Transformers, My Little Pony, Littlest Pet Shop, Tonka, Super Soaker, Milton Bradley, Parker Brothers, and Wizards of The Coast. The company's offerings encompassed a broad variety of games, including traditional board, card, handheld electronic, trading card, roleplaying, plug-and-play, and DVD games, as well as electronic learning aids and puzzles. Toy offerings included boys' action figures, vehicles and play sets, girls' toys, electronic toys, plush products, preschool toys and infant products, children's consumer electronics, electronic interactive products, creative play, and toy-related specialty products.

SMART UNION'S FUTURE

15 Ferris obtained Smart Union's latest financial statements, which were prepared under Hong Kong Generally Accepted Accounting Principles (HK GAAP) and certified by Pricewaterhouse Coopers (see **Exhibits 3** and **4**). He also was able to gather financial information on Nintendo Co. Ltd., Mattel, Inc., and Hasbro, Inc. (see **Exhibit 5**). He wondered whether Smart Union's recent profit decline was an ominous sign that the company's troubles might ultimately bring the company down. Although the company had declared and paid cash dividends in 2006, dividends were eliminated in 2007. The company's balance sheet indicated that bank borrowings of HK$240 million were current and due within a year. Would the company's cash flow generation enable the company to repay the loan, or would the bank be willing to refinance the debt at attractive terms?

[19] From Hoover's.

[20] Ibid.

EXHIBIT 3 **Smart Union's 2007 Financial Statements**

INDEPENDENT AUDITOR'S REPORT

TO THE SHAREHOLDERS OF SMART UNION GROUP (HOLDINGS) LIMITED
(Incorporated in the Cayman Islands with limited liability)

We have audited the consolidated financial statements of Smart Union Group (Holdings) Limited (the "Company") and its subsidiaries (together, the "Group"), which comprise the consolidated and Company balance sheets as at 31st December 2007, and the consolidated income statement, the consolidated statement of changes in equity, and the consolidated cash flow statement for the year then ended, and a summary of significant accounting policies and other explanatory notes.

DIRECTORS' RESPONSIBILITY FOR THE FINANCIAL STATEMENTS

The directors of the Company are responsible for the preparation and the true and fair presentation of these consolidated financial statements in accordance with Hong Kong Financial Reporting Standards issued by the Hong Kong Institute of Certified Public Accountants ("HKICPA") and the disclosure requirements of the Hong Kong Companies Ordinance. This responsibility includes designing, implementing, and maintaining internal control relevant to the preparation and the true and fair presentation of financial statements that are free from material misstatement, whether due to fraud or error; selecting and applying appropriate accounting policies; and making accounting estimates that are reasonable in the circumstances.

AUDITOR'S RESPONSIBILITY

Our responsibility is to express an opinion on these consolidated financial statements based on our audit and to report our opinion solely to you, as a body, and for no other purpose. We do not assume responsibility towards or accept liability to any other person for the contents of this report.

We conducted our audit in accordance with Hong Kong Standards on Auditing issued by the HKICPA. Those standards require that we comply with ethical requirements and plan and perform the audit to obtain reasonable assurance as to whether the financial statements are free from material misstatement.

An audit involves performing procedures to obtain audit evidence about the amounts and disclosures in the financial statements. The procedures selected depend on the auditor's judgment, including the assessment of the risks of material misstatement of the financial statements, whether due to fraud or error. In making those risk assessments, the auditor considers internal control relevant to the entity's preparation and true and fair presentation of the financial statements in order to design audit procedures that are appropriate in the circumstances, but not for the purpose of expressing an opinion on the effectiveness of the entity's internal control. An audit also includes evaluating the appropriateness of accounting policies used and the reasonableness of accounting estimates made by the directors, as well as evaluating the overall presentation of the financial statements.

We believe that the audit evidence we have obtained is sufficient and appropriate to provide a basis for our audit opinion.

OPINION

In our opinion, the consolidated financial statements give a true and fair view of the state of affairs of the Company and of the Group as at 31st December 2007 and of the Group's profit for the year then ended in accordance with Hong Kong Financial Reporting Standards and have been properly prepared in accordance with the disclosure requirements of the Hong Kong Companies Ordinance.

PricewaterhouseCoopers
Certified Public Accountants

Hong Kong, 23 April 2008

EXHIBIT 3 *(Continued)*

CONSOLIDATED BALANCE SHEET
As at 31st December 2007

	2007	2006
	HK$'000	HK$'000
ASSETS		
Non-current assets		
Property, plant and equipment	66,408	43,245
Land use rights	4,849	4,516
Intangible assets	2,967	632
Available-for-sale financial assets	2,342	5,120
Prepayments, deposits and other receivables	11,261	276
Deferred income tax assets	749	134
	88,576	53,923
Current assets		
Inventories	379,440	240,322
Trade receivables	165,438	104,029
Prepayments, deposits and other receivables	19,022	12,857
Derivative financial instruments	213	1,247
Convertible bonds	40,000	–
Current income tax recoverable	1,046	737
Pledged bank deposits	5,234	5,267
Cash and cash equivalents	101,584	64,882
	711,977	429,341
Total Assets	800,553	483,264

	2007	2006
	HK$'000	HK$'000
EQUITY		
Capital and reserves attributable to the Company's equity holders		
Share capital	34,248	24,000
Share premium	177,137	30,742
Other reserves	29,293	25,830
Retained earnings	76,112	85,832
	316,790	166,404
Minority interest	1,370	607
Total equity	318,160	167,011

(Continued)

EXHIBIT 3 *(Continued)*

	2007 HK$'000	2006 HK$'000
LIABILITIES		
Non-current liabilities		
Borrowings	201	2,749
Provision for long service payment	1,104	–
	1,305	2,749
Current liabilities		
Trade payables	195,631	158,837
Other payables and accruals	43,333	24,113
Borrowings	239,768	130,554
Derivative financial instruments	2,356	–
	481,088	313,504
Total liabilities	482,393	316,253
Total equity and liabilities	800,553	483,264

CONSOLIDATED INCOME STATEMENT
For the year ended 31st December 2007

	2007 HK$'000	2006 HK$'000
Sales	953,623	727,225
Cost of sales	(839,734)	(604,952)
Gross profit	113,889	122,273
Other income	12,320	1,906
Other (losses)/gains, net	(1,893)	1,804
Administrative expenses	(96,704)	(78,973)
Operating profit	27,612	47,010
Finance costs	(19,035)	(11,242)
Profit before tax	8,577	35,768
Income tax expense	(3,134)	(5,136)
Profit for the year	5,443	30,632
Attributable to:		
Equity holders of the Company	4,680	30,025
Minority interest	763	607
	5,443	30,632
Earnings per share for profit attributable to the equity holders of the Company during the year		
– basic (HK$)	0.02	0.15
– diluted (HK$)	0.02	0.15
Dividends		14,400

EXHIBIT 3 *(Continued)*

CONSOLIDATED STATEMENT OF CHANGES IN EQUITY
For the year ended 31st December 2007

	Attributable to the equity holders of the Company						
	Share capital	**Share premium**	**Other reserves**	**Retained earnings**	**Total**	**Minority interest**	**Total equity**
	HK$'000	**HK$'000**	**HK$'000**	**HK$'000**	**HK$'000**	**HK$'000**	**HK$'000**
January 1, 2006	**1,500**	**–**	**25,767**	**65,807**	**93,074**	**–**	**93,074**
Revaluation of available-for-sale financial assets	–	–	121	–	121	–	121
Currency translation differences	–		(58)	–	(58)	–	(58)
Profit for the year	–	–	–	30,025	30,025	607	30,632
Total recognized income for 2006	–	–	63	30,025	30,088	607	30,695
Net proceeds from issuance of new shares	6,000	47,242	–	–	53,242	–	53,242
Capitalization upon issue of new shares	16,500	(16,500)	–	–	–	–	–
Dividend relating to 2005	–	–	–	(10,000)	(10,000)	–	(10,000)
	22,500	30,742	–	(10,000)	43,242	–	43,242
December 31, 2006	**24,000**	**30,742**	**25,830**	**85,832**	**166,404**	**607**	**167,011**
January 1, 2007	**24,000**	**30,742**	**25,830**	**85,832**	**166,404**	**607**	**167,011**
Revaluation of available-for-sale financial assets	–	–	191	–	191	–	191
Gain on disposal of available-for-sale financial assets	–	–	30	–	30	–	30
Currency translation differences	–	–	1,721	–	1,721	–	1,721
Profit for the year	–	–	–	4,680	4,680	763	5,443
Total recognized income for 2007	–	–	1,942	4,680	6,622	763	7,385
Net proceeds from issuance of new shares	10,240	146,314	–	–	156,554	–	156,554
Share-based compensation	–	–	1,547	–	1,547	–	1,547
Issue of shares upon exercise of share option	8	81	(26)	–	63	–	63
Dividends relating to 2006	–	–	–	(14,400)	(14,400)	–	(14,400)
	10,248	146,395	1,521	(14,400)	143,764	–	143,764
December 31, 2007	**34,248**	**177,137**	**29,293**	**76,112**	**316,790**	**1,370**	**318,160**

EXHIBIT 4 **Selected Footnote Information from Smart Union's 2007 Financial Statements**

NOTES TO THE FINANCIAL STATEMENTS
2 SUMMARY OF SIGNIFICANT ACCOUNTING POLICIES

The principal accounting policies applied in the preparation of these consolidated financial statements are set out below. These policies have been consistently applied to all the years presented, unless otherwise stated.

2.1 Basis of preparation

The consolidated financial statements of Smart Union Group (Holdings) Limited have been prepared in accordance with Hong Kong Financial Reporting Standards ("HKFRS"). The consolidated financial statements have been prepared under the historical cost convention, as modified by the revaluation of available-for-sale financial assets, and financial assets and financial liabilities (including derivative instruments) at fair value through profit or loss.

The preparation of financial statements in conformity with HKFRS requires the use of certain critical accounting estimates. It also requires management to exercise its judgment in the process of applying the Group's accounting policies. The areas involving a higher degree of judgment or complexity, or areas where assumptions and estimates are significant to the consolidated financial statements, are disclosed in Note 4.

6 SEGMENT INFORMATION

The products and services provided by the Group are all related to the manufacturing and trading of recreational and educational toys and equipment and subject to similar business risk. No business segment information has been prepared by the Group for the year ended 31st December 2007.

The Group's sales are delivered to customers located in the following geographical areas:

	2007	2006
	HK$'000	HK$'000
Americas	638,708	503,866
Europe	208,916	154,419
Others	105,999	68,940
	953,623	727,225

The Group's total assets are located in following geographical areas:

	2007	2006
	HK$'000	HK$'000
Hong Kong	264,356	177,027
The PRC	536,197	306,237
	800,553	483,264

The Group's capital expenditures are located in the following geographical areas:

	2007	2006
	HK$'000	HK$'000
Hong Kong	952	481
The PRC	28,153	21,469
	29,105	21,950

EXHIBIT 4 *(Continued)*

7 PROPERTY, PLANT AND EQUIPMENT

	Group						
	Construction in progress	**Buildings**	**Leasehold improvements**	**Plant and machinery**	**Office equipment, furniture and fixtures**	**Motor vehicles**	**Total**
	HK$'000	**HK$'000**	**HK$'000**	**HK$'000**	**HK$'000**	**HK$'000**	**HK$'000**
Dec 31, 2006							
Cost	5,452	20,242	6,333	34,484	13,156	1,229	80,896
Accumulated depreciation		(202)	(5,099)	(22,540)	(8,788)	(1,022)	(37,651)
Net book amount	5,452	20,040	1,234	11,944	4,368	207	43,245
Dec 31, 2007							
Opening net book amount	5,452	20,040	1,234	11,944	4,368	207	43,245
Additions	21,474	562	540	4,451	1,544	534	29,105
Disposals		–		(53)	(37)		(90)
Transfers	(22,734)	21,106	1.628				
Depreciation		(1,099)	(1,404)	(4,994)	(1,075)	(212)	(8,784)
Exchange differences	335	2,333	7	245	12		2,932
Closing net book amount	4,527	42,942	2,005	11,593	4,812	529	66,408
Dec 31 2007							
Cost	4,527	44,291	8,510	37,586	14,567	1,762	111,243
Accumulated depreciation		(1,349)	(6,505)	(25,993)	(9,755)	(1,233)	(44,835)
Net book amount	4,527	42,942	2,005	11,593	4,812	529	66,408

Depreciation expense of HK$7,400,000 (2006: HK$5,753,000) has been charged in cost of sales and HK$1,384,000 (2006: HK$1,405,000) in administrative expenses. Motor vehicles include the following amounts where the Group is a lessee under finance leases:

	2007	**2006**
	HK$'000	**HK$'000**
Motor vehicles		
Cost—capitalised finance leases	850	316
Accumulated depreciation	(204)	(135)
Net book amount	646	181

(Continued)

EXHIBIT 4 *(Continued)*

8 LAND USE RIGHTS

The Group's interests in land use rights represent prepaid operating lease payments and their net book values are analyzed as follows:

	2007	2006
	HK$'000	HK$'000
At 1st January	4,516	–
Additions	–	4,593
Amortization of prepaid operating lease payments	(69)	(77)
Currency translation differences	402	–
At 31st December	4,849	4,516
Analyzed as:		
Land use rights in the PRC of between 10 to 50 years	4,849	4,516

9 INTANGIBLE ASSETS

	Group	
	2007	2006
	HK$'000	HK$'000
As at 1st January		
Cost	886	—
Accumulated amortization	(254)	—
Net book amount	632	—
Year ended 31st December		
Opening net book amount	632	
Additions	3,396	886
Disposals	(144)	
Amortization expense	(567)	(254)
Impairment	(350)	
Closing net book amount	2,967	632
As at 31st December		
Cost	4,138	886
Accumulated amortization and impairment	(1,171)	(254)
Net book amount	2,967	632

Intangibles represent capitalized toys development costs.
Amortization of intangible assets is charged to cost of sales.

13 INVENTORIES

	Group	
	2007	2006
	HK$'000	HK$'000
Raw materials	157,827	99,210
Work in progress	172,054	105,834
Finished goods	49,559	35,278
	379,440	240,322

EXHIBIT 4 *(Continued)*

The carrying amounts of inventories that were carried at fair value less costs to sell as at 31st December 2007 amounted to approximately HK$4,699,000(2006: HK$4,873,000). The cost of inventories recognized as expenses and included in cost of sales during the year ended 31st December 2007 and 2006 are as follows:

	Group	
	2007	**2006**
	HK$'000	**HK$'000**
Cost of inventories	835,953	604,196

14 TRADE RECEIVABLES

	Group	
	2007	**2006**
	HK$'000	**HK$'000**
Trade receivables	166,445	104,701
Less: provision for impairment of receivables	(1,007)	(672)
Trade receivables - net	165,438	104,029

The Group's trade receivables from its customers are generally with credit periods of less than 75 days. The sales to large or long-established customers with good repayment history comprise a significant proportion of the Group's sales. The Group has policies in place to ensure that sales of products are made to customers with an appropriate credit history to minimize the credit risk.

The maximum exposure to credit risk at the reporting date is the fair value of the trade receivables. The Group does not hold any collateral as security. The carrying amounts of trade receivables approximate their fair values.

The aging analysis of trade receivables as at 31st December 2007 and 2006 are as follows:

	Group	
	2007	**2006**
	HK$'000	**HK$'000**
0–30 days	112,063	78,737
31–60 days	19,890	5,670
61–90 days	15,201	11,394
91 days–1 year	17,226	8,633
1–2 years	2,065	267
	166,445	104,701

As at 31st December 2007, trade receivables of HK$1,107,000 (2006: HK$672,000) were impaired. The amount of the provision was HK$1,007,000 as at 31st December 2007 (2006: HK$672,000). The individually impaired receivables mainly relate to customers which are in unexpected difficult economic situations. The ageing of these receivables is as follows:

	Group	
	2007	**2006**
	HK$'000	**HK$'000**
Past due by:		
Up to 6 months	498	17
Over 6 months	509	655
	1,007	672

(Continued)

EXHIBIT 4 *(Continued)*

The details of provision for impairment of receivables are as follows:

	Group	
	2007	2006
	HK$'000	HK$'000
At 1st January	672	1,872
Additional provision	558	1,337
Reversal of provision	(223)	(1,190)
Write-off of provision	–	(1,347)
At 31st December	1,007	672

The creation and release of provision for impaired receivables have been included in "administrative expenses" in the consolidated income statement (Note 28). Amounts charged to the allowance account are generally written off when there is no expectation of recovering additional cash.

As at 31st December 2007, trade receivables of HK$97,371,000 (2006: HK$39,834,000) were past due but not impaired. These relate to a number of customers for whom there is no recent history of default. The aging analysis of these trade receivables is as follows:

	Group	
	2007	2006
	HK$'000	HK$'000
0–30 days	43,996	14,542
31–60 days	19,890	5,670
61–90 days	14,739	11,394
Over 90 days	18,746	8,228
	97,371	39,834

Trade receivables are denominated in the following currencies:

	Group	
	2007	2006
	HK$'000	HK$'000
Hong Kong dollars	112,737	43,104
US$	53,708	61,597
	166,445	104,701

As at 31st December 2007, the Group had factored trade receivables of approximately HK$7,097,000 (2006: HK$27,350,000) to banks on a non-recourse basis. As the financial asset de-recognition conditions as stipulated in HKAS 39 have been fulfilled, these factored receivables without recourse are de-recognized.

16 CONVERTIBLE BONDS

	Group	
	2007	2006
	HK$'000	HK$'000
Zero coupon convertible bonds	40,000	–

EXHIBIT 4 *(Continued)*

The bonds were issued by the Target at the principle amount of HK$40,000,000. Upon maturity, the bonds can be converted into 3,379 conversion shares of US$1.00 each in the share capital of China Mining Corporation Limited ("Conversion Shares"). Pursuant to the terms and conditions of the Agreement, the Target undertakes to and covenants with Smart Union Mining Investments Limited that (i) the Target will become the legal and beneficial owner of the 95% interests in the registered capital of Tiancheng on or before 30th April 2008 (or such other date as agreed in writing between both parties); and (ii) it will procure Tiancheng to obtain the mining license and any other necessary approvals and consents for the mining of the mine on or before 30th April 2008 (or such other date as agreed in writing between both parties) (the "Target's Undertakings"). In the event that the Target's Undertakings cannot be fulfilled on or before the maturity date, Smart Union Mining Investments Limited is entitled to demand the Target to redeem the Convertible bonds at its principal amount in full. In the event that all the Target's Undertakings have been fulfilled on or before 30th April 2008 (or such other date as agreed in writing between both parties), Smart Union Mining Investments Limited shall convert the convertible bonds in full at the conversion price and the Target shall allot and issue the Conversion Shares to Smart Union Mining Investments Limited.

The carrying amount of the convertible bonds approximates the fair value.

17 PLEDGED BANK DEPOSITS

The effective interest rate on pledged bank deposits as at 31st December 2007 was 3.8% (2006: 3.8%). These pledged deposits for bank borrowings are denominated in Hong Kong dollars and have an average maturity of 60 days (2006: 60 days) (Note 21).

21 BORROWINGS

	Group	
	2007	**2006**
	HK$'000	**HK$'000**
Non-current		
Bank borrowings, secured	–	2,650
Finance lease liabilities	201	99
	201	2,749
Current		
Bank overdrafts, secured (Note 18)	7,831	8,144
Short-term bank loans, secured	35,000	16,000
Trust receipt bank loans, secured	136,197	90,416
Current portion of non-current bank borrowings, secured	2,650	3,200
Factoring facilities utilized	57,929	12,730
Finance lease liabilities	161	64
	239,768	130,554
Total borrowings	239,969	133,303

Secured bank borrowings are secured by available-for-sale financial assets amounting to HK$2,342,000 as at 31st December 2007 (2006: HK$5,120,000) (Note 12), corporate guarantees executed by the Company and pledged bank deposits amounted to HK$5,234,000 as at 31st December 2007 (2006: HK$5,267,000) (Note 17). The maturities of the Group's borrowings as at 31st December 2007 and 2006 are as follows

	Group	
	2007	**2006**
	HK$'000	**HK$'000**
Within 1 year	239,768	130,554
Between 1 and 2 years	201	2749
	239,969	133,303

(Continued)

EXHIBIT 4 *(Continued)*

Finance lease liabilities—minimum lease payments:

	Group	
	2007	2006
	HK$'000	HK$'000
Within 1 year	185	74
Between 1 and 2 years	217	104
	402	178
Future finance charges on finance leases	(40)	(15)
Present value of finance lease liabilities	362	163

The present value of finance lease liabilities is as follows:

	Group	
	2007	2006
	HK$'000	HK$'000
Within 1 year	161	64
Between 1 and 2 years	201	99
	362	163

The effective interest rates of the Group's borrowings as at 31st December 2007 and 2006 are as follows:

	2007	2006
Bank overdrafts	7.4%	8.0%
Other bank borrowings	5.9%	7.5%
Finance lease liabilities	2.7%	3.3%

The carrying amounts of borrowings approximate their fair values, as the impact of discounting is not significant. The Group's borrowings are all denominated in Hong Kong dollars and subject to floating interest-rate within 6 months.

EXHIBIT 5 **Selected Financial Information for Nintendo Co., Mattel, Inc., and Hasbro, Inc.**

Income Statement Items	Nintendo Co Ltd		Mattel Inc.		Hasbro Inc.	
	(Displayed in USD Currency in Millions, Except per Share)					
	Y2007	Y2006	Y2007	Y2006	Y2007	Y2006
Sales	16,749.3	8,221.6	6,019.0	5,650.2	3,837.6	3,151.5
Cost of Goods Sold	9,698.6	4,787.0	3,010.0	2,872.0	1,477.4	1,236.1
Gross Profit	7,050.7	3,434.7	3,009.0	2,778.1	2,360.1	1,915.4
Selling, General, & Administrative Expense	2,097.5	1,461.3	1,998.4	1,859.8	1,673.9	1,392.3
Operating Income Before Depreciation	4,953.3	1,973.4	1,010.6	918.4	686.3	523.1
Depreciation, Depletion, & Amortization	73.7	50.8	170.1	170.2	156.5	146.7

EXHIBIT 5 *(Continued)*

Income Statement Items	Nintendo Co Ltd		Mattel Inc.		Hasbro Inc.	
	(Displayed in USD Currency in Millions, Except per Share)					
	Y2007	Y2006	Y2007	Y2006	Y2007	Y2006
Operating Profit	4,879.5	1,922.6	840.5	748.1	529.8	376.4
Adjusted Net Income	2,577.3	1,482.6	600.0	592.9	333.0	230.1
Balance Sheet Items						
Cash & Short-Term Investments	12,719.7	9,171.2	901.1	1,205.6	774.5	715.4
Net Receivables	1,458.3	746.7	991.2	943.8	654.8	556.3
Inventories	1,050.0	753.7	428.7	383.1	259.1	203.3
Net Plant, Property & Equipment	552.3	490.0	518.6	536.7	188.0	181.7
Total Assets	18,052.0	13,402.5	4,805.5	4,955.9	3,237.1	3,096.9
Long-Term Debt Due in One Year	0.0	0.0	50.0	64.3	135.3	0.0
Notes Payable	0.0	0.0	349.0	0.0	10.2	10.6
Accounts Payable	3,363.3	2,561.1	441.1	375.9	186.2	160.0
Long-Term Debt	0.0	0.0	550.0	635.7	709.7	494.9
Total Equity	12,317.2	9,372.9	2,306.7	2,433.0	1,385.1	1,537.9
Cash Flow Items						
Operating Activities - Net Cash Flow	3,328.8	2,336.1	560.5	875.9	601.8	320.6
Investing Activities - Net Cash Flow	2,335.6	(1,485.2)	(285.3)	(314.8)	(112.5)	(83.6)
Financing Activities - Net Cash Flow	(979.9)	(426.5)	(587.8)	(374.1)	(433.9)	(467.3)
Exchange Rate Effect	(530.1)	184.6	8.1	20.8	3.6	3.4
Cash and Equivalents - Change	4,154.3	609.0	(304.4)	207.8	59.1	(226.9)

Case 21

Teva Pharmaceutical Industries, Ltd

Tarun Khanna
Krishna Palepu
Claudine Madras

In Israel we have a 1970s song based on a poem from 1953 by Amir Gilboa about Theodor Herzl.[1] *It has a line in it about Herzl: "Suddenly a man rises in the morning, feels he is a people, and starts walking." That is exactly what Hurvitz did. Suddenly he woke up in the morning, feels he is a giant world class company, and starts walking. No one, aside from Herzl, has accomplished anything as remotely as impressive in this country as Hurvitz. It was impossible, a million to one odds at best, and he still did it. He woke up one morning and started walking.*

—*Ori Hershkovitz, equity analyst at Tel Aviv-based Leader & Company*

1 The markets had not been kind to Teva Pharmaceutical during the first half of 2006. The stock had plunged nearly 30% from January 1 to June 30, erasing billions of dollars from the company's market capitalization. Even good news, such as reports in July of Teva's wildly successful introduction of generic Zocor—the largest blockbuster drug ever to go off-patent—had failed to boost the stock significantly. Since nearly every retirement fund and mutual fund in Israel invested in Teva, this drop had been felt throughout the population, in effect amounting to every Israeli family losing NIS 3000, or $675.[1]

2 Teva was more than the world's leading producer of generic pharmaceuticals (see **Exhibit 1** for financials). It represented the gold standard of business in Israel. As the country's largest public company and first true multinational, it had avoided the traditional conglomerate model of early Israeli enterprises, choosing instead a highly focused approach embraced by later generations of successful Israeli firms. With revenues growing from $91 million in 1985 to an estimated $8.5 billion in 2006, the company had bred a new class of professional managers and scientists in the country. It had served as a bridge from Israeli science to the market and had been an important source of talent and capital for the growing biotechnology sector. It had also helped to catalyze the country's domestic capital markets by being one of the early companies to list on the Tel Aviv Stock Exchange in 1968.[2]

3 In 2005, Teva's $7.4 billion acquisition of Ivax catapulted the company to the top position among global generics in what one reporter dubbed "Generics' answer to Big Pharma."[3] Less than one year later, Teva filled 20% more prescriptions than Pfizer, the world's largest pharmaceutical company. It had a portfolio and pipeline twice the size of its next closest

Source: Professors Tarun Khanna and Krishna Palepu and Doctoral Student Claudine Madras prepared this case. HBS cases are developed solely as the basis for class discussion. Cases are not intended to serve as endorsements, sources of primary data, or illustrations of effective or ineffective management.

[1] The most important early advocate for the establishment of Israel.

EXHIBIT 1A **Teva Pharmaceutical Industries Income Statement (USD)**

	2001	2002	2003	2004	2005
Revenue	2,077.4	2,518.6	3,276.4	4,799.0	5,250.0
Other Revenue	—	—	—	—	—
Total Revenue	**2,077.4**	**2,518.6**	**3,276.4**	**4,799.0**	**5,250.0**
Cost Of Goods Sold	1,230.1	1,423.2	1,757.5	2,546.0	2,770.0
Gross Profit	**847.3**	**1,095.4**	**1,518.9**	**2,253.0**	**2,480.0**
Selling General & Admin Exp.	358.1	406.4	520.6	696.0	799.0
R & D Exp.	107.2	165.0	213.5	338.0	369.0
Depreciation & Amort.	—	—	—	—	—
Other Operating Expense/(Income)	—	—	—	—	—
Other Operating Exp., Total	**465.3**	**571.4**	**734.1**	**1,034.0**	**1,168.0**
Operating Income	**382.0**	**524.0**	**784.8**	**1,219.0**	**1,312.0**
Interest Expense	(46.9)	(54.5)	(45.2)	(42.0)	(34.0)
Interest and Invest. Income	20.7	17.8	24.4	27.0	45.0
Net Interest Exp.	**(26.2)**	**(36.7)**	**(20.8)**	**(15.0)**	**11.0**
Income/(Loss) from Affiliates	0.8	(2.7)	1.5	(1.0)	2.0
Currency Exchange Gains (Loss)	(5.4)	(22.8)	11.8	(14.0)	10.0
Other Non-Operating Inc. (Exp.)	4.0	35.4	4.0	55.0	(25.0)
EBT Excl. Unusual Items	**355.2**	**497.2**	**781.3**	**1,244.0**	**1,310.0**
Restructuring Charges	(15.7)	—	(7.4)	—	—
Merger & Related Restruct. Charges	—	—	—	(14.0)	—
Impairment of Goodwill	—	—	—	—	—
Gain (Loss) On Sale Of Invest.	1.6	(0.5)	—	—	—
In Process R & D Exp.	—	—	—	(597.0)	—
Legal Settlements	—	—	100.0	(30.0)	—
Other Unusual Items	—	—	—	—	—
EBT Incl. Unusual Items	**341.1**	**496.7**	**873.9**	**603.0**	**1,310.0**
Income Tax Expense	63.6	84.8	181.5	267.0	236.0
Minority Int. in Earnings	0.7	(1.6)	(1.4)	(4.0)	(2.0)
Earnings from Cont. Ops.	**278.2**	**410.3**	**691.0**	**332.0**	**1,072.0**
Earnings of Discontinued Ops.	—	—	—	—	—
Extraord. Item & Account. Change	—	—	—	—	—
Net Income	**278.2**	**410.3**	**691.0**	**332.0**	**1,072.0**

EXHIBIT 1B Teva Pharmaceutical Industries Balance Sheet (USD)

	2001	2002	2003	2004	2005
ASSETS					
Cash And Equivalents	768.9	809.9	1,057.3	784.1	1,276.0
Short Term Investments	21.2	235.7	322.1	256.8	935.0
Total Cash & ST Investments	**790.1**	**1,045.6**	**1,379.4**	**1,040.9**	**2,211.0**
Accounts Receivable	651.2	855.8	1,031.8	1,475.9	1,769.0
Other Receivables	166.4	218.9	300.6	398.4	—
Total Receivables	**817.6**	**1,074.7**	**1,332.4**	**1,874.3**	**1,769.0**
Inventory	570.2	781.1	1,004.6	1,286.3	1,114.0
Prepaid Exp.	—	—	—	—	316.0
Deferred Tax Assets, Curr.	—	—	—	—	95.0
Other Current Assets	—	—	—	—	—
Total Current Assets	**2,177.9**	**2,901.4**	**3,716.4**	**4,201.5**	**5,505.0**
Gross Property, Plant & Equipment	1,022.3	1,166.3	1,365.9	1,950.9	2,149.0
Accumulated Depreciation	(480.2)	(532.9)	(608.9)	(764.5)	(877.0)
Net Property, Plant & Equipment	**542.1**	**633.4**	**757.0**	**1,186.4**	**1,272.0**
Long-term Investments	141.9	277.3	396.7	806.5	278.0
Goodwill	466.1	560.3	647.5	2,572.4	2,462.0
Other Intangibles	103.0	158.4	269.1	695.2	635.0
Deferred Tax Assets, LT	—	—	—	—	76.0
Deferred Charges, LT	17.1	17.8	10.4	21.5	—
Other Long-Term Assets	12.1	78.2	118.8	148.5	159.0
Total Assets	**3,460.2**	**4,626.8**	**5,915.9**	**9,632.0**	**10,387.0**
LIABILITIES					
Accounts Payable	319.4	404.3	533.1	741.1	360.0
Accrued Exp.	50.6	63.7	86.5	120.9	587.0
Short-term Borrowings	202.8	176.1	291.7	390.0	264.0
Curr. Port. of LT Debt	3.7	566.5	352.5	170.4	111.0
Curr. Income Taxes Payable	24.4	141.0	179.8	190.6	205.0
Other Current Liabilities	137.2	172.6	251.3	590.9	733.0
Total Current Liabilities	**738.1**	**1,524.2**	**1,694.9**	**2,203.9**	**2,260.0**
Long-Term Debt	1,246.9	1,161.4	815.4	1,728.4	1,773.0
Minority Interest	2.2	4.9	6.7	10.9	8.0
Pension & Other Post-Retire. Benefits	10.4	13.8	13.7	16.9	11.0
Def. Tax Liability, Non-Curr.	39.0	43.7	34.6	212.3	219.0
Other Non-Current Liabilities	42.9	49.4	61.2	70.7	74.0
Total Liabilities	**2,079.5**	**2,797.4**	**2,626.5**	**4,243.1**	**4,345.0**

EXHIBIT 1B *(Continued)*

	2001	2002	2003	2004	2005
Common Stock	31.0	33.9	34.3	42.1	43.0
Additional Paid In Capital	480.6	481.5	1,159.3	3,035.0	3,369.0
Retained Earnings	970.4	1,345.7	1,960.3	2,171.4	3,081.0
Treasury Stock	—	—	—	—	(596.0)
Comprehensive Inc. and Other	(101.3)	(31.7)	135.5	140.4	145.0
Total Common Equity	**1,380.7**	**1,829.4**	**3,289.4**	**5,388.9**	**6,042.0**
Total Equity	**1,380.7**	**1,829.4**	**3,289.4**	**5,388.9**	**6,042.0**
Total Liabilities And Equity	**3,460.2**	**4,626.8**	**5,915.9**	**9,632.0**	**10,387.0**

Source: Capital IQ, https://www.capitaliq.com/main.asp, accessed February 18, 2010.

competitor.[4] With a 20% share of the U.S. generics market by revenue and number of prescriptions, it was by far the largest player in the world's largest market. Also, with the Ivax acquisition, Teva had gained the broadest geographic reach in the industry. One of the top players in Western Europe, it also had a significant operations in the fast-growing markets of Eastern Europe and Latin America, and had a presence in over 50 countries globally.

4 While Teva may have been Generics' answer to Big Pharma, Big Pharma was finally answering back. Novartis, one of the world's largest pharmaceuticals companies and the only one with a consistently strong presence in generics over the last two decades, had spent $10 billion on generics acquisitions since 2001. Novartis's generics unit, Sandoz, was now the second-largest generics company in the world. Other innovative pharmaceutical firms were aggressively fighting patent challenges through the legal process, through alliances with generics companies, and by moving to revive their own generics arms.

5 Low-cost firms from India, Eastern Europe, and elsewhere were also upping their game, emulating strategies that Teva itself pioneered over the last decade. Partly as a consequence, the pricing of generics in the U.S. market—the core of Teva's business for 20 years—had declined between 15% and 30% over the past three years.[5] However, the U.S. and worldwide markets continued to grow as aging populations and rising healthcare costs created pressure for lower-cost alternatives to expensive drugs.

6 In these industry conditions, could the company maintain its annual growth rate of 33% of the last five years, and, if so, how? Teva could keep its focus on the U.S. generics market, with major blockbusters set to lose their patent protection over the medium term, and take advantage of the glut of small firms to grow its share during the inevitable consolidation. Alternatively, the company could focus on the global generics market, either on the large potential markets that were slowly opening up to generics, such as Germany, France and Japan, or on the newer markets, such as Latin America or Asia. Teva could also continue to move up the value chain from low-cost generics into more specialized generics such as drugs with complex delivery systems or "biosimilar" versions of large-molecule drugs. Most aggressively, Teva could finally become serious about expanding into specialized innovative drugs, becoming one of the few pharmaceuticals companies to perform both functions in-house. While this strategy carried the company further from its core business, Teva had a long history of strong ties to local research talent, and had already successfully launched one blockbuster drug.[2]

[2] A "blockbuster drug" is defined to have annual sales of $1 billion or more.

7 In the meantime, Teva also needed to guard against the innovative firms and low-cost players to make sure that, as the incumbent, it did not allow creeping complacency to become fatal. The industry had changed significantly over the past five years; and the market leader needed to change with it.

THE GENERIC PHARMACEUTICALS INDUSTRY

Innovative Pharmaceuticals[6]

8 In 2006, the worldwide pharmaceutical industry totaled approximately $600 billion.[7] Globally, the six hundred publicly traded pharmaceutical and biotechnology companies had a combined market capitalization of over $1.5 trillion.[8] The industry had grown at approximately 12% over the last five years, with typical returns on equity of 20%, among the highest of any industry. Industry profitability depended on vigorous patent protection, particularly in the largest markets. Within the United States, the Patent and Trademark Office granted official protection for 17 to 20 years to new chemical entities. However, because the patent clock began prior to FDA approval, this protection translated into 10–12 years of effective patent life, as measured from the introduction of the drug into the market to expiration. During this period, gross margins on patented drugs typically ranged from 85% to 95%.[9]

9 Pharmaceutical firms were valued based on their pipeline of new drugs in pre-approval stages, as well as the projected lifespan of drugs currently on the market. In 2005 and 2006, drugs totaling $17 billion and $21.3 billion of annual sales had lost patent protection. Some industry participants were pessimistic about the future of the traditional (non-biotech) pharmaceuticals firms. They cited that more than 70 drugs were set to lose patent protection by 2010, including 19 blockbuster drugs, with few products in the pipeline to replace them.[10] As a consequence, annual industry growth was predicted to slow to 5% to 8% annually.

10 Pharmaceutical research was inherently a high-risk activity. One out of every 5,000–10,000 compounds tested became an approved drug,[11] and half of drug development costs were expended on drugs which never reached the market. Seven in every 10 marketed drugs did not produce revenues exceeding their R&D costs.[12] Drug development was a lengthy process, involving compound discovery, preclinical trials, three phases of clinical trials, and government approval. By the 2000s, the typical drug development duration from screening to approval was 10–15 years and cost $800 million, versus $140 million and $320 million in the 1970s and 1980s (in real terms). Research and development costs typically accounted for 14% of these firms' revenues, or between $30 and $50 billion per year for large companies.[13]

11 Once the drug was approved, it was marketed using the pharmaceutical firms' considerable sales forces. Sales and marketing costs varied by therapeutic category and potential market size of the drug, but on aggregate ranged from 30–35% of firm revenues. These costs included both "drug detailing," in which trained representatives visited hospitals and targeted prescribing physicians, and direct-to-consumer advertising, which had been liberalized in the United States in 1997.

Generic Pharmaceuticals

12 Generic pharmaceuticals refer to "bioequivalent" versions of their innovative counterparts. Most often in tablet and capsule form but also available in syringes, inhalers, and other delivery devices, generics in effect duplicated the active compounds developed by the original drug maker. These drugs were subject to the same regulatory standards and could

EXHIBIT 2 **Innovative and Generics Cost Structure Comparison (2005)**

	Teva	Barr	Sandoz	Mylan	Pfizer	Merck	Novartis[a]	Sanofi-Aventis
Net sales ($[b])	5.3	1.1	4.7	1.3	51.3	23.8	32.2	35.5
Net sales	100%	100%	100%	100%	100%	100%	100%	100%
Gross profit	47%	70%	51%	56%	83%	78%	72%	74%
R&D expenses	7%	12%	9%	7%	14%	14%	15%	14%
SG&A	15%	29%	26%	14%	33%	36%	36%	29%
Op income	25%	32%	13%	25%	22%	31%	19%	10%
Return on equity	19%	22%	Na	10%	12%	26%	19%	5%

Source: Bank of America Securities, Company 20F and 10K filings.
[a]Including Sandoz
[b]Market value of equity, priced mid-2006

only be manufactured and sold if the original drugs were not protected by patents. From a medical perspective, these drugs were largely identical to the versions of innovative firms and other generics producers.

13 Generics were typically priced significantly lower than their original versions because the drug makers did not need to recoup the massive costs of the initial research and development associated with drug discovery nor support the massive sales and marketing costs associated with introducing a new drug. See **Exhibit 2** for a comparison of the cost structures between innovative firms and generics firms. While the innovative and generics industries had both grown worldwide at around 9% to 10% annually since 2000 (see **Exhibit 3**), generics growth was expected to speed up to as much as 16% in major markets. Daniel Vasella, the CEO of Novartis, predicted that sales of generics would double to $100 billion worldwide by 2010 from the $52 billion in 2005.[14]

Generic Markets

14 **United States** The United States, by far the world's largest generics market, was the first major country to embrace unbranded generics with the enactment of the Hatch-Waxman Act in 1984. As a result of the act, generics penetration in the U.S. increased from 13% of the total number of prescriptions in 1983 to more than 50% in 2006 with prices close to 11% of the innovative products on a per-dose basis.[15]

15 The act contained two important provisions. First, it introduced the Abbreviated New Drug Application (ANDA) process which allowed generic drugs to shortcut the lengthy drug approval processes required by the Food and Drug Administration. Second, through its "Paragraph IV" provision, it allowed generics companies to challenge innovative drugs long before patent expiration. Crucially, it established a 180-day exclusivity period for the first company to submit an ANDA under a Paragraph IV challenge, providing incentives for generics competition. This exclusivity period set up a highly coveted duopoly for the first six months after the introduction of a generic drug. Paragraph IV had resulted in a vicious escalation in the legal battles between innovative companies and their generics counterparts, particularly with blockbuster drugs commanding multi-billion dollar markets.

16 During the exclusivity period, during which a generic drug faced competition only from its patented counterpart, the generic could be expected to capture up to 75% of the market by volume of prescriptions with discounts of 20% to 40% off the original drug price.[16] Gross margins during this period were typically near 70% to 90%, close to the innovator's margins

EXHIBIT 3 **Pharmaceuticals Industry Revenue and Growth**

Pharmaceuticals Industry Revenues

Revenues ($bn)	2000	2001	2002	2003	2004	2005	CGR (%)
Worldwide	362	395.1	431.3	470.8	513.9	561	9.2
North America	152	171.1	192.7	216.9	244.2	274.9	12.6
Europe	79.6	85.3	91.3	97.8	104.8	112.2	7.1
Eastern and Central Europe	7.2	7.9	8.6	9.4	10.3	11.2	9.2
Japan	57.9	59.7	61.5	63.4	65.3	67.3	3.1
East Asia and China	18.1	20.5	23.2	26.3	29.8	33.7	13.2
India	3.6	3.9	4.3	4.7	5.1	5.6	9.2
Latin America	25.3	27.6	30.1	33	36	39.3	9.2
Rest of World	18.3	19.1	19.6	19.3	18.4	16.8	−1.7

Generics Industry

Revenues ($, mm)	1998	1999	2000	2001	2002	2003	Past CGR (%)	Estimated Future CAGR[a]
Worldwide	27,180	29,750	32,600	35,900	39,400	43,300	9.8	10.0
United States	11,150	12,300	13,550	15,000	16,500	18,200	10.3	12.6
Western Europe	6,250	7,100	8,100	9,300	10,600	12,100	14.1	10.5
Japan	4,860	5,100	5,350	5,600	5,900	6,200	5.0	4.8
Rest of World	4,920	5,250	5,600	6,000	6,400	6,800	6.7	9.5

Source: Medical and Healthcare Marketplace Guide, 2004.

[a]Novartis estimates.

[b]Launched between 1997 and 2001.

Region Share of Pharma Market (2003)

North America	50.9
Europe	25.4
Japan	11.7
Africa, Asia, Australia	7.9
Latin America	4.1

Distrib'n of Sales of New Meds[b]	
United States	62%
Europe	21%
Japan	7%
Rest of World	10%

of 90% to 95%. After the 180-day period expired and other generics competition entered the market, the pricing of the 180-day generic drug decreased significantly, although the company often maintained a higher market share than the new generic entrants. In a typical scenario, the pricing would decline to 90% off the innovative price, while the market share of the 180-day holder would decrease from 70% to 75%, to 30% to 40%, with the corresponding sharp decline in margins. These numbers differed across products and with the number of competitors entering the market.

17 **Europe** The market for generics in the rest of the world varied greatly across countries. The European Union was slowly moving towards internal harmonization, although it was still far from achieving that aim. The United Kingdom and the Netherlands, the most competitive markets in the region, resembled the U.S. in their market structures. Pharmacists were free to substitute generic drugs for innovative versions at their discretion unless explicitly overruled by the physician, and prices were largely market driven. As a result, generic penetration was also high—49% of total prescriptions in the two countries in 2004—as governments, the public, physicians, and pharmacists generally accepted generics substitution.[17] The United Kingdom had a $2.9 billion generics markets that was expected to grow to $5.6 billion by 2008.[18]

18 Germany and France, like most other countries in the region, were "physician-driven" or "branded generics" markets in which pharmacists could not substitute generics at their discretion. Generics companies operating in these markets branded and marketed their drugs directly to physicians in the same manner as innovative companies and, as a result, incurred the costs of supporting much larger sales forces and marketing activities than in pharmacist-driven markets. Prices for both innovative and generic drugs tended to be government regulated in these markets; therefore, discounts associated with generic drugs generally were much lower than in liberalized markets. While these markets had lower penetration rates than pharmacist-driven markets—12% in France and 41% in Germany by volume in 2004[19]—they were still some of the largest markets globally both in size and potential. Germany had a $5.5 billion generics market in 2004 that was expected to increase to $9.7 billion by 2008. The $1.2 billion generics market in France was projected to grow even faster during the same period, to reach $3.3 billion by 2008.[20]

19 **Rest of world** Japan, the world's third-largest pharmaceuticals market, was also heavily regulated and had a generics penetration of approximately 10%.[21] Japan and other East Asian markets had various structural barriers to generics substitution, including a perception by patients and many physicians that generics were of inferior quality. Physicians also both prescribed and dispensed drugs, generating a portion of their income from pharmaceuticals. Given this dual role, they had little incentive to substitute the lower-priced generics. Over time, however, penetration in Japan, like all the large markets, was expected to increase as its population aged and health care costs rose.

20 Developing markets, such as Latin America, Eastern Europe, Russia, India, and China were becoming increasingly attractive markets for generics as governments moved to provide higher-quality care and middle classes emerged—though with budget constraints that led to a strong preference for less costly generic drugs. For example, in Poland, Lithuania, and Hungary, generics penetration by volume in 2004 was 87%, 73%, and 50%, respectively.[22] Many of these markets were physician driven, requiring all the corresponding sales and marketing activities, and were heavily government regulated.

Industry Players

21 Starting in the mid-1990s, the highly fragmented generics industry began to consolidate slowly and then a decade later, it experienced two competitive seismic shifts: the entrance of new types of competitors and the introduction of aggressive tactics by the innovative firms.

Low-cost players began to emerge from newly competitive markets such as India (Ranbaxy, Dr. Reddy's Laboratories, Orchid, among others), Eastern Europe (Pliva, Aegis, and Gedeon Richter), and Iceland (Actavis). Indian firm Ranbaxy was one leader of this generation. The Indian market had long been heavily protected and the government had de facto allowed local firms to circumvent international patent laws to manufacture drugs domestically, a practice which ended in 2005 with India's commitments as a full member of the World Trade Organization. With fierce domestic competition and very low consumer ability to pay, India had among the lowest pharmaceutical prices in the world. For example, the country had over 100 brands of generic ciprofloxacin priced at an average of 63 cents for 10 tablets of 500 mg each, compared to $51 for generic ciprofloxacin in the U.S.[23] (However, a large component of the price differences between generics in the Indian and U.S. markets could be attributed to additional costs which would have to be borne by all participants, such as obtaining federal approval and maintaining quality standards, as well as the pharmacy markup.) Ranbaxy had used its advantages to compete abroad: by 2005, the company generated 80% of its $1.2 billion revenues outside India. In mid-2006, Ranbaxy had the second-largest generics pipeline in the U.S. after Teva[24] and set itself the goal of surpassing Teva globally by 2012.[25] However, it was still significantly smaller on an absolute scale, and revenue was increasing at a rate of 19% over the previous five years compared to Teva's 33%. See **Exhibit 4** for competitor information.

22 Generic pharmaceutical companies also faced new competition from innovative firms. In 2005 Novartis acquired two generics companies, Hexal (Germany) and Eon (U.S.), and merged them into its generics arm, Sandoz, placing it temporarily into the top position in the generics industry. More significant than the relative size of the firm, this acquisition marked the first serious effort by an innovative company to compete in generics after a wave of failed attempts in the 1990s. Pfizer had also recently picked up activity with its Greenstone unit and others had recently signaled that they were reassessing the sector.

23 According to one observer, Sandoz had focused on developing a top-three presence in specific markets, namely Germany, much of the rest of Western Europe (with the notable exceptions of the United Kingdom, Ireland, and Italy), and the United States.[26] This approach—which emphasized the highly localized nature of pricing and regulations—was similar to that followed historically by Teva. In contrast, Ivax, another global generics firm since acquired by Teva, had expanded into a broad number of markets, but often with smaller market shares.

24 Another tactic by innovative firms affected the profitability of generics. Innovative giants such as Merck, Pfizer, and Eli Lilly increasingly released their own "authorized generic" version of their products during the 180-day exclusivity period, often by licensing production rights to a competing generics company. As a result, during this 180-day period, instead of facing only a branded competitor, the first-filer also competed with the authorized generic player, who had the support of the branded firm. This practice cut into the revenues of the first-filer by an estimated 50% to 60%.[27] While varying significantly across products, a representative generic drug which may have held 75% market share and 30% discount off the original price without authorized generic competition might have its share reduced to 50% and discounts rise to 60%. In 2004 and 2005, several high-profile antitrust cases emerged from these practices involving both Teva and Mylan as plaintiffs; however, given no signs of dampened competition in the industry—in fact, the opposite had occurred—no one expected the practice to be curtailed. Since 2003, every major drug with revenues over $1 billion going off patent had an authorized generic introduced onto the market.[28] As a result, generics companies could depend less on 180-day exclusivities

EXHIBIT 4 **Competitor Information**

Annual, 2005	Teva	Barr	Sandoz[a]	Mylan	Watson	Ranbaxy	Dr. Reddy's
Annual Sales ($ mil)	5,250.40	1,047.40	4,694.00	1,253.40	1,646.20	1,117.00	469.13[e]
Estimated U.S. generics revenues[b]	2,170.00	tbd	tbd	tbd	tbd	328.00	
Operating income	1312.9	330	342.00			41.9	21.75[e]
Employees	14,000	1,900	13,397	3,000	3,844	9,000	7,525[f]
Market Cap ($ mil.)	26,191.30	6,403.70	NA	4,626.50	3,247.60	3,249.00	832.70[g]
Strategic position							
Total Rx market share in U.S.[c]	18.0%	4.0%	10.0%	11.0%	9.0%	2.0%	
Number of US Rx (June 2006, '000)[c]	391	82	212	236	195	49	
Rx growth in U.S.[c]	17.4%	−2.9%	11.7%	8.3%	7.6%	27.2%	
Number of products in the U.S.	326	75	—	140	125		
FDA approvals[b]	43	16	—	22			
FDA applications (pipeline)[c]	201	35	—	41	35	59	
Para IV applications[c]	47	10	—	10	1		
Profitability[d]							
Gross Profit Margin	47.20%	73.30%	—	49.60%	48.20%	53.1%	52.00%
Operating Profit Margin	25.00%	35.90%	7.30%	24.30%	14.70%	4.00%	4.40%
Return on Equity	18.80%	21.90%	—	12.80%	6.40%	9.20%	6.10%
Return on Assets	8.20%	17.50%	—	9.80%	4.80%	2.30%	1.90%
Growth[d]							
12-Month Revenue Growth	9.40%	4.90%	—	−1.70%	0.30%	−3.10%	10.40%
12-Month Net Income Growth	222.90%	74.90%	—	−31.30%	−7.60%	−63.50%	50.80%
36-Month Revenue Growth	27.70%	9.50%	—	1.40%	10.40%	11.10%	7.60%
36-Month Net Income Growth	37.70%	15.50%	—	−14.70%	−7.60%	−22.9%	−29.40%

Sources: Company 10K, 20F, Hoovers, WR Hambrecht.

[a]Data unavailable

[b]Casewriter estimates

[c]IMS, June 2006

[d]Capital IQ, accessed August 28, 2007, including acquisitions

[e]Capital IQ, accessed August 28, 2007. Converted at historical exchange rate (12/30/2005), Rs44.97:$1

[f]Dr. Reddy's Laboratories, Annual Report 2005–2006. Data is as of March 31, 2006

[g]Derived from Capital IQ, accessed August 28, 2007 (12/30/2005 closing share price) and Dr. Reddy's Laboratories, 6K For the Quarter Ended December 31, 2005, published September 11, 2006

Converted at historical exchange rate (12/20/2005), Rs44.97:$

for profitability and many looked to other means of protecting their margins, such as entering profit-sharing alliances with innovative firms or with each other and focusing on niche drugs which attracted less competition.

Generic Products

25 Generics could be roughly divided into three categories of products: commodity generics, niche or "specialty" generics, and biosimilars. **Exhibit 5** shows several stylized scenarios of revenues and margins of drugs in these different categories.

26 **Commodity generics** Commodity generics, typically in tablet or capsule form, were generic versions of the small-molecule pharmaceuticals that made up the bulk of innovative firms' traditional businesses and consequently comprised the largest segment of generics. Examples ranged from generic versions of antibiotics Cipro and Zithromax to painkiller Oxycontin to cholesterol-lowering drugs Pravachol and Zocor. After the expiration of a 180-day exclusivity period, the margins on these drugs were typically lower than either niche generics or biosimilars, although this varied based on the number of competitors. For example, Eli Lilly's Prozac, one of the most successful antidepressant drugs in history, had both a very large branded market and was a relatively simple compound to synthesize. As a result, once the patent and the 180-day exclusivity period had expired, 18 competitors entered the market, collapsing prices and erasing profits.[29]

27 **Niche generics** Generic drugs could qualify as niche drugs if either their active molecules were difficult to synthesize or their delivery mechanism was non-standard. Respiratory drugs, for example, had patented inhalers and had to be branded and prescribed by physicians even in pharmacist-driven markets. Niche drugs could attract as few as one or even no generic version, depending on the difficulty and size of market. As expected, generic companies realized higher gross margins on these products than on commodity generics, while the capital required was greater than for commodity generics but less than for biosimilars.

28 **Biosimilars** The market for biosimilars was a multibillion dollar but largely undeveloped segment. Biosimilars were the generic versions of the so-called "biotech" drugs pioneered by companies such as Amgen and Genentech. The active compounds in these drugs were highly complex proteins or other large molecules that were far harder to replicate than traditional pharmaceuticals. While the worldwide market for biotech drugs was only $29 billion in 2002, it was expected to grow to $112 billion by 2012, a 12% annual growth rate, and take on increasing importance over the long term as the innovation in small-molecule drugs diminished and was replaced by this class of products.[30] Because of the complexity of the original drugs, the regulatory pathway for biosimilars was still undetermined in the U.S. and just appearing in Europe. However, the expected rewards were high as the prices of these drugs were expected to be discounted by only 10% to 20% off the branded prices, and the margins were correspondingly closer to innovative drugs than commodity generics.

29 Some estimated that the market could support only three to four companies competing in biosimilars because the capital and expertise required created significant barriers to entry. Predicted one industry analyst, "the companies that will be successful in [biosimilars] will be those that really have the resources to roll out a product launch. The biggest three that pharma needs to be worried about are Sandoz, Teva and Barr."[31] Others speculated whether the biotechs themselves would expand into this business. As of mid-2006, only Sandoz had launched a major biosimilar—a human growth hormone—in Australia and Europe, and both Teva and Barr had acquired companies to enter the field (Sicor and Pliva, respectively).

EXHIBIT 5 **Representative Revenues and Margins for Different Categories of Pharmaceuticals (relative to baseline of $1 bn innovative drug)**

	Patent-Protected Innovative Blockbuster	Commodity Generic in Substitute, or "pharmacy-driven," Market with Exclusivity (e.g., U.S.)	Commodity Generic in Substitute, or "pharmacy-driven," Market without Exclusivity (e.g., U.K., Netherlands)	Commodity Generic in Branded, or "physician-driven," Market (e.g., Germany, France)	Niche Generic Drug	Biosimilar Version of Biotech Drug
Approximate 12-month revenue (US$ m)	1,000	120	10	175	490	400
Approximate gross margin (US$ m)	930	60	4	140	392	340
Approximate operating profit (US$ m)	300	50	3	35	196	120
Assumptions:						
Market share by volume	100%	50% first 6 mos then 35%	10%	25%	70%	50%
Discount	0%	60% first 6 mos then 90%	90%	30%	30%	20%

Source: Casewriter estimates.

TEVA'S EARLY HISTORY

30 Teva's roots could be traced back to 1901 as Salomon, Levine and Elstein (SLE), a wholesale drug distributor based in Jerusalem to serve the local population and waves of immigrants from Europe during the first four decades of the twentieth century. During the 1930s, refugees from Nazi Germany came to British-Mandate Palestine and set up several small drug manufacturing plants, including one called Teva ("nature" in Hebrew). These early immigrants tended to be highly educated, and many had been scientists, physicians, and engineers in their home country. Because Germany was the birthplace of the pharmaceuticals industry and arguably had the top universities and scientific research institutions at the time, they brought many specialized skills required to set up pharmaceuticals cottage businesses in their new country.

31 In 1945, the newly created Arab League declared a general boycott against domestic and foreign businesses operating in the Jewish portion of Palestine, which was subsequently applied to all businesses dealing with Israel when the country was established in 1948. This boycott contributed to an economic structure in which foreign direct investment comprised less than 5% of all investment in Israel through the 1970s.[32] For the nascent pharmaceuticals industry, the absence of any large foreign pharmaceuticals company spurred a domestic industry of about 20 family-owned drug distributors and manufacturers each with annual revenues of approximately $1 million.[33] Together these family firms produced both the scale and, more significantly, the full portfolio of products required to serve the population of approximately 2 million people by the late 1950s. As a result, a community of chemists arose in the country with a broad set of synthesis skills, experienced in supplying drugs at a lower cost to serve the relatively poor home market. Also, since the patent-holding foreign firms would not conduct business directly in Israel, domestic firms could invoke the threat of "compulsory licensing" to pressure the patent holders into licensing the pharmaceuticals for use in the domestic market.[34] Compulsory licensing provisions were common in the legal codes of most countries, and could be invoked in certain situations in which good faith attempts to obtain a license under negotiated commercial terms failed for non-commercial reasons. While compulsory licensing was rarely invoked by these local pharmaceuticals companies, the threat increased their leverage to obtain voluntary licenses from the patent holders.

32 In the 1950s, SLE purchased Assia, a small pharmaceuticals manufacturing company. In 1962, Eli Hurvitz, a young employee of Assia, began the drive for consolidation of the fragmented industry. Hurvitz, born in Jerusalem in 1932, had started at Assia as a young economist in 1954. He had served as a private in the Israeli Defense Forces during the 1948 Arab-Israeli war and then obtained a degree in economics from Hebrew University. Hurvitz finished his active military service as a member of a generation of young Israelis dedicated to developing the new country. By 1962, both Hurvitz and Nachman Salomon, the head of the combined company, became convinced of the need to consolidate the industry. Salomon put Hurvitz in charge of negotiating the acquisitions. In 1963, after much discussion, they completed their first acquisition, of a company called Zori. Hurvitz reflected on his first major lesson in business:

> With these private, family-owned companies, they were not ready to dilute their ownership and lose control. We had to show them that mergers produce synergies, that they make money. We needed one example to prove that the result was not small at all but an order of magnitude. Only then could we convince the rest of them.

33 In 1968, he completed his second acquisition, this time of Teva, which had been publicly listed on the Tel Aviv Stock Exchange since 1951. The combined company officially changed its name to Teva Pharmaceutical Industries in 1976. That year, Hurvitz became the chief executive of the merged entity, the largest pharmaceuticals company in Israel with revenues of $28 million at the time.

The Billion Dollar Theory

34 By the early 1980s, having recently acquired Ikapharm, the second-largest remaining pharmaceuticals company in Israel after Teva, Hurvitz recognized that the company had grown as far as it could within its home market.[35] He hired Dr. Joseph Aleksandrowicz to head the strategic planning process for the company, which he continued to do until 1995. Aleksandrowicz recalled, "In the early 1980s, no company in Israel had any organized strategic planning. It was unheard of in the country at the time. Businesses were run more informally. Our production was best and FDA approved, we had marketing, computers, finance, and excellent, devoted people. But no one was used to creating a strategy."

35 Aleksandrowicz organized a two-year intensive program for the executive team, bringing in professors from leading American business schools to educate the leaders of the $50 million company. It was during one of these sessions in the mid-1980s that Hurvitz issued a challenge that became dubbed "The Billion Dollar Theory." Said one participant at the meeting, "Eli said to us: 'We have all the capabilities of a full-sized company. If we were operating in a large western market, we could be a billion dollar company, instead of the $50 million organization we are today. Now,' he asked us, 'how do we make that happen?'"

36 Hurvitz himself recalled the conversation:

> I remember in one planning meeting, I went around to each member of the executive team, asking what their growth goals were for the next year, five years. I heard 10%, 15% at the most. Everyone was thinking incrementally. I realized with that type of thinking, we would never grow to our potential. I had to break out of that thinking.

37 With the Billion Dollar Theory to guide them, the executive team recognized that they would have to expand beyond their home country and become the first Israeli company to enter a large, Western market. Dr. Aleksandrowicz recalled that, in addition to new markets, the group was occupied with the question of whether to be a focused company or a conglomerate and then, after choosing the focused approach—"extremely unusual for Israel at the time"—whether to be a chemicals or pharmaceuticals company:

> We decided on pharma, since it had more profits, we could collaborate with the scientific institutions in Israel, such as the Weizmann Institute, Hebrew University of Jerusalem, or the Technion, and we could export around the world. This path was so much riskier, but it also had a higher payoff if we were successful.

38 At the time, the company was partly owned by Koor Industries, the largest Israeli conglomerate controlled by the Histradrut, the powerful domestic trade union rooted in the socialist beginnings of the country. The board members from Koor in particular resisted this move as too risky for a company that employed so many people and served the basic health needs of much of the population. Hurvitz remembered:

> At the time, we had a $60 million market capitalization and it would cost us $20 to $25 million to enter the U.S. market. Now the decision seems obvious, but those numbers made it impossible to pass through the board. So I made them a pledge: I will not ever take a risk so big that it would jeopardize the company. I will risk quarterly or yearly profits, but never the company. I have always followed that. I managed the company for 100 quarters, not afraid to bet a year but never the company.

Expanding Abroad

39 Despite the close cultural and trade ties between Europe and Teva's home country, the executive team chose the U.S. market first. Europe was a still patchwork of regulation and

price controls, while the U.S. could be treated as a single market on the verge of uniform liberalization and market-based pricing. Teva entered the U.S. through a joint venture with W.R. Grace, a major American conglomerate, which gave them access to capital and contacts within the market. Chief Financial Officer Dan Suesskind said, "When we got together with W.R. Grace we said to them, 'We are willing to contribute to the partnership whatever we have, but money we don't ship over the ocean, of this they have enough in the U.S.' That's how we got to this arrangement."

40 Professor Elon Kohlberg, member of the board of the Teva's North America business, noted:

> Here comes Teva, a nothing company from a tiny country . . . and somehow, Hurvitz manages to structure a deal where Grace puts in over 90% of the capital for 50% of the joint venture. Who else could negotiate that kind of deal? . . . Grace was so much bigger than us at the time, and yet Mr. Grace himself used to come to the office just to spend time with Eli. He viewed him as an equal. That was part of the genius of Hurvitz.

41 In late 1985, the Teva And Grace (TAG) joint venture acquired Lemmon, a $20 million U.S. arm of Nattermann, a German company. From there, Teva entered the U.S. market and, just as in the Zori deal in Israel, once it had established a foothold, sales and market share steadily grew. Hurvitz built an internal team focused on acquisitions that earned a reputation in the industry for its systematic approach and successful outcomes. Teva became the most active acquirer in the industry, sometimes paying less than one times sales for a target company and rigorously executing the integration.

42 By 1993, the company had reached $502 million in revenues, halfway to its billion dollar goal, and North America had overtaken Israel as the largest contributor to the business. Teva continued to expand throughout the 1990s and 2000s, fueled by a series of acquisitions in North America and Europe (see **Exhibit 6**), and passed the billion dollar revenue mark in 1997. The geographic make-up of Teva's revenue changed dramatically as the company expanded. Israel accounted for the majority of the company's revenue until 1991, but that share had fallen to just 6% by 2004. During that same period, the North America share of revenue rose from 33% to 64% while the contribution from Europe and the CIS increased from 9% to 26%.

Developing Competitive Advantage

43 Over time, Teva became one of the largest suppliers to the growing segment of national pharmacy chains in the United States. In the mid-1980s, when Teva entered the U.S. market, the industry was dominated by wholesalers and distributors which had long focused on serving mom-and-pop pharmacies. Teva filled a vacuum for these national chains, enabling them to reduce their own internal costs by sourcing much of their formulary from a single company without use of a middleman. Teva provided not only a broad scope of products, but also inventory management, volume-based discounts and pricing bundles, services less valuable to the mom-and-pops but very important to the cost-conscious chains. Teva also kept its focus on low prices, acknowledging the commodity-like nature of the industry. Hurvitz reflected,

> Throughout the 1980s, everyone kept saying, "The Chinese are coming!" Everyone was terrified of this situation back then. So, we had to neutralize price as an issue for us. We spent a lot of time on our manufacturing and business model to ensure this, and always, always guaranteed the lowest price to our customers. If our competitors lowered prices after the contract was signed, we would give our customers credit. We were willing to forego part of our income in the short term for the long term. We knew back then that he who keeps market share will be the one who makes money in this industry.

EXHIBIT 6 **Teva Acquisitions from 1985 to 2005**

Date	Company Acquired	Location	Transaction Value (USD, M)	Value/Sales	Target Implied Price/Earnings	Teva Price/ Earnings
Jul-05	Ivax	United States	7,367	3.65	39.5	18.9
Aug-04	Dorom	Italy	85	2.33		
Oct-03	Sicor	United States	3,401	6.49	23.8	23.5
Jun-02	Honeywell Fine Chemicals	Italy	168	N/A		26.29
Feb-02	Bayer Classics	France	86	N/A		27.16
Dec-99	Novopharm	Canada	258	N/A		38.13
Aug-99	Copley	United States	220	1.77	39.7	33.14
May-98	Pharmachemie	Netherlands	87	N/A		26.45
Aug-96	APS/Berk	United Kingdom	53	0.81		41.41
Jan-96	Biocraft Labs	United States	296	2.12		38.97
Nov-95	Biogal	Hungary	25	0.36		33.13
Mar-92	Procintex and GRY-Pharm	Italy, Germany	23	N/A		25.38
1988	Abic	Israel	27	N/A		
1985	Lemmon	United States	21	N/A		

Source: Windhover's Strategic Intelligence Systems, Company 20F, Thomson Financial, Securities Data, Capital IQ.

44 This philosophy stayed with Teva in the subsequent years. According to Hershkovitz, "No one takes market share from Teva—no one. In the past, they have slashed their prices like nobody's business. This is a rule for the Indian companies: if you go into a Teva drug, you lose money, as simple as that."

45 Teva also sought to gain advantage through rigorous execution, including filing ANDA applications earlier and with fewer revisions than its competitors, backward integrating into active pharmaceutical ingredients, and efficiently managing its supply chain. As a result, Teva was able to sustain a large pipeline of Paragraph IV challenges as well as a broad portfolio of commodity generics, an elusive balance for its competitors.

Developing an Innovative Business

46 In the early 1980s, Teva decided to enter the innovative drug market, a move dubbed as "sheer chutzpah"[36] by Eli Hurvitz. By 2006, Teva's strong relationship with Israeli academic institutions yielded 150 to 180 proposals for new drugs per year. They had launched three drugs: two in partnership with Weizmann, including their blockbuster drug, Copaxone, in 1996, which became the leading treatment for multiple sclerosis. Teva relied on these external institutions for drug discovery, in contrast to Pfizer or other companies producing innovative drugs who had large internal basic research divisions. As a result, Dr. Irit Pinchasi, the VP of global innovative R&D, estimated that Teva's drug development cost for Copaxone amounted to approximately one-sixth to one-fourth the $1 billion typically required to bring an innovative drug to market.[37]

Mergers & Acquisitions

47 Since 1985 Teva had executed 14 transactions together worth over $12 billion, more than any other generics company, including Sandoz. It had built a reputation for successful mergers and fair treatment of employees, in part arising from the small community within Israel in which the consequences of treating employees poorly could be severe, and because it reflected deeply held values of Eli Hurvitz.

48 Many acknowledged the need for consolidation among generics companies. In the U.S., the top four firms controlled less than 50% of the market, the next six together controlled 20%, and none of the more than 40 firms in the remaining tail controlled more than 2%.[38] As Hurvitz stated,

> The market needs consolidation, globally. The more commoditized the market, the more this is true. And in this industry, the smaller players are the price leaders. . . . Mathematically we have a problem: we are already large. Today we are 20% of the [U.S.] market. How far can we go?

49 In 2002, Israel Makov succeeded Hurvitz as CEO, who, at 70 years old, remained in place as chairman. This event marked the first leadership handover within the company since 1976. The company continued its string of acquisitions, however. In 2003, Teva acquired Sicor which, at $3.4 billion, was eight times the deal size of its previous largest acquisition. Sicor offered not only additional scale, but also expansion into new customers, products, and technologies, selling injectable liquid products directly to hospitals rather than more traditional tablets to pharmacies. Some hailed the acquisition as an opportunity to expand and diversify away from commodity generics, particularly into biosimilars and the lucrative injectables business. Others cautioned that the businesses were too different and that the opportunity cost of choosing Sicor over other businesses had been high. Said one observer, "Focus had been the key to Teva's success over the years, during periods when other companies fell down trying to do too much. Sicor changed too many variables at once."

50 In 2005, Teva acquired Ivax for $7.4 billion, a move viewed positively by analysts for a variety of reasons. Some saw it as a tactical acquisition to gain access to Ivax's very strong first-to-file Paragraph IV pipeline in the U.S., which included generic Zocor and Zoloft (two of the largest blockbusters in history), at a time when Teva's own pipeline had softened. Others viewed the acquisition as more strategic, with Ivax's strong positions in global markets where Teva had little presence, particularly Latin America and Eastern Europe, as well as their innovative pipeline and niche generics in therapeutic areas new to Teva. Still others viewed the innovative and niche businesses positively, but were cautious of overexpansion into many small physician-driven markets.

Supply Chain

51 By initially limiting its markets to the U.S. and Israel and only slowly adding in new markets, Teva had maintained a rigorously low-cost culture and achieved greater scale benefits in its supply chain than any of its competitors. Said Eli Shohet, vice president responsible for the Ivax integration and the Central and Eastern Europe region:

> The bottom line is that we have scale advantages that cannot be matched by other companies at this time. Compare Ivax before the merger and Teva. In Teva, we have two plants in Israel that are currently capable of eight billion tablets and one in Canada with the same scale. One batch at Teva would have required five to six runs at Ivax, all in different locations. This is so much more expensive, and this is how most companies are set up. With our size, we can also source raw materials on a much larger scale than our competitors. You cannot just look at labor costs. First of all, they are not the only input and second of all, we are much more productive and capital intensive. And for labor intensive processes, we have operations in India.

52 Teva reconfigured its supply chain every several years since the early 1990s and after every major acquisition. The most recent integration with Ivax had been particularly challenging, as Ivax and Teva organized their worldwide operations very differently. Reflected Shohet,

> The culture of the two companies is the same, but the business model is different. Since 1995, Teva has operated as a global company. We localize the management and marketing in each region while having a global backend in R&D, manufacturing and APIs [active pharmaceutical ingredients]. The Ivax business model was an international company. It operated as a series of independent companies with very little cross-border interaction.

53 The backbone of Teva's supply chain was managed through several centers of excellence located globally to take advantage of differences in local labor skills and costs, tax provisions, and intellectual property regulations. The supply chain started with active pharmaceutical ingredient (API) production, a step which many of Teva's competitors at least partially outsourced, often to Teva. Teva's API division had sold $1.1 billion of ingredients in 2005, approximately evenly divided between internal and external use, and was one of the world's largest third-party suppliers of APIs. Once the APIs were produced, they were sent to pharmaceutical manufacturing facilities. The two largest of these facilities were in Israel, which primarily supplied the U.S. and Israeli market and had a capacity of 16 billion tablets, and in Hungary, which primarily served Europe. Teva estimated that it would produce 36 billion tablets in 2006. Teva reported unit-cost reductions of 30% in 2001-2005 due primarily to scale effects (see **Exhibit 7**).[39] Once the tablets were produced and packaged appropriately, they were shipped to their various markets and distributed locally. See **Exhibit 8** for a map of Teva's Israeli operations. Given the security risk associated with Israel's political situation, redundancies in the supply chain and extensive disaster planning had been conducted to mitigate disruptions associated with potential conflict within the country.

EXHIBIT 7 **Teva Cost and Output Trends (1998 to 2005)**

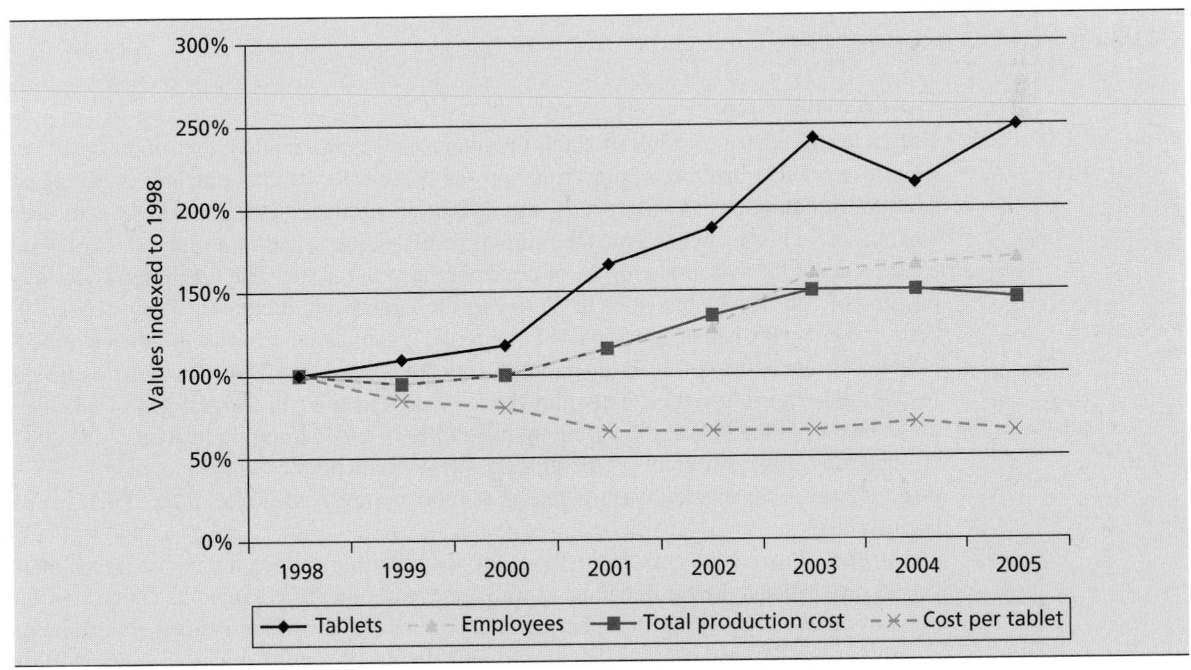

Source: Teva.

EXHIBIT 8 Teva Israel Production

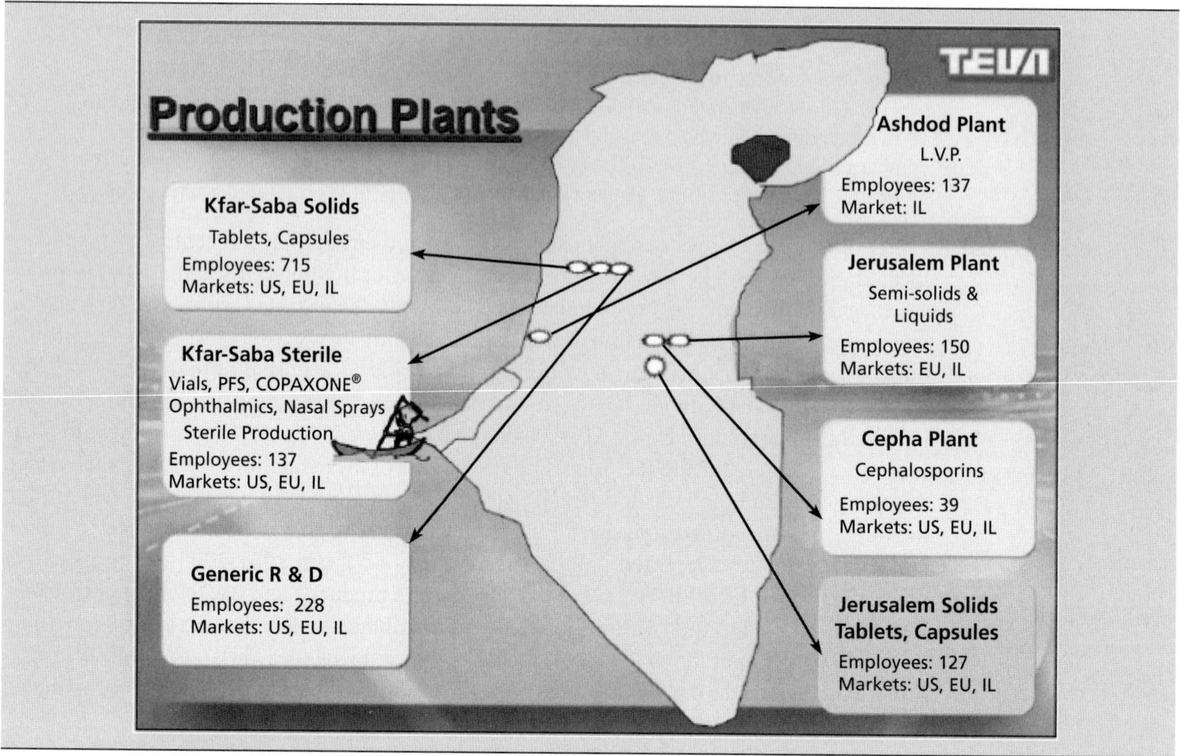

Source: Teva company documents.

TEVA IN 2006

Generic Markets

54 **United States** By the middle of 2006, Teva controlled approximately 18% of the base U.S. generics market by number of prescriptions (see **Exhibit 9**). Its total pipeline as of August 9, 2006, including the 180-day drugs, was 148 drugs products with branded sales of over $84 billion.[40] This segment formed the core of Teva's business, and some analysts expressed concern about the systemic erosion of prices in the U.S. market. The combined Ivax-Teva pipeline of 180-day exclusivities in 2006 was the largest in the industry. As of August 9, 2006, the company had 46 first-to-file Paragraph IV applications, covering drugs with $35 billion in branded revenues. From January through August 31, 2006, Teva had launched four drugs with exclusivities, including generic Zocor in June, the largest generics launch in the history of the industry covering branded sales of $4.4 billion. From January 1, 2004 through May, 2006, Teva had filed 24 Paragraph IV challenges compared to eight for Sandoz.[41] However, this market was tightening as more companies vied for a fixed number of exclusivities.

55 **Europe** Prior to the Ivax acquisition, Teva had focused on the pharmacist-driven markets in the U.K. and the Netherlands, as well as several other larger markets which showed signs of potentially moving to a pharmacy-driven model. It had maintained either low or no presence in the markets that remained dominated by physician-driven regulation, most notably Germany and Japan.

EXHIBIT 9 **Teva Total Generics Prescriptions**

Total Prescriptions in U.S. (June 2006)						
All Pharmaceutical Companies			**Generics Only**			
Company		**Growth**	**Company**		**Share**	**Growth**
Teva USA	393,014	17.3	Teva USA	390,845	18%	17.4
Pfizer	314,200	−9.1	Mylan	236,033	11%	8.3
Novartis (without Sandoz)	292,317	8.4	Sandoz	212,020	10%	11.7
Mylan	239,045	7.8	Watson	195,053	9%	7.6
Watson	195,060	7.6	Mallinckrodt	103,874	5%	23.9
Merck	137,545	9.9	Actavis	89,020	4%	−1.2
GlaxoSmithKline	128,982	−3.0	Barr	82,034	4%	−2.9
AstraZeneca	114,789	8.3	Par	71,767	3%	−2.8
Mallinckrodt	103,874	23.9	Qualitest	70,888	3%	−7.2
Actavis	89,022	−1.2	Ranbaxy	49,335	2%	27.2

Source: Teva, primary: IMS, June 2006.

EXHIBIT 10 **Teva and Ivax Geographic Mix, 2004**

Teva[a]		**Ivax**[b]	
North America	3,059	United States	860
% total	64%	% total	46%
Europe and CIS	*1,245*	*Europe*	*704*
% total	26%	% total	37%
Israel	*285*	*Latin America*	*316*
% total	6%	% total	17%
Other countries	*210*	*Other countries*	*0*
% total	4%	% total	0%
Total	**4,799**	**Total**	**1,880**

Source: WR Hambrecht.
[a]Teva 2004, 20F
[b]WR Hambrecht estimates

56 Europe comprised approximately 30% of Teva's 2005 revenues. Ivax gave Teva presence in the growing markets of the Czech Republic, Poland, Russia, and Slovakia (see **Exhibit 10**). Within Europe, Hungary, the U.K., and the Netherlands comprised approximately 75% of Teva's revenues, reflecting Teva's strength in pharmacist-driven markets and the legacy of Biogal, the company's acquisition in Hungary. Germany and France, the two largest physician-driven markets, together comprised slightly more than half of the remaining European revenues. Analysts differed on how Teva should approach these and other physician-driven markets. Teva could wait for the markets to adapt to a structure closer to the pharmacy-driven model in which Teva excelled. At the same time, other companies were already aggressively expanding into continental Europe, establishing dominant positions that could become difficult to displace later.

57 **Rest of world** In Japan and other Asian markets, Teva—like most other generics companies from outside the region—had adopted a wait-and-see strategy and had little presence. Ivax brought to Teva the leading presence in Latin America, which had contributed approximately 25% to Ivax's 2004 profits and was growing quickly.

Other Products

58 **Niche products and biosimilars** After the Ivax acquisition, Teva reorganized its internal operations and set up a separate specialty division to focus on niche products (such as hospital and respiratory drugs) and biosimilars. Teva expected $400 million in revenues from its respiratory franchise in 2006, growing to $1 billion to $2 billion by 2010.[42] It had not launched any significant biosimilars products in 2006, but expected this segment to be a high-growth area. However, some questioned whether Teva had focused too heavily on the U.S. market, which was bogged down in a regulatory impasse that was estimated to take five years or more to resolve. In contrast, Sandoz had focused more on Europe, working closely with the European regulatory authorities and had at least one marketed drug.

59 **Innovative pharmaceuticals** Copaxone had been Teva's first innovative drug, and had become the top treatment for multiple sclerosis in the world with worldwide total sales of $1.2 billion in 2005. It continued to grow at an annualized rate of 22% in 2006, compared to a combined rate of 13.5% for its competitors,[43] and had become an important contributor to Teva's overall profits. The cost structure for Copaxone differed from a typical innovative drug. In addition to lower research and development costs, sales and marketing expenses—typically two to three times the cost of R&D at large innovative firms—were lower for Copaxone, given the limited population of prescribing physicians. Furthermore, Teva had partnered with Sanofi-Aventis through 2008 to manage the sales and marketing of the drug, thus off-loading much of these costs from Teva. Most analysts estimated that Sanofi-Aventis passed on 50% to 60% of the revenues back to Teva. See **Exhibit 11** for an approximate breakdown of Teva's revenue between 2003 and 2005.

60 Azilect, a treatment for Parkinson's disease, had been released to the market in mid-2006. Dan Suesskind noted the importance of bringing this second drug to market: "At least [Azilect] showed that Copaxone was not a one-off. Having two marketed drugs is almost more important than having a pipeline." Teva also had a pipeline in other therapeutic areas with estimated potential sales of $6 billion by 2015.[44] Outside analysts estimated that this

EXHIBIT 11 Teva Estimated Revenue Breakdown, 2003–2005

	2005	2004	2003
Net Sales	5,250	4,799	3,276
Copaxone (@55%)	647	515	396
API	524	501	371
Other	23	22	20
Generics in U.S.	2,166	2,173	1,399
Generics in EU and ROW	1,890	1,589	1,091
Total generics sales	4,056	3,761	2,489
Number of generics prescriptions in U.S.	252	220	N/A

Source: Company 20F and casewriter estimates.

number could, in fact, be much higher and that, given the superior economics of innovative products, the relative proportion of innovative to generic drugs in Teva's revenue mix would steadily increase during the next decade. Others wondered whether four or five different therapeutic areas[45] was too much for Teva's limited research budget and limited experience bringing drugs to market.

Innovative vs. Generic

61 In 2006, Teva reported R&D expenses at an annualized rate of $500 million or approximately 6% of sales. Allocating resources between innovative and generics areas was one of the company's main challenges. The lead time for innovative drug development was 10 to 15 years, while generics development was three to five years, and the act of selecting and executing projects required very different skills and information. Reflected Dr. Ben-Zion Weiner, the head of Teva's research and development group:

> It is interesting how these two animals live under the same roof. On the one hand, we have low-risk products in generics, and then we have Copaxone and Azilect. The same person manages both and is responsible for dividing the resources. This is a very tricky decision making process. How do you trade off, say, investing in 10 low-risk generics drugs versus one high-potential innovative drug? This is a big part of our challenge.

62 Within the generics R&D division, Weiner's group had worked to create "an ANDA factory." Over the past decade, Teva had filed and won the greatest number of 180-day exclusivities in the industry, earning a reputation for quick ANDA filings and aggressive patent litigation. "Of course," said Dr. Weiner, "fifteen years ago, we were the entrepreneurs in this area. Since then, we have been studied by others and the gap has shrunk."

63 The innovative R&D group, on the other hand, had a different set of challenges. Said Weiner, "We are so small compared to the big guys. The consolidated research and development budget of the top 10 innovative firms is $45 billion. What can we do with a budget of [a few hundred million] against that? And that's just the top 10, the total budget of the industry is much bigger." In this context, the Teva team decided to leave the original research to external institutions, and to build research franchises in areas that did not require mass marketing to the general public and family doctors. With the addition of Ivax's research arm and existing pipeline, Pinchasi estimated that, by 2010, Teva would have a sufficient pipeline theoretically to launch one new innovative drug per year, in comparison to five per year of leading pharmaceuticals companies such as Pfizer.[46] Said Hershkovitz, "[Teva's innovative R&D group] is running way, way under the radar right now. They are currently running over 10 phase 2 trials, in addition to their phase 3 trials. And every month it seems as if we discover another clinical trial that they are involved in through equity in a startup."

64 Other companies, particularly Novartis, were tackling the same issue although from different corporate roots. Sandoz had achieved operating margins of only 7.3% in 2005 compared to 25% for Teva, and some employees commented on the issues with running a generics division within an innovative company, "In Novartis, if you sell the [branded] product one month later or not it doesn't make a big difference, because there is no other company to sell it," says Bedri Toker, Sandoz's top executive in Turkey, "But as a generic company I have to be first because there are many companies that can sell the same product. . . . The way of thinking is very different." Roche, another large innovative firm, had also considered entering the generics business three times over the last decade, but decided against it based on their belief that pure generics companies would always be able to underprice Roche. Hurvitz held similar views, saying, "It is very easy to manage a generic company when you are poor. It becomes very complicated when you are rich. It is impossible for

a rich company to act poor. As long as we remember this equation, and we do not become bureaucrats, and as long as we fight the fat culture, we will succeed."

65 Roche, like the other companies, also decided that is was too difficult to manage patent creation and challenging under one corporate umbrella.[47] This issue arose for both Novartis and Teva. Sandoz could not challenge any Novartis patents, and filed far fewer Paragraph IV challenges than Teva. On Teva's side, as they released more innovative drugs to the market, they anticipated greater challenges by other generics firms to these drugs. Responded Dr. Pinchasi to how they will manage these dual missions: "That will be interesting, no? We're now trying to learn what you have to do to make things hard for generic drug makers . . . After all, we know better than anyone how to challenge patents, but there's no guarantee we'll succeed. Yes, there are quite a few companies that would like to turn the tables on us, and challenge our patents."[48]

66 Many were watching whether either Sandoz or Teva could manage both businesses effectively under one corporate umbrella, particularly as they came from different roots but both sought growth in similar areas: generics sales in global markets, biosimilars, and niche innovative drugs.

CONCLUSION

67 After years of tremendous success competing against richer, Western companies, Teva was now the reigning incumbent in an increasingly competitive industry. New low-cost players were coming in behind them, having learned from Teva's success and hungry to capture a share of the growing market. The innovative firms had also finally woken up—vigorously protecting their hard-earned patents while also encroaching on the generics market. In front of Teva lay the complex world of global markets for generics, as well as the innovative drug market, both of which were large and growing but did not necessarily play to Teva's historical strengths. How should Teva grow in the next ten years? Should it focus on consolidating in the U.S. and other substitution-oriented generics markets, on further expanding into the global branded generics markets, or on gradually turning itself into a more specialized generics or even an innovative firm? Alternatively, did it need to focus on all three areas to succeed, and if so, could it manage such diverse goals under one roof?

END NOTES

[1] "Plummeting Teva stocks affect every household," Yedioth Ahronot, June 25, 2006.

[2] Alternately, the company could be viewed as listing in 1951, accounting for an antecedent company.

[3] "Teva/Ivax: Generics' Answer to Big Pharma", *In Vivo,* September 2005.

[4] Dan Suesskind, personal communication; Ranbaxy company documents.

[5] Casewriter estimates based on published financial reports and IMS data.

[6] This section has been adapted from "Strategy in the Twenty-First Century Pharmaceutical Industry: Merck & Co and Pfizer Inc.", HBS Case N2-707-487.

[7] IMS Health, "Global Pharmaceutical Sales, 1998-2005," IMS Health Company Web site, February 27, 2006, , cited in HBS Case 707-487, "Strategy in the Twenty-First Century Pharmaceutical Industry: Merck & Co. and Pfizer Inc. (RC Strategy)".

http://www.imshealth.com/ims/portal/front/articleC/0,2777,6599_77478579_77478598,00.html, accessed November 2006, , cited in HBS Case 707-487, "Strategy in the Twenty-First Century Pharmaceutical Industry: Merck & Co. and Pfizer Inc. (RC Strategy)".

[8] Peter W. Huber, "Of Pills and Profits: In Defense of Big Pharma," Commentary, Vol. 122, No. 1, July 2006, http://www.commentarymagazine.com, accessed August 2006, cited in HBS Case 707-487, "Strategy in the Twenty-First Century Pharmaceutical Industry: Merck & Co. and Pfizer Inc. (RC Strategy)".

[9] Henry Grabowski and John Vernon, "Longer Patents for Increased Generic Competition: The Waxman-Hatch Act After One Decade," Pharmacoeconomics, Vol. 10, Supplement 2, (1996): 110-123; Anita McGahan, Dale O Coxe, Greg Keller and John F. McGuire, "The Pharmaceutical Industry in the 1990s," Harvard Business School Case No. 796-058, Rev: July 18, 1996.

[10] "Healthcare: Pharmaceuticals," Standard & Poor's; Gray, "Our 7th Annual Report on The World's Top 50 Pharmaceutical Companies.", cited in HBS Case 707-487, "Strategy in the Twenty-First Century Pharmaceutical Industry: Merck & Co. and Pfizer Inc. (RC Strategy)".

[11] Bradley Weber, "The Pharmaceutical Industry.", cited in HBS Case 707-487, "Strategy in the Twenty-First Century Pharmaceutical Industry: Merck & Co. and Pfizer Inc. (RC Strategy)".

[12] Henry Grabowski, John Vernon, and Joseph A. DiMasi, "Returns on Research and Development for 1990s," cited in HBS Case 707-487, "Strategy in the Twenty-First Century Pharmaceutical Industry: Merck & Co. and Pfizer Inc. (RC Strategy) New Drug Introductions," PharmacoEconomics, Vol. 20 Issue 15 (Supplement 3), (2002): 11-29, via EBSCO, accessed September 2006, cited in HBS Case 707-487, "Strategy in the Twenty-First Century Pharmaceutical Industry: Merck & Co. and Pfizer Inc. (RC Strategy)".

[13] United States from 1963 to 1999," Clinical Pharmacology and Therapeutics, Vol. 69, No. 5, (2001): 286-296; Joseph A. DiMasi, Ronald W. Hansen, and Henry Grabowski, "The Price of Innovation: New Estimates of Drug Development Costs," Journal of Health Economics, Vol. 22, Issue 2, (March 2003): 151-185; "Personalized Medicine: The Emerging Pharmacogenomics Revolution," PriceWaterhouseCoopers, February 2005, http://www.pwc.com/techforecast/pdfs/pharmaco-wb-x.pdf, accessed September 2006. Another study, which included commercialization costs, put the figure of bringing a single new drug to market at about $1.7 billion; see Peter Landers, "Cost of Developing a New Drug Increases to About $1.7 Billion," The Wall Street Jouranl, December 8, 2003, p. B4, via Factiva, accessed September 2006, cited in HBS Case 707-487, "Strategy in the Twenty-First Century Pharmaceutical Industry: Merck & Co. and Pfizer Inc. (RC Strategy)".

[14] "Mixing Medicines: Betting $10 Billion on Generics, Novartis Seeks to Inject Growth," *Wall Street Journal,* May 4, 2006.

[15] Remarks by Lester M. Crawford. Acting Commissioner of Food and Drugs to the Generics Pharmaceutical Association, 26 February 2005, and WR Hambrecht estimates.

[16] Dr Joseph Aleksandrowicz, personal communication.

[17] European Generics Association; http://www.leaddiscovery.co.uk/datamonitor_shots/ BEST%20 Nov% 2016th% 20Generics%20Sample%20Pages%202.pdf.

[18] Ranbaxy Laboratories, Corporate Presentation, May 2006.

[19] European Generics Association.

[20] Ranbaxy Laboratories, Corporate Presentation, May 2006.

[21] Eran Ezra, personal communication.

[22] European Generics Association, http://www.leaddiscovery.co.uk/datamonitor_shots/BEST%20 Nov%201 6th%20Generics % 20Sample%20Pages%202.pdf.

[23] "Emerging Giants," *Businessweek,* July 21, 2006.

[24] Ranbaxy website, accessed August 28, 2006.

[25] "Emerging Giants," *Businessweek,* July 21, 2006.

[26] Dr Joseph Aleksandrowicz, personal communication.

[27] Teva internal communication (Dan Suesskind, August 28, 2006).

[28] Fenwick and West, November, 2005.

[29] Rouhi, "Generic Tide is Rising." Chemical and Engineering News, Volume 80, Number 38, CENEAR 80 38 pp. 37–51.

[30] Medical and Healthcare Marketplace Guide, 2004.

[31] http://news.monstersandcritics.com/health/article_1193475.php/ Analysis_ Biosimilars_to_ make_ ig_splash.

[32] meria.idc.ac.il/journal/2002/issue3/jv6n3a3.html as accessed on November 14, 2005.

[33] Eli Hurvitz, personal communication, November 2005.

[34] Dan Suesskind, personal communication.

[35] During the late 1960s, Teva had expanded briefly overseas to West Africa and Kenya, reflecting a period of close ties between the governments of these countries and the companies' recognition then of the need for expansion. However these markets proved limited in size and increasingly politically problematic and eventually Teva exited the region.

[36] "Nerve, gall or supreme self-confidence," *Merriam-Webster Dictionary,* accessed August 30, 2006.

[37] "Not just generics and Copaxone," Globes, 10 April 2006.

[38] Teva investor lunch, August 9, primary: IMS June data.

[39] Teva company documents.

[40] Q2 earnings call, August 8. 2006 and Hurvitz, personal communication.

[41] *Wall Street Journal,* May 4, 2006.

[42] Q2 earnings call, August 8, 2006.

[43] Teva company documents, IMS data.

[44] Teva company documents.

[45] Central Nervous System, immunology, oncology, hematology and respiratory.

[46] "Not just generics and Copaxone" *Globes,* April 10, 2006.

[47] *Wall Street Journal,* May 4, 2006.

[48] "Not just generics and Copaxone" *Globes,* April 10, 2006.

Case 22

The Ultimate Fighting Championships (UFC): *The Evolution of a Sport*[1]

Jesse Baker
Matthew Thomson

The UFC is the most exciting combat sport in the world because there are so many ways to win and so many ways to lose. . . . Boxing is your father's sport.

—*Dana White*

What makes UFC so great is that every single man on the planet gets it immediately. It's just two guys beating each other up.

—*Lorenzo Fertitta*

We're not for everyone, and we don't try to be. If you don't like fighting sports, great, this is America, that's your right. All we ask is that people understand what we are.

—*Dana White*

1 In early February of 2010, Bryan Johnston, the chief marketing officer for the Ultimate Fighting Championship (UFC), returned to his office at Zuffa LLC, the parent company for the UFC, in Las Vegas, Nevada. He was frustrated by the numerous athlete injuries that continued to plague scheduled events, most recently UFC 108 on January 2, 2010. This situation gave him cause to reflect on some much bigger issues he had been dealing with since leaving his role as vice president of partner marketing at Burton Snowboards to join the UFC and take full control of the organization's marketing activities in June 2009. Johnston was the first senior member of the firm who did not come from a background in boxing or television.[2] He felt a great deal of pressure to ensure that the UFC continued to meet the high expectations that had been set by its phenomenal early success.

2 The name UFC had become synonymous with mixed martial arts across North America. Over the past decade, the company had experienced unparalleled growth in the sporting industry and was now valued at more than $1 billion.[3] However, the competitive

Richard Ivey School of Business
The University of Western Ontario

Ivey Publishing

Source: Jesse Baker wrote this case under the supervision of Matthew Thomson solely to provide material for class discussion. The authors do not intend to illustrate either effective or ineffective handling of a managerial situation. The authors may have disguised certain names and other identifying information to protect confidentiality.

[1] This case has been written on the basis of published sources only. Consequently, the interpretation and perspectives presented in this case are not necessarily those of Ultimate Fighting Championships or any of its employees.

[2] Jon Show, "UFC Finalizes Team with CMO Hire," *Sports Business Journal,* June 1, 2009, page 25; available at http://www.sportsbusinessjournal.com/index.cfm?fuseaction=article.preview&articleid=62699, accessed August 8, 2009.

[3] Sean Gregory and James Osborne, "White vs. Fedor: Ultimate Fighting's Cold War Gets Hotter," *Time Magazine,* July 10, 2009; available at http://www.time.com/time/arts/article/0,8599,1909703,00.html, accessed September 3, 2009.

EXHIBIT 1 **Ispos-Reid Canadian Sports Monitor Study Results**

S3_11. (U.F.C. (Ultimate Fighting Championship)) Thinking about your interest in these sports and events in the past few years, would you say that you have less interest, the same interest or more interest than before? If you have never had an interest in the sport or event you can indicate that as well

Proportions/Means: Columns Tested (5% risk level) - A/B/C/D/E/F - G/H - I/J/K/L/M/N/O/P/Q/R/S - T/U * small base

	Total (Age)	18 to 34	18 to 49	25 to 54	35 to 54	45 to 54	55+
Base: Casual or avid fan	409	166	318	295	185	74	58
Weighted	431	208	354	315	176	64*	47*
	60	27	44	39	24	11	8
	14%	13%	13%	12%	14%	17%	18%
Less Interest							
	203	91	165	148	91	34	21
	7%	4%	47%	47%	52%	54%	44%
The Same							
	169	90	145	129	61	18	18
	39%	43%	41%	41%	35%	29%	38%
More							

Source: Ipsos-Reid Canadian Sports Monitor Study, Table 25.

landscape was changing quickly, and Johnston understood that he was running out of time to make important decisions on how to continue to grow the league while maintaining the UFC's competitive advantage that stemmed from its dominant position as the market leader.

3 The UFC had already begun to make strides in new international markets. According to the results of an Ipsos-Reid Canadian Sports Monitor Study, 22 percent of Canadian adults were interested in the UFC, which was fast approaching the Canadian National Basketball Association (NBA) fan base of 26 percent of Canadian adults.[4] Furthermore, 39 percent of those interested in the UFC said their interest had increased over the past few years, more than any of the 30 other sports surveyed in Canada, including hockey and the Olympics (see **Exhibit 1**).[5] Still, Johnston wondered about the long-term sustainability of the UFC's current strategy. In January 2010, a 10 percent stake in the company had been sold to Flash Entertainment, a Middle Eastern entertainment company and a wholly owned subsidiary of the Abu Dhabi government.[6] Johnston hoped that this move would allow the UFC to develop strategic partnerships in the Middle East and throughout Asia. However, if the UFC could not even deliver on the advertised fights within the United States, how would the company be able to deliver quality fights overseas? New international markets would dramatically increase the demand for talented main-event fighters.

[4] Ipsos-Reid Canadian Sports Monitor, "UFC (Ultimate Fighting Championship) Tops List of Sports Gaining Momentum in Canada," Toronto, ON, June 22, 2009.

[5] Ibid.

[6] Arnold M. Knightly, "UFC Sells 10 Percent to Mideast Company," *Las Vegas Review-Journal,* January 11, 2010; available at http://www.lvrj.com/news/breaking_news/UFC-sells-10-percent-to-Mideast-company-81192552.html, accessed January 22, 2010.

4 Johnston also wondered whether local talent would need to be identified and recruited to attract fans and fill seats in these new markets. The popularity of English-born fighter Michael Bisping was paramount to the success of UFC events in the United Kingdom. Would his popularity also hold true in other regions? Johnston was also wary of an expansion strategy that would compromise the company's core fan base, many of whom remained skeptical of the UFC's international initiatives. He remembered an interview he had seen recently, in which Marshall Zelaznik, the UFC's managing director of International Development, had reiterated the disappointment of many UFC fans, who feared that too many international events would dilute the quality of the events held within the United States.[7] Johnston did not want to alienate the UFC's primary market by stretching the resources too thin.

EARLY DEVELOPMENT

5 The concept of the UFC was originally developed in 1993, as a single-elimination, eight-man tournament called War of the Worlds by Art Davie, an enthusiast with an advertising background, and Rorion Gracie, a master in the martial art of Brazilian jiu-jitsu.[8] The concept developed as a tournament that would feature martial artists from different disciplines facing each other to determine the best martial art. Davie and Gracie formed WOW Promotions and founded Semaphore Entertainment Group (SEG) as a television partner.[9] The trademarked octagon design was developed for the enclosure in which the bouts were staged, and Davie and Gracie named the show "The Ultimate Fighting Championship."[10] The first event, later to be known as UFC 1, was held in Denver, Colorado, and proved to be a success from its inception, drawing 86,592 pay-per-view (PPV) television subscribers.[11] Following UFC 5, in April 1995, Davie and Gracie sold their interests in the organization to SEG.

6 Despite the UFC's early success, controversy surrounding the absence of any standard set of rules to govern the sport led to the sport being banned in 36 states.[12] One of many public figures who spoke out against the sport was U.S. Senator John McCain, who declared it to be "human cock-fighting."[13] s a result, the UFC was dropped from major cable PPV distributor, Viewer's Choice, and other individual cable carriers, such as TCI Cable.[14] The controversy also was a major barrier against obtaining official athletic sanctioning from state athletic commissions.

7 In the early 1990s, in fact, the UFC's tagline had been "There Are No Rules!" In reality, though, a limited set of rules did exist: no eye gouging and no biting. Other techniques such as hair pulling, head butting, groin strikes and fish hooking were frowned upon, but still permitted. These rules, or their lack thereof, were a major source of the controversy. Although the sport was appealing to some, until the sport was able to establish a clear set of rules to better protect fighters, opportunities were clearly limited for the sport's growth.

[7] Steve Cofield, Interview, Yahoo! Sports cage writer, *ESPN Radio 1100,* January 21, 2010; available at http://mmablips.dailyradar.com/video/ufc-112-marshall-zelaznik-talks-about-abu-dhabi-s/, accessed February 1, 2010.

[8] Clyde Gentry III, *No Holds Barred: Evolution,* Archon Publishing, Richardson, TX, 2001, pp. 38–39.

[9] Ibid., p. 41.

[10] Ibid., p. 29.

[11] John Paul Newport, "Blood Sport," *Details,* March 1995, pp. 70–72.

[12] Clyde Gentry III, *No Holds Barred: Evolution,* Archon Publishing, Richardson, TX, 2001, pp, 106, 123.

[13] David Plotz, "Fight Clubbed," *Slate.com,* November 7, 2009; available at http://www.slate.com/id/46344, retrieved October 3, 2009. A

[14] Staff, "John McCain — Enter the Opportunist & Sports Biggest Enemy," *MMAMemories.com,* December 14, 2007; available at http://www.mmamemories.com/2007/12/14/john-mccain-enter-the-opportunist-sports-biggest-enemy.html, accessed October 3, 2009.

8 In an attempt to gain more widespread acceptance and popularity, the UFC changed some rules and decided to increase its cooperation with state athletic commissions. On September 30, 2000, the UFC held its first U.S.-sanctioned mixed martial arts event in New Jersey. UFC 28 was sanctioned under the New Jersey State Athletic Control Board's "Unified Rules."[15]

ZUFFA LLC PURCHASE

9 Attempts to have the sport sanctioned across the United States eventually drove SEG to the brink of bankruptcy. In 2001, Frank and Lorenzo Fertitta, executives with Station Casinos, and Dana White, a boxing promoter, bought the UFC for $2 million and created Zuffa LLC (Zuffa),[16] a parent entity controlling the UFC.[17]

10 Lorenzo Fertitta, a former member of the Nevada State Athletic Commission, used his relationships to secure sanctioning in the state of Nevada in 2001. The UFC made its return to pay-per-view with UFC 33: Victory in Vegas. The UFC slowly began to regain popularity, and advertising and corporate sponsorships followed.[18] The UFC started generating higher live gates (i.e., ticket revenue) from hosting events at casino venues such as Trump Taj Mahal and the MGM Grand Garden Arena. The organization started to see PPV revenues as high as revenues before the political controversies in 1997.

11 The UFC secured its first television deal with Fox Sports Net (FSN). *The Best Damn Sports Show* aired the first mixed martial arts match in June 2002 at UFC 37.5, featuring as its main event Chuck Lidell vs. Vitor Belfort.[19] Later, FSN would also air one-hour highlights of the UFC's greatest fights.

12 The first major milestone came at UFC 40, when pay-per-view buys hit 150,000. The fight featured a grudge match between Tito Ortiz and UFC legend Ken Shamrock.[20] Despite this success, the UFC continued to experience financial deficits. By 2004, Zuffa had reported $34 million of losses since purchasing the UFC. [21]

THE ULTIMATE FIGHTER AND SPIKE TV

13 To avoid bankruptcy once again, Zuffa decided to take the UFC beyond pay-per-view and into cable television by creating *The Ultimate Fighter (TUF),* a reality-TV series that featured up-and-coming mixed martial arts (MMA) fighters competing for a contract in the

[15] Ivan Trembow, "New Jersey Commission Corrects Mainstream UFC Stories," *Ivansblog.com* (originally published by MMAweekly.com), July 21, 2006; available at http://www.ivansblog.com/2006/07/mixed-martial-arts-new-jersey.html, accessed October 3, 2009.

[16] Zuffa is Italian for "brawl," "scuffle" or "fight with no rules."

[17] Daniel Schorn, "Mixed Martial Arts: A New Kind of Fight," *60 Minutes* (website) (CBS News), December 12, 2006, p. 2; available at http://www.cbsnews.com/stories/2006/12/08/60minutes/main2241525_page2.shtml> accessed November 3, 2009.

[18] Todd Martin, "UFC Retrospective Series Part 3: The New Ownership, Todd Martin," *CBSSports.com,* June 1, 2009; available at http://www.cbssports.com/mma/story/11809856, accessed October 13, 2009.

[19] UFC Press Release, "Robbie Lawler vs. Melvin Manhoef, Joe Riggs vs. Jay Hieron set for Strikeforce: Miami Jan.30," prommanow.*com*, January 6, 2010; available at http://prommanow.com/index.php/2010/01/06/robbie-lawler-vs-melvin-manhoef-joe-riggs-vs-jay-hieron-set-for-strikeforce-miami-jan-30/, accessed January 11, 2010.

[20] Ivan Trembow, "UFC's Pay-Per-View Buys Explode in 2006," *Ivansblog.com* (originally published by MMAWeekly.com), July 13, 2006; available at http://www.ivansblog.com/2006/07/mixed-martial-arts-ufcs-pay-per-view.html, accessed November 12, 2009.

[21] Joel Stein, "The Ultimate Fighting Machines," *CNNMoney.com* (originally published by Business 2.0 Magazine), November 8, 2006; available at http://money.cnn.com/2006/11/07/magazines/business2/stationcasinos.biz2/index.htm, accessed December 3, 2009.

UFC. Several different networks rejected the concept, and not until Zuffa offered to pay the $10 million production costs was a partner found—in Spike TV.[22]

14 The show aired for the first time in January 2005, following *WWE Raw,* and it became an instant success. The finale for the first show featured fan favorite Forrest Griffin matched up against Stephan Bonnar with the winner receiving a six-figure contract with the UFC. Dana White had since credited this event with having saved the UFC.[23] A second season was aired in August of the same year, and two more seasons were aired in 2006. The success of the show led Spike TV to pick up more UFC content in the form of *UFC Unleashed,* an hour-long show that aired select fights from previous events, and *UFC Fight Night,* a series of fight events that debuted in August 2005. Spike would also feature *Countdown* specials to promote upcoming UFC pay-per-view cards.

15 In 2009, the 10th season of *TUF* featured a selection of heavyweight fighters, including the YouTube-famous, Kevin "Kimbo Slice" Ferguson.[24] This episode was an enormous success, drawing the highest ratings in the show's history with a household rating of between 3.7 million and 5.3 million total viewers.[25] The difficulty for Johnston lay in whether this success could be duplicated in foreign markets. The company's expansion strategy involved airing non-live UFC content, such as *TUF* and *UFC Unleashed* and *Fight Night;* however, given what he knew about the highly fragmented nature of his target audience, Johnston wondered whether these shows, which did incredibly well in North America, would experience similar success in other countries.

16 UFC's strategic partnership with Spike TV proved to be the ideal opportunity for the UFC to maximize exposure. These programs became the main outlets through which the UFC promoted its pay-per-view events, which allowed UFC to spend very little on advertising while targeting its core audience effectively. UFC was also able to generate significant sponsorship revenues through its television programming. The result was a dramatic increase in pay-per-view buys and an overall explosion in growth for the sport of MMA as a whole.

EXPLOSION OF PAY-PER-VIEW BUY RATES

17 UFC 52 was the first event to air after the first season of *TUF*. The event featured two future hall-of-famers, Chuck "The Iceman" Liddell and Randy "The Natural" Couture. The event doubled the last benchmark with pay-per-view audience of 300,000.[26] The second season of *TUF* was used to promote a rubber match between Liddell and Couture at UFC 57.[27]

[22] Ibid.

[23] Kevin Lole, "Trigg gears up for one more run," *Yahoo! Sports,* September 10, 2009; http://sports.yahoo.com/mma/news?slug=ki-trigg091009&prov=yhoo&type=lgns, accessed December 4, 2009.

[24] Kevin "Kimbo Slice" Ferguson is a street fighter with no formal training in any form of martial arts who became hugely popular through his impressive displays of bare-knuckle fighting in backyards and other illegal fighting circles. Videos of Kimbo featured on YouTube drew millions of views and earned him a spot on the 10th season of the *Ultimate Fighter*. He signed an endorsement contract with Tapout, an MMA retail clothing company, before he had ever won a single fight.

[25] Kelsey Philpott, "TUF 10 Breaks Another Ratings Record," *MMAPayout.com*, October 1, 2009; available at http://mmapayout.com/2009/10/page/8/, accessed October 5, 2009.

[26] Dave Meltzer, "UFC 52: Chuck Strikes Back," *Yahoo! Sports,* May 24, 2009; available at http://sports.yahoo.com/mma/news?slug=dm-ufcfiftytwo052409&prov=yhoo&type=lgns, retrieved December 4, 2009.

[27] A "rubber match" is the third fight between two fighters after the first two matches have been split. This third fight is meant to determine which fighter will have the winning record. The UFC has often used this term to create anticipation for upcoming fights and to increase the number of PPV buys.

This event drew an estimated 410,000 pay-per-view buys.[28] The next big milestone came in the same year when Chuck Liddell faced Tito Ortiz in UFC 66. The event drew more than one million pay-per-view buys, and the UFC's popularity continued to skyrocket.[29] In 2006, the UFC broke the pay-per-view industry's record for the most revenues in a single year with more than $222,766,000, exceeding PPV revenues from boxing and the WWE.[30] In July 2007, BodogLife.com, a gambling website, stated that, for the first time, the betting revenues from the UFC would surpass those from boxing.[31]

18 Playing a huge role in UFC's success was the organization's ability to promote its pay-per-view events through its cable television outlets, along with its ability to capitalize on the hype created by these shows, with much-anticipated fighter matchups following directly after. In the mean time, UFC had developed a self-sustaining positive feedback loop of publicly available material that served to promote the next pay-per-view event without having to draw on outside sources, resulting in favorable cost-efficiencies for the organization.

WORLD EXTREME CAGEFIGHTING AND PRIDE ACQUISITIONS

19 The UFC continued to expand its reach into new markets with the acquisitions of World Extreme Cagefighting (WEC) in December 2006 and PRIDE Fighting Championships (PRIDE) on March 27, 2007.[32]

20 WEC was a promotional company based in California that showcased fighters in lower weight classes than those featured by the UFC. This arrangement allowed the UFC to control a broader range of mixed martial arts entertainment within the United States (see **Exhibit 2**).

21 The acquisition of PRIDE, a struggling Japanese-based league cost less than $70 million and was intended initially to be run as a separate organization.[33] PRIDE had been the UCF's largest international rival and had featured many of the world's greatest fighters. Shortly after the acquisition, on October 4, 2007, the UFC closed the Japanese operations of PRIDE and began to rebrand many of the top PRIDE fighters under the UFC name.[34] When interviewed on ESPNEWS, Dana White remained vague about the reasons for closing the league, simply claiming that the model was not sustainable and that "PRIDE is a mess."[35]

[28] Kelsey Philpott, "UFC Establishes New Mark for PPV Buys in 2009," *MMAPayout.com,* December 28, 2009; available at http://mmapayout.com/2009/12/ufc-establishes-new-mark-for-ppv-buys-in-2009/, accessed January 3, 2010.

[29] Ivan Trembow, "UFC 66 Breaks Records; UFC Business Year-In-Review," *MMAWeekly.com,* January 6, 2007, available http://www.mmaweekly.com/absolutenm/templates/dailynews.asp?articleid=3235&zoneid=1, accessed November 27, 2009.

[30] Ivan Trembow, "UFC PPV Revenue Tops $200 Million in 2006," *MMAWeekly.com,* March 1, 2007; available at http://www.mmaweekly.com/absolutenm/templates/dailynews.asp?articleid=3520&zoneid=3, accessed November 24, 2009.

[31] John Hartness, Bodog says UFC will overtake Boxing," *gambling-weblog.com,* July 11, 2007; available at http://www.gambling-weblog.com/50226711/bodog_says_ufc_will_overtake_boxing.php, accessed December 5, 2009.

[32] Associated Press, "UFC Buys Pride for Less than $70M," *ESPN.com,* March 27, 2007; available at http://sports.espn.go.com/sports/news/story?id=2814235, accessed October 3, 2009.

[33] Ibid.

[34] Taro Kotani (translated by Korey Howard), "Pride Worldwide Japan Office Officially Closed," *MMAWeekly.com,* October 5, 2007; available at http://www.mmapower.com/news.asp?dismode=article&apage=2&artid=231, accessed October 4, 2009.

[35] Kris Karkoski, "Dana White: "PRIDE Is a Mess," *MMAFrenzy.com,* June 26, 2007; available at http://mmafrenzy.com/623/dana-white-pride-is-a-mess/, accessed October 23, 2009.

EXHIBIT 2 **List of Weight Classes for Ultimate Fighting Championship and World Extreme Cagefighting**

Ultimate Fighting Championship

Division	Upper Weight Limit	Champion	Title Defenses
Heavyweight	265 lb (120 kg)	Brock Lesnar *UFC 91*	1
Light Heavyweight	205 lb (93 kg)	Lyoto Machida *UFC 98*	1
Middleweight	185 lb (84 kg)	Anderson Silva *UFC 64*	5
Welterweight	170 lb (77 kg)	Georges St-Pierre *UFC 83*	3
Lightweight	155 lb (70 kg)	BJ Penn *UFC 80*	3

World Extreme Cagefighting

Division	Upper Weight Limit	Champion	Title Defenses
Lightweight	155 lb (70 kg)	Ben Henderson *WEC 46*	0
Featherweight	145 lb (66 kg)	Jose Aldo *WEC 44*	0
Bantamweight	135 lb (61 kg)	Brian Bowles *WEC 42*	0
Flyweight	125 lb (57 kg)	Vacant	-

Source: Case writer

Many people in the MMA community understood this rebranding as another step in the company's attempts to align the UFC's brand as closely as possible with the sport of MMA as a whole. It also revealed the UFC's intentions to buy out competitors and close their doors as a strategy to ensure its market position. The league followed this decision with a series of UFC events that served to unify the leagues under one name by pitting UFC and PRIDE champions against each other.[36]

22 Johnston was becoming increasingly concerned with the longer-term implications of the UFC's current business strategy. The league was undoubtedly the strongest it had ever been. However, limiting the number of avenues that young fighters could take to pursue careers in the sport of MMA seemed counter-intuitive, especially while simultaneously attempting to grow the organization. This strategy would undoubtedly require access to an increasingly large pool of talented fighters. Although ultimately the UFC's strategy had worked well in terms of ensuring its dominance in market share, Johnston was beginning to wonder whether these decisions would hinder the UFC's ability to jump into international markets. Despite the huge potential market that existed in Asia, he wondered how the UFC would be perceived given its previous decisions to close the doors of PRIDE and force its fighters to compete overseas in the UFC. PRIDE fighters were generally given very little time to adapt to the UFC's different fighting styles and rules. Many PRIDE fighters refused to accept the terms of the merger and felt they were not receiving a fair opportunity to establish themselves in the UFC. As a result, many fighters left the UFC for other smaller competing organizations.

[36] UFC 75: Champion vs. Champion featured UFC light heavyweight champion Quinton Jackson and PRIDE champion Dan Henderson; UFC 82: The Pride of a Champion featured UFC middleweight champion Anderson Silva and PRIDE welterweight champion Dan Henderson (at the time he held both PRIDE belts).

NEW COMPETITION EMERGES

23 Mixed martial arts had reached superstar status in the world of sport, and the UFC was capturing approximately 90 percent of the industry's total revenues.[37] However, many challenging organizations were emerging, each with a unique business model in attempts to become established in the market and to steal revenues from the MMA giant. The UFC had a simple strategy for limiting the growth of its competitors; it scheduled free counter-programming at the same time as their competitors with the intention of stealing revenues.[38] And although this approach was not profitable in itself, it worked by preventing new competitors from both achieving profitable operations and recouping their investments in high-profile fighters.

24 Although some competing organizations were airing live fights for free on cable television, an offering that the UFC was yet to make available on a regular basis, others were investing huge amounts to attract some of the world's best fighters. A key example was the world's number-one ranked mixed martial arts fighter, Fedor Emelianenko, who held the PRIDE Heavyweight Championship before the league was closed by the UFC, and who, despite being considered by most to be the world's best fighter, had never fought in the UFC. This situation was the result of Emelianenko's long-standing dispute with Dana White over the terms of a contract. Emelianenko was quoted as saying, "The bottom line was that the UFC was a one-sided offer, and you know, that's something that can never be acceptable."[39] Johnston recalled White's less than politically correct response to Emelianenko's accusations. "Let me put it this way. I've done fight contract with all the best fighters in the world . . . who the—is Fedor? Are you serious?"[40] Although Johnston understood that this attitude had played a crucial role in building the UFC brand with free publicity through Dana White's constant appearances in the media, he was also concerned with how this attitude could negatively affect other important relationships as the league continued to grow. Facing increased competition, Johnston wondered whether the organization might need to start rethinking the way it negotiated contracts with the league's fighters. He knew that the UFC would not be able to continue dominating the terms of contract agreements as it had in the past.

25 In 2008, Affliction Entertainment emerged as a promotions company, created by Affliction Clothing. The clothing company was looking to challenge the UFC in the United States after having experienced disputes with the UFC over royalties. Affliction Clothing, which had been one of the UFC's largest clothing sponsors, had been able to secure, with the financial support of Donald Trump, Fedor Emelianenko, considered by many to be the world's number-one ranked fighter.[41] The UFC reacted by banning fighters from wearing Affliction Clothing logos. The UFC also aired a last minute, free, live event on Spike TV, featuring one of the UFC's top fighters, Anderson Silva, to compete with Affliction Entertainment's pay-per-view event, *Affliction: Banned,* on July 19, 2008.[42] One year later, on July 24, 2009,

[37] Matthew Miller, "Ultimate Cash Machine," *Forbes Magazine,* May 5, 2008; available at http://www.forbes.com/forbes/2008/0505/080.html, accessed January 12, 2010.

[38] Interview, UFC fighter (name withheld), October 14, 2009.

[39] Sean Gregory and James Osborne, "White vs. Fedor: Ultimate Fighting's Cold War Gets Hotter," *Time Magazine*, July 10, 2009; available at http://www.time.com/time/arts/article/0,8599,1909703,00.html, accessed September 3, 2009.

[40] Ibid.

[41] Dan Arritt, "Showdown," *Los Angeles Times,* July 18, 2008; available at http://articles.latimes.com/2008/jul/18/sports/sp-mma18, accessed December 17, 2009.

[42] Ibid.

Affliction Entertainment announced that it would be closing the promotions business and Affliction Clothing would return to sponsoring the UFC.[43]

26 When Affliction Entertainment closed its doors, Strikeforce, a fighting league based out of California, signed Emelianenko and offered its first MMA fight on November 7, 2009, on live CBS. Strikeforce established sponsorship deals with Rockstar Energy Drink and found other partners to begin hosting fights in Japan. In June of 2009, Strikeforce also aired the first female championship on cable television.[44]

27 Other emerging competition included the International Fight League (IFL), which had a huge presence in overseas markets but was not well established within the United States. IFL was also not airing televised live fights. As well, EliteXC was challenging for market share, but the company had invested too much money in few main fighters and its business model did not appear to be sustainable. Mark Cuban, a well-known entrepreneur who also owned the National Basketball Association's Dallas Mavericks, was also pushing his way into the MMA market by partnering with organizations, such as Affliction Entertainment, and airing fights on his cable network, HDNet.[45]

28 DREAM was one of the UFC's strongest international competitors that emerged after the UFC's purchase and dissolution of PRIDE. The league contained numerous well-respected and talented fighters who would be competitive in U.S. markets but who had very limited exposure in North America. The style of the DREAM fighters and the marketing of their events differed greatly from the UFC. The league had established partnerships with HDNet, EliteXC, Strikeforce and M-1 Global, owned in part by Fedor Emelianenko.[46, 47, 48] Johnston expected this large network of increasingly integrated organizations would pose a serious threat to the UFC's ability to compete in new international markets.

FIGHTERS' SALARIES

29 With new competition in the United States and globally, Johnston wondered whether the company was doing enough to both retain the league's top talent and attract new fighters. He reflected on what he knew about original fighter payouts that often left first-time fighters losing money from their fights. To be cleared for a fight, the average medical bills for a fighter totaled approximately \$2,500,[49] which included magnetic resonance imaging (MRI) scan, computerized axial tomography (CAT) scan, blood work, an eye exam and a full physical examination. For first-time fighters, the actual payout was set at approximately \$2,000,

[43] John Morgan and Dan Stupp, "'Affliction: Trilogy' Event Canceled," *MMAJunkie.com,* July 24, 2009; available at http://mmajunkie.com/news/15621/aug-1-affliction-trilogy-event-canceled.mma, accessed January 4, 2010.

[44] Loretta Hunt, "Carano Shuns Freak Show One-Woman Act," *Sherdog.com,* June 18, 2009; available at http://sherdog.com/news/articles/carano-shuns-freak-show-one-woman-act-18045, accessed November 22, 2009.

[45] Dave Meltzer, "Ortiz vs. White Is UFC's Hottest Feud," May 16, 2008; available at http://sports.yahoo.com/mma/news?slug=dm-titodana051608&prov=yhoo&type=lgns, accessed November 22, 2009.

[46] Staff, "Mark Cuban's HDNET to air Japan's Dream," *MMAWeekly.com,* April 26, 2008; available at http://mmaweekly.com/absolutenm/templates/dailynews.asp?articleid=6167&zoneid=13, accessed October 11, 2009.

[47] Damon Martin, "Pro Elite & Dream Announce Partnership," *MMAWeekly.com,* May 10, 2008; available at http://www.mmaweekly.com/absolutenm/templates/dailynews.asp?articleid=6248&zoneid=13, accessed October 12, 2009.

[48] Steven Marrocco, "Strikeforce and Dream Formalizing 'Alliance'," *MMAWeekly.com,* August 2, 2009; available at http://www.mmaweekly.com/absolutenm/templates/dailynews.asp?articleid=9288&zoneid=4, accessed October 15, 2009.

[49] Interview, UFC Fighter (name withheld), October 14, 2009.

EXHIBIT 3 **Ultimate Fighting Championship: Number of Fights/Event, Average Gate Revenue/Fight, and Total Bonuses Paid Out to Fighters, 2006–2009**

Year	2006	2007	2008	2009	2006–2009
Average number of fights, per event	8.9	9.1	9.9	10.5	18.3%
Average Gate Revenue, UFC Events	$376,406	$614,077	$735,000	$898,375	138.7%
Average Gate Revenue, UFN/TUF Events	$170,250	$245,300	$321,833	$434,665	155.3%
Size of average bonus pool paid out by UFC event to fighters	—	$162,500	$196,667	$216,333	33.1%

Note: UFC = Ultimate Fighting Championships; TUF = The Ultimate Fighter; UFN = Ultimate Fight Night

with an additional $2,000 being awarded to the winner.[50] As a result, because of the medical bills alone, a first-time fighter who lost his fight would lose money overall. In reality, many other costs, such as training expenses, travel and fight preparation, would further compound the situation. If a fighter won his first fight, he might break even. If he continued to win, his earnings would increase incrementally (usually by $2,000 a fight).[51] The majority of fighters in the league, however, did not have large endorsements or high-profile contract agreements with the UFC; instead, they were barely scraping by. Johnston wondered whether this model provided enough real incentive for young athletes to join the sport. How was this model going to affect the long-term growth prospects for the sport? Did it make sense for an organization that had experienced such immense growth and success to take advantage of its talent?

30 Fighter compensation had been increasing along with company revenues, but Johnston realized that the UFC continued to lack significantly, compared with other major sports leagues.[52] Johnston examined an analysis of disclosed payouts and compared it with the UFC revenues over the past four years (see **Exhibit 3**). He wondered whether the current payout structure was enough, or did the UFC need to drastically change the way it compensated fighters?

31 The UFC also lacked any form of union to protect the interests of its athletes, although such unions existed in every other major sports league: the National Football League (NFL), the National Basketball Association (NBA), Major League Baseball (MLB), the National Hockey League (NHL) and the Association of Tennis Professionals (ATP). In the past, attempts to protect the athletes' interests had been actively resisted by the company's president, Dana White. The league had been criticized for refusing to negotiate contracts; as a result, in several instances, the UFC's most popular fighters had refused to fight, preferring instead to leave the UFC for smaller, competing leagues. For example, Tito Ortiz, a former light heavyweight champion and fan favorite, left the UFC over a dispute with Dana White.[53]

[50] Ibid.

[51] Ibid.

[52] Ibid.

[53] Dave Meltzer, "Ortiz vs. White Is UFC's Hottest Feud," *Yahoo! Sports,* May 16, 2008; available at http://sports.yahoo.com/mma/news?slug=dm-titodana051608&prov=yhoo&type=lgns, accessed November 22, 2009.

He later returned to the league and ended up fighting for less money than he had originally been offered.[54]

32 Johnston was uncomfortable with the way the UFC had, in the past, exploited what was essentially a monopoly in the North American market in order to bully fighters into what many believed to be unfair contracts. As new leagues emerged and gained momentum, he realized that achieving such favorable payment contracts with fighters might become increasingly difficult. The UFC had already seen many of its fighters leave, but had taken little action to rebuild these relationships. He wondered whether it was time to start paying more attention to this issue, but was unsure of how to go about making changes and how to gain buy-in from the rest of the leadership team, including White, who had seriously resisted the issue in the past.

33 Beyond the league's contract policies, the UFC also had final say on all sponsorship deals, including all forms of individual fighter sponsorships. Until recently, the UFC had not been able to control any sponsored images that appeared on the fighter's body.[55] However, in 2009, a new rule was established that required every sponsor to pay a licensing fee as high as $100,000 to the UFC for the right to sponsor a fighter. This fee made it substantially harder for up-and-coming fighters because sponsors were not willing to fund newer fighters who were more likely to fight on the undercard, therefore providing the sponsor with only limited exposure.[56] The licensing requirement also essentially locked out smaller or new companies from sponsoring the UFC because they could not afford to pay the required fees. Johnston believed that limited sponsorship competition might be harmful to the UFC and might adversely affect its long-term opportunities for sponsorship revenue.

34 The league had also just finished establishing a new set of corporate sponsors, including Harley-Davidson and Bud Light. Referring to the UFC's sponsors, Dana White was quoted in an interview as having said, "We don't need anybody."[57] Johnston understood the value of establishing strategic partnerships, and he was unclear about what exactly White had meant by this. Although White had also spoken about how the UFC was seeking strategic partners rather than blue-chip sponsors, Johnston was not sure whether the UFC's current sponsorship relationships reflected this preference.[58] Should the league be pursuing more cross-promotional advertising initiatives to push the UFC into new markets? Harley-Davidson was an expensive motorcycle brand that primarily targeted an older demographic. Was this choice of a corporate sponsor in line with the UFC's target audience of males aged 18 to 36?

INTERNATIONAL EXPANSION OPPORTUNITIES

35 The UFC was looking to follow up its recent partnership with Flash Entertainment by building a new arena at the Emirate Hotel in Abu Dhabi, a city that was emerging as the cultural and entertainment mecca of the United Arab Emirates (UAE). The new building would

[54] Dana White, Twitter.com, July 17, 2009; available at http://twitter.com/danawhiteufc.

[55] Interview, UFC fighter (name withheld), October 14, 2009.

[56] An undercard fighter is featured on a UFC card before the main advertised events are shown live on television. Often, the undercard fights were televised only at the end of the show, if at all, to fill empty air time when the main-event fights ended sooner than was expected. For example, all main-event fights featured first-round knockouts that ended the fight.

[57] Jacob Camargo, "Fedor, Kimbo Slice and Silva vs. Belfort and More," Interview, *fiveknuckles.com,* October 4, 2009; available at http://www.fiveknuckles.com/mma-news/Video-Dana-White-talks-Fedor,-Kimbo-Slice,-Silva-vs-Belfort-and-more.html, accessed November 13, 2009.

[58] Ibid.

be an outdoor arena with 10,000-plus seats and coliseum-style seating that preserved the trademark UFC atmosphere.[59] Johnston was still unsure about where to promote the event, but expected to see interest from across the UAE and planned to promote the event through the UFC's European, British and Asian partners.[60] When a UFC event had been held in Australia, fans had traveled from across the country to attend. Johnston wondered whether a similar response could be expected in the UAE, or whether the demand would be large enough within the city.[61]

36 Johnston also knew that the UFC had been working for years to tap into the huge boxing market in Mexico by developing young Mexican talent, such as Cain Velasquez and Roger Huerta. The UFC had also recently signed a television deal with Grupo Televisa S.A.B., the world's largest Spanish-speaking media company, and had debuted with a free, live broadcast of UFC 100, on July 11, 2009.[62] Other programming included live *UFC Fight Night* events, *UFC Countdown* shows and one-hour feature programs.[63] Johnston was eager to hold the UFC's first pay-per-view event in Mexico, but wanted to ensure that it would be a success.

37 The UFC had already experienced success through ESPN in the United Kingdom and Ireland, and on June 1, 2009, the UFC expanded into Portugal by showing UFC 98: MACHIDA vs. EVANS, on pay-per-view.[64] This event was followed by a Chinese TV Deal on June 29, 2009, which provided the UFC with one to four hours of UFC programming each week on Saturdays and Sundays, broadcast in languages specific to each province.[65] Inner Mongolia Television (NMTV) would air the events, which could reach a potential 240 million viewers in China.[66] Johnston was excited by the potential of this market, but he wondered what the next step would be. Was India the next frontier for the UFC? If successful, the UFC would see huge upside potential, but Johnston was not sure that the UFC had a product that was adequate to meet the needs of this market. He was not even sure he understood exactly what those needs were. The company was already busy trying to establish the UFC brand in Western Europe and America. Was the company perhaps moving too quickly?

38 Johnston also wondered how the UFC would market the events in new countries. He wondered whether he fully understood how the UFC was perceived in these new markets. Would it be enough to continue promoting the league in the same way as in the past? Would this approach be effective in foreign markets where the league did not receive free publicity through a huge range of media outlets? In Asia, for example, the league would be compared to Japanese fighting organizations such as PRIDE. These leagues featured different fighting styles and much more cultured traditions. Although Japanese events would still feature an elaborate show, many fans did not like the way the UFC had "Americanized" a sport that was seen in other countries to be worthy of much more elegance and respect.

39 The UFC's core fan base in North America resulted from converting fans from World Wrestling Entertainment (WWE) and boxing. Originally, the UFC's target audience had

[59] Steve Cofield, Yahoo! Sports Cagewriter, Interview, *ESPN Radio 1100*, January 21, 2010; available at http://mmablips.dailyradar.com/video/ufc-112-marshall-zelaznik-talks-about-abu-dhabi-s/, accessed February 1, 2010.

[60] Ibid.

[61] Ibid.

[62] Andy Samuelson, "UFC Inks TV Deal in Mexico," *LasVegasSun.com,* July 9, 2009; available at http://www.lasvegassun.com/blogs/sports/2009/jul/09/ufc-inks-tv-deal-mexico/, accessed February 1, 2010.

[63] Ibid.

[64] Josh Stein, "UFC Expands to Portugal," *MMAOpinion.com,* May 30.2009; available at http://mmaopinion.com/2009/05/30/ufc-expands-to-portugal/, accessed September 30, 2009.

[65] Jon Show, "UFC Expands TV Reach to China and Mexico," *Sportsbusinessjournal.com,* June 29.2009. http://www.sportsbusinessjournal.com/article/62917, accessed September 30, 2009.

[66] Ibid.

been perceived to be males aged 18 to 36. These assumptions were driving the organization's decisions on the sponsors to target and the event promotions to pursue. However, Johnston believed he was beginning to better understand the polarized and dynamic nature of the UFC's fan base.

40 In fact, not only men were drawn to the sport; Johnston also suspected that much interest was also generated in females aged 18 to 36. This female audience, he realized, would open up an entirely new sponsorship base. He wondered how he should go about examining the true nature of the UFC's audience and how he could best convey this audience sector to new potential sponsors.

41 The UFC also needed to consider an entirely new potential audience of fans who were neither MMA enthusiasts, nor fans of boxing or professional wrestling. These potential fans were general sports fans who had been introduced to the UFC through various media. Johnston wondered where these general sports fans fit into the existing categories of fans or whether they valued something altogether different. WWE fans tended to be more interested in the "show" and less concerned with the more technical aspects of the sport as compared with the boxing segment, which valued the fighters' athleticism and talent. WWE-rooted fans enjoyed watching rivalries develop in the media between the fighters and valued high-profile fighters with well-developed media personalities. Ultimately, these rivalries had been initiated to drive buys for PPV events. Johnston had recognized that the situation was unique in that the UFC was able to appeal to different customer segments that watched for different reasons. He also understood that a delicate balance was required when trying to meet the needs of these core fan bases. Regardless of the direction the company chose to pursue, it needed to ensure it continued to meet the needs of the existing fans.

42 The UFC had become a master in the art of generating free publicity through almost all media outlets, including television, radio, newsprint and social media networks. Much of the early success of the UFC could be attributed to the company's president, Dana White, who took a non-traditional role and became the organization's most crucial publicity machine. At various times, White had been scrutinized for his derogatory language and controversial comments. His loud personality and unorthodox role as an outspoken celebrity chief executive officer (CEO) was proving to be a unique and successful marketing strategy. Many fans related to his rough and aggressive attitude, which had been a strong driving force behind the growth and success of the league. In fact, many of his disputes with writers, athletes and public interest groups such as GLAAD[67] had been well documented by White himself through his Twitter account.

43 Frank and Lorenzo Fertitta owned the remaining 90 percent of Zuffa LLC. They had got their start in business as casino executives, and both shared a passion for mixed martial arts. They had allowed White to function as the organization's front man. When the company was founded, they wrote a legally binding clause into their contract that stated, in the event of a dispute between the two majority owners, a three, five-minute round, mixed martial arts fight would be used to determine the winner.[68] Recently, Lorenzo Fertitta had resigned as Station Casinos' president to work full-time as chair and CEO of the UFC to help the organization focus on its global expansion, which included "landing more big-name sponsors, particularly in countries other than the U.S."[69]

[67] GLAAD is an acronym for Gay & Lesbian Alliance Against Defamation.

[68] Joel Stein, "The Ultimate Fighting Machines," *CNNMoney.com* (originally published by Business 2.0 Magazine), November 8, 2006; available at http://money.cnn.com/2006/11/07/magazines/business2/stationcasinos.biz2/index.htm, accessed December 3, 2009.

[69] Staff, "Lorenzo Fertitta to Work Full-Time as UFC Chair and CEO," *Sportsbusinessjournal.com,* June 19, 2008; available at http://www.sportsbusinessdaily.com/article/121737, accessed February 4, 2010.

44 Another important personality of the league was Joe Rogan, a former martial artist and the former host of the popular TV reality show *Fear Factor.* Rogan had become one of the organization's most popular characters as the color commentator for all major UFC events. His seemingly infinite knowledge and incredibly accurate insights made him a fan favorite and one of the league's most valuable assets. In addition, Joe Silva served as the league's matchmaker and talent recruiter. He negotiated all contracts and played a key role in establishing the favorable deals the UFC was able to secure with many top fighters. Johnston wondered whether he should speak to Silva directly about his concerns.

FINANCIAL OVERVIEW

45 Standard and Poor's had released its latest credit report on Zuffa LLC, which documented the corporation's most recent financing activities. Zuffa's credit rating was reaffirmed at BB- (stable but not "investment grade").[70]

46 The company's 75 percent event-driven business model posed some concern to Johnston from a business standpoint. The company had recently made attempts to diversify its revenue streams by releasing a new video game, *UFC Unleashed,* and improved operating margins had been experienced on the company's U.K. operations.[71] Despite tremendous growth over the past year, Johnston understood that the company had really only been profitable for the last four years. Johnston wondered whether the owners would ever be interested in taking the company public, and, if so, when would be the right time to do so. He believed that if this option was to be pursued, the company's financial structure would first need to be re-evaluated.

47 Because more and more American states were moving toward legalizing mixed martial arts, Johnston knew that a huge potential for growth remained within North America. Currently, the 2010 fight schedule featured more international events than ever before. He wondered whether the company was moving in the right direction. Too much focus on overseas markets could leave the UFC vulnerable to the increasing competition within the United States; and a failure abroad could be devastating.

48 Johnston sat down at his desk and began to prepare his recommendations for the company's executive meeting later that week. He had not been with the organization for long and needed to carefully consider how to approach many of these issues. He knew that the executive could not alienate the organization's core fan base or dilute the quality of the UFC experience for its viewers. The massive potential of the European, Middle Eastern and Asian markets was an opportunity that could not be overlooked; however, moving into those international markets would not be as simple as duplicating the experience offered in the United States. Despite the company's strong financial position, the UFC could not afford to make significant investments in unprofitable new markets. To further complicate his job, Johnston realized that White and the Fertitta brothers did not operate their company in a typical manner; they had become enormously successful by trusting their instincts and gambling on their emotions. Johnston was concerned about the potential for this mentality to lead the company down the wrong path. White and the Fertittas had done a remarkable job at building the UFC brand, but Johnston's experience told him how quickly their success could change if they did not take the right steps to protect it. His decisions would play a crucial role in shaping the future of the organization.

[70] Standard and Poor's, "Zuffa's $100M Incremental Term Loan Rated 'BB-' (Recover Rating: 4); 'BB-' Corporate Credit Rating Affirmed," S&P Credit Research (Abstract), October 1, 2009; available at http://www.alacrastore.com/research/s-and-p-credit-research-Zuffa_s_100M_Incremental_Term_Loan_Rated_BB_Recover_Rating_4_BB_Corporate_Credit_Rating_Affirmed-749666, accessed November 2, 2009.

[71] Ibid.

Case 23

The Untsiya Company: *Business Development in Russia*

Galina Shirokova
St. Petersburg State University (Russia)
Gina Vega
Salem State College

1 In the frozen landscape of winter in St. Petersburg, Russia in 2008, Sergey Nikolaev, founder and CEO of the *Untsiya* Company (The Ounce), a leading tea shop chain in St. Petersburg, dropped into his Nevsky Avenue shop on his way back home to warm up with a cup of Russia's favorite hot drink. One question was uppermost in his mind—how could he use the limited space in his tea shops more effectively?

2 His eyes swept the room. He noted the marble tables and old-fashioned chairs where a few customers were sitting comfortably, enjoying some rare or premium tea. "What about starting a real café?" he wondered. "We've been considering bringing in a line of sweets for a long time. We could combine premium tea, high quality sweets and a small cozy café where customers could find comfort and exclusive products. Could the café be both comfortable and fast? Could it be delicious and still fast? Could we build a global brand like Starbucks, but leave the coffee to them and win our market with tea?"

3 Sergey took a look at the warm smile of the server bustling around a new customer. Sure, the idea of a café was not a bad one, but would his team be capable of handling several new business directions at once? There were many ways to expand: sweets, catering, tea production . . . but maybe he should concentrate all his efforts on the development of only one main business—selling exclusive tea in small exclusive shops?

THE RIGHT SHOP IN THE RIGHT PLACE

4 The first *Untsiya* shop opened in St. Petersburg in 2002. By 2007, there were 12 chain shops ranging in size from 15 to 30 square meters (160-320 square feet) operating in Russia's Northern Capital. They sold tea by the ounce. The average cost of 1.75 oz of tea was 120 rubles (USD 5.00). The average check in the tea shop was 390 rubles (USD 16.00). Each shop offered up to 220 kinds of loose tea from China, India, Ceylon, Taiwan, Japan, and Germany. Wholesale teas and related products were distributed to 45 regions of Russia. By 2007, the company employed 120 people. In 2006, the company revenues were USD 3.8M. In 2007 they had risen above USD 5M, an annual growth rate of roughly 75 percent (see **Exhibit 1**).

5 With old books and prints on the walls, dark oak cupboards, and a solid marble counter, the atmosphere in the *Untsiya* tea shop was reminiscent of a time long past. The muffled classical music and hundreds of clear glass jars filled with tea leaves on the shelves provided

Source: *The CASE Journal* 6, no. 1 (Fall 2009). This case is intended to be used as the basis for class discussion rather than to illustrate either effective or ineffective handling of a management situation. The authors would like to express their gratitude to Sergey Nikolaev, founder of the *Untsiya* Company, for his assistance in the preparation of this case study.

EXHIBIT 1 Company Revenue in February, 2007

February	Retail sales	Franchising	Wholesale	HoReCa	Corporate presents	Tea Club	Production	Total
Revenue (%)	48.0%	21.2%	22.0%	4.6%	3.3%	0.5%	0.4%	**100%**
Profit (%)	31.1%	34.3%	37.0%	5.3%	12.2%	−19.9%	0.0%	**100%**

Source: Company Records

a romantic backdrop for several young sales clerks who filled individual packets with tea and, dipping quill pens into an inkpot, inscribed exotic brands of tea on the paper bags. Their deftness captivated the customers who were waiting to be served. See **Exhibit 2** for a picture of a typical *Untsiya* tea shop.

THE RUSSIAN TEA MARKET

6 Russia has always been a tea-drinking nation, even in the 18th century, when one pound of tea delivered from China cost as much as 220 pounds of high-quality granular caviar. Although the proportions have changed, a cozy tea shop selling loose, premium tea has always been both a profitable and stable business.

EXHIBIT 2 A Typical Untsiya Store

EXHIBIT 3 **Tea Purchase Frequency as a Percent of Respondents**

Frequency	2006 (%)	2002 (%)
Once a week or more often	20	14
Twice or thrice a month	26	30
Once a month	26	25
Once in two or three months	6	8
Once in six months	3	2
Less than once in six months/never	20	21

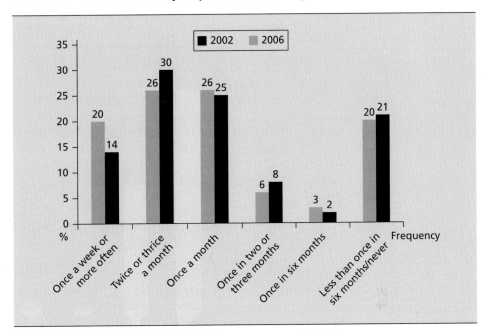

Source: Russian Tea Market Review at http://www.advertology.ru/article45552.htm

7 Tea-consumption was not limited to one demographic sector; it was enjoyed equally by both men and women irrespective of age, education or income.[1] Fully 98 percent of the country's population drank tea at least once a week in 2006; 80 percent drank it every day. The average annual per capita tea consumption was 3.3 lbs, making Russia one of the top ten tea-consuming countries in the world. Russia was the world's third largest market for black tea after India and Great Britain. In 2006, the market amounted to USD 1 B.

8 A 2006 survey conducted by *Levada-Center* revealed consumer preferences for tea brands, flavors and packaging. The survey questioned about 1600 Russians aged 18 and older. The majority of consumers (69 percent) bought tea at least once a month[2] (see **Exhibit 3**). An earlier survey conducted in 2002 among a similar representative sample showed similar results. Tea-drinking has long been a well-established tradition in Russia. The purchase and consumption patterns of the Russian consumer remained stable despite the introduction of new brands, changing from loose to bagged tea, from traditional black tea to more exotic varieties.

9 The majority of Russian respondents (65 percent) preferred loose tea over bagged tea (see **Exhibit 4**) in the 2006 study. However, bagged tea has grown in popularity, driven in part by office consumption, with a number of tea-breaks during a working day, and also by the convenience of bagged tea for busy people. Bagged tea consumers represented the most physically active population group: young people aged 18 to 24, single men and women with higher education, and relatively high income and social status.

[1] Romanova T. "Tata priglashaet na chai" (Tata invites for tea), in Vedomosti, 13.08.2007, #149 (1923), p. 5.

[2] Russian Tea Market Review at http://www.advertology.ru/article45552.htm (accessed September 5, 2009).

EXHIBIT 4 Consumer Preferences of the Type of Tea Packaging as a Percent of Those Buying Tea No Less Than Once in Six Months

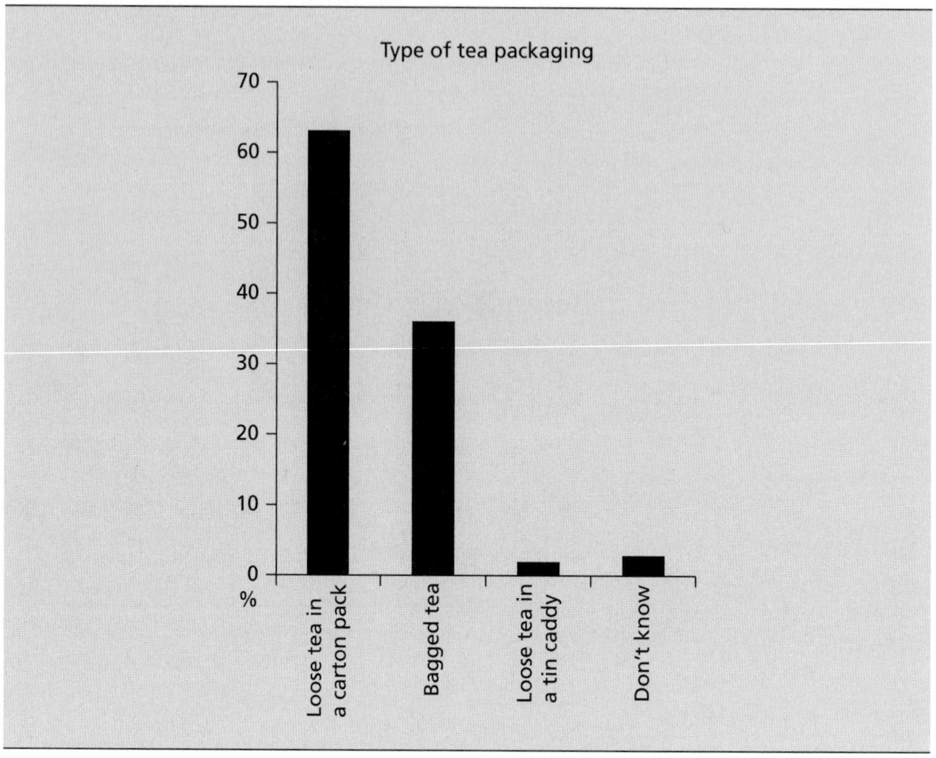

Type of tea packaging

70
60
50
40
30
20
10
0
%

Loose tea in a carton pack
Bagged tea
Loose tea in a tin caddy
Don't know

Source: Russian Tea Market Review at http://www.advertology.ru/article45552.htm

10 Russians were conservative when it came to consumer preferences for tea flavors with 77 percent of respondents traditionally preferring black tea (see **Exhibit 5**). What distinguished the younger, more financially secure and adaptable citizens of capital cities, especially Moscow, was that they more frequently chose bergamot or fruit tea as well as various green teas. As their income increased, Russian citizens gradually shifted their preferences to more expensive brands such as *Ahmad, Lipton,* or *Greenfield,*[3] leaving *Beseda* and *Lisma*[4] brands behind. Although regarded as a relative novelty on the Russian market, other teas (green and flavored tea, mate, oolongs, etc.) have also grown faster than the common black tea market.

11 Tea was most often sold pre-packaged in boxes or decorative containers in supermarkets or other food stores. But there was another, much less common way a seller could offer tea: a customer was first given a chance to smell the tea, and then purchased a bag filled with the desired amount. These specialized shops usually offered a choice of 50 to 100 different kinds of tea of higher than average quality. The bulk of available options comprised flavored teas (black tea blended with flowers, berries, and fruits bits) and premium teas (oolongs, mates, rooiboses, and flower teas). These teas were usually sold in specialized shops, specialized departments of department stores, or in small stalls within a supermarket (the shop-in-shop format).

[3] Russian Tea Market Review at http://www.marketcenter.ru/content/doc-0-6775.html (accessed September 5, 2009).

[4] According to research conducted by the *VladVneshServis* company. For more information visit http://www.marketcenter.ru/content/doc-0-6775.html (accessed September 5, 2009).

EXHIBIT 5 **Consumer Preferences of Kinds of Tea as a Percent of Respondents**

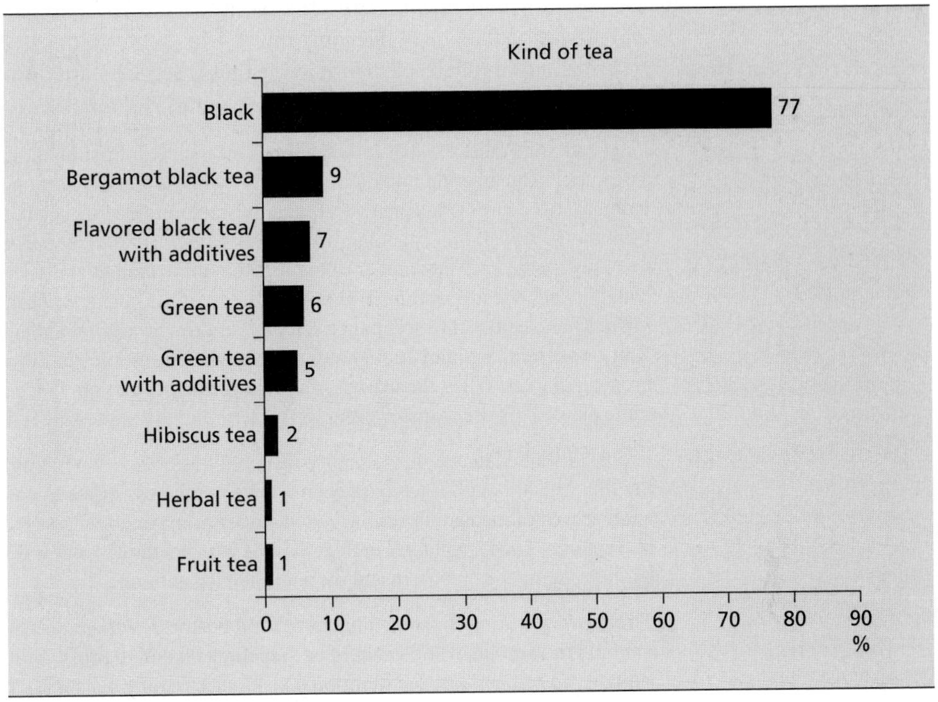

Kind of tea

Kind of tea	%
Black	77
Bergamot black tea	9
Flavored black tea/ with additives	7
Green tea	6
Green tea with additives	5
Hibiscus tea	2
Herbal tea	1
Fruit tea	1

0 10 20 30 40 50 60 70 80 90 %

Source: Russian Tea Market Review at http://www.advertology.ru/article45552.htm

COMPANY HISTORY: FROM A BUSINESS IDEA TO A NEW VENTURE

12 Aleksey Asvarishch and Sergey Nikolaev, co-founders of the *Untsiya* Company, were childhood friends. Before launching their venture, they worked in different fields: Asvarishch was in public relations, Nikolaev in radio. Mr. Nikolaev was famous in St. Petersburg as co-founder and the chairman of the board of the "*Modern*" radio station. Popular in the 1990s, this radio station was a launching pad for a network of DJs who then populated virtually all existing Russian FM stations. In 2001, Mr. Nikolaev and his partners sold the radio station to *Logovaz News Corporation* (currently owned equally by Boris Berezovsky and media tycoon Rupert Murdoch). The sale of the radio station brought its owners roughly USD 500,000.[5]

13 Alexey Asvarishch, a childhood friend of Sergey Nikolaev, made his career and wealth in political public relations. When Sergey offered him the opportunity to invest in a new business, he agreed without any hesitation because he always trusted his friend's entrepreneurial mind. They divided the shares in the new enterprise between them, with Nikolaev owning 60 percent and Asvarishch 40 percent.

14 Unlike the creative and energetic Nikolaev, Asvarishch was calmer and more stable. While Nikolaev was open and pleasant, Asvarishch was close-mouthed and taciturn. Nikolaev was the one who developed new ideas and initiated teamwork and creativity within the company. All new lines of business were the result of his efforts. Along with these characteristics, Nikolaev was people-oriented and interested in human relationships. It was important for

[5] Birger P. OtChayanny biznes (TeAmerarious Business) // *Expert North-West* magazine, # 21 (226), June 2005.

him to sustain a family climate in the company. Asvarishch was more results-oriented and he focused on fully implementing all projects initiated by his partner, paying close attention to the day-to-day operations of the company.

15 After selling his share of the radio business, Sergey started to look for another project, determined to find just the right business to enter.

> I just compiled a list of what I liked and what I disliked. First of all, I wanted to create a business in an emerging market. The radio business where I was operating right at the moment was depressed. When we started our radio project, the share of radio advertising in the national advertising spending budget was 17 percent, but by the time we sold it, the share was only 8 percent. The number of competitors grew dramatically. The market shrank. We couldn't generate any optimism about the future of the business. The investors who acquired my business expected to see 30 percent market growth, while I anticipated only 15 percent. And I was right, the market did not come anywhere near 30. But I preferred to act on a growing market. When the market is shrinking you have to run twice as fast just to stay in the same place. This is exhausting, and for what? I didn't want to stay in this mode.
>
> Second, I wanted to avoid personality-centered businesses. No more strong personalities in my life. And although I was overwhelmed with countless offers to come back into one or another area of media business, e.g. newspaper or magazine, I resisted them because I had had enough. I had spent ages in negotiations with celebrities and was completely sick of their endless attempts to get more and more money for nothing.
>
> Third, I was looking for something new, for a business without one single, limiting business model. I thought innovation should be somehow related to profitability. Now I think that actually we can perform old traditional tasks successfully even without inventing something new. But at that moment I was strongly oriented towards searching for a new business model.
>
> Also I wanted the business to be flexible, with plenty of options to shape it the way we wished. Look at the radio—there is only one profit center, the advertising department, and all other departments are cost centers no matter what you do. Everything is rigid and predetermined. It takes nine full months for an action to lead to real change because of the organizational complexities. You cannot quickly apply a new strategy because any move influences all the people involved. Actually you are rigidly tied to one business and there are no opportunities for growth or diversification. I was sick of that rigid business where you could not experiment and freely search for better practices.
>
> And one more reason—I didn't want to stay in the mass media business. Strictly speaking it is a weird business. If we compare the roles of status and wage in motivating an employee, we may see that people in that business are oriented basically to status. In other words, people are ready to work at a very low wage because they like the idea of being affiliated with show business and entering celebrity circles. I was really astonished. There were heads of departments with a monthly salary of USD 600 after eight years of professional employment. I did not want this bias towards fame at the cost of personal financial reward. This bias creates organizational distortion. People should be well-paid.
>
> Finally, I wanted my father to approve of my business. I wanted it to be socially beneficial. These are the criteria I identified in the very beginning.[6]

16 After defining these criteria, Nikolaev went in search of a business idea, starting with his friends. The ideas they suggested included ceiling production, commercial real estate development, and selling fresh fish, among others. Finally, one of his friends, Pavel Adadurov, complained that there was no good tea sold in the city. Nikolaev reacted immediately. Tea was a monoproduct, it had clear positioning, the rules of the game were straightforward, it

[6] From the interview with Sergey Nikolaev.

represented a new trend, and there was no ready-made business model. Moreover, tea was a warm comfort product that evoked diverse connotations: for each person it brought to mind either India or colonial settlements, tea clipper ships, or the traditional Russian tea-party. It meant family, friends, and informal socializing. More than that, it was characterized by a huge market, as tea was consumed by most of the country's population. Russia was the right place to launch a tea business. All in all, it was a lucky coincidence—the concept of the new business corresponded with all of Nikolaev's proposed requirements.

THE CONCEPT OF THE NEW BUSINESS: AFFORDABLE LUXURY

17 *Untsiya* was founded on the concept of "affordable luxury" which was built on three principles:

1. **Quality at a competitive price.** By 2007, *Untsiya* was a market leader providing high quality tea to the Russian customer. Besides purchasing pure black tea directly at auction in India and Ceylon (competitors in the premium tea market purchased tea in Germany, which meant that the tea arrived six months or even a year old), their price to the consumer was also highly competitive. Although price was secondary to quality, it was nevertheless an important issue because no matter how high the quality, the customer expected an attractive, competitive price.
2. **Special atmosphere.** The special atmosphere of *Untsiya* shops reassured customers that they had made the right choice by coming to that store and their selection would be a quality product. The owners paid a great deal of attention to the interior design of the shops, to their exclusive packaging, and to providing refined service. Every customer was able to consult a sales assistant on various kinds of tea and get *The Tea Leaf* newspaper, a special edition about tea issues.
3. **Distinctive Service.** The third principle was a special approach to clients. *Untsiya* customers were treated with respect. Sales assistants, trained to become experts, regarded their customers as individuals in search of information about a specific product. To assure consistent behavior, the company developed a system of personnel management that involved strict requirements for personnel selection, personnel training, examinations to evaluate field-related knowledge, intensive instruction, and tailored programs in personnel motivation and development. To maintain high quality, the company required compulsory certification of store managers and the individualized training programs for sales assistants.

18 Because of all these factors, one out of two customers was a repeat visitor to *Untsiya* shops. According to *Untsiya* customer surveys, quality service came in first or second among other factors of *Untsiya* shops' appeal.[7]

EARLY DIFFICULTIES

19 When he founded the *Untsiya* Company on August 15, 2002, Nikolaev couldn't imagine that it would be a tough task. However, the experience he gained during his years of managing the radio station did not help much during the formative years of the company. Problems cropped up nearly everywhere. (See **Exhibit 6** for information about doing business in Russia.)

[7] Untsiya—mera nastoyashchego (The Present is Measured in Ounces) // *Kupi Brend* (*Buy Brand*) magazine, # 4 (8), October, 2006.

firsthand the facts of import life. He explained, "My team was deeply shocked. It turned out that people in that business believed it was quite all right to arrange supply, deliver the first and then the second batch of goods and then absolutely unexpectedly and without warning set a different price for the second half of the order. That is, an invoice based on new prices was submitted after the tea was delivered. They also delivered the wrong tea. It was not that one or two kinds of tea arrived differently from the ones ordered, but 30 percent of the total order was wrong. All of that was accompanied by a low level of service, and a feeling that you were being deceived."

23 This was anathema to Mr. Nikolaev who, as a former media executive, was used to civilized communication. He commented, "Why is it so difficult to get a job on the radio? It is so because it attracts smart guys who want to become famous, because it is a community of educated and intelligent people. On the radio no one will try to conceal information if it is obvious that one can get it any other way. A person simply makes a call and asks for necessary information. It saves a lot a time. The tea market seemed something medieval to me. People talked about tea as if it were some miracle. Not in the sense that they loved tea so much, but with a shade of shamanistic reverence, 'It's tea, it's a miracle, you can't even imagine how difficult it is to buy it.' Later I understood that other countries also have similar problems with suppliers and this business is full of professional cheaters." The problems the founders faced with suppliers made them think about individual importing, which, in its turn, resulted in the development of wholesale and franchising business lines.

MAJOR PROFIT CENTERS

24 By January 2004, 18 months after the company's launch, according to Sergey Nikolaev: "It became clear that the strategy of developing a chain of specialized shops selling premium tea in St. Petersburg would be a success. The company established four profit-making shops and introduced a system of chain management which could easily control up to 20 points of sale (POS). It also became clear that for St. Petersburg it was reasonable to open 15 to 20 shops." Moreover they could easily predict its natural growth trajectory. They established seven profit centers:

1. **HoReCa.** The company entered the HoReCa segment (tea supply to **ho**tels, **re**staurants and **ca**fes). As the company sold premium teas and its image was perceived by restaurateurs largely through the activity of retail shops, *Untsiya* decided to concentrate on the upper-price segment. The HoReCa line did not compete with retail sales. The company employed sales representatives who looked upon tea as a special product and promoted it accordingly. Slowly, clients started asking if it was possible to sell *Untsiya* tea in cafes or other specialized shops.
2. **Wholesale.** The company launched a wholesale line which was originally part of the HoReCa subdivision. To avoid dilution of the *Untsiya* trademark, the company created the *Tea-Dealers Partnership* brand for the new wholesale line. This line started by selling loose tea to specialized tea shops, which turned out to be popular in some of the other areas of Russia such as the Urals, Siberia, and South Russia. To grow and extend this subdivision, the company participated in Moscow trade shows, which attracted new clients. By autumn 2006, they were supplying wholesale tea to 40 Russian cities.
3. **Franchising.** The city of Novosibirsk proposed that the company set up an *Untsiya* shop there. This gave them the idea of developing a franchising package containing terms and conditions, franchise selection criteria and pricing details. Novosibirsk decided not to participate in this project, but the company successfully presented the franchising

EXHIBIT 7 **Untsiya Locations in CIS and Russia**

Source: http://lib.utexas.edu/maps/commonwealth/commonwealth_pol_97.jpg (accessed online December 1, 2009)

package in Moscow where it gained popularity. The first franchised *Untsiya* shop opened in 2005. As of 2008, there were 20 such shops operating in 15 Russian cities. (See **Exhibit 7** for these locations.) Further expansion was expected as franchisees were committed by contract to open one shop per 300,000 citizens every 18 months.

4. **Packaging.** Another new subdivision selling packaged tea to supermarkets and retail chains appeared under similar circumstances. The company wholesale department received a request from *Globus Gourmet* (a 24-hour upscale grocery store founded in 2005) asking to let it sell *Untsiya* brand tea through their supermarket chain. It was stipulated that tea should be sold in traditional pre-packaged tea packs. Having emerged from the wholesale line, this subdivision controlled distribution channels to chain supermarkets, and the product bearing the in-house name *Packaging* was distributed through different channels, such as an in-house network and to franchise and wholesale clients. Sales started in March 2007.
5. **Coffee.** In autumn 2006, *Kafe Kult*, a new product specially developed for *Untsiya* by the HoReCa subdivision, appeared. As rivals offered both tea and coffee and *Untsiya* traded solely in tea, they decided to introduce a new product to overcome a competitive disadvantage. The choice fell on *Kafe Kult*, the German supplier. Coffee was distributed

not only through HoReCa channels but also through the in-house network, to franchise and wholesale clients.

6. **Moscow In-House Network.** In spring 2007, two in-house *Untsiya* shops opened in Moscow. A dual strategy was designed to make inroads into this market by opening both company stores and franchise shops. The company believed that its operations in Moscow would further develop such business lines as wholesale, franchising and packaging in other regions of Russia. At the end of 2007 there were 13 franchise *Untsiya* shops operating in Russian cities and CIS countries (Armenia, Azerbaijan, Belarus, Kazakhstan, Kyrgyzstan, Moldova, Tajikistan, and Uzbekistan). There were profit-making shops in Kaliningrad, Kemerovo, Tomsk, Kazan, Omsk, Kostroma, Ryazan and Saratov. New shops were to start in autumn 2007 in Tbilisi (Georgia), Novosibirsk, Novokuznetsk and Engels.[8] (See **Exhibit 7**.)
7. **Domestic Production Project.** In autumn 2006, *Untsiya* determined that its German supplier of flavored teas had breached its obligations under the exclusive agreement to supply *Untsiya* tea to Russia. While looking for another supplier, the company saw the possibility of launching domestic flavored tea production. Flavored tea, a blend of pure black or green tea, flowers (e.g. cornflower, sunflower), fruits, berries (strawberry, raspberry, pineapple, guava) and flavorings, was 70 percent of Untsiya's business by weight and 50 percent by revenue. Ninety-eight percent of premium tea was produced in Germany, which sold only ten times more in weight than *Untsiya* did alone in 2006. In addition, German production and logistics were considerably more expensive. Domestic production of flavored tea would give Russia more flexibility in satisfying consumer demand for the wholesale line. *Untsiya* stepped up its development of the *Domestic Production* project. By June 2007, they planned to rent a 1500 square meter production and storage facility. Commissioning was due to finish by August. By October, the company was planning to produce 30 kinds of flavored tea, and by spring or summer 2008, they intended to start producing its full range of flavored teas.

Company revenue in February, 2007 from these sources amounted to USD 421,000 (see Exhibit 1).

UNTSIYA'S ORGANIZATIONAL DESIGN

25 *Untsiya's* organizational structure has been subject to constant change. In January, 2003 it had a classical functional structure (see **Exhibit 8**). By 2007, the company's two major lines were each headed up by one of its founders (see **Exhibit 9**). According to Sergey Nikolaev, ". . . direct control is the major coordination tool the company employs. But we decided to divide the control among two owners because we both wanted to be in the company management." Thus, there were two systems exerting direct control.

Financial Controls

26 The first system involved monthly budgeting. This system permeated the company, i.e. each employee budgeted finances for the operations for which he was responsible and submitted the budget and financial report for approval to his immediate supervisor. These planning activities were regular and were performed on a monthly basis. The system proved to be effective not only when it came to issues of financial control. When composing a financial

[8] Untsiya – mera nastoyashchego (The Present is Measured in Ounces) // *Kupi Brend* (*Buy Brand*) magazine, # 4 (8), October, 2006.

EXHIBIT 8 **Organizational Structure as of January 2003 from company records**

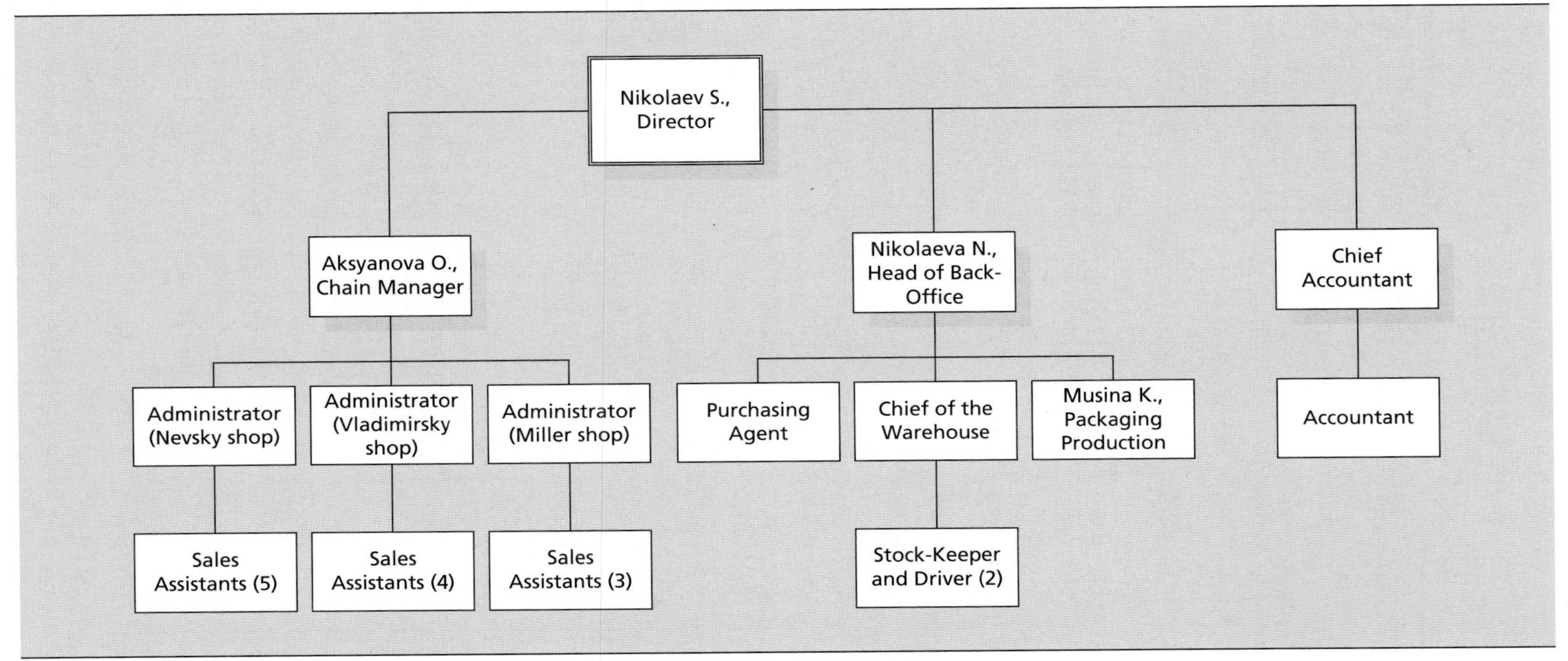

EXHIBIT 9 Organizational Structure as of February 2007 from company records

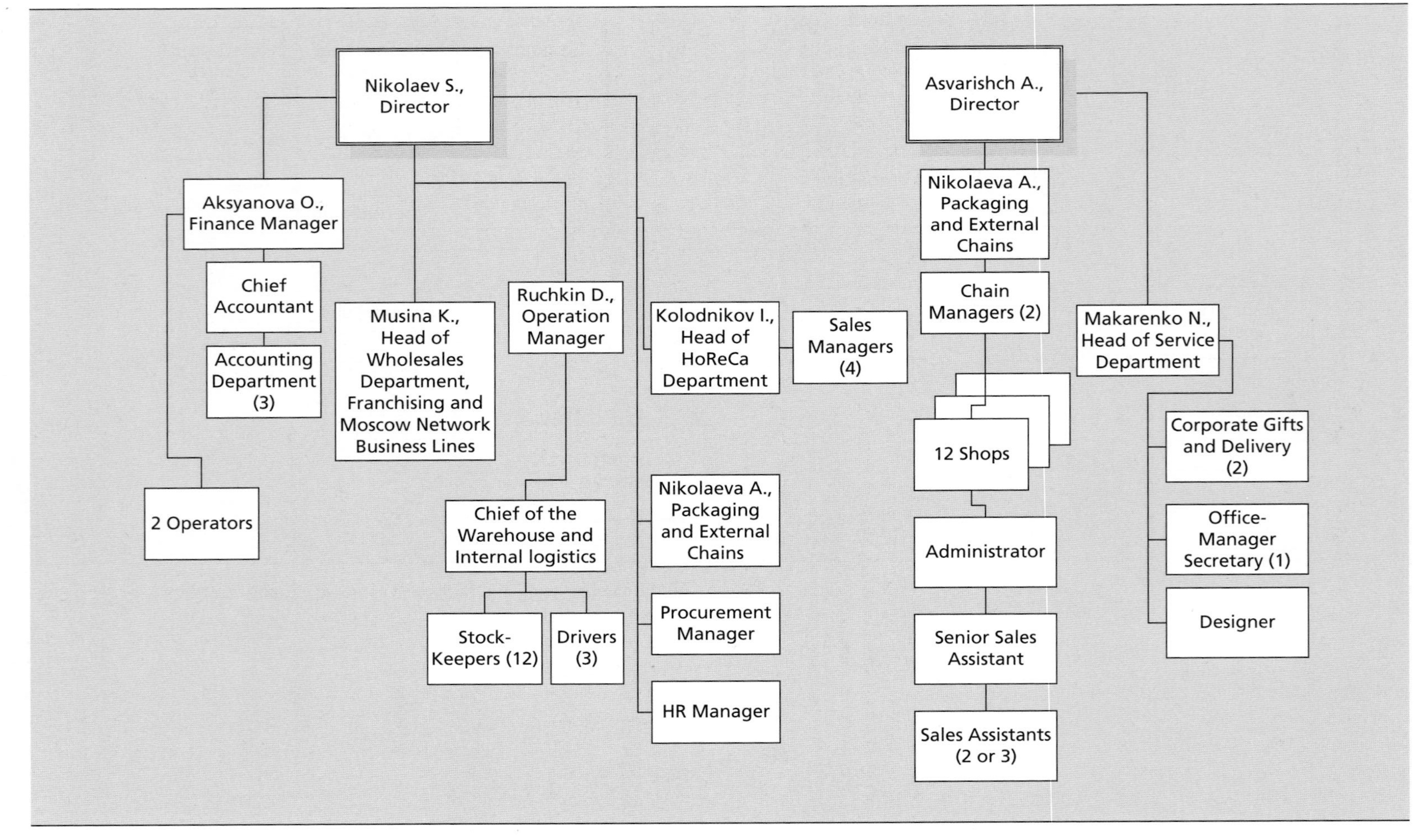

plan, the head of a subdivision also needed to plan and explain its activity and then report on work performance (e.g. if some of the expenses planned had not been spent, that may have been efficient from a financial standpoint, but ineffective from a performance standpoint).

Personnel Controls

27 The second system was a program of regular meetings. The idea behind it was that when a manager and his subordinate knew that they were to meet and discuss the current state of affairs and performance, they prepared for the meeting beforehand by gathering all the necessary information. Company experience showed that this format was convenient for both the manager and his subordinates. These meetings became less frequent as the planning horizon extended along with the company's growth. In 2004, meetings of directors and heads of departments were conducted weekly. In 2005, they were held every other week and in 2007, they morphed into so-called "strategic sessions" which took place once every six to twelve weeks. At these meetings, the company discussed different perspectives, set targets for the next three to six months, determined if some department or subdivision needed help from the head office, and planned further steps to be taken by management. There was always room for feedback and coaching. This system was moving towards less frequency and enhanced effectiveness.

The company's organizational structure in 2007 was characterized by the following features:

1. **Job expansion.** It was common practice for the company to expand job responsibilities. For example, Ms. Kseniya Musina, head of the wholesale department, franchising and Moscow network business lines, had held six positions by 2007. Musina started as a sales assistant, then, while still in that position, she simultaneously worked as a gift packaging designer, later taking charge of the gift packaging department. Following that, she worked in the procurement department. Then she supervised the wholesale project which later developed into the wholesale subdivision. After that, Musina took control over the franchising line. Later, without quitting her other jobs, she supervised the establishment of the in-house network in Moscow.

   Another example was Ms. Belokurova who joined the company in February, 2006 as the second accountant. In May, 2006 she entered the cross-functional team responsible for packaging design and revealed herself as a talented market analyst and good organizer. From September, 2006 until January, 2007, Belokurova was simultaneously employed as second accountant and deputy chief of the warehouse. From February, 2007 she worked as a project developer and chief of production at the storage facility.

   It was very often the case that there were several employees participating in job rotation. Within two and half years, rotation was conducted three times and affected senior positions involving up to seven employees at a time.

2. Another distinctive feature of *Untsiya's* organizational structure was that the company had two owners as its directors who, despite mutual respect, differed significantly in their approach to management. Asvarishch preferred a more structured approach to management, but Nikolaev felt that it was necessary to build a creative atmosphere in the company. This meant that for Asvarishch, the business was a source of wealth; for Nikolaev, the business provided an opportunity for self actualization. Consequently, they seldom interfered with each other's activities.

Collaboration

28 There were some significant collaboration aspects to *Untsiya*, including the interior design of the office. Most office staff worked in a bullpen, behind 1.5 meter (4 ½ foot) high partitions that separated the different departments. There were also two conference rooms, a kitchen and a smoking room. This structure facilitated more small meetings and communications in general (both effective and ineffective).

29 Temporary project groups were a second popular collaboration approach. These teams were set up to launch new projects and products (this was how, for example, the Packaging and Coffee projects were implemented) or to work on issues that concerned a number of the company's departments and divisions (e.g., significant changes to the company's website or semiannual inventory). Teams were usually cross-functional and operated within varying time frames—from several meetings up to six months. As a rule, teams were not hierarchical; all team members were equal and decision making was consensus-based. This approach was originally used to map out business processes (sales subdivisions forecasting; procurement planning; supply and delivery order placement; warehousing and inventory; distribution of scarce and slow-moving items between subdivisions), but the use of teams in this way failed.

30 The third aspect to collaboration was the *Club*, as it was popularly called. Every second Thursday at the end of the working day all those interested got together to listen to and discuss someone's report on a preannounced topic. These reports might be educational and deal with some business issues, such as *Jack Trout's Concept of Positioning* or *What Makes Japanese and European Management Different*. Or, some department might make a presentation focusing on its problems or plans after which the audience would discuss the issues covered. The format of these meetings was conversational rather than decision-making or a negotiation. No one expected consensus or a specific solution, although some decisions emerged through discussion. The second part of the *Club* meetings was an informal gathering with wine and a snack. These gatherings provided a venue for establishing a shared viewpoint. Such meetings gave employees a chance to discuss various cases from the company's practice or best experiences of other companies which led to reevaluation of company standards. On the one hand, such gatherings were quite popular as even retired employees asked for permission to visit or make reports. On the other hand, they occasionally grew into operations meetings conducted during off-duty hours, raising suspicions that some employees attended these meetings only because they felt they were supposed to.

31 The fourth aspect of collaboration was meetings of heads of departments at which directors/owners were not present. In 2007, this became an inconsistent tool as sometimes these meetings were conducted regularly, were chaired and minutes taken in turns, and sometimes they were called off. On occasion they were initiated by some concerned head of department, an approach that prevailed in conjunction with moving to a new office and holding a great number of minor operations meetings.

32 The final collaboration tool was in-house e-mail correspondence. Roughly 20 messages a week were addressed to all staff members with just a few of them coming from senior management. Much of this correspondence was an alternative to the usual operations meetings.

WHAT'S NEXT? POTENTIAL PROJECTS

Coffee Shops and Loose Tea

33 Nikolaev planned to have his experts analyze the effectiveness of setting up a coffee shop chain selling loose tea. Provided they developed a promising format, the chain could easily expand through franchising and establish operations in many regions of Russia. Expansion would resolve the problem of finding small selling spaces. Due to the scarcity of small retail spaces in the country, it was difficult to find appropriate locations of 20 to 35 square meters. Some company expenses (e.g. management and logistics) were connected with the number of points of sale, but not with the amount of selling space. Expenses per

EXHIBIT 10 **Timeline of Untsiya Events**

July, 2001	Sergey Nikolaev sold the radio station and started to search for a new business idea
August, 2002	The first Untsiya shop in St. Petersburg opened
Autumn, 2003	Three new Untsiya shops opened in St. Petersburg
January, 2004	The new HoReCa business line was established
February, 2004	Sergey Nikolaev formalized his business relationship with Aleksey Asvarisch
August, 2004	The wholesale department was established
June, 2005	The first franchising contract in Novosibirsk was signed
Autumn, 2006	The coffee line was created under the brand Kafe Kult
March, 2007	The new tea production project was launched
Spring, 2007	The first Untsiya shop was opened in Moscow

EXHIBIT 11 **Profit and Loss Statement 2007**

	Retail chain, St. Petersburg	Retail chain, Moscow	Delivery	HoReCa	Packing	Wholesale	Total
Sales, total	**$1 777 805**	**$ 67 443**	**$72 792**	**$166 380**	**$ 94 614**	**$1 686 577**	**$3 865 611**
Variable costs	$ 555 224	$ 21 086	$27 825	$ 46 924	$ 38 213	$ 982 595	$1 157 160
Fixed department cost	$ 707 032	$ 96 864	$10 953	$ 81 910	$ 65 645	$ 194 756	**$2 829 026**
Total costs	**$1 262 255**	**$117 950**	**$38 777**	**$128 834**	**$103 858**	**$1 177 352**	**$1 036 585**
Total profit	**$ 515 550**	$ (50 508)	**$34 015**	**$ 37 546**	$ (9 244)	**$ 50 9226**	$ 640 881
Overhead company costs	$ 351 857	$ 27 097	$ 7 890	$ 29 296	$ 22 016	$ 202 725	**$ 403 698**
Net profit	**$ 165 229**	$ (77 556)	**$26 215**	**$ 8 509**	$(31 053)	**$ 31 2354**	**$ 386 5611**

Source: Company Records

square meter of selling space were high. Moreover, it was impossible to decrease them by enlarging the company's tea range up to 300 brands, as customers were not likely to be able to select between that many types of tea. As Nikolaev said, "Creating a coffee shop chain seems rather an appealing idea because it involves similar key competencies." The project had not launched as of 2008 because the company already had a significant number of recently implemented projects. See **Exhibit 10** for a timeline of corporate developments and **Exhibit 11** for a Profit and Loss Statement for 2007.

New supermarket lines

34 It also seemed promising to expand the efforts of some of the already operating subdivisions. For example, with supermarkets as an important distribution channel, established

procurement and production processes facilitated the introduction of another tea line under a different brand, positioned in a slightly lower yet broader market segment. A second option would be to expand the efforts of the wholesale and production subdivisions to launch a less expensive line of high-quality loose teas.

New market segments

35 Sergey Nikolaev described the *Untsiya* company strategy as follows: "The company wants to grow large; it aims to be innovative; it pursues only related diversification; by entering new market segments, it tries to achieve market differentiation. I believe that it is possible to increase the company's revenues tenfold in five years, to USD 40M."

Further, Nikolaev said:

> We have reached that classical stage of setting new objectives. I love it. Some objectives have been reached, some not, some were slightly altered. So I'm thinking of what to do next. The company has a certain experience, it has learned something, and I have also learned something. People are different, people are talented and are ready to act. What I want is to come up with some idea which, provided it is amply financed (and I, thank God, do not have problems attracting funds), could develop into something special, some format based on our business, our knowledge which could be a real breakthrough, could become something really serious if not in the world, then within Russia. We are already leaders in the tea market. Our 100 shop chain is the greatest chain of tea shops in the world. But we want more. It is not clear yet if it is possible to create something new under the same brand expanding the tea shop format, or it should be something else which will make the business grow larger and more fundamental with capitalization of at least USD 100M. So far I don't know if I will manage to come up with some idea, but I want something special, something real.

Case 24

Tivo, Inc: *Tivo vs. Cable and Satellite DVR; Can Tivo Survive?*

Alan N. Hoffman, Rendy Halim, Rangki Son, Suzanne Wong
Bentley University

BACKGROUND

"With TiVo, TV fits into your busy life, NOT the other way around"

1 The evolution history of television started way back in 1939 with an original purpose of providing people with entertainment and enjoyment in life. It was then followed by an invention of the remote control in 1950 known as the "lazy bones". Perhaps this has been one of the biggest breakthroughs and most influential forms of entertainment we all have appreciated and enjoyed up until now. However, after the Lazy Bones was invented, the next generation of TV watching tools evolved, and one of them was TiVo, every couch potato's dream. Thanks to two Silicon Valley veterans with their creative and smart ideas, they took the initiative to recreate innovative and advanced technology developments in a radically different approach. TiVo was created not only just for entertainment, but "TV Your Way". Fundamentally designed, "With TiVo, TV fits into your busy life, NOT the other way around".

2 Now, many people may have heard the name TiVo . . . mentioned on popular TV shows, movies and many talk shows . . . even Oprah wonders in her September 2005 issue of her "O" magazine why life can't be like TiVo . . . but not so many know what TiVo really is about.

Source: The authors would like to thank Audrey Ballara, Will Hoffman, and Ann Hoffman for their research and contributions to this case. Please address all correspondence to: Dr. Alan N. Hoffman, MBA Program Director, LAC295D, Bentley College, 175 Forest Street, Waltham, MA 02452-4705, voice (781)891-2287, ahoffman@bentley.edu, fax (781)459-0335.

ONCE UPON A TIVO . . .

3 Pioneered by Mike Ramsay and Jim Barton, TiVo redefined entertainment in many other ways, delivering the promise of technologies that were much hyped. Incorporated in Delaware and originally named "Teleworld", the playback of TiVo started in August 4, 1997. As proposed, the original idea was to create a home network-based multimedia server where content to thin clients would be stream out throughout the home. In order to build such product, solid software foundation is much needed and that the device created has to operate flawlessly perfect, reliable and handle power failure gracefully for the consumers. At that time, both were still working in Silicon Graphics (SGI) and were very much involved in the entertainment industry. Jim Barton, though, was involved with on-demand video system. He was the executive sponsor of an effort to port an open source system called Linux to the SGI Indy workstation. Mike Ramsay was responsible for products that create movies' special effects for such companies as ILM and Pixar. With the combination of both worlds, these two SGI veterans thought Linux software would well serve TiVo as the operating system foundation. As for the hardware, it was designed solely by TiVo Inc and manufactured with the help of various OEMs including Philips, Sony, Hughes, Pioneer, Toshiba, and Humax. Combined they created a product that are very much interactive with real people, delivering a commitment where those people will be able to take charge of their own entertainment whenever they want to and wherever they need to.

From the Server Room to the Living Room

4 Swaying from their original idea to create a home network device, they later developed the idea to record digitized video on a hardware storage drive. Inside the Silicon Valley headquarters of TiVo in Alviso, California, both veterans created a so-called "fantasy living room", depicting a room full of executives' hope that will be a prototype for 100 million living rooms across North America. At that time, they both knew it would be so cool to exploit and develop the idea into an actual product with a promising future, a dream of most start-up companies. In the early days, Mike Ramsay said that they used to have thoughts of things like "Wow, you know, you can pause live television – isn't that a cool thing?" Jim Barton then got a computer to store a live TV signal and made it to play it back. Then . . . that was the start of TiVo—providing people with more than the original purpose of TV as just simply a tube to be watched, resulted with an invention to create the world's very first interactive entertainment network, where luxury of entertainment and control is in the viewers' own hands. As of March 31, 1999, TiVo shipped its first unit and because that day was a blue moon, an engineering staff code-named TiVo's first-version DVR as the "Blue Moon". Both Jim Barton and Mike Ramsay were psyched as the introduction to market a disruptive technology had just begun. Teleworld was then renamed TiVo in July 1999. Now that the living room is filled only with an oval coffee table and a comfy chair just like any other living rooms in the households, the only objects that can be distinctively seen and left is what's on the table surface—a telephone and TiVo's distinctive peanut-shaped remote control. The sofa and chairs all face an entertainment center containing a big-screen television that is linked to several TiVo boxes (a few are available; a few are works in progress).

TIVO ACCLAMATION

5 Now where the success of on-demand programs and online streaming are flocking TV networks, still many people have found DVR to be an essential part of their digital home entertainment center, catering more to people's viewing habits. Consumers would slip into stores such as big box retailers Best Buy, Circuit City, Target and Wal-Mart and sales people

would refer them to TiVo as TiVo has been commonly associated as the "DVR". Reminiscing back to the history of DVR, TiVo was actually never a beginner, but ReplayTV. The two early consumer DVRs, ReplayTV and TiVo, both launched their product in 1999 Consumer Electronics Show in Las Vegas. ReplayTV won the "Best of Show" award in the video category and was later acquired by SoniceBlue and D&M Holdings later in the years. However, it wasn't ReplayTV, the pioneer of DVRs in the DVR industry, the brand that made it to the world producing a cult-like product, but TiVo. TiVo's success also includes still currently being the only stand-alone DVR company in the industry. According to Forrester, from a scale of 1 to 5, TiVo's brand trust among regular users scores 4.2, while its brand potential among aspiring users scores A with 11.1 million potential users.

6 Spending approximately 13 months for full development of the first TiVo box, the wait was worthwhile as the revolutionary nature of TiVo won itself an Emmy award in August 19, 2006. This recognition was given to TiVo for providing innovative and interactive services that enhance television viewing to a whole new level. Other finalists for this particular Emmy award include AOL Music on Demand, CNN Enhanced and DirecTV Interactive Sports. With a cult-like product, TiVo has transformed into a verb. TiVo established a top-notch brand that has become the "it" word among its fervidly loyal customers and even noncustomers. In general, people would say "TiVo it", meaning to record or zap (make something disappear). A working wife, who has an important business dinner meeting that night and was rushing through the door, could speedily ask her husband, "Could you TiVo Desperate Housewives for me tonight dear?" On the other hand, TiVo felt that this verb transformation will jepordize TiVo and associate its products as a generic brand of DVR when people say, "I want two TiVos". However, with all the TiVo buzz, TiVo became public on September 30, 1999 at a price offering of $16 per share with a total of 5.5 million number of shares listed under the NASDAQ. On its way to the IPO, TiVo established one of the most rapid adoption rates in the history of consumer electronics. Quoted recently in an April 2007 article by PC World, TiVo became the third on the list of 50 best technology products of all time – saluted amazing products that changed our lives forever.

7 The acknowledgement has well served the young West Coast Company who is currently available in four countries which includes United States, United Kingdom, Canada and Taiwan. In addition, though it is not sold yet, TiVo's technology has been modified by end users so it could fit in another four countries such as Australia, New Zealand, Netherlands and South Africa. However TiVo has never come close to winning the number of customers (market share) nor generated a profit since it launched in 1997. Considered to be the best DVR system out there by variety of top-notch publications such as BusinessWeek, New York Times and Popular Science, TiVo hit a 3 million subscriber milestone only by February 18, 2005. Not long after, TiVo finally made its first profitable quarter. TiVo's subscribers include diverse and loyal subscribers from the infamous Oprah Winfrey, Brad Pitt and entrepreneur Craig Newmark (the owner of Craigslist). Though, the business philosophy of TiVo is relatively simple: TiVo connects consumers to the digital entertainment they want, where, and when they want it.

THE BRAIN INSIDE THE BOX

"It's not TiVo unless it's a TiVo"

The Surf & Turf

8 As people's daily life became busier and demanded more and more to attain the pleasure of watching TV digital video recorders became the tool to suffice that trend. The trend resulted in audiences wanting to have more direct allegiance with particular programs, TiVo then revolutionized that new way to watch TV with the introduction of the Digital Video Recording

system (DVR). Hard as it seems to be described in a sentence or two, the best way to describe what TiVo really is, is by the things that it does.

9 The DVR platform has created massive opportunity for TiVo to continue developing creative and sophisticated applications, features and services. Unlike a VCR (videocassette recorder), TiVo as a digital video recorder TiVo issues only Linux-based software and allows users to capture any TV programming and record them into internal hard disk storage for later viewing. Its patented feature "Trick Play", which allows viewers to stop, pause, rewind, and slo-mo live shows, is what TiVo is originally best at.

10 The TiVo device also allows users to watch their programs without having to watch the commercials if they don't want to. Users are exposed to promotional messages but are not forced to watch them. While this feature seems very attractive to consumers, understandably, not to television networks and advertising agencies. However, unlike ReplayTV that allows users to automatically and completely skip advertisements and was hit by several lawsuits by ad agencies and TV networks, TiVo managed to take a different approach.

11 With its inventive advertisement feature, TiVo offered to help, turning a difficult situation into a business opportunity, which has become TiVo's hallmark. TiVo surely knows that advertisements are a source of revenue, TiVo then started testing its "pop-up" feature. While recording or watching, there are some advertisements that pop up at the bottom of the TV screen. If a customer is interested in any of these advertisements, he has the ability to click to get more information about the product being advertised. People then have the choice to get advertisers' information or not depending on what they have interest in. "Product Watch" lets users choose the products, services, or even brands that interest them and it will automatically find and deliver the requested / relevant products straight to your list. Surprisingly, during the 2002 Super Bowl, TiVo tracked the viewing patterns of 10,000 of its subscribers and found that TiVo's instant replay feature was used more on certain commercials, notably the Pepsi add with Britney Spears, than on the game itself. As of today, TiVo has included 70 "showcase" advertising campaigns in its TiVo platforms for companies such as Acura, Best Buy, BMW, Buick, Cadillac, Charles Schwab, Coca-Cola, Dell, General Motors, GMC, New Line Cinema, Nissan, Pioneer, Porsche, and Target.

12 Beyond the key functions above, there are much more for users to surf throughout the integral functionality of a TiVo device. While a "Season Pass Manager" is to avoid conflict resolution such as overlapping recordings, a "Wish List" platform allows viewers to store their search accordingly to their specifics such as actor, keyword, director, etc. So far, no other companies have yet been able to match these two TiVo's recording features. In addition, the catchy remote control with its distinctive "Thumbs Up and Down" feature allows users to rate the shows they have watched purportedly for the use of others and themselves so that TiVo could assist and provide users with the movie similar to what they have rated. The remote itself has won itself design awards from the Consumer Electronics Association. Jakob Nielsen, a technology consultant of the Nielsen Norman Group, called the oversize yellow pause button in the middle of the remote "the most beautiful pause button I've ever seen." Steve Wozniak, the co-founder of Apple Computer mentioned "TiVo adjusts to my tastes and that its remote has been the most ergonomic and easy to use one that he has had encountered in many years".

13 In addition, being portable is now the hottest thing in television right now. Nowadays, that people have yet become more tech savvy, "TiVoToGo", its newest feature launched in January 2005, allows users to connect their TiVo to a computer with an internet or a home network, transferring recorded shows from TiVo boxes to users' PCs. Then, through a software program developed with Sonic, customers are able to edit and conserve their TiVo files. Later in August 2005, TiVo released a software that allows customers to transfer MPEG2 video files from their PC to their TiVo boxes to play the video on the DVR.

14 TiVoToGo feature also includes TiVo's "Central Online" which allows users to schedule recordings on its website 24/7, "MultiRoom Viewing" in order to transfer recordings between TiVo units in multiple rooms, download any programs in any format they want to into the TiVo box and transfer them into other devices such as iPod, laptop or other mobile devices such as cellular phones in order to provide a pleasure of viewing them anytime and anywhere the users desire to do so. On top of that, with the partnerships TiVo has established in regards to 3rd party network content, viewers now can access weather, traffic condition, even purchasing a last-minute movie ticket at Fandango.com and having the pleasure to enjoy "Amazon Unbox", allowing users to buy / rent the latest movies and TV shows to be download into the TiVo box.

"BEHIND THE BOX"—THE HARDWARE ANATOMY OF TIVO 101

So, many people would ask, how TiVo actually operates. "Even my mother can use TiVo with no problem!" This is the phrase that TiVo want their people to say.

15 Technically speaking, installing TiVo units have been pretty much self-explanatory because they are designed to be simple enough for everyone to install and operate. Parts that go into the device and its internal architecture have been made to be less complex. Online self-installation guide with a step-by-step pictured instruction has been the tool to suffice complete this request, however, options do come in handy, with a teamed up "door to door" professional installation service with Best Buy or a set-up appointment with 1-877—Geek—Squad.

16 In basic sense, TiVo is simply a cable box, with hard drive that gives the ability to record, and the fancy user interface. The main idea at the beginning, however, was to free people up from being locked by the network schedule. With TiVo, the watchers can watch anytime they want with extra features such as, pause, rewind, fast forward, slow motion, and many other great features, including the commercial-free watching experience.

17 Initially, the box will receive the signals coming from cable, antenna, or satellite. Then the signals received by the box will be divided into many frequencies and selected with the tuner that is built-in the box. The signals with the right selected frequencies will be sent

and encoded through the encoder, stored in the hard drive, and then decoded again for the watchers to view anytime.

18 TiVo's earlier model Series2 was supported with USB ports that have been integrated into the TiVo system to support network adapters which includes wired Ethernet and WiFi. It also provides the possibility to record over-the-air. The new TiVo series3 has been built with two internal cable-ready tuners and it supports a single external cable or satellite box. As a result, TiVo gives the ability to record two shows at once, unlike other DVRs. Moreover, the latest version of the TiVo box has a 10/1000 Ethernet connection port and a SATA port which can support external storage hardware[i]. It also has a HDMI plug which provides an interface between any compatible digital audio/video source, such as a DVD player, a PC, or a video game system. In other words, with the new TiVo box, customers don't even need their cable box anymore. Some recent models even contain DVD-R/RW drives which transfer recordings from the TiVo box to a DVD disc.

19 TiVo hardware can work as a normal digital recorder by itself. People might sometimes want to keep the hardware and cancel their subscriptions with TiVo, which is very damaging for the company revenue model.

WHAT THE HACK!

20 Where there is technology involved, there are incentives for hackers to challenge the system. Some people have hacked the TiVo boxes to improve the service, and to expand the recording capacity or/and storage. Others have aimed at making TiVo available in countries where TiVo is not currently available. In the latest version of TiVo, improved encryption of the hardware and software has made it more difficult for people to hack the systems.

THE TIVOPERATION—BEHIND THE SCENES . . .

". . . and I never miss an episode. TiVo takes care of the details"

MARKETING

Feel the Buzzzzzz—Hail Thy TiVo

21 When it comes to new technology, penetrating consumers markets are usually difficult as customers are slower to embrace new product than forecasters predict and opt to choose using old and easier technology like the VCRs. Mike Ramsay would get upset in the early days, when someone says, "oh, that's just like a VCR". He would then reply to them and say "no, no, no, no no. It's much more than a VCR, it does this, it does that, let's personalize it and all that stuff." At that point, it gets so difficult to describe what TIVo actually is, leading into five to ten minutes of a conversation instead of a 30-second TiVo pitch.

22 However, this problem has snot hindered TiVo from being a great product. Early on, TiVo has tried the traditional way of getting the product across with a result of repetitive stumbles in marketing its products. The millions of dollars spent on advertisements, did not help consumers understand what TiVo actually does. A customer claims, "I personally remember seeing Tivo ads on TV before I even knew what a TiVo was, and it took seven years for me to finally see one "in the flesh."

23 What makes TiVo DVRs different from other generic DVRs can only be felt and experienced and not seen even though the feature differences can be seen in **Exhibit 1**. According to Gartner analyst Van Baker, "For cable and satellite DVRs: the interface stinks. They do a

EXHIBIT 1

	TiVo Series2™ boxes	Leading cable service DVR*	Satellite DVR**	DIRECTV DVR with TiVo©
Record from multiple sources	**Yes combine satellite, cable, or antenna, depending on product.**	No Digital cable only	No Satellite only	No DIRECTV only
Easy search: Find shows by title, actor, genre, or keyword	**Yes**	Titles only-browsing only	title, subject, and actor only	Yes
Online scheduling: Schedule recordings from the Internet	**Yes**	No	No	No
Dual Tuner: Record 2 shows at once[1]	**Yes**	Yes	Yes	Yes
Movie and TV Downloads: Purchase or rent 1000's of movies and television shows from Amazon Unbox and have them delivered directly to your television.[2]	**Yes**	No	No	No
Home Movie Sharing: Edit, enhance, and send movies and photo slideshows from your One True Media account to any broadband connected TiVo box.[3]	**Yes**	No	No	No
Online services: Yahoo! weather, traffic & digital photos, Internet Radio from Live365, Podcasts, & movie tickets from Fandango	**Yes**	Limited	Limited	No
Built-In Ethernet: Broadband-ready right out of the box—connecting to your home network is a snap[4]	**Yes**	No	No	No
TiVoToGo transfers to mobile devices: Transfer shows to your favorite portable devices, laptop or burn them to DVD.[3,5]	**Yes**	No	No	No
Home media features: Digital photos, digital music and more	**Yes**	No	No	No
Transfer shows between boxes: Record shows on one TV and watch them on another.[3]	**Yes**	No	No	No

http://www.tivo.com/1.0.chart.asp

* Leading cable services compared to Time Warner/Cox Communications Explorer® 8000™ DVR and Comcast DVR

** Leading satellite services compared to DISH Network 625 DVR

[1] On theTiVo® Series2™ DT DVR, you can record 2 basic cable channels, or one basic cable and one digital cable channel, at once.

[2] Requires broadband cable modem or DSL connection.

[3] Requires your TiVo box to be connected to a home network wirelessly or via Ethernet

[4] Available on the new TiVo® Series2™ DT DVR and the TiVo® Series3™ DMR

[5] In order to burn TiVoToGo transfers to DVD you will need to purchase software from Roxio/Sonic Solutions.

Multiroom Solutions

	Digeo/Moxi	Motorola	Scientific-Atlanta	EchoStar	TiVo	Microsoft
Main DVR	Cable DVR*	Cable DVR†	Cable DVR†	Satellite DVR*	TiVo box	Media Center PC
Set-top box on additional TV(s)	IP terminal	Cable box‡	Cable box	None	TiVo box	XBox 360
How boxes share content	IP	IP	Digital broadcast	Analog broadcast	IP§	IP
Physical connection	Coax	Coax	Coax	Coax	Home network	Home network
Features available on additional TVs:						
Play back recorded programs	✓	✓	✓	✓	✓	✓
Record programs	✓	✓		✓	✓	✓
Pause programs	✓	✓		✓	✓	✓
View Internet content	✓	X			✓	✓
View personal digital content	X	X			✓	✓

*New product specifically designed for multiroom use "x" = Available, but operators have not yet deployed
†Standard cable DVR plus modifications for multiroom use
‡Requires additional IP dongle on standard digital set-top box
§Requires transferring files from one TiVo box to the other

Source: Forrester Research Inc., 2006

really bad job of it". TiVo would rally people to change their lives by continuously preaching its brand and products, creating cause and evangelism with a result of many people claiming TiVo have changed their lives. According to a survey reported on the TiVo website, 98% of users said that they could not live without their TiVo.

24 The one word that explicitly describes the cult-like product is "interactive" in many ways. So when TiVo subscribers feel the buzz, they show and tell, the story goes on and on and on. Between 1999 and 2000, TiVo's subscriptions increased by 86%. In addition to capitalizing on its tens of thousands of customer evangelists to move the product into the mainstream, TiVo's word-of-mouth strategy focuses on celebrity endorsements and television show product placement. The firm began giving its product away to such celebrities as Oprah, Sarah Michelle Gellar, Drew Bledsoe and many more, turning them into high-profile members of the cult, while Jay Leno and Rosie O'Donnell helped much influence TiVo's consumers in a very positive way.

THE MARKET RESEARCH TEAM

25 The need to create such unique emotional connection between people and this product is significant to TiVo. Another way for a firm like TiVo to always be a step ahead and develop ways to improve and measure promotions and viewer behavior is to do continuous intensive market research. TiVo's market research team is considered as one of its functional units that are driving the company which includes Lieberman Research Worldwide and Nielson Media Research. With Lieberman, the first ever DVR-based panel was established in August 2002. Internally, TiVo also has built a platform in their system that sends detailed information on its customers watching TV behavior back to TiVo. TiVo also fully embraced the community with its TiVo community and hackers programs so that TiVo research team know what people needs are, when and where they need them.

FINANCIAL

Fast Forward or Rewind TiVO's Stock?

26 TiVo started with a price of $16 during its IPO in 1999. TiVo reached the highest in its stock price history after its IPO at $78.75 with its first eye-catching ad, "Hey, if you like us, TiVo us" which then became its first milestone. After the rush of rapid growth, TiVo's stock price shoot down to a price as low as $2.25, the lowest in history around 2002. TiVo's stock price then started to pick up in 2003 when the FCC Chairman Michael Powell announced that he uses TiVo claiming TiVo is a "God's Machine" and when the White House Press Secretary Ari Fleischer was found too to be a loyal user of TiVo. Around mid 2003, TiVo hit its first 1 million subscribers, significantly increased its stock price to reach around $14.00/share then inches back down to a low $3.50 per share as a result of the resignation of its CEO, Mike Ramsay. With the new CEO in place, TiVo finally reached a 3 million subscribers milestone by mid 2005, reaching to a current average stock price of $6–$7 range per share. Now, the question is, how to appease investors without killing a feature that helps sell the product.

Deconstructing TiVO

27 Since it was founded in 1997, TiVo has accumulated more than $400M in losses. Looking at TiVo's revenues and costs structures in **Exhibit 2**, TiVo, an enigmatic company, have much divided its revenues and costs in variety of forms which includes service, technology,

EXHIBIT 2 **TIVO INC. CONDENSED CONSOLIDATED STATEMENTS OF OPERATIONS**
(In thousands, except per share and share amounts) (unaudited)

	Three Months Ended October 31,		Nine Months Ended October 31,	
	2006	**2005**	**2006**	**2005**
		Adjusted		**Adjusted**
Revenues				
Service and technology revenues	$ 52,616	$ 43,197	$ 160,605	$ 123,891
Hardware revenues	27,978	24,652	53,666	39,827
Rebates, revenue share, and other payments to channel	(14,934)	(18,234)	(32,932)	(27,860)
Net revenues	65,660	49,615	181,339	135,858
Cost of revenues				
Cost of service and technology revenues (1)	13,826	8,508	44,256	24,832
Cost of hardware revenues	31,925	24,667	68,678	48,006
Total cost of revenues	45,751	33,175	112,934	72,838
Gross margin	19,909	16,440	68,405	63,020
Research and development (1)	12,221	9,712	37,973	30,394
Sales and marketing (1)	10,123	10,006	25,856	24,410
General and administrative (1)	9,811	11,702	35,961	26,249
Total operating expenses	32,155	31,420	99,790	81,053
Loss from operations	(12,246)	(14,980)	(31,385)	(18,033)
Interest income	1,291	826	3,341	2,184
Interest expense and other	(133)	(10)	(165)	(13)
Loss before income taxes	(11,088)	(14,164)	(28,209)	(15,862)
Provision for income taxes	(4)	—	(35)	(51)
Net loss	$ (11,092)	$ (14,164)	$ (28,244)	$ (15,913)
Net loss per common share—basic and diluted	$ (0.12)	$ (0.17)	$ (0.32)	$ (0.19)
Weighted average common shares used to calculate basic and diluted net loss per share	91,930,061	84,200,655	87,680,571	83,362,402
(1) Includes stock-based compensation expense (benefit) as follows:				
Cost of service and technology revenues	$ 365	$ —	$ 1,035	$ —
Research and development	1,608	(6)	4,177	(131)
Sales and marketing	474	20	1,264	(20)
General and administrative	1,636	151	4,257	199

The accompanying notes are an integral part of these condensed consolidated statements.

EXHIBIT 2 ***(Continued)***

—	1998	1999	2000	2001	2002	2003	2004	2005
Consolidated Statement of Operations								
Data:								
Revenues								
Service revenues		$ 3,782	$ 989	$ 19,297	$ 39,261	$ 61,560	$ 107,166	$ 167,194
Technology revenues		$ —	$ —	$ 100	$ 20,909	$ 15,797	$ 8,310	$ 3,665
Hardware revenues		$ —	$ —	$ —	$ 45,620	$ 72,882	$ 111,275	$ 72,093
Rebates, revenue share, and other payment to the channel		$ (5,029)	$ (630)	$ —	$ (9,780)	$ (9,159)	$ (54,696)	$ (47,027)
Net Revenues		$ (1,247)	$ 359	$ 19,397	$ 96,010	$ 141,080	$ 172,055	$ 195,925
Cost and Expenses								
Cost of service revenues		$ 18,734	$ 1,719	$ 19,852	$ 17,119	$ 17,705	$ 29,360	$ 34,179
Cost of technology revenues		$ —	$ —	$ 62	$ 8,033	$ 13,609	$ 6,575	$ 782
Cost of hardware revenues		$ —	$ —	$ —	$ 44,647	$ 74,836	$ 120,323	$ 84,216
Research and development		$ 25,070	$ 2,544	$ 27,205	$ 20,714	$ 22,167	$ 37,634	$ 41,087
Sales and marketing		$ 151,658	$ 13,946	$ 104,897	$ 48,117	$ 18,947	$ 37,367	$ 35,047
General and administrative		$ 15,537	$ 1,395	$ 18,875	$ 14,465	$ 16,296	$ 16,593	$ 38,018
Total Costs		$ 210,999	$ 19,604	$ 170,891	$ 153,095	$ 163,560	$ 247,852	$ 233,329
% Costs over Revenues		−16921%	5461%	881%	159%	116%	144%	119%
Net Loss from operations		$(212,246)	$ (19,245)	$(151,494)	$ (57,085)	$ (22,480)	$ (75,797)	$ (37,404)

(Continued)

EXHIBIT 2 *(Continued)*

TIVO INC. CONDENSED CONSOLIDATED BALANCE SHEETS
(In thousands, except share amounts) (unaudited)

	October 31, 2006	January 31, 2006 Adjusted
ASSETS		
CURRENT ASSETS		
Cash and cash equivalents	$ 78,898	$ 85,298
Short-term investments	28,067	18,915
Accounts receivable, net of allowance for doubtful accounts of $121 and $56	27,300	20,111
Finished goods inventories	34,107	10,939
Prepaid expenses and other, current	4,327	8,744
Total current assets	172,699	144,007
LONG-TERM ASSETS		
Property and equipment, net	10,874	9,448
Purchased technology, capitalized software, and intangible assets, net	17,580	5,206
Prepaid expenses and other, long-term	597	347
Total long-term assets	29,051	15,001
Total assets	$ 201,750	$ 159,008
LIABILITIES AND STOCKHOLDERS EQUITY/(DEFICIT)		
LIABILITIES		
CURRENT LIABILITIES		
Accounts payable	$ 28,278	$ 24,050
Accrued liabilities	32,553	37,449
Deferred revenue, current	56,596	57,902
Total current liabilities	117,427	119,401
LONG-TERM LIABILITIES		
Deferred revenue, long-term	51,550	67,575
Deferred rent and other	2,208	1,404
Total long-term liabilities	53,758	68,979
Total liabilities	171,185	188,380
COMMITMENTS AND CONTINGENCIES (see Note 10)		
STOCKHOLDERS' EQUITY/(DEFICIT)		
Preferred stock, par value $0.001:		
Authorized shares are 10,000,000;		
Issued and outstanding shares—none	—	—
Common stock, par value $0.001:		

EXHIBIT 2 *(Continued)*

Authorized shares are 150,000,000;		
Issued shares are 96,922,295 and 85,376,191, respectively and outstanding shares are 96,841,792 and 85,376,191, respectively	97	85
Additional paid-in capital	753,373	667,055
Deferred compensation	—	(2,421)
Accumulated deficit	(722,335)	(694,091)
Less: Treasury stock, at cost—80,503 shares	(570)	—
Total stockholders' equity (deficit)	30,565	(29,372)
Total liabilities and stockholders' equity (deficit)	$ 201,750	$ 159,008

The accompanying notes are an integral part of these condensed consolidated statements.

hardware and shared revenues. Being a company that lives under a great shadow of Wall Street pessimism, the question then becomes what value can TiVo add besides hyping their latest technology developments. Service revenues for example, TiVo needs to know what is the actual value of TiVo-owned subscribers and not TiVo's partnerships subscribers such as to DirectTV and Comcast. Deconstructing the value of just this one particular matter then leads to other questions like how long does a TiVo subscriber remain a subscriber, how much do each of them pay and are willing to pay, how much advertising revenue do users produce for every tag they click, moreover, how long and how can TiVo maintain its subscribers to be TiVo-owned subscribers.

28 In one way, the chicken-and-egg problem may have been the bulk of the TiVo's hardware revenues problem where people would say "What, huh, TiVo, personalizing your own TV network? What the hell are you talking about?", but not being able to gain the economies of scale that it desires, it should be TiVo's point of concern. Even though rebates are being offered, still, TiVo has not reached its price point that really attracts people. TiVo offers three types of boxes depending on the hours of programming storage capacity which range from an 80-hour TiVo Series to 300-hour TiVo Series HD. For the basic TiVo Series2 box of 80 hours and 180 hours has a one-time fee of $99.99 and $199.99, while the HD TiVo box costs $799.99 with a 300-hours storage capacity.

29 TiVo also has been a heavy user of mail-in rebates which is reflected as one of their form of revenues shown in Exhibit 2. According to BusinessWeek, $5 million in additional revenue was recognized because nearly half of TiVo's 100,000 new subscribers failed to apply for a $100 rebate. This slippage type of strategy is known to marketers as the "shoebox effect" and this usage of promotional practice has caused a large positive impact for TiVo.

OPERATION

Research and Development – The "A" Team

30 Again, the word "interactive" is the buzz word. TiVo's R&D team makes sure that they build TiVo from the user's perspective and viewing habits. TiVo forms forums of communication through TiVo community.com and TiVo hackers. In this forum, criticisms are allowed and even encouraged, so long as they are constructive and help TiVo to grow.

Users and aspiring users of TiVo are allowed to say what they like and dislike and voices what they expect to see in TiVo in the future. Ideas generated through this forum will help TiVo's R&D team and developers to continuously be on hand and future innovates accordingly to the need of people's ever-changing lifestyle. TiVo is also concerned how its platform could actually be used the wrong way by kids these days. With this concern, TiVo has collaborated with parents to build a new feature called TiVo Parental Zone that allows parents to control what their kids are actually watching. Privacy concerns have also been an issue nowadays in the advance technology industry. TiVo manages to protect its community regarding privacy concerns by storing such information on a computer behind its "firewall" in a secure location, and often restricts the number of employees internally who can access such data.

31 Previously TiVo's R&D team only consisted of contract-based engineers. Now, TiVo makes sure that its R&D team consists of a diverse, utmost creative and detailed on-staff engineers. Its intensive research principle is that benefits must extend existing people's behaviors. The design team has every little detail of steps to follow to fit the needs of lifestyle. As an example of TiVo's meticulous product design process, TiVo created a remote control that combines personalization and interconnectivity. TiVo's remote has a feature of thumbs up and down to be clicked on for users to rate shows so that the TiVo will know what to record. In addition, TiVo allows the Braille ability on its remote for eye-impaired users. Other R&D processes includes product testing & development of its software and platforms, product integration of software to satellite system and product integration such as the integration of DVD burner and Tivo recorder. Besides developing its main products, TiVo R&D team also try to design platforms and technology that can be used with any other products and enhance the demand of TiVo's main products such as the ability to connect with computers, other home theater technologies and especially, cable and satellites.

32 Since intensified competition exists in this DVR industry, TiVo found the need to patent its advance software and technology platform. TiVo licensed its TiVoToGo software to chip maker AMD, digital media software such as Sonic Solutions and giant company such as Microsoft in order to enable video playback on pocket PCs and smart phones. As of today, TiVo has 85 patents granted and still 117 applications patents pending, which include domestic and foreign patents and further leave rivals scratching their heads. TiVo license its patents through several of its trusted partners such as Sony, Toshiba, Pioneer and Direct TV. TiVo believes that licensing its technology to third parties has been its best business model.

Executive Team & Management

33 TiVo's top management is always on hand with its operations and promotions. Former CEO, Mike Ramsay, would make overseas trip such as to Japan to conduct meetings and seminars with consumer electronic makers. This effort is as an attempt to convince the makers to embed TiVo's software into their products. In order to make sure everything goes well and accordingly, the ex-CEO has been focusing on maintaining partnerships. He would rarely be in his office, instead on the road talking to companies that can help TiVo build software and subscribers. However, many mistakes were made throughout his history being a CEO which includes twice employee layoffs in 2001:80 employees (approx. 25% of workforce) were laid off on 5th of April 2001 and 40 employees (approx. 20% of workforce) were laid off on 31st October 2001. TiVo's previous CEO, Mike Ramsay was just an engineer on the block. He knows how to be creative and build great machines, but didn't really know the industry very well, moreover manage the company and steer TiVo from drowning further.

As a result, Mike Ramsay resigned in mid 2005, a change of CEO was implemented, where the new CEO hired is the former president of NBC Cable, Tom Rogers, a new strength to TiVo's management.

34 In addition, TiVo's Board of Directors consists of individuals from very diverse backgrounds and companies, however, this actually pose as one of TiVo's concerns. TiVo needs more members that are from TiVo's industry-related background and can influence future DVR/Cable industry possibly they would make better decisions.

Sleeping with the Enemies

". . . So long, TiVo! Hello DVR! . . ."

THE INDUSTRY

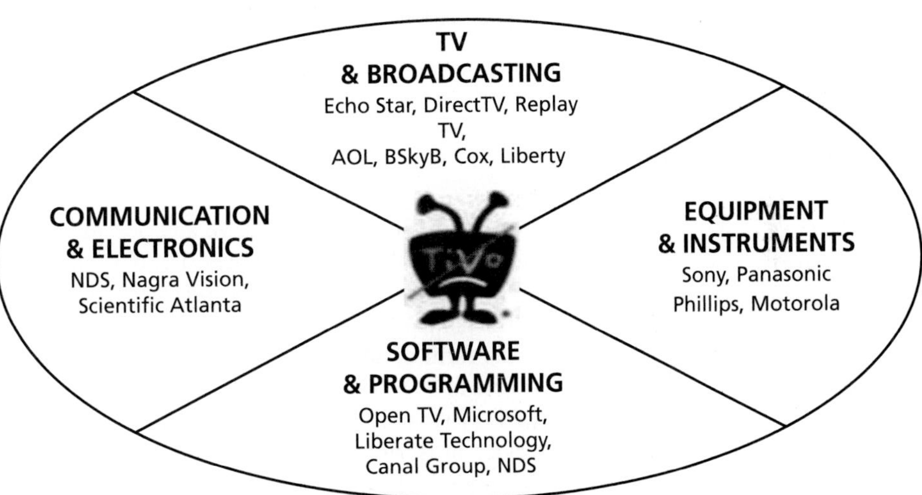

35 The Digital Video Recorder or Personal Video Recorder market is located at the convergence of these 4 established industries: Broadcasting and TV, Software and Programming, Electronic Instrument, and Communications Equipment.

36 For TiVo, introducing a disruptive technology into the industry was full of obstacles. When a digital video recording has the potential to be considered as a "disruptive technology", means that the technology creates something new which "usurp existing products, services, and business model." According to Mike Ramsay, the DVR phenomenon has established that "people really want to take control of television, and if you give them control, they don't want you to take it back." Though TiVo has innovatively added all the great software, platforms and services that a stand-alone TiVo DVR has to offer, the viewing will not work / be greater without a connection to a cable network or satellite signals. Therefore, users who want a TiVo DVR, will need to subscribe to TiVo, pay a onetime fee for the TiVo box and subscribe to companies that provides cable or satellite signals such as Comcast and DirecTV. Because this is the case, the TiVo DVR has made itself to be readily equipped with a built in cable-ready tuner for use with any external cable box or satellite receiver. TiVo has made many alliances and at the same time even competed with cable operators and satellite network. With cable, satellite, and electronics companies pushing to have their own DVRs, the DVR industry is expected to grow rapidly.

Market share wise, TiVo claim to cover the entire US market:

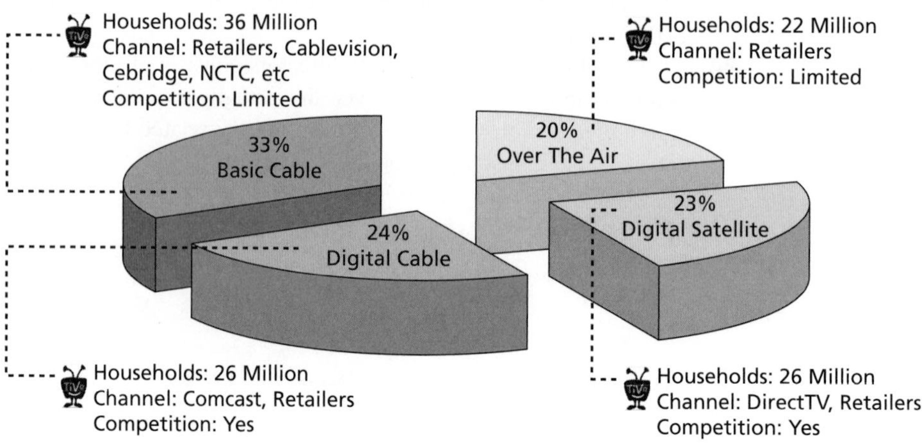

FRIENDS OR FOE?

37 In 2000, AOL invested $200 million in TiVo and became the largest shareholders of the company and one of its main service partners. The deal allowed TiVo to release a box that provided both TiVo's capabilities and AOL services. Aside from AOL, TiVo established other service partnerships. TiVo and Discovery Communication and NBC agreed on a $8.1 million deal in the form of advertising and promotional services. Later on, an additional $5 million was paid to NBC for promotions. It also collaborated on research and development and allowed TiVo to use a portion of its satellite network. AT&T helped TiVo to market and sell the service in Boston, Denver and Silicon Valley areas. BSkyB was the service partner for TiVo in the United Kingdom. Creative Artists Agency marketed and gave promotional support of the personal video recorder and was given in exchange 67,122 shares of preferred stock.

38 Despite all the partnerships that TiVo was able to enjoy, TiVo has actually been faced by a difficult challenge, that is cable and satellite operators who can be either TiVo's buddy or enemy—now that they offer digital video recorder-equipped set-top boxes of their own. Cable operators like Time Warner Cable and Cox Communications offer built-in DVR capability in set-top boxes and provide the equipment "free" to subscribers, and in late August 2003, Echostar announced a free DVR promotion, which was an unprecedented move in the industry. TiVo's fairly expensive retail priced unit could possibly jeopardize the company's ability to stay. There are relatively few cable and satellite providers, leaving TiVo with little power over them. These companies have the ability to dictate pricing of the TiVo technology because these huge cable companies can always develop or purchase their own generic DVR unit to market to their subscription base. Although TiVo had to give up a cut of profits to partners, still TiVo decided to have strategic relationships with competitors and cable companies for distribution and credit on its sales force.

39 Previously, DirecTV has been the backbone of TiVo, the service partner that has been fruitfully fueling most of TiVo's growth. In addition, TiVo's current 4.4 million subscribers have mostly come from its deal with DirecTV. As of early 2002, subscribers to TiVo service through DirecTV have increased from 230,000 to 2.1Million, representing more than half of all DVR subscriptions through satelite. Earlier when DirecTV began the talk with TiVo, the satellite provider was already equipped with a DVR service through its partnership with

Microsoft's Ultimate TV. For users to be able to watch their shows, subscriptions to DirecTV channels range from $29.99/month providing 40 channels to $65.99/month with over 250 channels.

40 Now that DirecTV is developing their own DVR device with the NDS Group and mentioned in 2005 that it would stop marketing and selling TiVo's digital recorders to its satellite TV subscribers starting in 2007, will TiVo become history? Though, DirecTV's DVR still costs users $299 onetime fee, but it includes unique features such as the ability to jump to a specific scene in the program as well as allowing users to pay for any downloaded pay-per-view movies only when they are being viewed. In 2006, TiVo and DirecTV reached a commercial extension agreement for three years. The agreement will allow existing DirecTV customers using the TiVo digital video recorder to continue to receive maintenance and support from DirecTV. As part of the agreement, TiVo and DirecTV also said they wouldn't sue each other over patent rights. Since the agreement with DirecTV was facing to expiration date, TiVo has been rushing to differentiate its product and struggling to strike other distribution deals.

41 In July 2000, Comcast, a cable operator, agreed to a trial offering TiVo boxes to its subscribers, hoping that the trial would lead to a bigger deal where Comcast would integrate TiVo software into Comcast cable boxes. After knowing it, Comcast balked and unwilling to concede. In April 2001, when another trial striked up to lead to a larger deal, TiVo laid off approximately 25% of its staff. November 2001, a full bloom of hope became hopeless when ATT Broadband agreed to offer TiVo DVRs to its customers with the fact that within a few weeks after, Comcast ended up killing the deal by acquiring the cable provider and its 14 million customers. In addition, in 2002, cable operators such as Comcast ended up developing their own DVR boxes with makes such as Motorola and Scientific-Atlanta. However, similar to DirecTV, Comcast, the nation's cable company, announced in March 2005, that it would offer its customers a video recorder service from TiVo and even will allow TiVo to develop its software for Comcast's DVR platform. Comcast and TiVo agreed working to make TiVo's DVR service and interactive advertising capability (ad management system) available over Comcast's cable network and its set-top DVR boxes. This agreement also included that under TiVo brand name, the first of their co-developed products would be available in mid- to late-2006.

42 Subscriptions to Comcast's basic or standard cable costs users $8.63 or $52.55. To want to have a DVR feature, users need to add $13.94 with Comcast in addition to the subscriptions to TiVo which ranges from $12.95 to $16.95 / month depending on the lifetime plan chosen that varies from one to three years. Due to the agreement with Comcast, TiVo's shares closed up nearly 75%, or $2.87 per share, to $6.70. Investors were positive about the news, some upgrading TiVo's investment rating from a sell to hold. Even though, sparking investors have concerned over TiVo's future, since DirecTV started using a second company, NDS, to provide DVR service, a deal with Comcast puts to rest some of those concerns by opening up a large new potential audience for TiVo's service. According to a filing with the SEC, TiVo receives an upfront payment from Comcast for creating a new DVR that works with Comcast's current service. TiVo also receives a recurring monthly fee for each Comcast subscriber who uses TiVo through Comcast.

43 Both TiVo's deal with a cable operator such as Comcast and a satellite broadcaster such as DirecTV were made merely because of the technological differences that can be tweaked around. Rolling out new technologies such as DVR, will be easier for satellite broadcasters because changes can be made in a central location. While as for cable operators, technology will have to be deployed gradually as they have different equipment in different areas. With all these deals, could TiVo's opportunities be beyond TV and that it help TiVo to become what it has always wanted to be: a software provider?

44 In addition, with the hype of being portable, lately, TiVo and BellSouth FastAccess DSL agreed on a variety of co-marketing. With strong southeastern presence and renowned customer satisfaction of BellSouth, TiVo can turn a DSL Internet connection into a pipeline for video content delivered directly to the television. To expand program recording to a cellular phone, its latest TiVo Mobile feature, TiVo struch up a deal with Verizon to bring the digital video recording pioneer's capabilities beyond its set-top boxes and the television, and directly to cellphones for the first time. In terms of contents, TiVo also has engaged in new partnerships with CBS Corp, Reuters Group PLC, and Forbes magazine, not to mention New York Times Co., National Basketball Association and some other firms are among the partners. This will make "news and entertainment programs available for downloading onto TiVos". International Creative Management are to recommend films, television shows and Internet videos that TiVo users can download onto their boxes. Finally TiVo has decided to open up to amateur videos through a deal with One True Media Inc., an Internet start-up that operates a Web service designed to help users easily edit their raw footage into slick home movies.

THE TALKATIVO

". . . Bring 'em on! We are talking the HD language now . . . Yeah!"

HD TREND

45 High definition sets in the entertainment industry are now the most important new consumer electronic items. HD products focus more toward quality of what is being seen and heard rather than the compactness like we saw a decade ago. High definition sets include HD TV, HD broadcasting, HD DVD, HD radio, HD photo and even HD audio.

46 In which TiVo is linked particularly to, high definition TV (HD TV) was first introduced in the United States during the 1990s and it is basically a digital television broadcasting system using a significantly higher resolution than the traditional formats such as NTSC, PAL and SECAM. The technology at that time was very expensive. Nowadays, as the prices have decreased, HD TV is going mainstream. A significant numbers of people have already bought HD TV; most people are planning to buy an HD TV soon. As of 2007, HDTVs are available in 24 million US households. By 2009, HD TV will have replaced all the old standard definition TV. With the price of the hard drive becoming lower and lower, and the increasing technology of HDTV, the demands for the HD products are also increasing multiple times. With HDTV, users are potentially being offered a much better picture quality than standard television, with greater picture on screen clarity and smoother motion, richer and more natural colors and surround sound.

HD TiVo

47 Lately, TiVo issued the TiVo Series3 which will allow customers to record HD television and digital cable. As people experience HD TV, TiVo service will be increasingly appealing. Once again, TiVo has set up the technological standards in the environment. With the TiVo Series 3, HD version, it allows the consumers to do many additional great things and deliver both the audio and visual in HD.

48 TiVo realizes that great quality videos need to be supported by great quality audio, thus, they put a lot of efforts in the audio development, and received the certification of being the first digital media recorder to meet their performance standard in HDTV. THX is very well known to have developed highest standard of audio mainly the surround systems in the entertainment as well as the media industry.

TiVo SERIES 3

49 The new Hi-Def TiVo Series3 which are being sold for $799, has the ability to record two HD programs simultaneously while playing back a third previously recorded one. It also has two signal inputs, it accepts cable TV and over-the-air signals. It replaces the existing as well as the 30-second commercial skip. In addition, the new HD TiVo is different because there is no lifetime membership anymore for the HD TiVo compared to the older DVR products. Is this the shift of TiVo revenue model? To aim at the subscription-based revenue stream.

50 Despite that the capability of TiVo being able to record and play back at hi-def level, there are still many considerations for people before buying the TiVo. The downside of the HD TiVo, however, the price tag that are overly expensive for most people especially when there are some DVRs being offered for free by the cable companies.

HD TiVENemies

51 Now that the HD trend is flocking the entertainment industry, TiVo competitors are also offering HD DVRs on their own and not just a DVR.

52 As for a cable operator such as Comcast, Comcast allows its subscribers to rent their DVR boxes for $13.94 / month as they do not offer to sell their DVR boxes to their customers. With their HD DVR boxes manufactured by Motorola and Scientific Atlanta, users are able to navigate their own preferences just like using a TiVo, except that TiVo may have better and more features built into the TiVo boxes. Then with the Comcast DVR boxes users will be able to watch the variety of cable channels offered by Comcast with an additional monthly subscription fee to cable channels.

53 Once a best friend, now may soon be a foe, DirecTV, a satellite operator, allows subscribers to add an additional DVR subscription service for $4.99 monthly on top of the chosen monthly subscription service package to DirecTV cable channels which ranges from $29.99 to $65.99. Same as Comcast not allowing users to keep their DVR boxes, if a user is in need of an HD DVR box, the user will need to pay an upfront cost of $299 with $100 rebate. As for the basic DVR, DirecTV charges $99.99 upfront cost.

REFERENCES

http://www.tivo.com/

http://en.wikipedia.org/wiki/TiVo

http://en.wikipedia.org/wiki/High-definition_television

http://egotron.com/ptv/ptvintro.htm

http://news.com.com/TiVo,+Comcast+reach+DVR+deal/2100-1041_3-5616961.html

http://news.com.com/TiVo+and+DirecTV+extend+contract/2100-1038_3-6060475.html

http://www.technologyreview.com

http://www.fastcompany.com/magazine/61/tivo.html

http://iinnovate.blogspot.com/2006/09/mike-ramsay-co-founder-of-tivo.html

http://www.acmqueue.org/modules.php?name=Content&pa=showpage&pid=53&page=7

http://www.internetnews.com/stats/article.php/3655331

http://thomashawk.com/2006/04/tivo-history-101-how-tivo-built-pvr_24.html

http://www.tvpredictions.com/tivohd030807.htm

http://www.tivocommunity.com/tivo-vb/showthread.php?threadid=151443

Case 25

TomTom: *New Competition Everywhere!*

Alan N. Hoffman
Bentley University

SYNOPSIS

1 TomTom, an Amsterdam-based company that provides navigation services and devices, leads the navigation systems market in Europe and is second in the US. Its most popular products include TomTom Go and TomTom One for cars, TomTom Rider for bikes, TomTom Navigator (digital maps), and TomTom for iPhone—its most recent release.

2 The company attributes its market leadership to its technology, large customer base, distribution power, and prominent brand image. But as the US and European personal navigation device market gets saturated, TomTom's sales growth rate declines. The company also faces increasing competition from other platforms using GPS technology like cell phones and smart phones with a built-in navigation function. Legal and environmental restrictions on the digital navigation industry make TomTom's future even more uncertain. Whether TomTom can keep expanding may well depend on whether it can become the prime mover in creating digital maps and navigational services for developing countries.

Source: The author would like to thank Will Hoffman, Mansi Asthana, Aakashi Ganveer, Hing Lin, Che Yii for their research. Please address all correspondence to Professor Alan N. Hoffman, Bentley University, 175 Forest Street, Waltham, MA 02452; ahoffman@bentley.edu. Printed by permission of Dr. Alan N. Hoffman.

TOMTOM: NEW COMPETITION EVERYWHERE!

3 TomTom is one of the largest producers of satellite navigation systems in the world, comprised of both stand-alone devices and applications. It leads the navigation systems market in Europe while stands second in the United States. TomTom attributes its position as a market leader to the following factors: the size of its customer and technology base; its distribution power; and its prominent brand image and recognition.[19]

4 With the acquisition of Tele Atlas, TomTom has become vertically integrated and also controls the map creation process now. This has helped TomTom establish itself as an integrated content, service and technology business. The company is Dutch by origin and has its headquarters based in Amsterdam, Netherlands. In terms of geography, the company's operations span from Europe to Asia Pacific, covering North America, Middle East and Africa.[19]

5 TomTom is supported by a workforce of 3,300 employees from 40 countries. The diverse workforce enables the company to compete in international markets.[4] The company's revenues have grown from €8 million in 2002 to €1.674 billion in 2008. However, more recently, because of the Tele Atlas acquisition and the current economic downturn the company has become a cause of concern for investors. On 22 July 2009, TomTom reported a fall of 61% in its net income at the end of 2nd quarter 2009.[3]

6 TomTom is in the business of navigation based information services and devices. The company has been investing structurally and strategically in research and development to bring new and better products and services to its customers. The company's belief in radical innovation has helped it remain at the cutting edge of innovation within the navigation industry.

7 The vision of TomTom is to improve people's lives by transforming navigation from a 'don't-get-lost solution' into a true travel companion that gets people from one place to another safer, faster, cheaper and better informed. This vision has helped the company to be a market leader in every marketplace in the satellite navigation information services market.[6]

8 The objectives of the company focus around radical advances in three key areas:

9 ***Better Maps:*** This objective is achieved by maintaining TomTom's high quality map data base that is continuously kept up to date by a large community of active users who provide corrections, verifications and updates to TomTom. This is supplemented by inputs from TomTom's extensive fleet of surveying vehicles.[6]

10 ***Better Routing:*** TomTom has the world's largest historical speed profile data base IQ Routes™ facilitated by TomTom HOME, the company's user portal.[6]

11 ***Better Traffic Information:*** TomTom possesses unique real-time traffic information service TomTom HD traffic™ which provides users with high quality, real time traffic updates.[6] These three objectives form the base of satellite navigation, working in conjunction to help TomTom achieve its mission.

TOMTOM'S PRODUCTS

12 TomTom offers a wide variety of products ranging from portable navigation devices to software navigation applications and digital maps. The unique features in each of these products make them truly "the smart choice in personal navigation."[19] Some of these products are described below:

TomTom Go and TomTom One

13 These devices come with a LCD screen that makes it easy to use with fingertips while driving. They provide 1,000 Points of Interests (POI) that help in locating petrol stations,

restaurants and places of importance. A number of other POIs can also be downloaded. Precise, up-to-minute traffic information, jam alerts and road condition alerts are provided by both these devices.[3]

TomTom Rider

14 These are portable models especially for bikers. The equipment consists of an integrated GPS receiver that can be mounted on any bike and a wireless headset inside the helmet. Similar to the car Portable Navigation Devices (PNDs), the TomTom Rider models have a number of POI applications. The interfaces used in TomTom Rider are user friendly and come in a variety of languages.[3]

TomTom Navigator and TomTom Mobile

15 These applications provide navigation software along with digital maps. Both of these applications are compatible with most mobiles and PDAs, provided by companies like Sony, Nokia, Acer, Dell and HP. These applications come with TomTom HOME which can be used to upgrade to the most recent digital maps and application versions.[3]

TomTom for iPhone

16 On August 17, 2009, TomTom released TomTom for the iPhone. "With TomTom for iPhone, millions of iPhone users can now benefit from the same easy-to-use and intuitive interface, turn-by-turn spoken navigation and unique routing technology that our 30 million portable navigation device users rely on every day," said Corinne Vigreux, Managing Director of TomTom. "As the world's leading provider of navigation solutions and digital maps, TomTom is the most natural fit for an advanced navigation application on the iPhone."[6]

17 The TomTom app for iPhone 3G and 3GS users includes a map of the US and Canada from Tele Atlas, and is available for $99.99 USD.

18 The TomTom app for iPhone includes the exclusive IQ Routes™ technology. Instead of using travel time assumptions, IQ Routes bases its routes on the actual experience of millions of TomTom drivers to calculate the fastest route and generate the most accurate arrival times in the industry. TomTom IQ Routes empowers drivers to reach their destination faster up to 35% of the time.

COMPANY BACKGROUND

Company History

19 TomTom was founded as 'Palmtop' in 1991 by Peter-Frans Pauwels and Pieter Geelen, two graduates from Amsterdam University, Netherlands. Palmtop started out as a software development company and was involved in producing software for hand held computers, one of the most popular devices of the 90's. In the following few years the company diversified into producing commercial applications including software for personal finance, games, a dictionary and maps. In the year 1996, Corinne Vigreux joined Palmtop as the third partner. In the same year, the company announced the launch of Enroute and Route-Finder, the first navigation software titles. As more and more people using PCs adopted Microsoft's operating system, the company developed applications which were compatible with it. This helped the company increase its market share. The year 2001 marks the turning point in the history of TomTom. It was in this year that Harold Goddijn, the former Chief Executive of Psion joined the company as the fourth partner. Not only did Palmtop get renamed to TomTom, but it also entered the satellite navigation market. TomTom launched TomTom Navigator, the first mobile car satnav system. Since then, as can be

EXHIBIT 1 **Company History**

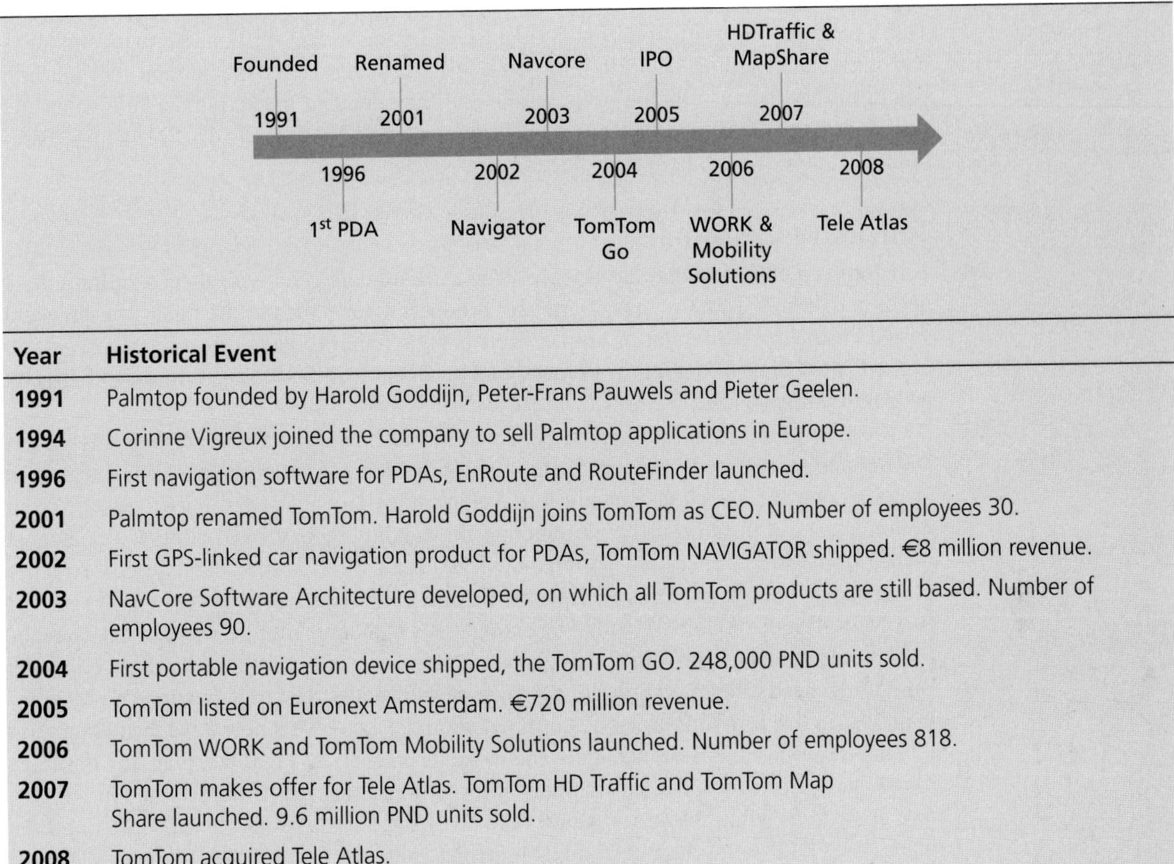

Year	Historical Event
1991	Palmtop founded by Harold Goddijn, Peter-Frans Pauwels and Pieter Geelen.
1994	Corinne Vigreux joined the company to sell Palmtop applications in Europe.
1996	First navigation software for PDAs, EnRoute and RouteFinder launched.
2001	Palmtop renamed TomTom. Harold Goddijn joins TomTom as CEO. Number of employees 30.
2002	First GPS-linked car navigation product for PDAs, TomTom NAVIGATOR shipped. €8 million revenue.
2003	NavCore Software Architecture developed, on which all TomTom products are still based. Number of employees 90.
2004	First portable navigation device shipped, the TomTom GO. 248,000 PND units sold.
2005	TomTom listed on Euronext Amsterdam. €720 million revenue.
2006	TomTom WORK and TomTom Mobility Solutions launched. Number of employees 818.
2007	TomTom makes offer for Tele Atlas. TomTom HD Traffic and TomTom Map Share launched. 9.6 million PND units sold.
2008	TomTom acquired Tele Atlas.

Source: http://investors.tomtom.com/overview.cfm

seen in **Exhibit 1**, the company has celebrated the successful launch of at least a product each year.[3]

20 In 2002, the company generated revenue of €8 million by selling the first GPS-linked car navigator, the TomTom Navigator to PDAs. The upgraded version, Navigator 2 was released in early 2003. Meanwhile, the company made efforts to gain technical and marketing personnel. TomTom took strategic steps to grow its sales. The former CTO of Psion, Mark Gretton, led the hardware team while Alexander Ribbink, a former top marketing official looked after sales of new products introduced by the company.

21 TomTom Go, an all in one car navigation system, was the next major launch of the company. With its useful and easy-to-use features TomTom Go was included in the list of successful products of 2004. In the same year, the company launched TomTom Mobile, a navigation system which sat on top of smart phones.[3]

22 TomTom completed its IPO on the Amsterdam Stock Exchange in May 2005. It raised €469 million ($587 million) from this offer. The net worth of the company was nearly €2 billion after the IPO. A majority of the shares were with the four partners.[5] From the years 2006 to 2008, TomTom strengthened itself by making three key strategic acquisitions. Datafactory AG was acquired to power TomTom WORK through WEBfleet technology, while Applied Generics gave its technology for Mobility Solutions Services. However, the most prominent of these three was the acquisition of Tele Atlas.[5]

23 In July of 2007, TomTom bid for Tele Atlas, a company specializing in digital maps. The original bid price of €2 billion was countered by a €2.3 billion offer from Garmin, TomTom's biggest rival. With TomTom raising the bid price to €2.9 billion, the two companies had initiated a bidding war for Tele Atlas. Although there was speculation that Garmin would further increase its bid price, in the end they decided not to pursue Tele Atlas any further. Rather, Garmin struck a content agreement with Navteq. Finally, TomTom's shareholders approved the takeover in December, 2007.[13]

TomTom's Customers

24 TomTom is a company that has a wide array of customers each with their own individual needs and desires. TomTom has a variety of products to meet the requirements of a large and varied customer base. As an example, their navigational products range from $100-$500 in the United States, ranging from lower end products with fewer capabilities, to high end products with advanced features.

25 The first group is the individual consumers who buy stand alone portable navigation devices and services. The second group is automobile manufacturers. TomTom has teamed up with companies such as Renault to develop built-in navigational units to install as an option in cars. A third group of customers is the aviation industry and pilots with personal planes. TomTom produces navigational devices for air travel at affordable prices. Another group of customers is business enterprises. Business enterprises refers to companies such as Wal-Mart, Target, or Home-Depot; huge companies with large mobile-workforces. To focus on these customers, TomTom formed a strategic partnership with a technology company called Advanced Integrated Solutions to "optimize business fleet organization and itinerary planning on the TomTom pro series of navigation devices". This new advanced feature on PNDs offers ways for fleet managers and route dispatchers to organize, plan and optimize routes and to provide detailed mapping information about the final destination. "Every day, companies with mobile workforces are challenged to direct all their people to all the places they need to go. Our customers appreciate having a central web repository to hold and manage all their location and address information," says Scott Wyatt, CEO of Advanced Integrated Solutions.[7] TomTom's last group of customers is the coast guards. They are able to use Tom-Tom's marine navigational devices for their everyday responsibilities.

Mergers and Acquisitions

26 TomTom has made various mergers and acquisitions as well as partnerships that have positioned the company well. In 2008 TomTom acquired a digital mapping company called Tele Atlas. The acquisition has significantly improve TomTom customers' user experience and created other benefits for the customers and partners of both companies, including: more accurate navigation information, improved coverage, and new enhanced features such as map updates and IQ routes which will be discussed in the scarce/unique resource section of the paper. Commenting on the proposed offer, Alain De Taeye, co-founder and CEO of Tele Atlas said:

> . . . the TomTom-Tele Atlas partnership signals a new era in the digital mapping industry. The combination of Tom-Tom's customer feedback tools and Tele Atlas' pioneering map production processes allows Tele Atlas to dramatically change the way digital maps are continuously updated and enhanced. The result will be a completely new level of quality, content and innovation that helps our partners deliver the best navigation products. This transaction is not only very attractive to our shareholders but demonstrates our longstanding commitment towards all of our partners and customers to deliver the best digital map products available.[1]

27 TomTom also formed a partnership with a company called Advanced Integrated Solutions, adding an itinerary planning and route guidance feature to the pro series of navigation devices to help businesses enterprises with large mobile-workforces. A few years ago they also partnered with Avis, adding their user-friendly navigation system to all Avis rental cars. This partnership began in Europe and recently the devices have made their way into Avis rental cars in North America as well many other countries where Avis operates. Harold Goddijn, chief executive officer of TomTom commented:

> Any traveler can relate to the stress of arriving in a new and unfamiliar city and getting horribly lost, with the availability of the TomTom GO 700 we're bringing unbeatable, full feature car navigation straight into the hands of Avis customers.[2]

28 TomTom has acquired several patents for all of their different technologies. By having these patents for each of its ideas, the company has protected itself against its competition and other companies trying to enter into the market.

29 TomTom prides itself on being the innovator in its industry and always being a step ahead of the competition in terms of its technology. On their website they say, "TomTom leads the navigation industry with the technological evolution of navigation products from static 'find-your-destination' devices into products and services that provide connected, dynamic 'find-the-optimal-route-to-your-destination', with time-accurate travel information. We are well positioned to maintain that leading position over the long-term because of the size of our customer and technology base, our distribution power, and our prominent brand image and recognition. By being vertically integrated and also control the map creation process TomTom is in a unique position to evolve into an integrated content, service and technology business."[6]

30 TomTom has a strong brand name/image. TomTom has positioned itself well throughout the world as the leader in portable navigation devices. It markets its products through its very user-friendly online website and also through large companies such as Best Buy and Wal-Mart. Recently TomTom teamed up with Locutio Voice Technologies and Twentieth Century Fox Licensing & Merchandising to bring the original voice of Homer Simpson to all TomTom devices via download. "Let Homer Simpson be your TomTom co-pilot" is just one of the many interesting ways TomTom markets its products and its name to its consumers.[9]

TomTom's Resources and Capabilities

31 The company believes that there are three fundamentals to a navigation system – digital mapping, routing technology and dynamic information. Based on these requirements three key resources can be identified that really distinguished TomTom from its competition.

32 The first of these resources is their in-house ***routing algorithms***. These algorithms enable them to introduce technologies like IQ Routes, that provides "community based information database". IQ Routes calculate your routes based on the real average speeds measured on roads at that particular time. Their website says, "The smartest route hour-by-hour, day-by-day, saving you time, money and fuel."[5]

33 The second unique resource identified was Tele Atlas and the ***digital mapping technology*** that the TomTom group specializes in. Having the technology and knowledge in mapping that the company brought to TomTom, has allowed them to introduce many unique features to their customers. Firstly, TomTom recently came out with a map update feature. The company recognizes that roads around the world are constantly changing and because of this they used the technology to come out with four new maps each year, one per business quarter. This allows their customers to always have the latest routes to incorporate into their everyday travel. A second feature they recently introduced is their MapShare program. The

idea behind this is that customers of TomTom who notice mistakes in a certain map are able to go in and request a change be made. The change is then verified and checked directly by TomTom and is shared with the rest of their global user community. "One and a half million map corrections have been submitted since the launch of TomTom Map Share™ in the summer of 2007."[5]

34 The third unique resource identified was ***automotive partnerships*** with two companies in particular; Renault and Avis. At the end of 2008, TomTom reached a deal with Renault to offer its navigation devices installed in their cars as an option. An article in Auto-week magazine said the following about the deal. "Renault developed its new low-cost system in partnership with Amsterdam-based technology company TomTom, the European leader in portable navigation systems. The system will be an alternative to the existing satellite navigation devices in Renault's upper-end cars."[8] The catch here is the new price of the built in navigation units. The cost of a navigation device installed in Renault's cars before TomTom was €1,500. Now with TomTom system it costs only €500. As talked about earlier in the paper, TomTom also partnered with Avis back in 2005 to offer its navigation devices, specifically the model GO700 in all Avis rental cars, first starting in Europe and expanding into other countries where Avis operates.

COMPETITION FACING TOMTOM

Traditional Competition

35 TomTom faces competition from two main companies. The first of these is Garmin which holds 45% of the market share, by far the largest and double Tom-Tom's market share (24%). Garmin was founded in 1989 by Gary Burrell and Min H. Kao. The company is known for their on-the-go directions since its introduction into GPS navigation in 1989. At the end of 2008, Garmin reported annual sales of $3493.1 million. Last year Garmin competed head-to-head with TomTom in trying to acquire Tele Atlas for their mapmaking. Garmin withdrew their bid when it became evident that it was becoming too expense to own Tele Atlas. Garmin executives made a decision that it was cheaper to work out a long-term deal with its current supplier than to try to buy out a competitor. Garmin's current supplier for map services is Navteq which was also acquired by Nokia in 2008.

36 The second direct competitor is Magellan, which holds 15% of the market share. Magellan is part of a privately held company under the name of MiTac Digital Corporation. Similar to Garmin, Magellan products use Navteq based maps. Magellan was the creator of Magellan NAV 100 that was the world's first commercial handheld GPS receiver which was created in 1989. The company is also well known for their award-winning RoadMate and Maestro series portable car navigation systems.

37 Together these three dominant players account for about 85% of the total market. Other competitors in the personal navigation device market are: Navigon, Nextar, and Nokia. Navigon and Nextar competes in the personal navigation devices with TomTom, Magellan, and Garmin who are the top three in the industry. But Navigon competes in the high-end segment which retails for more than any of the competitors but offer a few extra features in their PNDs. Nextar competes in the low-end market and its strategy is low cost. Finally, Nokia is mention as a competitor in this industry because they recently acquired Navteq who is a major supplier of map services in this industry. Along with that, Nokia has a big market share in the cell phone industry and plans on incorporating GPS technology in every phone making them a potential key player to look at in the GPS navigation industry.

New Competition

Cell Phones

38 Cell phones are a widely used technology by people all around the world. With the 2005 FCC mandate that requires the location of any cell phone used to call 911, phone manufacturers have now included GPS receiver in almost every cell phone. Due to this mandate, cell phone manufacturers and cellular services are now able to offer a GPS navigation services through the cell phone for a fee.

AT&T Navigator

39 GPS Navigation with AT&T Navigator and AT&T Navigator Global Edition feature real-time GPS enabled turn-by-turn navigation on AT&T mobile Smartphones (iPhone and BlackBerry) or static navigation and local search on a non-GPS AT&T mobile Smartphone.

40 AT&T Navigator features Global GPS turn-by-turn navigation—mapping and point of interest content for three continents, including North America (U.S., Canada, and Mexico), Western Europe, and China where wireless coverage is available from AT&T or its roaming providers. The AT&T Navigator is sold as a subscription service and costs $9.99 per month.

Online Navigation Applications

41 Online navigation websites that are still popular amongst many users for driving directions and maps are MapQuest, Google Maps, and Yahoo Maps. Users are able to use this free site to get detailed directions on how to get to their next destination. In today's economic downturn many people are looking for cheap, or if possible free solutions to solve their problems. These online websites offer the user free mapping and navigation information that will allow them to get what they need at no additional costs. However, there are downsides to these programs, "such as they are not portable and may have poor visualization designs (such as vague image, or text-based)."[12]

Built-In Car Navigation Devices

42 In car navigation devices first came about in more luxury, high-end vehicles. In today's market it has become more mainstream and now being offered in mid to lower tier vehicles. These built-in car navigation devices offer similar features to the personal navigation device but don't have the portability so you won't have to carry multiple devices but come with a hefty cost. Some examples of these are Kenwood, Pioneer, and Eclipse units all installed into your car. These units tend to be expensive and over-priced because of the fact that they are brand name products and require physical installation. For example, the top of the line Pioneer unit is $1,000 for the monitor and then another $500 for the navigation device plus the physical labor. When buying such products, a customer is spending a huge amount of money on a product that is almost identical to a product TomTom offers at significantly lower prices.

Physical Maps

43 Physical maps have been the primary option for navigating for decades until technology came around. Physical maps provide detailed road information to help a person get from point A to point B. Although cumbersome to use than some of the modern technology alternatives, it is an alternative for people who are not technically savvy or for whom a navigation device is an unnecessary luxury that they do not feel the need to spend money on.

POTENTIAL ADVERSE LEGISLATION AND RESTRICTIONS

44 In the legal and political realm, TomTom is facing two issues that are not critical now, but may have significant ramifications to not only TomTom in the future, but also the entire portable navigation device industry. TomTom's reactions to each of these issues will determine whether or not there is an opportunity for gain or a threat of a significant loss will occur.

45 The most important issue deals with the possible legislative banning of all navigational devices from automobiles. In Australia, there is growing concern over the distraction caused by PNDs and the legislature has taken the steps toward banning these devices entirely from automobiles.[26] There is a similar sentiment in Ontario, Canada where a law that is currently under review would ban all PNDs that were not mounted either to the dashboard or to the windshield itself.[27]

46 With the increase in legislation adding to the restrictions placed on PND devices, the threat that the PND market in the future will be severely limited cannot be ignored. All of the companies within the PND industry, not just TomTom, must create a coordinated and united effort to stem this tidal wave of restrictions as well as provide reassurance to the public that they are also concerned with the safe use of their products. An example of this opportunity comes from the toy industry where safety regulations are fast and furious at times. Many companies within the toy industry have combined to form the International Council of Toy Industries[23] to be proactive in regards to safety regulations as well as lobby governments on behalf of the toy industry against laws that may unfairly threaten the toy industry.[23]

47 The other issue within the legal and political spectrum that TomTom must focus on is the growing use of GPS devices as tracking devices. Currently, law enforcement agents are allowed to use their own GPS devices to track the movements and locations of individuals they deem to be suspicious, but how long will it be before budget cuts reduce the access to these GPS devices and then the simple solution will be to use the PND devices already installed in many automobiles?

48 This issue also requires the industry as whole to proactively work with the consumers and the government to come to an amicable resolution. The threat of having every consumer's GPS information at the finger tips of either the government or surveillance company will most certainly stunt or even completely halt any growth within the PND industry and that is why the industry must be on the offensive and not become a reactor.

49 Another alarming trend is the rise in PND thefts around the country.[22] With the prices for PNDs at a relatively high level, thieves are targeting vehicles that have visible docking stations for PNDs either on the dashboard or windshield. The onus will be on TomTom to create new designs that will help not only hide PNDs from would-be thieves but also deter them from ever trying to steal one. Consumers who are scared to purchase PNDs because of this rise in crime will become an issue if this problem is not resolved.

50 There is also a trend currently that is labeled the GREEN movement[29] that aims to reduce any activities that will endanger the environment. This movement is a great opportunity for TomTom to tout its technology as the smarter and more environmentally safe tool if driving is an absolute necessity. Not only can individuals tout this improved efficiency, but more importantly on a larger scale, businesses that require large amounts of materials to be transported across long stretches can show activists that they too are working to becoming a green company.

51 It is ironic that the core technology used in TomTom's navigation system, the GPS system, is proliferating into other electronic devices at such a rapid pace that it is causing serious competition to the PND industry. GPS functionality is virtually a requirement for all new smart phones that enter the market and soon will become a basic functionality in regular cellular phones. TomTom will be hard pressed to compete with these multifunctional devices unless they can improve upon their designs and transform themselves into just a single focused device.

52 Another concern not only for TomTom, but for every company that relies heavily on GPS technology, is the aging satellites that support the GPS system. Analysts predict that these satellites will be either replaced or fixed before there are any issues, but this issue is unsettling due to the fact that TomTom has no control over it.[24] TomTom will have to devise contingency plans in case of catastrophic failure of the GPS system much like what happened to Research in Motion when malfunctioning satellites caused disruption in their service.

53 Currently TomTom is one of the leading companies in the PND markets in both Europe and the United States. Although they are the leader in Europe, that market is showing signs of becoming saturated, and even though the U.S. market is currently growing, TomTom should not wait for the inevitable signs of that market's slowdown as well. TomTom needs to be proactive to the next big market instead of using its large resources to become a *fast follower*.

54 The two main opportunities for TomTom to expand, creating digital maps for developing countries and creating navigational services can either be piggybacked one on top of each other or can be taken in independent paths. The first-mover advantage for these opportunities will erect a high barrier of entry for any companies that do not have large amounts of resources to invest in the developing country. TomTom is already playing catch-up to Garmin and their already established service in India. Being proactive is an important and valuable opportunity that TomTom should take advantage of.

55 Globalization of any company's products does not come without a certain set of issues. For TomTom, the main threat brought on by foreign countries is twofold. The first threat which may be an isolated instance, but could also be repeated in many other countries is the restriction of certain capabilities for all of TomTom's products. Due to security and terrorism concerns, GPS devices are not allowed in Egypt since 2003.[28] In these times of global terrorism TomTom must be vigilant of the growing trend for countries to become overly protective of foreign companies and their technologies.

INTERNAL ENVIRONMENT

Finance

56 TomTom's current financial objectives are to diversify and become a broader revenue based company. The company not only seeks to increase the revenue base in terms of geographical expansion but also wants to diversify its product and service portfolio. Additionally, another important goal the company strives to achieve is to reduce its operating expenses.

57 ***Sales Revenue and Net Income***—In **Exhibit 2** it can be observed that from 2005 to 2007 there is a consistent growth in sales revenue and a corresponding increase in net income too. However, year 2008 is an exception to this trend. In this year sales revenue decreased by 3.7% and the net income decreased by 136%. In fact, in the first quarter the net income is actually negative totaling −€37 million. The decrease in sales can be accounted by the downturn in the economy. Actually, according to their 2008 annual report, the sales are in line with their expectations from the market. However, the net income plummeted much more than the decrease in sales. This was actually triggered by its acquisition of a digital mapping company – Tele Atlas, which was funded by both cash assets and debt.

1. **Quarterly sales**—In second quarter of 2009 TomTom received sales revenue of €368 million compared to €213 million in first quarter and €453 million in the same quarter last year (**Exhibit 3**). By evaluating quarterly sales for a three year period from 2007 till present, it is apparent that the sales do follow a seasonal trend in TomTom. With

EXHIBIT 6 Cash versus Long-Term Debt (in thousand €)

	12/31/2005	12/31/2006	12/31/2007	12/31/2008	6/30/2009
Long Term Debt	301	338	377	4,749	4,811
Cash Assets	178,377	437,801	463,339	321,039	422,530
Borrowings	0	0	0	1,241,900	1,195,715

EXHIBIT 7 Operating Margin

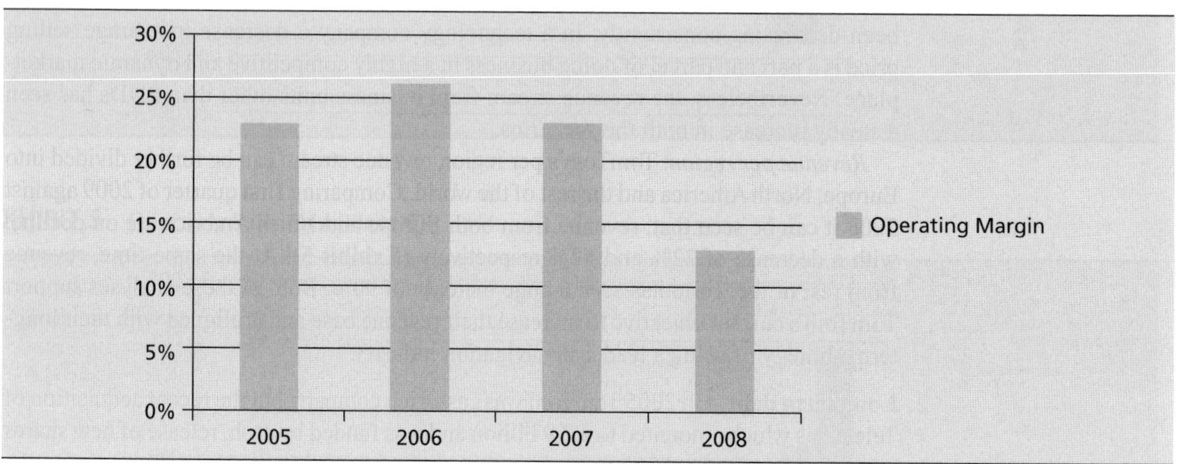

current customers are *early majority*, and hence, simplicity and ease alone could no longer provide it with competitive advantage.

59 Recently, to be in line with its immediate goal of diversifying into different market segment, TomTom is more focused on strengthening its brand name. In December 2008, TomTom's CEO stated – ". . . we are constantly striving to increase awareness of our brand and strengthen our reputation for providing smart, easy-to-use, high-quality portable navigation products and services."[19]

60 Along with Tele Atlas the group has gained the depth and breadth of expertise over the last 30 years, and this makes it a trusted brand. Three out of four people are aware of the brand of the TomTom business across the markets. The TomTom group has always been committed to three fundamentals of navigation – mapping, routing algorithm and dynamic information. Tele Atlas' core competency is the digital mapping database and TomTom's is routing algorithms and guidance services using dynamic information, and the group together create synergies that enable them to introduce products almost every year advancing on one or a combination of these three elements. Acquiring their long time supplier of digital maps, Tele Atlas, in 2008 gives them an edge with in-house digital mapping technology.

61 TomTom provides a range of PND devices like – TomTom One, TomTom XL and TomTom Go Series. Periodically, it tries to enhance those devices with new features and services, that they build based on the feedback from customers. Examples of services are IQ routes and LIVE services. While IQ routes provides drivers with the most efficient

route planning; accounting for situations as precise as speed bumps and traffic lights, LIVE services forms a range of information services delivered directly to the LIVE devices. The LIVE services bundle includes Map Share and HD Traffic – that is bringing the content collected from vast driving community directly to the end user.

62 These products and services accentuate effective designs and unique features, and require TomTom to work along with its customers to share precise updates and also get feedback for future improvements. Hence, effective customer interaction becomes essential to its long term goal of innovation. In 2008, J.D. Power and Associates recognized TomTom for providing outstanding customer service experience.[18] Although, it awarded TomTom for customer service satisfaction, J.D. Power and Associates ranked Garmin highest in overall customer satisfaction. TomTom followed Garmin in the ranking, performing well in the routing, speed of system and voice direction factors.[16]

63 As mentioned previously, when the navigation industry was still in its embryonic stages features, ease of use and high quality of its solutions gave TomTom products a competitive edge. Eventually, the competition increased in the navigation industry and even substitutes pose substantial threat to market share now. Currently, TomTom offers PNDs in different price ranges, broadly classified into high-range and mid-range PNDs, with an average selling price of €99. There are entry-level options that allow a savvy shopper to put navigation in his/her car for just over $100. Higher-end models add advanced features and services previously described.

64 TomTom sells its PNDs to consumers through retailers and distributors. After acquiring Tele Atlas it is strategically placed to gain the first mover advantage created by its rapid expansion of geographical coverage.[19] This is of key importance when it comes to increasing the global market share.

65 TomTom directs its marketing expenditure towards B2B advertising that is direct to retailers and distributors. TomTom also invested in an official blog website as well as search optimization which places it in premium results in online searches. This has enabled TomTom to do effective word-of-mouth promotion while keeping flexible marketing spending, in accordance to changes in the macroeconomic environment or seasonal trends.[19] Although, this approach gives it spending flexibility, it lacks a direct B2C approach. Currently only 21% US adults own PNDs while 65% US adults neither own nor use navigation.[14] By not spending on B2C marketing TomTom is discounting on the opportunity both to attract first-tier noncustomers and glean an insight of needs of second-tier noncustomers.[17]

Operations

66 The focus of operations has always been on innovation. More recently, TomTom's operational objective is to channel all the resources and core capabilities to create economies of scale so as to be aligned with their long term strategy. TomTom aims to focus and centralize R&D resources to create scale economies to continue to lead the industry in terms of innovation.[19]

67 Implementation of this strategy is well underway and the changes are visible. By second quarter of 2009 mid-range PNDs were introduced with capabilities from high-range devices, 50% of PNDs were soldwith IQ Routes Technology, first in-dash product was also launched in alliance with Renault and TomTom iPhone application was also announced.[19]

68 After aquiring Tele Atlas, to better support the broader navigation solutions and content and services, the group underwent restructuring. New organization structure consists of four business units, that have clear focus on a specific customer group and are supported by two shared development centers.

→ **TOMTOM GROUP**

TomTom B2C	Tele Atlas B2B	Work B2B	Automotive B2B
→ Consumers	→ PND → Automotive → Mobile → Internet → GIS	→ Commercial fleets	→ Car industry → Car industry suppliers
Dynamic Content & Publishing			
Shared Technologies			

69 TomTom's supply chain and distribution model is outsourced. This increases TomTom's ability to scale up or down the supply chain, while limiting capital expenditure risks. But, at the same time, it depends on a limited number of third parties and in certain instances sole suppliers, for component supply and manufacturing, which increases its dependency on these suppliers.

70 TomTom's dynamic content sharing model uses high quality digital maps along with the connected services, like HD Traffic, Local Search with Google and weather information, provides our customers with relevant real-time information at the moment they need it, and this is helping them deliver the benefits of innovative technology directly to the end user and that to now at affordable prices. Although, the network externalities previously mentioned are one of the advantages of TomTom's LIVE, it has also increased TomTom's dependency on the network of the connected driving community. Bigger the network will be, the more effective would be the information from the guidance services.

71 Furthermore, in order to reduce operating expenses and strengthen the balance sheet, undue emphasis has been placed on the cost cutting program. Currently the cost reductions are made up of reduction of staff, restructuring and integration of Tele Atlas, reduced discretionary spending and reduction in the number of contractors and marketing expenditures. However, if not executed wisely it could hamper TomTom's long term objective of being a market leader. For example one of the core capabilities of any technology company is its staff; reducing it can hinder future innovative projects. Likewise, reducing the marketing expenditures in a market which still holds rich prospects of high growth. There are still 65% of US adults who don't own any kind of navigation system either a device, or in-car, or that of phone.[14]

Human Resources

72 Like any other technology company success of individual employees is very important to TomTom. Additionaly, TomTom has a vision that success for TomTom as a business should also mean success for the individual employee. Therefore, at TomTom, employee competency is taken very seriously and talent development programs are built around it. There is a personal navigation plan that provides employees with a selection of courses based on competencies in their profile. In 2008 TomTom completed its Young Talent Development Program which was aimed at broadening the participants' knowledge, while improving their technical and personal skills.

73 TomTom's motto is to do business efficiently, profitably as well as responsibly. This underlines its corporate social responsibility. TomTom's headquarters is one of the most energy efficient buildings in Amsterdam. As mentioned before, earlier navigation was

oriented towards making the drivers arrive their their destintion without getting lost. TomTom was the pioneer in introducing different technology that actually helps drivers to make their journeys safer and more economical. This shows their commitment to their customer base as well as to the community as a whole.

ISSUES OF CONCERN FOR TOMTOM

74 First, TomTom is facing increasing competition from other platforms using GPS technology. Two main areas that come to mind are cell phones and smart phones. In the cell phone industry, Nokia is leading the charge in combining cell phone technology with GPS technology. They have a plan to put GPS technology in all their phones. Around the same time TomTom acquired Tele Atlas, Nokia also purchased Navteq, a competitor to Tele Atlas. With the acquisition of Navteq, Nokia hopes to shape the cell phone industry by merging cell phone, Internet, and GPS technology together.

75 As we see the Smartphone industry emerging with the IPhone and the Palm Pre, we also see a shift in how people are able to utilize these technologies as a navigation tool. A big trend in smart phones these days are applications. Because of the ease of developing software on platforms for smart phones, more and more competitors are coming to the forefront and developing GPS navigation application.

76 For TomTom, both of these sectors might signal major change is in the horizon and that there is no longer a need for hardware for GPS navigation devices. And that we're heading towards a culture where consumers want an all-in-one device such as cell phone or Smartphone that will do everything they need including a GPS navigation services. In a recent study done by Charles Golvin for Forrester, he believes that by 2013 phone-based navigation will dominate the industry. And the reason is due to Gen Y and Gen X customers who are increasingly reliant on their mobile phone and who will demand social networking and other connected services integrated into their navigation experience.[14]

77 The other problem TomTom is facing is a mature US & European personal navigation device market. After 3 years of steady growth in the PND market, TomTom has seen decreasing growth rate for PND sales. There could be many factors that are causing this such as the world wide recession but we felt that based on sales figures we're seeing the same trend in the US market as we have seen in the European market for TomTom. Initially entering the European market 12 months before entering the US market, TomTom has seen 21% dip in sales for the European market. Although, TomTom experiences some growth in the US market for 2008, they are noticing the growth rate has not been as good as the prior years.

APPENDIX

Google Drives into Navigation Market
REUTERS
Wed Oct 28, 2009 11:30am EDT

78 SAN FRANCISCO (Reuters)—Google Inc is adding Garmin Ltd and TomTom to its growing list of rivals as the Internet search giant weaves technology for driving directions into new versions of its smartphone software.

79 Google said its new Google Maps Navigation product will provide real-time, turn-by-turn directions directly within cell phones that are based on the new version of its Android software.

80 The navigation product, which features speech recognition and a visual display that incorporates Google's online archive of street photographs, marks the latest step by Google to challenge Apple Inc's iPhone and Microsoft Corp's Windows Mobile software with its Android smartphone software.

81 It also represents a direct competitive threat to companies like Garmin and TomTom which sell specialized hardware navigation devices. TomTom also makes a software navigation app for the iPhone that sells for $99.99 in the U.S.

82 Google executives told reporters at a press briefing on Tuesday ahead of the announcement that the company decided to offer turn-by-turn driving directions in its four-year-old maps product because it was the most requested feature by users.

83 CEO Eric Schmidt said that expanding into a new market with new competitors was not a part of Google's motivation.

84 "Those are tactical problems that occur after the strategic goal which is to offer something which is sort of magical on mobile devices using the cloud," Schmidt said.

85 The new navigation service will work with Google's forthcoming Android 2.0 software, the next version of the smartphone operating system developed by Google. The company announced development tools for Android 2.0 on Tuesday, but a spokeswoman said specific details about when Android 2.0 will be available should be directed to phone-makers and wireless carriers.

86 Google said the product, which will initially be limited to driving directions in the U.S., will be free for consumers.

87 Reporting by Alexei Oreskovic; Editing Bernard Orr

BIBLIOGRAPHY

1. TeleAtlas Press Release. <http://www.teleatlas.com/WhyTeleAtlas/Pressroom/PressReleases/TA_CT015133>.
2. TomTom press release. TomTom and Avis Announce the First Pan-European Deal to Provide TomTom GO.
3. Compare GPS Sat Nav Systems. <http://www.satellitenavigation.org.uk/gps-manufacturers/tomtom/>.
   Daniel, Robert. TomTom Net Fell 61%, Revenue Off 19%. <http://www.foxbusiness.com/story/markets/industries/telecom/tomtom-net-fell--revenue/>.
4. TomTom Challenge. <http://www.tomtomchallenge.nl/resources/AMGATE_400083_1_TICH_R76719135691/>.
5. TomTom NV. <http://www.answers.com/topic/tomtom-n-v>.
6. TomTom. TomTom, portable GPS car navigation systems. <http://investors.tomtom.com/overview.cfm>.
7. Advanced Integrated Solutions. TomTom and Advantage Integrated Solutions Partner to Deliver an Intelligent Fleet Routing Solution for Businesses. March 2009. <http://www.highbeam.com/doc/1G1-196311252.html>.
8. Auto-Week Article. Renault, TomTom promise cheap navigation. <http://www.autoweek.com/article/20080929/free/809299989#ixzz0MQ8bKdYo>.
9. Boston Business Article. <http://www.boston.com/business/ticker/2009/06/let_homer_simps.html)>.
10. Garmin Website. <http://www8.garmin.com/aboutGarmin/>.
11. Gis Development Article. <http://www.gisdevelopment.net/technology/lbs/techlbs008.htm>.

12. Magellan website. <http://www.magellangps.com/about/>.
13. Thomson Reuters. TomTom launches 2.9 bln euro bid for Tele Atlas. 19 November 2007. <http://www.reuters.com/article/technology-media-telco-SP/idUSL1839698320071119>.
14. Forrestor Research. "Phone-Based Navigation Will Dominate By 2013." 27 March 2009.
15. Hanstad, L. Anne. TomTom VP of Marketing Fletch. 27 September 2006.
16. J.D. Power and Associates. Garmin Ranks Highest in Customer Satisfaction with Portable Navigation Devices. 23 October 2008. <http://www.jdpower.com/corporate/news/releases/pressrelease.aspx?ID=2008221>.
17. Kim, W. Chan and Mauborgne. Blue Ocean Strategy. Boston: Harvard Business School Press, 2005.
18. Reuters . TomTom Inc. Recognized for Call Center Customer Satisfaction Excellence by J.D. Power. 7 January 2008. <http://www.reuters.com/article/pressRelease/idUS141391+07-Jan-2008+PRN20080107>.
19. TomTom AR-08. "TomTom Annual Report 2008." TomTom Annual Report 2008. December 2008.
20. TomTom Q2 2009. "Investor relations." TomTom Website. <http://investors.tomtom.com/reports.cfm?year=2009>.
21. Foley, Ryan. Chicago Tribune. 7 May 2009. 29 July 2009 <http://archives.chicagotribune.com/2009/may/07/news/chi-ap-wi-gps-police>.
22. GPS Magazine. GPS Magazine. 23 September 2007. 29 July 2009 <http://gpsmagazine.com/2007/09/gps_thefts_rise.php>.
23. ICTI. ICTI. 2009. 29 July 2009 <http://www.toy-icti.org/>.
24. Jones, Nick. Garnter. 5 January 2009. 29 July 2009 <http://www.gartner.com/resources/168400/168438/findings_risks_of_gps_perfor_168438.pdf>.
25. PriceGrabber.com. Price Grabber. April 2007. 29 July 2009 <https://mr.pricegrabber.com/2007_GPS_Pricing_Trends_Report.pdf>.
26. Richards, David. Smarthouse. 17 June 2009. 29 July 2009 <http://www.smarthouse.com.au/Automotive/Navigation/P4P3H9J8>.
27. Talaga, Tanya and Rob Ferguson. TheStar.com. 28 Oct 2008. 29 July 2009 <http://www.thestar.com/News/Ontario/article/525697>.
28. US News. US News. 14 October 2008. 29 July 2009 <http://usnews.rankingsandreviews.com/cars-trucks/daily-news/081014-GPS-Devices-Banned-in-Egypt/>.
29. Webist Media. Web Ecoist. 17 August 2008. 29 July 2009 <http://webecoist.com/2008/08/17/a-brief-history-of-the-modern-green-movement/>.

Case 26

Toyota: *The Accelerator Crisis*

Michael Greto
Andreas Schotter
Mary Teagarden

> *The root cause of their problems is that the company was hijacked, some years ago, by anti-family, financially oriented pirates.*
>
> *— Jim Press, former President & Chief Operating Officer (COO)*
> *Toyota Motor Sales, U.S.A., Inc.*

1 On February 24, 2010, Akio Toyoda, the grandson of Toyota Motor Corporation's founder, Kiichiro Toyoda, endured a grueling question-and-answer session before the U.S. House of Representatives Committee on Oversight and Government Reform. The committee represented just one of three Congressional panels investigating the 2009–2010 recall of Toyota vehicles related to problems of sudden acceleration and the company's delay in responding to the crisis.

2 Signs of the coming recall crisis began as early as 2006 when the National Highway Traffic Safety Administration (NHTSA) opened an investigation into driver reports of "surging" in Toyota's Camry models. The NHTSA investigation was closed the next year, citing no defects. Over the next four years, Toyota, known in the industry for its quality and reliability, would quietly recall nearly nine million Toyota and Lexus models due to sudden acceleration problems. Toyota's leadership, widely criticized for its slow response in addressing the problems, now had to move quickly to identify a solution that would ensure the safety of its vehicles, restore consumer confidence, protect the valuable Toyota brand, and recoup a plummeting share price.

3 Akio Toyoda testified:

> I fear the pace at which we have grown may have been too quick. I would like to point out here that Toyota's priority has traditionally been the following: First, Safety; Second, Quality; and Third, Volume. These priorities became confused, and we were not able to stop, think, and make improvements as much as we were able to before, and our basic stance to listen to customers' voices to make better products has weakened somewhat.
>
> We pursued growth over the speed at which we were able to develop our people and our organization, and we should sincerely be mindful of that. I regret that this has resulted in the safety issues described in the recalls we face today, and I am deeply sorry for any accidents that Toyota drivers have experienced.[1]

4 Exhausted from his testimony, Mr. Toyoda's mind surely reeled as he wondered what challenges led to the current recall crisis. Had the company lost sight of its long-term philosophy, a key principle behind the *Toyota Way?* Had Toyota sacrificed quality at the expense of extreme cost reductions? Were nonfamily managers to blame for "hijacking" Toyota? Was Toyota simply subject to the latest media witch hunt in the wake of the global economic crisis? Clearly, Mr. Toyoda had much to do to address the problems of the recent past and restore confidence in his company and the brand moving forward.

[1] http://www.toyota.com/about/news/corporate/2010/02/24-1-testimony.html.

THE GLOBAL AUTOMOBILE INDUSTRY

5 In 2008, the global automobile industry was estimated to be a US$1.9 trillion business. This represented a 19% decrease from a high of US$2.2 trillion in 2007, just before the global financial crisis. Global industry values are shown in **Exhibit 1**. The Asia-Pacific region accounted for the largest industry segment, with slightly more than US$644 billion in sales, 36% of the global market; followed by the Americas with a 31% share, or US$548 billion in sales. The European market held a 27% share, or US$480 billion, in sales. Despite the global automotive industry's fluctuating growth rates during the 2004–2007 period, the industry was expected to experience a fast recovery during the following years. Industry experts forecasted that the compounded annual growth rate (CAGR) would be at or above 4.5% during the 2008–2013 period.[2]

6 The global automotive market is highly concentrated. The top four manufacturers—including Toyota Motor Corporation with 12.8% market share, General Motors Corporation with 8.9%, Chrysler 8.1%, and the Ford Motor Company with 7.8%—dominated the global market (see **Exhibit 2**). Industry competition was intense, both at a global level and at the

EXHIBIT 1 **Global Automobiles Industry Value: $ Billion, 2004–2008**

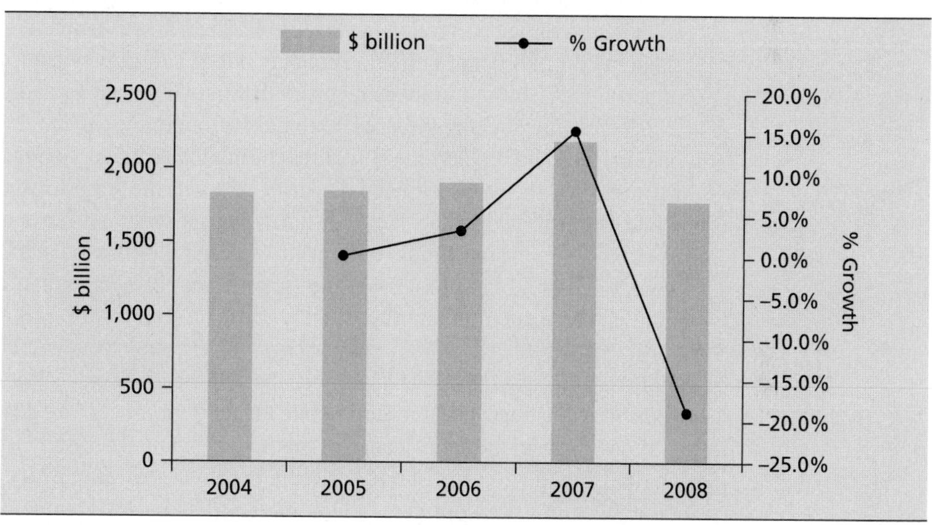

EXHIBIT 2 **Global Automobiles Industry Share: % Share, by Value, 2008**

Company	% Share
Toyota Motor Corporation	12.80
General Motors Corporation	8.90
Daimler AG	8.10
Ford Motor Company	7.80
Other	62.40
Total	100.00

Source: *Datamonitor.*

[2] Global Automobiles Industry Profile, *Datamonitor,* March 2009.

EXHIBIT 3 U.S. Automobiles Industry Share: % Share, by Value, 2009

Company	% Share
Toyota Motor Corporation	17.80
Ford Motor Company	17.50
General Motors Corporation	14.50
Honda Motor Company, Limited	11.80
Chrysler Group LLC	7.50
Other	30.90

Source: *IBISWorld.*

country level. The mature U.S. market was especially contested, with all manufacturers offering big discounts and low- to no-interest financing virtually year-round. By early 2009, the U.S had more than one car per capita registered.

7 While the U.S. auto industry historically dominated the global market, the "Big Three," as General Motors (GM), Chrysler, and Ford were referred to in the United States, had reported profit erosion since 2005. Unable to reduce skyrocketing debt, Chrysler and GM sought bankruptcy protection in early 2009. The U.S. government ultimately took a majority stake in GM in order to help the company out of bankruptcy protection. In April 2010, GM repaid US$8.1 billion in loans received from the U.S. and Canadian governments.

8 Meanwhile, the Japan-based automakers operating in the U.S. (Toyota, Honda, and Nissan) fared better than the Big Three during the global economic crisis. Industry analysts believed that the reason for the disparity between the American and Japanese automakers could be attributed to the fact that the Japanese were not burdened by legacy costs such as expensive pension funds, unionized workers, and the insistence that consumers would always demand big vehicles. At the same time, however, Japanese automakers produced smaller, more environmentally friendly compact cars for the U.S. market.

9 In 2008, Toyota took the number one spot in terms of new car sales, selling vehicles in more than 170 countries.[3] GM had been the historic global sales leader for more than 80 years. **Exhibit 3** illustrates the U.S. automobile industry's market share distribution. Both Toyota and GM downplayed the significance of this achievement. According to Toyota spokesman Steve Curtis, "Being No. 1 in volume has never been our goal. Being No. 1 in quality and customer experience has been our goal."[4] Despite the global sales volume gain, Toyota reported revenues of US$211 billion for 2009, a decrease of 19% from the previous year. This decrease was largely caused by the impact of fluctuations in foreign currency rates and decreased parts sales.[5] By 2010, China had overtaken the U.S. to become the world's largest automotive market. GM's China President, Kevin Wale, concluded, "It is not a blip…"[6]

TOYOTA MOTOR CORPORATION

10 Headquartered in Japan, Toyota Motor Corporation was established in 1933 as a division of Toyoda Automatic Loom Works under the direction of Kiichiro Toyoda. In 1934, the company produced its first Type A engine at the encouragement of the Japanese

[3] http://www.reuters.com/article/idUSTRE60A1BQ20100111.

[4] http://money.cnn.com/2009/01/21/news/companies/gm_toyota_sales/.

[5] Hoover's "Toyota Motor Corporation" Report, 2009.

[6] http://www.thetruthaboutcars.com/chinese-car-sales-break-sound-barrier/.

government, and two years later the company produced its first passenger car, the Toyota AA.

11 In 1937, The Toyota Motor Corporation was established as an independent company. During World War II, the company focused solely on truck production for the Imperial Japanese Army. Only after the war, in 1947, did Toyota resume production of passenger cars. By the early 1950s, Toyota was on the verge of bankruptcy until an order of more than 5,000 vehicles from the U.S. military for its war efforts in Korea revived the company.[7]

12 Recognizing a growing market in the United States, in 1957 Toyota established its first sales, marketing, and distribution subsidiary in the U.S., called Toyota Motor Sales Inc. (TMS). In the early 1960s, the U.S. introduced stringent import tariffs on certain foreign vehicles. In response, Honda and Nissan began building manufacturing plants in the U.S. In 1982, Toyota Motor Corporation formed a joint venture with General Motors, called NUMMI (New United Motor Manufacturing, Inc.). NUMMI established operations in a General Motors plant in Fremont, California, that was closed, and employed workers who had been laid off when the plant closed two years earlier. Toyota considered the NUMMI joint venture a learning opportunity.

13 Toyota Motor Manufacturing, U.S.A. (TMM) began production in the U.S. in 1988 and established new brands for this market. In 2009, TMM employed more than 8,900 people and supervised 14 regional offices throughout the 50 states.[8] Toyota produced 5.2 million cars in 58 production sites in 2000, and by 2009 they had the capacity to produce 10 million cars and had added 17 production sites. Basically, Toyota had added the capacity of a Chrysler-sized company. Over the years, Toyota diversified into several nonautomotive businesses, including aerospace, higher education, robotics, finance, and agricultural biotechnology. **Exhibit 4** illustrates Toyota's globalization timeline.

EXHIBIT 4 **Toyota Globalization Timeline**

	The Americas	Europe/Africa	Oceania/Asia/Middle East/China
1950s	1957: First Crown export 1957: Toyota Motor Sales, U.S.A., Inc. established 1958: Toyota do Brasil S.A. starts operations		
1960s			1962: Toyota Motor Thailand Co., Ltd. established
1970s	1973: Calty Design Research, Inc. established 1977: Toyota Technical Center U.S.A., Inc. established		
1980s	1984: Toyota-GM joint venture in the U.S., New United Motor Manufacturing, Inc. (NUMMI), starts production 1988: Toyota Motor Manufacturing, Kentucky, Inc. (TMMK) starts production 1989: Lexus dealerships established in the U.S.	1987: TMME Technical Center established	

(Continued)

[7] http://www2.toyota.co.jp/en/history/.

[8] Hoover's "TMS USA" Report, 2009.

EXHIBIT 4 *(Continued)*

	The Americas	Europe/Africa	Oceania/Asia/Middle East/China
1990s	1998: Toyota Motor Manufacturing Indiana, Inc. (TMMI) and Toyota Motor Manufacturing, West Virginia, Inc. (TMMWV) start operations	1990: Toyota Motor Europe Marketing & Engineering S.A. (TMME) established 1992: Toyota Motor Manufacturing (U.K.), Ltd. (TMUK) starts production 1998: Construction of new plant in France announced	1998: Tianjin Toyota Motor Engine Co., Ltd. (TTME) starts operations 1999: Toyota Kirloskar Motor, Ltd. starts operations (India)
2000–2005	2001: Toyota Motor Manufacturing, Alabama, Inc. (TMMAL) established 2002: Toyota Motor Manufacturing de Baja California S. de R.L. de C. V. (TMMBC) established (Mexico)	2001: Toyota Motor Manufacturing France S.A.S. (TMMF) starts production 2002: Toyota Peugeot Citroën Automobile Czech (TPCA) established 2002: Toyota Motor Manufacturing Poland Sp.zo.o.(TMMP) starts production 2002: Toyota Motor Industries Poland Sp.zo.o.(TMIP) established 2005: Production of the Toyota Aygo starts at TPCA (Czech Republic) 2005: Toyota Motor Manufacturing Russia Ltd. (TMMR) established	2000: Sichuan Toyota Motor Co., Ltd. (SCTM) starts production (China) 2002: Toyota Kirloskar Auto Parts Private Ltd. (TKAP) established (India) 2003: FAW Toyota Motor Sales Co., Ltd. (FTMS) established (China) 2004: Toyota FAW (Tianjin) Dies Co., Ltd. (TFTD) established (China) 2004: Toyota FAW (Changchun) Engine Co., Ltd. (FTCE) established (China) 2004: IMV series Hilux Vigo launched (Thailand) 2004: Guangzhou Toyota Motor Co., Ltd. (GTMC) established (China)
2006	Feb.: Opening of the NAPSC March: Agreement reached to subcontract production to Subaru of Indiana Automotive, Inc. (SIA) (production to start in spring 2007) April: Establishment of the TEMA May: TMMK, TMMI, and TMMWV celebrate 20th anniversary Sep.: Toyota Motor Manufacturing Canada Inc. (TMMC) celebrates 20th anniversary Oct.: TMMK starts production of the Camry Hybrid Nov.: Toyota Motor Manufacturing, Texas, Inc. (TMMTX) starts production of the Tundra	Jan.: Expansion of TME-TC Mar.: Opening of the E-GPC	May: Production of the Camry starts in Guangzhou, China Aug.: Establishment of Training Course at the AP-GPC

Source: *Toyota.*

14 In the spring of 2009, Toyota named 52-year-old, U.S.-educated Akio Toyoda, a member of its founding family, as new president. In announcing Mr. Toyoda's appointment, the company said it needed someone with a youthful perspective who could carry out changes and reverse the company's decline. In the company's recent past, Mr. Toyoda would have been seen by senior management, known for its conservatism, as too young and inexperienced to take the helm. This unprecedented move happened as the company faced what it thought was its biggest crisis in decades—sales were dropping around the world. Mr. Toyoda, a critic of the company's management, believed that they had allowed Toyota to overextend itself in relentless pursuit of unseating GM as the world's biggest automaker.

15 When Mr. Toyoda took over, the company was on the cusp of being the world's largest automaker. Industry analysts assert that this victory came at an enormous price. Aggressive plant and model rollouts in new markets from India and China to the U.S. and Brazil had strained the company's resources, led the company to misread the market, to produce faulty products, and to build underutilized plants.

16 Toyota's problems paled by comparison to other automakers that were all facing crippling challenges caused by the world's economic crisis and their own inefficiencies. In the face of declining sales, Toyota began operating in crisis mode and undertook penny-pinching measures, like turning down thermostats, curbing production, slashing management bonuses, and laying off thousands of temporary workers. The company anticipated that after the financial crisis, they would be positioned to assert global leadership in the automotive industry. Mr. Toyoda was expected to make swift changes, including a management shakeup, and committed to lead Toyota's comeback by putting customers first. "I will go back to the basics of the foundation of the company," said Mr. Toyoda. "I intend to exercise as much boldness as possible in pushing ahead with the reforms."[9]

The Toyota Way

17 From its humble family business origins, Toyota had revolutionized management, manufacturing, and production philosophies. Many business scholars praised its values and business methods and, as a result, the *Toyota Way* was adopted by many other businesses in a wide variety of industries. The *Toyota Way* mandates planning for the long term; highlighting problems instead of hiding them; encouraging team work with colleagues and suppliers; and, perhaps most importantly, instilling a self-critical culture that fosters continuous and unrelenting improvement. From the assembly line to the boardroom, Toyota's principles push employees to strive for perfection.

18 In 2001, the company officially launched the "*Toyota Way 2001*" that included 14 management principles in four broad categories, shown in **Exhibit 5**. In light of Toyota's global expansion, Koki Konishi, a company general manager, alluding to the difficulty Toyota could face, told the *New York Times* in 2007:

> There is a sense of danger. We must prevent the Toyota Way from getting more and more diluted as Toyota grows overseas.[10]

[9] John Murphy, Norihiko Shirouzu, "Corporate News: Toyota Management Heads Toward a Shakeup—Amid Sales Crisis, New President Promises 'Bold' Moves; Executives Are Viewed as Conservative, Bureaucratic." *Wall Street Journal.* (Eastern edition). New York, N.Y.: Jan 21, 2009. pg. B.3.

[10] Martin Fackler, "The 'Toyota Way' Is Translated for a New Generation of Foreign Managers," *The New York Times,* February 15, 2007.

EXHIBIT 5 14 Principles of the "Toyota Way"

Section I: Long-Term Philosophy

Principle 1. Base your management decisions on a long-term philosophy, even at the expense of short-term financial goals.

- Have a philosophical sense of purpose that supersedes any short-term decision-making. Work, grow, and align the whole organization toward a common purpose that is bigger than making money. Understand your place in the history of the company, and work to bring the company to the next level. Your philosophical mission is the foundation for all the other principles.
- Generate value for the customer, society, and the economy—it is your starting point. Evaluate every function in the company in terms of its ability to achieve this.
- Be responsible. Strive to decide your own fate. Act with self-reliance and trust in your own abilities. Accept responsibility for your conduct, and maintain and improve the skills that enable you to produce added value.

Section II: The Right Process Will Produce the Right Results

Principle 2. Create a continuous process flow to bring problems to the surface.

- Redesign work processes to achieve high value-added, continuous flow. Strive to cut back to zero the amount of time that any work project is sitting idle or waiting for someone to work on it.
- Create flow to move material and information fast as well as to link processes and people together so that problems surface right away.
- Make flow evident throughout your organizational culture. It is the key to a true continuous improvement process and to developing people.

Principle 3. Use "pull" systems to avoid overproduction.

- Provide your down-line customers in the production process with what they want, when they want it, and in the amount they want. Material replenishment initiated by consumption is the basic principle of just-in-time.
- Minimize your work in process and warehousing of inventory by stocking small amounts of each product and frequently restocking based on what the customer actually takes away.
- Be responsive to the day-by-day shifts in customer demand rather than relying on computer schedules and systems to track wasteful inventory.

Principle 4. Level out the workload (heijunka). (Work like the tortoise, not the hare.)

- Eliminating waste is just one-third of the equation for making lean successful. Eliminating overburden to people and equipment and eliminating unevenness in the production schedule are just as important—yet generally not understood at companies attempting to implement lean principles.
- Work to level out the workload of all manufacturing and service processes as an alternative to the stop/start approach of working on projects in batches that is typical at most companies.

Principle 5. Build a culture of stopping to fix problems, to get quality right the first time.

- Quality for the customer drives your value proposition.
- Use all the modern quality assurance methods available.
- Build into your equipment the capability of detecting problems and stopping itself. Develop a visual system to alert team or project leaders that a machine or process needs assistance. Jidoka (machines with human intelligence) is the foundation for "building in" quality.
- Build into your organization support systems to quickly solve problems and put in place countermeasures.
- Build into your culture the philosophy of stopping or slowing down to get quality right the first time to enhance productivity in the long run.

Principle 6. Standardized tasks and processes are the foundation for continuous improvement and employee empowerment.

- Use stable, repeatable methods everywhere to maintain the predictability, regular timing, and regular output of your processes. It is the foundation for flow and pull.
- Capture the accumulated learning about a process up to a point in time by standardizing today's best practices. Allow creative and individual expression to improve upon the standard; then incorporate it into the new standard so that when a person moves on, you can hand off the learning to the next person.

EXHIBIT 5 *(Continued)*

Principle 7. Use visual control so no problems are hidden.

- Use simple visual indicators to help people determine immediately whether they are in a standard condition or deviating from it.
- Avoid using a computer screen when it moves the worker's focus away from the workplace.
- Design simple visual systems at the place where the work is done, to support flow and pull.
- Reduce your reports to one piece of paper whenever possible, even for your most important financial decisions.

Principle 8. Use only reliable, thoroughly tested technology that serves your people and processes.

- Use technology to support people, not to replace people. Often, it is best to work out a process manually before adding technology to support the process.
- New technology is often unreliable and difficult to standardize and therefore endangers "flow." A proven process that works generally takes precedence over new and untested technology.
- Conduct actual tests before adopting new technology in business processes, manufacturing systems, or products.
- Reject or modify technologies that conflict with your culture or that might disrupt stability, reliability, and predictability.
- Nevertheless, encourage your people to consider new technologies when looking into new approaches to work. Quickly implement a thoroughly considered technology if it has been proven in trials and it can improve flow in your processes.

Section III: Add Value to the Organization by Developing Your People

Principle 9. Grow leaders who thoroughly understand the work, live the philosophy, and teach it to others.

- Grow leaders from within, rather than buying them from outside the organization.
- Do not view the leader's job as simply accomplishing tasks and having good people skills. Leaders must be role models of the company's philosophy and way of doing business.
- A good leader must understand the daily work in great detail, so he or she can be the best teacher of your company's philosophy.

Principle 10. Develop exceptional people and teams who follow your company's philosophy.

- Create a strong, stable culture in which company values and beliefs are widely shared and lived out over a period of many years.
- Train exceptional individuals and teams to work within the corporate philosophy to achieve exceptional results. Work very hard to reinforce the culture continually.
- Use cross-functional teams to improve quality and productivity and enhance flow by solving difficult technical problems. Empowerment occurs when people use the company's tools to improve the company.
- Make an ongoing effort to teach individuals how to work together as teams toward common goals. Teamwork is something that has to be learned.

Principle 11. Respect your extended network of partners and suppliers by challenging them and helping them improve.

- Have respect for your partners and suppliers, and treat them as an extension of your business.
- Challenge your outside business partners to grow and develop. It shows that you value them. Set challenging targets and assist your partners in achieving them.

Section IV: Continuously Solving Root Problems Drives Organizational Learning

Principle 12. Go and see for yourself to thoroughly understand the situation (genchi genbutsu).

- Solve problems and improve processes by going to the source and personally observing and verifying data rather than theorizing on the basis of what other people or the computer screen tell you.
- Think and speak based on personally verified data.
- Even high-level managers and executives should go and see things for themselves, so they will have more than a superficial understanding of the situation.

(Continued)

EXHIBIT 5 *(Continued)*

Principle 13. Make decisions slowly by consensus, thoroughly considering all options; implement decisions rapidly (nemawashi).

- Do not pick a single direction and go down that one path until you have thoroughly considered alternatives. When you have picked, move quickly and continuously down the path.
- Nemawashi is the process of discussing problems and potential solutions with all of those affected, to collect their ideas and get agreement on a path forward. This consensus process, though time-consuming, helps broaden the search for solutions, and once a decision is made, the stage is set for rapid implementation.

Principle 14. Become a learning organization through relentless reflection (hansei) and continuous improvement (kaizen).

- Once you have established a stable process, use continuous improvement tools to determine the root cause of inefficiencies, and apply effective countermeasures.
- Design processes that require almost no inventory. This will make wasted time and resources visible for all to see. Once waste is exposed, have employees use a continuous improvement process (kaizen) to eliminate it.
- Protect the organizational knowledge base by developing stable personnel, slow promotion, and very careful succession systems.

Source: J. Liker, 2004. *The 14 Principles of the Toyota Way: An Executive Summary of the Culture Behind TPS,* p. 37. Ann Arbor, MI: University of Michigan.

19 Developed by Toyota and incorporated in the *Toyota Way* is the Toyota Production System (TPS). TPS, commonly referred to as the precursor of "lean manufacturing" principles, was originally called "Just-in-Time" production, and is undergirded by the philosophy that "Good Thinking Means Good Product."

20 Company documents describe TPS:

> The Toyota Production System (TPS) was established based on two concepts: The first is called "jidoka" (loosely translated as "automation with a human touch"), which means that when a problem occurs, the equipment stops immediately, preventing defective products from being produced; the second is the concept of "just-in-time," in which each process produces only what is needed by the next process in a continuous flow.[11]

21 In essence, the system was designed to remove all unnecessary waste *(muda)* from the production and manufacturing process. More than just waste avoidance, it aimed to eliminate any excess interruption, misalignment, unnecessary work, or redundancies in the production process that add no value to customers. Specifically, TPS addressed seven kinds of waste: overproduction, operator motion, waiting, conveyance, self-processing, inventory, and correction (rework and scrap). Through TPS, Toyota had been able to significantly reduce lead time and production costs.

22 TPS evolved into a world-renowned production system, effectively injecting a new vocabulary and *modus operandi* into industries beyond automobile manufacturing. For example, companies in the construction and health care industries adopted and adapted the principles of the TPS for their own operations. The efficiency improvements caused by better logistics systems and a quality focus, resulting in significant cost savings, became standard practices in many Japanese and non-Japanese companies.

23 William G. Hunter, a professor and quality expert, visited Toyota and other leading Japanese firms in the 1980s to study what scholars called the "Japanese Miracle." His

[11] This section relies on two sources: http://www2.toyota.co.jp/en/vision/production_system/, and http://www.leanuk.org/downloads/general/leaning_toward_utopia.pdf.

EXHIBIT 6 **Toyoto's Management Structure as Depicted by William Hunter**

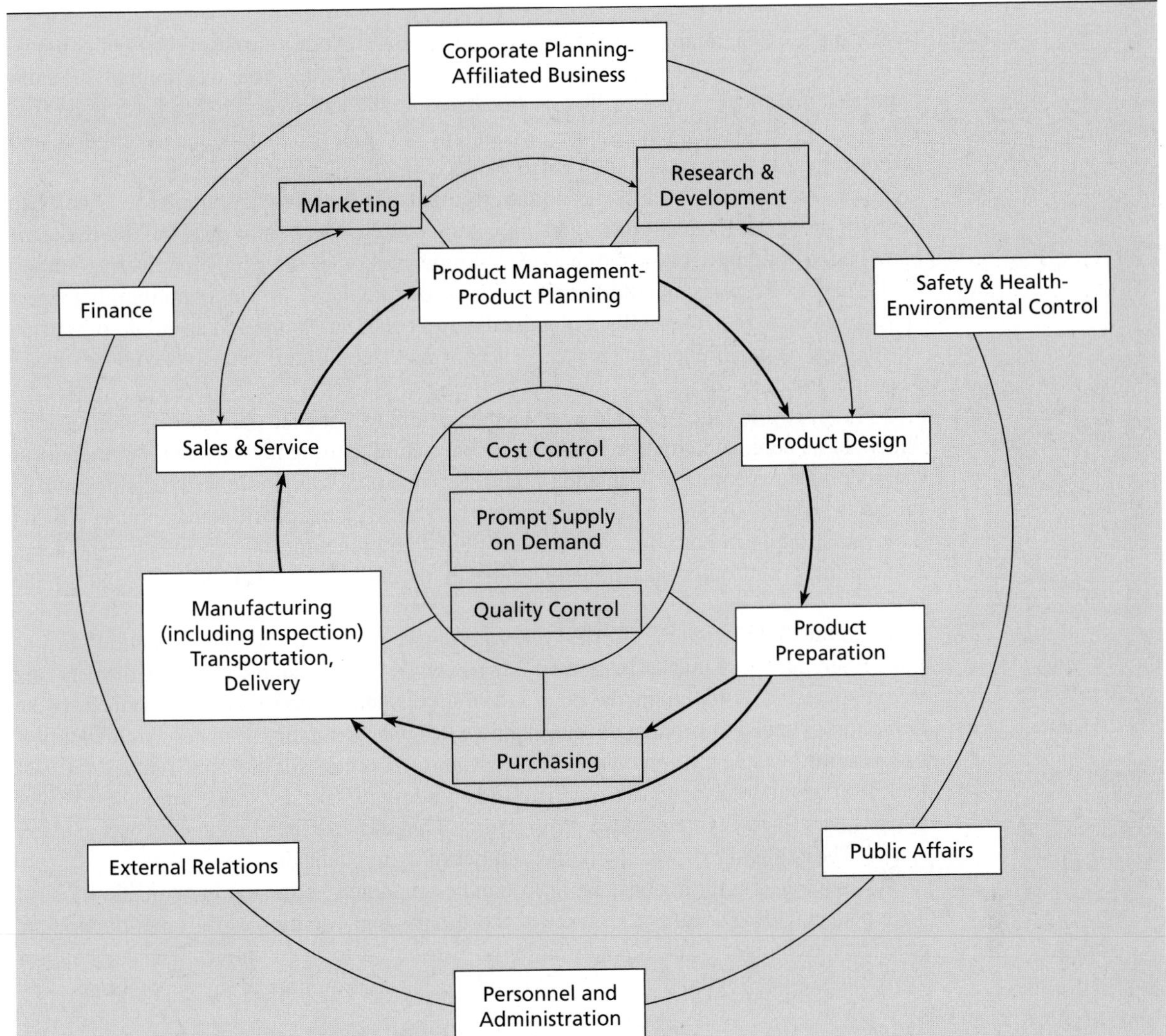

conclusions included: Japanese top management was absolutely committed to quality; Japanese view America's predominant management style, especially as it relates to quality and productivity, as being "pathetic, misguided, and somewhat comical" because of its focus on the inspection process. For more than 20 years, Japanese companies had understood that quality and productivity required a system. It had to be embedded in the corporate culture. It was not derived from a process as simple as inspection alone.[12] Hunter emphasized that the quality function was central and finance was an auxiliary function. Hunter's diagram of the early management structure at Toyota is shown in **Exhibit 6**.

[12] William Hunter, Center for Quality and Productivity Improvement, University of Wisconsin, Report No. 4, February 1986. Also published in *Quality Progress,* July 1987, pp. 19–26.

PEDAL TO THE METAL

24 Beginning in 1995, on the heels of 68-year-old Tatsuro Toyoda's stroke, a series of nonfamily members took the helm at Toyota. At the start of this transition, the company's health paralleled that of Mr. Toyoda's. Toyota was losing market share and risked posting its first loss since 1950 due to a weak Japanese economy, a strong yen that dampened exports, and increasing trade friction with the United States.

25 In the following 15 years, the nonfamily management was determined to accelerate Toyota's growth with an aggressive globalization strategy. As part of this strategy, the company began building factories in the U.S., Europe, and other markets, effectively doubling the number of overseas manufacturing facilities to more than 100. Under nonfamily leadership, Toyota revived financially and gained market share at "a kind of speed no other carmaker has ever experienced in the past,"[13] according to Koji Endo, an analyst with Advanced Research Japan in Tokyo.

26 In 1996, Toyota's then-CEO Hiroshi Okuda officially launched the "Toyota 2005 Vision" which, at its core, encompassed a strong global manufacturing network that targeted local markets from Argentina to Thailand to the U.S. The 2005 Vision followed the slogan "harmonious growth" through a "global master plan" and "global profit management." Okuda believed strongly in harmony between the global environment, the world economy, local communities, and other stakeholders, and that Toyota's growth can be beneficial to the world."[14]

27 From the "2005 Vision," a series of revolutionary management and production innovations emerged. Those innovations drove down costs by fundamentally changing the way cars were engineered. After taking the helm in 1999, President Fujio Cho often talked about the criticality of speed in product development cycles. Cho's mantra ultimately yielded a program dubbed CCC21, *Construction of Cost Competitiveness* for the 21st Century. CCC21 took lean manufacturing to extreme levels. According to Takashi Araki, a project manager at partsmaker and Toyota affiliate Aisin Seiki, "The pressure [was] on to cut costs at every stage." The explicit goal was to cut the number of components in a car by 50%.

28 One such example involved the grip handles mounted above the door inside most of Toyota's vehicles. Designers scrutinized these parts and, working closely with suppliers, reduced the number of parts required by 85% from 34 to 5. Initiatives like this enabled Toyota to cut procurement costs by 40% and the installation time of many components by up to 75%.

29 Never complacent, Toyota's strong growth and significant cost savings following the implementation of the "2005 Vision" led leaders to revise the plan in 2002, taking their cost leadership strategy one step further by adopting the "Global Vision 2010." Even more ambitious, this new plan targeted a 15% global market share by early 2010. By April 2010, the company had yet to reach the 15% mark, although the new vision had sparked an impressive string of achievements, including industry-leading operating margins of 8.6%, global sales growth of up to 600,000 additional vehicles per year, and the displacement of General Motors as the world's biggest automaker by unit sales.[15]

30 When Katsuabi Watanabe took the helm as president in 2005, he did not hesitate to share the results of CCC21 with New York's financial community: "Under CCC21 activities,

[13] Alan Ohnsman, Jeff Green, and Kae Inoue, "The Humbling of Toyota," *BusinessWeek,* March 11, 2010.

[14] http://www2.toyota.co.jp/en/vision/traditions/nov2008_feb2009.html.

[15] Norhihiko Shirouzu, "Inside Toyota, Executives Trade Blame Over Debacle," *Wall Street Journal,* April 13, 2010.

which I led, Toyota realized cost reductions of more than 200 billion yen (US$2.2 billion) a year on a consolidated basis."

31 Despite the savings of more than US$10 billion over the six years since CCC21's inception, Watanabe set out to achieve even more cost savings through the new "VI" *(Value Innovation)* strategy. Dubbed an "aggressive version of CCC21," *Value Innovation* promised greater savings by making the entire development process cheaper and faster, further trimming parts, production costs, and time to market.[16] According to company documents, the goal of Toyota's new vision was "to work hard towards making every dealer, plant, regional headquarters, design center, and supplier around the world, including TMC, the 'best company in town.' In other words, a 'company that is respected and admired by the communities we operate in and creates and shares a desirable future for all.' "[17]

32 Many industry insiders, including Takaki Nakanishi, an auto analyst at JPMorgan Securities in Tokyo, expressed reservations about Toyota's rapid growth. "Toyota is growing more quickly than the company's ability to transplant its culture to foreign markets," Nakanishi said. "This is a huge issue for Toyota, one of the biggest it will face in coming years."[18]

ENGINE OIL SLUDGE: A HARBINGER OF THINGS TO COME?

33 Even as Toyota pursued growth at breakneck speed, and at the same time vigilantly cut costs in order to reduce waste, its vehicles were seen as the gold standard for reliability and quality among consumers and car industry analysts. Two separate surveys conducted between 2000 and 2010 by J.D. Power & Associates (a global marketing information firm that conducts independent surveys of customer satisfaction, product quality, and buyer behavior in the automotive industry) revealed that Toyota's perceived brand image improved based on the declining rate of owner complaints.[19] Toyota's advertising and marketing strategy only bolstered the high-quality image. Unlike its domestic competitors, Toyota's marketing campaigns remained remarkably steady over the years, weavings its hallmark values of quality, safety, and reliability into its messages.

34 During its meteoric rise to the top of the global automobile industry, cracks in Toyota's reputation started to appear. In 1999, the company faced a setback that threatened to tarnish its stellar reputation for quality in the United States. As many as 3.3 million vehicles were affected when certain four- and six-cylinder engines in Camrys, Corollas, and other models became prone to oil gelling, or "sludging." This problem manifested itself by clogging the internal oil passages, ultimately causing the engine to seize—a problem only remedied by replacing the entire engine, which could cost more than US$8,000. Some of the engines that failed were only two years old and still under factory warranty.

35 Toyota refused to cover the repairs and denied warranty claims, claiming that the sludge was the result of user error, essentially accusing vehicle owners of not changing their oil in a timely fashion, or not having the oil changed at a dealership, or using the wrong blend of oil, or an inferior filter.[20] The company's response to the engine sludge problem was not well

[16] Alan Ohnsman, Jeff Green and Kae Inoue, "The Humbling of Toyota," *BusinessWeek,* March 11, 2010.

[17] http://www2.toyota.co.jp/en/vision/traditions/nov2008_feb2009.html.

[18] Martin Fackler, "The 'Toyota Way' Is Translated for a New Generation of Foreign Managers," *The New York Times,* February 15, 2007.

[19] Norhihiko Shirouzu, "Inside Toyota, Executives Trade Blame Over Debacle," *Wall Street Journal,* April 13, 2010.

[20] Richard Truett, "Oil Sludge Threatened To Smear a Good Name." *Automotive News* 82.(2007): 56. *Business Source Complete.* EBSCO. Web. 23 Mar. 2010.

received by its customers. Though the Internet was still in its infancy, Toyota customers, annoyed over the company's "maintenance issue" claim, mobilized against the company in chat rooms, on automotive Web sites, and through consumer organizations.

36 Toyota customers also hired lawyers and filed lawsuits against the company at an alarming rate. By 2002, some 3,400 warranty claims had been filed against Toyota. In response to this wave of customer complaints, Toyota's U.S. sales division sent letters to 3.3 million owners of 1997-2001 models offering to cover the cost of repairs for engine damages caused by the oil-sludge buildup.[21] The company regarded the action as a special policy adjustment, not a recall.

37 While never admitting to design or manufacturing flaws, the letter informed customers that Toyota was extending the engine warranty to eight years with unlimited mileage. However, many drivers had already paid for the repair and expected to be reimbursed. It was not until February 2007 that Toyota finally settled the remaining class-action lawsuits. Concurrent with the settlement, Toyota implemented a system that allowed some 7.5 million customers to be reimbursed for repairs and incidental expenses going back as far as the year 1999. At the time of the settlement, Toyota U.S. spokesperson Mike Michels told *Automotive News*:

> This is one of the first issues for Toyota where the Internet played a major role. Today, we closely monitor public discussion and compare how that correlates with information from dealers and warranty data. We compare them all…today, we're in a position to move faster. [22]

38 Unrelated to the oil-sludge crisis, Toyota recalls almost doubled, from 975,902 to 1,887,471 vehicles worldwide, during the period from 2003 to 2004. In 2005, in reaction to the surge in quality issues and recalls, then-president Watanabe implemented a high-level so-called *"Customer First"* management committee that had the task to coordinate engineering, production, sales, and service issues related to quality.[23] However, as Toyota became the leading automaker in the world, the initiative was never really pushed. Toyota scrapped the *Customer First* program in early 2009, perhaps under pressure from falling margins and declining sales (see **Exhibit 7**).

ACCELERATING RECALLS

39 On February 2, 2010, only three years after Toyota settled the oil-sludge class-action lawsuits, U.S. Department of Transportation Secretary Ray LaHood publicly criticized Toyota's response to rising consumer concerns over allegedly faulty accelerator pedals. He told the Associated Press that, "Toyota may be a little safety deaf."[24] This was a huge blow for the company's market perception of quality, safety, and reliability. LaHood made this comment about six months following the fatal crash of a Lexus ES 350 that killed an off-duty highway patrol officer and his family. Just moments before the crash, the driver called 911, reporting that his accelerator was stuck.

40 One month later, on September 29, 2009, Toyota recalled 3.8 million U.S. vehicles, claiming that floor-mat problems could cause the accelerator to be stuck. In a move reminiscent of the oil-sludge crisis, Toyota insisted that there was no vehicle-based cause for the problems. Over the next six months, Toyota announced several adjustment measures and,

[21] "Toyota to Cover Costs Of Repairing Engines Damaged by Sludge." *Wall Street Journal,* 12 Feb. 2002, Eastern edition: ABI/INFORM Global, ProQuest. Web. 22 Apr. 2010.

[22] Truett, "Oil sludge threatened to smear a good name."

[23] Hans Greimel, "Toyota's Quality Meetings Faded Away" (cover story). *Automotive News* 84.6398 (2010): 1-45. *Business Source Complete.* EBSCO. Web. 26 Apr. 2010.

[24] http://www.msnbc.msn.com/id/35240466/ns/business-autos.

EXHIBIT 7 **Toyota Motor Corporation's Annual Income Statements, March 2005–March 2009**

Toyota Motor Corporation
Primary Industry: Auto Manufacturing
NYSE: TM [ADR] **Tokyo:** 72030

Fiscal Year-End:
March

Annual Income Statement (All dollar amounts in millions except per share amounts.)

	Mar09	Mar 08	Mar 07	Mar 08	Mar 05
Revenue	211,023.5	263,028.2	203,218.7	179,731.8	172,318.7
Costs of Goods Sold	189,707.2	215,314.2	163,167.8	144,771.6	138,124.1
Gross Profit	21,316.3	47,714.0	40,050.9	34,960.2	34,194.6
Gross Profit Margin	10.10%	18.10%	19.70%	19.50%	19.80%
SG&A Expense	26,055.0	24,998.3	21,053.7	18,912.3	18,662.4
Depreciation & Amortization	15,368.9	14,919.0	11,732.5	10,348.4	9.267.9
Operating Income	–4,738.7	27,715.8	18,997.2	16,047.9	15,532.2
Operating Margin	—	8.60%	9.30%	8.90%	9.00%
Nonoperating Income	–1,944.2	3,174.7	2,297.0	2,571.3	1,611.0
Nonoperating Expenses	941.4	—	—	—	—
Income Before Taxes	–5,760.2	24,384.8	20,217.3	17,833.4	16,298.3
Income Taxes	–580.2	9,120.0	7,622.3	6,793.5	6,110.7
Net Income After Taxes	–5,180.0	15,264.8	12,595.0	11,039.9	10,187.6
Continuing Operations	–4,491.3	17,187.4	13,951.3	11,723.3	10.879.8
Discontinued Operations	—	—	—	—	—
Total Operations	–4,491.3	17,187.4	13,951.3	11,723.3	10,879.8
Total Net Income	–4,491.3	17,187.4	13,951.3	11,723.3	10,879.8
Net Profit Margin	—	6.50%	6.90%	6.50%	6.30%
Diluted EPS from Total Net Income ($)	–2.9	10.9	8.7	7.2	6.6
Dividends per Share ($)	2.1	2.8	1.9	1.7	0.9

in addition, recalled millions more vehicles with the aim of preventing the floor mat from causing the accelerator to get stuck. On January 16, 2010, Toyota informed the NHTSA that the pedals themselves had a dangerous "sticky" habit, thus revealing that the problem was not just the floor mats. Five days later, Toyota recalled approximately 2.3 million more vehicles because of stuck accelerator pedals.

41 Toyota told the government that it "thinks a friction problem in its accelerator pedal mechanisms may make the pedal 'harder to depress, slower to return, or, in the worst case, mechanically stick in a partially depressed position.' " At the same time, CTS Corporation, the Elkhart, Indiana, supplier that made the accelerator pedal mechanisms for Toyota, said that the friction problem accounted for fewer than a dozen cases of stuck accelerators, "and in no instance did the accelerator actually become stuck in a partially depressed condition."[25]

[25] http://www.msnbc.msn.com/id/35110966/ retrieved July 15, 2010.

42 On January 26, 2010, in a drastic move, Toyota suspended sales and production of popular models, including the Corolla and Camry, as it tried to find a workable solution to fix the accelerator problem. Over the next few days, Toyota expanded the recall of vehicles in the U.S. by another 1.1 million vehicles, bringing the total worldwide recalls related to the accelerator problem to 8.8 million. During the following weeks, Toyota did not seem to stay out of the press as a new safety recall emerged from the automaker on a nearly weekly basis. A detailed timeline of events is shown in **Exhibit 8**.

43 Despite the months and years that had passed since problems with the accelerator pedal first surfaced, Toyota's leadership appeared to be in no hurry to address the problem. At a news conference in Japan on February 5, President Toyoda finally apologized for the car recalls and promised to beef up quality control: "I apologize from the bottom of my heart for all of the concern that we have given to so many of our customers."[26]

44 Two weeks later, on February 24, 2010, Toyoda delivered prepared testimony before the U.S. House of Representatives Committee on Oversight and Government Reform. The transcript of Toyoda's full testimony is shown in **Exhibit 9**.

45 Transportation Secretary LaHood said Toyota *"put consumers at risk"* by failing to promptly notify authorities about potentially defective accelerator pedals. LaHood asserted that Toyota knew about the problem in late September but did not issue the recall until late January, violating a federal law that requires an automaker to notify the government of a safety defect within five business days.[27] As a result, on April 5, 2010, the NHTSA sent a letter to Toyota demanding that the company pay a US$16.4 million civil penalty—the maximum under the law—for its slow response to the sticking accelerator pedal. On April 19, the company agreed to pay the fine.[28] To former Toyota insiders, the mangled message had roots in the company's fractured organizational structure in the United States.

46 The government fine was not the only expense that Toyota had to worry about. Echoing its oil-sludge crisis, customers and shareholders filed multiple lawsuits, including three class-action suits, claiming company executives "deliberately misled investors and the public about the depth of accelerator problems in millions of its vehicles."[29] In addition to these potentially costly lawsuits, Toyota's market capitalization had fallen 21 percent, and its inventory position skyrocketed since the problems became public in late January 2010.[30]

47 To make matters even worse for the carmaker, the April 2010 issue of the popular Consumer Reports magazine, a commonly referenced source for car buyers, issued a "Don't Buy: Safety Risk" rating for the 2010 Lexus GX 460. The magazine argued that handling problems made the vehicle unsafe.[31] This was the first time in nearly a decade that the magazine had rejected a vehicle. Perhaps learning a lesson from the accelerator crisis, Toyota responded immediately by saying it would recall all 9,400 of the 2010 Lexus GX 460s that were sold since December 2009. Toyota, the worldwide benchmark manufacturing company for quality and the promotion of continuous improvement, had seriously stumbled. By spring 2010, a Consumer Reports National Research Center survey reported that American drivers felt that Ford had made significant improvement in its car safety and quality, while Toyota was perceived to have made a dramatic drop.[32]

[26] "Toyota President Akio Toyoda Apologizes for Global Recalls." http://www.huffingtonpost.com/2010/02/05/toyota-president-akio-toy_n_450665.html.

[27] http://www.ledger-enquirer.com/2010/04/19/1093175/moving-faster-toyota-recalls-suvs.html.

[28] http://pressroom.toyota.com/pr/tms/toyota-motor-corporation-agrees-157093.aspx.

[29] http://www.cbsnews.com/stories/2010/03/21/business/main6320021.shtml.

[30] http://finance.yahoo.com/q?s=tm, accessed April 28, 2010.

[31] http://blogs.consumerreports.org/cars/2010/04/consumer-reports-2010-lexus-gx-dont-buy-safety-risk.html.

[32] http://blogs.consumerreports.org/cars/toyota/.

EXHIBIT 8 2006–2010 Timeline of Toyota Recall-Related News

2006	September 14	NHTSA opens an investigation into driver reports of "surging" in Camry models.
2007	March	Toyota receives reports about accelerator pedal issues in Tundra model.
	April	NHTSA states that no defect was found in 2006 Camry investigation. It closes probe into "surge" problems in Camry model.
	September 26	Toyota and Lexus models recalled to secure floor mats, which were reported to slip and cause the car to accelerate out of control.
2008	January 31	NHTSA opens investigation of Tacoma truck models experiencing sudden acceleration problems.
	August 27	NHTSA closes investigation of Tacoma trucks stating they found no evidence to suggest a vehicle defect.
2009	April 21	In response to sudden acceleration reports, a Toyota spokesperson states that, "People are under so much stress right now, they have so much on their minds. With pagers and cell phones and IM, people are just so busy with kids, families, boyfriends, and girlfriends. So you are driving along and the next thing you know you are two miles down the road and you don't remember driving because you are thinking about something else."
	August 28	A family of four driving a Lexus ES 350 is killed. Moments before the crash, the driver called 911 to report that his accelerator was stuck.
	September 29	Toyota issues a safety notice for 3.8 million vehicles due to the crash risk posed by the gas pedal becoming caught under the floor mat. NHTSA calls for the recall of the 3.8 million vehicles.
	November 4	NHTSA accuses Toyota of providing owners with "inaccurate and misleading information" about its floor mat recall.
	November 25	Toyota recalls 4 million vehicles to reconfigure gas pedals and redesign floor mats due to the risk of floor mat entrapment.
	December 26	Four people die near Dallas when their Toyota Avalon accelerates off of the road.
2010	January 12	Toyota announces that it will install a brake override system in addition to the brake pedal redesign and floor mat reconfiguration.
	January 21	Toyota recalls 2.3 million vehicles to correct a separate problem that could cause the gas pedal to stick.
	January 26	Toyota suspends sales and halts production of 8 car models due to accelerator pedal problems.
	January 27	Toyota increases its floor mat recall to an additional 1.1 million cars. General Motors announces incentives for Toyota owners who want to swap their car for a GM model.
	January 29	Toyota expands its recall to models sold in Europe.
	February 1	Toyota says it has developed a fix for the sticking gas pedal issue and has begun shipping the new parts to dealers.
	February 2	U.S. Transportation Secretary LaHood criticizes Toyota's response to the problems with the gas pedals.
	February 3	Transportation Secretary LaHood warns consumers not to drive recalled cars, then claims this was a misstatement and consumers should contact their dealers. NHTSA claims to have received more than 100 complaints about braking system problems in the Prius.

(Continued)

EXHIBIT 8 *(Continued)*

February 4	Toyota says the recalls for gas pedal-related issues could end up costing the company US$2 billion. Toyota also confirms on this date that the recalls total 8.1 million vehicles. The automaker blames a software glitch for braking problems in its 2010 Prius. The NHTSA opens a formal investigation into the braking system of the Prius hybrid model.
February 5	Toyota president and CEO Akio Toyoda apologizes for the car recalls at a news conference in Japan and promises to beef up quality control: "I apologize from the bottom of my heart for all of the concern that we have given to so many of our customers."
February 9	Toyota recalls 437,000 hybrids worldwide over brake problems, bringing the total number of cars recalled to 8.5 million.
February 13	Toyota announces the recall of 8,000 Tacoma trucks in North America for potential defects in the front drive shaft of certain 2010 models.
February 16	Toyota announces plans to suspend production at two U.S. plants as sales slow following the company's massive recalls. NHTSA orders Toyota to provide documents showing when and how it learned of the defects affecting about 6 million U.S. vehicles.
February 17	Toyota president Akio Toyoda says he will not appear before U.S. lawmakers, and that the company will take steps to fix problems with its cars. The U.S. government plans to open an investigation to probe possible steering issues on about 500,000 Toyota Corollas.
February 18	Toyota president Akio Toyoda accepts a "formal invitation" to appear before a Congressional committee investigating unintended acceleration in Toyota cars.
February 21	In an internal presentation, Toyota staffers say the company saved US$100 million by negotiating an "equipment" recall rather than a "vehicle" recall.
February 22	Toyota says it has received a federal grand jury subpoena for documents relating to Prius braking problems.
February 23	*Consumer Reports* drops two of the four Toyotas that would have made its annual list of Top Pick cars because of a "stop sale" order.
February 24	Toyota president Akio Toyoda apologizes during a prepared testimony before the U.S. House of Representatives Committee on Oversight and Government Reform: "I'm deeply sorry for any accident that Toyota drivers have experienced," and pledges full cooperation as the investigation continues.
April 5	The NHTSA sent a letter to Toyota demanding that the company pay a US$16.4 million civil penalty—the maximum under the law—for its slow response to the sticking accelerator pedal.
April 8	Toyota Motor Sales (TMS), U.S.A., Inc., announced it has established a new **SMART** business process utilizing existing product engineers, field technical specialists and specially trained technicians to quickly and aggressively investigate customer reports of unintended acceleration in Toyota, Lexus, and Scion vehicles in the United States. The rapid-response **S**wift **M**arket **A**nalysis **R**esponse **T**eam will attempt to contact customers within 24 hours of receiving a complaint of unintended acceleration to arrange for a comprehensive on-site vehicle analysis.
April 14	Toyota asked dealers to temporarily suspend sales of the new 2010 Lexus GX 460 after *Consumer Reports* issued a "Don't Buy" safety warning on the SUV.
April 15	Toyota has announced that it will now check all of its SUVs for problems similar to the one uncovered by *Consumer Reports* in the Lexus GX 460 SUV.

EXHIBIT 8 *(Continued)*

April 16	Toyota to begin voluntary safety recall on certain 1998-2010 model year Siennas to address potential corrosion on spare tire cable.
April 19	Toyota announced that it has agreed to settle the civil penalty demanded in the NHTSA's April 5 letter related to the company's recall for slow-to-return and sticky accelerator pedals by paying US$16.4 million. Toyota announces voluntary recall on 2010 model-year Lexus GX 460 to update vehicle stability control software.
April 22	The international ratings agency Moody's Investors Service downgraded Toyota's credit rating to Aa2 from Aa1 because of concerns over product quality weakening the firm's capacity to repay long-term debt.
April 28	Toyota announces voluntary recall on 2003 model-year Sequoia to upgrade program logic in vehicle stability control system.

EXHIBIT 9 **Prepared Testimony of Akio Toyoda, President, Toyota Motor Corporation, to Committee on Oversight and Government Reform**

February 24, 2010

Thank you, Chairman Towns.

I am Akio Toyoda of Toyota Motor Corporation. I would first like to state that I love cars as much as anyone, and I love Toyota as much as anyone. I take the utmost pleasure in offering vehicles that our customers love, and I know that Toyota's 200,000 team members, dealers, and suppliers across America feel the same way. However, in the past few months, our customers have started to feel uncertain about the safety of Toyota's vehicles, and I take full responsibility for that. Today, I would like to explain to the American people, as well as our customers in the U.S. and around the world, how seriously Toyota takes the quality and safety of its vehicles. I would like to express my appreciation to Chairman Towns and Ranking Member Issa, as well as the members of the House Oversight and Government Reform Committee, for giving me this opportunity to express my thoughts today.

I would like to focus my comments on three topics—Toyota's basic philosophy regarding quality control, the cause of the recalls, and how we will manage quality control going forward.

First, I want to discuss the philosophy of Toyota's quality control. I myself, as well as Toyota, am not perfect. At times, we do find defects. But in such situations, we always stop, strive to understand the problem, and make changes to improve further. In the name of the company, its long-standing tradition and pride, we never run away from our problems or pretend we don't notice them. By making continuous improvements, we aim to continue offering even better products for society. That is the core value we have kept closest to our hearts since the founding days of the company.

At Toyota, we believe the key to making quality products is to develop quality people. Each employee thinks about what he or she should do, continuously making improvements, and by doing so, makes even better cars. We have been actively engaged in developing people who share and can execute on this core value. It has been over 50 years since we began selling in this great country, and over 25 years since we started production here. And in the process, we have been able to share this core value with the 200,000 people at Toyota operations, dealers, and suppliers in this country. That is what I am most proud of.

Second, I would like to discuss what caused the recall issues we are facing now. Toyota has, for the past few years, been expanding its business rapidly. Quite frankly, I fear the pace at which we have grown may have been too quick. I would like to point out here that Toyota's priority has traditionally been the following: First; Safety, Second; Quality, and Third; Volume. These priorities became confused, and we were not able to stop, think, and make improvements as much as we were able to before, and our basic stance to listen to customers' voices to make better products has weakened somewhat. We pursued growth over the speed at which we were able to develop our people and our

(Continued)

EXHIBIT 9 *(Continued)*

organization, and we should sincerely be mindful of that. I regret that this has resulted in the safety issues described in the recalls we face today, and I am deeply sorry for any accidents that Toyota drivers have experienced.

Especially, I would like to extend my condolences to the members of the Saylor family, for the accident in San Diego. I would like to send my prayers again, and I will do everything in my power to ensure that such a tragedy never happens again.

Since last June, when I first took office, I have personally placed the highest priority on improving quality over quantity, and I have shared that direction with our stakeholders. As you well know, I am the grandson of the founder, and all the Toyota vehicles bear my name. For me, when the cars are damaged, it is as though I am as well. I, more than anyone, wish for Toyota's cars to be safe, and for our customers to feel safe when they use our vehicles. Under my leadership, I would like to reaffirm our values of placing safety and quality the highest on our list of priorities, which we have held to firmly from the time we were founded. I will also strive to devise a system in which we can surely execute what we value.

Third, I would like to discuss how we plan to manage quality control as we go forward. Up to now, any decisions on conducting recalls have been made by the Customer Quality Engineering Division at Toyota Motor Corporation in Japan. This division confirms whether there are technical problems and makes a decision on the necessity of a recall. However, reflecting on the issues today, what we lacked was the customers' perspective.

To make improvements on this, we will make the following changes to the recall decision-making process. When recall decisions are made, a step will be added in the process to ensure that management will make a responsible decision from the perspective of "customer safety first." To do that, we will devise a system in which customers' voices around the world will reach our management in a timely manner, and also a system in which each region will be able to make decisions as necessary. Further, we will form a quality advisory group composed of respected outside experts from North America and around the world to ensure that we do not make a misguided decision. Finally, we will invest heavily in quality in the U.S., through the establishment of an Automotive Center of Quality Excellence, the introduction of a new position—Product Safety Executive—and the sharing of more information and responsibility within the company for product quality decisions, including defects and recalls.

Even more importantly, I will ensure that members of the management team actually drive the cars, and that they check for themselves where the problem lies as well as its severity. I myself am a trained test driver. As a professional, I am able to check on problems in a car, and can understand how severe the safety concern is in a car. I drove the vehicles in the accelerator pedal recall as well as the Prius, comparing the vehicles before and after the remedy in various environmental settings. I believe that only by examining the problems on site, can one make decisions from the customer perspective. One cannot rely on reports or data in a meeting room.

Through the measures I have just discussed, and with whatever results we obtain from the investigations we are conducting in cooperation with NHTSA, I intend to further improve on the quality of Toyota vehicles and fulfill our principle of putting the customer first.

My name is on every car. You have my personal commitment that Toyota will work vigorously and unceasingly to restore the trust of our customers.

Thank you.

Source: Toyota

STRUCTURAL CHALLENGES

48 As Toyota grew into a global powerhouse in the auto industry, the organizational structure that emerged was a centralized design "…that put key decision-making in the hands of executives in Japan. . ." Toyota built up a vast complex of engineering centers, test tracks, financial arms, sales offices, and manufacturing plants that spread from California to New York, spilling over into Canada and Mexico. Toyota did not have a U.S. headquarters; its units operated as fiefdoms that reported independently to Japan.[33] Some industry analysts

[33] This section draws quotations from http://articles.latimes.com/2010/feb/23/business/la-fi-toyota23-2010feb23.

pointed to Toyota's unique subsidiary structure as a contributing factor in the recall crisis and the company's delay in responding to the same.

49 According to former Toyota employees, "The complicated tasks of gathering information about sudden acceleration reports, analyzing the problems, and engineering fixes, as well as reporting the issues to federal safety regulators, were handled by different Toyota subsidiaries, each managed separately in many cases from Japan..." Documents released by the U.S. House of Representatives investigators show that some of the disjointed subsidiaries of Toyota had an explicit strategy to minimize safety recalls, saving the company hundreds of millions of dollars even while reports of fatal accidents were increasing.

50 Some believed that Toyota's structure in the U.S. ultimately impaired its ability to prevent the safety problems before they reached the crisis stage. In the midst of Toyota's recall crisis, several former insiders offered insights into the structural drivers of the recall crisis. John Jula, a former engineering manager at Toyota's technical center in Ann Arbor, Michigan, told the *Los Angeles Times*: "You know the joke that every bank branch has a president—well, every Toyota facility has a president, and one can't tell another what to do."

51 Jula, who left Toyota in 2003 after eight years with the company, described how he had only very limited interactions with the sales or dealership organizations responsible for collecting safety data from consumers. His experience was that this information went directly to Japan without ever being relayed back to the U.S. organization, and that all key engineering decisions came from Japan.

52 Another insider, Laurence Boland, who spent 25 years with Toyota in its sales organization based in Torrance, CA, observed: "They let Americans do what they do best, advertising and services, and in that area they left us alone. But when it came to money and technical matters, they kept the control in Japan."

53 Former Toyota attorney Dimitrios Biller supported the observation that no real decisions were made in the U.S. John P. Kristensen, an attorney in a lawsuit against Toyota, argued that:

> Toyota has used its structure to fend off lawsuits, forcing attorneys to file repeated requests for information to subsidiaries. You don't need an MBA to know that Toyota's American subsidiaries were intentionally created to keep consumers in the dark...the system was set up intentionally to work like this.

54 Though the majority of Toyota's key decisions came out of Japan, some Toyota insiders and industry analysts took another perspective, and maintained that Toyota had tried hard to become a local company in the U.S. Emphasizing Toyota's localization effort in 2007, Toyota Executive Vice President Tokuichi Uranishi stated:

> Local customization comes first, followed by model integrations, shared platforms, and common parts to reduce complexity. It should not be the other way around, nor should it be at the same time. A global company that surveys every potential market need and chooses one optimal solution will be very efficient, but along the way it sacrifices the creative potential of its employees in the local operations.[34]

55 In July 2002, as part of Toyota's internationalization efforts, the company established a Global Knowledge Center (GKC) in Torrance, CA, to pursue a dual strategy of localization and global integration. The objective of the GKC was to disseminate innovation from specific local markets into a global process to benefit the whole company. According to company documents, the GKC was a strategic resource for sharing innovative ideas and global

[34] Emi Osono, Norihiko Shimizu, and Hirotaka Takeuchi. *Extreme Toyota: Radical Contradictions That Drive Success at the World's Best Manufacturer.* John Wiley & Sons, Inc., 2008: 97.

knowledge of best practices in sales and marketing across multiple countries. Dedicated to collaborating with Toyota distributors, the GKC aimed to optimize growth and to leverage the Toyota brand globally.[35]

56 Until the GKC was established, Toyota was not organized for transferring customer knowledge across countries or sharing best practices in sales and marketing among different business units. In a 2005 interview Executive Vice President Yoshimi Inaba stated: "What we can do today is to provide local staff with a lot of ideas and examples based on our international experience so that they can adapt them to local requirements for greater market success."[36]

57 So how exactly does one of the world's best manufacturers, known for its profitability, strong engineering, and quality, manage its aggressive global expansion strategy? Akio Matsubara, Toyota's Senior Managing Director of Human Resource Management, offered the following answer:

> When we operate in other countries, we are sensitive to the needs and requirements of the countries and regions we have entered. For example, to get a sense of the true situation on the ground in the United States, we ran a test at [NUMMI] in California, a joint venture with GM. After that, we started factory operations in Kentucky. The issue then was how to successfully assimilate into the region. We tried to become an extremely local-friendly company, because in many cases our company significantly affects the local economy and the lives of the people in the region in question.[37]

A COMPLEX WEB

58 With more than 8,900 U.S.-based employees, 14 regional offices, and 1,500 dealerships across all 50 states, Toyota was one of the largest foreign companies in the United States. Despite size, Toyota struggled to effectively leverage its TPS standards due to the complexity of its far-reaching and complex global supplier and partner network compounded by its headquarter-centric decision-making processes.

59 A manufacturer has to design, engineer, build, buy, and then assemble more than 10,000 parts to make a car. As part of TPS, Toyota broke away from the Western supply-chain model, which saw carmakers sourcing in-house or awarding short-term contracts to the lowest-price bidders. Toyota refined supply-chain management by selecting certain suppliers as the exclusive suppliers of particular components. This led to intimate collaboration between Toyota and these long-term partners. Toyota classified its suppliers according to a three-tier system. Tier-one suppliers supplied large, integrated systems to the automakers, followed by tier-two suppliers who provided individual parts and/or assembled components, followed finally by tier-three suppliers who primarily provided single components for several tier-two suppliers.[38]

60 Toyota, along with many other Japanese companies, including Honda, had a business structure called keiretsu, essentially a networked, industry-specific, diversified conglomerate that resulted in the vertical integration of its supply chain. Akio

[35] https://www.toyotagkc.com/mvc/gkclanding/show.

[36] Osono et al., *Extreme Toyota: Radical Contradictions That Drive Success at the World's Best Manufacturer,* p. 118.

[37] Ibid., p. 96.

[38] "The Machine That Ran Too Hot." *Economist* 394.8671 (2010): 74. *Business Source Complete.* EBSCO. Web. 23 Mar. 2010.

Okamura, a partner at Roland Berger Strategy Consultant's Automotive Competence Center, observed:

> Japan's automotive industry from its inception was shaped by keiretsu, business groups that have bound banks, trading houses, and industrial firms into loosely knit conglomerates. Sticking together by holding shares in each other and buying each other's wares, foreign companies were largely prevented from gaining a foothold in this market.

61 Okamura, also commenting on the effects of globalization on kaizen practices, stated:

> As original equipment manufacturers (OEMs) move to share global platforms, suppliers are being asked not only to supply parts to Japanese OEM plants, but also to their partners' plants. Japanese suppliers also are being forced to search for foreign partners to supply overseas markets.[39]

62 While Toyota pursued its aggressive global growth strategy, its supply chain became dangerously stretched. The company began to depend increasingly on suppliers from outside of Japan and outside the *keiretsu* structure, non-Japanese suppliers with which Toyota did not have prior working experience. Toyota also struggled to find enough senior engineers responsible for monitoring these new suppliers. Nevertheless, Toyota leaned even more heavily on its single-source supply-chain approach, often using single suppliers for entire ranges of its cars across multiple markets—and reaping incredible economies of scale in the process. A senior executive at one of Toyota's tier-one suppliers told the *Economist*:

> If you don't want duplication of supply, you have to have very close monitoring, you have to listen to your supply base, and you have to have transparency. That means delegating to local managers. With Toyota, it works well at the shop-floor level, but things break down higher up.[40]

A LACK OF CONSENSUS

63 On April 14, 2010, the *Wall Street Journal* published an article chronicling the Japanese family versus nonfamily management infighting that had apparently been plaguing Toyota for some time. Jim Press, the former CEO of TMS and the highest-ranking non-Japanese executive ever employed at Toyota, told the WSJ that the root cause of [Toyota's] problems was that the company was hijacked, some years ago, by anti-family, financially oriented pirates.[41]

64 In March, Mr. Toyoda, while acknowledging that the ultimate responsibility for the recalls rested with him, seemed to agree with Mr. Press's comments when he stated at a news conference that the problems arose when some people just got too big-headed and focused too excessively on short-term profits only. In the context of Japanese culture, which was based on harmony, consensus decision-making, and blame avoidance, such comments were highly unusual. In Japan, the public debate of problems and explicit conflict negotiations were avoided at all costs, and conflict resolution was typically sought behind closed doors.[42]

65 Given Toyota's highly centralized Japanese management structure, some industry analysts wondered if the recall crisis would have been handled differently had it occurred closer to Japan.[43] The TPS's "go and see" principle suggests that to truly understand a

[39] http://www.autofieldguide.com/columns/0905strat.html.

[40] "The machine that ran too hot." Economist 394.8671 (2010): 74. Business Source Complete. EBSCO. Web. 23 Mar. 2010.

[41] Shirouzu, "Inside Toyota, Executives Trade Blame Over Debacle."

[42] "Cultural Orientation Inventory" by Cultural Navigator v6.6.2.1., Training Management Corporation (TMC), a Berlitz company.

[43] Author interview with Tejinder Grewal.

situation, one needs to go to where the work is done. Given Toyota's centralized management structure and increasingly complex web of suppliers, some analysts wondered whether this principle got lost among Toyota's foreign subsidiaries, especially in the United States. Some suspected that cultural differences between Japan and the U.S. were exacerbating the crisis and making it less manageable. Differences can be seen using the Cultural Orientation Indicator? comparing the United States and Japan. **Exhibit 10** provides an overview of these differences.

EXHIBIT 10 **Cultural Orientations Indicator® (COI)**

	United States	Japan
Characteristics of a good manager	Employees want to be treated fairly and with respect, with adequate and honest communication from their managers. As a society with highly egalitarian values, employees also want to be trusted that they will perform effectively and will not be micromanaged. For a manager to be effective, he/she should understand what motivates employees from various perspectives beyond only promotion and remuneration.	A Japanese manager is expected to be an excellent and skilled worker; to provide a great example to do the job; to help guide, support, and help employees in the right direction accordingly; is responsible for protecting and defending his or her subordinates to others or higher authorities when something happens on a project (especially when the subordinates face difficulties or made mistakes); a person who has good skills to coordinate the group as a team/family; and a good listener.
Motivation	Many U.S. Americans in the business world are motivated by monetary rewards and status, such as job advancement, material goods, or a nice office. U.S. Americans are also motivated by accomplishment of a job well done. A compliment from a manager is not only desired but is often expected by workers in this culture. U.S. Americans want to work hard for promotions, but are also self-motivated.	The Japanese tend to be motivated when they work as a group and experience an accomplishment and achievement as a group. However, in contemporary society, personal recognition is becoming more important than ever before. Many Japanese believe the following are key motivators: recognition, fair performance evaluation, and salary increase and promotion.
Decision-Making	As an egalitarian culture, the United States emphasizes decision-making at all levels of an organization, not only at upper levels of management, depending on the gravity of the decision being made. There tend to be lower levels of bureaucracy than in highly hierarchical cultures, and more empowerment for people to make decisions at multiple levels in a company.	The Japanese tend to make their decisions as a group. Furthermore, although they have a strong hierarchy orientation, on decision-making the bottom-up process is very common since many business proposals are created among lower-ranking managers.
Authority	Managerial power tends to come from one's hierarchical position in the organization, and also from alternative sources of power such as affiliation, technical expertise, as well as their personality and ability to motivate their team. Whether a	Although most Japanese companies maintain a strong hierarchical structure, the subordinates are more expected to have their own views with a sense of initiative or leadership. Japanese managers expect their subordinates to be able to find and create their own jobs/

EXHIBIT 10 *(Continued)*

	United States	Japan
	manager operates in a collaborative and participative manner or in an authoritative manner, most workers will air their disagreements in some way, even in a union environment.	projects and propose their own jobs to their managers.
Delegation	Managers delegate tasks readily in the United States, and are typically not as concerned about losing power in the delegation process. With higher tolerance for risk commonly found in the U.S., and also lower levels of hierarchy, there is not as much concern of failure when delegating, and there tends to be little micromanagement in the delegation process.	Fundamentally, tasks are delegated by the managers to their subordinates. However, the biggest difference between the Japanese task delegation style and many Western styles is that the members are expected to create their jobs and tasks proactively by understanding the circumstances. This skill is regarded as the most essential skill for the workers.
Information Sharing	Among many U.S. organizations, people and departments share information readily, depending on the need to know. However, information may not be shared readily among different departments, which can be a barrier to optimal efficiency and a sense of organizational teamwork.	Regular meetings and frequent personal contact among team members is common. The frequent communication system to share information (Report—Contact—Consult, or *Ho-Ren-So*) is practiced by everyone under this group work environment.
Structuring of Tasks	Generally, a manager in the United States will present a task and a general idea for how the task should be organized. Participant input is often solicited to help modify and change the task according to specific requirements. Managers typically enter with objectives, and employees in the United States will often help determine the tasks to meet the required outcomes.	In Japan, the big picture decisions are often decided by higher management, and they are brought down to the lower level. At the same time, the jobs according to the big picture are decided by the group members. The managers' roles are not to define and order the job areas and tasks. Rather, their roles are to grow and manage subordinates to be able to understand the vision and proactively plan their own jobs accordingly.
Conflict Management	In the United States, conflicts and disagreements are typically dealt with right as they arise, and discussed openly. Occasionally, indirect approaches, such as the use of a third party, might be needed in some situations, but this is the exception in the United States.	The Japanese like neither conflict nor debate in public. When they have a conflict during the negotiation, they try to solve the issues behind the scenes. Japanese often try to take advantage of a conflict in terms of building a firm relationship by overcoming it together.
Organizational Structure	Historically, U.S. businesses grew out of a "command and control" hierarchical management structure. Much of this legacy top-down hierarchical structure still exists, but this structure has changed dramatically over the past century with much flatter organizations, greater decision-making authority given to lower levels within an organization, and more autonomy in the workplace.	Most Japanese companies still follow a rigid hierarchical, pyramid structure. This system is based on seniority. However, the system does not reflect the simple top-down power relationship that is more common in several Western corporate systems.

Source: CulturalNavigator.com.

66 Additionally, Richard Johnson and William Ouchi, in their classic study of Japanese management styles, found that the practice of "decision-making by consensus" had costs. On occasion, the Japanese were so concerned with the desire for conflict avoidance that important issues failed to get full attention. Managers who disagreed with a certain proposal would sometimes remain silent rather than upset the relationships that they had so carefully developed.[44] Therefore, it was highly unusual when Toyota's nonfamily managers publically stated that Toyota's troubles were less a quality crisis and more a management and public relations crisis.

67 Mr. Okuda, nonfamily member and Toyota's president from 1995 to 1999, put an even finer point on this argument in 2000 when he told the *Wall Street Journal*, referencing family managers such as now-president Akio Toyoda, "Nepotism just doesn't belong in our future."[45] Other nonfamily managers argued that Mr. Toyoda was too focused on top-line growth and profits in order to overtake GM as the world's leading automaker, instead of making sure that the company's reputation as a quality manufacturer remained intact.

68 In Toyoda's Congressional testimony on February 24, 2010, he alluded to a return to these principles:

> I believe that only by examining the problems on site can one make decisions from the customer perspective. One cannot rely on reports or data in a meeting room. I will ensure that members of the management team actually drive the cars, and that they check for themselves where the problem lies, as well as its severity.[46]

MOVING FORWARD

We need not be concerned. We need only continue as always, making our improvements.[47]

Kiichiro Toyoda, Founder
Toyoda Automatic Loom Works

69 Could Akio Toyoda simply follow his grandfather's advice to focus on continuous improvement, especially given plummeting margins? Mr. Toyoda had to sort out what combination of structural, cultural, or strategic challenges led to the current recall crisis. Had the company lost sight of its long-term philosophy, a key principle behind the *Toyota Way*? Had Toyota sacrificed quality at the expense of extreme cost reductions? Were nonfamily managers truly to blame for "hijacking" Toyota?

70 What role had Toyota's supply chain and *keiretsu* structure played in the recalls? Thinking beyond Toyota's woes to the global industry, did Harvard's Michael Porter have Toyota in mind when he said that Japanese firms rarely have strategies because operational excellence alone is not strategy?

71 Was Toyota simply subject to the latest media witch hunt in the wake of the global economic crisis? Would *Consumer Reports*, which traditionally praised Toyota vehicles, really have issued a "Don't Buy" on the Lexus without pressures of the economic crisis and a media-driven campaign for Buy American? Ford and GM had both had more and larger recalls than Toyota (see **Exhibit 11**).

[44] "Made in America (Under Japanese Management)," *HBR*, 1974.

[45] Shirouzu, "Inside Toyota, Executives Trade Blame Over Debacle."

[46] http://www.toyota.com/about/news/corporate/2010/02/24-1-testimony.html.

[47] http://www.nytimes.com/2008/02/10/business/worldbusiness/10iht-10facts.9900222.html.

EXHIBIT 11 **Top 10 Largest Vehicle Recalls 1971–2009**

Company	Year	Problem	Number of Vehicles
Ford	1996	Ignition switch fires	7.9 million
GM	1971	Broken engine mounts cause sudden acceleration	6.7 million
GM	1981	Broken front suspension bolts result in steering problems	5.8 million
Toyota	2009	Shifting floor mats cause unintended acceleration	5.4 million
Ford	2005	Cruise control switch fires	4.5 million
Ford	2009	Cruise control switch fires	4.5 million
Ford	1972	Defective seat belts	4.0 million
GM	1973	Possibility of stones disabling steering gear	3.7 million
Volkswagen	1972	Faulty windshield wiper assembly	3.7 million
Honda	1995	Seat belt release jam	3.7 million

Source: M. O'Rourke, 2010. "Toyota's Total Recall." *Risk Management*, 57: 8–11.

72 Clearly, Mr. Toyoda had much to do to fix the problems of the recent past, and restore confidence in his company and the brand moving forward. More importantly, Mr. Toyoda had given his personal commitment in his testimony to the U.S. House Committee on Oversight and Government Reform: "My name is on every car. You have my personal commitment that Toyota will work vigorously and unceasingly to restore the trust of our customers."

Case 27

Veja: *Sneakers with a Conscience*

Kim Poldner
Oana Branzei

THE FIRST FIVE YEARS

1 Sébastien Kopp and François-Ghislain Morillion (see **Exhibit 1**), recent business graduates in their twenties, had traveled the planet looking for a cool way to do business.[1] In 2005, they

EXHIBIT 1 **Veja Founders**

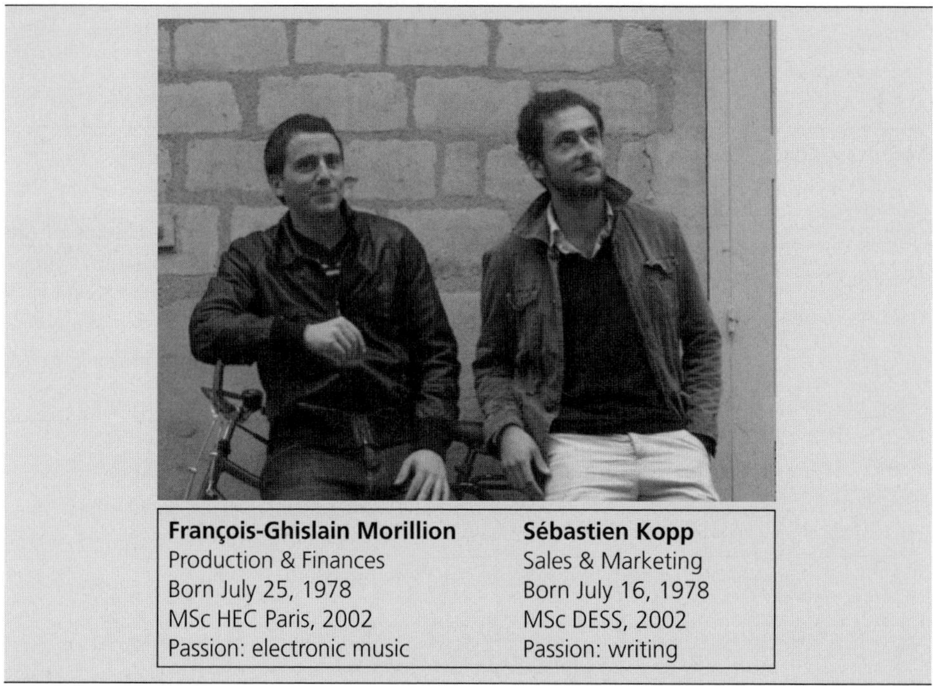

Source: Prepared by the case writer on the basis of company documents and interviews. Photo credits: Veja, used with permission.

[1] Their world journey is featured at the Juste Planet website; available at http://www.justeplanete.org/index.php, accessed on September 26, 2010.

settled in Brazil, where they founded Veja,[2] the first ethical sneaker company in the world. The Veja sneakers were made from wild latex sourced from the Amazon river area (Amazonia) to mitigate rubber tree deforestation, from Brazilian organic cotton to enhance biodiversity and from vegetable-tanned leather to prevent water pollution. These sneakers not only made consumers look good but also prompted them to take a closer look at bigger issues, such as the use of pesticides, genetically modified crops and fair-trade labor practices.

2 Kopp and Morillion had designed and produced several sneaker collections, had launched brand extensions (e.g., Veja Baby and Veja Kids), had opened offices in London and had established a distinctive presence online (see **Exhibit 2**). In 2005, the company started off aiming to sell its sneakers—with a conscience—in conventional stores, right next to iconic brands such as Nike. By 2010, Veja was selling more than 100,000 pairs annually, in 200 stores worldwide, including 80 in France. Customers included singer Lilly Allen and actress Angelina Jolie, whose baby had been recently photographed wearing Veja running shoes.[3] Veja sneakers had been on display at the Ethical Fashion Show (EFS) in Paris, the biggest eco fashion event that brought together 100 brands from around the world. Perhaps even more impressive, Veja had created, from scratch, a global chain that emphasized solidarity and the environment and linked small producers in Brazil to the European catwalks.

HOLD OR FOLD?

3 Kopp and Morillion had been at the forefront of a rapidly changing industry. Large companies wanted a share of the rapidly increasing market that valued ecologically and socially responsible fashion. Small ethical fashion brands such as Veja were hot buys. Since 2007, several small eco-fashion pioneers had been taken over by bigger brands. These deals enjoyed great media coverage and stirred vivid debates on the future of fashion.

4 New ethical fashion brands were popping up in attempts to copy Veja's successful business model.[4] For example, France-based Loic Pollet, the founder of Sébola,[5] who had launched his first collection in the fall of 2008, commented "Looking at success stories like Veja, we felt inspired to start our own brand." Since 2009, Canada-based Tal Dehtiar, founder of Oliberté, had begun working with producers in Ethiopia to launch a competing eco-sneaker.[6] In March 2010, the sneaker brand Sawa shoes launched its first collection, made in Cameroon.[7] Ethical fashion companies such as Simple Shoes[8] and Patagonia[9] had also added eco-sneakers to their offerings. Multinationals such as Nike and Adidas[10] had also recently launched their own limited editions. For example, Nike's Trash Talk sneaker, co-developed with Phoenix Suns basketball star Steve Nash, was made from

[2] In Brazil, Veja means "look." For the company, "veja" symbolized looking around to develop a conscience about what is going on in the world.

[3] Ana Santi, "From Fashion to Rubber," Born in Brazil: Bringing Brazil to the UK," blog entry, posted August 22, 2010; available at http://www.borninbrazil.co.uk/2010/08/from-fashion-to-rubber.html, accessed on September 26, 2010.

[4] Eco Fashion World, "Guide"; available at http://www.ecofashionworld.com/Brands-/listA.html, accessed on September 26, 2010.

[5] Interview with Loic Pollet, October 1, 2009, used with permission; further information at http://www.sebola.fr, accessed on September 26, 2010.

[6] Oliberté Limited, "This Is Africa"; available at http://www.oliberte.com/, accessed on September 26, 2010.

[7] Sawa, available at http://www.sawashoes.com/eng/, accessed on September 26, 2010.

[8] Simple Shoes, available at http://www.simpleshoes.com/, accessed on September 26, 2010.

[9] Patagonia, Inc., available at http://www.patagonia.com/web/us/search/sneakers, accessed on September 26, 2010.

[10] Kim Poldner, "Adidas Green," *Eco Fashion World*; available at http://www.ecofashionworld.com/Trends/ADIDAS-GREEN.html, accessed on September 26, 2010.

EXHIBIT 2 Veja Collections

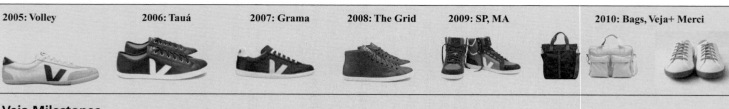

Veja Milestones

2005	2006	2007	2008	2009	2010
Feb: Launch Veja	Feb: Collaboration Agnes b.	June: launch Veja + Christine Phung	March: Launch Veja Kids	March: Launch bags+wallets	Jan: Launch Veja+Merci
Sept: Launch Veja website	July: Launch Veja blog	Sept: Veja @ Ethical Fashion Show (EFS)	Aug: London office open	Sept: Expo SP, Mon Amour	Feb: Veja+Bonpoint Merci
Nov: Launch Veja Baby	Nov: 1st rubber collection	Dec: Veja lands in Madrid	Oct: Launch online store	Nov: Launch Veja+ Cyclope	May: Snippet expo London

Ethical Fashion Milestones

2005	2006	2007	2008	2009	2010
Ethical Fashion Forum is founded in the UK	1st Esthetica in London	Organic Exchange turns 5 years old*	5th EFS in Paris	EFS launches in other cities like Milan	Messe Frankfurt acquires EFS
Launch of Made-By				Launch NY Green-shows and TheKey.to Berlin	

Source: Prepared by the case writer on the basis of company documents and interviews.

*http://cogent.controlunion.com/cusi_production_files/SISI_files/FL_011210114219_Market_Report_08-_Executive_Summary.pdf, accessed September 28, 2010.

factories' leftover materials.[11] Veja faced even greater competition for its accessories, such as Veja's newly launched bags (see Exhibit 2). The competitors were keenly watching Veja's next move.

ETHICAL FASHION DEALS

5 On December 4, 2006, Timberland acquired Howies Limited (Howies), an active sports brand created less than a decade ago to serve as "a voice and mechanism for communicating a core environmental and social conscience, to ask a different question and show the world that there is another way to do business."[12] Jeffrey Swartz, Timberland's president and chief executive officer (CEO) welcomed Howies to the family: "I want people to believe in the power of the marketplace to make things better."[13] Swartz also pledged that "Together we will leverage our complementary strengths to bring our brands to new consumers and new markets."[14] Timberland's media release commended the ethical fashion brand for innovation, authenticity and integrity. The co-founders of Howies, David and Claire Hieatt, had built a company they were proud of. They would stay onboard to help the Howies brand grow within Timberland, citing their commitment to "make better and lower impact products, to give a better service and to do more good as we go about our business. Those are our rainbows to chase. They always will be."[15]

6 On May 18, 2009, "the world's largest luxury conglomerate [the Louis Vuitton Group], paid an undisclosed amount to secure a minority stake in Edun, a prominent ethical fashion line"[16] founded just four years earlier by Ali Hewson and her husband, Bono, U2's lead singer and a political activist, with designer Rogan Gregory. Edun had used "star power and edgy designs to bring worldwide attention to important ethical fashion principles."[17] Although critics wondered whether the acquisition could "green" the conglomerate, Louis Vuitton soon created a special bag for Edun (which sold for US$4,900) and agreed to donate all proceeds from the bag sales to the Conservation Cotton Initiative—an organization advocating for the development of eco-friendly, organic cotton farming to improve incomes and increase economic growth.[18] The bag was adorned with charms—distinctive bunches of ebony and bone spikes—that were produced in co-operation with Made,[19] a fair-trade brand

[11] Nike, "Steve Nash and Nike Turn Garbage into Trash Talk," media release, February 13, 2008; available at http://www.nikebiz.com/media/pr/2008/02/13_Nash.html, accessed on September 26, 2010.

[12] David Hieatt, "Exciting News," December 4, 2006; available at http://www.howies.co.uk/content.php?xSecId=56&viewblog=557, accessed on September 26, 2010.

[13] PSFK, available at http://www.psfk.com/2006/12/ethical_entrpre.html, accessed on September 26, 2010.

[14] Fibre2fashion, "USA: Timberland Acquires Howies, UK-based Active Sports Wear Brand," December 4, 2006; available at http://www.fibre2fashion.com/news/company-news/timberland-company/newsdetails.aspx?news_id=27033, accessed on September 26, 2010.

[15] David Hieatt, "Exciting News," December 4, 2006; available at http://www.howies.co.uk/content.php?xSecId=56&viewblog=557, accessed on September 26, 2010.

[16] Ethical Style, "Louis Vuitton Buys Minority Stake in Edun," Ethical Style blog entry, May 18, 2009; available at http://ethicalstyle.com/2009/05/louis-vuitton-buys-minority-stake-in-edun/, accessed on September 26, 2010.

[17] Ibid.

[18] EDUN, "EDUN Launches the Conservation Cotton Initiative – Joining Forces with the Wildlife Conservation Society," news release, July 31, 2007, PR Newswire; available at http://www.prnewswire.com/news-releases/edun-launches-the-conservation-cotton-initiative---joining-forces-with-the-wildlife-conservation-society-52788817.html, accessed on September 26, 2010.

[19] Made, available at http://made.uk.com/, accessed on September 26, 2010.

of jewelry and accessories expertly finished by craftspeople in Kenya; these bag charms were Louis Vuitton's very first "made in Africa" product.[20] In exchange, Bono and his wife appeared in the latest Louis Vuitton campaign.[21]

7 On September 10, 2009, the Vivarte Group (known for such brands as Naf Naf and Kookaï) partnered with Les Fées des Bengales; Vivarte's share remained undisclosed. The ethical fashion brand Les Fées des Bengales had been founded in 2006 by two sisters, Sophie and Camille Dupuy, and their friend Elodie le Derf, after a voyage in poverty-stricken yet beautiful rural India. Sophie Dupuy recalled the trip as having been a revelation. She was captivated by the brightly colored saris and equally struck by the trying work conditions and the know-how she observed in the traditional workshops. Les Fées de Bengales was mainly set up to work with women in India.[22] Seventy percent of its output was produced in India but the company had recently acquired new partners in Portugal, Tunisia and France to grow its output. Post-partnership, both design and production remained in the hands of the founders: "We are continuing with our strategy and now we even guarantee the eco-friendly production line."[23]

THE ETHICAL FASHION INDUSTRY

8 The global apparel, accessories and luxury goods market generated total revenues of $1,334.1 billion in 2008.[24] In 2005, the industry employed approximately 26 million people and contributed to 7 percent of world exports.[25] Fierce competition and lack of supply chain transparency kept driving costs down—at a high social and environmental burden that included the use of child labor, unfair practices and disruption of natural ecosystems.

9 Ethical fashion was booming. Some predicted that, by 2015, certain practices, such as the use of organic cotton, would become mainstream.[26] Nearly every big label, including H&M, Guess and Banana Republic, had developed a "green" line. Nike and Adidas had integrated ethical principles into their core business, and leading retailers, such as Wal-Mart and Marks & Spencer, had made ethical sourcing a centerpiece of their new strategy.[27] For example, Wal-Mart had become the biggest buyer of organic cotton in the world. Although the quantity of organic cotton produced was still minuscule—in 2009, 175,113 metric tonnes of organic cotton were grown, representing 0.76 percent of the cotton production[28]—the organic cotton segment was growing at an impressive 20 percent per year.

[20] Trend Hunter Fashion, "Tribal Designer Bags: The Louis Vuitton for Edun Keepall 45 Duffel Is Stunning"; available at http://www.trendhunter.com/trends/louis-vuitton-for-edun, accessed on September 26, 2010.

[21] High Snobiety, "Louis Vuitton x Edun Keepall 45 Tavel Duffel Bag," September 20, 2010; available at http://www.highsnobiety.com/news/2010/09/20/louis-vuitton-x-edun-keepall-45-travel-duffle-bag/, accessed on September 26, 2010.

[22] Les Fées de Bengale, available at http://www.lesfeesdebengale.fr/v3/fr/la-marque/lhistoire, accessed on September 26, 2010.

[23] Barbara Markert, "Vivarte Partners with Les Fées de Bengale," *Sportswear International Magazine*, September 10, 2009; available at http://www.sportswearnet.com/fashionnews/pages/protected/VIVARTE-PARTNERS-WITH-LES-FES-DE-BENGALES_1877.html, accessed on September 26, 2010.

[24] *Consumer Goods: Global Industry Guide*, Datamonitor, March 2009, accessed on September 26, 2010.

[25] HM Customs & Excise, Provided by the British Apparel & Textile Confederation (2005) provided to Defra: www.defra.gov.uk, accessed on September 26, 2010.

[26] cKinetics, *Exporting Textiles: March to Sustainability*, April 2010; available at http://www.ckinetics.com/MarchToSustainability2010/, accessed on September 26, 2010.

[27] Organic Exchange, *Organic Cotton Market Report 2007–2008*; available at www.organicexchange.org, ccessed on September 26, 2010.

[28] Organic Exchange, *Organic Cotton Farm and Fiber Report 2009*; available at www.organicexchange.org, accessed on September 26, 2010.

10 Several established fashion brands were working together with non-governmental organizations (NGOs) to add organic fibers to their collections. For example, Vivienne Westwood[29] used her catwalk shows as platforms to campaign for less consumption and a more sustainable lifestyle. Since 2005, eco fashion designs had been shown during New York Fashion Week by such fashion brands as Versace, Martin Margiela and Donna Karan. Instead of using traditional fabrics, such as silk and cashmere, many fashion designers now preferred to use fabrics such as sasawashi (a Japanese fabric made from paper and herbs), hemp and peace silk (a silk produced in such a way that silk worms lived out their full life cycle).

11 In 2003, the Ethical Fashion Show (EFS) was launched in Paris. It was the first and biggest event to focus exclusively on ecological, socially responsible and environmentally friendly garment production. In 2008, EFS began expanding to other cities, from Milan to Rio de Janeiro. In April 2010, the Messe Frankfurt (also known as the Frankfurt Trade Fair)—the world's market leader in trade shows, which hosted 31 textile fairs around the world—took over the EFS. The acquisition meant that Messe Frankfurt, the combined fair and exhibition company, now covered the world's entire supply chain in the sector of textile fairs.

12 As the ethical fashion movement picked up,[30] it brought together like-minded stylists, activists, models, journalists, stores, celebrities and events. Eco boutiques on the web encouraged online shopping and drove change in the retail industry. Fashion schools stimulated their students to consider this issue through the introduction of special topics within the curriculum. Governments played their part by regulating destructive practices and transforming the mindset of consumers. NGOs developed systems to trace each item back to its origins. Others campaigned and lobbied to create more general awareness on ethical fashion and to help create eco fashion brands that could become successful examples of public–private partnerships.

13 The main actors in the ethical fashion movement, however, were the small eco-fashion brands, many of which had been born less than four years earlier. By 2010, more than 500 ethical fashion brands were in business around the globe. In the majority of the brands, the founder (and the founder's small team) worked directly with people in developing countries to source and produce socially and environmentally responsible fashion items. These ventures were no longer just designing an item to wear; they were crafting stories that signaled how individuals felt about big issues, such as poverty and deforestation. Wearing eco-fashions made a statement all right, but it was no longer just about the clothes—or shoes.

14 Eco-fashion was still in its infancy. Despite the financial crisis, sales of organic and ethical fashion were shooting up, growing by 50 percent each year.[31] Although the industry was small—eco-fashion represented just 1 percent of the sales in the broader fashion industry—it was growing momentum. Eco-fashion was particularly popular among a segment known as "cultural creatives,"[32] who were highly educated consumers who had an

[29] Vivienne Westwood is a well-known fashion designer, whose four decade career remains highly influential, http://www.viviennewestwood.com/flash.php, accessed on September 29, 2010.

[30] Entrepreneurs in ethical fashion were from a variety of backgrounds. They ranged from NGO workers to business people, and only a small percentage had been trained as fashion designers. Many of them had altruistic reasons for starting their brand, such as to help a specific community in a developing country. In the beginning, the focus of these brands was often not on design, but more on survival and philanthropic goals. This focus changed as an increasing number of entrepreneurs hired professional stylists who created ever more beautiful collections.

[31] Organic Trade Association, "Industry Statistics and Projected Growth," June 2010; available at http://www.ota.com/organic/mt/business.html, accessed on September 26, 2010.

[32] Cultural Creatives, available at http://www.culturalcreatives.org, accessed on September 26, 2010.

interest in spirituality, actively participated in society through voluntary work, advocated a conscious lifestyle and were motivated by a high need to strive for a better world. More than 50 million cultural creatives spent $230 billion on everything from yoga gear to organic apples to hybrid cars. This trend was evident not only in fashion-forward countries, such as France, the United Kingdom, Germany and the United States, but also in BRIC countries, such as Brazil, which were characterized by increasing numbers of customers seeking a green lifestyle.[33] Awareness for eco-fashion brands was growing rapidly: 18 percent of consumers had heard of eco fashion brands, three times the number four years earlier.[34]

BUSINESS MODEL

15 Kopp and Morillion started their company without a clue about the fashion industry. After graduating from Paris business schools, Kopp and Morillion took off for a one-year journey around the world. They visited and studied sustainable development projects in different industries, from Chinese factories to South African mines to the Amazon rainforest, witnessing first-hand problems such as deforestation, exhaustion of natural resources and labor exploitation. When they returned to France, they knew they needed to act and to act now. They first tried consulting and recommended to companies such as supermarket Carrefour: "Stop charity, but instead have a close look within your company at what is wrong in the countries where you work and try to do something positive about it."[35] Then they realized they had to do something themselves: "Let's pick a product and try to put as much sustainable development in it as we can."[36]

16 Both Kopp and Morillion were sneaker addicts. They knew from the start what they wanted to create: good-looking shoes that had a positive impact on both the planet and society, as opposed to the negative impacts that characterized the big sneaker manufacturers. The two friends took the path of fair trade because they felt it would be the most effective way to integrate environment and dignity into everyday products. They set out to "invent new methods of work."[37] Veja was built on three main values: using ecological inputs, using fair trade cotton and latex and respecting workers' dignity.

Getting Started

17 Kopp and Morillion's journey around the world had opened their eyes to the rich variety of countries and cultures. They chose to operate in Brazil. Kopp and Morillion loved Brazil, its climate, its language and culture, and they imagined themselves living in Brazil. Here, they had met many people from NGOs and social movements working collaboratively to protect the sensitive Amazonian eco-system; connecting with these players, they felt, would help them scaffold the entire value chain.

[33] Hartman Group, *The Hartman Report on Sustainability: Understanding the Consumer Perspective, 2007;* available at www.hartman-group.com, accessed on September 26, 2010. Consumers in many major markets want more green product choices. Studies show that 50 percent of women want mass retailers to carry more green goods, and 11 percent of these consumers see themselves as "extremely green" today, and 43 percent say that they will be "extremely green" in five years.

[34] Forum for the Future, "Fashion Futures 2025: Global Scenarios for a Sustainable Fashion Industry," February 24, 2010; available at http://www.forumforthefuture.org.uk/projects/fashion-futures, accessed on September 26, 2010.

[35] Interview with François Morillion, October 2, 2009, used with permission.

[36] Ibid.

[37] Veja, "Is Another World Possible?," available at http://www.veja.fr/#/projets/VISION-26, accessed on September 26, 2010.

18 After calculating the budget needed to produce their first sneaker collection, Kopp and Morillion were able to negotiate a bank loan. They then moved to Brazil, set up their company and began producing the collection. They presented their first sneaker collection at a conventional trade fair in Paris. Who's next?[38] always had extra space available to feature new designers, and Kopp and Morillion managed to secure a spot to showcase their new sneakers. They learned on the go:

> I remember running out the tradeshow to buy some paper on which we could write down the orders people placed. But then you talk to your neighbours and you pick up quickly how it works.[39]

19 It was a Cinderella story. Kopp and Morillion identified the stores where they wanted to place their sneakers and then invited those buyers to see their collection. People came, loved the product and started buying. Their product was so successful that the first collection sold out, and Veja was able pay back its bank loan within a year. Veja had enough money to produce a second collection. Since then, the company grew ten-fold by following the same approach: they took little risk, produced small quantities and focused on the product. Morillion commented:

> We had a plan for the first year, then we had a plan until we presented the shoe and after that we discovered a whole world we didn't know about. We basically went learning by doing, making many mistakes.[40]

20 Morillion was in charge of production and finances, and Kopp ran the commercial side of the company, but they did most of the work together. "We fight every day," [Morillion] confessed. In the first few years . . .

> . . . every day there was a new problem because we really had no clue about the shoe business. It was definitely the biggest challenge in building Veja, to learn how to make proper shoes.[41]

21 Kopp and Morillion initially spent half of the year in Brazil. Then they hired a shoemaker who had all the expertise they needed and who later became the manager of the Veja team co-located in Porto Alegre, the eleventh most populous municipality in Brazil, the centre of Brazil's fourth largest metropolitan area and the capital city of the southernmost Brazilian state of Rio Grande do Sul. The Brazil-based team took care of quality, administration, logistics (e.g., shipping) and the entire raw material process of buying and paying the cotton, rubber and leather. The founders were in touch with the Brazilian team daily, via Skype, and traveled to Brazil four or five times a year to meet with their Brazilian co-workers. In addition, the team manager traveled to Paris twice a year to see the new stores where the sneakers were sold and to meet customers and colleagues in the headquarters in Paris.

Distribution Chain

22 Since the beginning, Veja had aimed to place its product in trendy sneaker boutiques next to other (non-ethical) brands. Veja did not see the need to promote its ethical approach to customers who were already convinced about the importance of purchasing ethical products. Instead, the company wanted to inspire customers who were accustomed to buying trendy

[38] http://www.whosnext.com/, accessed on September 29, 2010.

[39] Interview with François Morillion, October 2, 2009, used with permission.

[40] Ibid.

[41] Ibid.

sneakers. Veja sneakers sold in premium venues, such as the Galeries Lafayette in Paris and Rien à Cacher in Montreal. Veja sneakers were available in selected shops across Europe and Canada, but most sneakers were sold in France, Spain and the United Kingdom.

23 In France, Veja collaborated with the Atelier Sans Frontières association (ASF), which facilitated work for socially marginalized people,[42] by helping them to build a new life and by promoting their social, professional and personal development. Since the founding of Veja, ASF had received all the finished sneakers from Brazil, stored them and prepared all the orders, which were dispatched to the retail stores where Veja sneakers were sold. ASF logisticians had recently started managing the functional portion of Veja's online store, the Veja Store.[43] ASF was in charge of printing, preparing, packing and sending all online orders.

Production

24 Veja sneakers were manufactured in a factory close to Porto Alegre. Most of the employees traced their roots to a community of German descendants who had arrived in Brazil at the end of the 19th century. All employees owned houses with running water and electricity, and 80 percent were union members. Sixty percent of the workers lived in the towns and villages surrounding the factory (the farthest being located 47 km away), while the remaining 40 percent live near the factory. The factory pre-arranged coach services ensure all employees could travel safely and comfortably to work.

25 Veja complied with the core International Labour Organization (ILO) labor standards but felt more was needed to guarantee dignity at work. For example, Veja cared about workers' freedom to gather and uphold their rights, their standard of living and purchasing power, their social benefits and their rights of free speech. The average wage of the factory workers was approximately €238 each month, 16 percent higher than Brazil's legal minimum wage for the shoe industry of €205 each month. In addition, Veja paid overtime and an annual bonus. The factory employees were entitled to four weeks of paid holiday, and they did not work on bank holidays. During the peak season, each employee worked a maximum of two hours extra per day, on average. Each employee contributed seven to 11 percent of their salary to INSS (Instituto Nacional do Seguro Social, Brazil's governmental pension scheme), which provided an additional safety net for the employees.

26 When Kopp and Morillion were in business school, had taken internships in investment banking and consultancy companies, where they learned about hard work and earning a lot of money. Morillion commented: "In these places, we saw how people were stressed and didn't like their jobs, but just came home happy because of the money. This is definitely not our culture."[44] At Veja, employees started their work at 9:30 in the morning and left the office before 7 p.m. On Friday afternoons, everyone went home at 4:30 p.m., and the founders themselves often went out of town for the weekend. Keeping the balance between work and private life was at the core of Veja's approach of creating a company that cared about the employees.

27 Each year, each new member of the Veja team was given the opportunity to travel to Brazil to meet the producers. For the founders, involving their employees in the entire Veja

[42] Beyond this partnership with Veja, ASF tried to involve its employees in other tasks, such as collecting old sports material and computers and repairing them. All the work is adapted to the people depending on their skills and experience. The aim is to aid the employees in (re)building their lives and careers.

[43] Veja, http://www.veja-store.com/, accessed on September 26, 2010.

[44] Interview with François Morillion, October 2, 2009, used with permission.

story was essential, instead of simply letting them work in an office in the center of Paris. Morillion explained:

> We travel a lot and meet many different people, but our employees don't get that chance. If we don't involve them in the whole process, they will get bored and might want to leave the company. [We created] different experiences for our employees and they loved it.[45]

Certification

28 As part of the fair trade certification process, the main shoe factory in Porto Alegre underwent two social audits. The different departments of the factory and the fabrication workshops (which housed the cutting, sewing, soles, assembling processes) were audited in 2008 and 2009, in accordance with the Fairtrade Labelling Organization–Certification (FLO-Cert) standard requirements. The auditor raised 52 non-compliances in May 2008 and 16 non-compliances in February 2009; in April 2009, the certification of the factory was officially confirmed.

29 While the fair trade certification was increasingly important to consumers, for it was a means to a greater end, a starting point in Kopp and Morillion's path to improve the bigger picture. Veja sought to establish higher standards and strive toward loftier social and environmental objectives. To help the farmers gain additional credibility, Kopp and Morillion supported the cooperatives in the process of obtaining certification, but their personal relationships with the farmers extended beyond certification. The founders cared about social equity, and saw their venture as one means to improve farmers' lives by supporting traditional livelihoods.

Supply Chain

30 Kopp and Morillion created a supply chain that was based on sustainable relationships (see **Exhibit 3**). They viewed the company's connection to its producers as one not just of trade but of cultural exchange. Whereas the fashion industry was accustomed to contracting new parties as soon as a factory could deliver on time or cut costs, Veja tried to improve living conditions and to work cooperatively with supply chain to jointly develop the best product they could imagine. Veja bought raw materials directly from producers. The company paid a fixed price, which, though higher than the market price, was calculated by the farmers and allowed them to live in dignity. Veja was happy to pay extra. Kopp and Morillion viewed fair wages as a means of re-establishing social justice.

Cotton

31 The canvas for the Veja sneakers was organic cotton. With help from Esplar,[46] an NGO that had been collaborating with Brazilian farmers for 30 years, Veja started working with 150 families to grow cotton under agro-ecological principles (i.e., without the use of agrochemicals or pesticides); Veja now sourced cotton from 400 families in the state of Ceará in northeastern Brazil.

32 Veja purchased 90 percent of the organic cotton it used from ADEC, a new association of rural farmers who followed agro-ecological principles. The strong interdependence made Veja vulnerable. Changes in weather and natural disasters, such as insect plagues and violent rains, could deplete the supply of organic cotton. Production needed to adapt to the availability of organic cotton, which still varied considerably. Depending on the extent of the harvest, Veja sometimes needed to reduce the quantities of sneakers ordered by retailers.

[45] Ibid.

[46] Esplar, available at http://www.esplar.org.br/, accessed on September 26, 2010.

tanning techniques. Veja had just started collaborating with other French-Brazilian brands, such as Envão and Tudo Bom, to work together on improving the supply chain and jointly sourcing raw material to be able to meet the quantity criteria. The Veja founders welcomed other small brands interested in sourcing from Brazil because Kopp and Morillion felt "it makes them stronger and reduces the risk for both them and their producers."[49]

Zero Ads

38 Generally, 70 percent of the cost of sneakers was dedicated to marketing. Veja, however, had a "no advertising" policy. Regardless, the company's products had been endorsed by the media and appreciated by the public since the company's creation. Veja benefitted widely from media coverage, blogs, forums and word of mouth. Morillion commented:

> That is really the most rewarding thing in running this company, to see people walking down the streets on our sneakers. Last week I saw someone with a Veja bag, which is a very new product just in stores. He was not even a friend of us, but a complete stranger who had already picked up this product![50]

Zero Stock

39 The popularity of Veja's products paid off: most outlets had fewer Veja sneakers than they could sell. Veja did not produce extra; it produced only according to orders placed six months in advance. Veja was not about large volumes but about profitability—with a conscience.

Environmental Footprint

CO_2 Emissions

40 Veja looked at every aspect of its supply chain and adjusted the company's methods of transportation, organization, production and distribution. All Veja shoes were transported by boat from Porto Alegre, Brazil, to Le Havre in France. Upon arrival in Le Havre, the shoes traveled in barges along the canals to the Parisian suburbs. Veja's packaging was made from recycled and recyclable cardboard and it used shoe boxes that were sized down to optimize efficiency. Finally, Veja's headquarters used Enercoop (a green electricity cooperative) instead sourcing electricity from Électricité de France (EDF, the French national nuclear energy supplier).

Limitations

41 Veja was open, both about its limitations and its work to overcome them. Kopp and Morillion were open about the remaining shortcomings of Veja's production processes and explained how they kept working to become more sustainable. For example, because production was still low, Veja did not need many pairs of shoelaces and could thus not afford to create the laces from organic cotton. The moss used to maintain the ankle was a synthetic, oil-based product. The shoes' sole contains between 30 percent and 40 percent of rubber, whereas the insole contained only 5 percent of rubber. The insole also had technical properties (i.e., comfort and resistance), which required additional components, such as synthetic rubber. The eyelets in the shoes did not contain nickel but were composed of metal whose origin was not controlled. The sneakers were shipped by boat from Brazil to France, but American and Asian stores and clients continued to be serviced by plane. Veja also aimed to recycle the sneakers, thereby further increasing their lifespan.

[49] Interview with François Morillion, October 2, 2009, used with permission.

[50] Ibid.

Message

42 Since day one, Veja had produced more than sneakers. It also crafted art events as a way of connecting to customers and inspiring its own employees. The company's communication team reached out, and Veja sponsored art installations made by local artists they befriended in the French and Brazilian urban art scenes.[51] For example, for the 2006 Fashion Fair "Who's next?" Veja invited the art collective Favela Chic to perform. In an example of Veja's own creativity, São Paulo's 2006 ban on advertising inspired Veja to create an installation in the window display of the Parisian store French Trotters.[52]

43 The most recent exhibition (in October 2009), suggestively titled "São Paulo, Mon Amour," showcased the vision of São Paulo artists on their city.[53] The pieces conveyed messages about social inequality and pollution in Brazil's capital (Brasilia) and raised awareness about these issues. The exhibition, which was held in a public space in Paris, attracted 3,000 people in two weeks' time and was jointly sponsored by the Brazilian Ministry of Culture and the Municipality of Paris. Veja chose a discreet approach to promote the event by inviting the company's contacts, who would thus associate the brand with an interesting and beautiful exhibition.

44 Art was also a driver in the various special collections Veja developed in collaboration with other companies and organizations. For example, in 2007, the company launched a collection designed by the young French fashion designer Christine Phung.[54] In July 2009, the Veja Kids, a line of sneakers for children, landed exclusively in Bonpoint stores around the world.[55] Using the motto "Sell your car, get a bike," the company launched the Cyclope collection in the Cyclope shop in Paris in November 2009.[56] In January 2010, the Veja+ Merci became exclusively available in the Merci store, a lifestyle and fashion emporium in Paris. All proceeds from the Cyclope collection were donated to charity.[57]

THE DECISION

45 When Veja had started, Kopp and Morillion were in their mid-twenties. They had never worked for anyone else, commented Morillion:

> By now I don't think we can ever work for another company, since Veja allows us so much freedom to do what we want and to strive for our dreams. [58]

46 They had many ideas, but took things step by step and try to take as little risk as possible. At the moment they were focusing on their first range of accessories, like bags, wallets and

[51] Although the event was a co-production between Veja and several other parties, the company deliberately chose to not be visible in the event's promotion and publicity.

[52] Veja, "Urban Archeology," March 25, 2009; available at http://blog.veja.fr/en/site/comments/urban_archeology/, accessed on September 26, 2010.

[53] Veja, "São Paulo, Mon Amour," blog entry, posted September 9, 2009; available at http://blog.veja.fr/en/site/comments/megapole_insensee_mon_amour/, accessed on September 26, 2010.

[54] Curitiba 75, "Veja," video clip; available at http://www.youtube.com/watch?v=h__qANp3g8U&feature=player_embedded, accessed on September 26, 2010.

[55] Veja, "Veja and Bonpoint, One to Watch this Winter," blog entry, posted July 17, 2009; available at http://blog.veja.fr/en/site/comments/veja_and_bonpoint/, accessed on September 26, 2010.

[56] http://blog.veja.fr/fr/archive/200912, accessed on September 26, 2010.

[57] Veja, "Vega + Merci," blog entry, posted January 12, 2010; available at http://blog.veja.fr/en/site/comments/veja_merci/, accessed on September 26, 2010.

[58] Interview with François Morillion, October 2, 2009, used with permission.

computer cases. In another five to 10 years, they could save enough to open their own flagship store.

> We're always thinking about the next project, but not really about the one after. It comes as it goes.[59]

47 Kopp and Morillion's social change ambitions held strong. Veja's website portrayed the company as one drop in the ocean, offering the following call to action:

> Day after day, prophets of all kind are pulling the emergency cord, the entire economy is turning green and sustainable-developementising speeches are spreading around.
>
> Actions remain scarce but words abound.
>
> Beyond movies about the environment, beyond multinational companies building green windows to hide disasters, beyond the Copenhagen speeches filled with words and political promise.
>
> And despite this green-fronted economy, let's try to offer a different vision which combines fair trade and ecology and links together economy, social initiatives and the environment.
>
> A vision that proposes cultural change.[60]

48 Kopp and Morillion's vision for social change had already extended beyond their company. Kopp and Morillion coached new eco-fashion brands, which then started men's collections; they tried to give them direction:

> Many people call us and we meet them and give them advice. What is lacking in the ethical fashion field, is strong men's brands and this is where Veja tries to make a difference.[61]

49 Kopp and Morillion also aimed to influence existing brands to convert to organic and fair-trade practices. Sometimes they felt it might be easier to change existing brands because they had already create the style that people wanted to wear, whereas ethical fashion brands often lacked the right aesthetics.

> I think the ethical fashion world is still missing a bit of fashion and that's why it doesn't grow as fast as we all hope. Our product came at the right time at the right place. If we would have done the same product without the fair-trade and organic [angle], it might have brought us the same success. It's sad, but I think it is true.

50 They had a lot of work ahead: "Right now I still haven't found cool ethical T-shirts and jeans and I just hope that I can wear only ethical one day."[62]

[59] Ibid.

[60] Veja, "Veja Is Just a Drop in the Ocean," http://www.veja.fr/#/projets, accessed on September 26, 2010.

[61] Interview with François Morillion, October 2, 2009, used with permission.

[62] Ibid.

Case 28

Wells Fargo: *The Future of a Community Bank*

Alan N. Hoffman

Bentley University and Rotterdam School of Management, Erasmus University

1 Wells Fargo, founded in San Francisco during the gold rush as a money delivery express, is now the fourth largest bank in the US and ranks number one in America's deposit market share. It achieved initial success by being a trustworthy custodian of its customers' wealth. By staying true to a customer-centric business model, it aims to fulfill all its customers' needs and help them succeed financially. After establishing itself as one of the best community banks in the US, Wells Fargo has expanded internationally as a global bank. It has also significantly diversified offerings in order to gain market share. Because of a comprehensive range of products, Wells Fargo is exposed to increasing risks and competition. During the global financial crisis, it was negatively impacted due to its large exposure to bad loans through acquisition of Wachovia. Although the combination of advanced online banking technology and its massive physical network makes Wells Fargo stand out from its competitors, it remains challenging for the company to gain or maintain a leading position. If not managed properly, the diversifying strategy may in the end endanger Wells Fargo's overall market share. The 2010 US financial reform legislation may limit growth potential for a large bank like Wells Fargo. How Wells Fargo can succeed in this increasingly regulated yet highly competitive industry is an open question.

COMPANY HISTORY

2 Wells Fargo was founded in San Francisco in 1852 by Henry Wells and William Fargo, two former express messengers. Before launching Wells Fargo, the two, together with several other pioneer expressmen, created the American Express Company. When the directors declined to extend the business westward to California during the gold rush, Wells and Fargo left American Express and created their own company to serve the western frontier.

3 Wells Fargo quickly expanded throughout the West. The two primary services it offered were banking and express delivery. Following Fargo's vision of a railway system that linked all of America, the company took on the motto of "Ocean to Ocean," connecting the commercial centers of New York and New Jersey through the heartland of America and across to the Pacific Ocean.

4 Wells Fargo was growing strongly when World War I began and the government nationalized the express network. With its express business gone, all that remained was its banking in San Francisco.[1] Wells Fargo Bank had formally separated from the express business in 1905 and thereafter survived the physical challenges of the San Francisco earthquake and

Source: The author would like to thank MBA students Andrew Longmire, Stephanie Mancuso, Paul Souppa, and Shanshan Zhou at Bentley University for their research.

RSM Case Development Centre prepared this case to provide material for class discussion rather than to illustrate either effective or ineffective handling of a management situation.

[1] https://www.wellsfargo.com/about/history/adventure/since_1852

fire, along with the economic hardships brought about by two world wars and the Great Depression.

5 Wells Fargo, in its current management structure, is primarily the result of an acquisition by Norwest Corporation in 1998.[2] The new company maintained both the San Francisco headquarters and the Wells Fargo name. Its management philosophy allowed it to help grow the West's new agricultural, film, and aerospace businesses. While remaining faithful to its history, Wells Fargo continued to add modern banking features such as automated banking, drive-up tellers, and phone access. It also expanded services to include express lines, credit cards, and online banking.

6 On 31 December 2008, Wells Fargo acquired Wachovia, one of America's largest financial service providers, after a government-forced sale of Wachovia to avoid a complete failure. Wells Fargo did accept US$25 billion "bailout" money from the US government to cover Wachovia's losses. These losses were due to failing mortgages mostly linked to its 2006 acquisition of Golden West Financial. The Wachovia purchase, at only US$7 a share, was pennies on the dollar even considering the government financial support Wells Fargo took on. After the merger, Wells Fargo became the fourth largest bank in the US by assets, after Bank of America, JP Morgan Chase, and CitiGroup.[3]

7 After the acquisition of Wachovia, Wells Fargo now has locations in over 130 countries around the world.[4] It is represented in 36 European countries and has been increasing its presence in emerging economies, especially the BRIC countries (Brazil, Russia, India, and China). In 2007, it teamed with HSBC to launch cross-border lending in China.[5] In 2006, it set up two offices in India to expand its technology and business processes.[6] In 2000, it acquired National Bank of Alaska to enter the Russian markets.[7] In Brazil, Wells Fargo now has four offices open in Sao Paulo, Rio de Janeiro, Sao Bernhard do Campo, and Joinville.[8]

INDUSTRY ENVIRONMENT

The Financial Crisis

8 The finance industry has been on a rollercoaster ride since 2005; financial institutions have experienced huge earnings and major revenue loss. Since February 2007, the industry has been the focus of ire and blame for the world's economic recession. In 2008 when the credit crisis hit the industry hard, almost all companies in the industry had declined revenue growth. The massive loan loss write-down as a result of the credit crisis caused the industry to contract overall by 25% between 2007 and 2009. Through US federal bailouts for the "too big to fail" banks and the collapse of over 200 small, middle, and large sized banks in the US alone,[9] the landscape of the finance industry has changed drastically.

9 Because of the severity of the financial collapse in the US, the finance industry is seeing more supervision than ever before. In July 2010, the US Congress passed the most

[2] https://www.wellsfargo.com/about/history/adventure/modern_times

[3] http://www.ffiec.gov/nicpubweb/nicweb/top50form.aspx

[4] https://wfis.wellsfargo.com/ProductServices/A%20to%20Z/WellsFargoGlobalBrokerNetwork/

[5] https://www.wellsfargo.com/press/20070502_tradebank

[6] http://www.naukri.com/gpw/wellsfargo/index.htm

[7] http://www.allbusiness.com/marketing-advertising/segmentation-targeting/1061261-1.html

[8] https://wfis.wellsfargo.com/ProductServices/A%20to%20Z/WellsFargoGlobalBrokerNetwork/WWNetwork/SouthAmerica/Brazil/Pages/default.aspx

[9] http://www.fdic.gov/bank/individual/failed/banklist.html

sweeping set of changes to the financial regulatory system since the 1930s, ending more than a year-long effort to pass legislation in response to the 2008 financial crisis. The bill aims to strengthen consumer protection, rein in complex financial products and head off more bank bailouts.[10]

10 As consumer confidence slowly increases and investors have begun purchasing the common stocks of major US banks, the finance industry seems to be on the way to recovery. From 2010 to 2015, industry revenue is expected to increase 6.6% annually, and the market should experience much less volatility with regulation changes.[11] The big banks are under tighter government control but continue to benefit from government support and try to diversify their products so as to be more competitive. Overall, it will likely take some time for the finance industry to recover and to re-establish clarity on consumer confidence and employment. The surviving banks are in a long transitional period from survival mode to growth mode.

Competition

11 The finance industry is competitive and increasingly so. Due to mergers and bankruptcies, particularly in 2009, the number of participants in the industry has declined. As a result, the ten largest commercial banks have captured almost 40% of the market share in the US. This figure is expected to further increase with market recovery. The top five financial institutions in the US include Bank of America, JP Morgan Chase, CitiGroup, Well Fargo, and PNC Financial Services.

12 *Bank of America,* one of the world's largest financial institutions, operates in all 50 states and in over 40 foreign countries. It serves about 59 million consumers and small business. It is also one of the world's largest wealth management companies and employs roughly 20,000 financial advisors with US$2.5 trillion in assets. After the purchase of Merrill Lynch in 2008, Bank of America became one of the largest financial service firms. With all these factors, the company has more cost advantage over other competitors.

13 Bank of America generates revenues through all different financial sectors. It managed to increase revenue by 33% in 2009 and expects to see an additional 6.7% increase in 2010. Throughout the years, the company has gone through several major mergers and acquisitions to maintain its leading position. The notable ones are ABN, FleetBoston, Countrywide and Merrill Lynch.

14 Like other financial companies, Bank of America was hit hard by the crisis and received US$45 million from the government in bailout money. But it was the second of the big four players to repay its funding, indicating an increased confidence of surviving without help from the government. Despite the financial trouble with Merrill Lynch, Bank of America is starting to regain traction in its recovery. There are plenty of businesses within the bank that could bounce back after the current recession is over.

15 *JP Morgan Chase,* one of the largest financial institutions in the world, operates over 5,100 branches, including 2,322 branches added after the acquisition of Washington Mutual. JP Morgan Chase is a diversified bank. Its revenue is divided among several different sectors including investment banking, retail financial services, card services, commercial banking, treasury and security service, and asset management and corporate. The company's comprehensive list of products puts it in a leading spot.

16 JP Morgan Chase has managed to experience steady revenue increases from 2007 through 2009 despite the recession. It had a total of US$38.4 billion revenue in 2009, a

[10] http://money.cnn.com/2010/07/15/news/economy/Wall_Street_reform_bill_vote/index.htm

[11] http://www.netadvantage.standardpoor.com.ezp.bentley.edu/NASApp/NetAdvantage/index.do

35.7% increase from 2008. Its strong balance sheet enabled it to attract customers and gain the top position in every major investment banking business in 2009. As a result of its strong financial position, JP Morgan Chase was one of the first financial institutions allowed to repay Troubled Asset Relief Program (TARP) funds.

17 Similar to Bank of America and Wells Fargo, JP Morgan Chase grew through external acquisition during the recession. The two major purchases are Bear Stearns in 2008 and Washington Mutual in 2009. The latter acquisition in particular gave JP Morgan Chase a huge revenue boost. Even though JP Morgan Chase has its hands full dealing with all the problem assets from Bear Stearns and Washington Mutual, in addition to its own troubled assets, it has a better chance to continue to outperform its competition due to its strong balance sheet.

18 *Citigroup, Inc.* has the world's largest financial services network, spanning 140 countries with approximately 16,000 offices worldwide. The company employs about 300,000 personnel globally and holds more than 200 million customer accounts. Citigroup operates through four major business groups: consumer banking, global wealth management, global cards and institutional client groups.

19 Compared to its competitors, Citigroup suffered the most during the financial crisis. Due to huge exposure to toxic mortgages, the company suffered heavy losses and received a massive bailout from the US government. It had negative 2.1% revenue growth in 2008 and negative 5% growth in 2009. In addition to poor financial performance, the acquisitions by Bank of America, Wells Fargo and JP Morgan Chase have severely hurt Citigroup's market share.

20 *PNC Financial Services* is the fifth largest bank in the US and the third largest provider of off-premise ATMs in the US. The company manages approximately US$290 billion in assets, has over 2,600 branches all over the country and employs about 60,000 workers across the US and abroad. PNC's total earnings increased from US$215 million in 2008 to US$1.2 billion in 2009, which reflects the acquisition of National City. Provision for credit losses was US$1.6 billion in 2009, an increase of US$1 billion from 2008. This was mainly driven by real estate, middle market, and the National City acquisition.

21 PNC's strategy of focusing on risk management has served it well in recent years. It has avoided most of the troubles in sub-prime mortgages and other high-risk loans. The company maintains a moderate risk profile with a diverse portfolio of commercial, mortgage, home equity, and real estate loans. PNC's latest strategy of cutting expenses and its ability to mark down a large portion of National City's loans has helped the company to save on costs, but its exposure to commercial real estate and business loans will probably continue to create problems in the later stages of the recession and recovery.

A COMMUNITY BANK

Customer Centricity

22 Wells Fargo says, "If you find one trusted provider that can satisfy all your financial services needs and save you time and money, why not bring all your business to that trusted provider?"[12] The company bases its business development on this premise. It tries to satisfy all its customers' financial needs, make it easy for them to arrange financial transactions, and allow them a volume discount.

[12] https://www.wellsfargo.com/invest_relations/vision_values/3

23 Wells Fargo has a two-pronged strategy. The first employs its national scope and depth of technology utilization to form a better understanding of its customer investment preferences, which enables it to cross-sell existing products to its current customer base. Furthermore, Wells Fargo expects to grow via the good will it has created and the networking element of loyal customers.

24 The second strategy is to continuously develop its reputation as a sustainable, trustworthy financial services provider. By maintaining close ties with customers, Wells Fargo is able to keep them on in the face of growing global competition. The company leverages its size and national reach to provide new financial products and better delivery systems. It hopes to maintain the friendly, community bank feeling in an increasingly globalized and impersonal marketplace.

Products

25 Wells Fargo products include banking, insurance, trust and investments, mortgage banking, investment banking, retail banking brokerage, and consumer finance.[13] It offers these products through banking stores, the Internet and other distribution channels in all 50 states of the US. These products cover three different operating segments at Wells Fargo–Community Banking, Wholesale Banking, and Wealth, Brokerage and Retirement.

26 The company understands that one product does not cater to every customer, so it creates many different vehicles that will meet the needs of every different type of customer at every different stage of his life. Due to the large value of assets under management, as well as the large volume of deposits that it holds, Wells Fargo maintains an economy of scale advantage over small and mid-sized banks. It is able to offer customers lower rates on loans and higher yields on investments, which further adds to its customer base.

27 Community Banking is by far the largest source of Wells Fargo's revenues, accounting for 71% of its 2009's total revenue. This segment includes Regional Banking, Diversified Products and the Consumer Deposits groups, as well as Wells Fargo Customer Connection (formerly Wells Fargo Phone Bank and Wachovia Direct Access). Wells Fargo has accounts where the minimum opening deposit is as little as US$100 and there are no monthly fees as long as the account is set up with direct deposit or there is a minimum of US$1,000 in the account. These accounts are targeted towards the lower net value customers.

28 Well Fargo's loan services include auto loans, mortgages, home equity loans, and loans for those with less than perfect credit (a service where customers can refinance existing debt that they already have).

29 The company also offers various insurances such as auto insurance, rental insurance, homeowner insurance, identity and credit theft insurance, life insurance, health insurance, pet insurance, and long-term care insurance for individuals to protect against the downside of bad health. In addition, it offers business owner insurance and workers' compensation.

30 Wells Fargo's investing services include planning for retirement, children's education and other financial goals. It also takes advantage of America's two major demographic changes–an aging population and a racially more diverse population, and tries to serve the two groups better. Its Elder Services program helps retiring baby boomers with healthcare management, financial management, legal matters, and everyday matters.[9] The company has won awards and recognition for this program from the American

[13] https://www.wellsfargo.com/downloads/pdf/invest_relations/wf2009annualreport.pdf

Society on Aging. It has also created Team Networks to better understand the cultures and the market of minorities. These networks include Amigos (Hispanic), Asian Connection, Arab Americans, Employees with Disabilities, Checkpoint (Afro-American), Native Peoples, PRIDE (Gay, Lesbian, Bisexual, and Transgender), and Persian American Connection.

31 With such a wide range of offerings at hand, Wells Fargo tries to cross sell its products to expand the number of products to which its current customers have access, gain new customers in extended markets, and increase market share with many businesses. With an aim of having an average of eight products per customer, it averaged 5.95 products per customer in 2009, while Wachovia had 4.65 products per customer. Wells Fargo believes there is untapped potential by increasing cross-sale opportunities with the Wachovia retail bank. In the meantime, only one out of every five of Wells Fargo's banking customers has a mortgage with the institution; only one-third of its mortgage customers have a banking relationship. Wells Fargo wants to make each one of its banking customers a mortgage customer, and vice versa.[14]

Technology

32 Wells Fargo sees its technology as one of its strengths and uses it to personalize services. Advanced technology allows the company to keep accurate information about account balances, transaction history, and life events. This helps Wells Fargo predict which products its customers will need at various times so that it can provide better services.[15]

33 Wells Fargo offers banking through all electronic channels including Quicken, Money, Prodigy and the Internet. The company launched its mobile banking services in October 2007. At the time, customers could only sign up for the service online and only utilize the service through text messaging. Since February 2010, Wells Fargo has updated its technology to allow customers to sign up for mobile banking through text messaging in order to gain access to customers who have smartphones, but who have yet to take to online banking. Wells Fargo is the first large bank to offer enrollment to mobile banking services through text messaging, and is the only one of the five largest US banks to earn a gold rating for the Javelin Mobile Banking scorecard for features, access channels, and marketing through mobile banking services.[16] The next step will be to offer alerts such as overdraft alerts, or check and deposit clearing alerts.

Social Responsibility

34 Wells Fargo believes it is important to act ethically and with integrity towards all customers, employees, vendors and stockholders because it reflects upon the company. It has a team member code of ethics and business conduct for all employees to follow. The team member code covers topics such as confidentiality, conflict of interest, insider trading, and sales incentive plans, and this is stated in writing with no gray area.

35 Wells Fargo also believes that if the communities are doing well, then its business will do well in turn. Its goal is to turn philanthropy into strength and reap the rewards by gaining customers.[17] In 2008 alone, it donated US$226 million to nonprofit organizations and educational institutions that address community needs. Its philosophy is to listen to local residents because they know what the community needs.

[14] https://www.wellsfargo.com/invest_relations/vision_values/9

[15] https://www.wellsfargo.com/invest_relations/vision_values/4

[16] http://www.javelinstrategy.com/blog/2010/02/06/wells-fargo%E2%80%99s-mobile-banking-tosses-away-the-crutch-of-online-only-enrollment/

[17] https://www.wellsfargo.com/about/csr/charitable/where

36 To help Wells Fargo build a strong reputation, management has launched a goodwill program. The company gives an average of US$618,000 per day back to the local communities it serves.[18] Employees of Wells Fargo give over 1.4 million volunteer hours to charities. This charitable giving and social goodwill encompasses the areas of education, human services, community development, arts and culture, civic services, and environmental issues. Wells Fargo is also environmentally conscious. It eliminated the use of envelopes at ATM machines, which saved more than 30 million envelopes over a two-year period.[19]

Finance

37 Wells Fargo aims to maintain a strong balance sheet and have a conservative financial position measured by asset quality, accounting policies, capital levels, and diversity of revenue sources.[20] Its total revenue grew at 61.25%, from US$34,898 million in 2008 to US$56,274 million in 2009 (see **Appendix 1**). This mainly is attributed to the acquisition of Wachovia, which was completed at the end of 2008. Community Banking, a growth area for Wells Fargo for many years, is where the company draws the most income. In 2009, 72% of Wells Fargo's revenue came from this segment alone. Wholesale Banking accounts for 21%, while Wealth, Brokerage and Retirement earns about 6% (see **Appendix 2**).[21]

APPENDIX 1 **Revenues per Quarter**

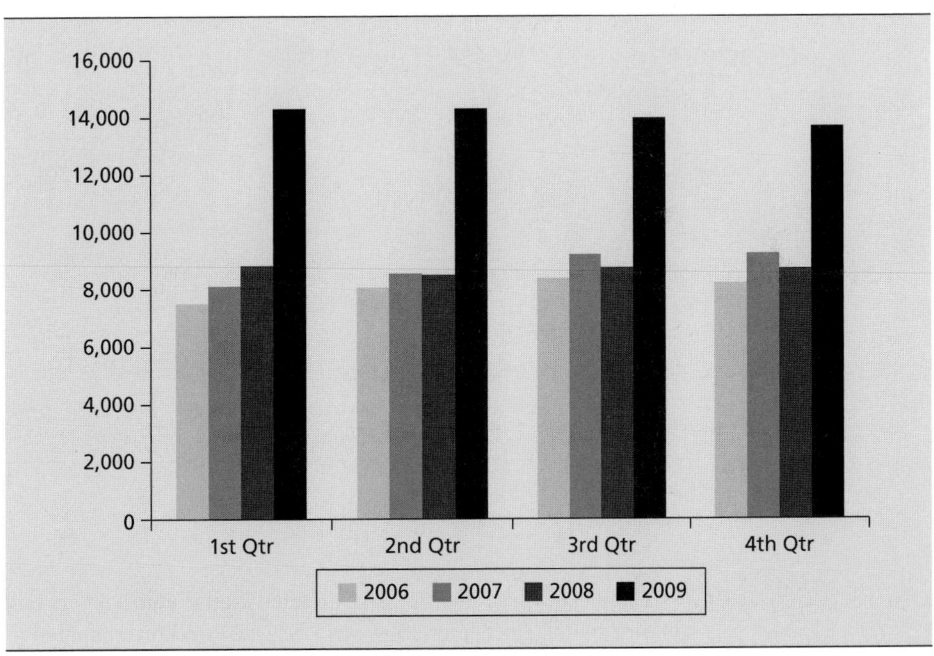

[18] Ibid.

[19] http://adobe.americanbanker.com/index.php?option=com_content&view=article&id=19

[20] https://www.wellsfargo.com/invest_relations/vision_values/5

[21] Wells Fargo 2009 Annual Report.

APPENDIX 2 **Distribution by Operating Segment**

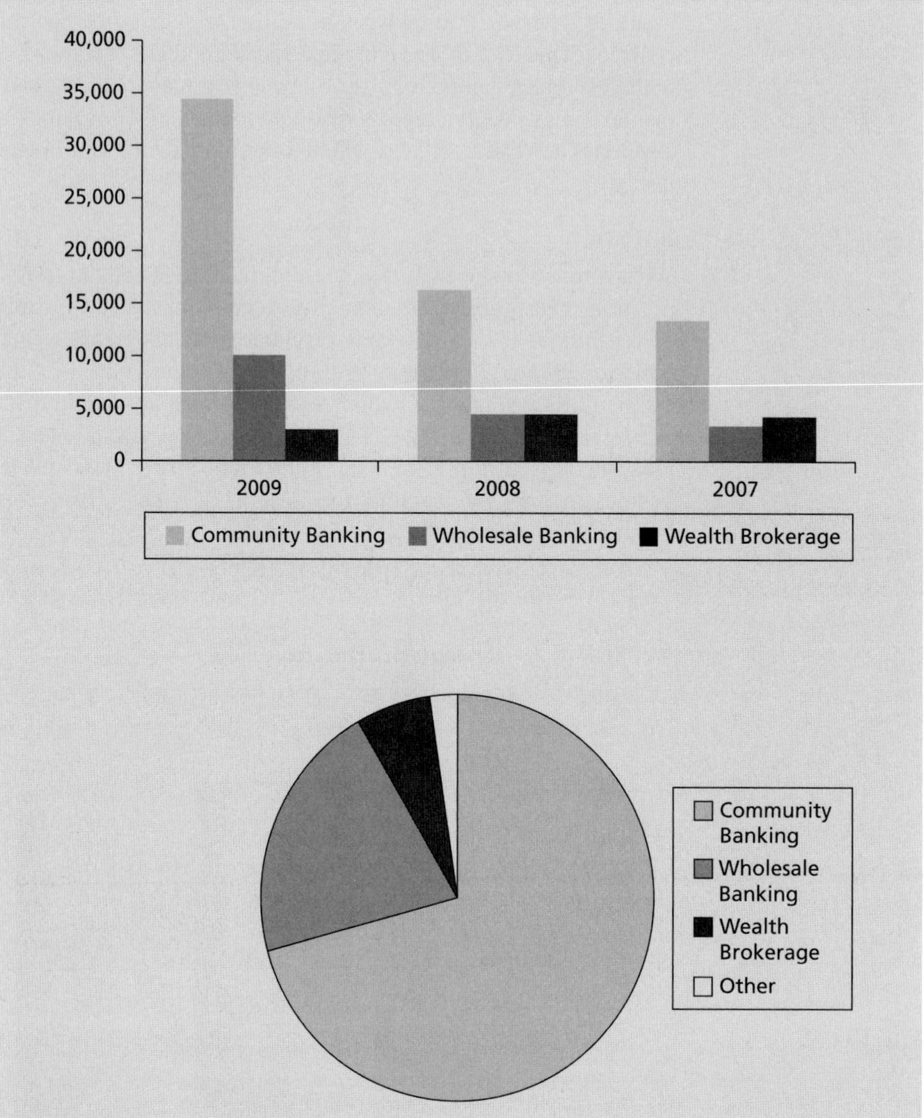

38 The Wachovia acquisition also affected Wells Fargo's net income. The net income for the quarter ending December 2009 was US$2,823 million compared to negative US$2,734 million for the same quarter in 2008–a greater than 200% increase (see **Appendix 3**). Overall, the net income for 2009 increased to US$12,275 million, up from US$2,655 million in 2008.

39 Wells Fargo faces significant credit losses, however. In 2007, its overall credit loss grew over 120% from the 2006, and in 2008 that number went up another 220%, followed by an additional 36% in 2009 (see **Appendix 4**). On a positive note, its elevated profits were able to cover the increasing credit losses by more than two times.

APPENDIX 3 Net Income per Quarter

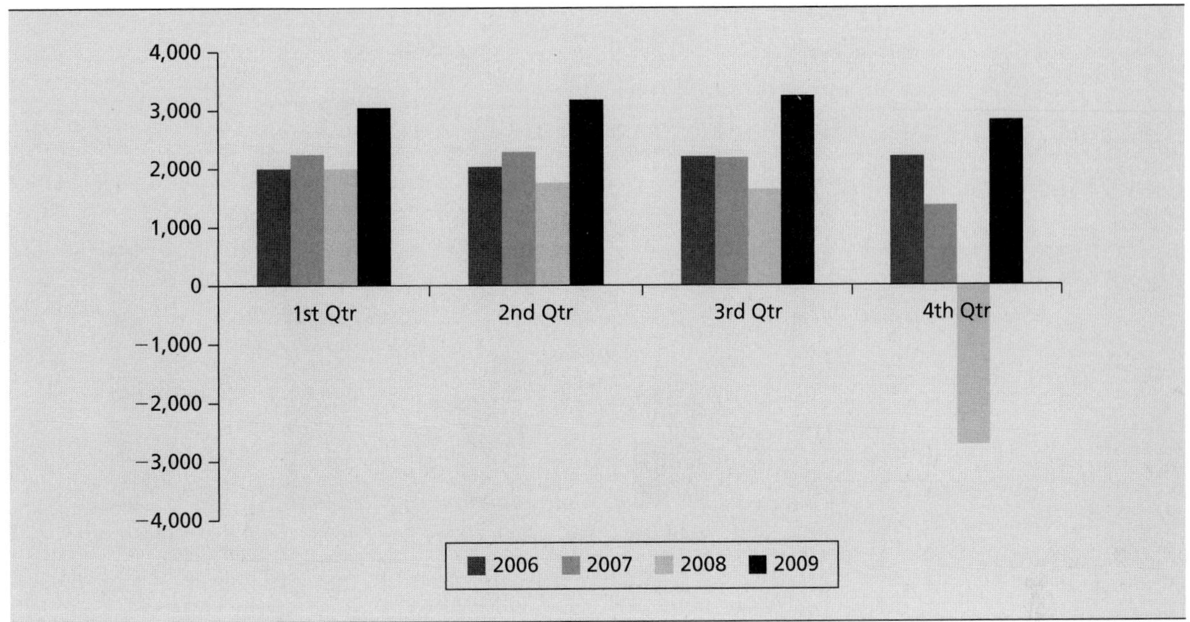

APPENDIX 4 Quarterly Credit Losses

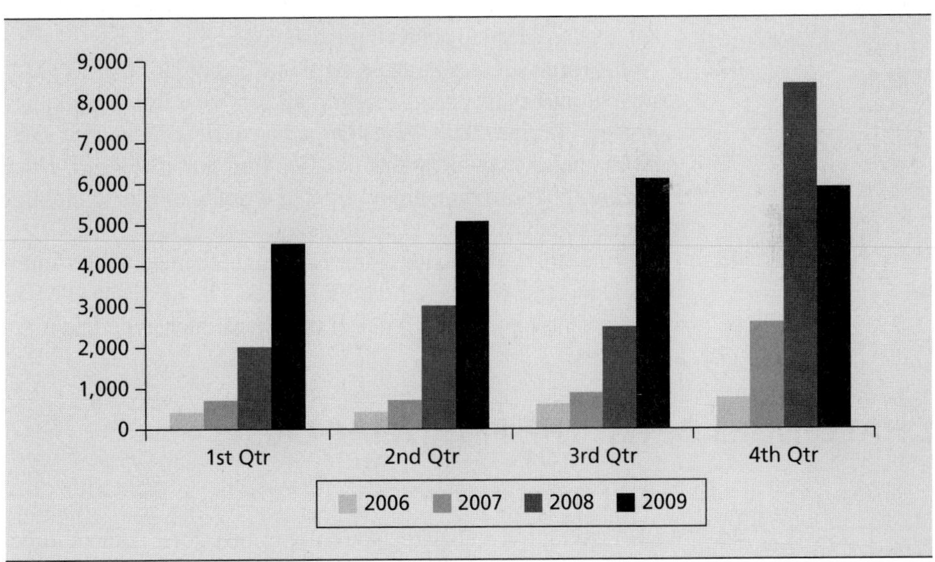

40 The company's long-term debt fell from $267,158 million in 2008 to $203,861 million in 2009 (see **Appendix 5**). In 2009, Wells Fargo repaid US$25 billion to the US Treasury for its TARP funds.

Marketing

41 Amidst all the financial scandals of recent times, investors are hesitant to trust advisors with their money. Wells Fargo's goal is to help customers become personally accountable

APPENDIX 5 Other Financial Info

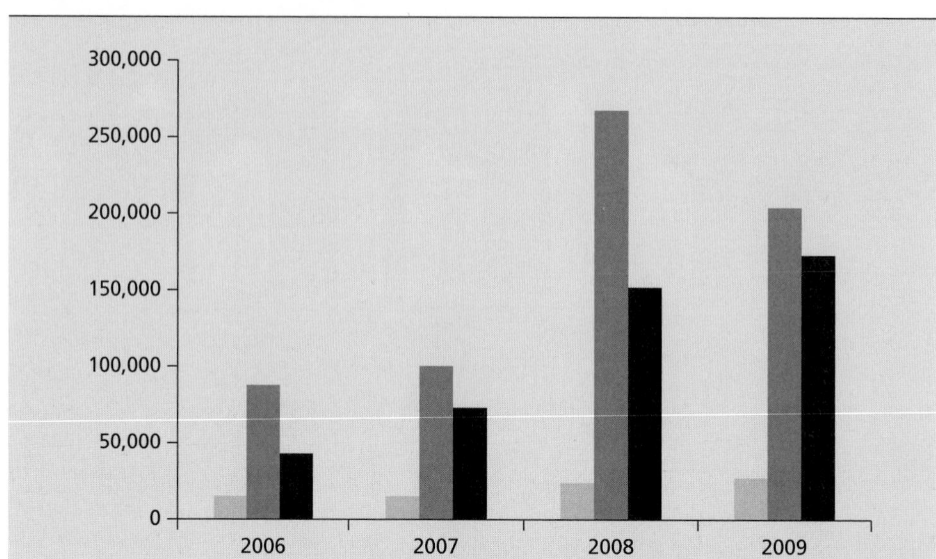

for their own financial well-being by assisting them to define their goals and then develop a plan that will lead to achieving those goals.[22]

42 Wells Fargo stresses in its promotional campaigns that its products "make everyday life easier." It pushes this slogan within all services, from checking accounts to investing, to mortgages. In June 2008, Wells Fargo began running its first ever national print advertisement campaign in publications like *The Wall Street Journal*, *The Economist*, and *The New York Times*.[23] These campaigns targeted wealthy clients to highlight their relationship with Wells Fargo advisors and to create brand awareness.

43 In June 2009, it launched a new campaign[1] themed, "With You When," that featured both Wells Fargo and Wachovia brand identities. The idea is to show how Wells Fargo can help customers throughout the course of their lives, such as getting married, retiring, and starting a business.[24]

CHALLENGES AFTER THE FINANCIAL CRISIS

Credit Rating

44 Wells Fargo has a stellar reputation with investors. Although the company's credit rating was lowered to AA- in light of the 2008 financial crisis,[25] it was the only US bank to earn Moody's highest credit rating in 2007. The company's strong credit rating has made it

[22] Ibid.

[23] http://www.iiwealthmanagement.com/articleFree.aspx?ArticleID=1945459

[24] http://charlotte.bizjournals.com/charlotte/stories/2009/06/01/daily9.html

[25] The Standard & Poor's rating scale is as follows, from excellent to poor: AAA, AA+, AA, AA−, A+, A, A−, BBB+, BBB, BBB−, BB+, BB, BB−, B+, B, B−, CCC+, CCC, CCC−, CC, C, D. Anything lower than a BBB− rating is considered a speculative or junk bond.

APPENDIX 6 **Five-Year Performance Graph**

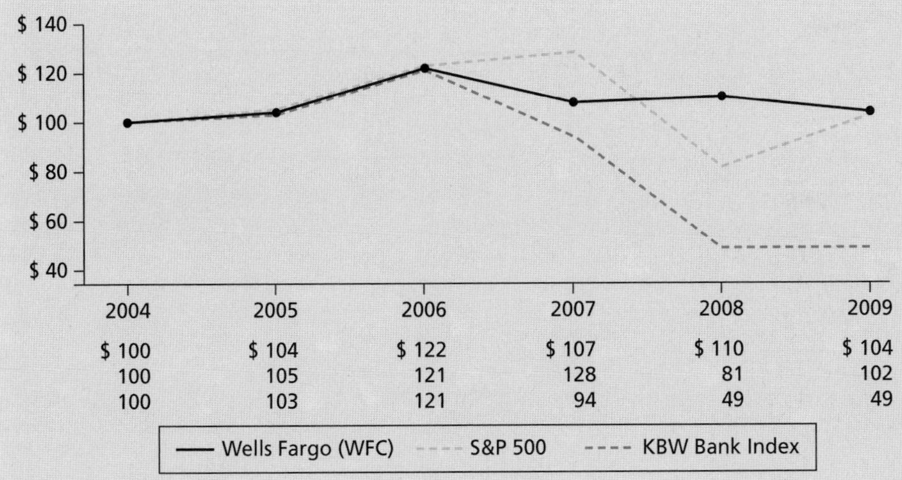

$ 140
$ 120
$ 100
$ 80
$ 60
$ 40

	2004	2005	2006	2007	2008	2009	5-year CAGR	
Wells Fargo (WFC)	$ 100	$ 104	$ 122	$ 107	$ 110	$ 104	1%	Wells Fargo
S&P 500	100	105	121	128	81	102	0%	S&P 500
KBW Bank Index	100	103	121	94	49	49	−13%	KBW Bank Index

—— Wells Fargo (WFC) - - - - S&P 500 - - - - KBW Bank Index

Source: Wells Fargo Annual Report 2009

attractive to customers (see **Appendix 6**). Its ability to attract low-cost deposits has allowed it to borrow more cheaply than the government during the financial crisis.

45 Yet, the company's good credit rating is not to be taken for granted. The biggest challenge Wells Fargo faces is that it has to deal with an increasing number of bad commercial and consumer loans. A large majority of these loans came from the 2008 acquisition of Wachovia. These loans were the primary reason why Wells Fargo had to take the US$25 billion bailout money from the federal government. Even though it has repaid the federal loan in full, the quarterly write-offs due to these loans have continued. First quarter 2010 results show that non-accruing loans increased 11% over the last quarter, while other major banks have reported decreasing numbers of non-accruing loans.[26] If the trend continues, Wells Fargo will become less attractive to investors than its competitors, which will result in falling share prices.

Diversified Products

46 Striving to be the best in community banking, Wells Fargo offers a comprehensive range of products with a strong national backing and global reach. If the company continues on its stated path to "meet all of its customers' financial needs," it may leave itself open to smaller, more focused companies picking off its valued customers.

47 In the first quarter of 2010, Wells Fargo's net income from Community Banking fell 25% from the previous year. Over the same period, its net income from Wealth, Brokerage, and Retirement also plunged by 60%, despite Wells Fargo stated initiative to be the most respected wealth, brokerage, and retirement service in the US. In addition to its 10,000 stores in North America (see **Appendix 7**), Wells Fargo also has many establishments in other regions it has to oversee. Developing a sound global strategy is compelling if the company wishes to maintain a leading edge over its competition.

[26] http://www.washingtonpost.com/wp-dyn/content/article/2010/04/21/AR2010042101634.html

APPENDIX 7 North America's Most Extensive Network for Financial Services

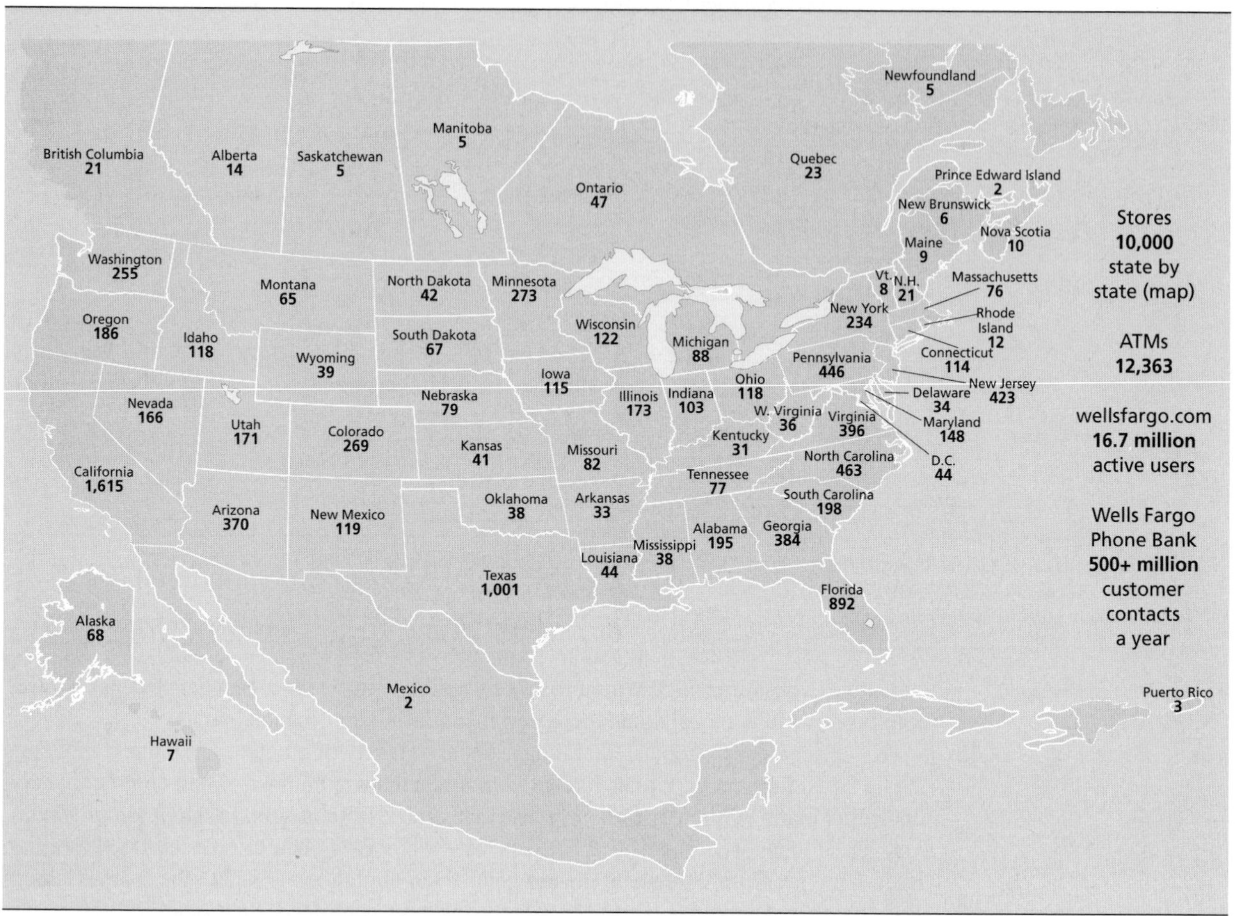

Source: Wells Fargo 2009 Annual Report

48 In improving its overall business lines by being all things to all customers, Wells Fargo is in the danger of losing focus. By trying to gain market share through a diversified product portfolio, it exposes itself to more risks and competition. Resource allocation and investing in R&D may also be challenging with limited capital. A lack of clear focus would make it more difficult for Wells Fargo to gain or maintain the number one position for its products, especially during a recession. These are serious concerns that Wells Fargo cannot overlook.

Wall Street Reform

49 In July 2010, the US Congress enacted sweeping financial reform legislation intended to avert another future financial crisis. The US government now has the power to shut down and liquidate any financial institution that could threaten the entire financial system. This legislation would also establish a Consumer Financial Protection Bureau inside the Federal Reserve that could write new rules to protect consumers from unfair or abusive practices in mortgages and credit cards. It creates a new council of regulators, led by the Treasury, that would set new standards for how much cash banks must keep on hand to prevent them from ever triggering a financial crisis. It regulates credit default swaps and derivatives to only being traded over exchanges or clearinghouses to fix the problem of not being able to effectively price these instruments.[27]

50 Although the regulation changes the playing field in the banking industry, it does so to all companies in the industry. Therefore this could be an opportunity for Wells Fargo to become innovative in its financial products and to use its relatively strong positioning within the industry to grab market share from the other banks. While Wells Fargo did take "bailout" money from the government, the money was mostly to cover the losses of Wachovia. Wachovia's losses were due to failing mortgages mostly linked to its 2006 acquisition of Golden West Financial.

51 The threat is that the new legislation may limit growth potential for a large bank like Wells Fargo. Large banks could be forced to sell off or spin off several of their businesses in order to comply with federal regulations. They might lose their economies of scale advantage over small and medium sized banks. How Wells Fargo can succeed in this increasingly regulated yet highly competitive industry is an open question.

[27] http://money.cnn.com/2010/07/15/news/economy/Wall_Street_reform_bill_vote/index.htm

Case 29

Whole Foods Market 2010:
How to Grow in an Increasingly Competitive Market?

Patricia Harasta
Alan N. Hoffman
Bentley University and Rotterdam School of Management, Erasmus University

1 Reflecting back over his three decades of experience in the grocery business, John Mackey smiled to himself over his previous successes. His entrepreneurial history began with a single store which he has now grown to the nation's leading natural food chain. Whole Foods is not just a food retailer but instead represents a healthy, socially responsible lifestyle that customers can identify with. The company has differentiated itself from competitors by focusing on quality as excellence and innovation that allows them to charge a premium price for premium products. This strategy has formed their success over the last 30 years but like any success story there are limits to how far it can go before a new direction is needed so that it remains successful for the next 30 years. While proud of the past, John had concerns about the future direction Whole Foods should head.

COMPANY BACKGROUND

2 Whole Foods carries both natural and organic food offering customers a wide variety of products. "Natural" refers to food that is free of growth hormones or antibiotics, where "certificated organic" food conforms to the standards, as defined by the U.S. Department of Agriculture (USDA) in October 2002. Whole Foods Market® is the world's leading retailer of natural and organic foods, with 193 stores in 31 states and Canada and the United Kingdom. John Mackey, current president and cofounder of Whole Foods, opened "Safer Way" natural grocery store in 1978. The store had limited success as it was a small location allowing only for a limited selection, focusing entirely on vegetarian foods. John joined forces with Craig Weller and Mark Skiles, founders of "Clarksville Natural Grocery" (founded in 1979), to create Whole Foods Market. This joint venture took place in Austin, Texas in 1980 resulting in a new company, a single natural food market with a staff of nineteen.

3 In addition to the supermarkets, Whole Foods owns and operates several subsidiaries. Allegro Coffee Company was formed in 1977 and purchased by Whole Foods Market in 1997 now acting as their coffee roasting and distribution center. Pigeon Cove is Whole Foods' seafood processing facility, which was founded in 1985 and known as M & S Seafood until 1990. Whole Foods purchased Pigeon Cove in 1996, located in Gloucester, MA. The company is now the only supermarket to own and operate a waterfront seafood facility. The last two subsidiaries are Produce Field Inspection Office and Select Fish, which is Whole Foods' West Coast seafood processing facility acquired in 2003. In addition to the above, the company has eight distribution centers, seven regional bake houses and four commissaries.

Source: The authors would like to thank Will Hoffman, Christopher Ferrari, Robert Marshall, Julie Giles, Jennifer Powers and Gretchen Alper for their research and contributions to this case.

Please address all correspondence to: Dr. Alan N. Hoffman, Department of Management, Bentley University, 175 Forest Street, Waltham, MA 02452-4705, voice (781) 891-2287, ahoffman@bentley.edu, fax (781) 459-0335.

4 "Whole Foods Market remains uniquely mission driven: The Company is highly selective about what they sell, dedicated to stringent quality standards, and committed to sustainable agriculture. They believe in a virtuous circle entwining the food chain, human beings and Mother Earth: each is reliant upon the others through a beautiful and delicate symbiosis." The message of preservation and sustainability are followed while providing high-quality good to customers and high profits to investors.

5 Whole Foods has grown over the years through mergers, acquisitions and new store openings. The $565 million acquisition of its lead competitor, Wild Oats, in 2007 firmly set Whole Foods as the leader in natural and organic food market and added 70 new stores. The Federal Trade Commission (FTC) focused their attention on the merger on antitrust grounds. The dispute was settled in 2009, with Whole Foods closing 32 Wild Oats stores and agreed to selling the Wild Oats Markets brand.

6 The organic grocer's stock plunged in 2008 as its sales staggered. Later that year the private equity firm Green Equity Investors invested $425 million in Whole Foods, thereby acquiring about a 17% stake in the chain. For the first time in its 29-year history, Whole Foods reported negative same-store sales in the quarter ended December 2008 as traffic in its stores fell.

7 Today Whole Foods is listed in the S&P 500 and ranked 284th in the Fortune 500. It is the world's leading natural and organic foods supermarket and is America's first national certified organic grocer. In 2009, it had sales of $8 billion and 289 stores; 273 stores in 38 states of the U.S. and the District of Columbia, 6 stores in Canada, and 5 stores in the UK. The company has grown from 19 original employees to more than 53,500 team members.[1]

8 While the majority of Whole Foods locations are in the U.S., European expansion provides enormous potential growth due to the large population and it holds "a more sophisticated organic-foods market than the U.S. in terms of suppliers and acceptance by the public." Whole Foods targets their locations specifically by an area's demographics. The company targets locations where 40% or more of the residents have a college degree as they are more likely to be aware of nutritional issues.

WHOLE FOODS MARKET'S PHILOSOPHY

9 Their corporate website defines the company philosophy as follows, "Whole Foods Market's vision of a sustainable future means our children and grandchildren will be living in a world that values human creativity, diversity, and individual choice. Businesses will harness human and material resources without devaluing the integrity of the individual or the planet's

[1] Hoover's Company Information, " Thomson Reuters Company in Context Report," 4/16/2009. Fast Company Magazine, December 2009.

ecosystems. Companies, governments, and institutions will be held accountable for their actions. People will better understand that all actions have repercussions and that planning and foresight coupled with hard work and flexibility can overcome almost any problem encountered. It will be a world that values education and a free exchange of ideas by an informed citizenry; where people are encouraged to discover, nurture, and share their life's passions."

10 While Whole Foods recognizes it is only a supermarket, they are working toward fulfilling their vision within the context of their industry. In addition to leading by example, they strive to conduct business in a manner consistent with their mission and vision. By offering minimally processed, high quality food, engaging in ethical business practices and providing a motivational, respectful work environment, the company believes they are on the path to a sustainable future.

11 Whole Foods incorporate the best practices of each location back into the chain. This can be seen in the company's store product expansion from dry goods to perishable produce, including meats, fish and prepared foods. The lessons learned at one location are absorbed by all, enabling the chain to maximize effectiveness and efficiency while offering a product line customers love. Whole Foods carries only natural and organic products. The best tasting and most nutritious food available is found in its purest state—unadulterated by artificial additives, sweeteners, colorings, and preservatives.

12 Whole Foods continually improves customer offerings, catering to its specific locations. Unlike business models for traditional grocery stores, Whole Foods products differ by geographic regions and local farm specialties.

EMPLOYEE AND CUSTOMER RELATIONS

13 Whole Foods encourages a team based environment allowing each store to make independent decisions regarding its operations. Teams consist of up to eleven employees and a team leader. The team leaders typically head up one department or another. Each store employs anywhere from 72 to 391 team members. The manager is referred to as the 'store team leader.' The 'store team leader' is compensated by an Economic Value Added (EVA) bonus and is also eligible to receive stock options.

14 Whole Foods tries to instill a sense of purpose among its employees and has been named for 13 consecutive years as one of the "100 Best Companies to Work For" in America by Fortune magazine. In employee surveys, 90% of its team members stated that they always or frequently enjoy their job.

15 The company strives to take care of their customers, realizing they are the "lifeblood of our business," and the two are "interdependent on each other." Whole Foods' primary objective goes beyond 100% customer satisfaction with the goal to "delight" customers in every interaction.

COMPETITIVE ENVIRONMENT

16 At the time of Whole Foods' inception, there was almost no competition with less than six other natural food stores in the U.S. Today, the organic foods industry is growing and Whole Foods finds itself competing hard to maintain its elite presence.

17 In the early to mid 2000s, its biggest competitor was Wild Oats. In 2007, Whole Foods put a bid on Wild Oats for $670 million[2], and drew an antitrust investigation from the FTC.

[2] Lambert, Thomas A. "Four lessons from the whole foods case: the antitrust analysis of mergers should be reconsidered." *Regulation.* 31.1 (Spring 2008): 22(8). General Business File ASAP. Gale. Bentley College-Solomon R Baker Lib. 4/10/2010.

The FTC felt that a merger of the two premium natural and organic supermarkets would create a monopoly situation, ultimately harming consumers. It was found that although Whole Foods and Wild Oats were the two key players in the premium natural and organic food market, they are not insulated from competition from conventional grocery store chains. With the decision coming down in favor of Whole Foods and Wild Oats, the transaction was completed. Although this eliminated Whole Foods most direct competitor, they still faces stiff competition in the general grocery market.

18 Whole Foods competes with all supermarkets. With more U.S. consumers focused on eating healthfully, environmental sustainability, and the green movement, the demand for organic and natural foods has increased. More traditional supermarkets are now introducing "lifestyle" stores and departments to compete directly with Whole Foods. This can be seen in the Wild Harvest section of Shaw's, or the "Lifestyle" stores opened by conventional grocery chain Safeway.

19 Whole Foods competitors now include big box and discount retailers who have made a foray into the grocery business. Currently, the U.S. largest grocer is Wal-Mart. Not only do they compete in the standard supermarket industry, but they have even begun offering natural and organic products in Supercenter stores. Other discount retailers now competing in the supermarket industry include Target, Sam's Club and Costco. All of these retailers offer grocery products, generally at a lower price than what one would find at Whole Foods.

20 Another of Whole Foods' key competitors is Los Angeles based Trader Joe's, a premium natural and organic food market. By expanding its presence and product offerings while maintaining high quality at low prices, Trade Joe's has found its competitive niche. It has 215 stores, primarily on the west and east coasts of the U.S., offering upscale grocery fare such as health foods, prepared meals, organic produce and nutritional supplements. A low cost structure allows Trader Joe's to offer competitive prices while still maintaining its margins. Trader Joe's stores have no service department and average just 10,000 square feet in store size.

21 Additional competition has arisen from grocery stores, such as Stop 'N Shop and Shaw's, which now incorporate natural foods sections in their conventional stores, placing them in direct competition with Whole Foods. Because larger grocery chains have more flexibility in their product offerings, they are more likely to promote products through sales, a strategy Whole Foods rarely practices.

A DIFFERENT SHOPPING EXPERIENCE

22 The setup of the organic grocery store is a key component to Whole Foods' success. The store's setup and its products are carefully researched to ensure that they are meeting the demands of the local community. Locations are primarily in cities and are chosen for their large space and heavy foot traffic. According to Whole Foods' 10K, "approximately 88% of our existing stores are located in the top 50 statistical metropolitan areas." The company uses a specific formula to choose their store sites that is based upon several metrics, which include but are not limited to income levels, education, and population density.

23 Upon entering a Whole Foods supermarket, it becomes clear that the company attempts to sell the consumer on the entire experience. Team members (employees) are well trained and the stores themselves are immaculate. There are in-store chefs to help with recipes, wine tasting and food sampling. There are "Take Action food centers" where customers can access information on the issues that affect their food such as legislation and environmental factors. Some stores offer extra services such as home delivery, cooking classes, massages and valet parking. Whole Foods goes out of their way to appeal to the above-average income earner.

24 Whole Foods uses price as a marketing tool in a few select areas, as demonstrated by the 365 Whole Foods brand name products, priced less than similar organic products that are carried within the store. However, the company does not use price to differentiate itself from competitors. Rather, Whole Foods focuses on quality and service as a means of standing out from the competition.

25 Whole Foods spends much less than other supermarkets on advertising, approximately 0.4% of total sales in the fiscal year 2009. They rely heavily on word-of-mouth advertising from their customers to help market themselves in the local community. They are also promoted in several health conscious magazines, and each store budgets for in-store advertising each fiscal year.

26 Whole Foods also gains recognition via their charitable contributions and the awareness that they bring to the treatment of animals. The company donates 5% of their after tax profits to not-for-profit charities. It is also very active in establishing systems to make sure that the animals used in their products are treated humanly.

THE GREEN MOVEMENT

27 Whole Foods exists in a time where customers equate going green and being environmentally friendly with enthusiasm and respect. In recent years, people began to learn about food and the processes completed by many to produce it. Most of what they have discovered is disturbing. Whole Foods launched a nationwide effort to trigger awareness and action to remedy the problems facing the U.S. food system. It has decided to host 150 screenings of a 12 film series called "Let's Retake Our Plates," hoping to inspire change by encouraging and educating consumers to take charge of their food choices. Jumping on the bandwagon of the "go green" movement, Whole Foods is trying to show its customers that it is dedicated to not only all natural foods, but to a green world and healthy people. As more and more people become educated, the company hopes to capitalize on them as new customers.[3]

28 Beyond the green movement, Whole Foods has been able to tap into a demographic that appreciates the "trendy" theme of organic foods and all natural products. Since the store is associated with a type of affluence, many customers shop there to show they fit into this category of upscale, educated, new age people.

THE ECONOMIC RECESSION

29 The uncertainty of today's market is a threat to Whole Foods. The expenditure income is low and "all natural foods" are automatically deemed as expensive. Because of people being laid off, having their salaries cut, or simply not being able to find a job, they now have to be more selective when purchasing things. While Whole Foods has been able to maintain profitability, it's questionable how long they will last if the recession continues or worsens. The reputation of organic products being costly may be enough to motivate people to not ever enter through the doors of Whole Foods. In California, the chain is frequently dubbed "Whole Paycheck."[4]

30 However, the company understood that it must change a few things if it were to survive the decrease in sales felt because customers were not willing to spend their money so easily. They have been working to correct this "pricey" image by expanding offerings of private label products through their "365 Everyday Value" and "365 Organic" product lines. Private

[3] "Whole Foods Market; Whole Foods Market Challenge: Let's Retake Our Plates!" Food Business Week, 4/15/2010.

[4] "Eating Too Fast At Whole Foods," Business Week (2005): Print.

label sales accounted for 11% of Whole Foods total sales in 2009, up from 10% in 2008. They have also instituted a policy that their 365 product lines must match prices of similar products at Trader Joe's.[5]

31 During the economic recession, restaurants had a severe impact. A survey conducted showed that adults were eating out 50% less than they were prior to the economic crash.[6] Whole Foods saw this as opportunity to enter a new area of business, the pre-made meals sector. They began selling pre-made dinners and lunches marketing towards those still on the go but interested in eating healthy and saving money. Offering the feed "4 for $15" deal, they were able to recapture some lost sales. In November of 2008, the stock fell to $7 dollars. After the pre-made meals were created, the stock increased to $28 dollars in September 2009.[7] If Whole Foods continues to come up with innovative ideas to still compete during a recession, there is much opportunity as the economy evolves and climbs up the economic life cycle into recovery, expansion, and boom states.

ORGANIC FOODS A COMMODITY

32 When Whole Foods first started in the natural foods industry in 1980 it was a relatively new concept and over the first decade Whole Foods enjoyed the benefits of offering a unique value proposition to consumers wanting to purchase high-quality natural foods from a trusted retailer. Over the last few years, however, the natural and organic foods industry has attracted the attention of general food retailers that have started to offer foods labeled as natural or organic at reasonable prices.

33 As of 2007, the global demand for organic and natural foods far exceeded the supply. This is becoming a huge issue for Whole Foods, as more traditional supermarkets with higher purchasing power enter the premium natural and organic foods market. The supply of organic food has been significantly impacted by the entrance of Wal-Mart into the competitive arena. Due to the limited resources within the U.S., Wal-Mart begun importing natural and organic foods from China and Brazil, which led to it coming under scrutiny for passing off non-natural or organic products as the "real thing." Additionally, the quality of natural and organic foods throughout the entire market has been decreased due to constant pressure from Wal-Mart.

34 The distinction between what is truly organic and natural is difficult for the consumer to decipher as general supermarkets have taken to using terms such as "all natural," "free-range," "hormone free," confusing customers. Truly organic food sold in the U.S. bears the "USDA Organic" label and needs to have at least 95% of the ingredients organic before it can get this distinction.[8]

35 In May 2003 Whole Foods became America's first Certified Organic grocer by a federally recognized independent third-party certification organization. In July 2009, California Certified Organic Growers (CCOF), one of the oldest and largest USDA-accredited third-party organic certifiers, individually certified each store in the U.S., complying with stricter guidance on federal regulations. This voluntary certification tells customers that Whole Foods have gone the extra mile by not only following the USDA's Organic Rule, but opening their stores up to third-party inspectors and following a strict set of operating procedures designed to ensure that the products sold and labeled as organic are indeed

[5] "As Sales Slip, Whole Foods Tries Health Push," Katy McLaughlin, 8/15/2009, Wall Street Journal.

[6] Ziobro, Paul. "Whole Foods Highlights Its Eat-At-Home Values," Wall Street Journal 2009, Web. 4/10/2010.

[7] Ibid.

[8] "Whole Foods Markets Organic China California Blend," YouTube, 4/10/2010. http://www.youtube.com/watch?v=JQ31Ljd9T_Y

organic–procedures that are not specifically required by the Organic Rule. This certification verifies the handling of organic goods according to stringent national guidelines, from receipt through repacking to final sale to customers. To receive certification, retailers must agree to adhere to a strict set of standards set forth by the USDA, submit documentation, and open their facilities to on-site inspections – all designed to assure customers that the chain of organic integrity is preserved.

OPERATIONS

36 Whole Foods purchases most of their products from regional and national suppliers. This allows the company to leverage its size in order to receive deep discounts and favorable terms with their vendors. It still permits store to purchase from local producers to keep the stores aligned with local food trends and is seen as supporting the community. Whole Foods operates ten regional distribution centers to support its stores. It also operates two procurement centers, four seafood-processing and distribution centers, a specialty coffee and tea procurement and brewing operation, five regional kitchens, and eight bake house facilities. Whole Foods largest third-party supplier is United Natural Foods which accounted for 28% of total purchases in 2009, down from 32% in 2008.

37 Product categories at Whole Foods include, but are not limited to:

- Produce
- Seafood
- Grocery
- Meat and Poultry
- Bakery
- Prepared Foods and Catering
- Specialty (Beer, Wine and Cheese)
- Whole body (nutritional supplements, vitamins, body care and educational products such as books)
- Floral
- Pet Products
- Household Products

38 While Whole Foods carries all the items that one would expect to find in a grocery store (and plenty that one would not), their ". . . heavy emphasis on perishable foods is designed to appeal to both natural foods and gourmet shoppers." Perishable foods now account for two-thirds of its sales. This is demonstrated by the company's own statement that, "We believe it is our strength of execution in perishables that has attracted many of our most loyal shoppers."

39 Whole Foods also provides fully cooked frozen meal options through their private label Whole Kitchen, to satisfy the demands of working families. For example, the Whole Foods Market located in Woodland Hills, CA that has redesigned its prepared foods section more than three times in response to a 40% growth in prepared foods sales.

40 Whole Foods doesn't take just any product and put it on their shelves. In order to make it into the Whole Foods grocery store, products have to under go a strict test to determine if they are "Whole Foods material." The quality standards that all potential Whole Foods products must meet include:

- Foods that are free of preservatives and other additives
- Foods that are fresh, wholesome and safe to eat

- Promote organically grown foods
- Foods and products that promote a healthy life

41 Meat and poultry products must adhere to a higher standard:

- No antibiotics or added growth hormones
- An affidavit from each producer that outlines the whole process of production and how the animals are treated
- An annual inspection of all producers by Whole Foods Market
- Successful completion of a third party audit to attest to these findings

42 Also, due to the lack of available nutritional brands with a national identity, Whole Foods decided to enter into the private label product business. They currently have three private label products with a fourth program called Authentic Food Artisan, which promotes distinctive products that are certified organic. The three private label products: 1) 365 Everyday Value: A well recognized and trusted brand that meets the standards of Whole Foods and is less expensive then the regular product lines; 2) Whole Kids Organic: Healthy items that are directed at children; and 3) 365 Organic Everyday Value: All the benefits of organic food at reduced prices.

43 Whole Foods growth strategy is to expand primarily through new store openings. New stores are typically located on premier real estate sites, often in urban, high-population locales. They do not have a standard store design, instead each store's design is customized to fit the size and configuration of the site selected. They have traditionally opened stores in upper-income, more urban neighborhoods that typically have a high percentage of college graduates.[9]

44 The Company tracks what it calls the "Tender Period" which is the time between when it takes possession of the leased space for construction and other purposes and the time when the store is opened for business. **Exhibit 1** shows the time and cost involved can be

EXHIBIT 1

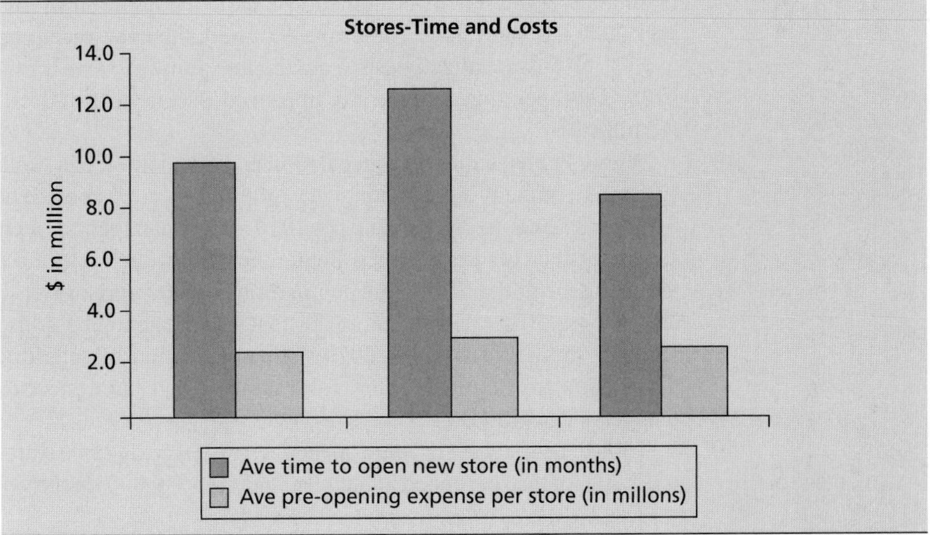

[9] Whole Foods Market, Inc. SEC filing, Form 10-K dated 9/27/2009.

significant with pre-opening expenses running between $2.5 to $3 million dollars and the time required ranging from 8.5 to 12.6 months. If Whole Foods opens 17 stores per year, this will consume $43 to $51 million dollars of its available cash each year.

45 When opening a new store, Whole Foods stocks it with almost $700,000 worth of initial inventory, which their vendors partially finance. Like most conventional grocery stores, the majority of Whole Foods inventory is turned over fairly quickly; this is especially true of produce. Fresh organic produce is central to Whole Foods' existence and turns over on a faster basis than other products.

FINANCIAL OPERATIONS

46 Whole Foods Market focuses on earning a profit while providing job security to its workforce to lay the foundation for future growth. The company is determined not to let profits deter the company from providing excellent service to its customers and quality work environment for its staff. Their mission statement defines their recipe for financial success.

> Whole Foods, Whole People, Whole Planet—emphasizes that our vision reaches far beyond just being a food retailer. Our success in fulfilling our vision is measured by customer satisfaction, Team Member excellence and happiness, return on capital investment, improvement in the state of the environment, and local and larger community support.

47 Whole Foods also caps the salary of its executives at no more than fourteen times that of the average annual salary of a Whole Foods worker; this includes wages and incentive bonuses as well. The company also donates 5% of their after tax profits to nonprofit organizations.

48 Over a period from September 2005 through January 2010, while total sales of Whole Foods have continued to increase, the operating margin has declined. With the acquisition of the Wild Oats the operating margin decreased significantly from 5.7% in 2006 to 3% in 2008 as Whole Foods struggled to handle the addition of 70+ new stores. The fiscal year 2009 has shown some improvement with the most recent operating margin back up to 3.9% on an annualized basis from the low point of 3.0% for the year ended September 2008. The operating margin has improved due to cost and efficiency improvements[10] (**Exhibit 2**).

49 Whole Foods' strategy of expansion and acquisition has fueled growth in net income since the company's inception. The total number of stores has increased from 175 at September 2005 to 289 in January 2010. They managed to open only a total of ten new stores for the two years ended September 2009. This was a result of their integrating the stores from the Wild Oats acquisition in 2007 and conserving cash in order to pay down some of the debt taken on in that transaction. The company did open five new stores in the first quarter of 2010 with a projection of an additional ten new stores for the remainder of the year. They forecast to open 17 new stores in each of the following two years (**Exhibit 3**).

50 Though new stores are being opened, average weekly same store sales have declined from $617,000 for the year ended September 2007 to $549,000 for the year ended September 2009

[10] "As Sales Slip, Whole Foods Tries Health Push," Katy McLaughlin, 8/5/2009, *Wall Street Journal.*

EXHIBIT 2

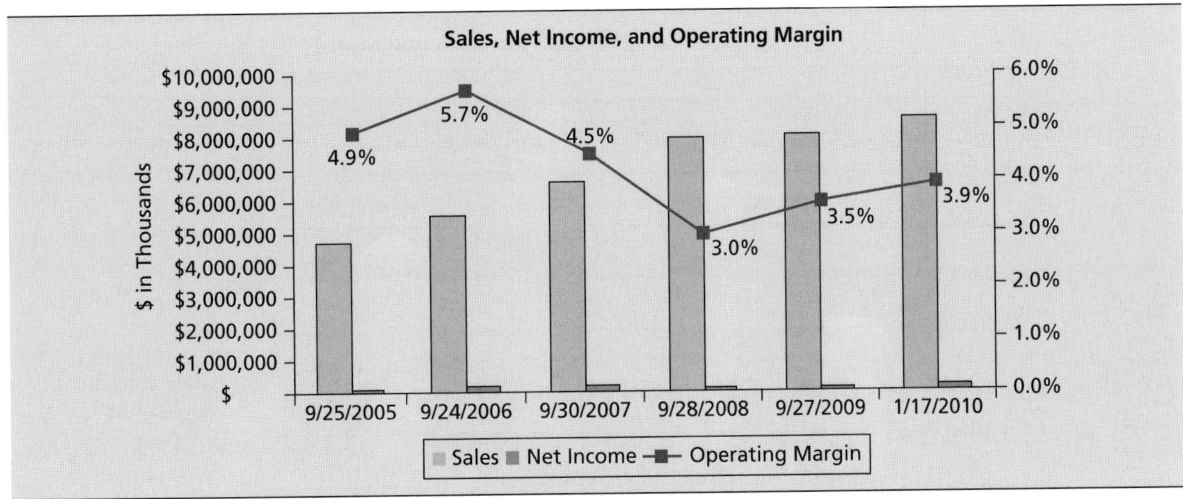

EXHIBIT 3

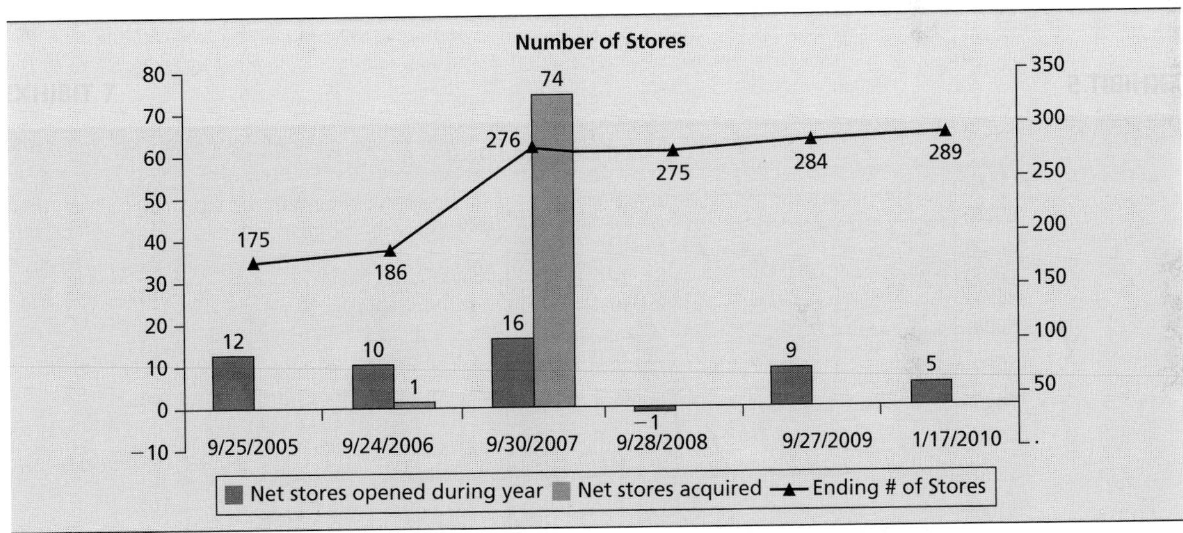

(**Exhibit 4**). The company's sales have been impacted by the recession and resultant pull-back in consumer spending as well as increased competition as more traditional grocery and discount chains expand their offerings of natural and organic products.[11]

51 Whole Foods has improved its balance sheet since the acquisition of the Wild Oats chain in 2007. Long-term debt has declined from $929 million at September 28, 2008 to $734 million as of January 17, 2010, a reduction of $195 million or 21%. Cash and short-term Investment balances for the same periods increased from only $31 million to $482 million, an increase of $451 million (**Exhibit 5**). The company's long- and short-term debt ratios are in line with industry averages and reflect a solid financial condition.[12] These

[11] "Wal-Mart vs. Whole Foods," Ben Steverman, 5/14/2009, Business Week.

[12] Market Edge Research Report, 4/12/2010.

the fact that overall sales have been increasing. It is likely that this trend will continue unless Whole Foods starts to focus on growing sales within the stores they have and not just looking to increase overall sales by opening new stores. It is also increasingly difficult to find appropriate locations for new stores that are first and foremost in an area where there is limited competition and also to have the store in a location that is easily accessible by both consumers and the distribution network. Originally Whole Foods had forecast to open 29 new stores in 2010 but this has since been revised downward to 17.

55 Opening up new stores or the acquisition of existing stores is also costly. The average cost to open a new store ranges from $2–$3 million and it takes on average 8-12 months. A lot of this can be explained by the fact that Whole Foods custom builds the stores which reduces the efficiencies that can be gained from the experience of having opened up many new stores previously. Opening new stores requires the company to adapt their distribution network, information management, supply and inventory management and adequately supply the new stores in a timely manner without impacting the supply to the existing stores. As the company expands this task increases in complexity and magnitude.

56 The organic and natural foods industry overall has become a more concentrated market with few larger competitors having emerged from a more fragmented market composed of a large number of smaller companies. Future acquisitions will be more difficult for Whole Foods as the FTC will be monitoring the company closely to ensure that they do not violate any federal antitrust laws through the elimination of any substantial competition within this market.

57 Over the last number of years there has been an increasing demand by consumers for natural and organic foods. Sales of organic foods increased by 5.1% in 2009 despite the fact that U.S. food sales overall only grew by 1.6%.[13] This increase in demand and high margin availability on premium organic products had led to an increasing number of competitors moving into the organic foods industry. Conventional grocery chains such as Safeway have remodeled stores at a rapid pace and have attempted to narrow the gap with premium grocers like Whole Foods in terms of shopping experience, product quality, and selection of takeout foods. This increase in competition can lead to the introduction of price wars where profits are eroded for both existing competitors and new entrants alike.

58 Unlike low-price leaders such as Wal-Mart, Whole Foods dominates because of its brand image, which is trickier to manage and less impervious to competitive threats. As competitors start to focus on emphasizing organic and natural foods within their own stores, the power of the Whole Foods brand will gradually decline over time as it becomes more difficult for consumers to differentiate Whole Foods' value proposition from that of their competitors.

[13] Organic Trade Association http://www.organicnewsroom.com/2010/04/us_organic_product_sales_reach_1.html

Case 30

Wynn Resorts, Ltd.

Victoria Page
Alan N. Hoffman
Bentley University

ROAD TO GOLD TIMELINE

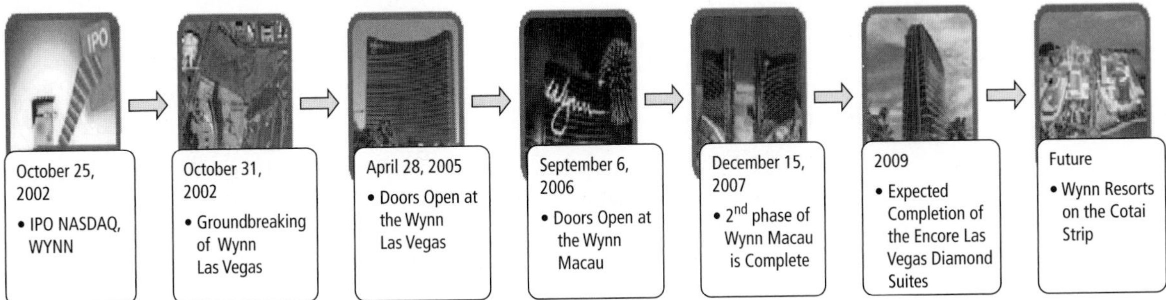
IPO
October 25, 2002
• IPO NASDAQ, WYNN
October 31, 2002
• Groundbreaking of Wynn Las Vegas
April 28, 2005
• Doors Open at the Wynn Las Vegas
September 6, 2006
• Doors Open at the Wynn Macau
December 15, 2007
• 2nd phase of Wynn Macau is Complete
2009
• Expected Completion of the Encore Las Vegas Diamond Suites
Future
• Wynn Resorts on the Cotai Strip

"KNOW WHEN TO HOLD 'EM, KNOW WHEN TO FOLD 'EM"

1 Millions of people travel to Las Vegas each year with big dreams of hitting the jackpot; most of them leave Las Vegas empty handed, heartbroken, and even further in debt. Very few people win big, and even fewer make their lives' fortune in 'Sin City'; Steve Wynn is one of the lucky few who has. From humble beginnings with a family run bingo parlor in Maryland, to Chief Executive Officer and Chairman of Wynn Resorts LTD, premium destination, world class Casinos and Resorts. Seen by many in the entertainment industry as a visionary, Steve Wynn has revolutionized the City of Las Vegas one casino at a time.[1]

2 From small stakes in the Frontier Hotel in 1967 as a newcomer to Vegas; to upping the ante with a complete renovation of the Golden Nugget from a dingy downtown Vegas casino to a four star resort and gaming facility. Mr. Wynn was not satisfied with his accomplishment of attracting high net worth clientele to downtown Vegas; he had dreams of expanding his casino empire, starting with a twin Golden Nugget Resort in Atlantic City a rival gambling destination. Also on his repertoire of great successes are the magnificent Mirage (1989), Treasure Island (1993), and the breathtaking Bellagio (1998). After what was considered the largest merger in the gaming industry's history, the Mirage became a part of MGM, Inc. for $6.4 million. Steve Wynn stepped down as Chairman and CEO and set his sights on developing his largest casino resort yet, the Five Diamond Wynn Las Vegas.

3 Wynn Resorts LTD owns and operates the Wynn Las Vegas, NV, and the Wynn Macau, a casino resort located in the Macau Special Administrative Region of the People's Republic of China. The company is in the process of developing an expansion to the Wynn Las Vegas,

Source: The authors would like to thank Khalifa Al Jalahma, Erin Cavanaugh, Sevgi Eason, Gary Held, Kelley Henry, John Kinnecome, Deb Lahteine, Antoinette Paone, and Farah Syed and Will Hoffman for their research. Please address all correspondence to Dr. Alan N. Hoffman, MBA Program Director, LaCava 295, Bentley College, 175 Forest Street, Waltham, MA 02452; ahoffman@bentley.edu.

[1] http://www.investingvalue.com/investment-leaders/steve-wynn/index.htm

called The Encore Diamond Suites. In addition, the company continues to explore opportunities to develop additional gaming or related businesses in other markets, both domestic and international.

4 The officers of the company include the following:

- *Stephen A. Wynn*
  Chairman of the Board and Chief Executive Officer
- *Marc D. Schorr*
  Chief Operating Officer
- *John Strzemp*
  Executive Vice President and Chief Administrative Officer
- *Matt Maddox*
  Chief Financial Officer and Treasurer

5 As mentioned, Mr. Wynn was previously the Chairman of the Board, President, and CEO of Mirage Resorts. In 1997 under his leadership, Mirage Resorts was ranked by Fortune magazine as the second most admired company among American companies; it was also rated in the top three for innovativeness and quality for their product and services. Steve Wynn is a man who is obsessed with details and continuously strives for perfection.

6 The Wynn Las Vegas Resort & Casino, which opened on April 28, 2005. The property, which encompasses 217 acres of land, is located at the intersection of the Las Vegas Strip and Sands Avenue. The resort not only features an 111,000 square foot casino with 137 table games, but also luxury hotel accommodations in 2,674 hotel rooms and suites, 36 fairway villas, and 6 private entry villas. The property offers its guests 18 restaurants, a Ferrari and Maserati car dealership, 76,000 square feet of high-end retail shops, recreational facilities including an 18-hole golf course, five swimming pools, full cabanas, a full service spa and salon, and lavish nightlife (nightclubs and lounge entertainment). The Wynn Las Vegas has been described on the strip as "intimate," since it is significantly smaller than some of its competitors' structures. Because of the demand for the services provided by Wynn Las Vegas, The Encore Diamond Suites are currently in development. Encore will be located on the Strip, adjacent to Wynn Las Vegas and is expected to be completed in 2009.

7 Wynn Resorts is constantly looking for additional locations and opportunities to expand both domestically and internationally. In addition, Wynn is currently looking at opportunities for possible resorts in the Philippines as well as expanding into new markets, such as horseracing.

WHO IS THE PIT BOSS?

8 The greatest operational strength of Wynn Resorts LTD is the founder himself, Steve Wynn. With over 30 years experience in Las Vegas, this man has contacts, alliances and knowledge that could not be easily replaced. As told by a bartender at Wynn Las Vegas, Mr. Wynn continues to be a very hands-on CEO. He can be seen regularly on the casino floor talking with customers and employees. His passion for perfection can be seen throughout Las Vegas, from the Golden Nugget on Fremont Street to the Bellagio, and including the Wynn Casino, which shares his name. When talking about the Wynn Macau and its scale in comparison to some of the other casinos, Mr. Wynn stated, "Bigger ain't better. Better is better." This is the idea that lays the foundation on which Wynn Resorts relies to differentiate their resorts from those in direct competition.

9 Many of the other senior executives joined Mr. Wynn when he left The Mirage. The management team at Wynn Resorts has a tremendous amount of experience with building quality resort casinos. As Wynn Resorts continues its growth, the combined experience of these individuals will ensure the resort continues to build world-class operations.

10 If Steve Wynn left the company for any reason other than death or a severe disability, the resort would lose all lines of credit. Although Mr. Wynn is an operational strength, the company's complete dependence on him is a significant weakness. *"Our ability to maintain our competitive position is dependent to a large degree on the efforts and skills of Stephen A. Wynn, the Chairman of the Board, Chief Executive Officer, and one of the principal stockholders of Wynn Resorts."*[2]

ACES WILD

11 "The US tourism industry is the third-largest retail industry after automotive and food stores, according to the TIA. Travel and tourism is also one of the nation's largest services export industry."[3]

12 The hotel/tourism industry has changed in the recent years, due to possible threats of terrorism and cutbacks in consumer spending on travel. Post September 11, the US was forced to introduce more strict visa requirements as well as more meticulous passport requirements. These requirements started on January 1, 2007. Recent escalating airline fuel costs have also brought airfare increases. These changes impact the number of people who choose to travel and vacation farther away from home, thus affecting the overall industry.

13 There are many opportunities in the gaming industry from a social and demographic vantage point. As the legalization of gambling is spreading in the US, the social acceptance of the pastime is beginning to spread as rapidly. In the past, gambling has been negatively tied to addiction and corruption, but today gambling is being seen more and more as a socially acceptable and fun recreational activity, especially among the elderly.

14 In 2006, the Las Vegas strip had 38.9 million visitors, and Wynn Las Vegas enjoyed 94.4% occupancy at its 2,716-room hotel, far exceeding the area's average.[4] Wynn Resort's brand is synonymous with luxury in the casino market, and it capitalizes on this reputation, appealing to the high-end market.

15 Based on demographic trends in the US, Wynn Las Vegas is in the right industry at the right time. In a report provided by *Mintel Research* on Casino and Casino-Style Gambling, they note that the population is aging, which is good news for the industry; as people get older, it is believed that they are more likely to gamble. "Overall, the US population is growing older . . . Casino gambling is very much a sport of a graying generation. Retirees and empty nesters typically enter casinos with a disposable income, financial security, and free time."[5] Currently in the US, the baby boomers are in the process of retiring, they are healthier and wealthier than earlier generations, and have greater spending power. As the boomers retire, they are spending more money on leisure and recreation, and they are piling into the casinos. This growing market segment represents an opportunity for the gaming industry and for Wynn Resorts more specifically.

[2] Schuman, Michael, "Egos Bigger than China," *Time,* Vol. 168, Issue 7, October 23, 2006.

[3] "The North America Hospitality and Tourism Sectors." *Mergent Industry Report.* October, 2006.

[4] "Wynn Resorts, Limited: Form 10-K" *United States Securities and Exchange Commission.* Filed 31 December 2006. Available Online. Thompson Research.

[5] "Casino and Casino-style Gambling-US-November 2006." Available Online. http://academic.mintel.com.ezp.bentley.edu/sinatra/oxygen_academic/search_results/show&/display/id=177167/display/id=247080

16 There are a few social and demographic threats that Wynn Resorts must watch and take into account. Firstly is that the social norms in the United States differ from those in practice in Macau and should not be universally applied. The occupancy rate at the Wynn Macau resorts is 80%, which is significantly less than that of the Las Vegas resort.[6]

17 Of those that visit Macau, only 25% actually stayed overnight. Those that did stay overnight tended to stay for a short period of time (1-2 nights). This is significantly different than the average visitor in Las Vegas. While Wynn is investing in expansion of the Macau facility, it is important to bear in mind this distinction. While Macau visitor behavior may change, analysts agree that it will not happen overnight. Investing in the hotel arena may not be a safe bet for Wynn and other casinos.[7] Wynn's ideal client is what is referred to as a "whale," aka the risk-friendly, deep-pocketed, high-roller gambler. With increased global competition, it will be imperative for Wynn Resorts to maintain its social status and high brand image to attract and retain the "whale" customers. If they go elsewhere, it will be a substantial loss for the company.

PUT ON YOUR POKER FACE

18 Within the gaming and resort entertainment industry there are many competing properties including, The Mirage, Las Vegas Sands, The Venetian, Paris, and The Bellagio, to name a few. Each casino has its own theme, which attracts a significant number of visitors and directly competes with the Wynn Las Vegas.

- *Ameristar Casino* has casinos in St. Charles, Kansas City, Iowa, Blackhawk, Vicksburg, Cactus Petes and Horeshu. They have established themselves as the premier gaming and entertainment facility in these areas.
- *MGM Mirage* owns featured resorts such as The Mirage, Bellagio, Mandalay Bay, and Luxor just to name a few.
- *Las Vegas Sands Corporation* is one of the leading international developers of multi-use integrated resorts. The company owns The Venetian Resort Hotel Casino, the Sands Expo and Convention Center in Las Vegas and The Sands Macau in the People's Republic of China (PRC) Special Administrative Region of Macau. The company has recently opened 2 new resorts in 2007, The Palazzo Resort Hotel Casino in Las Vegas and The Venetian Macau Resort Hotel Casino in Macau. They are also developing the Cotai Strip, a development of resort casino properties in Macau, and were selected by the Singapore government to build The Marina Bay Sands, an integrated resort scheduled to open in Singapore by the end of 2009.
- *Boyd Gaming Corporation* is one of the premier casino entertainment companies in the United States. They have operations in Illinois, Indiana, Louisiana, Mississippi, New Jersey and Nevada.
- *Harrah's* owns, operates, and/or manages about 50 casinos, Bally's, Caesar's, Harrah's, Horseshoe, and Rio just to name a few. The majority of the casinos are based primarily in the US and the UK. Operations include casino hotels, dockside and riverboat casinos, and Native American gaming establishments.

[6] "Wynn Resorts, Limited: Form 10-K" *United States Securities and Exchange Commission.* Filed 31 December 2006. Available Online. Thompson Research.

[7] Cohen, Muhammad. "No Sure Thing". *Macau Business.* December 2006. Available Online. http://www.macaubusiness.com/index.php?id=634

19 Steve Wynn feels unaffected by competition, as he believes his casinos cater to travelers who have higher demands. Wynn's main focus is to target high-end players with fancy new suites and baccarat tables. Wynn focuses on differentiating itself by concentrating on the atmosphere and design of the resorts and by enhancing customer service and luxury as a full service provider.

20 The timing could not be better for Steve Wynn to start something new. The $9.4 billion merger between Harrah's and Caesar's Entertainment along with MGM and Mandalay Bay coming together give Wynn several top managers to choose from when developing his casinos. In addition, due to such mergers, it could be expected that casinos like Harrah's, which traditionally target middle-market gamblers, will reduce their focus away from the Caesar's Palace high-end customer to target the middle-class gambler. Such a move could result in additional revenues for Wynn as such gamblers will look to Wynn Resort for higher-class amenities.

21 In general, rival casino operators say that new properties are good for Vegas because they create more reasons for people to come to town. Behind the scenes, however, they compete for the kind of gamblers who feel comfortable betting $10,000 or more per hand. MGM may already have launched its counteroffensive. "They're throwing tons of events, shopping sprees, baccarat tournaments, fishing trips," says Steve Conigliaro, an independent businessperson who hosts high rollers at various casinos. "Steve Wynn is going to take some business away. He knows what people like." "The idea of this building was to create extended spaces, to bring the outdoors inside, and to transport the guest into another realm," said spokesperson Denise Randazzo. "The real difference here is that we save all the really amazing features for the resort guests."[8]

LUCK OF THE DRAW

22 In the resort casino industry, the ability to find land and licenses in legal areas is very difficult as many countries have strict regulations around gaming resorts. Gaming licenses are difficult to obtain due to government regulations and limited availability. It is arguably more difficult to find a location that not only can support the size but also meets the legal requirements of that location. Today, Wynn Resorts LTD has a premier spot on the Las Vegas strip that is also home of the strip's only golf course. Wynn is also the holder of one of only four licenses in Macau. Having such scarce resources provides the company with a remarkable advantage.

23 Regulations regarding expansion in China remains questionable and could potentially be a barrier to entry. In Wynn Reports 10-K, they note certain risk factors for the company including the fact that their concession in Macau effectively expires in June 2017, at which time the government in Macau has the right to take over their operation. The company also notes that there are currently only three gaming concessions granted until 2009; if the government in Macau were to revise this situation by granting more concessions they would in essence alleviate this particular barrier to entry for other casinos and Wynn could potentially see more competition in the area.

24 Macau, an island located 37 miles southwest of Hong Kong and an hour ferry ride away, has become a popular gaming destination. At this time, there are 24 operating casinos in Macau with several others in the construction and development phase. Sociedade

[8] Freiss, Steve. "In Las Vegas, a $2.7b haven for high rollers." Boston Globe. April 29, 2005.

de Jogos de Macau (SJM) owns and operates 17 of these 24 casinos. "Most are relatively small facilities" and not on the high-end like The Wynn. However, they control three of the largest casinos in Macau: the Hotel Lisboa, The Greek Mythology Casino and the Jai Alai.[9]

25 Currently, Wynn Macau is charged a 35% tax on gross gaming revenue, and they are forced to contribute up to 4% of gross gaming revenue for the promotion of public interests, social security, infrastructure, and tourism in Macau.[10] If regulations were to change and taxes were lowered, Wynn Resorts would be able to retain more of its earnings.

26 Currently, the Chinese government does not allow casinos on its mainland, only Macau,[11] so the breaking of the casino monopoly in Macau has provided to be an enormous growth opportunity for Wynn Resorts.[12] The government of Macau is trying to turn Macau into the "tourist destination of choice" in Asia.[13] In 2002, the 'government-sanctioned' casino monopoly in Macau ended when the government granted concessions to three outside companies to operate casinos in Macau. Each of the three was allowed, with the approval of the government, to grant one sub-concession to another gaming operator.[14] If this legal situation were to occur in other areas of the globe, it could provide additional global growth opportunity for Wynn Resorts. Under the concession granted to Wynn Resorts, Wynn is able to develop an unlimited number of casino resorts in Macau with the government of Macau's approval.[15] This legal opportunity provides significant value for Wynn Resorts since they are one of a select few with such a right. In addition, since a limited number of companies have casino operating rights in Macau, Wynn is operating in a somewhat restricted competitive environment because they hold one of those six gaming licenses.[16]

27 Recently, Wynn Resorts was granted concession for its land application for 52 acres in Macau's Cotai Strip. This legal right is essential for Wynn Resorts future expansion plans. Stephen Wynn stated in Wynn Resorts third quarter 2007 conference call that he plans to build "the most beautiful hotel on the earth in Cotai." Currently, the designs include a 1,500 to 2,000 all-suite hotel to occupy all 52 acres, and Stephen Wynn stated this hotel will have things that have never been seen before; it will be expensive but "it will be an experience."

28 The Chinese government has and is expected to continue to relax restrictions on travel and currency movements between China and Macau. Thus far, by relaxing its currency and travel restrictions, Chinese citizens from certain urban and economically developed areas are able to visit Macau without a tour group, and they are now allowed to bring an

[9] "Wynn Resorts, Limited: Form 10-K" *United States Securities and Exchange Commission.* Filed 31 December 2006. Available Online. Thompson Research.

[10] "Wynn Resorts, Limited: Form 10-K" *United States Securities and Exchange Commission.* Filed 31 December 2006. Available Online. Thompson Research.

[11] Tan, Kopin. "Gambling on LVS, Wynn in Macau." 25 November 2007. Available Online. http://online.wsj.com/article/SB119594535268803103.html?mod=googlenews_wsj.

[12] "Macau Wow." *Economist.* 1 September 2007. Vol. 384, Issue 8544, Pg 62. Available Online. Business Sources Premier.

[13] "Wynn Resorts, Limited: Form 10-K" *United States Securities and Exchange Commission.* Filed 31 December 2006. Available Online. Thompson Research.

[14] Ibid.

[15] Ibid.

[16] "Wynn Resorts Ltd: Stock Report." *Standard & Poor's.* 22 September 2007. Available Online. www.etrade.com.

increased amount of money into Macau; this will possibly boost the profit potential for Wynn Macau.[17] If the Chinese government continues to loosen its restriction on travel and currency, tourism to Macau will grow and the profit potential for Wynn Resorts will increase.

29 In 1999, Portugal retuned Macau to Chinese control after 450 years of Portuguese control. Macau's legislative, regulatory, and legal institutions are still in a phase of transition since this change in control occurred less than eight years ago.[18] The long-term success of Wynn Macau will depend on the successful development of the political, economic and regulatory framework in Macau. Wynn Resorts could be affected if an unfavorable environment develops in Macau.

30 By doing business in an emerging market, there are significant political, economic and social risks for Wynn Macau.[19] For example, domestic or international unrest, health epidemics such as the bird flu, terrorism or military conflicts in China or Macau will drastically affect Wynn Macau by not only reducing the inflow of customers from a decrease in tourism, but also, by decreasing discretionary consumer spending and by increasing the risk of higher taxes and government controls over gaming operations.

31 Furthermore, under Wynn Resorts agreement with the government of Macau, the government has the right at any time to "assume temporary custody and control over the operation of a casino in certain circumstances."[20] The ability of the government to take control of the casino at any time it deems appropriate is a significant threat to the success of Wynn Resorts since it could lose control of its operations in Macau.

32 Additionally, Wynn Macau is subject to the strict regulatory controls by the government, which limits their freedom of operations and creativity. For example, one of the regulations requires them to have an executive director who is a permanent resident of Macau and holds at least 10% of the company's capital stock.[21] The Macau government must approve this executive director and any successor, and they have to approve all contracts for the management of the casinos operation in Macau. This is just one example of the type of restrictions and the level of control the government holds over Wynn Macau.

33 The Macau land concession poses additional threats to Wynn Resorts. Under the agreement, Wynn Macau is leasing the 16-acres from the government of Macau for 25 years. The government of Macau may redeem the concession beginning June 24, 2017 and Wynn Macau will be entitled to fair compensation based on the amount of revenue generated during the previous tax year.[22] If the government takes back the land, the long-term plans of Wynn Resorts would be derailed, possibly leaving them with high debt and no means to repay. However, if the government does not take back the land, the concession may be renewed but the semi-annual payments to use the land could substantially increase, taking away from Wynn's bottom line.

34 After April 1, 2009, the government of Macau has the right to offer additional concessions for the operation of casinos in Macau.[23] If additional concessions are granted, Wynn Macau will face further competition since these competitors already own land in Macau but do not have concession to build yet. In addition, if the efforts to legalize gaming in Thailand

[17] Ibid.

[18] Ibid.

[19] Ibid.

[20] Ibid.

[21] Ibid.

[22] Ibid.

[23] Ibid.

or Taiwan are successful, Wynn will face additional competition from the surrounding area.[24] This competition will draw away customers, it will reduce the level of potential profits, and Wynn Macau could lose key employees to more attractive employment opportunities elsewhere in Asia.

35 Another threat exists in the possibility of Wynn Resorts being unable to collect on its gaming debts. This could have a significant negative impact on Wynn Macau's operating results if the company cannot collect their earnings. In Macau, taxes are due on gross gaming revenue regardless of whether revenue was actually collected. In essence, Wynn Macau would have to pay taxes on money it never received if it was unable to collect on the debt.[25]

36 As the competitive environment in Macau increases, the available employee talent pool will decrease which could hamper future expansion plans in Macau. Wynn Resorts will need to petition the government to allow visas for more immigrant workers, and if they are unable to do so, they run the risk of having employees who cannot run the facilities. If Wynn is successful, the strict immigration laws will take time to change that could threaten Wynn's future in Macau.

37 Wynn Resorts has positioned itself well in the growing gaming markets, particularly in Macau. The development of a casino in this area is a strategic opportunity. From an economic standpoint, Macau's GDP has grown nearly 30% in the first two quarters of 2007. The growth in gambling has also resulted in increased foreign investment in the area. US exports to Macau have seen a tremendous increase as well.[26]

38 Macau's GDP growth is not likely to be sustainable. With increased competition in the region, Wynn's first-mover advantage will be diminished. Also, the company only has two casinos producing revenue, and with development efforts underway on their next projects, cash flow is undoubtedly going to be an issue.

PUT YOUR MONEY WHERE YOUR MOUTH IS

39 One of Wynn Resorts LTD's greatest marketing strengths is strategic development of its product. The product that Wynn sells is a luxury destination experience that makes the customers feel pampered and valued through high-quality amenities and customer service. This lavish experience allows consumers to justify spending significant amounts of money gambling, dining, drinking, shopping, and at the spas. The company strategically developed the Wynn brand name to be synonymous with high-quality goods and services. Continuous promotion of the brand is part of Wynn's overall company strategy.[27]

40 Steve Wynn is known for raising the luxury bar in Las Vegas. The packaging of Wynn's product is the glitz and glamour of its hotels, casinos, restaurants and shops (such as a Ferrari and Maserati dealership). As a customer enters the lobby of a Wynn hotel, they are instantly struck with grandiose decor. This feel extends throughout the hotel in the hallways, hotel rooms, suites, villas and private-entry villas. The casino takes flash and glitz to another level and a mere glimpse of the lights and sounds would make any customer excited to gamble. The casino floor is designed specifically for the high-end customer and contains

[24] Ibid.

[25] Ibid.

[26] "Macau." *BuyUsa.Gov*. 18 September 2007. Available Online. www.buyusa.gov/hongkong/en/macau.html

[27] Wynn 10k.

many private VIP areas and high roller tables. These special areas and tables further contribute to the high-end customer experience.

41 The resort is able to charge a premium price due to the clout of the Wynn name, the high-income base of its customers and the high quality of its products and services. In 2006, Wynn generated the highest room rate on the Las Vegas Strip. The average room rate for the quarter ending December 31, 2006 was $291, with the next highest being the Bellagio at $260 and then the Venetian at $243.[28]

42 Wynn is further segmenting the high-income customer market with the introduction of Encore at Wynn Las Vegas, an all-suite hotel with its own casino, restaurants, nightclub, pool and spa. This product layering allows Wynn to capitalize on the "celebrity" obsession with Las Vegas. Encore at Wynn Las Vegas will be superior to Wynn Las Vegas in luxury, amenities, and of course, price. This will serve to keep out people that cannot afford the price and will be attractive to elite customers who seek privacy as well as luxury.

43 Steve Wynn is by no means a newcomer to Las Vegas and he knows the importance of strategic placement on the Vegas Strip. Wynn owns 235 acres on the strip, which houses hotels, casinos and a golf course, the 'only' golf course on the strip. Wynn was also strategic in its purchase of land in Macau and Cotai obtaining significant portions of land in the middle of all the excitement.

44 Wynn has been successful in the past with direct marketing to its high-end target customer. This past year, it has expanded its promotion to include various media channels such as print media, radio and television.[29] Wynn Macau provides the opportunity for cross marketing with Wynn Las Vegas. Since the target market segment in both Wynn Las Vegas and Wynn Macau is high income, its customers have the resources to travel and vacation in other parts of the world, which can make cross marketing very effective. Wynn is the only gaming operator to target high-end customers in both Las Vegas and Macau.[30] Wynn Las Vegas already has a strong client base of Asian customers and Macau provides the opportunity to increase this customer segment. Wynn recognizes that the Chinese economy is on the rise and that the population is becoming increasingly educated and wealthy. The "premium customer" in China, those in the top income brackets, will increase to approximately 180-200 million over the next 10 years.[31]

45 Since Wynn has the highest rates on the strip, it would be tough to extend its customer base beyond high-end clients. In addition, the already high prices may cause Wynn to increase rates at a slower percentage per year than other hotels on the strip. For the quarter ended December 31, 2006, Wynn's average room rate increased 4.4% from 2005 to 2006 while competitors' rates increased from 5.0% to 9.5%.[32]

46 Wynn faces the challenge of understanding the customer in Macau and other global markets. In order to accomplish this, Wynn has marketing executives located in offices around the world. However, a sole marketing executive in strategic global locations may not be sufficient to conduct thorough market research and adjust the product as necessary. Lastly, focusing solely on the high-end market can be a marketing weakness in that Wynn is missing a large customer base of middle-income clients. This segment includes vacationers and younger people looking for a relatively inexpensive place to stay with the understanding that most of their budget will go to dining and entertainment.

[28] Kramer, Ron. *Wynn Resorts,* Bear Stearns Retail, Restaurants and Consumer Conference, March 1, 2007

[29] Wynn 10k.

[30] Kramer, Ron. *Wynn Resorts,* Bear Stearns Retail, Restaurants and Consumer Conference, March 1, 2007

[31] Ibid.

[32] Ibid.

47 When a customer pulls into the Wynn entrance off the Las Vegas or Macau strip, the feel is that of just being removed from a busy crowded city street and dropped into a tropical paradise. As you enter the casino, you are surrounded by beautiful flower gardens, and soothing sounds of water. Though close in the distance are the sounds of the casino floor, a gaming atmosphere is not the first to strike you. Wynn resorts makes their customers feel at ease by inviting them to relax and enjoy the serene surroundings. In the restaurants, specifically the Mediterranean themed Bartolotta's, the renowned chef comes out and interacts with the diners. Every moment in the casino and each interaction with staff are designed to be the ultimate customer experience. The staff is focused on giving the customer a luxury experience and quality customer service.

48 Wynn Resorts' goal is to attract high-end gaming customers. In August of 2006, Wynn Resorts, LTD. changed its tip pooling policy to include pit bosses and table supervisors. Operationally, this move made it feasible for experienced dealers to take positions as supervisors, who up until that point generally earned less than the dealers. The return on this new policy that the company expects is simply that as high rollers gamble more, the pit bosses, or "table supervisors" will have more at stake in making sure the customers are happy. They will give comps more, and in return, customers will stay longer and return more often. This tip pooling policy is an example of the kind of moves Wynn has made to further the luxury experience the customer receives.

SMALL BLIND—BIG BLIND

49 It is clear that Mr. Steve Wynn was successful at building and operating a casino resort empire that turned his personal worth into $1.6 billion. This feat was accomplished with his personal ambition, business savvy, and vision for what entertainment really means to the world. Although Steve Wynn appears to be, the epitome of casino resort gurus, this label does not hold the key for guaranteed future success of the Wynn Resorts LTD, there are many challenges that Wynn will have to face, and the future may throw some curveballs along the way. As it stands now there are three major challenges the firm will need to address in the future; the first being that they need to secure a way to maintain their competitive advantage as increased competition will be introduced both domestically and abroad into the gaming industry. Secondly, the Macau government reserves the right to take control of the Wynn casino in 2017, as mentioned above this would be detrimental to the profits for the company Wynn Resorts LTD, some solutions will need to be devised to ensure that the survival of the company is not majorly dependent on the revenues generated by the Wynn Macau resort and casino. Moreover, a third concern about future success, but certainly not the final concern, is the loss of Mr. Steve Wynn himself. If this loss was to occur, someone else with his expertise, passion and governmental ties (concessions and licenses) is a scarce resource. In the most likely scenario a loss of Steve Wynn may result in the sale of the firm to a competing company such as MGM, Inc. The Wynn Resorts, although not guaranteed future success, is certainly on the right track, and quite the remarkable company.

FINANCIAL STATEMENTS (February 22, 2008 10-K Edgar Online)

WYNN RESORTS, LIMITED AND SUBSIDIARIES
CONSOLIDATED STATEMENTS OF OPERATIONS
(amounts in thousands, except per share data)

	Year Ended December 31,		
	2007	**2006**	**2005**
Operating revenues:			
Casino	$1,949,870	$ 800,591	$ 353,663
Rooms	339,391	283,084	170,315
Food and beverage	353,983	309,771	173,700
Entertainment, retail and other	245,201	205,213	125,230
Gross revenues	2,888,445	1,598,659	822,908
Less: promotional allowances	(200,926)	(166,402)	(100,927)
Net revenues	2,687,519	1,432,257	721,981
Operating costs and expenses:			
Casino	1,168,119	439,902	155,075
Rooms	83,237	73,878	44,171
Food and beverage	212,622	194,403	118,670
Entertainment, retail and other	161,087	134,530	80,185
General and administrative	310,820	231,515	118,980
Provision for doubtful accounts	36,109	21,163	16,206
Pre-opening costs	7,063	62,726	96,940
Depreciation and amortization	219,923	175,464	103,344
Contract termination fee	—	5,000	—
Property charges and other	60,857	25,060	14,297
Total operating costs and expenses	2,259,837	1,363,641	747,868
Equity in income from unconsolidated affiliates	1,721	2,283	1,331
Operating income (loss)	429,403	70,899	(24,556)
Other income (expense):			
Interest and other income	47,765	46,752	28,267
Interest expense, net of capitalized interest	(143,777)	(148,017)	(102,699)
Distribution to convertible debenture holders	—	(58,477)	—
Increase (decrease) in swap fair value	(6,001)	1,196	8,152
Gain on sale of subconcession right, net	—	899,409	—
Loss from extinguishment of debt	(157)	(12,533)	—
Other income (expense), net	(102,170)	728,330	(66,280)
Income (loss) before income taxes	327,233	799,229	(90,836)
Provision for income taxes	(69,085)	(170,501)	—
Net Income (loss)	$ 258,148	$ 628,728	$ (90,836)
Basic and diluted income (loss) per common share:			
Net income (loss):			
Basic	$2.43	$6.29	$(0.92)
Diluted	$2.34	$6.24	$(0.92)
Weighted average common shares outstanding:			
Basic	106,030	99,998	98.308
Diluted	112,685	111,627	98,308

WYNN RESORTS, LIMITED AND SUBSIDIARIES
CONSOLIDATED BALANCE SHEETS
(amounts in thousands, except share data)

	December 31,	
	2007	2006
ASSETS		
Current assets:		
Cash and cash equivalents	$ 1,275,120	$ 789,407
Restricted cash and investments	—	58,598
Receivables, net	179,059	140,232
Inventories	73,291	64,368
Deferred income taxes	24,746	13,727
Prepaid expenses and other	29,775	30,659
Total current assets	1,581,991	1,096,991
Restricted cash and investments	531,120	178,788
Property and equipment, net	3,939,979	3,157,622
Intangibles, net	60,074	65,135
Deferred financing costs	83,087	74,871
Deposits and other assets	97,531	80,792
Investment in unconsolidated affiliates	5,500	5,981
Total assets	$ 6,299,282	$ 4,660,180
LIABILITIES AND STOCKHOLDERS' EQUITY		
Current liabilities:		
Accounts and construction payable	$ 182,718	$ 123,061
Current portion of long-term debt	3,273	6,115
Current portion of land concession obligation	5,738	7,433
Income taxes payable	138	87,164
Accrued interest	12,478	15,495
Accrued compensation and benefits	93,097	71,223
Gaming taxes payable	75,014	46,403
Other accrued expenses	18,367	10,742
Customer deposits and other related liabilities	177,605	127,751
Construction retention	16,755	15,700
Total current liabilities	585,183	511,087
Long-term debt	3,533,339	2,380,537
Other long-term liabilities	39,335	5,214
Long-term land concession obligation	6,029	11,809
Deferred income taxes	152,953	97,064
Construction retention	34,284	8,884
Total liabilities	4,351,123	3,014,595
Commitments and contingencies (Note 18)		
Stockholders' equity:		
Preferred stock, par value $0.01; 40,000,000 shares authorized; zero shares issued and outstanding	—	—
Common stock, par value $0.01; 400,000,000 shares authorized; 116,259,411 and 101,887,031 shares issued; 114,370,090 and 101,887,031 shares outstanding	1,162	1,018
Treasury stock, at cost; 1,889,321 shares	(179,277)	—
Additional paid-in capital	2,273,078	2,022,408
Accumulated other comprehensive loss	(2,905)	(94)
Accumulated deficit	(143,899)	(377,747)
Total stockholders' equity	1,948,159	1,645,585
Total liabilities and stockholders' equity	$ 6,299,282	$ 4,660,180

WYNN RESORTS, LIMITED AND SUBSIDIARIES
CONSOLIDATED STATEMENTS OF CASH FLOWS
(amounts in thousands)

	Year Ended December 31,		
	2007	**2006**	**2005**
Cash flows from operating activities:			
Net income (loss)	$ 258,148	$ 628,728	$ (90,836)
Adjustments to reconcile net income (loss) to net cash provided by operating activities:			
Depreciation and amortization	219,923	175,464	103,344
Deferred income taxes	68,152	170,321	—
Stock-based compensation	18,527	16,712	4,676
Amortization and writeoffs of deferred financing costs, and other			
Loss on extinguishment of debt	19,318	23,419	14,045
Provision for doubtful accounts	157	11,316	—
Property charges and other	36,109	21,163	16,206
Equity in income of unconsolidated affiliates, net of distributions	60,857	25,060	14,297
Decrease (increase) in swap fair value	481	(911)	(1,331)
Gain on sale of subconcession right	6,001	(1,196)	(8,152)
Increase (decrease) in cash from changes in:	—	(899,409)	—
Receivables, net	(75,029)	(72,927)	(104,418)
Inventories and prepaid expenses and other	(7,565)	(21,261)	(58,934)
Accounts payable and accrued expenses	54,093	164,287	159,578
Net cash provided by operating activities	659,172	240,766	48,475
Cash flows from investing activities:			
Capital expenditures, net of construction payables and retention	(1,007,370)	(643,360)	(877,074)
Restricted cash and investments	(293,734)	205,216	499,765
Investment in unconsolidated affiliates	—	—	(3,739)
Purchase of intangibles and other assets	(43,216)	(59,456)	(40,181)
Proceeds from sale of subconcession right, net	—	899,409	—
Proceeds from sale of equipment	21,581	—	109
Net cash provided by (used in) investing activities	(1,322,739)	401,809	(421,120)
Cash flows from financing activities:			
Proceeds from exercise of stock options	9,180	21,790	1,404
Proceeds from issuance of common stock	664,125	—	—
Cash distributions	(683,299)	(608,299)	—
Proceeds from issuance of long-term debt	1,672,987)	746,948	627,131
Principal payments on long-term debt	(297,321)	(440,929)	(121,933)
Proceeds from termination of interest rate swap	—	6,605	—
Purchase of treasury stock	(179,277)	—	—
Payments on long-term land concession obligation	(7,411)	(9,000)	(8,921)
Payment of deferred financing costs and other	(27,045)	(4,572)	(21,008)
Net cash provided by (used in) financing activities	1,151,939	(287,457)	476,673
Effect of exchange rate on cash	(2,659)	—	—
Cash and cash equivalents:			
Increase in cash and cash equivalents	485,713	355,118	104,028
Balance, beginning of period	789,407	434,289	330,261
Balance, end of period	$ 1,275,120	$ 789,407	$ 434,289
Supplemental cash flow disclosures:			
Cash paid for interest, net of amounts capitalized	$178,072	$133,850	$95,839
Cash distributions to convertible debenture holders	—	58,477	—
Cash paid for income taxes	79,168	180	—
Equipment purchases financed by debt and accrued assets	—	—	860
Stock-based compensation capitalized into construction	809	1,353	2,651

BOARD OF DIRECTORS
(http://phx.corporate-ir.net/phoenix.zhtml?c=132059&p=irol-govboard)

Stephen A. Wynn
Chairman of the Board and Chief Executive Officer

Kazuo Okada
Vice Chairman of the Board

Linda Chen
Director

Dr. Ray R. Irani
Director

Robert J. Miller
Director

John A. Moran
Director

Alvin V. Shoemaker
Director

D. Boone Wayson
Director

Elaine P. Wynn
Director

Allan Zeman
Director

Glossary

A

adaptive mode The strategic formality associated with medium-sized firms that emphasize the incremental modification of existing competitive approaches.

adverse selection An agency problem caused by the limited ability of stockholders to precisely determine the competencies and priorities of executives at the time they are hired.

agency costs The cost of agency problems and the cost of actions taken to minimize them.

agency theory A set of ideas on organizational control based on the belief that the separation of the ownership from management creates the potential for the wishes of owners to be ignored.

agile organization A firm that identifies a set of business capabilities central to high-profitability operations and then builds a virtual organization around those capabilities, allowing the agile firm to build its business around the core, high-profitability information, services, and products. Creating an agile, virtual organization structure involves outsourcing, strategic alliances, a boundaryless learning approach, and Web-based organization.

ambidextrous organization Organization structure most notable for its lack of structure wherein knowledge and getting it to the right place quickly is the key reason for organization. Managers become knowledge "nodes" through which intricate networks of personal relationships—inside and outside the formal organization—are constantly, and often informally, coordinated to bring together relevant know-how and successful action.

B

balanced scorecard A management control system that enables companies to clarify their strategies, translate them into action, and provide quantitative feedback as to whether the strategy is creating value, leveraging core competencies, satisfying the company's customers, and generating a financial reward to its shareholders. A set of four measures directly linked to a company's strategy: financial performance, customer knowledge, internal business processes, and learning and growth.

bankruptcy When a company is unable to pay its debts as they become due, or has more debts than assets.

barriers to entry The conditions that a firm must satisfy to enter an industry.

benchmarking Evaluating the sustainability of advantages against key competitors. Comparing the way a company performs a specific activity with a competitor or other company doing the same thing.

board of directors The group of stockholder representatives and strategic managers responsible for overseeing the creation and accomplishment of the company mission.

boundaryless organization Organizational structure that allows people to interface with others throughout the organization without need to wait for a hierarchy to regulate that interface across functional, business, and geographic boundaries.

breakthrough innovation An innovation in a product, process, technology, or the cost associated with it that represents a quantum leap forward in one or more of these ways.

business model A clear understanding of how the firms will generate profits and the strategic actions it must take to succeed over the long term.

business process outsourcing Having an outside company manage numerous routine business management activities usually done by employees of the company such as HR, supply procurement, finance and accounting, customer care, supply-chain logistics, engineering, R&D, sales and marketing, facilities management, and management/development.

business process reengineering A popular method by which organizations worldwide undergo restructuring efforts to remain competitive. It involves fundamental rethinking and radical redesigning of a business process so that a company can best create value for the customer by eliminating barriers that create distance between employees and customers.

C

cash cows Businesses with a high market share in low-growth markets or industries.

CCC21 A world-famous, cost-oriented continuous improvement program at Toyota (Construction of Cost Competitiveness for the 21st Century).

chaebol A Korean consortia financed through government banking groups to gain a strategic advantage.

company creed A company's statement of its philosophy.

company mission The unique purpose that sets a company apart from others of its type and identifies the scope of its operations in product, market, and technology terms.

concentrated growth A grand strategy in which a firm directs its resources to the profitable growth of a single product, in a single market, with a single dominant technology.

concentric diversification A grand strategy that involves the operation of a second business that benefits from access to the first firm's core competencies. A strategy that involves the acquisition of businesses that are related to the acquiring firm in terms of technology, markets, or products.

conglomerate diversification A grand strategy that involves the acquisition of a business because it presents the most promising investment opportunity available. A strategy that involves acquiring or entering businesses unrelated to a firm's current technologies, markets, or products.

consortia Large interlocking relationships between businesses of an industry.

continuous improvement A form of strategic control in which managers are encouraged to be proactive in improving all operations of the firm. The process of relentlessly trying to find ways to improve and enhance a company's products and processes from design through assembly, sales, and service. It is called *kaizen* in Japanese. It is usually associated with incremental innovation.

core competence A capability or skill that a firm emphasizes and excels in doing while in pursuit of its overall mission.

corporate lattice A concept based on research by Cathleen Benko and Molly Anderson suggesting that the working structure of an organization today is like a lattice—a three-dimensional structure extending infinitely vertically, horizontally, and diagonally. The work of a lattice-functioning organization is done in a virtual, dynamic, project-based manner resembling nodes on a network, each with the possibility of connecting anywhere and anytime to others to provide answers and ideas and to form teams or communities.

corporate social responsibility The idea that business has a duty to serve society in general as well as the financial interest of stockholders.

D

dashboard A user interface that organizes and presents information from multiple digital sources simultaneously in a user-designed format on the computer screen.

debt financing Money "loaned" to an entrepreneur or business venture that must be repaid at some point in time.

declining industry An industry in which the trend of total sales as an indicator of total demand for an industry's products or services among all the participants in the industry has started to drop from the last several years with the likelihood being that such a trend will continue indefinitely.

differentiation A business strategy that seeks to build competitive advantage with its product or service by having it be "different" from other available competitive products based on features, performance, or other factors not directly related to cost and price. The difference would be one that would be hard to create and/or difficult to copy or imitate.

discretionary responsibilities Responsibilities voluntarily assumed by a business, such as public relations, good citizenship, and full corporate responsibility.

disruptive innovation A term to characterize breakthrough innovation popularized by Harvard Professor Clayton Christensen; usually shakes up or revolutionizes industries with which they are associated even though they often come from totally different origins or industry settings than the industry they "disrupt."

divestiture A strategy that involves the sales of a firm or a major component of a firm.

divestiture strategy A grand strategy that involves the sales of a firm or a major component of a firm.

divisional organizational structure Structure in which a set of relatively autonomous units, or divisions, is governed by a central corporate office but where each operating division has its own functional specialists who provide products or services different from those of other divisions.

dogs Low market share and low market growth businesses.

downsizing Eliminating the number of employees, particularly middle management, in a company.

dynamic The term that characterizes the constantly changing conditions that affect interrelated and interdependent strategic activities.

E

eco-efficiency Company actions that produce more useful goods and services while continuously reducing resource consumption and pollution.

ecology The relationships among human beings and other living things and the air, soil, and water that supports them.

economic responsibilities The duty of managers, as agents of the company owners, to maximize stockholder wealth.

economies of scale The savings that companies achieve because of increased volume.

emerging industry An industry that has growing sales across all the companies in the industry based on growing demand for the relatively new products, technologies, and/or services made available by the firms participating in this industry.

empowerment The act of allowing an individual or team the right and flexibility to make decisions and initiate action.

entrepreneurial mode The informal, intuitive, and limited approach to strategic management associated with owner-managers of smaller firms.

entrepreneurship The process of bringing together the creative and innovative ideas and actions with the management and organizational skills necessary to mobilize the appropriate people, money, and operating resources to meet an identifiable need and create wealth in the process.

equity financing Money provided to a business venture that entitles the provider to rights or ownership in the venture and that is not expected to be repaid.

ethical responsibilities The strategic managers' notion of right and proper business behavior.

ethical standards A person's basis for differentiating right from wrong.

ethics The moral principles that reflect society's beliefs about the actions of an individual or group that are right and wrong.

ethnocentric orientation When the values and priorities of the parent organization guide the strategic decision making of all its international operations.

expert influence The ability to direct and influence others because they defer to you based on your expertise or specialized knowledge that is related to the task, undertaking, or assignment in which they are involved.

external environment The factors beyond the control of the firm that influence its choice of direction and action, organizational structure, and internal processes.

external interface boundaries Formal and informal rules, locations, and protocol that separate and/or dictate the interaction between members of an organization and those outside the organization—customers, suppliers, partners, regulators, associations, and even competitors.

F

feedback The analysis of postimplementation results that can be used to enhance future decision making.

formality The degree to which participation, responsibility, authority, and discretion in decision making are specified in strategic management.

fragmented businesses Businesses with many sources of advantage, but they are all small. They typically involve differentiated products with low brand loyalty, easily replicated technology, and minimal scale economies.

fragmented industry An industry in which there are numerous competitors (providers of the same or similar products or services the industry involves) such that no single firm or small group of firms controls any significant share of the overall industry sales.

functional organizational structure Structure in which the tasks, people, and technologies necessary to do the work of the business are divided into separate "functional" groups (e.g., marketing, operations, finance) with increasingly formal procedures for coordinating and integrating their activities to provide the business's products and services.

functional tactics Detailed statements of the "means" or activities that will be used by a company to achieve short-term objectives and establish competitive advantage. Short-term, narrow-scoped plans of functional areas that detail the "means" or activities that a company will use to achieve short-term objectives.

G

generic strategy A core idea about how a firm can best compete in the marketplace. Fundamental philosophical option for the design of strategies.

geocentric orientation When an international firm adopts a systems approach to strategic decision making that emphasizes global integration.

geographic boundaries Limitations on interaction and contact between people in a company based on being at different physical locations domestically and globally.

global industry An industry in which competition crosses national borders on a worldwide basis.

globalization The strategy of pursuing opportunities anywhere in the world that enable a firm to optimize its business functions in the countries in which it operates.

golden handcuffs A form of executive compensation where compensation is deferred (either a restricted stock plan or bonus income deferred in a series of annual installments).

golden parachute A form of bonus compensation designed to retain talented executives that calls for a substantial cash payment if the executive quits, is fired, or simply retires.

grand strategy A master long-term plan that provides basic direction for major actions directed toward achieving long-term business objectives. The means by which objectives are achieved.

grand strategy clusters Sets of grand strategies that may be more advantageous for firms to choose under one of four sets of conditions defined by market growth rate and the strength of the firm's competitive position.

grand strategy selection matrix A four-cell matrix that helps managers choose among different and grand strategies based upon (1) whether the business is operating from a position of strength or weakness and (2) whether it must rely solely on its own internal resources versus having the option to acquire resources externally via merger or acquisition.

growth industry strategies Business strategies that may be more advantageous for firms participating in rapidly growing industries and markets.

H

holding company structure Structure in which the corporate entity is a broad collection of often unrelated businesses and divisions such that it (the corporate entity) acts as financial overseer "holding" the ownership interest in the various parts of the company, but has little direct managerial involvement.

horizontal boundaries Rules of communication, access, and protocol for dealing with different departments or functions or processes within an organization.

horizontal acquisition A grand strategy based on growth through the acquisition of one or more similar firms operating at the same stage of the production-marketing chain.

I

ideagora A Web-enabled, virtual marketplace that connects people with unique ideas, talents, resources, or capabilities with companies seeking to address problems or potential innovations in a quick, competent manner.

implementation control Management efforts designed to assess whether the overall strategy should be changed in light of results associated with the incremental actions that implement the overall strategy. These are usually associated with specific strategic thrusts or projects and with predetermined milestone reviews.

incremental innovation Simple changes or adjustments in existing products, services, or processes.

industry A group of companies that provide similar products and services.

industry environment The general conditions for competition that influence all businesses that provide similar products and services.

information power The ability to influence others based on your access to information and your control of dissemination of information that is important to subordinates and others yet not otherwise easily obtained.

innovation A grand strategy that seeks to reap the premium margins associated with creation and customer acceptance of a new product or service. The initial commercialization of invention by producing and selling a new product, service, or process.

Innovation Time Out policy A policy implemented at Google and other firms allowing many employees to set aside a portion of their workweek, often one day per week, to examine and develop their ideas for new products or services the company might pursue. This concept is believed to help companies in two key ways—accelerating the creation of new product/service offerings or improvements in those that exist; and keeping employees challenged and engaged in ways that aid retention and keep staff learning and growing.

intangible assets A firm's assets that you cannot touch or see but that are very often critical in creating competitive advantage: brand names, company reputation, organizational morale, technical knowledge, patents an a unique "bundle of resources"—tangible and intangible assets and organizational capabilities to make use of those assets.

intrapreneurship A term associated with entrepreneurship in large established companies; the process of attempting to identify, encourage, enable, and assist entrepreneurship within a large, established company so as to create new products, processes, services, or improvements that become major new revenue streams and/or sources of cost savings for the company.

intrapreneurship freedom factors Ten characteristics identified by Dr. Gordon Pinchot and elaborated upon by others that need to be present in large companies seeking to encourage and increase the level of intrapreneurship within their company.

invention The creation of new products or processes through the development of new knowledge or from new combinations of knowledge.

isolating mechanisms Characteristics that make resources difficult to imitate. In the resource-based view context these are physically unique resources, path-dependent resources, causal ambiguity, and economic deterrence.

J

joint venture A grand strategy in which companies create a co-owned business that operates for their mutual benefit. Commercial companies created and operated for the benefit of the co-owners; usually two or more separate companies that come together to form the venture.

K

keiretsu A Japanese consortia of businesses that is coordinated by a large trading company to gain a strategic advantage.

L

leadership development The effort to familiarize future leaders with the skills important to the company and to develop exceptional leaders among the managers employed.

leader's vision An articulation of a simple criterion or characterization of what a leader sees the company must become in order to establish and sustain global leadership. IBM's former CEO, Lou Gerstner, described IBM as needing to become the leader in "network-centric computing" is an example of such a characterization.

learning organization Organization structured around the idea that it should be set up to enable learning, to share knowledge, to seek knowledge, and to create opportunities to create new knowledge. It would move into new markets to learn about those markets rather than simply to bring a brand to it, or find resources to exploit in it.

legal responsibilities The firm's obligations to comply with the laws that regulate business activities.

liquidation A strategy that involves closing down the operations of a business and selling its assets and operations to pay its debts and distribute any gains to stockholders.

long-term objectives The results that an organization seeks to achieve over a multiyear period.

low-cost strategies Business strategies that seek to establish long-term competitive advantages by emphasizing and perfecting value chain activities that can be achieved at costs substantially below what competitors are able to match on a sustained basis. This allows the firm, in turn, to compete primarily by charging a price lower than competitors can match and still stay in business.

M

market development A grand strategy of marketing present products, often with only cosmetic modification, to customers in related marketing areas by adding channels of distribution or by changing the content of advertising or promotion.

market focus A generic strategy that applies a differentiation strategy approach, or a low-cost strategy approach, or a combination—and does so solely in a narrow (or "focused") market niche rather than trying to do so across the broader market. The narrow focus may be geographically defined, or defined by product type features, or target customer type, or some combination of these.

market growth rate The projected rate of sales growth for the market being served by a particular business.

matrix organizational structure Structure in which functional and staff personnel are assigned to both a basic functional area and to a project or product manager. It provides dual channels of authority, performance responsibility, evaluation, and control.

mature industry strategies Strategies used by firms competing in markets where the growth rate of that market from year to year has reached or is close to zero.

milestone reviews Points in time, or at the completion of major parts of a bigger strategy, where managers have predetermined they will undertake a go–no go type of review regarding the underlying strategy associated with the bigger strategy.

modular organization An organization structured via outsourcing where different parts of the tasks needed to provide the organization's product or service are done by a wide array of other organizations brought together to create a final product or service based on the combination of their separate, independent, self-contained skills and business capabilities.

moral hazard problem An agency problem that occurs because owners have limited access to company information, making executives free to pursue their own interests.

moral rights approach Judging the appropriateness of a particular action based on a goal to maintain the fundamental rights and privileges of individuals and groups.

multidomestic industry An industry in which competition is segmented from country to country.

O

operating environment Factors in the immediate competitive situation that affect a firm's success in acquiring needed resources.

opportunity A major favorable situation in a firm's environment.

organizational capabilities Skills (the ability and ways of combining assets, people, and processes) that a company uses to transform inputs into outputs.

organizational culture The set of important assumptions and beliefs (often unstated) that members of an organization share in common.

organizational leadership The process and practice by key executives of guiding and shepherding people in an organization toward a vision over time and developing that organization's future leadership and organization culture.

organizational structure Refers to the formalized arrangements of interaction between and responsibility for the tasks, people, and resources in an organization.

outsourcing Obtaining work previously done by employees inside the companies from sources outside the company.

P

parenting framework The perspective that the role of corporate headquarters (the "parent") in multibusiness (the "children") companies is that of a parent sharing wisdom, insight, and guidance to help develop its various businesses to excel.

passion (of a leader) A highly motivated sense of commitment to what you do and want to do.

patching The process by which corporate executives routinely "remap" their businesses to match rapidly changing market opportunities—adding, splitting, transferring, exiting, or combining chunks of businesses.

peer influence The ability to influence individual behavior among members of a group based on group norms, a group sense of what is the right thing or right way to do things, and the need to be valued and accepted by the group.

perseverance (of a leader) The capacity to see a commitment through to completion long after most people would have stopped trying.

planning mode The strategic formality associated with large firms that operate under a comprehensive, formal planning system.

policies Broad, precedent-setting decisions that guide or substitute for repetitive or time-sensitive managerial decision making. Predetermined decisions that substitute for managerial discretion in repetitive decision making.

pollution Threats to life-supporting ecology caused principally by human activities in an industrial society.

polycentric orientation When the culture of the country in which the strategy is to be implemented is allowed to dominate a company's international decision-making process.

portfolio techniques An approach pioneered by the Boston Consulting Group that attempted to help managers "balance" the flow of cash resources among their various businesses while also identifying their basic strategic purpose within the overall portfolio.

position power The ability and right to influence and direct others based on the power associated with your formal position in the organization.

power curves A power curve is a depiction of a fundamental structural trend that underlies an industry.

premise control The systematic recognition and analysis of assumptions upon which a strategic plan is based, to determine if those assumptions remain valid in changing circumstances and in light of new information.

primary activities The activities in a firm of those involved in the physical creation of the product, marketing and transfer to the buyer, and after-sale support.

principles (of a leader) A leader's fundamental personal standards that guide her sense of honesty, integrity, and ethical behavior.

process The flow of information through interrelated stages of analysis toward the achievement of an aim.

product development A grand strategy that involves the substantial modification of existing products or the creation of new but related products that can be marketed to current customers through established channels.

product differentiation The extent to which customers perceive differences among products and services.

product life cycle A concept that describes a product's sales, profitability, and competencies that are key drivers of the success of that product as it moves through a sequence of stages from development and introduction to growth, maturity, decline, and eventual removal from a market.

product-team structure Assigns functional managers and specialists (e.g., engineering, marketing, financial, R&D, operations) to a new product, project, or process team that is empowered to make major decisions about their performance responsibility, evaluation, and control.

punitive power Ability to direct and influence others based on an ability to coerce and deliver punishment for mistakes or undesired actions by others, particularly subordinates.

Q

question marks Businesses whose high growth rate gives them considerable appeal but whose low market share makes their profit potential uncertain.

R

referent influence The ability to influence others derived from their strong desire to be associated with you, usually because they admire you, gain prestige or a sense of purpose by that association, or believe in your motivations.

regiocentric orientation When a parent company blends its own predisposition with those of its international units to develop region-sensitive strategies.

relative competitive position The market share of a business divided by the market share of its largest competitor.

remote environment Economic, social, political, technological, and ecological factors that originate beyond, and usually irrespective of, any single firm's operating situation.

resource-based view A new perspective on understanding a firm's success based on how well the firm uses its internal resources. The underlying premise is that firms differ in fundamental ways because each firm possesses a unique "bundle of resources"—tangible and intangible assets and organizational capabilities to make use of those assets.

restricted stock Stock given to an employee who is prohibited or "restricted" from selling the stock for a certain time period and not at all if the employee leaves the company before that time period.

restructuring Redesigning an organizational structure with the intent of emphasizing and enabling activities most critical to a firm's strategy to function at maximum effectiveness.

retrenchment A business strategy that involves cutting back on products, markets, operations, or other strategic commitments of the firm because its overall competitive position, or its financial situation, or both are not able to support the level of commitments to various markets or the resources needed to sustain or build its operations in some, usually declining or increasingly competitive, markets. Unlike liquidation, retrenchment would have the firm sell some assets, or ongoing operations, to rechannel proceeds to reduce overall debt and to support the firm's efforts to rebuild its future competitive posture.

reward power The ability to influence and direct others that comes from being able to confer rewards in return for desired actions or outcomes.

S

Sarbanes-Oxley Act of 2002 Law that revised and strengthened auditing and accounting standards.

self-management Allowing work groups or work teams to supervise and administer their work as a group or team without a direct supervisor exercising the supervisory role. These teams set parameters of their work, make decisions about work-related matters, and perform most of the managerial functions previously done by their direct supervisor.

short-term objective Measurable outcomes achievable or intended to be achieved in one year or less. Desired results that provide specific guidance for action during a period of one year or less.

simple organizational structure Structure in which there is an owner and a few employees and where the arrangement of tasks, responsibilities, and communication is highly informal and accomplished through direct supervision.

Six Sigma A continuous improvement program adopted by many companies in the last two decades that takes a very rigorous and analytical approach to quality and continuous improvement with an objective to improve profits through defect reduction, yield improvement, improved customer satisfaction, and best-in-class performance.

social audit An attempt to measure a company's actual social performance against its social objectives.

social computing The area of computer science focused on the intersection of social behavior and computational systems using blogs, e-mails, instant messaging, wikis, sharing information, and so on; creating or recreating social conventions and contexts via software and hardware as well as more computational-oriented offerings that leverage to collective opinion like online auctions, prediction markets, social choice, tagging, and social sentiment. Facebook, Groupon, Google+, Twitter, LinkedIn, and Farmville are a few examples of social computing.

social computing guidelines These policies, rules, or suggested guidelines are rapidly being put into place at most companies to guide employees' job-related involvement on social networking and computing sites for both personal and business reasons. IBM has pioneered formal social computing guidelines since it has a strategic priority of encouraging IBMers to engage in online social computing as a key way to keep IBM innovative and technology savvy.

social justice approach Judging the appropriateness of a particular action based on equity, fairness, and impartiality in the distribution of rewards and costs among individuals and groups.

special alert control Management actions undertaken to thoroughly, and often very rapidly, reconsider a firm's strategy because of a sudden, unexpected event.

specialization businesses Businesses with many sources of advantage. Skills in achieving differentiation (product design, branding expertise, innovation, and perhaps scale) characterize winning specialization businesses.

speed-based strategies Business strategies built around functional capabilities and activities that allow the company to meet customer needs directly or indirectly more rapidly than its main competitors.

stakeholder activism Demands placed on a global firm by the stakeholders in the environments in which it operates.

stakeholders Influential people who are vitally interested in the actions of the business.

stalemate businesses Businesses with few sources of advantage, most of them small. Skills in operational efficiency, low overhead, and cost management are critical to profitability.

stars Businesses in rapidly growing markets with large market shares.

stock options The right, or "option," to purchase company stock at a fixed price at some future date.

strategic alliances Alliances with suppliers, partners, contractors, and other providers that allow partners in the alliance to focus on what they do best, farm out everything else, and quickly provide value to the customer. Partnerships that are distinguished from joint ventures because the companies involved do not take an equity position in one another.

strategic business unit An adaptation of the divisional structure in which various divisions or parts of divisions are grouped together based on some common strategic elements, usually linked to distinct product/market differences.

strategic control Management efforts to track a strategy as it is being implemented, detect problems or changes in its underlying premises, and make necessary adjustments.

strategic intent A leader's clear sense of where she wants to lead the company and what results she expects to achieve.

strategic management The set of decisions and actions that result in the formulation and implementation of plans designed to achieve a company's objectives.

strategic positioning The way a business is designed and positioned to serve target markets.

strategic processes Decision making, operational activities, and sales activities that are critical business processes.

strategic surveillance Management efforts to monitor a broad range of events inside and more often outside the firm that are likely to affect the course of its strategy over time.

strategic thrusts or projects Special efforts that are early steps in executing a broader strategy, usually involving significant resource commitments, yet where predetermined feedback will help management determine whether continuing to pursue the strategy is appropriate or whether it needs adjustment or major change.

strategy Large-scale, future-oriented plans for interacting with the competitive environment to achieve company objectives.

strength A resource advantage relative to competitors and the needs of the markets a firm serves or expects to serve.

structural attributes The enduring characteristics that give an industry its distinctive character.

support activities The activities in a firm that assist the firm as a whole by providing infrastructure or inputs that allow the primary activities to take place on an ongoing basis.

SWOT analysis SWOT is an acronym for the internal Strengths and Weaknesses of a firm, and the environmental Opportunities and Threats facing that firm. SWOT analysis is a technique through which managers create a quick overview of a company's strategic situation.

T

tangible assets The most easily identified assets, often found on a firm's balance sheet. They include production facilities, raw materials, financial resources, real estate, and computers.

technological forecasting The quasi-science of anticipating environmental and competitive changes and estimating their importance to an organization's operations.

threat A major unfavorable situation in a firm's environment.

three circles analysis An internal analysis technique wherein strategists examine customers' needs, company offerings, and competitor's offerings to more clearly articulate what their company's competitive advantage is and how it differs from those of competitors while the strategists are in the midst of strategic analysis activities.

turnaround A grand strategy of cost reduction and asset reduction by a company to survive and recover from declining profits.

U

utilitarian approach Judging the appropriateness of a particular action based on a goal to provide the greatest good for the greatest number of people.

V

value chain A perspective in which business is seen as a chain of activities that transforms inputs into outputs that customers value. Customer value derives from three basic sources: activities that differentiate the product, activities that lower its cost, and activities that meet the customer's need quickly.

value chain analysis An analysis that attempts to understand how a business creates customer value by examining the contributions of different activities within the business to that value.

vertical boundaries Limitations on interaction, contact, and access between operations and management personnel; between different levels of management; and between different organizational parts like corporate vs. divisional units.

vertical acquisition A grand strategy based on the acquisition of firms that supply the acquiring firm with inputs such as raw materials or new customers for its outputs, such as warehouses for finished products.

virtual organization Corporations whose structure has become an elaborate network of external and internal relationships. In effect, a temporary network of independent companies—suppliers, customers, subcontractors, and businesses around the core, high-profitability information, services, and products. Creating an agile, virtual organization structure involves outsourcing, strategic alliances, a boundaryless learning approach, and Web-based organization.

vision statement A statement that presents a firm's strategic intent designed to focus the energies and resources of the company on achieving a desirable future.

volume businesses Businesses that have few sources of advantage, but the size is large—typically the result of scale economies.

W

weakness A limitation or deficiency in one or more resources or competencies relative to competitors that impedes a firm's effective performance.

Photo Credits

Chapter 2

p. 32: © AP Photo/Douglas Healey

Chapter 3

p. 60: © AP Photo/Gene J. Puskar; p. 69: © AP Photo/Fritz Reiss

Chapter 5

p. 141: © Jin Lee/Bloomberg via Getty

Chapter 6

p. 150: © Julie Cordeiro/Boston Red Sox

Chapter 7

p. 203: © AP Photo/Dave Koenig; p. 206: © Doug Kanter/Bloomberg via Getty

Chapter 8

p. 233 (left): © AP Photo/Paul Sakuma; p. 233 (right): © Kimberly White/Corbis; p. 242: © Yoshikazu Tsuno/AFP/Getty

Chapter 9

p. 272: © AP Photo/Gautam Singh; p. 277: © Norm Betts/Bloomberg via Getty

Chapter 10

p. 287: © Symantec Corporation; p. 293: © Monica M. Davey/Corbis; p. 307: © Tony Avelar/Bloomberg via Getty

Chapter 11

p. 337: © The McGraw-Hill Companies, Inc. All Rights Reserved

Chapter 12

p. 357: © AP Photo/Reed Saxon; p. 360: © AP Photo/Mark Lennihan

Chapter 13

page 386: © Mike Simons/Getty; p. 395 (top left): © AP Photo/Bell Atlantic; p. 395 (top right): © AP Photo/Paul Sakuma; p. 395 (bottom left): © Tom Uhlman/Bloomberg via Getty; p. 395 (bottom right): © AP Photo/Nati Harnik

Chapter 14

p. 401: Book cover of *Taiichi Ohno's Workplace Management,* © Gamba Press 2007, Photo of cover courtesy Wilson Publishing Services; p. 413: © InnoCentive, Inc.

Name Index

Page numbers followed by n refer to notes.

D

E

Q

R

S

Subject Index

F

G

T

U

V

W

Case Index